MW01055610

Affect Imagery Consciousness: The Complete Edition

By Silvan S. Tomkins

Affect Imagery Consciousness:
The Complete Edition

By Silvan S. Tomkins

Professor Emeritus
Department of Psychology
Livingston College
Rutgers University

With the editorial assistance of

Bertram P. Karon, Ph.D.

Book Two:

Volume III

THE NEGATIVE AFFECTS: ANGER AND FEAR

Volume IV

COGNITION: DUPLICATION AND TRANSFORMATION OF INFORMATION

The Silvan S. Tomkins Institute

SPRINGER PUBLISHING COMPANY
New York

Springer Publishing Company, LLC
11 West 42nd Street
New York, NY 10036–8002
www.springerpub.com

Acquisitions Editor: Philip Laughlin
Production Editor: Matthew Byrd
Cover Design: Mimi Flow
Composition: Aptara Inc.

07 08 09 10 / 5 4 3 2 1

Library of Congress Cataloging-in-Publication Data

Tomkins, Silvan S. (Silvan Solomon), 1911–1991
Affect imagery consciousness : the complete edition / by Silvan S. Tomkins.
p. cm.
Includes bibliographical references and index.
ISBN 978-0-8261-4404-1 (book one) – ISBN 978-0-8261-4406-5 (book two) – ISBN 978-0-8261-4408-9 (2-book set)
1. Affect (Psychology) 2. Consciousness. I. Title.
BF531.T58 2008
152.4–dc22 2007051043

Printed in the United States of America by Edwards Brothers, Inc.

CONTENTS

VOLUME II—THE NEGATIVE AFFECTS

BOOK TWO

VOLUME III—THE NEGATIVE AFFECTS: ANGER AND FEAR

VOLUME IV—COGNITION: DUPLICATION AND TRANSFORMATION OF INFORMATION

Part III Perception

Part IV Other Centrally Controlled Duplicating Mechanisms

Silvan S. Tomkins
1911–1991

PROLOGUE: AFFECT IMAGERY CONSCIOUSNESS

It is not unusual for the great minds to explore several paths before they pick up the scent of their future. Many roads diverge in the woods and it matters a great deal which we follow and when. Silvan S. Tomkins entered the University of Pennsylvania hoping to emerge as a playwright; he saw existence as sequences of scenes animated by emotion and linked to form stories about lives. He left with a Masters in Psychology and a doctorate in Philosophy, thence to postgraduate work at the Harvard Clinic studying Personology under Henry Murray. A lifelong passion for the racetrack led him to study the facial display of horses to correlate attitude and performance. During the Great Depression he made a good living picking horses for a betting syndicate; sheer joy overtook him when, near the end of his life, in his honor the local track named a race "The Professor." Most comfortable at the seashore, his son recalls that often he'd stand silently at the water's edge for hours on end "just thinking." None who knew him remembers a brief conversation, for everything led anywhere. Occasionally, for days at a time, he'd detach his telephone from its wall socket as protection from his compelling sociophilia.

The writings for which this essay is offered as a Prologue consumed him from the mid-1950s through the end of his life in 1991. Knowing it was his "lifework," Tomkins conflated "life" and "work," reifying the superstition that its completion would equal death and refusing to release for publication long-completed material. He knew the risks associated with this obsessive, neurotic behavior, and the results were as bad as predicted. The first two volumes of *Affect Imagery Consciousness* (*AIC*) were released in 1962 and 1963, Volume III in 1991 shortly before he succumbed to a particularly virulent strain of small cell lymphoma, and Volume IV a year after his death. This last book contains Tomkins's understanding of neocortical cognition, ideas that are even now exciting, but until this current publication of his work as a single supervolume, almost nobody has read it. The bulk of his audience had died along with the enthusiasm generated by his ideas. Big science is now more a matter of big machines and unifocal discoveries as the basis for *pars pro toto* reasoning than big ideas based on the assembly and analysis of all that is known. Tomkins ignored nothing from any science past or present that might lead him toward a more certain understanding of the mind. Every idea, every theory deserved attention if only because significant observations can loiter in blind alleys.

"Why are there no commas in the title ?" we all asked him. "Because there isn't any way to separate the three interlocked concepts. Affect produces attention that brings its trigger into consciousness, and the world we know is a dream, a series of images colored by our life experience of whatever scenes affect brought to our attention and assembled as scripts." *Affect Imagery Consciousness* is the label for a supraordinate concept. It fit his personality perfectly, this belief that something so complex as the person could only be encompassed by allusion and imagery no matter how many machines might be needed in order to prove individual ideas. It was inconceivable to him that his "book" could be "finished" because there was always so much more to learn. On his deathbed he was consumed with questions about the logic underlying the design of the hospital. He worked until he died, and left to his intellectual heirs the task of organizing and releasing what he dared not describe as "complete."

These years after his death few people know his personality, his sense of himself, how he hoped to be known or remembered. Surely he was one of history's most original psychologists, a tireless scientist who contributed much to that discipline. Yet the biggest clue was the balance of books in his library. Most important to him were philosophical concepts, the deepest possible musings about what it meant to be human and the role of the human in the world. Of perhaps equal valence were biographies of great leaders and thinkers, for concepts must derive from personhood. Front and central to him was the battle between Bertrand Russell (whose *Principia Mathematica* reduced all ideation to mathematical neatness) and Ludwig Wittgenstein (who said that books and formulae could neither embrace nor encompass the complexity of existence). Kant's *Critique of Pure Reason* was his totem, and Tomkins defined himself as a neo-Kantian. If, as Tomkins commented, Kant compared the human mind to a glass that imprinted its shape on whatever liquid was poured into it, our concepts of space, time, and causality must be understood as constructions that imposed the categories of "pure reason" on "things," thus disguising and pushing their ultimate nature beyond understanding. Kant's error of omission required repair by the theories of affect and script Tomkins was now to introduce: No matter how reasonable, the engine of analysis is engaged and focused where aimed and sent by emotion; human thought is never dispassionate. It is from this perspective that I ask the reader to consider the complex work that opens a few pages forward.

What of our demonstrable essence defines us as human, as different from other life forms? Imagine, if you will, the enormity of the task he took on. Tomkins claimed that the core, the critical element of the mind, whatever was to be our fundamental nature, derived not from the splendid neocortex that allowed critical thinking and enabled productivity of all kinds, but in the lowliest and most primitive of places—the face of the infant. Over and over he reminded us that "there is a taboo against looking at the face," a cultural rule that one should not stare at the face of another. But lovers stare enraptured into each other's eyes, almost addicted to joy. Babies literally search mother's face as if attempting to drain it of needed information, just as maternal attention to the face of the preverbal child is essential to their connection. The contrast between what seemed most attractive to babies and the rules promulgated to keep us away from that normal object of our fascination guaranteed Tomkins's curiosity.

He studied the face with unique equipment—including a specially built camera capable of taking 10,000 frames/second. ("It sounded like a canon when it went off," he laughed. "We had to keep it in the next room with a one-way mirror so the subject could be isolated from the noise. No one had ever seen that much detail in any affect display before.") But for what he thought would be one normal book, he had to do something different, something that would drive home to a new generation the importance of the face.

And so he compiled everything known about the face—musculature, enervation, characteristics of its skin, thermal response, microcirculation, and more. He postulated as yet undiscovered but unsought microreceptors in the skin of the face. Such receptors would allow sensitivity to subtle and almost microscopic movements of its musculature; the signals they picked up were made more salient by moment-to-moment alterations in facial circulation. For theories he could not yet prove, he adduced evidence from elsewhere in biology. To Tomkins, the skin of the face was favored as the receptor site for some of the most vital information imaginable. The face, he claimed, is the display board for what he termed "the affect system," a specialized neuromuscular system responsible for some of the most important functions in human life. Amplified by affect, anything becomes important. Affect, he said, "makes good things better and bad things worse."

The obvious is obscure because it is unexamined. From first hearing, the leitmotif of Molière's "Bourgeois Gentilhomme" became a pillar of my intellectual house: "Until today I had never heard of prose, and now I find I have been speaking it every day of my life." Poe's "Purloined Letter" was hidden safely in plain sight. Despite that wars are fought over access to water and legal battles engaged to protect the purity of what we drink and breathe, such elements are taken for granted until selfish interests move our society into zones of danger. Throughout history parents have chastised their children for their failure to control and contain their visible emotionality; a sobbing adult is mocked for "being emotional." Decades ago, in a hushed moment during the stage performance of a multi-talented film star, I saw a raptly attentive audience of thousands reduced to sudden, helpless hilarity when the unexpected brief scream of a baby co-opted our attention. "Never try to work a crowd with anybody under three," said the star to thunderous applause. Tomkins asked why we had emotions and why we paid attention to them.

Advanced life forms occupy only two kingdoms—plant and animal. He wondered how they differed, why they occupied two such distinct realms. The clue lay in their verbs, for animals are animated and plants remain where planted. "It was therefore possible to program into the genetic code of any plant the responses to any situation it might encounter." Leaves and roots contain cells specialized to identify a variety of stimuli and to transmit messages that engage life enhancing protocols. Daily we read that plant biologists have discovered ever more complex systems through which trees and other advanced members of that kingdom communicate with each other, send and interpret messages, and mobilize intricate defenses of their turf. But (so far) there is no evidence that any tree can learn, remember, or teach another what it has experienced, save for the species specific system of evolution through which whatever life form manages to survive some novel insult gets therefore the privilege of primacy until some new danger threatens that species.

Affect as a System

Mobility allows animals the ability to escape many situations they find noxious, but the survival of any individual creature is tightly linked to the sophistication of its ability to analyze new data and from any encounter to remember as many aspects as necessary for future utilization. Tomkins pointed out that the evolutionary sequence featured steady increase in the ability to receive and interpret signals that differ most in the rate at which they vibrate. The slowest forms of vibration are touch and movement, followed by sound, heat, and light. Success as a life form depends largely on the ability to process data of each type, and to retain in memory whatever was discovered in previous experiences.

Touch, sound, heat, light? They are constants, always present, always sources of information. How can any organism discriminate among or "make sense of" information flowing simultaneously to and from several organs and receptors? The ability to store and retrieve data from past experience is essential for the survival of the most advanced creatures, but how best should such information be managed? What aspect, what attribute of the information available to Animal's steadily increasing range of data acquisition might favor its best possible analysis? What brings, maintains, controls attention, and once it is engaged, what allows us to relinquish attention?

Over the decades of his research, Tomkins identified nine of these primary motivating mechanisms, the inborn protocols that when triggered encourage us to spring into action. Two feel different kinds of good and are known as "the positive affects." Four feel different kinds of unpleasant and are known as "the negative affects," and one other is a very brief neutral reset button for the affect system. Late in his career, he recognized two other stable forms of displeasure that he linked to innate mechanisms evolved to protect us when hunger or thirst might lead us to ingest potentially dangerous substances. So great is the importance of food and the hunger drive that on a symbolic level these became protective protocols that alerted us to interpersonal danger and were therefore called "auxiliary affects." Affect is motivating but never localizing; the experience of affect tells us only that something needs our attention. Other systems must be engaged in order to decide what must be done and how.

Most of us were taught in the language of Mowrer's 1938 dictum that every response was triggered by a stimulus, that life was lived as sequences of stimulus-response pairs, "S-R Pairs." Yet in real life, life as it is lived by organisms with affects, no stimulus can trigger a response unless and until it triggers an affect. It is the affect that brings the stimulus to the attention of the organism that then mobilizes a response. Life is not made up of "S-R Pairs." We live with S-A-R triads or "Stimulus-Affect-Response" sequences. Mood altering substances, whether in the form of medication or foodstuffs, are not needed by animals too primitive to have affects, but are essential accoutrements for those organisms that have an affective life. True to his romantic affinity to the theater, he gave these tripartite sequences the group name of "scenes."

Affect, Feeling, Emotion, Mood, Disorders of Mood

The affects are physiological mechanisms easily visible on the face of the newborn and although muted through the process of maturation, can be easily identified throughout life into senescence. The reader may find helpful the following terminology of affect-related experiences, all of which will be explained in greater detail below:

1) by the terms "affect" or "innate affect," we reference a group of nine highly specific unmodulated physiological reactions present from birth.
2) We use the term "feeling" to describe our awareness that an affect has been triggered.
3) The formal term "emotion" describes the combination of whatever affect has just been triggered as it is coassembled with our memory of previous experiences of that affect. Tomkins eventually dropped the term "emotion" in favor of the much larger category of these coassemblies that he called "scripts."
4) In general, the term "mood" or "normal mood" refers to a state in which some immediate experience has triggered an affect in such a way that the combination reminds us of an analogous historical experience, the memory of which re-triggers that affect. Such sequences may go on in the form of reminiscences that maintain the more-or-less steady experience of any affect. This kind of normal mood will vanish the moment some new stimulus triggers another affect and terminates the loop.
5) By "disorders of mood" we refer to biological glitches that produce the relatively steady experience of any positive or negative affect, affects that share neither the triggers nor the time constants typical of normal affective experience.

A good way to conceptualize this system of nine quite different alerting mechanisms is to view them as a bank of spotlights, each of a different color, each flicked on by its own quite individual switch, each illuminating whatever triggered it in a way highly specific to that light. We don't "see" any stimulus unless and until it is brought into our field of awareness as colored by affect.

The Drive System

As psychological mechanisms, the innate affects differ greatly from the biological drives that have for so long dominated the discipline of psychoanalysis and become part of our everyday language. As Tomkins explained them, nearly all drives have in common the property that they announce the need to move some substance into or out of the body and specify the site at which that action must occur. Breathing, ingestion, excretion, sleepiness, and sexuality are managed by instruction protocols that encourage an organism to initiate and complete specific actions at highly specific sites. Most of these instruction sets are fully functional from birth, although the sexual protocols don't ordinarily engage until their special organs have matured. All drive systems can operate without the need for instruction but can also be engaged intentionally. They are far more fractionated than usually considered, for we can become hungry not just for food in general but for specific nutrients recognized by the drive system as deficient. The drives provide localizing information, but derive all of their motivation from the affect system. Tomkins noted that, for example, "sexuality is a paper tiger" unless amplified by affect; sexual arousal cannot occur in the absence of affective amplification. Often we ignore hunger when preoccupied.

Pain

The only other inborn mechanism of attention is pain, and it is equally motivating and localizing. We hurt where there has been injury, and the various types of pain may be viewed as analogues of that injury: ripping, cutting, burning, tearing, breaking or bruising. Eyes and hands move quickly and precisely to what hurts and as soon as possible. Pain, drives, affects: Three interlocked but remarkably different systems of prewritten instructions. If pain initiates messages about injury, and drives are set in motion by the physiological need to move something into or out of the body, what attribute is shared by all of the innate affects ? What have they in common that allowed Tomkins to describe this group of nine mechanisms as a system ? The descriptions that follow are highly condensed statements about the nature of each affect, extended introductory sentences through which I hope to whet your appetite for the book itself. They are not ordered as you will find them in the book, but represent what I understand as the final form of his thinking on each subject.

The Nine Innate Affects

1) Surprise-Startle

Tomkins reminds us that everything must increase, decrease, or remain stable at some level. He suggested that the affects evolved as highly specific responses to such qualia – mechanisms sensitive to increases, decreases, or specific kinds of steady-state presentation, but neutral to the nature and function of the bodily system involved. Each affect might then be seen as an analogue of this specific aspect of its stimulus, regardless of whatever else that stimulus represented. Take, for instance, our response to the sharp report of a pistol shot: automatically, we blink, raise our eyebrows, inhale suddenly with the sound of "uhh," sometimes bend forward slightly at the waist, and then look around to see what might have "triggered" our reaction. Taken for granted is the quality most important to Tomkins – affect over the range from mild surprise to full startle (and to which he gave the formal range name "surprise-startle") clears the mind of whatever we'd been "thinking about" only a moment earlier. Freed from what might previously have been the subject of our attention, we are suddenly able to search for the cause of this freedom. "Sudden on, sudden off" is the neutral reset button for the attention system. It is equally likely to be triggered by something pleasant or unpleasant, but is "experienced" and remembered in terms of what we next recognize or assign as its triggering source. Despite their meaning to us, a pistol shot and the joyous shout "Surprise!" at a birthday party gain our attention from the same affect.

2) Distress-Anguish

Imagine next a noxious steady state stimulus (relentless noise, unpleasant ambient temperature, physical discomfort, hunger, fatigue) that turns on and simply won't turn off. The baby's cry of distress is an amplified analogue of a noxious, steady state stimulus, and a universally recognized output that signals clearly its helpless discomfort. It is accompanied by a highly specific facial display: the outer edges of the mouth turned down to form the characteristic "omega of melancholy," eyebrows arch, and eyes fill with tears. As she picks up the crying infant, the mothering caregiver checks quickly and reflexively for the most likely sources of steady state discomfort: cold, wet, hungry, lonely, sleepy, or in pain for some as yet undetermined reason. Some condition, some now quality of its existence has triggered an affect over the range from mild distress to sheer anguish, and it is the expression of that affect which draws mother to the helpless infant and throughout adult life operates as an amplified analogue of steady state discomfort. And since the cry of the infant is itself a steady state and quite relentless auditory signal, the cry of her baby triggers maternal distress-anguish by affective resonance.

It was the phenomenology of affective resonance that led me to read Tomkins's work and later work with him. Our training places young physicians in strange places, and I'd always been amused to watch the theater of the newborn nursery where the cry of one infant would like a wave course over other infants until all were crying in unison. None of us onlookers cried, which suggested that with maturity came the learned ability to maintain one's personal boundaries even in the presence of intense ambient affect. Furthermore, in my clinical work as a psychiatrist, I had often experienced within myself specific emotions that were coursing through but not expressed verbally by my patients. Each of the nine innate affects is an amplified analogue of its stimulus conditions, and (simply because it carries, amplifies, and extends the qualia of its original stimulus) is therefore capable of triggering more of that affect in oneself. The baby hears its own cry as a competent trigger for more, and more intense crying. Quite early, the infant also learns to get mother's attention by imitating its own innate cry, a process Tomkins called "autosimulation." No matter why triggered, the cry of distress-anguish acts as a significant trigger for the distress of others.

We are thus wired to react innately to the expressed affect of others as if it were our own, and therefore enabled to know a great deal about the inner world of those others. Infantile expression of affect is often an all-or-none phenomenon and has thus evolved as the most efficient possible system to guarantee maternal attention to baby's needs. We would forever live at the mercy of those who express affect with the most intensity save for the fact that each of us learns to protect and preserve variable degrees of inner peace in the face of others' affect. To be most receptive as audiences, and in certain social or sexual situations, we may suspend the operation of what I eventually termed an "empathic wall," but our ability to live in a complex world with all its intense experiences requires that we practice variable susceptibility to the affect of others. Twenty-five years ago we viewed it as an "ego mechanism"; now the empathic wall is understood as an affect management script. I suspect but cannot prove that the entire mythology of "mental telepathy" is a fanciful extrapolation of the far simpler physiology and phenomenology of affective resonance through which we really do know a great deal about the inner experience of the other person.

3) Anger-Rage

Babies, of course, do not merely sob quietly. The logical extreme of a steady state complaint is of course the cry of rage, the roar of dissent, the prolonged all-or-nothing scream that conveys the utter unbearability of its trigger. Tomkins gave this hot affect the range name anger-rage, and suggested that the circulatory changes associated with the infant's swollen, reddened face operated both as a highly visible sign of the innate affect and a feature that made even more salient whatever messages might be associated with the muscular part of its facial display. Muscles all over the body are recruited in the service of anger-rage—fists, arms, and legs tensed in isometric contraction, abdomen taut, mouth open at its widest. Said a friend observing his 6-week-old son rage on the changing table, "If he were 6 feet tall, that would be King Kong." Just as with any other of the innate affects elucidated by Tomkins, anger can be autosimulated and thereby recruited on demand—initially as a pale imitation of the physiological affect mechanism, but soon enough morphed into the real thing as art paves the way for the innate. The expression of our own affect triggers by resonance more of the same in both self and other—a demagogue can make rage as infectious as a comedian can generalize laughter. In the infant, a steady-state stimulus at one range of intensity triggers distress-anguish, whereas a steady-state stimulus at a higher range of intensity triggers anger-rage.

All innate affects are modified by experience and learning. Comparing the facial display of infants and adults, Tomkins asked us to consider geology. The fresh, new Rocky Mountains are sharp, craggy, and definite. Older mountains like the Catskills are rounded, weathered, smoother. Displayed on the face of the infant, innate affect involves every possible muscle and the maximal reactivity of facial microcirculation. The adult display of affect is muted, smoother, and subtle. Despite that the anguish of a baby is heart-rending and the sob of an adult is far more private, both involve analogic amplification of a higher than optimal steady-state stimulus. Despite that the entire body of an infant may be committed to the display of rage, an adult may learn to miniaturize the display of that same affect by momentarily tightening the jaw muscles or a fist hidden in a pocket. Analogues display qualia, not degrees of intensity.

4) Enjoyment-Joy

From the "on-off" quality of surprise-startle and the constant density qualities of distress-anguish and anger-rage, look next at the affects characterized by graded increases or decreases in stimulus density. Easiest to grasp is the affect responsible for laughter, the feeling of relief, the sense of "whew !" when a challenging situation ends, or the joy of victory. The gradual decrease in any stimulus will trigger a pleasant smile and a relaxation response, whereas rapid decrease in stimulus density will trigger laughter. There is nothing intrinsically "funny" about the punch line of a joke, but the suddenness with which an anecdote ends is quite analogous to an unexpected physical punch. In the world of professional comedians, "one-liners" are protocols in which the operator draws our attention with an interesting premise but terminates that attention unexpectedly by referencing an alternate meaning of that phrase.

The modal example of this genre is Henny Youngman's archetypal "Take my wife. Please." The initial phrase (the words as well as the tone in which it is delivered) prepares us for perhaps a minute's description of that beleaguered spouse, but the immediately following punch line shifts the meaning of "take" from "please listen to the following story about my wife" toward "remove my wife." It is only the suddenness with which we are forced to make this shift, accept that we were tricked, and recognize that the joke has ended, that triggers laughter. Despite that we laugh at jokes and consider them a major source of enjoyment, most of them "don't work" unless they contain at least some elements of novelty and surprise. ("I've heard that before.") If surprise-startle is triggered by the sudden onset and sudden offset of data acquisition, the guffaw is an analogous response to sudden or unexpected offset following a relatively slow onset. Tomkins gave this affect the range name "enjoyment-joy," thus referencing the wide spectrum of situations in which "stimulus decrease" brings pleasure. In the infant, it is seen as a moment of complete relaxation of all the facial muscles, the smile of contentment, and bright shining eyes. You will often see adults crowded around a baby in order to savor that wonderfully infectious affect, sometimes pleading aloud "Give us a smile." As adults, our personal world is often so complex that we search diligently for situations that allow the simple pleasure of even momentary relaxation and consequent enjoyment-joy.

5) Interest-Excitement

Recall, for a moment, Tomkins's basic premise about the affect system: Advanced animals cannot survive as individuals or as a species unless they are able to 1) select whatever turns out to be the most important source of information available at any moment; 2) develop the best method of handling that information; and 3) manage systems for the retention of and immediate access to what was so learned. Interest-excitement is the genetically scripted protocol that mobilizes attention to information that enters our neurological system at an optimally increasing rate of stimulus acquisition. So important, so compelling is this positive affect that adults will endure standing in line to see a new movie, purchase the latest fashion of anything, or embrace almost anything that seems both novel and safe. Although it is the most important affect associated with the normally disciplined learning in a classroom situation, its range name makes clear that the intensity of the expressed affect is related to the rate at which stimulus acquisition increases. Within limits, we are programmed to attend to novelty in an atmosphere of excitement.

Each of the nine innate affects is equally responsible for the attitude we call "attention," and the universal sense that attention requires some sort of effort or work leads us to claim that we "*pay*" attention to a stimulus. Yet I doubt that any concept introduced by Tomkins has produced as much confusion as his insistence that what we had always considered "normal attention" was itself a highly specific affect mechanism. In the infant, this is seen as the rapt face of "track, look, listen," and we take it for granted as the attitude of "pure" attention to novel information entering through any portal at an optimum rate of stimulus increase. The sheer ordinariness of this affect has precluded serious investigation for centuries. It is characterized by furrowed brow, head tilted slightly forward and perhaps a bit to the side as if favoring one ear, mouth slightly open, (in the infant) tongue protruded slightly and often to the non-dominant side. The childhood activity we call "spontaneous play" is almost always initiated by this affect, despite that normal playing almost always provides a wide range of other affects as difficulty, success, and failure are encountered.

6) Fear-Terror

Just as distress-anguish and anger-rage are negative affects that amplify or bring into awareness different levels of steady-state discomfort, thus increasing radically the possibility that it might be remediated by conscious action, affect over the range from mild fear to sheer terror calls our attention to some sort of information entering our system at a rate categorized as "too much, too fast." Whereas distress and anger identify steady state overload, fear-terror identifies rapidly increasing overmuch. The term "anxiety" usually references the milder forms of fear for which we cannot immediately assign a source. We all know fear-terror as the "alarm" that goes off when driving on a highway, we are alerted to what may be a rapidly approaching danger. In an automobile, we then swerve, brake, or increase our speed to avert whatever has triggered this alarm. Unlike the kind of attention associated with surprise-startle, conscious awareness of whatever has frightened us does not involve sudden clearing of our attention to whatever had been going on only a moment ago, but rather an increased intensity of and different type of concentration on something that has begun to happen uncomfortably rapidly.

If excitement and anger are hot affects, the worried attention of fear is a cold affect in which the face is turned a bit to the side, the cheek is blanched, and all muscles are held stiffly for a moment. It includes the cry of terror, eyebrows raised and drawn together, sometimes the corners of the mouth drawn back and (in extreme terror) contraction of the muscles underlying the skin of the neck. As fear is an analogic amplifier of something that is happening too rapidly, it also causes the pulse to race uncomfortably; the pounding heart of fear-terror itself can terrify the already frightened individual. The emergency reaction of acute terror is toxic even when quite brief. Affect always makes good things better and bad things worse.

7) The Protective Mechanism of Shame–Humiliation

Tomkins's analysis of shame differs from any ever propounded for this complex and inherently uncomfortable emotional experience. His description of the visible changes associated with shame fits what we already understood: in the moment of shame the head dips down and to the side, removing our gaze from whatever had been going on only a moment earlier. This is what is meant by the Chinese expression "losing face," for the visage of the acutely shamed person is removed from the previously consensual interchange. I've emphasized that shame affect causes a "cognitive shock," a momentary inability to think clearly. Acute vasodilatation accounts for the phenomenology of the blush, reddening the face and often the neck and upper chest, and therefore maximizing the degree to which others can perceive our discomfort and thus maximize it. Both Darwin and Tomkins commented that this terrible visibility of our own shame robs us of the very privacy that might have let us recover our composure. A hot negative affect that is responsible for much emotional discomfort, its function and logic have long been obscure. His own judgment fiercely dependent on the primacy of the drive system as the source of all wishes and needs, Freud declared that shame was well-deserved punishment for the wish to exhibit the genital. The psychoanalytic movement so deeply embraced this attitude that for several decades thereafter the appearance of ordinary embarrassment during an analytic or psychotherapy session was neither investigated nor interpreted.

Tomkins understood shame as a powerful system of reactions that set in motion a wide range of responses. Alone of the innate affects, he conceptualized it as a mechanism triggered when something interferes with the experience of positive affect—either interest-excitement or enjoyment-joy—but does not turn it off completely. Shame affect has evolved to call attention to the presence of some stimulus that distracts from the preexisting positive affect but does not displace it. "Aw mom !" is a typical and expected protest of the child whose excitement over a television program has been interrupted when mother demands attention and distracts from the obvious trigger for interest by standing in front of the screen. The exciting scene goes on, continuing to operate as the normal and expected trigger to interest, but her intrusion triggers the special response of shame affect. Other terms that involve shame affect include disappointment, dashed expectations, being declared the lesser in any form of comparison, and being jilted or taunted.

Shame affect can almost always be overridden by intentional concentration on the preexisting good scene with satisfying return of the original positive affect. As such then, affect over the range from mild shame to paralyzing humiliation is considered an "affect auxiliary," an affective experience that operates only as a limitation on what started as a good scene. As only one example, since one of the most powerful experiences of positive affect involves mutualized excitement or joy when staring into the eyes of one's beloved, the merest flicker suggesting that something has "gone wrong" triggers the full expression of shame. Sexual arousal (the drive is deeply dependent on its coassembly with excitement) is a fragile and highly vulnerable experience. Foreplay routinely involves sequences in which the arousal-excitement coassembly is challenged by moments of shame as self-consciousness, and then overridden by the conscious intent to resume and increase the original state of arousal until the desired state of mutual arousal is achieved and sexual congress begun.

My own studies suggest that shame is the dominant negative affect of everyday life, far more varied in its triggers and presentation than any other displeasure. Most of the problems of interpersonal life can be traced to shame-based issues; the majority of advertising and marketing campaigns are designed to deal with issues of self-esteem and the valence of personal identity. Just as each of us longs for pleasurable excitement and reasonable amounts of joy, the ubiquity of situations that interfere with the experience of positive affect makes shame—no matter how disguised—our constant companion. One of the factors that made shame so difficult to study until Tomkins offered this realm of explanation is the reality that each of us has different interests and a history of enjoying different scenes, the incomplete interruption of which triggered our own shame experiences. So deeply personal and uniquely individual are our own scenes of shame that (sadly) nobody else ever seems to "know" exactly what shame means to us. I dealt with this puzzle in the 1991 book *Shame and Pride: Affect, Sex, and the Birth of the Self*, which Tomkins regarded as the logical extension of his theoretical work on shame affect into the lived world of scripts.

8) and 9) The Drive Auxiliaries of Dissmell and Disgust

Small children are omnivores who would be at great danger of ingesting noxious and dangerous substances were they not protected by two inborn mechanisms. *Dissmell*, a neologism coined by Tomkins, makes us reject potential foodstuffs that carry an odor outside certain rigidly determined limits. From the early beginnings of extrauterine life, such substances trigger programmed reactions that include wrinkling the nose and upper lip, backward movement of the head away from the offending odor, and the vocalization "eoouuh." So powerful is this innate mechanism that it becomes a part of a "rejection before sampling" script with increasing importance as the child matures. Although it has evolved as one form of protection against potentially dangerous food, dissmell is the physiological mechanism underlying prejudice, in which we reject a person or a concept before trying or testing it personally.

Similarly, potential foodstuffs that trigger tastes outside a rather narrow realm of acceptability are rejected with *disgust*, in which from infancy on the offending material is spat out, the lower lip protruded, and the head thrust forward with the vocalization "ugh." This mechanism forms the basis of another script through which a person or experience once found "delicious" is now declared disgusting and worthy only of expulsion. The social/legal system of divorce may be understood as a process through which someone once loved is expelled as lawyers maximize and manage the affects of disgust and anger.

A System of Prewritten Affect Mechanisms Forms a Blueprint

The palette of nine innate affects, this universal set of prewritten instructions, controls and animates far more than the neat patterns of reaction sketched briefly above. Tomkins observed that the existence of this group of affects is a major factor in the formation of personality, of the habits and goals "natural" to all humans. We are, he said, motivated to accept, savor, and seek out the two positive affects because they are "inherently rewarding," and motivated to avoid, quash, and rebel against the six negative affects because they are "inherently punishing." Although the number of situations in which any individual might encounter these nine innate mechanisms is perhaps infinite, at least these experiences can be arranged in nine discrete categories. All life is "affective life," all behavior, thought, planning, wishing, doing . . . There is no moment when we are free from affect, no situation in which affect is unimportant, and the simple fact that these action protocols exist forces on each human a set of four highly specific behavioral requirements. Tomkins identified this group of inherently scripted rules as the Blueprint:

The Tomkins Blueprint for Individual Mental Health

1) As humans, we are motivated to savor and maximize positive affect. We enjoy what feels good and do what we can to find and maintain more of it.
2) We are inherently biased to minimize negative affect.
3) The system works best when we express all of our affects.
4) Anything that increases our power to accomplish these goals is good for mental health, anything that reduces this power is bad for mental health.

Psychiatrist Vernon C. Kelly, first Training Director of The Silvan S. Tomkins Institute, has a core interest in couples therapy and the specifically interpersonal manifestations of innate affect. Working carefully with Tomkins, Kelly developed a Blueprint for Intimacy, affect-based rules of the road for couples. Relationships are about the way we feel with others, and cannot prosper unless careful attention is paid to the affects experienced by self in the context of other. Their new Blueprint gave precedence to affective resonance as the core element of intimacy, and stated clearly that effective management of the affects experienced in the context of a relationship is the core task of intimacy:

The Tomkins–Kelly Blueprint for Intimacy

1) Intimacy requires the mutualization and maximization of positive affect.
2) Intimacy requires the mutualization and minimization of negative affect.
3) Central to intimacy is the requirement that we disclose our affects to each other.
4) Anything that increases our power to accomplish these three goals is good for intimacy, anything that reduces this power is bad for intimacy.

The clinical implications of these two blueprints have turned out to be quite rewarding. Much of our personal and interpersonal discomforts are affective, and few people find difficulty learning the "nine letters of the affective alphabet" in the service of understanding self and other. One is reminded of the scene in the movie "Batman" in which the evil Joker stares in growing rage at the easygoing goodness of the newly discovered "caped crusader" being interviewed on television and snarls "At last I know the name of my pain !" The attitude of Molière's naïve character becomes increasingly salient in direct proportion to the importance we assign to the universality of innate affect.

Script Theory

Return, for a moment, to Tomkins's adolescent dream of becoming a playwright. Life is a series of scenes (Stimulus-Affect-Response Sequences) loosely organized into segments called Acts; a life story can be made cohesive only if one discerns or assigns a unifying theme or purpose. But what is the minimal set of experiences necessary to establish such a theme ? Half a life later, he offered a stunning explanation for what we had taken for granted as the path of normal life, bridging the gap between the momentary innate affects easily identified on the face of the infant and the subtle complexity of adult psychology.

The trivial affords good examples of script formation. Imagine that you love some favorite specialty food (as in my daughter's affection for Brazilian hearts of palm) and learn that the local market is selling cans at a ridiculously low price, obviously to lure customers who will also purchase other goods. Immediately on reading this advertisement, you rush to the store only to find out that they're sold out of that product. You're disappointed, do purchase something else you needed, and return home blaming bad luck. If nothing like this ever happens again, this scene will never achieve "importance" beyond its place in the momentary annoyances of everyday life.

Not long after this scene, imagine next that your favorite clothing store advertises at vastly reduced price some article of clothing you'd admired but earlier rejected as too expensive. You rush there only to find that they're sold out of that product. Yes, you are disappointed. But something else happens, simply because the stimulus-affect-response sequence involved is almost identical to what happened when you rushed to purchase that delicious treat at the food market. Automatically, we link the two quite different scenes as examples of an affective process in which anticipatory excitement powered our trip to the store, and disappointed expectations triggered some degree of shame affect. ("I've been tricked.") Furthermore, we can now bundle in the mind these two experiences and mobilize the affect of disgust toward this new family of scenes because an expected good experience became quite distasteful. In the example given, from this moment forward we will operate within the bounds of a script through which a loss leader offer triggers protective disgust, mistrust, and perhaps contempt.

Tomkins defined consciousness as a state created by the assembly of an event (percept, cognition, scene retrieved from memory, etc.) with the affect it triggered, and postulated that only those states that achieved conscious representation would be stored in memory. But the storage system, the complex system of attributes that allowed us to assemble experiences with these special cognitive skills, was what he called script formation. The technology and equipment required to store, access, and cross-reference each experience as a separate datum would be far more massive and complex than a system that grouped memories on the basis of the affects with which they were associated. Individual stimuli are amplified into consciousness by affect, but in script formation the affect within families of similar scenes is magnified, making far more meaningful and tenacious whatever information is so bundled.

The "general features of all scripts" include sets of rules for the interpretation, evaluation, prediction, production, or control of scenes. Some of the enormously complex features he described include the idea that scripts are selective and always incomplete. They are in varying degrees accurate and inaccurate in these tasks, are continually reordered and capable of change, and tend to be more self-validating than self-fulfilling. If it is affect that amplifies its trigger enough to provide the amplification and conscious awareness of that trigger, it is through our lifetime of script formation that we live and "know" how we live. The application of Script Theory to clinical work, psychological experimentation, indeed to the understanding and betterment of our shared world, will be the job of the next generation of scholars and clinicians.

Therapeutic Disassembly of Scripts

I have been fascinated by one currently popular system of psychotherapy, which is perhaps best understood in the language of script theory. Psychologist Francine Shapiro developed the form of treatment she called EMDR (Eye Movement Desensitization and Reprocessing), and through an extensive network of training facilities, taught and licensed a great many therapists. At the suggestion of Tomkins Institute member and EMDR expert Marilyn Luber, PhD, Dr. Shapiro invited me to become trained in her system, interpret it in the language of Script Theory, and present my understanding to her own group. That training, and experience of this system with my own patients, has increased radically my understanding of scripts.

The trained EMDR therapist asks the patient to concentrate on a specific target image, usually the noxious scene (stimulus-affect-response sequence) that has either precipitated the request for treatment or is considered by the patient most representative of that person's dysphoria; one is instructed to allow into consciousness all of the negative affects associated with this scene. Next, the patient is instructed to outline the desired new image with its associated positive affects, an image of who and how one would like to be. When patient and therapist agree that these two constructs have been built and are held firmly in mind, the patient is asked to focus on and visually track a moving stimulus (finger, light, sound, touch). After a few repetitions of this process, the target noxious scene no longer operates as a trigger for negative affect. At this point, the operator asks whether another scene with similar affective tone has come to mind, and repeats the process until it, too, has been rendered relatively neutral. In some cases, one or two such sessions will produce significant reduction in the dysphoria that provoked the request for treatment; in cases characterized by significant and ongoing psychological trauma, treatment may take longer.

Observing both live and videotaped therapy sessions, I was able to demonstrate from the facial displays of each patient that this system of treatment worked best when shame was the negative affect most responsible for that patient's dysphoria. The therapeutic process asks the patient to hold in consciousness two contrasting images—the scene made painful by shame affect, and the desired outcome of a similar scene amplified by unimpeded positive affect—and while doing this, focus attention on a novel, moving stimulus. The facial display of each patient was clearly that of "track, look, listen," the modal face of the affect interest-excitement. The EMDR protocol "tricks" the mind by transforming old scenes previously amplified by the negative affect shame-humiliation to what are essentially new scenes when amplified by the positive affect of interest-excitement. Since the patients' scripts had been formed by the steady accretion of new scenes to an established sequence, as each painful scene was revisited therapeutically in the ambience of the positive affect interest-excitement, the established pathological script was sequentially disassembled and rendered ineffective. I suspect that script theory will become an increasingly valuable system for the explication of much that is now obscure.

Disorders of Affect

To the best of my knowledge and understanding, Tomkins ignored only one important aspect of affective life. His theoretical system defined the nine innate affects as neurobiological mechanisms that turned on when their switch was activated, and turned off as soon as the organism focused attention on the triggering event and began to deal with it. The depressive disorders are characterized by such aberrations of normal affect management as the inability to mobilize positive affect or to turn off distress-anguish. There are myriad situations in which an affect continues unabated unless or until we devise some way to turn it off. Psychologist Wesley Novak has taught our group to enter and by sympathetic attention often empty "the cave of tears" in which most "depressed" individuals store the anguish they cannot countenance. The system of cognitive therapy introduced by Aaron T. Beck teaches depressed patients how to think differently about their negative affect and so reduce the degree of emotional pain previously suffered. Such therapeutic approaches are based on the reality that many of us can benefit from education about affect management.

It is ordinary folk knowledge that shame is soluble in alcohol and boiled away by cocaine and the amphetamines, that opiates dull some dysphorias as well as pain, and that cannabis derivatives foster dissociative states that allow temporary freedom from certain noxious affects. I have read that of all the societies identified on our planet, only two isolated aboriginal cultures (tribes in Micronesia and Venezuela) have ever failed to "discover" caffeine, nicotine, and alcohol. Included in the wide range of affect management scripts possible for us humans are both psychological and chemical modalities. We are quite inventive in our ability to use devices and scripts of all sorts to quell or stimulate affect. Tomkins wrote eloquently about substance abuse and addiction; Tomkins Institute member Marsha Schwartz Klein has taught a generation of clinicians a wide range of therapeutic approaches based on his logic.

As a practicing psychiatrist, I am fascinated by the variable responses of patients to our currently available medications. There can be little argument that the Bipolar Affective Disorders are caused by genetic glitches (polymorphisms, or minor but significant alterations in the genes responsible for what we consider "normal mood"), and that the systems through which we now manage these disorders of affect metabolism are at best frail. Despite that the basket of antipsychotic, antidepressant, and antianxiety agents is wide and deep, I am aware of no single medication that attacks the cause of any "mental" illness. The contemporary pharmacopoeia is best understood as a holding action, a system of treatments that relieves only a fraction of the symptoms experienced by our patients.

Of perhaps equal importance is the fact that at this writing, most psychiatric ills bear names based on theories well known to be outmoded: No one believes that Borderline Personality Disorder represents a state poised on the border between neurosis and psychosis—it is clearly a disorder in which the psychology of shame is predominant. (Our entire culture works hard to disavow shame.) The entire concept of "impulsiveness" or "impulse control" should be scrapped in favor of language that recognizes which of the innate affects has become difficult to manage. "Attention-Deficit Disorder" and "Attention Deficit Hyperactivity Disorder" are less insulting to the patient than the term "Minimal Brain Dysfunction" that they replaced, but both are syndromes in which interest-excitement is inadequately mobilized and/or maintained, and hypersensitivity to shame-humiliation dominates the clinical picture. In my clinical experience, patients with "Conduct Disorder," "Oppositional Defiant Disorder," "Reactive Attachment Disorder of Infancy or Early Childhood," and "Social Phobia" all share features of unusual susceptibility to shame affect. "Anxiety" has become an overinclusive or nonspecific term referencing not fear-terror but pretty much any negative affect, and therefore increasingly useless as a descriptor. Generalized Anxiety Disorder ("GAD") is currently described as responding best to serotonergic medications that are otherwise used routinely to remediate clinical conditions characterized by unremitting shame symptomatology. When questioned closely, most of these patients seem to fear embarrassment. Tomkins was forever reminding us that there is a taboo against looking at the face, and indeed in most clinical conditions much can be learned by studying facial display. Disorders of affect metabolism render both blueprints inoperative, simply because individual wellness and the emotional health of a couple are deeply dependent on the ability not merely to recognize but to modify what feels wrong.

Cyclic Changes in the Public Display of Affect

Longevity favors the critical writer. I entered college during the early 1950s, when public protest was barely audible and alcohol the only known lubricant for playfulness impeded by anticipatory shame. These decades later I still enjoy the memory of a dozen couples kissing on couches in a fraternity commons room, the Boston accented voice of one young woman rising above the crooner's voice: "Oh, I'm having so much fun, this must be a sin !" This was an era of self-control, chastity, public display of morality; the average age of first intercourse for women was 20 and the menarche 16. Today, pregnancy in a 9-year-old no longer warrants mention in a medical journal. Public behavior is bawdy and loud, its scripts intertwined with a pharmacopoeia of hallucinogens, marijuana, cocaine, amphetamines, and other drugs known to magnify excitement and ward off shame. The early psychoanalytic movement described the young child as untrained in the limitations on behavior associated with maturity, and therefore "polymorphic perverse." Today, public nakedness is taken for granted, the internationally accessible electronic display boards allow anyone to advertise sexual availability and encourage desire, and all limitations on behavior are scorned. Sexual activity is regarded as more of a skill set than anything to do with the search for emotional intimacy, and there is no evidence that sexual freedom has reduced the frequency of heterosexual or homosexual rape.

From infancy through senescence we are sandwiched between conflicting instruction sets to "say what we really mean" and also "maintain a cool head." Screaming infants are shushed and the taciturn are encouraged to express their affect more vigorously so we know what they "really" think. Normal socialization and consensual downregulation of affective expression do incur some psychological costs: Just as emotional maturity seems inextricably linked with the ability to maintain reasonable control over our expressed affects, people really do need places where they can cheer, scream, and lust in safety and relative privacy. The entertainment world is designed for the maximal display of affect of all sorts, broadcast with visual and auditory support that allows us maximal opportunity to resonate with it. The enormously popular genre of horror movies allows its audience to experience maximal amounts of terror safely and recover from it quickly, just as the gambling casinos provide "games of chance" with carefully calibrated variations in perceived risk and danger. Love stories allow us to sit in relative comfort as we watch actors go through relational sequences that both resemble and far exceed our own personal experience; such films provide results that are analogues of what any viewer can hope to achieve. We can thus try on the identity of a war hero, business tycoon, a sexually or an athletically daring role model. We can laugh safely at a fool who is "nothing like me" and imagine ourselves responding perfectly to any situation. The world of athletic competition has become merely another arm of the entertainment industry, its heroes (like aging actors) discarded when they have been used up or injured so badly that they have difficulty finding employment when their public careers have ended.

Personal computer games and elaborate fantasy game systems for groups ask our youth to practice strategies for murder and lethal crimes that require total attention and prolonged immersion. Notwithstanding the constant disavowal of responsibility by their designers and distributors, it has become obvious to the casual observer of modern society that what is learned in games often finds its way into "real life." Kids now kill with far more frequency than we'd like to admit, and they do it in ways they've learned from their entertainments. There were over 400 murders in my city last year, crimes committed mostly by young men who killed because they owned guns and lived in a society that sees gun violence as a form of play that evidences competence and therefore produces healthy pride.

There are two problems most likely to trigger interference with a system in which entertainments and personal satisfaction are linked to the intensity of the affective experiences involved: Firstly, the biological nature of the affect system must eventually act as a brake on the steadily increasing density of whatever stimuli are manufactured. Too much of anything becomes unpleasant, not just because the audience protests that "we've seen this before," but because there is only a slim border between intense positive affect and negative affect. Secondly, there is an increasing likelihood that public disgust for increasingly violent entertainments will rise to the extent that our culture will follow the path of previous generations and build into our social systems the kind of structures and safeguards that will initially enrage the entertainment industry but actually save it from far worse attacks. No society can survive constant and unchecked increase in affective amplification. We don't tolerate it from children over the age of three, and I fully expect that within a few years of this writing our society will have withdrawn its support of the unmodulated expression of affect and sexuality now in vogue. We'll do it quite badly, because change of this sort only occurs as the result of scripts based in anger, disgust, and dissmell, and the subsequent retreat from social and political control will place us right back where we are today.

Tomkins on Cognition

"The human being confronts the world as a unitary totality. In vital encounters he is necessarily an acting, thinking, feeling, sensing, remembering person." In Volume IV, Tomkins rejoined the motivational and the cognitive systems he had separated for the purpose of investigation and explanation. Motivation, as summarized above, involves all of the mechanisms for amplification through which data is brought into consciousness. But he defined as cognition all of the ways raw information is acquired, and how it is transformed from the way it entered the system to however it gets to be used. Unlike the kind of transformation provided by the contemporary computer, cognition is much more than problem solving and the storage/retrieval of data. It involves matters as real and vague as knowing, understanding, sensing, and loving; it must explain aesthetics as well as the aiming of artillery. In *AIC*, Tomkins asked that we reclaim the almost archaic term "mind" for the combination of affect and cognition, and called that coassembly "the minding system."

"Cognitions coassembled with affects become hot and urgent. Affects coassembled with cognitions become better informed and smarter." Whatever is processed by the cognitive system must be amplified by the motivational system—pure transformation cannot matter very much without the special oomph provided by affect. Raw data amplified without transformation would bring little advantage to the organism. "The blind mechanisms must be given sight; the weak mechanisms must be given strength. All information is at once biased and informed." Intrinsic to humanness is this "minding" or caring about what we know. The special function of the minding system is the ability to convert the raw texts of affect and cognition into the compelling poetry of scripts, which provide the rules that turn data into language with grammar, semantics, and ways of living. Volume IV contains Tomkins's early vision of "human being theory," studies that he presented as incomplete and ambiguous simply because the elusive complexity of our many systems prevented the development of a unified theory.

His unique definition of cognition as the process of data transformation solved a problem largely ignored by previous thinkers. Even casual study of the brain reveals the integration of sensory and motor mechanisms with the regions traditionally considered cognitive. Eyes and ears transform vibratory information in the forms we term sight and sound, and which we consider as intrinsically separate realms of data acquisition. Yet our fellow mammal the bat and the avian owl produce maps of astonishing precision by transforming sonic data that allow precise localization of both prey and predator. To Tomkins, there is no separate mechanism that can be defined as specifically and distinctively cognitive, just as there is no separate mechanism that can be defined as purely motor or purely sensory. Kinesthesia provides the central assembly with data no less vital than sight or hearing. It is the gestalt, the totality of our attributes that makes us human. Data will always be transformed in the process of acquisition, and transformed data must be amplified if it is to be used. Cognition and affect must be separated for the purpose of study, but they must work together if we are to be whole.

The Reader's Quandary

There is a special sort of "nerve" or "guts" required for a close reading of Tomkins's overwhelming masterpiece. Even to know about *AIC* means that one has thought a great deal about the concepts of motivation and consciousness, and wondered whether there was some way to draw together all the disparate theories found in ordinary textbooks. I got here because a senior colleague suggested that a journal article on empathy by psychoanalyst Michael Franz Basch might inform my early musings about what I soon understood as affective resonance. His reference to a 1981 article by Tomkins led me to purchase Volume I of *AIC*, which I found so densely written that immediately I enlisted the aid of Dr. Kelly to form the study group that after Tomkins died became *The Silvan S. Tomkins Institute*. Under the direction of Dr. Kelly, we mounted public colloquia and developed an international system of study groups through which several hundred scholars have enjoyed guided entry into this compelling set of ideas.

As mentioned in the opening paragraphs of this Prologue, because of Tomkins's personal peculiarities the final pair of volumes that constitute *AIC* were released 30 years after Volumes I and II. Only one vendor, the Joseph Fox Bookshop of Philadelphia, maintained the entire set in stock and handled the needs of scholars all over the world for it as well as the other books written by our group. This present publication of the entire set as what we have come to call a supervolume has been made possible by a grant from the 1675 Foundation, which has taken special interest in our work. By allowing the Tomkins Institute to underwrite this publication and act as co-publisher, the new management of Springer Publishing Company has been able to make *AIC* both affordable and accessible to a large audience. Our gratitude to both organizations is great. Nevertheless, our experience with this material suggests that it is most easily learned in the company of others. We hope you will enjoy, learn from, and perhaps add your wisdom to the study of affect, imagery, and consciousness.

Donald L. Nathanson, MD
Executive Director
The Silvan S. Tomkins Institute

Volume III

The Negative Affects: Anger and Fear

To Irving E. Alexander

Silvan S. Tomkins received his Ph.D. in philosphy from the University of Pennsylvania. Following two years of postdoctoral work in philosophy at Harvard University with Quine, Sheffer, and Perry, he became a research assistant at the Clinic under the direction of Murray and White. He has taught at the Harvard Psychological Clinic. During this time he participated in the second decade of personological research at the Clinic under the direction of Murray and White. He has taught at the Harvard and Princeton Universities, the Graduate Center of the City University of New York, and Livingstone College of Rutgers University. He is currently Professor, Department of Social Systems Sciences, University of Pennsylvania. His long-term project is a general theory of personality.

PREFACE

It is thirty-five years since the general outlines of my theory were first presented at the fourteenth International Congress of Psychology, in Montreal in 1954. At that time I had intended to reopen issues which had long remained in disrepute in American psychology : affect, imagery, and consciousness. Today those issues are no longer in disrepute. They are now, indeed, at the center of our concern. The black box of behaviorism has been illuminated by neurophysiologists, biochemists, phenomenologists, cognitive theorists, and affect investigators. The heart and mind have been regained as the proper study of human beings.

It is twenty-eight years since the first volume of *Affect Imagery Consciousness* was published, 27 years since the publication of Volume 2. What was originally to have been a one-volume work has since grown into a multivolume treatise. The proliferation of fields of application of the theory has delayed the completion of the work. The growing cost of publication, along with the increasing diversification of fields of application, has prompted me to sacrifice the unity of presentation of the theory in favor of several separate publications. I will presently publish separate volumes dealing with script personality theory, psychology of knowledge and ideology, personality and the face, the addictive dependencies, psychotherapy, and a theory of value.

This third volume of *Affect Imagery Consciousness* includes such revisions of my theory of affect as the intervening years of research and thought by myself and others have prompted. It also includes the two primary affects which Freud made the cornerstones of psychoanalysis: anger and anxiety. I had originally intended to treat these affects in much less detail than I had the affects of excitement, enjoyment, shame, distress, disgust, and dissmell, which had been neglected by Freud. I have, as planned, given an abbreviated account of anxiety because of Freud's powerful analysis of its role and because of the massive accumulation of knowledge about it in the past several decades. However, the reader may be puzzled by the extended treatment of anger and violence in this volume. I have deviated from my original intention to treat this affect in reduced detail on two grounds. First, my development of script theory enabled a more searching analysis of anger than had been possible 20 years ago. Second, the problems of ideology and violence have grown increasingly strident and urgent at the international level, prompting me to increase the depth and scope of my inquiry. The consequence is that most of Volume 3 concerns anger and violence, while anxiety remains a smaller part of this theory of affect. Volume 4 will include the theory of memory, perception, consciousness, imagery, cognition, and action as these interact as a feedback mechanism. This part of the theory was originally the major part of the model presented in 1954. I was at that time more interested in what I called the theory of the human being than in the theory of personality. I felt then, and now continue to believe, that an understanding of the separate, but matched, components of the human being is a necessary foundation for understanding that more complex integration which we call personality. General, experimental psychology had, I felt, abdicated its responsibility to provide the theoretical base for the study of personality. It was my intention to provide such a base. This defined the scope of what I thought would be a one-volume work on a model of the human being. So as I became more acquainted with affect as a motivational mechanism, one volume grew into three volumes, and then these generated others in personality and social science. Paradoxically, the non-affect part of Volume 4 is what was originally the major part of the one-volume work, completed, but not published, in 1954. The observation of my son's face and affect during a sabbatical year in 1955 forced me to elaborate the treatment of affect and so delayed the publication of the first volume until 1962, eight years later.

My indebtedness, in the 27-year interval between Volumes 2 and 3 is to the many individuals who prompted me either to enlarge the scope of my inquiry or to deepen it. Whether they encouraged more intensive or extensive inquiry, they enriched my understanding beyond what I might otherwise have ventured.

I was fortunate to have been asked by Martin Duberman to recom- mend someone who might write a chapter on the psychology of the abolitionists for his book *The Antislavery Vanguard.* On scanning the historical material I volunteered to do the study myself. From this I developed a theory of commitment and a study of the lives of the major abolitionists. More importantly, it prompted me to learn more of what has since become the field of psychohistory.

From my student Kozuko Tsurumi I learned something of the culture of Japan and that my theory had some implication for the study of culture and society. These were reflected in her *Social Change and the Individual.*

Marion Levy extended my vision to the study of the sociology of the family by inviting me to consider the relevance of affect theory for his theory of the family. This appeared in A. J. Coale, L. A. Fallers, M. J. Levy, D. M. Schneider, and S. S. Tomkins, *Aspects of the Analysis of Family Structure.* I am further indebted to Marion Levy for his continued intellectual support and stimulation and his belief that my theory of affect was as important for an understanding of society as it was for the study of the individual.

I am indebted to the political scientist Robert North for asking me to provide him with an affect dictionary which he might use for the analysis of political documents. This took a few years to do and ended in failure, owing to the complexity and ambiguity of the language of affect. Nonetheless, from this failure I learned important lessons about the language of affect and the historical development of consciousness as it is reflected in the absence, presence, degree of differentiation, and mixtures of affect with non-affect meanings in different languages.

I am indebted to John William Ward, who asked me to join him one year, in the Special Program in American Civilization at Princeton University, on the topic "Sigmund Freud and American Culture." From this exercise I learned something of how seminal ideas gradually capture the imagination of everyman in contemporary society.

I am indebted to William Gilmore for deepening my knowledge of and interest in psychohistory. His scholarship and passion for ideas have held my attention in extended dialogues.

From my friend John Sinton, environmental scientist, I have learned much that I surely would have learned in no other way. To my astonishment, he sensitized me to the relevance of the biology and psychology of affect, to an understanding of its role in the ecosystem of earth, air, fire, and water. Because of his friendship I undertook long-term collaborative work with him which helped us both better understand the world we live in.

To my friend Edmund Leites, philosopher and ethical theorist, I owe an ongoing dialogue about the theory of value and a reawakened interest in the field I abandoned 45 years ago—a field to which I intend to return, as I now review it, in the light of affect theory.

To my friend John Demos I am indebted for a deepened understanding of the role of affect in American history, first in witchcraft and second in the critical shifts in the socialization of the affects of conscience in Puritan America and then in 19th-century America.

To my friend Russel Ackoff, also a former student of philosopher Edgar A. Singer, I owe the invitation to join his department of Social Systems Sciences at the University of Pennsylvania after I had retired. There I was exposed to the problems of social systems in the industrial and political setting and was able to enlarge the application of affect and script theory to the vital areas of work and political power.

When I first engaged the psychoanalytic community in dialogue in the late 1950s I encountered resonance from only Lawrence Zelig Freedman whom I first met as a fellow at the Center for Advanced Study in the Behavioral Sciences, at Stanford. We have continued that dialogue to the present, since I became a fellow of his Institute of Social and Behavioral Pathology. In the past decade there has been an increasing interest in affect theory within the psychoanalytic community. I am particularly indebted to Michael Basch for his sustained support as well as to Frank Broucek and Samuel Kaplan. Within the past five years Donald Nathanson has brought his own psychiatric and biological expertise to bear on this theory and will shortly publish his account of it. I am deeply indebted to him not only for a continuing searching dialogue but also for a friendship which has sustained me when my spirit was at its lowest ebb, shepherding me through the most serious medical crisis of my life.

This theory has been very substantially shaped and enriched by a most improbable friendship and dialogue between a Jewish son of an atheist and a truly Christian theologian, the Reverend David McShane. For over twenty years his deep excitement at the relevance of affect theory for understanding the religious impulse has prompted a resonance in me toward the Judeo-Christian tradition I could have experienced in no other way. His extraordinary love of humanity combined with his passion for ideas made it impossible for me to continue in my totally secular posture. When my energies were at their lowest ebb, I would be rescued time and again by his loving Christianity.

I am indebted to my neighbor, Bob Curtis, for rescuing this manuscript in the face of a hurricane swamping my beachfront home. I also owe special thanks to Dr. Robert Goldstine for helping me, time and again, through dental emergencies which had brought my work to a halt.

I am of course also indebted to many fellow psychologists. To Fred Emery and Eric Trist, then at Tavistock, I owe much. Their critical appreciation of my work reassured me deeply and inspired me to continue on the long road ahead. They published *Affect Imagery Consciousness* under the Tavistock imprint in England and invited me to address the Tavistock group, and Fred Emery engaged me in his standardization of the Tomkins-Horn Picture Arrangement Test on a representative sample of the British population. This represented the first time that a personality test had been standardized on representative samples in two societies, using standard polling techniques.

Jerome Singer joined me in forming the Center for Research in Cognition and Affect at the Graduate Center of the City University of New York. I was its first director; he was its second director. He has, more than any other psychologist, taught me some of the implication of affect theory for understanding human development, particularly cognitive development. He has created, through his pioneering studies in play and daydreaming, a critical bridge between cognition and affect—two fields which are capable of being centrifuged apart via hypertrophy of affect or cognition. It is a testament to the integration of his personality that he has sought to close this perennial gap.

Because of the stimulation of Daniel Horn, Director of the Clearinghouse for Smoking Information of United States Public Health Service, who posed me the unsolved but urgent problem of addiction to smoking cigarettes, I spent several years in intensive research on the problem of the addictive dependencies. To guide this research I constructed a model of smoking behavior, which was tested by Daniel Horn in several large-scale studies of the United States population. When this model was substantially confirmed, Fred Ikard and I, under a grant from the American Cancer Society, submitted the model to further experimental inquiry. These studies would in all probability have been further extended except for the tragic and untimely death of my young collaborator Fred Ikard. Our relationship had been an exceptionally close one, and the shock of his death created such a vacuum in my laboratory that these studies were never resumed after the publication of the final report of the completed studies.

I owe a deep personal and intellectual debt to David Loye, whose passion for the understanding of the role of ideology in society and whose appreciation of my theory sustained my own interest during long periods of time characterized by Bell as "The End of Ideology." His further empirical investigations and his development of the center position as a creative synthesis of the left and right inspired me to continue to develop the implication of my theory of ideology.

To George Atwood I am indebted for the application of my theory of nuclear scenes and the psychology of knowledge to an under- standing of the relationship between the personality of personality theorists and the nature of the personality theories which they generate. I am also indebted to him for his interest in and collaboration on the study of the face in relation to Rorschach and Thematic Apperception Test protocols.

To Paul Ekman and Carroll Izard, the two major investigators in the field of affect research, I owe several years of close contact and collaboration. Paul Ekman was the first American psychologist to respond to my work with a sustained program of empirical research to test and extend my early findings. Using some of the photographs I had developed for the study "What and Where Are the Primary Affects ?" he was able to demonstrate that the validity demonstrated in that monograph held across many cultures. We then collaborated on the development of FAST—a facial affect scoring technique. Since then he has, independently, developed an affect encyclopedia for the measurement of facial affect, which is a major contribution to the study of facial affect. Although I began by teaching him how to decode the face, he has ended by teaching me much, owing to his sustained investigation of the facial musculature. Shortly after I met Paul Ekman, I met Carroll Izard. We collaborated on the editing of *Affect, Cognition, and Personality*, and I have served as a consultant on his cross-cultural studies of facial affect. Using pictures of his own, but employing the same categories of affect that I did in "What and Where Are the Primary Affects?" he was able to demonstrate that there was a widespread consensus in the judgment of facial affect across many cultures. I learned from his results with the Japanese that their sensitivity to disgust photographs was so marked as to justify separating contempt from disgust, a conclusion which I had suspected from other data of mine in the study of ideology. We have also collaborated on the study of anxiety in Spielberger's *Anxiety and Behavior*.

To Seymour Rosenberg, colleague and dear friend, I owe the invitation to join him in forming the department of psychology at Livingston College—Rutgers University. Our association, both intellectual and personal, has been deeply rewarding and has sustained me during several years of varied Sturm and Drang. Further, his excitement at the frontier of personality at which he works has evoked my respect and, via contagion, a sense that personology is about to be reborn.

To Gershen Kaufman, pioneer in the study of shame, I am indebted for deepening my understanding of both my own theory and his theory.

To my good friend William Stone I owe a sustained interest and research program in my Polarity theory of ideology. He has also undertaken a restandardization of the Polarity scale which he revised with my cooperation. By his enthusiasm and energy he has revivified a lively interest in this theory among political psychologists and political scientists.

To my friend Donald Mosher I owe a stunning extension of script theory to an understanding of the macho personality, based on an integration of his many years of research in this area and a deep understanding of script theory, which he mastered by a deep investment of his unusual talent and energy.

I am indebted to Virginia Demos in many ways. She will edit some of my collected papers in the near future. Her sustained friendship combined with an understanding of my theory, which taught me about many of its implications I had not understood, and her creative use of it in a sustained program of research in infant affect development, all created a debt I gratefully acknowledge.

To Ursula Springer my debt is that of an author who promised, in what he thought was good faith, to meet deadlines which were endlessly postponed, so that in the end even he began to doubt whether this work would ever be completed. For her endless patience, goodwill, and support, I am forever grateful.

To Rae Carlson, founder of the Society for Personology, I owe twenty years of dialogue and friendship, as stimulating as it was supportive and critical, issuing in a systematic program of sustained research in script theory, which constitutes the most coherent corpus of theoretically informed investigation of the theory represented in this volume.

To my mentor Henry A. Murray, who died recently, I offer this belated gift to the founder of personology.

In the preface to Volume 1 I said that my greatest single debt was to Irving E. Alexander. The only error in that judgment was human—the inability to predict how much twenty-eight years would increase that debt. This volume is therefore dedicated to him.

S. S. T.
Strathmere, New Jersey

Volume IV

Cognition: Duplication and Transformation of Information

To Donald L. Mosher

PREFACE

As I wrote in *Computer Simulation of Personality,* "In the late 1930's I was seized with the fantasy of a machine, fearfully and wonderfully made in the image of man. He was to be no less human than automated, so I called him the humanomaton. Could one design a truly humanoid machine? This would either expose the ignorance or reveal the self-consciousness of his creator, or both." (Tomkins, 1963a, p. 63)

While pursuing this line of thought, I encountered Wiener's (1960) early papers on cybernetics. These fascinated me and encouraged me in my project of the design of a humanomaton. One could not engage in such a project without the concept of multiple assemblies of varying degrees of independence, dependence, interdependence, and control and transformation of one by another.

It was this general conception which, one day in the late 1940's resulted in my first understanding of the role of the affect mechanism as a separate but amplifying co-assembly. I almost fell out of my chair in surprise and excitement when I suddenly realized that the panic of one who experiences the suffocation of interruption of his vital air supply has nothing to do with the anoxic drive signal per se. A human being could be, and often is, terrified about anything under the sun. It was a short step to see that excitement had nothing per se to do with sexuality or with hunger, and that the apparent urgency of the drive system was borrowed from its co-assembly with appropriate affects as necessary amplifiers. Freud's id suddenly appeared to be a paper tiger since sexuality, as he best knew, was the most finicky of drives, easily rendered impotent by shame or anxiety or boredom or rage. This insight gave me the necessary theoretical base to pursue the nature of this system further.

The first public presentation of this model was at a colloquium at Yale University, in the early 1950's, under the title, "Drive Theory is Dead," delivered with fear and trembling in the stronghold of Freudian and Hullian drive theory. To my surprise, it was well received. In 1954, at the 14th International Congress of Psychology in Montreal, it was presented as "Consciousness and Unconscious in a Model of the Human Being." This paper was rejected for publication by every American journal of psychology. It was however translated and published in France, at the initiative of Lagache, one of the members of the symposium at Montreal, by Muriel Cahen as "La conscience et l'inconscient representes dans un modele del être humain" (pp. 275–586 in *La Psychanalyse,* Volume Premier, edited by Jacques Lacan, Presses Universitaires de France, Paris 1956).

This paper was a condensation of the original one-volume work, *Affect Imagery Consciousness,* completed in 1955. Chapter One of what was to be published as Volume I of that work represents a condensation of that original volume on human being theory, representing affect, imagery, and consciousness in equal portions. The major presentation of the cognitive model was deferred to the present Volume IV.

This occurred because of the birth of my son in 1955 when I was on sabbatical leave. This so fleshed out the role of affect in the model that it required three volumes in itself before the original model could be seen in perspective and so was deferred until the present time (1991).

Beginning shortly after his birth, I observed him early, for hours on end. I was struck with the massiveness of the crying response. It included not only very loud vocalization and facial muscular responses, but also large changes in blood flow to the face and engagement of all the striate musculature of the body. It was a massive total bodily response which, however, seemed to center on the face. Freud had suggested that the birth cry was the prototype of anxiety, but my son didn't seem anxious. What then was this facial response? I labelled it "distress." Next, I was to observe intense excitement on his face when he labored after the first few months of his life to shape his mouth to try to imitate the speech he heard. He would struggle for minutes on end, and then give up, apparently exhausted and discouraged. I noted the intensity of the smiling response to his mother and to me, and again I became aware that nothing in psychoanalytic theory (or any other personality theory at that time) paid any attention to the specificity of enjoyment as contrasted with excitement.

This volume thus became the fourth instead of the first and only volume, primarily because the unexpected riches of affect became salient in Volumes I and II, and the later development of Script Theory as a sequel to Affect Theory became Volume III. This is also the reason why the contemporary reader may find the bulk of it both new and unfamiliar and old and dated. It was written 40 years ago, and I found little reason to change it. In some quarters it will be as persuasive or unpersuasive as it would have been in 1955. With considerable hubris, I am as pleased with it now as I was then. It is not as radical a theory now as it was then, but I think it is no less true, and significant parts of it remain little explored and radical. I am pleased that 40 years have ravaged it so little. The only recent updating is to be found in the first chapter on cognition.

I am indebted to my colleagues and students at Princeton who shared with me their varied expertises in general experimental psychology. First to Irving Alexander, who was a Hullian and an auditory experimenter at that time, who via a decade of talk became a personologist under my guidance as I picked up a smattering of learning and sensory theory.

To Edward Engel, first as a graduate student, then as a consultant to the psychology department of the Philadelphia Psychiatric Hospital, I owe my knowledge of the phenomena and theory of steroscopic perception, particularly in conjunction with the application of the stereoscope to the study of depressive patients. Without his help this study could not have been initiated. To my former colleagues William Ittelson and William Smith I also owe thanks for what smattering I possess of the lore of visual perception.

To my former colleague Charles Reed I am indebted for a critical experimental test of my theory of visual perception.

To Mario Halle, Fellow at the Center for Advanced Study in the Behavioral Sciences, I am indebted for much rewarding discussion of ideas we had come to independently over different routes. I particularly profited from his conception of analysis by synthesis in which an idea first proposed by D. M. MacKay (1956), independently conceived by me, was also independently carried to a more powerful formulation by Halle. MacKay, Halle and myself, each unaware of the others' work, had arrived at the same solution to the problem of perception.

To Robert Abelson I am indebted for the clarification of some of my ideas on the nature of memory during a week-long discussion we had at the Center. We were both indebted to the Center for the financial support which made it possible for us to confer on the general problem of computer simulation.

I am indebted to Jerome Singer, who joined in forming the Center for Research in Cognition and Affect at the Graduate Center of the City University of New York. I was its first director. He was its second director. I have learned from his pioneering studies in play and day-dreaming the critical bridge between affect and cognition, a perennial gap that he, above every other theorist, has sought to close.

I am deeply indebted to David McShane for two decades of shared intellectual excitement about the ideas in this volume, communication which was frequent, enduring and wonderful.

I owe my life and final editing of this volume to my son and two friends, who gave generously of their time and love to nurse me round the clock through a perilous illness. These were Mark Tomkins, Corky Devlin and Amy Cook.

To Barbara Watkins, Senior Editor and Vice President of Springer Publishing Company, I owe a unique debt—an entirely rewarding and productive relationship in the editing of Volumes III and IV, altogether rare in my experience.

Finally, I dedicate this volume to Donald L. Mosher, with whom I have been working for the past decade on the integration of this volume with the previous volumes and new works of his own. This has been most productive for him and for me. I look forward to the several volumes of his which will result from this collaboration.

S. S. T.
Strathmere, New Jersey

ACKNOWLEDGMENTS

There are several persons without whom this fourth volume could not have been completed. The publisher, along with the author's son, Mark W. Tomkins, would like to acknowledge the dedication and hard work of the following individuals:

Lauren Abramson, Ph.D., for her extensive research contributing to the completion of the bibliography.

E. Virginia Demos, Ed.D., for her thoroughness in editing the page proofs and epilogue.

Walter "Corky" Devlin, whose friendship, devotion, and nurturance during the final year of the author's life made his attention to this project possible.

Donald L. Mosher, Ph.D., for his outstanding work on the epilogue.

Donald L. Nathanson, M.D., who generously provided his time as a contributing editor, and who also worked extensively on the bibliography.

Others deserving of our special thanks include:

Russell Ackoff, Ph.D.
Irving Alexander, Ph.D.
Rae Carleson, Ph.D.
Amy Cook
William Cowan, M.B.A.
Paul Ekman, Ph.D.
Reverend David McShane
Seymour Rosenberg, Ph.D.
Jerome Singer, Ph.D.
John Sinton, Ph.D.
Brewster Smith, Ph.D.
William Stone, Ph.D.
Barbara Watkins

Mark Tomkins would also like to extend a special thanks to Ursula Springer, Ph.D, Mary Grace Luke, Pamela Lankas, and the staff of Springer Publishing for the patience, confidence, and support that were required over a thirty-year period to make all four volumes possible.

Volume III

THE NEGATIVE AFFECTS: ANGER AND FEAR

Part I

MODIFICATIONS, CLARIFICATIONS, AND DEVELOPMENTS IN AFFECT THEORY

Chapter 24

Affect as Analogic Amplification: Modifications and Clarifications in Theory

The Theory presented in *Affect, Imagery, Consciousness* in 1962 has since been developed and modified in five essential ways. First, the theory of affect as amplification I now specify as analogic amplification. Second, I believe now that it is the skin of the face, rather than the musculature, which is the major mechanism of analogic amplification. Third, a substantial quantity of the affect we experience as adults is pseudo-, backed-up affect. Fourth, affect amplifies not only its own activator but also the response to both that activator and to itself. Fifth, I now distinguish nine rather than eight innate affects. Originally contempt and disgust were treated as variants of a unitary response. I now distinguish disgust from dissmell, both as innate and contempt as a learned analog of dissmell.

SUMMARY OF THE THEORY OF AFFECT AS AMPLIFICATION

I continue to view affect as the primary innate biological motivating mechanism, more urgent than drive deprivation and pleasure and more urgent even than physical pain. That this is so is not obvious, but it is readily demonstrated. Consider that almost any interference with breathing will immediately arouse the most desperate gasping for breath. Consider the drivenness of the tumescent, erect male. Consider the urgency of desperate hunger. These are the intractable driven states that prompted the answer to the question "What do human beings really want?" to be: "The human animal is driven to breathe, to sex, to drink, and to eat." And yet this apparent urgency proves to be an illusion. It is *not* an illusion that one must have air, water, food to maintain oneself and sex to reproduce oneself. What is illusory is the biological and psychological source of the apparent urgency of the desperate quality of the hunger, air, and sex drives. Consider these drive states more closely. When someone puts his hand over my mouth and nose, I become terrified. But this panic, this terror, is in no way a part of the drive mechanism. I can be terrified at the possibility of losing my job, or of developing cancer, or at the possibility of the loss of my beloved. Fear or terror is an innate affect which can be triggered by a wide variety of circumstances. But if the rate of anoxic deprivation becomes slower, as, for example, in the case of wartime pilots who refused to wear oxygen masks at 30,000 feet, then there develops not a panic but a euphoric state; and some of these men met their deaths with smiles on their lips. The smile is the affect of enjoyment, in no way specific to slow anoxic deprivation.

Consider more closely the tumescent male with an erection. He is sexually excited, we say. He is indeed excited, but no one has ever observed an excited penis. It is a man who is excited and who breathes hard, not in the penis but in the chest, the face, in the nose and nostrils. But such excitement is in no way peculiarly sexual. The same excitement can be experienced, without the benefit of an erection, at mathematics—beauty bare—at poetry, at a rise in the stock market. Instead of these representing sublimations of sexuality, it is rather that sexuality, in order to become possible, must borrow its potency from the affect of excitement. The drive must be assisted by an *amplifier* if it is to work at all. Freud, better than anyone else, knew that the blind, pushy, imperious Id was the most fragile of impulses, readily disrupted by fear, by shame, by rage, by boredom. At the first sign of affect *other* than excitement, there is impotence and frigidity. The penis proves to be a paper tiger in the absence of appropriate affective amplification.

The affect system is therefore the primary motivational system because without its amplification, nothing else matters—and with its amplification, anything else *can* matter. It thus combines *urgency* and *generality*. It lends its power to memory, to perception, to thought, and to action no less than to the drives.

MODIFICATION 1: ANALOGIC AMPLIFICATION

My original theory of affect as amplification was flawed by a serious ambiguity. I had unwittingly assumed a similarity between electronic amplification and affective amplification, such that in both there was an increase in gain of the signal. If such were the case, what was amplified would remain essentially the same except that it would become louder. But affects are separate mechanisms, involving bodily responses quite distinct from the other bodily responses they are presumed to amplify.

How can one response of our body amplify another response? It can do this by being similar to that response—but also different. It is an analog amplifier. The affect mechanism is like the pain mechanism in this respect. If we cut our hand, saw it bleeding, but had no innate pain receptors, we would know we had done something which needed repair, but there would be no urgency to it. Like our automobile which needs a tune-up, we might well let it go until next week when we had more time. But the pain mechanism, like the affect mechanism, so amplifies our awareness of the injury which activates it that we are forced to be concerned, and concerned immediately. The biological utility of such analogic amplification is selfevident. The injury, as such, in the absence of pain, simply does not hurt. The pain receptors have evolved to make us hurt and care about injury and disease. Pain is an analog of injury in its inherent similarity. Contrast pain with an orgasm, as a possible analog. If instead of pain, we always had an orgasm to injury, we would be biologically destined to bleed to death. Affect receptors are no less compelling. Our hair stands on end, and we sweat in terror. Our face reddens as our blood pressure rises in anger. Our blood vessels dilate and our face becomes pleasantly warm as we smile in enjoyment. These are compelling analogs of what arouses terror, rage, and enjoyment.

These experiences constitute one form of affect amplification. A second form of affect amplification occurs also by virtue of the similarity of their profile, in time, to their activating trigger. Just as a pistol shot is a stimulus which is very sudden in onset, very brief in duration, and equally sudden in decay—so its amplifying affective analog, the startle response, mimics the pistol shot by being equally sudden in onset, brief in duration, and equally sudden in decay. Therefore, affect, by being analogous in the quality of the feelings from its specific receptors, as well as in its profile of activation, maintenance, and decay, amplifies and extends the duration and impact of whatever triggers the affect. Epileptics do not startle, according to Landis and Hunt (1939). Their experienced world is different in this one fundamental way. If epileptics had in addition lacked fear and rage, their world would have become even more different than the usual humanly experienced world. They experience a pistol shot as sudden but *not* startling. A world experienced without any affect at all, due to a complete genetic defect in the whole spectrum of innate affects would be a pallid, meaningless world. We would know *that* things happened, but we could not care whether they did or not.

By being immediately activated and thereby coassembled with its activator, affect either makes good things better or bad things worse, by conjointly simulating its activator in its profile of neural firing and by adding a special analogic quality which is intensely rewarding or punishing. In illustrating the simulation of an activating stimulus (e.g., a pistol shot) by the startle response, which was equally sudden in onset, equally brief in duration, and equally sudden in decay, I somewhat exaggerated the goodness of fit between activator and affect to better illustrate the general principle. Having done so, let me now be more precise in the characterization of the degree of similarity in profile of neural firing between activator and affect activated. I have presented a model of the innate activators of the primary affects, in which every possible major general neural contingency will innately activate different specific affects. As I explained earlier, increased gradients of rising neural firing will activate interest, fear, or surprise, as the slope of increasing density of neural firing becomes steeper. Enjoyment is activated by a decreasing gradient of neural firing. Distress is activated by a sustained level of neural firing which exceeds an optimal level by an as yet undetermined magnitude, and anger is also activated by a nonoptimal level of neural firing but one which is substantially higher than that which activates distress. Increase, decrease, or level of neural firing are in this model the sufficient conditions for activating specific affects. Analogic amplification, therefore, is based upon *one* of these three distinctive features rather than all of them. It so happens that the startle simulates the steepness of the gradient of onset, the brief plateau of maintenance and the equally steep gradient of decline of profile of the pistol shot and its internal neural correlate—but that is not the general case. Analogic simulation is based on the similarity to the sufficient characteristic of the adequate activator—not on *all* of its characteristics. Thus, it is the decay alone of a stimulus which is analogically simulated in enjoyment. If one places electrodes on the wrist of a subject, permits fear to build, then removes the electrodes suddenly, we can invariably activate a smile of relief at just that moment. This amplifies (or makes more so) the declining neural stimulation from the reduction of fear. Therefore, enjoyment amplifies by stimulating decreasing gradients of neural stimulation. Interest, fear, and surprise amplify by simulating increasing gradients of neural stimulation. Distress and anger amplify by simulating maintained levels of stimulation.

MODIFICATION 2: THE SKIN RECEPTORS OF THE FACE ARE THE MAJOR LOCUS OF ANALOGIC AMPLIFICATION

The second modification in my theory concerns the exact loci of the rewarding and punishing amplifying analogs. From the start, I have emphasized the face and voice as the major loci of the critical feedback which was experienced as affect. The voice I still regard as a major locus and will discuss its role in the next section.

The significance of the face in interpersonal relations cannot be exaggerated. It is not only a communication center for the sending and receiving of information of all kinds, but because it is the organ of affect expression and communication, it is necessarily brought under strict social control. There are universal taboos on looking too directly into the eyes of the other because of the likelihood of affect contagion, as well as escalation, because of the unwillingness to express affect promiscuously and because of concern lest others achieve control through knowledge of one's otherwise private feelings. Man is primarily a voyeuristic animal not only because vision is his most informative sense but because the shared eye-to-eye interaction is the most intimate relationship possible between human beings. There is in this way complete mutuality between two selves, each of which simultaneously is aware of the self and the other. Indeed, the intimacy of sexual intercourse is ordinarily attenuated, lest it become too intimate, by being performed in the dark. In the psychoanalytic myth, the crime of the son is voyeuristic by witnessing the "primal scene," and Oedipus is punished, in kind, by blindness.

The taboo on the shared interocular experience is easily exposed. If I were to ask you to turn to another person and stare directly into his eyes while permitting the other to stare directly into your eyes, you would become aware of the taboo. Ordinarily, we confront each other by my looking at the bridge of your nose and your looking at my cheekbone. If our eyes should happen to meet directly, the confrontation is minimized by glancing down or away, by letting the eyes go slightly out of focus, or by attentuating the visual datum by making it ground to the sound of the other's voice, which is made more figural. The taboo is not only a taboo on looking too intimately but also on exposing the taboo by too obviously avoiding direct confrontation. These two strategies are taught by shaming the child for staring into the eyes of visitors and then shaming the child a second time for hanging his head in shame before the guest.

Only the young or the young in heart are entirely free of the taboo. Those adults whose eyes are caught by the eyes of the other in the shared interocular intimacy may fall in love on such an occasion or, having fallen in love, thereby express the special intimacy they have recaptured from childhood.

The face now appears to me still the central site of the affect responses and their feedback, but I have now come to regard the skin, in general, and the skin of the face, in particular, as of the greatest importance in producing the feel of affect.

In *Affect, Imagery, Consciousness,* (1962, Vol. 1, p. 244) I have described the affect system as consisting of thirteen components, beginning with the innate affect programs and including affect motor messages. My statement that I regard the face and voice as the central site of affect responses and their feedback must not be interpreted to mean that the whole affect system and its supporting mechanisms are found in the face. Analogically, one might argue for the importance of the thumb and fingers in man's evolution without specifying that there is a forearm, biceps, body, and brain which support the thumb.

Further, it is now clear, as it was not then, that the brain is sensitive to its own synthesized chemical endorphins which serve as analgesics and thus radically attenuate pain and all the negative affects which are recruited by pain on both innate and learning bases.

My original observations of the intensity of infantile affect, of how an infant was, for example, seized by his own crying, left no doubt in my mind that what the face was doing with its muscles and blood vessels, as well as with its accompanying vocalization, was at the heart of the matter. This seemed to me not an "expression" of anything else but rather the major phenomenon. I then spent a few years in posing professional actors and others to simulate facial affect. McCarter and I (1964) were rewarded by a correlation of + .86 between the judgments of trained judges as to what affects they saw on the faces of these subjects as presented in still photographs and what I had intended these sets of muscular responses to represent. This success was gratifying, after so many years of indifferent and variable findings in this field, but it was also somewhat misleading in overemphasizing the role of innately patterned facial muscular responses in the production of affect. I was further confirmed in these somewhat misleading results by the successes of Paul Ekman and Carroll Izard. Paul Ekman (1969), using some of my photographs, was able to demonstrate a wide cultural consensus, even in very primitive remote preliterate societies. Carroll Izard (1969), using different photographs but the same conceptual scheme, further extended these impressive results to many other literate societies.[1] The combined weight of all these investigations was most impressive, but I continued to be troubled by one small fact. The contraction of no other set of muscles in the body had *any* apparent motivation properties. Thus, if I were angry, I might clench my fist and hit someone, but if I simply clenched my fist, this would in no way guarantee I would become angry. Muscles appeared to be specialized for action and not for affect. Why then was the smile so easily and so universally responded to as an affect? Why did someone who was crying seem so distressed and so unhappy? Further, from an evolutionary point of view, we know that different functions are piled indiscriminately on top of structures which may originally have evolved to support quite different functions. The tongue was an organ of eating

[1] Izard's results were not quite so good as those of Ekman for, I think, two reasons: first, his photograph selection was guided primarily by empirical criteria rather than theoretically chosen; i.e., if subjects agreed that a face showed interest it was retained, despite the fact that the clue to such consensus might be that the subject was depicted staring at some object. Second, the critical distinction between innate and backed-up affect was not observed in Izard's picture selection.

before it was an organ of speech. The muscles of the face were also probably involved in eating before they were used as vehicles of affect—though we do not know this for a fact. It is, of course, possible that the complex affect displays on the human face evolved primarily as communication mechanisms rather than as sources of motivating feedback. My intuition was, and still is, that the communication of affect is a secondary spin-off function rather than the primary function. This is not however to minimize its importance *as* communication.

The primary importance of motivating feedback over communication, however, would appear to have been the case with a closely related mechanism—that of pain. The cry of pain does communicate, but the feeling of pain does not. It powerfully motivates the person who feels it, in much the same way that affect does. That someone else is informed of this is not, however, mediated by the pain receptors in themselves but by the cry of distress which usually accompanies it. I therefore began to look at affect analogs such as pain and sexual sensitivity and fatigue for clues about the nature of the motivating properties of the affect mechanisms.

I soon became aware of a paradox—that three of the most compelling states to which the human being is vulnerable arise on the surface of the skin. Torture via skin stimulation has been used for centuries to shape and compel human beings to act against their own deepest wishes and values. Sexual seduction, again via skin stimulation, particularly of the genitals, has also prompted human beings on occasion to violate their own wishes and values. Finally, fatigue to the point of extreme sleepiness appears to be localized in the skin surrounding the eyes. This area will sometimes be rubbed in an effort to change the ongoing stimulation and ward off sleepiness. But in the end, it appears to be nothing but an altered responsiveness of skin receptors, especially in the eyelids, which make it impossible for the sleepy person to maintain the state of wakefulness. He cannot keep his eyes open, though he may be powerfully motivated to do so. I then found further evidence that the skin, rather than "expressing" internal events, in diving animals led and commanded widespread autonomic changes throughout the body in order to conserve oxygen for the vulnerable brain. When the beak of a diving bird is stimulated by the water as it dives for fish, this change produces profound general changes such as vasoconstriction within the body as a whole. Investigators somewhat accidentally discovered that similar changes can occur in a human being putting his face in water (without total immersion of his body) (Eisner, Franklin, Van Citters, & Kenney, 1966). Then I examined (at the suggestion of my friend, Julian Jaynes) the work of Beach (1948) on the sexual mechanism in rats. Beach, examining the structure of the penis under a microscope, found that sensitive hair receptors of the skin of the penis were encased between what resembled the interstices of a cog wheel when the penis was flaccid. When there was a blood flow which engorged the penis, the skin was stretched smooth, and then the hairs of the receptors were no longer encased but exposed, and their exquisite sensitivity changed the animal from a state of sexual quiescence to one totally sexually aroused. The relevance of such a mechanism for an understanding of the affect mechanism now seemed very clear. It had been known for centuries that the face became red and engorged with blood in anger. It had been known that in terror the hair stood on end, the skin became white and cold with sweat. It had long been known that the blood vessels dilated, the skin felt warm and relaxed in enjoyment. The face, like the penis, would be relatively insensitive in its flaccid condition, its specific receptors hidden within surrounding skin. When, however, there were massive shifts in blood flow and in temperature, one should expect changes in the positioning of the receptors; and, pursuing the analogy to its bitter end, the patterned changes in facial muscle responses would serve as self-masturbatory stimulation to the skin and its own sensitized receptors. The feedback of this set of changes would provide the feel of specific affects. Although autonomic changes would be involved, the primary locus would now be seen to be in specific receptors, some as yet to be discovered. Changes in hotness, coldness, and warmth would undoubtedly be involved, but there may well be other, as yet unknown, specific receptors which yield varieties of experience peculiar to the affect mechanism.[2]

MODIFICATION 3: ADULT AFFECT IS BACKED-UP SUPPRESSION OF BREATHING AND VOCALIZATION OF AFFECT

The third modification of the theory concerns the role of breathing and vocalization of affect. I have not changed my opinion that each affect has as part of its innate program a specific cry of vocalization, subserved by specific patterns of breathing. It is rather one of the implications of this theory which took me some years to understand. The major implication, which I now understand, concerns the universal confusion of the experience of backed-up affect with that of biologically and psychologically authentic innate affect. An analog may help in illustrating what is at issue. Let us suppose that all over the world human beings were forbidden to exhale air but were permitted and even encouraged to inhale air, so that everyone held their breaths to the point of cyanosis and death. Biologists who studied such a phenomenon (who had also been socialized to hold their breath) would have had to conclude that the breathing mechanism represented an evolutionary monstrosity devoid of any utility. Something similar to this has, in fact, happened to the affect mechanism. Because the free expression of innate affect is extremely contagious and because these are very high-powered phenomena, all societies, in varying degrees, exercise substantial control over the unfettered expression of affect, and particularly over the free expression of the cry of affect. No societies encourage or permit each individual to cry out in rage or excitement, or distress, or terror, whenever and wherever he wishes. Very early on, strict control over affect expression is instituted, and such control is exerted particularly over the voice in general, whether used in speech or in direct affect expression. Although there are large variations between societies, and between different classes within societies, complete unconditional freedom of affect vocalization is quite exceptional. One of the most powerful effects of alcohol is the lifting of such control so that wherever alcohol is taken by large numbers of individuals in public places, there is a typical raising of the noise level of the intoxicated, accompanying a general loosening of affect control. There are significant differences in how much control is exerted over voice and affect from society to society, and Lomax (1968) has shown a significant correlation between the degree of tightness and closure of the vocal box as revealed in song and the degree of hierarchical social control in the society. It appears that more permissive societies also produce voice and song in which the throat is characteristically more relaxed and open. If all societies, in varying degrees, suppress the free vocalization of affect, what is it which is being experienced as affect? It is what I have called pseudo-, or backed-up, affect. It can be seen in children who are trying to suppress laughter by swallowing a snicker, or by a stiff upper lip when trying not to cry, or by tightening their jaw trying not to cry out in anger. In all of these cases, one is truly holding one's breath as part of the technique of suppressing the vocalization of affect. Although this is not severe enough to produce cyanosis, we do not, in fact, know what are the biological and psychological prices of such suppression of the innate affect response. I would suggest that much of what is called "stress" is indeed backed-up affect and that many of the endocrine changes which Frankenhauser (1979) has reported are the consequence as much of backed-up affect as of affect per se. It seems at the very least that substantial psychosomatic disease might be one of the prices of such systematic suppression and transformation of the innate affective responses. Further, there could be a permanent elevation of blood pressure as a consequence of suppressed rage,

[2] I would suggest that thermography would be one major avenue of investigation. I pursued this possibility about twenty years ago and was disappointed at the relative inertia of the temperature of the skin. It may, however, be that advances in the state of the art in recent years may permit a more subtle mapping of the relationships between changes in skin temperature and affect.

which would have a much longer duration than an innate momentary flash of expressed anger. French (1941) and the Chicago psychoanalytic group found some evidence for the suppressed cry of distress in psychosomatic asthma. The psychological consequences of such suppression would depend upon the severity of the suppression. I have spelled out some of these consequences elsewhere (1971, 1975). Even the least severe suppression of the vocalization of affect must result in some bleaching of the experience of affect and, therefore, some impoverishment of the quality of life. It must also produce some ambiguity about what affect feels like, since so much of the adult's affect life represents at the very least a transformation of the affect response rather than the simpler, more direct, and briefer innate affect. Such confusion, moreover, occurs even among theorists and investigators of affects, myself included.[3]

Thus, a face with lips tightly pressed together and with clenched jaws will be assumed to be an angry face. But this is *not* an angry face but one in which anger has been backed up. An angry face would be one with mouth open crying out its anger loudly. The appearance of the backed-up, the simulated, and the innate is by no means the same. While this may be generally recognized—so that typically we know when someone is controlling an affect or showing a pretended affect—with anger, the matter is quite confused. Because of the danger presented by the affect and the consequent enormous societal concern about the socialization of anger, what is typically seen and thought to be the innate is in actuality the backed-up. Finally, it is upon the discontinuity of vocalization of affect that the therapeutic power of primal screaming rests. One can uncover repressed affect by encouraging vocalization of affect, the more severe the suppression of vocalization has been.

MODIFICATION 4: AFFECT AMPLIFIES BOTH ITS ACTIVATOR AND THE RESPONSE TO AFFECT AND TO ITS ACTIVATOR

Fourth, I have maintained for several years that although affect has the function of amplifying its activator, I have been equally insistent that affect did not influence the response to the activator or to itself. I portrayed the infant who was hungry as also distressed but in no way thereby pushed in one direction or another in behavioral response to its hunger and distress. I was concerned to preserve the independence of the response from its affective precursor. It seemed to me that to postulate a tight causal nexus between the affect and the response which followed would have been to severely limit the apparent degrees of freedom which the human being appears to enjoy and to have come dangerously close to reducing both affect and the human being to the level of tropism or instinct. It seems to me now that my concern was somewhat phobic and thereby resulted in my overlooking a powerful connection between stimulus, affect, and response. I now believe that the affect connects both its own activator and the response which follows by imprinting the latter with the same amplification it exerts on its own activator. Thus, a response prompted by enjoyment will be a slow, relaxed response in contrast to a response prompted by anger, which will reflect the increased neural firing characteristic of both the activator of anger and the anger response itself. What we therefore inherit in the affect mechanism is not only an amplifier of its activator but also an amplifier of the response which it evokes. Such a connection is in no way learned, arising as it does simply from the overlap in time of the affect with what precedes and follows it. It should be noted that by the response to affect I do not intend any restriction to observable motor responses. The

[3] By this reasoning the finding that observers across cultures will agree in identifying affect from facial expression does not tell us whether the faces utilized depicted innate or backed-up affect, nor whether observers recognized the difference between the two. In these studies both controlled and innate responses were used as stimuli, but observers were not questioned about the difference between the two. It is my prediction that such an investigation would show a universal confusion just about anger, in which backed-up anger would be perceived as innate, and innate anger would not be recognized as such.

response may be in terms of retrieved memories or in constructed thoughts, which might vary in acceleration if amplified by fear or interest, or in quantity if amplified by distress or anger, or in deceleration of rate of information processing if amplified by enjoyment. Thus, in some acute schizophrenic panics, the individual is bombarded by a rapidly accelerating rush of ideas which resist ordering and organization. Such individuals will try to write down these ideas as an attempt to order them, saying upon being questioned that if they could separate and clarify all of these too-fast, overwhelming ideas they could cure themselves. Responses to the blank card in the TAT by such schizophrenics imagine a hero who is trying to put half of his ideas on one half of the card and the other half on the other side of an imaginary line dividing the card into two.

Via temporal overlap there may be produced S-S equivalences, S-R equivalences, and R-R equivalences, mediated by affect analogs which overlap with both S and R. So an obnoxious person can become an irritating and angering person and at the same time a hurtable person. The anger which follows, accompanies, and imprints the perception of the person also imprints the impulse to hurt as well as the aggressive act. Because of the equal imprinting by affect of stimulus and response, it becomes difficult to learn control over affectprompted overt responses. No less significant, it radically complicates the learning of the critical differences between the nature of the world we perceive (apart from its affective coloring), the remembered experiences and the newly constructed thoughts about this world (including affect-prompted expectations), and the overt responses to such a mixture.

What Piaget described as the child's sensorimotor schema is rather a sensori-affect-motor *fusion* in which an object is an exciting-to-be-scanned with eyes object, touched with open reaching hand object-to-be-scanned more by putting into the open mouth object. It is all of these experiences at once in rapid succession fused by excitement which is experienced *throughout* this sequence and thus connects and makes similar the sight of the object, the reaching for it, the touch of it and the taste and texture of it in the mouth. Excitement is the continuous *contour through time* which binds the seeable, reachable, touchable, tasteable object into a fusion with the affect. Later one can conceive the unified core behind all these variants, but at the beginning it must be the continuing affect which provides the psychic glue for the rapidly changing sensorimotor encounters.

What Freud described as primary process thought is ubiquitous. One cannot readily differentiate thinking from the affect which prompts it, nor differentiate affect from the thought which activates affect. If you make me angry, it is you who really seems angering and obnoxious; but if someone else has already angered me, you may seem no less obnoxious as I tell you so. What has been described by Freud, as the omnipotence of thought, when one fears one has killed a person one hates or feels guilty for a wish one never acted upon, is more accurately described as a derivative of the overlap in time of affect, perceptual, cognitive, and motor responses. This is a universal rather than a neurotic phenomenon. The differentiation of affect from what activates it, what accompanies it, and what follows from it as a consequence is at best a slowly learned skill. It is vulnerable always, under the pressure of intense and enduring affect, to confusion and dedifferentiation. If you make me fearful enough, the world and everything I do in it, alike, can become dangerous. If you make me sad and depressed enough, the world as well as my efforts in it can become worthless and meaningless. If you make me excited and happy enough, I will love you, the world, myself, and whatever I do. Indeed, the intoxication of sex and love, either or both, derives from just such experienced fusion. Who can tell who is who at the moment of orgasm? If the other is also beloved, the orgasm confirms and magnifies the fusion of the lovers. In the extreme case of the love-death, such fusion is frozen in time. Death is sought as a small price for union eternal, out of time. In religious mysticism such union is experienced with God. There is a medieval myth which tells that a man looking up at the heavens became so intoxicated that when his gaze returned to earth hundreds of years had elapsed. The theological quest, no less than romantic love, is powered by the passion for passion and its intoxicating obliteration of time and space and its boundaries. "Verweile doch, du bist so schön," Goethe implored the transient moment of beauty. This is just what intense affect does. His plaint was a testament to its transience.

The power of affect to fuse people, their ideas, and their acts has been exploited by charismatic leaders of all kinds to bind their followers together to a common leader in a common cause. This is the essence of charismatic leadership. In modern times Hitler best understood the psychological power of assembling thousands of people together, fused as one by the shared intense affect evoked by and imprinting his person, his intense speech, and their shared resonance in a thundering "Sieg Heil." It resembled a mass affective orgasm. Because intense affect is early on inhibited via control of the voice, his sanctioning of shared loud speech legitimated, expressed, and intensified long overcontrolled and inhibited affect.

Finally, we may understand ritual as resting upon the power of shared affect to fuse and bind together all those who act together in shared belief and feeling. When ritual becomes automatized and habitual, consciousness and affect alike become attenuated, and the power of ritual to hold any group together is at risk. It becomes the end of a honeymoon in which the ritual has lost its power.

The great German philosopher Immanuel Kant likened the human mind to a glass which imprinted its shape on whatever liquid was poured into the glass. Thus, space, time, causality, he thought, were constructions of the human mind, imposing the categories of pure reason upon the outside thing-in-itself, whose ultimate nature necessarily forever escaped us. I am suggesting that he neglected a major filtering mechanism, the innate affects, which necessarily color our every experience of the world, constituting not only special categorization of every experience but producing a unique set of categorical imperatives which amplify not only what precedes and activates each affect but which also amplify the further *responses* which are prompted by affects.

MODIFICATION 5: THE NUMBER OF PRIMARY AFFECTS IS DIFFERENTIATED INTO NINE RATHER THAN EIGHT

In the original theory, each affect was presented as a hyphenated pair. Thus, there were eight such pairs, as follows: interest–excitement; enjoyment–joy; surprise–startle; distress–anguish; fear–terror; shame–humiliation; contempt–disgust; anger–rage.

Biologically, dissmell and disgust are drive auxiliary responses that have evolved to protect the human being from coming too close to noxious-smelling objects and to regurgitate these if they have been ingested. Through learning, these responses have come to be emitted to biologically neutral stimuli, including, for example, disgusting and dirty thoughts. Shame, in contrast, is an affect auxiliary to the affect of interest–excitement. Any perceived barrier to positive affect with the other will evoke lowering of the eyelids and loss of tonus in the face and neck muscles, producing the head hung in shame. The child who is burning with excitement to explore the face of the stranger is nonetheless vulnerable to shame just because the other is perceived as strange. Characteristically, however, intimacy with the good and exciting other is eventually consummated. In contrast, the disgusting or dissmelling other is to be kept at a safe distance permanently.

These eight pairs of affects are meant to indicate differences in intensity. Thus, terror was presumed to be more intense than fear, rage more intense than anger, humiliation more intense than shame, excitement more intense than interest, joy more intense than enjoyment, startle more intense than surprise. However, in the case of disgust–contempt there was an ambiguity. It seemed evident that vomiting was a more intense response than spitting out what gave a bad taste in the mouth and that both were more intense than drawing the nose away from a bad smell; and so disgust and contempt could be regarded as a unitary pair, hyphenated to indicate intensity differences.

Despite these apparent differences in intensity which seemed to justify linking these responses together as a unitary phenomenon, I later became aware of several problems with this formulation. First, there appeared to be some independent variability of intensity *within* each type of response. Thus, a bad smell might be slightly bad or very bad. Old meat might be aged somewhat to give an added piquancy to a steak, which might please some but offend others. However, badly putrescent meat emitting a very strong odor would please no one because of the intensity of the odor. Similarly, a bad taste in the mouth might be slight or very bad. So the intensity of bad tastes and smells appeared to vary independently of each other. However, the nausea response still seemed to be the most intense response. There was, however, a problem here too. First, not all infants and not all animals appeared to regurgitate with extreme responses. For some it appeared a mild and not too disturbing response. Second, if it did not smell bad, nor taste bad, why had it been swallowed? Clearly the "judgment" of the stomach had been independent of the failed early warning mechanisms and appeared to be an all-or-none response which varied only in duration. It was, of course, possible (as in seasickness) for the response to continue to be emitted despite the absence of food in the stomach. Such differences are differences in duration or extensity rather than differences in intensity.

Not only were there differences in intensity within each type of response (smell, taste, regurgitation) which varied independently of each other, but they were also capable of being combined with each other in a mixed response. Thus, a bad-tasting food might also be a bad-smelling food, and a bad-smelling food might also contribute to a bad taste. If one has a cold which clogs the nasal passages, nothing has "taste." In the generalized smell and taste responses (when the bad object is a person and not a food) it is not uncommon for a person to lift both his upper lip (as though to a bad smell) and lower his lower lip (as though to a bad taste) and also to protrude his tongue, again as though to a bad taste. In the case of the other affects there could be no such mixtures because different intensities of the same affect do not lend themselves to such blends. Thus, it is not possible to combine fear and terror, anger and rage, interest and excitement, distress and anguish because one is a weaker form of the other, stronger form of the same affect. This is not to say that there may not be alternation or oscillation from one intensity to another. Clearly, a face which responds at the same time with an upper lip raise, nostril wrinkle, and a lower lip and tongue protrusion is giving a mixed response which together indicates an increase in intensity over each component; but the major difference is not in intensity but in some other dimension. It is the opposite of looking and listening at the same time. These are two different ways of taking in information as nose and tongue are two different ways of rejecting information. Just as one can look with varying intensity and duration, and listen with varying intensity and duration, so one may combine looking and listening with varying mixtures of intensity and duration. So too the bad smell and bad taste responses can be combined with varying intensities and durations with respect to foods, odors, and symbolic objects.

Not only does there appear to be a nausea response, a bad taste response, and a bad smell response, each capable of independent as well as mixed responses, but there is still another response in the family which I had not adequately differentiated. This is what I had somewhat ambiguously labeled the contempt response. The contempt response in my original conception included both the bad smell response and the sneer. I had assumed that the sneering response, which is typically a unilateral lifting of one side of the upper lip, was similar in meaning to the bilateral bad smell response in which the entire upper lip is raised. This overlooked a critical difference. In response to a bad smell one never raises one side of the lip, since the impulse is to pull the entire face and especially the nose away from the apparent source of the bad odor. The sneer, as I began to observe it more carefully, was clearly a learned response in contrast to the bad smell response which was originally unlearned. This is not to deny that most of the bad smell responses we observe which are bilateral (especially when emitted to people and symbols) are also learned. But we must distinguish two kinds of learning here. One kind of learning involves the response itself. Just as I may voluntarily simulate a smile I do not feel, I may voluntarily simulate smelling a bad odor I do not really smell. Such simulation can, but need not, closely resemble the innate response. If I have learned to simulate the real thing, I have the further option of learning to change it. Thus, I can learn to smile very fast to convey the message that I am not pleased. One may also use a voluntary bad smell response for exactly the same reason; for example, "Your idea smells bad."

Varying intensities of the bad smell responses range from a slight contraction of muscles which "ready" the muscles necessary to lift the upper lip, to actually lifting with varying speeds, duration of holding, and extent of upper lip raise. Varying intensities of the bad taste response vary from readying the neck (platysma) muscles to assist in lower lip lowering and/or protruding, to actually lowering the lower lip and or protruding it, to protruding the tongue. Further, the mouth may remain closed but the intensity of the internal bad taste response vary from small, as if bad taste in the front of the mouth, to large, as if bad taste including front and back of the tongue, to an internal wretching response which can vary from readying the appropriate muscles in the mouth and throat to actually emitting regurgitation responses of varying degrees of completeness. These responses may be registered on the face and neck in trace amounts.

DISGUST, DISSMELL, AND CONTEMPT

Instead of contempt–disgust as a unitary response varying only in intensity, I now differentiate disgust and dissmell as two independent innate drive auxiliary responses and distinguish both of these from contempt. First an apology for the neologism, dissmell. If disgust is an appropriate word signifying a bad taste, dissmell is its analog for a bad smell. Innately, one wishes to spit out the bad-tasting food and to draw the head and the body away from the bad-smelling object. Both are distancing responses which require no learning.

Although I have argued for the existence of nine innate affects, the theory of the innate activators of affect omitted shame, contempt, and disgust. I do not believe these three are innate affects in the same sense as the six already described. They have motivating, amplifying properties of affects but also have somewhat different characteristics and mechanisms.

Dissmell and disgust are innate defensive responses which are *auxiliary* to the hunger, thirst, and oxygen drives. Their function is clear. If the food about to be ingested activates dissmell, the upper lip and nose is raised and the head is drawn away from the apparent source of the offending odor. If the food has been taken into the mouth, it may, if disgusting, be spit out. If it has been swallowed and is toxic, it will produce nausea and be vomited out through either the mouth or nostrils. The early warning response via the nose is dissmell; the mouth or stomach response is disgust. If dissmell and disgust were limited to these functions, we should not define them as affects but rather as auxiliary drive mechanisms. However, their status is somewhat unique in that dissmell, disgust, and nausea also function as signals and motives to others, as well as to the self, of feelings of rejection. These readily accompany a wide spectrum of entities which need not be tasted, smelled, or ingested. Dissmell and disgust appear to be changing more in status from drive-reducing acts to acts which *also* have a more general motivating and signal function, both to the individual who emits it and to the one who sees it.

Just as dissmell and disgust are drive auxiliary acts, I posit shame as an innate *affect auxiliary* response and a specific inhibitor of continuing interest and enjoyment. Like disgust, it operates only after interest or enjoyment has been activated and inhibits one or the other or both.

The innate activator of shame is the incomplete reduction of interest or joy. Such a barrier or perceived impediment might be because one is suddenly looked at by one who is strange, or because one wishes to look at or commune with another person but suddenly cannot because he is strange, or one expected him to be familiar but he suddenly appears unfamiliar, or one started to smile but found one was smiling at a stranger. The response of shame includes a lowering of the eyelid, a lowering of the tonus of all facial muscles, a lowering of the head via a reduction in tonus of the neck muscles, and a unilateral tilting of the head in one direction.

Shyness, shame, and guilt are identical as affects, though not so experienced because of differential coassembly of perceived causes and consequences. Shyness is about strangeness of the other; guilt is about moral transgression; shame is about inferiority; discouragement is about temporary defeat; but the core affect in all four is identical, although the coassembled perceptions, cognitions, and intentions may be vastly different.

First, as I have already described, *both* disgust and dissmell could vary independently in intensity.

Second, they appeared to be capable of conjoint evocation with either one at different intensities, for example, mildly bad smelling and at the same time very bad tasting.

Third, the differences within disgust were qualitatively different as well as somewhat independent, so that something which had not tasted disgusting might nonetheless be regurgitated. Further, that bad taste on the tongue was sometimes differentiated from bad taste toward the back of the tongue.

Fourth, the sneer of contempt was unilateral, suggesting learning, in contrast to the bilateral innate response to an innate stimulus—e.g., a lifting of the upper lip, a flaring of nostrils, and a pulling back of the whole face—from a bad smell. We must distinguish two independent sources of learning—the activating stimulus may be innate or learned, and the response may be innate or learned, independent of each other. In the case of the bilateral dissmell response, we are suggesting that it can be an innate response to an innate stimulus but that it can also be an innate response to a learned stimulus, in which case one reacts to a "dirty" message from the other with an innate dissmell response (and even in the extreme case with innate disgust to the point of nausea). Further, it can also be a learned response to an innate stimulus (e.g., a learned tic to bad smells as well as to a variety of noninnate stimuli). The major difference between a tic, like dissmell, and an innate response is the origin of the response. In the case of the innate response to the innate stimulus there is no modulation of the response and there need be no generalization and no control of it. In the case of the learned response to an innate stimulus it has through learning become generalized to previously neutral stimuli even though the lip may be raised in precisely the same way as if it were an innate response. However, the learned bilateral response more commonly is a somewhat different response than the innate response. Its latency, speed, and duration may differ significantly.

As Landis and Hunt have shown with the startle response, however, differences between the learned and unlearned response may be so subtle as to be determinable only under microanalysis. Whether the learned response is identical or vastly different however, it is still different in neurological pathway in much the same manner as breathing via the carotid sinus reflex is different from voluntarily controlled breathing regardless of whether the latter is identical or different from subcortically controlled breathing. In part the similarity of the learned to the unlearned response depends upon the further distinction between voluntary and involuntary responses, which is orthogonal to the difference between innate and learned responses. A tic or habit may be a learned, yet involuntary response, even though it *may* once have been voluntary. In general, a voluntary learned response has a wider possible variance than either the involuntary learned response or the innate response. One may elect to voluntarily stimulate an innate response to either an innate or learned simulus, either exactly or in a somewhat modulated copy. Indeed, most of the affective responses we observe on the faces of most adults are learned modulations of the innate responses, representing a *blend* of both the innate and voluntary (or involuntary) learned responses. Thus, a person may lift his upper lip just a little to many learned stimuli, in a modulated, either voluntary or habitual involuntary response (which he may or may not be conscious that he is doing).

The sneer of contempt being, usually, unilateral, is a learned (either voluntary or involuntary) response to either innate or to learned stimuli. A person may sneer equally at bad smells and at learned presumed norm violations, or he may limit his sneers to the latter, and responds with an innate dissmell response only to the innate bad smell stimulus; or finally, he may emit an innate *blend* of an innate bilateral response but with a superimposed modulation which lifts one side of the lips more than the other side.

Fifth, dissmell was primarily a distancing response aiming at removing the nose and body away from the bad smell. In contrast, the unilateral sneering response appears to be a *mixture* of dissmell and anger in which the individual either stands his ground or even moves *closer* to the offending other with hostile intent to offend, to denigrate, to besmirch. It is as though the sneering adds "insult to injury." Rather than moving away from the bad-smelling other, he will rub the other's nose in his own shit. The language of the contemptuous sneering one is apt to be anal—*accusing* the other of smelling bad with the aim of further sullying him. He wishes to punish the other further just because he smells so bad—"You're full of shit" is the not uncommon verbalization which accompanies the unilateral sneer. I found, after seeing the difference between dissmell and contempt, that some previously puzzling findings in Tomkins and McCarter (1964) were now more understandable. Anger is most frequently confused (i.e., misjudged) as contempt–disgust. Contemptdisgust is also most confused with anger, but much less frequently—5 percent (disgust-contempt confused with anger) compared with 15 percent (anger confused with contempt–disgust). These posed photos unfortunately confused contempt, dissmell, and disgust both as facial responses and as categories for judgment (because I had not sufficiently understood these differences at the time of this study) and so render interpretation problematic. Nonetheless, they suggest that anger and contempt *may* be confused because they *are* in fact blended in facial response and in feeling tone. Further research is needed to evaluate the relationships between innate and learned (stimuli versus responses), voluntary and involuntary contempt, disgust, dissmell, and anger.

Sixth, while serving as a consultant to Carrol Izard in his crosscultural studies of judgment of facial affects, he confronted me with a perturbation in his data with Japanese subjects. Much more often than in any other of the societies he had studied they responded to a photograph of a smile as though it was a case of disgust. I observed one instance of this confusion very closely and determined that it appeared to be based upon a shadow which appeared in the crease under the somewhat open and protruding lower lip. Using this as a hypothesis I was enabled to detect most of the other cases of this confusion. Apparently the extreme sensitivity to the possibility of a disgust response had pushed Japanese subjects to such a vigilance that a smile could be dangerous if the lower lip had inadvertently cast a shadow suggestive of disgust. The centuries-old danger of such responses in Japan derived from the feudal period in which loss of face required ritual hara-kiri. This heightened the necessity to smile and reassure the other as it also magnified the vigilant scanning for the possibility of either contempt, disgust, or dissmell on the face of the other. This experience seriously undermined my assumption of the unitary nature of contempt–disgust, inasmuch as this was specifically a sensitivity to disgust rather than to contempt. I remained insensitive to the continuing ambiguity between contempt and dissmell.

POLARITY THEORY

Seventh, and perhaps most decisive, were findings from several years of investigation into my Polarity Theory.

This theory has been described previously (1963, 1965) and will be treated more fully in a later volume. I will here present a summary statement for the purpose of illuminating the significance of the distinctions between shame, disgust, dissmell, and contempt.

I have been concerned for some time with a field I have called the psychology of knowledge, an analog of the sociology of knowledge. It is a concern with the varieties of cognitive styles, with the types of evidence that the individual finds persuasive, and most particularly with his ideology. I have defined ideology as any organized set of ideas about which humans are at once most articulate, ideas that produce enduring controversy over long periods of time and that evoke passionate partisanship, and ideas about which humans are least certain because there is insufficient evidence. Ideology therefore abounds at the frontier of any science. But today's ideology may tomorrow be confirmed or disconfirmed and so cease to be ideology. In a review of two thousand years of ideological controversy in Western civilization, I have detected a sustained recurrent polarity between the humanistic and normative orientations appearing in such diverse domains as the foundations of mathematics, the theory of aesthetics, political theory, epistemology, theory of perception, theory of value, theory of child rearing, theory of psychotherapy, and personality testing.

The issues are simple enough. Is man the measure, an end in himself, an active, creative, thinking, desiring, loving force in nature? Or must man realize himself, attain his full stature, only through struggle toward, participation in, and conformity to a norm, a measure, an ideal essence basically prior to and independent of man? This polarity appeared first in Greek philosophy between Protagoras and Plato. Western thought has been an elaborate series of footnotes to the conflict between the conception of man as the measure of reality and value versus the conception of man and nature alike as unreal and valueless in comparison to the realm of essence that exists independently of space and time. More simply, this polarity represents an idealization of man—a positive idealization in the humanistic ideology and a negative idealization in the normative ideology. Human beings, in Western civilization, have tended toward self-celebration, positive or negative. In Oriental and American Indian thought, another alternative is represented, that of harmony between man and nature.

I have further assumed that the individual resonates to any organized ideology because of an underlying ideo-affective posture, which is a set of feelings that is more *loosely* organized than any highly organized ideology.

Some insight into these ideological concepts held by an individual may be obtained through the use of my Polarity Scale. The Polarity Scale assesses the individual's normative or humanistic position on a broad spectrum of ideological issues in mathematics, science, art, education, politics, child rearing, and theory of personality. Following are a few sample items from the scale. The normative position is A; the humanistic, B. The individual is permitted four choices: A, B, A *and* B, and *neither* A *nor* B.

	A	B
1.	A. Numbers were discovered.	B. Numbers were invented.
2.	A. Play is childish.	B. Nobody is too old to play.
3.	A. The mind is like a mirror.	B. The mind is like a lamp.
4.	A. To see an adult cry is disgusting.	B. To see an adult cry is pathetic.
5.	A. If you have had a bad experience with someone, the way to characterize this is that it leaves a bad smell.	B. If you have had a bad experience with someone, the way to characterize this is that it leaves a bad taste in the mouth.
6.	A. Human beings are basically evil.	B. Human beings are basically good.

I have assumed that the ideo-affective posture is the result of systematic differences in the socialization of affects. For example, the attitudes toward distress in the items above could be a consequence of the following differences in distress socialization. When the infant or child cries, the parent, following his own ideo-affective posture and more articulate ideology, may elect to convert the distress of the child into a rewarding scene by putting his arms around the child and comforting him. He may, however, amplify the punishment inherent in the distress response by putting himself into opposition to the child and his distress. He will require that the child stop crying, insisting that the child's crying results from some norm violation and threatening to increase his suffering if he does not suppress the response. "If you don't stop crying, I will give you something to really cry about." *If* the child internalizes his parent's ideo-affective posture and his ideology, he has learned a very basic posture toward suffering, which will have important consequences for resonance to ideological beliefs quite remote from the nursery and the home. This is exemplified by the following items from the polarity scale: "The maintenance of law and order is the most important duty of any government" versus "Promotion of the welfare of the people is the most important function of a government."

The significance of the socialization of distress is amplified by differential socialization of all the affects, including surprise, enjoyment, excitement, anger, fear, shame, dissmell, and disgust. Differential socialization of each of these affects together produce an ideo-affective posture that inclines the individual to resonate differentially to ideology. In the preceding example excitement and enjoyment are implicated along with distress, anger, shame, fear, dissmell, and disgust as it is the relative importance of the reward of positive affects versus the importance of the punishment of negative affects that is involved in law and order versus welfare.

What is less obvious is that similar differences in ideo-affective posture influence such remote ideological options as the following items from the Polarity Scale: "Numbers were invented" versus "Numbers were discovered"; "The mind is like a lamp which illuminates whatever it shines on" versus "The mind is like a mirror which reflects whatever strikes it"; "Reason is the chief means by which human beings make great discoveries" versus "Reason has to be continually disciplined and corrected by reality and hard facts"; "Human beings are basically good" versus "Human beings are basically evil." The structure of ideology and the relationships between the socialization of affects, the ideo-affective postures, and ideology are more complex than can be discussed here. I wish to present just enough of this theory to enable the reader to understand the relationship of the theory to the distinction between disgust and dissmell.

I have assumed that the humanistic position is the one that attempts to maximize positive affect for the individual and for all of his interpersonal relationships. In contrast, the normative postion is that norm compliance is the primary value and that positive affect is a *consequence* of norm compliance but not to be directly sought as a goal. Indeed, the suffering of negative affect is assumed to be a frequent experience and an inevitable consequence of the human condition. Therefore, in any interpersonal transaction, the humanist self consciously strives to maximize positive affect insofar as it is possible. The intercorrelations between all items are predominantly positive on a combined sample of about 500 subjects. Ninety-seven percent of all possible intercorrelations between items are positive when keyed as humanistic for one option and normative for the other. Further, the few negative correlations are very low, whereas the average positive intercorrelation is + .30.

In Item 6 above we have confronted the individual with one form of this question. "Human beings are basically good" versus "Human beings are basically evil."

If an individual agrees with the proposition "human beings are basically good" and disagrees with the proposition "human beings are basically evil," what else does he believe or say he believes? Using a criterion of a positive correlation of .30 or better, he agrees with 80 percent of all the other items keyed as humanistic if he thinks human beings are basically good, or with 80 percent of all the other items keyed normative if he thinks human beings are basically evil. That is, 80 percent of all the items in the test correlate .30 or better with this item. If we use as a criterion a positive correlation of .40 or better, he agrees with 55 percent of all the other appropriate items. If we use as a criterion a positive correlation of .50 or better, he agrees with 32 percent of all the other appropriate items.

If one believes human beings are good, there is a cluster of attitudes about science which stresses man's activity, his capacity for invention and progress, the value of novelty and the excitement of discovery, the value of immersion and intimacy with the object of study. If one believes human beings are basically evil, there is a cluster of attitudes about science which stresses its value in separating truth from falsity, reality from fantasy, the vulnerability of human beings to error and delusion, the wisdom of the past, the importance of not making errors, the value of thought to keep people on the straight and narrow, the necessity for objectivity and detachment, for discipline and correction by the facts of reality.

Second, there is an associated cluster of attitudes about government—that welfare of the people is the primary aim, that freedom of expression should be permitted even if there is risk in it, that democracy should strive to increase the representation of the will of the people, that anger should be directed against the oppressors of mankind, not against revolutionaries, and that punishment for violation of laws is not always to the advantage of the individual or his society.

If the individual believes human beings are basically evil, the associated cluster of attitudes on government is that the maintenance of law and order is primary, that offenders should always be punished, that freedom of expression should be allowed only insofar as it is consistent with law and order, that the trouble with democracy is that it too often represents the will of the people and that revolutionaries should be the targets of anger, not the oppressors of mankind.

Third, the individual who believes human beings are basically good is generally sociophilic. The human being who believes human beings are basically bad is generally sociophobic. One likes, trusts, and is sympathetic; the other dislikes, distrusts, and responds to the distress of the other with dissmell.

Fourth, there is particular sympathy and love of children and of childish play.

Fifth, there is a cluster of attitudes in favor of feelings as such. Their lability is valued, and they are presumed to offer a special avenue to reality.

Sixth, there is a bias in favor of pluralism and plenitude rather than of hierarchical selectivity.

Finally, a covert measure of taste versus smell correlates both with the more explicit ideological option as well as with its correlates. This item is positively related (+.49) with the belief in the goodness of human beings. This covert measure is related to all the expected ideological options in much the same way as the more explicit statement of ideological posture.

In this series of studies, we also compared the humanistic and normative ideological positions with the scores on the Tomkins-Horn Picture Arrangement Test. This is a broad-spectrum, projective-type personality test which has been standardized on a representative sample (1500) of the American population and which is computerscored. Separate norms for age, intelligence, and education permit us to compare the polarity scores of young and old, dull and bright subjects on a wide variety of personality measures.

The results for this group confirmed our theoretical expectations on the relationships between humanistic and normative ideology and personality. The humanistic ideology is significantly related to general sociophilia (key 97), whereas the normative ideology is significantly related to sociophobia, in which there is avoidance of physical contact between men (key 120), to the expectation of high general press of aggression from others (key 124), and finally to social restlessness (key 149).

Sociophilia is measured by the predominance of arrangement of three pictures which show the hero both alone and together with others so that in the last picture the hero is with others rather than alone. Sociophobia is measured by the predominance of the last picture showing the hero alone rather than with people. It should be noted that the humanistic orientation is much more generally related to sociophilia than the normative orientation is related to sociophobia, since it is physical contact with men (a special case of the more general sociophobia) which is elevated; whereas general sociophilia is elevated in the humanist orientation. The second finding sheds some additional light on this avoidance of contact since here (key 124) there is a predominance of arrangements in which the hero is placed in a final position of being insulted or aggressed upon.

Finally, the third finding, social restlessness (key 149) is measured by maximizing the number of changes from social to nonsocial situations, as in the sequences alone-together-alone or together-alone-together, rather than the sequences together-alone-alone (or alone-alone-together) or together-together-alone (or alone-together-together). This finding tells us that the individual cannot tolerate for long either being by himself or with others. It is in marked contrast to the general sociophilia found in the humanist orientation.

These more indirect measures of personality are entirely consistent with the structure of explicit beliefs defended by these subjects in the polarity scale.

In the final series of studies, the total number of subjects is 247, but we will discuss 167 of these, of which there were 87 high school students of both sexes and 80 normals, aged forty-five to sixty, of both sexes. In this procedure we first posed and took facial photographs of several professional models, both adults and children, to simulate the eight primary affects. We then presented a set of the sixty-nine best photographs to a group of untrained subjects, whose task it was to identify the affect in the photograph. The average intercorrelation between the judgments of the subjects and the affects which the models had been posed to simulate was .85 for all affects and all photos. These intercorrelations ranged from .63 for surprise to .98 for enjoyment. The best set of photos of all affects for any one subject, a young girl, was selected for presentation in a stereoscope. The same face, showing one of six affects (surprise and interest were excluded), was used throughout the experimental series. The subject was presented on each trial with one affect on the right eye and another affect on the left eye. In addition, each affect was also randomly presented simultaneously to both eyes as a check on how the face would be seen if it were not in conflict with a different face.

Each affect was pitted in turn against every other affect, so, for example, the sad face of the subject was presented to one eye while the other eye saw a happy face, on another trial an angry face, on another trial an ashamed face, on another trial a dissmelling face, and on another a frightened face. In all there were thirty-two pairs of stimuli shown to each subject. After the presentation of a pair of slides the subject was asked to describe the posed affect he had just perceived. Then one of the two slides was shown separately to him and he was asked whether it resembled the face he had just seen (when in fact each eye had been shown a different face). Next, the other slide was shown to him, and he was again asked whether it was like what he saw before or not. A score of 1 was given to the posed affect which the subject stated was more like his percept of the stereoscopically presented pair of affects, and a score of zero was assigned to the other posed affect. Whenever the two separate affects contributed equally to the combined percept, they each received a score of 1/2. Since each affect was matched once with the other five, it would thus earn five independent scores. Summing over all five generated a single score for each affect. These scores were then correlated with the humanist score and the normative score of each subject.

It was our assumption that the same attitudes which operate at the cognitive level in responding to the Polarity Scale and to the Picture Arrangement Test would also be activated in the resolution of the perceptual conflict in the stereoscope, when the brain is confronted with two incompatible faces, and thereby produce either a fusion of both faces or a suppression of one affect in favor of the other.

On the basis of our theory we predicted that the humanistic orientation would result in a dominance of the smiling face over all other affects. We predicted that the normative orientation would produce a dominance of the dissmelling face. Both predictions were confirmed. The correlation of the dominance of the smiling face with the humanistic orientation was .42 for both the young and older subjects. The correlation of the dominance of the dissmelling face with the normative orientation was .60 for the younger subjects and .45 for the older subjects. These findings are consistent not only with the structure of explicit ideology as it is affirmed within the Polarity Scale but also with the findings of sociophilia and sociophobia as revealed in the Picture Arrangement Test.

Another series of studies on the polarity theory was undertaken by Vasquez (1975). Here we tested derivatives of the theory for differential facial responses of subjects previously tested on the Polarity Scale.

The first hypothesis concerning the face was that humanists will smile more frequently than the normatively oriented, both because they have experienced the smile of enjoyment more frequently during their socialization and because they have internalized the ideoaffective posture that one should attempt to increase positive affect for the other as well as the self. The learned smile does not always mean that the individual *feels* happy. As often as not, it is a consequence of a wish to communicate to the other that one wishes him to feel smiled upon and to evoke the smile from the other. It is often the balm that is spread over troubled human waters to extinguish the fires of distress, hate, and shame. Vasquez confirmed that humanist subjects actually smile more frequently while talking with an experimenter than do normative subjects. There is, however, no such difference when subjects are alone, displaying affect spontaneously.

The second hypothesis was that humanists would respond more frequently with distress, and normatives would respond more frequently with anger. The rationale for this was that when an interpersonal relationship is troubled, the humanist will try to absorb as much punishment as possible and so display distress rather than anger—anger is more likely to escalate into conflict, being a more blaming extrapunitive response than distress. It was assumed that the normative subject will more frequently respond with anger because he or she is more extrapunitive, more pious and blaming, and less concerned with sparing the feelings of the other, as his or her internalized models did not spare his or her feelings. This hypothesis was *not* confirmed, but neither was it reversed. This failure may have arisen because the differences in Polarity Scale scores were not as great as we would have wished. In part, this was a consequence of a strong humanistic bias among college students at the time of testing and because of the reluctance of known normatives to volunteer for testing (e.g., very few subjects from the American Legion would cooperate with Vasquez). This is consistent with prior research, including my own, which indicates that volunteers are more sociophilic and friendly.

The third hypothesis was that humanists would more frequently respond with shame and that normatives would respond less frequently with shame but more frequently with disgust and dissmell. The rationale was that shame represents an impunitive response to what is interpreted as an interruption to communion (as, e.g., in shyness) and that it will ultimately be replaced by full communication.

In contrast, dissmell and disgust are responses to a bad other and the termination of intimacy with such a one is assumed to be permanent unless the other one changes significantly. These hypotheses were confirmed for shame and disgust but not for dissmell. Humanistic subjects, while displaying affect spontaneously, did respond more frequently with shame responses than did normative subjects; whereas normative subjects displayed significantly more disgust responses than did humanistic subjects.

In conclusion, it was predicted and confirmed that humanistic subjects respond more frequently with smiling to the good other and with shame if there is any perceived barrier to intimacy. The normative subjects smile less frequently to the other and emit disgust more frequently to the other who is tested and found wanting.

So much for the general texture of the theory and the general confirmation of it by intercorrelations between the theory and the Polarity Scale with personality test, stereoscopic resolutions, and facial responses. How do these findings support our assumption that what was formerly labeled contempt–disgust, as the eighth primary affect, should now be considered dissmell as Affect 8 and disgust as Affect 9, and contempt as a learned blend of dissmell and anger? The reader has to be troubled at this point because all of this theory and research *failed* to make just these suggested distinctions, and yet these distinctions are now suggested to be confirmed by research which disregarded them. My argument is surely post hoc and will require further support, some of which I have offered, some of which will require more research.

The general distinction between the significance of shame on the one hand and contempt–disgust, dissmell on the other is clear.

Shame–humiliation is the negative affect linked with love and identification, and contempt–disgust-dissmell are the negative affects linked with individuation and hate. Both affects are impediments to intimacy and communion, within the self and between the self and others. But shame–humiliation does not renounce the object permanently, whereas contempt–disgust does. Whenever an individual, a class, or a nation wishes to maintain a hierarchical relationship or to maintain aloofness, it will have resort to contempt of the other. Contempt is the mark of the oppressor. The hierarchical relationship is maintained either when the oppressed one assumes the attitude of contempt for himself or hangs his head in shame. In the latter case he holds onto the oppressor as an identification object with whom he can aspire to mutuality, in whom he can be interested, whose company he can enjoy, and with the hope that the oppressor will on occasion be interested in him. If, however, the predominant interaction is one of contempt from superior to inferior, and the inferior internalizes the affect of contempt and hangs his head in contempt from the self as well as in contempt from the oppressor, then it is more accurate to say that the oppressor has also taught the oppressed to have contempt for themselves rather than to be ashamed of themselves.

In a democratically organized society the belief that all men are created equal means that all men are possible objects of identification. When one man expresses contempt for another, the other is more likely to experience shame than self-contempt insofar as the democratic ideal has been internalized. This is because he assumes that ultimately he will wish to commune with this one who is expressing contempt and that this wish is mutual. Contempt will be used sparingly in a democratic society lest it undermine solidarity, whereas it will be used frequently and with approbation in a hierarchically organized society in order to maintain distance between individuals, classes, and nations. In a democratic society, contempt will often be replaced by empathic shame, in which the critic hangs his head in shame at what the other has done; or by distress, in which the critic expresses his suffering at what the other has done; or by anger, in which the critic seeks redress for the wrongs committed by the other.

The polarization between the democratic and hierarchically organized society with respect to shame and contempt holds also in families and socialization within democratic and hierarchically organized societies.

In the Polarity Scale I had wished to oppose shame to what I presumed to be the unitary contempt–disgust, and I further wished to disguise the choice as an indirect measure of the individual's tolerance for a rejection of human beings and of life generally. To that end I presented a choice *within* contempt–disgust which would be an analog to the choice between shame on the one hand and contempt–disgust (as unitary) on the other. The latter choice has two components, distance and permanence. Shame involves more tolerance for intimacy and closeness than does contempt–disgust. Shame also involves a temporary distancing rather than the permanent distancing of contempt–disgust. If one were to hold permanence constant and vary distancing, one could then use the different distancing *between* contempt and disgust as an analog for the combined difference between shame and contempt–disgust. This I did in item 5, which offers the choice between a bad experience leaving a bad smell versus a bad taste in the mouth. In both cases the individual is confronted with what is negative in his experience in general and in his interpersonal relationships. In one choice (bad taste) another human being or any bad experience has been permitted to come close, to enter the body through the mouth. In the other choice (bad smell) the bad-other-person experience has been kept at a distance. Therefore, the distance relationships between shame (close) and contempt–disgust (far) are analogous to the distance relationships between bad taste (disgust [nearer]) and bad smell (dissmell [farther]). Even though disgust and dissmell both *share* permanence in contrast to the temporary character of shame, yet the psychological significance of the choice between different distances (even though both are rejections of permanence) does in fact prove to be an indirect, disguised measure of the difference between shame and disgust–dissmell. This strategy worked because I had artificially restricted the choices offered to the subject. This is a perennial source of possible error in test interpretation, since under such conditions one does *not* know how he would have chosen had he been given a more extended set of alternatives. I was assuming that given the choice between disgust and dissmell, the one who chose disgust *would* have chosen shame had the alternatives been extended and that the one who chose dismell would have chosen disgust-dismell if these had been put into opposition with shame.

When this assumption appeared to be validated, I had then to confront an unexpected consequence—that the difference between bad tastes and bad smells had systematic correlations no different than those between shame and *both* of them. To be a taster was to being a smeller as the ashamed one was to both the smellers and tasters. It was then that I felt compelled to break the eighth primary affect apart into eight and nine.

Chapter 25

Affect and Cognition: "Reasons" as Coincidental Causes of Affect Evocation

The History of American psychology to date can in part be understood in terms of the preferential treatment of particular subsystems and psychological functions and of the imperfect competition of the conceptual marketplace, which overestimates some one function or set of functions to the detriment of others. Drives, affects, memory, perception, cognition, action, consciousness have in varying alliances tended to dominate our theoretical and experimental landscape.

After James's stream of consciousness and Titchener's introspection turned in upon itself, consciousness fell into deep disrepute in American psychology. It was caught in the crossfire between Freud's "unconscious" and "behavior," when behaviorism seized center stage in American psychology. Like any imperialist enterprise, behaviorism swept out of power not just one competitor—consciousness and introspection—but all its fellow travelers—cognition, motivation, memory, and perception—and replaced them with conceptual puppets. Thus, cognition was not banished but replaced by movements of the larynx. It remained for Skinner to empty entirely the black box of all organisms except for that of the benign can-do experimenter. But all theoretical imperialisms eventually begrudgingly suffer the return of the repressed. Just as psychoanalysis in its senility cleared a conflict-free sphere of the ego, and even celebrated its autonomy, so Skinnerian theory readmitted "coverants" to fill the vacuum of its own design. But theories improvised to rectify sins never have the vigor of their youth, and the neglected domains rarely flourish in the alien conceptual environment. Motivation prospered in psychoanalytic theory. Cognition and motor learning did not. Motor learning prospered in behaviorism; motivation and cognition did not. Perception, memory, and cognition prospered in Gestalt psychology; motivation and motor learning did not. Motivation and learning prospered in Hullian theory; cognition did not. Cognition prospered in Piagetian theory; motivation did not.

Psychologists have not been pioneers in the study of affect. In the long history of concern with the nature of affect, it is first the philosophers and then the biologists who have been most engaged. Beginning with Aristotle, the primary emotions and "passions" have been subjected to the closest scrutiny and theorizing for over two thousand years. In biology, Darwin's *The Expression of the Emotions in Man and Animals* (1872) is the classic statement of the evolutionary significance of the emotions. Since Darwin, Cannon, Selye, Richter, Gelhorn, Hess, Lorenz, and many others have continued to stress the centrality of this domain. Indeed, as Lorenz said in his preface to Darwin: "I believe that even today we do not quite realize how much Charles Darwin knew" (Lorenz, 1965, p. xiii). It should not surprise us that the biologically trained and philosophically oriented Freud and James should also have concerned themselves with affect as a central phenomenon. A deep concern with either mind or body, or both, appears historically to lead to concern with affect.

Psychologists interested in the body have paradoxically tended to stress the drives over affects, and psychologists interested in the mind have tended to stress cognition over affect. Psychologists interested in neither mind nor body have stressed the behavior, in the extreme case, of an empty organism.

Behaviorism, psychoanalysis, and cognitive theory each subjected affect to the status of a dependent variable. The cognitive revolution was required to emancipate the study of cognition from its cooptation and distortion by behaviorism and by psychoanalytic theory. An affect revolution is now required to emancipate this radical new development from an overly imperialistic cognitive theory.

In this chapter I will examine affect "sicklied o'er with the pale cast of thought," offering both a critique and a remedy. I will argue that cognition is one among many triggers of affect, that "reasons" are "causes" only coincidentally in this respect, but that "reasons" are more central and primary in what I have defined as magnification of affect.

I will now try to show that much contemporary theory and research about the nature of affect risks a radical oversimplification of a complex domain, misidentifies this mechanism with other mechanisms, most notably the cognitive mechanisms, and neglects its multiple functions within the total biopsychosocial system.

METHODOLOGICAL BIAS FOR SIMPLICITY VERSUS COMPLEXITY, ANALYSIS VERSUS SYNTHESIS, AND VERIFICATION VERSUS DISCOVERY

The radical increase in numbers of grant applications, papers, and book manuscripts in affect theory and research I have recently refereed testifies that the next decade or so belongs to affect. Having waited twenty years for this development, I am less than euphoric at what I see. It had been my hope that such a development might transform American psychology. Instead, the field of affect is, in part, being co-opted by the very fields it should have illuminated. So we have "cognitive" theories of depression, "behavioral" modification of anxiety, analytic methodologies which stress "manipulation" of facial muscles, factor-analytic studies which attempt to centrifuge affect as a distillate, analysis of variance procedures to decontaminate affect from other functions and to decompose and fragment the organized affect mechanism itself into its vocal, facial muscle, and skin components. I am not "against" cognition, behavior, experimental manipulation, factor analyses, nor analyses of variance. I am against co-optation, assimilation, and business as usual in the face of genuine novelty. It makes a great difference whether one regards an automobile as a new invention or as a horseless carriage which must be fed gasoline rather than hay.

Lest I appear more extrapunitive and more boorish than I am, let me begin with a confession of personal sin, an isolated lapse in an otherwise exemplary professional life. In directing the doctoral dissertation of Ernst Fried (1976) we tested the hypothesis that pupils would learn more from a teacher who showed positive rather than negative facial affect while teaching. The experiment was a statistical success. There was indeed a reliable difference in learning depending on whether the face of the teacher showed excitement or disgust to her class. But the differences were disappointingly small, even though reliably different. I was puzzled until I realized that I had been victimized via an identification with the aggressor, by a wish to "protect" my student from possible criticism by other members of his committee. Since it was facial affect that was hypothesized to mediate the difference in learning, all else had to be kept "constant" lest the results be ambiguous and contaminated. Above all, the voice had to be the same in quality, speed, and duration. We therefore dubbed into the videotapes of the two faces the same neutral, lifeless voice. So the students were observing an excited face with flat voice and a disgusted face with the same dull voice. It is a testament to the power of the facial information that the hypothesis was nonetheless confirmed. The differential effects, however, were greatly attenuated by removing the appropriate accompanying affect-laden voice. Affect normally is carried by correlated channels. In the interest of an analytical methodology of purity we violated the nature of the phenomenon, which owes its power to a massed, conjoint variance, biologically evolved to capture the human being in just this way.

At another time I spent a few years and several thousand dollars of government money in ultra-high-speed photography of the face. I assumed that at speeds of ten thousand frames a second, microanalyses of the face would yield "secrets" of affect and human nature analogous to those the microscope had revealed about biological structures. Although microexpressions of the face do reveal some important information, they also create great noise. At ten thousand frames a second the smile becomes an interminable bore, forfeiting much vital information which can be seen easily by the naked eye or by conventional slow motion photography. I had again violated the critical time-correlated relationships which the innate affect programs control, in the interest of greater experimental manipulation, and succeeded in throwing away more information than I gained. Although analysis and synthesis is a major mode of cognition, and experimental manipulation of dependent and independent variables a major mode of science, the pursuit of purity and decontamination of ambiguity is not without a serious price when it pulls apart what nature has joined together. There is a delicate balance between methods which aim at purity and methods which aim at power via modeling and testing conjoint variance. The choice of methods has been too often dictated by ideological preferences in favor of simplicity and purity or in favor of complexity and power, in favor of independence and dependence of variance or in favor of interdependence of variance. These biases derive not only from different theories about the nature of human beings but also from different tolerances for methods of simplicity and clarity within narrow limits, as against complexity and greater degrees of freedom and some ambiguity for broader scope of inquiry.

There have been a few experiments in which an attempt has been made to test my theory of the significance of the face in the experience of emotion. These generally have utilized voluntary simulation of facial affective responses. The most recent of these experiments is that of Tourangeau and Ellsworth (1979). In this experiment, subjects are required to voluntarily simulate facial affective responses and to hold these responses for a couple of minutes during which they observe affect-evoking films. Not surprisingly, the voluntary responses are ineffective in producing the experience of emotion. Such an experiment is seriously flawed in several respects.

Voluntary simulation does not guarantee the generation of the appropriate full-blooded sensory feedback. Not only are the requisite vocal responses and the autonomic changes mediated by the endocrine, cardiac, and respiratory systems bypassed in voluntary mimicry of the facial affective response, but no less important is the frozen, static quality of the stimulation they used. Thus, a smile is a sequence of motor responses, as is a startle, as is a cry of distress, and as is a sudden fear response. When one uses a static holding of the facial musculature in a fixed pattern selected from an organized series of responses which has distinctive features of rate and distance, one is *not* simulating the affective response, not even the learned simulation of the innate response. In a true voluntary simulation of a smile, in which, let us say, the individual uses his face to lie to the other, to pretend a friendliness he does not feel, his dissimulation succeeds only to the extent that the rate of the smile, and the distance over which the mouth is moved, approximate the innate smile. To the extent to which either of these parameters is not exactly simulated, the face fails to dissimulate affect and is diagnosed as a fake smile.

How much more faked it would seem if it were simply held static for a period of time. Indeed, as I have argued elsewhere (Tomkins, 1975), voluntary facial behavior is also used as a symbol. The paradox of such use is that such symbolism rests upon an assumed and generally true consensus about what an innate facial response is. The information in such symbolic use of the face is to be found in the direction and magnitude of the deviation of the simulated response from the innate response. Thus, a smile which is either faster or slower and/or more or less wide than an innate smile tells the other that one is really *not* amused. A surprise response which is *slower* than an innate surprise tells the other that one does not believe what the other is saying—i.e., that it is too surprising. One becomes uncomfortable in the presence of eyebrows which go up too slowly when one wanted to provoke astonishment at the tall tale one is trying to sell the other. The longer they remain up, as in this experiment, the more certain it becomes that the other is not surprised but is disbelieving.

I question the value of the Tourangeau and Ellsworth study apart from its irrelevance as a test of my theory. To explain why, I must first discuss the relationship of artificial intelligence and computer simulation of cognitive processes. It is generally recognized that these are concerned with quite different domains. Artificial intelligence is concerned with the production of smart programs which can do clever things. Whether it does this in the same way as a human being thinks is as irrelevant as whether an airplane has feathers. It *flies*. Whether it flaps its wings is of no consequence. It is an engineering triumph in its own right, as is any program conceived as artificial intelligence. Within the field of artificial intelligence the invidious comparison is *between* artificial intelligences, hardware as well as software. Thus, an adding machine is a very poor computer, and one computer is not as smart as the next-generation computer. One chess program is better than another chess program, but both programs may be better or worse than any specific chess player.

In computer simulation of intelligent behavior there should be nothing "artificial." Ideally, one would require a program to simulate human errors as well as successes. The relevance of the distinction between artificial intelligence and computer simulation to the evaluation of the usefulness of testing voluntary muscular facial responses is this: the fruitfulness of artificial intelligence is in the utility of the achieved programs. These are technological inventions which justify themselves in many ways. The fruitfulness of computer simulation is more theoretical. It is a way of both producing and testing models of human cognition—of problem solving which includes problem solution as a special case. What we hope to learn from such models is how the brain really works. We are not necessarily interested in its stupidity or in its cleverness since human cognition is as vulnerable to error as final output as to the correct "response." I would suggest that the hypothesis tested in the Tourangeau and Ellsworth study has *no* utility as an example of artificial affect and very little utility as a simulation of a complex series of affective responses, since it uses neither the appropriate neural pathways, nor the appropriate muscular *series* of responses, nor the appropriate full sensory feedback of innate affect responses, but rather a frozen moment in the wrong modality—and as such, it is a failure at simulation of innate affect. It is an exercise not in affect simulation but in artificial affect, without the possible benefits of its analog in artificial intelligence.

What is one to make of an experiment in which one opposes intense innate affect (evoked by films which have been designed to arouse such affect) with the countervailing effects of artificially manipulated voluntary muscular contractions on the face? Consider the logic of this in an extreme case. Suppose I ask you to put a smile on your face, and I then stab you. Would anyone suppose that the simulated "smile" would in any way compete with the instigated terror?

The difference between innate affect—triggered either by films, real life, or by thoughts and images—and the voluntarily innervated simulations and transformations of these responses is fundamental. It is a difference whose importance must not be attentuated in the interest of easier experimental designs.

The importance of this difference has been further amplified by the revisions of my theory, which assigns a primary role to blood flow, temperature, and altered sensory thresholds on the skin of the face in contrast to a more secondary role assigned to the facial musculature. These changes had not been published, when Tourangeau and Ellsworth did their study, but their study tests neither version of my theory.

It is my assumption that facial affective responses are neither necessary nor sufficient conditions for the conscious experience of affect. They are not sufficient because these responses may or may not be admitted into the central assembly, depending on competing messages which may succeed in prior entry and exclude affect messages from the face. In the same manner even extreme pain messages may be excluded (e.g., in combat) owing to intense concentration which limits competing pain messages. Neither are they necessary conditions for the *experience* of affect, which *can* be produced by messages retrieved from memory in the absence of facial feedback. Just as a proofreader's error is based on memory-guided imagery rather than on sensory feedback, and just as one can play blindfolded chess utilizing memory-generated arousal imagery, so affect imagery which was originally facial, and vocal, can be retrieved from memory and experienced as affect.

I would suggest that such experiments are a consequence of two biases. First is the perennial tension between the logic of verification and the logic of discovery. There is an ideological and temperamental difference between those who are excited by the possibilities of discovery and those who are excited by the possibilities of verification or disconfirmation. Just as the policeman dreads losing a criminal, and a judge dreads punishing the innocent, so scientists may lean toward discovery even at the price of ambiguity and error or toward certainty in verification even at the price of loss of information. If it becomes critically important to verify a theory, many experimenters are prepared to test more "testable" versions of a theory in the interest of combating error. These scientists enjoin us to let many exciting possibilities go lest we contaminate the house of science with one lie.

The second bias, which is often (but not always) conjoined with the first, is one toward simplicity rather than complexity, toward analysis rather than synthesis, toward sharp distinctions of independent, dependent, and interdependent variability. So, even though the theory asserts that the biological evolution of this system produced correlated programs of activation and response, one tries nonetheless to distill from this complex a simple distillate as the core of the phenomenon. In this view complexity is the low-grade ore which contains gold, which must somehow be centrifuged and decontaminated. I would suggest that such tests of my theory have thrown away more of the gold than they have reclaimed.

The complexity of the affect mechanisms lends itself to fragmentation and the posing of either-or questions in an adversary mode. Is affect in the voice, or in the skin, or in the muscles, or in the autonomic system, or in the hands and body? Since the study of any of these matters takes time, energy, and affect, it is not surprising that defenders of specific territories can become acrimonious, pious, and imperialistic.

COGNITIVE THEORIES OF AFFECT: THE SCHACHTER-SINGER THEORY

In 1962 Schachter and Singer offered a new theory of emotions which quickly became a classic in social psychology. Studies in psychology often become classic under two conditions: they need to be believed, and they are not read. For over a decade, addressing a couple hundred or so professional audiences, I was confronted with the rhetorical question, "But didn't Schachter and Singer demonstrate that there are no discrete emotions?" When I first answered this question with the question "Have you read this paper?" I was somewhat surprised that, with one exception, none of these psychologists had in fact read the paper. As a student of the psychology of knowledge, I had to ask myself, why did this theory need to be believed? The paper itself was seriously flawed, both empirically and theoretically, and yet it was not seriously challenged by social psychologists until almost twenty years later, by Maslach (1979). Empirically, it was an experiment without a statistically significant main effect, and the reported significant effects were small in size and not always in the predicted direction. Theoretically, it was no more persuasive. Only the trained incapacity of professionals, combined with a bias in favor of the counterintuitive, could have permitted acceptance of the theory. Surely no one who has experienced joy at one time and rage at another time would suppose that these radically different feelings were really the same, except for different "interpretations" placed upon similar "arousals." Only a science which had come to radically discount conscious experience would have taken such an explanation seriously. It is as reasonable a possibility as a theory of pain and pleasure which argued that the difference between the pain of a toothache and the pleasure of an orgasm is not in the stimulation of different sensory receptors but in the fact that since one experience occurs in a bedroom and the other in a dentist's office, one interprets the undifferentiated arousal state differently.

Further, if emotion depended upon an increased state of arousal, then nightmares and indeed any emotions in dreams would have been impossible since the state of sleep is a state of diminished and not increased arousal. The concepts of arousal and activation were at the outset simple and clear. Moruzzi and Magoun (1949) were able to awaken a sleeping animal by electrical stimulation of the reticular formation, which was accompanied by electroencephalographic (EEG) activation. This distinction between a sleeping and wakeful state correlated with EEG differences was an important first finding, but it soon became evident that the body was fractionated into many specific subsystems with respect to arousal and that correlations between subsystems were characteristically low. According to one investigator (Elliott, 1964), the highest intraindividual correlation between any two central and autonomic measures is .16 when the individual's performance is studied across a wide variety of tasks and situations.

Lindsley (1951) and Malmo (1959) assumed that autonomic responsiveness was essentially homogeneous, and therefore differences in activation, paralleling differences in "arousal" as demonstrated by reticular stimulation, could provide a basis for understanding both emotion and motivation. To some extent this was science based upon a pun, since if one became aroused in emotion and "aroused" and activated from sleep to wakefulness, it was concluded that perhaps they were one and the same phenomenon. It would have been better had the more neutral term "amplification" been used by Moruzzi and Magoun. It would then have not lent itself so readily to confusion with emotional arousal. Indeed, it was clear from the work of Sprague, Chambers, and Stellar (1961) that it was possible, by appropriate anatomical lesion, to produce a cat that is active by virtue of intact amplifier structures but shows little affect and, conversely, to produce a cat that is inactive and drowsy but responds readily with affect to mild stimulation. This, a lead article in *Science* (1961), was widely neglected by both Schachter and all arousal and activation theorists.

> Thus, it appears that after interruption of much of the classical lemniscal paths at the rostral midbrain, the cat shows . . . little attention and affect, despite the fact that the animal is wakeful and active and has good motor capacity. . . . These cats are characterized by a *lack of affect,* showing little or no defensive and aggressive reaction to noxious and aversive situations and no response to pleasurable stimulation or solicitation of affection by petting. The animals are mute, lack facial expression, and show minimal autonomic responses. . . . Without a patterned afferent input to the forebrain via the lemnisci, the remaining portions of the central nervous system, which include a virtually intact reticular formation, seems incapable of elaborating a large part of the animal's repertoire of adaptive behavior. . . . In contrast to this picture, a large reticulate lesion sparing the lemnisci results in an animal whose general behavior is much like that of a normal cat except for chronic hypokinesia or drowsiness and for strong and easily aroused affect to mild stimulation, (p. 169)

Finally, it was clear from the discovery of the "joy center" by Olds and Milner (1954) that there was an "arousal" system II which was part of the limbic-midbrain system described by Nauta (1958). The relationships between these two arousal systems has been the subject of much experimentation, most recently reviewed and integrated by Lapidus and Schmolling (1975). It is clear that the unidimensional homogeneous arousal system upon which the Schachter-Singer theory was based was an oversimplification of the neurophysiology of that time. Since then, the picture has become steadily more differentiated, as Lapidus and Schmolling have shown.

But if there were no reliable empirical findings, if it was strongly counterintuitive, and if it violated known neurophysiological findings, why was it so hugged to the bosom of social psychologists for almost twenty years? I would suggest the following hypothesis. For well over a decade before the appearance of this theory, learning theory had dominated psychology. There had been a deep polarization between Hull's conception of the importance of drives as primary motives and Tolman's more informational theory, stressing, as it did, cognitive maps. Animals learned either because they were "driven" or because they "thought" about what they needed to learn. Issue after issue of the *Psychological Review* was devoted to a running battle between the Hullians and the Tolmanians. With the death of Hull and the increasing interest in cognition on the part of many psychologists, Tolman seemed to have won the day. But Hullian theory, through Dollard and Miller (1941) and Mowrer (1950) had been able to integrate psychoanaltyic theory with Hullian theory. There was a sense in which the "victory" of cognition over drive theory was pyrrhic. Cognition of the Tolmanian kind was a little too "cold" to carry the entire motivational burden. What seemed needed was some way to heat up cognition. Because the battle had been joined as one between drives and cognition, affect as a primary biological motivating system was not an alternative. What seemed to be needed was something bodily and hot, but not too much of a competitor for cognition or else the victory over drives would only have been apparent, and the battle would have needed to be resumed between cognition and affect.

Given this theoretical vacuum, a theory which united the global, cognitively blind, but apparently "arousing" system with the more subtle cognitive apparatus, was irresistibly attractive. One was offered a neurophysiologically respectable Id, tamed and led by the cognitive soul, in the Platonic image of horse and rider. That there were several horses, each with a mind of its own, could be denied via the comfortable primitive and more docile reticular formation, led by a more competent cognitive governor. As a consequence, social psychology has been able to maintain the fiction that thinking really makes it so—even manufacturing our feelings. As one derivative, "attribution" became the central problem in motivation for social psychology. Social psychology rediscovered Descartes' "Cogito Ergo Sum."

Affect as Pure Cognition

The cognitive appraisal theory of activation of affects is a seriously restricted theory which fails to address the entire problem, but it is at least plausible. But the "cognitive revolution" is much more severely limited when it addresses the more general question of the nature of affect itself.

Many years ago the study of cognition itself was seriously impoverished by the behaviorist revolution. Thought was trivialized as a "behavior of the larynx." American psychology has been given to function imperialism such that it can rewrite thought as though it were action. We are now in danger of rewriting affect as though it were a form of cognition or a dependent variable of cognition. Thus, Averill (1980) suggests "an emotion may be defined as a socially constituted syndrome which is interpreted as a passion rather than an action . . . but there is no single subset of responses which is an essential characteristic of anger or of any other emotion." It is extraordinary that this can be asserted despite the overwhelming evidence of the universality of facial expression across cultures, among neonates, and even in the blind.

It was not true that John Watson did not know how to think, but this did not prevent him from identifying his own thought processes as laryngeal acts. It was not because he loved thought less but because he loved behavior more. Our present generation of cognizers do not love affect less, but they do love cognition more and love it not wisely but too well. The critical point is that the human being has evolved as a multimechanism system in which each mechanism is but one among many evokers of affect. Thinking can evoke feeling, but so can acting, so can perceiving, so can remembering, and so can one feeling evoke another feeling. It is this generality of evocation and coassembly which enables affect to serve for a system as complex and interdependent as the human being. No less important is its capability of evoking thought, memory, action, and perceptual scanning and imprinting these other mechanisms with its own gradients and levels of stimulation.

The affect mechanism is distinct from the sensory, motor, memory, cognitive, pain, and drive mechanisms as all of these are distinct from the heart, circulation, respiration, liver, kidney, and other parts of the general homeostatic system. Who would have supposed that the kidney could be "defined" as a heart, or that it was really a heart "interpreted" as a kidney?

Cognitive Theory's Answer to the Question: At What Age Do Affects First Appear?

The cognitive bias also influences the interpretation of the age at which affects appear. Since many psychologists think infants cannot think, they are inclined to believe, as Emde (1976) and Lewis and Brooks (1978) do, that some affects in earliest infancy are precursors rather than the real thing. They are explained away as "reflexes" without "consciousness" until the third month or "self-conscious awareness" around eighteen months. Thus, Emde speaks of endogenous smiles, thought to reflect internal psychological rhythms during REM sleep in early infancy, and of a gradual shift to exogenous smiles to social stimuli in later infancy. Lewis and Brooks argue that emotional experience is dependent on self-awareness and cognitive evaluation. "Without the I in 'I am . . . ' the verbal phrase and the emotional experience implied by it have no meaning for the Western mind." True emotional "experience," as contrasted with emotional "expression," is mediated by caregivers' verbal labeling of responses to expressive behaviors, plus a growing competence and self-awareness. Demos (1981) has shown that there are several assumptions in this position which are not supported by the existing data on early infancy. First is the assumption "that early affective expressions represent unlearned reflexive behaviors." Second is the assumption that self-awareness appears as a consequence of the child's growing ability to distinguish internal bodily changes from external environmental changes in making cognitive evaluations. She argues:

> There is an increasing body of data on early infancy which indicates that the human infant is capable and probably perceptually biased to make distinctions between self and environment, including other humans, right from the beginning. . . . Lewis and Brooks seem to be working from a model which assumes that development is a gradual process of going from initially global, undifferentiated entities to increasingly discrete, differentiated functions. An alternate model, adopting a systems approach, assumes the neonate possesses various differentiated functions organized in a rudimentary way, and that development involves successive coordinations and re-organizations of these discrete functions. The accumulating evidence on early infancy is more congruent with the latter model of development, (p. 558)

Next, Demos suggests that the emphasis of Lewis and Brooks on cognitive evaluation as a determinant of emotional experience is subject to the many problems inherent in the James-Lange theory—most notably, the paucity of evidence, despite several decades of physiological research, for patterns of bodily reactions specific to each emotion. Further, "the model founders on its inability to account for the speed of emotional responses."

Finally, Demos indicates that

> . . . the timetable for assigning cognitive "appraisals" of situations to infants would have to be moved back to the second week of life, and even in a few precious cases, to the first week. . . . Currently, physiologically produced affective expressions are called precursors to affect. But with the adjusted time table, these "precursors" would be occurring during the same period as true emotions, and thus such a designation becomes less useful, (p. 560)

Cognitive Theory's Answer to the Question: What Are the Primary Affects and How Many Are There?

The final question we address is what are the primary affects and how many are there? This is a basic question, primarily biological in nature, which is treated more and more as though it were a psychosocial question. Affect mechanisms are no less biological than drive mechanisms. We do not argue for a Chinese hunger drive and an American hunger drive as two kinds of hunger drives. Subserving these taste preferences, we speak of a small and limited number of taste receptors and do not invent new primary taste receptors with every new food recipe. Nor do we postulate new sensory color receptors with every new color combination in painting. Nor do we postulate new pain receptors with each discovery of a new disease or new instruments of torture. If each innate affect is controlled by inherited programs, which in turn control facial muscle responses, autonomic responses, blood flow, respiratory and vocal responses then these correlated sets of responses will define the number and specific types of primary affects. The evidence I have presented (1964), plus the cross-cultural consensus demonstrated by Ekman (1972) and Izard (1968), suggests strongly, if not conclusively, that there are a limited number of such specific types of response. There are, I believe, only nine such responses: interest, enjoyment, surprise, fear, anger, distress, shame, dissmell, and disgust. These are discriminable distinct *sets* of facial, vocal, respiratory, skin, and muscle responses. The decisive evidence for this will, I think, require conjoint, specific, patterned brain stimulation with moving and thermographic pictures of the face. This is a project for the future. In the meantime we must not assume that we can solve *this* problem by an analysis of the cognitions which are combined with each of these affects.

If, as I believe, each affect is mediated by specific sensory receptors in the skin of the face, the difference between the terror of a specific phobia and the objectless terror which Freud distinguished as "anxiety" is *not* a difference in the cold sweat and sensitized, erect hair follicles. It is rather a difference in the consciousness of what information has entered and been coassembled with the affect in a central assembly. In one case there is a perceived "cause" of the terror; in the other there is not. Although there are profound further consequences of such differences in experienced affect, it is theoretically important that we be clear about what is affect and what is affect-related information, which may vary independently of the affect with which it is coassembled. The number of different complex assemblies of affects and perceived causes and consequences is without limit. It is important that they be studied and labeled. Indeed, all languages are centuries ahead of psychology in having named very subtle distinctions in affect complexes, and one can use such linguistic distinctions to characterize critical differences in how each society experiences and transforms affects.

Some years ago I sought an analog of Homo sapiens for the title of a talk on feeling man, and was surprised to find that neither in Greek nor in Latin was there an exact word for feeling. The closest analog proved to be Homo patiens, from whence came "passion" in the sense of passive suffering. Languages have labeled affects per se and have also referred to them with varying degrees of prominence and clarity in combinations with other functions. Thus, in English "anger" labels a primary affect; "hostile" refers to affect, too, but with the additional connotation of a more extended and more complex feeling and cognitive state. "Irritable" refers to hostility which in response to provocation waxes and wanes, but with a permanently low threshold. "Rage" refers to anger of very high intensity compared to "annoyance." "Vicious" adds a qualitative moral normative judgment to a presumed intense anger, adding the complication of intention to hurt another. "Aggressive" also adds behavioral criteria to the affect but is less normative than "vicious." "Destructive" speaks not to the behavioral aspect but rather to the consequences and outcome of the behavior. A person may be destructive by action or by speech. He may be conscious of his destructiveness or not. But the word "destructive" may have nothing to do with anger, since one may kill accidentally and since guns and atom bombs are also destructive, as are hurricanes. Indeed, it is the ambiguity of language with respect to affect per se which defeated me in my attempt to create an affect dictionary. Several years ago the political scientist Robert North, who was then studying the circumstances preceding the outbreak of war by coding newspaper descriptions of prewar diplomacy, asked me to provide him a dictionary of affect words, coded according to my understanding of the primary affects. I studied several thousand English words for two years and had eventually to give up the attempt because of the great variety of admixtures of affect with cognitive, behavioral, and event references which made it impossible to code for an unambiguous affective reference. Despite the failure of the specific mission, the linguistic analysis of affect proved deeply revealing and should be further pursued.

As in language usage generally, one can tell a great deal about both the society and the status of affects in that society by the distinctions it has labeled verbally. Whether it distinguishes shame externally evoked from shame internally evoked, whether it distinguishes sadness from crying, whether it distinguishes aggression from anger, whether it distinguishes joy from excitement tell us whether conscience has been internalized; whether distress is sometimes suffered silently, sometimes not; whether anger is sometimes inhibited, sometimes acted on; whether different kinds of positive affect have been experienced sufficiently to be distinguished.

Important as subtle distinctions between affect complexes are, it is nonetheless critical that such complexes not be confused with the very restricted number of biological primary affects. Because there are an infinite number of the former, these are already forming the basis of competing classifications and lend themselves to adversary debate and magnification and theoretical confusion. The confusion arises because there is no theoretical basis for deciding between classifications of combinations—any more than one could define a limited classification of types of sentences, in contrast to a question of how many letters there were in any specific alphabet.

Thus, if one hangs one's head in shame, the total experience of this response is different if one has failed—in which case one speaks of "feelings of inferiority"—compared with the same response if one has violated a moral norm—in which case one speaks either of "feelings of guilt" if this is a response of the self to the self's immorality or, less commonly, that one is "ashamed of oneself." Contrary to some theoretical distinctions between shame and guilt as based on internalization versus externalization, the same affect may be internalized or externalized independent of whether the content concerns morality or inferiority. One may be internally sensitive to matters moral or achievement-oriented, or externally sensitive to either, as when failure shames because of others' contempt compared with self-contempt evoking shame. In each case the affective response is identical though the total complex experience is different, *despite* an identity of the affective component in the central assembly. It is yet another difference in experience if one hangs one's head in "shyness" as though naked in the face of scrutiny. One should not distinguish shame from guilt and shyness as affects but as affect complexes of shame plus varying perceived and conceived causes and consequences.

The number of distinctions one can draw between affect complexes is theoretically without limit. The affect may be perceived as having an object or as free-floating, a phobia versus objectless anxiety. Affect with an object may be perceived to originate either within or outside the individual, as in "he shames me" versus "I am ashamed of myself." Free-floating affect may later be emitted *to* an object or not, as in having awakened full of good feeling one simply savors this state per se, in contrast to expressing affection *to* one's wife and children and speaking of how beautiful a day it is. Because these responses *follow* the positive affect, they are less likely to be experienced as having been caused by the objects to which they are emitted. It is, however, also possible that the feeling which precedes *is* nonetheless perceived as having been *caused* by an object which *follows,* as in the case of the person who wakes from a sleep of nightmares, who finds fault with the first person he encounters and does not know that he was "looking" for an object. The affect may be perceived as having been caused by the other and having consequences for the self, versus having been caused by the other and having consequences primarily for the self's impression of the other, as in "he always cheers me up" versus "I like him." In both cases the other may evoke the affect of enjoyment, but the affect is conceived to have a different locus of termination.

The affect may be perceived to be about the past, present, or future. Thus, one has hope or despair for the future, regret or nostalgia for the past. It may be combined with varying degrees of ambiguity or clarity, as when one anticipates a meeting to be harrowing and it turns out well *or* poorly compared with what one expected. It may be combined with varying degrees of probability, as when one is excited about a meeting with a friend compared with a meeting which one expects and hopes to be rewarding but is less than certain it will turn out well. The affect aroused may be perceived as intended by the other or as unintended, as when someone accidentally steps on your toes. The origin of the affect may be perceived as produced by the self intentionally (as in proud achievement) or unintentionally (shame for a stupid error). It may be perceived as caused by social forces (taxation without representation) or by nature (drought) or by a combination (pollution) of social and natural forces. It may be perceived in the self or other as appropriate or inappropriate (e.g., justified anger vs. blind irrational rage, justified shame vs. irrational shame). It may be perceived as controllable or uncontrollable (e.g., excitement vs. seduction). It may be perceived as stable or labile (e.g., steady joy or sadness vs. sudden shifts from happy to sad). It may be perceived as slowly accelerating or rapidly accelerating (e.g., slow increase in distress vs. explosive grief, slowly increasing fear vs. rapidly growing panic, slow increase in anger vs. explosive rage). It may be perceived as graded or ungraded (e.g., from mild annoyance to more intense anger to rage vs. only weak annoyance, or only rage, or both). It may be perceived as homogeneous or heterogeneous in dyadic scenes (e.g., mutual enjoyment vs. I am excited—he is sad). The affects may be pure or mixed (e.g., happy vs. happy-sad). Mixed affects may be experienced simultaneously or in sequence (e.g., excited and disgusted vs. excited then disgusted). Affects may be differentially polarized (e.g., happy-sad vs. happy-disgusted). Affects may be described by the difference between movement away from negative affects and movement away from positive affects (e.g., relief affect vs. deprivation affect). Targets of affect may be perceived as negative, positive, both, or neither, as in "I like him, I don't like him, I like him but also dislike him, I don't have any strong feelings toward him."

Positive, negative, ambivalent, or neither may be targeted toward self or other as in "I dislike him" versus "I dislike myself"; "I like him" versus "I like myself"; "I'm ambivalent about him" versus "I'm ambivalent about myself"; "I don't have any strong feelings about him" versus "I don't have any strong feelings about myself." In other words, affects may be intra- or extrapunitive, intra- or extrarewarding, intra- or extraconflicted, intra- or extraimpunitive, not rewarding.

Affects may be described by success or failure (victory affects vs. defeat affects). Affects may be described by secondary affects to victory or defeat affects (e.g., positive celebration affects vs. negative celebration affects).

This is a sample of an indefinitely larger population of affect complexes. So long as they are recognized to be complexes, they provide valuable possibilities for the enrichment of personality and social psychology. Should they be presented as competing lists of primary affects, as different "systems" or "theories" of affect, then such richness can eventually impoverish and confuse our understanding of the affect domain because there is no theoretical basis for preferring one such set to another as classification systems. There are increasing signs that this elementary distinction is in danger of being disregarded and that the primary affects are being defined by the cognitively perceived causes and consequences of the affects, rather than by their own characteristics. It is as though the pain mechanism were to be defined by the varieties of instruments of torture. It is yet another unfortunate consequence of the hypertrophy of cognitive imperialism. The affect mechanism lends itself to endless mutual enrichment of drive, perceptual, memorial, motor, and cognitive assemblies, of every degree of dependence, independence, and interdependence. All these must be pursued and understood but not at the price of misidentification, co-optation, and special pleading for the primacy of thought.

These strictures on possible confusion between primary affects and the more complex blends of affect and cognition should in no way be interpreted as minimizing the psychological significance of the more complex combinations of affects and their even more complex integrations in scenes and scripts.

Awe and the sublime, envy and jealousy, love and hate, enchantment and disenchantment, seduction and betrayal, regret, hope, longing, nostalgia, compassion, forgiveness, atonement, trust and distrust, optimism and pessimism, intransigence, depression and elation, arrogance and humility, indignation, malice, pity, wonder—these are central phenomena; most of them were described by Aristotle two thousand years ago, and well described. We will address the problems in forthcoming volumes on script theory.

The Innate Activator Theory and its Relation to Cognitive Theory

Cognitive theory is in close accord with common sense in its explanation of how affect is triggered—too close, in my view. For some few thousand years everyman has been a "cognitive" theorist in explaining why we feel as we do. Everyone knows that we are happy when (and presumably because) things are going well and that we are unhappy when things do not go well. When someone who "should" be happy is unhappy or suicides, everyman is either puzzled or thinks perhaps there was a hidden reason or, failing that, insanity. There are today a majority of theorists who postulate an evaluating, appraising homunculus or, at the least, an appraising process which scrutinizes the world and declares it as an appropriate candidate for good or bad feelings. Once information has been so validated, it is ready to activate a specific affect. Such theories, like everyman, cannot imagine feeling without an adequate "reason."

Two thousand years ago Aristotle described the major affects and "explained" them in much the same language as contemporary cognitive theorists use today. Although Aristotle's physics would today be regarded as metaphysics, his theory of emotions has been unwittingly rediscovered by contemporary cognitive affect theorists. One could interchange Aristotle's language with what appears in our best introductory texts, and the difference would not be detected.

Thus, "the persons with whom we get angry are those who laugh, mock, or jeer at us, for such conduct is insolent. Also those who inflict injuries upon us that are marks of insolence." Aristotle's conception reflects the importance of pride for the Greek culture. What is in fact only one trigger of anger is exaggerated in its significance in what was still a warrior culture. It is not surprising that in the overachieving twentieth-century American society a majority of "aggression" experiments in social psychology regularly insult captive subjects to elicit anger.

Aristotle asserts that "fear is caused by whatever we feel has great power of destroying us, or of harming us in ways that tend to cause us great pain."

Every contemporary cognitive definition of each of the primary affects can be found in Aristotle. There are two alternative interpretations which are possible. First, such a consensus, over two thousand years, is a testament to the transparency of the phenomena. Therefore, any reflective individual will necessarily come to the same answer to this perennial question. Further, if one asks a child or a random sample of men and women on any street, *all* will agree that one fears harm and whatever is dangerous, that one becomes angry at insult, and so on. A second interpretation is that such an explanation is only a first approximation, which raises as many questions as it appears to answer. Aristotle knew that not everyone reacts emotionally as he "should" according to a reasonable definition of affect: "For those who are not angry at the things they should be angry at are thought to be fools, and so are those who are not angry in the right way, at the right time, or with the right persons."

Not only Aristotle but everyman, too, has always been troubled by the irrationality of affect, by its dark side, its uncontrollability, to the point of insanity, when one is insanely jealous, enraged, terrified, or excited in mania. The "reasons" for the irrational justifiably have a somewhat suspect status as supports for a cognitive theory of affect. The cognitive explanation of affect evocation is at best only partially persuasive.

What is the cognitive appraisal when one is anxious, but does not know about what, when one is depressed or elated but about nothing in particular? Even more problemantic for such theory is infantile affect. It would imply a fetus in its passage down the birth canal collecting its thoughts and, upon being born, emitting a birth cry after having appraised the extrauterine world as a vale of tears.

There must indeed be a cause or determinant of the affective response whenever it is activated. The critical question is whether the apparent "reason" is ever or always, that cause. I will argue that the apparent reason is *never* the cause in any case for the simple reason that the affect mechanism is a general one which can be "used" by *any* other mechanism, motor, perceptual, or memorial, or even by another affect. More importantly, however, I will argue that even when it *does* truly evoke an affect that it does so *coincidentally* via its abstract profile of neural firing rather than through its apparent content. In other words, it is neither the context of a joke which makes us laugh, nor its unexpectedness, but the sharp drop in rate of neural firing following the sharp increase in neural firing, which is correlated first with one expectancy and then by its violation. An immediate repetition of the joke, though it has the same content and the same sequence, now produces a much more compressed and flat profile of neural firing, correlated with our knowledge of what is coming. In no science do causes prove to be entirely transparent, and we should not be too surprised if the causes of affect evocation prove to be different than they appear to be. We are most likely to be seduced into thinking we understand causal relations in just those cases where common sense seems most obvious, because of the high correlation of an apparent cause with a true cause.

Consider the nature of the problem. The innate activators had to include the drives but not to be limited to them as exclusive activators. The neonate, for example, must respond with innate fear to any difficulty in breathing but must also be afraid of other objects. Each affect had to be capable of being activated by a *variety* of unlearned stimuli. The child must be able to cry at hunger or loud sounds as well as at a diaper pin stuck in his flesh. Each affect had, therefore, to be activated by some general characteristic of neural stimulation, common to both internal and external stimuli and not too stimulusspecific, like a releaser. Next the activator had to be correlated with biologically useful information. The young child must fear what is dangerous and smile at what is safe. Next the activator had to "know the address" of the subcortical center at which the appropriate affect program is stored—not unlike the problem of how the ear responds correctly to each tone. Next, some of the activators had not to habituate, whereas others had to be capable of habituation; otherwise, a painful stimulus might too soon cease to be distressing, and an exciting stimulus might never be let go—like a deer caught by a bright light.

These are some of the characteristics which had to be built into the affect mechanisms' *innate* activation sensitivity. In addition, these *same* triggering mechanisms had to lend themselves to be pressed into the service of *learning* and "meaning." It is very unlikely that the innate affect program would have evolved with two separate triggering mechanisms. Any theory of how we learn to become excited, afraid, or distressed must therefore account for the cognitive control of affect *via* utilization of the innate activating pathway, since it is extremely improbable that the infant's birth cry and early hunger cries are the result of his learning or thought processes.

I therefore examined all instances of the earliest infantile affect, observed by others and myself, for commonalities of the internal neural events which would be correlated with known external stimuli capable of innately activating specific affects. I believe it is possible to account for the major phenomena with a few relatively simple assumptions about the general characteristics of the neural events which innately activate affect and that these same assumptions can account for the later learned control of affect, whether that is via cognitive or motoric or perceptual mediation; I would account for the differences in affect activation by three variants of a single principle: the density of neural firing. By density I mean the frequency of neural firing per unit time. My theory posits three discrete classes of activators of affect, each of which further amplifies the sources which activate them. These are stimulation increase, stimulation level, and stimulation decrease.

Thus, any stimulus with a relatively sudden onset and a steep increase in the rate of neural firing will innately activate a startle response. As shown in Figure 25.1, if the rate of neural firing increases less

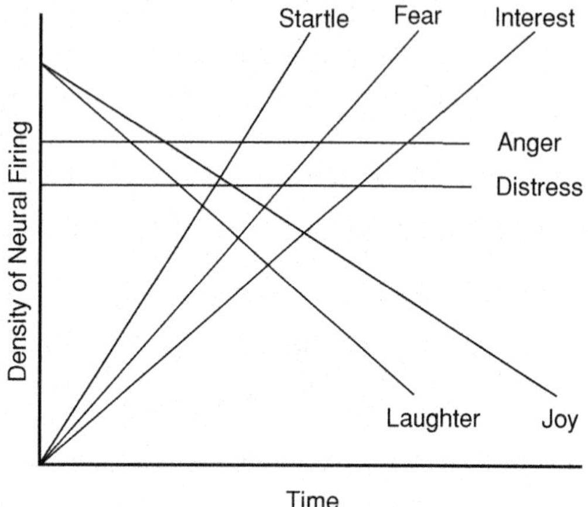

FIGURE 25.1 Innate activator model.

rapidly, fear is activated; and if still less rapidly, then interest is innately activated. In contrast, any sustained increase in the level of neural firing, such as a continuing loud noise, would innately activate the cry of distress. If it were sustained and still louder, it would innately activate the anger response. Finally, any sudden decrease in stimulation which reduced the rate of neural firing, as in the sudden reduction of excessive noise, would innately activate the rewarding smile of enjoyment.

With respect to the density of stimulation and neural firing, then, the human being is equipped for affective arousal for every major contingency. The general advantage of affective arousal to such a broad spectrum of levels and changes of levels of neural firing is to make the individual care about quite different states of affairs in quite different ways. It is posited that there are both positive and negative affects activated by stimulation increase but that only negative affects are activated by a continuing unrelieved level of non-optimal stimulation and only positive affect is activated by stimulation decrease.

How can such a theory account for *both* unlearned and learned activation of affect? Consider interest. Any sudden movement (which was neither sudden enough to startle nor sudden enough to frighten) which was steep enough in its acceleration to produce a correlated acceleration of neural firing could *innately* activate interest or excitement. Interest and excitement are the same affect, differing only in intensity. Consider now how the same neural profile could be produced by learning and "meaning" without the necessity of a homunculus or "appraisal" process. Suppose upon reading a book the novelty of an idea activates information processing at an acclerated rate. This would initially amplify and thus maintain "thinking" by *innately* activating excitement. If this now exciting implication keeps inferential processes alive at the same accelerated rate, the individual will then again be rewarded with a burst of excitement at each new expanding set of conceived possible implications of the original idea. So long as the combination of successive inferences and recruited affects sustains yet another inferential leap, the individual's interest will remain alive. When he runs out of new possibilities, he will also lose interest.

It is critical that such a theory be able to account for affect to all the varieties of voluntary responses other than purely cognitive responses. Thus, any sudden avoidance response to a presumed danger could become a self-validating response by *innately* evoking fear because of the sudden contraction of bodily muscles, whose pattern of neural firing could activate fear. The profile of neural firing of such a motor response is adequate to innately trigger fear even though the motor response itself is *not* innate but a consequence of an inference of possible danger.

Again, an individual who comes into a restaurant hungry might become distressed as the density of neural firing of the hunger signal increases to a level sufficient to trigger distress. But now he is subjected to the conjoint, elevated level of neural firing from two sources, his stomach in hunger and his facial and vocal muscles contracted in distress. It would require only a small additional contraction of his fist (occasioned perhaps by an inference of inequity upon seeing a waitress attend someone who came into the restaurant later than he did) to reach a level of neural firing adequate to activate anger. Such an arousal of anger is based on part drive, part affect, part inference, part contracted fist, conjointly adding up to the density level of neural firing required to innately trigger anger. To the extent to which such rates and levels of neural firings themselves become habitual and overlearned and located in either ideas *or* muscle movements, or both, they increase radically the frequency of specific affect activation.

If enjoyment is triggered by any sudden deceleration in the density of neural firing, it accounts readily for such innate phenomena as the smiling response to the sudden reduction of pain, but also to the sudden reduction of pleasure (e.g., at the moment of orgasm) and also to the sudden reduction of affect (e.g., enjoyment relief that one need not fear any longer). I demonstrated this latter in 100 percent of subjects by first strapping electrodes on their wrists and warning of electric shock for errors. After anxiety had developed, I suddenly took the electrodes off. In no case did the face fail to smile at that moment.

It can also account for cognitively mediated enjoyment. In experiments with infants, the infant will smile at the experimenter's face a few moments after it is exposed again to the infant after having been withdrawn from view. I would account for this by the sudden reduction of information processing which follows the affective sequence interest-surprise. This sequence of affects is prompted by the attempt of the infant to identify the face which now reappears. Upon recognition that the face is familiar, interest changes to surprise. Since surprise is like a square wave, sharply peaked in profile of neural firing, its sudden reduction in neural firing, conjoined with the termination of further perceptual scanning for the purpose of identification, innately activates the smiling response. As the perceptual and memorial skill improves in such a series of withdrawal and reappearance of the face, identification becomes more rapid, occasions less and less surprise and by the twelvth trial the smile ceases. Essentially, the same dynamic holds for the smile or laugh to humor. It is the sudden unexpectedness of the punch line which both surprises and terminates further increasing information processing. Although these are cognitive processes, it is their direction and rate of neural firing which mediate the triggering mechanism rather than their meaning or content.

Innate Activators and Music

The innate activator model has the further advantage of illuminating the affective import of music, which is opaque to cognitive interpretation. It is the sequences and mixtures of rising and falling gradients of sounds and varying levels of sounds which in my view are readily capable of evoking excitement, enjoyment, fear, distress, anger, and—in the obvious case of the Haydn symphony of that name—surprise. Several years ago Pratt (1942) showed that there was a restricted range of affective interpretation of specific musical works. This lead should now be pursued and the innate activator model tested against affective responses to rising and falling sequences of tones and to sustained increases of intensity of tones. Musical tones in this view are at once activators and analogs of rapidly changing feelings. It is the program music of the feeling life and, as such, as abstract as all objectless feelings. "Program" music is a cognitive corruption which requires that patterns of tones be translatable into patterns of light.

Innate Activators and Therapy

Psychopathology is, at the very least, an enduring unfavorable ratio of the density of negative to positive affect. There are important differential consequences of the cognitive theory and the innate activator model for psychotherapy. In the latter theory, insight therapy is likely to be of help only insofar as stable triggering of negative affect is coincidentally correlated with "reasons." However, insofar as dense negative affects are triggered by *combinations* of "reasons" and other triggers, insight would be of only limited value. Thus, learned hypertonus of the striped muscles would lower the threshold for distress or anger; learned styles of very rapid responses, motor, perceptual, or cognitive would lower the threshold for fear; or any increased level of neural firing due to variations in bodily temperature, noise, illness, or extreme ectomorphy all would lower the threshold for distress or anger and thereby increase and maintain psychopathology. In such cases relaxation techniques and/or drug therapy might be the preferred methods. It is difficult to account for the success of relaxation therapy, induced either by retraining or by drugs, on a cognitive basis. "Uppers" and "downers" clearly operate on the very general features of the internal environment rather than on specific cognitive transformations.

Innate Activators and Compression-Expansion Transformations

The cognitive "appraisal" theory tends to exaggerate the consciousness of appraisals and thereby also exaggerates the importance of insight in psychotherapy. I would stress the importance of compression-expansion transformations in "skilled" cognition. Skill in handling increasing amounts of information is characteristically achieved by reversible compression-expansion transformations. A familiar example is the relative inability of a skilled typist to say where the letter *N* is on a keyboard, without slowing down the process of typing a word like *now* and then scanning for where the finger would have gone. This is a *slower* expansion of what under normal skilled typing conditions is done quickly and without the benefit of consciousness via expansion at the slower rate. Suppose now that one has learned an equivalent skilled compression of signs of "danger," which are expanded quickly outside consciousness so that fear is innately triggered but without any "object." There is no difference in principle between these two skills. Both originally were learned for conscious reasons which are now unavailable to consciousness under the skilled fast expansion rate. The "reason" is now a congealed, compressed, unconscious instruction which cannot be dealt with so long as it remains "skilled." To such unconsciousness, secondary fear *against* consciousness would represent a baffling complication, but the fundamental dynamic of unconscious compression-expansion transformations must be distinguished from the motivated unconscious avoidance Freud discovered as repression.

I am suggesting that the innate activator model can account better than the appraisal model for the way in which compression and expansion of "instructions" can lock the individual into fears over which he has no conscious control.

CLASSIFICATIONS: AFFECT INTENSITY AND ACTIVATION

The innate activator model is *not* a model which explains differences in *intensity* of affect. Although I have distinguished interest from excitement and fear from terror and so on, I have not been able, as yet, to find an explanation for how differences in intensity of affect are innately activated. I have considered the following possibilities: First, it is possible that the affect program is at a uniform level of high intensity whenever it is first activated innately but that lower intensities represent successive habituation to repeated activation. This is indeed what happens in the case of the startle response. Here successive repetition results in an orderly dropping out of components of the total bodily startle, so that finally there is no more than an eye blink to a pistol shot. However, this component *never* habituates. Habituation would therefore occur via central inhibitory processes in response to massed repetition of the adequate innate stimulus which would differentially block more and more of the components of the total innate program. In this model intensity differences would represent an auxiliary subroutine activated by massed repetition of the adequate stimulus. A second possible model is that the innate gradients and levels of neural stimulation are *bandwidths* such that steeper gradients activate more intense affect and less steep gradients activate less intense affect; and higher-level neural stimulation activates more intense affect while lower-level neural stimulation, at the lower bound of the bandwidth, activates less intense affect. A third possible model would implicate the state and background support of each of the target organs of the total affective response. Thus, in the extreme case, depletion of body reserves, via either massed affect or massed physical exertion or stress, would render the heart, lungs, and endocrine support sufficiently depleted to "burn out" the affect even though the affect program was fully activated. Further, since a set of organs is involved, differential readiness of each of the members of the set for activation could contribute to varying rates of firing of each of the relevant organs. Accordingly, if the heart were already beating at a maximal rate when the instruction from the affect program was received, it would, paradoxically, slow down rather than speed up, according to the law of initial values.

These three possibilities are worthy of exploration, but I am not confident that they will prove to be validated, either singly or together.

CLARIFICATIONS: CONSCIOUS VERSUS UNCONSCIOUS ACTIVATION OF AFFECT

There is a critical feature of the innate activator model which was left ambiguous in Volume 1 in the hope that evidence might be found to decisively differentiate between three possible features of the innate mechanism. The critical questions are these: (1) can *any* neural firing trigger the affect mechanism, as I assumed in the original model, or (2) must the neural firing of the critical message have first been transmuted into a conscious "report," or (3) must the neural firing of the critical message be preconscious? Consider the implication of each of these possibilities.

If the neural firing of the critical messages which triggered the affect program had to be preconscious, then the added amplification from the activated affect would serve the purpose of increasing the probability of the combined affect and its trigger entering the central assembly and thereby becoming a conscious report. Such amplification of the trigger from affect would be dual in nature: first, an intensity increase and, second, an increase in the probability of becoming conscious. It would seem particularly important in the case of startle, since the main function of startle is to disassemble the central assembly and force a *change in consciousness* as an interrupter of whatever the individual was consciously attending. If it were necessary for the activating message to be conscious before it could trigger the startle, it might never be possible to interrupt any obsessive fascination which seized consciousness with the competing affect of excitement. It is to protect an individual against his own absorption and capture by excitement that the startle achieves its major function.

The advantage of restriction of affect to conscious reports would be that affect amplification would be selective, since the conscious messages are those which have already won out in the competition for entry into the central assembly and are by that criterion denser and more important to the individual. A further consequence of this model would be that one affect could trigger another affect only if the first affect itself were conscious—e.g., sudden reduction of conscious fear could evoke joy, but the sudden reduction of unconscious fear could not. The problem is complicated by the phenomenon of centrifugal attenuation of sensory input. Thus, if one works in a noisy environment, there is habituation to the noise based in part on centrifugal inhibitory messages which attenuate the sensory input at a distance. As a consequence, such noise does not become conscious nor does it characteristically recruit either distress or anger. If, however, there were no centrifugal inhibition *and* there were no recruitment of distress or anger, then one would have support for the model that the necessary condition for affect activation was a conscious report rather than a preconscious message.

This model generally leaves the individual much less vulnerable to the varieties of neural events going on of which he is unaware and over which he may have little control—e.g., shifts in diurnal temperature, muscle tonus, reverberating circuitry, reticular amplification, to name a few.

The advantage of the original model would be that differential amplification, whether conscious or unconscious, would lead to differential recruitment of more amplification from affect, thus making the loud message louder, the weak message weaker.

I am still inclined toward the original version of the model, particularly in view of more recent findings concerning night terrors. It now appears that objectless severe night terrors occur whenever the sleeper goes from a very deep stage of sleep to a lighter stage of sleep very *rapidly*. This is consistent with the innate activator model of a steep gradient of neural firing as the trigger of fear. It is clear that there could be little cognition in such dreamless sleep and little consciousness of any kind until the person reached the lighter sleep stage. The advantage of the original model is that it would permit both the night terror with minimal consciousness as well as terror which was evoked as a response to the conscious awareness of seeing an automobile approaching too quickly, or consciously inferring dangers which are not perceived.

Clarifications: Rate Versus Level of Neural Firing

A question has been raised concerning the mechanisms in gradient versus level effect activation. I wish to clarify this model by the analogous mechanism in the cochlea of the ear. In the case of both the affect mechanism and the ear we would invoke a resonating mechanism which was differentially "tuned" to specific *frequencies* of neural firing, holding time constant as the mechanism for triggering distress or anger, and different *rates* of *increase* or *decrease* of neural firing, holding time constant, as the mechanism for triggering surprise, fear, interest, or enjoyment.

Clarifications: Origin Versus Site of Trigger

Concerning another question which has been raised about the origin of the trigger versus the site of the trigger, I would cite the difference between a pistol shot and the cochlear response of the ear as two *origins,* as contrasted with the subcortical stored program for the startle as the *site* of the trigger of the affective response. In the case of epilepsy there is a disorder of the threshold of the trigger-site mechanism so that there is no startle response to a pistol shot despite no disorder of the cochlea of the ear as the origin of the trigger.

EVIDENCE FOR DISTINGUISHING AFFECT AND COGNITION

Zajonc, in his paper "Feeling and Thinking, Preferences Need No Inferences" (1980), was the first social psychologist to entertain the position I had urged for twenty-some years—that feeling and thinking are two independent mechanisms, that preferences need no inferences, that affective judgments may precede cognitive judgments in time, being often the very first and most important judgments. The paper was a brilliant one which has, I think, been influential in loosening the unthinking hold of thought on social psychologists. Together with the insistence of Abelson on the interdependence of affect and cognition, this demonstration of the independence of the mechanisms invited social psychologists to pursue the complex networks of relationships between affect and cognition as well as the larger matrices in which these are embedded.

AFFECT AS AMPLIFICATION VERSUS AFFECT AS "MOTIVATION"

The theory of affect as only coincidentally cognitive flies in the face not only of cognitive theory but also violates several assumptions of what has been called motivation theory, whether this is a cognitive, drive, or "need" theory of motivation. The concept of affect as analogic amplification has no counterpart in motivation theory, whether motivation theory is based on drives, perception, cognition, "need," or any combination thereof.

Contrary to Freud, it is extremely unlikely that any motivational mechanism could have been so blind and mismatched to reason and reality as the id. Contrary to cognitive theory, no motivational mechanism could have been so altogether docile and reasonable as we are being asked to believe. Affect is a loosely matched mechanism evolved to play a *number* of *parts* in continually changing assemblies of mechanisms. It is in some respects like a letter of an alphabet in a language, changing in significance as it is assembled with varying other letters to form different words, sentences, paragraphs.

In order to understand the nature of the affect mechanism there are several fundamental assumptions about both affect and about motivation which must be surrendered. One of these we have examined—that affect is necessarily cognitively activated.

Second is the assumption, in most theories of motivation, that motivation is best understood as involving means and ends and that ends are what means are "for." In behaviorist theories of motivation a further limitation was placed on this conception, stressing behavior as the critical end, as an "output" toward which the system was geared, as a factory is organized to manufacture a product.

In my view, the system as a whole has no single "output." "Behavior" is of no more nor less importance than feeling. Behaviorism applied to emotion has meant that *only* the *observable motor acts* (e.g., facial or vocal responses) qualify as legitimate behavior, ignoring the internal responses, both those that lead to and those that follow from the feedback of observable responses. More critically ignored was the awareness of these responses as "feelings." The concept of reinforcement used motivation as though it were a means to the end of guaranteeing learned behavior. This is a craft union's view of the matter, and a particularly American view of it. Everyman is and always has been more interested in just the opposite question—what must he do to guarantee that his life will be exciting and enjoyable? Affect is the bottom line for thought as well as perception and behavior. It is not as reinforcement theory had it, a carrot useful primarily in persuading us to perform instrumental acts, since instrumental acts are sufficient but not necessary to evoke rewarding affect. Affect is an end in itself, with or without instrumental behavior.

Motivation theory has characteristically, as in the case of Freud, attempted to discover the hidden agenda behind opaque behavior or, as in the case of Watson, attempted to delineate the instrumental nature of motivation. In part this can be understood as the perennial need of the scientist to deal with the problematic. If someone simply enjoys the act of eating or sex or is excited by the presence of the beloved, these appear too transparent to require "explanation" since the drive mechanism is so "obvious." Only if the love poetry could be seen as sublimated sexuality could it become interesting to Freud the theorist. Only if a rat would cross over an electrified grid to reach food or a sexual partner did the instrumental act become important as a measure of the motive. I do not wish to underestimate the significance of indirection in motivation, whether it be in the form of disguise or of an instrumental act. Rather I wish to affirm the existence of a problem which has not been appreciated to *be* a problem in motivation theory. This is the problem of the nature of experience which is an end in itself. One may persist in looking, remembering, acting, or thinking in the *same* way simply because it continues to evoke affective amplification and support. The mystery of *this* phenomenon appears when the exciting other ceases to excite, the frightening experience ceases to frighten, the enjoyable experience suddenly disgusts. Affective amplification is indifferent to the meansend difference. Sustained commitment characteristically requires affective amplification of both means and end but enables the pursuit of means endlessly without "reinforcement" of the end, so long as the means is supported either by reduction of negative affect or continuing evocation of positive affect. But no less important is the purely aesthetic appreciation of the true, good, beautiful, sublime, or religious, in art or science or human love and friendship. Without powerful affective amplication such experience would be pallid, drained of its enriching aura.

One of the tragedies of human existence is the loss of amplifying affect in what I have called "the valley of perceptual skill." Whenever the increase of skill in the compression of information enables the individual to handle a complex set of messages via compressed summaries, then there is a minimal drain on consciousness and the central assembly, since this is normally reserved for the new and problematic messages. Thus, we learn to drive an automobile with minimal "attention," but so, alas, do we learn to interact with our wives and husbands; so too can we barely "hear" a piece of music we have listened to a hundred times. Skill can attenuate consciousness and affect. Indeed, there can *be* no great skill without the coordinated compression and attenuation of conscious information. Not only does such skill cost us appreciation of the other, of nature, and of civilization, but it also produces the paradox that we necessarily value least that which we do best, which we execute as daily rituals (e.g., daily shaving).

There are several other assumptions in motivation theory which are contested by amplification theory. One of these is that affect and motivation are necessarily "about" something. Another is that motives necessarily eventuate in some kind of "response," usually behavioral. Another is that motivates are either "pushy" or "pully," that even when one does not "respond" to them, one is pulled to or pushed to respond because of motives. Another is that the inertia and urgency of motives severely limits their degree of transformability. Hence, the contrast between ego and id, cognition and affect. Another is that motives are limited in their degree of abstractness in contrast, for example, to concepts. Thus, hunger as a motive is about food, pushing and pulling the individual to eat and only to eat, or to do whatever is instrumental to the consummatory response. Another is that there is an identifiable internal organization which is motivational.

In contrast to these assumptions I will argue that what we ordinarily think of as motivation is not a readily identifiable internal organization resident in any single mechanism but is rather a very crude, loose approximate conceptual net we throw over the human being as he lives in his social habitat. It is as elusive a phenomenon as defining the locus of political power in a democracy. Is political power in the executive, legislature, or judiciary, or in the mass media, or in the people, or in big business, or in big labor, or in the universities, or in the states or cities? The answer is that both motivation and political power are everywhere and nowhere and never the same in one place for very long.

The affect mechanism has evolved to perform multiple vital functions in continuing assemblies with other vital mechanisms. Because of the principle of "play" it is imperfectly adapted to serve these multiple functions, but by virtue of the satisficing principle of good enough matching, affect "works" biologically, psychologically, and socially. It works by virtue of the *conjunction* of several major characteristics: its *analogic, urgent, abstract, general,* and *imprinting* features. It is insistent and urgent in a very abstract way—that "something" is increasing rapidly or decreasing rapidly or has increased too much. In its generality it is capable of very great combinatorial flexibility with other mechanisms which it can conjointly imprint and be imprinted by, thereby rendering its abstractness more particular and concrete—so that it can become an automobile that is coming too fast and too frightening rather than a more abstract awareness of "something" too fast. This imprinting of the perceived object is favored because of the analogic quality of the fear. The abstract acceleration is more likely to be connected to and imprinted on the perceived automobile because its perceived acceleration is an analog of the perceived acceleration of the fear response itself. This is, however, never guaranteed. In free-floating anxiety the "something" is never particularized.

Further, the same analogic and general characteristics will imprint themselves on *any* response which occurs under the pressure of fear. So the pedestrian will jump *quickly* out of the way of the frightening automobile. Thus, "stimuli" and "responses" become abstractly analogous and so coordinated. In addition, the possibilty of being without a cigarette can generate scenes of longing which accelerate so quickly that fear is evoked and recruits a frantic search whose rate is itself imprinted by the continuing fear, so the quick response to the fear evokes further fear.

Let us examine these conjoint features more closely. We have already described the urgency of the affect in its role as amplifier, as well as its analogic quality, and its capacity to imprint both its own activator and the response to its activator. In addition to these descriptions we should also remember that its urgency is further guaranteed by its syndrome characteristics and by its involuntary characteristics. It is a complex response, a syndrome, so organized neurologically and chemically via the bloodstream that the messages which innervate it innervate all parts at once, or in very rapid succession; hence, it offers great resistance to control (like a sneeze or orgasm). Second, they are aroused easily by factors over which the individual has little control, are controllable with difficulty by factors which he *can* control, and endure for periods of time which he controls only with great difficulty if at all. They are in these respects somewhat alien to the individual.

The *abstract* nature of the urgent, analogic characteristic requires further clarification in the light of some criticisms of this theory which assume that the biological nature of affect forecloses both generality and abstractness, as inherent in, or even possible for, the affect system.

Affect amplifies, in an *abstract* way, any stimulus which evokes it or any response which it may recruit and prompt, be the response cognitive or motoric. Thus, an angry response usually has the abstract quality of the high-level neural firing of anger, no matter what its more specific qualities in speech or action. An excited response is accelerating in speed whether in walking or talking. An enjoyable response is decelerating in speed and relaxed as a motor or perceptual savoring response. In acute schizophrenic panics, the individual is bombarded by a rapidly accelerating rush of ideas which resist ordering and organization. In each of these cases, the abstract profile of the amplifying affect is imprinted on the recruited responses. In a theory of memory (1971) I have demonstrated that memory retrieval itself can be controlled by distinctive features of acceleration and level of neural firing of information. So one can recover early handwriting by having the individual write slowly. One can recover early affect by requiring the individual to shout loudly. In each case specific rates and profiles of neural firing were isolated by new organizations that were faster in the case of handwriting, softer in the case of socialized affect.

The primary function of affect is urgency via analogic and profile amplification to make one care by feeling. It is not to be confused either with mere attention as such nor with mere response as such but with increased amplification of urgency—no matter how abstract the interpretation of its stimulus and no matter how abstract or specific the response which follows. The appropriate minimal paradigm here is the miserable, crying neonate who neither knows why he is crying nor *that* there is anything to do about it; nor, if he thinks that something might be done, does he know *what* he can do about it. It is *not* a "motive" in the sense in which psychology has used that concept, though it provides the core of what may become a motive. Without affect amplification nothing else matters, and with its amplification anything *can* matter.

So much for the abstractness of the affect mechanism. Its additional feature of *generality* is defined by its transformability, or degrees of freedom. By means of flexibility of coassembly the abstract features of affect are made more particular and concrete; and the more urgent features can also thus be made more modulated. In the game of Twenty Questions it is the relatively abstract partioning of the domain by such a question as "is it organic?" which contains the greatest information gain over all the succeeding questions. The final question, which solves the problem, is indeed the least informative single step in terms of possibilities excluded. The affect mechanism similarly invests its urgency first of all at just such an abstract level. Other information, either simultaneous or sequential, acts like a zoom lens to specify more concretely the vital area which has first been magnified by affect. It is because the innate activators are not specific releasers that such complex organization becomes possible. All the resources of the differentiated mechanisms can be brought to bear on the solution of human problems by virtue of the matched combinability of these separate mechanisms.

By way of contrast, consider the relative transformability of the drive, pain, and affect mechanisms. The drive mechanism is specific with respect to time and place—that the problem is in the mouth in the case of hunger. This information has been built into the site of consummation, so the probability of finding the correct consummatory response is very high. Hunger is also specific with respect to time. It tells us when to eat and when to stop eating. If the hunger receptors were instead in the palm of the hand, and if they contained no specific time information, we would spend our short lives rubbing the palms of our hands vigorously, endlessly, over any rubbable surface. The drive supplies vital information of where and when to do what. It normally requires additional affective amplification to make this specific information urgent.

The pain mechanism is like the drive system in its place specificity. When one pinches the skin, it hurts *there* (excepting referred pain). But unlike the drive system, the pain mechanism is time-general. We may never experience pain in all our lifetime or we may suffer constant intractable pain. Contrary to the imposed time rhythms which are structural in the drives, the pain mechanism is structurally timegeneral. It imposes no time constraints on whether or how often it must be activated.

The affect mechanism, in contrast to both drive and pain mechanisms, is both space- and time-general. One can be anxious for a moment, an hour, or a lifetime—anxious when a child, happy when an adult, or conversely. It is general with respect to its "object," whether that be its activator or what is responded to. In masochism one loves pain and death. In puritanism one hates pleasure and life. One can invest any and every aspect of existence with the magic of excitement and joy or with dread or fear or shame or distress. Affects are also capable of much greater generality of intensity than drives. If I do not eat, I become hungrier and hungrier. As I eat, I become less hungry. But I may wake mildly irritable in the morning and remain so for the rest of the day. Or one day I may not be at all angry until quite suddenly something makes me explode in a rage. I may start the day moderately angry and quickly become interested in some other matter and so dissipate anger. Affect density (the product of intensity times duration) can vary from low and casual to monopolistic and high in density—intense and enduring. Most drives operate within relatively narrow density tolerances. The consequence of too much variation of density of intake of air is loss of consciousness and possible death.

It is by virtue of its structurally based generality of space and time that it can readily coassemble with and therefore impart its urgency and lend its power to memory, to perception, to thought, and to action no less than to the drives. Not only may affects be widely invested and variously invested, but they may also be invested in other affects, combine with other affects, intensify or modulate them, and suppress or reduce them. Neither hunger nor thirst can be used to reduce the need for air, as a child may be shamed into crying or may be shamed into stopping his crying.

The basic power of the affect system is a consequence of its freedom to combine with a variety of other components in what I have called the central assembly. This is an executive mechanism upon which messages converge from all sources, competing from moment to moment for inclusion in this governing central assembly. The affect system can be evoked by central and peripheral messages from any source, and, in turn, it can control the disposition of such messages and their sources. Thus, it enjoys generality of dependence, independence, and interdependence. It is well suited for membership in a feedback mechanism since, from moment to moment, its role in the causal nexus can shift from independence to dependence to interdependence. It is free of the unidirectionality of billiard ball causal sequences (as would happen in a reflex chain, or to some extent in a drive chain). Affect can determine cognition at one time, be determined by cognition at another time, and also be interdependent under other circumstances. This permits one person to become truly more "cognitive" and another to be much more "affective" via the differential affective magnification of other mechanisms, including affect magnifying itself.

The same generality of combinatorial coassembly permits the differential magnification of biological, psychologocial, social, cultural, or historical determinants of affect. The recalcitrance of affects to social and cultural control is no more nor less real than their shaping by powerful cultural, historical, and social forces. I have distinguished excitement from enjoyment cultures and civilizations in which change or sameness, powerfully magnified by different cultures, captures and supports the appropriate families of affects which are necessary for living in a society which changes rapidly or slowly.

Next, by being coassembled with both activators and responses to affect and activator, and imprinting stimulus and response equally, in both an abstract and urgent way, the range of connectedness of experience is radically increased. Thus, via temporal overlap there may be produced S-S equivalences, S-R equivalences, and R-R equivalences mediated by affects and affect analogs. A pleasant person becomes a relaxing, warm, enjoyable, helpful person. An angry person becomes an angering, hurtful person. As affect density increases, it provides an increasingly viscous psychic glue which embeds very different phenomena in the same affective medium.

Finally, its generality is not time-dependent. Affective amplification is brief. To extend the duration and frequency of any scene, its amplifying affect must also be extended in duration and frequency. I have defined this as psychological magnification—the phenomenon of connecting one affect-laden scene with another affect-laden scene. This I have described as script theory (1980), and we will consider it briefly in the next chapter.

The conjoint characteristics of affect's urgency, abstractness, generality, analogic, and imprinting features thus together produce both match and, in varying degrees, mismatch between affect and other mechanisms, making it seem sometimes blind and inert, other times intuitive and flexible; sometimes brief and transient, other times enduring and committing; sometimes primarily biological, other times largely psychological, social, cultural, or historical; sometimes aesthetic, other times instrumental; sometimes private and solipsistic, other times communicative and expressive; sometimes explosive, other times overcontrolled and backed up.

Chapter 26

Affect and Cognition: Cognition as Central and Causal in Psychological Magnification

I have sharply contrasted the coincidental role of cognition in the evocation of affect as an amplifier, and its more central and causal role in the magnification of affect. Psychological magnification necessarily presupposes affective amplification, but amplification does not necessarily lead to magnification. Because affect is inherently brief, it requires the conjunction of other mechanisms to connect affective moments with each other and thereby increase the duration, coherence, and continuity of affective experience. Cognition plays a major role in such magnification.

The set of innate linkages between stimulus affect and response which I attribute to the affect mechanism suggests that human beings are to some extent innately endowed with the possibility of organized if primitive scenes or happenings somewhat under their own control, beginning as early as the neonatal period. In script theory, I define the scene as the basic element in life as it is lived. The simplest, most primitive scene includes at least one affect and at least one object of that affect. The object may be the perceived activator or the response to the activator or to the affect, and in a very special case the object of affect may be reflexive (i.e., affect about itself), for example, "What am I afraid of?" "Why am I afraid?" "Will my fear abate?" In such cases, the affect of interest is generated by the affect of fear.

If our experience must be amplified in its urgency by affect in order for any scene to be experienced, but affect itself can be as brief as a startle to a pistol shot, how can scenes themselves be amplified? To extend the duration and frequency of any scene, its amplifying affect must also be extended in duration and frequency. I distinguish the affective magnification of a single scene from psychological *magnification*—the phenomenon of connecting one affect-laden scene with another affect-laden scene. Psychological magnification necessarily presupposes affective amplification of sets of connected scenes, but the affective amplification of a single scene does not necessarily lead to the psychological magnification of interconnected scenes.

The concept of psychological magnification can be illustrated by two contrast cases. First are what I have defined as transient scenes. These are scenes which may be highly amplified by affect but which remain isolated in the experience of the individual. An automobile horn is heard unexpectedly and produces a momentary startle. It is not elaborated and has minimal consequences for any scenes which either have preceded this scene or which follow it. I may accidentally cut myself while shaving one morning. Unless I am severely neurotic, this is not experienced as a deepening sense of defensive self-mutilation in response to the threat of castration. It does not heighten a sense of helplessness and does not become a self-fulfilling prophecy. Or I listen to a very funny joke and laugh. Though the scene may be intensely rewarding because of the cleverness of the joke, it may remain a transient scene. No decisions on life work, on marriage, children, or friendship will ever be based on such an experience. The experience is unlikely to haunt me. Unless I am a professional raconteur, I am not likely even to repeat it to anyone else, or to myself. Lives are made up of large numbers of transient scenes. All experience is not necessarily interconnected with all other experience. Psychologists have not stressed such scenes because their interest is in understanding the interconnectedness of experience and the deep structures which subserve such connectedness. Nonetheless, if one were to summate the total duration of transient scenes in the lifetime of any individual, that sum might not be inconsequential. The total quantity of banality and triviality in a life may not itself be a trivial phenomenon but rather a reflection of the failure of the development of competing magnified scenes.

Second in contrast to psychological magnification are scenes which are neither transient nor casual but rather are recurrent, *habitual scenes,* which we have commented on before. These are subserved by habitual skills, programs which represent much compression of information in such a way that it can be expanded effectively but with minimal consciousness, thought, and affect. Every day I shave my face in the morning. When I finish, consider how unlikely it would be for me to look in the mirror, beam at myself, and say, "What a magnificent human being you are—you have done it again!" The paradox is that it is just those achievements which are most solid, which work best, and which continue to work that excite and reward us least. The price of skill is the loss of the experience of value—and of the zest for living. The same kind of skill can impoverish the aesthetic experience too often repeated, so that a beautiful piece of music ceases to be responded to. A husband and wife who become too skilled in knowing each other can enter the same valley of perceptual skill and become hardly aware of each other. Skills may become temporarily magnified whenever they prove inadequate, or permanently magnified as a result of brain damage from a stroke, when the individual must now exert himself heroically to relearn and execute what had once been an effortless skill.

Consider another type of habitual scene which I have called the "as if" scene. Everyone learns to cross streets with minimal ideation, perceptual scanning, and affect. We learn to act as if we were afraid but we do not, in fact, experience any fear once we have learned how to cope successfully with such contingencies. Despite the fact that we know there is real danger involved daily in walking across intersections and that many pedestrians are, in fact, killed, we exercise normal caution with minimal attention and no fear. It may remain a minimally magnified scene despite daily repetition over a lifetime. Such scenes do not become magnified, just because they are effective in achieving precisely what the individual intends they should achieve. Though we have said they are based on habitual skills, they are far from being simple motor habits. They are small programs for processing information with relatively simple strategies, but one may nonetheless never repeat precisely the same avoidance behaviors twice in crossing any street. These simple programs generate appropriate avoidant strategies for dealing with a variety of such situations, and caution is nicely matched to the varying demands of this class of situations, with a minimum of attention and affect. It should be noted that many highly magnified scenes are usually based upon and include habitual skills but *in addition* require intense vigilance—cognitive, perceptual, affective, and motoric—in order to transform the skilled programs to meet the ever-new demands of constantly changing situations. Such would be the case for professional tennis players in a championship match. Their skills are almost never entirely adequate until and unless they are continually rapidly transformed to meet the novelty of each encounter. Under such conditions, there is increasing psychological magnification of their tennis scenes on and off the court in rehearsal of the past and anticipation of future encounters of the same kind.

If a life was restricted to a series of transient scenes, punctuated by habitual scenes, such a life would be fatally impoverished by virtue of insufficient psychological magnification. It would resemble the actual life of an overly domesticated cat who never ventures outdoors and by virtue of having totally explored its restricted environment spends much of its adult life in a series of catnaps.

AUTOSIMULATION AND THE BEGINNING OF MAGNIFICATION

How and when does psychological magnification begin? Let us look now at the earliest examples of psychological magnification. We are born human beings. As such we inherit all the standard vital equipment which enables us to survive. But we also inherit a complex system of mechanisms which have evolved to make it extremely probable that we will become a person. In computerese, this is the difference between the hardware and the software. In language, this is the difference between the syntax and the semantics. Psychologically, it is the difference between the innate and the learned.

Consider one of the earliest human scenes, the hungry infant in the arms of his mother. As a human being, he carries as standard equipment the rooting reflex, by which he turns his head from side to side in front of the breast, and the sucking reflex, by which he manages to get the milk from his mother's breast once his lips have found and locked onto her teat. By any conception of the good life, this is a good scene. He appears to himself, as to his mother, to be utterly competent (and that without even trying) to make the world his oyster, to reduce and appease his hunger, and at the same time to reap the rewards of drive satisfaction. As a bonus, this reward is further amplified by bursts of the positive affects of excitement followed by the positive affect of enjoyment at satiety.

Is there any reason to expect trouble in such a paradise? Everything is in the best imaginable working order. And yet the newborn infant is *not* fundamentally happy with this state of affairs. His behavior, soon after birth, seems to tell us, "I'd rather do it myself! I may not be able to do it as well as those reflexes do it, but I might be able to do it better, and I'm going to try." The experiments of Jerome Bruner (1968) have shown that, very early on, the infant will replace the reflex sucking by beginning to suck voluntarily, and this is discriminably different from reflex sucking. If he succeeds, he will continue. If it doesn't work too well, he falls back on reflex sucking. This is a prime example of what I have called *autosimulation* or imitation of one's own reflexes. The same phenomenon occurs with the orienting reflex and the several supporting ocular motor reflexes. Although the eye is innately equipped to track any moving stimulus in a reflex way, I have observed apparently voluntary moving of the head and neck very early on to bring visual tracking under voluntary control.

Psychological magnification begins, then, in earliest infancy, when the infant imagines, via coassembly, a possible improvement in what is already a rewarding scene, attempts to do what may be necessary to bring it about, and so produces and connects a set of scenes which continue to reward him with food and its excitement and enjoyment, and also with the excitement and enjoyment of remaking the world closer to the heart's desire. He is doing what he will continue to try to do all his life—to command the scenes he wishes to play. Like Charlie Chaplin, he will try to write, direct, produce, criticize, and promote the scenes in which he casts himself as hero.

There is a deep mystery at the heart of the earliest attempts at simulation, whether that be of the other or of the self. Meltzoff and Moore (1977) have recently shown that neonates will imitate the facial responses of others they see for the first time. Contrary to Piagetian expectations, such early initiative in imitation and command of the earliest scenes, both of others and of the self, must be powered by emergents of the conjoint interactions of the several basic mechanisms which are standard equipment for the human being. It seems extremely improbable that the earliest hetero- and autosimulation could be wired in preformed software or hardware. It is also improbable that such an intention could be located in either the perceptual, cognitive, affective, or motoric mechanism. The idea of imitation, the intention to imitate, and the execution of imitation is not an inherited idea located in the cognitive mechanism, certainly not in the eye, certainly not in the affect programs, and certainly not in the hand and fingers. In order to imitate the other or the self, infants must somehow generate the idea that it would be something to do, generate the requisite affective interest first in the phenomenon and then in its imitation, guide the mouth, fingers, and hands in a feedback-controlled manner, and stop when the intention has been achieved (which in the case of imitation of the other they cannot see). In the case of autosimulation, the idea which they must generate of doing voluntarily what they have experienced involuntarily is nowhere present as a possible model. It represents an extraordinary creative invention conjointly powered by primitive perceptual and cognitive capacities amplified by excitement in the *possibility* of improving a good actual scene by doing something oneself. These are real phenomena, and they appear to be highly probably emergents from the interaction of several basic human capacities. This is why I have argued that we have evolved to be born as human beings who will, with a very high probability, very early attempt and succeed in becoming persons. There are some additional assumptions which are necessarily involved in such precocious achievements, but we will not examine them here.

The most basic feature of psychological magnification appears, therefore, in the first day of life—the expansion of one scene in the direction of a connected but somewhat different scene.

But if psychological magnification, as we have observed it in autosimulation, is heroic, it is not always, nor necessarily so. Even in infancy, the scenes may be more tragic than heroic. Fries (1944) experimented with infants by taking the nipple of the bottle away. Though many infants continued to struggle to recapture it, and gladly accepted it when offered again, some infants not only went to sleep but actively resisted efforts by the experimenter to reinsert the nipple into the mouth. These infants apparently judged the scene a bad one with which they wanted no more experience at that time. Negative affect proved stronger than the hunger drive. The quality of life, as these infants first encounter it, is poor.

We have contrasted transient scenes which are not magnified, whether they occur in infancy or at any time, with the earliest instances of heroic magnification on the part of the infant. This impression of the infant's readiness for initiative and magnification should now be tempered by another formidable aspect of human development—the infant's extremely limited capacity to relate experiences which occur at time intervals of any duration. Although infants are capable not only of relating scenes which follow quickly one upon the other but even of generating new scenes in response to immediately experienced scenes, they are not capable during the first six months of life of connecting what has happened before with what happens much later, as that interval increases.

LIMITED MEMORY AND LIMITED MAGNIFICATION

An investigation by David Levy (1960) gives a classic account of the limited ability of the six-month-old infant to relate one scene to another even when the scenes involve intense affective amplification. Such scenes are likely to remain transient scenes and to exercise little influence on development before six months of age. Six-month-old infants who had cried in pain at an inoculation they had received were observed on their second visit, a few months later, to the same doctor in the same clinic. Such infants show no sign of being afraid or distressed as they see the doctor in the white coat come at them with needle in hand. Though they do cry as soon as they feel the pain of the needle, they appear neither to remember what happened before nor to anticipate a repetition of the bad scene before. The pain of each inoculation is indeed amplified by the cry of distress, but nothing new has been added. It is presumably no worse than the first time because there has been no *anticipation* amplified by the affect. A few months later, they will *cry* at the sight of the doctor and the needle, as well as at the actual inoculation. This is psychological magnification, the phenomenon of connecting one affect-laden scene with another affect-laden scene. Through memory, thought, and imagination, scenes experienced before can be coassembled with scenes presently experienced, together with scenes which are anticipated in the future. The present moment is embedded in the intersect between the past and the future in a central assembly via a constructive process we have called coassembly. It is the same process by which we communicate in speech: The meaning of any one word is enriched and magnified by sequentially coassembling it with words which precede it and which follow it. So, too, is the meaning and impact of one affect-laden scene enriched and magnified by coassembling and relating it to another affect-laden scene. In infancy, therefore, magnification begins with immediately sequential experience but is severely limited in magnification potential whenever experience is separated in time.

MAGNIFICATION ADVANTAGE

I define magnification as the advantaged ratio of the simplicity of ordering information to the power of ordered information times its affect density:

Magnification Advantage

$$= \frac{\text{Power of Ordered Information} \times \text{Affect Density}}{\text{Simplicity of Ordering Information}}$$

The concept of magnification advantage is the product of information advantage and affect density (Intensity × Duration × Frequency). Information advantage, as I am defining it, is that part of the above formula minus the affect. It is fashioned after the concept of mechanical advantage in which the lever enables a small force to move a larger force, or as with a valve by which small energy forces are used to control a flow of much larger forces, as in a water distribution system. Informational advantage is an analog. Any highly developed theory possesses great informational advantage, being able to account for much with little via the ratio of a small number of simple assumptions to a much larger number of phenomena described and explained, which constitutes its power. The helix possesses very great informational advantage, capable as it is of vast expansion properties of guidance and control.

But information advantage is not identical with magnification. Consider the difference between the information advantage of what I have described as the valley of perceptual skill—the ability of an individual to "recognize" the presence of a familiar face at varying distances or directions—and varying alternative small samples of the whole. To see the chin, or the nose, or the forehead, or any combination is quite enough to enable skilled expansion of these bits of information so that one "knows" who the other is. It is "as if" information, with minimal (but accurate) awareness *and* minimal affect. All habitual skills operate via *compressed* information with minimal ratio of conscious reports to messages and with minimal affect. Thus, one may cross a busy intersection "as if" afraid, looking up and down for possible danger from passing automobiles, but characteristically without *any* fear and with minimal awareness of scanning. Contrast the informational advantage of a husband and wife "recognizing" the face of the other with the recognition of the same face in the midst of their initial love affair. When the lover detects the face of the beloved as a figure in a sea of other faces as ground, there is no less informational advantage involved in that recognition of the newly familiar face, but there is a radical magnification of consciousness and affect, which, together with all the significances attributed to the other, make if an unforgettable moment.

In our proposed ratio for script magnification, the denominator represents the compressed (smaller) number of rules for *ordering* scenes, whereas the numerator represents the expanded (much larger) number of scenes, both from the past and into the indefinite future, which are *ordered* by the smaller number of compressed rules. In the numerator there are represented both the scenes which gave rise to the necessity for the script and all the scenes which are generated as responses to deal with the initial coassembly of scenes, either to guarantee the continuation of good scenes, their improvement, the decontamination of bad scenes, or the avoidance of threatening scenes. The compressed smaller number of rules guide responses which, in turn, recruit amplifying affect as well as samples of the family of scenes either sought, interpreted, evaluated, produced, or expanded.

Because there is a *mixture* of informational advantage and affect-driven amplification, the individual is characteristically much less conscious of the compressed rules than of their expansion scenes, just as one is less aware of one's grammar than of the sentences one utters. Although the compression of rule information in the denominator always involves information reduction and simplification, there may be varying quantities of information in the number of coassembled scenes which gave rise to the scripted responses in scenes yet to be played, as well as varying intensities, durations, and frequencies of affect assigned to these scenes and to the scripted response scenes. Thus, a low-degree-of-magnification script may involve a small number of scenes to be responded to by a small number of scripted scenes with moderate, relatively brief affect. In contrast, a high-degree-of-magnification script may involve a large number of scenes to be responded to by a large number of scripted scenes with intense and enduring affect. The magnification *advantage* ratio of either script might nonetheless be low or high, depending on the ratio of ordering rules to rules ordered.

Further, any of the values in such equations are susceptible to change. Thus, in the midst of a heart attack (in a case reported by an English physician about himself), there was a rapid review of many scenes of his past life, their relationship to the present and future, a deep awareness that his life could never again be quite the same, and gradually a return to the status quo in which that whole series of reevaluations became attenuated and eventually segregated to exert diminishing instructions on how he conducted his life. Again, a central much magnified script involving someone of vital importance may be first magnified to the utmost via death and mourning and by that very process be ultimately attenuated, producing a series of habitually skilled reminiscences which eventually become segregated and less and less retrieved. Mourning thus retraces in reverse the love affair and is a second edition of it, similar in some ways to the mini-version of these sequences in jealousy, when a long quiescent valley of perceptual skill may be ignited by an unexpected rival.

The most magnified scripts require minimal reminders that the present is vitally connected to much of our past life and to our future and that we must attend with urgency to continually act in such a way that the totality will be as we very much wish it to be and not as we fear it might be. Between such a script and scripts I have labeled "doable" (in which one may pay one's bills as a moratorium in the midst of a task which is critical but, for the time being, "undoable" by any conceivable path) are a large number of scripts of every degree of magnification and type, which we will presently examine in more detail.

It should be noted that the measure is somewhat ambiguous in the sense that the volume of an object is ambiguous; that is, it is a product which may be the same though varying in its components. Thus, magnification might be the same between two scripts but vary in the intensity, duration, or frequency of affect density, or vary in the relative number of scenes coassembled versus scenes scripted for response versus the number of compressed rules for the governance of scenes.

Inasmuch as the degree of magnification varies, it is also a relative measure defined as differential magnification. Just as an individual's weight may vary so that he is heavier in the evening than in the morning, heavier at age thirty than at age ten, heavier than one friend and lighter than another, so he may be more or less differentially magnified and scripted for addictive dependency, strength of commitment, relative magnification of excitement versus enjoyment within and between scripts, at varying times or conditions or with respect to varying reference groups. Inasmuch as there are an indefinite number of such possible comparisons between the differential magnification of one script versus another within and between individuals, times, and conditions, I have conceptualized differential magnification as a special case of plurideterminacy, which is the continuing change in causal status of any "cause" by the variation of conditions (including its "effects") which succeed it and embed it in the nexus of a connected system, not excluding anticipations of possibilities in the future which can and do either further magnify and or attenuate different features of the origins of any scripted set of scenes.

SOME GENERAL FEATURES OF SCRIPTS

In my script theory, the scene, a happening with a perceived beginning and end, is the basic unit of analysis. The whole connected set of scenes lived in sequence is called the *plot* of a life. The script, in contrast, does not deal with all the scenes or the plot of a life, but rather with the individual's rules for predicting, interpreting, responding to, and controlling a magnified set of scenes.

Although I am urging what appears to be a dramaturgic model for the study of personality, it is sufficiently different in nature from what may seem to be similar theories to warrant some brief disclaimers. By scenes, scripts, and script theory, I do not mean that the individual is inherently engaged in impression management for the benefit of an audience, after Goffman. Such scenes are not excluded as possible scenes, but they are very special cases, limited either to specific individuals personality who are on stage much of their lives or to specific occasions for any human beings when they feel they are being watched and evaluated. Nor do I mean that the individual is necessarily caught in inauthentic "games," after Berne, nor are these necessarily excluded. Some individuals' scripts may indeed be well described as a game, and any and all individuals may on occasion play such games, but they are a very special kind of scene and script. Nor is script theory identical with role theory. Roles seldom completely define the personality of an individual, and when this does happen, we encounter a very specialized kind of script. The several possible relationships between roles and scripts, such as their mutual support and their conflicts, as well as their relative independence of each other, provide a new important bridge between personality theory and general social science. Indeed, what sociologists have called the definition of the situation and what I am defining as the script is to some extent the same phenomenon viewed from two different but related theoretical perspectives—the scene as defined by the society or as defined by the individual. These definitions are neither necessarily nor always identical, but they must necessarily be related to each other, rather than completely orthogonal to each other, if either the society or the individual is to remain viable. If the society is ever to change, there must be some tension sustained between the society's definition of the situation and the individual's script. If the society is to endure as a coherent entity, its definition of situations must in some measure be constructed as an integral part of the shared scripts of its individuals.

The closest affinity of my views is with the script theoretic formulation of Robert Abelson (1975) and Schank and Abelson (1977). Although their use of the concept of script is somewhat different from mine, the theoretical structure lends itself to ready mapping one onto the other, despite terminological differences which obscure important similarities of the entire two theoretical structures.

Before examining specific scripts I will now present some of the general features of all scripts:

1. Scripts are *sets of ordering rules* for the interpretation, evaluation, prediction, production, or control of scenes.
2. They are *selective* in the number and types of scenes which they order.
3. They are *incomplete* rules even within the scenes they attempt to order.
4. They are in varying degrees *accurate* and *inaccurate* in their interpretation, evaluation, prediction, control, or production.
5. Because of their selectivity, incompleteness, and inaccuracy, they are *continually reordered* and changing, at varying rates, depending on their type and the type and magnitude of disconfirmation.
6. The coexistence of different competing scripts requires the formation of *interscript* scripts.
7. Most scripts are *more self-validating than self-fulfilling.* Thus, a mourning script validates the importance of the lost relationship, but in the end it frees the individual from that relationship. A nuclear script which attempts to reduce shame validates the self as appropriately shameworthy more than it succeeds in freeing the individual of his burden. A commitment script validates the importance and necessity of the struggle, but the achievement of the commitment may erode it or require its redefinition to continue. A hoarding script validates the danger of insufficiency more than it guarantees against its possibility. A power script validates the danger of powerlessness more than it guarantees the adequacy and perpetuation of power. A purity script validates the impurity of the individual more than it guarantees his purity.

8. The incompleteness of scripts necessarily requires *auxiliary* augmentation. This may be gained via *media mechanisms* (e.g., vision) which provide relevant contemporary information which cannot be entirely written into any script except in a general way. Even the simplest habitual skilled scripts, such as shaving, requires a mirror; driving a car requires constant monitoring no matter how skilled the driver. One cannot begin to use any script without much information which cannot be scripted in advance. Further, one normally requires auxiliary media information gained by use of the arms and legs, to reach further information as well as to alter perspectives. Again, one requires speech and/or written language as auxiliary sources of information, past as well as present. These are also media mechanisms but culturally inherited media. Next one requires as auxiliaries, compressed information in the form of *theories,* lay and professional, about causal relationships, signs or omens, intentions and consequences. Next, one requires the memorially supported *plot,* which is a sequentially organized series of scenes of the life one has led and the lives others have led. Then one requires *maps,* which are spatiotemporal schematics which enable the plots to be handled more economically. We possess maps of varying degrees of fineness of texture, normally generated by their usefulness for different scripts. The difference between a duffer and a professional tennis player is reflected not only in the differences between their families of tennis scripts but also in the detail of the maps of their opponents' past performances. Finally, one script may use another script as auxiliary. Thus, Calvinism used the entrepreneurial activity of the economic competition script to increase the probability of grace in warding off the hell fires of their vivid version of the life hereafter.
9. Scripts contain *variables as alternatives.* Variables are those rules which as alternatives depend on auxiliary information to further specify. A script thus may, for example, differentiate strategy and tactics, conditional upon variable auxiliary information. Thus, Hitler gave orders to his generals to march on the Ruhr but to retreat at any sign of resistance from the French. A child may learn to script a relationship with a parent in which he extorts as much as possible just within the limits of the patience and power of the indulgent but irrascible other. The auxiliary information need, however, not be limited to external information. An otherwise deeply committed individual may nonetheless exempt himself from his major concern should he become ill or seriously disturbed or depressed. Very few scripts are conceived as completely unconditional, since they are designed to deal with variable selected features of selected scenes. When unanticipated conditions are encountered, the individual has the option of further adding to the script "not when I'm sick" or "no matter what, I must keep at it." Indeed, as we shall presently see, it is just such encounters and their absorption which are critical in the deepening of a commitment script.
10. Scripts have the property of *modularity.* They are variously combinable, recombinable, and decomposable. The separate scripts may be aggregated and *fused,* as when a career choice combines scripts which enable an individual to explore nature, to be alone, and to express himself through writing, as in the case of Eugene O'Neill, who chose to live at the ocean's edge in solitude as he wrote his plays. Compare such a set of component subscripts with that of a lumberjack who enjoys nature but in the company of others and also exercising his large muscles. Contrast both with an archeologist who is enchanted with the rediscovery of the past, with others, in very special remote nature sites. Not only is each component of a single script endlessly combinable and recombinable, but so are scripts themselves, as when addictive scripts for smoking, eating, and drinking are combined in a bottoming-out nuclear script.

Scripts may also be *partitioned,* as in the classic neurotic split libido and in the characteristically French separation of family and mistress—one cherished for enjoyment and continuity, the other for novelty and excitement.

LAURA: AN EXAMPLE OF CHILDHOOD MAGNIFICATION

Let us examine how a set of scenes may become magnified sufficiently to prompt the generation of a script. The case we will use is that of Laura, a young girl studied by Robertson in connection with a study of the effects of hospitalization on young children when they are separated from their parents. Laura was hospitalized for about a week. During this week away from her parents she was subjected to a variety of medical examinations and procedures and also was photographed by a moving picture camera near her crib. Like many young children, she missed her parents, was somewhat disturbed by the medical procedures, and cried a good deal. The quality of her life changed radically that week from good to bad. But what of the more permanent effect of these bad scenes on the quality of her life? First, the answer to such a question will depend critically on the degree of magnification which *follows* this week. How many times will she rehearse these bad scenes? Will such rehearsals coassemble the scenes in such an order and with such spacing that they are experienced as magnifying or attenuating the negative affects connected with these scenes? Further, apart from her own imagination, what will be the quantity of good and bad scenes she experiences at home when she returns? Will her parents further frighten or reassure her, or in attempting to reassure her give her an implicit message that she has been through hell? Further, will this be the beginning of further medical problems, or will it be an isolated week in her life?

What is important from the point of view of script theory is that the effect of any set of scenes is *indeterminate* until the future either further magnifies or attenuates such experience. The second point is that the consequence of any experience is not singular but plural. There is no *single* effect, but rather there are many effects, which change in time—what I have called the principle of *plurideterminacy.* Thus, when Laura first returned home, she appeared to be disturbed. Therefore, the effect, if we had measured it then, was deleterious. But in a few days she was her normal self again. Now if we assessed the effect, we would say that over the long term it was *not* so serious. However, some time later, when Robertson visited her home to interview her parents, she became disturbed once again, so the magnification of the bad scene had now been increased. This illustrates a very important third principle of psychological magnification and script formation: Scenes are magnified not by repetition but by repetition with a *difference.* It is, as in art, the unity in variety which engages the mind and heart of the person who is experiencing a rapid growth of punishment or reward. Sheer repetition of experience characteristically evokes adaptation which attenuates, rather than magnifies, the connected scenes. In the case of Laura, it is the very fact that Robertson now unexpectedly has invaded her home—the fortress of love and security—that has changed everything for the worse. Up to this point the main danger appeared to be that her parents might take her from her home and leave her in an alien, dangerous environment. But now her parents appear to be either unwilling or unable to prevent the dangerous intrusion into what was, till then, safe space. Indeed, they may appear to have become more problematic. Yet in a few days all is again well, and we would be tempted to think that the affair has been closed, that the long-term effects of the hospitalization are not serious.

All goes well for some time. Then Laura is taken to an art museum by her parents. They wish to see an exhibition of paintings. They leave Laura in a white crib which the museum provides. What will be the effect of this? Once before, they took her to a hospital and left her in a white crib. Will she become disturbed and cry? She does not—so we have been correct in supposing that the experience in the hospital is limited in its long-term effects. She has been left by her parents in a white crib, but the deadly parallel escapes her. A few minutes later, however, a man comes by with a camera and takes a picture of her. And now she does cry. The family of connected scenes has again been critically enlarged. This man is not Robertson. He has a camera, not a moving picture camera. It is an art museum, not a hospital—but it smells like danger to Laura, and her own crying becomes self-validating. The scene, whether dangerous or not, has been made punishing by her own crying. Any scene which is sufficiently similar to evoke the same kind of affect is thereby made more similar and increases the degree of connectedness of the whole family of scenes. Just as members of a family are not similar in all respects, yet appear to be recognized as members of the same family, so do connected scenes which are psychologically magnified become more similar as members of a family of scenes. The scene in the hospital, at home, and at the museum will now be sufficiently magnified to generate a script. What will this script be like?

First, it should be noted that this series of scenes involve little action on the part of Laura. She responds affectively to the hospital and museum scenes but is otherwise passive. She has not as yet developed action strategies for avoiding or escaping such threatening scenes. We do not know for sure that—or how much—she anticipates or rehearses these scenes. Therefore, our examination of the dynamics of script formation in the case of Laura is limited to script formation which is primarily interpretive and reactive and is a simplified case of what normally includes more active reaction to and participation in the generation of scenes and scripts. It is, however, useful for us at this stage of our presentation of script theory to deal with the simplest type of script which emphasizes the attainment of understanding of what is happening in a scene, since more complex scripts necessarily always include such understanding before coping strategies can be developed.

A complete understanding of the formation of scripts must rest on a foundation of perceptual, cognitive, memory, affect, action, and feedback theory. Needless to say, none of these separate mechanisms has been entirely satisfactorily illuminated at a theoretical level, and their complex modes of interaction in a feedback system is an achievement far from realization. Yet an understanding of the complexities involved in interpreting and perceptually and cognitively ordering constantly shifting information from one scene to the next requires just such a missing theory. I will present my theories of perception, cognition, memory, and feedback mechanisms upon which I have based script theory in Volume 4. I will use some of these assumptions in an illustrative but incomplete way in the following attempts to understand script formation.

The perception of a scene, at its simplest, involves a partitioning of the scene into figure and ground. The figural part of the scene, as in any object perception, is the most salient and most differentiated part of it, separated from the ground by a sharp gradient which produces a contour or connected boundary which separates the figure from its less differentiated ground. Such a figure becomes figural characteristically as a conjoint function of sharply differentiated gradients of stimulation (of shape, texture, or color in the visual field, of loudness, pitch, or rhythm in the auditory field), internal gradients of experienced affect (so that, e.g., it is the object with contours which excites, and is experienced as "exciting" rather than the ground), correlated gradients of experienced internal images and/or thoughts and/or words so that the object is experienced as fused with recruited images or imageless compressed thoughts or is fused with a word (e.g., "mother") and with actions taken or with action potentials (e.g., that object is touchable, can be put in the mouth, or dropped to make a sound). These separate sources of information, converging conjointly in what I have called the central assembly, interact intimately and produce an organization of a simple scene into a salient figure differentiated from a more diffuse background.

Differentiation of a scene involves shifting centration away from one figure to another aspect of the same scene which now becomes figural. The first figure characteristically becomes a compressed part of the ground but capable of later expansion so that it may produce a more complex awareness of the now more differentiated scene. Ultimately, the whole scene is compressed and perceived as a habitual skill so that very small alternative samplings tell individuals all they think they then want to know about a repeated scene. After achieving some knowledge of the general characteristics of a scene with respect to its beginning (what started the scene), its cast (who is in the scene), its place (where it is), its time (when did it take place), its actions (who did what), its functions (did I see it, dream it, think about it, move around in it), its events (what happened—e.g., it snowed, there was an accident), its props (what things are in the scene—e.g., trees, automobiles), its outcomes (what happened at the end of the scene), and its end (what terminated the scene), the individual, through memory and thought, is then in a position to compare total scenes with each other—to coassemble them and to begin to understand their several possible relationships to each other. Such comparisons between two or more scenes may go on in a third scene quite distinct from the scenes being compared, or the preceding scenes may be recruited simultaneously with another apparent repetition of one or more of the earlier scenes, in an effort to understand the similarities and differences between the present scene and its forerunners.

The human being handles the information in a family of connected scenes in ways which are not very different from the ways in which scientists handle information. They attempt to maximize the order inherent in the information in as efficient and powerful a way as is consistent with their prior knowledge and with their present channel capacity limitations. Since the efficiency and power of any theory is a function of the ratio of the number of explanation assumptions in the denominator relative to the number of phenomena explained in the numerator, human beings, like any scientist, attempt to explain as much of the variance as they can with the fewest possible assumptions. This is in part because of an enforced limitation on their ability to process information and in part because some power to command, understand, predict, and control their scenes is urgently demanded if they are to optimize the ratio of rewarding positive and punishing negative affect in their lives.

In their attempt to order the information and produce a script from a set of scenes, they will first of all partition the variance into what they regard as the major variance and the residual variance—the big, most important features of the set of scenes and the constants of their script equation as differentiated from the related, more differentiated variables of their script equation. In this respect, the procedure resembles factor-analytic procedures, whereby a general factor of intelligence is first extracted, followed by more specific factors which account for less and less of the variance. It resembles analysis of variance procedures in its strategy of first asking if there is a main effect and then asking about more specific interactions.

What is the general script factor or the main-effect script question likely to be? It is characteristically determined by three conjoint criteria: (1) What is experienced with the most dense (i.e., the most intense and enduring) affect? (2) What are experienced as the sharpest gradients of change of such affect? (3) What are the most frequently repeated sequences of such affect and affect changes? Whenever these three criteria are conjointly met in any series of scenes, they will constitute the first major partitioning of the variance within and between scenes. The most repeated changes in dense affect may occur either within any scene or between scenes or both. It should be noted that any one of these principles might operate in the organization of a *single* scene. An individual would, of course, pay attention to anything which deeply distressed him, to anything which suddenly changed, or to anything which was repeated within a scene. When, however, the task shifts to ordering a complex set of changes, both within and between scenes, his ability to deal with the totality of such information is sharply reduced. It is for this reason, I think, that the criteria for judging what is most important become more selective by requiring that conjoint conditions be met in a hierarchical order. The big picture must first be grasped before it can be fleshed in. An important, repeated change is the general script factor. This includes internal repetition, in past rehearsal and future anticipation.

Let us examine how this may operate in the case of Laura. The most repeated, most dense affects, which change most sharply, are those in going from home to hospital, from positive to negative affect; in going from hospital to home, a much slower change from negative to positive affect; in going from being at home with parents to the intrusion of Dr. Robertson, sharp change from positive to negative; in going from his intrusion back to being alone again with her parents, a slower change from negative to positive; and finally, in going from home to the art museum, a sharp change from positive to negative affect. The most general part of her script, therefore, can be described as a sequence of repeated dense, positive-affect scenes which suddenly change into dense, negative-affect scenes and then more slowly change back into dense positive scenes via a set of mixed positive and negative transition scenes. If we were to diagram it, it would look like this: $+ - \mp + - \mp +$. In Laura's case the relative time of the dense positive scenes is characteristically much longer than that of the dense negative scenes. The duration of the mixed transition scenes from negative to positive we do not have enough information to describe precisely. Such a regular alternation as occurs in this case is by no means the rule in the experience of human beings. Much change within and between scenes may be perceived as random or without any sharp gradients. Many series of scenes need not invoke very intense or enduring affect. Much change within and between scenes may involve little apparent repetition. Further, the relative density of positive and negative affect and the direction of change within and between scenes need not be as they appear in this case.

Having extracted and partitioned this main variance, let us now examine the residual more specific, more differentiated variance. This script, like any processing of information, will change in time as new evidence accumulates. Based upon the first change in scenes, the residual variance would have been partitioned in the following way. There are two contrasting, correlated sets of distinctive features which account for the general variance of alternation of positive- and negative-affect scenes. The good, positive-affect scene is characterized by *place* (at home), by *cast* (with parents), and by *action* (conversation, playing, etc.). The bad, negative-affect scene is characterized by the same distinctive features—place, cast, and action—but with the place the hospital, the cast a doctor and a moving picture cameraman, and the action medical procedures. Such a neat set of contrasted correlated features could not be sustained the moment the doctor appeared in her home. In this scene, the bad member of the cast still remains the same, but place (the home) is no longer totally safe, and action (the doctor speaking to parents) is no longer the same as a medical examination or moving picture taking but is nonetheless disturbing. In the third scene the place is at first a good place, but, eventually becomes a bad place even though it is neither home nor hospital. The cast is also not the same but someone like the moving picture cameraman. The action is not the same but somewhat similar, having a still picture taken.

At the end of this set of scenes, the residual variance which accounts for the general variance can be understood by the theory of the family of scenes. If we think of a set of scenes composed of features $a\ b\ c\ d\ e\ f$ and their contrasting features, $a'\ b'\ c'\ d'\ e'\ f'$, then if $a \ldots f$ is contrasted with $a' \ldots f'$ as correlated variance which produces $-$ to $+$ affect changes, versus $+$ to $-$ affect changes, then, in general, any contrast subsets of these two families become capable of producing the same contrasting general variance.

So, for example:

$$\begin{array}{lll}
\phantom{\text{or}}\ a\ b\ c & \phantom{\text{or}}\ \text{vs.} & a'\ b'\ c' \\
 & \text{or vs.} & \ b'\ c' \\
\text{or}\ b\ c\ d & \phantom{\text{or}}\ \text{vs.} & b'\ c'\ d' \\
 & \text{or vs.} & b' \ d' \\
\text{or}\ c\ d\ e & \phantom{\text{or}}\ \text{vs.} & c'\ d'\ e' \\
 & \text{or vs.} & c'\ d' \\
\text{or}\ a\ d\ e & \phantom{\text{or}}\ \text{vs.} & a'\ d'\ e' \\
 & \text{or vs.} & \ d'\ e'
\end{array}$$

would by virtue of family resemblances become capable of producing the same shifts from $+$ to $-$ affect or from $-$ to $+$ affect as the fuller, more tightly correlated set might have done originally.

Indeed, psychological magnification would continue to grow by virtue of incremental subtractions, additions, and transformations of distinctive features which expanded the family without violating it. It is a mechanism similar to what in fact happens in the recognition of a remote member of a family one sees for the first time. One may note that he has the family chin and nose but not the usual hair color. One now has an expanded knowledge of *that* family. When Laura can experience the same disturbance in three different places—hospital, home, and museum—with two different members of the cast—Dr. Robertson and the photographer at the museum—and with three different actions—medical examinations, Dr. Robertson talking to her parents, the photographer taking a still picture—there is nonetheless enough overlap of similar contrasting subsets to account for the critical affect shifts while at the same time she learns to be disturbed by the same people in a new place or by new people in new places doing somewhat new things. As these variants grow in number yet continue to produce the more general changes in dense affect, psychological magnification increases. One should also note that such growth is at first quite discriminating. There is what I have called a critical *interscene distance,* which itself changes with magnification, which determines how different a scene can be and still be responded to as if it were much the same. Thus, when Laura was taken out of the home to the art museum and left alone in a crib very similar to the one in the hospital, this was not sufficiently similar to evoke the critical general shift in affect.

I presume that each scene has a specific address in the nervous system and that such an address has one or more "names" which know that address and will retrieve that scene. I also presume the existence of names of names, that is, messages which know or direct processing to another name. For example, most individuals have two separate programs for handwriting. One of these is for slow handwriting and one is for fast handwriting. One name for the slow handwriting is the instruction "write very slowly." Under this instruction one can recover early handwriting. But the same program can be reached by the instruction "write on the blackboard in letters two feet tall." Since this is an entirely new task, the individual ordinarily writes slowly, and such large letters are characteristically written in the early way. Magnification of scenes also grows in this fashion if the scene being experienced calls upon a unique older scene for guidance in interpretation and action by virtue of being a name of a name of a unique scene. The theory of the varieties of types of names which will know the address of unique scenes in the brain will be described in the chapter on memory in Volume 4.

Laura, therefore, now has a script which sensitizes her to scan for sudden possibilities of danger—but danger which will slowly subside and return her to safety and well-being for a time, the cycle to be repeated again and again depending on how much this script is further magnified. In the early stages of magnification, it is the set of scenes which determine the script; but as magnification increases, it is the script which increasingly determines the scenes. How this can happen we will now consider.

Such a script as the one generated by Laura may or may not be further magnified in the future. All persons are governed by a multiplicity of scripts generated to deal with particular sets of scenes of varying degree of magnification. Some scripts wax and wane in importance, e.g., those subserving interpersonal relationships which themselves are magnified at one time and atrophy or lie dormant at another time. Some radically magnified scripts dealing with beloved parents, mates, or children may explode in magnification upon the death of the other to become radically attenuated just by virtue of that specially intense magnification involved in mourning. Some scripts subserve habitual skills, which occasionally become magnified briefly when unexpected changes tax the adequacy of the habitual skill, as when a carpenter has to deal with new building material of unusual recalcitrance to cutting. Other scripts are continually magnified by ever-changing demands on achieved skills, as in the practice of law or medicine. Even more magnified are those skills involved in competitive sports, where the peak moments of glory are few and transitory and restricted to that sector of the life span when one is in prime physical condition. Some scripts continue to be magnified even though the affects change their signs radically, as when friends become enemies, or enemies friends. Some lifelong commitments become attentuafed either through perceived attainment of major goals or because of erosion through intolerable cost. Some scripts show continued but intermittent growth throughout a lifetime, such as a friendship which is maintained despite spatial separation. Some scripts are highly magnified, enslaving the individual to dependencies in eating, drugs, or cigarettes which he cannot either control nor renounce, as in either physiological or psychological addiction. These scripts have a finite impact on the individual because they have very specific behavioral acts which, if performed, reduce the affect and consciousness of the addiction and thereby limit the degree of magnification. In the extreme instance, an individual may hoard many cartons of cigarettes in order never to encounter the experience of painful addictive deprivation. Smoking can then be treated as a habitual skill and done with minimal affect and awareness.

NUCLEAR SCRIPTS

The major variance in most human beings cannot be understood through such scripts even though one cannot understand much of personality structure if one does not know the extent and strength of such varieties of scripts within any particular personality. The numbers and varieties of such segmental and partially stabilized scripts is an important part of the total personality structure. But the central phenomena in any human being are those scripts we define as the nuclear scripts, which govern that large and ever-growing family of scenes we define as nuclear scenes. A nuclear family of scripts, and their underlying nuclear scenes, are defined by their rate and continuity of growth. They are the scripts which must continue to grow in intensity of affect, of duration of affect, and in the interconnectedness of scenes via the conjoint promise of endless, infinite, unconditional ends, of more positive affect and less negative affect, with endless conditional necessity to struggle perpetually to achieve (against lack), to maintain (against loss or threat), and to increase (against deflation and adaptation) the means to such a magnified end. They matter more than anything else, and they never stop seizing the individual. They are the good scenes we can never totally or permanently achieve or possess. If they occasionally seem to be totally achieved or possessed, such possession can never be permanent. If they reward us with deep positive affect, we are forever greedy for more. If the good scenes are good, they may never be good enough, and we are eager for them to be improved and perfected. If they punish us with deep negative affect, we can never entirely avoid, escape, nor renounce the attempt to master or revenge ourselves upon them despite much punishment. If they both seduce and punish us, we can neither possess nor renounce them. If they are conflicted scenes, we can neither renounce wishes of the conflicting nor integrate them. If they are ambiguous scenes, we can neither simplify nor clarify the many overlapping scenes which characteristically produce pluralistic confusion. These are the conditions par excellence for unlimited magnification. These nuclear scenes and scripts are relatively few in number for any individual, but they are composed of very large numbers of families of such scenes.

Let us examine some classic instances of nuclear scenes and nuclear scripts. What is it which guarantees that human beings will neither master the threats to which they are exposed nor avoid situations which they cannot deal with effectively? Mortality (death) is one paradigm for such a state of affairs because it cannot be mastered, nor can it be avoided. Another paradigm is the classic triangular scene (either due to the arrival of a sibling or the presence of the father) in the family romance. The male child who loves his mother excessively can neither totally possess her (given an unwanted rival) nor totally renounce her. He is often destined, however, to keep trying and, characteristically, to keep failing. Why does he not learn then that he would be happier to make his peace with both his mother and with his rival? Many human beings do just this, but to the extent to which the male child can neither possess nor renounce, he remains a perpetual victim.

VARIANTS AND ANALOGS

There are many additional magnifications of the wish for possession on the one hand and the inability to renounce the wish on the other, which we will not examine here. What we will examine is the paradox of how such victimage is perpetuated by reason as well as by affect. In order to understand this, we must distinguish two different ways in which we think. One is by the principle of variants; the other is by the principle of analogs. A variant is a way of detecting change in something which in its core remains the same. Thus, if one's wife is wearing a new dress, one does not say to her, "You look very similar to my wife" but rather, "I like the new dress you're wearing." Scenes which are predominantly positive in affect tone thus become connected and grow through the classic principle of unity in variety. So a symphony is written and appreciated as a set of variations on a theme. The enjoyment and excitement of such experience depends upon the awareness of both the sameness and the difference. So an interest in any skill or in any friend can grow endlessly by increasing variations on an underlying core which does not change. It is of the essence of friendship to enjoy the rehearsal from time to time of a long, shared past history.

Contrast this mode of reasoning with the principle of analog formation which, though it is used in dealing with positive affects too, is much more frequently and powerfully used in dealing with negative affect scenes. Let us first illustrate the nature of this mechanism on a neutral task. The great art historian Gombrich (1960) demonstrated that if one asks that a series of contrasting words (e.g., "mouse" vs. "elephant") be categorized as to which one would properly be called a *ping* and which one a *pong,* then it is remarkable that over 90 percent of all subjects agree that a mouse is a ping and an elephant is a pong. This is an extraordinary consensus on an absurd task, without any communication or collusion among subjects. I repeated the experiment and studied it further and discovered that although most subjects agree that a mouse is a ping and an elephant is a pong, they do not, in fact, all use the identical thought processes in arriving at their conclusion. Thus, some subjects thought that since a ping seemed small and a pong seemed large, then a mouse would be a ping since it is smaller than an elephant. However, other subjects thought that a ping sounded like a higher-frequency sound and a pong sounded like a lower-frequency sound; therefore, since a mouse has a squeaky voice and an elephant a low roar, a ping is a mouse and a pong is an elephant. Whichever reasons were used, however, the basic mode of thought was analogic and, as often as not, somewhat unconscious. Many subjects said, "I don't know why, but a mouse just seems more like a ping to me and an elephant seems more like a pong." In fact, the individual was responding to imagined relationships between shared dimensions.

Such analogic constructions become the major mechanism whereby a negative affect scene is endlessly encountered and endlessly defeats the individual when the ratio of positive to negative affect becomes predominantly negative. Consider the following example: A man is driving his automobile on a lovely spring day on a brand-new, justopened interstate highway. He looks at the lush greenery all about him and at the shiny, white new highway. An unaccustomed peace and deep enjoyment seizes him. He feels at one with beautiful nature. There is no one else. He is apparently the first to enjoy this verdant and virginal scene. Then, as from nowhere, he sees to his disgust a truck barreling down the road, coming at him and entirely destroying the beauty of the setting. "What is that truck doing here?" he asks himself. He becomes deeply depressed. He can identify the apparent reason, but he senses that there is more to it—that his response is disproportionate to the occasion—and the depression is deep and enduring.

This is an account of an individual who suffered severe sibling rivalry as a first-born, whose deep attachment to his mother was so disrupted by the birth of a sibling that he became mute for six months and who never, thereafter, forgave his mother for her apparent infidelity. This scene was one of hundreds of analogs which he constructed and imported into scenes which would have quite different significances for individuals with different nuclear scripts. It is because he can neither renounce nor forgive, nor possess his mother that he is destined to be victimized by endless analogs which repeat the same unsolved scene—seducing him to continually try to finally settle accounts with his hated rival and his beloved but faithless mother, and to restore the Garden of Eden before the fall.

He characteristically does not know why he feels as he does (any more than why a mouse seems like a ping and an elephant like a pong). He is victimized by his own high-powered ability to synthesize ever-new repetitions of the same scene without knowing that he is doing so.

This is one of the reasons why insight psychotherapy so often fails to cure—because no amount of understanding of the past will enable this individual to become aware of his new analogs before they are constructed. At best, he may become more self-conscious, after the fact, that he has been unconsciously seduced into yet another ineffective attempt at a "final solution" to his nuclear script. This often may abbreviate his suffering, so that his depression will not last six months but perhaps only six minutes. But there is no guarantee that yet another analog may not seize him within the hour.

This represents a major mechanism whereby a disproportionate ratio of negative to positive affect can become stabilized. There are other mechanisms no less powerful which serve the same purpose. Thought, like any powerful instrument, will serve any human purpose. Once enlisted in the service of powerful negative nuclear scripts, it becomes a formidable adversary which can be coped with only through the most heroic strategies. Here, insight *can* come to play a major constructive role. To the extent to which intense negative affect can be recruited *against* the repetition of self-defeating scenes, our individual may be persuaded that the suffering entailed in the renunciation of his excessive wish for revenge may be less than the price he is paying for insisting on reentry into a heaven which never quite existed and punishment for a criminal rival who was never quite so criminal as believed.

Contrast the luxuriant growth potential of analogs compared with variants, even when both are concerned with intense negative affect. In the case of Laura, a member of the bad cast, her doctor, had to actually come into her home to produce magnification. At the museum, there was no magnification even when she was left by her parents in a crib similar to that in the hospital until a person came with a camera similar to the camera in the hospital (i.e., an analog) made Laura anxious about a possible repetition of the bad scene. Variants do not lend themselves to the same rate of growth as analogs because the latter lend themselves to an increasing skill in similarity detection.

Consider another way in which a nuclear scene may grow endlessly. Any nuclear script organizes residual variance in three different ways. It may *exclude* variance as in a contrast family of scenes which by contrast and opposition heighten the nuclear script (as occurred in the case of Laura). Second, it may *satellize* other variance, using it as instrumental to the major variance. Third, it may *absorb* it and neutralize it by denying its essential quality, in order to preserve the apparent power of the nuclear scenes.

In the latter case, we are dealing not simply with analogs but with theoretical derivations from an assumed *paradigm.* Just as any general theory of personality (e.g., psychoanalysis) has a set of constants, of assumed laws about the theoretical structure of personality, so may a nuclear script possess the characteristics of a scientific paradigm which enables the individual to extrapolate explanations for apparently remote and contradictory phenomena consistent with the paradigm.

Consider the case of a man who, having suffered excessive humiliation over a lifetime, is confronted by unexpected praise from another man. How does his script absorb and neutralize such evidence? First, the sincerity of the judge may be questioned. Second, "He praised only this work of mine because he knows that everything else I have done is trash." Third, "He may be sincere, but he is probably a fool." Fourth, "This is a temporary lapse of his judgment. When he comes to his senses, he will have all the more contempt for me." Fifth, "What I have done is a fluke which I can never do again." Sixth, "He is trying to control me, holding out a carrot of praise. If I eat this, I am hooked and I will thenceforth have to work for his praise and to avoid his censure." Seventh, "He is exposing how hungry I am for praise and thus exposing my inferiority and my feelings of humiliation." Eighth, "He is seducing me into striving for something more which I cannot possibly achieve." So may defeat be snatched from the jaws of victory by a predominantly negative affect nuclear script. Such a script can be produced only by a long history of failures to deal effectively with negative affect scenes. It is not a consequence of suffering per se but rather of suffering which again and again defeated every effort of the individual to reduce his or her suffering. Indeed, many extraordinary personalities have grown strong and full of zest for life by dealing more and more effectively with formidable misfortunes. There are many different avenues to predominantly positive- or negative-affect nuclear scripts. The crucial features are the repeated sequences of scenes which end either in joy or despair. These depend variously upon the different combinations of the benign or malign environments and upon the strong or weak inner resources to deal with such opportunities and constraints.

We have thus far considered the generation of families of variant scenes, families of analogs, and families of paradigms or systematic theories as generators of nuclear scripts. These are some of the more important kinds of nuclear scenes and their scripts but in no way exhaustively describe all the varieties of possible theoretical structures.

CONTRAST BETWEEN NUCLEAR AND NONNUCLEAR SCRIPTS

Ideological scripts, like nuclear scripts, address the full spectrum of good scenes and bad scenes, of heavens and hells. Like nuclear scripts they too address cyclical as well as linear trends—of paradise, paradise lost, and paradise regained—as well as a description of the dangers of losing one's way and of going to hell rather than to heaven. Like nuclear scripts, too, they do not necessarily guarantee that the world will be exactly as we would like it. However, ideologies differ from nuclear scripts in their *coherence* and in their attempt to balance the good and the bad in *favor of heaven* against hell and thereby enlist the *faith* of the ideologist, be he Christian, Marxist, or scientist. Contrary to nuclear scripts, ideological scripts tend to be both self-validating and self-fulfilling, whereas nuclear scripts are primarily self-validating. Thinking, believing, and living ideology makes it so. Thinking, believing, and living nuclear scripts only fulfills the nuclear scene, not the nuclear script. This is not to minimize either the awful prices paid in ideological conflict or the illusory elements in ideological idealization. But on balance ideology makes life appear to be more worth living than not. Nuclear scripts, in contrast, appear *to the individual* to have robbed him of what might otherwise have been a possible better life.

Damage reparative scripts include nuclear scripts as one type of script which originates in a good scene turned bad, but differs in including other types of reparative scripts which in fact succeed in repairing the damage. Thus, in a depressive reparative script, an individual who has failed to meet the expectations of a beloved other both knows how to do so and wishes to do so and often succeeds, thereby repairing the damage and lifting the depression.

Limitation-remediation scripts resemble nuclear scripts in addressing those aspects of the human condition perceived to be imperfect, or insufficiently satisfying, and to which some long-term response must be made. The nuclear script also addresses imperfection and insufficiency to which some response is felt to be necessary. The differences are in the kinds of responses as well as in the kinds of scenes. In limitation scripts the scenes perceived to be imperfect do not characteristically or necessarily represent a *change* from a good scene to a bad scene. They are usually scenes which have been and promise to continue to be unsatisfying and imperfect.

One type of limitation-remediation script is the *commitment* script, which, like nuclear scripts, addresses the limitations of the human condition. These are often the imperfections condemned by ideological scripts. In contrast to nuclear scripts which are conflicted and ineffective, commitment scripts are unambivalent, evoking courage and negative-affect absorption rather than cowardice and negativeaffect intimidation, and are well defined and limited in purpose rather than ill defined and unlimited in greed; they are *cumulative* in their progress rather than *oscillating* between progress and retrogress.

Other limitation scripts may elect to *accept* the limiting scenes and try to profit as much as possible within these limitations, as in the English Victorian script described by the philosopher Bradley as "my station and its duties." Another type of limitation remediation may elect a *resignation* script, such as might occur in conditions of slavery, where resistance would have been perceived as guaranteeing death. The limitation script might elect an *opportunistic* script, as in the case of a peasantry which perceives itself to be exploited and intimidated but capable of exploiting its limited freedom in the interstices of a feudal society via effective cunning. The trickster is another example of such limitation scripts. A later-born child who is governed by primogeniture, actual or psychological, might also elect an opportunistic script.

A limitation script need not represent passivity or acceptance alone. It may combine these with *hope,* the great engine of the religions of the oppressed from the days of the early Christians in Rome through the plantations in the American South. The opiates of Christianity offered not only the promise of a life hereafter but a counterculture and a countersociety in the here and now. Limitation shared becomes limitation attenuated under such circumstances.

Finally, a limitation script *may* include actual *struggle* against the socially inherited limitations which are judged unfair and intolerable, and even against the existential inherited limitations. In the latter case, even death, perceived as grossly unfair and intolerable by the Greeks, prompted the hubris-driven script for some degree of immortality via struggle in warfare, which plucked enough fame to guarantee one would continue to live in the minds and hearts of Greek warriors to come. In a more mundane version of struggle against *socially* inherited limitation is the American Horatio Alger story of economic ascension via unremitting commitment and hard work.

Whether one adapts to limitation by commitment, by hope, by struggle, by resignation, by acceptance, or by opportunism, such scripts offer some measure of coherence and effectiveness. None of these scripts is a recipe for the endless incoherent ineffective Sturm and Drang of the nuclear script, which promises everything and delivers very little.

Decontamination scripts deal with barriers, conflicts, ambivalences, and plurivalences which arouse deep disgust. Like nuclear scripts these bad scenes may once have also been good scenes, as in the case that an idealized parent becomes a drug addict. Decontamination may succeed by either distancing the self from the contaminated other or by accepting the contamination. Similarly, if the self suffers disgust at the self, there may be successful purification of the self or self-acceptance. In either case the individual may successfully avoid or reduce continuing conflict.

Antitoxic scripts resemble nuclear scripts inasmuch as they are addressed to scenes of such toxic negative affect as terror, dissmell, and/or rage that they are opposed, excluded, attempted to be attenuated or defeated, avoided, or escaped. They differ from nuclear scripts in their *lack of ambivalence* and in their relative *effectiveness.* The same parent who might be alternately wooed and fought, both as variant and as analog, and neither effectively loved nor defeated in a nuclear script can be effectively opposed in an antitoxic script which may define that other as clearly toxic, one whose influence is to be minimized as much as possible. Here there are no regrets, whether or not that parent may have once been loved. Similarly, in the renunciation of now toxic addiction, the cold turkey, antitoxic script can be effective so long as the umbilical cord to the seductive cigarette can be cut.

Even if the effectiveness of reducing a toxic threat is minimal, it is nonetheless not complicated by additional aims as in a similar strategy in a nuclear script. Thus, a child who suffers massive intimidation at the hands of an alcoholic father who often beats him may retreat to a defensive introversion, seeking to hide from and to avoid or escape dreaded violence. In an antitoxic script the child could become very withdrawn to the point of catatonia, but that timidity is not betrayed by *also* attempting a dangerous counteractive defeat of that father, nor an equally dangerous reparative script in which he attempts to woo the dangerous other or entertains fantasies of loving reunion.

Change-review scripts are those which address radical changes in the self or other or the world which require confrontation and review of the consequences of change for the rules of a script or of several scripts. Conversion, enchantment, disenchantment, and mourning are some script types of responses to perceived radical change. Inasmuch as a nuclear script is a response of a specific change from a good scene to a bad scene, how does it differ from change-review scripts? The major differences are not in the scenes but in the scripted responses, which in turn reinterpret the scenes differently in nuclear and change scenes.

In what I have defined as change-review scenes, the *responses* are predicated upon the assumption that the changes are both radical and real and that life will never again be the same and therefore substantial script modification must be made. The beloved who died is really dead, and mourning contrasts that painful actuality with the new consequences entailed. Old wasted possibilities are reviewed with deep regret, and future possibilities which can never become realities are reviewed and negatively celebrated as the character of the mourned is positively celebrated. It should be noted that such mourning at the death of the beloved need not be undertaken. Such a death may indeed become nuclear and incapable of being accepted or renounced. The delayed grief reaction has consequences not unlike those of the nuclear script for those who would not and who could not grieve. Indeed, even at the beginning of mourning the individual *believes* he cannot live without the beloved. We do not wish at this point to explicate the mechanisms whereby the bereaved is enabled to become free of his dependence but rather to contrast the mourning script with the nuclear script, which characteristically never frees the individual from either the loss of the good scene, from its contamination, or from its ambiguity. Even in mourning (as revealed in my study of reactions to the assassination of President Kennedy, Tomkins & Izard, 1965) there is often experienced an "unreality" about the death as a consequence of the coassembly of vivid images of the past and the present. The nuclear script is *neither* mourning or delayed mourning. It is rather an awareness and insistence on *life* and *death* and *resurrection*. It is at *once* an acknowledgment of deep hurt, that it is over, but that it can be *attempted* to be brought back to life, to be purified, to be clarified, because it is intolerable to live with the nuclear scene.

The nuclear script is quite different than any of the varied types of change scripts. A change script of *enchantment* partitions the life space *firmly* between life as it has been lived and as it now promises in vidious contrast. In *disenchantment* the scripting is similar, but the contrast is invidious. In *conversion* there is both enchantment and disenchantment, but the partitioning is also firm rather than labile as in the nuclear script. Although some conversions to fascism from socialism were in themselves quite labile, such lability did not continue to swing back and forth between polar opposites.

Power scripts resemble nuclear scripts in their exaggeration and *compulsive* directives. They magnify means which are perceived to be instrumental to many ends into ends in themselves. Money, purity, security, achievement are some of the species of power scripts. Nuclear scripts are equally exaggerated and compulsive in their attempt to guarantee power. The differences between the nuclear and power scripts are, first, that a power script is *unitary* not multiple. The nuclear script may contain a large family of power scripts, attempting not only to become endlessly wealthy but also equally pure, equally achieving, equally loved, equally esteemed, equally secure. Second, the unitary focused power script lends itself to *cumulative progress* in spite of the unlimited appetite which may drive it. The hidden agendas of the same power script embedded in a family of nuclear scripts guarantees a recurrent cycle of *progress and retrogress*. The bifurcation of the nuclear script guarantees that if he is *not increasing* his power he has lost it, in contrast to a more continuous series perceived in varying rates of increase in power in a power script which is not nuclear.

Addictive scripts are essentially sedative power scripts which have transformed a sedative into an end in itself. The cigarette addict exaggerates the necessity of smoking a cigarette for his well-being as the miser inflates the necessity of money. The addictive script resembles the nuclear script in its *magnification of vigilance and monitoring* and in the radical increase in negative affect whenever the *bad scene* is reexperienced. The difference is that there is a specific scene or *response* which is a *certain antidote* for this poison. The cigarette delivers what it promises, at least for a while. The nuclear panic has no such quick fix.

Negative-affect sedative scripts, like nuclear scripts, address troubling scenes but differ from nuclear scripts in several respects. First, they address *any scene* with *negative affect,* whether or not it represents a *shift* from a positive affect scene. Second, it is *not* concerned with the scene as a whole or with its *remediation,* as is a nuclear script, but only with its negative affect. The sedative aims primarily at the attenuation or reduction of that negative affect. Third, because of its limited aim it is more likely to be *effective* than any nuclear script. Fourth, if it is effective, it may permit the scene to be confronted and/or dealt with more effectively. In contrast, the nuclear script is impaired in its effectiveness. Fifth, even when a sedative is effective in reducing negative affect, the recruitment of a nuclear script *interpretation* of sedation not infrequently reduces that sedation by experiencing it as an analog of the nuclear scene. Thus, such a reliance on a cigarette to sedate distress may be experienced as a demonstration of the helplessness of the self to live without a crutch or of the cruelty of the world which makes it necessary to save the self again and again.

Cost-benefit-risk scripts address systematic trade-offs, in specific scenes or for all scenes, about what relative quantities of probability, payoffs, and costs of enactment and/or consequences are to govern planning, decisions, or choices. Nonnuclear scripts of this kind include *satisficing* scripts, in which the individual intends to enact scripts which are *high* in probability, relatively *low* in positive-affect *payoff,* and relatively *low* in negative-affect *costs.* Another nonnuclear script of this type is the *optimizing* script, which may, for example, attempt to equalize probability, costs, and benefits at a *moderate* level so that one is *most likely* to optimize *both* positive-affect rewards and possible negative-affect costs. In this case, in contrast to the satisficing script, one is willing to take greater risks for more rewards *and* more negative-affect costs. In a *maximizing* script one is willing to try for the greatest possible affect gain, no matter how improbable and no matter what the negative-affect costs. In a *minimizing* script one intends the least possible negative-affect costs, no matter how improbable, no matter how little positive-affect payoff is entailed.

There are also many varieties of mixed types of such scripts. In *gambling* scripts one is prepared to risk a small amount of money and loss for a possible, but improbable, large amount of money and *gain.* In *insurance* scripts one is prepared to risk a small amount of money for protection against a possible, but improbable, large *loss.* In both gambling and insurance one is risking *small* amounts for *improbable large amounts* of *either* protection against *loss* or acquiring *gain.* In *"doable"* scripts one invests small positive affect at low negative cost for the certainty of doing extremely probable things. In *ideality* scripts (e.g., belief in God) one invests for high positive-affect payoff against the negative-affect cost of an indifferent cosmos, with no regard for probability. Although the existence of God may be affirmed in such a script, evidence is not required, and probability in effect is not scripted. This is revealed more clearly in the conception of utopia in which it is the ideal positive features which are salient and constitute a utopia whether it exists or not. It is in the nature of ideality scripts that they must meet positive payoff criteria above all else.

Nuclear scripts meet *none* of these types of cost-benefit risk scripts since they are best described as conjoint *mini-maximizing* scripts. The conjunction of greed and cowardice requires positive-affect ideality with no negative-affect costs. By virtue of double maxima it is guaranteed that both strategies fail.

Celebratory scripts resemble nuclear scripts in addressing scenes of such very high affect density that it is believed and felt some affect and/or action *must* be *expressed* or *communicated.* These may be either social or individual or dyadic *rituals* for death, or victory or defeat, or progress or retrogress. They may be limited to curses or thanksgivings. The nonnuclear celebratory script is not intended to sedate affect but to express and celebrate either its wonder or its horror. It is essentially aesthetic in function. It is a singing by the self to the self or to the other, or with the other, as in the opening lines of Virgil's *Aeneid.* It represents the self as judge, as historian, as commentator, as playwright. When it is socially defined as a ritual, it serves a critical role in the bonding of a group, whether it represents a victory or a defeat, a festivity or a mourning. It may serve the same function for a dyad in the sharing of remembered experience in a long friendship. What is the difference between nonnuclear and nuclear celebratory scripts? The nuclear script also ordinarily includes celebratory scripts in its family of scripts. These, however, tend to be primarily analogic of a nuclear scene long forgotten but kept alive by repetitions of the breakdown of the nuclear scripts or by the temporary antianalogic "victories." Nuclear celebrations are perennial, more often negative than positive, and proving the same thing over and over. The positive antianalog nuclear celebrations are neither as frequent nor as enduring or robust as the nuclear negative-analog celebrations. Further, they are extraordinarily labile but primarily in one direction. Great celebratory antianalog excitement or enjoyment characteristically gives way too readily to replays of analogic distress and shame. As an example, an unexpected visit may provide an extraordinary lift for an individual with a nuclear depressive script, but the same guest's departure may nonetheless deepen a nuclear depression substantially. Such an individual will be made worse just because he celebrated a gratuitous reward. It is just such a "difference" which now evokes a much deeper depression than might have continued in the absence of mutuality disconfirmed.

Finally, nuclear scripts are radically different than *affluence* scripts, which address neither the damages, the limitations, the contaminations, nor the toxicities of the human condition, but rather those scenes which promise *and* deliver intense and/or enduring positive affects of excitement or enjoyment. These script the sources of the individual's zest for life.

They may specify that one *respond* positively to particular scenes by savoring them whenever they occur, as on the occasion of a conversation, a dinner, or a flirtation in separate scenes or in one scene. They may specify that one *seek* particular scenes for excitement or enjoyment, as in travel, the theater, or in reading. They may specify that one attempt to *produce* rewarding scenes, as in hobbies, pleasing a friend, wife, or child, or decorating one's house. Such scenes may be narrow or broad in range, specifying one or more psychological functions (e.g., thinking, perceiving, remembering, acting, drivesatisfying), one or more people, places, times, or settings. Within any class of such rewarding scenes, satisfactions may be scripted as focal or diffuse, as in one or many friends, one or many hobbies, one or many arts.

Despite great varieties of scripts of affluence they share important commonalities which distinguish any of them from nuclear scripts. First, they *deliver what they promise.* Second, when they cease to deliver excitement or enjoyment, they are relatively *easily abandoned* for alternatives, compared with nuclear intransigence. Third, in contrast to the *ungraded, bifurcated* ordering of nuclear scripts, these are *graded* and continuous in order of intensity, frequency, and duration. Some are more intense, some are more frequent, some are more enduring than others, while all are rewarding in *varying* ways rather than *bifurcated,* as are the all-or-none nuclear analogs versus nuclear antianalogs. Differences in reward quantity and quality do not in themselves generate negative affect of invidious comparison. The individual does not demand of each such scene more than it can deliver. Fourth, the *bias* in these scripts is in the direction of *positive* rather than negative affect. Neutral or negative affect is characteristically reduced or attenuated by these scripts as relief, contrast, balance, or compensation. However, this is not characteristically nor necessarily their origin nor function; thus, in the special case of affluence scripts, the savoring of substances rather than the sedative or addictive dependency on substances: one smokes a cigarette to *enhance* reward rather than relieve suffering. Fifth, they are *gradual* rather than *labile* in their transition scenes. Their graded, continuous ordering permits more active control and choice rather than the volatile uncontrolled swings from nuclear antianalogs to nuclear analogs. Sixth, in contrast to the contamination, conflict, and confusion of the nuclear script, scripts of affluence are capable of generating complexity of *discrimination* which is *enriching* rather than frustrating, conflicting, or confusing. Seventh, they are capable of *benign* rather than *malignant growth.* Such growth may be cumulative or orthogonal or simply variable. Each enjoyable dinner may be responded to as a separate scene, as one of many rewarding scenes of all dinners, with or without cumulation or connectedness or vidious or invidious comparison either with other dinners or with other types of drive or nondrive satisfactions.

Eighth, they are capable of *optimizing* rather than mini-maximizing strategies. A good scene may vary in intensity or duration and yet be rewarding for what it is rather than for what it might have been or might yet be. Ninth, the degree of *magnification* of affluence scripts may *vary* radically between individuals and between different periods of the life of a single individual, in contrast to the necessarily *high degree of magnification* of a nuclear script. So long as one is in the grip of a nuclear script, one suffers an entropic malignancy which threatens the integrity of the personality. Affluence scripts can and do coexist with nuclear scripts, offering an alternative vision to nuclear intransigence, to addictive servitude, to the rigors of reparation, limitation, decontamination, and antitoxic scripts. Their role is an interdependent function of the overall ratio of positive to negative affect in the economy of the individual.

Part II
ANGER AND FEAR

Chapter 27
Anger and its Innate Activation

All the negative affects trouble human beings deeply. Indeed, they have evolved just to amplify and deepen suffering and to add insult to the injuries of the human condition in several different ways. Terror speaks to the threat of death to life. Distress is the affect of suffering, making of the world a vale of tears. Shame is the affect of indignity, of defeat, of transgression, and of alienation, striking deep into the heart of the human being and felt as an inner torment, a sickness of the soul. But anger is problematic above all other negative affects for its social consequences. My terror, my distress, and my shame are first of all my problems. They *need* never become your problems, though they may. But my anger, and especially my rage, threatens violence for you, your family, your friends, and above all for our society. Of all the negative affects it is the least likely to remain under the skin of the one who feels it, and so it is just that affect all societies try hardest to contain within that envelope under the skin or to deflect toward deviants within the society and toward barbarians without. We will presently examine the several innate as well as learned features of anger which determine its great toxicity for any society.

INTERDEPENDENCE OF THE SOURCES OF ANGER, THE RESPONSES TO ANGER, AND THE DIFFERENTIAL MAGNIFICATION OF ANGER SCRIPTS

Anger, like any affect, has numerous sources. In its generality, there are an infinite number of possible sources of anger, but because of the nature of the innate activating mechanism, not all possible sources are equally probable sources of anger. The probable sources of anger are a complex function not only of the varieties of the vicissitudes of scenes the individual actually encounters but also of the relative magnification of anger vis-à-vis other affects in the total set of scripts which govern the individual. The sources of anger, the responses to anger, and the differential magnification of anger are partially independent, partially dependent, and partially interdependent. In the beginning, scenes determine scripts. In the end, scripts more and more determine scenes. In the beginning, the infant's anger scenes are a function of the source of the anger and of the infant's response to both the source of anger and to the anger itself. This can be a momentary cry of rage or a sustained tantrum, depending primarily on the intensity and duration of the provocation and the willingness and capability of the mother to reduce the source, to distract or otherwise nurture the angry infant. The "response" to anger, initially, is little more than the anger itself. Ultimately, however, the response is embedded in the matrix of the entire personality. While the innate activating mechanism sharply constrains the probable sources of anger, it exerts much less constraint on the probable further responses to anger. The "angry" response inevitably becomes much more complex than a simple response to anger. The angry individual is also a loving, excited, enjoying, fearful, ashamed, distressed, disgusted person as well as an angry person. How much his affects are positive relative to how much they are negative and how much he is angry relative to how much he is distressed will determine his responses to anger as much as the perceived sources of anger and the felt anger itself.

The interdependencies between the perceived *source of* anger, the multiple *responses* to anger, and the differential *magnification* of anger scripts are complex and will be treated at length. Before doing so however, we will consider each of these, insofar as it is possible to do so, as somewhat independent phenomena.

What Is the Response of Anger?

Anger is an innate affective response which consists of deep and rapid breathing, a loud, sustained cry, the mouth opened, the jaw clenched, and the eyes narrowed, with a reddening of the face which stimulates the heat receptors and makes anger a hot affect. The latter is a by-product of the elevation of blood pressure which accompanies anger. The general autonomic response in anger depends on the intensity and duration of the anger; its profile has not yet been determined with certainty. The core of anger in man is the breathing, vascular, vocal, and facial responses which have been known ever since our early ancestors glowered at each other. According to Darwin,

> Rage will have been expressed at a very early period by threatening or frantic gestures, by the reddening of the skin, and by glaring eyes, but not by frowning. For the habit of frowning seems to have been acquired chiefly from the corrugators being the first muscles to contract round the eyes, whenever during infancy pain, anger, or distress is felt, and there consequently is a near approach to screaming; and partly from a frown serving as a shade in difficult and intent vision.
>
> It seems probable that this shading action would not have become habitual until man had assumed a completely upright position, for monkeys do not frown when exposed to a glaring light.

The interpretation of the anger response in infancy has been contested. Darwin observed that with his four-month-old child "there could be no doubt from the manner in which blood gushed into his whole face and scalp that he easily got into a violent passion." However, Valentine (1956) has pointed out that most of the symptoms in infants which have been attributed to anger, such as violent crying, reddening, kicking, and so on, "are general to any kind of distress." I would agree that crying and kicking appear in distress as well as anger; however, these are more intense in anger than in distress.

According to Ambrose (1960), by the second half of the first year, crying from anger is sudden in onset, with intense expirations, varying irregularly between long-drawn-out and very rapid; rasping vocalization; reddening of the head; sudden, rapid, uncoordinated limb and trunk movements; and general muscular tension.

Localization of the subcortical sites of the affect programs subserving anger has been reported. De Molina and Hunsperger (1959) have shown that growling and hissing can be produced by electrical stimulation of particular subcortical structures. Control of affective reactions in the cat has been localized by them to a system extending from fibers of the stria terminalis from their origin in the amygdaloid nucleus to their projections on the preoptic and perifornical zones of the hypothalamus.

With respect to the autonomic responses in anger, compared with fear, anger has been reported by Ax and Funkenstein to be associated with a greater increase in diastolic blood pressure and less elevation of systolic blood pressure and heart rate. Peripheral resistance was found to be elevated by anger but decreased by fear. Oken (1960) reported significant correlations between anger and both diastolic and systolic pressures (*r*, .75 and .72). He also reported that subjects who suppressed anger had a higher diastolic and a lower systolic pressure than those who expressed it when feeling angry. He also found that this anger-suppressor group also had lower mean levels of consciously experienced, motorically expressed, and total expressed anger. Thus, the general quality of constraint or inhibition of anger was associated with physiological differences consistent with an elevated peripheral resistance. Physiologically, in the absence of heart rate changes, diastolic blood pressure is primarily a function of peripheral resistance, while systolic blood pressure is more closely related to cardiac output. The higher systolic levels found in the more expressive group, suggesting a greater cardiac output, may simply reflect (Oken suggests) a reflection of greater physical activity consequent to their greater motor display of anger.

The empirical determination of the nature of the anger response has been complicated by the universal confusion of the experience of backed-up affect with that of biologically and psychologically authentic innate affect. No societies encourage or permit the individual to cry out in rage whenever or wherever he wishes. Although there are large variations between societies, and between different classes within societies, complete unconditional freedom of affect vocalization is quite exceptional. The consequence of the control over breathing and vocalization of affect is to produce a pseudo-, or backed-up, affect. The individual who tightens his jaw trying not to cry out in anger is learning not only to control anger but also to transform it and ultimately to confuse the backed-up affect with authentic affect experience. Innate affect requires the feedback of the innate cry of anger and the accompanying facial vascular and motor responses and the stimulation of the skin and muscle receptors. Thus, a permanent elevation of blood pressure, which can be a consequence of backedup rage, would have a much longer duration than an innate momentary cry of rage.

The more serious theoretical problem is that we do not know the exact differences between innate affects and backed-up affects. The cyanosis which is a consequence of holding one's breath is *not* inherent for the breathing mechanism but is peculiar to the voluntary interruption of breathing. Pseudo-, backed-up affect is also interrupted breathing and vocalization. Psychosomatic disease is but one of the possible prices of such systematic suppression and transformation of innate anger. The psychological consequences of such suppression would depend upon the severity of the suppression. Even the least severe suppression of the vocalization of anger must result in some distortion and bleaching of the experience of anger and some ambiguity about what anger really feels like. Such confusion also occurs in the look of the anger of the other. Since the closed mouth, with tightly pressed lips and clenched jaws, is one universal form of backed-up anger, we tend to share a worldwide illusion that this *is* the appearance of innate anger and that the other is really angry when in fact he is experiencing backed-up anger. To be "boiling mad" is *not* to be angry, either in the appearance to the other or in the experience of the self. It is in some as yet indeterminate way more than anger, and in some way less than anger, and, most critically, in some way different from anger. Most of the physiological research on the effects of "stress" is contaminated by the confounding of innate and backed-up affect in general and of backed-up anger in particular. The only way to determine what is innate in the anger response would be to examine it in earliest infancy, before it suffers the imposed control which backs it up.

The Function of Anger

The primary function of anger is to make bad matters worse and further to increase the probability of an angry response. It does this by amplifying both its own stimulus and whatever response is prompted by anger. It guarantees not only that bad matters are made worse but that *any* response, aggressive or *otherwise,* will be imprinted with the same density level and vigor of the combined stimulus and its evoked anger. An "angry" response may or may not be an aggressive response.

There is no *necessary* connection between anger and aggression, as a directed response. The infant may thrash about with flailing arms and limbs, as he may also do so, with less intensity, in distress. But there is no evidence of any innate coordinated action intended to aggress upon the source, of the anger.

The function of anger is like the function of any affect: to amplify and increase the urgency of *any* possibility, in an abstract way. It conjoins *urgency* with *generality* and with *abstractness.*

Analog Amplifier: The Urgency of Anger

Anger is the *most* urgent of all affects since it combines the highest level of sustained neural firing of the activator of anger with its analogous, equally high and toxic, level of neural firing of anger itself, plus an especially punishing quality of sensory stimulation.

Anger, like any affect, is an analog amplifier of whatever activates it. Our face reddens as our blood pressure rises in anger, and our breathing deepens as our cry of anger rises in intensity.

The combined feedback of these correlated changes in breathing, vocalization, blood pressure, and increased heat from our receptors on the skin of the face, together with the sensory feedback from the receptors stimulated by the massively contracted muscles of the throat and face, radically increase the dense neural stimulation which innately activates anger. Such increases in stimulation are, of course, not identical with the pain of a stubbed toe which might have triggered the anger, but it is *similar* in a fundamental way, which is why I label it an analog amplifier of the pain. It should be noted that the pain is itself also an analog but an analog of the *injury* which activates the pain. In this case, the original stubbed toe might have been perceived as an injury and judged to be something which should be attended to but without the urgency the pain receptors uniquely add to the experience. Because the stimulation of the pain receptors produces intense, nonoptimal neural firing, it in turn, via evocation of anger, adds to the compelling urgency of *both* injury and pain. Anger is an analog amplifier in two respects. First, its quality is toxic, not rewarding (just as pain is toxic in comparison with the pleasure of an orgasm). No less important, its toxicity mimics the *profile* of activation, level, and decay of its activator. It is equally intense in its level of stimulation, and it endures as long as its activator maintains its nonoptimal level of stimulation. In this respect it is similar to distress, which is however, at a somewhat lower level of stimulation. It is markedly dissimilar to startle, fear, excitement, and enjoyment since these mimic the profile of sharply peaked *gradients* of stimulation rather than *levels* of stimulation.

Anger thereby makes bad things worse by conjointly simulating its activator in its profile of neural firing and by adding a special analogic *quality* that is intensely punishing, as well as doubling the *quantity* of nonoptimal neural stimulation.

The Generality of Anger

Anger is not only urgent and abstract but is general in its degrees of combinatorial freedom. Its generality is such as to enable us to be capable of anger at what we perceive, at feelings we or others experience, at what we imagine, what we conceive, what we remember, what we plan, what we decide, what we do, what we anticipate, people we know or have known, places we inhabit or have inhabited, times we remember or experience as present or imagine in the future, scene settings, or scene events.

One can be angry for a moment, an hour, or a lifetime. One can be an angry child but a happy adult or a happy child but an angry adult. It is general with respect to its "object," whether that be its activator or what is responded to. Anger is also general with respect to intensity. If I do not eat, I become hungrier and hungrier. As I eat, I become less hungry. But I may wake mildly irritable in the morning and remain so for the rest of the day. Or one day I may not be at all angry until suddenly something makes me explode in rage. I may start the day moderately angry and quickly become interested in some other matter and so dissipate anger. Anger density, the product of intensity and duration, can vary from low and casual to monopolistic, intense, and enduring.

By virtue of its structurally based generality of space and time, anger can readily coassemble with and therefore impart its urgency and lend its power to memory, perception, thought, and action no less than to the drives. Not only may anger be widely and variously invested, it may also be invested in other affects, combine with other affects, intensify or modulate them, and suppress or reduce them.

Anger also enjoys generality of dependency, independence, and interdependency. It is thus suited for membership in a feedback mechanism, since from moment to moment its role in the causal nexus can shift from independence to dependence to interdependence. Anger can determine conviction at one time, recruiting selfvalidating angry thoughts; be determined by cognition at other times, becoming angry when one discovers that the other has offended; and be interdependent under other circumstances, as when somewhat irritable, one becomes enraged at discovering that the other has offended. Whether and how much one's anger is reactive, or selffulfilling, or interactive, and how variable or stable such causal dependencies are, depends upon the relative magnification of anger and other affects and other mechanisms. However, the possibility of such variations ultimately depend on the generality of combinatorial coassembly of the affect and other mechanisms.

The Abstractness of Anger

Anger is *abstract* in that it does not inform us of the particularities of its activator, since these may be very different from each other and one *may* not even know why one is angry; and it does not inform us of the particularities of the response to anger, since these may be very different under different provocations and one *may* do nothing about what one is angry about. In its abstractness it tells us primarily that our experience is too much, too dense, and too punishing, whatever else it may be in its particulars, be it the stimulus to anger or the response to anger, either or both of which may be imprinted with coassembled anger. In the event that the stimulus is not perceived *and* there is no further response to anger, we are nonetheless made aware of the abstract and urgent fact that we are being bombarded with too much punishing *stimulation* from anger alone, no matter what else of a more particular and less abstract nature is going on. In anger we need not *know* its activator to know that *something* is lexically stimulating, whatever else is happening.

Just as there may be free-floating fear which is deeply punishing whether or not one knows *what* one fears, so free-floating anger is also punishing in and of itself with or without an "object."

The appropriate minimal paradigm here is the crying enraged neonate in the midst of a tantrum who neither knows why he is enraged nor that there is anything to do about it beyond flailing his arms and legs.

Any further response to anger usually has the abstract quality of the combined high level of neural firing of anger and of its activator, apart from what its further specific qualities in speech or action might be. In contrast, an excited response is accelerating in speed whether in walking or talking. An enjoyable response is decelerating in speed, and relaxed, as a motor or perceptual savoring response. In acute schizophrenic panics, the individual is bombarded by a rapidly accelerating rush of ideas that resist ordering and organization. In each of these cases, the abstract profile of the amplifying affect is imprinted on the recruited responses, whether they be cognitive or motoric.

The Relationship Between Generality and Abstractness

The generality of anger, its freedom to combine with any stimulus or any response, requires not only a structural transformability and the freedom of flexibility of coassembly, but also requires that anger be abstract. Consider three possible objects of anger: angry because very hungry, angry because of stubbing one's toe, and angry because another offends politically. It is obvious that the *response* to each of these sources of anger must be tailored to the concrete particularity of each grievance. If anger itself were not abstract but concrete and specific, it might result necessarily in the same specification for different sources of anger, so that one might, for example, physically hit the cook, the chair on which one stubbed one's toe, and the political opponent. This is not to say that such a possibility is necessarily excluded, but it is clearly not required simply because it is the same anger which is activated in each case. The response to the perceived source of hunger, hurt toe, and political opposition *will* be vigorous, imprinted by this abstract feature of anger, but it will *in addition* have differentiating specific features which reflect some of the particularities of hunger, hurt toes, and political opposition.

Paradoxically, this particularity of response to different sources of anger is expedited by the abstract characteristic of the anger which is activated by each source. But the generality of anger requires not only an abstract imprinting of the response to the source of anger but also an abstract coupling with its perceived source. If I am to be able to be as angry to hunger as to a stubbed toe or as to a political opponent, then that *common* affective response must not be too specific or it will swamp and mask the uniqueness of each source. Generality of combination of anger with hunger, toe, or politics requires that each of these be experienced as both abstractly similar in being excessively stimulating in a toxic way (i.e., angering) and *also* as being so in three *different* ways. Because the cook angers me and the political opponent angers me, I experience them as similar in some way and dissimilar in other ways. Only because anger is abstract can it also be general in its degrees of freedom to combine with quite different objects. It is in this respect like a letter of an alphabet or a word in a sentence, each of which can combine *differently* with different letters to form different words, or with different words to form different sentences.

If anger *were* less abstract but yet general, we would be quite different human beings. In such a case anger might make one interpret *all* sources as having the specific characteristic of making one feel like hitting the perceived source and prompting one to, in fact, strike out at all sources of such anger.

If, on the other hand anger were abstract but less general, we would be capable of feeling overstimulated in a toxic way but only to specific sources (e.g., to hunger or sexual privation but not to political opposition) or only for specific periods of time (e.g., for a few minutes and then it would dissipate) or only for specific densities of provocation (e.g., only for extreme long-lasting offenses but not for minor annoyances). In fact, we are capable of feeling angry in an *abstract* way *combined* with the *particularities* which perception, cognition, memory, and action permit about anything in the most *general* way.

By being coassembled with both activators and responses to anger and activator, and imprinting stimulus and response equally in both an abstract and an urgent way, the range of connectedness of anger experience is radically increased. Thus, via temporal overlap there may be produced S-S equivalences, S-R equivalences, and R-R equivalences mediated by anger and anger analogs. An angry other person can become an angering and hurtable person. As anger density increases, it provides an increasingly viscous psychic glue that embeds very different phenomena in the same angering, hurtable medium. In extreme rage, as with any dense affective experience, the separateness of the self and other, of affect and action are dissolved into unholy mutually destructive fusion. Thus are produced many of Freud's "primary process" phenomena.

The Social Toxicity of Anger and Rage

We have said that anger is problematic above all other negative affects because of its social consequences. This is derivative in part from the innate nature of anger, in part from its close (but not inevitable) linkage to violent action, and in part from the learned consequences of the free expression of either anger or violent action, or both, for any society.

The social toxicity of anger and rage is a consequence of the conjunction of several innate characteristics of anger. First is the innate high intensity of anger. It is very intense because it is an analogic amplifier of its activator, which is the highest *level* of neural firing, most deviant from the optimal level. Inasmuch as it mimics that nonoptimal level, it is more intense than distress, which is also activated by a nonoptimal elevation of neural firing but at a level lower than that of anger.

Second, in combination with its innate activator the total density of nonoptimal neural firing is doubled. The individual who suffers the pain of stubbing his toe suffers still more when anger is added to his consciousness. In this instance there is the triple amplification of the injury to the skin, the added stimulation from the pain receptors, and the further anger added to both the injury and to the pain.

Third, the summated intensity may be endlessly prolonged in time, thus radically increasing the total density of negative stimulation. Anger, unlike excitement, fear, surprise, and enjoyment, does not habituate. The affects which are activated by rising or falling gradients of stimulation mimic these gradients of neural stimulation and thus are ballistic in their profile of sudden rise, peak, and sudden decline, as in the square wave of the startle response which mimics in analogic amplification the pistol shot which activates it. Unless the pistol shot is repeated, one does not repeat the startle. Further, even if the pistol shot is repeated, the startle characteristically habituates by dropping out components of the total bodily response until finally only an eye blink remains as resistant to habituation. Excitement, fear, and enjoyment also require repeated activation and also appear to habituate. In contrast, anger, like distress, is activated by a level of neural firing rather than by a gradient of neural firing. Anger may be aroused just as quickly as a startle or fear, and it *may* stop just as quickly as its stimulus. Thus, if one sits down on a tack, one howls in pain and anger, both quickly but also momentarily, as soon as one stands up in reflex escape from the pain. However, if the pain itself (or any other activator of anger) is sustained, the anger will endure. It need not and characteristically does not habituate. The possibility of the innate activation of prolonged anger (in contrast to gradient-activated affects such as fear) multiplies the density of both the intensity of the activator and the intensity of the anger, so the total toxicity may grow indefinitely. Distress shares this characteristic with anger, so one may be distressed endlessly; but since the intensity of both the activator and of the affect are at a lower level of neural firing, the total density, holding time constant, is less than in the case of anger.

Fourth, the responses *to* anger are innately imprinted with the doubled intensity of activator and anger. This means that *whatever* the individual does when he is both angered and angry will be as intense and vigorous as the total state which prompts the response. If it is a motor response, it may be tantrum-like and explosive whether or not it is sustained. Anger *need* not result in aggression or destruction if the stimulus is brief. It *may* result in no more than a brief howl or growl and a flailing of arms and legs or a banging of the fist on a table. But it is very likely to be intense, however brief. If intensity of stimulus and anger is prolonged, however, the probability of aggressive, destructive motor action is increased if there is *any* action at all. At the least the decibel level of speech will rise, imprinted by the high density of stimulus and anger. I am *not* supposing that anger necessarily leads to *aggressive* behavior, since clearly such behavior may be inhibited by fear of consequences, by shame or guilt, or be aggressive but turned against the self in self-mutilation or suicide. I am arguing for the innate imprinting of anger's characteristics on *whatever* is the further response to anger, so long as anger continues during the response to anger.

Fifth, such imprinting of activator and anger on the response to anger radically increases the difficulty of controlling both anger and aggression. As the duration of such intensity increases, the difficulty of control also increases, and a person is both less able to turn anger off and less able and less willing to control or inhibit explosive aggressive behavior. In this respect anger is not unlike *any* intense affect, but it is more so because its combined intensity and duration potential is higher than is the case for any other affect. Perhaps the closest non-affect analog of the innately difficult to control state is that of intense long-lasting pain. It is widely known that there are limits to the tolerance for such stimulation. Because of the innate victimage of the individual by intense, enduring negative stimulation, physical torture has been used over many centuries to persuade and to control human beings against their own wishes.

Sixth, the expression either of anger or of aggression, or of both, is innately *contagious*. The loud voice or a physical attack which hurts is innately capable of evoking anger and aggression from the victim. This is because of the innate match between the activator of anger and the affect of anger. Since anger is an analogic amplifier of *its* activator, it has the level of intensity necessary to evoke anger in the other. In this it resembles distress, since the distress cry of the infant is innately capable of evoking the distress of the caretaking mother.

Seventh, the innate contagion of anger to anger is innately capable of sustaining the continuation of mutual contagion and thereby of effecting the *escalation* of both anger and aggression. It is as difficult for any angry dyad to control and inhibit anger and aggression as it is for either individual to inhibit or control his anger in the first instance. This is why third-party intervention is often necessary to separate angry, fighting individuals.

These are some of the innate characteristics of anger and aggression which sensitize all societies to the inherent dangers of this affect and which therefore prompts universal vigilance and sanctions against its free expression. No less problematic are several additional characteristics and consequences, some real, some illusory, some self-fulfilling, which are dependent upon sustained social experience, learning, and reflection.

First, anger and aggressive acts often produce lasting and irreversible social damage. Murder, assassination, rioting, rebellion, revolution, and war may result in the loss of life, the destruction of property, and the destruction of crops and stores of food. Whole peoples may be forced to flee their homes and wander helplessly in quest of shelter and safety as refugees. These are not always nor readily reversible consequences of anger and aggression. These complex social phenomena are not simple derivatives of anger and aggression, but neither are they totally free of admixtures of anger and aggression. One may kill in the name of Jesus or of nation or of ideology without a trace of anger, but sustained aggression ordinarily requires the passion and fire of anger as well as the excitement and enjoyment of combat.

Second, any expression of either anger or of aggression may properly be regarded as a threat to the stability of any social order. Even when that social order inflicts great suffering on a majority of the individuals living under its governance, violence in the interest of remedial action nonetheless adds to that suffering some increment of threatened or actual disorder. As in any therapeutic enterprise, the toxicity of the cure may be as great or greater than the disease it destroys. Whether the long-term benefits of violent aggressive social action exceed the costs of destroying a society which is itself violent or unjust is necessarily uncertain and depends in part on who is asking the question. The sacrifice of one generation for the benefit of succeeding generations *may* be equally devoutly wished for and rewarding to all concerned, parents, children, and grandchildren for several generations (excepting only the vanquished, tyrannical, native ruling class, or colonial imperialists). More often it is or is believed to be of greater benefit to future generations than to those whose lives are disrupted by violence. Nor is it rare that the violence of revolutionary action does not change the general level of violence or injustice in the society but rather changes the cast of who is hurting and exploiting whom. Because of the known ambiguity of the consequences of remedial violence, it is regarded with *some* ambivalence by all societies, over and above the self-serving conservatism of those who monopolize political power.

Third, highly developed societies have characteristically monopolized the use of violence as legitimate only for governmental exercise. The state and the state alone may legitimately punish and even kill any individual or group within its own jurisdiction or, as in the case of war, external to its authority. The private use of violence (e.g., for familial revenge feuds) was not surrendered readily in modern times, even when there existed strong central governmental authority. Nor were multiple sources of political power readily subordinated to central political authority. Aristocratic classes have always been loath to surrender political power, including the right of the sword, as in the right of the samurai feudal Japan to decapitate those who offend. It is in part the awareness of the power of anger contagion and escalation and magnification (e.g., in the feud) which supports the acquiescence of the governed to the government as the exclusive exerciser of legitimated violence.

INNATE AND LEARNED ACTIVATION OF ANGER

How is anger activated? How is it related to the other major mechanisms—the motor, cognitive, drive, and perceptual mechanisms? Cognitive theory is in close accord with common sense in its explanation of how anger is triggered. For some few thousand years Everyman has been a cognitive theorist in explaining why we feel angry. Everyone thinks he knows that we become angry when the other does something “outrageous.” If a person becomes enraged for no apparent “reason,” Everyman is either puzzled or thinks that perhaps there was a hidden reason, or failing that, supposes the other may be insane, or some mixture of such reasons, as in "insane" jealousy.

But Everyman has never been far from the theories of the most subtle philosophers in this respect. Over two thousand years ago Aristotle described the major affects in much the same way as does everyman and as contemporary cognitive appraisal theorists do: "The persons with whom we get angry are those who laugh, mock or jeer at us, for such conduct as insolent. Also those who inflict injuries upon us that are marks of insolence." Aristotle's conception reflects the importance of pride for Greek society, thus exaggerating what is in fact only one possible trigger of anger, in the sociocentric way to which most cognitive theorists are vulnerable.

Aristotle faced the same difficulty that confronts Everyman and contemporary cognitive theorists. How is one to deal with the "exceptions"?

According to Aristotle, "For those who are not angry at the things they should be angry at are thought to be fools, and so are those who are not angry in the right way, at the right time, or with the right persons." Aristotle would be at home with those contemporary theorists who postulate an evaluating, appraising homunculus or, at the least, an appraisal process that scrutinizes the world and declares it as an appropriate or inappropriate candidate for anger. Once information has been so validated, it is presumed ready to activate anger. Such theorists, like Everyman, cannot imagine feeling angry without an adequate reason. The passionate disputes among philosophers concerning the role of "reason" versus "causality" in human affairs give no sign of diminution in some two thousand years of controversy. This dispute is in part ideological. It is the implied affirmation of the dignity of the "rational" human being versus the implied diminution of such dignity in the causal explanation of our behavior and of our feelings, which is just under the surface. Thus, Aquinas affirms "those who are so drunk that they have lost all rational capacity do not become angry; they are angered when they are slightly drunk, capable of reasoning, at least imperfectly."

There must indeed be a cause or determination of anger when it is activated, and one should not exclude the possibility that the determinant *might* be exclusively a reason, it might be a reason *and* a cause together, it might be a cause which is *coincidentally* accompanied by an apparent reason, or it might be exclusively a cause entirely unrelated to any apparent reason.

The problematic nature of the cognitive theory of appraisal as the sufficient condition for the activation of anger arises first of all when we encounter objectless, free-floating irritability and anger, when one is angry but about nothing in particular. Second is the problem of the earliest infant rage—the tantrum which neither the infant nor its mother can understand or control. Whether the birth cry is a cry of distress or rage or whether it varies with different infants has yet to be decisively determined. But surely it is not the outcome of an appraisal of the extrauterine world upon its emergence from the birth canal. Third are those rages which surprise the adult who feels them, surprising either because they are appraised *after* the fact as inappropriate or as inappropriately intense, so they are experienced as "unreasonable" and thus somewhat alien.

Cognitive theories address, at best, only half of the problem—those circumstances in which the "reason" for anger is known by both the one who experiences the anger and by the theorist who observes the angry one and who agrees with the explanation offered. But such a consensus between Everyman and scientist may nonetheless be a folie a deux if, as I think, a general theory must be a unitary theory, capable of explaining by one and the same mechanism both learned anger, rational or not, and innate, sometimes rational, sometimes irrational, and sometimes objectless anger. Further, a general theory must also be able to account for anger which is activated by mechanisms other than the cognitive mechanism, since one may be angered directly by excessive noise, by pain, or by hunger whether these are cognitively "interpreted" or not. It seems very unlikely that the innate affect program would have evolved with two separate triggering mechanisms. Any theory of how we learn to become angry must account for the apparent cognitive control of anger via utilization of the same activating pathway as occurs in *unappraised, innate, or learned* triggering of anger.

It is my belief that cognitive processes *can* and *do* activate anger, but primarily through their level of neural firing rather than through their meaning or content. Content, therefore, is *coincidental* to the level of neural firing. Thus, a *variety* of different appraisals would be capable of triggering anger so long as they occurred at the appropriate level of neural firing. The generality of anger—the possibility of being angered by insult, by excessive noise, by hunger, or by muscular tension—depends upon each of these firing neurally at a high level. A cognitive theory could account for such generality of anger only by assuming some "meaning" invariant in loud sounds, insults, contracted muscles, and hunger. This is not inconceivable, but the homunculus who so appraised the fitness of every possible source of anger would have to have achieved an extraordinary universal common denominator in all the varieties of cultures which locate many outrages in what appear to be vastly different loci.

Even more problematic for such to-be-achieved invariances of meaning would be those cases where there is a *summation* of several different sources which together trigger anger. Thus, an individual who comes into a restaurant hungry might become distressed as the density of neural firing of the hunger signal increases to a level sufficient to trigger distress. But if now that individual is subjected to the conjoint, elevated level of neural firing from multiple sources, the stomach in hunger and the facial and vocal muscles contracted in distress, it would require only a small additional contraction of the fist (occasioned perhaps by an inference of inequity on seeing a waitress attend someone who came into the restaurant later than he did) to reach a level of neural firing adequate to activate anger. Such an activation of anger is based on part drive, part distress affect, part inference, part contracted fist, conjointly adding up to the density level of neural firing required to innately trigger anger. To the extent to which such levels of neural firings themselves become habitual and overlearned and located in ideas *or* in muscle movements, they radically increase the frequency of anger activation.

But such a summated combination of diverse sources of anger has no obvious underlying meaning or content apart from its being "too much," the verbal equivalent of the overly dense level of neural firing. Indeed, it is just this quantitative characteristic which *is* often referred by the angry one to himself and to others as the "reason" for his anger, as in the commonplace "straw that broke the camel's back." But this same person will, however, on other occasions *also* give quite different accounts to himself and to others for his anger—for example, that the other was inconsiderate, selfish, insulting, or indifferent. Although the phenomenology of anger only occasionally refers to the quantitative aspect of the activating stimulus, it is nonetheless the case, I am arguing, that it is the *only* invariant in all these apparently diverse reasons for anger. Paradoxically, Everyman finds the quantitative feature much easier to understand in the case of distress than in the case of anger. One is more prepared to believe that an infant may cry in distress because sounds are too loud, hunger is too intense, pain too intense, lights too bright, than that any of these might be a general explanation of anger, given an *increased* level of neural firing. In part our differential resistance to such simple causal explanations of anger, compared with distress, arises from the greater social toxicity of anger and therefore its greater threat both to society and to our image of human nature. To the extent that we may be angered *whenever* the density of neural firing exceeds an optimal level, independent of our values, independent of our reason, we appear to diminish the stature of the human being. The affect mechanism is a wonder of the evolutionary process in its conjoint abstractness, urgency, and generality, but there is nonetheless a price for its extraordinary fitness for evolution. It is not endlessly docile and assimilable to every other human purpose and capacity. There is inevitably some "play" in the best of systems, be they evolved or consciously designed. If it is to be urgent and abstract and general, it cannot also be weak and particular and specific, as would be required if it had always to be first validated by reason before it was permitted to be activated. Reason and appraisal would have required it to be differentiated in its urgency, to be differentiated in its abstractness and particularity, and to be differentiated in its generality and its specificity, so that we could cognitively *choose* whom to be angry with, how much to be angry, how long to be angry, for what reason to be angry, and how to respond to anger once aroused. Because anger is at once abstract *and* general, we are able to be angry in the *same* way to an insult as to the pain stubbing our toe. Abstractness in such cases enables one to respond in the same way to sources of anger which are quite different. In order, however, to *also* respond *differentially* to insult and pain, the more *specific* distinctive features of the two sources must also be conceived, and the cognitive mechanism *has* the requisite complexity to deal *simultaneously* with similarity and difference. The density and urgency of the anger response can and frequently does swamp the awareness of the distinctiveness of different sources of anger, in the absurd case where one kicks the object on which one has stubbed one's toe, as though *it* was a responsible person. In this case the abstractness of anger combined with the urgency has swamped and dedifferentiated the cognitive zoom lens which would normally add sufficient specific texture to the ensemble of features in the central assembly so that one would feel both the similarity of anger to pain and insult, as well as the distinctive features of pain and insult, and therefore the necessity to respond in anger in somewhat similar ways but also in somewhat different ways.

We do, of course, try to modulate all these common and distinctive features by thought, and the wonder is how much we *can* tame this mechanism in the interests of social living. We must not, however, confuse the self as internal advisor with the innate activating mechanisms, lest we think the etiquette of manners in eating is a complete account of the hunger drive. Because the innate activating mechanism operates via a more abstract and simpler code than our phenomenology of affect, anger will always remain a somewhat alien force in our private life space and in our shared social world. The phenomenology of affect is necessarily misleading as a basis for decoding the nature of the innate activating mechanism.

IMPLICATIONS OF INNATE ACTIVATOR MODEL

Infinite Number of Possible Sources of Anger, Finite Number of Probable Sources of Anger

Anger is *always* activated via the resonance of the triggering mechanism to a nonoptimal bandwidth of neural firing. That neural firing may be produced innately, as in pain stimulation, *or* through learning, as in the *learned* stiffening of striped muscles to insult. But whether the *source* of the trigger is itself learned or innate or some combination of both, the *triggering* mechanism itself is an innate one. As one consequence one may learn to become angry about anything under the sun. In this sense it shares with all other affects the critical feature of generality of combinatorial assembly. This is not to say that any kind of stimulus is an equally *probable* source of anger. Drive pleasure is a much less probable candidate for anger activation than is drive pain. A slap in the face is a much more probable candidate than a caress or a kiss. But a slap on the face is always a possible source of joy rather than anger, and a caress or a kiss is always a possible source of anger. It must be emphasized that although the innate activation of anger requires a dense level of neural firing there is *no* requirement of extended duration of the trigger. I assume that the triggering mechanism is similar to the ear in its millisecond sensitivity to differential *rate* of firing (for level stimuli) and to differential *change* of *rate* of firing (for gradient stimuli). A slap in the face would *immediately* trigger anger and universally produce anger unless, for example, it suddenly produced a *learned* general relaxation of muscular tension which then innately triggered joy at the same time. Since the target organs of anger and joy are the same and since the slap on the face is a focal zone of increased neural firing and the general muscular relaxation is a more diffuse zone of *decreased* neural firing, there will be competition at the site of the affect organs (face, throat, voice, chest) between the simultaneously triggered anger and joy programs of instruction to these affect target organs. Under certain conditions the learned, activated, innate joy response will mask and interfere with the unlearned, activated, innate anger response. Suppose, as an example, that a man was about to be executed by a firing squad and at the last moment was slapped on the face as he was told there had been a stay of execution. Such a message would produce such a diffuse relaxation of muscle tonus that the preceding fear and simultaneous anger from the slap would be radically attenuated by the deep and *more enduring* joy from the relief mediated both by the relaxation of striped muscles and the recruited joyful cognition. Although the slap was *over,* the recruitment of joy-activating cognition and motoric relaxation would produce a phenomenal field of joy, not anger, despite the fact that both programs had been activated simultaneously toward the same target organs.

In contrast, the kiss or caress bestowed upon an ideological puritan would produce sufficient violation of central values to recruit, for example, stiffening of the entire musculature and body armor to innately enrage the individual against the kisser.

Because any object may be *learned* to serve as an innate activator of any affect, empirical investigations of perceived sources of anger have minimal importance for understanding the nature of the activating mechanism. But they *are* important in the delineation of learned loci of anger, their quantity relative to other affects and particularly their cross-cultural class, sex, and other demographic correlations. It is of critical importance to know that one individual is rarely angry and that another is always angry and that the same is true for different cultures, ages, sexes, body types, noise levels, air ion density, and so on. But these differences are orthogonal to the nature of the affect activating mechanism.

Ambiguity of the Phenomenal Experience of Anger

Because the critical activator of anger is quantitative and abstract, there is always some ambiguity in the experience of anger, both of what one is angry about and why one is angry.

One may or may not know who or what one is angry about. Anger may, like any other affect, be free-floating and objectless if, for example, it was muted or avoided and returns after a delay.

One may know who one is angry at but not why, or not why so angry. Some anger may seem justified, but the angry person may sense that he is angrier than he *should* be, that his anger is disproportionate either in its intensity or in its duration.

Given some ambiguity about who or what angers, one's certainty typically varies so that the more phenomenal clarity, the greater the certainty. If one does not *know* who or what one is angry toward, one necessarily lacks phenomenal certainty. In the case of what appears disproportionate anger, phenomenal certainty is typically undermined.

In addition to the *experienced* ambiguity of anger about who or what or why, there is the more typical *incomplete* and or *inaccurate* attribution of the source of anger. These are not altogether independent criteria. If one knows accurately who one is angry at but only incompletely, then one is partially accurate and partially inaccurate insofar as one is ignorant of the total causal matrix. If the ratio of unknown determinants far exceeds the known sources of anger, then such incompleteness of knowledge can radically undermine accuracy of attribution, even when one is typically "correct."

Consider also that if I am angry at you for very minor "reasons," compared with the total quantity of stimulation which is bombarding me, that I am vulnerable to confirmation of my attribution because anger is both self-validating and self-fulfilling. It is self-validating in that if I *think* I am angry at you there is a nontrivial sense in which that cannot be disconfirmed. You *have* angered me if I so experience it, no matter how much of a delusion this might prove if I had better understood what was happening. But experienced anger is not only self-validating, it is also self-fulfilling in that my anger is likely to be sufficiently contagious to make you as angry at me as I am at you and thereby to produce further escalation of mutual anger.

The awareness of the true object is further complicated by the fact that anger itself is entirely capable of activating more anger with or without additional support. The role of anger in perpetuating anger is, however, usually masked by the subordination of the anger to its perceived object. So, in addition to self-validation by misattribution and self-fulfillment by contagion and escalation, there may be further deepening of self-delusion by anger feeding on and increasing the duration and intensity of anger, since anger is a sufficient activator of more anger, quite apart from its perceived source.

Because the innate activator of anger is abstract and quantitative, accurate and complete knowledge of the nature of such overstimulation is the exception rather than the rule. This is not to say the individual typically has no idea of what in fact makes him angry, and no accuracy, but rather that, at best, he only approximates a complete and accurate knowledge of the dynamics of his felt anger.

Although many individuals, sometimes intuit that their rage is more abstract and quantitative than specific and qualitative in nature, this is not the rule. Occasionally, the quantitative elevation of neural firing will find sufficient phenomenal representation that the individual will realize that he is the victim of excessive "pressure" from which he must "escape." The anger diagnosed as due to the "rat race" or against someone who is "a bit much" may provide a phenomenal isomorphism with the abstract level of neural firing. But more often the diagnosis is at best approximate, as in confusing moral outrage with the combined low-grade bombardment of fatigue, the excessive noise level, and the elevated muscle tonus—all of which may summate to require only the smallest addition of a minor human foible to produce an explosion of rage. Again, a minor affront suffered in the morning may be cumulatively added to a minor affront in the afternoon and these two cumulated upon returning home in the evening to yet another minor unexpected affront. Given such multiplicative cumulation, the potentially minor annoyances of an easily absorbed unpleasant scene can evoke towering rage. Any sequence of angering scenes from the remote past may be cumulatively coassembled as simultaneous, and thereby radically magnified in anger, independent of daily sequences of angering scenes. The residues of such sequences may then be transformed by compression and provide a faint background context for the interpretation of future scenes. If such a compression transformation is specifically and fully expandable and recoverable, then past scenes may be rapidly recovered, expanded, coassembled, and imported into any present scenes so that the individual is again bombarded with an increasing family of bad scenes in his response to any present single scene.

Unconsciousness or partial consciousness of who one is angry at and why one is angry is a consequence of two quite different sources, one motivational and the other structural. One may be powerfully motivated *not* to know about one's anger, either *that* one is angry or *who* one is angry at or *why* because of a variety of anger binds. If the feeling of anger threatens shame, or terror, or guilt, or disgust, or distress in sufficient density, singly or in combination, the individual can be motivated to minimize the awareness of anger and its expression. In such a case the individual neither knows nor wishes to know the sources of his anger and might become angry or anxious at anyone who tried or threatened to raise such consciousness. This source of unconsciousness is independent of the anger-activation mechanism.

That mechanism *is* related to the second type of unconsciousness of anger. Because quantity of neural stimulation can *summate,* either sequentially or simultaneously, slowly or rapidly, by small quantities or large quantities, the variety and complexity of such patterns can readily escape the attention of the individual until a critical mass is reached and the anger program is activated. Consider that the phenomenology of anger is typically embedded in a complex sequence of scenes which includes much which is *not* angering as well as much recruited information of the past history of similar scenes and *their* perceived causes and outcomes and further consequences. The awareness of the stimulus to anger is influenced by several independent sources: the perceived stimulus to anger, the variety of expected consequences of that kind of *stimulus* in general as well as of that specific stimulus, the expected *consequences* of *anger* in general as well as to that kind of stimulus, the expected *consequences* of anger-prompted *further responses* (in general, as well as to that stimulus), and the variety of non-anger affects which may be activated by the perceived stimulus to anger. What one thinks one is angry about is a very complex resultant of the actual present scene and the further recruited information and further responses it evokes. This information is embedded in a centrally assembled mixture so complex and viscous, that the individual's judgment about these complex dynamics is at best a rough approximation of what might have angered him, even in the most favorable case that he is not powerfully motivated to avoid and escape consciousness of anger. Fortunately, in one sense, unfortunately in another, he does not have to "know" as a scientist knows in order to activate anger.

Positive Affect and Drive Pleasure as Paradoxical Sources of Anger

The innate activator model distinguishes gradients from levels of neural firing and, within levels, different degrees of nonoptimal levels. The generality of this model is such that no distinction is drawn between pain and pleasure or between positive and negative affects as sources of neural firing. This means that if one experiences *too* intense sustained drive pleasure or too intense and/or sustained excitement, one could, paradoxically, thereby evoke anger simply because the level of neural firing exceeded an optimal level despite the intensely rewarding quality of the neural sensory stimulation.

This paradox illuminates sado-masochistic sexuality, play-interruption anger, and crowd excitement anger. The heightening of both sexual pleasure and excitement via the inflicting of pain, in anger, paradoxically can also add enjoyment to this complex. We do not ordinarily regard anger as a source of joy as well as of excitement because we mistakenly assume that the density of nonoptimal neural firing is totally incompatible with either sexual pleasure or with simultaneous excitement or joy. We must remember that each affect program is independent and capable of activation by specific triggers either simultaneously or in very rapid succession. There *may* be incompatibilities between the innate affect programs at the sites of the target organs (chest, face, vocal cords, heart, blood vessels), which may then produce complex mixtures of affects and/or refractory periods, but these incompatibilities must be sharply differentiated from the openness of the *triggering* mechanisms of the several affect programs.

Sexual sadism consists in the conjoint heightening of anger, excitement, and joy, as well as sexual pleasure. Sexual masochism is the mirror image of such a complex, in which one ordinarily identifies with the role of *both* victim and victimizes There is usually, though not necessarily, a collusion between sadomasochistic partners such that double identification is shared at the same time that each also plays a distinctive complementary role. They need each other to share the total scene *and* to play distinctive roles of angry aggressor who inflicts pain and victim who suffers pain. Humiliation and degradation may, in addition, be conjoined with pain and suffering. If so, the sadist is excited by his disgust and or contempt of the self and of the to-be-degraded other, and the masochist is excited by the identification with the contempt of the other and by the experience of being hurt, disgusted, humiliated, and degraded. Some sadomasochistic sexual relationships may magnify humiliation primarily rather than the inflicting of pain, with or without anger. The texture of sadomasochistic sexuality varies, therefore, with the ratios of anger and humiliation, excitement and enjoyment, and sexual pleasure versus inflicted pain. Further, the added titillation of fear and/or shame or guilt can increase the density and urgency of the whole complex, to heighten the probability of anger evocation, in either sadistic or masochistic sexuality.

Sadomasochistic sexuality, then, need not include anger as a salient feature if humiliation and degradation are the primary currency of sexual victimage. However, anger is readily fused with intended humiliation and degradation in sadomasochistic sexual scenes.

Another type of sadomasochistic sexuality which is similar but not identical with humiliation and degradation is that which features absolute control and submission in bondage victimage, as in the case of "O," in which one inflicts complete control and the other willingly submits. Again, this may appear without anger, or it may be combined with anger so that control is accompanied and enforced by beating. A special case of sadomasochistic sexuality in which control and submission is involved is collusive rape, in which victim and victimizer equally require each other to play complementary roles.

Collusive rape may emphasize control and submission, but it need not. There are many varieties of collusive rape in which control and submission are not salient. Such rape may provide the vehicle for expression of self-assertion and aggrandizement combined with a variety of types of flaunting behavior such as guiltlessness, shamelessness, anguishlessness, or fearlessness, in varying combinations with anger.

The victim of rape may of course be entirely innocent of playing the complementary collusive role. It is collusive when *both* require complementary roles. A collusive rapist who encounters a too enthusiastic "victim" can be as frustrated as a truly collusive "victim" who has to seduce the attacker.

Such sexual sadomasochism is as varied in its texture as is personality. The sadist may angrily demonstrate his fearlessness by inflicting his sexuality on the masochist, who is at once timid and excitedly identified with the brave recklessness of the other.

The sadist may angrily demonstrate guiltlessness in inflicting an immorality on the masochist, who is at once "pure" and excited by the violation of that purity.

The sadist may angrily demonstrate shamelessness in inflicting an act of self-assertive boldness upon a masochist, who is at once equally shy and excited by the assertion of self-confidence by the other.

The sadist may angrily demonstrate freedom from the anguish of suffering; sexual and otherwise, in inflicting an act which gives pleasure, rather than suffering, deprivation, and anguish, upon a masochist who is at once equally distressed and freed from suffering by the identification with the self-assertive one who has broken the chains of bondage of distress from herself and thus for him. Such a sadist is excited by the masochist who cries out in orgasm how much he has "wanted" it. It may be uttered as an affirmation against too long delayed sexual experience and its frustrating distress and consequent intensification of present desire and pleasure. Such an affirmation can, however, vary radically in its meaning. It may be uttered as an affirmation against felt shame, in which case being forced to avow desire is to assert both shame and shamelessness. If the affect of shame has the connotation of immorality (rather than distance and shyness), then the forced avowal of "want" has the significance of assertion of both guilt and guiltlessness which excites.

The sadist may angrily demonstrate freedom from disgust in inflicting, for example, an oral and or anal pleasure on the masochist, who is at once disgusted and excited by the enforced disgusting act. The expression of "wanting" such experience is a conjoint avowal of the excitement of disgust and disgustlessness.

The sadist may intend primarily to demonstrate the freedom to feel and show *anger* in inflicting an act which combines sexuality with the expression of anger upon a masochist who is at once inhibited in his own anger and excited by the assertion of anger by the other. Such anger can vary in its manifestations from showing that one *feels* angry, or in its *communication* to the other, to its overflow in *action* (e.g., in hurting the masochist), depending on where in the socialization of such a chain inhibition has been imposed most severely.

Sadomasochistic rape may then be the vehicle of collusion in the sharing of sadomasochistic avowal of both the burden of inhibited affects, as norms, and the relief and excitement of flaunting such taboos.

In such flaunting sadomasochism, the emphasis may be primarily on flaunting one's own norms, on flaunting the norms of the other, or on both. Thus, if I am guilty about my sexuality, I may inflict pain angrily upon the other to demonstrate to myself and to the other that I can break the bondage of conscience or to demonstrate to the other that she cannot make me feel guilty. I can do this latter either by inflicting my guilty sexuality upon her or by forcing her to be sensual and avow her guilt and her guiltlessness, or by the shared flaunting of guilt in guiltless sensuality. These types of flaunting sexuality may, however, not be possible for a male with too severe sexual guilt, unless the script is played with a surrogate, sensual whore-mother who, in flaunting *her* free-flowing sensuality, legitimates the sensuality of her now liberated son. Such a scene may have the added significance of revealing not only the hidden but suspected sensuality of the mother but also of revealing her preference for her son over her husband, in an idealized version of the Oedipus triangle. Not only is the son given license to be as free as his father in such a script but also to surpass him. It may, however, be the vehicle of the radically different intention of vengeance, a special form of recasting, of reversing the role of the actors so that the victim who suffered punishment becomes the victimizer who inflicts just that specific punishment on his oppressor or on a substitute oppressor. In these cases the rapist who has been made to cry and suffer excessive distress wishes to make the other cry as he was forced to cry. This is a quite different kind of crying than the violation of distress as a result of sexual frustration in the shared avowal of how much sexuality has been "wanted" and now brazenly flaunted in collusive rape. The rapist who has been terrorized can, in recasting vengeance, be satisfied only by the screams of terror of his victim. The rapist who has been shamed requires his victim to suffer and express shame. The rapist who has been made to feel guilty requires his victim to avow guilt *at* being raped. The rapist who has been made to feel disgusted requires his victim to feel and avow disgust at the enforced humiliation. The rapist who has been made to feel impotent rage requires analogous cries of helpless outrage at being violated.

In all of these cases the imposed negative affect is satisfying to the punisher only insofar as it is *unilateral*. In contrast, collusive rape may involve the imposition of the same affects (e.g., making the other avow guilt or shame for imposed sexuality), but all affects are experienced vicariously by sadist *and* masochist, especially with respect to the heightened sexual pleasure and excitement from the conjoint avowal of such past suppressed affects as norms and their present wished-for and enjoyed violation.

Sadomasochistic sexuality ordinarily engages the nuclear scripts, those scenes which cannot be permanently solved and also cannot be renounced. Because of the tragic nature of such scenes they haunt dreams and fantasy in general as well as sadomasochistic sexual fantasy and activity. Such sexuality has much the same function which Aristotle attributed to Greek tragedy. In such nuclear script–derived sadomasochistic sexuality, the individual confronts and gives expression to the turbulence of the multiple yearnings he can neither entirely consummate nor renounce, and he gives expression to the suffering this entails. Sexual nuclear scripts characteristically have their origin in early childhood nuclear scenes which are *not* sexual scenes. Because sexuality ordinarily conjoins some degree of constraint with intensity of affect and drive pleasure, it readily becomes a vehicle for imagined solutions for problems which were originally neither soluble, nor renounceable, nor sexual in nature. If the nuclear scene is ordinarily asexual, the nuclear script is rarely entirely asexual. Sexuality is one major locus for the attempted solution, in fantasy, of an otherwise insoluble imperative. Although a nuclear scene often originally confronts a child with presumably impermeable barriers to the attainment of the heart's desire, the nuclear scripts which are generated in attempted solutions of the nuclear scene usually add dualistic conflict and pluralistic ambiguity to monistic frustration. The yearning, frustrated child readily becomes an angry, ashamed, guilty, and frightened child as he wrestles unsuccessfully with the variety of unsuccessful and often conflicting attempted solutions to a contaminated scene. Masturbatory sexual fantasies and, later, sexual encounters are used to experiment with the varieties of turbulent affects generated by such nuclear scripts to produce subsets of specifically sexual nuclear scripts. I have encountered numerous instances of a complex sexual nuclear script repeated daily and sometimes several times a day for many years. The individual appears to be compelled to repeat endlessly a complex sequence of interactions between himself and another which invariably ends in orgasm. I have also found similar sequences, with and without sexuality, generated again and again in the stories for Thematic

Apperception Test pictures by the same individuals who were compelled to act out these scripts sexually, either in masturbation or in sexual encounters.

The Interruption of Play

Next, the innate activator model illuminates the phenomenon, first described by Redl (1951), of the extreme anger and aggression evoked by the interruption of play of "children who hate." This phenomenon has been attributed to ego weakness and to an intolerance of normally absorbable frustration. While both of these explanations are probably true, the phenomenon can be further understood as the resultant of a conjunction of a very exaggerated level of neural firing of unusually intense and prolonged excitement on the one hand and the very intense muscular tonus which arises conjointly from the excited wish to resume play, the readiness for physical attack, and the characteristically motoric form of protest of jumping up and down. These appear to be children who have taught themselves to become angry very readily via the dense, added self-stimulation following interruption of any game which had already increased the level of neural stimulation via recycled excitement.

Crowd Excitement

Finally, there is also some illumination from the innate activator model of the dynamics of large-crowd behavior, whether it be primarily in political demonstrations, economic protests (e.g., strikes), sports arenas, or rock concerts. Anger and violence are commonplace whenever large numbers of people assemble to observe in excitement or to demonstrate strongly held beliefs. It appears irrelevant whether the occasion is primarily negative, as in protests, or positive, as in rock music concerts. If feelings run high and the affect contagion evoked in large crowds in turn evokes affect escalation, the potential for anger and for violence is ever just below the surface. The police and army are always alert to such a potential. Although this is not an inevitable phenomenon and does not characteristically involve the whole membership of a crowd, it is common enough to call for some explanation. In recent years the widespread use of drugs, particularly at large rock concerts, has in all probability reduced rather than increased the frequency of violence and riots at a presumably rewarding shared experience; since marijuana and other commonly used drugs increase relaxation, which decreases the level of neural stimulation and therefore the probability of anger. Riots from excitement occur not because human beings are so violent but because, first, too-long-sustained excitement is capable of also innately triggering the anger program. Second, such sustained excitement, whether political, economic, athletic, or aesthetic, can also trigger anger via the recovery of infantile and childhood rage. We will examine how this can occur in some detail in Volume 4, on memory. Briefly, we will demonstrate that early memory can be recovered via discontinuous distinctive features which isolated earlier memories from later variants. Thus, by instructing an individual to write his name slowly it is possible to recover early handwriting, which is distinctively slower than the adult signature. It is possible to evoke early anger by instructing the subject to shout *loudly,* "No I won't" or even by shouting alone, without a specific linguistic reference. Just as rate was a distinctive feature of early handwriting, so is loudness a distinctive feature of early affect in general and of early anger in particular. In large crowds, both the performer (politician, union leader, or rock star) and the audience are encouraged and permitted a lifting of the taboo on the loud voice, and indirectly, therefore, a lifting of the taboo on infantile and childhood affect. The individual under such permissive conditions can be captured by deep excitement and rage he has not given expression since the nursery. Intuitive political leaders have both engaged and controlled such affect for their own purposes by the skilled orchestration of their own loud, impassioned voice and the answering chorus from the audience. Hitler's excited, enraged voice was contagious and was escalated by the thousands of voices which chanted "Sieg Heil" in full-throated loyalty, communion, and pious enraged protest against the enemies of the Reich.

Limitations of Interpretation Psychotherapy

The implications of this theory for professional therapeutic "interpretation" of anger, psychoanalytic or otherwise, are substantial. It would caution against seduction by the exclusive concern with the apparent "meaning" of the anger. Despite the fact that a therapist who has become very familiar with his client's sources of anger is much less likely to be overinfluenced by the apparent immediate sources of anger and much more likely to understand the more remote and usually unconscious sources of his client's anger, nonetheless, most theories of interpretation are ultimately excessively cognitive in their attempts to trace the sources and objects of anger. The client and therapist are equally vulnerable to a folie à deux in this respect. Because neither is usually aware of the abstract quantitative nature of the activating mechanism, each is equally vulnerable to confusion when one and the same sources sometimes anger and sometimes do not anger, depending on simultaneous and sequential quantitative cumulations. The implications for what kinds of "insight" are therapeutic are also radically different. One must sensitize the client to the abstract quantitative features of his rage more than to their apparent content, though that content must *also* be understood as contributing to the level of stimulation. Therapist and client alike must be ever vigilant that the "same" provocation will be harmless if there is no summation but can become unbearably toxic and enduring if the sequencing summates rather than attenuates via spacing, whether that spacing be from the outside, from internal sources, or from both.

Equally important for therapist and client alike is the search-and-destroy mission for the many overlearned sources of internal elevations of neural firing, be they either episodic or sustained. Another example is a learned, sustained hypertonus of the body, as in Reich's "body armor," which can add a load of background neural firing which requires little additional stimulation to evoke anger. A related case is the more episodic focal hypertonic muscular responses. Thus, I observed countless male patients in my father's dental chair tightening various muscles in an effort not to cry out in pain. The pain of dental procedures summating with intense muscle contractions would often evoke muted anger responses on the face. Highly overlearned habits of muscle contractions in the hands, arms, toes, thighs, stomach, and chest occur in response to others, to imagined scenes, to memories, and contribute substantially to the level of neural firing sufficient for the triggering of anger. One is pursuing a will-o'-the-wisp in the quest for interpretive insight as to the sources of anger if one does not search out and attenuate such massive, usually unconscious supports for anger. Such habits of response can be attenuated through learned relaxation techniques, through drugs, or through competing rhythmic stimulation, as in warm baths, sunning, swimming, running, music of certain tempos, or massage. Centuries ago, psychotic rage was attenuated via warm baths which induced muscular relaxation. It "worked" without, however, contributing to our understanding of the nature of the activating mechanism. Everyman, in an attempt to escape his distress and his rage, intuited that relaxation was somehow necessary for relief and so sought it in alcohol, in meditation, in sunbathing, and in the rhythmic stimulation of massage, of music, of running, and of the soft caress.

The musculature is a critical site for increasing neural firing, but the therapist and client must also search out the information processing styles and habits which are capable of increasing the level of neural firing sufficiently to anger, independent of meaning. Just as individuals learn to characteristically walk and move their limbs slowly or rapidly, with great or low energy, so too do they learn to process information at varying rates and at varying levels of neural firing. The style of thinking, speaking, or moving very rapidly predisposes the individual to frequent evocation of excitement or fear. The style of thinking, speaking, gesticulating, or moving with great energy can elevate the level of neural firing sufficiently to predispose the individual to frequent evocation of anger. Therapeutic intervention for the excessively angry person will then require vigilance, not only into his overly intense use of his striped muscles but also some attenuation of the density of his perceptual, memorial, imaginative, and cognitive processes so that they are each less continuous and more spaced in time, less intense, with less simultaneous coassembly of different sources of information processing. Such a one needs to be encouraged to partition his cognitive processing rather than to do too much at once or too long. He should *not,* for example, try to use his senses to find evidence to support simultaneously his thinking through a problem, making a decision, planning, or imagining what the outcome will be as he remembers how similar ventures fared in the past. Such a person is constantly overstimulating himself to the brink of anger. Not only will such information processing make him vulnerable to anger from neural overstimulation, but it will also so overload his information-processing skills that the probability of cognitive confusion becomes yet another source of anger as he attempts to simplify overly complex, simultaneous cognitive demands upon himself. The classic phenomenon in psychoanalytic free association—that too many things come to mind at once to say anything—is not necessarily a sign of resistance. It is as often a derivative of an overreaching cognitive style born out of neurotic helpless anger.

Such cognitive self-overstimulation can also interfere with going to sleep and with staying asleep. A secondary consequence of insomnia and troubled sleep is fatigue, which will add yet another vulnerability to anger. Such an angry individual suffers from informational greed. He must have too much information too quickly. Anyone or anything that slows him down in any way is likely to add to his acquisitive anger, as in the case of a motorist trapped behind a slow driver on a crowded highway. As a cognitive overreacher, he is as likely to be continually angered by the opaque, the puzzling, the incomplete, the time and care demanded for cognitive organization and clarity as by any purely external impediment to cognitive mastery. His cognitive greed will guarantee that he will insistently strive for multiple carrots sufficiently beyond his reach to guarantee overstimulation, confusion, and helpless rage.

Such informational greed may, of course, be the consequence of excessive shame, which demands mastery; excessive guilt, which demands purity; excessive fear, which demands security; excessive disgust, which demands order and cleanliness; excessive distress, which demands serenity; any or all, however, so overloading the cognitive mechanism that rage is inevitable as excessive demands defeat the very mastery, security, purity, order, and serenity so desperately sought.

We have so far examined *informational* greed as a source of enraging self-stimulation. But self-stimulating greed which enrages is in no way limited to stable cognitive styles of information processing. Consider first *action* greed. Such a person, while on the telephone, may also continue to prepare dinner, pick up something which has fallen on the floor, and rearrange place settings on the dinner table, all the while looking for new fields for motor activity. Failing any new possibilities, he may drum his fingers in a rhythmic beat against the wall. While attempting to avoid the possibility of the sin of idle hands, he is providing a background of self-stimulation which may require little from his partner on the telephone to add an irritable edge to his voice. The inflated need to be "doing" something, anything, may arise out of anger, or evoke it or maintain it endlessly.

Next is *perceptual* greed in which the individual is constantly starving for more intense sensory and perceptual input. Such a one may carry with him his own very loud music, which he forces not only on himself but on anyone who happens to be in the same bus or train, or store, or street corner. Not infrequently his auditory pollution of the environment will evoke the anger of those whose space has been so invaded and may result in mutual violence. Perceptual greed may also prompt the quest for intense auditory experience in rock music. Here, although the quest is for excitement, the consequences may ultimately be fatigue and anger and, in the long run, hearing loss. The same quest for perceptual overstimulation occurs in the discotheque where the combination of loud sounds, constantly changing and moving colored lights, and the intense motoric activity in dancing seen in others and felt in the self as sensory feedback evoke and sustain first, excitement, then fatigue, and finally anger. Sustained perceptual excitement always has the potential of evoking rage, depending on its density, that is, the product of its intensity and its duration.

Next is *production* greed. In this the individual seeks not to maximize information processing, nor action, nor perceptual stimulation but rather to achieve specific *products* in the world. Such products may be books, paintings, money, buildings, children, institutions. If one *must* produce and produce too much, too fast, then one will necessarily eventually suffer the rage of the "rat race." Individuals do not characteristically seek such rage, but neither do they necessarily cease and desist from the compulsive and excessive quest for productivity which regularly overwhelms them. Interpretive psychotherapy which examines the sources of such frenetic quests is incomplete without equal attention to the inevitable consequences of the excessive quantity of self imposed overstimulation.

Next is *affect evocation* greed. Here the individual insists on evoking attention and positive affect from the other to himself. Like an actor he is always "onstage." Because a perennial audience cannot be guaranteed without excessive effort, he too is involved in a punishing "rat race," evoking rage from fatigue and the indifference and absence of a responsive or sufficiently responsive audience. The sources of such a magnified need for "mirroring" are often the shame, depression, and rage which are felt when the other looks away, as though the self is in perpetual potential rivalry with an unknown other.

Next is *control* greed, in which the individual insists on controlling the behavior and the consciousness of others. Because others usually insist on some degree of self-governance, the individual who is greedy for such control must exert himself excessively to monitor the behavior of the other and to shape it in the Skinnerian mode. The combination of effort, fatigue, resistance, and inevitable partial failure guarantees episodic or sustained anger. Interpretation of the sources of such control greed must be supplemented by an analysis of the price of excessive effort combined with the resistance of the other, and its inevitable consequence of partial failure, all cumulating to excessive self-stimulation and rage.

Finally, there may be a generalized *mini-maximizing greed.* Here an individual insists on minimizing negative affect and maximizing positive affect, conjointly. He insists on the best of all possible worlds. Whether it is information processing or action or perception or production or affect evocation or control or any of the great varieties of possible idealized scripts which human beings may seek, here the individual's criteria of success and failure are such as to guarantee rage. Effort is not only sustained and heroic, but the perpetual distance between the actual and the ideal which powers such effort together bombard that hero sufficiently to also evoke sustained anger.

Mini-maximizing greed aspires to reduce the distance between the ideal and the actual in every respect, whether it be in action, in perception, in production, in affect evocation, in control of others, in self-control, in understanding, in imagination, in decision, or in planning. Any barrier, imperfection, flaw, conflict, or ambiguity in the self or in the other can fuel unending rage in this type of greed.

Anger can also result from extreme narrowing of the cognitive field to a single channel endlessly repeated. Excessive repetition of a single stimulus or single response is extremely satiating and punishing and finally angering. Chinese water torture, of a drop of water on the head of the victim repeated endlessly at the same interval, produces an enforced attention and overstimulation which is extraordinarily toxic. Satiation first evokes distress and then anger, whether one has to listen or feel the same thing over and over—to say the same words again and again or to listen to the same words over and over again, whether it be one's own monologue, the monologue of the other, or an endlessly repeated and boring dialogue between the self and the other, in fact or in memory or both in sequence. Nor does it matter entirely whether such monologue or conversation is exciting or boring. The endless real or imagined repetition of praise or of sweet nothings can in the end become as satiating and enraging as the repetition of insults exchanged with real or imaginary adversaries.

Cognitive hypersimplicity and the narrowing of the cognitive field is not limited to exact repetition. Hypercomplexity is just as readily characteristically imprinted on the narrowest and simplest of questions as on the sweep of the broadest, multiple concerns. The greedy neurotic can readily alternate between a focus on the most elementary particles of his internal landscape as on the most cosmic concerns from its big bang origins to its possible entropic heat death. Such overlearned skills and styles of information processing can become sufficiently general that they are imprinted upon a wide variety of nondemanding and relatively trivial scenes. I am not arguing that trivial scenes are here necessarily overburdened with symbolic significance, as in an obsessive neurosis, but rather that increased density of self-stimulation can become both wished for and finally skilled, independent of the toxic consequences of such a style of information processing, so that the individual victimizes himself. Thus, at the beginning of a day such a person may review what is to be done and accomplished that day. The first half hour may be spent in thinking of the varieties of tasks of the day in exhaustive and exhausting detail. Then some attention may be given to ordering such a series in hierarchical priorities. What is the *most* important of the tasks? Next, the relationship of importance to effort demanded may be examined. Perhaps the easiest, most certain, and in a sense the most trivial tasks should be done first and thus gotten out of the way, leaving the rest of the day free and clear for single-minded concentration on what is most important and most demanding.

A case may then be entertained for the reverse order. Why not use oneself most heroically at the beginning of the day, leaving for the end those routine tasks which can be done just as well after one has spent oneself in heroic struggles with the most demanding problems? But a self-overstimulator can now see an even better possible strategy, that of a graded increase in difficulty. Perhaps he should start out with a very trivial task, like paying his bills; then step up to a slightly more demanding task, like shopping for food, which requires more time and effort; then answer his mail, which requires more thought, and then at last be ready for the supreme tests of the day. By now his head may be spinning, and spinning, moreover, in a turbulent sea of impotent rage. He may then seize upon that type of script I have called "doing the doable," which combines a high probability of problem *solving* with *some* guaranteed excitement and enjoyment, as in a game of solitaire. But as he plays the game of solitaire, he is *also* aware of the mail he has not answered, some of which has been too long delayed, of the shopping he *must* do because he is now completely out of food, of a very interesting TV program which he would like to watch *if* there is time and he has done what he has to do; but most insistently, and with alternating shame and rage, he cannot keep from his thoughts that in playing solitaire he is *not* doing either what he should be doing or even what *would* be much *more* enjoyable if he could permit himself to indulge himself. Simultaneity of multiple information processing thus radically interferes with the possibility of wholehearted commitment to any single scene through segregation of competing scenes. There is a continuing interpenetration of scenes, which both bleaches and complicates every scene, all competing for simultaneous attention.

Thus, such a neurotic can alternate between endless *repetition* of the simplest task, endless *complication* of *simple* phenomena, return to *single-minded,* mildly challenging *doable* tasks, endlessly intruded upon by remote, plural, complex, demands.

Such a cognitive style may be illuminated by a comparison with the more focused creativity of the productive individual. Several years ago I studied the work habits of productive and creative scientists and artists. I found a variety of styles, but the predominant one was the exact antithesis of the one we have just examined. Characteristically, a period of the day was *routinely* set aside for sustained, uninterrupted work—most often the first three or four hours of the morning. In one case, that of a philosopher, he rented a room in the city of the university where he taught. This room was known to no one, not even his wife. It had no telephone. He worked *every* day, from 8:30 to 12:30, writing four or five pages without fail. Characteristically, these individuals did many things after their most demanding and most sustained daily effort, but these were regarded as dispensable or optional or variable, depending on circumstance. They typically included many deeply rewarding scenes, but scenes not so controlled as those involved in their professional commitment. Thus, the theater, music, conversation, nonprofessional reading, sex, eating, playing with their children—all deeply engaged one or another of these individuals but were subordinated to a self-imposed strict regimen of hard work as required *before* they could permit themselves to nurture and indulge themselves to experiences which they also regarded as rewarding ends in themselves. This is not to say that their work was not experienced as a deeply rewarding end in itself. Many of these individuals said that the three or four hours during which they did their daily creative work were the peak moments of their lives. In marked contrast to the characteristic failure of segregation of the self-overstimulating angry person, these individuals were capable of unusual immersion in and focus on whatever engaged them.

I wondered whether it might be possible to modify the obsessiveness and alternations and intrusiveness of hyperfocus and hyperscope of such informational styles by using the contrasting style of the creative, productive individual as a model for the ineffective, enraged individual. I was fortunate at about that time to be asked for help by two graduate students at Harvard. In each case the individual worked all day long and far into the night but very inefficiently and very ineffectively. Despite very high intellectual ability they felt unable to meet the demands they imposed upon themselves and the demands the department of psychology imposed on them. They were in imminent, real danger of losing their supporting fellowships and teaching assistantships, and they faced the dread and shame of failing as candidates for the doctorate. I had then neither the competence nor the time to use depth psychotherapy, but I experimented with a very directive type of therapy.

After hearing their descriptions of their problems and the resultant distress, shame, self-disgust, and anger, and their sense of desperate hopelessness about completing the requirements for the Ph.D., I explained my strategy for changing their style of working. I emphasized the contrast between their style and that of the more productive workers in the study I had just completed and put them on a strictly rationed daily period of study time. They were to work *no more* than three hours each day, and they were to do this each day upon awakening. If as they did this, their minds wandered and they consequently did not finish their allotted assignments for that day, they had nonetheless to resist *adding* any more time to that work day. They were not only free to do whatever they wished for the remainder of the day, but this was *obligatory.* They *must* do that which they *most* wanted to do, exempting only the finishing of unfinished work. Further, if they found their minds wandering back to this, they were to reassure themselves that they would have another opportunity the next morning, but not before then. Next I asked them whether in their recent experience there had been any occasions when they had been able to use their time effectively and efficiently. In each case, the few hours just before having to take an examination seemed to draw forth the most heroic concentration of attention. Under these conditions, these otherwise disturbed individuals were quite capable of using their high capabilities.

I then suggested that each three-hour morning work period be regarded by them as issuing in just such a test—but a self-administered test which would give them evidence of how well they had used their opportunity and would also enable them to monitor whether from day to day they were improving their competence to profit from the use of their minds. I suggested they keep a written self-rating record which could enable them to plot long-term trends in their performance as well as sustain their motivation and provide appropriate rewards as well as punishments for backsliding. It was my intention to use their obsessiveness for their advantage rather than their disadvantage in such record keeping. It was also my intention to both limit and to intensify their informational greed by focusing it to such a limited part of their day that they *could* in fact realistically use themselves heroically and effectively and so give them a daily taste of the well-earned psychic profits of sustained hard work and whet their appetite for even greater concentration and achievements. As this began to be possible, I expected that they would be better equipped both to enjoy later nonwork scenes and to segregate one kind of scene from another. Indeed, just these outcomes were achieved. They remained, I know, still somewhat neurotic, disturbed human beings, but they were also quite different in nontrivial ways. They achieved their academic aims then and continued to enjoy rewarding professional careers after finishing the doctorate.

It may be objected that overly acquisitive, inclusive self-stimulation and obsessive rumination, alternating with excessive repetition of a too narrowly focused consciousness, are but symptoms of deeper causes which must be understood before the symptoms can be attacked. I am not disputing the necessity nor the desirability of such understanding but rather arguing for the equal necessity of interrupting overlearned cognitive skills because of their toxic capacity for evocation of rage, apart, from both their present meaning and more remote sources. It is not unlike the problem of freeing an individual from psychologically based addictive dependency. One can, for example, cure, via interruption, addictive dependency on cigarettes by having the person watch TV or moving pictures continually for a couple of days and nights. At the end of a couple of days of such enforced abstinence through distraction, the individual for the first time experiences the possibility of a *choice* which he has not experienced before. He may or may not then elect to exercise that possibility of stopping, or having chosen to stop, he may later again be swamped by addictive craving and backslide to his customary dependence. However, the possibility of choice is nonetheless a real and new alternative (no matter how weak or transient) which illustrates by contrast the role of interrupted compared with continuing sequences of learned self-stimulation in psychological addiction. In short, the overlearned habits and styles of cognitive self-stimulation require therapeutic intervention designed to free the individual from the toxic rage-evoking informational greed which has become so skilled that the individual can experience it only as ambivalent victim rather than as actor.

Psychopathology is much too complex to yield to simple remedies. I am not suggesting that an understanding of the innate activating mechanism of anger is sufficient to enable the cure of neurosis or psychosis. First, anger is but one affect among many, and psychopathology derives as much from problems of terror, guilt, shame, disgust, and distress as from anger. Second, even if anger were the *only* or major affect problem, a knowledge of the *immediate* triggers of the innate mechanism would not be sufficient to enable control of the complex networks which are recruited to produce the immediate trigger. Third, the abstract nature of the triggering mechanism is at the same time *particularized* by non-affect mechanisms which must also be understood and controlled either by the client or by the therapist. Nonetheless, "interpretation" psychotherapy *without* knowledge of or attention to the nature of the innate activating mechanism is as blind as any other kind of unconsciousness. The finer the texture of understanding of the complexities of psychopathological processes, the more effective therapeutic procedures can become. Interpretation will be radically enriched if it is embedded in an understanding of the causal matrix of the innate affect-activating mechanism.

COMPLICATIONS AND AMBIGUITIES FOR TESTING ANY AFFECT-ACTIVATION THEORY

If, as we think, the affect programs are stored in subcortical areas of the brain, then any theory of the trigger mechanism needs to address the nature of the neural transmission at that site rather than along the entire neural pathway. The known complexities of neural networks guarantee that the rate or density of neural firing at any one point in the pathways of neural transmission may or may not be preserved at another point. Thus, in sleep there is a general reduction in amplification of the sensory messages via reduction of the activity of the reticular formation, accounting in part for the particularly vivid characteristics of the remaining internally recruited sensory analogs in dream imagery. In selective attention to one sensory modality there appears to be centrally innervated attenuation of sensory messages at the periphery from competing sensory modalities, so one may not hear a message if one's attention is concentrated on what one is looking at, or the converse. However, if one severs a nerve which is transmitting intractable pain, the pain impulses eventually appear to route themselves over alternate lines of transmission, radically complicating the efficacy of surgical intervention in dealing with chronic intractable pain.

In contrast, for some peripheral sources of pain (e.g., from a sprained ankle) a temporary novocaine block will permanently stop the transmission of pain messages despite continuing trauma in the injured area. Further, pain impulses from widely distributed areas of the body do not summate at the central assembly and thus spare the individual consciousness of his possible total pain. He is characteristically aware only of his most intense pain. Thus, an individual who fears the pain of a dental drilling can mask that pain by inflicting a more intense pain upon himself, for example, by pinching his own skin or digging his fingernail into his skin. Since the central assembly appears to act on a principle of admitting only the most dense of the competing messages, it has been possible to mask dental pain by very loud sounds. In such a case, presumably, there has been no attenuation of the pain messages themselves prior to entry into the central assembly, but they are eliminated by exclusion in favor of more dense messages so that the dense messages become denser and the less dense become even less dense. But there are limits even here because if the individual is bombarded with pain which is "too" dense, the central assembly appears to shut off and disassemble all conscious messages. In such a case the individual faints and falls unconscious, as under extreme torture.

Further, there appears to be backward inhibition and masking so that a visual stimulus which is transmitted later (in milliseconds) can sufficiently attenuate an earlier visual stimulus so that only the later stimulus will be seen.

Next are the phenomena of habituation. Any individual will respond to the innately adequate stimulus of a pistol shot with a startle response. But the startle characteristically habituates if the shot is repeated again and again so that finally only an eyeblink remains as a milder "surprise" response. Such habituation is gradual, with more and more segments of the original response dropping out. We do not know whether the habituation of the startle is dependent on a correlated habituation of the auditory messages from the pistol shot. However, there is abundant evidence for sensory habituation in general. In any event the density of both the activating stimulus and the density of the affect response itself are both vulnerable to some degree of habituation and attenuation upon repetition.

Another source of ambiguity in the activation of anger arises not at the site of the affect programs but at the more remote sites of their target organs in the face, chest, heart, skin, and striped muscle. Even in the event that anger has, in fact, been activated by an adequately dense neural firing, the effect of the anger program itself on the several target organs is variable and conditional, in varying degrees, on the state of these target organs. Thus, if the heart is already beating very fast, an additional acceleration instruction, according to the law of initial values, may have the paradoxical effect of slowing it down. More seriously, a thoroughly depleted and exhausted body may be incapable of one more tantrum no matter how "instructed" by the anger program. The capability of the body's response is also conditional upon its internal temperature and its diurnal variation. Thus, a dull, repetitive lecture which would enrage an alert captive audience in the middle of the day might produce somnolence in the late afternoon when the body's temperature characteristically drops, requiring relatively little more repetitive stimulation to produce sleep.

Further, if two different affects, such as fear and anger, were activated at the same time in response to two different sets of recruited responses (e.g., enraged at being slapped but also frightened at the danger of further injury), the target organs might be incapable of responding simultaneously with fear and anger; so if one affect captured the target organs, the other affect might be radically attenuated. Depending upon the specific affects involved, there might be a resultant response or an alternation. In any event, the correlation between the density of neural firing and the observable affect would be reduced.

Still another attenuation of correlation between the affect stimulus and affect response would occur when the target organs have already been captured by one program and are continuing to be bombarded by repetitions from that affect program at the same time that a different affect program is targeted on the same face, voice, chest, heart, and striped muscles. So if a child has a continuing pain which distresses enough to produce sustained crying, the slap on the face from a parent who wishes thereby to persuade the child to stop crying may trigger rage; but the child may be unable to express rage because the sustained pain continues to activate distress which captures the facial and vocal apparatus in such crying, effectively blocking the cry of rage.

With very few exceptions, no single neural message is an island sufficient unto itself. It characteristically encounters or recruits allies which may summate with it and competitors which may attenuate or inhibit it. The sensory messages from the periphery are but one set of messages among many internal messages which bombard the affect-activating mechanisms. These stimuli may compete, summate, or inhibit each other before they reach the affect-activating mechanisms. This radically complicates the test of any theory of affect activation, but it does not make it impossible. It is at this point that we must complicate the relatively simple picture of the rise and fall of neural transmission at a moment in time to look at the neural consequences of the more complex and the more stable and enduring structures we have called scripts. We assume that these complex structures are stored in the brain and are in continuous interaction with the varieties of neural messages which bombard the individual. Any stimulus may be treated as a sign or analog, not only of what is "out there" at the moment but, just as critically, as a moment in a family of scenes from the immediate and remote past extending into the future, immediate and remote. The present scene may be interpreted to be identical, a variant, an analog, or opposite as antianalog, or simply different from the past and with correlative similarity or difference with respect to the future. Such imported possibilities may summate with the sensory messages from the periphery and together activate the same affect that the original message would have activated in any event.

Thus, a slap in the face may equally enrage a relatively unknowledgeable infant and an adult, but the adult may recruit sufficiently enraging past scenes, as well as similar future possibilities, to both increase the intensity of the neural stimulation and prolong it in time, thus transforming what is a momentary anger for an infant to sustained warfare for the adult subjected to an identical "stimulus." Less obviously, the density of the neural firing from the momentary slap may be taken as a sign of a dangerous attack still to come, which recruits avoidance responses of such a sharp gradient of increasing neural firing that fear rather than anger is activated, by masking or attenuating the neural transmissions from the slap on the face.

By script recruitment a relatively "weak" message, lacking the requisite density of stimulation to activate anger, may be joined in a neural summation which readily activates anger. The gentle laughter or smile of joy of another can readily enrage anyone who is prompted by the invidious comparison of the injustice of one's own suffering and the gratuitous happiness of the other, or of the injustice of the suffering of an exploited class compared with the invidious affluence of those who profit from such exploitation. It is by the recruited changes in muscle tonus, in the quantity of recruited memories of similar scenes, and in the quantity of further ideas prompted by such coassembled invidious comparisons that the relatively weak stimulation of the smile which is seen on the face of the other can produce explosive consequences. On the other hand, if such an invidious comparison has been experienced very often in the past and enraged the individual each time, it need not continue to cumulate over time without limit. It may instead become increasingly compressed and become conscious in that increasingly skilled way which produces habituation and attenuation rather than magnification. In such a case the individual continues to "recognize" the injustice, but there is insufficient detail, urgency, and novelty in consciousness to prompt expansion of such compressed information, and he shrugs his shoulders in mild disgust.

BOUNDARIES OF IMPLICATIONS OF THE INNATE ACTIVATOR MODEL

Having examined some of the implications of the innate activator model, we will now address the boundaries and limitations of such a model. These arise because the anger-activating mechanism is one mechanism among many. One must be able to perceive, remember, think, and act to be angry at all, and the variety of ways in which perception, memory, thought, and action are shaped necessarily influence anger, as anger in turn influences what and how we perceive, remember, think, and act. Further, anger is but one affect among many. How often we are angry, with what intensity and for how long, depends significantly on how often we are happy, sad, afraid, or ashamed as upon the anger-activation mechanism alone. Anger, like any other mechanism in the total system, is somewhat independent, somewhat dependent, and somewhat interdependent, as a function of variations in the state of the total system and in the state of its environment. Anger as independent can swamp otherwise persuasive constraints. Thus, a very angry person may impulsively do or say something he will regret a moment later. But if he becomes even more angry, he may not act at all, for fear he may kill the other. Paradoxically, the most extreme anger may become interdependent with fear and with the anticipated possible consequences of acting out of anger. Such inhibition of behavior may in turn either attenuate the intensity or the duration of the anger or further magnify it, depending on secondary reactions to the restraint, such as how much it is believed to be ego-syntonic or enforced upon the self as alien. Finally, anger may be experienced as directly dependent upon either external or internal sources. In one case one may be angered by sounds that are too loud; in the other, by the same scene as remembered, or as remembered and further elaborated because one did not either feel angry, or feel angry enough, or complain about it, or complained about it but did not otherwise act with sufficient aggression. Anger may be dependent not directly on the unmediated source but rather on the interpretation of the source, as in the difference between intentional and accidental harm by the other. In this case even a direct response of anger may be attenuated—if the interpretation of the other's intention changes later. It may be dependent on the interpretation of the consequences of becoming angry. Thus, in feudal Japan one often smiled to a possible affront to say to the other, as well as to the self, we are not angry with each other because if we were one of us might die. In this case the salience of the possible consequences of anger is the decisive factor in inhibiting both the external communication of anger and the internal response itself by activating fear, which can prevent both the activation and magnification of anger. This contrasts with anger and fear as interdependent, when both are activated, or alternate with each other in interaction.

The innate activator model tells us that the trigger of anger must be dense in its neural firing rather than increasing or decreasing in density. What it does not tell us is just how this stimulus is itself produced and the sequence of events which produce such a sufficient stimulus. Nor does it tell us completely what further memories and thoughts and other affects are recruited and brought to bear on the overt response to anger. It is in some respects like an account of a murder which is limited to an explanation of the pulling of the trigger of the gun. Pulling the trigger is not a trivial part of a murder, nor is it the whole of it. The gun is in the hands of someone with a history, who wishes and intends to kill a specific person, and his act has extensive consequences for himself, his victim, and for society. So too anger is a moment in a series of scenes which precede and follow the acts prompted by anger. Any model of the mechanism of the immediate activation of anger is neither trivial nor a complete account of anger and aggression. Both anger and aggression are embedded in complex personal, sociocultural, and historical matrices. It is some of these more complex problems that we will next address. We must turn then from anger as innately endowed amplifier to anger as magnified by learning. As we have noted in Chapter 3, magnification occurs by ordering sets of scenes and sets of responses to sets of affects, which together constitute scripts of varying degrees of magnification.

INNATE SOURCES OF ANGER VERSUS COMPETING LEARNED SOURCES OF OTHER AFFECTS

Because of the generality and abstractness of the anger mechanism one can become angry at anything under the sun, or at nothing. One can be an angelic saint or a satanic fallen angel. The immediate activating trigger of anger does not illuminate the nature of the range of possible sources of anger. There is an interdependent network such that anger may be a source of further anger, that recruitment may be a further source of anger, and that one's own hostile act may become a source of further anger. Finally, the consequences of one's acts may become a source of further anger.

To understand the sources of anger we must also understand the sources of competing negative affects and the sources of competing positive affects. A very happy person is much less likely to be a very angry person, and a very anxious person is much less likely to be a very angry person, though, of course, these are not excluded as possibilities by virtue of the independence of the separate affect mechanisms. Because each affect is orthogonal to every other affect, any single source which is preempted by another non-anger affect reduces the possibility of that becoming a source of anger. To the extent that I find human beings sources of excitement and enjoyment, the probability of their angering me diminishes, which is not to say I may not love and hate everyone in equal amounts, or love some and hate others. Similarly with my work; it too might be a love-hate relationship, or I might love some aspects and hate others. But as the ratio of the density of positive to negative affect increasingly favors positive affect, stable equilibria are created such that the minority affect is "absorbed" as adding to the challenge, zest, and celebration of love and work. Similarly with the ratio of non-anger negative affects to anger: The more timid, the more distressed, the more ashamed or guilty, the more disgusted, or dissmelling, the more likely anger is to be a diminishing response and to be "absorbed" by one or another of the competing negative affects. Thus, if I am very tired or guilty, such anger as I may feel is readily neutralized by virtue of the possible dangerous consequences of anger, or by virtue of the blameworthiness the angry person feels of himself.

The possible sources of anger are indeed infinite and any "list" would have to include any and every violation of whatever human beings have valued. Further, the very same list might be equally useful, or useless, for cataloging sources of distress, fear, shame, guilt, disgust, or dissmell. What makes some element of such a list an important source of anger for one person rather than another, or for one society rather than another, or a source of distress for one person and a source of anger for another person is both general and particular. It is the quantity of the value violation, that it is excessive, that makes noise a source of anger for one person, and a lesser quantity of stimulation from noise which makes it a source of distress for another. If, on the other hand, both listen to the same noise with similar ears but one is a relaxed endomorph and the other a taut ectomorph, the noise which distresses the jolly one may enrage the one who is more tightly strung, because the same noise is embedded in quite idiosyncratic psychosomatic networks. Some sources are much more likely to anger, some more likely to excite; but there is no a priori basis on which we can exclude candidates for either anger or excitement—such is the generality of the affect system. Many texts and treatises purport to sample the many sources of anger. They are at once incomplete and too numerous. They fit no one precisely, and if they did today, they might not tomorrow. We will examine some of the major varieties of the differential sources of anger as part of our examination of the varieties of different types of anger which involve sources embedded in varying networks of anger and other affects, responses, consequences, and ultimate targets of anger.

Let us consider briefly how a simple stimulus, innately adequate to activate anger by virtue of the density of its stimulation, might be transformed and attenuated by being embedded in different recruited scripts and thereby evoke affects other than anger.

Consider the case of a slap on the face. Since the face is the most richly innervated organ of the human body (exceeding the sensitivity even of the genital organs when these are put into simultaneous competition), the combined intensity of the simultaneous stimulation of several receptors should produce an internal set of stimuli adequate to activate anger. Indeed, this is certainly the most probable case if all else is equal and we view the human being as a tabula rasa innocent of both past and future. However, the slap is also sudden and may be unexpected enough so that the combined quick acceleration of the stimulation of the slap, summated with an equally quick acceleration of muscle response from the intention to avoid a repetition, with rapid memory recruitment for interpretation and rapid thought about what is happening, plus rapid perceptual scanning to investigate further, would innately trigger startle or surprise. This would occur on the basis of the square wave profile of rapid rise, brief maintenance, and rapid decay of the stimulation, arising equally from the slap, from muscles, further from perceptual scanning, from memory, and from thought. Clearly, however, surprise is a most improbable response to such a slap if it is repeated in rapid succession. It would now be expected rather than unexpected, and the intention might change from one of avoidance to one of counterattack, thus summating with the succeeding slaps to enrage rather than to surprise.

But the steep acceleration of the slap might activate fear rather than surprise if the acceleration of the external stimulus recruited and coassembled correlated perceptual, motor, memory, and cognitive responses with a slightly less steep gradient of acceleration than the slap itself and if the summation of these masked or attenuated the stimulation from the external stimulus. This would be most probable in the event that fear had become differentially magnified in the scripts of the individual, if he were a more timid person than either angry or surprisable, or excitable or joyful, or shameable or distressable or disgustable.

If he were very timid, any sudden stimulus of a wide bandwidth of acceleration would have been learned to be a possible sign or analog of danger and would have magnified the probability of recruitment of motor avoidance and escape response, memories of past fearful scenes, accelerating perceptual scanning and cognitive transformations aimed at understanding the potential danger in the situation and how to deal with it. More frequently, the very timid follow any innate startle (e.g., to a pistol shot) with a *secondary* fear response. Landis and Hunt found this occurred with schizophrenics. Because some of the autonomic components of fear are slower than the startle, even the simultaneous activation of startle and fear may be *experienced* as startle followed by fear; for example, when we stumble walking downstairs, there is often an unpleasant which continues to increase after the initial startle.

Alternatively, if the slap on the face occurred in the midst of an anxiety attack, the inertia of the target organs might successfully block the anger response even in the event that the anger program had been activated.

If the slap on the face comes from a lover or friend, the recruited motor, memory, perceptual, and cognitive responses might trigger surprise; but if the slap occurred in the context of an interesting conversation, it would be just as probable that the recruited responses would be prompted more by an attempt to understand why one was slapped than by an attempt to avoid or escape in fear or in surprise. In such a case one might quickly scan the face of the other for possible clues about the meaning of the slap but not as quickly as when one senses danger. The acceleration of looking, remembering, thinking, or acting in such a case would be less steep than the square wave of the adequate startle stimulus and also less steep than the panic-inducing trigger. Alternatively, a chronic intellectual with an overly magnified interest in understanding, as such, might react to a slap on the face from anyone in the same way someone else would respond to a slap from a friend.

The reader may be troubled by the assumption that responses which follow in time might mask and compete with messages which precede them in time. We are speaking in these cases of millisecond intervals, and it has been well established that it is possible to *backward-mask* an earlier visual stimulus by a later visual stimulus so that *only* the latter becomes conscious, so long as we are in the order of magnitude of milliseconds. The suddenness of the slap, while adequate as a stimulus to *innately* activate surprise response and dense enough to innately activate the anger response, is *also* a *sign* or *analog* of possible novelty for one whose interest or excitement has been much magnified. I am assuming that this sign or analog in turn prompts perceiving, remembering, and acting at a rate innately adequate to excite rather than surprise, frighten, or anger.

Under what circumstances might the slap trigger joy rather than anger? If the individual were in the midst of terror that the other might kill him and quickly intuits from the slap that the other is angry but not so angry that he intends to murder, then the conjoint relaxation of muscles and steep decline in neural firing from the reduction of terror and its correlated motor escape responses, the reduction of recruited memories of danger, the reduction of perceptual scanning for signs of danger, and the reduction of rapidly mounting, panic-driven ideation would innately trigger deep joy and not anger. Another circumstance might be a lovers' quarrel in which each withdrew from contact and communication with the other, producing shame, disgust, distress, and anger which together produced a very high level of neural stimulation. If one then is slapped by the previously distant, noncommunicating other and if such a slap is interpreted as a reopening of communication, albeit punishing, and a cessation of intolerable distance, then such a sign can further suddenly reduce the punishing negative affect to create paradoxical joy at being slapped.

Less probable, but possible, is the case in which the slap occurs in the midst of sustained joy, so intense and enduring from an experience which precedes the slap (e.g., from the announced birth of a child) that it is quite easy to turn the other cheek because of the inertia of the intense but relaxed joy which blocks access to face, body, and autonomic system even if the affect program has been activated by the slap. Even though the affect programs are independent, so that anger and joy can be simultaneously activated, the target organs of face, body, and autonomic system are not readily capable of opposite responsiveness—for example, of relaxation and contraction of facial or striped muscles.

The slap might activate shame rather than anger if it comes from a beloved or respected other and is interpreted as a temporary and partial barrier to excitement or enjoyment which in turn reduces but does not entirely extinguish positive affect. In such a case the eyes are lowered, the head is lowered, or the hands cover the face so that seeing and being seen is temporarily interfered with. Memories of past shame scenes and shame-relevant thoughts flood consciousness. The skin of the face may blush rather than become red in anger. Since shame is an affect-auxiliary response rather than a primary affect, in my view, there are no general patterns of neural firing which innately activate it. Rather it is the perceived partial impediment to interest which is its activator, and so one must look to the attenuators of interest to account for shame (or for guilt, a special type of shame restricted to the violation of moral norms).

It is unclear whether attenuation of interest has a general neural activator. I have not been able to find such. It appears that interest is attenuated in response to learning which provides some impediment or contamination which then blocks interest but does so only partially and intermittently. I take this still to be an open question which requires further investigation. Recent evidence from Demos (1986, personal communication) has shown that an infant confronted with a mother's face which is altogether and unexpectedly unresponsive will alternate in looking toward and away from the same face with an elevated frequency compared with looking at that same face under normal conditions.

Anton Chekhov was a classic case of just such hypersensitivity to shame in response to daily beatings by his father. He viewed his whole life's quest as an attempt to rid himself of that enforced shame and servility. Rather than anger, the beating and slaps on the face are responded to as an insult which alienates those who otherwise love each other. "How could you?" is the question which the beating raises for the child who loves the one who so offends him and who is confident enough of the love of the other so that he is neither frightened nor enraged by the physical attack. In such a case, even if anger is momentarily activated by the slap, it fails to be maintained and further magnified because of the differential magnification of positive over negative affect toward the other.

Finally, the slap would activate disgust or dissmell in the event that either the act or the personality of the other, or the nature of the relationship or the nature of the self, produced images of contamination and intensification of the wish to increase the distance between the self and the other or between one part of the self and another part of the self. In the case that the slap arouses disgust, it may do so simply on the basis that such action violates norms about what is minimally acceptable behavior from anyone. However, it might arise more particularly because it violated an image of the nature of the offending person. Again, it might arise because it violated an image of the nature of the interpersonal relationship between the self and that other. In such a case this behavior might be generally acceptable and might even be acceptable from that other if he slapped others, so long as he did not slap oneself and thus violate a relationship which was judged to be invulnerable to such behavior from the other. Finally, the slap might arouse disgust not because of concern about the other or even about the relationship but primarily because of the resultant tarnished image of the self. I cannot but be disgusted with myself for having permitted myself to be trapped into being degraded. Such contamination responses to a slap on the face are, of course, not mutually exclusive. They are often readily compounded so that the other will be accused of violating minimal decency, so that the slap can be seen to expose unsuspected character flaws and unsuspected vulnerabilities of the privileged nature of the relationship, as well as reflections on the wisdom of the self in having been so trusting. The greater the number of assaults implied by the act, the more magnified the disgust may become, though this is not necessarily the case since the intensity and duration of any affect is to some degree independent of the number of its sources.

Disgust and dissmell are drive-auxiliary responses, in my view, evolved to protect us against bad smells at a distance and bad taste if such a distance early warning system (dissmell) has been penetrated. Nausea and vomiting are the ultimate disgust response if all else has failed. Although they mimic primary affects, they appear to have no general profile of neural firing which activates them. They are much more activated by analogs of bad tastes and smells than by abstract patterns of level or gradient of neural firing. In the cases we are considering, such analysis must intervene and override and swamp the dense stimulation of the slap which would normally activate anger. It should be noted that although the activator is an analog and the response is also an analog, inasmuch as the slap is not experienced as either a bad smell or a bad taste, nonetheless the deepest disgust response may be indistinguishable from the innate drive-auxiliary response of nausea and vomiting. Thus, an individual who is told he has just unwittingly eaten something which violates a serious taboo (e.g., eating human flesh) may nonetheless truly empty his stomach and vomit forth the bad food. This can also happen as a consequence of the violation of moral taboos independent of oral behavior (e.g., incest). He can feel nauseous and vomit because of guilt or shame about something which was not orally ingested. Theoretically, a slap on the face could disgust sufficiently to produce either anorexia or vomiting or both, if disgust itself had been greatly magnified by supporting scripts.

Whether one reacted to a slap on the face with dissmell or disgust would depend on how much and how permanently the self wished to distance its self from the offending other, or from its own offending self. If the rupture was conceived to be total and permanent and to retroactively tarnish the whole past as well as future of the relationship, then the response would be one of dissmell, and the other (or the rejected part of the self) would be totally transformed and devalued. In this case the self has finally seen the truth. The other, in such a case, is now seen to have no redeeming features and indeed to never have had any in the past. In contrast, if there is an insidious comparison between the past and the present, in which the good other, the good scene, or the good self has *become* a disgusting other, a disgusting scene, or a disgusting self, this represents a transformation of what once was good. It is analogous to the food which smelled good enough to eat but which turned out to have a bad taste, in contrast to badsmelling food which has no redeeming features and which is therefore totally and permanently rejected.

VARIETIES OF TYPES OF ANGER

The Scene as a Nested, Simultaneous, Sequential Set

In order to understand the varieties of types of anger or of any affect, we must examine the nature of the scene as the basic unit of analysis of script theory. One does not become angry in a space-time moment, nor in a vacuum. Something precedes, something accompanies, and something follows anger. Psychologists with a bias toward analysis rather than analysis-synthesis tend to describe causality in the manner of a billiard ball sequence. Compact, dense aggregation with impermeable boundaries "hit" equally compact entities which in turn fall into an intended pocket and there come to rest. What this attempts is a spatial flow diagram in which time can be represented spatially, and the complexity of an experienced scene can be represented as a "stimulus" resulting, after collision with another entity, in a "response." This is our continuing, sometimes conscious, sometimes unconscious heritage from too many years of behaviorism. Such a conception, as we will illustrate in the chapter on cognition, in Volume IV does not even well describe the neuronal transmission from axon to dendrite.

The angering stimulus not only precedes anger, but it may continue on, during, and after anger has subsided, in fact or in imagination. That stimulus may remain the same or change radically during and following the anger of the self. Such change may or may not be perceived and if perceived may be accurate or inaccurate.

The source of the angering stimulus may be external, internal, or both. It may be perceived or not and, if perceived, may be perceived accurately or not. What that angering "stimulus" is may be the whole external scene or any part of it or some interaction, as when excessive noise adds to the angering quality of an insult; or the whole internal scene or any part of it, as when one remembers that insult with or without the excessive noise in that scene; or the whole external and internal scene or any part of either, or any interaction, as when one is insulted when very tired. The perceived angering quality of the scene may change from part to whole, as when one vows never to set foot again in a house where one was insulted, though the house was not insulting, nor to visit a country ever again because one was angered there by an isolated outrage. Further, the stimulating scene is not a point in time. Even a brief insult, a slap on the face, takes some time, and the angering insult may be the "last straw" in a series of innuendos of increasing aggressiveness over several minutes, days, weeks, months, or years. Any momentary scene is nested with a preceding set of scenes, a continuing set, and a following set, in fact and in consciousness, perceived and/or imagined. The present scene as experienced is never a razor's edge. It has extension in time through recruited memory of the immediate as well as remote past, through anticipation into the immediate and remote future, and through perception into the continuing, expanding present, which includes one's own as well as the other's responses, affective and motor, to the angering stimulus. But the scene with the angering other is nested not only in the history, immediate and remote, of scenes with that other but also in the history of the self's angry scenes with all other adversaries.

When I refer to the nesting of one scene within a larger family of scenes, I do not mean to imply that all possible comparisons and orderings of the present, past, and future scenes are continually generated but rather that some sampling of these possibilities is obligatory. It is not unlike what is required for engaging in any conversation. One may not remember precisely all the sentences in their exact sequences, but some integration across time must occur by both parties if communication in conversation is to be possible. One often only barely summarizes the intended meaning of the other and as often distorts that meaning by stressing some implications more than had been intended by the other. Yet if there is not also some coherent sampling and integration across time, we could not achieve such community of meaning as we in fact do. Some of the varieties of types of anger depend critically on the varying styles of sampling of the family of nested scenes. We will examine these presently, but for the moment we will continue our more abstract, more synoptic view of the ways in which anger is nested.

The Response to Anger

What are the responses to anger? We are accustomed to think of these as overt and "aggressive." The relationship between "response" and any affect is rarely either simple or transparent. As we have seen, considerable interpretation may be required to specify just what it is which angers us, nor is that attempt necessarily successful. To the extent that we are angry without a known or knowable "reason" our response becomes limited in its aim to reduce our anger as such, with or without a blameable source, as in kicking or pounding the fist on the self, a table, or anyone convenient. The aims of any response to anger are sufficiently complex to make the diagnosis of these component aims from the observed responses ambiguous. "Behavior" has been seductively oversimple for centuries. Behaviorism exaggerated what was already a cultural conspiracy of oversimplification. Whenever these culturally shared simplifications are violated, there is at hand a shared additional simplification to account for the violation of the assumed known reasonable linkage between anger and behavior. The individual who kills in a culturally exceptional way is adjudged "insane" or "possessed" by some special demon or spirit whose nature it is to act in just that way or to cause his victim to so act. Societies collectively as well as individually abhor a motivational vacuum. One "must" understand why the self and others act as they do in general, and this is particularly urgent when that action is highly toxic. But a theory of personality need not be so constrained. Were it not for the exaggeration of measurement and methodological criteria, with their insistence that it is better to be safe than sorry, we would not have been encouraged to prefer verification to discovery and to have regarded aggressive behavior as the unambiguous bedrock upon which we could build theories of anger and aggression.

The responses to anger are neither singular, simple, overt, nor necessarily "aggressive." Consider first the question of the overtness of a response to anger. If I had been a black American slave on a Southern plantation, feeling the pain of the lash of the whip, I might have wanted to express my anger in kind or to repay the debt in full and then some, or beyond that to kill the oppressor for all past suffering and to ensure freedom for the future. This would have entailed my own death, but I could have responded with an imagined scene in which vengeance is fully and richly taken and celebrated. And such fantasies could have led to sharing such possibilities through knowing glances with fellow victims who had also suffered the lash of the whip. Such fantasies and the planning they prompted did in fact lead to shared, secret communication which led eventually to uprisings and bloody massacres. The southern plantation owner was, in fact, ever vigilant about just such possibilities. He knew that the observed response of servility masked another response that was ever present as a threat. The "imagined" aggressive response was in fact taken quite seriously.

Intimidation, whether political or economic, does not aim only at controlling overt responses but also aims at thought control and affect control. It is known by those who wish to exert behavioral control that the precursors of overt behavior must also be controlled. From time immemorial authority has exacted not only deferential overt behavior but also deferential affect and deferential thought, whether covert or overtly expressed. Does a covert fantasy of revenge "satisfy"? It may satisfy more than passively suffering helpless rage and yet not totally satisfy. Much would depend on the complex interdependence of rage, pride, and guilt. Such a fantasy might reduce anger through increasing guilt. It might also reduce anger through reducing shame and restoring the pride of the shamed, wounded self. However, depending on the particularities of the relevant scripts, such a fantasy might increase anger if it exposed the gap between how one wanted to respond and one's enforced passivity confronted by the power of the other to enforce his will. Here the increase of shame would increase anger to the *same* fantasy that in the other individual conjointly decreased shame and anger when the imagined scene is interpreted as possible vengeance rather than enforced make-believe.

Anger cannot be "satisfied" in isolation. It is normally felt as one demand among many. In the full flush of hot anger its demands are peculiarly strident, but it remains one voice among many, within. Further, anger from a permanently provocative scene may be temporarily reduced by a covert fantasy until the next provocation, the next beating, when the victim must again address the unsolved problem. A fantasy of revenge which reduced anger once may not do so under repeated provocation, in which case the individual is driven either to "real" revenge, to permanent helpless rage, or to magnified saintliness and love for his enemies.

If the responses to anger are not necessarily overt because of feared sanctions, neither overt nor covert responses to anger are necessarily "aggressive." If it can be too dangerous to kill the oppressor, it can also be too dangerous to think of doing so and too dangerous to think of his dying, or too dangerous to have any thought which might reflect anger in any way. If imagined mutiny is still too dangerous as a covert response to anger which threatens to spill over into lethal violence, one may escape both the anger and the danger of the fantasied response by modifying the nature of the covert fantasy. Christianity offered the oppressed American slaves more rewarding fantasies—of a present, and particularly of a future heaven, in which all was to be eternal love and not hate, except for those who have sinned. At one fell swoop the angry black and the angry white were consigned to hell, where each got his just deserts. There was more than an opium for the masses. These were "uppers" for the good, black or white, and "downers" for black and white sinners. Not having aggressive thoughts, not having angry feelings, not acting aggressively were all to be rewarded eternally and their opposite punished eternally. The Christian paintings, churches, sermons, and doctrine provided the internal furniture for covert responses to anger whenever anger was aroused in spite of all the defenses which were designed to prevent its arousal. Like Jesus before them, they turned the other cheek and begged forgiveness for those who knew not what they did, even as they were crucified and about to return to heaven.

These are complex responses to anger, no less "responses" because they are covert, and no less so because they are loving, hopeful imaginings rather than angry, punishing fantasies. Covert, nonaggressive responses *can* be made to anger. Whether such responses aim at reducing anger or succeed in reducing anger are yet other questions. When one is angry, one does not necessarily wish to "reduce" anger. Just as often one wishes to aggress against its perceived source—the oppressor. In such a case the reduction of anger is a by-product, a bonus which may be celebrated or not, compared with the celebration of victory over the oppressor. Further, such victories may whet the appetite for more anger and for more aggression. Now, having put that other down, let us turn to the main event, the unfinished business of nuclear unappeasable rage and destroy all our enemies, past as well as possible future enemies. The excesses of revolutions, right and left alike, are based on nuclear scripts of attempted "final solutions" to what are intuited to be at once urgent and inherently insoluble scenes. So six million Jews were exterminated to guarantee the purity of German blood. So the blood of French aristocrats flowed to rid the body politic of France of its cancer in 1789. So the Huguenots were massacred to preserve the true Christian faith. Nuclear power is but the most recent instrument of extermination in the service of solving the urgent but insoluble nuclear scripts which haunt human and social aspiration.

We must not assume that a response to anger is to be judged by its effectiveness in reducing that anger. By such a criterion the murder which results from a fistfight which escalates in the course of a fight and which so increases the anger that the murderer now looks for new victims, would not involve aggressive responses. If the response to anger increases the anger, we do not hesitate to label it an aggressive response. Nor do we think it any the less aggressive a response if, immediately following, the anger subsides. Any response to anger, aggressive or nonaggressive, may reduce the anger, increase the anger, or leave it as it was prior to the response. The response to anger may or may not aim at the reduction of anger, and it may or may not succeed in its intention. Thus, I may *wish* to hurt someone whether I wish to become less angry, more angry, or don't care, so long as I hurt the other. Even though I do not aim at becoming less angry, I may in fact become less angry after I have either tried to hurt the other, or after I have succeeded in hurting the other, or after the other has suffered hurt at the hands of someone else or has dropped dead from natural causes.

The interactions between the intentions of overt responses, their outcomes, and the affect which prompted the intentions are complex, and we will presently examine them in more detail. The reason we are inclined to believe that a utopian fantasy is not a response to anger is that we think anger "requires" an aggressive response and, like hunger, will "insist" and persist until it is "satisfied." This overlooks several critical differences between affects on the one hand and "motives," including drive motives, on the other. The pure affect has no necessary "aims" as it has no necessary "objects" or triggers. I can be happy without being happy about anything in particular, and that feeling may last or it may be fleeting without any action on my part. When it has a known "cause" and when it generates a known "aim," the inferred cause may be accurate or not, the intended aim may be attained or not, and the consequences for the affect may be quite different than what had been aimed at and expected. I may intend to kill the other and discover that I am still angry about what I do not know or that I really loved the other and am now guilt-stricken. When a slave substitutes a vision of heaven for his earthly hell, we suspect that the anger which has been cooled lies in wait to be rekindled, or that it is smoldering unbeknownst to the Christian self. Here we are involved with the interface between theologies, Christian and Freudian. If there can be no guarantee that the Christian faith will extinguish anger and aggression once and for all, neither can there be a guarantee for the eternality of anger if it is responded to with love and faith. Anger, like any affect, is a ballistic response of the body. It must be triggered to be kept alive. It is no more eternal than love. If one engages competing affects via competing fantasies, then anger which might have continued indefinitely may not be renewed as long as its competitors seize center stage.

Consider the case in which someone steps on our toes in a movie theater. The anger evoked by the clumsiness of the other is readily dissipated by not being recycled by fantasy if the other apologizes. We do not think it strange that such a message terminates the momentary anger, intense and real as it may have been. Nor do we think it strange if it results in hours of rage when we detect a trace of a smile on the face of the offender, who, though he apologizes, nonetheless raises a question in our mind concerning his intentions. The covert Utopian fantasy of love and faith, Christian or otherwise, can simply terminate anger by supporting nonangry thoughts and feelings. Whether this proves permanent or not should not be prejudged in a theological way, either Christian or Freudian.

Independence, Dependence, Interdependence of Sources, Anger, Recruitment and Overt Responses, and Targets

Like any affect, anger is characteristically triggered by a source, further interpreted by recruited internal responses, and finally responded to by overt responses aimed at targets. Source, affect, recruited responses, overt responses, and targets are mediated by independent separate mechanisms which are also dependent and interdependent upon each other and upon other mechanisms.

Whether a source is a source of anger depends both on its own independent characteristics and also on the scripted characteristics of anger, other scripts, and the scripted overt responses characteristic of the individual. The source of anger as an independent set of features depends on how intrusive and insistent that angering source is. An unrelenting heckler as agent provocateur or an overtly pious, self-serving exploiter who continues to insist one act as he demands are more angering both in intensity and duration than is a piece of furniture on which one stubbed one's toe, thus evoking a momentary cry of pain and anger. These characteristics are inherent in the nature of the stimulus source of anger no matter who is being angered. Thus, too, a brief stab of pain is less angering than a long continuing pain of the same intensity. The anger, like the source, may be of the same intensity in both cases, but the character of the anger would increase as a function of the duration of the pain as independent source.

But the source of anger is both independent and dependent. What may be reacted to as a source depends not only on the independent features of that source but also depends on the scripted status of anger within the personality, on the status of other recruited scripts, and on the status of the scripted readiness to respond to a source of anger with an overt response.

The status of anger may remain homogeneous and unmodulated, may be radically magnified or attenuated by defense, or may be differentiated in varying degrees. Such variations in the scripted status of anger have differential consequences for what may become a source of anger.

If I have never learned to modulate my anger in any way, one consequence is that one source may become as angering as any other source. I will then become as angry at a trivial affront as at a vicious affront, at stubbing my toe as at a vital threat to life. This would be a consequence not of the failure to discriminate between these sources but rather the failure to learn to modulate anger itself.

If, however, my anger has been radically magnified, I will respond with anger more frequently and with more intensity, duration, and total density to any and to all sources, compared with someone whose anger has been less magnified; for example, one whose excitement rather than anger has been radically magnified, who experiences the world as much more exciting than angering.

If, on the other hand, my anger has been radically magnified but has not been differentiated in intensity, so that I characteristically respond with explosive anger if I respond with any anger, then the sources of anger may have to carry an excessive burden of differentiation to protect me from being angered unless the source "justifies" the ungraded explosive anger which is the only kind of anger I am capable of emitting.

Such compensatory source differentiation may also be required whenever anger remains homogeneous and unmodulated, no matter what its degree of magnification, since anger as an innate amplifier is inherently intense, apart from any additional magnification. This principle of compensatory differentiation for rectifying reduced degrees of freedom in any part of the entire network of source, affect, script, and response is a general one for optimizing the average degrees of freedom for the system as a whole. Thus, not only may the source be highly differentiated to protect against a lesser differentiation of the affect, but the source may be equally differentiated to protect against a lesser differentiation and reduced degrees of freedom of the expected consequences of responding overtly in anger to an angering source. In this case fixing the consequences of overt aggression as toxic may require minimizing source, affect, and recruited scripts together. If one is unwilling to fight, one may also have to learn to differentiate and attenuate both anger and the supporting scripts which together sensitize the individual to the anger-aggression potential in any stimulus source.

Just as the source is in part independent and in part dependent on the status of anger, recruitment, and response, so too is anger in part independent and in part dependent on source, recruitment, and response. Thus, anger, to the extent that it is independent, imprints its vigor on the source, making it more "angering," on the recruitment process itself, and on the overt response, guaranteeing high energy imprinted on whatever the individual does when angry. Although the innate anger response is characteristically intense and ungraded, some degree of differentiation and modulation of intensity and duration is required in all societies. The degree of modulation and gradation in the intensity and duration of anger varies radically from individual to individual and from society to society. Some individuals are taught, by self and by others, to be capable of mild annoyance, intense, brief anger, enduring moderate anger, sporadic towering rage, and many intermediate values of intensity and duration of anger. In contrast some learn only the differentiation of weak anger and strong anger, or no anger and explosive rage. Because the individual soon learns about his own competence in anger modulation per se, his further learning about sources, scripts, and overt responses necessarily is dependent on this relative incompetence to grade and modulate the anger itself as a relatively autonomous and formidable force in his life space. Just as an epileptic may learn to orient to the ever possible storm within, so too may unmodulated anger come to dominate the entire landscape of an individual who knows that if and when he is angered at all it is a force which seizes and dominates him.

But, in contrast, the anger may be "bound" by recruited scripts which threaten punishment for feeling angry or for displaying it on the face or for expressing it vocally or for communicating it verbally or for physically attacking or for all of these. But anger may bc radically increased rather than bound by recruited scripts and by overt physical responses, which in turn provide both high density of neural firing feedback which maintains or increases the anger, and by counterattack from the enemy which further escalates the anger. In such a case once anger has been aroused, one cannot predict its ultimate destiny without reference to its source, its recruitment, and its overt responses.

Next, the recruitment of magnifying scripts is also partly independent and partly dependent. The more magnified the script, the more independent it is of specific sources, of the status of anger, or of overt responses, all of which are more dependent on the script itself than the recruited script is dependent on them. In the extreme case, the paranoid's recruited scripts guarantee a broad spectrum of angering sources providing fuel to ignite, sustain, and escalate anger and overt hostile responses against ubiquitous persecutors. But the recruited-anger-relevant scripts may, in contrast, be finely tuned to a set of distinctive features of the stimulus sources such that many conjoint conditions are required for recruitment. Then only occasionally will such a script be recruited in support of anger and overt response to anger. The anger-relevant scripts may, however, be recruited not to the stimulus source but rather to the feeling of anger itself. Under these conditions it is not what the other does or says that is the distinctive cue for the anger script, but rather it is the conscious experience of anger alone which is the necessary and sufficient condition for recruiting the scripts. Irl this case so long as the individual remains "cool" under fire, his anger scripts can remain sleeping dogs despite source provocation. Finally, the anger-relevant scripts may be recruited neither to the stimulus source nor to the feeling of anger but only to the overt response itself. In such a case the conflict may remain localized even though the enemy has angered one, so long as one does not lay heavy hands on the other. Once the attack is launched, scenes of lifelong victimage, calling for retribution at last, can convert a trivial dispute into murder.

Finally, the hostile act, while most frequently dependent on the nature of the stimulus source, on the intensity and duration of anger, and on the type of recruited script, can also become relatively independent insofar as learned scripts differentially magnify or attenuate the weight assigned to action relative to source and anger. Thus, if action is given a positive high weight in a script in any anger scene, sources may be sought rather than passively awaited. The individual may seek out and create scenes which promise aggressive action. He may continually recruit further scripts which justify fighting and/or his anger may be regarded as sufficient justification for fighting. In contrast, if, in a script, action is given a very negative weight, sources of possible anger or fighting may be attenuated or denied.

Anger itself is cooled quickly lest it lead to fighting. Scripts justifying pacifism are recruited in interpreting and responding to scenes of potential conflict. The hostile act may also be independent in the case that having acted overtly in a hostile way, the source, now having been hurt becomes either more or less angering. Anger may now turn to fear or guilt or more intense anger. The scripts which are now recruited are relevant to the consequences of hostile actions as these were experienced before rather than to the hostile act as such. Such consequences of the act, as an independent influence on source, anger, and recruitment, are nonetheless usually preceded by influences from source, anger, and recruitment. Thus, one's script may prompt one to disregard a trivial insult and act on a more serious one, or the reverse, to act on a trivial insult but disregard a more serious insult if there is a fear of serious hostility but not of graded hostile acts. A script may dictate that one may act on enduring or intense anger but not on brief or weak anger, or the reverse. One may act on one recruited script which represents the scene as outrageous and not act on another recruited script which represents the scene as a temporary disagreement.

The recruited may be experienced as distinct from the present scene but "relevant," or as so fused with it as to be almost identical, in which case the hostile act may aim at retribution for both past and present at once. I may, in short, murder the other because he enraged me, because he was the straw that broke the camel's back, the last scene in a series of outrages, or because once I started to attack I saw him differently, I became more enraged, and I remembered all that I had suffered, singly or together. Thus, whether an individual becomes assaultive may depend on critical distinctive conditions or from any one of such conditions. In the latter case, more common in psychoses, the probability of assaultive behavior is very high because anytime another person is provocative or the self is tired or the psychotic is already angry, has recruited a bad scene, or has expressed some physical violence, there is an increased probability of more violence. Clearly, the more distinctive the critical features of either source, affect, or script necessary to trigger the overt response, the lower the probability of violence. This probability diminishes even more sharply the more conjoint critical features of source and affect and script are necessary to evoke violence.

The same relationships hold for suicidal violence against the self. Suicide is as rare as it is not only because the anger cannot be expressed against others but also because of the extreme improbability of the conjoint sources of anger which simultaneously evoke explosive uncontrollable anger and recruitment of a rush of similar scenes from the past. These together cry out for justice against the slings of outrageous fortune even at the cost of self-destruction, rather than overt destruction of the other. The destruction of the self then appears characteristically the only feasible way to hurt the other, as Karon (1964) has shown.

I am not suggesting that suicide is characteristically explosive and compulsive, since it is often carefully planned and executed without anger, and even with joy. But such a detached and serene suicide is frequently the last scene following a decision which was prompted by the conjunction of dense critical features and affect cumulation which I have described.

In summary, the degrees of freedom between any "stimulus," any anger, any script, any response, and any consequence of a response are very great in varying independence, dependence, and interdependence. Which part of such a network controls which other parts cannot be understood as a "chained" sequence in which, once the sequence is set in motion, the rest follows. Nothing necessarily follows and anything may follow from any point in the network, depending primarily on the specifics of the anger-aggression scripts which have been constructed to order just which nodes are critical and in which order.

I may script specific scenes as "angering" but not sufficient to act on. I may script how to find good fights. I may script scenes as ones in which one must control one's anger, but if one cannot, then one may or must become aggressive. I may script scenes in which one must become neither angry nor aggressive, but if physically attacked must respond with anger and counterattack. The varieties of such scripts are very great, and the individual may script some scenes of anger and aggression in very similar ways but script other scenes in more differentiated ways, as in fighting about small insults, medium insults, or only large insults in the same way, or proportional to the seriousness of the affront, or to fight only at medium affronts but at neither trivial nor at deadly insults.

Chapter 28
The Magnification of Anger

We will be concerned primarily with the magnification of anger and with the magnification of anger-driven violence, not with the total problem of violence which primarily implicates affects other than anger.

Aggression as intended violence must first be distinguished from unintended hurt inflicted. If one kills a pedestrian because the car one is driving suddenly accelerated out of control due to a fault in the design of the car, there need be no violence intended and no anger involved. If the driver is intoxicated and drives recklessly, there may be no violence intended and no anger involved. If the driver is sober but daydreams and fails to see the pedestrian, there is no anger necessarily involved in inflicting death on the other. If a surgeon kills a patient through insufficient skill, there need be no violence intended and no anger.

Even if one intends to kill the other in merciful deliverance from intolerable pain and suffering, there need be no intention of hurting and no anger. A child may intend to terminate the life of an insect in order to pull it apart to see how it is constructed. A butcher may intend to kill a turkey and cut it up to make a living as a butcher, with no anger. A distressed individual may intend to kill a fly that is distracting his attention, with no anger. I have known gunmen for hire who kill without anger or guilt or fear, as required by their profession.

But one may be angry and intend no violence, or intend violence out of affects and motives other than anger, or intend violence with anger modulated in varying ratios by other affects which precede and or follow anger.

If I stub my toe on a piece of furniture I did not see, I may hit it, without intending to damage it, to do "something" to express my anger, or even hit myself as stupid enough to have injured myself. Whatever I do impulsively in anger will bear the imprint of that affect, but this does not necessarily involve the intention to hurt, either as taking an eye for an eye or as permanently eliminating the perceived source of the anger in an excess of overkill. There is such a phenomenon as pure affect, such as anger without further response, just as there is pure excitement, joy, distress, or free-floating terror without a perceived object. Anger, like any affect, may have no perceived object, as in awakening irritable from the combination of a bad dream and fatigue from insufficient sleep. It is difficult to inflict violence on an unknown source but not impossible. A perpetually irritable person can find someone and sometimes many others to hurt, to appease his anger. It is, of course, common to find scapegoats for anger one either does not understand or finds too dangerous to deal with directly. But it is also common for the individual to become angry and wait for it to cool down; to smoke a cigarette to sedate the anger; to feel guilty for being angry; to be concerned at how he angered the other unintentionally; to cease to be angry at discovering the other is blind and so unknowingly bumped into him; to become afraid of his own anger and of the anger of the other; to try to repair the damage experienced by the self and or other. In short, anger may be short-circuited and produce nonviolent responses to the extent to which it is embedded, as it often is, in a larger matrix of other affects and other scripts. Because anger is one affect among many, it need not evoke a violent response, either overtly or covertly. Just as one may be too loving, or too timid, or too guilty to hurt, so too may one be similarly constrained to imagine, or to "wish," to hurt because of the differential magnification of competing affects. This is not to say that if or when such competing affects are weakened or absent (as under the influence of alcohol) such anger may not become much bolder and more prominent. We will presently examine the consequences of just such alteration in the strength of anger and its competitors. Here we wish only to argue that affect competition may either totally inhibit or attenuate anger enough to prevent violence as either an overt or covert intended response.

But if one may be angry without intended violence, one may also be violent and intend to hurt or kill from affects other than anger. One may kill out of terror; the scene is interpreted as a zero sum game in which there can be only one survivor. One may kill out of greed, as a crime syndicate kills its competitors for a lucrative market. One may kill out of dismell and disgust, as when Hitler killed millions of Jews to purify the Aryan blood of the German superrace. One may kill to better control possible enemies by shooting civilians in an occupied country. One may kill for scarce resources of food, water, or gold, as when empires use military power to extend economic exploitation. One may kill out of piety against heretics within and against foreign barbarian Satans. One may kill political opponents out of the wish for power or to maintain and increase political power so that it may become perpetual power. Even men of otherwise goodwill, philosophers, artists, and scientists may intend to and succeed in hurting those whose visions of the true, good, and beautiful are judged invidiously untrue, bad, or ugly. Indeed, no violence is greater than ideological violence. In no other way can so much hurt be transformed into so much believed good.

But if one may be angry and not violent, and violent and not angry, the majority of intended violence nonetheless is a mixed compound of anger and other affects and other scripts. The ratio of anger to other affects in violence may vary from zero anger to all anger, and that ratio itself may vary before, during, and after violence and between scenes of violence for the same individual. Thus, the hot moral outrage which first attracts the radical to a revolutionary movement may become much cooler when commitment has been transformed into strategy and when strategy has settled into long-term and shifting tactics.

Further, anger may wax and wane in such anger-modulated adversarial games as boxing, wrestling, football, soccer, and ice hockey, when, responding to failure, the contestants or the audience violate the rules of the game and become violent. However, the role of anger, even here, is always ambiguous and problematic, since love, identification, and wounded pride loom large in such rage. For some, such scenes recruit very remote analogs of idiosyncratic scenes from the earliest family romance. Thus, the defeated home team is for one the self as displaced first-born. For the equally enraged depressed fan at his side it is the self as cheated second-born, reexperiencing yet again his entry into a world in which another has been favored even before he arrived. For others the defeat is yet another replay of their lower class, lower caste, lower race, lower sexual preference, lower vigor, lower ability, lower life expectancy, lower beauty, lower health, lowered standard of living. With so many different enemies, it is entirely possible for a soccer game to produce violence out of a nonexistent consensus among strangers whose only shared bond is the rage which accompanies a pool of very diverse affronts and insults, in the analogs of defeat.

Because anger and violence so often implicate affects other than anger, our exclusion of non-anger-driven violence may at times be a difference which makes very little difference, although at other times and places, it makes all the difference. The magnified intransigence of greed, of piety, and/or of terror-driven violence may or may not include the magnification of anger.

HOW IS ANGER MAGNIFIED?

Anger is not necessarily magnified by virtue of being angry frequently. Thus, an irritable, sickly infant may cry in anger throughout his first months of life, suffer severe independent amplification of the cry of anger each time he suffers hunger or any other pain, and nonetheless fail to connect one angry scene with another and so fail to script anger and fail to magnify it. He may remain quite innocent that his body and his world are too repeatedly angering. He thus never "repeats" anger consciously, and so it cannot grow and become magnified. As we noted before, in David Levy's observations on infants receiving repeated injections, there was no anticipatory distress or anger crying before a second injection before the age of six months. Previous pain of the first injection did not provide any warning that the same white coat in the same room, in the same clinic, accompanied again by his mother, would again hurt him. After six months of age, repeated injections did begin to be reacted to as if they were distressing *before* the injection as well as during and after it. Also, the shorter the interval between injections, the more probable the anticipatory cry.

Ordering one scene to another scene, at a different time, is the minimal necessary condition for magnification to begin. The ordered scenes need not be identical repeated scenes. One might be more so, or even different from the other scene, and yet prompt coassembly and further affect to the set and to the future. Thus, if the second injection hurt more than the first injection, the ordering scripting might well become "watch out for increasing pain." If the first injection did not hurt and the second did, the ordering scripting might be "what will the next one be?"

Affect is a change-amplifying mechanism, making change "more so." If we are to understand magnification, we must understand the relationship of amplifying change to magnifying change, as a derivative. Consider the analog in Newtonian physics. Had Newton remained at the level of velocity he might never have discovered the law of gravitation, which required that the derivative of change in velocity—namely, the change of change, or acceleration—was the invariant with distance.

Magnification is to amplification as acceleration is to velocity. In magnification a perceived order between affect-amplified scenes itself evokes further ordering and further affect to that further ordering. There is no identity or necessary similarity between the affectamplified changes in the coassembled scenes and the affect-magnified scripted scenes in response to that ordered set. Thus, if an individual has at one time been shamed by the indifference of a parent, and at another time been distressed by the same parent's overcontrolling dominance, this set of two, differently punishing scenes might, on coassembly, evoke anger which then prompted exhibitionistic disobedience calculated to remedy both the shaming indifference and the distressing overcontrol by the parent. Although this might be the beginning of an anger-driven script, the observable response might not be overt anger. If this response evoked still more dominance from the parent and even more shaming, now by expressed disgust at the child, the next coassembly of these three scenes might evoke more anger, but yet another experiment in counterattack, this time by staying away from home till a very late hour, in the hope of turning the tide of the battle in his favor and extorting regret and shame from the parent and more loving attention toward his own needs. In this case the scripted response has now become more complex. It is still an anger-driven response whose immediate target is to punish, but with a more remote target of evoking both regret and shame and then more loving attention. He wants the other to pay for his offense and to reform and be a more loving parent. Clearly, the logic of this sequence of scripted scenes is a psychologic. The initial two scenes might, in another child, have prompted quite different affects and different scripted responses. One child might have responded with an overt tantrum rather than angry exhibitionistic disobedience. Another child might have responded with fear lest the relationship deteriorate still further and responded with appeasement behavior. The changes between the coassembled scenes characteristically demand further changes, first in affect and then in responses designed to reach that affect's scripted target. Such magnification by scripting may be a one-trial learning or it may continue for a lifetime, continuously or discontinuously, at slow or fast or variable rates depending on the perceived effectiveness of the script.

What is essential for magnification is the ordering of sets of scenes by rules for their interpretation, or production, or prediction, or their control, which scenes *and* their rules are themselves amplified by affect. There are three questions implicit in the question of how anger is magnified. First, how is *any* anger script ordered so that the individual does not face each instance of anger de novo, as an infant is innocent of the future? Second, how is the future biased toward more or less of an angry future rather than toward a future of positive affect or toward a future of negative affect but not an angry future? Third, what is the overall profile of the differential magnification of anger and the variety of types of scripted anger which together constitute a profile of the personality?

How Is an Anger Script Ordered?

Let us continue in our attempt to answer the first question. How is any script ordered, and specifically any anger script? We must remember that not all scripts contain the same number of components, nor necessarily the same type, any more than any sentence contains every type of word in the same general sequence in all languages. Consider the differences between an anger-avoidance, an angerescape, or an anger-last-resort script and an anger-seeking script.

Anger-Avoidance Script. In an anger-avoidance script a critical type of ordering which must be scripted is remote vigilance for the possibility of anger and a set of rules for further evasion of such anger should the possibility be detected, and further monitoring to determine whether the danger has been warded off. In learning to magnify anger by such a script, each component may be learned either simultaneously or in varying sequences. Thus, in the hypothetical case we have already considered, that of the angry disobedient child, he has *not* thus far considered it necessary to avoid either his own or his parent's wrath. Let us suppose that his adversarial angry disobedience results in an escalating contest of wills, in which he is painfully defeated by a show of superior force. At some point he might arrive at the conclusion that prudence was the better part of valor and begin a scripting of vigilant scanning for any possible repetition of the sequence of scenes which had ended so disastrously. But this alone might well prove inadequate to protect him from a repetition. He might well see it coming in advance but be unwilling or not know how to appease his adversary sufficiently to successfully avoid a repetition of what he has been trying to avoid. After a repetition of an angry confrontation he may do one of two things: either increase the remoteness and fine-grained texture of his scanning for anger and or adopt rules of disengagement as well as of rules of vigilant scanning. In such a case, he begins to attempt appeasement before the conflict is joined.

Let us suppose that the next time he detects possible conflict he exhibits signs of appeasement but still suffers an abrasive confrontation with the other. At this point a third type of ordering might be added to the script: postappeasement monitoring for whether there has been a reduction in the possibility of the dreaded scenes. If this is successfully achieved, the all-clear signal is sounded, and the script may be turned off. Should it be turned off prematurely, however, and he experiences yet another failure of avoidance, he might introduce a modified vigiliance rule of increased duration of continuing avoidance as well as increased remoteness of scanning for possibilities. Should this continue to fail, he might then further modify the vigilance rule to the status of the necessity of a perpetual alert. Further, as he continues to experience repeated failure of his avoidance script, each component might become extreme in his efforts to appease and in his monitoring whether he had in fact changed the attitudes of others sufficiently to reduce the danger. Ultimately, he may so compress these rules as a skilled script that they are run off with minimal consciousness, in much the same way an addict "knows" he has a cigarette in his mouth and knows when he needs another and how to hoard enough so that he does not run out of cigarettes. As with an addict, he may panic if all these learned scripted skills should occasionally break down, but his script also contains specific rules for damage control when avoidance and appeasement fail.

Anger-Escape Script. Consider next the learning of an anger-escape script. Suppose our disobedient child had, after suffering repeated defeats of his counterattacks, elected not to avoid any possible repetitions but to reduce his losses by escaping the bad scene sequences by similar appeasement. He would have defined the "solution" not as avoiding defeat but as limiting his losses. How much appeasement, and for how long, to terminate the script would depend on interdependent anger of both adversaries. Should any show of appeasement cool down the parent, then the script might stop at a very elementary level. Should the parent be relatively vengeful and unforgiving, the attempted appeasement rules would have to become more extensive, as would the postappeasement monitoring for change, particularly if the parent characteristically oscillated in his after burning wrath, so that he continued to be angry off and on despite conciliatory efforts by the child.

The strategy for escape need not, however, be scripted in the mode of appeasement. We suggested this to contrast an avoidance and an escape script in related modes. However, this child may have elected instead to literally escape the presence of the parent as a calculated strategy of escape until the other has changed and until the self is no longer angry. It is entirely possible for an individual who has a highly skilled anger-avoidance script to be entirely engulfed in deadly confrontations should his avoidance appeasement rules fail to appease someone who does not respond as his parents did. This is because he has no escape rules and no gradation of anger to deal with scenes of escalating anger other than through appeasement at a distance before anger becomes very dense. This is how overly anger-avoidant, timid, unaggressive individuals sometimes commit violent murders. They have overlearned avoidance at the expense of escape, thus isolating ungraded dense anger as a foreign, ungovernable force.

There is another type of anger-escape script, which is based on compliance rather than either appeasement or walking away from confrontation. In one such case I studied, whenever the child became increasingly angry in response to his mother's anger, the mother would effectively terminate the scene by a display of dense, angry disgust: "Stop it. You're being childish." Inasmuch as this mother was (in the eyes of her child) an insufficiently affectively responsive mother, he would try several different ways to evoke affect from her, including anger. So, although he would become very angry with her, her counteranger and disgust was in part not altogether unwelcome and did in fact offer an escape both from his own anger and from further anger from her should he stop his anger. But this had the paradox of producing an anger-escape script in which he required the special intervention of the other to terminate his anger, thus foreclosing the learning of self-control of his anger. In marriage this proved a serious mismatch of anger scripts. His wife failed to control his anger in this special way, so he had no learned script by which to turn off his escalating anger whenever their relationship turned adversarial and confrontive. His script had accepted termination rules defined by the other as ego-syntonic. He continually needed the other to help him control anger and escape from it when it became very dense. The role of the other may be central in any script formation or it may be secondary to the strategies of the individual's construction, or both.

An Anger-as-Last-Resort Script. In an anger-as-last-resort script the individual has contructed a set of rules which is neither avoidant nor escapist in aim. In this script anger plays a secondary role as auxiliary to other affects. Whatever the primary aim of the script, be it a positive affluent enjoyment or excitement, a shame-damaged attempted repair, a distress-limited attempted remediation, a disgustcontaminated decontamination, or a dissmell toxic antitoxic script, the individual scripts a contingency rule that if the major script fails to work effectively, then anger and/or aggression is the only way out. Because his primary aim is nonangry and nonaggressive, he does not include a vigilance-scanning avoidance rule. Nor is it his aim to escape confrontation, so there are no escape rules in such a script. Such a script employed in the enjoyment of a game of basketball might induce the individual to anger and/or to fight his opponent should he judge the other was being unfair or overly aggressive. He may, depending on the behavior of the other, rarely become angry or aggressive in such games but nonetheless be scripted as a last resort should all other alternatives fail.

Similarly, in intimate relations with spouse or children, whatever the scripted scene, whether affluent or damaged or limited or contaminated or toxic, there may be included a last resort to anger as an invariant backup to all other rules. In other individuals such a backup rule may be restricted to decontamination scripts because of identification with a parent who resorted to force whenever he judged his child had violated a major moral norm. Such a restricted access to anger may prove to be a liability in the political arena. Thus, in Walter Mondale's campaign for the presidency of the United States the only occasion when he was an effective warrior against his opponent, Ronald Reagan, was when he had detected a possible lie by his opponent. So effective was his pious wrath that Reagan became flustered and was generally believed to have been defeated, surprisingly, by his usually more temperate rival. In an interview on television prior to this debate Mondale had told of the rare occasions when his father had whipped him, namely, when he had been discovered to have told a lie. Via identification with that father he was enabled to script justifiable anger and aggression as a last resort when otherwise good scenes turned bad in just this way. The next Democratic candidate for president, Michael Dukakis, paid an even heavier price for failing to have even a minor last resort to anger when asked how would he respond to someone who had raped or killed his wife. Successful Democratic candidates, such as Roosevelt, Truman, and Kennedy, have combined compassion with angry toughness, especially in wit. Compassion with insufficient toughness has been a liability on the American political scene, most notably in the case of Carter. This is a consequence of a conjunction of Christian and individualistic warrior, capitalistic ideology.

How will such an anger script be constructed and magnified? First the scenes and script must be primarily concerned with affects other than anger—either excitement or enjoyment, or shame, or distress, or disgust, or dissmell, or surprise, or terror. Second, there must have been some experience, either by the self or witnessed in a significant other, of anger as effective and/or justified in dealing with some failure of scripted non-anger scenes. The self or the other wins a significant victory in a game by resorting to anger or aggression. The self or the other successfully repairs a damaging shaming insult by responding angrily *after* other attempted reparative strategies have failed. The other does not apologize if the self is humble or avoidant or walks away from the abrasive scene or is conciliatory, but suddenly yields when the victim expresses his anger. Further, this must be an *exceptional* state of affairs; otherwise the learned script would be an anger-driven counteractive or antitoxic script in which *any* evocation of negative affect was immediately evocative of anger, which in turn was expressed in aggressive behavior. In our hypothetical case of the disobedient child the last-resort rule might have been added to an anger-escape script in which the child typically attempted to conciliate his parent and did so effectively as a rule. However, if occasionally the parent continued to distress and shame him, *and* the child in effect cried "enough" and had a tantrum which made the parent back off and become more conciliatory, then the child might have learned that when the customary way of dealing with the angering other does not work, he has a backup, last-resort contingency upon which he can rely. If the other gives way too frequently or too easily, then anger may move up in the hierarchy of rules for when to use it. In the extreme case it becomes the preferred response of first rather than last resort—whatever other affects may evoke anger. In such cases he is quick to anger whether he is excited or joyful, ashamed or distressed, disgusted or dissmelled, surprised or terrified.

Anger-Seeking Scripts. Next, consider how an anger-seeking script might be constructed. In such a script, in contrast to an angeravoidance script, there is also a rule for remote vigilance scanning for the possibility of anger or aggression, but for the purpose of meeting it head on or of creating it rather than turning it down. One may construct such an anger-seeking script for different reasons: to test the self, to face down opposition, or to enjoy fighting, or any combination of such aims. In a masochistic anger-seeking script, it is the punishing anger of the other which is exciting and sought. In another type of masochistic anger-seeking script it is the anger and aggression of the other which is sought to punish the self for its own anger or other sins. In yet another type of nuclear anger-seeking script it is the anger and aggression of the other which is sought to attempt to reverse the good nuclear scene's loss by a desperate attempt to extort reform and love from the angry, rejecting other. Finally, an angerseeking script may be included in a power-expanding script, in which anger and aggression are used to diminish the power of anyone who contests one's own growing wish to expand one's dominion over others for economic, political, moral, aesthetic, religious, truth, or security monopoly. In such a script, every time I successfully fight a competing powerful other I diminish his power and expand my own in a zero sum game.

How Is an Anger-Seeking Script Constructed?

To construct an anger-seeking script, anger is conceived to be a means to some other valued end or to be a mixture of that other end and anger as also valued, or that anger is valued as rewarding in and of itself accompanied and or followed by excitement or enjoyment as derivative of anger and aggression.

In our later discussion of affluent anger scripts we will consider in more detail the construction of the macho script, which combines anger and aggression seeking as a conjunction of testing the self, demonstrating one's power to enjoy fighting and success in facing down one's opposition as well as in demonstrating prowess in seductive sexual encounters.

But any one of these criteria may separately prompt an angerseeking script. Thus, if either parent or sibling or peers requires the willingness and/or ability to fight as a major criterion of the value of a human being, then the least aggressive individual may be required to pass a rite de passage, a trial by fire, to be admitted into the adult world as a first-class member of the human tribe. Those who back off such tests are adjudged second-class citizens, wimps, or effeminate. Such a criterion may be a purely sociocultural or class- or genderinherited criterion, but it need not be so constructed. Any human being who has suffered at the hands of a hostile other can readily come to be disgusted at the self who accepts such outrage passively. Further, this may be experienced vicariously, as happened to Freud when he learned that his father had not responded more heroically to an anti-Semitic child's insult to his father. How magnified such a script becomes, how broadly and frequently it is necessary to test the self's adequacy in this respect, will depend upon the perceived decisiveness of the outcomes, the density of actual and/or perceived provocations, the adequacy of the self in respects other than anger and aggression, and the differential ratio of positive to negative affect in the general life space of the individual. A very dramatic fight which the individual wins decisively may establish his position in a dominance hierarchy once and for all, as sometimes occurs in animal dominance trials. Within the family-sibling rivalries a later-born may seek and win a decisive contest with his arrogant first-born rival, or perpetually seek such contests outside the family if he cannot overcome his lower status within the family. If he is a first-born who perceives his parents as rivals impossible to defeat, he may move to extrafamilial turf in business, science, or the military to continue to test the strength of the embattled self. Clearly, to construct such a script, both avoidance and escape and their rules of vigilance and response are excluded as further threats to the value of the self. Even anger as a last resort would be hazardous to a self so defined by willingness to anger and aggress. In the event that one parent shames the child for insufficient anger and another parent shames for excessive anger, this child is impaled on the dilemma of an impossible decontamination script: how to both seek anger scenes and to avoid or escape them.

If the primary aim of the anger-seeking script is to face down opposition, clearly anger must be ego-syntonic, at least to the extent that it is valued as critically instrumental in opposing those who oppose the self. It may begin with a later-born who judges he has inherited an unjust world in which those born before him inherited gratuities for which he has to fight. It may also originate in anyone whose class, wealth, ability, age, nationality, gender, race, or religion are perceived to be a basis for unjust prejudice or discrimination against him. Further, he must, on a variety of grounds, have rejected many alternative means of remedying the limitations he feels have been unjustly visited upon him. The other must be in fact, or be perceived to be, unwilling to correct inequities either because he thinks them just, or because he is too excessively self-serving to surrender any of his prerogatives or simply indifferent to the other or too hostile to be accommodating. Further, such a script conceives that if the other is successfully opposed, the self will in some ways suffer less or henceforth not at all, and live the rest of his days free of such distress and rage, at least from oppositional others. Such oppositional other or others may be restricted to one person and some surrogates, or to many people and many surrogates, and variously conceived to be possible to change in one brief trial or only partially changed as a result of a lifetime of struggle, to which the self commits itself totally. Such scripts may also be generated on an altruistic basis when a beloved other is believed to be unjustly oppressed, prompting heroic salvation scripts. Such altruistic scripts may also be generated when there has been vicarious identification with any group of oppressed others, as in the case of the abolitionists, as well as in the case of Karl Marx, both of whom we will examine in more detail later.

In order for such a script to be sustained there must be a willingness and a capacity to absorb and to neutralize the rigors and suffering which any oppositional anger-seeking behavior usually evokes from the opposition. This may begin in contests with parents or with siblings or peers, especially in adolescent gang fights. But no matter how magnified such oppositional scripts, they are, like all scripts, vulnerable to burnout and erosion if and when the prices of sustained angry opposition reach a critical density of punishment which exceeds the individual's capacity for absorption because of declining energy and vigor or reduced reward or both.

Next, in the case of the anger-seeking script for the excitement and enjoyment of fighting, such an affluence script is often generated in either families or subcultures which idealize and practice such fighting: warrior military classes, adversarial economic classes who exult in hostile takeovers, adversarial religious groups who thrive on the hostile nailing of the sinner to the cross, academics who thrive on uprooting contaminated theory or data or art, politicians who exult in defeating their opponents, the pious who thrive on hostile gossip, the artist who thrives on oppositional artistic creations and the destruction of conventional art, the lover who thrives on each new oppositional seduction, the athlete who thrives on defeating presumably superior athletes, the sinner who thrives on self-flagelation.

Such anger-seeking scripts may vary radically in the relative quantity of excitement and enjoyment and the density of anger and other negative affects. Some of these scripts may be much more positive than malicious, others equally so, and still others primarily intent on angry damage to the other with only minimal derivative enjoyment as a function of the quantity of hurt inflicted. Angry wit and humor parallel these differences. Some humorists enjoy their piercing wit more for the excitement and laughter they evoke in others, as well as in themselves, than for the anger which prompts their wit. Others have a sharper edge to their wit, while a much smaller number skate on the thin edge of humor and satire by the bitterness of their fun.

This depends in part on the modeling of humor and teasing and attack within the family and the fun and satisfaction and pride as well as the anger displayed by parents and others in putting down sinners and fools. Putting down fools is likely to be less malicious than attacking the family sinners, though not necessarily so. Chekhov as a young man dearly enjoyed mimicking members of his family, a script which served him well as a playwright and short story writer. It should be remembered that he was beaten daily by his father and that some of the sharp edges of his art reflects this anger. When parents lay heavy hands on older children with some evident excitement and enjoyment, this may not be reciprocated, but it is a small step to mimicking the parent with the next weakest sibling, especially when that sibling had informed on the older one to the parent for some sin. Some fathers take their sons on shooting expeditions (as in Hemingway's case) and teach their sons the excitement and enjoyment of killing animals, identifying it also as a ritual of manhood.

The dynamics of script construction by identification and modeling are, of course, quite different than those involved in anger-avoidance and escape scripts. More generally, anger or any other affect may be magnified by the scripted ordering of scenes in radically different ways. We have here examined only a few of those ways. The only commonality in such dynamics is the ordering of affect and response target changes to coassembled affect-laden scene changes which evoke such changed responses.

Chapter 29

The Differential Magnification of Anger

Anger may be a major magnified affect in the life of the individual or achieve very minor magnification. What are the chief determinants of these differences?

Anger is least magnified in the personality when its competitors are most magnified. Either excitment and or enjoyment are so magnified they effectively attenuate the magnification of anger, or negative affects other than anger are so magnified they effectively attenuate the magnification of anger.

Anger is most magnified when the ratio of negative affect to positive affect is radically negative, and the ratio of anger to other negative affect is radically biased in favor of anger; third, when such positive affect as is magnified is conjoined with anger, and fourth, when non-anger negative affect which is magnified is also conjoined with anger.

Consider first the conditions under which anger is minimized via the disproportionate magnification of positive over negative affect and how this is achieved and maintained.

HOW THE RATIO OF POSITIVE TO NEGATIVE AFFECT GETS FIXED

First let us briefly address the question of how varying values of the density and ratio of positive to negative affect may be fixed. There is no royal road to psychological affluence or poverty, although there are many alternative roads. Neither the biological inheritance of a vigorous, healthy, agile, beautiful, intelligent nervous system and body will guarantee a happy life, nor their opposite a miserable life. Neither the psychosociocultural inheritances or achievements of individual and national economic wealth, political status and privilege, social privileged status, knowledge and literacy, social stability and tolerable rates of change, openness of opportunity for age, gender, and class, or rewarding socialization via optimal mutuality, modeling, and/or mirroring will guarantee an optimal balance of positive over negative affect, nor will their opposites guarantee the reverse ratio.

One must, however, inherit and achieve *some* gratuities in sufficient numbers and quantities to attain a critical mass for a good and rewarding, or bad and punishing, life or for some intermediate mixture thereof. But the correlation between a good life and a rewarding life and the correlation between a bad life and a punishing life is variable. This is because of the variable interdependence of judgments of evaluation and effectiveness (by the self and by others) and the experienced ratio of the density of positive and negative affect. If one has enjoyed one's life, it is more probable that one (and others) will also judge that it has been good, effective, and fulfilling. But nothing is more common than the judgment and evaluation of a life as good and effective but that it failed to yield the expected and believed-deserved rewards of excitement and enjoyment. Similarly, if one has suffered excessively, one is likely to judge one's life ineffective and bad, but one may judge one's life to have been relatively ineffective and bad but not to have suffered negative affect in equal amount. Hence, suicide among the "affluent" and joy among the "impoverished" is by no means rare, whether that affluence be measured in economic, political, social, psychological, or biological terms. Not only must there be an optimal *set* of inheritances and achievements of affluence of many but not all kinds, but there also must be an optimal interdependence between "causes" and "effects" of affluence or of poverty. The rich must learn to *become* and *remain* richer, as the poor must learn the other skills. This is a special case of what I have called plurideterminacy, that the effects of any cause are indeterminate until they are continually validated by further magnification or attenuated. Any gratuity must be built upon to reward in the long run, any threat must be elaborated by further action to become traumatic. Thus, a mugging may be shrugged off as transient or built upon as a way of life if one elects to hire a bodyguard. Thus some of the major kinds of modular script components (e.g., the clarity of distance and direction, the quantity strategies of optimizing versus satisficing, versus mini-maximizing) are at once criteria of positive and negative scripts as well as their causes and supports. When, however, the density of the ratio of positive to negative affect reaches a critical level, then it can become a relatively *stable equilibrium,* both self-validating and self-fulfilling. At that point the possibility of radical change, though always present, becomes a diminishing probability requiring ever more densely magnified countervailing forces of positive or negative affect.

Let us now briefly examine the consequences of affluence over poverty for a sample of the major varieties of scripts.

All human beings require and generate scripts of *orientation* consisting of abstract spatiotemporal *maps,* more dense *theories* and special *instrumental skills* of how to talk, move, persuade, construct, what we must do to live in the world whatever its reward or punishment. The more affluent we are, however, the more such instrumental skills, maps, and theories are rewarding rather than punishing and the more positive features of that world are differentiated in texture and generalized in scope. Because scripted sources of orientation are more positive in reward, they also enable the development of greater skill. It is much more difficult for the very frightened, ashamed, disgusted, distressed, or enraged to write, speak, move, manipulate, or observe with great skill.

Consider next scripts of *evaluation.* All human beings in all societies must not only acquire orientation but also discriminate moral, aesthetic, and truth values—what to believe is good and bad, beautiful and ugly, true or false. These are *ideological* scripts, widely inherited, first of all, as religious scripts as well as a variety of national secular ideologies. These are scripts of great scope which attempt an account, guidance, and sanctions for how life should be lived and the place of human beings in the cosmos. They conjoin affect, values, the actual and the possible in a picture of the "real." As such they represent *faith,* whether religious or secular.

Since all ideologies contain evaluation, sanctions, *and* orientation and delineation of both positive and negative scenes, their relative salience in the life of the affluent is biased toward the positive components compared with the life of the impoverished, even when they inherit the *same* ideology. Some Calvinists were more certain they would be elected and others more certain that they would suffer eternal damnation. Still other Christians believed themselves destined for the midway of purgatory before entering heaven.

Next are *affect* scripts, concerned primarily with the control, management, and salience of affect. No society and no human being can be indifferent to the vicissitudes of affect per se, quite apart from other human functions and other characteristics of the world in which we live. This is because of their extraordinary potency for amplification and magnification of *anything,* their seductiveness, their threat, and not least their potentiality for contagion and escalation. *Affect-control* scripts regulate the consciousness of affects, their density, display, communication, consequences, and their conditionality. The affluent are characteristically the recipients of rewarding socialization of both positive and negative affects which is tolerant rather than intolerant toward consciousness of affect, toward the density of affect rather than its attenuation (e.g., "simmer down"); toward the display of affect rather than its suppression (e.g., "stop whining"); toward the communication of affect rather than its suppression (e.g., "don't ever raise your voice to me"); toward affect-based action rather than its suppression (e.g., "don't ever hit me again"); toward the tolerable consequences of affect-based action rather than the intolerable consequences (e.g., "when you get so angry you give Mommy a headache"); toward their specificity and conditionality rather than their abstractness and generality (e.g., "don't get too loud and angry when we have guests" versus "nobody likes an angry noisy kid").

In *affect-management* scripts, negative affects are sedated by specific actions quite apart from their instrumental consequences. Thus, cigarettes are smoked to "feel better" whether they help otherwise or not. As sedation becomes more urgent, it is transformed into an addictive script in which smoking becomes an end in itself and displaces all its original sources as the primary source or deprivation affect. As the density of negative to positive affect grows, such dependences shift from purely positive savoring scripts to sedative scripts to preaddictive scripts (e.g., I cannot answer the telephone without a cigarette) to addictive scripts, with fateful consequence for their compulsion and freedom to relinquish.

Affect-salience scripts address the questions of how directly or indirectly one should aim at affect and how much weight one should assign to affect in the whole family of scripts. When affect per se becomes focal as a script, we seek "kicks" or "peace" or try to avoid "terror" or "rage" or "sadness." Persons and activities are judged primarily by their affect payoff. In contrast, in derivative affect scripts, a person, a place, or an activity is rewarding *because* that one is a competent or nurturant or good person, because that activity is socially productive, because that place has extraordinary vistas or architecture. In affect-systematic scripts, affect becomes one of *many* criteria for script guidance, and many scripts are considered as part of one system for evaluation. As affluence increases, focal affect scripts are subordinated to derivative affect scripts, which are in turn subordinated to affect-systematic scripts.

All individuals enjoy some scenes via scripts of affluence, repair some scenes of shaming damage, remedy some scenes of distressing limitation, decontaminate some scenes which disgust and combat some toxic scenes which either terrify, dissmell, or enrage, via antitoxic scripts. When the ratio of positive affect to negative affect is great, the ratio of scripts of affluence exceeds scripts of damage repair, which exceeds scripts of limitation remediation, which exceeds scripts of contamination-decontamination, which exceeds toxic-antitoxic scripts. Although this is generally true, it is not a completely regular set of correlations because the nonaffluent scripts also have varying ratios of positive to negative affect, depending on their relative effectiveness, so that *some* of the ratio of positive to negative affect is constituted by reward in reparative or remedial, decontamination or antitoxic scripts. We will presently consider one such case in which affluence scripts are few but in which remediation via hard work becomes the central locus of deep and sustained positive affect.

TYPES OF AFFLUENCE SCRIPTS

Let us now consider some varieties of scripts of affluence and their interaction with a high ratio of dense positive over negative affect. As this ratio becomes more positive, it becomes a more stable equilibrium so that scripts of affluence assume a central influence in the personality. Empirically, this is a relatively rare state of affairs, as is its mirror image, the inverse ratio and the consequent centrality of scripts of toxicity for some individuals.

There are numerous types of affluence scripts, apart from their varieties of specific positive affects and apart from their varieties of specific loci of positive affect investment. A very high density and magnification of positive affect could *not* be achieved from a life lived as a series of unconnected transient positive, even "peak" scenes, since magnification, in contrast to amplification, requires coassembly of *sets* of scenes and scripted *further responses* to them, either to be repeated, to be sought, to be improved upon, or to be produced or created anew. Magnification of scripts of affluence can consist of neither isolated scenes nor of scenes sought exclusively for pure positive affect, such as pure excitement or pure enjoyment without regard to their source. The irrelevance and absence of evaluation (other than pure affect as critical) would impoverish the critical and discriminating skills of the individual to such an extent that the magnification of positive affect would itself be jeopardized. Such a one could only say, I know what excites or pleases me but not exactly why, or why it ceases to excite or please if and when it does so. Such an individual would be too easily uninterested, bored, or displeased to sustain a high density of positive to negative affect. It would be analogous to the difficulty of producing experimental neuroses in some the simple animals used in laboratory experimentation. They could not sufficiently connect and elaborate "traumatic" conditioning to become "neurotic."

By the same logic, an *exclusive* reliance on particular, scenederivative positive affect would not sustain a stable equilibrium of high positive over negative affect, since it would inevitably confront the individual with underrepresented scripts in his personality. Such an individual would be like a romantic lover who disregards too much and too long his other scripts of affluence, such as his parents, his children, his career, his friends, his health, his zest for food, for music, for travel, for nature, even for his daily routines, pallid though they seem in the midst of his obsession. The maintenance of a stable high positive affect over negative affect might *include* both pure affect scripts and scene-derivative affect scripts but must also include systematic interscripts, scripts of affluence, so that the scope and depth of the varieties of reward are guaranteed against either excessive diffusion and unconnectedness or against excessive concentration and alienation from the remainder of the inner and outer world.

From the viewpoint of strategy, the individual must attempt neither to minimize negative affect nor to maximize positive affect nor satisfice but attempt rather to optimize positive affect to achieve an optimal stable equilibrium. The distance between the ideal and the actual must not be so great as to demoralize, nor so small as to trivialize.

Some balance must also be achieved between the several basic functions of perceiving, thinking, remembering, feeling, and acting, lest serious underdevelopment jeopardize the more magnified specialized functions which necessarily require all functions as auxiliaries at the very least.

Every differential magnification of scripted affluence is capable, if unbalanced, of jeopardizing the system of affluence scripts. Unless excitement affluence is balanced by some compensatory relaxation of enjoyment (as in the suburbs or wilderness, against overstimulation from the city) the individual is in jeopardy of being drained. Unless enjoyment affluence is balanced by some compensatory risk and excitement (as in the tendency to introduce gambling into predominantly stable enjoyment societies), the individual will become restive and bored in his excessive enjoyment. Similar constraints appear with respect to affluence scripts located in different time frames. There cannot be fixation on the past, present, or future or on brief durations, middle durations, or long durations without some compensatory balance, lest the system of scripts of affluence be at risk.

Excessive breadth or depth of interest must be balanced by compensation at the least, though both might be optimized if neither is maximized. Scripts of affluence must be optimized rather than maximized since the *exclusive* magnification of scripts of affluence is vulnerable to serious disruption by what might have been easily absorbed except for *too little* exposure to, and immunization against, negative affect. The classic case is Buddha, the overly affluent prince, completely traumatized by his first exposure to the illness and suffering of an old man he happened to encounter by chance. The maintenance of affluence demands the capacity to understand and absorb negative affect when it *is* encountered. One cannot afford excessive specialization even of rewarding affluence without some capacity for the compensation of and absorption of the confrontation with the inevitable suffering by the self and by others. Indeed, what I have called the "rewarding" program of the socialization of affect (Tomkins, 1963) requires that the child be exposed to quantities and varieties of negative affect in sufficiently graded doses that he can learn both to confront them and to discover how he may find his way back from such bruising encounters.

Specialization of affluence is the rule but is ever vulnerable to disregard of neglected and underrepresented specialization unless there is provision for *some* compensatory magnification, even though it continues to be a minor script. The other alternative consistent with a stable equilibrium of high postive over negative affect is a more even, optimized balance between plural scripts of affluence.

There are numerous varieties of affluence scripts, and a stable high ratio of positive affect requires *many* such scripts. These include *repetition* scripts in which the individual seeks to reexperience either what was once rewarding or what has (sometimes years later) *become* rewarding. Such scenes as an attempt to revisit the past (which may indeed have been and as still remembered as having been painful) may become deeply rewarding as a possible reexperience from the vantage point of adulthood. These may, in fact, disappoint but nonetheless be compelling as a unique scene which one must recover in its particularity. One may discover, with Wolfe, that one cannot go home again but nonetheless cherish the experience. It represents the perennial fascination of human beings with "origins."

These scripts are somewhat different from *repetition with exploration* scripts. The young man who wishes to see the young woman he has just met, once again, and then again, wishes to repeat for the exploration of more of the same. Any budding interest requires for magnification further acquaintance and exploration. When such exploration has run its course, such scripts enter what I have called the valley of perceptual skill, in which the once beloved is daily *recognized* but without affect. Any affluence script of repetition with exploration is vulnerable to such attenuation if it is not magnified by continuing, further exploration in repetition or by further shared enjoyment or celebration or anticipation or posticipation.

There are also *repetition-with-improvement* affluence scripts, in which the major aim is to increase one's skill, not to a plateau but to continually redefined peaks, common among professional athletes and performing artists. Such improvement scripts include affluence commitment scripts in which the individual is excited by and enjoys the development of his talents and his skills of discrimination and of generalization, whether as a connoisseur or gourmet or gourmand or as a critic, a mathematician, a composer, conductor, or linguist. In many such cases the individual early on is excited by inherited talents for special kinds of achievement and becomes committed to their development on a purely positive affect basis. This is to be distinguished from commitment scripts of limitation remediation, in which the individual feels he must remedy a scene which is punishing as a felt lack or loss, evil, or false, or ugly.

There are also affluence *production* scripts in which one attempts to produce, again and again, a rewarding scene. A comedian or actor's major script may consist in the successful evocation of audience response to the scene *he* has *produced.*

There are also affluence *creation* scripts which aim at the creation of a product and/or a response toward that product by the other and/ or by the self. It is the uniqueness of the product and of the response to it which is criterial in such scripts. This is notably involved in the sensitivity to priority in artistic and scientific creation or discovery.

There are also affluence *responsiveness* scripts in which the aim is not to seek rewarding experiences, but rather to be open *to* them should they occur or recur. These sometimes occur poignantly among the elderly, who feel they have cheated themselves of what they might have found exciting or enjoyable in their youth and attempt a first, never-experienced childhood.

These shade imperceptibly into *responsiveness quest* scripts in which the individual travels or frequents places where he believes he is more likely to be the target of others who will evoke deep positive responses in himself which he is incapable of either seeking directly or of initiating. Art, especially drama, is sought by many as one form of a responsiveness quest for a "good cry," as well as for excitement or enjoyment. Some will even seek the possibility of an attack for the enjoyment and excitement of the release of suppresed rage, distress, terror, or shame. These may be considered affluence scripts *if* the excitement or enjoyment is the primary aim and the released negative affects are the instrumental vehicle for such rewards. Just as puritanical scripts seek to punish for pleasure, sadomasochistic scripts may seek pleasure and excitement or enjoyment from punishment.

There are also *positive celebratory* affluence scripts, in which there may be rituals for birth, recovery, progress, or victory or for anniversaries of beginnings or memorable scenes, or for rehearsals, as with old friends, or for revisiting cherished places or people or commenting on some admirable characteristic or behavior by the self or other or by a dyad or groups. Next are *instrumental-aesthetic* affluence scripts. These address the enrichment of the purely instrumental with varying admixtures of the aesthetic, beginning with singing at work, socializing at work, embellishing one's work, taking pride in it, savoring and celebrating it. Next are *positive anticipatory* affluence scripts in which the individual neither celebrates nor rehearses but scripts future-oriented scenes of great reward which offer the *bonus* of positive affect in the present, in a manner similar to the bonus of good scenes remembered. Next are *cross-referenced interscripted* affluence scripts which order relationships between scripts advantageously. Thus, a career may be scripted as a way of supporting a family and hobby and travel and self-development and contribution to citizenship, while the family may be scripted as a way of training and preparing for future careers or citizenship or hobbies or personality development.

There are, finally, also *aggregation* affluence scripts in which multiple sources of positive affect are conjoined in new scripts such as the choice of a mate, friend, career, residence. When the individual has achieved a stable positive over negative affect equilibrium he is capable of increasing his demandingness so that his choice of a mate, or friend, or career, or place to live is based upon the *conjoint* several features of scenes he finds most deeply rewarding. Thus, such a choice will not represent a partitioning of values but an aggregation approaching a summum bonum in which he not only aggregates what kind of a person he will marry, what kind of a friend he will cultivate, what kind of career he will pursue, what kind of place he will choose to live in, but also insists that these most wanted choices themselves be aggregated so that he lives with his mate in a place they cherish, surrounded by mutual friends they cherish, pursuing shared or complementary careers together in a family and friend business or profession.

In the Middle Ages the convergence on the building of great Christian cathedrals often represented the aggregation of the deepest motives and best energies of all members of a community in a celebratory, sacred, aesthetic, educational enterprise.

When the ratio of positive over negative affect is great, there are not only an abundance of types of rewarding scenes, but there is a general strategy of optimizing costs, benefits, and probabilities so that such affluence is not only achieved but maintained at a stable equilibrium. Disadvantageous shifts in costs, benefits, or probabilities are countered by scripted shifts in tactics to maintain the optimizing strategy against both overweening demands and unavoidable disappointments.

When the ratio of the density of positive affect over the density of negative affect is very high, the major scripts are scripts of affluence, of positive affect scenes as ends in themselves. But because life can not be lived in a world entirely free of negative affect, a stable equilibrium requires effective scripts for dealing with the inevitable damages of shame, the limitations of distress, the contaminations which disgust, and toxicities which terrify, enrage, or dissmell. Such scripts must be both effective *and* relatively low in magnification. It would be very difficult to lead a life of predominantly positive affect were one forced to confront massive daily scenes of shame, distress, disgust, terror, dissmell, or rage, no matter how effective the individual was in ultimately reducing them daily, only to confront more of the same every day. In the limiting case, an individual living in scenes of social disorder, in a Hobbesian war of all against all, might effectively win every battle every day at the price of killing at least one enemy each day but fail to maintain a preponderance of positive over negative affect, even though his daily survival in a deadly zero sum game rewarded him with intense excitement followed by dense joy at escaping death in killing yet another enemy.

IMPEDIMENTS TO A PREDOMINANCE OF POSITIVE AFFECT

There are two impediments to preserving a favorable ratio of positive affect. One is the quantity and density of negative affect. As that increases, the individual's effectiveness in neutralizing, absorbing, and reducing it declines. Second is the quality of negative affect. We must distinguish varying degrees of malignancy among the several primary negative affects. Although it is a function of negative affect to amplify a punishing state of affairs, to make it more so, to preempt attention and insist on urgency of some action, yet because the gravity of the punishing state of affairs itself varies in quality, so too does the affect it activates. Independent of the quantity of affect (holding density constant) shame is the least malignant, distress next, disgust next, and dissmell, rage, and terror most malignant and punishing. Because shame is evoked by and constitutes a partial interruption and reduction of positive affect, it readily lends itself to scripted reparative responses which return the scene to its positive quality. For this reason high positive-affect density is first of all vulnerable to damage by shame but also most readily repaired when this occurs in the midst of an otherwise primarily rewarding life. This is not to say that severe magnification of shame may not radically limit the effectiveness of reparative scripts when the overall ratio of negative affect to positive affect is reversed in favor of negative affect, or even when the ratio is more nearly equal.

Second, high positive affect density is also vulnerable to the ubiquitous limitations of the human condition, whether this distress be in interpersonal relationships or in work. But though distress is distressing, it is a much more benign affect than its more toxic counterparts, anger and terror. This is because its more moderate activating punishment and its more moderate amplifying characteristic permit longterm confrontation, experimentation, and ultimately effective remediation of both the distressing scene and the distressing affect. As we have noted before, an infant may cry in distress for months with "colic" and survive, whereas months of sustained terror or rage would more severely damage and possibly kill the infant. But so too with the adult. Sustained terror and rage are as malignant as sustained pain. The body was not designed to tolerate such states for long. That is why torture can kill. Terror and rage were designed to amplify the toxic states and make them worse, goading the individual to heroic emergency antitoxic responses.

Disgust is more malignant than either shame or distress and powers intense scripted decontamination responses. In its original role as auxiliary to hunger, the bad food is spit out, or vomited if it has passed into the stomach—a much more extreme response than hanging the head in shame at an interrupted, possibly contaminated, good scene. In shame there is every intention to return to the good scene, whereas in disgust the good scene has become unambiguously malignant and is to be spit out or vomited forth. Without serious and presumably difficult decontamination, no one would wish to try again the disgusting food or scene as analog of disgusting food. Dissmell is still more malignant and is not only not capable of decontamination but must be kept at a safe distance permanently in an antitoxic script. For these reasons we have supposed that there is a continuum of increasing malignancy from shame to distress to disgust to dismell to rage and terror and that shame and distress may be coupled as the more benign negative primary affects and prompting the more benign scripts of reparation and remediation in contrast to the coupled disgust, dissmell, anger, and terror as the more malignant negative primary affects which prompt the more malignant decontamination scripts and antitoxic scripts.

If the ratio of positive to negative affect is high, one of both the consequences *and* ways in which such a favorable ratio may be maintained is by a diminishing density of malignant negative affects and their correlated scripts and a higher density of the more benign negative affects and their correlated scripts. It is entirely possible to invest positive affect in major scripts of affluence and also to earn strong positive affect in the repair of shame-damaged scripts and the remediation of distress-limited scripts. As we noted before, positive affect would be at considerable risk if there were no competence whatever in confronting the many damaging and limiting conditions inherent in the life of any human being. This would also include some competence in decontaminating disgust and in antitoxic responses to dissmell, anger, and terror, which are also necessarily confronted in any life.

But as the density of the more malignant affects and scripts increases, the ratio of positive to negative affect would become increasingly vulnerable, much more than if the density of shame or distress were to increase equally, because of the more inherent difficulty of maintaining positive affect in the face of the more malign negative affects than when coping with the more benign negative affects. More specifically, it is extremely improbable that any individual could maintain a high density of positive over negative affect in the long run if he were vulnerable to massive and sustained rage, compared with the same duration and intensity of distress (as for example in mourning). We will later examine in more detail the general question of the relations between anger and *all* of the different types of scripts. At this point we wish to treat only those kinds of anger which occur in antitoxic scripts and secondarily in decontamination scripts, and to contrast these two types of scripts as jeopardizing high positive over negative affect ratio more than the reparative and remedial scripts jeopardize higher positive than negative affect density.

ANGER ATTENUATION IN REMEDIATION SCRIPTS

In damage-reparative scripts a good scene has been damaged, and if the primary affect to this damage is shame, that will tend to neutralize, absorb, or reduce any secondary anger which might also have been aroused at the damage to a good scene. Every effort will be made to restore the positive scene, and to the extent to which the positive negative ratio is favorable, will generally succeed.

As we have noted before in the comparison between nuclear and limitation-remediation scripts, these latter address those aspects of the human condition perceived to be imperfect, to which some enduring long-term response *must* be made and which it is believed *can* be remedied, with varying degrees of success, risk, effort, costs, and benefits. These scripts involve an optimizing strategy, though compared with scripts of affluence the positive benefits won involve much more absorption of negative affect as a necessary risk and cost of benefits. They are relatively clear in distance and direction, with little conflict or plurivalence. They bifurcate scenes into good and bad scenes and know which are good and which are evil and that one must strive for one at the same time one strives against the other. Limitation-remediation scripts range from scripts of *commitment* to *acceptance* to *conformity* to *opportunism* to *hope* to *resignation.*

Commitment scripts involve the courage and endurance to invest and bind the person to long-term activity and to magnify positive affect in such activity by absorbing and neutralizing the various negative costs of such committed activity. Commitment may be altruistic or narcissistic or both. These scripts may be economic, political, artistic, religious, scientific, familial, or self-improving. Although these scripts of remediation vary radically in the apparent quantity of remediation over risks and costs and in their pretensions to making the world closer to the heart's desire; nonetheless, when the individual's ratio of positive to negative affect is advantageous (though never so much as in scripts of affluence), even the resignation involved in willing the state of slavery when it becomes obligatory—which one may have inherited and which one accepts because it is a choice of living against dying—may provide the rewards of hope (e.g., in a Christian heaven), of evoking some positive affect for being a "good" slave, of a rewarding family life, of sharing a common fate with other slaves. Further, even the most miserable wage slavery of the very poor, as described by Oscar Lewis (1961) in *The Children of Sanchez,* reveals that the culture of poverty may coexist with some psychological affluence in the opportunistic remediation of severe limitation. Thus, Jesus Sanchez regards very hard work for very little money as much better than being without money or being given welfare. He is quite prepared to give up play and games and his "childhood" in preparation for the severities of life he anticipates from seeing how hard his own father works. Though he has had little education, he sees some opportunities for learning in the course of discharging his duties as an employee. He wishes to be like his father, who also had no one to help him. Like his father he is not given to showing affection to his own children, since they too must be prepared for the same hard work. He likes his work and he likes his boss (who "permits" him to work overtime on holidays).

His reasons for liking his work are multiple. First, he must work if he is to eat and to support his family. Second, he is neither passive nor controlled. Third, he is not abandoned when he has money, nor is he spoiled. Like his father he exhibits his endurance and perseverance through his work. Fourth, it provides him with such education as he has ever had and develops his skills in buying. Also, it satisfies his wish to be with many different kinds of people and to work for an admired father surrogate. Fifth, it enables generativity in providing him with some money to build a house which he can leave as his inheritance to his children. Finally, as he describes it, it is his "medicine," making him forget his "troubles." This "poor man" is psychologically very rewarded by his forced labor through which he remedies an inheritance which he has accepted but determined to remedy within the limits of possibility as he perceives them.

In the case of Jesus Sanchez we have a very high ratio of positive to negative affect despite two unusual conditions. First, the number of pure affluent scripts is minimal. He does not believe in "play." Life is too grim and serious for that. But his work scripted as limitation remediation is nonetheless deeply rewarding in very many different ways and sustains the highly favorable ratio of positive over negative affect. Second, as a member of a macho culture, Jesus Sanchez defends his honor by fighting, often, which he enjoys more than he is enraged by it or more than he fears it. It is not for him so much an antitoxic script but resembles more an affluence script, much more rewarding than punishing; such anger or fear as he experiences, being minimal, adds spice to his excitement and enjoyment.

So much for the attenuation of anger via the maintenance of a high density of positive over negative affect. Let us now consider the alternative mode of attenuation of anger via the maintenance of a high density of negative affect over positive affect, in which the negative affect is competitive with, and so contains and inhibits, anger. Any one negative affect or combination of negative affects may converge to make this possible.

Consider first the individual who is entirely oriented toward the ever-present possibility of damage by shame. He may magnify such contingencies by a family of scripts in which he becomes vigilant at a great distance and over great breadth of scenes to any remote possibility of shaming damage to good scenes, to which he responds with heroic measures to avoid or reduce such intuited possibilities. Should these avoidance-prompted responses fail, he will also have multiple backup responses to repair the shaming damage. These may range from apology through appeasement, ingratiation, persuasion, jollying, promised reform, negative celebration, to crying or, after making excuses for the self, escaping and leaving the scene until the other cools down, then to return and resume the customary scripted affluence scene—anything but expressing anger at the other *or* at the self. In such magnification of shame, anger is believed too toxic and threatening to be included in the possible responses to damage which must be repaired. This is not to say such an individual may not resort to self-disgust or even self-dissmell as an intrapunitive response to satisfy the rejecting other, that he too appreciates he deserves to have been shamed. He may also respond to such threats with distress and terror as well as shame, each of these secondary and tertiary affects further magnifying the damage and the felt urgency of recovering the good scene. In the prefeminist era married women were indeed enjoined to, expected to, and did comply with the stratification of the primary affects into the masculine and feminine affects, whereby they could be joyous, distressed, afraid, or ashamed but not angry. A low divorce rate was in part maintained by the attenuation of feminine anger and the magnification of masculine anger. The sad, humble, happy female was required, at the least, to hide her anger and ideally not to be angry. In this way the burden of reparation for any disturbance to the good family scene fell heavily on the shamed female.

Another way in which anger may be attenuated is by the differential magnification of distress in limitation-remediation scripts. In such a commitment script the individual may elect to be a helper rather than a reformer. The latter necessarily requires a more aggressive and angry adversarial script against limitations believed immoral and unjust. In the helper script of commitment the same scene is responded to primarily with empathic distress rather than pious outrage. There may also be secondary shame at the plight of the distressed other and even disgust at the indifference of those who may have contributed to the limitation scene. There may also be empathic fear for the future of the distressed if there is no help. This is again a scene which is defined as a "feminine" one, so prominent in the definition of the helping professions.

But this is not the only way in which anger may be attenuated by the differential magnification of distress. Whether scripted as conforming, as opportunistic, as accepting or resigned, life may be believed (and with good reason) to be deeply distressing and therefore to be accepted and worked at with dignity, with occasionally some negative distress celebration of how much it hurts but with overall acceptance of whatever rewards may from time to time lighten the enduring burden of being underprivileged by the inherited human condition. Such scripts were much more common before the eighteenth century. Pre-eighteenth-century poverty was either ignored, accepted, or ennobled. In the eighteenth century, poverty and limitation began to be seen as a "problem." This happened only when its eradication was perceived as possible as well as desirable. In England, from 1780 to 1850 there was a phase of self-sustained economic growth and wealth at the same time as there was a population explosion, an increased corps of journalists, newspapers, and reading public, as well as ideologists on capitalism, the nuclear family, and on emotion. Slavery was contested in the era of "good feelings," and individualism was glorified, especially in novels of "character." At the same time there was the rapid growth of knowledge and science in the "enlightenment." This was not time for humble acceptance of limitation but rather an idealization of endless knowledge, power, wealth, population growth, travel, and exploration as well as the idealization of the individual in his nuclear family, with its increased stress on affection in the family and increased respect for the child as well as for the aged. There was also, in marked contrast to the devastating epidemics of previous centuries, an increase in longevity and decline in the associated fear of death by plague.

All these improvements reduced the acceptability of distressing limitation and increased angry and confident demandingness for reform and revolution. Although it has been described as an era of good feelings, it would more appropriately be described as an era of righteous rising expectations which is only now approaching an asymptote in our belated awareness of the limits of growth.

Needless to say, many individuals the world over have continued to be left behind in this explosion of affluence, even in the United States with its hordes of impoverished homeless people who today live on the streets of one of the wealthiest nations in the world. So long as individuals must confront distressing limitations to which they cannot respond either with anger or with effectiveness, their magnification, celebration of distress, and glorification of their enforced acceptance will serve to attenuate anger in the service of extorting from their limitations some modicum of reward.

ANGER ATTENUATION IN DECONTAMINATION SCRIPTS

Yet another way in which anger may be attenuated is by the differential magnification of disgust in contamination-decontamination scripts. Such disgust may be directed at the other, at the self, or at both self and other. While such disgust readily recruits anger as a secondary or mixed response, it is also possible that it excludes and attenuates anger because of either countervailing remaining positive affect or because one is disgusted at one's anger as well as other opposing negative affects. Consider a decontamination escape script. In response to a deep disenchantment with a beloved mother who became drug-addicted, Eugene O'Neill ran away from home. Anger was experienced, but anger could not change his mother (or his father or his brother, who also aroused his disgust), and further his love for her was too strong to support intransigent anger. He had eventually to return to the scene and "bury his dead," as he described it. He was at once too loving and too disgusted to either escape permanently or so magnify his anger that he could free himself of his contaminated love.

Similarly, if disgust is magnified self-disgust, about sexuality and/ or anger, then anger must be attenuated in order to script effective decontamination. This is despite the frequent magnification of anger in support of self-disgust in which the individual kills himself in an enraged failure of decontamination. In the attenuation of anger by self-disgust the individual both negatively celebrates his own disgustworthiness and positively celebrates his successful attempts to purify himself, by chastity and/or meekness and love rather than hate. Asceticism may but need not necessarily magnify anger. Such attenuation of anger is, however, vulnerable to magnification against *other* sinners, who do not purify themselves as the sainted self has now done. In order to sustain a purification script of love and chastity it is easier if the source of self-disgust is primarily sexual rather than anger. The double burden is more daunting and given to requiring that other sinners reform and validate the sanctity of pious outrage. To the extent that the self can dedicate itself unambivalently to decontaminating its disgust of itself it is quite capable of so magnifying this type of script that previous anger is contained and attenuated. It should be noted, however, that even when the self-disgust is primarily directed against sexuality there remains an ever-present vulnerability to the magnification of disgust and anger in piety against those who continue to indulge themselves rather than to pay the price the self has extorted from itself.

Finally, anger may be attenuated by either terror or dissmell, or by both, in antitoxic scripts. One of the time-honored means of controlling both anger and aggression, over many centuries, has been by intimidation. While anger and terror are independent affects, each capable of independent activation, there is a chilling effect on anger whenever it is also experienced simultaneously or sequentially with terror if terror is linked as a punishment for anger. We will later present the TAT of a case we called Z, who had suffered physical abuse at the hands of his father. Two things were clear. First, he had been intimidated out of both feeling and acting on anger. Second such anger as he was capable of feeling had been so attenuated there was little "return of the repressed," but nonetheless it was not entirely eliminated. He was still capable of "imagining" anger and aggression toward tyrants under very special, remote conditions.

Dissmell, if greatly magnified, is also capable of attenuating anger by increasing the distance between the self and the bad-smelling other, as with the untouchables in a caste society. Such magnified dissmell depends, however, on the other's keeping his distance. If those others refuse this, then anger is characteristically recruited as a backup to dissmell, to punish the other for not staying in his place and becoming too intimate. In a less extreme case, an individual who has become excessively critical and dissmelling to many others, in a more democratic society, is likely to evoke counterdissmell and/or anger and so provoke anger in the overly critical dissmelling one. In such a case the magnification of dissmell would not be compatible with an attenuation of anger. Should the magnification of dissmell prompt the individual to exclude others by withdrawal from much social and interpersonal communion, it would be possible for the individual to maintain such an antitoxic script without anger but which nonetheless alienated him from a world he found increasingly unrewarding and intolerable.

This sometimes occurs as a tragic accompaniment of the aging process as the individual loses many of his dearest friends, family, and associates, and his place in the world of work, in retirement. Dissmell under such conditions may become much more lethal and corrosive than rage, especially as it is accompanied by an accelerated rate of cultural change which segregates and eventually isolates cohorts from each other. It was Margaret Mead, over fifty years ago, who was the first to intuit that as sociocultural change accelerated, individuals who were in cohorts no more than ten years older and younger than each other would find it more and more difficult to communicate with each other. Thus, the aged today, who lived through a deep economic depression in the 1930s in the United States and who fought a world war against Hitler's German fascism, may find quite alien a generation that can accept a two-tier society, led by leaders who regard the support of military dictatorships as a small price to pay for combating "Communists," in defense of the overprivileged against their exploited underclasses. Magnified dissmell is an alienation deeper than rage, which is still hot and engaged in the preservation of hope. Such terminal dissmell is perhaps the deepest sickness of the human spirit.

SUMMING UP HOW ANGER IS OR IS NOT MAGNIFIED

In summary, anger may be attenuated by the differential magnification of excitement or enjoyment. It may be contained by the differential magnification which damages by shame, which limits by distress, which contaminates by disgust, and which is toxic by intimidating terror or by the alienation of dissmell.

Anger is magnified by the inverse differential magnifications, first, when the ratio of negative affect to positive affect is radically negative; second when the ratio of anger to other negative affect is radically biased in favor of anger; third, when such positive affect as is magnified is conjoined with anger; and fourth, when non-anger negative affect which is magnified is also conjoined with anger.

Clearly a prime necessary, but not sufficient, condition for the magnification of anger is the radical attenuation of the zest for living represented by the absence or loss of excitement and enjoyment. This becomes a sufficient condition whenever, in response to no excitement and no enjoyment, competing negative affect does not inhibit anger, and anger becomes the primary response both to the absence or loss of excitement and enjoyment and to the varieties of damage, limitation, contamination, or toxicity of bad scenes, with or without the other negative affects. Finally, in the magnification of anger even excitement and enjoyment become biased as rewards, vehicles and opportunities for the further magnification of anger, in which anger and/or aggression is either exciting or enjoyable.

Anger may be maximally magnified in somewhat different ways. It may be *concentrated* in one type of script, or *distributed* among different types of scripts, or *concentrated and distributed.* In the first case the individual magnifies one type of script much more than any other type, and the family of such scenes is primarily goverened by anger. These may be pure antitoxic scripts, as when an individual falls into romantic hate with one supremely hateable object, as in *Moby Dick,* in which the bad other is hateable via a convergence of all other affects. He is represented as without any redeeming features which might evoke excitement or enjoyment. He is worthy of being hated not only because he angers but because he also distresses, shames, surprises (badly), disgusts, dissmells, and evokes terror, all of which converge to produce romantic hate in a manner similar to romantic love when the other is idealized as exemplifying the most excitement and joyworthiness and no features which might ever evoke distress, shame, disgust, dissmell, terror, or anger. In this way damage, limitation, contamination are collapsed as separate scripts into one much magnified antitoxic script. Such concentration of anger may, however, converge on a decontamination script rather than on an antitoxic script. In such a case disgust becomes secondary to rage against the sinner or sinners, as in an inquisition to rid the church of its disgusting heretics; to rid the body politic of its disgusting, immoral radicals, right or left; to rid society of its contamination of blood as in Hitler's extermination of Jews; as in academic or theoretic holy wars, to rid a science of disgusting myths and superstitions; or as in an artistic holy war to purge art of its disgusting conventionality, its remoteness from conventionality, its disgusting classical constraints or its disgusting romantic excesses. The responses to such holy wars are often equally belligerent as in the violence of the protests against an exhibition of Dadaism in Paris.

Concentration of anger may converge on a limitation-remediation script. In such a case distress becomes secondary to rage against those who are perceived responsible for the distressing limitations of human freedom, as in the case of reformers (as contrasted with helpers). Some such committed reformers become more engulfed by outrage than by distress, as in the case of John Brown, compared with some of the less militant American abolitionists. The storming of the Bastille became a potent symbol of the French Revolution and the impulse to aggressively remedy the intolerable constraints of imprisonment. "You have nothing to lose but your chains" became a potent symbol of the Marxist revolutionary strategy. In all of these cases angry revolution has swamped the original slower remediation of distress at enforced and unjust limitation. Not only is anger implicated in the time required for overdue change, but it is also implicated in the demanded quantity of change. As both the quantity and the speed of change demanded are increased, so is anger as both interdependent cause and effect of increased demandingness against unwanted limitations.

The hostile limitation remediation script may take the form of assaultive robbery, in which one forcefully takes from the others in revenge for what he has felt was an unjustified inheritance of poverty. This should be distinguished from robbery or burglary which explicitly avoids assault or even confrontation, from assault which is not primarily aimed at reversing wealth injustices, and from confidence men who appear to combine a wish to interact with others to skillfully seduce them into being swindled. The remedial script may take the form of hostile opportunism, in which the individual becomes blatantly self-serving by virtue of his feeling that his rage has been justified. It may take the form of a hostile conformist script—a sullen, overzealous clerk, bureaucrat, teacher, judge, critic, who uses the rules to punish violators in the discharge of his "duties." It may take the form of either a hostile reform or a hostile revolutionary commitment script. It may take the form of a hostile resignation script in which comfort is taken at holding others responsible for one's own resignation. It may take the form of a hostile overachievement script in which one attempts to do better than others to punish them, to excel to produce enraged distress in others, to bankrupt his competition to reduce them to the poverty which he has overcome, or to take over and absorb his competition, making them his satellites as he had been their satellite; in interpersonal relations he may relentlessly squeeze the other in order to limit and diminish him, to undo his own felt limitations and, by recasting, to reverse roles.

As a consequence of painful invidious comparisons when distress at limitation is swamped by anger, the individual may become outraged at being poor or becoming poorer; at being second best; at having less power than others; at having more conformity demanded of him than of others; at being less attractive, less intelligent, or physically weaker than others, less robust than he once was, shorter or taller than others, fatter or thinner than others, less knowledgeable than others, more controlled than others, an object of more indifference than others, more sickly than others, older or younger than others, of higher or lower class than others; more alien in linguistic incompetence or illiteracy than others, of more unfavorable gender than others, of less favorable nationality than others, of less favorable ethnicity than others, of less favorable skin color than others, less extroverted or introverted than others, less rational or more rational than others, more effective or less effective than others, too actionoriented or too inactive; too decisive or too indecisive, too much or too little given to planning, too impulsive or too inhibited, or having too much or too little anger, distress, dissmell, disgust, surprise, fear, excitement, or enjoyment. Any of these features may be experienced as damaging an otherwise good scene, as contaminating it, or as making it intolerably toxic, but in this case the interpretation is of an enduring limitation which evokes outraged distress which must be remedied rather than repaired or decontaminated or detoxified.

Concentration of anger may also converge on a damage-reparative script, thereby producing a deeply litigious personality. Such a one may also be shamed at what he experiences as violations of his just privileges and deserts, but this may become quite secondary to the repeated scripting of damages as "outrageous" and justifying punitive damages against successive offenders. He finds his way to legal battles again and again, seeking to undo outrageous damages by extortion of reparation. But his outrage and angry demands for reparation may be exhibited in an endless series of small abrasive encounters, in vying for space to park his car, for his place in a line or his seats at a theater, for failures of others to attend to his needs promptly or thoroughly, for invidious attention to less deserving others. Although these may have begun in acute or chronic shame, in the anger-magnified reparative script that is no longer the critical issue. He must now, again and again, have his pound of flesh. He is long past being a sullen, humble mouse.

In his more intimate interpersonal relations he is likely to demand apologies at the same time he refuses to accept any blame for any rupture in a relationship. Failing this, he is relentlessly unforgiving and continues to needle the other for any past damage, however small and even though the offense occurred only once. His memory is elephantine and keeps his rage endlessly alive as he replays the scene now made increasingly intolerable through the large number of rehearsals which cumulate as though there had been multiple offenses.

Further, he indulges in repeated recasting reversals in which he seeks to visit upon the offending other the shame-rage he has suffered from that one.

Just as magnified anger may be concentrated on any type of script rather than limited to its primary sphere, the antitoxic script, so too may it be widely *distributed* among various types of scripts, rather than concentrated.

Thus, an individual may limit his scripts of affluence to sadistic sexuality or to observing wrestling matches for the fun of seeing others inflict pain and injury on each other. The same individual might limit his damage-reparative scripts to the law of talion, an eye for an eye, a tooth for a tooth. He might earn a living as an overly zealous policeman, ever ready to use his authority to punish offenders by freely using his club to subdue them at the slightest show of insubordination. His decontamination scripts would elect him as the pious critic and enemy not only of lawbreakers but of all those godless, evil, ugly proponents of alien Communist ideologies, imported from the "evil empire" about which he had been warned by his president.

There may be widely distributed anger-magnified scripts of all types in such a case, but there may also be a wide distribution of targets of such magnified anger. Thus, he may have anger-driven affluence scripts which reward him with excitement or enjoyment as in telling off his wife, children, friends, associates, or strangers. He may enjoy sadistic sex from pornographic films, wife, mistress, prostitutes, and chance encounters. He may enjoy disciplining his dog and his children.

His reparative scripts of anger and aggression toward anyone who offends him momentarily are in no way limited to intimates or casual acquaintances or to strangers. He is quick to be offended and quick and insistent that all wrongs be righted, with an undercurrent of readiness for force should reparations be less than overgenerous.

His remediation scripts on the interpersonal level mimic his role as a policeman. He is ever ready to angrily remind all offenders and curb what he perceives as enduring limitations in the character and behavior of wife, children, and friends. No one ever succeeds in quite pleasing him as wife, child, friend, or associate. Despite providing a sanctioned outlet for his anger, his role as policeman angers him because of the increasing restrictions on the use of excessive force against those he feels are being coddled by the bleeding hearts.

His decontamination scripts on the interpersonal level are primarly extrapunitive and aggressively moralistic. The other does not only occasionally damage him and enduringly disappoint him by severe character flaws but especially do others arouse pious, self-righteous rage. Although there may be a deep undercurrent of disgust, his primary response is a rage at the immorality of his wife, children, friends, and associates. The restraints under which he works as policeman are felt to be deeply wrong, enraging to himself, a model of virtue, handcuffed by an immoral law which protects the criminals and punishes the defenders of law and order, allowing them to be released before paying for their crimes. But his rage at sinners is in no way limited to those he encounters on the streets. He is frequently outraged by his overpermissive wife who permits their children to get away with murder and guarantees they will grow up to be criminals. He frequently lays heavy hands on these children to impress upon them that sin is not without cost.

In his antitoxic scripts anger and aggression are the primary responses not only to the anger of others but also to terror and dissmell. An offender who also possesses a gun in a shootout with the police evokes terror and dissmell as well as anger, but anger predominates and justifies giving himself the benefit of the doubt in the often dangerous discharge of his duties. Whether it be as policeman or as citizen, in a toxic scene he is quick to anger and to aggress and to counteraggress. He will never back off a hostile encounter, less because he may be frightened or repellingly dissmelled, but primarily because his anger feeds on his anger. These are the individuals who may have been equally abused by their parents and who abuse their own children in delayed repayment.

Such an individual is capable of responding with some enjoyment, some excitement, some distress, disgust, dissmell, shame, terror, and surprise but in insufficient densities to compete with a predominant magnification of anger which swamps and engulfs the life space. This is, of course, as rare as its inverse, the stable equilibrium of an individual so positive in his magnification of excitement and enjoyment that all competing negative affect is neutralized, contained, or absorbed.

Much more common than the flat profile of distributed anger we have just explored is a combination of concentration in one major type of script, with some overflow and generalization to one or two other types of anger-driven scripts.

Thus, as we will later explore in more detail, the enemy may be delineated as conjointly toxic, terrorizing and dissmelling and angering, and also contaminated, immoral, and disgusting, and must therefore be angrily defended against, both his contamination and his toxicity. This was the posture of the Reagan administration and of Oliver North in their clandestine operation against the Nicaraguan Communist government. Neither shame nor distress was implicated. It was rather the density of the more malignant affects of disgust, dissmell, and terror which served to magnify and justify anger and aggression as the higher morality. Both North and Reagan could thus at the same time be protectively compassionate to all possible victims of the Communists, including the contras and all *loyal* anti-Communist Americans. It only heightened the perceived heroism of a loving father and husband, boss and friend, and loyal soldier. In bifurcating the world sharply into the good and the evil, anger is readily contained from overgeneralization.

Consider another type of concentration and limited distribution of anger and aggression, that of an opportunistic power script in which an individual seeks to remedy a socially inherited poverty via leadership of a criminal drug empire. This need not require the wish or the freedom to quick and massive anger and aggression, but clearly this may be required to rise in the hierarchy of organized crime. There are many adversarial competitors in such a business in addition to the legally constituted adversaries. Such a script will sooner or later require a readiness to magnify an antitoxic script as auxiliary to the opportunistic limitation-remediation script, so that ruthless gunning down of those who threaten the monopoly of his turf or who must be eliminated to extend his turf is willingly and angrily scripted as instrumental to the consolidation of power.

But such concentration of an anger-driven limitation-remediation script and auxiliary magnification of an anger-driven antitoxic script is in no way limited to role-scripted generalization. Thus, any individual who compares himself invidiously with others and who attempts to remedy this by angry recasting in which he seeks to better himself by hostile defeat of his betters will be vulnerable to both imagined and actual counteranger and aggression as a toxic threat which not only threatens his attempted efforts at remediation but which may also threaten his perceived safety and security.

Further, it has been a commonplace for those whose limitation remediation is vulnerable to the vicissitudes of shifting economic fortune to go from anger at their failed work-remediation scripts to antitoxic destruction of the machines in the early stages of the industrial revolution to the public destruction of Japanese automobiles by American General Motors workers who see their economic future vitally threatened by Japanese automobiles. The same dynamic is involved, worldwide, in the violence directed at "foreigners" who rob "natives" of their jobs or who work for lower wages, thus depressing wages generally. The same dynamic is involved when either younger or older will work for less or displace workers or when women will be used to either displace men or to depress wage scales. Similarly, whenever race or color is employed differentially in what is perceived to be unfair economic competition, violence is an ever-present possible response. Again, the use of nonunion labor in a previously unionized industry is an invitation to violence. The threat to limitation remediation is paradoxically reacted to most violently by the most privileged and by the least privileged. In the former case it is an expression of plenitude of power. In the latter case, less frequent, it is an expression of the extremity of felt powerlessness. This is therefore more likely to be blind fury and the other to be a more effective counterattack in defense of threatened privilege. Southern slaves often had no recourse to improve their condition except by uprising in massacres. Peasants in feudal regimes only had recourse against excessive taxation by open revolt and aggression.

In such cases anger did not drive the limitation-remediation scripts but was rather the consequence of the failure of their remediation efforts, which then evoked magnified anger and further antitoxic scripting.

Such a concentration of an anger-driven limitation-remediation script may implicate an anger-driven decontamination script. In this case the limited self prompts not only anger against those he envies but also disgusted anger at the immorality of those whom the gods favored and whom he holds responsible for their immorality as well as their counterfeit superiority. Such a husband is involved not only in cutting his wife down to size but also expresses his fury and disgust at her continuing sinning, demanding she reform and become as virtuous as he himself is in his justified anger.

Should his envious anger not permit such further generalization of his anger, he may nonetheless magnify it further by turning it against himself in angry self-disgust for the envious hostility he cannot control. In the extreme case this may transfer to a magnified antitoxic script in which he directs that anger against himself in self-mutilation, psychic or physical, or in suicide, imagined or attempted. Should his anger be located in the preservation of the environment, it might similarly move from a remediation script in which he aggresses upon those who threaten the environment to an auxiliary anger-driven decontamination script in which he bitterly condemns the pollution of character of those who pollute the environment, to an antitoxic anger-driven script in which the pollution and the polluters are represented as threatening the safety of the planet, thus justifying the most heroic violence to oppose such dangers. Pollution not only robs us of our inheritance but it is wrong and life-threatening, a triple threat. For such pollution, the polluters must first be made to remedy and undo the limitation and at the least pay for such remedies. Second, they must be punished and imprisoned if they will not reform, and in the extreme case no price is too high to stop them from their rape of the good earth. Angry disgust has been magnified to angry dissmell and terror.

In a more extreme case of magnification of anger-driven limitation remediation, "life" becomes increasingly limited in its perceived possibilities of remediation, which in turn drives anger into disgust, as well as distress, in decontamination scripting. And should this fail, increasingly it will prompt the most serious toxic dissmell and alienation from life and/or terror at the extremity of his terminal human condition, all combined with rage, not to go gently into the night.

In the case of activist antiabortionists we have a conjunction of magnified anger in an antitoxic script against the supposed murder of the fetus in which terror and alienated dissmell prompt violence against the murderers and also an anger-driven decontamination script which delineates the pro-choice woman as deeply immoral and disgusting, thus adding to the severity of the crime of abortion. The enemy is first life-threatening and terrifying and dissmelling and angering and therefore disgusting and immoral as well.

Yet another closely coupled anger-driven set of scripts, in which one may be more concentrated and the other a secondary derivative, are the damage-reparation and limitation-remediation scripts, when either becomes a vehicle for anger over the more customary negative affects in those scripts. When the self is shame-damaged to the point of towering rage which can be appeased only by the extortion of recasted shaming of the other or by an apology and or a promise by the sinner never again to wound the self, the individual often begins to find increasing evidence that these occasional lapses by the other have a deeper source in the more enduring flawed character of the other. When this occurs and episodic damage is increasingly interpreted as enduring limitation of the other, and of the relationship to the other, he is inclined to signal this by a transformation of each previously isolated affront into an accusation of the form "you always do that." Such an "always" is often more a consequence of the affect density of sustained rehearsal than of an accurate estimate of relative frequency of offense. It is not only a self-validating script but tends also to become self-fulfilling in that the repeated angry accusations are likely to anger the other into becoming more frequently and more enduringly hostile, so that a much less serious reparative effort does now in fact require more difficult and sustained remediation if the relationship is to be sustained. Because the anger of the aggrieved one now grows faster than the anger of the limited one, and because the relationship tends toward increasing polarization, the remedial anger becomes the dominant script and swamps the reparative script in degree of magnification; and whatever affluence now remains is at increasing risk, since what might once have been experienced as a damage to a scene of affluence becomes increasingly yet another instance of an enduring limitation of the other and the relationship which angers more than it shames or distresses and becomes self-fulfilling in that both parties become more strident and less accommodating to each other.

Conversely, a much magnified anger-driven limitation script, such as an opportunistic one, is capable of displacing increasing anger to a damage-shame-angered reparative script such that every unintended transient affront from anyone becomes capable of becoming a field of battle, to compensate for nagging ineffectiveness of the major limitation-remediation script. This is not uncommon among creative young writers as they struggle for recognition and become increasingly angry at the absence of appreciation. I have known such poets who became increasingly vulnerable to very trivial encounters, which they magnified to affairs of honor. Had they lived a few centuries earlier, they might have met their death in a duel. When the major remediation script provides much more rage than satisfaction, the minor reparative script is vulnerable to deadly exaggeration. Failure or the ambiguity of status need not, of course, lead to a magnification of vulnerability to anger damage. It is the combination of anger as a prime motive in the remediation script, combined with further affect as a consequence of the lack of success of the script, which prompts the displacement to another scripted domain. When remediation is less dominated by anger, commitment and absorption of its negative costs is much more readily maintained.

In honor societies the duel to death was an ever-present possibility whenever damage which shamed occurred. Thus, scripts of reparation led directly to antitoxic scripts. They were very closely coupled and mutually magnifying. Violation of honor demanded reparation via imposing death on the other or on the self, and in some societies this debt could never be repaid, and successive generations of families carried this burden into the indefinite future.

We have thus far examined the magnification of anger and the attenuation of anger as a function of the ratio of the density of positive and negative affect and the ratio of the density of anger to other negative affect. This is an exercise akin to the value of the properties of the frictionless plane in physics, illuminating as a limiting concept for the interpretations of deviations from the ideal simplest case.

As soon as we examine these deviations, as we will presently do, the complexity of the dynamics of the real cases increases exponentially, since the increasing degrees of freedom of independent, dependent, and interdependent variability defines the essential features of any system, physical or biological or psychological, as its complexity increases from stronger to weaker forces, coincident with its growing dimensionality, as Weisskopf labeled the quantum ladder in physics.

Consider first that anger may be magnified by being combined simultaneously with another negative affect, as in the cases when damage arouses both shame and anger, limitation arouses both distress and anger, contamination arouses both disgust and anger, toxicity arouses both terror and anger or both dissmell and anger. Second, anger may be combined sequentially rather than simultaneously, under the same conditions.

In such instances the scripted responses are characteristically designed to deal with both affects.

In a damage-shame-anger reparative script the individual is less likely to be confrontive than in the purely anger-driven scripts we have already examined. The options for such a conjunction will depend not only on the general ratio of positive to negative affect and the ratio of anger to all other negative affects but also on the overall differential ratio of the density of shame to anger, prior to the dynamics of any new scene in which any script may be subject to radical review for possible script changes. Further, any scene may be damaging and evoke varying ratios of affects other than shame or anger, which shift from scene to scene. In this case damage from an insult may evoke more shame than anger; damage from indifference may evoke equal quantities of shame and anger and distress. From one person an insult may anger more than it shames; from another, it shames more than it angers, but also frightens. From insult among intimates, more shame; from insult from strangers, more anger but also dissmell; from insult among equals, more anger than shame; from insult from superiors or inferiors, more shame and disgust than anger, or conversely. Such conditionally is without limit and must be examined in each specific profile of the entire family of scripts.

These dynamics become more complex yet when we consider the sequential as well as simultaneous coupling of anger and shame, anger and distress, anger and disgust, anger and terror, and anger and dissmell. In the case of a damage-reparative script for the sequential arousal of shame and anger, one must know how intense and how enduring the shame might be; how long the interval before anger was evoked; how intense that was compared with the shame; how long it lasted at what intensity; what degree of overlap for how long, at what differential intensity of the two affects as they might vary over time; as well as the possibility of additional negative affects under specific conditions which might summate with or conflict with either shame or anger. Further, sequential affect itself may be scripted quite differently from individual to individual. Thus, in one such reparative script anger may be absorbed and controlled with some degree of continuing resentment despite conciliatory reparation. In another script anger adds a sharper edge to the predominantly conciliatory reparation, with a warning that the other not repeat his offense or the relationship might not be able again to be so readily repaired. It also makes a considerable difference whether anger is an invariant sequel to damage-shame or conditional as a first, middle, or last resort, depending on how reasonable the other is in repairing the scene or the relationship. Thus, for some, the moment the other fails immediately to apologize, the scripted response is to become furious rather than remain ashamed. For others this does not occur until the middle stages of such a scene, and for still others it is a last resort to be used very sparingly only when, despite attempted reconciliation, the other has proved beyond any doubt that he deserves the angry response. Yet another variation on the recourse to anger may be scripted as conditional, not upon the further response of the one who has offended but rather on the initial gravity of the damage and the density of the shame, scripting a further resort to anger either when the initial offense has been very serious or less serious. Yet another variation recruits anger to shame, not as part of the reparative script but rather as an unscripted consequence of a failure of affect-control scripts. Should such control scripts bifurcate affect into relatively ungraded, very intense anger or very mild anger, with few graded densities of anger, then the reparative script may become vulnerable to invasion of rage by virtue of the failure of anger control to provide fine enough gradations of anger to make a more graded response to damage-shame possible. This is a special case of the difficulties of diagnosis of the scripted rules for any scene, since any scene may recruit intersection of scripts with widely differing rules and targets.

Chapter 30
The Socialization of Anger

We have argued that differential magnification of positive over negative affect and the differential magnification of anger over other negative affect are critical determinants of the magnification or attenuation of anger. Clearly then, the socialization of anger can only be understood as part of the socialization of all the primary affects. We have thus far described the rewarding and punishing socialization of excitement, enjoyment, distress, shame, and disgust and dissmell. In the next chapter on terror, we will describe the rewarding and punishing socialization of that affect. We will now address the socialization of anger, which should be compared with the socialization of each of the primary affects inasmuch as no affect is an island. Bear in mind also that the description of these techniques of socialization addresses more than the problem of how anger is magnified or attenuated. I have studied socialization of affect as an explicit attempt to prepare a child for ideological partisanship according to the predominant ideologies of his nation, class, ethnic, gender, and religion, as well as the idiosyncratic biases of his parents.

SOCIALIZATION OF AFFECT AND THE RESULTANT IDEO-AFFECTIVE POSTURES WHICH EVOKE RESONANCE TO THE IDEOLOGICAL POLARITY

Let us now consider how the socialization of affect produces those ideo-affective postures which in turn make the individual resonate to the right, left, or middle of the road in the ideological polarity. We will consider in turn the socialization of each of the affects. Before we do this, however, we will present an overview of the matter.

What might be the origins of such a duality in man's view of himself? Consider the basic alternatives open to parents interacting with their children. At one pole is that return of the parent to his own golden age through identification with the child in play and shared delight. The child's zest for life and obvious joy in simple human interaction and in elementary curiosity and attempted control over his own body and the world in general can revitalize the adult personality. Such a parent bestows on the child the feeling that he is an end in himself and that shared human interaction is a deeply satisfying experience. Further, such a parent will not puncture the child's conception of his ability to control his parent. Eventually, such a child must come to the awareness that the world presents endless opportunities for the experience of varied positive affects—joy, excitement, love of people, of places, of activities, and of things. He becomes addicted to creating satisfaction for himself and for others.

There is another possibility open to any parent. This is the conjoint opportunity and obligation to mold the child to some norm. The norm may be a moral norm, a norm of "manners," a norm of competence, a norm of independence. In any case, the parent sets himself in opposition to the child and bestows upon the child the sense that positive satisfaction is necessarily an epiphenomenon, consequent to effort, to struggle, to renunciation of his own immediate wishes. His own feelings and wishes are devalued in favor of some kind of behavior which is demanded of him. When the child wishes to do one thing and the parent wishes him to do another, the normative parent must set himself in opposition to the child's wishes. He must convey to the child that what he wants to do is of no consequence when it is in opposition to the norm. What is expected of him, in opposition to his own wishes, may be presented with all possible attractiveness and positive sanctions, but the fundamental necessity of renunciation and devaluation of his own wishes, thereby of his self, cannot in a normative socialization be sidestepped.

In a middle-of-the-road socialization there are three distinct options. First, one parent socializes according to the left and the other parent socializes in the right-wing manner. Such an individual is exquisitely aware of the clash of ideologies, living as he does at the intersection of opposites. As such he is likely to be much concerned with the reconciliation of opposites. He is concerned too with the problem of communication between his divided selves and between the left- and right-wing ideologists who have little or no understanding of each other and who therefore cannot communicate.

The second type of socialization which produces a resonance with the middle-of-the-road ideology is by parents who are mixed in their own ideo-affective posture or in their own ideology. Such parents may swing from loving and playing with the child to a very stern, demanding insistence on norm compliance.

In the third type of socialization the parents do not swing from the right to the left but stiffen their left-wing attitudes with right-wing overtones and temper their right-wing strictures with left-wing softening. Thus, such a parent may say, "You and your friend can play and have as much fun as you would like so long as you don't make too much noise. If you do, you will have to stop and your friend will have to go home." Again, "I want you to clean up your room, and I'm not going to let you do anything else until you do that. Do you understand? I know that you and your friend have a date to play together this afternoon, and I would hate to have you miss that, but if you hurry and finish up with your room, I'll take you over to see your friend."

WHAT IS SOCIALIZED?

The socialization of anger is characteristically vigilant, insistent, strident, and pious, because of its real and believed toxicity. Given its potential for harm, no society can be indifferent to its socialization. Whether anger is to be in the service of a warrior or of a peace-loving society, anger must be tamed and disciplined, against cowardice and fear in the warrior society, against aggressive self-assertion in the society which aims at peaceful and harmonious coexistence. We cannot enumerate the entire range of types of the socialization of anger, since there are as many idiosyncratic variations within any society as between societies. We will address some of the more important options in anger socialization in the hope of increasing the degrees of freedom of choice in such socialization in future generations, as well as to construct a more fine-grained model of the socialization of affect in general.

We will emphasize the parent-child socialization of anger because the conjoint impact of primacy for the child and exposures to the high density of affect of the parent is peculiarly magnifying in the case of anger. There are nonetheless several ambiguities in the concept of socialization of anger, or of any affect, which we must clarify. First, we will not limit the meaning of the socialization of anger to what it is the parent does to the child. Instead, it is a sequence of scenes which we will take as the unit of analysis. Instead of describing a socialization of anger as involving physical punishment for a display of anger or aggression, we would include both the sequence of interactions which led up to such punishment and, most critically, the immediate and delayed responses by the *child* to the punishment, as well as the further responses of the parent to the child's responses. An adequate model of affect socialization in script theoretic terms involves the specification of general but nonetheless finegrained families of interactions. By the child's responses we mean not only the readily *observable immediate* responses but also the *internal* responses and the *delayed* responses. A child who has experienced a tantrum which was terminated by a physical attack on his person may continue to alternate between fear and backed-up anger which eventually invades his sleep as a recurrent nightmare. These are a properly considered part of the socialization process as what the parent did or intended to do. The process of magnification critically depends on the child's responses to the parent's responses as much as on either alone. Later the child may have quite different encounters with anger with his peers, with those more aggressive and with those less aggressive than he is. Later there are also the ubiquitous aggressive others watched for endless hours on the television screens, who may provide quite different models of anger and aggression.

Third, there are also other affects' socialization implicated in the socialization of anger. A very punitive socialization of anger has very different consequences when that parent also punishes any display of excitement and enjoyment, as well as cries of distress or fear, compared with a punitive socialization of anger which is attenuated by much tender loving care with respect to any affect other than anger.

Fourth, there are many critical structures, functions, and processes other than affect implicated in the vicissitudes of anger socialization. These include variations in children's intelligence and education, in somatotype, in strength and beauty. Thus, in a study of a representative sample of the United States population (Tomkins-Horn Picture Arrangement Test) I found both intelligence and education to be inversely related to anger and to aggression. The more intelligent and the more educated the individual, the less angry and the less aggressive. Being very strong or very weak and being very sensitive or insensitive to physical pain cannot be trivial factors in the long-run readiness for fighting or inhibition of aggression or of anger. As with any other single factor it is also unlikely that its effects can be entirely independent. Thus, a very bright, well-educated very strong mesomorph might not be as belligerent as a very dull, uneducated mesomorph. But both might nonetheless be much more aggressive in a warrior society or subculture than in a peace-loving society. There are not only innate, genetically endowed differences which modulate anger socialization but also accidental rewards and punishments independent of anger socialization. For example, an individual who is incapacitated (and apparently punished) by childhood diseases or by accidents which require long periods of enforced rest in a hospital may suffer inhibition of general activity and of the use of his muscles generally, including anger displays and fighting. Contrast this with a young boy's defeating a widely hated and feared bully in a fair fight, which leads to his becoming an idolized leader of his clique or of a gang.

Fifth, there is an ambiguity concerning the duration of the socialization process. It is my belief that the socialization of any affect is never completed but is rather a lifelong process which may continue to deepen the impact of early socialization, to attenuate it, to introduce conflict or ambiguity, or, in the unusual case, to reverse it. When, for example, a nation is defeated in war, as happened to Japan and Germany in World War II, the next generation may become much more pacifistic than their early socialization of anger would have suggested. A model child reared most gently, as in the case of Karl Marx, may much later set himself in deep hostile opposition to his beloved father and to capitalist society after that father unexpectedly turned "bourgeois" and demanded his son become self-supporting.

THE MAJOR TECHNIQUES: PUNITIVE VERSUS REWARDING SOCIALIZATION

The critical question in the socialization of anger, as in the socialization of the child in general, is whether the parent regards the child as an equal, as an end in himself, or whether he regards anger and aggressive behavior as an alien entity which must be controlled by the parent so that the child will be socialized according to the norms of the society in which he lives and so that his own authority and comfort are in no way jeopardized. If he empathizes with the child, then the child's anger is experienced not simply as an affront to his authority and to society, and a discomfort or danger to his own wellbeing, but as a feeling of the child which is at once as disturbing to the child as it seems urgent.

In what we define as a rewarding socialization of anger, the parent makes every effort to minimize the experience of anger in the child on the assumption that it is an essentially destructive experience, or at least that it creates a world for the child which is less than ideal. So whenever constraints must be imposed on the child by the parent, this is done in such a way as to minimize the arousal of anger. The chief factor here is the communication of the parent's anger. Anger, like most affects, is contagious. There is no better way for me to make you angry than to show you I hate you. The parent therefore enjoys the greatest initiative in the arousal of the anger of the child, by whether or not he elects to communicate his own anger when the child has offended him in some way. If the parent wishes to minimize the child's experience of anger, he will muffle his own anger and impose constraints on the child's behavior in such a way as to produce the least possible distress and anger. Requests to turn down the volume of a record or the TV or a game will be communicated with a tone of confident neutrality accompanied by a rationale: "I'm speaking on the telephone, dear. Would you do me a favor and turn the TV down just a bit, please?" If it is possible, he will move into another room if the child and his friends are enjoying themselves with a deafening hilarity. The child's needs will be weighed against those of the parent, by the parent, and in this court of justice there will be an attempt to minimize injustice.

In the punitive socialization of anger, the parent is an unconscious agent provacateur. At the slightest provocation, which grows slighter and slighter as the day wears on and as mutual irritability mounts, the parent's eyes flash and the tongue lashes out at the offender. "*Will* you turn that damned thing down—I'm sick and tired of it!" What is requested of the child is essentially identical except that now anger is almost certain to be aroused in the child. There are, however, many ways of arousing anger in the child other than the show of anger itself. In the punitive socialization of anger the parent may maximize the experience of anger in the child in a number of different ways. He may continually insult the child: "How stupid can you be, you clumsy oaf?" He may anger the child by frequently physically hurting him. He may anger the child by threatening to physically hurt him. He may anger the child by teasing him to the point of tears. He may anger the child by his indifference to the child's requests for help or attention. He may anger the child by continually interfering with his excitement and enjoyment in numerous activities and interpersonal relationships with his peers. He may anger the child by isolating him and locking him in his room or by depriving him of supper or privileges. He may anger him by saying he no longer loves him. Any of these actions by the parent may or may not anger the child. The child may respond to insult by shame, to anger with fear, to withdrawal of love by distress, and so on; but when there is a punitive socialization of anger, there is also an undercurrent of irritability on the part of the parent which accompanies these other negative sanctions, which enhances the probability of the child's responding to the complex of anger and other affects with anger. More often than not, the parent who is in effect an agent provocateur is convinced that it is the child's anger and willfulness which evokes his reactive anger.

Once the anger of the child has been aroused, whether in response to the parent or not, the parent, in the rewarding socialization attempts to attenuate the child's anger as much as possible. He tolerates it as a protest and an implicit plea for help on the part of the child. He may literally absorb the physical punishment of being struck by the child who is in a blind rage, without retaliating, on the assumption that it will be self-limiting if it is not fanned by counteraggression and on the assumption that he can control his own anger better than the child can control his. Further, he hopes to demonstrate to the child that his blind rage is not as physically destructive to the parent as he might fear, nor as destructive of the underlying love relationship as he might also fear, nor as likely to evoke massive retaliation as he might have feared. In the punitive socialization the parent regards the child's anger as an act of insubordination which must be defeated at any cost. Despite the fact that such a parent is often the primary cause of the anger of the child, he pictures himself involved in a holy war in which he is the representative of the forces of light and the child the forces of darkness. Fire must be fought with fire. In punitive socialization the initial contagion of anger from parent to child is fanned into wildfire by a sequence of angry outbursts, each of which intensifies the anger of the other until heroic measures are necessary to bring the inferno under control. In such a destructive competition the will of the parent may finally be imposed by either a reign of terror, of shame, or of distress, by a complete withdrawal of love, or of privileges, and by a redefinition of the nature of the interpersonal relationship between the parent and the child. In its most extreme form the hostile intention is to completely break the will of the child so that he will never again show anger to the parent. Such a hostile intention may be dictated purely by the anger evoked from what is regarded as insubordination, or it may be fortified by ideology. Thus, in the report on the Hutterite community, by Eaton and Weil, from early infancy most parents and teachers are engaged in an effort to break the child's will so that he can grow up into a "good" person. The most valued characteristics are a strong conscience, the submission of impulsive wants to community expectations, and the repression of rebellious attitudes against the authority of the mores and of individuals in positions of power.

Next, in the rewarding socialization of anger not only does the parent tolerate the anger of the child, but he attempts to teach the child to both tolerate and to control his anger. He does this in part by providing a model through his own tolerance and rolling with the punches of his child, and through providing love after the anger is spent, thus disproving the child's fears that he may have destroyed the parent or their relationship. He also teaches control by encouraging a complete catharsis of anger, which not only gets at the root of the problem but produces a series of more and more graded forms of anger and thus ultimately enables a finer modulation of anger than the dichotomy of blind rage and submission. Further, the parent encourages verbalization of the affect of anger, so that the mute, blind, slashing flailing of arms and legs can be translated into the verbal expression which he must eventually learn for the adult communication of anger.

In the punitive socialization of anger the child is taught to control his anger but not to modulate it, nor to tolerate it. He is taught essentially that the open expression of full anger toward the parent must end in his defeat. He is also taught that the weak are not only defeated but are appropriate objects of anger. In rewarding socialization the child is taught that the weak should be helped. In punitive socialization the child is taught that the weak—beginning with himself—are the prime targets for the discharge of anger. He also learns, however, that if he can find someone weaker than himself, he too can exercise punitive authority.

Next, in a rewarding socialization of anger the parent attempts to teach the child to cope with the sources of anger, as well as to tolerate and modulate his own anger. This includes coping with the parent himself who has made the child angry. The parent informs the child how and why the entire sequence was generated and what might be done about it in the future. If the source is an impersonal one such as the anger of the child because he is not able to do something as well as we would like, the parent helps the child to do better, to try again, and to control his anger lest this increase his incompetence. If the source is another child who is bullying him, the parent encourages him to defend himself against unwarranted aggression.

In the punitive strategy the parent's instruction in coping with himself as the source of the child's anger is limited to making the child play the entire game according to the parent's rules. If the source is impersonal, as in failure-induced tantrums, there is no instruction in the source but rather a repression of the tantrum. In dealing with the unwarranted aggression by peers the parent is more likely to encourage counteraggression insofar as he identifies with his own child and then regards the other child as insubordinate and willful.

Next, in the rewarding socialization of anger, such restrictions as the parent may have to impose on the child's anger and aggression is taught through empathy and identification. The child is taught that when his anger hurts others, it feels just as he feels when he is hurt by someone's anger and that this is why care must be exercised lest we create needless suffering in the expression of anger. He is taught by the golden rule. In the punitive socialization of anger he is taught essentially by negative sanctions and by norms whose rationale he cannot understand except that they are uttered with piety and enforced by the superior power of adults.

Finally, in the rewarding strategy when the parent does evoke anger, he softens its impact by offering some future restitution: "I know you hate staying in the house when we have to go out, but we'll play together tomorrow afternoon." In the punitive strategy no apology or restitution is necessary or considered desirable: "We're going out now, and I want you to go to bed, and I don't want to hear any arguments, do you understand?"

The differential consequences of the rewarding and punitive socialization of anger are considerable. The consequence of a rewarding socialization is an adult who is capable of being angry, absorbing anger, and fighting with others but who has a high threshold of arousal of anger because it has not played a major role in his life. When he feels angry, it is an anger which is graded in intensity correlated to some extent with the severity of the occasion. It is not preceded, accompanied, or followed by a host of other crippling negative affects such as fear or shame or distress. Most important, his self is not split into a bad, angry self and a good, loving self, nor are others divided sharply into nice, loving people and bad, hating people. He is capable of seeing himself and others whole. After intense anger he knows the way back to the pre-anger self and the pre-anger relationship. To show anger and to aggress upon someone can be followed by physical survival for both parties, by mutual love between both parties, by mutual respect between both parties, by excitement and enjoyment once again. In short, anger can be an incident and accepted for what it is, a temporary flash of lightning which may sear and burn but which may also illuminate and clear the air, which has been oppressive. This individual might also sustain anger if the cause is just and the sources are deep and stubborn and require a lifetime of revolutionary activity to uproot.

The consequences of a punitive socialization of anger we have to some extent examined in the paranoid posture and in Dostoevsky's *Notes from the Underground*. The whole spectrum of psychopathology is intimately linked with the punitive socialization of anger.

There is no affect whose punitive socialization can more jeopardize human development. Depending on the particular negative sanctions employed, the experience or the possibility of the feeling of anger can come to evoke utter humiliation or guilt, or anguish or overwhelming terror. There are single and multiple anger binds depending on whether the anger of the child was contained primarily by one or another negative affect or withdrawal of positive affect. Thus, there are anger-shame binds, anger-fear binds, anger-distress binds in which the child is finally reduced to the tears of impotent rage. There are also the multiple binds such as the anger-shame-fear-distress bind, in which anger led in turn from contempt, which produced shame; to another outburst against the parent, which was countered by a threat of a beating, which produced fear; to a final challenge to parental authority, which was punished with a slap on the face, which produced further shame at being beaten, fear at the possibility of a more severe beating and tears of anguish at the impotence against overwhelming force.

Every socialization of anger is idiosyncratic with respect to the cohort of parent and child. A parent whose own socialization of anger occurred during a war, hearing his parents sanctioning aggression, socializing a child when both are vicitims of a deep economic depression and experiencing helpless anger produces quite special attitudes toward anger, compared with a parent socialized during a period of harmony and affluence when anger is weak and spasmodic, socializing a child when both continue to experience the security and optimism of an affluent society at peace. Such cohort differences are especially poignant in times of radical social change for oppressed but militant minorities. Thus, a black child socialized by a submissive black father and mother is subjected to special strains when his peers challenge white supremacy and he is caught between love and respect and disgust for his fearful, passive parents as he is angry, excited, frightened, and joyous in joining the civil rights movement. Similarly for liberated young women. This is not to say that earlier socialization is either completely undone or unmodifiable but rather that the particularities of such historical sequences must be considered in any general model of the socialization of any affect.

According to my concept of *plurideterminacy,* it is not theoretically possible to determine the effect of any event in the life history of the individual because there *is* no single effect but rather there are *many* effects, which *change* in time. Further, the aftereffects of particular socialization scenes are plurideterminate with respect to time's arrow. A perfectly real effect of early experience can be later *reversed* or *attenuated* or made *conflicted* or *ambiguous* rather than further magnified cumulatively. If the process of socialization of affect is never ended, then the question of the effects of the early socialization of anger must be viewed in a more complex way than psychoanalytic theory suggested.

If there are as many degrees of freedom as I have suggested in the socialization of anger with respect to sequences of scenes, with respect to the number of models, with respect to the number of other affects, with respect to other structures, functions, and processes, and with respect to the never-ending length of the process as well as its reversibility in time, then how is one to deal with such complex interdependencies? The theory of magnification was devised to give a general answer to such difficulties. Magnification is a systematic biasing of complex sequences by connecting affect-laden scenes by "operators" which "order" some sets of scenes with other sets of scenes selectively and which cumulate some variance and swamp other variance, and thus both increase some of the theoretical aftereffects of experience while decreasing other possible aftereffects.

Finally, we must confront the inherent ambiguity of the implicit ideology and value judgments in any assumption that some modes of socialization of anger are better or worse or more rewarding or more punishing than other modes. What is rewarding depends critically on what we value for the individual and for society.

First, there are pluralisms of different values which may be orthogonal rather than conflicted or hierarchical in their relationships with each other. To be an aggressive or nonaggressive farmer may be no better or worse than to be an aggressive or nonaggressive scientist or politician or artist. There may, however, be *minimal* aggressiveness required to perform any role and *maximal* aggressiveness at an upper limit beyond which the individual's performance of social roles is in equal jeopardy. A farmer may have to destroy animals who threaten to destroy his crops. But an overly aggressive politician may not be able to govern because he cannot command sufficient loyalty from his potentially loyal opposition.

Further, different social roles within the same society may place varying premiums on aggressiveness. An unaggressive warrior or soldier is as anomalous as a very aggressive healer or social worker.

More serious is the perennial tension between values defined for the individual and for the single society and for the international community. A pacifist in a warlike nation surrounded by peaceloving neighboring nations is as problematic as a militant in a peaceloving nation surrounded by hostile neighboring nations.

Individual, national, and international criteria for appropriate anger and aggression are at the very least in varying degrees of harmony and tension in different historical periods, and there is neither total consensus nor total disagreement on the values of aggression and nonaggression for either the individual, his society, or the larger human community. Is it ultimately good for individuals and for societies to be totally nonaggressive and stable and unchanging and bad for them to be totally aggressive and continually expansive and changing, or is there some optimal rate of change which sets limits at both the upper and lower bounds of assertiveness and aggression? What prices are paid for excessive violence or for minimal violence? How much violence is, in fact, required for fundamental social change? Is a Gandhi or a Martin Luther King, Jr., less effective in freeing a colonial India or a caste-ridden American racist society of intolerable social conditions compared with the unrelenting class warfare of a Lenin, Trotsky, or Stalin in ridding Russia of one repressive regime to replace it with a better and well intentioned but equally repressive regime?

There appears to be no universal consensus possible on what is an optimal degree of *difference* between the values of the individual, the society and the total social community. If all individuals are in total harmony but the society stagnates, how shall we value this circumstance compared with one in which revolutionaries jeopardize commonly held values in the interest of future generations' enjoyment of a better society? Was the adversarial and transcendental ferment of Western civilization redeemed by its progress in science and technology compared with the stability and shared community of Chinese civilization?

Anger and violence is also engaged in the critical interpretation of the past, present, and future. Whig historians have been impaled on the dilemma that to attack the past is to encourage present disorder and anarchy, while to sentimentalize the past is to impoverish progress. To sentimentalize the future is to threaten the present no less than to attack it directly. Nostalgia for either the past or the future serves the violent radical purposes of reactionaries and revolutionaries alike, who are united in their intolerance of the present. The liberal has also been intolerant of his own society but is more mindful that the center may not hold as it is being transformed closer to the heart's desire.

There never has been nor is likely to be a consensus concerning fundamental values in the theory of value. Even when all constraints are lifted from imagination, as in the construction of utopias, the range of ideals closest to the heart's desire reveals the same varieties of constructions and controversies which plague mundane conflict. At the heart of such conflict are the great varieties of potential differential magnification of the plural apparatuses of the innate primary affects. So long as you deeply cherish the excitement of risk and change and combat and I cherish equally the enjoyment of communion, reunion, and reduction of stimulation, we have grounds for anger, disgust, dissmell, and violence. We would then deeply disagree on what should be considered an appropriate and "healthy" socialization of anger.

Having confronted the deep, unresolvable value conflicts inherent in the socialization of anger, we will nonetheless argue that there yet remain some nontrivial directives for considering some aspects of anger socialization that are better and more rewarding than their opposed, more punishing modes of anger socialization. Such would include any learned incapacity to detect anger in the self or other, as well as any learned incapacity to detect the presence of non-anger. It is equally critical that one neither deny nor exaggerate the presence of anger in the self or in the other.

Again it is critical that one be capable of *feeling, expressing,* and/or *acting* on ego-syntonic anger so as to be capable of *not* feeling, *not* expressing, and *not* acting on anger to the extent that the individual's values and circumstances dictate such control.

Further, it is critical that anger and its expression and its action be capable of being *differentiated,* graded, and modulated. This is a learned skill since the innate anger appears to be relatively crudely differentiated if at all. The importance of this lies in the extent to which the lesser innate differentiation imposes restrictions in possible degrees of freedom for the entire system. The modulation of anger extends the possibilities both in the direction of more finely nuanced anger appropriate to varying degrees of seriousness of the problematic and in the direction of more sustained and deeper violence against violations of central values. In contrast an infant is much less capable of being either mildly annoyed or of sustaining hostility.

Such modulation is also critical in the ability to move from positive affect to anger and from anger back to positive affect through a graded series rather than in volatile explosive affect. However, increased differentiation *also* includes and does not surrender such primitive volatility and explosiveness under circumstances judged appropriate for heroic anger or violence.

We will next address the nature of ideological scripts and their role in the interpretation, evaluation, and sanctions of anger.

Chapter 31
Ideology and Anger

IDEOLOGICAL SCRIPTS

Ideological scripts attempt to provide general orientation of the place of human beings in the cosmos and in the society in which they live, an account of their central values, guidance for their realization, sanctions for their fulfillment and for their violation, and justification and celebration of how life should be lived from here to eternity. Though it begins in cosmology and religion, it ends in social criticism. Although ideology reaches for coherence and consensus, shared ideologies, as in religion or politics, are at the same time fractionated and partitioned into conflict and polarity.

Ideological scripts are those we inherit by virtue of being a member of a civilization, a nation, a religion, a gender, an age, an institution, a class, a region, a family, a profession, or a school. They represent the various faiths by which human beings live and, alas, die. They are the chief agents of bonding and of differentiation and division.

They are the most important single class of scripts because of their conjoint scope, abstractness and specificity, stability and volatility, past, present and future orientation, shared and exclusive features, spatial as well as temporal references, guidance as well as rewarding and punishing sanctions, actuality and possibility concerns, and above all because they endow fact with value and affect. The ideological script deals not only with truth per se but with the domain of the "real." As such, it is a matter of faith, without which human beings appear unable to live. It is the location of actuality and of possibility in a world of affect and value. These scripts are at once self-validating and self-fulfilling. They are lived out as if true and good against others as false and bad, though just how tolerant they may be of competitors is generally included in the ideological script.

Twenty-some years ago (Tomkins,1963b,1965) I presented a theory of the structure of ideology in Western thought and a theory of the relationship between ideology and personality. I traced a recurrent polarity between the humanistic and normative orientations, between left and right, in fields as diverse as theology, metaphysics, the foundations of mathematics, perception, theory of value, theory of child rearing, theory of psychotherapy, and the theories of personality and personality testing.

This polarity appeared first in Greek philosophy between Protagoras, affirming that "man is the measure," and Plato, affirming the priority of the realm of essence. This polarity represents an idealization, positive idealization in the humanistic ideology and negative idealization in the normative ideology. Human beings in Western civilization have tended toward self-celebration, positive or negative.

I further assumed that an individual resonates to any organized ideology because of an underlying ideo-affective posture (or script, as I would now call it) which is a set of feelings and ideas about feelings which is more *loosely* organized than any highly organized ideology. An example from my Polarity Scale would be the items "It is disgusting to see an adult cry" versus "It is distressing to see an adult cry." I further assumed that the script or ideo-affective posture was the resultant of systematic difference in the socialization of affects, in which affects were more punitively socialized on the right and more rewardingly socialized on the left. I outlined a systematic program of differential socialization of each of the nine primary affects, which together produced an ideo-affective posture which inclined the individual to resonate differentially to ideology.

The postulated relationships between personality and ideology have proved reasonably robust over several years of systematic research (Tomkins, 1975, 1982) in which quite different methods were employed on samples of subjects varying broadly in age, educational status, intelligence, and sex, as well as normality and pathology. The consistent finding is that the ideological humanist is positively disposed toward human beings in his displayed affect, in his perceptions, and in his cognitions. The ideological normative is negatively disposed toward human beings in his displayed affect, in his perceptions, and in his cognitions.

We (Tomkins & McCarter, 1964) first standardized a series of posed affect photographs in accordance with my theory of the nine primary innate affects. These produced an average intercorrelation of .86 between intended judgments and the obtained judgments. Many of these same photographs were later used by Paul Ekman (1972) to demonstrate a worldwide, pan-cultural consensus in the recognition of affect from posed photographs, thus reconfirming with more sophisticated methods what Darwin (1965) had demonstrated a century before. Using these photographs, we selected one face showing the different affects, for presentation in a stereoscope. The subject was presented, in each trial, with one affect on the right eye and another affect on the left eye, in conflict with each other. Each affect was pitted in turn against every other affect; for example, the sad face of the subject was presented to one eye while the other eye saw a happy face. When the brain is thus confronted with two incompatible faces, the response is either a suppression of one face, a fusion of both faces, or a rivalry and alternation between the two faces. We predicted and confirmed that the left-oriented subjects would unconsciously select a dominance of the smiling face over all other affects (correlation, .42; N, 247). We predicted and confirmed that right-wing subjects would unconsciously produce a dominance of the contemptuous face (correlation of .60). The ideological orientation had been tested by use of my Polarity Scale.

Next, in a series of studies of five hundred subjects, we compared the humanistic and normative positions with the scores on the Tomkins-Horn Picture Arrangement Test. This is a broad-spectrum, projective-type personality test which had been standardized (Tomkins & Miner, 1956) on a representative sample (1500) of the American population. This was designed to be computer-scored, with separate norms for age, intelligence, education, sex, and a variety of demographic characteristics. The results again confirmed the same predictions we had made for stereoscopic resolution. The humanistic ideology is significantly related to general sociophilia, whereas the normative ideology is significantly related to sociophobia, in which there is avoidance of physical contact between men, an expectation of general aggression from others, and finally, an elevated social restlessness, which maximizes the number of changes from social to nonsocial situations.

Finally, Vasquez (1975) predicted and confirmed differential facial affective responses in left- and right-wing subjects. The videotaped subjects were previously selected on the basis of their Polarity Scale scores. The questions here tested concerned the use of the face, whether conscious or unconscious, whether voluntary or involuntary, as a communication of affect. Again we predicted that humanists would smile more than normative subjects. It was confirmed that humanist subjects actually smiled more frequently while talking with an experimenter than do normative subjects. There is no such difference, however, when subjects are alone, displaying affect spontaneously. Our prediction was based not only on the previously confirmed dominance of the smiling face in the resolution of stereoscopic conflict and on the dominance of general sociophilia over sociophobia in the Picture Arrangement Test but also on the grounds both that they have experienced the smile of enjoyment more frequently during their socialization and that they have internalized the ideo-affective posture that one should attempt to increase positive affect for the other as well as for the self. The learned smile does not, of course, always mean that the individual *feels* happy. As often as not, it is a consequence of a wish to communicate to the other that one wishes him to feel smiled upon and to evoke the smile from the other. It is often that which extinguishes the fires of distress, hate, and shame.

We also predicted that humanists would frequently respond with shame and that normatives would respond less frequently with shame but more frequently with disgust and contempt. Our rationale was that shame represents an impunitive response to what is interpreted as an interruption to communion (e.g., in shyness) and that it will ultimately be replaced by full communication. In contrast, contempt and disgust are responses to a bad other, and the termination of intimacy with such a one is assumed to be permanent unless that other changes significantly. These hypotheses were confirmed for shame and disgust but not for contempt. The humanist subjects do respond more frequently with shame if there is any perceived barrier to intimacy. The normative subjects not only smile less frequently but display disgust on their faces more frequently to the other who is tested and found wanting.

Thus, whether we put the question to the brain faced unconsciously with conflicting perceptual information or to the fully conscious subject asked to decide in what order to place three, different scenes to make sense of them, or whether unbeknownst to the subject we take moving pictures of his complex and ever-changing facial displays, the individual continues to respond as though he lives in one world, consistent in behavior, cognition, perception, and affect. It is, however, one world which is systematically different if he views it from the left or from the right.

I (Tomkins, 1965) have demonstrated a deep coherence between the differential magnification of specific affects and quite remote ideological derivatives.

Thus, if you believe it is distressing to see an adult cry rather than disgusting to see an adult cry, you also believe human beings are basically good rather than evil, that numbers were created rather than discovered, that the mind is like a lamp rather than a mirror, that when life is disappointing it leaves a bad taste in the mouth rather than leaving a bad smell, that the promotion of social welfare by government is more important than the maintenance of law and order, and that play is important for all human beings rather than childish.

This polarity did not exist before social specialization and stratification. If one is primarily an herbivore, one has no need either of massive energy output nor of ferocity nor of cunning. Thus, the Semang, who, according to Sanday (1981) have a "plant oriented mentality," wander through their forest "light-footed, singing and wreathed with flowers" (p. 19) searching the treetops for game or honey. Women gather wild plant food which is the dietary staple. Men occasionally hunt small game but not large game, nor do they engage in any kind of warfare but are more involved with their families and with child rearing. Everyone joins in harvesting fruit. They place a high value on freedom of movement and disdain the sedentary life of agriculture. The deities are male and female. There is sexual differentiation without stratification. According to Sanday, "The earth mother is perhaps closer to human affairs and the sky father more distant. He makes the thunder and she helps the people to appease him. She is the nurturant figure and he the commanding figure" (p. 21). Under such benign physical and cultural conditions, there is both a zest for life and no stratification either between the affects or between the sexes. Both the excitement of mobility and the enjoyment of cyclical seasonal harvest are valued, as are men and women.

I would suggest that this polarity, which I have traced over a two-thousand-year period, is a sublimated derivative of social stratification and exploitation. The left represented, then as now, the oppressed and exploited against their warrior oppressors.

Over time this debate shifted to classes which protested their inferior status, who looked to expropriate the expropriators: aristocrats against kings, bourgeoisie against landed gentry, proletariat against bourgeoisie, peasants against all.

The most important ideological transformations in civilization occurred when small game hunting became large game hunting and nomadic and when gathering became settled agriculture. In one, origins and deities became masculine, skyward-transcendent, aggressive, possessive, intolerant, competing with men, taking sides in covenants with elected men against their enemies, punishing their favored men whenever they contested for divine power. In the other, origins and deities became immanent earth or sea mothers, indulgent if sometimes capricious, a plenum which contracts and expands slowly (rather than quickly and destructively), more fixed than mobile, more conservative than radical and discontinuously creative, more cyclical than linear. In one, men dominate the society. In the other, women dominate. One represents a magnification of excitement, the other a magnification of enjoyment.

The ideological magnification of excitement versus enjoyment did not occur because the sexes differed in their preferences but rather because two very different ways of acquiring food became more and more differentiated.

When the relatively undifferentiated hunter-gatherers split into predatory big-game hunters and sedentary agriculturalists, differentiation ultimately became increasingly specialized and finally stratified into warrior nomads who subjugated peasant agriculturalists in the formation of states, empires, and civilizations.

According to Rustow (1980), "where conquering drivers or mounted nomads ran into a population of sedentary plow-peasants, they installed themselves as the ruling stratum and thenceforth lived on the labor, dues, and services of the subjugated" (p. 29). The conquerors "now needed only to devote themselves to ruling, to fighting, and to the knightly way of life" in the castle as "petrified horse" and the horse as "an itinerant castle." It was further elaborated as part of religious ideology "as in heaven also on earth," as Genghis Khan said, "one God in heaven, one Ruler on earth." Nomads were sometimes transformed into conquerors by religious enthusiasms. Thus, the Bedouins of Arabia had for centuries led a circumscribed existence until they were electrified into domination and conquest as a religious duty of Holy War by Muhammad about 650 A.D. They set the patriarchy of the stock breeders in the place of the matriarchy of the plow peasants. The settled peoples characteristically lamented the barbaric crudeness and rapacious aggressiveness of the nomads, who rejected the culture of the settlers as degenerate and seductive, as well as overly invested in arduous physical labor.

As Tacitus (1901) had said of the German invaders, "they think it base and spiritless to earn by sweat what they might purchase with blood."

This indivious comparison was much magnified by the appearance of the war chariot and the horse. The rider appeared on the stage of history as a new breed of man, terrifying in his intoxication with speed and his ability to effect concentrated mass formations in concert with his fellow horsemen. Their superiority over the panicked settled peasantry was enormous and irresistible.

It was the intensification of violence and warfare, first against big game animals and then against human beings which ultimately produced the now universal bifurcation, polarity, and stratification of the innate affects into excitement, surprise, anger, disgust, and dissmell versus enjoyment, distress, shame, and fear. This polarity in families of affects not only appeared in cosmology and the nature of the gods but also in the relationship between the sexes and finally in secular ideological conflict.

The major dynamic of ideological differentiation and stratification arises from perceived scarcity and the reliance upon violence to reduce such scarcity to allocate scarce resources disproportionately to the victors in adversarial contests. Nor is this a uniquely human phenomenon. Many animals begin stratification in contests between males for exclusive *possession* of females. The paradox in this is that the prize of the contest is diminished to a position of lower status.

Sanday (1981), in her survey of 150 societies, found balanced authority and power between the sexes in the absence of forces perceived to threaten social survival. Invidious stratification of the sexes appears to begin in environments perceived to be unfavorable (e.g., famine) and responded to by masculine violence. There appears to be a close link between using enemy *others* violently and stratification *within,* beginning with gender stratification and then spreading to age and class stratification.

Consider what must happen when the world turns more negative than positive. First, feeling as such is confused with the predominant, unwanted negative affects. To the extent that anger and violence appear to offer the favored solution to a world turned bad, many other consequences follow. The first is that of the believed benefits of slavery from warfare. One can thereby convert enemies to means to one's own happiness, as well as rob the other of whatever territory, property, or food he may possess. Second, anger is increased because the innate determinant of anger is a considerable increase in neural firing, which is prompted by a variety of nonoptimal scenes of the now problematic world. Third, the conjunction of superior masculine strength and superior life-bearing feminine capabilities predispose the male to violence and death and predispose the female against it. If the die is cast toward violence, then excitement and risk taking must be elevated against the more pacific relaxation of enjoyment and communion. Fourth, surprise must be elevated against fear. Fear is a deadly affect for successful warfare, being the most serious enemy within. It is assigned to the enemies to be defeated. One should try to terrorize one's enemy. Fifth, anger must be elevated above distress. Distress must be born manfully. A man must not weep but rather make his enemy cry out in surrender. Sixth, the warrior must above all be proud, elevating disgust, dissmell, contempt (the fusion of anger and dissmell) above the humble hanging of the head in shame. Shame is what the proud warrior should inflict on his enemy. He as warrior should rather die than surrender in shame.

Notice that we have now partitioned the full spectrum of the innate affects into two and that these sets are now individiously stratified. The successful man warrior is excited, ready for suprise, angry and proud, contemptuous and fearless. The loser has given up and is relaxed in dubious enjoyment, crying in distress, terrified and humble and ashamed. It is a very small step to assign these demeaned affects to women inasmuch as they are readily defeated by men in physical combat. It is also a small step to regard children as little slaves and women and to regard lower classes in the same way. Boy children then must prove themselves to become men in rites of passage. A variety of trials by fire involve the mastery of the masculine over the feminine affects. I am suggesting that social stratification rests upon the affect stratification inherent in adversarial contests.

Women and lower-status individuals are then pictured as loving, timid, distressed, shy, and humble. An effeminate man is a loser, but even warriors capable of seizing and possessing women necessarily remain deeply ambivalent about mothers and mother surrogates who are loving and tender rather than risk taking, capable of distressed empathy rather than hostile, modest and shy rather than judgmental and distancing in disgust, dissmell, and contempt, timid and fearful rather than competitive and dangerous. The very powerful magnification of the warrior affects guarantees that the feminine affects will become as alien as they are seductive. An overly masculine female becomes as repellent as an overly effeminate male.

Large-scale societies are necessarily stratified to the extent that they require government from centralized authority. The origin of both state and government appears to have been primarily adversarial in recorded history. Most large societies began either in subjugation or much less frequently in confederation against the threat of it. The resultant stratification, though responsible for high culture and civilization, has exacted severe prices from the exploited populations, ranging from the terror of mass killings through severe privation and distress, the shame of caste and class derogation, the reduction of autonomy and freedom of expression via imprisonment, to the reduction of opportunity for self development via reduction of social mobility and the acceptance of the exploiters as "superior" and of the exploited as "lower."

Stratification has inevitably generated a polarity of ideologies in defense of itself and in protest against itself. The defensive ideologies vary as a function of the nature of the society they defend, and so change as these societies are changed via ideological challenge. These are the normative, right-wing ideologies. Locked into polarized conflict with them are humanistic, left-wing ideologies, which also change as societies change. They inevitably address three somewhat independent, somewhat interdependent problematic social conditions. First of all, they emphasize the intolerable *costs* in one or another negative affect of the prevailing ideology. There is too much violence, too much terror, too much distress, too much shame, too much disgust or dissmell. Second, they place the blame for the problematic on the established normative authority, which must then change itself or be changed by those who suffer. The ideological polarity arises because the normative ideology places the blame for the problematic squarely upon those who suffer and complain. It is thus the welfare "cheats" who are to blame for their own problems. Third, they inevitably represent not only the protests of those defeated in adversarial contests and who wish to win but in varying degrees the feminine affects diminished by the adversarial stratification. The left is constituted in varying ratios of outraged masculinity and suppressed femininity, the militants and the flower children. The right is much less complex, apologist as it is of primarily masculine, adversarial stratification, buttressed by "tradition." If it isn't broken, don't fix it.

Since different societies vary in their degrees of stratification, in the costliness of exploitation, in the type of cost, and in their degree of modulation and mixture of the masculine-feminine principles, the normative humanistic polarity is *both* universal and idiosyncratic for each society and historical moment.

Hertz (1973) and Needham (1973) have shown that this polarity has appeared in many preliterate societies. The left and the right appeared to be a distinction about a family of analogs with a very large number of members. Left was widely believed to be related to right, as woman is to man, as profane is to sacred, as impetuous is to reflective, as dark is to light, as death is to life, as sin is to virtue, as falsity is to truth, as hell is to heaven, as the sky is to the underworld.

Every society and every civilization confronts somewhat distinctive sets of problems with a family of shared assumptions, which is a larger family than the polarized differences in projected solutions to these shared problems. Variations and contest are around the major central tendency. Civilizations and their ideologies are at once orthogonal to each other in their central values and similar to each other in the range of polarized alternative solutions to these central problems.

We turn now to some of the relationships between anger, violence, and power and ideology. We will argue that the magnification of anger and of violence as instrumental increases radically as the transformation of the instrumental to power as end in itself idealizes anger—violence as power. Second, the magnification of anger as aesthetic increases as that anger is idealized as romantic hate versus romantic love. Third, anger and violence and power are still further magnified when the conjunction of idealized power and romantic love and hate are transformed into the sacred, as exemplifying both the idealized power to create as well as destroy by an idealized god who is eternal and the object of idealized love and who defines his own violence as sacred, against profane violence, and who provides by the demand for sacrificial violence against the self a bridge between profane sin and atonement.

Thus, anger as amplification is increased first by magnification, then by idealization, as means turned end and as end turned into romantic hate, and finally to the ultimate by sacralization, in which the sacred unites both idealization of power and glory.

ANGRY VIOLENCE AND ULTIMATE UNIVERSAL WEALTH AND POWER IN THE HUMAN ECONOMY OF SCARCITY

Before barter and before money as media of exchange there was, and remains, a more universal and more fundamental bottom line in remedying perceived scarcity. This is to lay heavy hands on the body and spirit of the other, to defeat and intimidate, to rob, to enslave, and to enjoy the fruits of his labor as one's own. Nor is this limited to the human animal. Many other male animals fight for the exclusive possession of females as well as for other privileges and thus establish dominance hierarchies. The human master-slave relationship is, however, the most violent form of barter, which results from one warrior defeating another warrior, who trades his life for slavery to the victor, to whom, as ever, go the spoils.

As we have seen, not all human societies have suffered scarcity sufficient to prompt violence for the remediation of that perceived scarcity, but there has been and continues to be no scarcity of violence itself, between either nations, groups, or individuals. A slave is clearly a form of wealth, and indeed slaves were bought and sold for centuries. A more muted form of such wealth from successful violence was the power to tax the defeated adversaries, whereby imperial power was consolidated and maintained without the necessity of actual slavery but with the same ultimate threat of extermination should there be resistance to paying the victor. If the slaves or taxes are forms of wealth, then how much greater is the wealth which redeems, through the power to threaten and to intimidate and to defeat, not only some specific other but any and all others. An allconquering army has unlimited credit. It is as good as the gold which redeems any money. Indeed, anger is the credit of violence in much the same way as money is the credit of gold. Even the threat of anger can serve as the threat of violence, which in turn can serve as the wealth of the fruits of exercised violence.

Indeed, credit is most powerful either as money or as political power; the more credible it is, the less it requires continual redemption by the reserves of backup gold or by the display of force. Violence which must be continually exercised is inflated money and power. Successful intimidation is the most valuable species of violence.

THE TRANSFORMATION OF VIOLENCE AS INSTRUMENTAL TO VIOLENCE AS END IN ITSELF

Any means which is successfully exercised for one purpose may be used for additional other purposes. When a one-one means-end is employed as a one-many means-end, the magnification of the means is thereby increased. The greater the number of commodities any money will buy, the greater the value of that money. Money was thus radically magnified as a medium of exchange, over barter, because of its greater generality and abstract transformability. Not only could it be used to buy any one of many commodities, but it could be used to satisfy changing preferences should one wish to exchange one commodity for a different commodity. Since affects are also abstract and labile, an abstract one-many medium of exchange is the perfect medium for satisfying whatever and whenever the heart so desires.

The paradox of so perfect a vehicle of exchange, in the case of violence as means for reducing scarcity, is that the magnified means to many ends is readily transformed into a magnified end in itself. In such a transformation there is created a new, synthetic scarcity which far exceeds the original scarcity which prompted its remediation by instrumental violence. Any all-purpose means will be transformed into an end in itself by the perception of any barrier to its exercise, by the perception of any scarcity of the means to reduce all other scarcity. So the antidote to scarcity becomes the major source of possible scarcity and is thereby magnified as an end in itself, to be zealously guarded against any threat to itself and to be continually expanded against any possible attenuation or obsolescence. The wealthy now become miserly and greedy for more and more wealth—in this case, for the security of more power for violence. As we will see later, the same dynamic of magnification can transform a cigarette from an instrumental sedative to an addictive dependence in which any threat of scarcity of a cigarette is more terrifying than any misery the cigarette once sedated.

The essential dynamic of such a transformation is twofold. First, there must be an increasing effective reliance on violence as a means for reducing many types of scarcity. Second, there must be one or more dramatic, much magnified threats to the continued successful exercise of that now powerful, necessary violence. If this threat is responded to with increased, intransigent violence to counter violence, then the power of violence itself is transformed into the most central, most magnified end in itself, apart from its original purposes. Thus, the revolt of a peasantry against excessive taxation is put down ruthlessly more because of its threat to the power of violent authority to tax than because of the scarcity of the loss of that particular tax money.

Such threats to monopolistic violence have engaged capitalists and proletariat alike in collusive master-slave violence from the beginning. The threat of job insecurity has made the worker as worshipful of job and money as ends in themselves as it has made the employer worship Mammon and the redemptive violence necessary to enforce his monopoly of both wealth and force. Both capitalist and proletariat have transformed money into an end in itself because of the threat of scarcity, but the capitalist has also transformed the monopoly of violence and power into an end in itself to enhance and increase the security of his capital. As labor organizes, it too eventually values its militancy and power over the benefits for which it struggles.

Violence which was originally invoked for the remediation of scarcity lends itself, readily though not necessarily, to greed for violence itself, apart from its original utility.

THE MAGNIFICATION OF POWER AND ANGER AND VIOLENCE AS IDEALIZED ENDS IN THEMSELVES ALSO INCREASES THE IDEALIZATION OF AESTHETIC ANGER IN ROMANTIC LOVE AND HATE

Not all anger is instrumental. However, the idealization of anger, violence, and power is frequently accompanied by an idealization of noninstrumental anger in romantic love and or hate. Those who hold a monopoly of power are not only envied but may also be further idealized in romantic love and or in romantic hate. Further, those who are diminished or oppressed by their superiors may also become the objects of romantic love, by other inferiors or by their masters, or the objects of romantic hate by those above or below them in the power hierarchy. Ordinarily, power holders generate an ideology which encourages a view of themselves as altogether lovable, and their adversaries as well as their inferiors as eminently hateable.

Romantic love and romantic hate are characteristically focused on one individual but may be toward a class or an ideology, as in anti-Semitism or anticommunism.

I consider it a further magnification by idealization because its object is regarded as having a monopoly on many, if not all, good or bad qualities. The hated one not only distresses but equally frightens, enrages, shames, disgusts, dissmells in various ways. The other is made the incarnation of good and evil. No evidence or example is too remote or too improbable. Further, evidence of opposite qualities are readily integrated in either romantic love or hate. The otherwise negative feature becomes "lovable" in one case, while the otherwise positive feature becomes despicable and suspicious in the hated one. In hated minorities their "difference" is hated, but their attempts at assimilation are viewed as hatable "uppityness" or trying to "pass." Some are viewed as too lazy, while others work too cheaply, too long hours. Some are too materialistic, while others are too spiritual. Romantic love or hate is not only self-validating but also self-fulfilling.

Romantic love may be quite independent of romantic hate, but they are frequently yoked, so what is most hated are those accused of being nigger-, Jew-, Communist-"lovers." Nothing offends the romantic hater more than the danger of "loving" what should be hated and hating what should be loved. In recent years the assassins have targeted those who have appeared to love those they should have hated, beginning with Lincoln and including Sadat, the Kennedys, and King.

THE MAGNIFICATION OF GREEDY, ANGRY VIOLENCE EVOKES AN INTRANSIGENT WAR OF ALL AGAINST ALL AS UNSTABLE AND RISKY ECONOMY OF SCARCITY AND WEALTII

The initial magnification of greedy, angry violence creates as many problems as it solves. It creates, at best, an unstable and risky economy of wealth and scarcity in the war of all against all, so vividly described by Hobbes. Life becomes "nasty, brutish and short." Neither the victorious nor the defeated gain any permanent wealth or security. Great violence first of all generates great terror, of slaves for masters but also of masters for slaves. The strong fear the weak as much as the weak fear the strong, and with good reason. Order based on force is forever entropic, verging on disorder.

Second, great violence generates great distress.and suffering, not only for its many victims but for those identified with its victims and for the survivors, whether victors or losers. Violence is costly to all adversaries, even though more costly to the losers. The winners rarely achieve victory without serious cost to themselves in suffering and loss of life and wealth. The greatest distress, however, is that enforced by the inequality of distribution of resources upon the defeated.

Third, great violence generates great shame, disgust, and dissmell via the humiliation imposed upon the defeated. But the victorious too live under the shadow of possible defeat by other adversaries or defeat by rebellion of the humiliated. In many stratified societies rituals of reversal permit annual celebrations of license as a safety valve against such tensions and threats.

Fourth, great violence generates great guilt (immorality shame) in the hearts of the victors for their greedy violence against their adversaries. Even the earliest hunters have left evidence of rituals designed to attenuate the guilt felt for the killing of animals. But the vanquished are also vulnerable to guilt for their wishes to avenge their defeat and humiliation and exploitation. The magnification of anger and violence always constitutes a threat to self-control which evokes both shame (at loss of control) and guilt (at the consequences of intransigent engulfing anger). Although all affects are contagious and capable of increasing escalation, anger is particularly dangerous by virtue of its toxicity once it becomes contagious and escalates into an increasing round of violence and counterviolence. The social and personal costs of the disorder of the war of all against all have always prompted urgent and desperate efforts to reduce the severity of the several costs of violence become greedy and intransigent.

THE STABILIZATION OF VIOLENCE AS WEALTH

If the magnification of greedy angry violence evokes an intransigent war of all against all and produces an unstable and risky economy of scarcity and wealth, how have human societies been able to control, tolerate, and modulate such toxicity of the human condition?

I would suggest that there have been three major strategies variously implicit and explicit in the major ideologies, religious and secular, which have attempted the interpretation and evaluation of the role of anger and violence in the cosmos and in human affairs.

First is a double mini-maximizing strategy of attempted minimizing of negative affect and maximizing of positive affect by distinguishing and idealizing good and powerful anger and violence from bad and weak anger and violence. Second is an optimizing strategy of moderation in all things, including anger and violence. Third is a satisficing strategy of reducing all desire, including anger, to an acceptable minimum through varieties of asceticism.

Positive and Negative Idealization of Anger and Violence via Monopolization, Sacralization, and Stratification

Because magnified anger and violence is never totally effective and secure, because it entails severe suffering for all and so is judged bad and immoral, and because it becomes increasingly intransigent and difficult to turn off once it begins to escalate in contagious adversarial encounters, it perennially cries out for heroic remediation.

The most heroic attempted solution has been the mini-maximizing strategy of distinguishing good violence from bad violence and of exaggerating that difference. Consider that magnified violence is at best only half good in both senses of good. It is only partly effective and is only partly just. The human victor is neither omnipotent nor all good (or even good at all for his victims). Nor is there any apparent limit to either his violence or the violent resistance he evokes. The mini-maximizing solution has been to conceive of a force that is at once all-powerful and all-good which is capable of and justified in containing forces which are at once both weak and all bad. If all that is good in violence and all that is bad in violence are to be differentially idealized and sacralized, then there must also be a monopolization of the good to one locus and a stratification between the good and bad violence so that such a monopoly of force is both firmly located and guaranteed by a stratification of the lesser power (but evil force) beneath the monopoly of good violence. The distinction between good and evil anger and violence must not only be idealized and sacralized but guaranteed a monopolistic, stratified, appropriate distribution of both power and virtue so that there remains no question about who and what will ultimately prevail in the struggle between good and evil.

In fact the master is no saint and the slave is no sinner, but by the psychologic of the mini-maximizing solution, master becomes also a saint and slave becomes also a sinner through requiring that the violence of the victor, as master, be positively idealized and the violence of the loser, as slave, be negatively idealized. Power and virtue are not only conjoined but invidiously bifurcated and stratified. The master becomes more saintly, and the slave becomes more immoral. But monopolization of the good force requires not only a monopoly of effective force and a monopoly of virtue in its exercise but a further aggrandizement of the powerful in all respects and a further invidious degradation of the powerless in all respects. It would not serve the psychologic of this solution to posit an assortment of attractive features and powers to the sinner and an assortment of unattractive features and powers to the master-saint. That one must also have a monopoly of wisdom and information so that he is omniscient as well as omnipotent, while his counterpart is foolish and stupid as well as immoral and lacking in the power of violence. The monopoly of good violence must also be in the hands of the most beautiful creature, in invidious comparison to his most ugly adversary. Not only are the good, the true, and the beautiful in the invidious possession of the monopolist of violence but he is also assumed to enjoy every variety of possible advantage and heavenly delight including awe, reverence, and even envy from his underprivileged counterpart. Bad violence, in this solution, can only be killed by overkill, by monopolistic and stratified sanctification not only of violence but of all things good and bad, true and false, beautiful and ugly, wonderful and awful, by which good violence is made as different from bad violence as it is possible to conceive. The contrast between the vidious and invidious is systematic and complete.

It should be clear that so stark a contrast in the idealized solution to the many problems inherent in human violence was a major source of the religious impulse and the religious imagination. The intractable problems of violence, scarcity, slavery, and, above all, death, whether by violence or by destiny, cried out for understanding, compassion, and forgiveness and remediation. There were, of course, a variety of gods, appropriate to the variety of perils and promises of the varieties of ways of human life: hunter-gatherers, hunters, nomads, agriculturists, free, enslaved, and variously regimented and controlled, impoverished and wealthy in resources, money, and military power. It is not surprising that there arose a variety of religions and a richly textured pantheon of gods specialized to represent and remedy all the varieties of special pleading of the human imagination. Despite major differences in religions and their deities, especially in their degree of demandingness and recommendation of mini-maximizing versus optimizing versus satisficing strategies, there is nonetheless a remarkable consensus in the religious imagination. The consensus is in the belief that there is an ideal order, in which human existence is located and by which it should be governed. The discrepancy between the ideal and the actual may be great or small, and its possible remediation may be great or small and depend on great heroic effort or sacrifice, or smaller effort, or be inherited as grace; but somehow, some kind, and some quantity of remediation is hoped for, demanded, expected, and promised. Life is to become less violent, everlasting, more abundant, more ideal, and more godly, be that god transcendent or immanent. Despite the ubiquity of the severity of the problems of violence, slavery, inequity, scarcity, and death, the religious solutions, like the secular ideological solutions, vary both in their demandingness and in the extravagance and extremity of promise of immortality, justice, and universal love.

In the ideological solution of minimizing of negative affect and the maximizing of positive affect, whether the ideology is religious or secular, the gap between the ideal and actual is at a maximum, and the promised remediation is also at a maximum. God is totally ideal, and his children will inherit that kingdom and be cleansed of their anger, their guilt, their terror, their distress, and their shame, in everlasting excitement and enjoyment. In order for that to be possible there had to be constructed a role model who not only exemplified the ideal way of life for all, for all eternity, but was also a judging, evaluating, all-powerful, just avenger, critic, guide, and helper who would help his erring children to find their way. So the master and saint are combined and opposed to the slave and sinner. Power and morality are fused as legitimated authority and opposed to weakness and sin and are further exaggerated in vidious and invidious contrast by the attribution of everything positive to God and everything negative to his sinners. Now there can be no doubt about who has the right to exercise legitimated good violence and who is sinning by the exercise of bad violence, nor is there any doubt about who will prevail in the adversarial confrontation between God and humanity. Divine authority not only ought to prevail against bad violence but has the power to do so.

Not only has God been granted a monopoly of good violence and all other ideal attributes but there has been a stratification of both lesser power and more evil violence as well as an exaggeration of the remaining negative and positive affects. Humanity is not only cursed with sin rather than righteousness but also with shame, with distress, and with terror for eating of the tree of knowledge. Its excessive excitement has been judged sinful, and only its enjoyment is innocent. The affects appropriate for humanity are the passive ones, enjoyment, distress, terror, and shame. Anger, disgust, dissmell, and excitement are reserved for God. The affects have thereby been partitioned into righteous divine affects and into willfull, sinful, childlike affects. Only childlike enjoyment and adoration of God remain innocent and untainted. Humanity, in its mini-maximizing religious solution of the problem of violence, reduced itself to the status of erring child to parent who possesses a monopoly of wisdom, virtue, and violence, and so reintroduced the earlier partitioning of the affects in adult society. This is the essence of the Islamic-Judeo-Christian religious solution of the children of Abraham. Good violence is monopolistically possessed by an omnipotent, omniscient, all-loving but judging God, who punishes his sinning children for all their many vices, including their evil violence, for their pride in emulation and competition with their God, for their worship of false gods, for their consorting with Satan, for their improper lust for knowledge and for everlasting life. Indeed, eating of the tree of knowledge was occasion enough for the expulsion from the Garden of Eden, just in time before eating of the tree of life, which would have enabled Adam and Eve to live, like God, forever.

Many of the still older religions testify to the intense lust of humanity for immortality, to remedy the most serious scarcity against which the human being struggles. There is abundant evidence from many of the early myths (e.g., the legend of Gilgamesh) that heroic men contested with their gods for possession of the secret of everlasting life, only to learn that man was created mortal, solely to serve the gods. Even before the Egyptian burial of the pharoahs for everlasting life, the earlier megalithic religions projected a life after death through the exaltation of the ancestors as identified with the stones (as in the Stonehenge). A stone substituted for a body built for eternity.

Despite the variety of religions and their gods, the centrality of the problem of intransigent violence is revealed by a nearly universal reliance upon sacrifice for appeasement of the gods. Although sacrifice varies in its prescriptions and in its origins, I believe there is nonetheless one feature of it which is human and pan-cultural. That is the control of intransigent anger and violence by turning it against the self and thus affirming love and fidelity and atonement for hate. A derivative of sacrificing the self is the sacrifice of one's dearest, most notably in God's demand that Abraham sacrifice Isaac. One of the most extraordinary features of Christianity was the sacrifice of the son of God in the passion of Christ, thereby tilting the ideal away from a more wrathful God toward an idealized God of love. This was a consequence of the attempt to modulate the exclusiveness of the covenant between God and his chosen people which had guaranteed that God would smite the enemies of the Israelites in return for their fidelity. In Christianity the covenant is less exclusive and more loving and thereby provided a purer and more universal love as model and as ideal for all.

The conjunction of the monopoly of power, good violence, and saintliness, and the contrasting stratification with invidious weakness, bad violence, and immorality, as a mini-maximizing religious solution to the problem of violence was fateful both for secular ideology and for the self-serving rationalization of the power of the politically and economically privileged over the underprivileged. Nor did it lose any of its influence as authority was more and more vested in the will of the majority. The "people" could impose their will, as the general will, upon minorities with as much piety and force as they themselves had suffered under the divine right of kings. Monopolistic power not only corrupts but positively idealizes itself as it negatively idealizes its adversaries in collusive stratification of resources, classes, genders, information, and affects. To the extent to which the monopolistic, mini-maximizing religious solution continues to exert its hold on ideology and the exercise of political, economic, social, political, and informational power, the haves and the have-nots are locked into an uneasy, collusive tension which masks the naked reliance on violence as the bottom line of privileged power by attributing more wisdom, more goodness and religious piety, more beauty to itself than to those assumed to lack wisdom, to be immoral, ugly, and either lacking in religious faith or having the wrong faith. Mini-maximizing ideology is not only divisive and adversarial but self-glorifying. It is an inherently unstable solution to the problem of intransigent angry violence.

The modern nation-state does indeed possess a monopoly, not only of force but of many of the prerogatives formerly attributed to God. It can require sacrifice of life in the defense of the state. It can imprison or execute for many varieties of crimes, especially of infidelity to the national interest as "treason." It can exact tribute in the form of taxation. It can require deference to its symbols, such as in saluting its flag. It can monitor and put under surveillance any individual or group judged to be dangerous or subversive of its power. It can collect many varieties of information about its citizens and at the same time restrict their freedom of access to privileged information. It can restrict freedom of movement within its borders as well as outside its borders and regulate such mobility via passports. It retains the power of eminent domain by which it can condemn the private use of property when judged to conflict with the larger interest. It can seize private property and nationalize some or all of the means of production. It can outlaw religious worship or declare one religion as the national religion. It can designate a judicial authority as the "supreme court," from which there is no further appeal, thereby attempting to sufficiently sanctify a secular branch of government to put an end to hostile, intransigent controversy which might otherwise endanger the authority of the state if it were permitted to be endlessly contested. It is the perennial danger of intransigent, escalating angry violence which has engendered a quasi-religious solution in the guise of an all-wise supreme court. The American separation of church and state is a more mundane attempted solution for the perennial danger of religious warfare as a threat to the power of the nation-state. The state can control the education of its citizens. It can control the practice of medicine. It can control a variety of welfare programs. It can control the arts and the sciences. It can control the practice of agriculture. It can control the practice of various professions via licensing.

It is not difficult to imagine how much more totalitarian modern society might become.

Indeed, as the world becomes more populous, more interdependent, more capable of surveillance and information control and increasingly capable of using lethal force, the pressure for the formation of one megastate may become irresistible. Whether such a one-world would be more or less benign or malignant would depend heavily upon its dominant ideology.

We turn now to an overview of the secular ideological solutions to the problems of anger and violence. In the mini-maximizing secular ideologies, the debate has centered on the locus of value and reality. Is "man the measure" as Protagoras represented the humanistic polarity? Or is it the realm of essence which exists independent of space and time, prior to man, which is the locus of reality and value, as Plato represented the normative polarity? Although Protagoras and Plato are poles apart, with fateful consequences for the problem of violence, and although this polarity has dominated Western thought for over two thousand years, it nonetheless masks an implicit consensus which is only revealed when we compare both of these adversaries with other ancient theorists both in Greece and in the Orient. That consensus is a mini-maximizing strategy. These secular ideologies are at a very short remove from the religious version of the mini-maximizing strategy. Both Protagoras and Plato are extravagant in their conceptions of reality and value. Theirs is an overweening pride in the power and glory of humanity or of the realm of essence. The implicit question behind their actual questions is the question, is man really a god as he is (the "measure"), or does he have within himself, in his reason, a capacity to contact the eternal realm of essence? Both are overreachers with a lust for the absolute, differing only about its locus.

Compare both Plato and Protagoras with the optimizing ideology of moderation of Aristotle. In his *Rhetoric,* virtue is conceived as a balance between excess and defect, "free from the extremes of either." Men in their prime

> have neither that excess of confidence which amounts to rashness, nor too much timidity, but the right amount of each. They neither trust everybody nor distrust everybody, but judge people correctly. Their lives will be guided not by the sole consideration either of what is noble or of what is useful, but by both; neither by parsimony nor by prodigality, but by what is fit and proper. So, too, in regard to anger and desire; they will be brave as well as temperate, and temperate as well as brave. . . . [A]ll the valuable qualities that youth and old age divide between them are united in the prime of life, while all the excesses or defects are replaced by moderation and fitness.

This is, of course, but one of many systematic differences in their visions. I have used it only as a vivid contrast to what is common in the positions of both Protagoras and of Plato.

Consider another, centrist, optimizing position of moderation, that of Confucius.

The range of responses to social disorder and violence is, in part, similar the world over and might be interpreted as supporting the theory of polarity between humanist and normative positions. Thus, in early China, from the eighth to the third centuries B.C. there was increasing social anarchy with the collapse of the Chou dynasty. Whole populations were put to death in mass executions. The problem forced upon Confucius and others was, how can such violent human beings live together? The major responses were, first, the classical right-wing position of the legalists, or Realists. Han Fei Tzu's answer was massive and certain use of law and force. Human beings are inherently evil, but they can be contained by a large militia and effective police force. Second was the classic left-wing response of Mohism. Mo-Tzu proposed love not force. Five hundred years before Christ, Mo-Tzu argued "But whence did these calamities arise? They arise out of want of mutual love. . . . It is to be altered by way of universal love and mutual aid." Confucius rejected both love and force, defending what appears to be the classic middle-of-the-road position. Both *jen,* the source of good-heartedness in the person, and *li,* order, are needed for individuals to live together in harmony. Harmony is the primary aim for both the individual and the society. Only via great respect and love and filial piety in the family can inner greatness and outer greatness be achieved. The good life is a hard-won achievement which results from the cultivation of the tradition which had existed in China's past, in the period of Grand Harmony.

Here we have, then, a humanistic left-wing position, a normative right-wing position, and a centrist position of moderation. However, all of these ideologies shared the same basic central problem of how to restore harmony to a society which had been torn asunder by violence and great disorder, which was *not* the problem addressed by Protagoras, Plato, and Aristotle. Further, the Chinese were concerned primarily with the social and the finite and with the immanence of this world, not with the transcendence of the infinite and otherworldliness and the realm of essences.

Finally, it is a concern with the maintenance of tranquility, enjoyment, and stability, not with the guarantee of excitement, risk, competition, growth, and progress.

The Chinese conjoined the affect of enjoyment with its investment of sameness, particularity, and tradition in contrast to the Western investment in excitement, abstraction, transformation, and change. They loved the here-and-now and particularly the land which they inherited from their ancestors, who had loved it before them. Their science was applied to satisfy present needs rather than pursuing a remote, never-to-be attained final truth. Their worship of learning stressed the mastery of particular texts. Their gods were their ancestors, not remote and out of space and time. Their interpersonal relations stressed the importance of affection and piety for their parents, their mates, and their children rather than the quest for the perfect romantic love and lover. Similarly, their political life included rebellions, but not revolutions in the Western sense. They would kick the rascals out, but expect no utopia as a result.

In radical contrast the shared consensus in the United States is individualism, egalitarianism, freedom, the pursuit of money in a capitalistic competitive economy, coupled with the transcendental Christian good works for those who fall behind and the Christian sense of sin for both winners and losers, as well as the endless hot pursuit of the infinite and the transcendental in science, politics, love, and religion. The left-right polarity now centers on the relative importance of big business versus big government, the relative importance of the environment versus the need for economic growth, the relative importance of military power versus peace, the relative importance of caring for the sick, and aged, and the poor versus selfhelp or turning the responsibility over to business, presumably more efficient than government.

If one examines the ideologies of the major civilizations, one can map the Western humanist normative polarity onto every civilization. When I first did this, I was excited by what appeared to be a universal in the structure of ideology. I was further encouraged that the same dualism had appeared in preliterate societies, according to Hertz (1973) and Rodney Needham (1973).

After the heady excitement about the apparent generality of this polarity subsided, I was confronted with the following paradox. If societies as different as the Zuni, the Muguwe, China, India, Greece, France, and the United States all agree that the left and the right is a fundamental polarity, then how does it happen that these are also radically different cultures, societies, and civilizations? It then became clear that the polarity concealed as much as it revealed. If the United States and ancient China both had a left, right, and center which were similar in some fundamental way, then they must also be different, in an equally fundamental way and perhaps, as I will argue, in a *more* fundamental way.

I will argue that every society and every civilization confronts somewhat distinctive sets of problems with a family of shared assumptions, which is a larger family than the polarized differences in projected solutions to these shared problems, and that variation and contest are around the major central tendency. Civilizations and their ideologies are at once orthogonal to each other in their central value and similar to each other in the range of polarized alternative solutions to these central problems. The polarity between the humanist and normative ideologies appears to function as a universal moderator of otherwise widely differing ideologies. The variations within ideologies which are what are best described by the polarity.

Thus, in marked contrast to the problem of social violence which Confucius confronted, Buddha, in India, experienced a sudden confrontation with individual suffering, the ravages of disease, old age, and death. His ideological response was a deeply introversive one. One hundred years after his death Buddhism divided into a left- and right-wing schism of Theravada versus Mahayanna Buddhism. One group argued that Buddha had been a deeply compassionate man, while the opposed group represented Buddha as a disciplined man. The humanistic-normative polarity here developed within the context of distress and suffering rather than aggression; within the context of the individual's problems, rather than the society's problems; and within an introversive rather than an extroversive mode. And so China resisted the intrusion of the deeply introversive Buddhism for some time until it had been tailored to meet the Chinese concern with the more social problems.

Satisficing Asceticism

The third type of ideological solution to the problem of anger and violence is the strategy of satisficing, of a radical reduction in what one demands from life, via varieties of simplicity and asceticism. These strategies are orthogonal to the normative versus humanistic polarities. Asceticism may be opposed to excessive complexity, or to quantity of demand, or to quality or impurity of demand.

In China there was an alternative centrist ideology to Confucianism. There was another middle-of-the-road position in Taoism. Taoism, like Confucianism and Mohism and Realism, was for harmony and against strife, but it was *also* against Confucianism and its emphasis on regulation and tradition. It was for Nature and the easy way. The ideal life is the simple life, not the cultivated life. There is a harmony and perfection in nature. Both man and society must be in tune with Nature.

If Taoism is the asceticism opposed to excessive cultivation and complexity, Stoicism is the asceticism opposed to the quantity of overweening demandingness. Thus, Seneca:

> There is but one chain holding us in fetters and that is our love of life.... A person who has learned how to die has unlearned how to be a slave.... So the spirit must be trained to a realization of its lot. It must come to see that there is nothing fortune will shrink from, that she wields the same authority over emperor and empire alike and the same power over cities as over men. There's no ground for resentment in all this. We've entered into a world in which these are the terms life is lived on—if you're satisfied with that submit to them, if you're not—get out, whatever way you please.... In the ashes all men are levelled. We're born unequal, we die equal.... Devotion to what is right is simple, devotion to what is wrong is complex and admits of infinite variations. It is the same with people's characters; in those who follow nature they are straightforward and uncomplicated, and differ only in minor degree, while those that are warped are hopelessly at odds with the rest and equally at odds with themselves.... What we can do is adopt a noble spirit, such a spirit as befits a good man, so that we may bear up bravely under all that fortune sends us and bring our wills into tune with nature's.... They should assume that whatever happens was bound to happen and refrain from failing at nature.... Let fate find us ready and eager. Here is your noble spirit—the one which has put itself in the hands of fate: on the other side we have the puny degenerate spirit which struggles, and which sees nothing right in the way the universe is ordered, and would rather reform the gods than reform itself.

Taoism and Stoicism follow nature, but for one it is the easy way, for the other it is a noble struggle against a self-indulgent over-demandingness, which is petulant and resentful.

Finally, there is an asceticism of purity and quality, as in Tolstoy, who struggled for chastity and sexual purity against his lust, for poverty against his own wealth, for the simplicity of the life of the peasant against his own aristocratic heritage.

So much for an overview of the place of anger and violence in some of the varieties of religions and secular ideologies.

Chapter 32

Anger-Management and Anger-Control Scripts

AFFECT-MANAGEMENT SCRIPTS: SEDATIVE

Although these models were developed to understand substance dependency, I have since generalized them to deal with the management of any negative affect. I will present them therefore both in their specific application to cigarette smoking and to the scripted management of anger or any negative affect in any scene.

Because affect-control scripts are imposed on all individuals to "socialize" affect, one inevitable consequence is the production of backed-up affect, which may be more problematic to the individual then the original problem which activiated anger or distress or terror or shame or disgust. Therefore, in most societies affect-control scripts generate affect-management scripts to deal with the toxic side effects of the affect-control scripts. It is not unlike a second medicine one must take to cure or modulate the side effects of the first medicine.

A sedative script is one which addresses any problematic scene primarily as though the first order of business was to attenuate or to reduce entirely the negative affect which that scene has evoked. The script may or may not address the further problem of dealing with the nature of the scene which is so troubling. The individual may use the sedative primarily as instrumental to further problem solution or as an end in itself, quite independent of the source of the negative affect. Further, the attempted sedation may or may not be successful. A cigarette may enable an individual made angry to be less angry, one made fearful to be less fearful or entirely calm. Quite independent of its effectiveness as a sedative of the negative affect, the cigarette may enable the individual to be more effective in dealing with the problematic scene or not. Thus, he may be helped just a little to be less fearful, but this small affect difference may make all the difference in dealing with the scene. Or he might become entirely free of fear via the cigarette and either give up on solving the problem of the scene itself or try and fail despite having become much less fearful because of the cigarette. Sedation refers to the intention to reduce the negative affect (whether successful or not), not to solving the problems which may be the source of the negative affect. This is not to exclude the individual generating a sedative script which is *intended* to be instrumental to problem solving. This is not uncommon with some sedative cigarette smokers who rely heavily on such sedation to help them solve their problematic scenes rather than simply to sedate themselves. I will refer to a script as a sedative to the extent it intends attenuation or reduction of negative affect per se, independent of its further role as instrumental to problem solving.

Clearly, a cigarette is but one type of sedative act. One may attempt self-sedation via alcohol, drugs, eating, aggression, sex, travel, driving, walking, running, TV watching, conversation, looking at nature, reading, introversion, music, or a favored place. It should be noted that none of these are sedative if they are used to *avoid* negative affect (though they may be so used).

It should also be noted that negative affect need not evoke a sedative script. Attention may be so riveted on the problematic scene and the urgency of dealing with it that the negative affect remains as background while the scene proper is figural. Thus, an approaching atuomobile apparently out of control rarely prompts attempted sedation. The individual in such a situation is likely to devote full attention to driving his own automobile so that he avoids the threatened danger rather than attempt to nurture himself.

Sedative scripts are unlikely when threat is perceived as mobile and urgent in demand of nonaffective remediation. They are also unlikely when there are normative ideological constraints against sedation, whether by the self or by others. It is for such reasons, I believe, that cigarette smoking in general is much less common among engineers, who tend to be somewhat uncomfortable with their own affects and sufficiently "impersonal" to be intolerant of "babying" the self.

Sedative scripts occur also under a limited range of the ratio of density of positive to negative affect. One will have no need to generate sedative scripts if that ratio is greatly biased toward positive affect because the individual suffers very little negative affect and therefore has not achieved sufficient density to become salient enough to prompt strategies for negative affect remediation as such. Further, the basic optimism which is a general derivative of such positive affect bias usually makes attempted coping with problematic scenes both salient and effective. Such an individual *may* sedate himself on the occasion of intractable negative affect scenes (e.g., the death or serious illness of a loved one or the experience of intractable pain from toothache or disease), but these are not scripted; rather they are conditional, impromptu responses to isolated, densely punishing scenes.

Further, sedative scripts do not ordinarily occur when the ratio of positive to negative affect is extremely biased toward negative affect. Under these conditions sedative scripts are characteristically transformed into addictive scripts. Therefore, if we know that an individual is governed by sedative scripts or by addictive scripts, we possess critical knowledge of some basic parameters of his personality.

Sedative scripts are also conditional scripts. They are quite different in this respect from addictive scripts. They are used *only* to sedate experienced negative affect and therefore vary in frequency and duration of activation dependent on the experienced frequency and duration of negative affect. As a consequence, the frequency of sedative acts is dependent not only on what I have defined as source affect (e.g., the affect prompted by a scene rather than by the outcome of a response to a scene) but also on the relative effectiveness of the scripted sedative, be it smoking a cigarette, an angry claustrophilic introversive response, or a claustrophobic extroversive response, as in a flight to being with others. If such attempted sedation is effective, the sedative response is terminated and its general frequency reduced. If, however, the sedative act is relatively ineffective, it will be repeated, and the general frequency of sedative responses will increase. Paradoxically, sedation increases as a conjoint function of the density of source affect and of the *ineffectiveness* of the sedative affect. Sedative smokers who smoke as frequently as addictive smokers (but who are nonetheless *not* addicted) are individuals whose overall density of negative affect is high and for whom the attempted sedation is relatively ineffective. To some extent such an individual suffers a phenomenon similar to biochemically based drug habituation. He needs more and more of the drug as it becomes less and less effective as a sedative. Indeed, most sedative scripts suffer the difficulty that their capacity for reducing and attenuating negative affect is limited and diminishes as the density of negative affect increases.

We can also determine the characteristic loci of negative affect by noting the types of scenes in which the individual resorts to sedation. Thus, some smokers are surprised to learn that although they smoke only when they are alone, some smoke only when they are surrounded by others, some smoke only when in the bosom of their family, and others smoke only when working at their business, whereas many smoke under all circumstances. Because of the specific conditionality of the sedative script and the unconditionality of the addictive script, one can reliably differentially diagnose these scripts by asking whether the individual smokes (or invokes other sedative acts) when he is on vacation. The addictive smoker is surprised by the question, responding immediately that he does. The sedative smoker may also be surprised by the question but also by the answer which is evoked. He often discovers, for the first time, that he does *not* smoke at all at such times. This illustrates an important feature of many scripts, that the "rules" may be so overlearned and skilled via compression that their presence becomes visible only by their effects.

In the mother-child relationship, sedative scripts may require the presence of the mother or a knowledge that she is near or readily available whenever the child feels distressed, afraid, angry, or tired but *not* otherwise. Such a child may be able to play endlessly without access to or wish for maternal comforting so long as all goes well.

There are sedative scripts which are equally opaque to the individual as to the personologist. Thus, what I have labeled doable scripts may be employed as sedatives to reduce or attenuate anger (e.g., by kicking furniture or by hitting the self) whenever anger is activated. Such responses are not meant to "hurt" anyone (even though the individual may hurt himself by such acts) but rather, hopefully, to attenuate or reduce the anger. It need not be effective to be so scripted, any more than smoking a cigarette guarantees negative affect sedation. In the case of one individual I studied in depth, he dealt with otherwise unreducible rage first by alcohol, then by provocative behavior toward the police who would then beat him into unconsciousness. As he was being beaten, rage would be displaced by enjoyment because, as he described it, he had gotten "even" and he had gotten it out of his "system." He was more than willing to pay the price of punishment since it reduced *both* his anger and his guilt. These scripts were replayed every weekend. The sedative script in such a case becomes collusive, requiring as it does that the other act in such a way that the intolerable anger is finally reduced. This script was one of a family of nuclear scripts in the counteractive mode. The sedative script need not, however, be a nuclear script.

To summarize, sedative scripts require that negative affect become sufficiently differentiated and salient from the scene in which it is embedded that it can become the primary target for attenuation or reduction, independent of its possible further instrumental function. In order for this to occur the density of the ratio of positive to negative affect must be neither so positive as to reduce the need for sedation nor so negative as to prompt an addictive script. Further, the individual must believe in the *possibility* of reducing negative affect, rather than experiencing himself as a totally helpless victim or as one who can do no more than celebrate his own misery. Further, he must believe in the *desirability* of reducing his own negative affect rather than be constrained by ideological norms against comforting himself. He must also favor the *self* as agent of sedation rather than seeking help from others to reduce his suffering.

Although any individual may script a cigarette or alcohol or dope as a regular sedative for anger and/or any negative affect, he may also script a favorite place or person or kind of activity (e.g., walking) as a repeatable sedative which is resorted to quite exclusively for "calming down" the rage which otherwise would consume. Thus, one parent may be used as a sedative to neutralize overly toxic contacts with another parent.

Eating also lends itself to sedation of anger. This occurred in one case I studied in which a distraught mother had repeatedly used food to calm her angry child.

We have thus far considered backed-up anger as requiring and prompting sedation. We will next consider the case in which anger is used to sedate other negative affects and at the same time reduce itself. In such cases anger itself is the opiate for backed-up intolerable affect.

DIFFERENTIAL SEDATIVE EXPLOSIVE RESPONSES

To the extent to which there has been major magnification of distress, of terror, of shame, of disgust, and of dissmell and none of these can be directly resolved and reduced except through rage and/or aggression, then these may become differentially magnified as sedative but explosive responses to what is perceived as excessive suffering. This is not to say that these are, or are perceived to be, solutions to life's problems, but rather that as the quantity of negative affect mounts and their attempted solutions prove abortive, the individual is more and more vulnerable, first to the passive, reactive triggering of rage and then to the equally reactive aggressive response to that rage. The aggressive response under these conditions is impulsive and explosive—pounding his fist on the table, kicking, throwing something to break it, shouting obscenities, hitting himself or anyone at hand. Its major aim is to feel and express the anger with the hope that it will reduce the excessive suffering which prompted the rage. Anger in this case can serve as a sedative which displaces and masks other negative affects, despite the fact that anger itself represents an increase in neural stimulation and in suffering. It serves such purposes in much the same way that an individual may inflict pain on himself in order to mask pain passively experienced (e.g., under medical or dental procedures). The pain he inflicts on himself is greater than the externally inflicted pain, yet it is preferred because the recruited affects to such pain, characteristically fear and shame, together with the pain, are worse than greater pain voluntarily inflicted which is initiated by anger, pride, and recruited positive affects against the passively recruited fear and shame of helpless victimage. Explosive anger and aggression can serve as an attenuator and reducer of any excessive and passively suffered distress, terror, shame, or disgust whenever it is ego-syntonic and identified as the self's own true feeling against imposed suffering.

I have observed one extraordinary case in which such moral outrage terminated a schizoaffective psychotic episode. This was a patient with a manic-depressive history whom I had to hospitalize, when, following a year's enforced passivity due to a back injury, he became manic in denial of his enforced passivity and "failure," as he had experienced lying on his back for a year. This was a man who had been a very active and successful professional most of his life. When he lost most of his money during the Great Depression following the crash of the stock market in 1929, he seriously entertained suicide. His mother had been a manic-depressive. Two of his brothers were also manic-depressives. They did take their own lives at that point. He did not, as he told me, because of his concern lest his wife and children suffer too much if he were not alive to care for them. As he entered the mental hospital, he said to me, "This is punishment for a life long of sin." During his manic phase he had relived, with hallucinatory vividness, his running away from the battlefield during the Russo-Japanese war in order to see his beloved mother once again. The Oedipal nature of this hallucination was suggested by the importation into this scene of a brutal officer who "beated me." This individual ordinarily spoke faultless English. Under the pressure of the manic attack he reverted to his earlier, more primitive use of the English language. I presumed that this scene evoked shame at his desertion as a soldier, excitement and enjoyment at the prospect of reunion with his mother, and guilt and terror at the hands of the brutal surrogate father who might and, as he hallucinated did punish him for the conjoint offenses of desertion and seeking his mother.

This was an individual whose self-esteem rested in large part on counterphobic sexuality, on successful activity and achievement, and on free-flowing anger and aggression. Failure and passivity were lethal for him and exposed him not only to the deepest shame but also to overwhelming guilt and terror, both in connection with moralistic and punishing males whom he saw as forbidding his access to females. Hospitalization was experienced as justified punishment for his sinful sexuality. He now felt guilt-ridden, ashamed, and terrified, and the preceding manic episode had been so florid that I had felt hospitalization was necessary for his protection. During the course of his hospitalization he spent long hours writing at great speed in order, as he expressed it, to "clarify his thoughts." This is not an atypical response to the turbulent excitement and terror-prompted rush of ideas found in both schizophrenic and in manic episodes.

His condition continued to deteriorate, and as a result the psychiatrist in charge moved him into a part of the hospital which housed the most deteriorated psychotics. When this happened, his wife asked me if I would accompany her to visit him. When we arrived, he appeared ashamed and in anguish. The moment he saw the both of us there was a radical transformation in affect and in thought. In place of shame, distress, and terror there was now a towering rage—moreover, a moral outrage. "How *dare* you put me in with people like *this?* What gives you the *right?* Let me *out* of here." I could scarcely believe what I saw and heard. He appeared to be in total remission. Not trusting my own judgment completely, I sought out the psychiatrist in charge, saying to him, "I know this sounds entirely improbable, but I think my patient is now suddenly quite well. Would you come and give me your judgment?" The psychiatrist returned with me and was equally astonished at the apparent recovery and immediately had him transferred to another ward where he would stay briefly and then be released.

However, this move into a more pleasant ward plunged the patient back into his former condition, but now with some attenuation of its severity so that he was later permitted weekends away from the hospital in the custody of his wife. On his first weekend away from the hospital he again reasserted his authority and refused to return to the hospital. The psychiatrist at the hospital insisted he return and warned the wife that her husband was in serious danger of suicide and that she was endangering his life if she did not return him to the hospital. Again the patient responded with such insistent moral outrage that his wife, intuiting again that her husband appeared to be his normal self, acquiesced. She proved right in that her husband never again fell mentally ill despite many severe stresses, including major surgery and five years of pain in a long terminal illness.

In attempting to reconstruct and understand what had happened, I assumed that his success in achievement and in his sexuality had justified, in his eyes, his own volatile temper and his equally impulsive aggression, as well as his sexual experimentation and his harddriving professional competitiveness. When he suffered a back injury and its enforced passivity, he was robbed of his achievement, of his sexuality, and of his anger and aggression. As a passive victim he first denied his loss of professional status by manic extravagant purchases of all kinds—clothing, securities, automobiles—to reassert his former affluence. These had been bought on credit and had to be returned. He had gotten into a serious fight with a taxi driver who he felt was cheating him, was put in jail, and had to be released on bail. Aggressive as he was, he would never, in his normal state, have fought seriously enough over a taxi fare to have been incarcerated. There then followed a long enduring and very florid manic celebration of the power of the human mind, which he thought could do "anything" it wanted to and also that he too shared in this general power. This manic celebration alternated with hallucinations of his youth, particularly of his flight from the battlefield to his mother and his fear of punishment by his superior officer. When I hospitalized him, the manic bubble was cruelly deflated and exposed him to "punishment for a life long of sin." The shame of passivity and failure was transformed into that shame which is experienced as "guilt" by virtue of interpretation of the same affect as the consequence of immorality rather than of failure. Freud long ago noted that suicides during economic depressions are often the consequence of the superego having been kept at bay by successful achievement. It then overwhelms the overachiever when fortune no longer smiles on him so that failure turns to guilt. In my formulation of this dynamic the underlying affect, shame, is identical in failure and in immorality, but the totality of failure and shame is experienced quite differently than is the combination of immorality and shame, labeled guilt.

When this load of shame from failure and from immorality was added to by what he perceived to be the irrational and unjustified exercise of authority ("How *dare* you—what *right* do you have to put me in with people like this?"), then his justified *moral* outrage swept away *both* his *guilt* at his immorality and failure and his shame at his failure. He felt, at that moment, neither a bad human being nor a failure. Although both guilt and shame had summated at immorality and failure, it was, in my judgment, the reduction of guilt which was decisive in his sustained recovery, since neither then nor in the years which followed did he ever recover his former success or affluence.

We will not consider the other types of affect management scripts, the preaddictive and the addictive, because these are cases in which sedation has been so radically magnified as ends in themselves that they are no longer used as instrumental for the sedation of anger or any other negative affect. In addiction the major affect involved is the learned deprivation panic at the absence of the addictive substance or response itself. The cure for that panic is the overlearned addictive response. Therefore, anger is no longer critically involved in addiction other than as a secondary response to any one or any circumstance which might block one's access to the addictive fix.

AFFECT CONTROL SCRIPTS: CONSCIOUSNESS, DENSITY, DISPLAY, EXPRESSION, COMMUNICATION, ACTION, CONSEQUENCES, CONDITIONALITY, SPECIFICITY

Scripts for the control of affect are both socially inherited, transmitted via family, as well as transformed via idiosyncratic influences in the family, and further transformed by the individual. Because of the phenomena of affect contagion and affect escalation, and their conjoint urgency and pressure on action, few societies fail to script affect control.

Such scripting may be general, specific, or both. Societies and individuals vary in the toleration of affect in general and with the toleration and promotion of specific affects. Thus, Levy has shown that in Tahiti there are a large number of rules and sanctions for teaching youngsters early on that one must control both anger and aggression. When a child *has* violated these rules, there are follow-up rules whereby later unrelated suffering (e.g., an injury from an accidental fall) will be "connected" with the previous aggression as evidence of the consequences of the previous violation of the rules.

Affect-control scripts may address, first of all, the question of consciousness of affect. Societies and families may teach the individual to become unaware of his feelings by a studied unawareness of their obvious presence. If the other acts *as if* you are *not* angry or not distressed, you may not learn either to label such feelings or to be aware for very long *that* you're angry or distressed. Thus, if every time a child cries out in either anger or distress, the parent immediately rushes to either distract the child or to solve the problem, attention may be diverted from those feelings to other feelings or to the source of the feeling as the critical focus of remedial action. Not infrequently, normative socialization of distress transmits a taboo on and/or minimizing of awareness of distress in favor of "doing" something about it, whether by the person himself or by the savior, who often loves "humanity" much more than he does any specific suffering human beings. Such minimizing of consciousness may be further scripted by ideological prescriptions against feeling specific affects: Don't be "gloomy"; you should be ashamed of yourself for crying, for being afraid, or angry, or disgusted, or too excited, or laughing too loud.

There are also frequent script rules governing affect density, its intensity, its duration, and its frequency. "Enough is enough"; "Simmer down"; "You always cry at the least little thing"; "You're too emotional" are prototypic affect-density-control scripts. Adults are not infrequently surprised to hear themselves admonish their own children with the same long-forgotten rules inherited from their parents.

There are also specific script rules for the display of specific affects on the face and in the voice: "Wipe that smile off your face"; "I don't want to hear any more whining"; "Don't you *ever* frown at me again." Display rules are independent of consciousness rules, so that the child may be taught that it is permissible to feel sad or angry but that "we" don't cry or pout. Feelings are, in such cases, to be "kept to oneself." These are the prime conditions for the production of what I have defined as backed-up affect, which creates confusion about what, in fact, innate affect feels like, similar to the difference between holding the breath and breathing.

There are specific script rules for the vocal expression of anger, independent of either its display or its verbal communication. "Don't you *ever* raise your voice at me again" is a threat against the decibel level of anger independent of its facial display or its verbal expression or *ito* consciousness. The child may suffer no inhibition on the conscious feeling of anger, on the facial display of anger, or even on its verbalization (e.g., "I hate you") so long as his voice is not strident.

There are further rules governing the communication of affect over and above its vocal expression or its display. This arises when displayed affect is linked to verbal communication. The child who cries out in distress or anger may be disregarded by a parent, who nonetheless explodes in anger at the verbalization of the same affect. "I hate you" will evoke sanctions ranging from "nice little boys don't say such things" to "I don't want to ever hear that again" to a sharp slap on the face to leaving the child alone.

Almost universal are rules for the control of action. Serious as the consciousness of anger may be, its display or vocalization or its verbal communication are trivial compared with the response to direct physical attack on the parent or on a sibling. Fire is, in this case, most often met with fire. Further, the massiveness of the counterattack is often overkill, in the attempt to stamp out once and for all the insubordination of the child against the authority of the parent, the state, and the larger normative order. During the heyday of Calvinism explicit scripts for "breaking the will" of the erring child were developed and enacted. For an upper-class, honor-governed society, however, it may be the failure of the child to be sufficiently brave in his aggression which is overloaded with shame and terror. Thus, the child is taught to fear cowardice more than the dangers of anger and aggression.

Next the consequences of affect may be linked and scripted: "When you're angry, Mommy is unhappy"; "When you get so angry, you give Mommy a headache." This need not be verbalized but rather demonstrated by a look of distress to the felt anger of the child or to the noisy excitement displayed by the child. In such ways the script rule is generated: "If I feel unhappy or angry or happy, I make others feel unhappy."

Finally, rules vary not only with respect to whether they apply to all affect or to specific affects, but also with respect to their conditionality. It may be taught (unwittingly) that there are certain times of day, or privacy or publicity (e.g., when there are guests versus when there are not), or who else is in the scene (sibling or other parent present or not), or when the parent is happy or unhappy, which determine differential appropriateness of specific affect consciousness, density, vocalization, communication, action, or consequences. Such rules may also be quite explicit. Thus: "No loud games when we have guests"; "When Mommy is tired, be quiet"; "You ought to show a better example to your little brother"; "Wait till I tell your father."

Anger-control scripts are always prominent in affect socialization, but they are not necessarily learned as rules which the individual himself controls. We will later consider an example of an individual whose anger was effectively controlled by a mother who could terminate her son's anger by dismissively saying, "You're childish." Years later, in his marriage, his wife could not turn off his anger, unmindful of the magic formula, nor could her husband, equally unconscious of the rule which governed him, and he was therefore victimized by mounting rage he did not know how to turn off.

The specificity and degree of magnification of control over the various independent features of anger have fateful consequences for the kinds of problems the individual suffers with the control of anger.

Thus, he may require that his anger be controlled exclusively by himself or by others. He may have problems with anger only under specific conditions, either when intimate with others or when in public places. He may become sensitized exclusively to the effect of his anger on others and so be free to express anger with others who are also angry or who do not respond negatively to anger. He may become sensitized primarily to the anger-powered act but otherwise quite free to verbalize his anger. He may, however, be entirely inhibited in verbalizing his anger but free to hit someone in anger. He may become free to verbalize or act on his anger so long as he keeps his decibel level under control. He may shout in anger but not frown, or frown but not shout. Finally, he may be inhibited in awareness of his own anger and/or that of others even though he reflects anger on his face, in his voice, in his words, or in his actions. As a result of such differential magnification of the independent features of anger, he is likely not only to be quite specific in his inhibitions of anger but also to be seduced by just such forbidden forms of anger. Thus, one who is free to feel anger but not to shout in anger is not only vulnerable to fear or shame about shouting but also is fascinated and seduced by the forbidden elevation of the decibel level of his voice in anger. Yet another, who is free to shout, finds most seductive the wish to physically hit the other in anger. There is no aspect of the complex totality of the affect of anger which may not suffer the twin problems of fear of loss of control and fascination with violation of control.

Chapter 33
Anger in Affluence and Damage-Repair Scripts

ANGER AND SCRIPTS OF AFFLUENCE

Anger may be incorporated into a script of affluence whenever it is constructed as a necessary part of achieving excitement and or enjoyment. This is to distinguish it from anger which is scripted primarily to hurt the other or to defeat the other (e.g., in an athletic game) and, when having achieved that scripted aim, there is positive celebration and joy and or excitement. Thus, in the sadomasochistic sexuality we considered before, inflicting and/or receiving aggressive punishment was scripted as the major or the only way in which sexual excitement or enjoyment could be achieved. An affluence script is defined as one in which the primary aim is positive affect, and the principal ways in which that aim can be achieved are also scripted. Thus, a timid person who fears social contact might be very happy to reach the safety of his home after attending a lecture or a cocktail party, but such joy would not define an affluence script. It would be defined as an antitoxic (against fear) script to escape fear by seeking escape to particular places defined as safe from fear. In a more extreme case of an antitoxic avoidance script, the individual would not have attended the lecture or the party.

In the case of aggressive athletics (e.g., professional boxing or wrestling) there is a paradox in the motives of those who participate in them and those who watch them. The participants need not be scripted for affluence through anger or aggression. Many champion boxers and wrestlers were distinguished for their skill and coolness under fire, taunting their opponents into anger in order to make them more impulsive and less skillful. However, those who regularly watch professional wrestling do script this sport as angry fun, urging their favorites on to greater mayhem and returning week after week in response to explicit billing by management that these matches are grudge matches and matches of revenge and violence. This should be distinguished from bullfights in which a ritual confrontation of death is celebrated. The aim is not to witness the bullfighter vent his anger on the bull but to see him display his skill and bravery under the threat of death by permitting the bull to come very close to him before he kills it. Although this is a central ritual in the macho culture of Spain, and although the macho script utilizes the dangerous fight as a test of machismo, it should nonetheless be distinguished from the macho script as defined by Donald Mosher. I am indebted to Donald Mosher for his explication of the macho script as it appears on the contemporary American scene. The reader is referred to Mosher and Tomkins (1987) for a more complete account of what I will next summarize.

The heart of the macho script, as defined by Mosher, is "(1) entitlement to callous sex, (2) violence as manly, and (3) danger as exciting."

The ideological script of the macho man is socially inherited within a macho culture by virtue of being a male. It "exalts male dominance by assuming masculinity, virility, and physicality to be the ideal essence of real men who are adversarial warriors competing for scarce resources (including women as chattel) in a dangerous world."

The ideology of machismo is a particular variant of normative ideology. In Spanish, *machismo* means the essence or soul of masculinity. To be scripted to be a "real man"—thereby to exaggerate the stereotypic qualities of *masculinity*—requires socialization that differentially magnifies the "superior, manly" affects of anger, excitement, surprise, disgust, and contempt in contrast to the "inferior" and "feminine" affects of distress, fear, shame, and relaxed enjoyment.

There are at least seven socialization dynamics required to differentially magnify the masculine affects of a macho script. First, distress is intensified by the socializer until it is transformed into anger. Second, fear expression and fear avoidance are inhibited through parental dominance and contempt until habituation partially reduces them and activates excitement. Third, shame over residual distress and fear reverses polarity through counteraction into exciting manly pride over aggression and daring. Fourth, pride over aggressive and daring counteraction instigates disgust and contempt for shameful inferiors. Fifth, successful reversal of interpersonal control through angry and daring dominance activates excitement. Sixth, surprise becomes an interpersonal strategy to achieve dominance by evoking fear and uncertainty in others. Seventh, excitement becomes differentially magnified as a more acceptable affect than relaxed enjoyment, which becomes acceptable only during victory celebration. For a further explication of how the innate affect dynamics are used to enhance these learned transformations the reader is referred to Mosher and Tomkins (1987).

Next consider the macho rites of passage during adolescence. Three ritual scenes require physical action to test a real man: the fight scene, the danger scene, and the callous sex scene. You must first fight your way into the subculture of macho youths. You have to have "heart." The fight, dangerous and exciting, tests the triumph of anger over distress while pride and shame and self-disgust and other disgust hang in the balance.

The danger scene is another test of masculine fearlessness, often a needless risk of life and limb. The challenge of the dare looms large in invitations to danger. These have specific rituals in particular locales—to climb the watertower, to race your car, or to steal dangerously. In the callous sex scene the 4-F philosophy—"find them, fool them, fuck them, and forget them"—epitomizes machismo's sexual ideology. Mosher reports: "The not-so-funny joke has it that no one climaxes during their initial experience with sexual intercourse, the boy gets his orgasm the next day when he tells his friends."

These three scenes constitute part of the enculturation process which supports the primary socialization of affects. Another type of enculturation is the ritual of celebration as the informal celebration following the formal military parade ritual of completing boot camp in the military.

> The recruit, shorn of his civilian dignity and hazed as a coward, a faggot, a mama's boy, and the like, undergoes an ordeal. If successful, he leaves the status of recruit behind to assume his new military identity as a warrior. In ritual celebration, the new soldier, sailor, airman, or marine *must* with his buddies, go to the bar, get drunk, get laid, get into a fight with an outgroup member, and do something daring.

Whereas celebration involves a resonance based upon action, vicarious resonance requires only audience participation in a variety of myths and dramas of prototypical idealized macho scenes.

A third process of enculturation is by interaction and complementation with women and by interaction and identification with men. Macho scenes that elicit complementary responses from women validate the macho script as much as do macho scenes with men, be they scenes of identification or battle, or both.

The resonance between the scripts of macho personality and ideology validates the self, justifies the macho life-style, celebrates the macho ideology, and provides a basic understanding of the self in the world.

The macho script can and usually does change in time. Because of its emphasis on physicality it is a young man's script. From adolescence to midlife, macho physicality reaches its zenith and slowly wanes. As his vigor declines, the demands of the script can become excessively burdensome, and he discovers that he is no longer invulnerable to the feminine affects of shame, distress, fear, and enjoyment. His defensive script now turns to substance abuse. Under alcohol the lure of just "nodding out" becomes increasingly seductive. According to Mosher, "when the ratio of positive to negative affects resulting from living a macho life style has reached its nadir, the macho man still hopes for a heroic rescue of his failed life. He believes that he can save the meaning of his life by heroically losing it" in a pseudo-reparative script. Macho men fantasize going out in a blaze of glory just as Phaeton did in the archetypal male myth. His epitaph was

> Here Phaeton lies,
> Who drove his father's chariot: if he did not
> Hold it, at least he fell in splendid daring.

"Death before dishonor" forbids the macho male to embrace a truly reparative script of affirming the long-suppressed feminine affects. We will later examine the inverse of this struggle in Tolstoy, who so rejected his own masculinity and sexuality that he embraced poverty, chastity, peace, simplicity, and love.

DAMAGE-REPAIR SHAME-ANGER SCRIPTS

In damage-repair scripts, scenes which are enjoyed or exciting are damaged and interrupted and evoke shame as the primary response. Depending on the general differential density of positive over negative affect, and the differential density of the benign over the more malignant negative affects, the response to shame will be both reparative in aim and with minimal secondary other negative affect. Should the general and more specific affect ratios be more malignant, shame will recruit secondary and tertiary distress, disgust, anger, dissmell, and terror which in varying ratios complicate reparation or swamp it completely, requiring that one deal with the damage as if it were a more permanent distressing limitation, or a disgusting contamination, or a toxic source of dissmell, rage, and/or terror. In such recruitments to shame, the magnification of an otherwise repairable damage into a more serious affront may be relatively transient, restricted to non-overt responses, or acted on impulsively and then regretted and atoned for via apology or guilt or reform. However, it may be buttressed by more permanent scripts which bypass repair altogether, in which the possibility that the other was himself governed by a minor transient is entirely discounted. We may illustrate the inherent ambiguities of interpretation of any damage by a recent example from the United States campaign for the presidency in the case of candidate Gary Hart. His candidacy was compromised by the publicity attending an extramarital sexual encounter. This might have been absorbed as a transient shameful lapse indicating transient impulsivity or transient poor political judgment, a symptom of a more enduring character limitation or a more serious moral contamination which was permanently disgusting, or as a most serious toxicity which repelled by dissmell, enraged by the magnitude of the offense, or terrified by the prospect that a whole country might be put at risk should such a flawed individual be in control of the awesome power of the presidency.

In reparative scripts anger may play varying roles vis-à-vis impunitive reparative scripts. These vary from minuscule shades of anger, to delayed anger, to angry demands that the other apologize before good relations can be resumed, to a permanent reserve, that the relationship will never again be as trusting as it was before, with constant vigilance for signs of repetition of damage. These latter may mark the beginning of the end of a marriage—after a fight or the discovery of a sexual infidelity or the forgetting of an anniversary.

We will examine a few of the varieties of shame-anger-driven damage-repair scripts: (1) the ambivalent reparative script of Anton Chekov, (2) the redemptive reparative script of Karl Marx, (3) the reparative nuclear script of damage by sibling rivalry, and (4) the typical accommodative reparative script of the shame-anger-ridden depressive.

CHEKOV: OPTIMIZING AFFLUENCE, SHAME-ANGER DAMAGE REPAIR, HEALER REMEDIATION, CRITIC DECONTAMINATION, AND ANTITOXIC SCRIPT

Chekhov lived the first years of his life in the face of daily humiliation. His father whipped him almost every day, forbade him to play, and forced him to work. In the second half of his life he lived in the shadow of death. He became aware of the tuberculosis, of which he was to die at the age of forty-four, as early as his twenty-fourth year. And yet, despite the beatings which might have activated terror and humiliation sufficient to produce a paranoid script, Chekhov's primary response to these beatings, and to the real threat of death he later faced, was reparative and remedial. He felt robbed of the good life but hopefully and tenaciously clung to the possibility of the good life, despite frequent depressions, and was capable for long periods of great zest and love of life. His love of human beings and his capacity for excitement and joy in work were as intense and deep as was his contempt and hatred for "despotism" and "insincerity." Though the image of the oppressor contaminated his love of human beings, it never so seriously threatened him as to extinguish his zest for life. Rather, his awareness of the promise of life was heightened, its beauty made more poignant, if more fragile, by his awareness of the enduring imminence of ugliness and evil.

The question of how Chekhov was able to live with the awareness of his progressive tuberculosis yet never developed depression severe enough to require hospitalization is of considerable interest. The answer cannot be altogether certain. It was the relative balance of negative and positive affect in his early socialization which appeared critical. As we will see, Chekhov was much more concerned with avoiding and escaping humiliation by direct confrontation than with the quest for achievement and love per se or as antidotes for humiliation. Although his father insisted that his son work hard, he did not appear to evoke sufficient love from Chekhov to produce a loveshame bind. The major problem during Chekhov's childhood thereby became one of overcoming humiliation. The young Chekhov developed great fortitude, first in tolerating his humiliation and then in throwing off his servility. He developed sufficient distance from others and sufficient backbone in the face of rejection that the tie of love and achievement to his father and to the state of humiliation and depression never became so intimate that he became vulnerable to that utter hopelessness which is psychotic depression. He did, on the contrary, develop the capability which he was to prize so much—"iron in the soul"—sufficient to produce a script which is much more concerned with coping with humiliation by resistance and countercontempt than by love and achievement as appeasement to the shamer. This is not to say that he did not long for love and think of it as a counter to humiliation, nor that he did not view work both as a prime cure for humiliation and as a precondition of love, but rather that in addition to these, and to some extent prior to these, he early developed extreme pride and fortitude against oppression and depression rather than appeasing the humiliator entirely through love and good works.

As with Dostoevsky, the insult to his pride generated anger and countercontempt rather than the humiliation and terror which power the paranoid fantasies of grandeur and persecution. Unlike Dostoevsky, however, he was not consumed and trapped by his hatred and scorn for his oppressor. He returned contempt for contempt, but he also had a vision of a life dedicated to love and work which neutralized his humiliation, his anger, and his countercontempt.

There is another reason for his relative resistance to depression: the split between the humiliator and the love object. Whereas in psychotic depression it is ordinarily one and the same person who loves the child and who humiliates him, here it was a relatively benign mother and sister who were his objects of love, thus enabling him, to some extent, to keep his love objects distinct from his oppressor.

As we will see, this difference was not absolute, but rather one of degree.

This socialization of Chekhov, plus the continuing awareness of death, made for frequent depressions throughout his life, but also for less severe depressions and for a reduced capacity for intimacy and love as well as a reduced capacity for sustained work. Although he was capable of hard, long-sustained work and was extraordinarily productive, he was also plagued by the lure of idleness and passivity. Although he could not live without the presence of others, neither was he ever able entirely to break through the encapsulation of his self to reveal himself to others completely.

Chekhov's Relation to Father

Chekhov's grandfather, his father's father, had come from a long line of serfs. By dint of a driving ambition he succeeded in buying his freedom, emancipating himself and his family. He was forty-two by the time he had scraped together the 3,500 rubles which purchased their freedom. Indeed, he could not buy the freedom of his daughter, but her freedom was thrown in, as a generous bonus. He had learned to read and write and had seen to it that his three sons also had learned these skills. Once free he was determined that his sons should exploit their new status and rise above their social origin. He was a stern father, who nonetheless conveyed to them his close identification with them—that they should achieve at least as much as their father and hopefully much more. He set them an example of great energy and industry and busines success. He finally attained the high position of steward of a large estate near Taganrog. To Taganrog he sent his son, Chekhov's father, to work in the countinghouse of the merchant Koblyn. This was a lowly status among the Russians in Taganrog. Chekhov's father worked long hours for a pittance, had to be fawning and servile to all those just above him in status, and also suffered occasional beatings from his superiors. This training in harshness and servility completed the equally punitive education he had received at the hands of his dominant father. And yet there was another, softer side to Pavel Yegorovich which was expressed in an intense love for art, for music and painting. As a boy he had learned to sing, to play the violin, and to paint. His great religiosity was, according to Simmons, "a manifestation of his devotion to the beauty of the ritual and of his passion for sacred music—which he later participated in professionally."

Pavel Yegorovich, like his father before him, smarted under his bondage to the rich merchant for whom he worked. After years of toil and saving he managed to open his own grocery store. Chekhov's father, now his own master for the first time, inflated himself to the dignity to which he and his father before him had so long aspired. He began to refer to himself as a "merchant" and to his unpretentious store as a "commercial enterprise." But six children born in ten years placed a great financial burden on this enterprise, and Pavel Yegorovich was never the provider he wanted to be. Indeed, after years of struggle he was unable to pay the five hundred rubles he had borrowed to help build his house and had to declare himself bankrupt. Facing debtor's prison, he stole out of town and escaped to Moscow. This was the ignominious end to thirty years of struggle to raise the social and economic status which he had inherited from his own upwardly mobile but more successful father.

One of the reasons for the failure of his business, paradoxically, was his success as a social and civic leader. He did indeed earn a position of respect in Taganrog, but not as a merchant. He assumed many civic duties, attended many religious ceremonies, and directed a choir of his own. He had achieved the trappings of a man of high station but in part at the cost of his business. He had to force his children to neglect their studies and to spend many hours taking care of his store while he was engaged in creating a shining image of himself in the community.

Chekhov's relationship with his father was a highly ambivalent one. His father in many ways represented what Chekhov loathed and hated most, and yet he was also tied to him by strong feelings of filial affection and some respect as well as by a strong identification with his father against which he was to struggle for many years.

First and foremost, he resented the almost daily beatings at the hands of his father. Many years later, when he was thirty-four years old, Chekhov wrote to his friend Suvorin: "I began to believe in progress in my early childhood, because of the tremendous difference between the time when I was still whipped and the time when I was not."

When Chekhov's mother protested against her husband's beating of the children, he gave the classic reply: "I was brought up in this manner and, as you can see, I'm none the worse for it."

In Chekhov's story "Three Years" there is an autobiographical passage:

> I remember father began to teach me, or to put it more plainly, whip me, when I was only five years old. He whipped me, boxed my ears, hit me over the head, and the first question I asked myself on awakening every morning was: will I be whipped again today? I was forbidden to play games or romp. I had to attend the morning and evening church services, kiss the hands of priests and monks, read psalms at home. . . . When I was eight years old, I had to mind the shop; I worked as an ordinary errand boy, and that affected my health, for I was beaten almost every day.

Chekhov as a little boy refused to believe that a school friend of his was never beaten.

Nemirovich-Danchenki, his friend and director of the Moscow Art Theatre, said that Chekhov remarked, "Do you know, I can never forgive my father for having whipped me as a child."

However, Chekhov began to refer to his unhappy childhood only after he had achieved fame as a writer. His pride was such that he could not admit these past insults to his dignity until he was able to hold his head sufficiently high that he could tolerate these memories.

His two brothers, Alexander and Nicholas, revolted against such treatment from their father by becoming alcoholic and ultimately by running away from home. Chekhov confronted his problem more directly. As far as we can tell, he responded to these beatings and to other physical assaults on his body by his peers, not with fear but with shame. Out of his struggle with his deep sense of shame for these and other affronts to his dignity, he slowly evolved an indomitable pride, which eventually he summarized in a letter to his uncle Mitrofan: "People must never be humiliated—that is the main thing."

How early Chekhov minimized his fear of physical assault and defended his dignity in coping with these threats to his pride may be seen in a reminiscence of his brother Alexander, who recounts how his younger brother Anton stood up to a beating from him by not telling their father and thereby asserted his independence of him.

In a letter to Chekhov many years later, Alexander reminded him of an incident which illuminates the development of the young Chekhov:

> I remember the first manifestation of your independent character and my first realization that my influence over you as your older brother had begun to disappear. . . . To make you submit to my authority again, I hit you over the head with a tin. . . . You left the shop and went home to father. I was expecting a good whipping, but a few hours later you walked majestically past our shop on some errand and deliberately did not even glance in my direction. I followed you with my eyes for a long time and—I don't know why myself—burst out crying.

The father's despotism was by no means limited to whipping his sons. The second great grievance in Chekhov's childhood was his enforced labor in his father's grocery store.

The store was open from five in the morning to eleven at night. Taking care of it was the duty of Alexander, Nicholas, and Anton. It was repugnant to Anton on many counts. First, it interfered with his studies, and he worried about the reprimands he would receive from both his teacher and his father for his failures in school. Second was the cold. There was little difference between the temperature in the unheated store and outdoors, and the young Anton would shiver, numb with cold for hours as he tended the store and intermittently tried to prepare for his lessons for school. When he stuck his pen in the inkwell, the point would scrape on ice.

A letter from Alexander read: "Thus Antosha served his time in the store which he hated. There he learned his school lessons with difficulty or failed to learn them; and there he endured the winter cold and grew numb like a prisoner shut up in four walls, when he ought to have been spending his golden school days at play."

Further, the young Anton detested and was disturbed by the combination of constant fawning on the customers and stealing from them, both of which were then accepted rules among the mercantile community.

Chekhov's description of his father in his letters was "Father used to smile at his customers even when the Swiss cheese in the shop made him feel sick."

Among the tricks of the trade was short-weighting the customers. Anton could not understand how his God-fearing father could be a thief, and he confronted his mother with his doubts. She would reassure Anton of his father's fundamental honesty. For his father there was no conflict between religion and conscience on the one hand and business on the other. The two had nothing to do with each other. But for Anton, this heightened his distaste for working in his father's grocery store.

When their mother protested that Anton was being overburdened, her husband would reply, "He's got to get used to it. I work. Let him work. Children must help their father." When his mother protested, "But he's been sitting in the store all week. At least let him take Sunday off to rest," Pavel replied: "Instead of resting, he fools around with street urchins. If one of the children isn't in the store, the apprentices will snitch candy, and the next thing will be money. You know yourself that without one of us there the business will go to pieces." This ordinarily brought the argument to a close.

When Anton complained to his father about his servitude, he was told: "You can't run about because you'll wear out your shoes.... It is bad to fool around with playmates. God knows what they'll teach you. In the shop at least you'll be a help to your father." When Anton complained that he could not get his lessons done, the reply was "Why, I find time to read over two sections from Psalter every day, and you are unable to learn a single lesson!"

Thus did he come to his conclusion, voiced as an adult, "There was no childhood in my childhood."

In addition to the beatings and his daily tour of duty in the store, his early relationship with his father was contaminated by that one's passion for music and the church, both of which he continually forced on his reluctant children. He never wearied of trying to implant in his children his own love of music and art. He was quite prepared to whip his sons into an appreciation of music and religion. He had an exceptional musical ear and cuffed his children whenever they sang off key.

Not only was Anton whipped into music appreciation, but homework, play, and sleep were all sacrificed to his father's passion for music and the church. Anton often said to his brothers, "What an unhappy lot we are! Other boys may run, play, visit their friends. We can only go to church." Most of the beatings he received were for poor singing or for misbehaving during religious ceremonies.

Chekhov's father was assistant director of a church choir, but because he so prolonged the musical part of the service, he was dismissed from this position. He then decided to organize his own choir. He organized a choir with his children and the townspeople, mostly blacksmiths, and gave many concerts. Alexander described the impact of this on young Anton as follows:

> Poor Anton who was still a small boy with an undeveloped chest, a thin voice and a rather poor ear for music, had an awful time of it. He often cried bitterly during choir practice which went on till the late hours and which deprived him of the sleep which was so necessary to his health. Father was meticulously punctual, strict and exacting about everything that had to do with church services. If his choir had to sing at morning mass during the high festivals, he would wake his children at two or three o'clock in the morning and go to church with them regardless of the weather. His children had to work hard on Sundays and holidays as well as on weekdays.... Father was as hard as flint, and it was quite useless to try to make him change his mind. Besides, he was a passionate lover of church music and could not live without it.

The long-term impact of this religious training was later described by Chekhov in a letter to Suvoren:

> When, as a child, I was given a religious education and made to read the lesson at church or sing in the church choir, and the whole congregation gazed admiringly at me, I felt like a little convict, and now I have no religion. Generally speaking, so-called religious education can never do without, as it were, a little screen behind which no stranger is allowed to peep. Behind that screen the children are tortured, but in front of it people smile and feel deeply moved. It is not for nothing that many divinity students become atheists.

Not only did his father beat him and force him to work, to sing, and to attend church, but he also not infrequently aroused the anger and contempt of Chekhov by virtue of numerous traits which repelled his son. We noted before that Chekhov was shocked by his father's fawning on his customers, as well as by his stealing from them.

Chekhov was also repelled by his father's vanity. His father was an extraordinarily vain man who delighted in such profundities as "Why is the snow lying here and not there?" Above all, Chekhov found it hard to tolerate his father's peasant-like rudeness to his mother. To Alexander he wrote, "Despotism and lies so disfigured our childhood that it makes me sick and horrified to think of it. Remember the disgust and horror we felt every time father made a scene at dinner because there was too much salt in the soup or called mother a fool."

The total crushing impact of his father's character, his harshenss and dominance, and his son's long, painful struggle to overcome this impact Chekhov communicated many years later in the now classic letter to Alexey Suvorin:

> Could you write a story about a young man, the son of a serf, a onetime shop assistant, choir boy, schoolboy and university student, brought up to fawn on rank, kiss the hands of priests, accept without questioning other people's ideas, express his gratitude for every morsel of bread he eats, a young man who has been frequently whipped, who goes to give lessons without galoshes, engages in street fights, tortures animals, loves to go to his rich relations for dinner, behaves hypocritically towards God and man without the slightest excuse but only because he is conscious of his own worthlessness—could you write a story of how this young man squeezes the slave out of himself drop by drop, and how, on waking up one morning, he feels that the blood coursing through his veins is real blood and not the blood of a slave?

Yet despite the nagging preoccupation with his own servility he did not become a Dostoevskian "Underground Man." The key to his development must be sought in the positive features of his relationship with his father, his mother, and his brothers and sisters.

Let us first consider the more positive aspects of his relationship to his father.

It is clear that his father was much more than an ignorant, cruel tyrant, both in fact and in the eyes of his children. Indeed, Chekhov himself said, "We get our talent from our father and our soul from our mother." Both his father and his mother lived for, and through, their children, consumed with ambition for them, hoping that their children would not only better themselves but that their children would enjoy a life better than they themselves had ever known. They lived vicariously through their children, and though such commitment can never be selfless, neither can it fail to communicate its intensity and sincerity. Such parental concern and identification with their children may be stifling, but it is also rewarding. It is just this consuming overidentification which ties the child to the parent no matter how much the child may also wish to extricate himself. All human beings are drawn to those who love them.

It was the combination of love and the insistence on work, on music, on religion, and on learning in general which was largely responsible for the generally high level of achievement by all six children. It was, as Simmons has suggested, "little short of a miracle . . . in a family only one generation removed from serfdom, that all six children should have received a higher education." Moreover, they all flourished. Alexander became a journalist and successful writer; Nikolai, an artist and illustrator; Ivan, a pedagogue; Mikhail, a jurist and writer; Mariya, a teacher and artist; and Anton, one of Russia's greatest dramatists and short story writers.

Their father taught them to read music, to sing, and to play the violin and also employed a teacher of the piano and a teacher of French. Further, there were many evenings at home when group singing and playing of piano and violin were a rewarding experience which delighted them all and heightened their awareness of themselves as a family group. Helped also by the warmth of the mother, they repeatedly had the experience of a strong and warm family group, united by a common interest in the arts.

There were also domestic theatricals which were produced by the Chekhov children. Anton was the star of these. At first he would imitate at home the characters he saw on the stage. Later he wrote and acted scenes about life in Taganrog. The interest of all the children in stories and dramas was nurtured by their mother's tales of peasant hardships in the old days of serfdom and of the bombardment of Taganrog during the Crimean War. Also, their nurse, Agatha Kumskaya, fascinated the children with her gothic stories of witches, monsters, and ravished princesses.

There was then laughter and excitement and the shared intimacy of a strong family group centered on the arts to relieve the austerity of the despotic Pavel Yegorovich.

It was not only Chekhov's mother who buffered the harshness of his father. His brothers and sisters also relieved the austerity of his father's despotism. Theirs was the cameraderie of all who share a common suffering at the hands of the same oppressor. They shared not only suffering but also much fun in playing together. In the summertimes there were occasions, despite the ever-demanded chores, when the children were permitted the luxury of play and sports together. They fished, swam at the seashore, and walked in the public garden. They also enjoyed tremendously their occasional vacations at their grandfather's.

In addition to the development of a strong group feeling between his brothers and sisters, Anton developed very strong separate dyadic relationships with each of his brothers and sisters.

And too, his father also had his good-humored and witty side, even though this appeared more often under the influence of alcohol than at any other time:

"My father and grandfather sometimes got very drunk when they had visitors, but that never interfered with their work or prevented them from going to morning mass. Drink made them good-humored and witty."

The strength of the family feeling may be seen in Michael's account of their reunion in Moscow: Chekhov, alighting from a cab, said,

> "How are you, Mikhail Pavlovich?" It was only then that I knew it was my brother, Anton [he had not recognized him because his brother had grown to be over six feet tall], and with a scream of delight I rushed downstairs to tell mother. A gay young man entered our flat and everybody rushed to embrace him. I was sent off to the post office at once to send a telegram to father about Anton's arrival. Soon Zembulatov and Savelyev came and, after their rooms had been made ready for them we all went out sightseeing together. I acted as their guide and took them around the Kremlin, showing them everything, and we were pretty tired by the time we returned home. In the evening father came, we had supper in a large company, and we were as happy as never before.

Not only were there numerous occasions of shared excitement and enjoyment by the family as a whole, but Chekhov's father was capable of displaying intense pride in his children's success. Many years later, when Chekhov received the Pushkin Prize, he wrote proudly: "Mother and father talk awful rot and are indescribably happy." Throughout Chekhov's letters there are innumerable references to his father's display of pride at all the minor as well as major successes of his children.

Chekhov's father was very ambitious that his children become rich or at least wear an official uniform. His was the peasant's respect for a uniform. Chekhov wrote to his brother Alexander, when the latter got a job as a customs official:

> Father tells everybody that you have a wonderful job. When tipsy he talks of nothing else except your uniform. Please, describe your uniform to him, and

> add at least one account of how you stood in the cathedral among the great ones of the world.

When Ivan became a teacher, Chekhov wrote, "Father is very happy: Ivan has bought himself a cap with a cockade and ordered a schoolmaster's frock-coat with bright brass buttons."

When, four years later, Chekhov's brother Michael became a tax assessor, Chekhov wrote, "Michael has had a civil service uniform of the sixth class made for him and tomorrow he is going to pay visits in it. Father gazes at him with tears of admiration in his eyes."

As we have noted before, Chekhov's first references to his unhappy childhood occur only after he had become famous. At seventeen, in contrast, he was quite aware of how indebted he was to his father for his education.

Thus, when he was seventeen, in a letter to his cousin he wrote:

> When you see my father tell him that I have received his dear letter and that I am very grateful to him. He and mother are the only people in the world for whom I shall never be sorry to do anything I can. If I ever achieve a great position in the world, I shall owe it entirely to them. They are good people and their great love for their children puts them above all praise, makes good all the faults they may have acquired in the course of a hard life and prepares that quiet haven for them in which they believe and on which they pin their hopes as only few people do.

Twelve years later, however, in a letter to Tekhonov, the editor of a Petersburg periodical, he wrote,

> Thank you for your kind word and your warm sympathy. As a little boy, I was treated with so little kindness that now, having grown up, I accept the kindness as something unusual, something of which I have had little experience. That is why I should like to be kind to people, but don't know how: I have grown callous and lazy, though I realize very well that people like us cannot possibly carry on without kindness.

The fact of the matter was that his father was both kind and unkind, so it is not altogether surprising that his son could not easily achieve a consistent picture of him.

Though he spent much of his life freeing himself of the unwanted consequences of his relationship to his father, some of Chekhov's cardinal traits, wanted and unwanted, were based upon identification with his father rather than upon his struggle against that identification.

First was his father's stubbornness. Chekhov had described him "as hard as flint and you won't be able to make him budge an inch." Chekhov too was stubborn.

Then there was his father's temper. Though Chekhov suffered much as a result of his father's temper, he also developed a similar readiness to tongue-lash those who displeased him.

Chekhov was, as he described himself, "naturally hot tempered," but he said that over the years he had learned to control himself as he believed every decent man should do.

Next was his father's belief in hard work, discipline, and the ability to tolerate both. He incorporated these ideals despite his complaints against his father.

To Yozhov he wrote:

> If you do not train your mind and your head to discipline and forced marches now, you will find that in three or four years it will be too late. It is my belief that you and Gruzinsky must force yourselves to work for hours every day. You work too little—both of you. If you go on writing so little, you will write yourself out without having written anything.

As part of his father's idealization of toughness, there was a taboo on crying. This, too, Chekhov internalized. His father had not only frequently made his children cry but at the same time had forbidden them to cry, on the pain of further punishment. When they lived in Moscow, he had tacked on the wall the following:

"Work Schedule and Domestic Duties to Be Observed in the Household of Pavel Chekhov in Moscow." Each of the children was assigned a time to get up, to go to bed, to eat, and to attend church and told what they should do in their free time. At the end of this schedule there followed: "Failure to fulfill these duties will result in a stern reprimand, then in punishment during which it is forbidden to cry." Chekhov had internalized this contempt for the open expression of distress: "To be able to deal adequately with such a subject one must be able to endure suffering but our modern writers only know how to whine and slobber." He also said: "The child is bawling! I have just made a resolution never to have any children."

Next was his father's fawning and servility, which his son loathed so much. Yet he required, as he himself said, a lifetime to free himself from his own servility.

As an example of his own problem, he fawned on Grigorovich, putting their relations on a master-disciple basis. He was extravagant in his praise of Grigorovich, bracketing him with Gogol, Tolstoy, and Turgenev, and said that he would not be forgotten "so long as there are woods and summer nights in Russia and plover and snipe utter their cries." Chekhov, however, soon grew to resent Grigorovich's constant advice and assumption of the role of the wise older man toward him. Finally, he wrote to Suvorin that he thought Grigorovich was a fraud.

According to Magarshack, it was Chekhov's own unwanted need to please which he saw in Grigorovich and which finally disgusted him.

> I am very fond of Grigorovich, but I do not believe that he really is anxious about me. He is a tendentious writer himself and only pretends to be an enemy of tendentiousness. I can't help thinking that he is terrified of losing the respect of people he likes, hence his quite amazing insincerity.

Next was his father's preoccupation with money. This too became Anton's preoccupation.

Chekhov was very ambivalent about money. He complained that he had grown up "in an environment in which money played a disgustingly large part." Nonetheless, like his father, he was seduced by the fantasy of sudden riches and gambled all his life on the state lottery tickets and on roulette. To Michael Chekhov he wrote, "I am well and that means that I am alive. I have only one secret illness which torments me like an aching tooth—lack of money." At the end of his life he sold his works for what he thought was a very large sum of money, but in this too he soon discovered he had deceived himself.

The paradox of such a close identification with a parent who threatened his individuality and independence through beating him and humiliating him may be partially accounted for by a special set of circumstances which both attenuated his father's direct influence and at the same time demanded and permitted the growth of Chekhov as an adolescent.

When Anton was sixteen years old his father became bankrupt and had to leave town to avoid debtor's prison. All the family soon joined his father in Moscow, with the exception of Anton. Anton was left on his own. He had three years of study to complete before he could attend the university at Moscow. He was at last free of his father, of tending the shop, of the choir, and of going to church. But he was now also alone and penniless. He lived now as a lodger in the house which had once been his home and belonged to his parents. Further, he was continually begged to send money to support his family. His mother wrote him virtually as though he were the head of the family and responsible for their welfare.

The combination of freedom from his father, plus the demands for help from his family in Moscow, surely accelerated his individuation from his father and the growth of his independence and self-reliance. Paradoxically, however, it also fostered the internalization of many of his father's cardinal traits, as we have seen. He became not only independent and self-reliant but stubborn, quick to anger, disciplined, impatient of those who were soft, servile, ambitious, and acquisitive. Freed of his father, he became a better student, too, and was awarded a small scholarship to medical school, awarded by the town after he graduated from the gymnasium at Taganrog. His identification with his father became complete three years after his father had been forced into bankruptcy and had to flee to Moscow to escape debtor's prison, and Anton inherited his father's role of provider for the family.

The strength of his identification with his father may be seen in his readiness to assume his father's role after his father became bankrupt and the family had moved to Moscow. At this time his father lived where he worked, some distance away from Moscow and visited his family only on Sundays. The family lived in great poverty.

Anton found them in the twelfth apartment they had been forced to move into since they left Taganrog. Nine people occupied a basement apartment located in a region notorious for its licensed brothels. The only certain source of income was what their father could spare from his very meager pay. Nikolai occasionally sold a painting or gave some drawing lessons. Alexander lived apart and was able only to support himself as a university student. The younger children needed help. Ivan was studying for his teacher's diploma, and Mosha and Misha also needed help if they were to continue their schooling.

Anton at that time had earned a scholarship to medical school and could have, like his brother Alexander, rented a room apart from his family and so earned his medical degree. But the prospect of five years of study in these grim circumstances, while at the same time caring for and partially supporting his destitute family, did not discourage Anton. He was prepared to take over these heavy responsibilities at the same time that he studied to become a doctor. His identification with his father and his love of his family was such that he felt compelled to elevate his family at the same time as he was attempting to rescue himself from the poverty, ugliness, and coarseness of the way of life which bankruptcy had forced upon them all. This responsibility as head of the family, which he willingly assumed at the age of nineteen, he was to carry for the rest of his life.

His aims were to guarantee the education of his younger brothers and sisters, to rescue his father from his menial, humiliating employment, to make his mother's life less austere and more secure, to help his older brother, Alexander, realize his potential as writer and to help Nikolai to become a great painter. All of these his father had struggled to do for his family. Anton would not permit this paternal vision to suffer defeat.

But most important was the new corrective factor now added to the identification with his father. Although his father had provided the basic identification as a harsh, overdemanding model for the socialization of Anton and his brothers, its excessive harshness had all but crushed his two older brothers so that they were now unable and unwilling to rescue the family. One was on the way to alcoholism, and the other was a somewhat schizoid and irresponsible painter. What Anton added to his identification with his father was a radical correction—"People must never be humiliated—that is the main thing." His father's socialization had been interiorized to the extent that he had been molded into identification with an overdemanding model but with this correction. Like his father before him it became his mission to assume the responsibility for the destiny of others. But because his father's overdemanding identification with his son had been so painfully humiliating, his son was dedicated to improving upon his father's way of saving souls. Much of his father's dominance, harshness, and piety remained, but they were now subordinated to the achievement of new norms—one must not lie, one must not be unfair, and above all, one must not humiliate others. It is one of the ironies of such identification that new corrective ideals will often be generated by such a socialization but will be unconsciously imposed in the same manner as the original model imposed them, which was itself responsible for the reformer's new ideals.

Thus, the new ideals were imposed with strictness and harshness as well as with love. Anton exercised considerable dominance and would lose his temper on the slightest provocation. His brother Michael described him as follows:

> Anton's will became the dominant one in our family. Harsh and brusque remarks I had never known him use before began to be heard, such as, "That's not true," or "One must be just," or "One mustn't tell lies," and so on.... Anton's views were accepted as law, and who knows what would have happened to our family after Alexander and Nicholas had left it if Anton had not arrived just in the nick of time from Taganrog. The need of earning money at all costs made Anton write stories, and Nicholas, who had returned to the bosom of his

> family, drew cartoons, for the humorous journals. Ivan soon became an elementary-school teacher, and little Michael began copying students' lectures and diagrams. Our mother and our sister Mary worked hard too. It was, indeed, a touching reunion of all the members of the family, who rallied round one person—Anton—and who were bound to each other by ties of sincere and tender affection.

Just how domineering and strict Chekhov could be may be seen from a letter he wrote at this time to his elder brother Alexander. When Chekhov found himself the head of his impoverished family, he tried to wean his brother Alexander from his alcoholism. He wrote him the following letter:

> Alexander, I, Anton Chekhov, am writing this letter while entirely selfcomposed and in the full possession of my faculties. I am resorting to this schoolgirl's expedient in view of your express desire that I should not talk to you again. If I won't allow my mother, sister or any woman to say a wrong word to me, I shall certainly not allow it to a drunken cabby. Even if you were a hundred thousand times dearer to me than you are, I should refuse on principle, and on anything else you like, to put up with any insults from you. If, however, contrary to all expectations, you should like to make your usual excuse and put all the blame on your "irresponsible state," I, for my part, should like you to know that I am perfectly well aware that "being drunk" does not give you the right to——on anyone's head. I am quite willing at any time to expunge from my vocabulary the word "brother" with which you tried to frighten me when I left the battlefield, and that not because I have no heart, but because in this world one must be ready for anything. I myself am afraid of nothing, and I should like to advise my brothers to be the same. I am writing this in all probability to save myself in the future from all sorts of unpleasant surprises and, perhaps, from being slapped in the face, for I realise very well that on the strength of your most charming "but" (which, let me add parenthetically, does not concern anyone) you are capable of slapping anyone's face anywhere. Today's row showed me for the first time that the delicacy of feeling which you extol so much in your story "Somnambula" would not prevent you from slapping a man's face and that you are a most dissembling fellow, i.e., a fellow who always consults his own interests first, and therefore, I remain your most humble servant, A. Chekhov.

Here we see Chekhov rejecting his brother because he is acting too much like their father, but the irony is that he is doing it in much the same harsh way as their father might have acted. This was not to be the last time that Chekhov was to remind Alexander that he was acting like their father. To his brother Alexander he wrote, after a visit to him and his new mistress:

> What made me so indignant the very first time I came to see you was your *horrible* and absolutely inexcusable treatment of Natalie and the cook. I hope you will forgive my saying so, but to treat women, whoever they may be, like that is unworthy of a decent man. What heavenly or earthly power gave you the right to make them your slaves? Language of the foulest kind, shouts, reproaches, rows at breakfast and dinner, constant complaints about your hard life and your damnable work—are these not the expressions of the coarsest despotism? However worthless or culpable a woman might be, however intimate your relations with her might be, you have no right to sit in her presence without trousers, or be drunk in her presence, or utter words which even factory workers would not use in the presence of women. . . . Nor will a man who respects a woman allow himself to be seen by his parlour-maid without trousers, and shout at the top of his voice "Katya, fetch the chamber-pot!" . . . You claim that decency and good manners are prejudices, but one must have some regard at least for something, a woman's weakness or one's own children. . . . You can sink as low as you please, but you must take care that your children do not get hurt. You can't use foul language in their presence with impunity, or insult your servants, or shout viciously to Natalie, "Go to hell out of here! I'm not keeping you."

Chekhov went on to remind his brother that this was how their own father treated their mother.

Chekhov's corrective to his father's rule was not altogether lost in its effect on his father. At the beginning there was a brief struggle between the new and the old leaders of the family. Chekhov's father sensed that his authority, which had been steadily undermined by his failure, was now being eroded rapidly. He resented Anton's assumption of leadership and authority, but in time he submitted to Anton's authority. His son made it clear that there were to be no more "Work Schedules and Duties" and no more beatings. Indeed, eventually, his father had second thoughts on the wisdom of his former harsh ways.

Chekhov's Relation to His Grandfather

Chekhov's commitment to work was also reinforced by his beloved grandfather. The role of grandparents in the socialization process has in general been grossly underestimated. It is our impression that their influence as models is often great because they show much love to their grandchildren without admixture of that punishment and dominance which so often attenuates the love of the child for his parents. Grandparents can afford to leave discipline to the parents, and confronting their own death more directly, they cling more tenaciously to life and love in their strong and intimate relationships with their grandchildren. Few grandchildren fail to respond to such a show of affection, and Anton was not an exception. In addition, his grandfather was, and also appeared to Anton to be, a much stronger personality than his own father. Anton and his brothers loved to visit him because he was so kind to them. Yet he too considered it a duty to work and made them work hard. Chekhov later wrote to Suvorin: "In my childhood, living at my grandfather's on the property of Count Platov, I had to work from dawn to dusk."

Because his grandfather was a beloved and revered kindly old man, we must suppose that work was now further endowed with the meaning of evoking love and respect for the one for whom one worked.

Chekhov's Relation to His Mother

Whereas Chekhov's father had been quicker to whip and dominate than to show his love for his son, his mother had been more loving than corrective. Had her influence been more monopolistic, Chekhov might have developed with that greater dependence which is characteristic of the depressive. As it was, she was responsible for the softer side of his personality and for some of the security which enabled him to stand up to his father. His more completely positive relationships with his mother and brothers and sisters permitted him to individuate himself from his father. He was able to recognize how much he loathed his father in part because he enjoyed the love of his mother and his siblings. He was able to develop "iron in his soul" to cope with his father and all those surrogates who later seemed to threaten to humiliate him, in part because his affective investment in his father was more negative than positive and because of his relatively greater positive affective investment in his mother and siblings. But it must not be forgotten that this was possible too because his father was not a purely negative influence in his life. Had his father been only harsh and coercive, he might well have crushed altogether the fragile spirit of independence which later became so characteristic of the adult Chekhov.

Chekhov himself thought that he owed his more active, driving achievement and his ability to his father and his gentler side to his mother. "We got our talent from our father and our soul from our mother." Anton's mother, Eugenia Yakovlevna Morosova, was a gentle, kind, and somewhat educated and cultivated woman. Her father had been a cloth merchant, and she had received some education at home. Despite the ill-mannered arrogance of her husband she returned warmth and good humor for his abuse. She helped create a pleasant home despite the tyranny of her husband, and time and again she intervened to protect her children from the assaults of their father.

Near the Chekov house was a scaffold with a post for the flogging of prisoners. These floggings were visible from the Chekhov house. His mother was very distressed at the suffering of these prisoners and kept crossing herself while they were being flogged. She was bitterly opposed to serfdom and, in the words of Michael, "inspired in us a love and respect for all who were less fortunate than ourselves."

Anton was drawn to his mother not only by virtue of her own positive qualities but also because she suffered the same humiliation at the hands of his father as he himself did. There are innumerable references to his contempt for his father because of his father's insults to his mother and because of his father's failure to adequately take care of her. As we noted before, he was incensed with his brother Alexander's treatment of women, reminding him that this was how their own father treated their mother. His identification with and concern about his mother's humiliation are revealed also in his dreams. "When I feel cold I always dream of a venerable and learned canon of a cathedral who insulted my mother when I was a boy."

Chekhov is referring here to a quarrel with Pokrovsky, the chief priest of the Taganrog cathedral. Chekhov's father had infuriated the priest by correcting him during the services whenever he thought the ecclesiastical rules were being violated. Pokrovsky's indignation extended to the children, and since he was also the scripture master at the secondary school, he marked the Chekhov children down and quarreled with Chekhov's mother, predicting that no good would come of the children.

Anton was early capable of vicarious insult, not only with his mother but at school. As a student he was quick to sense and to resist insult to others as well as himself. Thus, when L. F. Volkenstein was expelled for slapping the face of another student who had insulted him by calling him a "yid," Chekhov forced the administration to rescind the expulsion by organizing his classmates to threaten to refuse to attend classes. But the classroom was not only the scene of vicarious humiliation but also of his own direct humiliation. The same disturbance he felt when his father humiliated his mother was also generalized to his teachers and examinations. He tells of the terror he endured at the prospect of being called on when he was unprepared. In a letter he wrote: "I still dream of my school, an unlearnt lesson and fear that the teacher might call me out." In another letter he described nightmares in which his teachers figured:

> When my blanket slips off my bed at night I usually dream of huge, slippery boulders, cold autumn water, bare banks of a river—all this rather indistinctly, as though through a mist, without a patch of blue sky; depressed and gloomy, as though I had been abandoned by the whole world or lost my way, I keep staring at the stones and I get the curious feeling that I must cross that deep river; at the same time I see tiny tugs hauling enormous barges, floating tree-trunks, rafts, etc. Everything is very grim, depressing and damp.... And when I start running away from the river, I come across crumbling cemetery gates, funeral processions, my former school teachers.... It is then that I am filled with a peculiar nightmarish chill which is never experienced by people who are awake but only by those who are asleep.

Examinations were a great trial for Chekhov. As he wrote in a letter to his cousin Mikhail, "I nearly went off my head because of these wretched exams.... I forgot all my pleasures and all the ties that bound me to this world during those days of constant worry and anxiety."

He was concerned for his mother not only because she suffered humiliation from his father but also because his father could not provide adequately for her. After his father became bankrupt and the family moved to Moscow, Chekhov was deeply concerned for his mother's welfare. To his cousin Mikhail he wrote: "Please go on comforting my mother who is physically and spiritually broken.... In this unhappy world there is no one dearer to us than our mother, and you will greatly oblige your humble servant by comforting his mother who is more dead than alive."

Not only was she gentle and kind and a fellow sufferer, but she also was responsible in large part for her children's interest in storytelling and in acting and the drama. She was very receptive to the theatricals which her children produced in their home and was particularly appreciative of the star of those performances, her son Anton. She was herself, as we noted before, an excellent storyteller, and her children would listen, spellbound, to her stories. Thus, she reinforced the interest in art which her husband tried to impose in his more heavy-handed way.

Chekhov's mother was, in fact, not altogether unlike his father, despite her much gentler nature. She was, first of all, equally ambitious for her son, equally demanding that he be industrious, that he make something of himself, and that he work for her. His mother was quite prepared to make serious demands on her son for support:

> We have received two letters from you and they were all full of jokes, while we had only four copecks to buy bread and candles, and we were expecting to get some money from you, and we are in a terrible plight here, and you don't believe us, and Mary has no winter coat and I have no warm shoes, and we sit at home.

She also has some doubts about his industry which she is not reluctant to communicate in the same letter:

> Every day I pray to God that you should come, but your father says that when Anton arrives, he, too, will go to parties and do nothing, while Fenichka [her sister Feodossya who had joined her in Moscow] argues with him and says that you are an industrious boy who prefers to sit at home, and I don't know which of them to believe.

Finally, his mother's ambition and her dominance over her son, though not as harsh as that of his father, were nonetheless strident and insistent:

> Hurry and finish your Taganrog schooling and, please, come to us soon; I'm impatiently waiting. And as you respect me, mind that you enter the Medical School; it is the best career. . . . And I want to tell you, Antosha, if you are industrious you will always be able to find something to do in Moscow to earn money. . . . I can't help thinking that it will be better for me when you come.

Nor was she incapable of identifying and communicating her perception of what she took to be serious faults in her son's character. Thus, Chekhov's mother said that he possessed "an inborn and inveterate spite."

She was, in short, a more gentle but nonetheless somewhat overdemanding model, who both reinforced his identification with his father and also provided a model for a corrective to that identification.

After Anton assumed the role of the provider for the family, his mother's nurturance could be given freer expression. She was delighted to be able to care for her family and all her guests in a manner her husband had never been able to afford. She loved to feed everyone well, and she worked night and day to nurture everyone. At night, for one of Anton's woman friends she would provide a bedtime snack "in case, child, you should suddenly become hungry." She anticipated every wish of her favorite son. If he came out of his study glancing at the clock, she would drop whatever she was doing and rush to the kitchen crying, "Oh dear! Antosha wants his dinner!"

Chekhov's Relation to His Sister

Just as Chekhov's mother provided a haven from his father's tyranny, so whatever was less than completely satisfying to Anton in this relationship was remedied by his loving sister Masha.

The mutual intensity of feeling between Chekhov and his sister was reminiscent of that between Wordsworth and his sister Dorothy and between Freud and his daughter Anna. In both cases the depth of the relationship was such that sister and daughter did not marry. Tenacity is one of the marks of the creative genius, and it is not surprising that the great intensity of feeling of such men should communicate itself to siblings or to children in their family and produce a tie that binds. The same intensity of feeling and tenacity which ties the child or sibling to the creator equally binds the creator to the beloved child or sibling. The importance of such relationships in the life of a creative genius cannot be exaggerated. Because his work demands on himself are so great, because he lives on the brink of uncertainty and defeat, and because he has so often suffered early, painful wounds to both his pride and trust in others, his appetite for constant, unconditional and unlimited love and respect is usually insatiable. To the extent to which a daughter or a sister can provide constant reaffirmation of love and respect, the Promethean spirit can be sustained.

There can be no doubt that Anton's sister Masha provided just such support for her beloved brother. Their relationship is illuminated by a reference in Alexander's letter to his brother Anton following a visit: "Of one thing I'm convinced. Your relations with Sister are false. A single tender word from you with a cordial note in it—and she is all yours. She is afraid of you and sees in you only what is most praiseworthy and noble."

Indeed, their letters to each other are love letters. Listen to Masha's complaints about her brother's absence: "Without you, the Yalta house is empty and boring. If you would only come home for Easter, it would be wonderful! The sun pours into your study and makes it cozy and cheerful. I'm very sad at leaving! I kiss you affectionately."

Masha's love for her brother Anton was such that she could not bring herself to marry and "deprive him of the conditions for creative work." After having received a proposal of marriage from Alexander Smagin she told her brother, "Well, Anton, I've decided to get married." As she recalled the scene, many years later:

> Brother, of course, understood who the man was, but he said nothing. Then I realized that this news was unpleasant for him, since he continued to remain silent. But what, in fact, could he say? I understood he could not confess that it would be hard for him if I left for the home of another, for a family of my own. Yet, he never pronounced the word "No."

She left him, deeply distressed and unable to reach a decision. She waited for him to speak:

> I thought much. Love for my brother, my ties to him, decided the matter. I could not do anything that would cause unpleasantness to my brother, upset the customary course of his life, and deprive him of the conditions for creative work which I had always tried to provide. I informed Smagin of my refusal, which caused him suffering. He sent me a sharp letter filled with reproaches.

Chekhov, in a letter to Suvorin at this time, describes both his own and his sister's reluctance to marry. Chekhov, however, was unprepared to recognize the critical role which his relationship with his sister played in both of their reluctances to marry:

> My sister's marriage did not take place, but the romance, it seems, continues through correspondence. I understand nothing about it. There are guesses that she refused, at least this time. She is an unusual girl who sincerely does not wish to marry.... Now about myself. I don't want to marry, nor is there the woman. But the deuce with that. It would bore me to fuss about with a wife. However, it would not be a bad idea to fall in love. Without real love, life is dull.

The depth of his relationship to his sister can be seen not only in his refusal to marry until three years before his death, but also in the nature of his attraction to his wife. There can be little doubt that some of the attraction of Olga Knipper for Anton Chekhov was her striking physical resemblance to his sister Masha. A group picture taken in Yalta of Chekhov, his mother, his sister, and Olga Knipper is reproduced in Magarshack's *Chekhov.* It reveals clearly the physical basis of this attraction in the extraordinary resemblance between the two women.

That this physical resemblance excited Chekhov sexually seems likely when one considers both how important sexuality was for him and how little attracted he had been to women before he met and married Olga Knipper, three years before he died. In response to his brother Misha's prodding him to get married he had replied:

> Concerning my marrying, on which you insist—how can I explain it to you? To marry is interesting only when one is in love; to marry a girl simply because she is attractive is like buying something unnecessary at a bazaar merely because it is nice. The most important thing in family life is love, sexual attraction, being of one flesh—all the rest is unreliable and dreary, no matter how cleverly we may have calculated.

But about Olga Knipper he had told Suvorin: "Nemirovich-Danchenko and Stanislavsky have a very interesting theater. Beautiful actresses. If I were to remain there a little longer, I would lose my head. As I grow older the pulse of life in me beats faster and stronger."

When Chekhov did marry, he did so rather suddenly and without preparing either his mother or his sister in advance.

When Chekhov did not hear from his sister immediately after announcing his marriage, he wrote her:

> That I'm married, you already know. I don't think the fact will in any way change my life or the conditions under which I have lived up to now. Mother is no doubt saying God knows what, but tell her that there will be absolutely no changes, that everything will go on as before. I will live as I have hitherto, and Mother as well; my relations with you will remain as unalterably warm and good as they have always been.... At the end of July I'll be in Yalta, where I shall live until October, then in Moscow until December, and then back again to Yalta. That is, my wife and I will live apart—a situation, by the way, to which I'm already accustomed.

The next day he received his sister's reply to an earlier letter in which he had casually mentioned the possibility of marriage. This letter had been delayed in reaching him because of his traveling. He suddenly realized, if he had not before, how much he had wounded his sister by his marriage. In her letter she suggests that Olga continue to be her brother's mistress but not become his wife:

> Now let me express my opinion on the score of your marriage. For me personally this course of action is shocking! And in your case these emotions are superfluous. If people love you, they will not abandon you, and there is no question of sacrifice on that side nor of egoism on yours, not in the slightest. How could that have entered your mind? What egoism?! You will always be able to get married. Pass that on to your Knipshits [one of Chekhov's pet names for Olga Knipper]. To begin with, you need to think about the state of your health. For God's sake don't imagine that selfishness directs me. For me you have always been the nearest and dearest person and your happiness is my only concern. I need nothing more than for you to be well and happy. In any case, act according to your own judgement, for perhaps I am showing partiality in this situation. And it is you who have taught me to be without prejudices! My God, how hard it will be to live without you for two whole months, even in Yalta! If you would only permit me to visit you while you are taking the kumiss treatment, even if it were only for a week. Write more often, please.... If you don't answer this letter right away, then I'll be ill. Greetings to "her."

Chekhov was disturbed by this letter, and he responded to it with a letter to Masha which she chose to conceal from the world, according to Simmons. Thus, it did not appear in her six-volume edition of Chekhov's letters (1912–1916). In 1951 she turned it over to the Manuscript Division of the Lenin Library, writing: "I request that it not be published." Hence, it was not included in the *Complete Works and Letters,* published 1944–1951. In 1954, however, she published her own *Letters to Brother A.P. Chekhov* and included the letter we have just quoted, of May 24, and, in a note, part of Chekhov's answer of June 4. After Masha's death in 1957 it became possible to publish this letter in full for the first time (1960).

This letter was as follows:

> Dear Masha, your letter, in which you advise me not to marry, reached me here yesterday from Moscow. I don't know whether or not I'm mistaken, but the principal reasons I married are: in the first place, I'm now more than forty years old; secondly, Olga's family is a good one; thirdly, if I have to part with her, I will part without any let or hindrance, just as if I had not married; she is an independent person and lives on her own means. So an important consideration is that this marriage has in no sense changed either my form of life or that of those who have lived and still live with me. Everything will positively remain as it was, and as formerly I will continue to live in Yalta alone.... When I told Knipshits that you were coming, she rejoiced.

In addition, in order to save her waiting until this letter was delivered, he sent her the following telegram: "I'm sending a letter in which I propose a trip together on the Volga. Well. You are agitated to no purpose, all remains as of old. Greetings to Mother. Write."

Masha, once having learned of her brother's marriage, felt guilty at her letter of May 24, and wrote him the following letter on May 28 (before receiving his letter or telegram):

I go about thinking, thinking without end. My thoughts crowd one another. How terrible I felt when I learned that you had suddenly married! Of course, I realized that sooner or later Olga would manage to get close to you, but the fact that you got married somehow at once disturbed my whole existence and compelled me to think about you and myself and about our future relations with Olga. And they suddenly change for the worse and how I fear this. I feel more alone than ever. Don't think there is malice in me or anything of that sort, no, I love you more than before, and with all my soul I desire every happiness for you, and for Olga, also, although I don't know how she will regard us and I cannot now give an account of my own feeling toward her. I'm a little angry with her because she said absolutely nothing to me of a marriage, and it could hardly have happened impromptu. You realize, Antosha, that I'm very sad and low in spirits, I am good for nothing and everything sickens me. I want only to see you and no one else.

Masha did not join her brother on his honeymoon but did respond to her brother about a letter from her sister-in-law as follows:

Dear Antosha, Olga writes me that you were very distressed by my letter. Forgive me for being unable to restrain my disturbed state of mind. I'm sure that you will-understand and forgive me. This is the first time that I've indulged in such frankness and I regret that it has distressed you and Olga. If you had married someone other than Knipshits, then I would probably never have written you a thing, for I would have hated your wife. But the present situation is quite different: your wife was my friend to whom I had grown attached and we had experienced much together. That is why I was filled with various doubts and fears, perhaps exaggerated and to no purpose, but I sincerely wrote what I thought. Olga once told me how difficult it was for her to live through the marriage of her oldest brother, so it seems to me that she should all the more readily understand the situation and not scold me. In any case, it makes me unhappy to have distressed you and I'll never, never do it again.... So don't be angry with me and remember that I love you and Olga more than anything in the world.

It is of interest that this triangle is between two younger sisters for an older brother who is an actual older brother for one and a surrogate older brother for the other, who had "lost" her beloved older brother to another woman.

Masha was to reveal the full intensity of her "murderous mood" and her "wretchedness" not to her brother but in a letter to Bunin, a mutual friend of Anton and herself. She confided:

I'm in a murderous mood and constantly feel the wretchedness of my existence. The reason for this partly is Brother's marrige. It happened so suddenly.... I've long been emotionally upset and keep asking myself: Why did Olechka have to allow a sick man to take such a beating, and even more so in Moscow? But it seems that the affair has ended all right.... I've begun to think about my own marriage, and so I ask you, Bukishonchi. find me a bridegroom, and may he be rich and generous! I've no desire to write but I would talk with you with great satisfaction. Write me some more. I've very broken up over Antosha and Olechka.

It is also clear that Chekhov's marriage to Olga Knipper did not by any means radically weaken his relationship with his sister. As a result it was inevitable that there would be serious rivalry between his wife and his sister. His wife, Olga, was angered when she learned by chance that Masha was privy to confidences from Chekhov of which she knew nothing. There were numerous conflicts between Masha and Olga. Indeed, Masha often acted as an informant on her sister-in-law during the period when they shared an apartment. Thus, Masha wrote from Moscow to her brother, then in Yalta:

It has become dull for me in Moscow, especially since I'm unwell and am always sitting alone, grieving over you at home for I almost never see Olga. Yesterday we nearly quarrelled. I tried to keep her from going to Morozov's ball but she went nevertheless and got back only by morning. Today, of course, she was all worn out when she went to rehearsal, and tonight she has a performance.

Olga felt a rivalry between herself and her sister-in-law which again and again had to be smoothed over by her husband;

Your letter is very, very unjust, but what has been written with the pen can never be effaced; there's

> no help for it. I say again, and assure you on my word of honor, that Mother and Masha invited both of us, and not me alone, and that they have always felt warmly and cordially toward you.

Olga also resented other intimacies between her husband and his sister. The care which Anton accepted from his sister he would not so readily tolerate even from his wife. Indeed, his wife complained of this in a letter:

> Why is it that when I'm there it is always difficult? Why do you torment me and never do anything?... But as soon as I go away, or as soon as you leave me, then remedies are prescribed and you begin feeding up, and Masha can do anything for you.

Perhaps the most telling evidence of his enduring tie to his sister was his will. Chekhov left to Masha the major part of his estate: "Dear Masha, I bequeath to you my Yalta house for possession during your lifetime, and the money and income from my dramatic productions; and to my wife Olga Leonardovna my dacha at Gurzuf and five thousand roubles. If you wish you may sell the real estate." Nothing was left to his mother since he assumed Masha would take care of her.

The multiple family of scripts which developed from this matrix were distinguished by a general strategy of moderation. Life seemed to Chekhov to be neither extraordinarily punishing nor rewarding and the possibilities of changing the world were neither hopeless nor Utopian. "I have very little passion.... Only people with equanimity can see things clearly, be fair and work." He had, of course, intense affect, especially shame. What he meant by saying he had little passion was more a reference to his governing scripted responses rather than to all the affects he had known in the critical scenes of his life. He was midway between a pragmatic and progressive liberal, always mindful that the human condition was a mixed affair, that the villains had redeeming features, the saints had serious flaws, and that he himself was not exempt from the limitations and contaminations he saw all around him. As a consequence, revolutionary radical utopianism of both the left and the right, which was endemic to late-nineteenth-century Russian culture, repelled him. Better to leave one's books to a town library, feed starving peasants, give medical care to the sick, protest injustice in the prisons at Sakahlin. Better too to expose the smugness of the pious as artist and critic and to reveal some of the less obvious good qualities of those in whom one would least expect it.

From a deep script of shame and anger-driven damage repair he would first attempt to salvage his own self-respect by stiffening the iron in his soul, against his humiliating father. He would oppose that damage by recasting, by humiliating the humiliators, but would try very hard (and not always successfully) not to humiliate others. Indeed, as one who had suffered so much he was very quick to experience shame vicariously. One hundred years before his time, he therefore was a strong defender of the dignity of women *and* the protection of the environment. Not only should both sexes be treated without discrimination but nature, too, in its beauty, should be appreciated and not violated. As a physician he lived his life as a healer of the limitations of the body and as a repairer of the damages it suffered.

The price he paid for the shame and anger he had suffered was a conjunction of recasting, in countercontrol and in distance maintenance. Although dedicated to never humiliating others, he could never quite trust others (with the exception of his sister) enough to reduce the distance between himself and them so that deep face-to-face intimacy could be achieved. In part this was magnified by the punitive socialization of his own distress. He became a kinder and gentler version of his father and mother but always with an undercurrent of distancing dismell, as in his affectionate term for his wife, "my little cockroach," whom he kept at a safe distance much of the time in Moscow. He had had half-serious love affairs with many women whom he had successfully transformed, always, into "friends" to turn off their passion.

In summary his scripts dictated that one repair as much shameanger damage as possible for the self and for others, that the same modest goals be used to remedy life's enduring limitations, that one expose all those who are piously self-serving and humiliating, as well as those who are lazy, boring, taking rather than giving, insensitive, vulgar, vain, ineffective, self-indulgent, overly pious, opportunistic, fawning, and servile. One should also expose the corruption of power in high places which dehumanized prisoners in Siberian Sakahlin. Chekhov preceded Solzhenitsyn by a century. Further he preceded the protest against discrimination against women and the pollution of the environment by many years.

Finally, he scripted a defense against intimacy, that one avoid being shamed and angered by a conjunction of controlling others, keeping them at a safe distance. In short one must heal self and others, purify the self of shame, expose the corrupt and insulate the self against too great vulnerability to shame, all done with optimal moderation and awareness of the limitations of the human condition.

THE CASE OF SCULPTOR: REPARATIVE NUCLEAR SCRIPT OF SIBLING RIVALRY SHAME-ANGER DAMAGE

We will here present a summary of the case of Sculptor, which has been presented in greater detail in Tomkins (1987). In that presentation the nuclear script based on reparation was assumed to be the general case. I have since generalized the theory of the nuclear script, so the reparative nuclear script is now conceived to be a special case. What is now the general case is any magnified negative affect scene which generates sufficient greed for relief, conjoined with sufficient intimidation and cowardice which blocks both enduring and effective attenuation of the family of problematic scenes at the same time that one cannot relinquish the increasingly excessive greedy demandingness. In the case of the reparative nuclear script, a good scene has turned bad. In the case of other nuclear scripts there may never have been a good scene but only an excessively damaging one, or an excessively limiting one, or one excessively contaminated one, or one excessively toxic which demands solution but cannot command it.

If ideology is a faith in a systematic order in the world and commitment is the courage and endurance to bind the self to an enhancement of a segment of that order, nuclear scripts speak to the conjunction of greed and cowardice in response to seduction, damage, limitation, contamination, confusion, and intimidation. Nuclear scripts represent the tragic rather than the classic vision.

A nuclear scene is one or several scenes in which a very good scene turns very bad. A nuclear script is one which attempts to reverse the nuclear scene, to turn the very bad scene into the very good scene again. It succeeds only partially and temporarily, followed invariably by an apparent replay of the nuclear scene in which the good scene again turns bad.

Nuclear scripts arise from the unwillingness to renounce or mourn what has become irresistibly seductive and the inability to recover what has been lost; to purify or integrate what has become intolerably contaminated or conflicted; to simplify or to unify what has become hopelessly turbulent in complexity, ambiguity, and rate of change; and to diminish the intolerably toxic.

It is the seductiveness of the good scene which magnifies the intolerability of its loss and the intransigence of the relentless attempt at reversal of the bad to the good scene. It is the intimidation, contamination, or confusion of the bad scene which magnifies the hopelessness and ineffectiveness of that reversal.

Thus, there is produced a conjunction of greed and cowardice. By greed I mean the inflation of positive-affect seductiveness. By cowardice I mean the inflation of negative-affect intimidation, contamination, or confusion.

The self victimizes itself into a tragic scene in which it longs most desperately for what it is too intimidated to pursue effectively. That part of the personality which has been captured by a nuclear script constitutes a seduction into a lifelong war which need never have been waged against enemies (including the bad self) who were not as dangerous or villainous as they have become, for heavens which never were as good as imagined, nor, if attained, would be as good as they are assumed to be. Nuclear scripts are inherently involved in idealized *defenses* against idealized *threats* to idealized *paradises.*

They represent an entropic cancer in which negative affect increasingly neutralizes positive affect and does so by the varieties of mechanisms of magnification and growth which are co-opted by the nuclear script, which invades the life space of the more positive affect possibilities governed by other types of scripts. Growth and magnification are thereby excessively pressed into the service of psychological warfare on behalf of a beleagured personality.

How could such improbable scripts have been constructed and, having been constructed, never relinquished? Briefly, several conjoint conditions, both simultaneous and sequential, had to have occurred. First, both good scenes and bad scenes had to be magnified through *repetition* and *aggregation* rather than repetition and attenuation. Second, such magnification must have become *reciprocally defined* rather than orthogonal. The good scene must have become more seductive by vidious contrast to the bad scene, made worse by its invidious contrast to the good scene. Reciprocal simultaneous contrast magnified both the good and bad scenes. Third, such reciprocal definition and magnification must have been *multidimensional,* thus further enhancing the magnification of both. Fourth, the *directionality* of *sequence* must have been *biased* from positive to negative rather than in the opposite direction and rather than random. Fifth, such biased directionality must have magnified an intention to *reverse* that bias rather than modulate it, accept it, or habituate to it. The nuclear script formation begins with this intention to reverse the magnified nuclear scene. Sixth, nuclear script magnification begins with the *reciprocal* definition of nuclear scene and script, since that script is defined as the rules by which the nuclear scene can be reversed. Seventh, the nuclear script is *multidimensional,* both in the varieties of dimensions of the nuclear scene to be remedied and in the varieties of strategies to be employed in reversing each dimension. Eighth, the nuclear script is *biased* in the *directionality* of its *sequences,* beginning with analogs of the bad scene which are reversed into *better* scenes as antianalogs, which invariably turn into replays and analogs of the bad nuclear scenes. Thus, a nuclear scene positive-negative sequence is transformed into a nuclear script negative-positive-negative sequence. Ninth, good and bad scenes are *bifurcated and intense* rather than continuous with gradations of degree. One is safe or in danger, victorious or defeated, loved or rejected. Strategies of the nuclear script are therefore judged entirely effective and ineffective. Tenth, nuclear scripts employ a *minimize*-negative-affect—*maximize*-positive-affect strategy rather than optimizing or satisficing strategies. Eleventh, nuclear scripts are further magnified by *biased uncontrolled lability* in which rapid uncontrolled shifts from positive to negative scenes, from antianalogs to analogs, occur more frequently than shifts in the negative positive direction. These are more controlled but slower and more arduous. Such lability is in contrast to scenes which are *stable* and *polarized,* or segregated; or orthogonal; or scenes which *change* but do so *slowly* with effort or at a *controlled rate,* as in any skilled performance.

Nuclear scene and script are interdependent not only in their reciprocal *definition* of heaven and hell, but, more important, they are locked into *reciprocal magnification.* Many scripts become autonomous of their origins, but a nuclear scene as origin in heaven-turned-hell and a nuclear script as hell with terminal in heaven collude not only in keeping each other alive but in providing the luxuriant soil for their reciprocal growth and magnification. Each *requires* the other to thrive. It is only the *repeated* intensely rewarding vision of heaven and the equally punishing replay of that heaven-turned-hell—in unending, varied, but nonetheless inevitably recurrent sequences of scenes of delight and anguish—which validates the nuclear script and prompts the lifelong pursuit of certain defeat amid uncertain, partial, and temporary victories.

How such collusive reciprocal definition and magnification of nuclear scene by nuclear script may occur we will now examine in the case of a creative sculptor. This was an individual whose life was at some risk in his first year. He suffered protracted hunger because of an inability to digest milk, to which he responded with violent projectile vomiting. His mother gave him to a wet nurse for breastfeeding, who described the infant's oral greed as "killing" her. This provided the earliest repeated mode of a good scene, the pleasure of feeding, turned suddenly and unaccountably bad, shaking the whole body in frightening, painful projectile vomiting. Because he was troubled with intestinal problems, he was given, on the advice of his mother's brother (an experimentally minded physician) high colonic enemas of argyrol. These were no less painful, nor less terrifying than the vomiting. Together they evoked a vivid sense of himself as a battlefield with concurrent explosions at both body orifices. Further, food and feces were fatally connected by his mother's insistence on giving him an enema to "clean" his body whenever he ate food she feared might be bad for him. In this way the good scene of oral pleasure was turned bad, not only by vomiting but by intentional maternal invasion of his body by high colonic enemas. To this day he remembers the terror of the threat of the enema. But he was bound to his oppressor by the intense love she displayed, by her constant reassuring, hovering attention, by her soothing bathing of him, by her constant feeding of him (after his first year's projectile vomiting had stopped), and not least by her remaining by his side when he went to bed, permitting him to hold her hand so that he fell asleep in her arms. If it was hell to be ripped apart at the mouth and anus, it was heaven to look at her, to be looked at, to be fed, to be bathed, and to be held in her arms.

If too often she appeared to wish to torture him, that only heightened those moments when she became his savior, and those moments became more continuous and sustained after his digestive problems diminished. The distinction between good food and good mother, and bad food and bad mother, bad vomiting and bad enema was to become a permanent script in which he was to be forever vulnerable to the good turning bad as a nuclear scene. Even at this early date the sequences were at least two-dimensional. He was not simply the passive victim of his savior. He also knew that to be ravenously hungry and taking into his body meant that he would have to give up and give back what *he* had greedily sought and taken in and that, if he did not, it would be taken from him by force. Distress, pain, pleasure, and terror were tightly fused.

Taking in was then further contaminated by a severe whooping cough which left a residue of inhibited, shallow breathing, discovered and disinhibited thirty years later in the course of psychotherapy.

When he was three years old, his precarious hold on life via his mother's eyes and hands was suddenly and violently shaken by the arrival of a baby girl. His mother's eyes and hands and whole being were now riveted on that intruder and away from him. His own account of that scene is consistent with the account his mother gives.

For six months he retreated to his own room, and he spoke to no one. His mother reported that he appeared angry. This primary initial response of defense by retreat is one of the universal first nuclear subscripts to the shock of the good nuclear scene turned bad. However, it must be insisted that this is nuclearity by reciprocal definition and magnification. Had Sculptor not been so sensitized by the prior reciprocal magnification of the good and bad mother, he might well have weathered the reduced attention from his mother.

If he could have modulated his anger and distress and shame, the scene would have not been nuclear, and the script would not have become nuclear. It is the reciprocal density of positive and negative affect which is critical in the reciprocal magnification of paradise lost and which must be escaped, fought, for and recovered.

If his scripted *response* to this scene had not been to run away and hide and be mute, then that bad *scene* would not have been so intolerable. It was in *part* made more intolerable by his attempt to make it *less* so. In that very attempt he characterized it as a scene which *must* be escaped. Second, the conversion of a scene to a nuclear scene via a nuclear scripted response is never totally or permanently successful and so becomes a replay, an analog of the very scene the individual is trying to master. To run away and become mute is *not* to radically diminish his aloneness, but to exemplify it, no matter how much better it seems than continuing to passively suffer the scene of betrayal. A scene is made nuclear, and the scripted response to it nuclear when the response *must* be made *and* does not *effectively* deal with it. Nuclear scripts conjoin ineffectiveness with compulsion in contrast to the addictive script which is equally compelled but effective. The nuclear script response ultimately results in an analog for the intolerable nuclear scene, even when it is temporarily or partially effective. We will defer a discussion of Sculptor's other nuclear subscripts.

The nuclear script not only magnifies the nuclear scene by reciprocal definition but also by bifurcating the good and bad nuclear scenes into the starkest idealization and invidious contrast between the good scene and the good scene turned bad. Such a polarization excludes many degrees of freedom as possible alternatives. Strategies for remediation are therefore similarly bifurcated and perceived to provide safety or danger, victory or defeat, reunion or exile. The self or the other is regarded as clean or dirty, conflicted or decisive, affluent or poor, confused or single-minded. In the case of Sculptor he is either hungry and greedy in eating or vomiting or being robbed and invaded by enema. He is either in total possession of his mother or he has entirely lost her. He must therefore hold her hand tightly or withdraw, mute, and hide in his room. There are no gradations in nuclear script space, and this radically diminishes the possibilities of graded responses which might deal more effectively with the good scene turned bad. Such bifurcation leads directly to action strategies which are equally radical.

With respect to their general strategies, nuclear scripts are typically two-valued, requiring minimization of negative affect and maximization of positive affect rather than optimizing or satisficing strategies. Greed requires a maximum of reward. Cowardice requires a minimum of punishment. Clearly, a double maximum cannot be achieved, and the nuclear script consequently fails in *both* respects. It neither attains the prize nor escapes defeat. It is a game which must be played even though the player knows the dice are loaded against him.

There is a reciprocal relationship between the bifurcation of nuclear scenes and the minimizing-negative and maximizing-positive-affect strategy. To the extent that Sculptor is confronted with either totally losing or keeping his beloved mother, he is caught between greed and cowardice. He must have everything. He must lose nothing. He is necessarily forever suspended between heaven, which he can never reach, and hell, which he can never escape, by pursuing a double minimizing-maximizing strategy.

Nuclear script formation is magnified by the *multidimensionality* and by *multiple ordering* of the family of nuclear scenes and nuclearscripted responses to them. Because the change from a very good to a very bad scene is so momentous, all the cognitive powers of the individual are inevitably brought to bear on it. The individual is totally engaged in trying to understand what has happened, why it has happened, what might have prevented it, how it might be prevented from happening again, how serious the consequences might be, how long such consequences might last, what he might do to mitigate these consequences, how much this is possible, whether this change means he will have to change his understanding of the other or of himself or of their relationship, how responsible he was for what happened, how responsible the other was or both were, what he should do about it and what are the consequences of every response, how he can discover the optimal response, whether he should try to defend himself, to avenge himself, or to recover the good scene. These are but a sample of the multidimensional *possibilities* he now generates and with which he must come to terms by way of response. For every possible interpretation of what happened and what might further happen there are *many* possible remedies he is forced to entertain and to act on. The more biased and ineffective, or partially or temporarily effective, these prove to be, the more other possibilities he is forced to try. Nor will such experimentation ever come to a complete halt in his lifetime of seeking a final solution to these, his most urgent and central problems. In contrast to the increasing discrimination and enrichment of nonnuclear scripts by *convergent differentiation,* here *generalization* increases complexity in ever-divergent nonconverging possibilities. It is like a strategy in a game of Twenty Questions in which possibilities are continually increased rather than decreased through differentiation and convergence.

Because of the multiple ordering of interpretation and responses to interpretation, it is not possible to enumerate all the theoretical possibilities in all nuclear scripts. We can nonetheless enumerate four of the more general types of nuclear subscripts ordinarily generated in any family of nuclear scripts. First are a set of positive and negative *celebratory* scripts. These describe, explain, and celebrate the nuclear scene which was once so wonderful and then turned so bad *and* the continuing family of scenes which has been repeated again and again and which casts a long shadow over the future as ever-present possibilities. These celebratory scripts power continual monitoring of ongoing experience for signs of *either* good scenes, (antianalogs) or bad scenes (analogs) or possible sequences of good scenes which will become bad scenes. These celebratory scripts also then guide responses and celebrate their successes and failures, separately as well as sequentially. Thus, the individual who has just won an apparent nuclear victory by defeating his enemy will react as an omnipotent hero. The same script may dictate the surrender to total ignominious defeat moments later, to be followed by the negative celebration of the sequence of how the mighty have fallen.

The second general type of nuclear subscript is the script of *defense.* This may take one of several forms of avoidance or escape in which the individual attempts primarily to minimize the negative affect of the nuclear scene by, for example, running away from home, becoming introverted, being alone, becoming mute. The negative affects usually involved in these scripts are terror, shame, or distress—the "feminine" affects.

The third general type of nuclear subscript is the *counteractive* script, in which the individual attempts to reverse the sign of the affect in the scene by changing negative to positive affect or by reversing the casting of the scene via recasting. In the latter case the individual who had been terrorized would attempt to terrorize the other; if humiliated, would attempt to humiliate the other; if distressed, would attempt to distress the other; if enraged, would attempt to enrage the other; or if disoriented, would attempt to disorient the other. The negative affects involved are usually the "masculine" affects of anger and disgust and dissmell. Recasting is, however, one type of counteraction. Thus, a loss may be counteracted by trying to understand how it happened or by action designed to give it "meaning," as in the case of the head of the gun lobby who elected to prevent the further use of guns after his son was killed. Counteraction may take the form of atonement for guilt, or increased skill to reduce shame, or toughening of the self better to endure distress. Counteraction may take the form of simplification of the lifestyle in an attempt to deal with the turbulence of the pluralistic nuclear script, to get away from the "rat race." Counteraction may take the form of hostile identification in which one attempts to make the other envy the self by surpassing the other.

Finally, there are *reparative* scripts in which the individual attempts to reach the good scene, rather than to hide or to avenge himself. It is an attempt to recover excitement and enjoyment, not via belief, not via revenge, but directly. This may take one of several forms, either an attempted recovery of the preproblematic good scene before all the trouble started or a new scene projected into the future as a Utopian scene which will *undo* all the problems created in part by *both* the nuclear scene and by the nuclear script. In some versions the sinners must pay an appropriate price to be reinstated, and that sinner may be the self, the other, or both. Reparative scripts may be restricted to the level of fantasy and yearning or may be expressed in political manifestos and political activity in favor of a future Utopia, or in helping behavior in which one enacts an idealized good scene, "saving" both the self and the other.

Because the individual is continually being reexposed via analog formation to the contaminated nuclear scene, it appears to *him* (and to observers) that he is really trying to *recover* the good scene and to *minimize and escape the bad scene.* We are saying, however, that the nuclear scripts do *not* aim at recovering the original good scene but rather aim at recovering or producing an idealized good scene which has been magnified by contrast with an idealized contamination of the good scene, by double simultaneous contrast.

Consider how Sculptor generated these types of nuclear subscripts. In his celebratory scripts he continually detected analogs of scenes of betrayal and antianalogs of lovers who were pure of heart and faithful until death did them part. He also found recurrent sequences of the apparently faithful turning treacherous. He was alternately attracted to the good beloved, repelled by the bad beloved, and crushed by the saint becoming a whore.

He fled the betraying mother in a defensive set of nuclear subscripts which included mutism and hiding in his own room so that he would not have to look at his mother breast-feeding his sibling rival. But he also attempted several counteractive strategies. He hit the sibling and made her cry. His counteractive attempts to assert his rights to hurt his rival, to exhibit his own superior virtues failed to displace the other from center stage. Then he experimented with becoming his mother, walking around with an extended belly in simulation of his mother's pregnancy, evoking more laughter than joy. Then he attempted to become his own mother by feeding himself and overeating as he watched the mother lovingly feeding her new love.

Next he became increasingly curious about his extraordinary rival. What was it about such a toothless, hairless wonder which could turn that all-wise, all-loving mother's face away from his own, to that face? There is evidence of much more than curiosity and uncertainty. A year later he remembers an overwhelming excitement at the story of Genesis, of how God created the world out of "nothing," as he put it. Had his mother not earlier exhibited just such incredible creativity? Further, his mother often admiringly spoke of his sibling as perfectly "sculpted." Thus, I think, were the foundations laid for a counteractive nuclear subscript of creativity as a sculptor, perfectly suited to emulate and compete with his mother as creator. His sculpture, alas, did not breathe life into his creation, but it was the best he could do.

Then he attempted to be a better mother by feeding and caring for her child continuously, never once looking away and so never threatening her. At the same time he would hit his mother if she attempted to displace him in his counteractive script.

Finally, he would alternate mutism, withdrawal, and counteraction with numerous direct and indirect *reparative* quests for resuming his interrupted communion with his mother. He would ask to be bathed because then he would be cared for. He would pretend to be sick because then he was immediately again his mother's beloved. He would ask to be fed by his mother. He would insist that his mother hold his hand as he went to sleep, guaranteeing at once her attention and the displacement of his rival. He attempted to do clever things to evoke her attention and then repeated them endlessly to hold that attention, guaranteeing the ultimate loss of her attention.

None of these experiments was ever abandoned. I was able to trace their continuation and elaboration over many years. They constituted the basis for a lifelong family of partitioned nuclear subscripts.

It should be noted that the partitioning of the nuclear script into many varieties of celebratory, defensive, counteractive, and reparative subscripts introduces genuine novelties into the original nuclear scene responses. The individual never stops inventing new ways of celebrating, defending, counteracting, and repairing both the original nuclear scene and succeeding *derivatives* over a lifetime. Thus, when an individual tried to escape the original nuclear bad scene, he might or might not have attempted that in the original nuclear scene; and if he does in the derivative nuclear subscript successfully escape an experienced threat of the nuclear bad scene, this constitutes a genuine antianalog *victory* over *that* defeat. When that victory is attenuated or habituated and he begins to feel lonely again, this is characteristically experienced as a *double* defeat. It is in one case a defeat of the nuclear subscript of escape inasmuch as he may no longer feel "safe." In the second case it is *also* a replay of the original nuclear scene, in that he experiences the attenuation of victory as equivalent to being alone again as he was in the nuclear scene. Finally, the sequence possible threat of the nuclear scene–successful escape–attenuated escape is also an analog replay of the entire original nuclear good scene turned bad. In this whole sequence the positive-negative nuclear scene hovers over the nuclear subscript threat defense-victory-failure as a double repetition of positive turned negative and negative turned positive turned negative. A dual sequence has been overcome in a triple sequence, but this *also* repeats the dual sequence as a *part* of the triple sequence. Every nuclear subscript success is also a specific failure *and* a repetition of the original nuclear scene failure. In one case his victorious escape has turned "weak," into loneliness. It has also turned back into the original loneliness he intended to escape. The paradox of such magnification of the original nuclear scene is that it is produced by the partial success and subsequent failure of the responses intended to weaken that original defeat.

At the same time that possibilities are multiplied by the generation of these four types of nuclear subscript, further magnification of the nuclear script requires the learning of many new skills of analog formation of auxiliary theories and of generalized nuclear script space-time maps.

KARL MARX: REDEMPTIVE, REPARATIVE SCRIPT

In the depressive script of reparative atonement the individual alternates between heaven and hell, between paradise lost and paradise regained, by atonement through good works. He must work by the sweat of his brow to make his peace with his creator, whom he has offended and disappointed. In the redemptive script there is also the Garden of Eden and paradise lost, but now paradise is not regained through atonement but is redeemed, for God and his children, by his wonder children. It is not God's chosen people who must atone for having displeased their creator; but rather it is these wonder children who will lead God and themselves back to the Garden of Eden and the recovery of their collective innocence in heaven. In this version of the fall of man, it is God who has sinned against his children and made them sin, but it is by them that he *and* they must be saved—a little child shall lead them. As in the depressive script, good works are also necessary to regain paradise, but these are not to please God. God is now a fallen angel who must be punished and shown the error of his ways so that all may be saved and return to heavenly communion.

There is here a magnification, a purification and idealization, of both heaven and hell and of the heroic strategy necessary to defeat Satan and regain paradise. In such a script the positive and negative poles constantly grow more polarized at the expense of all other competitors. Consequently, such a posture tends toward a lifetime of creeping polarities. More and more is learned to be bifurcated into special instances of the basic polarity. In the case of a creative genius of the stature of Karl Marx we must expect the generation of a large array of concepts which will confront an equally large array of concepts—each one of which will be pitted against its own enemy on the other side of the barricades. Such turns out to be the case. Capitalist and proletariat constitute but one dyad of a large set of such dyads.

Another critical feature of Marxism and of the redemptive script in general is the sharp division between strategies of redemption and the intolerance of meliorism.

Marx spent most of his life in neither his heaven nor his hell but rather in a transition state, deeply committed to the strategy of changing hell into heaven and as such committed to instrumental activity, but at the same time utterly intolerant of any suggestion of meliorism. In the case of the redemptive script no meliorism can be tolerated because it is feared that if paradise is not to be totally regained it will remain utterly lost. In contrast to the world view of Freud, here the world once was a wonderful nursery, and it can and must be redeemed; indeed, it must and will become even better than it was before. It will be an adult nursery in which everyone will do as he pleases, in which every human potentiality will be realized. It will be a heavenly community of human gods in which there is excitement, enjoyment, love, and respect, more than enough for all. With so exciting a prospect any suggestion of compromise is a betrayal of the potentialities of humanity. Despite the fact that no compromise short of total redemption is acceptable, there is at the same time a complete commitment to do whatever is necessary no matter how difficult or how painful or how long it will take to achieve redemption for humanity. The redemptive script is as uncompromising in its insistence that love shall prevail as is the paranoid script in its uncompromising vigilance against the oppressor and its demand for revenge. Marx, as we will see, could be as unrelenting in his opposition to the oppressor as any paranoid, but revenge never becomes an end in itself because Marx's vision is of a completely idealized *dyadic* relationship rather than revenge for the individual alone or for the oppressed class alone. In the end both the oppressor and the oppressed will be saved so that their once perfect communion can be regained.

Marx, not unlike many other creative geniuses, enjoyed the blessings of an extended golden age. He was regarded as a "wonder child" and at the same time was early introduced by his father into the world of arts and letters, so the young Karl experienced maximal excitement and enjoyment while being educated by his father and later by Baron von Westphalen, who was to become his father-in-law. Education was fun for Karl Marx. The world of arts and letters was altogether exciting and satisfying. It combined rewarding intimacy with his beloved father at the same time that Karl evoked respect from him for his precocious accomplishments. His father loved him, respected him, and was ambitious for him while at the same time he guided, stimulated, and educated him. This was, for some time, a father-son relationship which had been made in heaven. Marx enjoyed the same kind of relationship with Ludwig von Westphalen, who played the role of cultivated, benevolent grandfather to his future son-in-law. Moreover, both of these men were liberals who taught Marx to venerate humanism, freedom, and independence and thereby encouraged his youthful pride and rejection of irrational authority.

As Marx grew into manhood, his father's guidance grew increasingly burdensome—became, we think, the famous "chains." Marx had always been quick to respond to censure with shame and anger. It was easy for Marx to respond to contempt in general with countercontempt and anger, but when the contempt came from his beloved father, it was not so easy to respond in kind. He was never able altogether to do with his father what he was to advise the proletariat to do with their oppressors.

The difficulty for Marx grew out of the oscillation between the unadulterated shared excitement and enjoyment which continued from the past and the negative phases in which his father censured him. It was the invidious comparison arising from the coexistence of the entirely acceptable past and the not entirely acceptable present, contaminated by varying admixtures of censure and contempt and unwanted advice, that forced Marx to construct a new script. In this new script the positive past was magnified and idealized and the somewhat contaminated present was purified of its positive components, leaving as a residue a magnified humiliation incarnate which could then be responded to with total self-righteous anger and contempt. We are assuming that Marxism was a theoretical solution not only for the problems of society, as Marx understood them, but also for his own dilemma. He never, in fact, behaved as a Marxist toward his own father. Although some creative artists and scientists literally project the structure of their own past history into their creations, it is much more common that the creator achieves a *solution* which is *new* rather than a simple restatement of his personal struggle with his own destiny. We should not exaggerate either the continuity or the discontinuity of personal development. If the creative projection is a new solution rather than an unsolved old problem, it is nonetheless usually an attempted solution to a persistent personal problem even when it is objectified and writ large. To the extent to which there are commonalities between his own problems and those of humanity at large, his new solution may be more or less relevant to the general human condition. In the case of Marx the long enjoyment of the Garden of Eden followed by the later exclusion generated a militant self-confident humanism which was to provide the major ideology for the oppressed who had no memory of a golden age but who were now to live in the hope of redemption.

Marx's solution of his problem, then, was to magnify the difference between the positive and negative state and to commit himself to the struggle to recover the golden age against his oppressor so that both could once again enjoy each other. Paradise lost was conceived as a state of alienation, in which both the oppressor and the oppressed suffered alienation from their true selves and also from each other.

If we look back at Heinrich Marx's strictures we can see that everything which he objected to has been maximized in his son's vision of Utopia. His father had warned against his son's "silly wandering through all the branches of science," and his son's version of the classless society permitted complete freedom of choice. Indeed, not only could the future citizen wander through any and all branches of science, but his freedom from specialization was such that he could do one thing in the morning and another thing in the afternoon.

Heinrich Marx had also warned against his son's disregard of the value of money and had urged him to become "well fixed." Karl Marx's reply was that money was a false god, and in the Utopian society there would be no need of money.

Heinrich Marx had also warned his son against too "poetical fantasies" and that he should settle down to "make his name rise high in the world" and give up his idea of becoming a poet. In Utopia, all would be beautiful and artistic. Even the factory foreman would perform like an orchestra conductor.

Heinrich Marx had warned his son against the excessive "goodness of your heart." In the Utopian classless society, all was based on love and the mutual regard for the highest development of every human being. Every activity and relationship is humanized so that man attains his highest reach.

But Marx did not simply reject his father's values. Even as he rejected some of his values he maintained critical others. In his strategy for attaining utopia Marx was in large part identified with his father. His father had censured him for his "otherworldliness" and for his inability to separate fantasy and imagination from reality. Marx was to censure Hegel for his subjectivism, and to distinguish sharply between "reality" and "imagination." The basic strategies for dealing with the transformation of slavery into freedom are also based upon identification with both his censorious and his loving father.

Karl Marx faced the personal problem of redeeming both himself and his father from a relationship which had grown mutually more more and more unsatisfactory. Redemption could not be conceived in purely individualistic terms by Marx because he was too fond of his father and had enjoyed too much with him to renounce the rewarding dyadic relationship; and he had internalized the humanitarian ideology of both his father and von Westphalen, so *all* of humanity had to be saved if he and his father were also to be saved.

Marx was incorrigibly social because he had found fulfillment in communion which had both stimulated and rewarded his individual development. There could be for Marx no purely personal solution for the problem of alienation. His personal dilemma had to be filtered through his ever-expanding knowledge of history, philosophy, science, and art. Given his great intellectual gifts and his vast store of knowledge, it was inevitable that his personal problem had to be writ very large if it was to be solved to the conjoint satisfaction of his intelligence and his sensibilities. It is an oversimplification to suppose that a person of such erudition, with such an active intelligence, could be entirely satisfied with either *a* purely personal solution to his own dillema or with a purely "objective" reading of human history. His interest in man was an interest in himself, his father, *and* all of humanity, albeit conceived in categories learned from his own experience. It is our conviction that man's affective and cognitive capacities being what they are necessarily generate motives which impel human beings to try to understand the human condition as they experience it. The requirement that intellectual clarity and generality be achieved is prompted *both* by affect *and* by cognition. Human beings *feel* the necessity of seeing the truth, of intuiting the real structure of the world quite as poignantly as they feel the need to enjoy the mutual love and respect of communion. The human being is capable of understanding what he does not *wish* to be true. The engagement of his cognitive capacities by affect orthogonal to his intelligence, in the case of an individual with high intelligence, is more subtle than mere rationalization. It is rather to be seen in the generation of the problems, the categories of analysis, and the general direction of what will seem plausible solutions to these problems. The "solution" may be wish-fulfilling or it may be masochistic, but in any event it is ordinarily the outcome of a creative synthesis—for the individual, a new solution to an old problem.

Marx's strategy for redemption was essentially bipolar, reflecting again an identification with his ambivalent father. His father had oscillated from contempt and anger for his son to loving, respecting, and at the same time educating his son. Marx was to employ identical affects and affect investments in his strategies for redemption. It is our argument that organized Marxism, like organized Christianity, has tended to stress the more militant component of the bipolar strategy but that the pole of love and respect was the more fundamental one to both Christ and Marx.

Here, in contrast to the depressive script, contempt and anger is not directed against the self as a strategy of atonement. It is an important theoretical question why a bipolar socialization should in one case be directed against the self and in the other, directed outward. The answer to this is not certain, and it is likely to prove to require more than one answer. In general, however, we think that in the more intrapunitive posture, love and respect have been offered in a more conditional manner, and the price of love and respect has been taught very clearly by the consistent use of contempt and loss of love as punishment for failure or sin, as well as the consistent use of love and respect as reward for atonement for failure or sin, through good works. Not only are sanctions used consistently, but, perhaps more important, their relationship to each other and to the behavior which offends and which pleases is made very clear and at the same time amplified through dramatic reward and punishment. In contrast, in the case of Marx, in the letters written by his father there's the oscillation from deference toward his son to contempt and back to deference mixed with contempt against himself rather than his erring son. Thus, he decries his own inconsistency, his own reluctance to censure his son, then does censure him harshly, and finally, acknowledges his son's intellectual powers as being superior to his own. There is missing here any firm insistence on atonement or any statement of the conditionality of his love on his son's atonement. It is rather an attitude of free-floating censure and displeasure with a *hope* that his son will reform rather than an insistence that his son change his ways if he is to recover his father's love and esteem. It is an unconditional love (if not an unconditional respect), which has been contaminated for the father, but there is no suggestion in his letters to his son that the father *could* withdraw his love even though he might continue to censure and despise *some* of his son's behavior.

Not only is there, in the socialization which produces the redemptive script, a split between unconditional love and semiconditional respect, but there is an absence of total negative affect for the total self of the erring child. At no point does Marx's father completely reject the total personality of his son. It is always a censure for some limited sin rather than for a total depravity. Further, there is a limitation on the *time* of censure as well as its extent. In comparison with the depressive father, Marx's father cannot sustain his contempt entirely even during the writing of a single letter.

But if contempt was limited in scope and in duration, it was nonetheless amplified in a way which undermines the possibility of atonement. Marx, stung to the quick by his father's growing dissatisfaction with him, sought at first to cope with his humiliation by an omnivorous, devouring, Faustian quest for omniscience. He ranged broadly and desperately over the wide reaches of philosophy, art, and the sciences in quest of his identity. It was this very quest, however, which evoked still more contempt from his father. In the case of the depressive, the road to salvation is made clear to the sinner. In the case of the redemptive script, the quest for relief from censure evokes more censure and so further contaminates the golden age and makes impossible both atonement and meliorism. There is in the redemptive script both more mutuality and more independence than in the case of the depressive script.

It is the combination of the mixture of contempt and love, the unconditional love with the conditional respect, the lack of insistence on atonement and the lack of total rejection for the whole personality of the sinner as well as the relatively brief time of censure, and finally contempt heaped upon contempt, which, together with the earlier preponderance of positive affect expressed toward and evoked from his son, prompt shame and anger and countercontempt rather than contempt against the self followed by atonement. It should be noted, however, that his love for his father did not permit the ready, direct expression of contempt and anger toward his own father but rather prompted its deflection onto capitalists, proletarians, and fellow revolutionaries. We have seen that Marx was concerned lest, in breaking the "chains" of his conscience, we break "our hearts."

In the alienated state the proletarian was told what to do; was forced into specialization of labor; lost most of what he created which was of value; was driven by hunger, thirst, and sex like an animal; was servile; lacked money, the new false god in capitalist society; was made insatiable in his envy and greed; and lived his life in ugliness without appreciation of beauty.

In the future classless society man would do exactly as he pleased; he would be surrounded by beauty—even a foreman in a factory would be like an orchestra conductor; he would be entirely creative and moreover keep what he produced or give it to others out of love since there would be no money; hunger, thirst, and sex would be humanized; he would be proud rather than servile; and he would be in harmony with himself, with others, and with nature.

Marx conceived two major strategies for effecting the transition from one state to the other: First, one responds to contempt with contempt. The humiliated worker must be made angry and contemptuous of his oppressor—he has only his chains to lose! Second, and for Marx more important, we think, the children must educate the parents—the proletariat must teach *all* of mankind how to live, in love and in freedom. Marx is a Christian who will *not* turn the other cheek and a Hebrew prophet who *will* eat of the tree of knowledge.

It should be noted that both of these tactics are based on identification with the loving father who both educated and censured Marx. Marx replies to censure with countercensure, but this is subordinated, as it was in his own socialization to education and to redemption.

Residues of the Golden Age in Marx's Relationship With Engels

Further evidence for the assumption of a golden age in Marx's early development may be seen in his lifelong relationship with Engels. After his father's death, Karl Marx became intimate with Engels as a collaborator, as a friend, and as a patron. Though in his relationship to Engels he assumed the dominant position in the intellectual sphere, he made himself dependent on Engels, as he had on his father, in accepting and in demanding that he be financially supported.

Marx called upon Engels again and again and again for money. The following letters written within six months reveal his continuing insistence on financial support:

> With the last money you sent me I paid the school fees, so that I might not have to pay two terms' fees in January. The butcher and the grocer have forced me to give them notes of hand. Although I do not know how I shall pay those notes when they fall due, I could not refuse without bringing the house down about my ears. I am in debt to the landlord, also the greengrocer, the baker, the newspaper man, the milkman, and the whole mob I had appeased with installments when I came back from Manchester; also to the tailor, having had to get the necessary winter clothing on tick. All I can expect to receive at the end of the month will be 30 pounds at most, for these infernal devils of the press are only printing part of my articles.... What I have to pay (including interest to pawnbrokers) amounts to about 100 pounds. It is extraordinary how, when one has no regular income, and when there is a perpetual burden of unpaid debts, the

old poverty persistently recurs, despite continual dribbles of help.

These "dribbles of help" from Engels added up to not a small sum, and Engels's reply is in part a complaint:

This year I have spent more than my income. We are seriously affected by the crisis, have no orders, and shall have to begin working half time next week. I shall have to pay the 50 pounds to Dronke in a month, and during the next few weeks a year's rent for my house falls due. This morning, Sarah (be damned to her) stole the money out of my coat pocket. I am now living almost entirely at Mary's, to keep down expenses as much as possible; unfortunately, I cannot get on without a house of my own, or otherwise I should remove to her place altogether.

But Engels's self-denial did not stop Marx from continuing to demand more and more help from him. In four months Marx was asking for more money again:

It is sickening to have to write you in this way once more. Yet what can I do but pour my miseries into your ears again? My wife says to me every day that she wishes she were with the children in the grave, and I really cannot take it amiss of her, for the humiliations, torments and horrors of our situation are indescribable. As you know, the 50 pounds went to the payment of debts, but did not suffice to settle half of them. Two pounds for gas. The pitiful sum from Vienna will not come in before the end of July, and will be damned little, for the dogs are not printing as much as even one article a week now. Then I have had to meet fresh expenses since the beginning of May. I will say nothing about the really desperate situation in London, to be without a centime for seven weeks, since this sort of thing is chronic. Still, you will know from your own experience that there are always current expenses which have to be paid in cash. As far as that was concerned, we got on for a time by pawning again the things we had taken out of pawn in the end of April. For some weeks, however, that source has been so utterly exhausted that last week my wife made a vain attempt to dispose of some of my books. I am all the more sorry for the poor children seeing that we are so short in this season of exhibitions, when their acquaintances are amusing themselves, and when their one terror is that any one should visit them and see the nakedness of our poverty.

When Engels's common-law wife, Mary Burns, died, he wrote to Marx:

Dear Mohr: Mary is dead. Yesterday evening she went to bed early. When Lizzy went up to bed towards midnight, she was dead already. Quite suddenly. Heart disease, or a stroke. I did not hear of it till this morning; on Monday evening she was perfectly well. I simply cannot tell you how I feel about it. The poor girl loved me with all her heart.

But Marx so identified Engels with his father that he paid little attention to his friend's deep grief. It may be that Marx's hostility to his own mother was here projected onto his friend's wife, or it may have been jealousy for a rival or nothing other than overconcern with his own problems. In any event his response to Engels was in complete indifference to his friend's grief.

Dear Engels: The news of Mary's death has both astonished and dismayed me. She was extremely good-natured, witty and much attached to you. The devil knows that there is nothing but trouble now in our circles—I myself can no longer tell whether I am on my head or my heels. My attempts to raise some money in France and Germany have failed, and it is only to be expected that 15 pounds would not hold off the avalanche more than a week or two. Apart from the fact that no one will give us credit any more, except the butcher and the baker (and they only to the end of this week), I am harried for school expenses, for rent, and by the whole pack.

The few of them to whom I have paid a little account, have pouched it in a twinkling, to fall upon me with redoubled violence. Furthermore, the children have no clothes or shoes in which to go out. In a word, there is hell to pay. . . . We shall hardly be able to keep going for another fortnight. It is abominably selfish of me to retail all these horrors to you at such a moment. But the remedy is homeopathic. One evil will help to cancel the other.

Marx knows he is being "selfish" and demanding of help from his best friend just at the time when that one has suffered a great personal loss. What are we to make of this?

First is Marx's insatiable need for the love and respect of the other. When Marx is confronted with his friend's grief, it was first of all a threat of loss of love for himself. If Engels is so disturbed by the loss of Mary Burns, then he has so much the less time and attention left for me. As if to insure himself against such a contingency, Marx presses his own claims for love, attention, and, above all, money.

When Marx had suffered the grievous loss of his favorite son Edgar, he had turned to Engels for support.

> The house is desolate and orphaned since the death of the dear child, who was its living soul. I cannot attempt to describe how we all miss him. I have been through a peck of troubles, but now for the first time I know what real unhappiness is. As luck would have it, since the funeral I have been suffering from such intense headaches that I can no longer think or see or hear. Amid all the miseries of these days, the thought of you and your friendship has kept me going, and the hope that you and I will still find it possible to do something worth doing in the world.

Engels was shocked at Marx's callousness about Mary and could not bring himself to answer at once. It was five days before he penned the following reply:

> You will find it natural enough that on this occasion my own trouble and your frosty attitude towards it have made it impossible for me to write you sooner. All my friends, including acquaintances among the philistines, have on this occasion, which indeed touches me shrewdly, shown more sympathy and friendship than I could have anticipated. To you it seemed a suitable moment for the display of your frigid way of thinking. So be it.

It should be noted that Engels either misinterpreted Marx or was giving him a graceful way out since Marx had indeed shown sympathy and not frigidity, but for himself rather than for his friend.

In a few days Marx replied:

> It was very wrong of me to write you that letter, and I repented it as soon as it was posted. My wife and children will confirm me when I say that on receipt of your letter I was as deeply moved as by the death of my own nearest and dearest. But when I wrote to you in the evening, I had been driven desperate by the state of affairs at home. The brokers were in; I had a summons from the butcher; we had neither fire nor food; and little Jenny was ill in bed. In such circumstances, I can, generally speaking, only help myself out by cynicism.

Engels was relieved:

> I felt that when I buried her, I buried with her the last fragment of my youth. Your letter came before the funeral. I must tell you that I could not get the letter out of my head for a whole week, could not forget it. Never mind, your last letter has made up for it, and I am glad that in losing Mary I have not at the same time lost my oldest and best friend.

Immediately following the crisis in their relationship which had been occasioned by Marx's apparent lack of concern at the death of Engel's common-law wife, Engels was again under pressure from Marx for money. This time he "borrowed" a hundred pounds on account of the firm, without consulting his partners. Marx had threatened to go into bankruptcy, and Engels's heroic attempt was made because he wrote Marx: "I cannot bear to look on while you carry out your plan. Still, you will understand that after my exceptional efforts . . . I am absolutely cleaned out and that therefore you will not be able to count on anything from me before June 30th."

Engels played the role not only of the good father but also that of the demanding, censorious father.

In summary, the damaged relationship with the father was never totally damaged because the bond was too deep and too mutual despite mutual anger and dissmell. The shared unconditional love exceeded the conditional respect. Instead of depressive atonement for damage, Marx responded not only in anger but in redemptive love. It would be necessary to take over power in a dictatorship of the proletariat (while acknowledging the good the bourgeoisie had contributed), but this would pass and the state would "wither away."

Despite his extraordinary historical erudition, Marx was able to persuade himself that in the future Utopia, while there might be preserved some role differentiations, *no one* would be *permanently* assigned and chained to any role. The chains would be gone forever, so if he wished, he could go fishing in the afternoon and conduct a symphony orchestra that very evening. This would in no case prejudice how he spent the next day and all his succeeding days. He would be the wonder child who saved not only himself but his bourgeois father.

Chapter 34
Anger in Depressive Scripts

THE DEPRESSIVE SCRIPT: SHAME-ANGER REPARATIVE ATONEMENT AND COVENANT REMEDIATION

The depressive script is based on a covenant between parent and child which makes him a "chosen" child so long as he obeys the commandments of that agreement. It is not altogether unlike the covenant between God and his chosen people, nor is it identical.

The depressive is one who has found both heaven and hell on earth. Further, he is one who knows only heaven and hell. Hell may be the price of either immorality or failure, or both. In either event it is a fall from grace for a violation of a parental dictate. It is also a dyadic heaven and hell. It is always the other and the self who together enjoy heaven or suffer the torments of hell. The depressive believes that the other shares both his triumphs and his despair, that the other is not only censorious but is also as deeply disappointed as the one who is thereby depressed by the censure and disappointment of the other. In contrast to the paranoid, the depressed one has not been driven out of the Garden of Eden by the flaming sword of the guardian angel, by terror. He has rather been lectured and reproved by a more loving but more ambitious God, who has tried to show him the error of his ways and who has expressed not only his scorn but his deep disappointment in his favorite son. This god wishes to make man in his own image, to form his will, not to break it, to inspire love and respect and identification with himself rather than to forbid complete identification. Rather than the God of the old testament who requires innocence and, failing that, fear and awe, this one requires complete identification, even to the point of realizing ambitions which God himself failed to achieve. This God needs his mortal son to achieve immortality, just as the human race needed Jesus to achieve perfection.

Therefore, the favorite son cannot be driven out of the Garden of Eden but must be shown the way to achieve the state of beatitude and holy communion in which God will love and respect his favorite son. Unlike the paranoid, he not only can recover the state of grace but both the sinner and his God are dedicated to the recovery of their love affair, by restitution, atonement, and good works.

Contrary to the psychoanalytic interpretation of depression, the drama is not essentially an oral one in which one is fed and the other feeds, or in which the depressive oscillates between oral dependence or greediness and oral guilt. If we were to use oral imagery, it would be the case that the child feeds himself by feeding the parent, who feeds the child in gratitude and who instructs the child on what is good and what is bad food; when the child has given the parent bad food, the child also both loses his own appetite and has to somehow provide better food for the parent before he too can enjoy eating and the act of being fed by the parent. But this is not really the nature of the drama. The depressive is not interested in eating per se, nor in feeding the parent. He *is* interested in maximizing the twin affects of excitement and enjoyment simultaneously in others and in himself and in minimizing the anguish and humiliation and the attenuation of all effort which occurs when the positive communion is ruptured. He maximizes excitement and enjoyment not by being fed nor by feeding others, but by doing something which holds the other in rapt attention in excitement and enjoyment. He is exhibitionistic and also demanding, but he will work hard and long to keep the loving eyes of the other on himself. His disorder is self-limiting and episodic because he is excessively vulnerable to the fall from the state of grace whenever he loses the love and respect of the other, in fact, or whenever he loses the love and respect of the other who has been internalized and who lives under his skin. Indeed, he is vulnerable to the loss of *either* love or respect. If the other respects him but does not love him, or loves him but does not respect him, he is driven into that corner in the Garden of Eden which is hell in heaven. Not only is either loss of love or loss of respect a hell, for anguish and humiliation and reduction of nonspecific amplification, but any great reduction in energy is also a part of depression.

This is one of the reasons why, we think, depression is more frequent in old age and at the menopause and after the birth of a child. In all of these conditions there is a reduction in free energy available to the individual. Since such a reduction of available free energy is ordinarily followed by a subjective awareness of being "tired" and since such a bombardment of what is essentially low-level pain is an innate activator of distress, the combined loss of amplification and distress readily act as an activator of shame and self-disgust, and the individual is thereby "depressed." This is also why those with depressive scripts are daily vulnerable to minor depressions in response to the ebb and flow of the diurnal rhythms of internal temperature.

Because of these specific vulnerabilities—that he must be loved, that he must be respected, that he must be full of energy at all times—the depressive generates specific idealized scenes. In one of these he is loved for himself alone. He has "true" friends who will love him no matter what. Thus, in Mark Twain one finds the recurrent theme of the "Prince and the Pauper"—that when the prince has no fine clothes and is mistaken for a lowly pauper, he finds his true friend who loves him as he is, despite his low status.

In another idealized scene which the depressive constructs he is given unconditional respect—whether he is loveworthy or not. When this assumes psychotic proportions, it is the manic state, in which the self can do no wrong and cannot fail. The manic state is interesting in contrast to its paranoid analog, the delusion of grandeur. In both disorders the importance of the self is affirmed, but one is the impulsive boastfulness of a child who has been made to feel too much like an insignificant child. He recovers his self-esteem by feeling and acting big. He will therefore, in fact, undertake actions to fit the fantasy. He will buy expensive clothes and automobiles and gamble, on credit and impulsively. In contrast, the delusion of grandeur is a colder, more ideational affair which the paranoid will not test by impulsive action. Indeed, he will use it primarily as a weapon against the other delusion, that of persecution. In contrast to the manic, the delusion of grandeur has no affective or action payoff. It is a joyless delusion which brings no real comfort. The manic, in contrast, feels, for the moment at least, that he is important, even though he is desperately fighting off the state of depression and total defeat. The manic, if one scrutinizes him carefully, can be seen to be depressed the moment there is an interruption in his mania. This particular type of affirmation of the importance of the self is forced alike upon those with depressive psychosis and those with the depressive script because of the excessive demands of a socialization which has tied love to excellence, or achievement, or morality. Because of the inherent difficulty of always meeting both demands at once, there necessarily emerges a fantasy in which the individual becomes so godlike in stature that love is guaranteed as a by-product. Just as the prince finds true love as a pauper, so the manic finds true respect whether he is loved or not. But these are imperfect and at best transient solutions for the depressive. He must in the end become a prince who is also truly loved. He cannot remain a pauper even with love, and he cannot remain a prince without love.

Indeed, great achievement per se can become as dangerous as failure for the depressive if it is perceived as entailing loss of love and intimacy. The depressive may fear success lest it alienate the leader from the led. In contrast to the paranoid fear of the evil eye of the envious, however, it is not a fear that the weak and envious will seek to turn the tables on the strong, to kill and dispossess the strong. It is rather a fear that the envious will have contempt for and turn away from one who has risen so high that he has lost the common touch, that he has ruptured the communion and intimacy which once they enjoyed together. The depressive also fears lest in his quest for achievement he surrender communion and intimacy with the other, not only because the other may turn away but because he himself must turn away from the other for long periods of time if he is to guarantee great achievement. Even those depressive individuals whose career choice guarantees continuing contact with the other—such as actors and among these the individual performers, particularly the comics—must spend much time in disciplined hard work away from the audience they need and love.

What is the nature of the censure from the other and the humiliation which is evoked in depression? We have previously distinguished shame from disgust and dissmell on the ground that in shame the object, whether it be the self or the other, is not relinquished, whereas in dissmell the object is entirely rejected. In depression there is shame, disgust, dissmell, self-disgust and self-dissmell. The parent characteristically evokes both shame and self-disgust in the child by displaying disappointment as well as disgust and dissmell for the child who transgresses. Since, however, he also displays love as well as distress and disgust and dissmell, the impact is never as totally rejecting as it might otherwise be despite its distancing potential. The depressive internalizes the disgust and dissmell of the parent as well as the parent's distress, but to this internalized face and voice he responds with shame and the wish to recover the smiling, excited face of the parent. Although disgust and self-disgust are somewhat attenuated by the buffering shame response, nonetheless the depressive is one who has forever lost his innocence. Though he has not been driven out of the Garden of Eden to live by the sweat of his brow in fear of his God, nonetheless he knows what it means to be driven into that corner of Eden which is hell; and having internalized disgust and dissmell, he is now capable of judging others as he has been judged. Like his parent, he now both loves and wishes to control others and wants others to realize their best potentialities. In his relationship with his own child, as well as with others, he has a low threshold for feeling ashamed *for* the other and *with* the other, and he is quick to express both his disappointment and his disgust as well as his love and respect. In contrast with the paranoid, however, he is not afraid of the sinner or of the weak but rather suffers with them as well as censuring them. There but for the grace of God go I.

The depressive, like his parent before him, is not altogether a comfortable person for others with whom he interacts. As a friend or parent or lover or educator he is somewhat labile between his affirmations of intimacy and his controlling, judging, and censuring of the other. His warmth and genuine concern for the welfare of others seduces them into an easy intimacy which may then be painfully ruptured when the depressive readily finds fault with the other. The other is now too deeply committed and too impressed with the depressive's sincerity to disregard the disappointment and censure from the other and is thereby seduced further into attempting to make restitution, to atone, and to please the other. When this is successful, the relationship is now deepened, and future ruptures will become increasingly painful—both to tolerate and to disregard. So is forged the depressive dyad in which there is great reward punctuated by severe depression. The depressive creates other depressives by repeating the relationship which created his own character. The depressive exerts a great influence on the lives of all he touches because he combines great reward with punishment, which ultimately heightens the intensity of the affective rewards he offers others. One finds the depressive particularly among the great actors, the great educators, the great jurists, the great statesmen, the great writers—in short, among all those who are concerned conjointly with communion with man, with control of man, and with excellence in goodness or in achievement which excites man. The depressive is concerned not only with impressing, with pleasing and exciting others through his own excellence, but also that others should impress him, should please him, and should excite him through their excellence. Since he combines genuine warmth and concern for the other with the demand that the other realize his best potentialities, his influence on others is profound. We are speaking now primarily of those with the depressive script, but this includes the psychotic depressive in his nonpsychotic state.

The classic psychoanalytic theory of depression suffered from the absence of the affect of shame. Indeed, in Abraham's case material from which he derived his theory of depression it is clear that there was not only distress but also shame involved, as well as aggression as a secondary reaction to the suffering produced by an unfaithful love object.

Thus, in one case

> His analysis showed that his mother had been "unfaithful' to him and had transferred her "favours' to his younger brother, i.e. she had nursed him at the breast. This brother occupied for him the position of father in his Oedipus complex. In each symptom of his various depressive periods he faithfully repeated all those feelings of hatred, rage and resignation, of being abandoned and without hope, which had gone to colour the primal parathymia of his early childhood.

In another case he stresses

> how much the child longed to gain his mother as an ally in his struggle against his father, and his disappointment at having his own advances repulsed combined with the violent emotions aroused in him going on in his parents' bedroom. Unable either to achieve a complete love or an unyielding hatred, he succumbed to a feeling of hopelessness.

In both these instances Abraham correctly stresses the love and hate which is provoked by jealousy but fails to interpret the affect of shame which is evoked by the turning of the love object to what appears a more esteemed and love-worthy competitor.

THE DEPRESSIVE POSTURE IN THE COMIC PERFORMER

We will now examine the depressive posture in two contemporary performers, one of them a comic and one primarily an actress and singer: Jackie Gleason and Judy Garland. Before we examine these actors let us consider briefly how the theater provides a medium for the expression of the depressive script.

Drama and Acting as Mimicry, Countercorrective Identification, Expression of Depression, and Achievement of Communion

The theater provides for the playwright and actor alike a unique medium for the communication of thought and feeling. Both wish desperately to tell something, with feeling, and to evoke thought and feeling from their audience. Both must indeed communicate their thoughts and their feelings if a deep communion between writer, actors, and audience is to be achieved in the theater. Not all dramatists nor all actors have the depressive script, even though many do.

For the depressive, the theater provides the opportunity of expressing and experiencing vicariously the state of depression in all of its despair; its bittersweet longing; its soul-searching penetration; its half-plaintive and half-angry regrets for sin, for failure, and for the loss of innocence; its demands for rescue; and its imperious insistence on love and respect. It can provide also for writer and for actor, if the play is a success, the magic and balm of achieved communion in which the depressed one is lifted from hell to heaven. Finally, the theater provides a medium for countercorrective identification in mimicry.

In mimicry one holds the mirror to life, and the dramatist and the actor are first of all mimics. It is our belief that depressive socialization both employs and teaches mimicry. The depressive parent not only disapproves of his beloved child but also holds the mirror for the child, describing exactly how the child offends.

In corrective identification the parent expresses surprise, disappointment, contempt, or anger at the child's deviation from the parental norm, at the child's failure to realize his own best potential, and at his deviation from his own past better behavior. Although such a parent may be quite harsh, there is also conveyed, either then or at some other time, the close identification of the parent with the deviant child.

Such a parent teaches the child not only a set of norms for his own behavior but also a general mode of interpersonal relatedness. Such a child is being taught both to have contempt for and to concern himself closely with others and to hold up a mirror so that others may see themselves as they are seen. Among other things he is being taught to mimic and satirize the other, to both criticize and help the other. Such a mode of interpersonal relatedness is readily pressed into use to express countercontempt per se as well as love and identification. Whereas another child may be taught by a physically punitive parent to respond to others by physical hostile counterattack to any assault on themselves, the depressive child is essentially being taught to respond to affront by countercontempt.

Mimicry is the method of choice of any child who is at once close to others but who has also been humiliated by them. It is a prime way of the depressive for expressing contempt and concern at one and the same time. Such mimicking contempt may take many forms. It is either based upon an identification with the parent's contempt, now turned toward the self or away from the self toward others, or it may be directed against the parents and involve a correction of the corrector. In the latter case, countercorrection may be no more than a turning of the tables on the parent, as when Chekhov criticized his aged father for being lazy (having been earlier humiliated by his father in the same way). But correction of the corrector may also involve a new norm directed against the parent, as when Chekhov insisted that his aged father stop beating and humiliating his brothers. In this case the general mode of corrective identification which has been learned from the father is retained, but it is reversed against the father because now the parental norms themselves become the object of contempt. Chekhov, as we have seen, used mimicry when he was a child as a weapon against all who oppressed and humiliated him.

It is our belief that the humor and the mimicry of the comic are born of contempt and love. The comic is one who wishes to be loved and respected for the loving contempt which he turns on himself, on his audience, and on others generally. He holds a bittersweet mirror to his audience by means of which he hopes to evoke that complex of feelings peculiar to the depressive script. His humor is gentle and loving, biting and contemptuous, at once. He destroys and punishes out of love.

The relative balance of outraged angry contempt and forgiving love may vary widely from humorist to humorist and from comic to comic, but when anger and contempt entirely crowd out love, humor is also being squeezed out. Humor which is entirely savage is almost indistinguishable from the tragic.

Let us turn now to an examination of a contemporary American comic.

Jackie Gleason

Jackie Gleason, in his "Apology at Bedtime," presents an almost identical oscillation from contempt to love:

> Listen, son, I'm saying this to you as you lie asleep, one little hand crumpled under your cheek, blond curls on your forehead. I've just stolen into your room, alone. A few minutes ago, as I sat reading my paper in the den, a hot, stifling, wave of remorse swept over me. I couldn't resist it and, guiltily, I came to your bedside.
>
> These are the things I was thinking, son. I had been cross. I scolded you as you were dressing for school because you gave your face just a dab with a towel. I took you to task for not cleaning your shoes. I called out angrily when I found you had thrown some of your things on the floor. And at breakfast too I found fault. You spilled things. You put your elbows on the table. You spread butter too thick on your bread. As you started off to play and I made for my car, you turned and waved your little hand and called, "Goodbye, daddy," and I frowned and said in reply, "Straighten your shoulders."
>
> And then it began all over again in the late afternoon. As I came up the hill, I spied you down on your knees playing marbles. There were holes in your stockings and I humiliated you before your boy friends by making you march ahead of me back to the house. "Stockings are expensive, and if you had to buy them, you'd be more careful." Imagine that, son, from a father. Such stupid logic! And, do

> you remember, later, when I was sitting in the den, how you came in softly and timidly with a sort of a hurt look in your eyes, and I glanced up over my paper, impatient at the interruption. You hesitated at the door. "What is it you want?" I snapped. You said nothing but ran across, in one plunge, and threw your arms around my neck and kissed me again and again, and your small arms tightened with an affection that God had set blooming in your heart and which even neglect could not wither, and then you were gone, pattering up the stairs.
>
> Well, son, it was shortly afterward that my paper slipped from my hands and a terrible, sickening, fear came over me. Suddenly I saw my horrible selfishness and I felt sick at heart. What was habit doing to me? The habit of complaining, of finding fault, of reprimanding. All of these were my reward to you for being only a small boy. It wasn't that I didn't love you; it was that I expected too much of you. I was measuring you by the yardstick of my own age, and, son, I'm sorry. I promise never to let my impatience, my nervousness, my worries, ever again muddle or conceal my love for you.

The father is guilt-stricken because he violated the loving communion between father and son by holding too high standards for his son, whose love for his father had been unconditional in the face of insult. Gleason represents the father as making restitution for this rupture of their relationship. The parent is guilty of "expecting too much of youth," the depressive tension between love and contempt.

Judy Garland

Judy Garland was an actress and singer whom we have chosen to illustrate the depressive posture among actors other than comics. The following material is based upon interviews reported in *Look* magazine.

First let us examine the characteristic intimacy with children, which oscillates between anger, guilt, and love:

> My children are the most special thing in my life. They are very portable. I've uprooted them, dragged them from one country to another, because I'll never leave them in the care of servants. They are happy as long as their mother and daddy are with them. You try to keep them as long as you can and prepare for the day when they'll leave. You have to be ready not to be an idiot about it when they do leave, because they will. They must have a life of their own.
>
> But, right now, we're just a family of baggy-pants comedians. We have lots of fun, lots of love. Even at our lowest moments, we are really very funny together. The kids are even amused by Momma's bad Irish temper. They think it's funny when she explodes and apologizes the next minute. At least, I don't sulk and get ulcers.

Note that it is the mother, Judy Garland, as it was the father in the case of Jackie Gleason, who makes restitution to the children for having violated the intimacy and communion which they had enjoyed. Note also the characteristic depressive ambivalence toward holding onto her children and making them independent enough to leave.

Next let us examine the norms by which she is governed:

> It *may* be my power of concentration. I really mean every word of every song I sing, no matter how many times I've sung it before. But then in Paris and Amsterdam, I didn't sing in French or Dutch, and the same audience uproars took place. So I really don't know what it is. Something wonderful takes place between me and all the people out there. It's like a marvelous love affair. All you have to do is never cheat and work your best and work your hardest, and they'll respond to you. Such satisfaction can't apply to many other things in life.

She must work her "hardest," not cheat, give her utmost concentration, and then she will evoke from her audience the love and intimacy which is "a marvelous love affair." This is one variant of the depressive script in its purest form: I will work for you and we shall be as one!

Such an actress captures her audience because she communicates her love, her passionate need of their response, and her utter willingness to work for her audience.

There is also terror—the terror of evoking contempt rather than love and respect, and so being plunged into hopeless depression:

> It's a great thing to lose fear. I had an unreasonable block against television, and I had to break through

> this final block in my life. My previous TV shows were utter chaos to me, because I was so frightened. In those shows, I'd blow up like a fish—you know, the kind of fish that expands if you tickle its tummy?

This fear, we think, is the fear of that complex which leads to depression. Stagefright is, of course, by no means restricted to such fear. The unknown audience is a blank screen which can be endowed with whatever type of threat seems most imminent and most dangerous to the performer. Although the depressive is vulnerable to fear in the face of an unknown and uncertain audience, ordinarily such fear is the fear of contempt, of loss of love, and of the state of depression. It is for this reason that fear is readily reduced by the positive responsiveness of the audience. This is quite a different fear than that of the paranoid actor who fears a physical attack which humiliates as it hurts.

There was however a faint trace of such a fear in Judy Garland's response to the crowd:

> There's a trick about handling crowds. If you try to push your way through in a panic, they'll mob you. The psychology is to walk very slowly, talking and joking as you walk. Then they are nice and sweet, nobody gets hurt or pushed, or mad at you—and we all end by loving each other."

This fantasy ends on a depressive rather than a paranoid note, and it would appear to be a faint residue of the projection of the angry "explosions" for which she apologizes to her children—her Irish temper. An angry depressive will expect anger which may "hurt" more often than will a depressive whose primary negative affect is dissmell rather than anger.

THE DEPRESSIVE SCRIPT IN THE EDUCATOR

Those who assume the depressive posture may continue to seek a parental audience to work for, or they may come to play the parental role and seek substitute children whom they may alternately reprove and reward. Nor are these two roles necessarily mutually exclusive. They may also alternate between the role of the depressive parent and the role of the depressive child. Whichever of these strategies the adult depressive elects, he will be powerfully drawn to the role of educator. I wish to distinguish sharply the role of educator from the role of scholar and investigator. The scholar and the investigator are committed to the pursuit of knowledge as such, and although such a commitment does not infrequently attract the depressive, our concern is rather with the educator, who may or may not be committed to the pursuit of knowledge as such.

The educator is primarily concerned with the communication of knowledge to others rather than to the pursuit or discovery of knowledge. Educators in general are motivated in quite different ways. The educator may be an obsessive concerned with tidying up the minds of the young so that they may be clean and orderly. He may be a paranoid who converts the classroom into a trial by fire in which he terrorizes as he humiliates, not sparing the rod lest he spoil the child. It is only relatively recently that the use of physical punishment has ceased to be a method of instruction in elementary schools. He may be an educator only accidentally because he is an investigator who is also expected to teach.

Though the motives which draw people into becoming educators are varied, surely the call to the depressive must be peculiarly compelling. The classroom permits the depressive parent-child reproofreward theme to be repeated again and again with endless variations. The teacher not only uses the students as substitute parents who are to be impressed, to be excited by their common interest and to thereby achieve intimacy, but their boredom, their censure and their turning away constitute an enduring threat and challenge which convert the classroom into a theater in which the depressive teacher, because he can never be sure of his audience, is put on his mettle to convert the audience to him and to his ways. He oscillates between good and bad performances in which he and his students are alternately transported and depressed. This is one way in which the depressive drama is performed. But it may also be performed with the children playing the role of children, not of parents. The teacher's children now represent him as a child, and he will play the role of the parent. In this role he will censure his beloved children for their ignorance, and he will love and respect them for their efforts to meet his highest expectations. Common to either role the teacher elects will be their mutuality and communion on the basis of achieved excellence. In one case it will be the excellence of the teacher which excites the students, and in the other it will be the excellence of the students which excites the teacher. In either event both teacher and student will feel drawn into intimacy through the shared adoration of excellence.

SOME CROSS-CULTURAL EVIDENCE CONCERNING THE NATURE OF DEPRESSION

Eaton and Weil's (1955) study of the Hutterites provides further supporting evidence for our view that depression is a consequence of the conjoint presence of that kind of love and dominance which ties the child to the parent in love and shame through atonement, restitution, and good works.

Among the Hutterites, depression is the most common reaction to stress in the sect. Patients with a manic-depressive reaction constituted 73.6% per cent of all Hutterite persons diagnosed as psychotic.

In a population of 8,542 Eaton and Weil found 9 schizophrenics and 39 manic depressives, or 4.33 times as many depressives as schizophrenics. In the United States, the incidence is approximately 15 to 1 in favor of schizophrenia, with 31.2 schizophrenics per 100,000, according to Malzberg's data on first admission in 1950 in the state of New York.

Eaton and Weil reported that in ten other populations, geographically widely distributed over Asia, Europe, and North America, there were more schizophrenic than manic-depressive patients. The highest ratio of schizophrenic to manic-depressive reactions was 46 to 1 in the area of Northern Sweden.

They report a virtual absence of severe personality disorders, obsessive-compulsive neuroses, and psychoses associated with syphilis, alcoholism, and drug addiction. There was little free-floating anxiety, acting out, or projection. Nearly all patients, even the most disturbed schizophrenics, lived up to the strong taboo against overt physical aggression and physical violence. Paranoid, manic, severely antisocial, or extremely regressive symptoms were uncommon. Equally rare, or completely absent were severe crimes, marital separation, and other forms of social disorganization.

This group is both genetically and culturally inbred because of the distinctive and separatist orientations of the Hutterite way of life, as well as the strong kinship ties. Hutterite religion forbids marriages with nonmembers of the church. They have a strict moral code, which is enforced. Adolescents are carefully watched, and in addition conscience and parental control reduce the possibility of sexual relationships outside the Hutterite group. Eaton and Weil report that they did not encounter a single case of a woman reputed to have been made pregnant by an outsider.

Hutterites believe in the communal ownership and control of all property. Christ and the Bible are their chief guides. They live under economic communism in which the community assumes a major responsibility for everyone. No wages are paid, but everyone is expected to work. They eat their meals in the community dining room, and the meals are prepared by different women in rotation. The Hutterite way of life provides social security from the womb to the tomb, according to Eaton and Weil. In sickness, the colony pays for all necessary care. In the case of male death, widows and dependents have no financial worries. The Hutterite religious creed also promises absolute salvation so long as one follows its precepts.

The source of depression among the Hutterites is not from failure to work or achieve but rather from immorality. With respect to achievement no one is pushed to exert himself beyond what he himself regards to be his capacity. Everyone is expected to do the best he can, but he is not subjected to unusual pressures in this domain. Censure and shame occur primarily in the moral realm rather than in the achievement realm. In contrast to most depression in contemporary American society, love is conditional not upon achievement but upon goodness.

It is particularly the control of anger and sexuality which is tightly joined with the threat of loss of love. The Hutterite child is not censured or shamed for incompetence or laziness so much as he is for not "minding," for being disrespectful, for being aggressive, for questioning the existence of God, and for masturbating. If he violates any of these social norms he is censured and humiliated, but if he atones, makes restitution, and mends his ways, he is again beloved. The affects involved are identical with those we postulated in the case of the union of love and achievement. When it is the control of sex and aggression which is the focus of socialization, the affects of shame and self-disgust are experienced as "guilt." While we believe that guilt is in fact the affect of shame focused on the self-control of sex or anger or any other impulse the culture defines as immoral, the conscious awareness of the totality in the central assembly can appear to the individual to be quite different from the experience of shame for failure. In short, shame for failure and shame for immorality are experienced as two quite different complexes despite the fact that the affect in each complex is identical, in our opinion.

It is clear that in America generally, as well as among the Hutterites, there are depressions which are guilt depressions and those which are achievement depressions. In both cases love has been tightly tied to censure, shame, and self-contempt. The only difference consists in the specific conditions under which love is gained or lost. Common to both types of depression is the tenacity of both parties in maintaining the love relationship despite disappointment and censure.

There is then both harshness and love, balanced and coordinated to produce the desired Hutterite adult. Let us consider first the censure and the negative aspect of Hutterite socialization.

Andreas Erenpreis, the Hutterite elder, wrote the following admonitions against permissiveness in child rearing in 1652:

> Just as iron tends to rust and as the soil will nourish weeds, unless it is kept clean by continuous care, so have the children of men a strong inclination towards injustices, desires and lusts; especially when the children are together with the children of the world and daily hear and see their bad examples. In consequence they desire nothing but dancing, playing and all sorts of frivolities, till they have such a longing for it, that you cannot stop them anymore from growing up in it. . . . Now it has been revealed that many parents are by nature too soft with their children and have not the strength to keep them away from evil. So we have a thousand good reasons why we should live separated from the world in a Christian community. How much misery is prevented in this way!

These admonitions still guide the thinking of contemporary Hutterites about child rearing, although Eaton and Weil also note a diffusion of more permissive philosophies in some families and communities.

From early infancy most parents and all colony schoolteachers are engaged in a conscious effort to "break the child's will" so that he can grow up into a "good" person with a strong conscience, submitting impulsive wants to community expectations and suppressing rebellious attitudes against the authority of the mores and of individuals in positions of power. Masturbation and aggression are both suppressed.

The consequence is considerable stress in childhood at home and at school. Tears were not infrequent in Hutterite kindergartens and schools. They are regarded as a necessary evil. It is expected that children will rebel and that they must be scolded or spanked to learn to mind. Four hundred forty-five young Hutterites and their teachers were tested by Eaton and Weil, and additional ratings were obtained from Hutterite religious teachers. Two thirds of the children were rated by the public school teachers as "poorly adjusted, with a tendency to depression." The Hutterite teachers included more than four in five of their pupils in this category.

As an example of the strict discipline by which the Hutterite child is controlled, Eaton and Weil recount the following incident:

> A young staff member, who is very spontaneous with children, started to play tag with a group that had gathered around him. The tagging progressed into hitting, and our field worker was soon preoccupied warding off shouting boys and girls who were competing in the effort to get a lick at him. The

> staff member enjoyed the "game" and encouraged it. Suddenly the shrill voice of an elderly lady came out of an entrance door of the communal kitchen across the courtyard: "Geht Heim!" (Go home!). As if hit by lightning, the children froze, stopped and dispersed. One remark from a respected adult was enough to curb them, although the woman was not the parent of any of them. Later, she and several other adults apologized profusely to the staff member for the behavior of the youngsters explaining "They are awfully bad."

Nearly all patients, even the most disturbed schizophrenics, lived up to the strong taboo against overt physical aggression and physical violence. Paranoid, manic, severely antisocial, or extremely regressive symptoms were uncommon. Although Hutterites showed evidence of aggressive feelings in projective tests, they were not expressed overtly.

So much for one side of Hutterite socialization. We have stressed in our theory of depression the importance of sufficient love to make both parties to the conflict eager to heal the rupture of intimacy. Let us examine first, in this connection, the insistence on reformation by the sinner and forgiveness by those sinned against:

The Hutterites still follow the principles laid down by Andreas Erenpreiss in 1652, in his epistles on the Hutterite creed:

> Christ teaches us therefore to deal with small and petty things between man and man by means of a brotherly warning and admonition. But if a man is stubborn and does not want to take brotherly advice, he should be brought before the whole community. If he does not listen to the whole congregation, neither will he comply nor obey, he should be regarded as a heathen man and a publican, who has been cut off and excluded. It is better that the evil member be cut off, than that the whole body, namely the congregation, becomes confused and spoiled by such mean people, as we have said in part already above.
>
> Now such warnings and punishments *must lead to reformation and not to damnation.* [Italics mine.] If a member pollutes himself with coarse and heavy sins and becomes guilty before God, he should be punished and put to the blush before the whole congregation, in order to make the matter serious and set an example. Everyone who is taken into the community promises to accept brotherly warning and punishment, wherever it may be needed. It amounts to this: If a member falls into sin, as may easily happen, he should not abandon his hope and faith, go his way and give up everything; but he should bear his punishment in tears before God, recognize his own sin and repent like David, the servant of God, or repent in suffering like the prodigal son. The saints shall also pray for his forgiveness and the angels in heaven rejoice over the sinner who repents; following an honest repentance he will be gladly received back into the congregation.

Here the emphasis is more upon reformation than upon forgiveness, but in contemporary Hutterite socialization and community life there is evidence of great reserves of goodwill not only toward the erring child but toward the adult sinner and toward those who have become mentally ill.

Eaton and Weil's summary of the ambivalent socialization of the Hutterite child fits exactly what we have assumed to be specific for producing the depressive script and psychotic depression. "Children are generally wanted, they experienced a great deal of affection and acceptance by parents and most other people in a colony, but they were subject to a great deal of rigid and consistent discipline." There is a high degree of agreement among the Hutterites about what is "right" and what is "wrong."

The Hutterite community, as described by Eaton and Weil, suggests that each member of the community receives intimate, loving support along with considerable directive dominance, to which he is expected to conform, and censure if he violates social norms. It is, we think, just this combination of love, dominance, and censure which prevents a high incidence of alienation and schizophrenia and guarantees a continuing vulnerability to depression. The group will not let the Hutterite become estranged but neither will it tolerate serious infractions of the moral code. They show the children much love. The culture encourages parents to be permissive toward the physical and intellectual limitations of children at various stages of development. There is strong identification with the children. They are the only wealth an adult may call his own. There are few competing values, no professional ambitions or status aspirations.

Consistent also with our hypothesis of the importance of restitution and a way back to the strong positive relationships which have been ruptured by norm violation is the characteristic leniency of the Hutterite toward the adult offender.

There are two kinds of crimes for the Hutterite: aggression and social withdrawal. A Hutterite who serves in an army is violating Jesus' admonition against violence. To some Hutterites, a soldier is almost a murderer, who is inviting eternal damnation on himself. A Hutterite who leaves the colony to live "in private, on the outside" also is damned because he "refuses to live in community as did Christ and his apostles."

Despite their strictness in these matters, Hutterites are very tolerant toward these sinners. They will take them back with no more than a token ritual punishment excommunication for a number of days or weeks. "Deserters" are also welcome to visit their families, even for extended periods. Deviants are hardly ever rejected as persons. Family ties are maintained and often succeed in bringing the "stray lamb back to the fold." Hope is never given up, unless the deserter marries an outsider.

Not only are offenders treated leniently, forgiven, and taken back, but those who are incapacitated by mental illness are treated very gently. When a Hutterite became mentally ill, the entire community showed love and supported the patient. They were treated as sick rather than psychotic. There was no stigma attached to psychotic episodes to hamper recovery.

Hutterites refer to a depression as an *Anfechtung*—a "temptation by the devil." They regard the disorder as a spiritual or religious trial by God. Several patients mentioned the Book of Job, in which God tests the sincerity and the strength of a man's belief and trust in him. They believe that depression happens to good people. Manic-depressives are not ashamed of their episodes and speak freely about them. They are generally well integrated into the community. According to Eaton and Weil, they include a somewhat larger proportion of leaders and their wives than would be expected by chance.

There is thus both great censure and harshness in the socialization of the Hutterite child and in the treatment of the adult offender and equally great goodwill and leniency if and when the offender reforms. It should be noted that these two variables are theoretically quite independent one of the other. It is quite possible for socialization to be permissive and loving until an offense has been committed and then for the parent to be unrelenting in his hostility and condemnation of the child. Similarly, a society may be generally rewarding and positively disposed toward its members but excessively harsh and unforgiving of violations of its laws. Again, socialization may be generally harsh at all times, neither rewarding the child for good behavior nor forgiving the child for norm violations, even if he reforms or atones for his offenses. Finally, socialization may be generally rewarding so that the child is showered with love and excuses readily made whenever he violates parental norms.

In depressive socialization as we find it among the Hutterites there is much love and much censure combined with a readiness to forgive if there is reformation and atonement.

DEPRESSIVE PSYCHOSIS: HUMILIATION, ANGUISH, AND REDUCTION OF AMPLIFICATION

The depressive psychosis is two parts affect and one part attenuation. The depressive cries in anguish. His head and eyes are lowered in shame, and the tonus is gone from his body. Moving picture analysis of his posture, his walking, and his movements reveal that along with shame and anguish there has been a serious reduction in nonspecific amplification of all neural messages, especially involving the motoric. His arms do not swing much when he walks. There is little waste motion in any of the movements of the body which normally are executed with verve. He crosses his legs slowly. He lights a cigarette listlessly. His speech may be quite retarded. X-ray analysis reveals a sluggish movement of a barium meal through the intestines. The body acts as if it were incapable and unwilling to support normal tension in the muscles and unwilling to burn energy at a normal rate. It is the body of one who has been defeated, who is nursing his wounds.

The manic-depressive has, like the paranoid, also been deeply shamed but, unlike the paranoid, has at the same time suffered great distress rather than terror. Further, he has ordinarily been shamed for a reason and for something he can do something about.

The parent of the depressive, while he has humiliated the child and exerted considerable dominance in bending the child to his will, has also loved the child and exhibited strong positive as well as negative affect—hugging, kissing, smiling at and with the child, in short maximizing the positive affects of human communion. Such a parent is also idealized by the child as a strong but warm parent. The critical difference here is that there is a way back from the bottom of despair and shame suffered at the hands of such a parent. The way back may be immediate—as when the parent, having discharged contempt or distress or hostility against his child, and full of sympathy for the child he has just pained, opens his heart and arms in a gesture of loving reunion. It may be a delayed recovery and even a very delayed recovery if the parent's displeasure calls for atonement or restitution by the child for behavior which has offended, but even then the child and parent are both anxious to reestablish a close and warm relationship, and eventually there is a reconciliation.

In contrast to the paranoid, such an individual's deepest hope is to achieve communion with others, to be as close physically as possible, to talk with others, to excite them, to please them, and to do what will evoke both love and respect from them. Perhaps the clearest difference is found in the attitudes toward the eyes. One is afraid lest human eyes see him; the other is afraid lest human eyes *not* look at him.

Love and achievement are tightly bound together in depressive psychosis because the parent and the child are both caught up in the mutual enjoyment of exciting the admiration of the parent for something which the child is doing, just as both are bitterly disappointed and ashamed when the child does something which destroys their communion.

Let us turn now to our studies with one hundred depressives using the Picture Arrangement Test. Our control group was a subset of our representative sample of 1,500 cases. All in all we compared approximately 800 pathological cases with our representative normal sample of 1,500 cases. The reader is referred to Volume 2 (pp. 560–580) for pictures of the Picture Arrangement Test.

First, the paranoids were reliably elevated over normals on *Low Self-Confidence* such that they believe the hero will fail to win approbation from the group (Key 168). In a set of situations showing a man talking to a large audience the paranoid ends more frequently being booed than applauded and also ends with smaller rather than larger audiences. This indicated an expectation of being humiliated. Manic-depressives, by contrast, are elevated compared with normals on the opposite key—*High Self-Confidence: Win Approbation from Group* (Key 160),—in that they respond with the hero being applauded by his audience and with larger rather than smaller audiences. Manic-depressives do not expect to be humiliated. They see their own efforts as evoking praise from others. They not only wish to be looked at, in contrast to the paranoid's fear of being looked at, but their fear is often of *not* being looked at. In radical contrast some of the paranoids were apparently so threatened by a picture of the hero exposed to so many human beings at once that they denied the nature of the crowd situation altogether and distorted the faces of the audience into apples and oranges which were on the hero's pushcart.

More generally, Levin and Baldwin have reported a significant correlation of -.44 between an inventory designed to measure exhibitionism in children and an inventory designed to measure anxiety about facing audiences. Although negatively correlated, there were children who both sought an audience and were also afraid of audience visibility. They reported that boys who receive most reward and least punishment from their parents are most exhibitionistic, enjoy facing an audience, and are least anxious about performing before an audience.

Further evidence for the difference in the nature of the interpersonal relationships of paranoid patients and depressives comes from the elevation of Key 142, *Dependence—Continuing Support as End State—Dominance or Instruction,* in paranoids. In these plates the hero is placed in a final situation in which he is told how to do something by a foreman and in another case is hypnotized by a psychiatrist or hypnotist. In contrast, the manic-depressives are elevated on the more general of these keys, No. 139, *General Dependence—Continuing Support As End State,* in which, in addition to Dominance and Instruction, the hero is also placed finally in a situation where he is given *assistance* and *praise.*

In Volume 2 (pp. 560–580) are shown the additional plates and sequences in plates 2, 5, 17, and 21 in which assistance and praise are added to plates and sequences involving just dominance and instruction. These are added to plates 9, 17, and 23, which constituted the key which was elevated in paranoids (142): *Dependence—Continuing Support As End State—Dominance or Instruction.*

Thus, on plate 2 the hero is placed in a final situation in which he is being cared for by a nurse rather than being alone. On plate 5 the hero is placed in a final position in which he is being praised and patted on the back by a foreman for a job well done.

Among paranoids, irrespective of the position in which the praising foremen is put, there is a characteristic denial of body contact and of praise. The foreman is represented as lighting a cigar for the worker or giving the worker a banana, but direct physical contact between male and male is often denied. On plate 17 he also ends on being praised or instructed, whereas the paranoids are elevated on ending on instruction. On plate 21 the hero ends on being taken care of by the doctor. There are also some overlapping responses between the paranoids and depressives on plates 9, 17, and 23, in which the hero is being instructed or hypnotized.

It is the difference between these two keys which is most illuminating of a socialization which is dominating and controlling but also rewarding, contrasted with one which is simply dominating and controlling. Further evidence of the more positive components comes from the elevation of two sociophilic keys (108 and 111) showing a preference for physical contact. In these plates the hero is selected as continuing a situation in which he achieves body contact with one or more people of either sex.

These are shown in addition to plates 2, 5, 17, and 21, which were in Key 139 above, those plates which, added to the ones in Key 139, constitute Key 108. These are plates 10 and 22. In plate 10 the hero and heroine end on an embrace. On plate 22 the hero ends surrounded by the largest group of people with the closest physical proximity. Key 111 is a subset of Key 108 in which it is physical contact with just one other person which is selected.

Consistent with the importance of shame and the counteractive work interest is an elevation of work motivation for both paranoids and manic-depressives. It is our supposition, however, that for one group achievement supports the individual wish for independence from others' control, whereas in the other it is a royal road to commanding love and respect. Despite these important differences, there is, we think, a commonality insofar as achievement is a specific antidote for the affect of shame and the consequent damage to selfesteem.

Another characteristic which both paranoids and manic-depressives appear to share somewhat is a general *lability of affect* (Key 202). It is very pervasive among paranoids, rather than among manic-depressives, in whom it is found less elevated. Again, although apparently somewhat sharing a characteristic which distinguishes them from normals, it nonetheless appears to be a somewhat different finding when we examine it further. Not only is it not as general a finding among manic-depressives, but in addition there is no other evidence for its exerting pressure, whereas among the paranoids it is accompanied by an elevation on Key 200d, *General Restlessness—Tendency to Move from One Environment to Another,* and Key 150, *Social Restlessness—Sociophilia.* This latter is indicated by the sequence together-alone-together, the former by such sequences as the hero together with a group, at home alone, and then walking somewhere, or at home, with the group, and then walking. Both findings taken together indicate a restlessness which moves the individual toward and away from social interaction with an inability to sustain either being alone or with people. In contrast, the manic-depressive, though his affect may be somewhat labile, is constant in his wish to be with people.

We come now to our evidence for the fear of aggressive attack. We have already noted the elevated wish for body contact by the manic-depressive. In the paranoid the significance of the increased distance which he wishes between himself and others is illuminated by a very marked denial of physical aggression. On plate 4 of the PAT a group of men are shown in a free-for-all fight. This picture is unambiguous to most people. Denial, which is scored only when this picture is described in a manner which clearly does not involve physical aggression, occurs in only 4% of normal subjects. Approximately 20% of paranoids deny this aggression. Other schizophrenics deny this aggression 10%, and manic-depressives deny it 5.9% which does not differ from the normal frequency.

Although the manic-depressives are not elevated on the denial of physical aggression, they were, unexpectedly, elevated in the percentage of denial of injury on plate 16. Whereas normals deny injury 5.9%; paranoids, 25.4% (reliable at the .01 level); and schizophrenics in general, 1.1%; manic-depressives deny injury 17.6%, which is reliable at the .05 level, compared with normals. The manic-depressives are elevated on Key 171, *General Hypochondriasis,* above every other pathological group. We had originally related this denial and hypochondriasis to the fear of aggressive attack and the denial of aggression. Our assumption was brought into question by two findings. First, the failure of the manic-depressives to be elevated on denial of aggression, combined with their unexpected elevation on denial of injury, made the assumption that fear of injury was a consequence of fear of aggressive attack improbable. Second was the converse finding by Karon that among the Southern Negroes there was denial of aggression without denial of injury.

There are at least the following possible interpretations of the elevation of denial of injury among manic-depressives. One is that there is indeed a strong anxiety in addition to shame and distress among this group, which, when heightened, produces the agitated depressive and the schizoaffective disorder. Another is that the hypochondriasis of the paranoid is the fear of aggressive attack, whereas the hypochondriasis of the depressive is a cry of distress and an appeal for help.

Some evidence to support this interpretation is the elevation on the hypochondriasis key which is specifically concerned with proneness to injury, on which paranoids are elevated but depressives are not. Some further evidence comes from Nesbitt's study of values, in which he found hypochondriasis elevated among college students whose primary values were sociophilic and whose underlying character structure was similar to that of manic-depressives.

A third interpretation is based on our analysis of the changes in the strength of sociophilia, achievement, and hypochondriasis from adolescence to senility, which we have examined before. In a representative sample of the American population we found that hypochondriasis was inversely related to achievement and positively related to sociophilia. Further, we found peak elevations in hypochondriasis at the two critical transition points, late adolescence from (14 to 17) and late maturity (from 55 to 64). In the first case, despite optimal physical health, there is intense preoccupation with and pessimism about the body just before one is to enter the labor force and the assumption of adult responsibility. In the latter case, hypochondriasis reaches an absolute peak just before retirement, when one is to leave the labor force for good. It is the imminence of any radical change in status and its threat to the sense of identity which we regard as the common factor in these two crises. In both cases hypochondriasis drops sharply once the new status has been consolidated. From eighteen to twenty-four, when achievement motivation reaches its peak, hypochondriasis is second lowest of any period in the individual's life. Turning the attention outward to work apparently cures the hypochondriasis of the average American. The absolute low point of hypochondriasis comes, however, immediately following its absolute peak (ages 55 to 64) in the period of retirement from sixty-five on. Paradoxically, when the body is most vulnerable to death (65+), the person is least hypochondriacal, and when the body is least vulnerable (14–17), the person is most hypochondriacal. The lowest hypochondriasis for the average American comes with retirement. The second lowest period (18–24) is at the time of the assumption of adult responsibility and entering the labor force. It is not, therefore, work itself which is the cure for hypochondriasis but rather, we think, a firm commitment to any new status, whether that be active or passive. It would seem then that the hypochondriasis of our depressive patients may be essentially a reflection of a radical identity threat produced either by failure in achievement or communion, or both.

Finally, there is also evidence, not only for this interpretation of the difference in meaning between the denial of injury in paranoid schizophrenia and in the manic-depressive psychosis but for our general theoretical position, in two studies of early memories, one by Friedman and Schiffman and one by Jackson and Sechrest. The latter reported that the early recollections of depressed patients were more often characterized by themes of abandonment than was true for normals, anxiety neurotics, obsessive-compulsives, and gastrointestinal cases.

Freidman and Schiffman used preliminary studies at the Philadelphia Psychiatric Hospital on paranoid and depressive patients as a guide for predicting the differential contents of early recollections in paranoid and psychotic depressive patients. Their hypotheses were as follows. Early memories of paranoid patients will show

1. Absence of positive affects.
2. Unmitigated fear, terror, and/or horror.
3. Concern with bodily harm other than that caused by illness or aging.
4. Absence of persons, or personal relations that are negative or neutral, at best.

Early memories of psychotic depressed patients will show

1. Positive affects.
2. If negative affects, then tragic ones, such as sadness, distress.
3. Concern with physical illness and aging but not with other bodily harm.
4. A strong but generalized desire to be emotionally close to others.
5. Work and/or achievement orientation.

Friedman and Schiffman presented these hypotheses as rules to naive judges and secretarial workers for deciding whether an early memory had come from a paranoid patient or from a psychotic depressive. These rules constituted the only guide these naive judges had with which to make these decisions. The first experiment used two such judges, and two months later the experiment was replicated using two other, also naive, judges.

The judges were particularly effective in selecting the early memories of depressives. In Experiment 1, they agreed and were correct (by the criterion of independent diagnosis by the hospital staff of the Philadelphia Psychiatric Hospital and two additional psychiatrists) on 16 of 20 cases of depression; in Experiment 2, on 15 of 19 cases.

They did poorly, however, on the paranoid schizophrenics. In Experiment 1 they were in accord and correct in 3 out of 10 cases and in Experiment 2, in 2 out of 7 cases. There were more occasions in which the sets of judges agreed but were in error (in 9 additional cases). These decisions by naive judges required approximately five minutes per decision. Clearly, the hypotheses on depression are more valid than those on the paranoid early memories, though the critical hypothesis concerning fear was validated. Fear was absent in the early memories of depressives but appeared frequently in the early memories of paranoid schizophrenics. It should also be noted that the paranoid schizophrenics were selected from the files of two institutions and had not been as carefully screened, as were the depressives, by staff and by two additional psychiatrists.

THE SELF-REPORT OF PSYCHOTIC DEPRESSIVES TREATED PSYCHOANALYTICALLY

O. Spurgeon English has presented the verbalizations of six cases of manic-depressive psychosis which he treated by intensive psychoanalytic or psychotherapeutic interviews. We present selections from these cases as further, independent evidence for our theory of psychotic depression. Our interpretation of this evidence departs in several respects from that of Spurgeon English. Contrary to him and to psychoanalysis in general, we take the depressive's reports more nearly at their face value.

First, there is a recurrent association between the need to be loved and respected at the same time. Thus, one depressive described his illness as follows: "In a depression period I am lost in a negative impression of myself. I can't feel that I am worth anything to anyone. Because I cannot feel *loved and accepted* [italics mine] nothing I have ever done matters or can comfort me."

It is noteworthy that the depressive does not complain simply of being unloved or simply of not being accepted but requires the conjoint presence of both love and acceptance.

Again, another patient also verbalized the intimate connection between being perfect and being loved as follows: "If I am less than perfect, no one will want to have anything to do with me." Note that imperfection is responded to not simply as a fault or as a source of shame or self-contempt but as a source of loss of love.

Again another patient expressed the same idea as follows:

> To fail to come up to the expectations of people makes me want to die. If what I do or say has not been accepted unconditionally, I feel it has been absolutely worthless. I know this reacts against me, but it seems to be all or nothing. Either I'm wonderfully right or I'm dead wrong and ostracized. . . . No amount of accomplishment can overcome a feeling of inferiority unless there is warm praise and recognition of the effort.

Note again that accomplishment without "warm praise" will not cure the feeling of worthlessness.

Another patient verbalizes the same idea as follows: "How lucky the child who is allowed to feel that he is loved by his parents and is important to them. Then disappointments could never pull you down into those awful depressions."

Again, it is not enough to be loved or to be important—done without the other. Only this conjoint set of parental attitudes together would, in the mind of the depressive, give the protection which is necessary to tolerate "disappointments" without "those awful depressions."

The capacity of the depressive to experience both intense negative and positive affect, to oscillate between heaven and hell, was beautifully expressed by one of English's patients: "I can't tell you of the exuberance of having someone care about you—nor of the despair of finding out that they do not."

Because the exuberance of the state of loving and being loved always gives way to the "despair of finding out that they do not," some depressives try to preserve some distance between themselves and their love objects as a defense against hurt. Thus, one of English's patients said: "I never let myself love completely. I fear ridicule, criticism, rebuke, rebuff. I fear exploitation. I fear I become putty in someone else's hands and that I can no longer shape my own destiny. To love someone is an invitation for that person to hurt me."

Again another patient expressed the same idea: "When I start feeling love, I feel defenseless; I feel myself vulnerable to attack from people."

Although the depressive feels that others blame him and reject him for his imperfections, his exquisite sensitivity to being shamed combined with his empathy for the other make it all but impossible for him to reply in kind. Thus, one patient said: "I'd rather suffer the pain of criticism myself than inflict it upon someone else."

Again, another says: "I would rather regard myself as weak or inadequate than to blame another."

Notice that hostility takes the very special form of contempt, of criticism, of blame rather than the inflicting of physical harm. As Spurgeon English noted, the depressive will often criticize someone but then make an excuse for this person. Further, in his depression he blames himself still more for any efforts made on his behalf, to which he cannot respond in kind.

When the depressive is so depressed that he cannot respond to the other, this is a secondary source of shame and guilt. Thus, one depressive described this dilemma as follows:

> When I was depressed neither my mother nor my father could be of any comfort to me. I felt so guilty that they were trying to give me so much and I could give so little. I felt such a complete failure and what they tried to do made me feel worse.

Further, in the depths of his depression the depressive is troubled more generally by his inability to invest his affect in anyone but himself: "The pain was so great in my depressed state that I had to give all my feeling to take care of that pain. I couldn't love or hate. I had no strength left for anything."

Not only does he find it difficult to invest his affect in others in this state, but the interest of others, which is ordinarily exciting, is radically attenuated in its significance: "When I am depressed I hurt so much all over that anyone's friendship or love doesn't matter to me."

Chapter 35

Anger in Disgust-Decontamination Scripts

We turn now to a sample of disgust-anger-driven nuclear decontamination scripts in which disgust is the primary affect but with anger as a strong secondary affect. We will present the cases of Tolstoy, Wittgenstein, and Hemingway in which the internal problem of masculinity-femininity was very prominent. We will also look at Freud and O'Neill, for whom disgust was more outwardly directed and magnified-for Freud, generalized to both mother and father; for O'Neill, not only generalized but reciprocated in a *folie à quatre*.

TOLSTOY: NUCLEAR DECONTAMINATION SCRIPT OF DISGUSTING SEXUALITY AND NUCLEAR ANTITOXIC SCRIPT OF TERROR OF DEATH VIA FEMININE AFFECTS AGAINST MASCULINE AFFECTS

Tolstoy was haunted intermittently all of his life by self-disgust, shame, guilt, and rage at his ungovernable sexuality and by a preoccupation with and terror of death and self-destruction, of his own death, of his mother's death, and of the death he might inflict on others via his own sexuality, thus linking sexuality and death together with disgust, shame, guilt, and terror. For long periods of his life he was able to attenuate the severity of these scripts, but always in the background was an enduring struggle with these formidable adversaries. He was much more successful in the first half of his life in facing these dangers, by a wholehearted acceptance of the feminine affects of enjoyment, distress, and shame, which helped keep terror modulated and which attenuated the overweening pride and demandingness of the masculine affects of excitement, anger, disgust, and dissmell. But in the second half of his life he was buffeted by a decline in enjoyment and acceptance of his wife, his family, and his art, by intrusive excitement and sexuality coupled with a vivid intrusion of terror at the possibility of his own death. This resulted also in a radical increase in disgust and guilt and rage, not only at his own sexuality but at his own and others' wealth and greed, at the coercive force of government and the church, at the military, and at social convention in general. Evil became a much more formidable reality as his scripted rules for containment were breached, forcing him into more extreme warfare against the forces of evil within himself and others. This cost him a decade of artistic productivity as he engaged in good works to save himself and others in a double attempt at decontamination and antitoxic struggle against immorality and against death.

We will first examine his early development and his more effective scripting for truth through joyful acceptance of the world as it really is and for an acceptance and approbation of the feminine affects of enjoyment, distress, shame, and terror against the masculine affects of excitement, anger, surprise, disgust, and dissmell.

He was haunted from childhood by the search for happiness and truth. Indeed, for him they seemed often to be the same. At the age of five or six Tolstoy had told his brothers that he knew the secret of universal love, happiness, and harmony for all peoples and that the secret was written on a green stick buried on the side of a ravine about a quarter of a mile from the house at Yasnaya Polyana. Tolstoy was buried at that spot as he had requested.

In an early diary entry he had written: "I shall always say that consciousness is the greatest moral evil that can afflict man." This is because it confuses subjective reality with objective reality. The cure is a consciousness that reflects the whole rather than a part.

Grief especially reflects a desire for reality to be other than it is. Virtue consists in accepting death and the world the way it is. Vanity is the belief that one can control the universe, and particularly death. This was learned very early by Tolstoy at the death of his mother, in the contrast between her dying and when he saw her for a second time when she was dead. Despite his realistic recording of the sights, smells, and sounds of the scenes, he cannot help remembering her as alive, vital, and joyous. The contrast between this remembrance and the pale, lifeless, and ugly face of death was not only to haunt him the rest of his life but to provide his basic philosophy of life and his enduring quest for what he regarded as the deeper meaning and reality of life, usually covered over by convention, by society, by the state, by institutions, by the church, even by art. But Tolstoy believed that though the mind may cheat us into confusing wish with reality it can also be made more moral and disciplined in the everlasting insistence on truth and reality. His last spoken words were: "Truth . . . I love much . . . As they . . . "

Tolstoy believed early that indifference and joy, rather than grief and compassion, should be the response to the death of a human being—like the peasants who are humble, uncomplaining, and accepting in contrast to the aristocrats, for whom the world exists as an appendage to their longings and fears and makes them not only overdemanding but manipulative and overcontrolling and in the end necessarily failing to bend reality to their wishes.

The death of a tree, in contrast, is real and beautiful "because it doesn't act up, doesn't fear, and doesn't pity," as he wrote in a letter to his cousin.

As he will later represent this in *War and Peace,* one possesses the world by giving it up, by permitting it, in all of its complexity, to seize one's consciousness. Freedom is not abstract but particular, to let life be what it is. Men need not be in disharmony with the world.

Isaiah Berlin's classic characterization of Tolstoy as being like the fox (who, according to Arsilochus, "knows many things") who desires to become the hedgehog (who "knows one big thing") was prefigured in his diary at the age of seventeen: "Train your reason to be in keeping with the whole, with the source of everything, and not with a part, with the society of men; then your reason will be united with this whole, and then society, as a part will have no influence on you."

His message is the sanctity of the individual against the coercion and corruption of the government, the military, private property, modern art. All of these are deceitful, self-serving coercive forces which corrupt the reason of the inviolate individual. No one needs teachers, priests, government officials or even one's fellow man.

Instead of many "rules" by and for a weak and selfish person, one ought to live simply and naturally and for and with others, not within and for that weak and selfish person. In one of Tolstoy's early works, *The Cossacks,* the character Eroshka says:

> God has made everything for the joy of man. *There is no sin in anything.* Take the example of animals. They live alike in Tartar thickets and in ours. What God bestows, that they eat. But our people say that instead of enjoying this freedom we are to lick hot plates in hell for that. I think that everything is a cheat. You die, and the grass grows: that is all that's real.

When he was twenty-seven, he noted in his diary:

> Yesterday a conversation about theology and faith suggested to me the colossal thought, the fulfillment of which would take a lifetime of devotion. The thought is the following: to establish a new religion in harmony with the development of mankind, the religion of Christ, but purified of belief in mysteries, a practical religion, one that does not promise a future bliss, but one that brings such harmony on earth.

It was critical for Tolstoy to find and to know the meaning of life. When articles of appreciation were written in 1910 on the sixth anniversary of the death of Chekhov, Tolstoy, though he liked Chekhov personally, could not conceal his disgust at his failure to find the meaning of life. "The fact that he didn't know and had never found the meaning of life strikes them all as being somehow special—they see something poetic in it!" (Bulgokov, 1971). Previously he had written: "He is always vacillating and searching . . . therefore he is incapable of teaching anything."

In a letter written shortly after Dostoevski's death to his friend N. N. Strakhov:

> It seems to me that you have been the victim of a false and erroneous attitude—not on your part but on everybody's part—towards Dostoevsky. . . . He is touching and interesting but one cannot sit on a pedestal for the edification of posterity a man who was all struggle (Christian, 1978). So it was not enough to struggle like Dostoevski and certainly not enough to never arrive at the answer, like Chekhov.

If one is joyous, humble, hardworking and simple, like peasants, and one lives in holy matrimony with a beloved wife and cooperates in raising a family, this is heaven on earth, real Christianity. This was his formula for the acceptance of the truth and reality of the world which would oppose the self-centered vanity of the aristocratic way of life he had inherited. It would dissipate the excitement-powered demands for complexity; for endless striving for mastery, for wealth, and, above all, for sensuality and for danger; and overweening pride in control.

His earliest script for the resolution of the conflict between lust and love was holy matrimony, dedicated to procreation, and to hard work in the service of humanity, shared with a woman who was equally dedicated to these, his own, ideals. Marriage became for him, as for Levin in *Anna Karenina,* "the central thing of life, from which all its happiness depended." He had described his vision of marriage as "toil, self-denial, and love." This formula for decontaminating and sanitizing his sensuality gave him peace for the first ten years of his marriage.

Concerning his future wife he had written in his diary: "Not love, as before, not jealousy, not even compassion, but similar to, to something sweet—like a hope (which cannot be). . . . But a beautiful evening, good, sweet feeling." A few days later: "Never had life with a wife presented itself to my imagination so clearly, joyfully, and peacefully." A few days later, in a letter to his sister: "Old fool that I am, I have fallen in love. I say this and don't know whether or not I have spoken the truth." He was married a couple weeks later. Four months after marriage he notes in his diary: "Domestic happiness has swallowed me completely."

We should note that this philosophy of acceptance and joy in life as it really was flew in the face of a long-standing struggle against self-disgust at his self-control failures, sexual and otherwise. There was a generalized disgust about the weakness of the self and its inability to govern itself. In his diary he had written: "I'm twenty-four and I haven't done anything yet. I feel that I've been fighting doubts and passions for eight years and to no avail. What am I destined to do? The future will tell." Earlier, when he was nineteen, he had written in his diary: "During this whole time I did not conduct myself as I wanted to conduct myself." In the same year: "I suddenly wrote down many rules and wanted to follow them all; but I was too weak to do so." Six years later, when he was twenty-five: "I am so weak! I must fear idleness and disorderliness as I fear gambling." At age twenty-seven the load of distress, shame, and self-disgust had become so magnified through cumulation that he became sufficiently enraged to turn against himself: "I shall destroy myself unless I improve myself." He must live more for others and less for himself, he felt, but in fact it was his picture of himself as lazy and vain that most concerned him in his early adulthood. To save others was to save the helpless self as well.

Because his script required both self-control and selflessness, any enforced escape from freedom proved temporarily helpful. Thus, his struggle for self-governance was temporarily aborted when he joined the army at the age of twenty-four. In a letter he confessed he was happy to be no longer free because freedom had caused all his faults.

Although his marriage gave him relief from sexual self-disgust, guilt, and rage for a decade, eventually the dreaded affects reappeared even with his beloved wife, whom he came to experience as a seductive whore.

This is not to be confused with projection, in which the self is protected from contamination by attributing one's own evil only to the other. Tolstoy again and again experienced his own degradation. He knew that he was not innocent, but he also knew that he had been tempted by someone who was as impure as himself, and he was as enraged at that other as at himself.

Sexuality offended Tolstoy for several reasons. First, it too often violated the need for self-control and so evoked shame. Second, the demands of the flesh evoked guilt because of his belief that it was selfish and immoral as well as intractable. Third, to be seduced into an immorality combining shame and guilt evoked deep self- and other-disgust at the invidious comparison of an ideal way of life and these contaminations. Fourth, the combination of shame, guilt, and disgust evoked rage against himself and his seducer. If he could not improve himself, he might destroy himself and the other, or that immoral seducer might destroy herself.

Fifth, sexuality had become linked with guilt at the death of the beloved through the arrogant overconfidence, coupled with a possibly unconscious rage-prompted "clumsiness," as Tolstoy depicted it in Vronsky's unintentional killing of his beloved mare Frou-Frou.

In such a case sexual guilt and self-disgust at contamination might flow not from sexuality per se but by its having become toxic rather than simply contaminated, by the fusion of dismell and anger with sexuality, making it a much more threatening concern. If such had happened, we can better understand Tolstoy's (and Vronsky's) horror at having clumsily so shifted his weight as to have killed Frou-Frou. Tolstoy makes it quite clear, by referring to Vronsky's trembling jaw as he stands over the mare he has destroyed, that it has the same significance in the seduction scene with Anna, when the same description of Vronsky and his open trembling jaw is given following his conquest of Anna. If this were so, it could explain why ten years of happy marriage to a loyal wife might turn into degrading, seductive intercourse with a whore. Tolstoy had, when younger, indulged himself with women he might have treated sadistically in sexuality.

His anger might have been more magnified than his sexuality at this time for several reasons. First, he complained of a loss of vitality and interest and productivity. Second was the intensification of his fear of death.

At the age of forty-nine, in a hotel in Arzmaz, Tolstoy for the first time experienced "indescribable" terror at the prospect of death. Six months later there is the first reference to *Anna Karenina.* Tolstoy's wife refers in her diary to a conversation with her husband in which he tells her of imagining a feminine type from the highest society who destroys herself.

Four years later Tolstoy wrote to A. A. Tolstoy that he would like to throw away the novel *Anna Karenina* and that he was not pleased with it. A month later he wrote to Golokhvasrov that the writing of *Anna Karenina* was repulsive to him. He did finish it two years later. From first conception in 1870 it took until 1876 to finish it.

A year later (1875) Tolstoy in a letter to Strakhov: "My God, if only someone would finish Anna Karenina for me. Unbearably repulsive." In a letter to his brother at that time he wrote: "I think it is time to die." Four months later (1876) he said in a letter to Fet: "The end of winter and the beginning of spring are always my most fruitful time for work, and I have to finish the novel, which is boring to me."

There is a hint, also in *Anna Karenina,* that Vronsky's disaffection with Anna is in part prompted by his attachment to his mother. This bond, as for Tolstoy himself, was one which dominated the marital bond. He should have treated his wife better, but he could not and felt guilty.

Six years after his conversion he admitted in a letter to Chertkov: "Never have I entreated her with tears to believe in the truth or told her all simply, lovingly, softly. . . . She lies beside me and I say nothing to her, but what ought to be said to her I say to God."

His earliest memory was of the death of his mother: "The room was nearly dark. It was hot and it smelt of mint, eau de Cologne, camomile and Hoffmann drops. Whenever I remember it, imagination brings back every smallest detail of that frightful minute." This did result in a nuclear reparative subscript, in which he hungered for what he had lost, sought it endlessly, but which he could not permit himself to accept even from his ever-loving wife because of a more serious contamination of sexuality by guilt-ridden disgust. At the age of seventy-eight he wrote poignantly of how he "longed to press myself against some loving, sympathizing being, to shed tears of love and affection and to feel myself being consoled." So the feminine affects were not simply a defense against the masculine affects, although they were that, but more important, they represented a paradise he had known and lost so painfully so early in his life, when he was in effect orphaned by the death of both of his parents.

It may well be that the ultimate source of his overwhelming guilt and self-disgust at this sexuality is a consequence of his idealization of his beloved mother, which made any relationship less powerful than that intimacy inauthentic and degrading. It is suggestive of an equally invidious contrast in machismo cultures, which combine contempt and disgust for women as sexual conquests with an equally intense Maryolatry, in which the Virgin Mary is worshipped.

The connection between excitement, mastery, masculinity and femininity, death and sexuality, and disgust and guilt is communicated most vividly in *Anna Karenina.*

Vronsky is riding Frou-Frou, his favorite mare, in a steeplechase. He is an expert rider, even arrogant in his record of wins. "He felt that the mare was at her very last reserve of strength" yet he was certain she would make one more, the last ditch.

> She flew over it like a bird, but at the same instant Vronsky, to his horror, felt that he had failed to keep up with the mare's pace, that he had, he did not know how, made a fearful, unpardonable mistake in recovering his seat in the saddle. All at once his position had shifted and he knew something awful had happened.

Frou-Frou fell. "She fluttered on the ground at his feet like a shot bird. The clumsy movement made by Vronsky had broken her back." Looking down at Frou-Frou's "exquisite eyes," her "speaking eyes," Vronsky calls her his "poor darling" and cries out, "What have I done?"

Vronsky stands for Tolstoy and his judgment that sexuality between men and women kills the women we so love. We clumsily break their backs, shoot our birds, put out their exquisite eyes because they have given for us more than their last reserves. Although Tolstoy made this a tragedy of the consequences of an illicit love affair, and although Vronsky is depicted as immoral in taking Anna away from her husband, we know also that the sanctity of marriage which promised the healing of the sexual disgust and guilt did so for only a limited time for Tolstoy. The family was already in jeopardy because of Tolstoy's own return of that form of sexuality which disgusted and enraged him.

In my view, Anna is compulsively and self-defeatingly overpossessive, repelling Vronsky, who is more and more influenced by his mother over the passion of Anna. This is, I think, a derivative of Tolstoy's aching wish for his long-lost mother, in opposition to Anna, whom he sees as an improper mother.

Tolstoy had always seen rational intelligence as a male quality; he found educated women affected, "emancipated" women obnoxious. He wanted women to be admired for qualities of feeling especially in connection with the maternal instinct, which would complement male rationality. When sexuality even in marriage became disgusting, he reduced women to less than human status. He vented his rage on his wife for seducing him after each seductive sexual intercourse. In his diaries, which his wife copied, she would encounter further insults: "There is no love, there is only the physical craving for intercourse and the rational need of a life companion." He had advised his sons that "a sound healthy woman is a wild beast."

Tolstoy had always been jealous and overpossessive, not only about his wife but also about his daughters and even about his sons. Tatanya Tolstoy, the second-born child, in *Tolstoy Remembered* (1978) includes a memoir by her daughter, Tatyana Albertini, about Tolstoy in which she says that he "would have liked all his daughters to remain spinsters and told them so." Alexandra, the youngest child, in *The Tragedy of Tolstoy,* reveals his jealousy at the thought that men should take his daughters away from him.

He was both overprotective and overpossessive of his children of either sex. Illya Tolstoy (1971), his son, tells that *Tolstoy's terror of sex made him insist that his sons should never mingle when young with the village children, from whom "things" might be picked up.* "We used to go tobogganing in the village, but when we began to develop friendships with peasant boys *papa* was quick to notice our enthusiasm and put a stop to it. So we grew up surrounded by the stone walls of English governesses, tutors, and various teachers."

A touching passage relates Tolstoy's extreme anxiety lest his son should have the same early experiences with prostitutes that he himself was so ashamed of. He encouraged Ilya's early engagement, and entered as rapturously as his son into the arrangements for it. Before the marriage Ilya went into his bedroom to find his father sitting there writing.

> Hearing my footsteps he spoke without looking round.
> "Is that you, Ilya?"
> "Yes."
> "Are you alone? Shut the door. Now no one can hear us, and *we can't see each other, so we won't feel ashamed. Tell me, did you ever have anything to do with women?"*
> When I said "No," I suddenly heard him start to weep, sobbing like a child. I too cried; and for some time, with the screen between us, we continued to shed tears of joy; and we were not ashamed *but were both so glad that I consider the moment one of the happiest of my entire life. The tears of a father of sixty can never be forgotten, even in a moment of the greatest temptation.*

After Tolstoy's spiritual crisis he was locked into what he described in his diary as a "struggle to the death" with his wife, Sonya.

The convergence of a contamination of his sexuality, a diminution in his interest in writing, and an increase in his terror of death produced a crisis and a radical increase in his asceticism and in his condemnation of masculine affect and all its derivatives, behavioral and institutional.

Tolstoy longed for the humble life of simplicity and acceptance and renunciation with its chastity, poverty, simplicity, humility against wealth, greed, immorality, the state, the government, the church and the military, all instruments of mastery and overcontrol. In 1891, at the age of sixty-three he renounced the copyrights of everything he had written since 1881.

After his spiritual crisis he finally returned to his art but wrote mostly about death and sex, purity and corruption. "The Death of Ivan Ilych" was his first work after his conversion. He castigates Ivan for his life as a series of evasions of love and self-knowledge by a conventional overly materialistic life. He now begins to notice that when he is dying no one really cares that he is in pain. Death, for Tolstoy now, is the model for solidarity. Only through shared consciousness of its significance can one reach the communion of true brotherhood. Death is the true tie which binds.

Only when Ivan begins to feel pity for his crying son and then for his wife that he turns from pseudo-justifications of his life does he see the truth of his life.

> He was sorry for them, he must act so as not to hurt them: release them and free himself from these sufferings. "How good and how simple!" he thought. "And the pain?" he asked himself. "What has become of it? Where are you, pain?"
> He turned his attention to it.
> "Yes, here it is. Well what of it? Let the pain be." "And death . . . where is it?"
> He sought his former accustomed fear of death and did not find it. "Where is it? What death?" There was no fear because there was no death.
> In place of death there was light.
> "So that's what it is!" he suddenly exclaimed aloud. "What joy!"
> To him all this happened in a single instant, and the meaning of that instant did not change. . . .
> "Death is finished," he said to himself. "It is no more!." He drew in a breath, stopped in the midst of a sigh, stretched out, and died.

The "truth" of death is in the long-deferred love and communion which reveals the brotherhood and sisterhood of humanity.

Nine years later he was to explore in "Master and Man" the redemption possible in confronting the truth of death in a more poignant fashion. In 1895 he wrote "Master and Man." The main characters get lost in the wildness of a Russian storm. The merchant Vasili and his servant Nikita are trapped in this storm because Vasili cannot tolerate missing a day of business.

At the beginning of their journey they meet a choice point. One road is well marked, the other unmarked but shorter, and Vasili chooses that one, lest buyers from the town forestall him in making a profitable purchase. His servant had recommended the longer, well-marked road. They get lost several times and find themselves back in the same village. They are invited to stay the night, but Vasili declines. "I can't, friend. Business. Lose an hour and you can't catch it up in a year." Soon they are lost again. Nikita says they must spend the night in the storm and unharnesses their horses and stands the shafts on end in front of the sledge so that "when the snow covers us up, good folks will see the shafts and dig us out." In the sledge Vasili lies awake thinking of pride with the one thing that gave meaning to his life, of how much money he had made and might still make. He looks at his servant Nikita wrapped in his miserable worn out cloth coat. "If only that peasant doesn't freeze to death! His clothes are so wretched I may be held responsible for him. What shiftless people they are—such a want of education." In the middle of the night he gets on the horse and rides away. For Nikita "it's all the same to him whether he lives or dies. What is his life worth?" But in the storm his horse falls, and Vasili jumps off. He follows the horse's tracks in the snow and is led back to the sledge where he finds Nikita half-frozen. Then suddenly, quite unexpectedly, he brushes the snow off Nikita and lies down on top of him,

> covering him not only with his fur coat, but with the whole of his body, which glowed with warmth.... There ... lie still and get warm, that's our way.... No fear, we shant lose him this time! he said to himself, referring to his getting the peasant warm with the same boastfulness with which he spoke of his buying and selling.... And he remembered his money, his shop, his house, the buying and selling ... and it was hard for that man called Vasili Brekhunov, had troubled himself with all those things with which he had been troubled.... "Well, it was because he did not know what the real thing was" he thought, concerning that Vasili Brekhunov. And again he heard the voice of the one who had called him before. "I'm coming! Coming!" he responded gladly, and his whole being was filled with joyful emotion. All around the snow still eddied. The same whirlwinds of snow circled about, covering the dead Vasili Andreevich's fur coat, the shivering horse, the sledge now scarcely to be seen, and Nikita lying at the bottom of it, kept warm beneath his dead master.

We see here a replay in the counteractive and reparative mode of the death scene with his mother, whom he could not keep alive. As an excitement-driven son, he had forgotten the real wealth and loss which gave tragic meaning to his life. What he had desperately really hungered for was redemption in the warmth of her life-giving body in deep communion. The excitement of greed was disgusting, masking what was really vital, the equally greedy need for the peace which came from mutual love and enjoyment; even at the cost of death. Death in the arms of love loses its terror. These are the feminine affects of enjoyment, distress, and shame taming even the terror of death.

LUDWIG WITTGENSTEIN: NUCLEAR DECONTAMINATION SCRIPT FOR SEXUALITY, DISGUST, AND ANGER

Wittgenstein, like Tolstoy, was haunted by self-disgust at his uncontrollable sexuality and by the anger coupled with disgust and sexuality which, when directed at the self, prompted suicidal impulses.

Like Tolstoy he inherited very great wealth and was an aristocrat, born into one of the most eminent families of Vienna. He was the youngest of a family of eight. His father, Karl Wittgenstein, was the creator of Austria's prewar iron and steel industry and a patron of the visual arts and of music.

When Ludwig talked of suicide incessantly, his sisters were terrified because three of his four brothers had already committed suicide, and two were known to have been homosexual, according to Bartley (1973), whose biography I have used in this analysis. Wittgenstein had also alarmed Bertrand Russell with talk of suicide.

As we have noted before, it is a small step from the malignant decontamination script to the more malignant antitoxic script. What is more unusual is a later-life transformation in the other direction to a distress-limitation-remediation script. This series has been described by Wittgenstein himself in the following way:

> Whenever you are preoccupied with something, with some trouble or with some problem which is a big thing in your life—as sex is, for instance—then no matter what you start from, the association will lead finally and inevitably back to that same theme. Freud remarks on how, after the analysis of it, the dream appears so very logical. And of course it does. . . . An "Urszene" . . . often has the attractiveness of giving a sort of tragic pattern to one's life. It is all the repetition of the same pattern which was settled long ago. Like a tragic figure carrying out the decrees under which the fates had placed him at birth. Many people have, at some period, serious trouble in their lives—so serious as to lead to thoughts of suicide. This is likely to appear to one as something nasty, as a situation which is too foul to be a subject of a tragedy. And it may then be an immense relief if it can be shown that one's life has the pattern rather of a tragedy—the tragic working out and repetition of a pattern. (Bartley, 1967, pp. 50–51)

In the case of Wittgenstein, as with Tolstoy, the self-disgust and anger in ungovernable sexuality contaminated not only his sex life but spread to the whole range of the masculine affects. Not only was excitement outlawed, but also anger, disgust, and dismell, all centered upon sexuality but spreading to other loci so that their care, as with Tolstoy, led to a more feminine, Christian asceticism, leading to chastity, poverty, goodwill, service, simplicity, community. Wittgenstein not only read Tolstoy but was deeply moved by him and in part modeled himself on him and on Christ. And yet it must be remembered that Tolstoy's sexual guilt was that of heterosexuality and Wittgenstein's that of homosexuality. Despite this important difference the decontamination nuclear script recommended the same rituals of purification. These in the end cured neither nuclear script. Their strong sensuality, magnified by disgust and by guilt broke through their attempted control again and again, leaving them with punishing guilt and self-disgust and rage and dismell.

At one point Wittgenstein wrote to his friend Paul Engelmann:

> Things have gone utterly miserable for me lately. Of course only because of my own baseness and rottenness. I have continually thought about taking my own life, and now too this thought still haunts me. I have sunk to the bottom. May you never be in that position. (Engelmann Letters from Wittgenstein, p. 32)

Ten months later, after further homosexual encounters, he again wrote to Engelman:

> I have been morally dead for more than a year. . . . I am one of those cases which perhaps are not all that rare today: I had a task, did not do it, and now the failure is wrecking my life. I ought to have done something positive with my life, to have become a star in the sky. Instead of which I remained stuck on earth, and now I am gradually fading out. My life has really become meaningless and so it consists only of futile episodes. The people around me do not notice this and would not understand; but I know that I have a fundamental deficiency. Be glad of it, if you don't understand what I am writing here.

Wittgenstein's homosexuality was not directed toward "nice" boys but rather to lower-class, rougher, blunter boys in the area called the Prater. The more refined young men frequented the Sirk Ecke in the Kärtnerstrasse. He found to his horror he could not resist going to the more dangerous zone. Similarly, Bartley reports the same pattern years later in England. He fled the fashionable and intellectual young men in favor of the company of tough boys in London pubs.

We do not know the exact nature of his sexual excitement, the degree to which it was sadomasochistic and/or degrading in his eyes, but it is clear he suffered a split libido such that he could use young men with "nice faces," as he put it, in platonic relationships to help him control his lust for what he considered "vile" but seductive sex. Thus, a series of close friendships developed with good-looking young men of sweet and docile disposition to whom he could become very attached. This included some of his favored Cambridge friends and students.

Although, as we will see later, Wittgenstein was capable of considerable anger and some cruelty, yet it appears these affects were secondary to self-disgust and even to self-dissmell. Thus, he has written:

> A man can bare himself before others only out of a particular kind of love. A love which acknowledges, as it were, that we are all wicked children.... Hate between men comes from our cutting ourselves off from each other. Because we don't want anyone else to look inside us, since it's not a pretty sight in there.
>
> It's difficult to think *well* about "certainty," "probability," "perception," etc. But it is, if possible, still more difficult to think, or *try* to think, really honestly about your life & other people's lives. And the trouble is that thinking about these things is not *thrilling*, but often downright nasty. And when it's nasty then it's *most* important. (Wittgenstein 1944, p. 159)

"It's not a pretty sight in there" suggests more self-disgust and/or dissmell than either anger or guilt. It's "nasty" means it's most important. He had in another connection written that he "would above all abhor anybody inquiring into his personal life." Further, he had said he would not want to undergo a training analysis since "he did not think it right to reveal all one's thoughts to a stranger."

In his letters to Engelmann the words he uses most frequently to refer to himself are *indecency, badness, filthiness, baseness, vileness.*

At the end of his service in World War I, Wittgenstein had a dream he labeled as his "first dream," followed about two years later by one he called his "second dream." The first dream was as follows:

> It was night. I was outside a house whose windows blazed with light. I went up to a window to look inside. There, on the floor, I noticed an exquisitely beautiful prayer rug, one which I immediately wanted to examine. I tried to open the front door, but a snake darted out to prevent me from entering; I tried another door, but there too a snake darted out to block my way. Snakes appeared also at the windows, and blocked my every effort to reach the prayer rug.

Wittgenstein's interpretation was a classical Freudian one:

> *The prayer rug,* symbolized that for which he had sought for years in vain and for which he was to continue to search for most of the rest of his *life: an integration of his libido,* a *sublimation, for intellectual and spiritual purposes, of his sexual drives.* For what does a prayer rug look like? Its central feature is a *form rather like that of an erect penis.* But this tremendous energy, transformed into a work of art, is *contained within strong and beautiful borders.* Wittgenstein's own situation was not that depicted by the rugmandala, that goal for which he searched. Rather, at that time his own spiritual progress was checked and thwarted by the loose, ugly, *uncontained serpents which haunted both his waking and his dreaming hours.*

The second dream:

> I was a priest. In the front hall of my house there was an altar; to the right of the altar a stairway led off. It was a grand stairway carpeted in red, rather like that at the Alleegasse. At the foot of the altar, and partly covering it, was an oriental carpet. And certain other religious objects and regalia were placed on and beside the altar. One of these was a rod of precious metal.
>
> But a theft occurred. A thief entered from the left and stole the rod. This had to be reported to the police, who sent a representative who wanted a description of the rod. For instance, of what sort of metal was it made? I could not say; I could not even say whether it was of silver or of gold. The police officer questioned whether the rod had ever existed in the first place. I then began to examine the other parts and fittings of the altar and noticed that the

> carpet was a prayer rug. My eyes began to focus on the border of the rug. The border was lighter in colour than the beautiful center. In a curious way it seemed to be faded. It *was, nonetheless, still strong and firm.*

Wittgenstein was uncertain about how to interpret this dream, but he thought it important, and it was one source of his conviction that he had been "called" and that he ought to become a monk. The prayer rug appears in both dreams. Without Wittgenstein's full associations the interpretation must remain problematic. However, some differences between the two dreams are of interest. In the first the dreamer is outside looking in, and his entrance is blocked by many snakes. He cannot therefore reach the rug. In the second dream he is inside, as a priest, but now the threats are from the outside and consist of theft of the rod of precious metal. The difference between snakes as barriers to his inspection and thieves who rob the insides of their precious objects, whose value is then questioned by the police, is suggestive since between the two dreams he had in fact moved out of the family house referred to in the second dream and rented more modest quarters of his own. But it was in these quarters that his attraction to the seductive young men had radically increased, so this second dream might point to a wish for more parental and religious control than he was himself capable of exercising. This might be the meaning of the change in the containing borders of the prayer rug, "faded" but nonetheless strong and firm. Shortly after experiencing this dream he acquired a walking stick, which he carried constantly for many years. Is this the phallic rod that had been stolen? Some reason to think so was a comment he made many years later about religion. Religious customs, he said, are instinctual responses to an inner need for release and satisfaction, unconscious and with no other purpose. "When I am angry about something I sometimes beat on the ground or against a tree with my cane. But I do not, for that matter believe that the earth is guilty or that beating is of any help. I ventilate my anger. And all rites are of this sort. Such actions could be called instinctual."

Why he may have "beat" on Mother Earth in anger may be illuminated by one of the very few references he makes to a woman:

> One story he used to tell his elementary school pupils in Trattenbach as early as 1921 goes like this:
>
> Once upon a time there was an experiment. Two small children who had not yet learnt to speak were shut away with a woman who was unable to speak. The aim of the experiment was to determine whether they would learn some primitive language or invent a new language of their own. The experiment failed.

Here the woman must play a vital role in the language of children but is unable to speak, and so the children cannot invent a language of their own.

Elsewhere in discussing religion he had also stressed the difficulties of understanding an unknown language as "explorer into an unknown country with a language quite strange to you . . . when we try to learn their language we find it impossible."

Further, "one human being can be a complete enigma to another" since each form of life is in varying degrees a different "game." Wittgenstein, in his later life and work, completely undoes his early theory, thus attenuating some of the sting of his earlier beliefs and conflicts. Now religious beliefs were outside of philosophy as one more grammar or form of life which a philosopher could describe but not validate nor invalidate. The importance of religion for Wittgenstein personally, and also for others, he thought derived from wonder at the existence of the world, the experience of feeling absolutely safe, and the experience of guilt, that God disapproves of one's conduct. If Wittgenstein could have convinced himself of the absolute validity of the supernatural, then he would have had to feel terror for his safety at the certain condemnation by God of his uncontrollable lust. But there are no absolute grammars or languages, and his game remains a privileged one alongside the religious one. We see here yet another similarity to Tolstoy, who was also haunted with the fear of death and who connected it with his sexuality and with his general way of life. Indeed,

Wittgenstein reduced religious belief to experience which points to something but leads to nonsense by intending to go beyond the factual and beyond significant language to point to the supernatural. "My whole tendency, and I believe the tendency of all men who ever tried to talk about Ethics or Religion was to run against the boundaries of language." No knowledge can come from it, "but it is a document of a tendency in the human mind which I personally cannot help respecting deeply and I would not for my life ridicule it."

The family of decontamination nuclear scripts developed in defense, celebration, and counteraction against a disgusting, angering, guilt-ridden, uncontrollable sexuality was, as we have said, not dissimilar from that of Tolstoy, nor from the almost universal ascetic shift from the stratified masculine affects to the feminine affects from the Hebrew patriarchal God who demanded sacrifice to the Christian more feminine God who sacrifices his own son out of his love for his children, in the passion of Christ.

The first script was attempted ascetic control of his sexuality by the cultivation of pretty, nice, rather than rough, disgusting and disgust-exciting, young men in the higher realm of intimate but platonic friendships. This affect- and drive-control script was at best partly effective and, in its most nuclear characteristic, ineffective, thereby continually enlarging and magnifying the nuclear script.

Second was the withdrawal from a major source of excitement pride, his excessive inherited wealth. Wittgenstein, according to a companion in the prisoner of war camp in World War I, thought himself following the gospel according to Matthew "If thou wilt be perfect, go and sell what thou hast, and give to the poor, and thou shalt have treasure in heaven: come and follow me." He appeared suddenly at his banker's one morning insisting he wanted nothing more to do with his money and it must be disposed of immediately. His sister Mining writes: "He gave it all to us, his brothers and sisters with the exception of our sister Gretl, who at that time was still very wealthy, while we had forfeited much of our wealth." It was at that time one of the largest fortunes in Europe.

Third was a nuclear script of identification with the simple versus the complex, with the peasant versus the urban aristocrat, with the life of simple enjoyment rather than complex excitement and risk and mastery, of giving rather than of taking, of identification with children rather than with adults and parents. He implemented this by teaching elementary school in Lower Austria. He had Tolstoy's romantic vision of the noble serf in mind. Upon arriving at the dreary little village of Trattenbach he was excited. To Bertrand Russell he reported: "A short while ago I was terribly depressed and tired of living, but now I am slightly more hopeful." Three weeks later in a letter to his friend Engelmann he wrote: "I am working in a beautiful little nest called Trattenbach. I am happy in my work at school, and I do need it badly, or else all the devils in Hell break loose inside." A year later he wrote to Russell: "Still at Trattenbach, surrounded, as ever, by odiousness and baseness. I know that human beings on the average are not worth much anywhere, but here they are much more good-for-nothing and irresponsible than elsewhere." Wittgenstein had expressed his disgust with city life and for the "half-educated" corrupted by the popular press and so had anticipated a peasant virtue magnified by invidious contrast to what he had left behind. He was not prepared for the realities of what he found, to which he then responded by a subscript of counteraction to "get the peasantry out of the muck"—Nuclear Script 4. This engaged him passionately for six years in an attempt to rescue the disgusting contamination of the noble peasant, which had itself been a counteractive script against the disgusting urban "half-educated." As is characteristic of the ineffective nuclear family of scripts, any failure of defense or counteraction replays the original source as a newer version of the good scene turned bad and, in this case, disgusting. Counteraction or defense must then begin again at the sight of the dreaded antianalog turned analog.

In the end his effort to reform the peasantry through educating their children failed. They eventually ran him out of town. But according to Bartley, who interviewed some of his former students, Wittgenstein did have a profound positive effect on the peasant children whom he taught, and they on him. Yet in the end adults remained "wicked children," disgusting and enraging themselves, their parents, and their God.

HEMINGWAY: NUCLEAR DECONTAMINATION OF FEMININE AFFECTS BY ANTITOXIC MASCULINE AFFECTS

In Hemingway we have a nuclear script which is the inverse of Tolstoy. Tolstoy defended himself against excessive masculinity by femininity. Hemingway defended himself against excessive femininity by masculinity. Both are decontamination scripts in origin which spread to antitoxic scripts. Both are nuclear in their intransigent, ineffective unwillingness and inability to either completely renounce, purify, or integrate the scenes and their adversarial affects.

I have based this analysis primarily on Kenneth Lynn's (1987) biography.

Grace Hemingway, Ernest's mother, kept her son in dresses and shoulder-length hair longer than customary. He wore "pink gingham gowns with white Battenberg lace hoods, fluffy lace-tucked dresses, black patent leather Mary Janes, high stockings, and picture hats with flowers on them." Beside one photo of him, his mother wrote "summer girl." She paired him with his older, somewhat intimidating sister Marcelline, treating them like "twins of the same sex" (sometimes male, sometimes female), pressing him to be and not to be a "real" boy. He was caught between his mother's wish to conceal his masculinity and her wish to encourage it.

The younger children were also sent confusing signals. His younger sister Ursula wore a Rough Rider costume and was nicknamed Teddy. Like her father and brother Ernest, Ursula eventually committed suicide. She and Ernest appear to have engaged in androgynous and incestuous fantasies.

Grace Hemingway's husband endured the sexual humiliation of a lesbian relationship between his wife and their housekeeper. Dr. Hemingway finally screwed up his courage and threw the woman out of the house. Ernest sided with his father in this and was strongly identified with his henpecked father and resented his domineering mother.

Lynn has traced much of the impact of this early socialization on his later development:

> To be a boy but to be treated as a girl. To feel impelled to prove your masculinity through flat denials of your anxieties . . . and bold lies about your exploits. To be forced to practice the most severe economy in your attempts to "render" your life artistically, because your capital of self-understanding was too small to permit you to be expansive and your fear of exposure too powerful. To make a virtue of necessity by packing troubled feelings below the surface of your stories like dynamite beneath a bridge.

The evidence he has presented is substantial, and the reader is referred to what will certainly be the definitive biography for some time to come. We will presently sample some of it but will center more on the analysis of the complex network of affects and subscripts in this almost stereotypic macho script. It is not really such a script if we compare it with an effective macho script of the kinds described by Mosher. It is rather a pseudo-macho nuclear script which is at best only partly macho.

To begin with, there is a deep ambivalence about sexual identity. He was left not only with disgust, shame and dissmell, anger and terror but also with excitement and enjoyment in cross-sex games with women. Thus, he recorded in 1953, annotating his fourth wife's diary:

> She has always wanted to be a boy and thinks as a boy without ever losing any femininity. If you should become confused on this you should retire. She loves me to be her girls [sic], which I love to be, not being absolutely stupid. . . . In return she makes me awards and at night we do every sort of thing which pleases her and which pleases me. . . . Mary has never had one lesbian impulse but has always wanted to be a boy. Since I have never cared for any man and dislike any tactile contact with men except the normal Spanish abrazo . . . I loved feeling the embrace of Mary which came to me as something quite new and outside all tribal law.

He is therefore not only disgusted by the ambiguity of his sexual identity, as well as angry, dissmelling, and terrified in counteracting it via both decontamination and antitoxic nuclear scripting, but seduced by his own attachment to reproducing the games of his childhood. It is not surprising that out of this same menage both he and his father and the younger sister he loved committed suicide. How does one renounce what excites as it disgusts, as it dismells, as it terrifies, as it enrages?

The extraordinary outcome is that there was *any* authenticity and achievement besides the outrageous lying, posturing, degrading of others, impotence, cheating, self-serving inflation, and sadism. The legendary Hemingway is apparently almost entirely fraudulent.

It must, however, be remembered that he was at rare moments capable of both candor and courage, as when he once wrote to Scott Fitzgerald: "We're all bitched from the start and you especially have to be hurt like hell before you can write seriously. But when you get the damned hurt use it—don't cheat with it. Be as faithful to it as a scientist."

Lacking stable paternal, maternal, and sibling models he could identify with, he lived in a vortex of mixed excitement at cross-sex games and the most turbulent mix of labile negative affects, which might have driven a less robust individual to an earlier suicide. Consider the multiple turbulences to which he was vulnerable: (1) excitement versus disgust and dissmell, (2) disgust versus dissmell, (3) disgust and dissmell versus terror, (4) terror versus rage, (5) disgust versus rage, (6) dissmell versus rage, (7) terror versus excitement.

Each of these affects would recruit subscripts to defend himself against, to counteract, to celebrate positively and negatively in multiple decontamination and antitoxic scripts. Given such a multiplicity of turbulent affect-driven nuclear scripts, the observable behavior becomes more intelligible.

He must avoid exposure above all, for multiple reasons: terror, shame, disgust, dissmell, and rage. He must inflate and lie about his courage, his connoisseurship, his wounds, his suffering, his ability as a sportsman, his grace under pressure, his boxing skill and fairness, his skill in the number of animals he killed, the number of fish he caught, the use of guns to shoot fish, his knowledge of bullfighting.

Next he must degrade, diminish, hurt anyone whom he defines as a competitor and attribute to them his own self-inflationary tactics.

Next he must attack physically those who question any of his boasts or his reputed performances. Thus, he physically attacked Max Eastman. "What do you mean accusing me of impotence?" Eastman had guessed at Hemingway's actual impotence.

Next he must continually test for a variety of unwanted scenes. Will he be exposed? Will he be seduced? Will he not be seduced? Will he become disgusted or not? Will dissmell keep disgust at a safe distance? Can he dissmell the other before he is dissmelled? Can he be angry without being terrified? Can he be dissmelling without terror? Can he be exposed and not terrified? Can he suffer and complain and not become disgusting and dissmelling? Is he really brave? Is he really a man? What will happen if he fights, if he tries to seduce a woman, if he runs away, if he goes hunting and kills no animals while others do? The number of bad scenes possible when multiple malign negative affects are at risk is without limit. This is specially so when decontamination scripts recruit antitoxic scripts, as in this case.

O'NEILL: NUCLEAR DECONTAMINATION OF RECIPROCATED DISGUST AMONG FATHER, MOTHER, AND SONS

Eugene O'Neill's life was governed by a shared nuclear script of mutual recrimination and disgust. In contrast to Freud, who generalized a deep disgust toward his mother, then toward his father, and finally toward the anti-Semitic society in which he lived, O'Neill's magnification of disgust grew as a *folie à quatre* among mother, father, older brother, and himself.

Because his mother had become addicted to morphine, the impact on the tightly knit small family was massive and shared, in disgust and rage and, to some extent, in terror. However, the father proved equally disgusting and flawed in character, and inevitably the two sons could not escape becoming both victims and victimizers, each disgusting all in a network of mutual recrimination which contaminated their entire lives, both as shared and as they tried to avoid and escape each other. Inevitably, they were alternatively repelled and drawn to each other over their entire life courses. In contrast to shame, there is no easy road back to shared enjoyment and excitement. In contrast to dissmell there is no easy road permanently away from the repellent other. Disgust is the most inherently nuclear affect in that the good scene cannot be readily renounced, but its contamination cannot be readily purified and healed. The other has now become enduringly flawed, and to the extent to which the self is the object of disgust, either reducing or increasing the distance between oneself as positive and the flawed self becomes extraordinarily difficult.

With respect to permanent character flaws such as his father's excessive stinginess, his boasting, and his waste of his talent, a nuclear script cannot be reparative in the same sense as we saw it in the case of Sculptor, who wished to return to the time before the arrival of the sibling who took his mother's attention away from him, since there is no purely good scene to which to return. This is not to say there may not be any purely rewarding scenes in even the most disturbed families, but they are very vulnerable to intrusive damages, limitations, contaminations, and toxicities. Therefore, efforts at reparation under such conditions are frequently sought via avoidance or escape or by achieving some distance from intimate family interaction—even if it is limited to retiring to one's own room.

For Eugene O'Neill, his mother's morphine addiction had been experienced as a rather permanent character flaw, despite the fact she had before his birth been free of it. The sibling rivalry he experienced at the hands of his older brother was also something experienced as an enduring part of his life. Therefore, all of the disgust evocation from father, mother, and brother had no sharply segregated positive scenes which might have been experienced as a predisgust scene. At best there were scenes of relief, and of *some* contrast, but scenes ever vulnerable to negative intrusion.

For much of his life he sought relief, purification, avoidance, and escape from the scenes which disgusted. As with any nuclear script he generated families of subscripts of defense, of counteraction, of decontamination (rather than reparation) and scenes of positive and of negative celebration.

Thus, there was a recurrent quest for the ideal place to live. He invested his considerable royalties in finding just the right place, in the Caribbean, then on the California coast, each promising in the beginning endless beauty and peace, only to become disenchanting after a while, the whole sequence to be repeated throughout his life. He could go home again, but he could not find a home that would heal the nuclear disenchantment. No matter how breathtaking the setting, he would ultimately find that it was not what he had thought it was and what it had promised to be. In part this was produced by unavoidable habituation; the once exciting beauty of the ocean became so habitual and so skillfully perceived that there ceased to be consciousness and rewarding affect, and hence it was readily further transformed into the analog of disenchantment, as though the mundane ocean site had once again become the O'Neill home by the ocean in New London, with its familiar flawed father, mother, and brother. This is a familiar example of the vulnerability of antianalogs to transformation to analogs which they had been intended to better.

Not all of O'Neill's escapes to the sea were always vulnerable to habituation and transformation. In *Long Day's Journey into Night,* Edmund (who stands for Eugene) speaks of the sea as the one place he belonged "without past or future, within peace and unity and a wild joy, within something greater than my own life, or the life of man, to Life itself! To God, if you want to put it that way." On a boat he had a "saint's vision of beatitude." He should have been born a fish; as a man he will "always be a stranger who never feels at home, who does not really want and is not really wanted, who can never belong, who must always be a little in love with death."

One must remember the words he had attributed to his mother in this connection: "You were born afraid because I was so afraid to bring you into the world . . . afraid all the time I carried you. I knew something terrible would happen. . . . I should never have borne you. It would have been better for your sake." He was convinced that it was his birth that had made his mother into a morphine addict. In *Long Day's Journey into Night* she stresses that she was "so healthy" before he was born, and "I was so sick afterwards." But there was in this case, as in all others, blame for all, by each. Eugene blamed his father for his stinginess in casually choosing a quack doctor to save on medical costs. It was this doctor who presumably prescribed morphine for his mother. In the play the mother also complains, implicitly blaming her husband as well as her son: "That ignorant quack of a cheap doctor. All he knew was I was in pain. It was easy for him to stop the pain."

Answering his son Eugene, who had accused him of neglect in failing to recognize his mother's addiction and miserliness in not getting expert medical help, his father protests: "[H]ow was I to know then? What did I know of morphine? It was years before I discovered what was wrong. I thought she'd never got over her sickness, that's all."

A major feature of disgust is the implicit invidious contrast between what it once was, how good it was that was expected to be repeated, and the bad taste now experienced. As experienced at the hands of those held responsible, each victim in the O'Neill family is exquisitely skilled in recreating the invidious contrast between how good life was before the guilty one made it bad. Each holds all others responsible for the same kinds of invidious bad tastes compared with what was good before, or for the violations of expectations and hopes.

The disgusting invidious contrast is not only blamed on the other, but in this family each blames all, and even forgiveness may be used as a further weapon for impaling the disgusting other to the cross. Since each is blaming all others for the same bad scenes, each is caught in several cross fires and must continually alternate between attack, defense, and counterattack in a very complex network of shifting warfare, moving the scripts quickly back and forth between decontamination and antitoxic aims as blame for disgust arouses dismell and rage and terror.

Thus, Mary (the mother) remembers having had in her childhood a "real" home in contrast to what she now has. She idealizes her father. But her husband reminds her that her home was ordinary and her father drank. But she wanted to join a convent and live a simple, virginal existence. Her love for her husband has violated her wish for purity. She complains not only about her husband but more generally:

> None of us can help the things life has done to us. They're done before you realize it, and once they're done they make you do other things until at last everything comes between you and what you'd like to be, and you've lost your true self forever.
>
> The past is the present, isn't it? It's the future, too. We all try to lie out of that but life won't let us.

She associates her Catholicism with her need for morphine, to still the pain in her arthritic hands. These hands once played the piano; she studied music in the convent. "I had two dreams. To be a nun, that was the more beautiful one. To become a concert pianist, that was the other." But her marriage and family responsibilities stopped all that.

Then she is reminded of her guilt at failing to take care of her child who died, which now is blamed on her husband:

> I know why he wants to send you [Eugene] to a sanitorium—to take you away from me! He's always tried to do that. He's been jealous of every one of my babies! He kept finding ways to make me leave them. That's what caused Eugene's death. He's been jealous of you most of all. He knew I loved you best because.

Yet, as we have seen before, this does not stop her moments later from blaming Eugene for her dope addiction and blaming him for being born.

The father was dominated by the fear of the poverty-stricken past, and like his wife, is disgusted at having lost something valuable in the past. About his stinginess he wonders: "What the hell was it I wanted to buy?" He had had a real potential as a great actor which he had wasted by doing over and over again the same play, presumably to make money to support his family. Implicit is some blame for his wasted talent. His reward is a first-born who is an alcoholic: "A sweet spectacle for me! My first-born, who I hoped would bear my name in honor and dignity, who showed such brilliant promise!"

O'Neill's brother in the play confesses to hating him because "it was your being born that started Mama on dope." He dates his own decline from the day he first saw her injecting herself with morphine. "Christ, I'd never dreamed before that any women but whores took dope." When she later appeared to be beating the habit, "meant so much, I'd begun to hope, if she'd beaten the game, I could too." When he realizes she has slipped again, he goes to the local brothel and goes upstairs with the least attractive of the whores, Fat Violet, who drinks so much and is so overweight that the madam has determined to get rid of her.

> By applying my natural God-given talents in their proper sphere, I shall attain the pinnacle of success! I'll be the lover of the fat woman in Barnum and Bailey's circus! Pah! Imagine me sunk to the fat girl in a hick town hooker shop! But you're right. To hell with repining! Fat Violet's a good kid. Glad I stayed with her. Christian act. Cured her of her blues. Hell of a good time. You should have stuck with me, kid. Taken your mind off your troubles. What's the use of coming home to get the blues over what can't be helped. All over-finished now-not a hope!-
>
> If I were hanged on the
> highest hill,
> Mother o'mine, O mother o'mine
> I know whose love would follow me still.

O'Neill, in writing *Long Day's Journey into Night,* was involved in a review of his life in order both to better confront it, as he had done only tangentially and abstractly before, as well as to give some well-formed shape to that life, a self-therapeutic effort not uncommon in old age. It was a variant on mourning, which is also a review of a radical change in a relationship. This differed from mourning in addressing primarily his own ambivalent past rather than the idealized past of mourning, similar to the review of a divorce rather than a death. It cost him very dearly, and we are the heirs of his finest play and the raw material for understanding the creativity of a great artist.

FREUD SCRIPT: NUCLEAR DECONTAMINATION AND THE GENERALIZATION OF DISGUST AND ANGER

In Volume 2 we examined Freud's relation to his mother and to women in general as he had projected it in his chapter on the psychology of women. Briefly, we found a nuclear script occasioned by sibling rivalry which was characterized by a sense of deep betrayal and intransigent disgust and anger at his mother's lack of conscience in turning away from him. His conviction that the world was no nursery was coupled with a pervasive pessimism, accompanied by a more specific disgust at women's failure to develop a superego.

We wish now to supplement this picture of his nuclear script as much more heavily decontaminated in nature than reparative, in contrast to the case of Sculptor, who also suffered a severe sibling rivalry. Sculptor held tenaciously to the reparative subscript of the family of nuclear scripts. Freud appeared less certain such would be possible, in part, I will argue, because disgust became more generalized, first toward his father, then toward the anti-Semitic society he encountered, and finally toward all those who would attempt to contaminate "reason" and science. This latter came eventually to jeopardize his relationship with Jung. Not unlike Tolstoy, who was a seeker of "truth" all his life, against the idealization of reality by consciousness, Freud became the Hebrew prophet as Tolstoy became the prophet of a radical Christianity which aimed at the liberation from the false consciousness of conventional religion.

Freud was confronted not only with a betraying, angering, disgusting mother but also with masculine models who were, in varying ways and to different degrees, disgusting and angering as models for dealing with the rabid anti-Semitism which angered and disgusted him and which stood athwart his hope to advance in his professional life as well as threatening his self-respect and dignity.

Consider the flawed options which confronted Freud as a Jewish prophet exiled in the wilderness, surrounded by anti-Semites who held him and his people in bondage. He had four possible models: his father, Hannibal, Moses, and Joseph.

His father had early on disillusioned him and disgusted him. At the age of twelve he was walking in Vienna with his father, who told his son how much better it had become for a Jew in Vienna than it had been in the *shtetls* of Galicia. He told his son about the time in Tysmenitz when a gentile had knocked his hat into the gutter, taunting him: "Jew, get off the pavement." When his indignant son asked him, "What did you do?" the reply was "I stepped into the gutter and picked up my cap." Freud was deeply disgusted, comparing his cowardly father invidiously with Hannibal, the Semitic warrior who avenged his people against the Roman oppressors.

These were the two poles of the possible responses to anti-Semitism in Freud's mind, either craven submission or aggressive defiance and vengeance. Freud was too proud, too disgusted, and too angry to identify with cowardice, but he did identify powerfully with the messianic avenger Hannibal. For this dangerous fantasy, which included not only vengeance against the Romans but rescue of mother Rome, he paid the price of a deep-seated inhibition against travel to Rome, which he finally was able to resolve.

He did not give up the Hannibal dream readily. His anger- and disgust-driven resonance to the heroic, messianic script was too seductive, despite, and in part because of, its danger. Even as a scientist he had envisioned himself as a conquistador. Anti-Semitism continually fanned the fires of the embers of rage and disgust at the maternal betrayal.

If he could not be the cowardly father nor Hannibal, what options remained? There were two and a half: Moses and Joseph were the two, and reason in science was the ambiguous half.

Joseph was the interpreter of dreams who eventually rose to become the chief minister to the Egyptian pharaoh. Moses was the patriarch who had the strength to lead his people out of bondage to the promised land. Freud himself became an interpreter of dreams, but as we will see, this science distinguished reality from dream, made ambiguous the dream of the promised land, and at the same time raised the question of whether Moses was really a Jew or an Egyptian, a preoccupation which haunted him to the end of his life. I believe these ambiguities reflect the nuclear intransigence of unresolvable decontamination and damage repair, stemming from the enduring problem of betrayal by his mother, disgust at his father and at anti-Semitism, and the cold comfort of reason as a completely acceptable resolution of the gap between reality and passion. This science left one with a less disgusting vision of reality than the hopeless dream of a return to the nursery of his mother; the hopeless dream of a return to the promised land, via Zionism; the hopelessly sentimental and more disgusting attempt to pretty-over reality by spiritualism, à la Jung; the cravenly disgusting cowardice of his father; the assimilation of Joseph to the Egyptians; or the ambiguous identity of Moses as a Jewish leader or as an Egyptian. Further, it was less disgusting than confusing wish with reality, as in the theory of sexual seduction by the father, which was "really" a function of projected wish, as the exaggeration of anti-Semitism was in part a function of Semitic intransigence, which exaggerated the significance of the oppressor.

His (partly disgusting) resolution to all his problems was to bite the bullet and accept the deep limitations of the general human condition, as well as the more specific insults of having been born a Jew, by the ennobling trust in reason in science. "Where Id was there shall Ego be." Small as the voice of intellect might be, it would in the end be heard against the voice of the maternal, conscienceless id and against the equally strident intimidating voice of the paternal superego. The best reason could offer in the battle against neurotic anxiety was the distress of normal human misery, but this was better than the unknown and unameable terrors and it was better than the religious opium of the masses or the spiritualistic opium of Jungian mysticism. Better though not best to know the truth and suffer than to drug oneself, as indeed Freud did with his own terminal cancer, resisting sedatives lest his reason be clouded.

The rabid anti-Semitism confronting Freud seriously compromised both his career and his dignity as well as the possibility of solving the problem of Jewish identity via assimilation. Freud had written Fliess after attending a play, *The New Ghetto,* by the future Zionist leader Theodor Herzl "about the future of one's children to whom one cannot give a country of their own." In an interview between Freud and the son of Theodor Herzl, the founder of Zionism, Freud had said, "Your father is one of those people who have turned dreams into reality. This is a very rare and dangerous breed.... I would simply call them the sharpest opponents of my scientific work." In rejecting Herzl, as well as Moses and Hannibal, he is not entirely identifying with Joseph in his assimilation with the Egyptians through his dream interpretation. For Freud he has chosen his characteristic way: the rough, hard, but least disgusting road. He is too proud to "pass." Disgust and anger are too deep in him to take the easy way and become another Joseph in the court of the pharaoh, even though he will pursue the Talmudic driven inner quest of dream interpretation.

What then, of Moses? Moses could not be an altogether satisfactory identification figure for Freud, for a number of reasons. First was Freud's intransigent denied longing for the betraying, conscienceless, whore mother. He could neither forgive her nor entirely forget her. Moses, however, had identified with the jealous patriarchal God who, in a covenant with his warlike, nomadic chosen people, promised them a return to their homeland, to smite their enemies, in return for their unconditional loyalty to him. The crux of this loyalty was the idolatry of the earth goddess by the Israelites, turned into pacifist agriculturalists, who hungered to be fed by the good mother earth goddess. Moses' rage at their violating the "law" and the Ten Commandments in their idolatry of the rival female goddess frightened not only the Israelites but also Freud, who fainted in fright confronting the representation of this scene. I would suggest that this terror was occasioned more by Moses and Jahveh as "real" fathers than by Jacob, for whom he had more disgust than fear, in their denunciation of the idolatrous worship of the golden calf. It was beyond a strictly sexual incest a deep oral hunger for the seductive mother, whom he could not and would not renounce in favor of a less than heroic father and a mythic Moses and Jahveh.

Further, although Moses led his people to the promised land, he did not himself enter it. Freud's response to the promised land was plurivalent. It attracted him in different ways, but he also had reservations, as we have seen, both about Hannibal and about Herzl's Zionism, the latter as attempting to dangerously force "dreams into reality" and as such the "sharpest opponents of my scientific work." In this respect Moses was no more realistic than either Herzl or Jung in his mysticism and wish-fulfilling "spiritualism," which was disgusting and even dissmelling "mud." In the end Freud could neither reject nor entirely accept Moses, nor satisfy himself that he was a Jew or an Egyptian, since Freud could neither totally accept or reject his own Jewishness nor totally accept or reject the "Egyptians" among whom he spent his life. His solution as a man of reason gave him dignity but not warmth, the price of intransigent disgust and anger generalized.

Chapter 36
Antitoxic Anger-Avoidance Scripts

ANTITOXIC SCRIPTS

We will next address that family of scripts in which anger is one of the primary affects, rather than a secondary or tertiary affect. This is in contrast to affluence scripts in which anger may be secondary to excitement or enjoyment and in contrast to reparative scripts in which anger may be secondary to shame and the reduction of damage to an affluent scene. It is in contrast to limitation-remediation scripts in which anger may be secondary to reducing enduring limitations which primarily distress. Finally, it is in contrast to contamination-decontamination scripts in which anger is secondary to contaminations which primarily disgust.

We have labeled the most malignant trio of affects—terror, dissmell, and anger—as the primary constituents of toxic scenes which demand antitoxic scripts, in which fire is fought with fire. Terror may be fought by anger, dissmell, or terror. Anger may be fought by terror, dissmell, by anger. Dissmell may be fought by terror, anger, or dissmell. It may be elected to avoid, escape, express, counteract, exert power, or destroy the toxic other by any combination of anger, dissmell, and terror or by any single countertoxic anger, dissmell, or terror. Anger or dissmell or terror may be that of the other or of the self or both. If your anger terrifies me, that is a toxic scene to which I may respond secondarily with a mixed terror, dissmell, and anger and script either avoidance, escape, or aggressive counterattack. If your dissmell infuriates me, that is a toxic scene to which I may respond with a mixed angry dissmell by keeping you at a distance in a recasting script to make you feel furious and distanced. Although anger or dissmell or terror is each primary and sufficient to constitute a toxic scene and thereby prompt an antitoxic script, each frequently recruits the other toxic affects in complex mixtures. This generates complex families of antitoxic scripts with varying ratios of anger, dissmell, and terror in and for the self and other. Further, anger may be the preferred scripted remedy for either the anger of the other, his dismell of me, or his terror of me.

But although an antitoxic script is the most malignant type of script—for the individual, for his adversary, and for society—its malignancy is nonetheless independent of its differential magnification. This depends on the spectral density of all the individual's family of scripts. It is quite possible (though not common) for an individual to wish for, or welcome, or imagine, or even plan the death of a toxic other but to primarily lead a life of affluence and/or good works and goodwill in repair or remediation of the damages or limitations of his life space. We will illustrate such variation in four cases, each of which entertains the death or murder of toxic adversaries with varying degrees of differential magnification of competing, less malignant scripts.

We will present, through an analysis of their TATs, three cases which we have called X, Y, and Z and which will illustrate three general statuses of anger, the condition of isolation, the condition of coexistence with competitors, and the condition of being bound.

In the first case, X, anger and shame are in constant ferment and competition with positive affects, each coexisting, competing, and alternating with each other.

In the second case, Y, anger is quite isolated and seems to exert no residual intrusive pressure from the return of the repressed. In the third case, Z, anger proved so dangerous as it was magnified that it had to be bound and kept under tight control by assuming an entirely submissive attitude toward a father who constantly provoked anger.

The TAT provides an opportunity to assess the degree of isolation and/or of repression of any wish. Let us consider some examples. If the TAT of an individual portrayed a son submissive to his father and to every other male figure in all his stories but one, and in this story was a hero under the influence of alcohol and in prehistoric times destroyed some physical property in a blind rage, we would assume that the magnification of the repressing affects was very great. We would assume this since it forbade the expression of any aggression except under the most unusual and remote conditions of this story and then only toward a nonliving object. If the same individual had also given us a story of a hero who attacked the prehistoric monster of card 11, we would have said that the magnification of repressing affect was somewhat less, since it permitted aggression toward living organisms. If in addition the hero had rescued a princess from this monster, we would suppose that there was somewhat less repression, inasmuch as a *human being* had been introduced as the reason for this aggression. If the individual had portrayed all his heroes submissive in face-to-face relationships but in one story the hero led a revolt against the government, we would assume that the repressing affect had been still weaker because it sanctioned aggression against human agencies. If in addition there had been stories of the hero's hatred of policemen, we would assume still less magnification of the repressing affects because the impersonality of authority had been concretized in the person of the policeman. Less repression would have permitted some herpes to aggress upon other adult males with whom they had a more personal relationship. Finally, if the individual had also told stories in which the hero behaved submissively toward his father in the face-to-face relationship but nursed private and unexpressed wishes for revenge, we would assume that the magnification of the repressing fear operated only to prevent the overt expression of the wish but did not prevent awareness of the wish.

It is our assumption that the remoteness of conditions under which antisocial wishes may be expressed is a function of the relative magnification and pressure of repressing and repressed affects. As the magnification of repressing affect increases relative to the magnification of the repressed affect, the conditions under which the latter may be given expression in TAT stories become more and more "remote." As this ratio approaches equality, the expression of the repressed affect will appear under less and less remote conditions in the stories.

Since we will employ "remoteness" as an index of repression, let us consider in more detail the varieties of remoteness. There is remoteness of object—the wish may be directed toward a parent who is usually the original object of the repressed wish, or toward a parent surrogate, policemen, the law, government, animals, or physical objects. This represents a typical series of increasingly remote objects for the displacement of repressed wishes. There is remoteness of time—the present, the immediate past or future, the remote past or future. There is remoteness of place of setting—the individual's customary habitat or geographically remote settings, ranging from other countries to other planets. There may be remoteness of function level, ranging from behavior to wish, memories, daydreams, nightdreams, and special states. Finally, there may be remoteness of conditions ranging from the hero's everyday conditions to states of extreme fatigue, frustration, or anxiety, and so on. A story may be extremely remote in one respect but not in another. For example, normal individuals occasionally murder their parents in their TAT stories. This represents a minimum of remoteness of *object* but some other dimensions will usually be extremely remote—the individual will depict either the parent or the hero as suffering some special condition. The parent may be represented as particularly brutal because he is under the influence of alcohol, or the hero may be particularly frustrated or "queer."

By means of these criteria we may estimate, crudely, differences in remoteness of expression of repressed wishes between one protocol and another.

Let us now turn to the cases of X, Y, and Z.

The Case of X

X is a young woman who describes her father as a quite refined man with many gifts and a fine personality. She is admittedly much fonder of her father than of her mother but feels sorry for her mother because her life has been a hard one, and X feels her mother deserved a better fate. It is evident from her stories that her hostility toward her mother is marked. In the face-to-face situation her heroine feels this hostility but suppresses it.

> This woman is trying to talk some sense into this girl. She is reading a perceptual passage to her, but the girl's mind is far away. She does not want to listen to this woman [her mother] because she associates most of her previous humiliating experiences with her. She wants to get away, to be free. She has mixed feelings of self-pity, aggression, and a desire to start out on her own. However, she makes an effort and suppresses this mood and listens to what her mother is reading.

On the basis of this story we would expect to find further evidence of aggression directed toward other females and would predict that remote displacement would not be required, since the existence of hostility is freely admitted into the consciousness of the heroine in the face-to-face situation.

In the following story we see the transference of this affect to other women.

> This woman is jealous of the other woman because she has a sweeter disposition, etc., etc., and men seem to prefer the company of Woman 2 because she is so gay and charming, even though not one fifth as intelligent as Woman 1. "I don't care," says Woman 1 and returns to her book. Little by little the woman becomes absorbed in her book, and the petty jealousies, etc., seem to fall off. In fact when she puts the book aside, she feels very friendly toward the whole world and even goes out of her way to be good to Woman 2.

There is a continuation of hostility and jealousy toward other females, and the reasons are similar—she feels that she is inferior to her mother and other women in competition for the attention of men. We are told, in addition, that she has learned to control this aggression, which she could do no more than suppress in childhood, by turning to books, which enables the petty jealousies to "fall off." In the following story there is the same attempt to manage the anger born of frustration and feelings of inferiority by immersing herself in something which removes her from her own bitterness.

> That hideous woman at the back is this woman's evil nature which she has long suppressed. This woman wasn't really evil when a child but things went against her. She felt frustrated on every hand. Now, however, she wants to restore her own mental health by attaching herself to some great and selfless cause. The more she strives in this direction, the fainter and fainter grows the woman at the back. Eventually, the finer qualities in her are completely reinstated.

These are the conditions of her mental health: identification with and dedication to something which will make the anger grow "fainter and fainter." This mechanism must be distinguished from reaction formation. She does not "pretend" to be more friendly than she really is. In the previous story she "went out of her way" to be friendly toward the woman she hated because she had been able to overcome her anger through absorption in something which interested her, and this diminished the feelings of inferiority which aroused her anger. In this story her attachment to a noble cause is the instrument of dissipating the anger and inferiority at the same time. As a result the anger fades. It can be reduced in intensity and extensity because it is not an end per se but the consequence of her intolerable feeling of humiliation and inferiority. For this reason reading, in one case, and dedication to a selfless cause, in the other, can at once dissipate the feeling of both inferiority and anger which results from it.

We are also told, indirectly, how her mental health might be irreparably shattered. If her feelings of inferiority were for any reason to increase beyond a critical point, with no possibility of overcoming them, we might predict that she would be overwhelmed by the anger which would result from her humiliation. This happens to one of her heroines, and the aggression is directed against the original object, the mother.

> The woman who is strangling the other woman is crazy. She used to be a pretty girl once but she developed a physical deformity—her hand became swollen and ugly. She was so distressed by this fact that her whole personality changed. She felt

> nobody cared for her anymore. She became morose and suspicious of others even when they were being genuinely nice to her. Little by little this neurotic trend grew till she became positively dangerous. Her mother loved her and wanted to protect her so she would not hear of the girl being sent to the asylum. However in one of her fits the maniac caught her mother by the throat as she was coming down the stairs and strangled her. The rest of the family rushed in, but it was too late. They did not punish her, of course, but they put her in a mental home.

The presence of an inferiority which cannot be overcome results in a feeling of humiliation and suspicion of the attitude of others toward her, which leads ultimately to an overwhelming "fit" of aggression against her mother.

That the joint problems of inferiority and resultant anger and aggression are the principal concern of this young woman is further indicated by the following three stories.

> This woman is pleading with this man to leave his work for a while and relax. She offers herself to him. The man here seems to be hesitating between his duty and his love, but actually he knows which really matters to him. Besides he will soon grow tired of the woman, and the temporary pleasure is nothing compared with the rewards of his work. So he fools around with her for a while and then throws her off without a remorse because after all she got what she wanted, and he gave as much as was his to give. The woman takes it badly at first, but she recovers and throws herself into her own work with greater determination. She is thrilled to find how well she makes out on her job.
>
> This woman is blissfully happy because she has found someone who returns her affection with equal intensity. The man is here a little amused at her childish clinging because he had thought her so mature and self-contained. She, on her part, is happy because she can cling to him as much as she likes without fear of his ceasing to respect her on that score; she wants to feel thus protected and cherished always so that she might in turn be a source of strength and faith. A year ago she despaired of ever meeting such a person. Now she laughs because she had doubted her destiny. The two work together and make great contributions to the welfare of humanity. They are a sort of combination of Einstein and Madame Curie.

In these stories the conditions necessary for her happiness in love and work are presented. She can be happy if she can be dependent without fear of losing self-respect or the respect of her lover. Through the secure gratification of this dependency she is enabled to offer something in return, and the couple working together make great contributions to the welfare of humanity. But if the superior male rejects her and makes her feel inferior, she will turn to work to escape her misery. She is "thrilled to find how well she makes out on her job," but she does not make "great contributions to the welfare of humanity." Nor is she a "Madame Curie."

This young woman suffered acute feelings of shame and rage, and much of her energy was expended in coping with these feelings, controlling the anger she felt, repressing its more intense and primitive components. Evidence from the TAT is congruent with this fact. Approximately 75 percent of her stories are concerned either with the wish to be respected and loved or the wish to aggress upon those who humiliated her. We have rated the remoteness of expression as low since she is aware of these feelings in the face-to-face situation with her mother, although she suppresses the overt expression of these feelings. She continues to be aware of these feelings throughout the stories, although the most intense aggression is *expressed* under more remote conditions—by a "maniac" in a "fit." We have rated this remoteness as low (but not very low) because of the continuity of the expression of aggression from face-to-face normal conditions and remote conditions. In such a case the individual's mental health is capable of being shattered through the intensification of the strength of the repressed shame-anger. As in the story told by X, she might lose her sanity if she suffered sufficient increase in her feelings of shame to intensify the anger which results from intolerable humiliation. She might, however, become a "Madame Curie" if she found a man who made her feel both loved and *respected.* Under these conditions she would be capable not only of trust and dependence, but she could, in addition, offer nurturance to such a man, and together they would make great contributions to the welfare of mankind. This case illustrates very clearly the unstable equilibrium characteristic of her conflicts. Although her suppressed aggressive wish presents a real problem and might conceivably produce a psychotic state, it is not in and of itself the primary problem. It is the resultant of feeling inferior and unloved by the father surrogate. For this reason the vicissitudes of her love and work can, as they vary from day to day, intensify or completely do away with her feelings of anger so that the relationship which we have assumed to exist between the repressing affect and the repressed affect is true only under certain specific conditions of frustration. When these are increased or decreased, the relationship between repressed anger and repressing affect may change radically.

Her shame and anger may be repaired when she suffers damaging shame either from a rival or from indifference from her husband by reading a book in the first case or by "throwing" herself into her own work with greater determination in the second.

Longer-term remediation, however, requires the love and respect of her co-worker in an "Einstein and Madame Curie" relationship through which they make great contributions to the welfare of humanity.

Anger and shame are ever threatening to damage and limit her world, but she is capable of repairing and remedying both affects under specially favorable conditions. Whenever she is confronted with irreparable damage or unremediable inferiority, she will kill her adversary in an antitoxic script.

The Case of Y

Y is a young woman, twenty years of age, whose attitudes, as they were expressed in interviews, were not dissimilar to those of X. Y adores her father but feels much less tenderness toward her mother, although she tries to be fair: "I realize that she's that way and apparently cannot overcome it, so I think nothing of it." There are, however, important differences: Y's father reciprocates her feelings: "He is especially friendly toward me and is happy if I am happy." "The respect which my father has for me is very great, and to me this is very important because unless I am worthy of his respect we could not be close friends as we are." This latter is reminiscent of X's need to be respected by the idealized father who elicits her respect.

Despite the great similarity of the basic personalities of X and Y, the differences are profound. Y has achieved the relationship which might save X from being overwhelmed by humiliation and rage. Y's worship of her father has not interfered with her plans for marriage. She has transferred to her future husband the adoration which she has felt toward her father and seems destined to achieve a happy marriage.

The TAT stories told by her are what we might have expected. In the following story she tells us again of her adoration of her father.

> Frank's father was a well-known violinist, and Frank worshipped him. His main ambition in life was to be a great musician, as proficient as his father, but he doubted if anyone else could be so talented. He has had only a very few lessons and sits, pondering over the violin. Frank cannot visualize just how such beautiful music can come from such an instrument and wonders whether he should give the whole idea up or if, after many years, he could attain the goal he wants to set for himself. He concluded that even though he's young he is somewhat like his father and he too can be a musician.

In her second story her somewhat ambivalent but not overly intense feelings toward her mother are delineated.

> Ethel had always gone to a country school and was interested in getting an education. Ethel's mother had very little education but was happy with what she had been accustomed to and could not understand why Ethel must have more than a high school education. Ethel does not like to go against her mother's wishes but tries to explain that many changes are taking place in the world today and that she cannot be satisfied with the insignificant life she had led thus far, and she wants to go to school, get an education, and see what is really going on in the world.

Finally, the transference of her love from her father to her future husband, as well as her fulfillment in maternity, is expressed in a wish-fulfillment fantasy.

> Mary and John had been married just a year ago, before he joined the Navy. He had been home on leave two months ago and was now at sea. Mary loves him deeply and naturally misses him but tries to keep her mind occupied and not to worry about him. On this particular night, however, she's restless and cannot sleep. She tries reading but can think of nothing but Johnny. She walks out in the hall and stands by the window, dreaming of Johnny and the day he'll be back. Mary doesn't feel well the next morning and goes to the doctor, to learn that she is going to have a baby. After this she is very busy, making preparations for the baby, and the time passes very quickly. Johnny gets another leave and is with Mary when the baby is born.

These three stories are typical of the entire protocol and indicate that there is no discrepancy between her overt behavior, her publicly expressed attitudes, and her private world. She is not an individual divided against herself or one whose behavior exemplifies any pathogenic mechanism which we could detect. She is entirely free of neurotic symptom formation and of neurotic anxiety.

Her stories were all like this, with the *one* exception which follows.

> As much as Richard disliked it, he was becoming quite accustomed to having his father come home in a drunken condition, but this evening when, in addition to being highly inebriated, he was angry and started beating his wife, it was too much for Richard, who was very fond of his mother. Richard tried to control his temper but with no avail. He was certain that his father did no good for his family or anyone, and before he realized just what he was doing, he reached for the revolver and shot him. Richard has now decided that even though he must give himself up, it is much better this way than having his mother tortured the way she has been for the past two years.

The murder of parents in TAT stories is an extremely rare phenomenon in normals. Had we found any evidence of such a wish, we would have expected it to be directed against the mother, although there were no indications of hostility of such proportions. That this story could be told by an individual who loves both her father and future husband so deeply and is apparently so free of ambivalence is very puzzling when one is accustomed to expect all antisocial wishes which suffer repression to press toward expression and to produce symptoms if they are not expressed. To the best of our knowledge this story is an isolated fragment in the total picture of an otherwise well-adjusted individual. What it represents one can only guess. It is conceivably a residue of accidentally witnessing the primal scene—seeing the father, who was distinguished for his kindness and even temper, excited and passionate and apparently hurting the mother. But whatever its meaning it is clear that the father is seen to be different from his normal self. He is pictured under the influence of alcohol, and the aggression which he displays is given a finite course—two years. Presumably, this represented a change of character in the father. Consonant with our hypothesis that this fragment produces no pressure symptoms is the hero's lack of remorse for this murder.

We have said that in Y's conflict the remoteness of expression of anger was high. But in this case we have rated the pressure of repressed anger as very low because this anger appears in only one story. Although its intensity is very high in this story, the total estimate of magnification (based on its intensity and extensity throughout the protocol) would be very low, since there is no other evidence of the wish. We would rate the remoteness of expression as high since there is no continuity between the face-to-face normal relationship with the father and the murder of the father under remote conditions. We would have rated it as very high if the hero had instead murdered an animal or an adult other than the father.

We have said that a conflict between a high and very low magnified wish should not permit a return of the repressed wish or sequelae which are pathogenic. This hypothesis would appear to be supported by the evidence from this case. The positive love of the father and future husband exerts sufficient magnification to contain this repressed fragment of hostility and at the same time permit the individual no awareness of its presence. It is as remote from the personality as it is isolated within the microcosm of the TAT.

It is the relative density of positive over negative affect in this case which permits affluence and remediation scripting to isolate and contain the rare antitoxic script.

The Case of Z

The case of Z is that of a nuclear script which differs from the nuclear script of Sculptor in stressing remediation, decontamination, and antitoxic scripts rather than reparative scripts. In the case of Sculptor a good scene turned bad, and the nuclear script was targeted on repairing that damage and recovering the beloved mother in an affluent reunion. In the case of Z the problem is more classically Oedipal. The father will not permit the family romance. He is the villain who diminished his son by intimidation. It is a nuclear script because Z will not give up his mother but neither can he possess her, nor avenge himself on his father.

Z is a young man of nineteen whom I studied intensively over a ten-month period. He was given four successive administrations of the TAT at three-month intervals. He was also presented with other pictures daily. He told over four hundred stories during this period.

Not unlike X and Y, Z was also much possessed by the family romance. He had, in many respects, a classical Oedipus conflict. He loved his mother dearly, respected his father, and was deferent to him. The TAT revealed aggression toward his father less repressed than in the case of Y but more repressed than in the case of X.

Let us examine first those stories in which we see the hero in a face-to-face relationship with his father.

> This fellow has had amnesia and they are now taking his measurements. By these measurements they will discover that he is the son of a wealthy man. He goes to live with his father, who is a sadist, and because of the treatment he runs away, getting another attack.

The son is submissive to the sadistic father and runs away, to suffer another attack of amnesia. In the next story we are told of the enduring consequence of his father's severity.

> These children have been told by their father definitely not to leave the house. Their friends are at the window coaxing them to come out and play. They shake their heads but after a long while sneak out. They are caught and severely punished, and this is the way their childhood is spent. When they grow up, they become strict disciplinarians, except the boy, who will be very gentle, almost effeminate.

The consequence of this severe paternal discipline is that the boy "will be very gentle, almost effeminate." This again is the relationship in the face-to-face situation. But as the pictures and stories lead into general social relationships and away from the family this picture changes.

> This picture is supposed to represent a person hypnotizing another. This person is an older fellow sitting there. He is an insane person. He has great illusions about himself. He thinks he can cause the will of another to snap into his own will and make him do whatever he wants. This person has gone to sleep and pays no attention. This upsets him and he goes back to the insane asylum.

The father surrogate is still portrayed as an omnipotent figure, but he is insanely so, and the younger man refuses to comply with his wishes. There is here no overt aggression or even overt rebelliousness but a passive resistance—he has "gone to sleep and pays no attention."

As the stories increase in remoteness, there is a gradual change in the hero's reactions.

> This old guy. I hate him. He is the most disgusting individual. He is a bourgeois capitalist, and he spies on his friends, sees things they don't want him to see. His life is not complete unless he observes his friends unaware. Such a low individual has been completely summed up. Somebody will catch him spying and shoot him through the heart.

In this story the older male adult is a more remote object of displaced anger, inasmuch as he is seen as a representative of a *class* of men who are rejected. The hero's reactions have, as a function of this increased distance, changed from passive resistance to a feeling of disgusted hatred, but there is still no overt aggression. The father surrogate is still portrayed as someone who exercises too much dominance over the lives of others and who "spies on his friends." Although the hero does not express his hatred, the story ends with the possibility that "somebody will catch him spying and shoot him through the heart." This is the first act of overt aggression against a father surrogate, although it is not the hero's doing.

With more remoteness, there is a change to overt aggression.

> This man has been blinded by tear gas and is now being led by a friend out of a group that is being dispersed by the police. His activities in this group were innocent; he now becomes a cop-hater. This may sometime lead him to get in an argument with a policeman and strike him. For this there would be a jail sentence and further rooting of his dislike for the police.

This story represents one further step away from the father in that the policeman is not the representative of a class but the representative of the law and society at large, and he envisions a possible overt expression of aggression toward policemen. In addition, the punishment for this act of aggression will intensify his hatred.

In this story he was "innocent" at the beginning. In the next story he is less innocent.

> The man in the picture is a laborer. He has just been to a labor agitation meeting. Now he is being forcibly exited. The result of this is that he will become more antisocial than ever. He will become more stubborn, perhaps run up against the law and go to jail. Any way you look at it, this fellow's life will become less and less satisfactory to society.

Here he becomes "more antisocial than ever" and "more stubborn." The implication is clear that he went to the labor agitation meeting in the first place with antisocial intent. The hero is still portrayed as the victim of persecution. The "law" and "society" are no less sadistic than the father, but we see him turning more and more openly against these paternal surrogates. His role is becoming less and less passive.

The following story represents the underlying wish displaced to the object at greatest remove from the father.

> The man is an instigator of a revolt. Having laid his plans, he now has gone home and, standing at the window with the room darkened, he watches the explosion in a gov't building, which is a signal for the revolt to begin. Mingled emotions are experienced by him at this instant, fear for an instant then excitement and joy—trust of his companions.

This is the clearest expression of the underlying wish to get rid of the omnipotent and ubiquitous father. The object is remotely displaced. It is the impersonal force of authority represented by the established government. It is of further interest that this revolt is not punished. It would appear that the cooperation of trusted allies had made a successful holy war of this revolt. But although revolt may call for the cooperation of the oppressed and although it may be successful against the "government," it is not so successful when the parent surrogate is a less remote and more concrete tyrant.

> An eclipse—colored slaves are unloading a boat. The wife of the foreman is on the bridge looking for the law for the men are bootlegging. The Negroes will take the eclipse as a sign of revolt and kill their master. The wife will run away, the slaves will be caught and sold again—all because of the eclipse.

Here the condition of revolt is the pact of slaves against the master. This is the most open aggression expressed toward the father figure, albeit at some distance, but although there is a group responsibility for the act, the whole group is caught and sold again. This aggression is less remotely displaced insofar as the object of aggression is a "master" rather than the more impersonal government.

If these feelings of anger are as intense as they seem to be, we would expect that the sadism embodied in the father's behavior toward the son might well engender sadistic impulses of revenge by the son. We have as yet seen no evidence of a purely sadistic enjoyment on the part of the hero. He has expressed hatred, he has struck a policeman, overthrown the government, and with others killed his master. We would assume that the conditions necessary for the full expression of this sadistic wish would be an extreme degree of remoteness of the displaced object of his aggression. Such is the case in the only story of its kind told to over four hundred pictures:

> This man has just set fire to a stable full of horses, but he couldn't resist the temptation to stay around and watch the agony of the animals. While he was doing this, a watchman catches him and he is taken to prison.

This is at once the most remotely displaced object of his aggression and the most open expression of the depth of his feeling. The conditions of this story are remote in two senses. First, aggression is expressed toward animals rather than human beings, and second, the objects of his aggression are helpless victims who are incapable of counteraggression. Under these joint conditions of remoteness he can aggress, torture, and enjoy the agony of his victims.

We should expect that any harm which befell the father would in no way be the responsibility of the son. The following story is an example:

> Bringing home the groceries, a father slipped and sprained his ankle. It hurt, and so he got into the bathtub and turned on the hot water. This caused increased swelling, and the man lost two weeks from work besides much sleep.

The father suffers an "accident," but the son is in no way responsible. Another story of the same variety follows:

> The man's son is leaving on the train after spending a week's furlough with him. This is the last time that the man will see his son. Within a week the man is dead.

The father dies after seeing the son, but the son is by that time far away and is clearly not responsible for his father's death. The death of the father, for no apparent reason, is testament to the remoteness of the death wish from the individual's consciousness.

In order to evaluate the magnification of this repressed wish we will have to consider at some length the other wishes expressed in this protocol. We are fortunate in finding in this individual another important wish which is also repressed. The comparison of two repressed wishes within the same individual will allow us a test of the dynamics of repression.

There is much evidence for a repressed wish for the exclusive and complete possession of his mother. The fusion of the wish for love and sex from his mother has created serious problems. It has been further complicated by a fusion of sex and aggression. In the face-to-face relationship with the father we saw no evidence of any trace of the repressed anger. In the face-to-face relationship with the mother, there is evidence of his love for his mother in the following rescue script.

> This woman heard someone in the living room, and thinking it was her son and friends, she has opened the door to say good night before she retires. Instead it turns out to be robbers who turn a gun on her and force her to tell where the valuables are. As they are leaving, her son comes in and, being an impetuous person, attacks them. They shoot him and escape. She immediately goes to aid him. Does he die? No, it's only a severe flesh wound.

This classical theme is apparently close enough to consciousness and of sufficient magnification and acceptability to be projected into the mother-son relationship rather than toward some more displaced object. Individuals in whom this wish is more repressed express it under more remote conditions, such as a response to card 11 about a prince who rescues the fairy princess from the dragon.

More striking than this manifestation of his wish is the following story in which a fusion of sex and aggression is attributed to the mother:

> The person on the left is the boy's mother. While fondling the boy, she all at once bit off part of the

> boy's ear. After this she became a perfect wreck and had to be separated from the boy, who became very afraid of her. Later she died in an insane asylum.

We are told in effect that "fondling" between mother and son may lead to loss of control, in a fusion of sex and aggression, and this may lead to her death.

This story, with modifications, is repeated with the brother as the hero, rather than the mother.

> There has just been a murder committed. The man has killed his sister and, dazed and stunned, stumbles out and stubs his toe. Gangrene sets in, and his toe is cut off. Then he is hung.

This story was told to card 13, the picture of a naked woman in bed and a man standing near by. It is important in the interpretation of this story to know that this subject has no sister but that he considers his mother more of a sister than a mother to him. From material which will be presented later, it is clear that this picture of a naked woman incited the same fusion of sex and aggression which seized the mother above when she was fondling her son. It is no less dangerous an act for the son than the mother. The consequences are peculiarly severe—he "stubs his toe. Gangrene sets in, and his toe is cut off. Then he is hung." It is interesting to compare the punishment suffered by heroes who aggressed upon paternal surrogates and this punishment, which presumably stems from the same source. Aggression against father figures received relatively light punishment—the slaves were caught and sold again for killing their master, the hero was jailed for his antisocial behavior toward the policemen and toward the horses, and when he revolted against the government there was no mention of punishment of any kind. But for the murder of his "sister," no single punishment is severe enough. And the consequence of similar behavior on the part of the mother is insanity and death.

In another response to the same card in another administration of the test, he told the following story.

> The man is very drunk. In this condition he has gone to see the woman shown here. She has gotten undressed and into bed and is now pretending to pay no attention to him and to be disinterested. He is getting undressed in order to get into bed with her. In the moment thinking how wrong it is to do the thing he has contemplated. Immediately, however, liquor will cloud his mind and his body will take control. Afterwards, he will probably be very upset about it.

In this response, where the remoteness of the object and condition is increased—he is "very drunk"—he is able to consummate the sexual act. We see a third type of remoteness in this act in that he disclaims responsibility for it—"immediately, however, liquor will cloud his mind and his body will take control." Concomitant with this increased remoteness, there is a decrease in the severity of punishment. He "will probably be very upset about it" but suffers nothing more severe. This is a page from the subject's past history. Previous to the period of testing he was involved in one such episode, very much under the influence of alcohol, and suffered remorse afterward.

His heroes are generally tortured by the problem of the control of their sexual impulses and the serious consequences of the loss of such control.

A typical example of this conflict appears in the following story.

> The scene is an English churchyard at night about a century ago. The man is a clergyman, and he is worshipping at the grave of a woman whom he loved deeply but never revealed his emotion. The struggle between celibacy and his natural desire has ruined his health. Now he is thanking God that the struggle is over and he can sublimate his passion by loving her memory.

It is clear from this story that Z suffers no split in his libido. His sexual and love wishes are directed toward the same object.

In the following story the typical sequel to actual loss of control is given.

> The man, while suddenly kissing the girl on the cheek, bit her cheek. He apologized profusely. He could [slip?] tell why he had done it. No avail—their acquaintanceship was broken off.

This story was written, and the words "could tell why" probably present a slip of the pencil, again indicating the pressure of the repressed wish and the relative weakness of the repressing affect. We see again the fusion of oral aggression with sexuality that was first noted in the story of the mother who bit off part of her son's ear. The consequence of this loss of control is less serious than the loss of control on the part of the mother. The relationship is broken, but there is no insanity following loss of control.

In the following story the same theme is repeated.

> This couple are dancing together. They have been old friends for a long time. Now the man tells the woman that he loves her. He kisses her lightly on the lips. Then she'll tell him that she doesn't love him and not to put her in a position where she'll have to forfeit his friendship by not allowing him to see her.

It is of some interest that where the hero suffers either the disruption of the relationship or external punishment, there is no guilt or remorse; and conversely, where the hero suffers guilt, there is no punishment. But some form of punishment, either exogenous or endogenous, is present in all his love stories.

In the following story there is an interesting denial of sexual wishes.

> The woman has just gone through a harrowing experience. She has come to tell her friend about it, but at the memory of it she faints as is shown. That he is not making undesired advances to her is shown by the way he holds her. Of interest is the semicircle near his forehead, which may either be a lock of hair or part of the door, and also the picture which doesn't seem centered or significant in such a large frame.

Notice that the statement "that he is not making undesired advances to her is shown by the way he holds her" creates sufficient anxiety to disrupt his story and lead him to describe small details of the picture. This was a rather typical response to terror which was incited by his own stories. We see again that the repressed sexual wish is sufficiently powerful to generate terror at the thought of it breaking through. Stories of his repressed aggressive need did not result in such small-detail response to terror.

Arising from the fact that his love object and his sex object are one and the same person and that his love and sex need have a passionate oral-aggressive component, there is such a generalization of these repressed wishes to more remote love and sex objects that he cannot, in his stories, allow any consummation of marriage.

The following story is typical of this inhibition.

> The woman has heard some very sad news—perhaps a person close to her has died. She turns to the man, a close friend, perhaps a lover, and seeks consolation. . . . In another way, depending on how the girl's eye interprets emotion to the observer, the girl might be dancing with the boy. She acts very sophisticated and he seems amused, perhaps at something she'd said. They will be good (not close) friends but won't ever marry.

"Good" friends are typically not "close" friends. In the following story there is further evidence of the repressing affect:

> Both these people are married [crossed out] working, and they have made it a point to get time off together and go for a bicycle trip during the summer. This has now become almost a tradition and will go on for years. They are friends and never show any warm feelings for each other.

He began the story about a married couple and then penciled over it to make them friends who "never show any warm feelings for each other." Again, good friends are not close friends.

In the following story the same logic determines the nature of the relationship.

> These two people had been in love in their youth but had separated. The woman is a widow, and now in their old age they enjoy each other's company calmly and dispassionately.

Where there is mutual passion, the couple is separated and allowed to reunite only after they are capable of a more calm relationship.

Another example of the same theme is the following:

> These two children play together often. The little girl learns that her family is to move away. She tells the little boy nothing about this but kisses him good-bye. She joins a nunnery when she grows up and doesn't see the boy again until she is very old, when she is visiting a dying man in the poor district. He smiles, and she follows an impulse to kiss him although she does not recognize him. He begins to get better but then dies suddenly.

Although there is the reunion here of two lovers who still are capable of passion, the man after a brief improvement "dies suddenly."

Or the couple may be separated by the premature death of one of the lovers.

> When a young boy, Roger Rollins brought his girl, Mary Caudry, to this tree and carved their initials on it. Later, in her teens, Mary died, and Roger every year makes a pilgrimage to this tree.

The following two stories are typical of a series of similar stories, showing the destiny of those who are brave enough to marry.

> This couple has been traveling on their honeymoon, and now they are tired of hotels and are talking about the new house they are going to move into next week. On the morrow he will be called into service and she will go back to her mother—the house sold.
>
> This couple are quite poor, but they have decided to stop worrying about it and go to Florida. They have come back from a vacation in Florida; he, unable to support his wife in a satisfactory manner, joins the army, and she goes back to her folks.

Marriage is typically dissolved shortly after its inception, primarily because the hero is unable to provide for his wife in a satisfactory manner. The hero generally joins the army; he is not drafted. At the time of this testing the draft was not a serious concern of this subject.

Now let us consider the repressed sexual and aggressive wishes. The sexual wish is fused with oral aggression in this record, and the consequence of its expression can be compared with the consequences of expressing aggression toward the father.

Of approximately four hundred stories, about three hundred, or 75 percent, deal with the conflict of either sex or aggression so that this individual is under relatively high pressure from both of these wishes. Of these three hundred stories, approximately one hundred dealt with anger and aggression and approximately two hundred with love and sex. Hence, we would expect more pressure from the latter conflict than the former.

In the case of the aggressive wish we rated its pressure as low, since it does not appear at all in the face-to-face father-son stories and only gradually increases in intensity in the remaining stories. There is clearly less pressure to the aggressive wish in this case than in the case of X but more pressure than in the case of Y. It is not so remote as in the case of Y, but it is more remote than in the case of X.

The pressure of Z's love-sex wish, however, is higher than that of his aggression, since it appears in the face-to-face situation and has both high intensity and extensity in stories involving love objects other than the mother. The conflicts of the hero concerning the control of sex are equivalent in pressure to those of X in attempting to control aggression. The love-sex wish is also low in remoteness of expression, appearing as a wish to rescue the mother, as an act of aggression toward the sister, and as undisguised passion toward love objects at one remove from the mother. In both cases the individuals are chiefly concerned with the *control* of the wish—in one case, the aggressive wish; in the other, the love-sex wish. But in the case of Z's aggression there is no indication that any hero ever *feels* hostile toward the father in face-to-face relationships—he either runs away or becomes very gentle and effeminate. Whenever a hero struggles with the control of a wish, we may be certain the storyteller is repressing the wish with considerable difficulty and that there is a delicate unstable equilibrium between the magnification of repressing affect and the repressed affect.

How can we test these derivations? There is a relatively simple method available. If we could generally weaken the repression, we would be able to test whether a differential effect was produced by this weakening of repression. We would assume from our estimation of the relative differential magnification of affects that some decrease in the repression should allow Z's love-sex wish freer expression in face-to-face relations in TAT stories than the aggressive wish, since the ratio of the repressive affect to the love-sex wish is smaller than the ratio of repressive affect to the aggressive wish. In order to test this we administered the TAT to Z while he was under the influence of alcohol. It was our prediction that in this state his stories would become frankly incestuous in theme but the aggression toward the father would not appear so openly. Following are two of the stories pertinent to this prediction.

> This poor little dope is looking at a violin. He plays—what does he play? Sonata on a G String. And all the kids call it on a G string. It must be by Rachmaninoff. My mother stood right next to Rachmaninoff. She touched him. She went to a concert by him and she stood right beside him. She almost swooned. This poor little dope. No doubt he is taking music lessons. Just the way they've got his hair cut into bangs. Still, he is a plump little chap. No reason why he doesn't play football. Somewhere back in his mind he wants to study, but he doesn't want to be forced to study. The meeting having agreed that he doesn't want to be forced to study, we'll say that he will be a very good violinist but not a professional. Maybe he will go into engineering as a reaction. Well, the poor little guy has got to be an engineer, but music will be very close to his heart.
>
> This naked woman is the man's sister. I am forced to say that because I have said she is his lover for so long that it becomes trite. She is his sister, and she has had what is considered by the rules of modern society an inappropriate relationship with him. What's that? Incest applies to mother and son as well as sister and brother. A broad term. So much more than pure physical love. A soul and a mind. Incest—society shudders at the word. Why? Why? Society has set up barriers. On a certain island it is indecent to be seen eating with a woman. Incest or any other relationship is not considered indecent. So here is this woman in love with her brother, her brother in love with her. So they have this baby. And this other woman, the aunt, is brought up in a Victorian school. She is insulted. She is very angry. In her anger she kills the baby. Through projection of her hate for her nephew-in-law and her niece, she kills the baby. Life is snuffed out. How do perverted relationships differ from normal?

Our predictions have been confirmed. In the first story the Oedipus triangle appears more openly, but the father, in the role of Rachmaninoff, is the master who is capable of making his mother swoon. The sexual meaning of this music is indicated by a pun "all the kids call it on a G string." The hero in comparison is "this poor little dope" who has had his "hair" cut. The hero is clearly envious of the father's virtuosity and, although oppressed and inferior, thinks there is really no reason why he could not play a more masculine role—"No reason why he doesn't play football." He thinks "he will be a very good violinist, but not a professional" (i.e., he will never be able to achieve his father's virtuosity). But then even this is qualified, and in the end he "has got to be an engineer, but music will be very close to his heart." In other words, though aspiring to the father's place, he does not see how he can achieve it. This is a discussion of his feelings toward his father, which had never before appeared so openly. But despite this weakening of the repressive affects against his aggression, there is yet no indication here of actual aggression against the father. In the second story the incestuous wish toward the sister is given frank, poignant expression. He does not understand why it is considered inappropriate. The sister-brother relationship is thought to be no different than the mother-son relationship—"Incest applies to mother and son as well as sister and brother. A broad term." He is then reminded of the oral nature of his wish—"On a certain island it is indecent to be seen eating with a woman." But on the same island it is thought that incest, if it does not involve oral wishes, is permissible. But then conscience in the form of a "Victorian" aunt kills the baby that is the fruit of the consummation of their love. The story ends on a pathetic note, "How do perverted relationships differ from normal?"[1]

If so much appears in the TAT, under the influence of alcohol, one may ask whether the repressed affects are *ever* sufficiently weakened to permit the expression of overt aggression toward the father. We have found no evidence that this ever happens. Dreams over a ten-month period revealed fantasies very similar to the TAT stories under alcohol. This would be consistent with the theory that there is some reduction of vigilance in dreams but that the forces of repression are by no means completely vanquished.

The following two dreams are typical of those recorded daily for ten months.

> I was stripped to the waist when my mother came in. I was glad I hadn't put on my shirt. Mother didn't seem to pay much attention to me. I embraced my mother. The other woman said, "So he didn't go overseas." Then I started looking at a pocket-sized notebook with a dark green cloth cover and black printing hardly noticeable on it. This had been dropped beside me by a man who came in with my mother. I then realized it was a passport, and it was my father's. I looked up, and the man was my father whom I hadn't recognized till then.
>
> My mother and I were cleaning floors. We both had mops. First her mop got tangled in my hair, which caused very little commotion, and then my mop got tangled in her hair, which upset everyone. I felt very unhappy.

The first dream is not unlike the first TAT story told under alcohol, except that embracing the mother reveals overt expression which was achieved only in the second TAT story told under alcohol. The father is recognized belatedly and is the apparent cause of the mother's indifference to the son. This also repeats the relationship between Rachmaninoff and the son. But as in the TAT story there is no aggression toward the father. In the second dream the sexual significance of hair appears thinly veiled as it did throughout his TAT stories. No one is alarmed by the mother's advances toward the son, but everyone, including the hero, is unhappy when he makes advances toward the mother.

The relationship between these dreams, interpreted on the level of manifest content, and his TAT stories is significant. We have seen that his deeply repressed wish to kill his father appears in the TAT displaced to remote objects but that it does not appear in his dreams, insofar as their manifest content is concerned. This would seem to indicate that the censorship which Freud postulated as operating in the dream life is probably correct. There would appear to be some relaxation of vigilance, but the affects which control repressions have not been completely inhibited. The TAT seems to offer the individual greater distance and more opportunity for the displacement of deeply repressed wishes to very remote objects. That this type of displacement occurs in dreams is also certain but in this case the wish, because of low pressure and higher counterpressure, could not be projected into the manifest content of dreams. The latent content of the dream revealed through association to elements of the dream stands in the same relationship to the manifest content as remote stories to face-to-face normal stories. Thus, if we regard such a normal story as if it were a dream and ask the individual to freeassociate to it, we not infrequently arrive at the content of the more remote stories.

In this case we have found further evidence that the return of the repressed is a function of the total magnification of the conflict and the relative magnification of opposed affects. The sexual conflict was of greater magnification and more evenly balanced than that concerning his anger and aggression toward his father. For both of these reasons he suffered more terror from his incestuous wishes than from his aggressive wishes, even though the source of

[1] The affect of this individual while telling these stories was intense and massive. It must not be supposed that it was entirely the consequence of the alcohol per se. The subject had insisted that the examiner drink with him, and this I did. My intoxication matched that of the subject's. Previous experience with alcohol administered to subjects in a "scientific" manner had convinced the examiner that a large part of the reduction of inhibition resulting from alcohol intoxication was a consequence of the social atmosphere. An experimenter who dispassionately tests and observes the behavior of an individual who has been asked to drink 50 cc of alcohol will not achieve a reduction of high-pressure repressive affects.

punishment in both cases was the father. His stories also indicate that the punishment for incest or sexual expression in general is much more severe than the punishment for the expression of aggression. The consequence of this difference in the strength of repression, for his love life and general social relationships, is noteworthy. Because the incestuous wish is so close to the surface and countered by a relatively high fear, there has been a widespread generalization of both the wish and the fear to other possible love objects. Because the aggressive wish is relatively weaker and under greater counterpressure than in the sexual conflict, this wish has not suffered the same degree of generalization to social relationships. Therefore, Z can be more aggressive to other males than he can be tender or passionate to other females.

Z had in fact suffered physical abuse at the hands of his father. Although he had not been able to defend himself against his father, he did maintain a defensive posture against other males lest he be compromised as he had been by his father. This was an anger-aggression-avoidance antitoxic script of nuclear magnification. Toward women (other than his mother) he was quite vulnerable, finding them at once both seductive and terrifying, to the point of severe anxiety attacks before, during, and following sexual intercourse. Analog formation toward mother surrogates was driven by his strong but relatively unconscious pursuit of his beloved mother. Analog formation toward father surrogates was much more contained and bound by his more conscious and effective avoidance of his known adversary, which shielded him both from that person and, no less critical, from any conscious awareness of his intense anger toward and terror of his father, converting that script into an "as if" avoidance in the way we may cross a heavily trafficked street as if it were dangerous but with no fear. Most effective avoidance scripts are transformed into skilled, relatively unconscious, affectless performances. Had he been willing and able to also avoid sexual encounters, there might have been no observable sequellae of the nuclear script, and indeed the nuclear script would have then been transformed into a double avoidance and renunciation of both his deepest excitement and most dreaded terror and rage.

IDEOLOGY, TERROR, DISSMELL, AND ANGER

The fourth case of an antitoxic script is one driven by each of the malignant affects and by an anticommunist ideology in the covert Iran-contra sale of arms to Iran by Oliver North. In his public testimony before the United States Congress he defended both his covert activity and his lying to Congress and shredding of government documents to conceal evidence. He believed the Communist enemy to be aggressive and dangerous and therefore to be feared and aggressed against. Further, that enemy was not only enraging and terrifying but also dismelling, representing an alien ideology as offensive to American ideology as it was dangerous. No effort should be spared in defeating that alien conspiracy, and it should be prevented from gaining a foothold in Nicaragua lest it spread and contaminate the Western Hemisphere and ultimately invade the United States of America. This is the latest version of the two-hundred-year-old American myth of the chosen people in the promised land, blessed but innocent and vulnerable to the corruption of and by the Old World.

He therefore could defend his activity as inspired by terror, by anger, and by dissmell. But if his heart was pure and the nation was in jeopardy, why should he not have shared this knowledge with Congress? Why did it have to be kept secret? In his testimony before Congress he defended secrecy on the ground of terror—that were it to become public knowledge, lives would have been lost. Further, he accepted a security system to defend his home, his family, and himself against these terrorists who threatened him and his family. In bifurcating the world into pure but innocent Americans and badsmelling, evil, aggressive, and terrifying Communists, North was forced into secrecy and into lying to the U.S. Congress for the good of the nation, including that very Congress itself. He chided Congress for endangering the lives of innocent people unwittingly by not understanding the gravity of the threat and the necessity of covert counteraction against this foul enemy. When a battle is joined, those who are not with us are against us, whether they know it or not, whether they intend it or not.

Though the alien dismelling aspect of the foreign ideology was salient in North's mind, the terror appeared to be even more threatening, inasmuch as he based his defense of secrecy on the threat to life rather than the threat of the foreign ideology as such. There is little question that North's ethical sense would not have permitted him to lie, to shred evidence, and to so testify to a worldwide audience that he was proud to have done so, had he not believed that the greater evil would have been to sacrifice the lives of the good innocent victims to the evil, conscienceless advocates of communism. Conceivably, he might have defended his action on the ground of preserving democracy against subversion by communism—a not uncommon defense by the defenders of one ideology against another ideology—but he did not do so. It is for this reason that I judge his antitoxic script to be compounded of terror, rage, and dismell but of terror above all. However, in contrast to the nuclear script of Z, terror does not prompt an avoidance antitoxic script but rather a conjoint, counteractive, and destructive antitoxic anger-, dissmell-, terror-, and ideologically driven script.

This antitoxic script dominates and co-opts all the other types of scripts of Oliver North. Thus, the major decontamination scripts consist in rooting out the pollution of Communist influence wherever it appears and in exposing the folly of those who do not understand either the danger or the evil of their activity. Those who leak vital secret information are to be condemned as immoral and must be deceived and prevented from learning government secrets.

Limitation-remediation scripts are defined by commitment to the defense of capitalistic democracy and to the holy war against its enemies. North publicly thanked God for those who contributed money to the holy war and helped organize such efforts.

Damage-reparative scripts are defined by any change from capitalistic democracy toward communism. The red tide must be pushed back wherever it has damaged a previously good society. This includes defeating those Representatives and Senators who have infiltrated the American government and who have opposed the secret war against Nicaragua. The holy war must be waged on many fronts—exposing the corrupt, remedying the limitations, repairing any damages.

Such a script should be distinguished from a paranoid script, which is also characterized by terror but terror deepened by delusions of persecution. Oliver North was attempting to rescue hostages who had in fact been captured by terrorists who threatened their lives. Further, paranoids conjoin terror with humiliation, which they attempt to counteract by delusions of grandeur. North responded with courage, dedication, and aggressive counterattack rather than with delusions of grandeur.

North's script should also be distinguished from the macho script in which the defense of honor is conjoined with much selfaggrandizement. What made North so heroic a figure in the eyes of many Americans was his selfless commitment to the welfare of the nation, as well as his protectiveness toward his wife and children.

For North we live in an evil and dangerous world which threatens our good way of life. Under these conditions, awareness, courage, and protectiveness become the cardinal virtues. It is a strictly bifurcated vision of relentless warfare between heroes and villains who are aided and abetted by some fools (in Congress and elsewhere) who do not understand our mortal danger, who leak information, who stand in our way, who oppose me and my safety as well, who judge me and our cause rather than helping me and the nation win the war. This is neither a paranoid nor a macho vision. This is prudential, pious, self-sacrificing heroism for the higher good and the higher morality. It is but a step removed from the sacred violence of God and Abraham.

ANTITOXIC ANGER SCRIPTS

In contrast to anger as affluent, damaged, or reparative, limiting or remedial, contaminating or purifying, antitoxic anger scripts address anger as either unalloyed threat or as a response to unalloyed threat, or both. Whereas affluence scripts are for and about excitement or enjoyment, which may include anger in defeating an adversary or in punishing him or in enjoying his misfortune, anger-reparative scripts are intended to return a damaged scene to its previous affluence. Anger-remedial scripts are intended to punish and defeat adversaries judged limited and imperfect, not for fun but for remediation—to make the world better, to either improve or to interfere with the adversary or to make the world better for his victims or for oneself or for both, or to reduce anger to more tolerable levels. That imperfect adversary might include the self who needs to be punished for his anger, or for his lack of anger, so that he may become less proud or more proud.

In anger antitoxic scripts, in contrast to anger-decontamination scripts, it is either the anger of a scene or what evoked anger which is bad in itself, and purely bad, being neither disgusting nor conflicted nor the result of a good scene turned bad which it is hoped can be reversed. It is rather dissmelling than disgusting, or terrorizing rather than distressing or shaming. Nor is it conceived possible to remedy and correct, nor to enjoy in any way, nor to reduce to a more tolerable level. It is, of all scenes and their scripts, the most purely punishing and with the fewest possible degrees of freedom.

Any scene may be toxic and not so perceived, or conversely, or have degrees of freedom for remediation, for purification, for reversal, or even for affluence, and not be so perceived. Thus, many Jews in Hitler's Germany refused to believe they were in danger and were in fact exterminated. Conversely, many "enemies" could be appeased, compromised with, persuaded to reform or to relent, cooled down and jollied out of their malevolence, or in fact be misunderstood as to their malevolence but nonetheless be scripted for a sustained antitoxic response which is at once self-validating and self-fulfilling. However, it is also the case, and not infrequently, that threats are real and antitoxic scripts deal with them effectively. In between such alternatives are many gray scenes which might or might not have been more effectively scripted.

The historical record is nonetheless not reassuring. Millions of human beings have for many centuries been exiled, imprisoned, tortured, assaulted, killed, starved, robbed, degraded and humiliated, deceived, betrayed, intimidated, discriminated against, abandoned, exploited, and enslaved. Such violence has begotten violence in kind—sometimes in less, sometimes in equal, and sometimes in greater measure—increasing the already massive toxicity of the human condition. And yet without the justified violence against unjustified violence there might have been substantially less justice and less tranquility than we now enjoy. It is a complex calculus in which better possibilities have had to grow in social soil less nutritious for life than for death.

Antitoxic scripts are inevitably nested within larger moral, secular, and religious ideological scripts. They are also constrained by affect-control scripts and softened by affect-management scripts. No individual and no society is able or willing to live value-free. We are not only Cartesian thinking animals but also feeling and therefore valuing animals. Value may be defined not only as any object of any affect but also as any experience of any pure affect per se, as its own "object." It is enjoyable to enjoy. It is exciting to be excited. It is terrorizing to be terrorized and angering to be angered. Affect is selfvalidating with or without any further referent, as is pain or drive pleasure.

Antitoxic anger scripts are not only necessarily value-laden but are also specifically moral. Their rules confront the perennial problem of evil in the human heart as well as in the cosmos. What kind of world is it and what kind of all-powerful, all-knowing, all-good, and loving deity could have created or, once created, could have tolerated so much misery and evil in the world? The covenant between Jahweh and the Hebrews was one answer. There are two kinds of anger and suffering in the world for the chosen people. God's anger is always righteous; and if his children keep the faith and obey, he will reward them by smiting their enemies. If they disobey and worship false idols, particularly the earth-mother goddess of the agriculturists, or if they try to compete with him as devils, he will purge them of sin either by exile, by flood, or by Babel. Thus were two kinds of anger created: self-righteous, good anger, either by God against bad Hebrews or by Hebrews against their bad enemies, and the bad anger of the disobedient chosen people and of their godless enemies. Such a conception was flawed as a general solution to the problem of evil in the world by its exclusiveness and its particularism.

Christianity was an inevitable generalization of the deity of the Old Testament. This God's covenant was with all his children. No one was excluded, but there was still sin and sinners and so justified suffering in the world. However, whereas Jahweh had demanded sacrifice from the faithful as a sign of their faith, this deity sacrificed his own son as a sign of *his* faith, thus turning anger and violence against himself as a sign of his love for his children. The linkage of sacrifice, suffering, and love of the Old Testament is at once preserved and generalized. Not even the deity is exempt from sacrifice as a sign of love and faith. God and Jesus now introduce a radical extension of the idea of the difference between good and evil.

Christianity became a powerful universal religion in part because of its more general solution to the problem of anger, violence, and suffering versus love, enjoyment, and peace. It was more general in two senses. Anyone might be a child of God and saved. Second, the same principle of good and evil applied to God as well as to his children. He thus became a more feminine, loving, forgiving god, and in the later Maryolatry he became the object of just such worship as had inspired the wrath of Jahweh against the worship of the golden calf and the earth-mother goddess. Jesus and this God both provided a model of goodness by turning the other cheek in love, not hate. Although hate remained in the world, Jesus and his God now provided a good example of the possibility of redemption through universal love, rather than in unilateral sacrifice by a chosen people to a wrathful masculine deity who demanded more sacrifices, loyalty, and love than he himself exemplified.

Thus was introduced into the heart of Western humanity an agonizing gap between the reality of the pluralism of the biological inheritance of potentialities for love and for hate, for life and for death, and for the potentiality for romantic love of the saint against the hate of the sinner. Both Judaism and Christianity were concerned with the feelings of both gods and their children rather than simply with their behavior. Even sacrifice need not be carried out if Jahweh were convinced it was a sign of a loyal and loving worshipper. The Hebrew and Christian prophets, up to and including Marx and Freud, have captured the heart and soul of humanity by exposing the true feelings of the saint and sinner alike.

As we have seen before, this intransigent Western dualism of love and hate is not worldwide. Confucianism and Taoism handled the problem of violence and anger by the middle way of moderation and cultivation or by the simple way of living close to nature, thus avoiding the corruptions of more complex social orders.

No treatment of antitoxic anger scripts for Christians or for Jews or for Moslems, all children of Abraham, can escape the severity of the split between love and hate and between good and bad anger. We live with the permanent bad conscience of sinners who would be saints. The psychic reward for such a burden of guilt is a reassurance against an even greater terror of evil anger unlimited, uncontrolled, and unpunished, in which they and not the meek will inherit both heaven and earth. Against just such violence coupled with greed has Marxism offered itself as a variant of Christianity. The money changers are to be driven from the temple to redeem humanity's potential for universal love.

If we had no affects adversarial against anger, the most probable scripts which would be generated as anger antitoxic scripts would be entirely extrapunitive. Lacking terror, guilt, and love we would nail the sinner to the cross, crucify, and kill him in pious self-protective, self-serving, justified anger. Or if the other were much less powerful, one would kill as easily and effortlessly as an annoying fly or bug is exterminated. This might indeed be done without any anger, since not all toxic scenes necessarily evoke anger—some are frightening, some dissmelling, with or without anger. Not all violence is driven by anger. Professional gunmen may be quite cool, interested only in getting the job done. I have nonetheless witnessed one such professional, flushed with anger, threatening to kill someone, who had uttered an obscenity within hearing distance of his wife, if the offender did not shut up.

Because we are of at least two minds about toxicity and anger, antitoxic scripts may be partitioned into two quite different sets. One kind of anger antitoxic script primarily intends to eliminate the scene which provokes the anger. The other kind of anger antitoxic script primarily intends to eliminate or stop the anger which is provoked. There is an additional type of such script which combines these intentions. In this case the primary intention is to eliminate both the scene and the anger which it provokes but with no conflict between these intentions.

Let us now consider some of the varieties of scripts which are intended to eliminate or stop either anger, its provocation, or both.

ANTITOXIC ANGER-AVOIDANCE OF INTIMIDATING NEGATIVE AFFECTS

In anger-avoidance scripts the "enemy" is not primarily the one who angers nor the affect which secondarily evokes anger (e.g., disgust which then angers), nor the internal source of the anger (e.g., the pain of stubbing one's toe), nor even the mixture and conjunction of anger and another negative affect (e.g., disgust and anger), but rather it is the experience of anger itself which prompts the generation of scripts which attempt to avoid the experience of anger. This is a shortcut to safety in which a very toxic scene's threat is shifted from that scene as a whole to that part of it which is believed most threatening. The psychologic of such a script is that it is safer to avoid the anger than to confront the angering scene as a whole. One consequence of such a shift is that a much larger and more remote set of toxic scenes may now become unwittingly threatening, since one is now monitoring for signs of anger rather than for signs of the originally angering scenes. Consider an analog of an individual who fell asleep while driving his car and who narrowly escaped death. Such an individual might shift his concern from possible accidents to any sign of fatigue or somnolence. In the extreme case his shift of fear might be to his driving his car, or finally, to riding in a car driven by anyone. The abstractness and generality of affects readily permit the shift from the immediate source of an affect to that affect itself as the "effect" of the other possible sources, and so shift the affect to those possible sources, away from the original actual sources. This is why insight into the "real" causes of anger or of fear or of both can be so ineffective in reducing toxic affect. It is similar to telling a cigarette addict he really doesn't need a cigarette because the original need no longer exists. Insight into origins is therapeutic only in those cases where scripts are concerned primarily with origins which have become unknown and when there is no other present danger in confronting such origins.

Why should anyone turn the other cheek and return good for evil? Anger-avoidance scripts assume that whatever angered is less important and less threatening than the evoked anger itself. Secondarily, such a script might be prompted by the assumption that the avoidance of anger will also have the desired effect of prevention of reexperience of the scene which evoked the anger, but in such a case we are dealing with a combined anger- and anger-provocation-avoidance script.

The plasticity of the affect system permits any affect or set of affects to be so differentially magnified that other affects are radically and differentially attenuated. How may anger become so toxic that one would rather avoid anger than directly counterattack who or what angered?

Although we have stressed the centrality of moral values in the control of anger, we should now broaden that conception. It may become necessary to avoid anger because of any one of a very broad spectrum of intimidations.

Any one affect of any set of affects or all other affects may be taught or self-taught as reasons and sanctions against anger. One may be terrorized out of anger. One may be made too guilty to be angry. One may be shamed out of anger, as impotent and weak rather than bad. One may be distressed out of anger by costly and enduring loss of privileges for the display of anger. One may be disgusted out of anger by identification with a parent who turns from love to disenchantment and disgust at a child's temper. The message in such a scene is "I am disgusted with my little boy. What happened to the nice good boy I loved?" One may be dissmelled out of anger by identification with a parent who turns from love or from neutrality to distancing dissmell. The message in such a scene is "You are a dirty, bad-smelling little boy." There is in such a case no necessary invidious contrast with a beloved good child who is expected to return to favor. In becoming the object of dissmell there is always the possibility of being permanently banished to a remote distance, to psychological Siberia, whether or not there is reform and atonement, just as a murderer need not be readmitted to society just for later good behavior. Someone dissmelled out of anger may be forced into permanent second-class citizenship despite every avoidance of anger. Further, one may be intimidated out of anger by the withdrawal of or threat of withdrawal of either excitement or enjoyment, by the other in the self or by the other for the self. In the first case the other might simply turn away from the angry child. The message in such a scene is "I don't like you. I am not interested, and I don't enjoy seeing you angry." In the second case it is rather "There will be no toys for you. It is your excitement or enjoyment which is at risk, not mine."

The further sources of and combinations of the affects by which anger may be made toxic are both unlimited and idiosyncratic to the nature of the socializers and the one socialized. Thus, a frail child might be frightened out of anger by a severe beating, whereas a more rugged mesomorph might be stimulated to counter anger or to shrug it off. Still another child might be shamed out of anger by a beating if the relationship was both deeply rewarding and also fragile. A child who may shrug off a beating may nonetheless suffer severe inhibition of anger if that same parent were to shift interest and enjoyment to a rival sibling whenever the child became angry. What is critical in the inhibition which prompts anger-avoidance scripts are the magnified disadvantageous risks, costs, and benefits of anger versus the other affect or affects opposed to anger, by whatever particular scenes the affects are differentially magnified.

It should be noted that there is no inherent inhibiting effect of any specific affect on anger. Thus, the same disgust which may inhibit anger may also prompt revenge on the other, in recasting in which the other is made to feel disgust. Again, that disgust may come into conflict with anger in a decontamination script in which one may oscillate between anger and self-disgust, or prompt a remediation script to improve the disgusting angering scene, or prompt an affluence script in which black humor is used to have fun at the expense of the other.

It should also be noted that the intention to avoid anger necessarily presupposes that one has freed oneself of anger, either by escape, by attenuation, by suppression, by repression, or by displacement by another negative affect (e.g., too afraid to continue to be angry or too guilty to continue to be angry). Further, it presupposes that one is not governed by any wishes for revenge, or even protest, which might keep resentment alive. Otherwise, the major effort to deal with evoked anger would first have to address the problem of how to escape the troubling anger before strategies of avoidance could become a major intention of an antitoxic anger-avoidance script.

As we have seen before, the teaching of anger control, as in the Puritan breaking of the will of the child, often involved a long series of punishing scenes calculated to magnify avoidance of anger through obedience against all its possible competitors.

Antitoxic Conformity as Instrumental to Avoidance of Own Anger and Aggression of Others

The generalized conjoint dangers of own anger leading to the aggression of others may be scripted for avoidance at a distance, not by monitoring either for signs of aggression from others or for signs of possible anger in the self but rather by a generalized decision to do whatever the aggressive other wants one to do. This may or may not entirely solve the problem inasmuch as the punitive other may be sufficiently hostile to require no provocation from his victims. If such is the case, an additional script may be needed to meet such a contingency, namely, a script of submission if and when conformity or any other strategy fails.

Antitoxic Submission as Instrumental to Avoidance of Own Anger and Aggression of Others

Submission as a response to the aggression of the other and/or to the possible anger of the self in response to that aggression may be scripted independently if the frequency and duration of attacks has been low. If attacked very often and with greater brutality, however, the individual may be forced into a generalized conformity as a way of reducing the provocation of attack, supplemented by a submission script, if and when, despite every effort at appeasement, the other renews his attacks. This is seen classically in slavery, where conformity is enforced, but submission to further punishment is also the price of avoiding being killed.

Antitoxic Anger Avoidance as Instrumental to Avoidance of Aggression of Others

If a child has responded to the aggression of a parent by anger and counteraggression and then been beaten severely for it, until he displays neither anger nor aggression, he may generate an antitoxic anger-avoidance script which intends to avoid any further aggression from the other by avoiding any show of his own anger (as well as any show of aggression). Such a script is often produced in conformity to the dictates of the child abuser who verbalizes just such a script for the child. "Don't ever let me catch you raising your voice to me again or I'll teach you a lesson you'll never forget." That child abuser not infrequently had heard just that message from his own abusing parent.

Although such a script may be limited to a particular oppressor, it is a prime candidate for generalization to others, at the slightest show of negative affect from others, because of the density of intimidation and the presumed severity of consequences of being in terror, either by the self or about the other. Such an individual lives in a mine field where danger is ever present but unknown.

Although such scenes may have also included fears of one's own impulsive aggression as well as anger, or fears of actual aggression against the parent which attempted to flaunt the authority of the other and which were severely punished, this script is primarily generated by the linkage of avoiding one's own anger as the only way of avoiding the aggression of the other. As we will presently see, a very similar scene may generate differences in scripted responses which magnify differentially, the danger of one's own close coupling of anger spilling over into possible aggression, in one case, versus the danger of the repetition of actual anger-aggression scenes which were punished. Each of these three scripts rests upon the ultimate threat of the aggression of the other but with varying salience of what is most immediately to be avoided, whether it is any feeling and show of anger, or any anger which might become aggressive, or any anger which would repeat a past aggression which had been punished.

In the present script the formula is more general: "no anger, no beating" versus "no anger, no possible aggression, no beating" versus "no anger, no repetition of aggression, and no repetition of beating."

Antitoxic Anger Avoidance as Instrumental to Possible Aggression Avoidance

The unmodulated rage which engulfs may prompt another type of anger-avoidance script, as instrumental to the avoidance of one's own murderous aggression which, it is felt, one may not be able to control. In such a case it is the close coupling of anger and uncontrollable impulsive aggression which prompts avoidance of anger. It should be noted that, although the individual is in this case most troubled by the possibility of his own impulsive aggression, yet he may diagnose his own anger as most necessary to avoid. This exemplifies a critical feature of any script construction: the loose relationships between the perceived sources of reward or toxicity and their adopted remedies. Inasmuch as any avoidance strategy necessarily operates at a distance, what is scripted as necessary to be avoided is often quite distinct and remote from its ultimate target. That remoteness varies as a function of how severe the threat is presumed to be, what resources the individual presumes he possesses to control it, the safety factor willing to be tolerated, the presumed consequences of error, the presumed stability of the life space, and a variety of other possibilities which are believed relevant to consider the more serious the threat appears. In general, the distance to be preserved in avoidance varies directly with the perceived mobility and toxicity of the threat and inversely with the perceived ability and willingness to escape or to confront and counteract the threat should avoidance fail.

Such an individual may or may not be fully aware of his ultimate target of avoiding his own aggression. He may become unaware of it, as anyone who has a strategy may become unaware of it when the tactics for a strategy become more and more figural and, in the extreme case, transformed into ends in themselves rather than means to ends. Such is the case with the transformation of sedative scripts into addictive scripts, when a cigarette once used to sedate negative affect becomes urgently necessary to sedate the deprivation affect of being without a cigarette per se, independent of any other negative affect which would before have been the rationale of sedative reliance on the cigarette.

A second condition under which the ultimate target of an instrumental avoidance of anger may become unconscious is the case in which such consciousness would arouse negative affect against such a motive. For example, an individual who prides himself on his fearlessness might well repress his unwillingness to confront the consequences of his aggression in comparison with a greater tolerance of his wish to avoid his own anger. This could have been produced by socialization either by a parent or by peers or by the society at large, in which humiliation and loss of face is much greater for backing down and away from fighting than from avoiding becoming angry. The script rationale in such a case is, it is better to avoid fighting by avoiding anger than by having to escape fighting, but also better to rest one's case on anger avoidance exclusively by avoiding exposure, either to the self or others, that aggression avoidance is also operative. Avoidance of consciousness is only a special case of avoidance scripts in general and may be superimposed as an additional aim on any avoidance script. In such a case one has rules for the avoidance of one danger and separate rules for the avoidance of awareness of the avoidance rules themselves. Either set of rules may be entirely effective or intermittently ineffective. Thus, were the avoidance of anger to fail, one would then also have to confront the failure of the avoidance of awareness, of having attempted to deny avoidance of aggression as an additional target of anger avoidance.

Antitoxic Anger-Avoidance As Instrumental to Avoidance of Negative Affect of Others

If a child has responded to the negative affect of his parent by anger and then been subjected to more severe negative affect until he displays no more anger, he may generate an antitoxic anger-avoidance script which intends to avoid such increased density of negative affect from the other by avoiding any show of his own anger. This is not intended to avoid all negative affect from the other. This, the child may realize, is not possible from the other, who may continually criticize or overcontrol, but in a low key so long as the child does not respond with anger. It is rather the more strident, more punishing quantity of negative affect, evoked by the child's angry protest or resistance, which is intended to be avoided by the avoidance of anger. It resembles some bad marriages in which one of the dyad curbs his or her temper to lower the decibel level of a steady stream of unwanted verbalization of negative affect. Such a script may be expanded to include a variety of appeasement behaviors toward the same end of controlling the negative affect from the other.

It should be noted that such a script is similar to but also different than anger-avoidance of internalized negative affect (e.g., in which the child has been made too guilty or too terrified to counteraggress). In such scripts it is primarily one's own negative affect which inhibits anger. In instrumental avoidance of the negative affect of the other it is primarily the threatening angry or dissmelling face of the other which prompts the avoidance of anger as instrumental to the avoidance of the threat. Such a script is much less likely to be generalized than the avoidance of internalized negative affect and anger, since these are much more abstract and less tied to particular persons, even though it was a particular person who was the origin of the intimidation.

Antitoxic Anger-Avoidance as Instrumental to Failed Aggression Control

In this case it is not the fear of possible loss of control of aggression from impulsive anger which is at issue but rather the attempt to prevent the repetition of an impulsive aggressive attack which has occurred and which has been punished severely. In the preceding script it was avoidance of the possible loss of control of anger over impulsive aggression which was primary. In this script it is not simply this possibility which is at issue but rather the past actual loss of such control which is dominant. In one the message is "I might do it;" in the other, "I might do it again."

Thus, an anger-avoidance script may be generated, not in response to an original provocation which angers but in response to severe punishment for aggression rather than for anger as such. A child who hits his mother or father in anger may be beaten for his aggression—"never hit me again"—but respond, not with scripting avoidance of aggression, but with scripting avoidance of anger if he believes that the control of anger in the future is the only way he can control his aggression or if he believes he was punished for anger *and* for aggression. The Puritan's breaking the will of the child aimed at guaranteeing obedience but often guaranteed an anger avoidance instead, as an unintended byproduct.

Such a script may arise from a mixture of motives, in part dread of being beaten for loss of control of anger leading to loss of control of aggression and in part dread of whatever interpretation such socializers added to the lesson accompanying beating. One child may be beaten more in sorrow than in anger, with the moral that such aggression distresses the socializer even as it hurts and terrifies the offender. Yet another parent who lays heavy hands on the sinner may express deep disgust at the good boy turned unexpectedly unlovable, all the while being urged to reform because otherwise he will both lose the respect and love he has forfeited and he will be beaten as a bonus to help persuade him. The overly sharp distinctions which have been drawn between internalized versus externalized guilt and shame do not adequately represent the heterogeneity of motives which are attempted to be inculcated to control anger and aggression.

For yet another physically punishing parent, dismell and terror are added to pain. This parent banishes the offender from the human race and at the same time threatens even more severe beatings should the offense be repeated. The only reward which may be offered is cessation of physical pain and of terror, without any reduction in continuing rejecting dissmell. The child has been labeled a bad apple, once and for all, who must be contained by force.

An aggressive, punitive, but shame-ridden parent may label the beating as providing an opportunity for the shameful and shaming child to atone and reform and permit the once-loving relationship to be resumed. Such a parent hangs his head in shame as he lays heavy hands on the shameful one. He may then send him to his room, excluding him from family life until he has had the time to reflect on his shameful behavior and to resolve never to repeat the scene, at which time normal life in the family may be resumed. The beating is administered with the impression that it shames and hurts the parent as much as it should shame the child.

Such an anger-avoidance script we classify as an antitoxic script because of the large admixture of physical punishment in its formation. A child whose anger is entirely controlled by threat of loss of love through shaming would be properly described as a damagereparative or limitation-remedial script rather than an antitoxic script, inasmuch as such a child would inhibit his anger or his aggression in the hope of restoration of an interrupted good scene rather than as an avoidance of physical threat per se.

Antitoxic Anger-Avoidance of Unreducible Anger

Anger may prompt avoidance scripts not only because of its inhibition by other affects but also by virtue of the vicissitudes of anger itself. Consider the plight of an enraged child who, in the midst of a tantrum, is left to scream it out on his own. Quite apart from the consequent interpretation of this scene as abandonment, he is given no help either in modulating that anger nor in finding his way back to the parent who enraged him. He is left with an increasingly toxic rage he does not know how to reduce, nor necessarily wish to reduce. It is experienced as an epileptic attack may be experienced, as an alien seizure which engulfs him and which he cannot control. The only scripting which may be possible for him is to guarantee avoidance of any possible repetition of the dreaded uncontrollable and selfpunishing tantrum without end. Such a scene is a special case of a more general condition for the generation of avoidance scripts, namely, the failure of the individual, for whatever reason, to perceive or construct alternative possibilities for coping with a toxic scene. Any individual who is sufficiently punished by a scene with or without anger may be prompted to escape when he sees no other possibilities. Later he may generate an avoidance script so that he does not have to reexperience either that scene or his enforced escape. Being happy to have escaped the punishing other he has no wish to see that one again and will thenceforth give him a wide berth to avoid him. But in the case we are now considering, such attenuation of anger by escape has not been possible and is deemed unlikely to be possible if reexperienced in the future. Therefore, the urgency of scripted avoidance is greatly magnified. Should avoidance fail occasionally and the individual reexperience the dreaded toxic unlimited, inescapable, and irreducible rage, there will be a further magnification of the necessity for avoidance and an increased vigilance in monitoring increasingly remote signs of its possible repetition. Not only can there be no guarantee that any script will always work, but neither can the individual always correct the failures of a script to work, any more than a golfer can guarantee elimination of all errors in his skill. He may try endlessly to avoid anger and fail repeatedly despite increasingly heroic measures.

In the case of particularly energetic and high-spirited infants and children, I have observed sustained rage for some hours terminated only by complete exhaustion. In such cases avoidance scripts may concern the end state of exhausted affectlessness more than the sustained rage which produced it. In the extreme case a schizoid introversive avoidance script might be generated, not against rage, not against affectlessness, but rather against any wish for social contact which comes to be identified as too toxic because it may become the precursor of the dreaded sequence of rage and exhaustion. Rage which has prompted avoidance because it was unmodulated, uncontrollable, and inescapable is also a prime candidate, if it should fail to be avoided and be provoked again, of prompting uncontrollable aggression and murder of the original persecutor. This is how it can happen that very well behaved, overcontrolled individuals will sometimes surprise themselves and all who know them by a single outburst of murderous aggression, as described most recently by Muriel Gardiner.

John Bowlby and James Robertson observed children, aged 18 months to 3½ years, who had been placed in a hospital or residential nursery for a week to several months. They observed that the children suffered great longing, crying, and searching continually for their missing mothers. Then they seemed depressed, appearing to lose hope, and finally became indifferent, to the point of failing to recognize their mothers (despite recognition of their fathers). They described these phases as progressing from protest through despair to detachment. From the descriptions Bowlby and Robertson have given it would appear that these phases are characterized first by anger and distress (violent crying), next by distress and shame (depressed), and finally by anger and interest avoidance (in the recognition of the father but failure of recognition of the mother). One cannot be certain that such avoidance of both anger and interest does not also contain an indirect display of angry blame at the abandoning, now reappearing mother, but it is certainly a cool rather than hot blame, if indeed it is also a blaming response as well as a double avoidance response. Bowlby, of course, minimizes the rage of the child, in contrast to Klein, as he also minimizes the ambivalence of the child in contrast to Freud. What hurts most, and therefore is most needed for Bowlby, is defense against separation and detachment, since attachment is for him the central motive in the life of the young child, and separation is a real rather than a neurotic threat overly magnified by Kleinian greedy rage and by Freudian ambivalence. In my view these three phases are three interdependent but separate scripts: first, ambivalent excitement and enjoyment contaminated by anger and distress; second, a reduction in anger and an increase in shame and distress in depression; third, an increase in avoidance of excitement and avoidance of anger in the differential recognition of the father and indifference to the mother.

Antitoxic Avoidance of Anger as Delayed Dependent on Scenes Which Terrorized and Shamed

Anger may be magnified as a much delayed response to a set of scenes which evoked dense negative affect other than anger. Consider the classic scene of *l'homme escalier,* the humiliated one, smarting from defeat, who belatedly invents the clever remarks which would have crushed his opponent and now partially appeases the anger which he did not feel while being humiliated by the contemptuous adversary. It is the cumulative density of the rehearsed, remembered, imposed shame, coupled with the distance from the bad scene, which belatedly angers.

Much more serious is the coupling of terror and shame, which so engulfs that anger can be evoked and felt only under more remote space-time conditions, which permits sufficient security to evoke rage and to generate fantasies of revenge for the dense fear and shame which had been imposed by the brutal other.

But the same differential magnification of terror, shame, and anger which had prevented the victim from becoming angry and fighting with his attacker in the first place may also in varying degrees blunt and attenuate the secondary anger experienced as a delayed response to the bad scene. Now it is his own secondary anger and fantasies of revenge and recasting, and especially of much magnified wishes of destroying the other as a "final solution" for his victimage, that recruits not only the terror and shame of the scene as victim, but of much more shame and terror, which would be experienced in projected scenes of more serious acting out of his hatred and wish to kill the dangerous enemy. The longer anger is delayed, the harder it becomes for the worm to turn because it is experienced as increasingly dangerous, terrorizing, and humiliating. This is a self-validating script inasmuch as the magnification of such anger would in fact provoke more dangerous aggression in counterattack from his intended victim. His enemy, who had intended only to intimidate and humiliate him, is now feared as a murderer who would be justified to kill him, not only in self-defense but also because he had been made much more angry by being counterattacked.

To the extent to which terror and shame are more magnified than anger, the avoidance of anger will be scripted as scene-dependent. Any sign of the remote possibility of an attack will be monitored and responded to with varieties of distancing the self from such danger and of appeasing the dangerous other to ward off such a threat. This may include ideological defenses proclaiming the ideals of peace and the essential goodness of human beings.

Further, the dangerous scene may also be scripted in an even more remote way by monitoring for possibilities of one's own anger, lest that anger get out of hand and result in a fight to the death. Such a one may have to smile constantly to inform all others and the self that there will be no anger and no fight. Secondarily, these may also be combined with a perpetual smile, a head inclined to one side or slightly lowered as an appeasement gesture that one is still as humble and passive as one was when one was originally victimized. The head may also be bowed in immorality shame as an atonement for the bad anger which one feels was wrong even though provoked. It is in this case a testament to the power of the Christian dictate to turn the other cheek rather than to counteraggress. In such a case two sources of shame conflict with and contaminate each other. The indignity of acquiescence in one's victimage shames and cries out for the justice of revenge and recasting, the law of talion, but the Christian gloss on talion cries out for guilt for anger and for love of one's enemy. This is a deep division between the Judaic and the Christian, between the Old and New Testament, between a God who demands sacrifice and who avenges and a God who sacrifices himself.

Closer to home, such guilt for counteranger and counteraggression to a punishing attack which shames and terrorizes is readily evoked when the attacker is a parent who is beloved. Indeed, just such love may have been the critical inhibitor of anger to anger in the first place. This would have been compounded if such a parent combines the laying of heavy hands on the child with a pious moral sermon justifying the severity of the attack. Initially, such a child would combine terror, indignity, shame, and immorality shame, and his later anger would evoke still more immorality shame for his anger rather than the demanded atonement for his original offense. In this case anger is inhibited not only by the terror and indignity shame of the original scene but by the conjoint immorality shame of the original sermon and of the deeper guilt which would accompany the further flaunting of parental authority by counteractive anger and aggression against the very source of moral authority.

Anger-avoidance scripts may be either antitoxic scripts or decontamination scripts. Whenever the object of anger is dangerous and/or humiliating alone, then avoidance is a type of antitoxic script. Whenever, in addition, the target of anger is also regarded positively, then avoidance may also be an avoidance of a contaminated scene, lest an already contaminated relationship be made worse.

Antitoxic Anger-Avoidance by Blaming for Distress

If anger is too intimidating to express but too deep to relinquish entirely, it may be displaced via a thinly veiled extrapunitive script in which the self is presented as suffering distress rather than anger, while others are blamed and held responsible for such suffering. Blame is meant to hurt without the risk of anger and aggression, even as the self gains in goodness as a long-suffering victim of an angry heartless other.

The voice of such complaint is primarily the voice of distress, punctuated by intrusions of muffled anger. Originally, such a script may have been generated in the hope of evoking sympathy and turning off the anger of the other, but as that fails to happen, the suppressed anger increasingly appeals to others for sympathy against the bad other.

Antitoxic Anger-Avoidance by Blaming /or Terror and Danger

It is not uncommon that when an individual is aggressed upon that he is both terrified and enraged, together, or in the sequence terrorrage or rage-terror. When it is the case that even the possibility of anger itself evokes terror, then the aggressive attack of the other becomes more terrifying by the conjoint terror of the aggression and the terror of one's own angry response to the aggression and/or to the terror evoked by that aggression.

Under such conditions there may be generated an anger-avoidance script with the intention of blaming the other for terrorizing by endangering the self. The other is represented as a monster in invidious comparison to the utterly nonangry, nonaggressive, fearful self, thereby avoiding both the anger and the wish for aggressive revenge on the other.

Such unconsciously hostile pacifism may be concentrated on the original enemy or be continually generalized, first to the military-industrial complex and its threat of nuclear destruction and or finally to human nature as no damned good, with the one notable exception of the endangered self.

Such a script should not be confused with the pacifism of either pure terror or pure goodwill. What is distinctive of this type of script is the indirection of the anger and its expression through the attribution of blame.

Antitoxic Anger-Avoidance via Critical Disgust or Dissmell

Anger which is combined with dissmell or with disgust may be masked and avoided by exaggerating criticism, in disgust or dissmell, of the other, who is represented as suddenly disenchanting or exposed as altogether lacking in redeeming features. One then need not confront one's own rage or one's own intent to aggress. One can inflict great damage by attribution of bad-tasting or bad-smelling features to the other, from a privileged distance from which one descends to deliver a pious judgment, sufficient perhaps to evoke the anger or aggression of others but for which the self is not responsible. This is not to argue that disgust or dissmell is inherently safer than anger for all individuals. For some, an explosive, relatively brief outburst of anger may be much less toxic than any display of disgust or dissmell which might imply that the beloved other has been weighed and found wanting and is perhaps irretrievably imperfect and disappointing. Such a threat might be masked by a cleansing explosion of anger which can later be more readily repaired.

Antitoxic Anger-Avoidance by Cool Protest and Criticism

Anger may be avoided by scripts which intend to hurt others by cool, objective criticism and protest of "outrages," which do not enrage the critic but which are intended to evoke rage from others as well as from those who are the objects of protest and criticism. Such individuals are sometimes so successful in avoidance of their own anger that they are surprised at the anger their objective evaluations often evoke. They will protest that it was not their intention to arouse "emotions" but to correct a problem. They may objectify all their feelings, in which case the avoidance of anger is but a special case of a generalized affectlessness. Such individuals use the word "emotional" as equivalent to irrational, bordering on the psychotic or neurotic. The contrast between "reason" and "emotion" as good and bad, perfect and imperfect, divine and all too human, is of course a many-centuries old, hallowed, if not hollow, distinction in philosophical and theological thought. The attempt at self-governance by the bridling of the emotions is itself largely affect-driven, but from the underground, as in this scripting of "cool" objectivity in criticism.

THE DEGREE OF MAGNIFICATION OF ANTITOXIC ANGER SCRIPTS

No matter what kind of response is scripted to cope with toxic anger scenes, whether avoidance, escape, expression, counteraction, or destruction, its degree of magnification is nonetheless independent of its type.

In the extreme case an anger-avoidance script may be limited to one person, a father or a mother, in one type of scene, who is known to be punitive about particular privileges such as playing with toys whenever that is very noisy and there are guests in the house. The script generated under such limited circumstances need not be generalized to any other scenes, nor even to playing with toys in general if that is done quietly or at some distance from the guests. It is only the noisy play with toys when there are guests which offends and which angers the parent, which then angers the child, and which results in the punishment of loss of love conjoined with loss of exciting fun playing with toys. If the offender is willing and able to modulate both his anger and his noisy play, he may readily learn the simple script: when there are guests, avoid noisy excited play with toys and don't get angry. On the other hand, should he become intransigent and flaunt his defiance and provoke a contest of wills—which ends in humiliating defeat before the entire family and their embarrassed guests, followed by a long lecture and beating after the guests have left and by an enforced, enduring loss of further privileges, plus a decided chilling of customary affection previously enjoyed—the lesson to be scripted becomes a candidate for much more remote, extensive, and serious anger-avoidance scripting.

Now noisy excitement may have become closely coupled with anger, and both have been uncoupled from toys, guests, and parents. Now he may script extensive monitoring for remote signs of noisy excitement and/or anger in himself for whatever reason, in whatever kind of scene, to be retreated from to a safer, quieter, unangry scene. Between two such extremes there are many possible alternative anger-avoidance scripts in which such rules are limited to the punishing person rather than to anyone, to any scene in which that person shows signs of irritability, whether about noisy playing with toys or not, to either parent rather than the original parent, or to any parent surrogate. It may be monitored in connection with any future playing with toys whether there are parents or guests present or not, in connection with any type of play in the future whether with toys or not, or whether by the self or by others so that noisy TV shows now create uneasiness as analogs of the offending scene. Once analog formation is magnified, it is a ready candidate for further magnification by self-validation as well as by self-fulfillment. To the extent that turning away from a noisy TV show reduces signs of fearful excited anger, it is at once self-validating, self-fulfilling, and a condition for further defensive analog formation. The engine of such increasing remoteness of monitoring is not escape from the dreaded affect but rather its avoidance and the avoidance of signs of its possibility.

Further, such scripts are also vulnerable to analogic magnification by other actors in other scenes. Thus, a child so sensitized may be prompted to further magnify such a script by the constraints and sanctions imposed in the schoolroom against noise and sometimes against even speaking to other children when the teacher is speaking. Such an atmosphere for such a child may conjointly stimulate both anger and its avoidance. Playful excitement becomes a candidate for seductive but toxic rebelliousness. His future vocational choice may come to require he work either alone or in remote nature sites or in quiet concentration, free of supervision. He may also require a wife, and particularly children, who do not violate the boundaries of decent decibel levels of sound.

The same range of variation in degress of magnification, independent of type of script, occurs with counteractive anger scripts. Consider the same scene of noisy, angry playing with toys when there are guests but with a less formidable parent and a more formidable child. This child is more adversarial and more successfully combative, and this parent is less adversarial, and less insistent, and less effective in driving the excitement and the anger of the child underground.

In response to his parent's angry embarrassment at the child's noisy play, which appears to disturb guests, this child opposes anger to anger in a defiant flaunting of parental authority calculated to demonstrate that the demand is angering and not only will not be obeyed but will be disobeyed as angering, and therefore the playing will be done with louder excitement and anger in an openly provocative manner. If the parent declines this invitation to a contest of wills, the child has learned a simple but limited defiance script. When there are guests and your father (or your mother) becomes unreasonably intrusive and demanding about the noise you make in playing with toys, you can and should continue playing but must first demonstrate your anger and your right to oppose the anger of the other, who in this situation may be overly controlling and intrusive. There need be no further generalization of such a script either to the other parent or to peers, to parent surrogates or to other kinds of demands in other kinds of scenes. Such a child may quite willingly go to bed when so requested that same evening even when he may not wish to and even when the parent is quite strident in his insistence. Further, conformity to the more preferred parent may temporarily, visibly increase, as a consequence of heightened opposition to one parent in one scene. Should such a scene not recur, this miniscript may atrophy from later disuse and irrelevance.

Contrast such a limited script with an increasing magnification of the same type of script. Now the parent whose authority is in jeopardy before his guests elects to fight fire with fire. "Stop that immediately" is accompanied by a sharp slap in the face. The scene is no longer concerned with playing with toys or with disturbing the guests. It is now anger confronting anger. Both the parent and the child now become committed to teaching the other a lesson. What before succeeded in teaching the child to avoid future displays of anger now fails. The lesson this child learns is that if he is defiant enough, long enough, he can wear his adversary down, both to have his own way and to punish his adversary. This child may lose some battles, but if he is sufficiently determined to win the war, and his parent's resolve is ambivalent, he may prevail; and his oppositional script may be firmly validated and increasingly generalized to many parent surrogates who oppose his provocative behavior. He has taught himself and his adversary how the will of the other may be broken.

Chapter 37

Antitoxic, Anger-Driven Expressive and Counteractive Scripts

BASIC PSYCHO-LOGIC OF THE ANTITOXIC, ANGER-DRIVEN SCRIPTS

In antitoxic anger-driven scripts the basic psycho-logic is "You have done something excessively toxic to me (and or mine), and I must feel angry, or express it, or communicate it, or protest and blame you, or flaunt you, or counteract it by doing to you what you did to me, or more, or oppose you, or stop you, or prevent you from doing it again, or avoid or escape you, or demonstrate that I am capable of responding and coping with you, or injure, or in the extreme case destroy the you or your family, allies, property, honor, power."

We will presently examine in some detail the major varieties of antitoxic anger-driven scripts as distinguished from the antitoxic anger-avoidance scripts. We intend here only to contrast these differences.

First are what we have labeled anger-expressive scripts. These range from backed-up anger scripts, in which the individual struggles not to express his anger but nonetheless not to avoid being aware of it either, to the full verbalization and vocalization and facial display of anger. It stops short of other action against the source of anger. The counteractive-anger scripts range from identifying the other as perceived source, through criticism, through doing to the other what the other did to the self, through doing more than that, to demonstrating that the self can stop, prevent, and/or punish the angering other. The destructive-anger scripts go beyond both expression and counteraction against provocation in their intention to inflict serious and permanent injury on the other, over and above what he may have done to the self or to others with whom the self is identified, allied, or attached.

These antitoxic anger-driven scripts may also vary independently in their modes of interrelatedness.

ANTITOXIC, ANGER-DRIVEN SCRIPTS: EXPRESSIVE, COUNTERACTIVE DESTRUCTIVE; INDEPENDENT, DEPENDENT, INTERDEPENDENT; VARIABLE DEGREE OF MAGNIFICATION

Anger-avoidance scripts, in which anger itself is regarded as more toxic than its source, must be sharply distinguished from those varieties of antitoxic anger scripts in which the intention is to feel and or to express anger toward, to counteract against, or to destroy its source. Different as these two classes of anger scripts are, it is quite possible for each of them to govern the same individual confronted with different sources of anger or with different densities of anger under different conditions or at different periods of his life. Thus, an individual who inhibits and avoids anger toward his father or his older, stronger brother may express and displace it on a younger, weaker brother. Or he may avoid his anger toward his mother out of guilt but express it toward his father as counteractive against felt angry shame. Further, he may express intense rage but avoid expressing less intense anger, or express mild irritability but draw back from the expression of more intense anger. Again, he may avoid anger when sober and energetic but express it when intoxicated or tired or sick, or the reverse. He may avoid anger as a child and become belligerent in his old age, or be a rebellious child but an anger-inhibited adult.

The distinctions between types of scripts may or may not be a distinction between types of personalities. It may become a distinction between types of personalities whenever one person is governed exclusively or primarily by one type of anger script and another is governed by a different type of anger script, so one primarily avoids becoming angry whereas another never does so but is often extremely destructive.

These distinctions between the toxicity of anger per se versus the toxicity of sources of anger vary independently of the degree of magnification of the script, as we have noted before. Thus, an anger-avoidance script may have to contend with ever-present, dense, possible rage or with occasional minor irritability. A destructive script may be an occasional response to an unusual provocation or a constant way of life in which the individual seeks out enemies to destroy.

The distinctions between types of scripts and their degrees of magnification are also independent of their mode of interrelatedness, in dependence, independence or interdependence. Thus, an avoidant script may avoid anger whether it has been provoked (dependent upon an attack by the other), independently wells up within himself, or confronts him as the result of a complex conflict between two scripts, neither of which he can renounce (e.g., demands from a job versus demands from his family). No matter what the perceived source of his anger or how dense it may be, an avoidance script intends to keep it as distant as possible to minimize anger.

Under the same circumstances a confrontive, combative script would oppose the perceived source of anger, dense or slight, whether it was provoked by the other, was experienced as coming from within as independent, or was experienced as the result of competing pressures from work and from family. His aim is confrontation rather than the minimizing of anger. His formula is don't get mad, get even.

Anger scripts which are not anger-avoidant as such may nonetheless be anger-expressive but aggression-avoidant in varying degrees. Anger scripts which are counteractive against the perceived source of anger may also be aggression-avoidant in varying degrees. Even anger-destructive scripts may be aggression-avoidant to some degree even though primarily aggressive in intent. Thus, such a script may intend to wound but not kill or to kill one person but not many (as in hand-to-hand combat in war as opposed to indiscriminate nuclear attack).

In anger-independent scripts, anger is both the origin and the target of responses to cope with anger. Anger has become relatively independent of the many scenes in which it has been evoked. Thus, in an anger-management script, an anger-sedation script will prompt recourse to a cigarette to either attenuate or to reduce that anger, no matter what else may be problematic in the scene. It is not intended to deal with the source of anger as such. In an affect-control script, the response to either muffle or to express the cry of anger may be independent of the nature of the scene or what else to do about it. In an ideological-anger script, the response may be to condemn or to praise any experience or display of anger, whether one can control it or not and whether it is one's own anger or the anger of someone else or both. In pure affect-salience scripts, anger as such, apart from its scene dependencies and interdependencies, may be sought and fused with excitement for pure affect "kicks," in which anger serves the function of a spice, converting a negative affect into varying ratios of mixed positive and negative affect to heighten excitement and enjoyment. It may be fused with sexuality, requiring anger for sexual excitement and enjoyment. Affect-salience scripts for pure anger as such may also prompt avoidance, escape, expression, counteraction, or destruction, not for the intention of dealing with angering scenes but rather solely for the purpose of dealing with anger as such.

Anger-independent scripts may intend to express anger, to counteract and confront it, or to act on it and destroy its source, to satisfy pure anger as such. The payoff in such a script need not be the elimination of the adversary as source of anger but the demonstration to the self or other that one is anger-aggression-capable. In secret societies such an act may be required as the price of admission as a sign of commitment to the group. Such a script may prompt a life as a soldier of fortune in anyone's war to give free expression to freefloating anger or to test one's ability to do so, or both. Such testing often is also prompted by varying ratios of terror, shame, and guilt for anger.

In anger-independent scripts the rules concern neither what angers nor precisely what to do about angering scenes as such but rather intend to instruct the individual on what to do with his anger. The specific anger-independent script may require he avoid or escape it at any cost, express it, or struggle with another or destroy another no matter what the cost once he has been angered. In such a case it may be deemed better to die in combat than to swallow one's anger. However, the independence of anger scripts does not necessarily require such behavior, since it may require only the display of an angry face or a verbalization of anger as appropriate response to any anger. In short, anger-driven independent scripts messages may be "If and when you get angry, let them know it, or get even, or destroy them," no matter who or what the anger is about.

In anger-dependent scripts it is not anger per se which is the origin and terminal of the scripted responses. It is rather that which evokes anger which controls the scripted responses. So a child may be angered by a scene in which he has been scolded by a parent for shameful behavior. The scripted responses to such scenes may be either avoidant or confrontive and counteractive. In the former case he will script behavior intended to avoid offending the parent. In the latter case he might script behavior intended to flaunt the authority of the parent. Both scripts are equally dependent on the scene as origin and terminal, rather than on anger as such, independent of the rest of the scene. The anger-dependent script need not be dependent on the entire scene, nor exclusively on external events in the scene. An anger-dependent script might concern only the anger of the other, to be avoided or fought, or one's anger at discouragement, scripted for reaction against one's own angry discouragement by trying harder. In this latter case we have a remedial rather than an antitoxic anger script since the aim is more to correct what provoked anger than to be destructive or expressive.

Any anger-dependent script not only defines the nature of the scene which angers and the nature of response which is to cope with the scene but also often defines the degree of vigilant orientation responses appropriate either generally or in restricted circumstances. An individual may be always on the alert for possible trouble which may anger or only when confronting particular types of threatening places or people. Anger-dependent scripts are differentiated by the degree of distribution versus concentration of scenes which anger. If a child is angered by one parent, the child may generate a tyrant script oriented toward learning exactly when the tyrant must be appeased and how, or be opposed and how, and when it is a safe scene, as well as how to deal with each of many variants of scenes which anger. In contrast, if a child becomes the scapegoat victim for the whole family, for peers, and for strangers outside the family, as well as for a variety of impersonal sources (e.g., illness, losses, and accidents), then such a variety of sources may produce either massive avoidant or combative responses which may appear to the observer to be anger-independent even though in fact they are anger-dependent but on a very widely distributed set of scenes as alternative sources.

Interdependent anger scripts are special cases of systematic salience scripts, as contrasted with pure affect scripts and with affectworthy, affect-derivative scripts. In these scripts not only is anger one element among many which require scripting, but any single script may also require further interscripting whenever two scripts deal with overlapping elements in different ways. In such scripts responses attempt to meet multiple purposes; that is, they may have conjoined and alternative, delayed, partitioned, or conditional responses which are continually open to changes as sources appear to change and as the consequences of scripted responses appear either to change or require reinterpretation from varying newly revealed perspectives. In such scripts, anger is neither a dependent affect of some scene, such as an aggressive attack from another, the control of which reduces anger, nor an independent cause which can aim at its own reduction by simple expressive, destructive, counterattack, or sedative or control responses. In interdependent anger scripts anger is one affect among many from many sources, which may fuse and magnify each other (as in angry, exciting sexuality) and also conflict with each other, so that such a mixture may also evoke shame or guilt, all embedded in a larger matrix of estimated interdependent risks, costs, and benefits; such scenes may be sought as moral "holidays," as compensations for overly severe affect-control scripts which govern everyday life. Many societies set aside specific times and places to give expression to such conflicted orgiastic wishes or to reverse social roles which are oppressively hierarchical. After such cathartic license, social life is scripted to return to normal.

In anger-interdependence scripts there is a "conversation" between anger and other affects and scene features and scripted responses, rather than a one-way communication in which anger either "listens" to its determinants, as effects, or "talks" to its audience as a one-way cause. In such scripts, if I am angered, I am neither monologic passive victim nor intransigent avenger but dialogic negotiator and conversationalist.

Whether one elects to avoid anger or to express it, to counteract it or to destroy its source is independent, however, of whether such anger is experienced as dependent, as independent, or as interdependent. One may "negotiate" but yet script avoidance or expression or counteraction or destruction, but it is always open to renegotiation.

We will now examine in more detail some of the varieties of expressive, counteractive, and destructive anger scripts.

Antitoxic Conjoint Anger-Avoidance and Anger-Driven-Avoidance Scripts as Expressive and Communicative or Counteractive

A highly generalized introversive avoidance script may be generated by the conjunction of two quite separate sources of avoidance. The same individual may be prompted to avoid different scenes by the same response but for different reasons. Thus, the same parent who inspires fear of being beaten for any display of anger may prompt an introversive avoidance of contact with him in order to minimize any possibility of the display of anger. However, the same individual may also continue to feel resentment toward that same punishing parent, which prompts an anger-driven script of avoidance to give that parent a sign of and a communication of his anger, an expression and communication he indicates by avoiding contact as much as possible by both physical isolation and by introversive withdrawal.

This is a special case of one of the more general mechanisms of magnification, of generating responses which are capable of satisfying different wishes at the same time or at different times. In this case one avoids the dangers of anger while at the same time enjoying the indirect expression of anger in an attenuated form which tells the other he has not totally surrendered to him. The one-many ordering of means to ends magnifies any response which may singly serve many purposes, either conjointly, at once, or alternatively at different times.

In the case we have just considered, there is conjoint response, both against the expression of anger and for the expression and the communication of anger at the same time. A similar magnification of an avoidant-introversive response may occur as alternative rather than conjoint means to different ends. Consider the case in which one parent terrorizes a child out of anger while the other parent evokes anger by threatening withdrawal of love for the display of anger; "I don't want to see you when you're bad." Such a scene is sufficient to generate a counteractive anger-driven avoidance script which attempts to recast the scene by doing unto the other what was done to the self. This introversive withdrawal intends to punish the other in the same way the other punished the self. By employing the same scripted response for counteraction as for denial, such a response is thereby further magnified. It is not unlike the magnification of the value of money by the purchase of a variety of desired objects. Each purchase increases the desirability of money up to and including, eventually, the conversion of money into an end in itself, as the supremely desirable object. So as the introversive response is scripted to serve an increasing number of conjoint or alternative purposes, it may become more magnified, finally, than any of the single purposes it served.

Counteractive Versus Expressive Versus Communicative Antitoxic, Anger-Driven Scripts

In expressive scripts anger is limited to telling the self alone (as in backed-up anger) or to displaying anger on the face (without vocalization of anger). In communicative scripts expression is used to inform and motivate the other that he has angered the self, but it stops short of counteraction against the other or intended destruction of the other. In counteractive scripts anger prompts further effects on the other designed in various ways to blame, protest, oppose, flaunt, stop, reduce, prevent, avoid, escape, or demonstrate the self's power against the other and to revenge oneself on the other, short of the most toxic reprisals of serious and enduring injury and destruction of the adversary.

Since the intention of counteractive-anger-driven scripts is deeply hostile, it is not uncommon for them to further magnify the toxicity of any scene and of the life of the aggrieved one and his adversaries. Thus, in a counteractive blaming script which insists on apology from the other, that other may detect the greater wish of the aggrieved one to humiliate him than to restore equity in the relationship. Counteractive-anger-driven scripts are thereby very likely to be more self-validating of the need for counteraction but less self-fulfilling of the scripted responses in correcting that need.

Antitoxic, Anger-Driven, Backed-Up, Self-Expression Scripts

This is the minimal form of anger-driven antitoxic scripts. In it the individual is harshly constrained against any show of anger on the face, in the voice, or by gesture, words, or action. The classic case is the slave, who dares not display either anger or rebellion, on the pain of death or, at the least, the lash of the whip. Similar brutalization of the individual may occur in neurosis or in psychosis by many varieties of intimidation which produce varieties of cowardice. The scripting of backed-up anger may represent both heroism and cowardice. It is cowardice in its surrender of open affect expression by facial display, vocalization, verbalization, gesture, or overt angry and aggressive action. It is heroic in its resistance to the complete denial and extinction of anger which may be demanded. Like Dostoevski's underground man, he will not be altogether good and compliant but remain sullen to the end, intransigent in feeling backed-up anger even if he cannot openly express it. It is a crippled form of self- and affect expression in which the intimidated but resentful self attempts to preserve its integrity by resisting the demand for complete subordination, by permitting and preserving and by nursing anger in its distorted backed-up mode by holding one's breath, one's tongue, one's voice, one's facial muscles, and one's arms, fists, and limbs. This readily becomes a self-perpetuating magnified script, since the muscular tension required to control these varieties of expression creates an elevated level of neural firing sufficient to reactivate continuing anger, which then requires more sustaining muscular tension to control such anger from further expression. In such a script vigilant monitoring is exercised not for the detection of the source of anger but primarily for the detection and control of any change in any of the musculature of the face, voice, and limbs which might otherwise permit backed-up anger access to the face, voice, speech, or gesture or to the arms and limbs in aggressive attack. The real enemy has been offered almost total surrender and been displaced by the body of the self as the ever-present enemy and danger.

Antitoxic, Anger-Driven, Facial-Display Scripts

In this type of anger-driven script, the constraints on anger are less than for the backed-up anger script but nonetheless quite substantial. Such an individual does not feel free to vocalize anger, verbalize it, or act on it, but he does feel safe enough to permit it silent expression on his face. He may script a frown, a clenched jaw, tight lips, narrowed eyes to appear on his face whenever he is angered. It should be noted that (with the exception of the frown) these displays of anger do not represent the free expression of innate anger but are rather a compromise between that and backed-up anger. Most individuals, and even many investigators of facial affect (including myself early in my investigations) are so accustomed to suppressing the angry voice and the angry face that they do not realize that a facial display of tight lips and clenched jaws and slit-like eyes is a defense against the innate expression of the loud angry voice with mouth open and with eyes open. Because of this there arises the paradox of wide agreement among judges that such a face is "angry" and more frequently judged to be so than is a photograph of wide-eyed, fullblooded, full-throated anger. We know, correctly, that the tight-lipped other is angry, but we err in identifying that backed-up, silent transformation as the real thing. We would less readily confuse the holding of the breath with uninhibited breathing. We have the concept of holding the tongue and of biting the tongue but not the concept of holding the breath of anger.

Such a scripted facial display of backed-up anger may vary in its degree of magnification from an occasional pout to a perpetual sullen frown. It may be a pure anger response or one mixed with disgust or dissmell or with shame, either simultaneously or in regular scripted sequences. When anger and dissmell appear together, their message is one of complete outraged dissatisfaction with others as bad-smelling, as in caste or racial unrelenting prejudice. When there is a sequential facial display, from disgust to anger, there is the scripting not of a sustained unrelenting hostile distancing from the other but rather of an invariant expectation that the other will be ultimately found distasteful and to such a degree that anger is the final scripted inevitability, as in the message "That's a bit much." In contrast, if the facial displayed sequence is regularly from anger to disgust, such a script assumes that whenever a positive relationship turns negative in sufficient quantity of negative features it will first arouse anger but eventually lead to a more permanent distaste and distancing of the self from the other. Thus, in the mixed facial display of anger and dissmell there is a permanent hostile distancing. In the sequence disgust-anger there is a temporary disenchantment which infuriates from time to time. In the sequence anger-disgust there is too much which punishes to preserve intimacy and enchantment for very long. In one I am angry because I have been disgusted; anger is about disgusting imperfection. In the other I am disgusted because I have been angered; disgust is about love turning to hate.

The permissible scripting of facial anger may or may not be scripted as both expressive and communicative. It is possible for it to be scripted as non-communicative but expressive only when the person toward whom one feels anger is not confronted. It is also possible that the presence of the other is compatible with the display of facial anger so long as there is no vocalization, verbalization, gesture, or action. In part this depends on the severity of affect-control socialization. Some parents will permit pouting so long as it is silent and not too flaunting. Others will forbid facial anger display in their presence, but not if the child moves away and displays anger in the presence of the other parent or at some distance, in a more wounded and pathetic than provocative display.

There is a gray area between facial anger display as expressive per se and as communicative to the other. In the script we describe here the intention is limited to expression and varies only in how compatible such expression may be with the presence of the angering other, or how much distance there must be to permit the display of silent facial anger. This difference depends on whether the socializer interpreted any display as a communication or permitted silent display as expressive but not communicative, so long as it remained silent.

Antitoxic, Anger-Driven, Density-Display Scripts

These are anger-driven expressive and/or communicative scripts which define the permissible limits of anger display in terms of its density as constituted by the product of its intensity, duration, and frequency.

To the extent to which such density rules require severe limits on either the intensity or duration or frequency of expressed or communicated anger, the individual is also limited in any future encounters with scenes which may be much more toxic than those encountered in his early socialization. So a child socialized against very intense, or long-lasting, or frequent display of expressive or communicative anger may later be severely handicapped in dealing with warfare, whether on the battlefield or on the streets, in business or in the professions, or in his marriage.

Conversely, to the extent he is early exposed to very high density of anger displays, to which he responds in kind and which he scripts as permissible at very high density of anger levels, he too may be severely limited in any future encounters with scenes which may be much less toxic than those encountered in his early socialization.

It should be noted that what is experienced as toxic depends in part on what is really toxic, in part on what is so perceived, and in part on how effectively one can cope with these scenes. A truly toxic scene may not be so perceived but become so, and a safe scene may be perceived as toxic and be responded to less effectively than it might have been had it not been believed to be so toxic.

Therefore, an individual who has become accustomed to very toxic scenes and who scripts very high levels of anger as permissible will be advantaged in coping with very toxic scenes but more likely to be disadvantaged by overreacting to non-toxic scenes with too ready anger. Conversely, an individual who has been socialized against the display of dense anger may escape needless confrontations but suffer needless defeat and submission in the face of unexpected and exaggerated toxicity.

One individual may thus be too gentle to live in his future real world and the other too hostile for his future real world. In part this is a highly probable outcome of changes in society and in social and class roles which cannot be altogether predicted or controlled. Simpler and more stable societies are better able to socialize the anger (and other affects) of their young for their probable future life, though they too suffer varying mismatches between prescribed permissible anger density and constitutional differences in those they attempt to shape via culturally shared scripts.

Quite apart from future social changes, early affect-control socialization which attempts to shape permissible affect density levels is inherently limited in how much differentiation can be taught, and if taught learned. Affect socialization is at best a gross affair. Neither the teachers, nor models, nor students are altogether capable, knowledgeable, willing, or eager to learn highly differentiated anger-control scripts which describe or model, with any precision, exactly what density of anger is appropriate and just how to achieve such levels of control. It is much more probable that attempted rules will be overdone and underdone than matched exactly. Anger in particular is rarely modeled by a parent whose own anger is completely free of other problematic negative affects. Further, he is very likely to be engulfed by the felt anger of the child toward his own person, rather than to be governed by an awareness of all the probable future scenes for which the child is to be shaped. Even if he were so aware, it is not clear that either parent or both together can be adequate models for all the varieties of scenes the child may encounter during his life as an adult. There is no obvious way in which such matches might be guaranteed apart from a totally insulated and stable society. For much later learning there is no urgency or necessity to equip the child during his early years with all the skills he might later need. The shaping of and scripting of anger, however, is peculiarly vulnerable to the effects of primacy and early experience. If one enrages and or terrorizes the infant or young child with sufficient density, the resultant scripts are candidates for self-validating magnification or attenuation, which become increasingly monopolistic and resistant to effective competition from more differentiated scripts for permissible affect-density levels. This is not to argue the impossibility of later differentiation but rather for its increasing difficulty and improbability. It is not unlike accent in later, second-language acquisition.

We have thus far contrasted two extreme types of affect-density scripting. The majority of such scripts are neither so inhibited nor so free-flowing in their definition of permissible affect density. One variety of such scripts defines the density of permissible anger expression as proportional to the toxicity of the scene. What is prohibited in such a script is a tantrum for a trivial affront or a mild anger for a serious insult. The anger should fit the crime is the rule.

Another variety of such scripts is the reverse rule. It is permissible to blow off steam at trivial annoyances but not at more toxic scenes, lest these escalate into life-and-death threats to both adversaries. Such scenes call for cool negotiation.

Another variety of such scripts specifies a middle level of density for a restricted range of affronts. One must avoid expressing anger at either very trivial affronts or very serious affronts but respond with moderately dense anger to middle-level toxic scenes.

Antitoxic, Anger-Driven, Anticipated-Anger-Expression Script

As anger increases in demandingness, either preemptive in its claim for attention and/or urgent in its claim for expression against adversaries, and when the present scene offers no possibilities for appropriate expression of anger, one common option is to turn unrequited hate to the future. Fantasied imagery offers rich possibilities for anticipated telling off the hated one which also has the bonus of any as-if scene in that it is experienced both in the future and at a distance and in the present. In this respect it shares the aesthetic mode with any drama which enacts scenes both as real and as if. Just as one may feel truly sad for the death of a hero and truly angry at the villain in a tragedy, while at the same time knowing the actors have really not killed or been killed, so in generated fantasy may hate be given expression which is at once gratifying and yet also unreal in some respect. Fantasy is more often than not as constrained as the actual scene might be constrained. Thus, the individual who would be constrained from counteraction or destruction in his adversarial encounters would commonly be so constrained in fantasy as well, and therefore anticipated anger may be channeled into expression but not into further action or destruction.

The scripting of anticipated anger expression can coexist with actual uninhibited anger expression toward the same person or toward others when the opportunity occurs, in much the same way as a lover may have fantasies of expressing love to his beloved and also do so when opportunity occurs. It is but one of the auxiliary scripts generated whenever any affect is magnified but not always readily given direct expression, for whatever reason.

Such scripts may also be shared and provide a basis for bonding between any individuals who share a resentment, for example, to a political leader, a political party, an ethnic or caste group (upper or lower), or an occupational group. Thus, a study of janitors revealed that they shared a fantasy of telling off their tenants, uniformly believed to be overdemanding toward janitors and utterly unreasonable. To the extent that any role differentiation evokes angry polarization in who has disappointed whom, we should expect the emergence of antitoxic anticipated-anger expression as a bonding agent between us against them or between them against us.

Such anticipations of anger expression may, under varying conditions, either increase the magnification of anger when it is finally expressed or decrease its magnification, depending on the specific nature and phase of the fantasied expression and its perceived appropriateness in the later face-to-face confrontations. Such fantasies may have either attenuated the anger by the time the opportunity for expression occurs, by virtue of having peaked, or be magnified by continuing recruitment and aggregation of past offenses, generating an ever-growing debt which the other has unwittingly incurred. In this respect it is similar to the dynamics of mourning, which increases in intensity as more and more scenes are rehearsed, but which finally is attenuated by virtue of having explored to the full all the possible hurt of the invidious comparison between the good scenes with the beloved and their impossibility now and into the indefinite future. Just as grief work is not necessarily infinite, so is anger work capable of complete exploration and attenuation if it is pursued and worked through, first to its bitter end and finally to its bleached end. Both grief and anger work are explorations of possibilities superimposed on already magnified scenes of love or hate. These possibilities often are experienced as endless but are in fact finite, even if large, unless the exploration of such possibilities is interrupted, inhibited, or prevented from being completely explored, in which case they remain consciously apparently endless, without limit, and as such both self-validating and self-fulfilling.

ANTITOXIC, ANGER-DRIVEN EXPRESSION AND COMMUNICATION SCRIPTS

In antitoxic anger-driven communication scripts the individual feels free to deal with toxic scenes which evoke anger by both expressing his anger by vocalization and by communicating it by verbalization in face-to-face confrontation with the angering other. This is to be distinguished from explicit blaming and/or cursing and or threatening of the other. In this type of script complete freedom of expression and communication is either satisfied in telling the other one is angry, and in assuming this will result in controlling the other, or is inhibited in going further and blaming, censuring, cursing, demanding, or threatening the offending other. Restriction to the communication of anger as sufficient may be based on modeling of a parent who used such communication sparingly but effectively because the parentchild relationship was primarily rewarding, needing no more than an occasional display and communication of anger toward the child to control whatever was the child's offending behavior. Such a child may later adopt the same script for turning away angering others. There is, of course, no guarantee that the other will respond to him as he responded to his parent, in which case the script may then be reviewed for possible changes.

Such a script may, however, be limited to the communication of anger and inhibited in any additional confrontation whenever the socialization of anger encountered tolerance of communicated anger but severe punishment for any additional tantrum, aggressive flaunting, blaming, demanding, cursing, or aggressive physical attack.

ANTITOXIC ANGER-DRIVEN COUNTERACTIVE SCRIPTS AS ACTIVE, INTERACTIVE, OR REACTIVE

Counteractive anger scripts share with all scripts variations not only in their degree of magnification and in their dependence, independence, and interdependence but also in their degree of activity, reactivity, or interactivity.

In reactive anger-counteractive scripts, the individual may punish his adversaries but only in response to their specific offenses whenever these occur. In active anger-counteractive scripts, the individual takes considerable initiative in seeking out and punishing offenders. In interactive anger-counteractive scripts, the individual is midway between responding only to immediate offenses and seeking out offenders for punishment. He elects to monitor possibilities for offenses, so the probability of his seeing in any present scene an angering offender who deserves punishment is radically increased. He does not seek out known offenders but is ever alert to the possibility that there is a guilty other where one might not expect one. Analogs of possible offending scenes permit recruitment of additional information to be imported, so the probability of any particular scene becoming offensive is increased proportionally to the conjoint magnification of analog formation and monitoring.

Antitoxic, Anger-Driven, Anticipated-Counteraction Script

Whenever an individual is engaged in continuing long-term adversarial relationships, whether in the context of work, family, interpersonal relationships, political affairs, or warfare, there may be generated fantasies and plans to inflict defeats upon the adversaries. These arise not from any avoidance or cultivation of anger in these relationships but from the fluctuations in relative success and failure between the contestants. To the extent that one was defeated in one encounter it is likely that a counteractive reversal of such a defeat will be devised and anticipated in response. However, the same logic dictates a counteractive script even when one has defeated the other, who is expected to try harder to reverse the outcome in the next encounter. In games of sport competition, such alternations of plans and anticipations routinely occur, not only within each encounter but between renewals of games. Getting even in competition haunts victor and defeated alike. This is one of the rationales for scripting a record number of wins, which will resist defeat in the future by an as yet unknown adversary. The history of nineteenth- and twentieth-century European and American international rivalry is replete with anticipated growth of military strength by adversary nations which then lock in the victors to matching such anticipated growth. Indeed Lebow, in an examination of wars anticipated and fought, as compared with wars anticipated and not fought, has revealed a stereotypy of escalating projections in either case. Warfare has come to be a continuing preoccupation and intention of offense and defense, of planning and imagining as well as of waging war.

Similarly with the individual, warfare of varying densities comes to be waged in the mind, in between adversarial encounters ever pointed toward the future. Angry escalation is inherent in adversarial relationships, and anticipation is a major theater of mutual counteraction and deterrence, whether between business, political, or academic rivals or between hostile husband and wife.

ANTITOXIC EXPLOSIVE-ANGER RESTRAINT SCRIPTS

Antitoxic explosive-anger restraint scripts are generated when anger appears not so threatening as to require avoidance but sufficiently problematic to be mobilized explosively only in extremis, as a last resort, when all other alternatives have failed. Anger is regarded as bad and to be avoided at most, but not all costs. If the other is truly bad or utterly unreasonable, he may legitimately be regarded as worthy of fury and so becomes infuriating. The reasonable one is slow to anger, but when the bounds of rationality are violated by the other, then counteractive explosive, offensive anger is scripted as legitimate. Such anger is characteristically full-blooded and dense, in part because such individuals have not learned to grade and modulate intensity or duration of anger but only to hold it in check, to be used only for scenes in which it can be given full expression. Such a script may be learned from a parent who patiently tolerates many transgressions of his norms by his children until an invisible limit has been exceeded, at which such a parent explodes in self-righteous wrath.

The degree of magnification of such a script may vary with respect to frequency and duration of anger and what are considered justifiable provocations, as is true of any script.

In contrast to anger-restraint escape scripts, in which the magnification of anger is constrained by leaving the scene which has angered, here the same effect is scripted by employing only explosive anger and only in extreme cases.

In contrast to antitoxic anger-driven expressive and communicative scripts, such explosive anger is not limited to expression and communication but also permits counteraction of varying degrees of severity, such as blaming, demanding, cursing, or threatening, but stops short of physical attack and injury and destruction.

Antitoxic Anger-Restraint Escape Scripts

Antitoxic anger-escape scripts are generated when anger appears problematic but not so threatening as to require avoidance. It is neither repressed, suppressed, nor displaced by other negative affects, and it is hot enough to recruit wishes for vengeful action, aggressive fantasies, open display of facial anger, increased loudness of speech, or verbal protest, but anger is also sufficiently restrained and constrained by competing affects, competing assumed disadvantageous risks and costs over benefits, that one intends in the end to back off and escape one's own anger and thus restrain it rather than to magnify and nurse it and/or to translate it into counteractive or destructive aggressive action. Such escape scripts may dictate leaving any scene which has aroused too much anger, with the intention of turning the anger off or down. This may be particularly necessary if the other is experienced as an agent provocateur. If literal escape from the scene is impossible, the individual may teach himself how to turn off his attention to his anger by relaxing his muscles, by shifting his attention to other concerns. In one case I discovered an individual who had taught himself to fall asleep quickly in scenes in which he had become too angry. These are similar in intention to sedative scripts which attempt to soften and reduce anger but different in employing leaving the scene either literally or psychologically.

In contrast to anger scene escape as expressive, counteractive, or destructive anger, here escape is scripted as putting limits on the potential for endless escalation. This is in marked contrast to the scripting of escape as a mode of telling the other one is angry, or escape as a way of defeating one's adversary by interrupting his anger, or escape as a way of seriously injuring one's adversary, who believes the relationship is too strong to be broken. In disturbed marital relationships the angry one may leave to turn off his own anger, to defeat and stop the anger of the other, to deeply wound the other, or all of these, in which case escape responses become highly magnified as all-purpose solutions.

ANTITOXIC ANGER SCENE ESCAPE AS EXPRESSIVE AND COMMUNICATIVE ANGER AND/OR COUNTERACTIVE ANGER AND/OR DESTRUCTIVE ANGER

One may script escape from angry scenes not because one is inhibited in anger but because one uses escape as a sign to the other that one is sufficiently angry that one wants no more to do with him. Such a script may or may not further include avoidance of the angering other. It is often learned from parents who have expressed their anger in this way toward their child with or without a further moral attached to leaving the child alone, such as a lecture that the parent will return when the child cools down, apologizes, or sees the error of his ways, singly or together. Or the escaping parent may combine escape with a wounding expression of a significant change in feelings toward the child: "I don't like you any more"; or a more limited change: "I don't like you when you're like that." Escape may be combined with any of a large variety of additional meanings of varying severity, duration, specificity, or ambiguity. These may be sufficiently magnified as threats to the self so that they are then scripted as weapons against others who anger the self with or without further explicit meanings and references to the other as one leaves his presence.

Escape, therefore, may be used simply as a communicative sign of anger expression, to inform the other that one is displeased, but it may also be additionally (or exclusively) weighted with the intention to counteract and/or to destructively punish the other. This can occur only when either the parent or the child has either been taught or self-taught the lesson that nothing is more hurtful than the contamination of a rewarding relationship by the appearance of anger in either member of a dyad. This may then be used counteractively to defeat the other or to punish him severely and destructively by psychological exile of the offender by escape.

ANTITOXIC, ANGER-DRIVEN AVOIDANCE SCRIPTS AS END IN SELF, OR AS EXPRESSION, COMMUNICATION, COUNTERACTION, OR DESTRUCTION

Antitoxic, anger-driven avoidance scripts are generated by hatred of others rather than by avoidance of anger per se. Such scripts may be limited to one particular hated person, to a class of such persons, or to all persons. Some such nature lovers are more in hate with human beings than in love with nature.

Such anger may be fused with disgust or with dissmell, having been disenchanted with one or more once-beloved people or having early on had such unrewarding experiences with one or more others that one is too angry to wish to be with others. Whether some autistic children become autistic in this way is still debated, but there is less question that some varieties of extreme introversive scripts are powered by anger and dissmell or disgust. Further, such anger-driven avoidance scripts are at least as old as the beginning of social class and caste differentiations. Badsmelling, inferior, and sometimes dangerous lower classes or castes have been excluded and avoided for several thousands of years. Anger, terror, or dissmell do not necessarily become visible unless the bad other intrudes into one's private space.

Anger which prompts avoidance is not limited to disgust or dissmell. It may be generated by any negative affect which evokes anger. I may avoid you in anger because you have made me feel guilty because you are so poor, so sick, or so underprivileged and I am so rich, so healthy, or so overprivileged. I may avoid you in anger because you have made me feel afraid of you by threatening to attack me. I may avoid you in anger because you have made me feel ashamed of myself for envying you. I may avoid you in anger because you have made me feel too distressed about your troubles.

In each of these cases my anger prompts avoidance, not because I cannot tolerate that anger but because the anger is directed against the person who evoked negative affect other than anger, to such a quantity that anger was also evoked in such a fashion that there was more satisfaction in never again confronting that scene than in expressing that anger or in counteracting it or in destroying the other. One rather wishes to be rid of the source of anger than to fight it or express it or even to destroy it, in part because one is not that much involved with the other to make the effort which might be required to confront the source and to struggle with that other or with those others. One may become divorced not only from a wife or a husband out of hate but also from the society one once loved if and when the sources of anger become too numerous to express in any way other than avoidance and withdrawal.

As in divorce, anger-driven avoidance scripts may also be generated in order to give a sign and to communicate, as well as to express one's anger toward the hated other, and/or in order to interrupt and counteract the angering attitude of the other, and/or to deeply injure the other by avoiding the other one had previously loved.

Such a generalized magnified avoidance should be distinguished from the same type of script which combines introversion with avoidance. In the present type of avoidance there may be considerable positive extroversion coexisting with a highly magnified but discriminating avoidance of hated others, whether introverted or simply avoidant.

Antitoxic, Counteractive, Anger-Driven Flaunting Scripts

Flaunting scripts intend to counteract anger when the other's attempted control or evaluation of the self is resented and intolerable enough to generate behavior which is specifically designed to assert the self's independence of the other. The type of behavior required is essentially reactive and defined by the actor's interpretation of the constraints the adversary is demanding and by the actor's interpretation of what might add further insult to the demonstration of independence. Negativistic behavior is a special case in which one scripts behavior which is the opposite of what the other wishes, as when a child will not give up a toy demanded by a parent but runs off with it. The more general case of flaunting would be an increase in the noise of playing with toys when a parent asks for less noise. Certain types of delinquent and criminal behavior represent flaunting scripts. In special cases flaunting may represent both antitoxic and affluence scripts, in which the delinquent or criminal is rewarded by excitement and/or enjoyment as well as defiant anger in flaunting the authority of the police and society.

Flaunting scripts require an individual with sufficient self-confidence and self-assertion to oppose the other and sufficient positive affect for the other not to wish to recast and control the other or to seriously hurt the other. Indeed, the flaunting may have varying ratios of fun in teasing the other and of anger in self-assertion against the other. A parent who makes a game of flaunting behavior by mock anger may indeed undercut the anger sufficiently to convert flaunting behavior into an affluence script.

Antitoxic, Counteractive, Anger-Driven Oppositional Scripts

In counteractive oppositional scripts it is the intention to oppose the other's attempted control and/or evaluation of the self. In contrast to flaunting scripts, there is less insistence on the self's assertion of its own wishes and value and more anger at the wishes and values of the other. Such an individual loves both himself and the other less than in flaunting behavior. It is a more purely antitoxic script, in which an angry *no* is the response either to demands for behavior or to demands against behavior. Whatever it is the other wishes, the self is certain it will oppose.

If such a script is greatly magnified, self-assertion is more and more defined by opposing any perceived source of demand or of prohibition. The self is seduced into unwitting abandonment of endopsychic sources of affluence other than those defined by anger-driven antitoxic opposition. Such enjoyment or excitement that may be won comes to depend more and more on successfully opposing others, whose demand and prohibitions consume the unwilling victim.

Such a script is often socially inherited from an overcontrolling parent who was himself overcontrolled and oppositional but sufficiently identified with the parent to repeat the entire scene with his own child, to his ambivalent surprise. While he insists on controlling the child, he often is covertly excited by the spectacle of himself in his oppositional child. "He has my temper" he will tell his spouse, with mixed pride and anger.

It is not only overcontrol which generates such oppositional scripts but also an overloading of the significance of oppositional behavior by the socializer, who says explicitly, in response to protests or demands for a rationale, "You do it because I said so." It is such a definition of the scene which leads readily to the transformation "I will not do it because you said so," thereby excluding large numbers of possible alternative interpretations of the scene. Such interpretations reduce dyadic interactions to the simple alternative of who will insist and who will oppose that insistence. This is how the oppositional child can become an overcontrolling parent.

Antitoxic, Anger-Driven, Counteractive Blaming-Protest Scripts

In this form of counteraction we move to a variety of responses designed to focus blame on the offender. When someone has been angered, sufficiently enough to script counteractive blaming responses, he is confronted with several options which we will now consider.

First is a generalized protest against "outrage." In this, the immediate offender is less important than the scene he is responsible for. He is one of a number of offenders, and the offending scene is but one of a family of outrages. "Did you hear the latest?" is the hostile blaming of a spouse, a political party, an ethnic group, a class, or a nation presumed to be the source of continuing outrages, of which the latest is but a special case which is presumed to be neither the first nor the last. The fact that it has occurred again and will recur again and again, gives the present protest its hard, long-suffering edge. There is enough blame to go around, in both space and in time. Nor is such blame necessarily ineffective as a counteraction. In our increasingly televised and polled society, a report that a majority of citizens disapprove of a measure, an executive, judge or representative, or a party is not without substantial consequences.

The more reactive the blaming, the greater is the emphasis on the present instance. The more active the blaming, the more the individual seeks out outrages to celebrate and protest. The more interactive the blaming, the more probable any scene is likely to be seen as outrageous, since monitoring for just such possibilities is itself magnified, of which the individual is likely to be unaware because of the compressed skill of such networks, which operate silently until they find the relevant analog. One has thereby taught oneself the skill of detecting outrageous grievances and celebrating them in protest, without knowing how, in much the same manner as one exercises any skill.

The abstractness and generality of the affect system permits blaming to become a preferred end in itself as a counteractive expression of anger, without requiring anything further from the offender. The blamer intends primarily, in these antitoxic counteractive scripts, to somewhat wound the other without either destroying him, preventing a repetition, punishing him, or extracting restitution. Despite the fact that blame may stridently assert the other should be punished, the primary intention is to punish by blaming itself. We are not accustomed to take seriously the fact that anger, or any affect, may be combined with any response to become an end in itself, independent of the verbalized intention of the angry blaming.

Blaming as a type of counteraction is radically different than recasting as a type of counteraction. In the latter case one does intend to do unto the other what the other did to the self.

Antitoxic, Anger-Driven, Blaming, Responsibility-Attribution Scripts

In these blaming scripts it is not the bad scene which is salient. It is rather the offending other, who is held responsible for the scene, who is angrily blamed. "You did it" is the counteraction. It is the one who did it which is critical, rather than the outrage for which he is responsible, which is salient. "Et tu Brutus" is the classic case. This form of blaming, which is very general if not universal, is learned very early on by any child singled out for blame whenever he offends a parent. It may be exaggerated when further punishment follows swiftly upon such attribution of responsibility. This teaches the child that if he is held responsible, he is necessarily in further trouble; but if he is not, he escapes two bad scenes at once. Responsibility and punishment combined tend to attenuate the significance of the specificities of his offenses. So a sibling witnessing some damage to a prized possession of a parent by a rival may gloat, "You're going to get it" when both know that the sequence responsibility-punishment is an unavoidable fate.

A child sensitized to such a sequence readily acquires the scripting of blaming by responsibility attribution as a weapon against his own enemies. He is less a grievance collector than a one-man posse.

Antitoxic, Anger-Driven, Counteractive Blaming-Evaluation Scripts

In counteractive warning-evaluation scripts, the offending other is not held responsible for the specific offense but rather is blamed by more general evaluation of the offense and/or evaluation of the offender. Not "You did it" but "That was a bad thing you did," or "You're bad"; or "That was a stupid thing to do" or "You're stupid"; or "That was an ugly thing to do" or "You're ugly"; or "What you said is not true" or "You're wrong" or "You're a liar" or "You're ignorant"; or "That was unchristian" or "You're not a Christian."

It is the violation of norms—moral, aesthetic, truth, or religious—which is the focus of angry evaluative blaming, whether focused on the act as a special case or on the actor as having the kind of personality which commits such norm violations, or both.

This is, of course, one of the most widely used methods of socializing the affects and behaviors of the young, and it is as readily learned to be used as a weapon as it is to be dreaded as a weapon directed at the self by others, either in fact or in memory or in anticipation, or as in internalized alter ego or superego. The generalizability of such a script is much more probable than is the case with blaming for responsibility for a specific case.

It should also be noted that such a script need not demand or require that the other change his behavior or atone or reform, since the primary intention of this type of script is to inflict a special kind of wound on the other independent of any further outcomes. Indeed, for many, reform of the other or apology by the other would constitute a frustration, an unwelcome impediment to free-flowing pious hostile evaluation. In part this is inherent in any magnified script, since the function of a script is to deal with a selected set of scenes by a selected set of responses. Exceptions to magnified scripts are constantly encountered and assimilated to the script, but there is also a vested interest in economizing the degree of work in altering the major outlines of the rules. As we will presently see, a blaming script which requires the other to reform or apologize may be equally hostile and magnified, but it is nonetheless a script with quite different rules for expressing anger.

Antitoxic, Anger-Driven, Counteractive Blaming-for-Punishment Scripts

In blaming-for-punishment scripts, anger is counteracted by blaming the other as punishment-worthy. In contrast to the salience of evaluative moral culpability or to the salience of responsibility, here it is the appropriateness and deserving worthiness of the offender for harsh punishment for the crime which is at issue. The other must not be permitted to escape retribution. Such a script often begins in an invidious comparison between the punishment meted out to the self and to sibling rivals in the family. The child who suffers excessive punishment for his crimes, who sees his rival forgiven similar offenses, sees insult added to injury and insists that the other be punished. As such a script becomes magnified, the individual is less and less concerned about the nature of the crimes, about characterizing them or their authors as immoral, or protesting outrages, and more concerned about the angry expression of the wish that offenders deserve to be punished and should not get away with murder. The irony of such scripts is that actual punishment of the offender need not be intended and would, in fact, frustrate the one who blames in this way. Because one has again and again witnessed the self as punished and others as escaping punishment, there is increasing anger at such scenes, real or so believed, but less and less belief that their toxicity can be corrected in fact. If such a one cannot in fact punish the other, or believes he cannot or does not try to, but cannot attenuate or relinquish his impotent anger, he may nonetheless blame others by crying out that a pound of flesh is owed as a counteraction against the other, which is intended to wound the other even as he realizes the other will nonetheless escape the full retribution and punishment he deserves. This is a sullen mouse who wishes to wound an aggressive cat by telling him he should be punished.

It is generally ineffective either in reducing the anger of the aggrieved or the aggression of the offender.

Antitoxic, Anger-Driven, Counteractive Cursing Scripts

Cursing scripts are expressive and communicative of anger but are distinguished by their additional intent to use these as also counteractive by conjoining them with more active and denser hostility so that the verbalization of wish and hope, in addition to anger, increases the hurt of the other. In contrast to blame scripts, in which there may be protest, attribution of responsibility, negative evaluation, or even deserved punishment, here the offended one goes beyond holding the other responsible or punishment-worthy. He in fact attempts to provide punishment by the severity not only of his anger but by his expressed wishes and hopes for retribution for the other. In the extreme case the expressed wish may be for the most extreme counteraction, the destruction or serious and permanent injury of the other. "I hate you. I hope you drop dead" goes well beyond the expression or communication of anger per se. Such scripts may in fact go still farther in sorcery, as in sticking needles into a reproduction of the other to hasten the destruction of the other. In cultures where magic is widely used, the boundary between the curse and magic is a permeable one, so curses are used more sparingly because of their believed greater toxicity.

Curses have a very long history. They constituted one of the earliest forms of law in ancient treaties, in which a sovereign conjoined blessings for loyalty in his vassals with correlative curses for infidelity. It is now believed these provided the model for the later covenant between God and the Israelites. Curses are here equivalent to more than wishes and hopes. They are threats of sanctions God will visit on the chosen people if they are unfaithful and worship false gods. Thus, in Joshua, "Then afterward he read all the words of the law, the blessing and the curse, just as it all was written in the book of the law" (Joshua 8:34).

Antitoxic, Anger-Driven, Counteractive Demanding-Punishment Scripts

In contrast to blaming scripts, we now describe a series of equally toxic counteractive scripts which intend to demand action from and/ or against the other rather than simply to blame or evaluate the offender. These scripts are generated by individuals who are more self-confident and whose models typically followed through in their socialization of the anger of their children.

Demanding-punishment scripts, in contrast to blaming punishment scripts, intend and insist that the other be punished, whether by the self or by society. These punishments are not only wished but intended, planned, and in varying degrees executed. They may also blame, but the primary intention is to punish as well as to communicate that demand. Such punishment may include censure, ostracism, fines, or imprisonment but stop short of destruction or serious enduring injury of the other.

Antitoxic, demanding, anger-driven scripts intend primarily to hurt the other. This is often masked by the nature of what is demanded, especially when it is the avowal of guilt rather than punishment which is demanded. Thus, if one demands that the other accept and confess that he is a bad person who has done a bad thing, this may be confused with a remedial demanding script. In the latter script a very moral parent may be outraged that the child is aggressive without guilt, and demand the child acknowledge that he is bad. His intent may be partly to vent his own self-righteous wrath, but its ultimate intention is to produce a child with a well-developed conscience; and when that child displays true guilt in the face of the demand, the ambivalent parent may smile and hug the child to reward him and to strengthen the ties that bind. Both now bask in the glow of righteousness. In the present antitoxic demanding scripts such remedial intentions are relatively weak or absent compared to the wrath of self-righteousness. It is hell, or purgatory on earth, which is intended for the sinner, under the guise of correcting and remedying his evil character by demanding he avow his own badness.

Further, the demands for acceptance of responsibility of a self which is norm-violating is in no way necessarily limited either to the violation of moral norms nor to one type of norm violation. The parent, and later the author of angry, demanding scripts, may demand acceptance of any variety of negative normative violations. The child may be coerced into acknowledgment and acceptance of the self as having offended the parent and angered him by violation of aesthetic norms, "Yes, I am a slob. I will try to keep my room neater"; by violation of achievement norms, "Yes, I don't try hard enough. I will try to improve my grades"; by violation of truth norms, "Yes, I am careless about the facts. I'll try to do better on my next paper." The whole self may be damned angrily in invidious comparison with a beloved and envied sibling: "Why can't you be more like your brother? He is so good, so beautiful, so intelligent. He never gives me the trouble you do." The only reply which will get the victim temporarily out from under the tongue lashing is "I'm just no good. I'll try." This moves him no farther than from hell to purgatory at the moment as he continues to twist under the hurt and terror and shame of the angry, disgusted face of the harshly disciplining parent. He has, however, also learned the beginning of a script of this type as a weapon against angering others. He has learned how to skin the other alive by the construction of moral stockades which lock others into avowal and acquiescence in their own unworthiness.

Neither blaming nor demanding anger-driven scripts aim at their avowed verbalized intentions when counteraction is primarily anger-driven.

Antitoxic, Counteractive, Anger-Driven Demand-for-Restitution Scripts

In contrast to the demand for apology, in the demand-for-restitution script what is extorted is repayment for presumed damages to the self. The intent is to force the other to make it up to the wounded angry self by extortion which is intended to hurt the other more than to help the self. This is evidenced in litigations for defamation of character, when the successful plaintiff, having won a large sum of money, conspicuously donates that money to a charity. It is also often explicitly stated that legal suits will be filed in order to bankrupt the offender, or to teach him a lesson he will not forget.

This may begin in the family by demanding the child pay for his offenses by loss of his allowance or by the surrender of enjoyed privileges as restitution to the offended parent. Such a child in such a family is provided a model of an exchange economy, in which one offense can be paid off in a variety of ways—for example, by money, privileges, or effort—so he must do some distasteful chore for a period of time or not be permitted to watch television for a period of time proportional to the gravity of the offense, as well as by losing money otherwise regularly paid him as an allowance.

This should be distinguished from exploitation as such, in which a defeated other is made to pay tribute or, in the extreme case, is made into a slave. In the demanded-restitution script, what the other must be made to give is in proportion to the hurt he has inflicted, presumably by taking something of value, which must then be repaid, if not exactly, then by something of equivalent value. This is one of the bases for imprisonment for crimes when it is presumed to be a repayment of a debt to society at large. In the extreme case the life of the other may be demanded for having murdered, as a demanded restitution of one life for another life, though such punishment may, alternatively, be viewed as a pure destructive-revenge script.

In such a script there is not only an interpretation that the offender has robbed the victim of something of value but also that the offender has it in his power to reverse that loss and to make some exact or equivalent restitution for what he has taken. Rivalry scenes, either between siblings or between the child and his parents, as in Oedipal rivalries, are prime candidates for such scripts. Crimes of passion for infidelity are based on similar scenes but different scripts in that the murder of the rival or the unfaithful one would be an anger-driven, destructive script rather than an anger-driven, counteractive, demanding-restitution script.

In rivalry scenes, when the individual is angry at both a parent and a sibling, or at both parents, for robbing him of exclusive possession of a loved parent, then he may, for example, partition his anger into two different kinds of scripts, demanding restitution from the most beloved one and blaming the rival.

It should also be noted that insofar as restitution is demanded, compared with apology, there may be some quantities of positive affect as well as hate involved, inasmuch as one is demanding not only that the other suffer for having robbed the self but also that the robbed self be made better by the return of what was taken. In contrast, when apology is demanded, the primary enjoyment extorted is from the humbling of the offender in venting anger. In this respect, depending on the ratios of the mixture of positive affect and anger, a restitution-demanding script might be more or less remedial in intent as antitoxic in intent.

Further, as we have seen before, a nuclear script may also demand restitution from the lost beloved as a type of decontamination of a good scene turned bad.

Antitoxic, Anger-Driven, Counteractive Demanding of Acceptance of Responsibility

In this type of anger-driven counteractive script it is the intention to demand that the offender acknowledge and accept the responsibility of having angered and hurt the self. This is in contrast to a blaming attribution-of-responsibility script. The major difference is that in the latter case the individual anger is satisfied in hurting the other by exposing him as responsible. It is assumed that such an attribution is deeply wounding because the other tried to keep it secret. In the present type of script the individual's anger requires that he coerce the other into an unwelcome and punishing acceptance and acknowledgment of responsibility. Presumably, the other has made no secret of his behavior but denies responsibility for having hurt the other, asserting, for example, that the other is exaggerating.

Such a script may begin in sibling rivalries in which one sibling complains to a parent that the other has hurt him, demanding first that the other be punished for his aggression. If the other denies he really did any damage and/or had no intention of doing so, then the injured party may become outraged at the attempt by the other to rewrite the history of the damage—"You did too"—and demand that the least the sibling can do is to accept the responsibility for what he did. This is quite different than a blaming script in which the first major aim is to expose the offender, upon which it is assumed punishment may automatically befall the offender. In the present case the other may admit he pushed the victim, but it really didn't amount to much, or if it did, it wasn't intentional. In one case the aggrieved one is exposing an offense. In the other he is demanding that the other confess and take the consequences that clearly belong to him.

In the present script the integrity of the other is in question and can be restored only by demanding that the offender accept responsibility. One angrily forces the other to be good rather than simply exposing him as bad. Both intentions are aimed at counteractive hurt to the other, the hurt of exposure versus the hurt of acceptance of responsibility. This script demands and insists that the other live by an internalized conscience. It is similar to a parent who demands from a child a stage of development which is beyond his present state. Having been so socialized, that child will respond to aggressive others as if they were underdeveloped children who must be made more moral. In such a script the affront is at least as moral as it is hurtful and angering in other ways. Consider the scene in which an individual discovers his automobile has been damaged while parked in a shopping mall. In a blaming script the individual spares no effort to find the offender, and if he succeeds, his response is to insist the offender pay for the damages. In a demand-of-responsibility script, damages might also be sought, but full compensation would require that the other confess that responsibility. Without such acceptance of responsibility this individual would continue to feel anger, and that anger would grow. In the blaming script the combination of exposure plus damages would satisfy. There is no demand for a conscience in the other.

Antitoxic, Anger-Driven, Counteractive Demanding of Acceptance of Negative Normative Evaluation

In a script which demands acceptance of negative normative evaluation, more is involved in transgression than the acceptance of responsibility for a transgression. The other must be coerced not only into being morally responsible for a bad act but coerced into accepting a more general attribution of immorality of his character as a whole.

The specific bad scene is typically embedded in a much larger context in which this transgression is represented as the inevitable consequence of the kind of immoral human being he is, and the intended wounding of the other is to force him to accept that characterization of himself, that he ought to be better than he is.

This kind of script can be generated by having been so coerced into painful confessions by an overly zealous parent whose own conscience was not too firmly internalized. Such scripts appeared prominently in nineteenth- and twentieth-century Russia. They were superimposed on Marxist ideology in the coerced confessions in the political trials of dissidents after the Russian revolution. Indeed, one of the most striking differences between the individualism of Western culture and the more collective community-bonded Russian culture is to be found in the magnification of the right of the individual not to incriminate himself in a court of law, as compared to the magnification of the right of the community to coerce and exact confession of guilt from the offending individual.

The tension between the individual and the collective is, of course, as old as the history of human society, and it is paralleled in every nuclear family in the tension between parents and children, since the parents attempt to transmit the norms of the collective to the next generation through their socialization of their children. Since these parents reflect, in varying degrees, the ambivalences and ambiguities of their own childhood and their own tension with their parents, there is always some ambiguity between the child as later parent confronting his own child, which parallels the ambiguity between the individual and the collective.

This tension is particularly acute in the socialization of anger and aggression, and insofar as we bifurcate anger into good anger and bad anger, there will be a continuing vulnerability to generate scripts of anger-driven, counteractive demanding of negative normative evaluation, in which the offender is intended to be wounded by accepting his own bad angry self in invidious comparison with the angry, offended, and therefore good other.

Antitoxic, Counteractive, Anger-Driven Demand-for-Apology Scripts

In demand-for-apology scripts it is not punishment of the other, nor acceptance of responsibility for an angering act, nor confession that the self is bad that is demanded but rather an angry insistence that the other apologize to the victimized but angry self. He intends to extract such apology not for the good of the other, not for the restoration of a rewarding relationship, but to vent the anger by inflicting a particular kind of psychic wound with the intention of diminishing the other, by forcing him to humiliate himself.

Such scripts are often learned from parents who had learned it from their parents. Although apology may be demanded for remedial intent, either for the other or for the dyad, it need not be so motivated. It is one of a variety of ways in which human beings practice extortion on each other. Extortion need not be anger-driven, whether tribute is exacted legally by taxes, imposed by an invading oppressor, or threatened by organized crime syndicates, which offer protection against further violence from themselves by extorted payoffs. But extortion may be compounded of greed and anger or issue primarily from anger, as in the case of the present scripts. It resembles criminal extortion in that the demanded apology gives reward to the self as it hurts the donor.

Apology demanding, like any script, may be magnified to any degree; it may be concentrated on one person or one group or be diffuse; it may be entirely reactive only to immediate offense or active in particularly litigious personalities; or it may be interactive in a constant monitoring of scenes for possibilities of affronts which may demand the extortion of apology from the presumed offender. It may be limited to a narrowly defined particular type of offense which angers or evoked by a broadly defined set of angering scenes.

Antitoxic, Anger-Driven, Counteractive Independent-Aggressive Scripts

Independent-aggressive scripts are those in which whenever the individual is angered he characteristically aggresses, physically, on the most appropriate object. If there is no one present, he may hit a door or wall in his rage and sometimes inflict damage both on his surroundings and on his own fists. This type of script is independent in that its trigger is not the provocation of the other or anything peculiar to the angering scene, but rather to the anger evoked, whatever its source. It may be scripted conditional upon a range of density of anger—for example, to strike out whenever anger reaches a high level of intensity, frequency, or duration, or any combination thereof. However, this script need not be conditional on density, particularly when the characteristic density level of anger is high and largely ungraded and unmodulated. Indeed, knowing one's own script may lead to another script which is directed to the avoidance of anger to defend against his inability to control his own anger once activated. Further, he may employ another, more extrapunitive script of warning or threatening others against angering him, lest they become the inevitable targets of his own uncontrollable rage and aggressive attack. However, in the present case he does in fact translate anger into aggression whenever that anger has been aroused, for whatever reason. The one he attacks need not be the one he holds responsible for his own anger. Indeed, he may later defend his action by reminding the other that he had been warned to stay out of his way because he was in an ugly mood.

Such scripts may have been learned from models from whom one received frequent attacks for little or no reason, creating a climate of violence as customary, in antithesis to a climate of love and nurturance frequently displayed in smiles and hugs, equally unprovoked by the behavior of the self.

These scripts may also be learned by having had anger sufficiently magnified, by repeated and cumulative provocation, that anger is translated into aggressive attack against the enemy so frequently that the script is compressed into the simpler formula when angry: hit; don't wait to be hit.

Antitoxic, Anger-Driven, Counteractive Anticipated-Aggression Scripts

In anticipated-aggression scripts one responds to the anticipated aggression of the other rather than to one's own anger as independent. One's own aggressive attack may be scripted as required, either when one sees signs of the imminent possibility of the aggression of the other or immediately upon being attacked by the other. In either case the intention is neither to win opportunistically nor to vent one's own anger but to defend oneself against the aggression of the other, to stop it and to limit the damage to the self. One may be prepared to inflict heavy costs on the other and even to absorb heavy costs on the self in order to prevent what is anticipated to be a possibly more damaging outcome. When such intentions are scripted, there is no guarantee that such counteraggression will not in the end be more costly to all, as in any warfare, no matter whether offensive or defensive in intention.

Antitoxic Anger-Driven, Counteractive Instrumental-Aggressive Scripts

In instrumental-aggressive scripts one hits first and early whether the cue is one's own anger or the anger of the other. It is a response to the probability of a fight. This is part of the lore of street smarts, that fights are most often won by the one who gets in the first punch. Such a script is not primarily about anger or about violence per se but about opportunistic advantage in the adversarial climate of the ghetto. Indeed, the maintenance of one's cool is favored not only in the ghetto and the culture of poverty but also in the culture of the warrior elite, as among the Japanese samurai, who prided themselves on cool, fearless, and angerless combat effectiveness. In one Japanese fable, an attempt on the life of a warrior is turned against the adversary with the slightest of responses. Similarly, the quality of a matador is judged by how close he permits the bull to come and how gracefully and calmly he kills the bull. In contrast to the ghetto, where aggression is more purely instrumental, the warrior and the matador have added an aesthetic criterion to aggression and violence.

Antitoxic, Anger-Driven, Counteractive Threat Scripts

Threat scripts are generated with the intention of stopping or preventing the repetition of angering scenes against offenders who are believed capable of being so influenced. The threats may be physical, indicated by physical gestures to communicate intended physical aggression as a threat, or by verbalized intentions of physical attack or by threat of death. Threats may vary from intended legal action to harm of the other's family to economic threats (e.g., to bankrupt) to political threats (e.g., as threatened political loss of support) to threats of shaming by exposing hidden immoral behaviors to threats of loss of love or respect. A threat script ordinarily is based on two assumptions. First is an assumption of shared values, that both the self and the offender agree that the threat is not trivial but represents something which matters very much to both. Second is an assumption that the behavior of the offender is not as important to the offender as is the threat, so the offender can be deterred by the greater damage inherent in the threat than in what he is doing which so offends and angers his victim.

Such scripts arise in parent-child relationships in which purely positive affect motivation is insufficient (or so believed) to control the behavior of the child which angers the parent. Depending on the ratio of positive to negative affect in parent and child, threats, even though negative in themselves, nonetheless vary substantially in whether they are more positive or negative in intent. Thus, in parentchild relationships in which the affect ratio is more positive than negative, the threats will intend to deter by withdrawal or by loss of love, respect, or privileges the child is known to enjoy. In cases where the ratio of positive to negative affect favors the negative, threats are also more negative, relying more on inflicting of pain, injury, or sustained negative affect, especially backed-up negative affect such as rage, distress, or dissmell. The parent in these cases intends to impose more impotent backed-up anger and disgust or dissmell on the child than that evoked in the parent, more painful than whatever might be the rewards for the child in angering his parent.

The climate of control by threat requires both credibility of backup sanctions combined with relatively infrequent translation of threat into follow-through. In this respect it has the properties of any exchange mechanism which uses credit or money. There must be gold or valued products to redeem money on demand, but such a system would degenerate into a barter system—or, in the case of threat scripts, into pure aggressive scripts—if proof were continually required to redeem threat. Further, if the parent is too harsh in his occasional translations of threat into severe punishment, he may generate excessive intimidation which discourages identification sufficiently so that the child as adult is too intimidated to script threat against others as an antitoxic, anger-driven counteraction.

Antitoxic, Anger-Driven, Counteractive Struggle Scripts

Counteractive, anger-driven struggle scripts intend neither to simply threaten nor to aggress upon the offender but to confront and engage the adversary and to divert him sufficiently in the struggle to stop whatever evoked the anger. The exact tactics will depend on the nature of the offense more than on one's own anger. These may range from a withering look or a verbal challenge—"What the hell do you think you're doing?"—to political protest demonstrations, to militant picket lines in support of strikes, to long-sustained punitive legal battles by litigious personalities.

In the case of political or economic struggle behavior, such scripts may be mixtures of committed remediation scripts and counteractive anger-driven struggle scripts, and the ratio of intended remedy versus angry struggle may vary widely. This is also the case in extended legal battles. In the present script the intent is primarily anger-driven, to struggle with the angering other rather than to remedy a bad situation per se. The litigious personality is more driven by anger than by the dollar award in a legal damage suit, and he will soon find others to take to court, whether he wins or loses each lawsuit. Attorneys, too, are sometimes equally litigious, enjoying the legal battle for its own sake and giving vent to anger as well, both in the struggle and in defeating the other. This interest in the law may be also compounded of varying ratios of intent to play a rewarding game, with limitation-remediation of wrongs committed, plus the additional reward of developing and sharpening one's own adversarial skills as in any long-term committed skill of either affluence or limitation remediation.

Struggle scripts may originate in parent-child struggles in which an overcontrolling hostile parent is frequently angered by a self-assertive child who is constantly challenged to stop and justify his behavior, which is labeled offensive again and again. If the child is not intimidated, he is taught both to become frequently angered and to counteract the angry intrusiveness of the other and thus to generate a struggle script.

Even if he is too intimidated to respond in kind against his parent, he may yet experiment with such a script against less formidable adversaries among his siblings or peers or, in the extreme case, many years later as a type of recasting against his own children.

Chapter 38

Antitoxic, Anger-Driven Power and Recasting Scripts

In anger-driven recasting scripts it is the intention to satisfy anger in a very particular way by replaying the scene exactly but with the victim now the victimizer and the offender now the victim. This is a type of revenge in which not only reciprocity is achieved but, equally important, so is the particularity of the scene preserved, with the critical exception of who plays which role. In recasting it is not enough that the punishment fit the crime in an abstract equivalent way, for example, by paying money or serving a prison sentence. It is akin to romantic love and romantic hate. Just as one may love a particular person so that there are no alternative persons who are appropriate replacements for a lost love object, so one may hate a particular person in a very particular way, thus requiring an idiosyncratic type of revenge for satisfaction.

This is one of the most important derivatives of script theory, that scripts vary not only in the content of their scenes but also in the degree and mixture of their abstractness and particularity

I assume that what is learned and what is remembered is a scene rather than a simple "response." Suppose that when a parent frowns, hollers "no, no," and at the same time slaps the hand of a child for reaching into a cookie jar the child responds with shame at the interruption, both in the dyadic relationship and in the act of reaching, and then with distress at the pain of the slap. I am suggesting that *both* the affect of the parent, manifested conjointly in face, voice, and slap, and the affect of the child are learned and remembered. Further, not only is the entire scene experienced as an organized totality at a moment, but so is the sequence of scenes in time in much the same way as a conversation must be experienced as a *dialogue in time* if it is to be a dialogue at all. This assumption is quite different than the theory of interiorization of good and bad objects. I assume that the human being lives "in the world" from the beginning and that the frown, the loud voice, and the slap interrupting his reaching, and the shame and distress, though it occurs as a sequence, is nonetheless experienced as *one* continuous scene. When it is remembered, the other is as salient as the self, and the excited reaching is as salient as the interruption and its consequent shame and distress. Although such a sequence of scenes may be limited in both their detail and complexity as well as their temporal reach, in infancy and childhood the compactness and spatial as well as the temporal coherence of scene sequences is nonetheless crucial for later extension of such learning and memory.

The same dynamic appears in the development of linguistic competence. The earliest comprehension contains very abbreviated strings of words, with evidence of severe selection and compression of information for both what the child hears and speaks. Nonetheless, these primitive strings are coherent both for the self and the other and across time. On the basis of such a fundamental or somewhat limited and primitive organization, it is possible later to increase both the amount and connectedness of linguistic information.

Since it is a sequence of scenes which is experienced and later remembered, the individual can later operate on the set of scenes in a variety of different ways. At this point we will examine that type of operator we have called recasting. In recasting, the scene is decomposed and recomposed so that the original actors are recast to play different roles than they played in the original scene. The remainder of the scene is, however, conserved and *not* transformed. Any scene may be operated on by any operator, just as any series of numbers might be reversed in order, added, multiplied, or averaged. We are not arguing that recasting is the only or even the most important type of scene transformation. A scene might be recast and also transformed to have a better or worse outcome, but the recasting refers exclusively to the shifting of who plays which part in the scene.

We will now examine how recasting can produce anger at the other or at the self in the scene we are considering. We have assumed that in this scene the child is *not* angry but that the parent is angry and angry in a particular way, combining voice, frown, and slap. If the child used the recasting transformation, his own voice, his own face, and his own hand would slap the hand of the parent as that parent reached for the cookie; he would yell "no, no" and frown at the parent. This is the law of talion, an eye for an eye, a tooth for a tooth. One does to the other what the other did to the self. One need not, in this case, assume more than the power to imitate and reverse roles. One need not here assume any interiorization of another self. Both the other and the self are equally transparent, as are the setting, the props, the place, time, actions, and events in any scene. What is the motive for recasting? Does the reversal require that the recipient of affect experience the *same* affect as the one who expressed and imposed that affect upon the self? Must the child be angry at the angry parent to yell, frown, and slap his parent? If he is angered, why would he respond in kind rather than in his own idiosyncratic way, for example, by having a tantrum? Clearly, if the infant or child were terrified or deeply shamed or distressed by the parent's anger, we would not expect any *immediate* recasting. Both the original wish to reach out and any thought of the possibility of retaliation might be swamped by overly dense nonangry affect.

There are several possible motives for recasting. The primary one is reciprocity. Consider the case in which one wishes to return a favor. Here the gift must be approximately equal in value to the gift one received. If one has been paid a compliment, reciprocity calls for the return of a compliment. If one has been insulted, reciprocity calls for the return of the insult. Reciprocity, however, does not require an *identical* response but one of equivalent value. Recasting from the motive of reciprocity *would* use the same response to equalize the bestowal of either postive or negative affect. The aim of reciprocity is to produce symmetry in a scene. If the child was shamed rather than angered by the parent and the child felt this to be grossly unfair, he might recast for a particular kind of reciprocity, to make the other know how it feels to be shamed by a slap on the hands. The paradox here is that the *response* of the child need not arise from his own felt anger but from his hurt from shame. See how it feels to be slapped? Aren't you now ashamed that you slapped me? His wish is here to inflict the same shame affect from an angry slap and thus to achieve equity and reciprocity. It may also be further motivated by the wish to express and to *communicate* to the parent his own disorientation at the sudden unexpected change in their relationship as well as to induce such disorientation in the other.

Recasting, then, as a special type of reciprocity need not arise from felt anger. But if it need not, it often *does* arise from felt anger. When this is so, the anger may be the only response to the anger of the other, or one among many affective responses. If it is the only affective response to the anger of the other, the child might respond to the other's anger in his own way, quite independent of the anger of the other. Such an angry response, (e.g., a tantrum at being interrupted in his wish to have a cookie) does not involve recasting. It is his major intention to have the cookie. To the extent that the child yells, frowns, and slaps the hand of the parent it is a recast scene. In this case the original wish has had to be relegated to the background of consciousness. He wants first of all to even the score with the other. The cookie can wait. Indeed, he may know that his parent doesn't really want the cookie, so his recasting is limited to slapping a hand which is not even interested in reaching for a cookie. He may or may not include in his conception of recasting his former freedom to reach for what he wants to eat. In order to achieve total symmetry he would have required a parent who continued to eat even as he denied his child the same privilege and then stopped the parent from eating as he recovered his own freedom to eat what and when he chose.

Recasting from anger alone, in contrast to recasting without anger, aims at inflicting on the other *both* the angry response by the self and the induction of anger in the other. It need not include satisfaction of the frustrated wish for the self, nor frustration of that wish for the other.

Recasting from anger combined with other negative affects (e.g., shame) aims at inflicting on the other the angry response by the self and the induction of the other negative affects in the other as well as the induction of anger in the other. It need not include satisfaction of the frustrated wish for the self, nor frustration of that wish for the other. It might include such a criterion if the parent had made the invidious comparison salient and had taunted the child with his own enjoyment of the cookie at the same time he prohibited the child's eating it.

The anger which prompts recasting need not have been experienced in the original scene. A child traumatized by the anger of an overwhelming parent may experience a long delayed anger at any time after the scene, particularly as the result of repeated beatings, which increase the density of the evoked anger. This is seen most frequently in cases of serious child abuse, which appears to be a socially inherited scene capable of being transmitted over several generations, from father to son. The child who was beaten beats his own child. Here we have a delay and a displacement in anger and aggression so that recasting is both delayed in time and displaced until the son becomes a father. Such delayed and displaced recasting is often experienced as surprising and totally alien to the son become father, especially if that son had suffered terror, distress, and shame more than anger. A second cousin of such recasting is the less physical fusion of disgust and anger in the unexpected utterance of disgusted, pious, angry clichés one had suffered at the hands of a parent, now directed at one's own child. "Money doesn't grow on trees, you know" can suddenly engulf both parent and child with equal surprise and alienation. The parent can remember only his own shame or disgust at being so assaulted. He did not recast this scene against his own parents but apparently waited until a more opportune moment, much to his surprise and often selfas well as other disgust.

We have seen before that the neonate is early on capable not only of imitation of the other but also of autosimulation of reflex-endowed acts. If we assume that the initial reversal of roles is entertained, but suspended or blocked because the child loves the parent or is afraid of the parent or excessively ashamed, then a further recasting transformation similar to that in autosimulation would split the self in two. Now one self, possessing one hand, would frown, yell at, and slap the other hand, thus preventing the overeaching hand of the greedy self from reaching the cookie. In such a case it is important to realize that *two* bad selves have been created. One is modeled on the angry parent; one is modeled on the greedy child. The child, by a *double* recasting, has learned to be angry at and to hate himself. Whether he transformed the original recasting of the parent, against himself out of love or fear or shame, has further differential consequences we will not examine here. What we wish to emphasize at this point is the dependence of that learning on the specific features of the original scene. It is the specific facial frown, the specific loudness and quality of the angry voice, and the specific intensity of the slap and the pain it causes which will be simulated. It is not necessarily a superego, ego ideal, or bad or good object which is interiorized but rather a specific simulation of how the other responded to the self—in this case via face, voice, and hands—which is transformed in recasting the scene.

This is not to deny the possibility of further, later transformations which change the original scene in much more complex and abstract ways. As in any dialogue, the person is capable of preserving *both* the original words and their more remote and more abstract implications as well as the capability of radical *compression* of scene and dialogue in further summarizing transformations. Much more often than we realize, however, critical scenes remain very vivid, very intense, and very particular. Insofar as our anger is recast, your anger may be centered on the angry face and mine on the angry voice as we experienced it from an offended parent. In our concern for measurement of variables we have been motivated to minimize the particularity of conjoint scene variance. In our concern for a general personality theory we have also been motivated to be too ready to label general structures which are presumed to operate at the same level of abstraction that would be ideal for the construction of a general theory of personality. I am urging that the person can and does operate at varying levels of abstraction and particularity, not uncommonly at both levels at the same time, and that scientists and theorists, because they have a vested interest in the abstract and general, have a perennial vulnerability to minimize what is often at the heart of a personality.

Characteristically, the more dense the affect—that is, the more intense and enduring—the more particular it is. The most "memorable" moments in any person's life are those very particular, very intense, very enduring scenes which become unforgettable just because they are at once rare and distinctive, occurring but once and engulfing consciousness with dense affect. So it is one cannot forget one's first kiss, the birth of one's first child, the death of one's mother or father. None of these scenes can either be forgotten or confused with similar scenes.

COUNTERACTIVE NEGATIVE-AFFECT-EVOKED-ANGER RECASTING SCRIPTS

In negative-affect-evoked-anger recasting scripts, it is the intention to make the other experience both anger and the specific negative affect or affects which had evoked anger.

Thus if I am insulted-angry, I wish to humiliate the one who humiliated me. If I am terrorized-angry, I wish to terrorize the one who threatened me. If I am distressed-angry, I wish to frustrate or distress the one who frustrated or distressed me. If I am hurt and pained-angry, I wish to physically hurt the one who hurt me. If I am joyless-angry, I wish to rob the one who robbed me of my happiness. If I am excitementless-angry, I wish to impoverish the life of the one who took away my zest for living. It will not do if I insult someone who hurt me, or if he insulted me that I hurt him.

The other must be made to feel exactly what he imposed on me. In recasting, the angry one is the phenomenologist par excellence since what matters most to him is not that the other be punished per se but that his conscious suffering be identical with the consciousness he produced.

COUNTERACTIVE, ANGER-EVOKED SCENE RECASTING

In anger-evoked scene recasting the salience of the intended recasting shifts away from the affects evoked to those features of the scene which the offended one is most insistent the other be repaid. It is assumed that if this is achieved the other will necessarily experience the evoked accompanying affects as well.

Thus, if one has been angered by a punch in the jaw, one must punch the other in the jaw, assuming the other will experience pain and anger. If one has been terrorized and angered by the same kind of punch in the jaw, one may punch the other in the jaw, under the possibly mistaken assumption that the same response will also terrorize and anger the other.

If one has experienced anger at a scene sequence of excitement of the other turning to indifference, this scene sequence may be recast by exciting the other and then exhibiting conspicuous indifference, assuming that the other will also experience the affects evoked in the self, despite the probability that the other now will not.

If a child has been angered by being sent to his room, he may recast this in a delayed use of such insistence when confronted with anger evoked by his own children.

Lower-caste individuals who are excluded from intimacy and contact with the upper caste may vent their anger at those they consider weaker and more inferior by excluding and keeping them at a distance. In some cases there may be a social inheritance of such exclusion from shared space by parents driving their children out of the house when they anger their parents.

COUNTERACTIVE RECASTING-PLUS SCRIPTS

In recasring-plus scripts, the principle of reciprocity and particularity is preserved but enlarged on.

If the other angered me by his indifference, I elect to repay him in kind, plus a bonus, by intending never to speak to him again, so that his suffering will not only be identical with mine but also much magnified in intensity, frequency, and in duration.

If the other angered me by humiliating me, I will humiliate him, not simply as he humiliated me but again and again without limit so that he experiences angry humiliation to the end of his days.

If he made me angry by robbing me, I will take his money and will see to it that he is bankrupted and never again able to get a job and earn money and so angered endlessly.

If he terror-angered me, I will not only threaten him with terror in kind but will haunt him night and day so that he lives with dread of perpetual danger and terror which also angers him.

If the pain angered me, I will return that pain plus much more severe and enduring torture, which also angers him.

COUNTERACTIVE ANALOG-RECASTING SCRIPTS

In anger-driven analog-recasting scripts, a much magnified recasting script which originated and may or may not continue with a toxic angering other is further magnified by monitoring for and finding others and other scenes which evoke anger by appearing to be sufficiently similar to original sources to require similar responses.

This is not, strictly speaking, a type of projection, even though the individual may be relatively unaware of his own contribution to the construction of analogs. He is not projecting an imaginary attack but rather sees possibilities for repetition of toxic scenes that someone without his past experience might not have detected. Further, it need not be, in every case, entirely mistaken. Thus, an individual who has suffered violent physical attack as a child may well more accurately detect such possibilities in present high-crime areas, even though he may physically attack someone in such a scene who has only accidentally bumped into him. The sting of physical pain is quick to generate a toxic analog for which he has an equally toxic counterattack. Such an accident may have been really an accident, or it may have been a testing of his will or a distraction which masked an accomplice who robbed him as he was being bumped. Should he have a recasting-plus script and carry a gun for such occasions, he may in fact kill or injure the other, who may have had no hostile intention or who may have intended to rob him at gun point and might have used that gun if his victim resisted. The ambiguity of these scenes of muggings does not permit us today to identify with any certainty when violent self-defense is an inappropriate misreading of the potentialities of a scene for further violence.

A more common, but no less hostile type of analog recasting is the readily wounded critic whose nose is ever alerted to other critics, to whom he responds with dissmell and anger, intending to humiliate the other by commenting that he should clean up his own act before being so contemptuous of others.

However, it is also possible, and not infrequent, that all or most of an individual's anger is either avoided or expressed in scripts which diverge sharply in their intentions with respect to whether the toxicity of anger is located in the affect itself or in its sources.

COUNTERACTIVE POWER SCRIPTS VERSUS RECASTING SCRIPTS

In recasting scripts anger is directed toward counteraction by enforced reciprocity, to do unto the other what the other did to the self. In power scripts the anger-driven intention is not reciprocity of suffering inflicted but rather the exact opposite, to guarantee an inequality of control between the self and the other, either for the control of scarce positive resources for the self or for the control of unwanted scenes for the other, rather than for the self. Who does and can do what to whom is the question, rather than, as in recasting, getting exactly even, in which both suffer. In power scripts it is intended that the self suffer as little as possible and that if there is to be any suffering it will be the self who controls it for the advantage of the self against the other's attempted control. It is not defined by relative advantage per se but by the perceived ability to control advantage. Indeed, in some power scripts the advantages may be very secondary compared with the believed importance of control per se, particularly in the case that the issue of power is transformed from its instrumental role into a magnified end in itself.

COUNTERACTIVE ANGER-POWER SCRIPTS

In an anger-power script, power concerns the control of anger itself. The issue has become who may and can display anger at whom. In such scripts the intention is to achieve the power either to make the other angry, helplessly so, or to forbid the other the right to display anger, equally helplessly, and/or to achieve the power to prevent the other from either making the self angry or forbidding the self to display anger. Further, such scripts intend the self to be able to freely display anger very generally against any possible control, either by conscience or by reproof from others. Such a script may be directed against the power of an overly pious self as well as against the piety of others.

The origins of such a script are scenes in which the other—parent, sibling, or peers—defines the scene as anger-controlling, to the disadvantage of the self, in a hostile way. Thus, the other may taunt the self, "I got your goat," and equally forbid the self to respond with counteractive anger or control: "Don't you try anything on me." Insult is added to insult. The other defines himself as possessing a monopoly of the privilege of anger display. I can be angry at you, and you cannot be angry at me. If the parent or sibling or peer is successful in intimidation, no similar anger-power script may be possible. However, the script may be rewritten as possible and desirable against weaker adversaries and/or delayed until such conditions are encountered as an adult against weaker others, including one's own children.

COUNTERACTIVE AGGRESSION-POWER SCRIPTS

In aggression-power scripts, it is the power to aggress rather than simply to display anger which is intended. Now the question is who controls the power to inflict hurt on whom. In feudal Japan the samurai possessed such a monopoly of the power of the sword against commoners. When they lost this right in modern times, they felt sufficiently helpless and weakened in power that they resorted to judo and similar martial arts.

In contrast to anger-power scripts, the origin of these scripts is in scenes which are defined by parents as displaying a monopoly of power to inflict aggression on the helpless other without the possibility of counteraction by the other. If aggressive counteraction is severely punished, such an aggression-power script may never be generated, or may be delayed or displaced, or may give rise to wishful fantasies but without intention to execute and without plans.

COUNTERACTIVE ANGER- OR AGGRESSION-POWER-DEMONSTRATION SCRIPTS

In anger- or aggression-power-demonstration scripts the intention is less in the general actual power of the self over others than in the dramatic demonstration of that power. Such demonstration may be intended for the self, for the other, for a wider audience, or for all of these. Insofar as power is monopolistic, the less it must be demonstrated and contested the more monopolistic it is. It lends itself to verification most vividly if it can be demonstrated where it is least probable and least justifiable. In this respect it is like a crucial experiment in science in which a counterintuitive prediction in support of a theory is confirmed.

This is violence as theatre. It was used by Kennedy against Khrushchev in the Cuban missile crisis. The question was defined as "who would blink first?" Humiliation of the powerless one is critical in such anger- or aggression-power-demonstration scripts. You may not threaten me, but I may threaten you and in a way particularly humiliating to you by demonstrating that in a contest of wills it is you who must give way. We may place our missiles surrounding the perimeter of your country, but you may not do this to us. There can be no reciprocity in the sharing of power when demonstration is at issue.

When such a script is magnified, the individual or nation becomes an agent provocateur, seeking out opportunities for the demonstration of power. Since monopolistic power is always at risk and since such demonstrations are provocative, this type of script is self-validating, but it may in the end be self-defeating by provoking the same script in more and more adversaries, who may finally in alliance defeat the arrogant other. The arrogance of such power has within it the seeds of its own destruction.

COUNTERACTIVE INSTRUMENTAL-POWER SCRIPTS

In instrumental-power, anger-driven scripts it is not the power for anger display or aggression which is at issue. It is rather the angry intention to have the power to control one's access to a good scene or to minimize or escape a bad scene, either in general or in competition with an adversary who wishes to achieve the same scenes to his own advantage against the self. It is a contest for the control of turf, not for the power to show anger or to humiliate the other. Such contests need not in fact be anger-driven at all, but neither do they necessarily escape a heavy imprint of anger on otherwise purely instrumental power wishes. Anger will be manifested in instrumental power quests by overloading with a secondary intention to hurt the other. This may be seen in competitive games, when victory per se is not enough, even when a monopoly of power over competitors has been achieved. Thus, a football team which is angry as well as competitive aims not only to win but to inflict hurt on the other as well, by making the defeat as painful as possible, physically and psychologically. This is my turf, and don't you dare contest it, or you will be sorry. The intention is instrumental—to win the championship—but in a way which is hostile as well as powerful.

Such scripts originate in scenes in which a parent forces the child against his inclination to do whatever the parent wants done. This is an overdemanding rather than an overly intrusive, overly aggressive, or overly evaluative parent. He angrily, constantly, demands that the child serve his needs, in effect denying that the child is an end in himself. It is a variant of psychological slavery. Criticism of the child centers on any failure of the child to be useful to the parent. "What are you good for?" is the question. The other has been transformed into a commodity as beasts of burden have been used. Exploitative power need not be angry so long as exploitation is served, but anger is quick to be mobilized in the face of any diminution in compliance or usefulness or competitive self-assertion.

There are psychological plantations at some distance from those of classical slavery. They are found in industry, in nursing homes, in the military, in the political sphere, and even in the groves of academe, when others are used to serve one's own purposes, with anger in varying degrees of display for violations of usefulness or against competitive self-assertion—when, for example, a research assistant publishes a reinterpretation of an experiment by his mentor to his own advantage.

COUNTERACTIVE POWER-AS-END-IN-SELF SCRIPTS

In anger-driven power as an end in itself, the script intends to force total compliance for power as an end in itself rather than as instrumental. Any means may be transformed into an end in itself. One may work for money because it is useful for many purposes or become a miser who counts his money as though it were valuable in and of itself. Such transformations are ordinarily produced by dramatic scarcity. For many children of the Great Depression both money and jobs, the means to money, became transformed into ends in themselves. In the present case it is a more general power which has been so transformed. This power will command money as well as much which money cannot command. Power as an end in itself becomes in the extreme case godlike in intent. It is generated either out of a sense of deep powerlessness or out of overweening, overprivileged overindulgence. Both are angry but in the former case also terrified and humiliated, as in paranoid delusions of both threat and omnipotence. In the latter case power is compounded of anger and disgust or dissmell. How dare you disobey, or disappoint me, or oppose me is the angry scripted response.

The origin of such scripts is either the parent as tyrant, who humiliates and terrifies as he angers, or the parent who overindulges the child and gives in to the occasional tantrum by the child, who has long exercised his overprivileged position and has no intention of ever being thwarted by the parent.

Such an overprivileged aristocratic power script may be either acted out or played out covertly, even as he acts out the role of the intimidated one. Further, such scripts are sometimes transformed from wishes or fantasies into overt behavior in adults who are the recipients of unusual praise and respect, whether in political office, in the arts, in the economic domain, in the military, in athletic competition, or in science. Such reward has not infrequently destroyed political and other leaders who have come to believe they possess divine privileges and attempt to act out power as an end in itself; others are conceived to exist primarily to mirror and reflect their glory. When the other fails to pay sufficient tribute, the self in this script responds, in one case, with disgusted outrage; in the other, with terror and shame at the threat of powerlessness now experienced.

Such a script is not limited to lapses in power from the behavior of others. It also includes any sign of loss of power in the self, from any invidious comparison of the present self with a previous self. A present self which is less attractive, strong, wealthy, extroverted or introverted, competent, healthy, affectful, sexy, ambitious, or curious may generate either a sense of terrifying humiliating powerlessness or of powerless outraged disgust, or both. It may radically complicate childhood, in sibling rivalry; old age, in declining vigor; and midlife, in the contraction of possible horizons.

When a nation enjoying excessive imperial privileges elects such a script, it may for some time be self-fulfilling and successful in the attempt at world dominion. But it also ordinarily succeeds in overextending the boundaries it must govern requiring an evergreater diversion of resources to the military, which undermines the center in the attempt to control the periphery.

Similar disasters often befall young industries which attempt too rapid expansion of their market shares and so bankrupt their resources.

It is also a commonplace of military strategy traps, especially in the invasion of very large countries, as both Napoleon and Hitler learned in Russia. The limits of power exceed the hunger for power, which becomes an end in itself.

Chapter 39

Antitoxic, Anger-Driven Destructive Scripts

DESTRUCTIVE SCRIPTS VERSUS COUNTERACTIVE SCRIPTS

We have just examined some of the more extreme scripting of counteraction through revenge, which inflicts on the other what the other inflicted on the self, as well as the added assaults which go beyond reciprocity in their intention to give satisfaction to anger which has been greatly magnified and so calls for punishment going beyond the immediate crime.

Destructive scripts cross such boundaries. It is their intent to inflict the most enduring and most severe injury, in the destruction of the other and/or his honor, his property, his works, his family, his friends, his religion, his political power, his freedom, his place, his home, or his memory. By destruction I mean the destruction of life but also the destruction of anything of great value to the other, or so believed by the destroyer.

What is targeted for destruction is interdependent with why one intends to destroy. If it is instrumental to preserving my own life against the threat by another, it might require the life imprisonment of the other or his death. If it is in the interest of my political career, it might require the destruction of his honor or his perceived moral integrity or his reputed competence. If I were a Greek a few thousand years ago, I might have had to kill a valiant warrior in battle if I wished not to be forgotten after I had died. In all of these cases anger as such may vary radically in its degree of magnification, but whether it is out of fear, ambition, or fame, anger is also there.

If what one must destroy depends on why one must destroy, why must one destroy or believe one must destroy? The belief in the necessity or desirability of destruction is itself complex and various. It may be deemed undesirable but necessary, for example, to protect society from further murders by imposing life imprisonment or execution. It may be deemed desirable but not necessary, for example, to impeach or to imprison a political leader and remove him from political life for serious violation of his office in order to protect the integrity of the office. It may be deemed necessary because of the quantity of his offenses, ranging from corruption to torture, imprisonment, and the execution of many innocent people. It may be deemed necessary because of the terrible quality of his one offense, for example, that he took delight in hacking to death a defenseless child or an aged, venerated person. Further, theories and beliefs, cultural or idiosyncratic, play critical roles in the scripting of destruction both necessary and desirable. These range from beliefs in the dangers of black magic, the evil eye, Satan, witchcraft, heaven through martyrdom, blood-sucking vampires, possession, Jews, Communists, atheists, revolutionaries, and fundamentalists of all kinds. Indeed, in the eyes of theory-driven adversaries, there are very few demonic forces exempt from either the desirability or the necessity for destruction in the name of salvation in this or the world beyond. When such theories are not culturally shared, they are labeled paranoid. When they are shared only by segments of a society, they are labeled as extremist. But when they are culturally shared, they constitute a variety of holy wars against the unholy, normally located outside the self-righteous destructive society.

Although fear and anger and theories which support destruction are interdependent and collusive, yet they are also somewhat independent. To what extent it may be possible to extirpate destructive theory and ideology and so attenuate the magnification of the anger and other negative affect which support destructive scripts we cannot know until the experiment has been completed. The experiment cannot be an altogether crucial one because theory and ideology is but one source, albeit a major one, in the provocation of destructive scripts. So long as there remains competition for scarce resources, either real or so believed (e.g., for land, water, fame, or power), there will remain the possibility of the generation of destructive scripts independent of ideology. So long as there remain real or believed hurts and injuries which human beings inflict on each other, through intent, negligence, or accident, scripted counterdestruction will remain a possibility.

If rage is a universal, biologically endowed, ever-present possibility, is aggression an equally probable possibility? If aggression is so, are death and destruction also equally possible or probable? In the heart and mind of anyone who has experienced dense outrage is a potential murderer. It is not an impulse inherently foreign to the human being, even though it is in no way a necessary consequence of the affect mechanism itself. We are born potentially angry to any degree of magnification, from zero to perpetual, as we are also born potential murderers and killers, from zero to a way of life labeled warrior or military or criminal. The connection between the innate potential for anger and the potential for scripting that anger to destruction or to murder is, however, not innate but learned, though that learning itself too frequently finds ready students. Rationalizations for destruction are as numerous as they are pious. Jehovah was the supreme warrior, bestowing blessings and curses in equal measure: blessings for loyalty and for good warfare, curses for disloyalty by his chosen people.

Let us examine briefly what is required for antitoxic rage to be transformed into destructive rage. Since there are a variety of antitoxic scripts and a variety of destructive scripts, some conditions necessary or sufficient for one kind of destructive script formation may vary somewhat from another type of transformation from avoidance or from counteraction to destruction. Thus, what turns romantic jealous hate into murder is not identical with what transforms an aggressive, expansive power script into a destructive power script which requires the death of those who oppose the quest for power.

The question we raise here is a special case of the more general one of the nature of magnification. As we have noted before, there is no one royal road to magnification or to its transformation, though there are many roads. Consider that there are three major classes of determinants of magnification and of its changes, either in magnitude or in direction. First is the magnitude and stability of the support networks which magnify any script. Second is the magnitude and stability of the support networks which magnify inhibition of alternative scripts. Third is the magnitude and stability of the support networks which magnify alternative scripts. What is for any script, what is against changing it, and what alternatives are there for changing it? Any change of any script is a complex resultant of these three classes of determinants. One would kill, then, if everything were for it, nothing against it, and no alternatives appeared as good.

If we ask, then, what would prompt an angry rejected lover to become a killing lover, or what would prompt an ambitious, angry, power-hungry political leader to become a killing political leader, we would have to consider changes in either how strong the need is for the beloved or for power in the first place and how stable an equilibrium there is in the face of competitive alternatives and in the face of the erosion of inhibitions against destructive alternatives. Because any script is a system of sets of rules embedded in a system of other scripts, each of which is variously interdependent or dependent or independent, it is rarely possible to specify the consequences of changing any single determinant of a script independent of the remainder of the system within that script and between that script and other scripts. Thus, if the magnitude of magnification of inhibitory rules about murder is very great, the rejected lover or the defeated political leader would be restricted in the alternative directions open to him no matter how great an increase in rage and other negative affect had occurred, or no matter how ineffective his present angry script (e.g., of counteraction) may have proved. The beloved may not have been moved at all by his angry outbursts or by his attempted counteractive rejection of the other. The defeated political leader's angry outbursts may have evoked only derision or indifference, but assassination may not be a possible option either because of his personal inhibitions against destruction or because of a very strong political tradition against such violence as a response to defeat.

Neither the demonstrated ineffectiveness of an existing antitoxic anger script, nor increasing rage and provocation to violence, nor a weakening of inhibitions against extreme violence either singly or together would necessarily transform an aggressive script into a destructive script. In part this is because every society recognizes the toxicity of anger and of violence and very early on begins to subject it to systematic sanctions to ensure both its inhibition and its magnification and expression for ends deemed socially desirable. But although the culture for violence varies widely, there are very few societies or groups which sanction entirely unregulated and uninhibited violence. The distinctions between friends and enemies may sometimes become fuzzy or attenuated, but the loss of such distinctions can rarely be tolerated for long. But extreme violence is neither rare nor universal and endless. It tends to be a self-limiting phenomenon, both for the individual and for society.

The theoretical task is to specify both the direction and magnitude of changes and their conjoint patterning, which together generate the fateful transition from anger to aggression to destruction. Because there are, in principle, an indefinitely large number of such possible transformations, we will here limit ourself to a sample of ideal types of such transformation. Just as physics has at times found it profitable to define empirical phenomena as deviations from idealized counterparts (e.g., degree of inertia as deviation from a frictionless medium), so I propose to illuminate the transformation of empirical anger aggression scripts into anger-destructive scripts by an idealized swamping of the variance.

One set of conditions favoring destructive-anger scripts would be a set of scenes (either in the home or at large, or both) in which dense anger was sufficiently frequently provoked to justify destructive violence as an appropriate response, in which there were unusually weak inhibitions against violence, both personal and/or social (as in honor societies), and in which destructive violence appeared to be the most effective means of seeking redress against all other alternatives. Everything favors it against alternatives; nothing inhibits it.

Another set of conditions favoring anger-destructive script formation is one which bifurcates scenes into sharply opposed very positive and very negative ones in an invidious comparison. Violence may then be justified as the only possible way of decontaminating the bad scene and recovering or attaining the good scene. In such a script there is not generalized weak inhibition against violence, nor are other alternatives rejected in general. It is believed that once the source of evil has been eliminated, life will either return to normal, or become normal for the first time. Once the tyrant has been killed, the body politic will be normal. The quantity of suffering and rage is invidiously contrasted and magnified by the prospect of liberation and salvation, thereby diminishing both perceived alternative and their possible effectiveness.

We have thus far delineated chronic scripts of destruction. But some destructive scripts are generated under more acute provocation. We will consider two such cases. In one the major determinant is an acute increase in provocation. In the other there is a regressive dedifferentiation of anger control.

Some children who have been abused for many years and who have become accustomed to living with backed-up anger, lest they be further beaten, will, on occasion, kill their persecutors. This can occur for a very small increment of abuse which is responded to by a quantum leap in rage and action, seemingly disproportionate to every similar scene suffered over many years. I believe that such quantum transformations occur whenever the scene is coassembled with the past and with the future so as to constitute grounds for radical review. It is similar in its essential dynamic to mourning or to any deep sudden enchantment or disenchantment. Whenever the individual believes something has changed radically and significantly he is driven to generate review scripts. The moment one learns of the death of a beloved other, one is usually propelled into an in-depth review of the changes which one must now confront as past scenes and future scenes are coassembled and reevaluated from the present, now altered perspective. This is the grief work, I suggest there is also rage work which may be generated equally quickly whenever, and for whatever reason an already chronically enraging situation is perceived to have radically changed.

However, in this case the other has not died but is suddenly believed worthy to be killed. The self is not necessarily either more angry or less inhibited (though one may be both). I am suggesting that it is sufficient to suddenly see someone in an entirely new way to produce a new script. Thus, a very small increment in perceived positive attribute may generate the beginning of a romantic love, a romantic hate, or destruction. The formula in all these instances is "I did not realize that." "That" may be any attribute or any call to action. It is, of course, not a transformation which can occur without much preparatory script work. It is in this respect similar to any scientific discovery which appears suddenly after years of wondering about the nature of a domain.

Finally, we consider a different type of acute anger destruction script which depends not as much on radical reorganization of the scene but upon dedifferentiation of overcontrolled rage. If an individual's anger has been punitively socialized in such a way that his anger has been first overstimulated and then driven underground, he has thereby been robbed of the necessary skill to feel or to express or to act on modulated, graded anger. He learns a type of anger- and aggression-avoidance script as a defense against his now dangerously magnified anger. He has been taught to be not angry and not aggressive lest he kill. Any set of circumstances which attenuates that inhibition leaves him vulnerable to murderous rage. This may occur under the influence of any drug, extreme fatigue, extreme pain, or provocation which exceeds his previous experience in successfully absorbing and denying provocation. Such an individual may be quite as surprised by his sudden destructiveness as any of those who knew him to be an unusually gentle person.

Let us now examine further these and other types of anger destructive scripts.

DESTRUCTIVE RECASTING SCRIPTS

Destructive recasting scripts intend to repay destruction by the other with reciprocal destruction. These differ from counteractive recasting scripts that intend reciprocity against the offender, in which the offense is less serious. In destructive recasting, as in the family feud, one death must be paid for by another, which in turn must be repaid, endlessly, on and on. This differs from a remedial script in response to a senseless death (e.g., by a drunk driver or by a mugger with a handgun) in which a bereaved parent may commit himself to organize others in a program of education and political action to prevent the repetition of such destruction in the future.

Destructive recasting scripts were for a long time, and in many parts of the world continue to be, serious impediments to political democracy. Elias and Dunning have shown that the eighteenth century in England was a period of pacification and domestication of the landed classes following the end of civil strife and dissensions. The threat of civil war had subsided, though memories of it lingered and many feared its recurrence. But they had also become tired of the violence. As we have seen before in the case of China, fear of and disgust with severe violence is sometimes a precondition of a period of unusual pacification and stability.

In England the administration and utilization of the monopoly of physical force and taxation did not fall to any one group, as it had in other countries. In France it was the king and court which inherited such power. In England power was distributed, following the civil war, among several competing ruling groups. No one group could successfully dominate all other groups. They agreed on a set of rules according to which they could take turns in exerting governmental power. There were at first serious clashes, till the middle of the eighteenth century. Gradually, according to Elias and Dunning, "the fear that one of the contending groups and its followers would physically injure or annihilate the others receded." They came to agree not to use violence for governmental power but to compete by words, votes, and money, and this began to hold. This in part occurred because no one, including the king, had unrestricted control of a standing army. There lingered the fear that whoever held governmental power, would stop playing by the rules and use the power of the government to destroy their opponents. How could one be sure that if the group in power lost the next election they would surrender the very attractive resources of physical power and the power of taxation and permit the victors to take them over? Elias and Dunning believe that it was just this successful pacification among previously destructive political groups which permitted the development of representative government and at the same time transformed the more violent pastimes of the landed classes into the more rule-governed games we have labeled "sport" in modern times.

Whenever, as is still the case in many countries, military power can either seize governmental power or be used by a political party to consolidate its power, representative democratic government cannot be consolidated, or if consolidated be anything but fragile and at risk. More subtly, whenever industry, the military, and the government share power collusively, representative government is also at risk. The threat of destructive recasting scripts in the latter case is the rationale for the collusive draining of major resources into preparation for wars of annihilation, depicted as destructive recasting. We must kill them before they kill us, which we know they intend to do, since they have already done it to others with whom we are allied. In such scripts, destructive recasting is often conjoined with a zero sum rationale in which it becomes a choice between who will live and who will die, without any alternatives as possibilities.

DESTRUCTIVE ZERO SUM SCRIPTS

In the antitoxic, anger-driven, destructive zero sum scripts, it is believed that the self and the adversary, or the family and its adversary, or the nation and its adversary, or the religion and its adversary cannot in fact coexist. The only alternatives open concern who will live and who will not. One must destroy or be destroyed.

Inasmuch as the history of civilizations testifies to the ubiquity and continuity of lethal violence, in which many millions of human beings have in fact been destroyed as well as imprisoned, tortured, exiled, robbed, degraded, or excluded, such scripts cannot be regarded as exceptional in any way. The socialized, acculturated civilized human being is clearly the most destructive animal on earth, as well as the most constructive. But in the zero sum script it is often the believed impossibility as well as intolerability of coexistence of rival constructions which compels the most severe destruction. Thus, despite the obvious fact that communism is a variant of capitalism, and despite the fact that mixed forms of private and state capitalism do in fact coexist, the shared scripts of the adversaries call for mutual destruction of the alternative society and its mode of economic organization.

Similarly, despite the fact that Protestantism is a variant of Christianity, Protestantism and Catholicism waged a relentless war for centuries, aimed at the destruction of the adversarial form of the same religion.

Because the human animal is so deeply ideological an animal, the zero sum script is frequently not only an expression of a belief in the impossibility of coexistence of adversaries but in addition a conviction of the undesirability and intolerability of the existence of the adversary. We cannot coexist with them, and further we should not, by all that is sacred. It is commonly magnified not only by disgust and by piety but also by fear as well as by rage, the most volatile and explosive mixture to which human beings and their societies are vulnerable.

This is not to minimize the severity of minimally ideological, lethal, adversarial conflict for truly scarce commodities. An exiled people who return to their promised land may displace and exile or subordinate those who have occupied the land for centuries. Whose land is it? Does Israel still belong and should it belong to the Jews? Does the United States still belong and should it belong to the American Indians? What violent conquest can do once can be endlessly repeated and reversed when it is, like land or water, a scarce commodity which is contested. As worldwide interdependence increases such contests will increase within and between nations. Does and should California possess the water which it diverts from distant states or which southern California diverts from northern California? Should the United States be permitted to send acid rain to its northern neighbor, Canada? Should Russia be permitted to pollute the atmosphere by accidents of its nuclear energy generators? Should countries which profit from the production and sale of addictive drugs, such as cocaine, be permitted to flood world markets? The scarcity of wanted commodities and the plenitude of unwanted commodities will, as the world becomes more and more interdependent, prompt the generation of increasingly anger-driven, destructive zero sum scripts when final, absolute solutions are sought in the face of mutual intransigence.

Returning to zero sum scripts generated by individuals, their dynamic may be continuous with centuries-old struggles such as that between the Irish and the English, or in feuds between families, or between Jews and Christians, Moslems and Christians, Hindus and Moslems, blacks and whites, or Turks and Armenians.

A more idiosyncratic zero sum destructive script may arise out of child abuse by a brutal parent, who, by inflicting physical pain again and again, magnifies anger in the child, sufficient to generate a zero sum script in which the child intends to destroy the other. This may begin with the wish to counteract and recast the beating as the child is being beaten. It may subside when the beating is over, but it becomes reactivated again and again as the physical abuse is repeated. But later the anger may cumulate via rehearsal between such scenes, and the wish may be transformed into more vivid images and fantasies of intending to attack the parent rather than simply wishing to do so. Such fantasies may begin as reactive scenes, in which the child imagines the parent's attack as so punishing as to warrant a justified counterattack in kind. But the gap between the child's power and that of the parent, when next he is beaten, may well evoke more fear than anger, just because he had considered counterattacking the other. The longer such scenes are imposed with no possible escape or avoidance, the more likely it is that the fantasy of intentional counterattack will be transformed into a plan and not only into a plan to counterattack but a plan to destroy the enemy. This might be prompted by the conviction that a counterattack would be followed by even more brutal attack from the other so that it would be safer, as well as more effective, to rid himself of the enemy once and for all. Such a plan would in all probability be opportunistic in nature rather than highly organized because of the unequal power between the adversaries. So he would bide his time, waiting patiently for the opportune moment.

The irony of such a script is that the time he must wait is very long, sometimes only appearing many years later when he is an angry father confronting his own son. But some abused children are engulfed, on occasion, by such overwhelming rage that they seize upon any available lethal weapon, such as a hammer or kitchen knife, and kill. In some cases this appears to have been primarily governed by a previously planned revenge, whereas in other cases it appears to be primarily a response to the density of rage which exceeds tolerability and pain of previous experience, and in still other cases it was scripted as a response should the other exceed certain limits on the painfulness of attack or certain limits on the frequency of such attacks. Some children appear to decide on a quantum of abuse they can or will tolerate, in terms of either frequency or force of attack.

The paradox of the unequal power of the brutalized child versus the parent is that it is the perceived danger of counterattack against the aggressive parent that is believed will surely be followed by even more severe retaliation that pushes some victims into the necessity of destroying the other and then of intending it, either whenever the opportunity makes it possible or with more specific plans if the child is less intimidated. This is a type of zero sum script in the sense that although his adversary does not so define it, the child eventually does so define it. The child plans eventually to kill or be killed, not because he and the other so regard the scene but because he comes to regard the scene as intolerable, leaving only the option of one survivor for a life that can be tolerated. The child may, in fact, have other alternatives, such as escape, but may be too intimidated to think it possible.

Even in cases when the child had no intention, nor any plan, to murder but does murder, apparently impulsively, under the press of extreme provocation and great rage, it is my belief that in those brief moments a zero sum destructive script is in fact generated and prompts the destruction. It must be remembered that script formation occurs primarily when sets of scenes of the past and possible future scenes are coassembled in the present, and the responses that are scripted are to that set but primarily future oriented. Just as a mourning script may be started the moment one learns of the death of the beloved, so a destructive script may be generated the moment one learns of the intolerability of the existence of the hated one if there has already been a cumulation of past toxic scenes with that other.

DESTRUCTIVE BOUNDED ZERO SUM SCRIPTS

In the bounded zero sum scripts, the adversary and the self are locked into mutually destructive intentions by one or the other, administering or suffering severe injury in a contest in which only one party can win. This is a bounded zero sum script insofar as the severity of the violations and of the inflicted injuries stop short of death. The other is permitted some right to exist so long as he has suffered severe defeat and injury in the scenes of greatest relevant conflict.

DESTRUCTIVE ROMANTIC-HATE SCRIPTS

Romantic-hate destructive scripts are of two kinds, pure and derivative, reactive. In the derivative, reactive, destructive romantic-hate script, romantic love turns to hate when the other appears to turn from love to indifference, rejection, or hate. The most dramatic such scripting is in the crime of passion, when the unfaithful beloved is murdered by the outraged betrayed lover. This is not necessarily a simple recasting since the unfaithful one may continue to avow love for the betrayed lover. The variety of components of such a script range from enraged revenge through wounded pride, intolerable aloneness, and disenchantment to the wish to stop the intolerable sight of the beloved in the arms of a rival and so to deny it and be freed from the consciousness, memory, and anticipation of it. Whatever other affects and wishes are coassembled in such a script, it is clear that the hate is no less romantic than the romantic love which inspired its transformation.

The second type of such a script is pure romantic hate which is also destructive. Just as romantic love need not turn into romantic hate, so romantic hate need not be reactive to romantic love. However, there can also be pure romantic hate which is not necessarily destructive, as we have already seen. The difference between counteractive romantic hate and destructive romantic hate lies in a complex of greater quantity or quality of hate such that counteraction against the much-hated other is insufficient, or because failed counteraction adds to that quantity, or because of added outrages from the hated other, or because of a difference in conscience or the believed sanctity of life which forbids murder no matter what the provocation in the case of counteractive romantic hate and a diminished sense of the sanctity of human life in the case of destructive romantic hate. Indeed, some who script destructive romantic hate will do so on the basis of much lesser quantities of provocation of hate than those who script a counteractive romantic hate. As we have noted before, the transformation of a script into a destructive script will depend on the exact quantities and patterning of interaction effects between component rules. In a macho society in which the beloved is more often an extension of the male's honor, killing of the unfaithful lover or lovers requires much less provocation, much less justification, and many fewer alternatives, as well as a requirement that diminished honor be reclaimed through destruction.

The most critical feature of romantic hate, destructive or otherwise, is the conjunction of massing of hated characteristics converging on one individual who is uniquely hateable and, in the destructive script, uniquely necessary to be destroyed, in contrast to the reciprocity of recasting or the opposition of zero sum scripts.

DESTRUCTIVE POWER SCRIPTS

The destructive power script which is anger-driven is instrumental to the achievement, maintenance, or expansion of power. The destructive power script need not be driven by anger at all. One may kill to aggrandize one's power, or the power of one's class, religion, or nation, without anger. But it is not uncommon for the adversary whose power is contested to be angered in resistance and to evoke and to escalate anger even if the original quest for power was not an angry one. A power struggle is rarely anger-free at the end, no matter its beginning.

In comparison with a zero-sum destructive script this one aims to eliminate any and every barrier whenever and wherever found. The destruction of one rival is not presumed to rid the field of future struggles, as in the zero sum script which divides the spoils between the self and the other in a decisive contest.

In comparison with a destructive romantic-hate script, this script does not focus on one hated object since the power-threatening other is seen as only one-dimensional rather than wicked in all ways. It tends for the same reason to be more realistic in its estimates than does the romantic-hate destructive script.

In comparison with the destructive recasting script, the other may have inflicted no damage which evokes the need for reciprocal damage. Indeed, the other may not even know his power is coveted and at risk until he is under attack.

In comparison with invidious destructive scripts, power-destructive scripts are concerned with the instrumental rather than with aesthetic ends in themselves and rather than with moral values. In invidious destructive scripts the other is envied for his good and admirable attributes, abilities, skills, or possessions. One would wish even to be that other. In the power-destructive script such issues are irrelevant to the seizure of the power the other commands.

Although the power script is essentially instrumental in nature, as opposed to aesthetic or moral or truth values, it may under certain conditions also be transformed into an end in itself by magnification. This transformation does not transform it into a moral, aesthetic, or truth value as such, but it does increase its centrality versus all other competing values. In such a case it remains no longer merely instrumental. Power becomes so magnified, as money does for a miser, whenever it is structured as a one-many means for all other ends, when it has been radically threatened and then redefined as more important than any and all of the ends to which it is the one indispensable means. Whenever power is so transformed, the probability of ruthless destructiveness is also enhanced in the defense of power itself, now defined as vital rather than instrumental.

DESTRUCTIVE WILLPOWER SCRIPTS

In the anger-driven, destructive willpower script, it is not power as instrumental nor power as an end in itself which is at issue. What is at issue is whose "will" will prevail when there is a confrontation and contest between the self and another or others. Such a will is a hypothetical entity whose existence and sanctity often begins in a struggle between parent and child in which the parent asserts the primacy of his own will and the intention to break the will of the willful child. If such a child asks why he must surrender to the will of the parent, he is told that he must do so because the parent says so, commands it, and will punish the child for disobedience. At issue here is not any instrumental power or any macho conception of honor, but rather the scene is defined as sheer willpower of one will against another will. Such a will does not require further justification or rationalization. It is will as an end in itself. The ability to hurt or destroy the other is but one of many ways in which such will may be tested and exhibited.

It is just such a conception of the self's strength which has, for centuries, made the value of life appear to be extraordinarily cheap. Human beings have killed each other over such very trivial confrontations as accidentally bumping into each other, who has the right of way on the sidewalk, on the highway, or for a parking space for horse or automobile. It is the felt outrage at the challenge itself against the sovereignty of one's own will which is at stake in such overblown confrontations. The strength of the jeopardized will is in no way limited to destructive personal encounters. Athletes of strong wills will hold their fingers to a flame to reassure themselves that their will is sufficiently vigorous to tolerate the experience of pain. Compared with running athletes who wish to reassure themselves about the vigor of their bodies, here an injury to the body becomes a sign of the health of the will.

DESTRUCTIVE HONOR SCRIPTS

As we have noted before, honor and its defense involve a complex code which may include destructive duels and other confrontations but is not so restricted, nor does it necessarily include destruction either as a primary aim or means of defense. However, in honor societies the surrender of the right to avenge honor by killing and the granting of a monopoly on the use of violence to the centralized government came slowly and reluctantly. Long after duels of honor had been declared illegal they continued, to preserve the identity of the aristocracy against the lower orders.

Many societies have placed supreme values above the value of life per se and have used the willingness to sacrifice life as a critical test of commitment to such values. Honor societies are in no way exceptional in using the willingness to sacrifice one's life as a test of one's commitment to a central value. Even in the capitalist society, dedicated as it is, presumably, to profit, there arose in response to the threat of communism, the slogan "better dead than Red."

The readiness to correct insubordination and the dishonor of the threat to rituals of deference by killing arises, I believe, from its origin in warrior classes. A warrior who lives by the sword must be ever ready to kill or be killed. That readiness is not only a major component of his honor and status but also a guarantee that he will not need so often to defend that honor. In this it is similar to the reputation of a bank or a currency that it will be redeemed whenever requested. To the extent that there is a question about such readiness, there is certain to be a test of it and thereby often a self-fulfilling prophecy. Honor, like the value of currency, is a credit phenomenon, which is threatened by the very phenomenon of being threatened. If a soldier refuses to salute his superior officer, he has, by definition, dishonored not only that officer but the entire institution and so must be dealt with by severe sanctions. Because honor is defined, among other things, as commanding deference, any failure to so command has the property of a crucial experiment, in which one disconfirmation is sufficient to disconfirm the entire network of theoretical assumptions.

DESTRUCTIVE-PURIFICATION SCRIPTS

The destructive-purification script is based upon a conjunction of disgust or dissmell and anger, with or without fear. In extreme nausea the good food turned bad is vomited. In extreme dissmell the totally bad other is distanced. In destructive purification the polluting other must be dealt with more harshly and killed in the interests of purification and of serving notice against any others who might come too close and pollute, as in the lynching of blacks in the American south. In Hitler's Germany, Jews were exterminated to rid the society of its blood polluted through intermarriage of Germans and Jews. Although scripts of honor and pollution may be conjoined by virtue of their modularity, there remain important differences between them. Honor is defined by the conjunction of attributes and behaviors by the self which are supported and confirmed by the deferential behaviors of others toward the honorable one. One must act honorably and be responded to as though one were honorable in one case. In pollution, behavior is secondary to the distance between the pure self and the polluting other. So long as the polluting other keeps his distance, the purity of the self is not threatened. The remote bad smell cannot pollute. The remote bad taste cannot pollute by disgust. This is why sexuality or intermarriage become peculiarly threatening when either occurs with one of a lower caste or a lower race, or even of a lower class in some cases. The idea of pollution is a vivid bodily one, even when it is generalized, as it has been to the environment, as Mother Earth. The polluter is readily imagined to have raped the pure Mother Earth, who is then defiled.

The pollution based on dissmell evokes unambivalent rage inasmuch as the presence of the pollution threatens the purity of the self. The pollution based on disgust, however, is much more ambivalent, since such a pollution emanates from another who was believed pure, with whom one became intimate but who ultimately left a bad taste as an aftermath. The rage is as much at the self, for having been trusting, naive, then disappointed and betrayed, as at the disgusting other. The destruction of such a one might be even more vengeful but also more bitter—more bitter because once so sweet. Nor is such destruction always entirely extropunitive. Painters who have struggled long and hard to complete a cherished painting, and who finally become disgusted with their accomplishment have on occasion slashed their painting in a rage of revulsion at their failure, at attempted beauty turned ugly. Indeed, depressions which end in suicide are often compounded of just such disgusted rage, literally turned against the self—in protest, in varying ratios of disgust and rage—at the other, at the dyad, at the self, or at a good world turned very disgusting, disgusting and angering enough to be destroyed.

DESTRUCTIVE INVIDIOUS-COMPARISON SCRIPTS

Destructive invidious-comparison scripts are generated by differences between the self (and its allies) and others, which are experienced as sufficiently intolerable to necessitate destroying or killing the envied other.

The classic cases of such scripts occur in class warfare, when the privileges of a ruling class are both resented and envied sufficiently to generate revolutionary destruction, and when such a besieged ruling class resents such challenges sufficiently to generate counterrevolutionary destruction. Although such struggles often also involve struggles for power, invidious-comparison destruction need not necessarily concern power as such if it is the envy of privilege or the loss of privilege which is felt as outrageous. Such invidious comparison may enrage in part because it is deemed immoral for there to be such contrasts in wealth and poverty by the lower classes and deemed equally immoral by the upper classes that they should be robbed of their inheritance or of what they believe they deserved or earned by virtue of either their nobility or military prowess. Power supports privileged inequality but is not thereby identical with it. Vested interests typically accumulate the true, the good, and the beautiful to their possession and especially to their possessors, producing a deep piety both for and against such inequalities of status in both upper and lower castes and classes, which erupt from time to time in bloody rebellion and revolution and counterrevolution.

FANTASIED-DESTRUCTION, COUNTERACTION, OR EXPRESSION SCRIPTS

Whenever an individual or a group or a nation has suffered an intolerable quantity of damage, hurt, or suffering but is too intimidated either to express anger, or counteract it or to destroy the enemy and too intransigent in anger to relinquish or to avoid it, then there may be scripted fantasies of either destroying the enemy or of counterachng the enemy or of expressing anger toward him, or all of these. Such scripts include wishes and fantasies but not plans. One would enjoy destroying the other, would wish it, hope for it, imagine it, but without any intention of doing it and without any plan to do so. What one intends is to imagine the possibility and to never relinquish it. Such anticipations are magnified not only by the seriousness of the hurt inflicted but especially by any felt inability to retaliate. It is then that such fantasy is likely to be most severe since felt helpless rage adds deep insult to injury. To be both injured directly and too weak to retaliate is to overload images of wished-for retaliation in the future with backed-up rage, which is as punishing as the original crime upon the self and further magnifies the demand for vengeance. In some such cases the other is, in fact, murdered, followed by suicide. Such murders are impulsive, surprising, and engulfing, in contrast to the cooler planned murders of the planned anticipated-destruction scripts in which one waits for a favorable moment in which to translate the wish into action.

Such fantasy scripts are entirely ego-syntonic and may occasion covert celebration of any sign of damage to the hated other and overt celebration should the other die or be defeated. They are not avoidant of consciousness or of affect expression or even of affect communication to trusted others. They avoid only communication to the enemy, and counteraction and destruction, usually out of prudential fear.

ANTITOXIC ANGER IN PLANNED ANTICIPATED-DESTRUCTION SCRIPT

Whenever an individual or a group or a nation has suffered an intolerable quantity of damage, hurt, or suffering, there may be scripted a plan of destroying or very seriously limiting the power of the other to continue such damage or to ever repeat it. This is also inevitably present in the recasting destructive feud, as we have noted, whether individual or familial or societal. These are not helpless rages. The principled revolutionary, the principled resistor to the invader or to the oppressive regime, may be possessed by an effective hot rage, which in the end translates the anticipated destruction of the enemy into a deserved retribution and a new beginning.

Anticipated-destruction scripts concern continuing suffering which is intolerable, in contrast to anticipated counteractive scripts which concern continuing but intermittent and tolerable adversarial relationships which are also in varying degrees cooperative, as in competitive sports or work or family relationships. In contrast to both of these, anticipated-anger-expression scripts typically concern intermittent enmities toward absent, somewhat distant enemies when unfinished and recruited anger cannot be directly and immediately expressed but may be expressed in imagery as well as in later face-to-face confrontation.

DESTRUCTIVE-ANGER SCRIPTS

In destructive-anger scripts, the individual intends, whenever enraged, to destroy the offending other whoever he might be. Such intention may also evoke intense conflicting or inhibitory affect, such as terror, disgust, shame, or guilt, either concurrent with, preceding, or following the rage-driven wish and/or intention to kill, but this script nonetheless disregards such complications.

This script should be distinguished from the crime of passion in which the justification is presumed to arise from the conjunction of the extremity of the provocation and the extremity of the uncontrollable rage. It is because the betrayed lover is presumed to be justified in his rage that he is also presumed to be both impulsively driven and justified in killing. In destructive-anger scripts there is a related but somewhat different psychologic. In this case there is no scripting of the provocation of anger, only a scripting of the predetermined response to rage, once and whenever and for whatever reason it has been provoked. Indeed, it is quite generally understood that the provocation of intense anger per se, whatever the reason, carries with it serious and dangerous possibilities, quite apart from this particular script.

Such a script may be learned within any family which is itself located within a culture of violence. Children are then exposed to stories of killings out of rage, in which explanations are in terms of anger provocation rather than in terms of what the fight was about. This may then be further amplified by scenes in which an irate parent lashes out in extreme rage and violence for what may seem to the child insufficient reason other than the parent's rage. Part of the lore among the siblings in such a family about a parent is "don't go near him when he's mad," quite independent of whatever might have angered him.

What additional magnification may be attributed to daily exposure to such aggression on television cannot be readily determined because such exposure will vary radically in its effects as a consequence of the variety of other sources which converge on the generation of such a script. Simple exposure to the culture of violence alone is insufficient to produce such a script. This requires not only models as necessary conditions but also victimization by brutal attack, which produces an intransigent rage and wish for revenge that exceeds either simple recasting or even recasting-plus scripting, and generates over and above wish and fantasy an intention to respond with extreme destructive aggression whenever enraged. The individual must also be resistant to intimidation, both in the scenes in which he has been victimized and enraged and in any projected possible future scenes, to avoid inhibiting his destructive intentions by virtue of conscience, fear of counterattack, or fear of legal punishment, including his own execution. His resolve is a general one: "I'm not going to be made enraged and let the bastard get away with it even if I have to kill him." This is a much rarer destructive script than most others because of its generality and abstractness. It is much more frequent in the less destructive form, "Nobody's going to push me around." It should be noted that by scripting the sufficient source as one's own anger an important generalization has occurred away from specific sources. It is no longer the origin of the anger which is at issue, so the probability of murder is radically increased. This angry one is much more dangerous than anyone who destructively scripts a specific family in a feud, a specific person in destructive romantic hate, or a principled political destructive script.

It may be better understood as a magnified analog of the more common anger-destructive script involved in killing an annoying house fly. Many have no hesitation nor guilt in routinely killing a fly which continues to settle on one's skin and so angers and is killed. Such a script is sometimes expressed in the formula "Don't get mad, get even," when "even" is equivalent to ridding oneself of the agent provocateur rather than recasting. In this case one does not care who or what is involved so long as one gets rid of it and the rage which has been evoked. It should also be distinguished from similar responses in honor scripts, where the angered one is overly quick to avenge his honor. This individual does not feel dishonored but simply irritated in the extreme when that is scripted as justification enough for the extremity of aggressive response.

It should also be distinguished from destructive-power scripts, which require that anyone who angers by getting in the way of what one wants be destroyed, as in organized crime's deadly warfare against those who contest for the same territory. Here too there may be no hesitancy in wiping out the angering other, but it is a more discriminating response in that murder is not a general response to anger as such but to anger which is evoked by threats to power.

DESTRUCTIVE WAR SCRIPTS

Perhaps the most destructive scripts are those generated by modern nation-states. Their peculiar destructiveness derives from the engagement of mass armies for long periods of time, utilizing and destroying the best human and material resources of all parties to the warfare. The most recent addition, nuclear destructive weapons, is a continuation of a still growing trend, over several centuries, to put more and more resources at risk of destruction.

How can a nation mobilize and maintain the morale of millions of its citizens in sustained all-out exercise of death and destruction? First, it should be noted that the wholehearted enduring commitment of a nation to war is never entirely successful, and if successful is rarely sustained indefinitely at a maximum level. Indeed, success or failure in modern warfare is most often a function of which of the national contestants first loses its collective zest for the battle. The most formidable enemy is the most determined enemy, and such an enemy fights the war with an aggregated script. An aggregated script may be primarily antitoxic, affluent, limitation-remedial, or decontaminating, but it is further magnified by also recruiting and satisfying secondary scripts as it achieves the purposes of the dominant script. The more these secondary purposes are shared, the greater is the magnification of the collective effort, even if different groups contribute quite different skills and achievements to the shared effort.

What are some of the aggregated scripts which may magnify a dominant war script? One is the defense and preservation of a shared way of life. This may include a common language, a common territory, a common history, a common form of government, a common form of economic production, a common form of education, a shared religion, shared forms of art, science, and entertainment, shared forms of marriage and family, shared modes of dress, manners, and morals. There may be aggregated shared scripts concerning freedom, honor, national power, and achievement. Since most nations also regard themselves as better than any other nation, while at the same time harboring some doubts, warfare provides a contest which will confirm the nation's narcissism as it tests and hopefully puts to rest the pretensions of the hostile adversary.

Such a contest is also seen as a vehicle of stretching the energies, will, abilities, and skills of all to the maximum, exposing and confirming hidden reserves and potentialities. Further, it is seen as ennobling in its call for courage and sacrifice of each for all in loyalty and new-found friendships on the battlefield. There is seen also a welcome relief from the boredom, trivialities, and pettiness of everyday life in the heroic, dangerous, shared excitement of the battle. Battle generates not only excitement and enjoyment but also rage and disgust and dissmell at the other, who threatens not only one's own life but the lives of one's comrades, one's family, one's friends, one's fellow nationals, and the allied civilized nations. Such a rage is untroubled by shame or by guilt and offers a theater for the catharsis of the less pious and more conflicted and more banal anger of everyday life. Further, one may satisfy one's dependence proudly in combat. One is never entirely alone there. It is, in brief, a promised cure for the psychopathology of everyday life, albeit at the possible cost of the life of the self and others. And in the end it is seen as having won "peace." Even such an unlikely warrior as William James longed for the moral equivalent of war.

DESTRUCTIVE SACRED SCRIPTS

According to Eliade, the early invention of tools, and the transformation of stone into instruments for attack and defense produced a universe of mythico-religious values. Above all, it was the mastery over distance gained by the projectile weapon that gave rise to mythologies such as lances that pierce the vault of the sky and thus make an ascent to heaven possible (later seen in Jacob's ladder and the tower of Babel). Primitive hunters regarded animals as similar to men but endowed with supernatural powers, that a man could change into an animal and vice versa, and that mysterious relations exist between a certain person and a certain animal. There were divinities of the type Supreme Being Lord of Wild Beasts, which protects both the game and the hunters. Further, killing the animal constituted a ritual.

Killing, sacrifice, divinity, and the idea of the transcendent sacred appear to have gone hand in hand with the utilitarian early toolmaking. Nor is there any trace of attenuation of the equation between killing, sacrifice, purification, and the divinity of the sacred in the Western Judeo-Christian civilization to the present day. Demonstration of love, whether by God to his chosen people or to all people, or by them to God, requires sacrifice through death. The same idea is central in Islam. Today we still witness the sacrifice, in a holy war, of thousands of Muslims who expect, by their martyrdom, to reach heaven through their death in battle.

This is more than a linkage of central aggregated values to killing and to death such as we find in the wars of the modern secular nation-state. In secular war the preservation of life, of the self, and of the nation is central. It is only the enemy who is to be destroyed. In the holy war for the sacred, life on earth is invidiously contrasted with the eternality of the divine and sacred. The same idea appeared in some American Indian warrior cultures in the depiction of the happy hunting ground in the sky. This conception of the sacred is not universal, but it is extremely widely distributed and has lent extraordinary vigor to the proselytizing religions of the Christian and Muslim children of Abraham, as well as to the Israelites. Any ideology which demands unconditional commitment, including the sacrifice of life upon the altar of the sacred over all other values, is at once the most seductive and the most dangerous threat human beings have yet generated to cope with their hunger for eternal bliss and immortality through denial and devaluation of their fear of anger, aggression, and death by their glorification and sacralization through sacrifice and death for God. Life and death thus come full circle. Nor has the secular nation-state been altogether reluctant to march to war to the beat of the distant celestial drum.

Chapter 40
Fear and its Socialization

FEAR-TERROR

Human beings are, at once, the most violent and the most anxious of animals. As told in Genesis, the price of the unholy lust for excitement and knowledge was the fall from innocence to shame, from plenty to insufficiency and the necessity of the distress of hard labor by the sweat of one's brow, from enjoyment and love to anger and aggression, and not least, from everlasting life to the terror of death, whether as inherited inevitability or the consequence of brother murdering brother.

When Freud underlined the centrality of the yoked twins, aggression and anxiety, in the death instinct, he gave us a variant of Genesis. The anger that murdered was but a turning outward of the death instinct that aimed ultimately at our own self-destruction. Our deepest anxiety therefore was properly of ourselves. Freud was, in this respect, only the most recent of the long line of Hebrew prophets who addressed the problems of civilization and its discontents.

Ours has been called the age of anxiety. From Darwin, Cannon, Selye, Richter, and Crile, to Pavlov, Miller, and Skinner, and from Kierkegaard to Sartre, anxiety has, appropriately, assumed a more and more central significance in the study of man and other animals.

Yet there remain deep ambiguities about the nature of fear and anxiety. Two thousand years ago Aristotle wrote: "Fear is caused by whatever we feel has great power of destroying us in ways that tend to cause us great pain." Freud thought it was a "signal" of danger that the ego used to warn itself. This is an even more cognitive theory than Aristotle's inasmuch as Aristotle stressed the "power" of destroying us as the cause of fear, whereas Freud had reduced that power to its "signal" characteristics. In this respect it would be similar to someone yelling "Fire!" in a crowded space. That signal is *not* an affect. It is not fear but fear-provoking. To confuse fear with its activator is one ambiguity. To confuse its activator with its cognitive signal properties is to compound the ambiguity. Present-day cognitive affect theories revert to more strictly Aristotelian theory in that some form of cognitive "appraisal" is believed both necessary and sufficient to evoke affect.

Freud was also responsible for failing to differentiate distress and anxiety by suggesting that the birth cry was the prototype of anxiety. By confusing distress and anxiety, the latter term was given an initial connotation which made anxiety equivalent to psychic suffering of all kinds. By a further extension, everything which caused suffering or frustration of any kind became a cause of anxiety. Therefore, it was a brief step to the general postulate that any kind of "stress" or nonoptimal circumstance might produce "anxiety" in children and later, via generalization, in adulthood.

Freud further confused the analysis of anxiety by his initial theory that it was a biochemical by-product of inhibited sexuality. This theory was based upon his observation that couples who overstimulated each other sexually and who did not consummate their interaction in intercourse and orgasm often suffered anxiety. This gave some credence to the later assumption by Miller and other learning theorists that anxiety was a "learned" drive.

The usage of the word *anxiety* has come to include every variety of circumstance which is capable of evoking any variety of negative affect (be it distress, shame, guilt, disgust, dissmell, surprise, or contempt) excluding anger. Hence, contemporary measures labeled tests of anxiety would more properly be named tests of negative affect exclusive of anger. It was the great authority of Freud in partitioning the negative affects into anxiety and aggression which prompted these ambiguities.

Like all concepts which "succeed" and are taken into too many bosoms, anxiety has become a weasel word, meaning all things to all men. The common denominator of these meanings is some kind of "stress," which all animals will signal by some kind of "avoidance." It will be our position that the original meaning of the word has suffered such attenuation that we propose that the intense form of fear now known as anxiety be replaced by the word *terror,* which has not yet lost its affective connotation. We have so debased the word *anxiety* that it has in the extreme case become equivalent in meaning to the word *wish,* as in the usages "he is anxious to see that play" or "he is anxious to please."

Further, we propose that Freud's distinction between fear as conscious and anxiety as unconscious be dropped and that terror be recognized as the same affect whether its object is known or not. Just as Freud distinguished the aim of a drive as independent of the drive itself, so that a homosexual object choice was not a different sex drive than that in a heterosexual object choice, he should also have maintained the distinction within anxiety between different loci of anxiety as well as different degrees of awareness of these loci. He revolutionized the theory of drives by stressing the independence of the drive from its objects. He remained more conventional in his cognitive theory of anxiety and in his insistence on accepting phenomenological differences as fundamental. In this he was similar to those who believed in the distinction between "normal" and "perverse" sexuality.

The Fear Response

In *The Expression of the Emotions in Man and Animals,* Darwin said:

> . . . we may likewise infer that fear was expressed from an extremely remote period, in almost the same manner as it now is by man; namely, by trembling, the erection of hair, cold perspiration, pallor, widely opened eyes, the relaxation of most of the muscles, and by the whole body cowering downward, or held motionless.

Darwin properly includes autonomic and skin responses as well as motor responses. He should also have included the cry of terror, the raising and drawing together of the eyebrows, the tensing of the lower eyelid as well as opening of the eyes, the stretching of the lips back as well as the opening of the mouth, and finally, the contraction of the platysma muscles of the neck in extreme terror.

The Functions of Fear-Terror

As in the case of any affect, the primary function of terror is to amplify its activator by simulating its profile, of rapidly increasing neural firing and adding an appropriate analog, in this case of special toxicity. In contrast to startle, also an amplifier of accelerated neural firing, which is designed simply to sufficiently amplify its activator so that it serves as an interrupter of ongoing neural firing in the central assembly, terror is designed to punish rather than to interrupt. It is not uncommon for startle to be followed by terror, but it may be followed by excitement depending on the outcome of poststartle scanning. In contrast to excitement, which also amplifies accelerating neural firing, terror is activated by and simulates gradients of neural firing midway in rate of acceleration between startle and excitement. The added analog to excited neural firing is designed to reward rather than to interrupt or to punish. It is as though the affect system had been designed in one case to say, in the case of startle, what is happening is important but indeterminate and must be paid attention. In the case of excitement the messages are that something is happening quickly, and it is rewarding. In the case of terror the messages are, it is faster than excitement, too fast and punishing, but not so fast as startle, which is more indeterminate and more interrupting than punishing.

Further, terror also imprints its own profile (and that of its activator) and of its own analog on whatever response is going on and on whatever responses are recruited while terror is activated. It was Nina Bull who first called attention to the biphasic nature of the responses to terror and the responses to excitement. Inasmuch as these responses amplify by increasing rates of neural firing, one would expect the terrorized person to move rapidly, as does the startled and the excited individual, but there is also, as Bull noted, a period of immobilization after startle, excitement, or terror. This is accompanied, after the initial cry of surprise, excitement, or terror, by a breathless moment, of varying duration, in which one is riveted in attention to the surprising, the exciting, and the terrifying. I would suggest that the increased neural firing both precedes and follows this immobilization and that in the case of terror there is a potential conflict between the analogic sensory feedback responses of terror and its profile of increased acceleration of neural firing and immobilization of responses. Such conflict can occur via that quality of the feedback from the skin receptors made sensitive to terror by variation in blood flow to the face and by the stretching of the skin to expose the hair on the face to the total terror messages. The increased neural firing of the evoked fear program comes into complex interaction with this changed sensory feedback from the now-exposed affect skin receptors, which tell the individual that he is experiencing cold and sweat and hair standing on end. These messages represent the unpleasant analog of terror, which may prompt alternation between immobilization of further responses and increased speed of further responses. This may also be the reason for the combination of immobilization and trembling of the limbs and of the face. It may also be seen in the eyes, which alternate between a frozen stare and brief rapid sidelong glances, as though to escape with the eyes if one cannot do so with one's legs.

Terror is a response that is very toxic even in small doses. Terror is an overly compelling persuader designed for emergency motivation of a life-and-death significance. In all animals such a response has the essential biological function of guaranteeing that the preservation of the life of the organism has a priority second to none. The biological price of such a response is high. Physiological reserves are squandered recklessly under the press of terror, and the magnitude of the physiological debt which is invoked under such duress has only recently come to be entirely appreciated. We have seen before, in the phenomenon of voodoo death, that continuous terror sustained for only a few days is sufficient to produce death.

In man the multiple linkages of such a toxic affect to a variety of internal and external cues makes possible the chronic anxiety neurosis independent of continuing terrorizing harm. This disease is a consequence of one of the mistakes of the evolutionary process. Fortunately, the human infant is spared this danger of the experience of excessive, prolonged terror in the absence of harmful stimulation since its memory and anticipatory skills take considerable time to develop.

It is also extremely difficult to make the lower forms suffer chronic terror in the absence of continuing traumatic stimulation in the way in which it is possible for this to occur in a human being. There were more than a couple hundred attempts to produce an experimental neurosis in the rat, which failed, though it has been possible to experimentally produce such neuroses in cats and dogs. Presumably, there must be a sufficient cognitive complexity to enable the animal to create a matrix of anticipations independent of the actual presence of the originally terrifying scene. The rat does not appear to possess the requisite cognitive powers, though he is quite capable of recognizing and being frightened again by a scene in which he has been previously hurt.

The evolutionary solution to the problem of excessive toxicity of affects was to coordinate the toxicity of the self-punishing response to its duration and to the probable duration of its activator. Thus, in the terror response we are endowed with an essentially transient response of high toxicity evoked by presumably equally transient gradients of increasing density of neural stimulation, whereas in the distress response we are endowed with a more enduring self-punishing response of lower toxicity ordinarily evoked by a more enduring level of nonoptimal neural stimulation. This is not to say that the cry may not be transient, as to a stab of pain, or that terror may not be enduring, as in an animal being hunted by a predator who is continually gaining ground in a pursuit.

But generally speaking, the distress response is more likely to be evoked for a longer time in part because it is a response to a continuing level of stimulation rather than to a gradient of stimulation and in part because its lower toxicity does not provoke such urgent, emergency responses that distress will be as quickly terminated. In general, terror is likely to be of briefer duration because it requires repeated bursts of gradients of neural firing to continue to activate it and in part because its toxicity is such that the individual is more likely to act immediately to reduce terror.

The major function of terror's toxicity and urgency is similar to that of pain—to reduce the toxic state as quickly as possible. This is ordinarily achieved in two steps. First, similar to startle, the central assembly is cleared of most competing information and entirely captured by terror and its object. Any further action which might decrease the distance between the self and the object is stopped, and the individual is frozen in terror, immobilized. This is the major mechanism of avoidance. It guarantees that the terrorized animal will not move toward the source of danger, just as intense pain ordinarily guarantees that the individual will be motivated to quickly terminate contact with the source of pain. But terror can misfire for the animal who is so immobilized that he is eaten before he can flee the predator. For man too the frozen immobility of terror may cost him his life rather than save it. Less dangerous, but no less crippling for effective escape or counteraction is the panic of stagefright, in which the public speaker confirms his own dreaded prophecy by standing mute before his audience.

If the terror response is transient or if it slightly abates, then the second phase may be initiated—flight and escape from the dreaded object. The difference may be seen in the face in the frozen straightahead stare of terror and in the rapid movement of the eye to the right or left to escape the sight of the dreaded object.

Despite the toxicity of the terror response it is biologically and psychologically functional if it is activated by truly emergency situations, if the terror is a transient response, and finally, if it prevents further contact with the source either through immobility or through flight. If immobility results in death or in an increase of threat, it has misfired. Even terror-driven flight may misfire. Thus, many individuals have died in fires when all tried to escape at once, and so trampled each other to death. Terrorized flight ordinarily so taxes the channel capacity of the individual that he is capable only of the most primitive responses. Ordinarily, in a state of nature, most animals which were terrorized were in fact doing what was useful by wild, headlong flight from a predator. It is an open question whether the capacity for gross terror, incompatible as it is with the concurrent exercise of complex cognitive functions is still as useful for an animal such as man.

THE EVOLUTION OF FEAR

As we have noted before, an animal's way of life and adaptation to its environment influences the affects it is capable of emitting. As Crile has shown, the autonomic and endocrine systems of animals are systematically correlated with the way of life of the animal. He predicted and found evidence that the adrenal gland—celiac ganglion dominance was most marked in the cat family and the rodents in which both attack and defense depend on outburst energy. Crile found that the more highly specialized an animal is for a rushing attack, the more the adrenal glands and the celiac ganglia dominate, so that energy may be mobilized quickly. On the other hand, following such a convulsion of activity, there is rapid exhaustion. The cat family in general has no great endurance.

Crile proposed that constant energy is mobilized by the hormone of the thyroid gland. He expected, therefore, that in animals adapted to the long chase, either as pursuer or pursued, the adrenal gland—celiac ganglion dominance should be less marked, and these animals should have larger hearts and thyroid glands. He examined the dog family, especially the wolf and the impala, and compared the relative weight of heart, brain, and adrenal and thyroid organs with those of a member of the cat family of about the same size and weight, the jaguar. As predicted, the dogs had a larger thyroid and smaller adrenal than the jaguar, as well as a larger heart. The adrenal was still slightly larger than the thyroid, whereas in the cat family it is much larger. Crile also found the same relationship to hold between the eagle and the vulture and between horses bred for speed compared with horses bred for endurance. In the case of the thoroughbred race horse, an animal bred for sudden discharge of high energy, it is notable that a by-product has been a radical increase in both aggressiveness and fearfulness. They are given both to blind panic and to extreme savageness, both of which can be so pronounced that it unfits the thoroughbred for racing. Crile was able to do a postmortem on a horse who was a prototype of the extreme emotional volatility which can be a by-product of breeding for pure speed. This animal never reached the races because it could not be properly trained, such was its volatility. Crile found in this animal the largest adrenal gland that he had seen in any horse.

In the five hundred primates and particularly the anthropoid apes that Crile dissected, he found a larger ratio of brain to body weight than in any other wild or domestic animal of comparable size, but the ratio of thyroid to adrenal gland was not like that in man but rather with an adrenal dominance. Crile suggests that one has only to consider the stealthy, tree-climbing leopard, the enemy of the primates, to realize that if they had had the thyroid-adrenal balance of man, they would have been more intelligent but too slow to escape the leopard—and would have left no progeny.

In man, the thyroid is relatively larger than in any other land animal and is larger than the adrenal in comparison with the ape and virtually all the wild land animals who have a larger adrenal than thyroid. In the fetus and human infant the adrenal gland is larger than the thyroid. At the time of birth there begins a gradual decline of the adrenal gland dominance, which continues until the twentyfirst year, at which time the thyroid is $2\frac{1}{2}$ times the size of the adrenal glands. Crile attributes some of the volatility of the infant to this early, more primitive endocrine balance.

In 1948 Tular and Tainter showed that, in addition to adrenalin, the adrenal medulla secreted another hormone, which they called noradrenalin and which has only the effect of stimulating the contraction of small blood vessels and of increasing the resistance to the flow of blood. Von Euler found that specific areas of the hypothalamus caused the adrenal gland to secrete adrenalin and that other areas of the hypothalamus cause the adrenal gland to secrete noradrenalin. Euler compared the ratio of adrenalin and noradrenalin secretion in different wild animals and found that aggressive animals such as the lion had a relatively high amount of noradrenalin; whereas animals such as the rabbit, which depend for survival on flight, have relatively high amounts of adrenalin. Animals both domesticated and wild that live very social lives, such as the baboon, also have a high ratio of adrenalin to noradrenalin. Hokfelt and West established that in children the adrenal medulla has more noradrenalin, but later adrenalin becomes dominant.

These later findings supplement those of Crile concerning the dominance of the adrenal gland in the human infant. Together they suggest that the human infant compared with the adult is both more volatile in general and more aggressive than fearful.

Richter's study of the domestication of the Norway rat and the effects of selection for docility and laboratory manners on the size of the adrenal gland has also supported Crile's report on the atrophy of the adrenal gland in captive lions and the general co-variation of the adrenal with "wildness."

The Norway rat was first brought into the laboratory about the middle of the nineteenth century and has thus been domesticated for over a century for a very restricted way of life.

Richter found that in the domesticated Norway rat the organs which become smaller are those which Crile implicated as energy-controlling organs: the adrenals, the liver, the heart, the preputials, and the brain. The adrenals may be one third to one tenth as large as in the wild rat; the brain, one tenth to one eighth smaller.

Behaviorally, the domesticated rats are less active, more tractable, less suspicious, and less aggressive, and they show less tendency to escape than do wild rats.

In brief, an animal's way of life exerts, through natural selection, a profound influence on the nature of the affects it will be capable of emitting. How it gets its food and how it defends itself depend on the structure of its body, which determines both the kind of affect it is able to emit and the kinds of behavior this affect will mediate.

Not only are some animals more aggressive and fearful than others, as Richter has shown, but the specific profile of arousal, maintenance and decline of the *same* affects may be of decisive importance, as we can now see from Crile's work. This difference in profile of arousal and maintenance of anger or fear between the cat and dog family, for example, would appear to be a function of the way the animal stalks its prey and the way it defends itself. It would seem unlikely that an animal whose aggression is closely coordinated to a sudden rush against its prey would be capable of very graded aggression and fear. The "spit" of a cat resembles the profile of a sneeze in its sudden arousal and reduction. Both the fear and anger of the dog family, on the other hand, appear to be capable of both a slower and a more graded buildup and a more sustained arousal. This more modulated characteristic of the affect system in the dog family may indeed account for this animal's capacity for general amiability and domestication. We would suppose also that its more graded fear and anger enable it to explore interaction with a variety of animals in addition to its domesticator.

We have seen in both Crile and Richter's work a persistent correlation between aggressiveness and tearfulness. There is a suggestion in Crile's evidence that this correlation is due to utilization of overlapping organ systems. The horse becomes both more aggressive and more fearful as it evolves into a race horse. The cat is capable of both great fear and aggression, each of which is emitted suddenly and massively. There is a persistent line of evidence in Crile that the more reasonable and tractable animals, such as the Arabian horse, the dog, and adult man, have become so through a diminution in the dominance of their adrenal glands over their thyroid. The volatility of the human infant, on the other hand, he attributes to the dominance of the adrenal over the thyroid gland.

As we have seen, the more recent evidence on adrenalin and noradrenalin would argue that differences in the predominance of one hormone or the other would favor predominance of fear or aggression. However, these findings are not inconsistent with the further possibility that the relative predominance of adrenal over thyroid might favor both intense and ungraded aggression and fear and the predominance of thyroid over adrenal favor the more graded control of fear and aggression.

The close correlation between fearfulness and aggressiveness is particularly marked in the rat, whose change from the wild to the domesticated state reduced both timidity and aggressiveness.

RELATIONSHIPS BETWEEN INNATELY PROGRAMMED FEAR AND THE EXPERIENCE OF FEAR

Although innately activated fear is, as Darwin thought, relatively invariant for some thousands of years, this is not necessarily the case for the experience of fear.

Lacey has shown that there are somewhat idiosyncratic ways in which each individual eventually comes to express fear. In an investigation of the phenomenology of fear I have also found that the experience of fear varies radically from subject to subject. Thus, one individual may characteristically feel fear in his face and stomach another in an apparent tightening of his throat, another in an apparent band around his head, another in dizziness in his head, another in a weakness in his knees, another in a feeling of fear in his genitals, another in a feeling of fear in his anus, another in an accelerated heart rate, another in trembling of his face and limbs, another in a stiffening of all his muscles, another in sweating. We suppose that such variability of experienced fear is based upon either selection or accretion or variation in the source of fear, or variation in intended instrumental strategies of fear avoidance or reduction.

This is due, first, to the variable interdependency between affective response and the awareness of affective response. Due to limitations of channel capacity there may be selection in which only some components of the total fear response are transmuted into conscious reports. The face may, in fact, be cold and sweaty, but the individual is aware only of the trembling of his facial muscles and his limbs. Another may be aware only of his racing heart or the butterflies in his stomach. In all of these cases the entire set of facial and autonomic responses may be emitted, but only a subset may be included in the central assembly and transmuted into conscious experience. In such a case there are unconscious component fear responses, in those components of the total set which are emitted but which do not reach awareness.

Quite apart from the variability of what reaches consciousness as fear, the same report of fear may vary radically, depending upon what is reported concurrently with it in the central assembly.

The fear which is experienced as a single affect will appear to be quite different when it is experienced concurrently with anger or shame or contempt or distress. The fear which is experienced as caused by a visible threat will be experienced differently when it is experienced as a free-floating experience without an apparent object. The fear which is experienced as caused by something which is remembered will be experienced differently when it is experienced as caused by a present or a future threat. The fear which is experienced passively before a threat which one is helpless to resist is experienced differently than before the same threat which one is certain one can successfully confront. One must not confuse the component fear or terror response with the other components, perceptual, cognitive, and motoric, with which it is coassembled. It may indeed be an identical component of different central assemblies and yet be experienced in radically different ways, just as a group of letters (e.g., *i t*) will be experienced differently as subsets of different words (e.g., *it, bite, bitter*). The dependence of perceptual parts upon the total particular field in which it is embedded holds for the perception of affect as for any other component of the central assembly. The familiar distinction between fear and anxiety, in which fear is differentiated from anxiety on the basis of the presence or absence of an "object" or on the basis of consciousness or unconsciousness of its object, is, we think, inadvisable. It is inadvisable because it makes one distinction when many need to be made and because the distinction properly applies to combinations of affect and other components of the central assembly rather than to the affects themselves.

We have seen before, in our analysis of the use of electric shock as a stimulus to evoke fear in human subjects, how difficult it is to evoke fear and only fear by what seems an appropriate stimulus. Electric shock is always something more than the experimenter intends. We saw that the threat of electric shock may be experienced as punishment, as unprovoked aggression, as an object of curiosity, as a biting oral attack, as something exciting, as an attempt to produce caution, as an attempt to test the courage of the subject, or as an attempt to humiliate the subject. Further, there are great variations in the interpretation of the probable duration, intensity, and frequency of electric shock during any experimental series.

Finally, there are other affects which are characteristically incited along with fear in many subjects. For some subjects there is anger and guilt for anger, in some distress and shame over distress, and in others pride lest one betray fear, or humiliation for cowardice.

Because the threat of electric shock may be interpreted so differently, there are equally great variations in further responses to these presumed threats. It is not that fear is not ordinarily excited by such a threat but rather that it is not all that happens nor even necessarily the most central affective response. Although before receiving a shock fear is general for all subjects, there are marked differences in fear after receiving the first shock. Some subjects are so frightened by the shock that there is marked further deterioration in the ability to learn under the threat of further shock. For other subjects, the actual shock comes as a relief which dissipates further fear.

Thus, one subject observed calmly, "So that's what the shock feels like," and improved his performance from that point on. Other subjects are momentarily unnerved but are eventually able to recover.

The threat of shock also frequently involves pride, and a proud subject can become more afraid of exposing his fear than of the electric shock itself. With nearly all subjects there is an apology for the expression of fear when this expression is uncontrolled. One subject asked, "Is this supposed to make me cautious?" and proceeded to improve his performance under the threat of shock. When he received the shock, he explains "Ouch, that startles you . . . didn't hurt." The cost of controlling the display of fear was considerable, however, inasmuch as he was one of two subjects to hallucinate electric shocks. The affront to his pride was finally repaired in the postexperimental period: "I enjoyed it very much. The shock startled you. But I forgot all about it."

Some Consequences of the Innate Activator Theory

In contrast to anger's dependence on the quantity of neural stimulation at a fixed level of change of rate of neural stimulation which exceeds an optimal base line, fear is critically dependent on the rate of acceleration of change in neural firing exceeding an optimal base line. All the primary affects are change amplifiers. The major distinctions concern the direction of such change, whether increasing or decreasing, and whether that change is a fixed quantum or a rate of change (similar to the critical difference in physical theory between speed and acceleration).

A major consequence of this theory is that it radically enlarges the sources of fear at the same time that it permits both the self-validation and self-fulfillment of the believed sources of any particular fear. Because of the conjoined abstractness and amplification of fear, even free-floating objectless fear is self-validating; that is, it is frightening enough to experience fear that one is prompted either to attempt escape or avoidance of continuing or repeating the experience. Whatever we do in such a case is likely to be sufficiently imprinted with the accelerated neural firing of both the activator of fear and of the fear profile itself that it too will be done rapidly. Such rapid responses are quite capable of reactivating fear, prompting the individual to feel helpless in the face of continuing fear or of repeating his escape attempts still more quickly and desperately. We are as frightened by our own too quick responses as, for example, by the imminent head-on collision we attempt to avoid by turning the steering wheel rapidly and by jamming on the brakes rapidly. We should expect that not only external rapid stimulation will frighten us but also that a great variety of sudden internal events to be capable of activating fear. These include the feedback of sudden muscular contractions, as in avoidance responses, the rapidly accelerating retrieval of information from storage, the rapidly accelerating construction of future possibilities via imagery or cognition, the rapid change of rate of any internal organ or system, such as the heart, circulatory system, respiration, endocrine system. The unexpected complication which arises from this model for the interpretation of fear is that many of the former criteria of fear now appear to be possible activators of fear rather than simply evidence of fear. Thus Schiff, Caviness, and Gibson have reported persistent fear responses in the Rhesus monkey to the optical stimulus of "looming."

They have argued that the rapid approach of a solid body is a natural source of danger for most animals and that the optical stimulus arising from the approach of, or approach to, a body indicates an impending collision. Gibson has proposed that the expansion of a closed contour in the field of view is specific to relative approach. Symmetrical expansion of any silhouette means a collision course, and when magnification comes to fill the entire 180-degree frontal field of view, a collision occurs. This optical stimulus Gibson has called looming.

Using an optical apparatus designed to provide the optical equivalent of an impending collision, a silhouette was made to undergo magnification or the reverse. This resulted in a visual experience of a dark circular object approaching or receding in a large luminous field at a constant high rate of speed. Schiff et al. report that this produces a clear three-dimensional perception. They compared this with a control of a simple lightening or darkening of the screen produced by raising or lowering a shutter just in front of the lamp This does not produce a three-dimensional perception for an observer.

In response to the stimulus of looming, six of eight infant Rhesus monkeys and thirteen of the fifteen adult animals withdrew abruptly or "ducked" in response to the stimulus; that of contraction led to exploratory responses in nineteen of the twenty-three animals. In only one case did an animal retract, duck, or flinch in response to the latter stimulus. Darkening led to a few slight flinching responses, but these were much milder than those observed in the looming condition and occurred only when the darkening followed a looming trial. This was interpreted to mean that darkening per se is not sufficient to produce a withdrawal response but that it may evoke a partial withdrawal response through learning or sensitization. The condition of lightening produced exploratory responses similar to those observed with the stimulus of contraction.

Because there were no differences in response between the infants and adults, and because the response did not habituate, Schiff et al. regard it as probable that this response is independent of learning, or else such learning must occur at a very early age: "We conclude tentatively that looming is a sufficient stimulus for withdrawal responses in Rhesus monkeys."

We would agree with this conclusion but would interpret it somewhat differently. Looming is one of a larger class of stimuli, we would propose, which would be sufficient to evoke the fear response. This is because it is sufficient (under many, but not all conditions) to produce a rising gradient of neural firing of sufficient density to activate the fear response. Although "preliminary informal observations indicate that the event remains effective over a range of speeds, the limits of which are yet to be determined," it would be our prediction that the speed of the expanding stimulus is critical in evoking fear and that if this speed is exceeded, there would be startle rather than fear; and that if this critical speed is not attained, there would be interest and exploratory behavior rather than fear; and finally, that if the speed necessary to evoke interest is not attained, the stimulus will evoke no attention. We would interpret the exploratory behavior evoked by the contracting stimulus as a function of a gradient of neural excitation sufficiently rapid and dense to evoke interest but not fear and would predict that even such a contracting stimulus, if sufficiently intense and rapid enough in its rate of change of shape would be as sufficient as looming to evoke the fear response, or even startle if the change were sudden and massive enough.

Whether or not the response will habituate must be left an open question. Only two animals were tested by a succession of fifteen looming trials spaced about ten seconds apart. When one considers that the startle response to a gunshot will habituate (with the exception of the eye-blink component) and that even abdominal reflexes habituate, it seems improbable that the fear response to looming will not habituate.

The basis of such habituation is, however, not simple. It is our belief that any fear response or any other affect activated by an increasing gradient of neural stimulation will upon repetition, become either sensitized or desensitized but cannot remain the same.

We would interpret the few "flinching" responses under darkening as possible startle or weak fear responses produced by a partly adequate stimulus plus internal previously learned fear responses, the feedback of which produce sudden stimulation.

One way of testing for the effect of avoidance behavior itself upon the resistance of the response to habituation would be to test the animal under tranquilizer or sedative so that the stimulus could be peceived with minimal avoidance response to fear response and then tested again in the normal state.

Another consequence of this theory of innate fear activation concerns the effect of drugs on fear. It follows that any radical change of the internal environment by drugs can either increase or decrease the threshold for fear by increasing or decreasing the general neural rate of firing. We would suggest that the time-honored effect of alcohol on the release of inhibitions is through its relaxation of the skeletal musculature and of the blood vessels lying close to the skin. The muscles relax, and the face becomes warm and tingles from vascular relaxation. The combined effect is to radically reduce the possibility of activating fear. A warm bath is similarly disinhibiting, and hydrotherapy has been used successfully to control acute anxiety through essentially similar mechanisms.

Perhaps the most serious consequence of this theory for psychopathology is the power of overlearned compression-expansion transformations, whereby we silently recognize many alternative parts, similarities, or signs of families of scenes which are capable of suddenly "looming" in our consciousness sufficiently rapidly to evoke terror and which may or may not be accompanied by any other conscious source. They may be experienced as garden variety daymares or as day-terror, analogs of their nighttime brothers. The pity is that once such skills are learned, origins and what they are "about" may become irrelevant because of the nature of the affect-triggering mechanism which is set off, not by content per se but by the abstract profile of neural firing, with or without further meaning.

This theory also permits us to understand both the unusual intensity of night terrors and their lack of content compared with the less frightening but more lucid dreams occurring during the relatively light Stage I REM sleep. The night terror typically begins in Stage IV sleep that is characterized by slow brain wave activity, regular heart beats, and deep, even breathing. Night terror occurs during sudden intense arousal from this slow-wave Stage IV sleep. Suddenly, there would be sharp body movement, a rise in the heart rate and rate of breathing, accompanied by mental confusion, lack of body coordination, and retrograde amnesia. Such individuals tend to have relatively fast heartbeats during Stage IV sleep. It has been possible to reduce the frequency of such night terrors by tranquilizer drugs. It has also been possible to experimentally produce such night terrors by sounding a buzzer during Stage IV sleep. It would appear to be the suddenness of transition between the deepest sleep and wakefulness which both terrifies with unusual intensity and leaves the individual confused and without "content" for his terror. This is in stark contrast to the lucid nightmares occurring in the light Stage I REM sleep which happen in an organized detailed bad scene.

There is a minianalog of the night terror which occurs as one is about to fall asleep, when one is unusually relaxed and one's leg or arm contracts rapidly and involuntarily. Suddenly, one is precipitated into a hyperalert state by a very brief but intense flash of terror, which also has no "content."

THE MAGNIFICATION OF FEAR

Relationship Between Fear Scripts and Fear Magnification

Although magnification occurs through the generation of families of scenes and families of responses to these scenes, so that there is no affect magnification (as distinguished from affect amplification) without scripts, magnification may nonetheless vary independently of the type of script. In affect management scripts a sedative type of script for fear may achieve little, moderate, or great magnification, depending on the frequency, intensity, and duration of experienced fear. Whenever fear is experienced, a sedative script requires recourse to an act or scene which has the capacity to reduce the fear. But such a script might result in one cigarette being smoked occasionally or once a day, or once an hour, or all day long every day. Whatever the frequency of the response, the script remains a sedative script. We do not define the distinctive features of any script by its degree of magnification per se.

Therefore, the magnification of fear-terror is a complex function of the type of script and the frequency, duration and frequency of the component affects, of their instigators, and of the responses to them. Some scripts prove to be self-limiting (e.g., mourning scripts); some scripts specify everlasting duration (e.g., commitment scripts); some scripts specify occasional brief responses (e.g., doable scripts); some scripts specify continuing duration with variable magnification (e.g., addictive scripts). But mourning scripts may vary in their affect intensity even though self-limiting. Commitment scripts may vary in intensity even though they specify everlasting duration. Doable scripts, though characteristically brief and occasional, may nonetheless vary in frequency. Addictive scripts may be renounced, even though scripted for continuing duration.

Determinants of the Magnification of Fear-Terror

One cannot specify the determinants of the magnification of fear-terror independent of the determinants of the magnification of the entire spectrum of affects. First, how fearful anyone may be depends critically on how much excitement and enjoyment is magnified. The better the world appears to be, the safer and less dangerous it will appear to be. Second, how fearful anyone may be depends on how angry, how ashamed, how distressed, how dissmelling, and how disgusted one is. Although any negative affect may coexist with any other negative affect, either simultaneously or sequentially, so that one may be angry and afraid; nonetheless, as the overall density of the non-fear negative affect ratio increases over the overall density of fear, there is an increasing stability of such an equilibrium, for reasons similar to the stability of the density of the positive-negative affect ratio whenever that approaches an extreme value in either direction. So a very timid individual is very improbably an angry person, and a very angry individual is very improbably a timid person.

More specifically, as the density of positive affect increases, the density of affluence scripts increases, the density of limitation-remediation scripts decreases, the density of contamination scripts decreases more, and the density of antitoxic fear or other negative affect scripts is at a minimum. As the density of negative affect increases, this order is reversed, with antitoxic scripts (of fear or any negative affect) at a maximum and affluence scripts at a minimum.

As the density of fear over other negative affects increases, avoidance scripts increase over escape scripts, and these increase over confrontation and counteraction, antitoxic scripts. In affect-management scripts, addictive scripts increase over preaddictive scripts, and these increase over sedative scripts. In affect-control scripts, ungraded and backed-up-affect scripts predominate over graded affect-control scripts. In ideological scripts, the less militant forms of either the humanistic or normative scripts increase with increasing fear density. Because the density of magnification of fear-terror scripts is an interdependent function of the entire matrix of positive and negative affects as well as of the variety of scripts in which affects are embedded, we will examine these determinants in the context of some of the varieties of fear scripts and their magnification, which we will sample.

Magnification and the Socialization of Fear

The socialization of fear, as of any affect, is not restricted to infancy and childhood. Sociocultural dicta concerning fear are continually being generated and exhibited by everyone of all ages, classes, roles, subcultures, and nations. Peer attitudes toward fear and cowardice may be quite different than those of parents. When a nation goes to war no one is exempted from judgment concerning the control of fear. Although a conscientious objector may be exempted from military service, he is not exempted from invidious judgments concerning his "difference." When a nation is defeated in war, a whole society may be exposed to questions about the role of fear in its defeat. When the role of violence increases dramatically in a society, so too does the salience of fear. In short, the socialization of fear, the social definition and shaping of fear, is a never-ending process and as such a substantial part of the magnification of fear. To live under the constant threat of violent attack is to experience a constant possibility of magnification of fear for all. There are societies in particular historical periods when the fear of death is ubiquitous and where living is redefined as learning to die with dignity, as in periods of great violence in Japan, or where scapegoats must be found to blame for plagues which threaten to exterminate a society, as in Europe in the fourteenth century. In seventeenth-century New England there was widespread socially shared terror of witches.

To be exposed to such contagious terror, whether as a child or as an adult, was to be socialized in terror and to suffer its magnification. But the most florid overt manifestations of this terror in the Salem witchcraft trials was neither the beginning nor the end of the feelings of terror about witches. As we have noted earlier, the idea of the "evil eye" and the terror it generates is as old and as contemporary as the affects of fear and anger. Neither the idea nor the fear has ever died out. It appears only to wax and wane in the more enlightened segments of society, but it has continued its robust existence as an underground phenomenon, particularly among the less educated, from the beginning of recorded history to the present. This is not to say that the Christian Satan has always been implicated as the source of malevolence and terror, but rather that someone or some social group has always been found to inspire terror and rage and that there is little evidence that it is any less true today than it ever was. Counterrevolutionaries, Fascists, infidels, the American Satan, Communists, Zionists, blacks, are very much alive and well as sources of terror and counteranger over the world today. There are important differences in *who* represents evil and danger for whom, but the more important invariance is the everlasting terror of the danger from the malevolent other. There is a deep "paranoid" strain in both human nature and in human society and culture which makes it both self-validating and self-fulfilling.

We must not assume that the socialization of fear in childhood can be very independent of either the ideology of the larger society or the events of international relations. Nor are these interrelationships either simple, readily demonstrable, or unchanging.

The socialization of fear—important, ubiquitous, and everlasting as it is—is nonetheless not identical with the magnification of fear. Socialization properly refers to the *social* influences on affect, be they transmitted through, parents, peers, families, social classes, roles, social institutions, or international influences. These many social influences do not exhaustively describe all that goes on in the development of the individual human being. Despite the pervasive social environment the individual is nonetheless a somewhat unique subsystem within the larger matrix. The magnification of terror remains the construction of each separate individual, no matter how similar such constructions prove to be. Societies vary significantly in how much homogeneity and individuality they encourage or inhibit, but there is necessarily considerable slippage which arises as a result of the heterogeneity of experience even in the most homogeneous of societies. Magnification refers *equally* to the individual and social construction of terror. It is therefore a process which must be understood in terms of both socialization and individualization. The ordering of terror scenes, connecting past with present and future possibilities, which constitutes magnification, includes the "social" but transcends it via the construction of unique terror scenes and scripts. There is a nontrivial sense in which no two human beings have ever confronted the universal terror of dying in exactly the same way.

THE EARLY SOCIALIZATION OF FEAR

The varieties of types of socialization of fear are great, depending on cultural and class determinants and on the idiosyncratic interactions between parent and child. Thus, the same punishing type of fear socialization from a macho alcoholic father will be much less toxic for a rugged mesomorphic child who fights back than for a sickly, relatively weak, small, ectomorphic child who cowers in terror before every assault. Again, such a child may be spared the further magnification of terror by a comforting mother but at the price of excessive maternal dependence. He has unwittingly been taught that he cannot cope with fear without maternal "protection." Should that mother be equally punishing and intrusive or indifferent, he would suffer increasing magnification of terror which he had not learned to avoid or escape. Such was the history in one case I studied: a catatonic who, as an adolescent, set his whole body in rigid contraction and perpetual vigilance for the expected attack. Whenever his therapist came dangerously close, he would hit him—in terror, however, rather than in rage, as any terrorized animal will do whenever cornered.

Further, the possible aftereffects of such a punitive socialization of fear will also depend on the space of free movement available to the victim. In the case of a lower-class family in a city ghetto, compressed into perpetual interaction by living in one or two rooms, there may literally be no place to hide or to run away to for relief. In contrast the same child, living on a farm, might be able to find both safety and reward in isolation with Mother Nature. Again, such a victimized child possessing high intelligence may be able to construct imaginary worlds closer to his heart's desire at the cost of varying combinations of introversion and withdrawal and loss of contact with reality. Should such a set of scenes occur in a child less blessed with internal resources, the only introversion available may be the more primitivized schizophrenic stereotypies of compressed, idiosyncratic, endlessly repeated pseudo-communications to the self and to others.

Because of the plurideterminacy of any script formation it is not possible to specify "the" effects of any type of socialization of fear. It is only the convergence of many determinants over time which magnify or attenuate the socialization of any affect.

Nonetheless, there are sets and families of socializations guided primarily by ideology, variously normative and humanistic, masculine and feminine, punishing and rewarding, which do bias the degree and types of magnification of fear.

Socialization of fear which will produce scripts resonant with left wing ideology will include one or more of the following components.

The experience of fear is minimized. The child is exposed to a parent who refrains from terrorizing the child. Even when the parent himself may be frightened for the safety of the child, he tries to protect the child without communicating his own fear. The parent believes and communicates to the child that fear is noxious and not to be invoked except under emergency conditions.

There is a verbalized ideology exaggerating the noxiousness of fear. The child's exposure to fear is not only minimized, but he is also exposed to a verbalized ideology which exaggerates the noxiousness of fear and which is in some measure self-defeating since the child is made more timid about fear than he need be. However, the general benevolence of the intention somewhat limits this secondary effect.

The parent makes restitution for fear. If the parent has willingly or unknowingly frightened the child, he atones for this by apology or explains that this was not his intention. He also reassures and reestablishes intimacy with the child.

Tolerance for fear per se is taught. If the child becomes afraid, the parent attempts to teach the child not to be overwhelmed by the experience, to accept it as a part of human nature, and to master it. This presupposes a parent who is somewhat at home with his own fear, who can tolerate it in himself and others sufficiently to teach tolerance of it to his child. In particular the masculinity of the father must not hinge excessively on shame about being afraid.

Counteraction against the source of fear is taught. Not only is the child taught to tolerate the experience of fear, but he is also taught to counteract the source of fear while he is experiencing fear. Such a technique was used in World War II to prepare combat troops to face fire. They were required to crawl forward while being shot at just above their heads. The child is similarly taught to confront various sources of fear, first with the aid of the parent as an ally and then gradually more and more on his own. Visits to the doctor and dentist, confrontation of bullies among his peers, confrontation of parental authority are all occasions for learning to counteract fear by going forward rather than retreating; and in the type of socialization we are describing theses steps are graded to the child's ability to master them.

There is concern that the child not become chronically anxious. The parent, upon detecting any signs of anxiety in the child, attempts some type of therapy or refers the child to a therapist. Anxiety is regarded as an alien symptom and is treated as any other problem might be treated, with speed and concern. He is generally concerned lest the child's spirit be broken.

Socialization of fear which will produce scripts resonant with right-wing ideology will include one or more of the following components.

The experience of fear is not minimized. The child is exposed to a parent who relies upon terror as a technique of socialization. When the parent himself is frightened, he communicates this to the child. The parent may be chronically anxious, so the child becomes anxious through identification. When the socialization is normative, terror may be used to guarantee norm compliance. The child may be threatened into goodness or manners.

There is a verbalized ideology minimizing the noxiousness of fear. The child is exposed to a parent whose verbalized ideology minimizes the noxiousness of fear, which has a double consequence. On the one hand the child is made less afraid of fear through identification with such a parent, but he is also made more anxious because this parent has no hesitancy in using fear frequently as a way of socializing him.

There is no restitution for the use of fear. If the parent has willingly or unknowingly frightened the child, he makes no restitution. There is no apology nor explanation that this was not his intention. Nor does he attempt to reassure or reestablish intimacy with the child. If the fear has taught the child norm compliance, the parent regards it as entirely justified.

Tolerance for fear is not taught. If the child becomes afraid, tolerance for fear is not taught. Either the child is permitted to "sweat it out" alone, or the burden is increased by shaming the child for its fear. Some normative socializations, especially those aiming at toughness or independence, do attempt to teach the child to overcome his fear, but this is frequently done by invoking shame and other negative sanctions for cowardice. Other types of normative socialization emphasize the value of fear as a deterrent, so there is no motive to attenuate the experience of terror.

Counteraction against the source of fear is not taught. When the child shows fear, counteraction against the source of fear is not taught. It is either disregarded or derogated. If it is derogated, the parent may also force the child to counteract his fear by such humiliation that the child would rather be still more frightened than suffer further humiliation. The child so socialized may seem on the surface similar to the one who has been taught to counteract fear by graded doses and with the parent as an ally, but the difference is quite deep and will become evident under those circumstances in which counteraction proves impossible, for example, in response to terminal illness. Under these conditions the individual socialized through contempt will suffer deep humiliation, whereas the one socialized by an ally will not.

There is no concern about anxiety in the child. The parent characteristically is insensitive to signs of anxiety in the child and disregards or minimizes them. He deprecates as an alarmist anyone who suggests the child might need help. So long as the child is meeting the norm, the parent is not concerned with the hidden costs.

Socialization and the Archaic Infantile Taboos Ignored by Psychoanalysis

As we noted in the analysis of distress, there is a very archaic set of taboos concerning crying, utterly inappropriate for any adult by most cultural norms and ordinarily outgrown in normal development. These are the taboos frequently appropriate to preserve the life of the very young or the comfort of his parent. The same taboos may be learned not only through punishment which produces crying in the infant but also through the arousal of fear or terror. It is a fine line which sometimes separates the spanking which produces crying and the spanking or verbal assault which produces terror. In large part it depends upon the suddenness or unexpectedness of the assault, as well as upon its future promise of rate of increase.

1. The taboo on *curiosity.* A child may be spanked and made afraid for showing curiosity. The very young child sometimes must be restrained in his explorations into the nature of things lest he destroy himself and the objects of his curiosity. The overly timid parent may unwittingly terrorize the infant out of curiosity and exploratory behavior. This is particularly likely if the exploration has involved a near miss, such as when a child runs into the street

after a ball in disregard of an approaching automobile which nearly hits him. Under such provocation I have seen terrorized parents terrorize their careless children by severe beating and verbal assault.

2. The fact of *self-injury.* A child may also be punished for self-injury. Whenever a child has in fact injured himself, many parents add further punishment lest the child not appreciate how he might avoid what he has done to himself. Particularly when the parent is very frightened about the child's self-injury and imagines future, more serious repetitions is he likely to communicate his own terror and activate it in the child through overly severe assault, physical or verbal or both.

3. The impulse to *cooperate and help his parents.* The child may be terrorized out of cooperativeness and the wish to help the parents whenever the offered "help" to an overburdened mother who is cleaning the house so slows her down that she is overly severe in punishing the child for his misguided help.

4. The *identification impulse.* The child may be frightened out of identification with his parents. There is no single wish possessed by the normal child that is stronger than the wish to be like the beloved parent. Such a wish, however, produces a great variety of behaviors which may jeopardize the child's life or discomfort his parents. Punishment for such behavior is not intended to punish the identification wish itself as far as the parent is concerned. To the child, however, such punishment can end in terror and a taboo on his deepest wish.

5. The *smile and laughter of joy.* Because the child's delight is characteristically noisy and boisterous, it is a prime candidate for punishment and thereby for terror.

6. The generation of *noise* in general. Apart from explosive laughter, there are numerous occasions when the child's spontaneous high decibel level discomfits his parents, who may respond with punishment sufficiently sudden, severe, and unexpected to produce terror.

7. The taboo on the most intense form of curiosity, *staring into the eyes of the stranger.* Although the child is initially shy in the presence of the stranger, once he has overcome this barrier, he is consumed with the wish to explore the face of the new person. Since this is a source of discomfort both to the parents and to their guests, this is sometimes forbidden with sufficient severity to induce terror in the child.

8. *Shyness or shame in the presence of strangers.* Just as often as a child is made to cry because he insists on staring at strangers, so he may also be punished severely for his shyness when confronting either strange peers or adults. A child can be made to feel terror because he feels shy and will not shake the hand of the guest or play with the child of the guest. Ordinarily, the parent may increase the intensity of the shyness or shame in the presence of the stranger and later, when the guest has left, evoke terror by severe punishment for his display of shyness.

9. The *linkage of the display of terror to more terror.* A child who is afraid to go down a dark hall into his dark room may be severely spanked so that showing fear is learned to be a source of terror. He is taught to be more afraid of showing fear than of experiencing it. Or he may be shamed for his fear, the parent acting as if the harmlessness of the animal who frightens the child is really foolish, denying the significance of the child's experience.

10. The *taboo on crying* itself. A child who cries about anything, including punishment, may then be punished much more severely till terror inhibits crying.

11. The terrorizing of *celebratory exhibitionism.* Nothing pleases the triumphant child more than to exhibit his prowess in achievement and to be mirrored by loving parents who take joy and pride in what he has been able to do. Indeed the important distinction made by Kohut between idealization and mirroring may be combined in the mind of the child who wishes to be applauded for exhibiting achievements which make him more like his idealized parents. To turn away, to ridicule, to be lukewarm, or to frighten about possible dangers for such exhibitions may kill both the idealization of parents and the wish to be mirrored by them at once, enforcing a protective introversion against both shame and fear.

SOCIALIZATION AND AFFECT-CONTROL SCRIPTS

The socialization of fear is governed not only by general ideological dictates but also by quite specific strictures on the circumstances in which it is appropriate and inappropriate to have feelings of fear, to display them, to express them vocally, to communicate them verbally, to act on them, and to produce fear generated consequences. Such socialization is intended to and customarily does produce a variety of affect-control scripts which target the control of fear within any scene rather than the control of the totality of features of the various scenes in which fear is embedded and is but one among many distinctive features. Thus, in contrast to affect-control, socialization for a script which targeted either the avoidance of or the confrontation with physical danger might be silent on coping with whatever fear might be generated in such scenes. If one were driving an automobile that was about to be hit by another automobile, attention would characteristically recruit skills and scripts dealing with action that would avoid the imminent collision. Should terror freeze such action, it might also freeze any fear-control scripts that would have been recruited under less severe emergency conditions, so that a scream of terror might occur despite affect-control scripts which forbade the vocalization of fear.

The relationships between general ideological influences on affect-control and more specific affect-control scripts depend, first, on the scope and specificity of the ideology. Religions have varied radically in both how detailed and how broad their scope, how immanent and how transcendent their guidance, and how much such guidance is magnified by assumed sanctions in the here-and-now compared with a remote day of reckoning. Early American puritanism, for example, was unusually vivid and severe in implanting a fear of death and its attendant possible punishment by God for sin. By the nineteenth century this was no longer a fear to be reckoned with on a daily basis. Further, there are idiosyncratic variations in which parts of a culturally shared ideology are magnified by a particular parent. One Christian parent may insist more on the love of Jesus than on the terrors of hell for having sinned. Because many individuals are governed by secular as well as religious ideologies, one Christian may emphasize good work in capitalist enterprise more than good works as the favored gateway to heaven. Such a child may be taught to fear indolence and poverty as a more severe threat than evil and sin.

Further, the class or caste location of parent and child may determine radical differences in how much and what to fear. The son of royalty is taught to inspire fear in the governed. The son of a slave is taught to fear the master and all who are not slaves. There are also strong idiosyncratic differential affect magnifications in any parent, which may determine that his child is as impressed as he is with the danger of living and the necessity for prudence and cowardice. Another parent, a prouder slave, teaches his children opportunistic courage in the face of the overwhelming power of the master. In less dramatic ideological variations, some parents will indoctrinate children into fearless opposition to different varieties of norm violations, to stand with the majority or to stand against it as an opposition of one for the sake of principles.

The idiosyncratic personal variations in the differential magnification of fear account for the varying degrees of consistency or inconsistency as well as the varying degrees of identity, overlap, differentiation, or orthogonality between the ideological socialization of affects and the more specific affect-control scripts taught in early socialization. Thus, a particularly timid parent may, by example, very early convey a sense of the tearfulness of the world in general or of a particular source of fear. In one case of a dog phobia I investigated, there was social transmission by a mother who had, as a child, herself been bitten by a dog. Whenever she saw a dog, her whole body tightened in fear, which her child experienced as she tightened her hold on the child. He remembers himself as very early coming to duplicate her sudden stiffening and so frightening himself into a fear of dogs. But just such a parent, who is counterphobic for his child if not for himself, may exert himself to guarantee the child does not inherit what he is ashamed of as a character flaw, urging the child to become exceptionally brave in the mastery of fear. Such a parent may unwittingly magnify the fear of shame of cowardice as he attenuates the fear of animals or impersonal dangers. To preserve his parent's respect and love he must not fear dogs, but he may thus be taught to fear the shame of cowardice more than the fear of dogs. Another parent who loves dogs may ridicule his child's sudden fear of an overly eager dog, thus teaching both that dogs are fearful and that such fear itself is shaming and ultimately an additional source of fear in coping with dogs.

Finally, affect control group scripts are generated not only by social transmission but by all the complex pluridetermінate transformations of inherited ideological and affect-control scripts which are characteristic of script formation in general.

Affect-control scripts address first of all the question of the consciousness of affect. Societies and families may teach the individual to become unaware of his fear by a studied unawareness of its presence so that the child does not learn to label fear or to be aware for very long that he is afraid. Every time such a child shows signs of fear, the parent rushes to either distract the child or remove the child from the source of fear, thus diverting attention either to other feelings or to remedial action, away from attention to fear. In addition there may be strictures against feeling afraid ("Don't be such a scaredy cat").

There are also frequent script rules governing the density of fear and its intensity, duration, and frequency ("Enough is enough," "Simmer down," "You're always scared").

There are also specific rules for the display of facial fear ("Lighten up") for the vocalization of fear ("Shut up," "Stop crying or I'll give you something to really cry about"). There are rules for the communication of fear, particularly for the verbalization of fear, which may be independent of the rules against vocalization ("We don't talk about it"; "Don't tell me your troubles"). Such a parent may permit vocalization of fear, walking away and permitting the child to cry it out after refusing to listen to his verbalization of fear.

There may be rules favoring avoidance or escape from dangerous frightening scenes or, in contrast, punishing what is regarded as cowardice, quite apart from the rules governing fear itself. In these scripts, fear-governed action is the chief target of fear-control scripts. This may be done by coupling fear, action, and other affects ("Cowards are disgusting"; "Foolhardy kids think they're smart alecs. Don't be too big for your britches.")

Next, the consequences of fear-based action may be scripted for the child ("The next time you run out on the street chasing a ball you won't be so lucky—you'll be hit by a car"). Such lectures may be accompanied by a beating, to magnify terror against action which is prompted by excitement but which the parent wishes to link with dangerous consequences so that the child will become more cautious.

Fear-control scripts also govern the generality and specificity of conditions under which the rules for fear, its consciousness, display, vocalization, verbalization or action, or consequences are required. In the extreme case there is some socialization in honor societies which requires the maintenance of honor even at the cost of death, whether in battle or by suicide in disgrace. In such cases, fear and even death is scripted as less punishing than dishonor, and it is the fear of dishonor which is invariant. There are no specific conditions which make it possible to tolerate fear if honor has been violated. A person who has been timid and dishonorable deserves to die or to be killed or enslaved. Ordinarily, however, there are many specific conditions scripted for permissible fear, as in submitting to overwhelming forces, be it in a mugging on the street or at the hands of an angry parent whose child has committed an unforgivable offense after having been warned many times. Such a parent may exempt the child from fear-control scripts which apply in general when he has exceeded the boundaries of his parent's patience. Again, the child may be taught that he must be on his best behavior at special times ("Be quiet when mommy is tired"; "Behave when we have guests").

Affect-control scripts may in some individuals be special subscripts of more general ideological scripts, with varying degrees of overlap, mutual support, conflict, ambiguity, or independence of each other. However, affect-control scripts are also influenced in varying ways by all other scripts. Thus, an otherwise brave individual, scripted as forbidden to display any sign of fear, may suddenly panic uncontrollably at a diagnosis of terminal illness of his child, in part reliving his own helpless fear as a child before he had learned to muffle his own cry of fear. An otherwise timid adult may grow suddenly fearless and courageous in the defense of his child who has been threatened and intimidated. Love can make cowards of the brave and heroes of the timid since affect-control scripts coexist with the totality of all other scripts within the personality.

Chapter 41

Fear Magnification and Fear-Based Scripts

THE MAGNIFICATION OF FEAR-TERROR

As is the case with any affect, there are many degrees of freedom in the magnification of fear. The same density of fear may occur with varying ratios of intensity, duration, and frequency. One individual is vulnerable to constant low-grade fear. Another is frequently bombarded with slightly more intense fear but enjoys much positive affect in his fear-free intervals. Another is intensely afraid but with only moderate frequency. Yet another is entirely engulfed by terror; although these scenes occur only rarely, they generate moderate anticipatory fears of possible repetition much more frequently.

Independent of the density and magnification of consciously experienced fear is the degree and frequency of fear at a distance of varying remoteness that may prompt either constant vigilance against a dreaded possibility, frequent testing, or only occasional monitoring for possible feared scenes. In none of these scripts may conscious fear be experienced or it may be experienced with varying densities. Nonetheless, if there is a script which calls for continual monitoring of the possibility of fear, it represents a substantial magnification of the possibility of fear that may radically attenuate the magnification of either excitement or of enjoyment or of other negative affects. Just as a miser counts his money for protection against poverty rather than for the fun of using his money, so the power to keep fear at arm's length may become the only enjoyment of relief the hoarder of safety may know.

Magnification of fear may also vary independently of the effectiveness of scripts in either avoiding or escaping or reducing fear. One individual may be quite effective in reducing fear by smoking a cigarette whenever he is afraid but nonetheless often suffer fear. Another may be relatively ineffective in reducing fear, but the frequency of his fear is sufficiently low so that his failure to attenuate or reduce it does not result in further magnification. Yet another is very effective in avoiding conscious fear but pays an excessive price in constant vigilance against imaginary remote possibilities. Another is constantly monitoring for the possibility of fear but is at the same time continually afraid that he will suffer even more fear despite his vigilance, such as a hypochondriac seeking continual testing and medication for possible illness. Compared with the manifest hypochondriac is the equally vigilant but much less fearful jogger whose daily jogging appears to him to effectively keep the doctor away and to reward him with a bonus of good health against possible illness.

Magnification of fear may also vary independently of the concentration or distribution of loci of sources of fear. One individual is afraid of everything under the sun but only with moderate intensity and duration. Another is afraid of only one scene, of one person, of one possible failure by the self, or of one physical disease (e.g., heart, if he is from a family where all have died young of heart attacks), but this scene may engulf him constantly or frequently or occasionally and may then be able to be escaped or limited or continue to grow until it burns itself out.

Magnification of fear may also vary independently of the concentration or distribution of loci of recruited scenes and sources of fear. One individual afraid of only one scene (e.g., an aggressive father) deals with each scene, with minimal further magnification, as posing a specific threat of how to minimize the danger in this scene. He may confront variants of such scenes every day but continue to deal with one scene at a time and win some and lose some. Another individual continually magnifies the same daily assaults by importing many past scenes which ended disastrously and many future possibilities of even greater threat, as well as many additional possible scenes which might add to this fear; for example, a possible invasion of a virus epidemic others had experienced a year ago, which would leave him even more vulnerable to the dangerous father.

Another individual with the same script may import endless analogs in dealing with his father and also with father surrogates. In the extreme case the tear of the father is endlessly magnified by retroactive importation of surrogate fathers in adversarial roles in which he had suffered defeat. It is now his defeat by his boss which inflates a fear of his aged father—or even of his dead father.

The magnification of fear may also vary independently of the concentration or distribution of loci of responses to fear or of the loci of perceived consequences of responses. One individual is most frightened of having to escape from fear. So long as he can avoid dangerous confrontations, he suffers minimal fear, although he may have to magnify his vigilant monitoring of such possibilities. Once he has failed to avoid such scenes, however, he becomes terrified and is unable either to escape or to reduce his terror. Another does not script avoidance responses, dealing more effectively with confrontation scenes but also suffering considerable fear in the process. However, such fear does not prompt the formation of avoidance scripts. He may continue his somewhat impulsive aggressiveness even though the fights he provokes continue to evoke fear as well as anger.

Another individual is less concerned about whether he should attempt to avoid or escape fear than what will be the consequences of his responses. If he is frightened and hits the agent provocateur, he may be afraid he will be provoked to kill him and afraid of the further consequences of his fear-provoked aggression. Another individual, governed by a code of honor, may become afraid he might be killed in the defense of his honor. In feudal Japan the exaggerated and synthetic smile became a stereotyped mutual appeasement gesture lest the loss of face result in death. Such possibilities of trivial encounters producing fear-laden outcomes may be concentrated by phobias for place, rank, social class, or race or be widely distributed as if to materialize Hobbes's war of all against all. Such concern about possible outcomes of one's own responses may or may not be combined with a fear of external sources as frightening per se. Thus, a police officer may become afraid of random violence with or without becoming afraid that he might kill in dealing with such violence, depending in part on how much his choice of this profession was determined by fear and guilt about his own anger and aggression.

His fear may be concentrated and restricted to the consequences of his killing someone or be distributed more broadly to the consequences of any type of aggression on his part, including nonaggressive responses such as criticism which he fears might hurt others irreparably. This might even include his own self-assertiveness had he been socialized by punitive, overcontrolling parents or by an overpossessive mother who could not tolerate any show of independence by her beloved son. In one case he might fear intensification of control should he assert himself. In the other he might fear the anguish of his overpossessive and overdependent mother should he leave her or even declare his own individuality.

In summary, magnification of several features of fear scripts may vary independently of each other. Conscious fear itself may vary in intensity, duration, and frequency in different degrees and patterns of density and magnification. Independent of the consciousness of fear is degree and frequency of vigilance and monitoring for dreaded scenes. Independent also is the relative effectiveness of avoiding or escaping or reducing fear of the frequency and density of conscious fear. Magnification may also vary independent of the concentration or distribution of loci of sources of fear, of recruited scenes of fear, of responses to fear, or of perceived consequences of his responses. The varieties of patterned combinations of these somewhat independent features of magnification generate a very large number of different kinds of fear scripts of equivalent degrees of magnification.

MAGNIFICATION VIA INDEPENDENCE, DEPENDENCE, AND INTERDEPENDENCE

The magnification of fear may occur in many ways through the construction of a variety of scripts. Some of these concern themselves exclusively with fear, as both the origin and target of responses to cope with fear. Fear in such scripts has become relatively independent of the many scenes in which it has been evoked. A fear script of sedation will prompt recourse to a cigarette to either attenuate or reduce that fear, no matter what else may be the problem in the scene. It is not intended to deal with the source of fear as such. In an affect-control script the response independent of scene source may be to muffle the cry of fear. In an ideological fear script the response may be to condemn any experience or display of fear whether one can control it or not and whether it is one's own fear or the fear of anyone else.

In affect-salience scripts, fear as such, apart from its scene dependencies and interdependencies, may be sought and fused with excitement, for pure affect "kicks" in which fear serves the function of a spice, converting a negative affect into varying ratios of mixed affect to heighten excitement and enjoyment. It may be fused with sexuality, requiring fear for sexual excitement and enjoyment. Affect-salience scripts for pure fear as such may also prompt avoidance, escape, or confrontation, not with the purpose of dealing with frightening scenes as such but solely for the purpose of dealing with fear, to avoid it at all costs or to escape it or to confront it and destroy it. Thus, one individual seeks to avoid being drafted into combat primarily lest he become afraid rather than to avoid death or injury. Another escapes and deserts from the battlefield because he cannot tolerate his fear rather than because of fear of death. Another enlists as a soldier of fortune in anyone's war to evoke fear and to tolerate it as a test of his ability to master an otherwise alien, overwhelming terror. He is not trying for "honor" or for "bravery" but to test and demonstrate affect mastery per se. He may even risk death and die attempting to confront his fear as his chief enemy.

In fear-dependent scripts it is not fear per se which is the origin and terminal of the scripted responses. It is rather that which evokes fear which controls the scripted responses. So one may be frightened by an entire scene in which one has been scolded for disobeying a warning to be careful lest one be hurt. The major affects may be shame and distress. The major loci may be an ambivalent mother who threatens loss of love if the child disobeys one more time. The fear of such a scene is strictly derivative and dependent, and though an adult faced with analogs of such a scene might have recourse to fear sedation, he primarily concerns himself with the future avoidance of repeating the bad set of scenes. He may indeed run away in attempted escape from intolerable fear as such, but if it is scripted as scene-dependent fear, he will ultimately have to deal with the source of that terror in the scene which evokes it. He might even keep running, but for the purpose of permanently escaping such scenes rather than as an attempted sedation of fear alone. He might be prompted into interscript conflict—to run away from his fear alternating with the possibility of scripted, interscript conflict. The fear-dependent script need not be dependent on the entire scene, nor on external events in the scene. A fear-dependent script may concern the source of fear in one's own uncontrollable anger or in the uncontrollable anger of the other. What else might be going on in anger-fear scenes might be of no consequence in such fear-dependent scripts. The script zeroes in on the perceived source as cause. If this can be avoided or escaped, it is assumed that there will be the fringe benefit of experiencing no such fear. Another type of fear-dependent script is the magnification of vigilant orientation responses. In this type of script the main purpose is to accurately identify and understand just what are the distinctive features of a scene which frightens. This is particularly magnified in free-floating terror, in contrast to phobic scripts. To be terrified and not to know what terrifies powers a magnification of the search for clues and orientation.

Fear-dependent scripts may be further differentiated by the degree of distribution versus concentration of scenes which frighten. If a child is terrorized in many ways by one parent, a tyrant script is ordinarily generated that is oriented toward learning exactly when the tyrant must be appeased and when it is a safe scene, as well as how to deal with each of many variants of scenes which frighten. In contrast, if a child becomes the scapegoat victim for the whole family, for peers and for strangers outside the family, as well as for a variety of impersonal sources (e.g., thunderstorms, illness, and accidents), then the problem of identifying and coping with such a variety of sources may be sufficiently forbidding to generate a generalized introversive avoidance script. One may also generate an introversive avoidance script to deal with a single tyrannical terrorizer, depending on how many terror-free scenes are perceived possible. However, such an introversive script may be combined with a terror-free or sedative-extroversive script with other members of the family and with peers and strangers.

Interdependent fear scripts are special cases of systematic salience scripts as contrasted with pure affect scripts and with affect-worthy, affect-derivative scripts. In these scripts not only is fear one element among many which require scripting, but any one script may also require further interscripting whenever two scripts deal with overlapping elements in different ways. In such scripts, responses attempting to meet multiple purposes have both conjoined and alternative, delayed, partitioned, conditional responses, which are continually open to changes as sources appear to change and as the consequences of scripted responses appear either to change or require to be reinterpreted from varying newly revealed perspectives. In such scripts fear is neither a dependent effect of some scene—such as an aggressive attack, the control of which eliminates fear—nor an independent cause, which can aim at its own reduction by simple sedative (or control) responses. In interdependent scripts fear is one affect among many which may fuse and magnify each other, as in fearful, exciting sexuality, and also conflict with each other, so that such a mixture may also evoke shame or guilt all embedded in a larger matrix of estimated interdependent risks, costs, and benefits; such scenes may be sought as moral "holidays," as compensations for overly severe affect-control scripts which govern everyday life. Many societies set aside specific times and places to give expression to such conflicted orgiastic wishes or to reverse social roles which are oppressively hierarchical. After such cathartic license, social life is scripted to return to "normal."

In interdependence scripts there is a "conversation" between fear and other affects and between other scene features and scripted responses, rather than a one-way communication in which fear either "listens" to its determinants as effect or "talks" to its audience as a one-way cause. In such scripts if I am frightened, I am neither monologic passive victim nor intransigent avenger but dialogic negotiator and conversationalist. We next consider some of these varieties of fear scripts in more detail.

MAGNIFICATION OF FEAR AS SPECIFIC AFFECT DEPENDENT

Fear may be magnified by any specific affect as an independent evoker of fear. In this case one is afraid after evocation of a specific affect which had been terminated by sudden punishment rapid enough to trigger massive fear lest it be repeated.

One may become anger-afraid by one or a series of scenes in which the expression of anger in a tantrum is terminated, for example, by a sudden slap on the face, rapid and massive enough to stop the tantrum by evoking terror as a competing affect and maintaining terror by continuing attacks and threats that any repetition of the tantrum will be met by more severe punishment; so anger is attenuated by a new and greater problem of avoiding or escaping from terror and from the attacks which evoke it. The more frequently and longer the rehearsal of such a scene is repeated with terror and projected as a possibility into the future and acted on as a possible real and present danger, the more magnified such fear may become. It is important to note that it is not necessarily the pain of the slap which is critical but rather its suddeness. If it were the pain and distress which were critical, one might be taught to be anger-distressed rather than anger-afraid. If it were the pain and shame which were critical, one could be taught to be anger-ashamed—as happened to Chekhov, who was beaten by his father again and again. These assaults did not frighten Chekhov but did humiliate him for a lifetime. The question for him was "How could you?"

But anger may magnify terror by any sudden reaction which substitutes terror for anger. Thus, a sudden look of contempt, of distress, or of shame; a sudden looking away from the child; more dramatically, leaving the child alone with his tantrum; suddenly sending the child to his room; suddenly holding the child rigidly; putting one's hand over his mouth; or a sudden command such as "Just stop that" may, depending on the nature of the child and his relationship with the parent, be capable of interrupting anger and evoking the terror, for example, that he is losing the love of the parent because of his anger. In the further magnification of such scenes attention may be unequally focused, or alternately focused, on the anger, the terror, and the specific transition trigger, be it a slap, a leaving of the room, the change in the face or voice of the parent. In order for anger-fear magnification to occur it is necessary only that one is taught or teaches oneself that it is one's own anger rather than the parent's sudden response which is to be feared. Of course, one might also learn to be afraid of the trigger as much as or more than the anger or be afraid only of the slap, missing altogether in the further elaboration of such a scene that one was slapped for the tantrum. Much depends on what one elects to script as avoidance or escape responses.

Thus, if the child elects an escape response for future anger scenes for which he may be punished, he may run away from any scene in which he begins to feel angry lest he again feel terror. In contrast, if the child elects an avoidance response for future anger scenes for which he may be punished, he may become sensitized, at a distance, to various possibilities for anger or fighting and avoid such scenes in advance. As the degree of magnification of terror increases, so may the remoteness of avoidance responses, producing in the extreme case a complete repression of anger against any possibility of terror. There is the further option of the extent to which it is anger of which one has become afraid or whether it is terror itself which has become an independent source of terror. This option we will examine later. Our concern here is with fear as a dependent magnification rather than as an independent magnification. For this, much depends on the later reconstructions of such a scene and what one scripts as requiring coping responses. In the case we are considering it is one's own anger which is scripted as the source of terror rather than what produced the anger or how that anger was punished and followed by terror. The scene has been reduced to a simpler formulation.

Consider now the terrorizing of distress. The dynamics are similar to those for becoming anger-afraid. If a child cries out in distress and the parental response is predominantly punitive, verbally or physically, or ridiculing, or leaving the room to let the child cry it out, and any one or any subset of these nonrewarding responses is sufficiently massive and sudden enough to evoke fear, then the set of such scenes may be further transformed into a simple script: Crying is terrifying; therefore, let me not cry lest I experience terror.

Distress is a negative affect of much less toxicity than terror and so enables the human being more easily to confront and solve his problems. Distress is also ubiquitous, whereas fear is properly an emergency reaction. If I may feel like crying many times during every day—when I am confronted with very difficult problems whose solution is not at once apparent, when I feel tired or sick, or when I am criticized or rejected—then if under all of these circumstances I were to become terrorized rather than distressed, I would be severely disturbed. Under such conditions it would become very much more probable that I would quit trying to solve difficult problems, that I would dread the normal diurnal variations in energy as if they were mortal illnesses, and that I would become very cautious about trusting and liking human beings. Avoidance or escape of the distress experience itself would become a much more likely script than attempting to control the sources of distress. A generalized pessimism would be the consequence of the terrorizing of distress.

Since the human being responds innately to pain from his body with the cry of distress, the terrorizing of distress radically increases the problem of physical courage. Although pain is not easy for the human being to tolerate, it becomes much more intolerable when terror is added to pain and distress.

The terrorizing of distress would produce a weak ego incapable of tolerating frustration, whether this be met in trying to solve problems, in fatigue or illness, or in deprivation or discipline of any kind.

The terrorizing of distress would increase the difficulty of achieving individuation and a sense of identity and the toleration of loss of love. It is difficult, because it evokes distress, to tolerate the threat of loss of love and communion. But this is part of the price of achieving a firm sense of one's own identity, and of becoming individuated from one's parents, from one's wife and friends, and from humanity in general. The addition of terror to distress favors more radical strategies of submission and conformity, or rebellion and deviance, lest one experience the terror of loneliness and difference.

Further, an individual who is distress-terrorized may become vulnerable to any sign of distress in others. Any attempt at communion through the expression of distress will evoke from the distress-sterrorized listener not sympathy but terror.

Finally, such an individual may be forced into massive defensive strategies lest such experiences be repeated. Thus, a person who is distress-terrorized may deny that he or others are ever tired or sick, are ever defeated or seriously challenged in competitive striving and problem solving, or that he or others are ever lonely. Such a linkage may also power compulsive athleticism or withdrawal from the risks of life, compulsive achievement or passivity, and compulsive communication or isolation.

Next consider the terrorizing of shame. If a child has been deeply shamed and then abandoned, or hit, or the target of further ridicule, and if he is then prompted to terror, either from the rate of punishment, from its rapidly perceived possible implications for the preservation of the relationship, or from the rate of his own running away from the scene, or from all of these, then the simplified script may be generated: Lowering your eyes and head is terrifying; therefore, let me walk tall always, lest I experience terror.

DEPENDENCE OF FEAR ATTENUATION ON THE DIFFERENTIAL MAGNIFICATION OF COMPETITIVE AFFECT

As we have noted before, the magnification of any script is independent of what type of script it is. One may sedate fear as a preferred mode of dealing with frightening scenes but may have to do this occasionally or continually, depending on the density of experienced fear.

We have been considering the magnification of fear as dependent. We will now briefly examine how the dependence of fear on other affects may attenuate rather than magnify fear.

Fear may be radically attenuated, either in specific scenes, or for a lifetime, by the differential magnification of competing positive or competing negative affect. As the zest for life increases, the possibility of evocation and magnification of terror decreases. Danger and such fear as this may evoke serves primarily to increase both excitement and enjoyment by heightening challenge and its mastery. Further, great excitement will prompt boldness and insensitivity to possible danger. If positive affect does not completely attenuate fear, it may nonetheless diminish its toxicity.

As we have noted before in Harlow's experiments with young monkeys, those reared without benefit of the affection and solace of the surrogate mother ran in terror from the frightening object. Those who had enjoyed the benefits of mother love ran to her for protection, and after experiencing the reassuring contact, shortly thereafter turned to explore and do battle with the object which had a moment before paralyzed the young monkey.

Other negative-affect magnification may also attenuate fear. If anger, dissmell or disgust are magnified in outrage, the individual may become too insistent on punishing the other to become afraid of the other. Indeed, even otherwise extremely timid children and adults have committed murder when long-suppressed anger is momentarily magnified in outrage so that they are engulfed in explosive violence. One of the crimes of passion which is sometimes offered as a legal defense in the extenuation of murder. But such magnification need not be episodic. Anyone with deep-seated anger may spend a lifetime exacting revenge even at the cost of his life, with or without any fear. Any principled martyr will fly in the face of possible danger and fear.

If one may be too outraged to be afraid, so too may one be too deeply distressed and saddened. Just as the mourner might have been terrified at the imminent death of his beloved, yet he cannot be afraid at the cemetery. It is over; he is engulfed in anguish. Mourning need not be limited in object or in time. To the extent that one magnifies a generalized mourning script, life may be experienced as a perpetual vale of tears, the present and future constantly invidiously compared with a past golden age or a wished-for better world closer to the heart's desire which is now scripted as forever impossible, having been based on wishful illusion. This is not an uncommon dynamic in marriage based on romantic love idealization. When there begin to appear signs of disenchantment in the self, other, or both, there may be a growing fear of further possible discontent. When mutual disenchantment is acknowledged and divorce has occurred, there may be a long period of mourning in which distress completely attenuates the previous fear of rupture of the cherished relationship. Such a sequence may, however, eventually further magnify fear in a script which vigilantly monitors for possible repetition of analogs of tragic love and hate and mourning. In such a case, much will depend on how nuclear such scenes may be, how preponderant the ratio of positive to negative affect may be, and how much such a sequence of scenes is scripted as limited in particularity with respect to person and time rather than generalized to "marriage," to "women," to "human nature," or to "society." Generalization need not be based on the fear of possible repetition. That expectation of repetition might equally occur from a much magnified disgust or even shame at the self, other, or both, which powers an expectation which contaminates any possible future marital relationship. One need not fear such a possibility if one convinces oneself that it would necessarily be disgusting or humiliating if repeated with any other person.

Finally, the magnification of a shame script may attenuate the possibility of terror. In the extreme case the resolutely humble slave masters possible danger and fear by putting aside any thought of challenge to the complete authority of the other. In a less extreme case women have, for many centuries, been cast in the role of humble and loving servants of men, powerless to aggress, and either timid or so completely acquiescent as to minimize both anger and fear. The magnification of humble shame ordinarily begins in so terrorizing the victim for willfulness that the "will" is broken in order to magnify shame over resistance, anger, and fear. There need be no magnification of fear if there can be an enduring magnification of humility and shame.

MAGNIFICATION OF FEAR AS SCENE DEPENDENT

In contrast to the magnification of fear as a response to one's own affect (e.g., fear of one's own anger) or as a response to the other (e.g., fear of the anger of the other), the scene as a whole may be magnified as fear-evocative. In this case it is the conjunction of both the other's behavior and the response of the self that eventually evokes fear that may then be further magnified over time.

A child who hurts himself and is scolded by an anxious mother who condemns him for having disobeyed his mother's warnings to be "careful" and who then hangs his head in deep guilt (immorality shame) for having violated his mother's wishes and warnings, may then further respond with fear at the possibility that he has already or may in the future lose his mother's love. Should such a scene be repeated with increasing displeasure and impatience from that condemning mother, the hypothesis of possible loss of love may be confirmed and further magnified, evoking a growing fear not only of his own carelessness but also a fear of accidents and physical injuries over which he has no control. Then any sign of the possibility of such scene repetition, as in witnessing accidents, muggings, deaths from terrorist bombs, famine, or warfare, may quickly and relatively unconsciously evoke the theory-powered conviction of an increasing spread of dangerous violence in general, and thence to the analogpowered repetition of the feared scene in which it is the self which has been injured and it is the loving mother who now turns against him, adding the deeper insult of guilt to injury. Further, any similarity or any part of the original scene (e.g., in any physical hurts, toothaches, back pains, or reductions in energy either from diurnal variations in energy or as a consequence of aging) can become analogs of rapid but relatively unconscious compression-expansion transformations that evoke uneasy fear or panic at exactly what he does not know. As magnification increases, he is more and more vulnerable to signs, parts, and similarities. Now a visit to the doctor, dentist, or attorney may be dreaded lest he again be "lectured" and exposed as the corrupt, willful one who is responsible for his own injuries because he had not exerted the prudence demanded by the loving judging other.

Further, he may be prompted not only to avoid such a scene, but also to counteract it by fearful building of his body's health by jogging several miles every day, by suntanning for the glow of health, by dieting, by multiple vitamin overkill, by weightlifting. Further, he may attempt a reparative script by counterphobic frequent medical checkups for any early warning sign of threat to physical integrity and to demonstrate to that mother surrogate that he is really mindful of her concerns and that he really is good and worthy of her continuing love and respect. Such a one may suffer very little fear so long as he daily exorcises the condemning other by exercising. Deep-seated, much magnified fears of guilt and loss of love are, however, not necessarily diminished by such action at a distance but are rather the major source of magnification. If the individual can be persuaded of the desirability and continuing necessity to avoid or escape any dreaded scene, such a scene is thereby magnified as escapeor avoidance-worthy, whether it is successfully avoided or escaped or not.

The only way in which such fear might be attenuated, rather than magnified by an avoidance script, would require the development of sufficient skill and effectiveness to be governed by a habitual, skilled as-if script, in which the whole set of scenes are primarily controlled by messages which are relatively unconscious, bypassing the central assembly and thereby not being transmuted into conscious reports, and by messages whose coordination is sufficiently smooth to avoid gradient triggering of fear. It is thereby transformed into an as-if avoidance script, as happens daily with those who walk or drive across a traffic intersection where one might be killed if one did not sufficiently scan for possible dangers but which one does scan without either great conscious concentration or fear. Everyday examples of the same phenomenon are abundant. If one trips walking down a set of stairs, one becomes afraid again, becomes much more "careful," and then lapses into the customary as-if script of walking quickly up or down stairs without fear and with minimal but effective monitoring via a small ratio of conscious reports to messages. Fear, as a gradient-activated affect is peculiarly self-validating by any rapid response against any rapid set of possibilities, be they perceptual, motoric, or cognitive.

It should be noted that the same set of avoidance-defensive behaviors may be scripted as responses to quite different scenes. One cannot deduce the scene origin of any script from the terminal responses of the script. The fearful athleticism and dread of physical problems may have origin scenes of physical abuse by a brutal father or mother or sibling or peer, as a result of which there is a magnified power script dedicated to preventing any possible repetition of helplessness in the face of physical attack and ultimately to the counteractive scene in which one will do to the other what has been done to the self, as occurs with abused children who become abusing parents of their own children. Such a one may fear a visit to a doctor because he is anticipating a beating rather than a scolding. He jogs and lifts weights for safety, not for purity of spirit. He hopes to strike terror into the heart of any assailant, not recover and redeem love from an ambivalent other.

In our previous discussion of the dynamics of humiliation we presented evidence of yet another source of hypochondriasis in the Picture Arrangement Test responses of a representative sample of the population of the United States.

There are peak elevations in hypochondriasis at the two critical transition points, late adolescence (from 14 to 17) and late maturity (from 55 to 64). In the first case, despite optimal physical health, there is intense preoccupation with and pessimism about the body just before one is to enter the labor force and the assumption of adult responsibility. In the latter case, hypochondriasis reaches an absolute peak just before retirement, when one is to leave the labor force for good.

It is the imminence of any radical change in status and its threat to the sense of identity which we regard as the common factor in these two crises. In both cases hypochondriasis drops sharply once the new status has been consolidated. From eighteen to twenty-four, when achievement motivation reaches its peak, hypochondriasis is second lowest of any period in the individual's life. Turning the attention outward to work apparently cures the hypochondriasis of the average American. The absolute low point of hypochondriasis comes, however, immediately following its absolute peak (ages 55–64), in the period of retirement from sixty-five on.

Paradoxically, when the body is most vulnerable to death (65+) the person is least hypochondriacal, and when the body is least vulnerable (14–17) the person is most hypochondriacal. The lowest hypochondriasis for the average American comes as noted above, with retirement. The second lowest period (18–24) is at the time of the assumption of adult responsibility and entering the labor force. It is not, therefore, work itself which is the cure for hypochondriasis but rather, we think, a firm commitment to any new status, whether that be active or passive.

It may be that the open acceptance of dependence and passivity in senility is as therapeutic as the acceptance of responsibility is in early maturity. Indeed, the problem of death is in part the problem of the change of status associated with retirement and the shame provoked by the enforced, unwilling surrender of lifelong commitments in work.

In such hypochondriasis the individual asks himself, "If I am retired, what will happen to my body?" In the previous script the question was, "If something happens to my body, what will happen to my relationship with my beloved?"

A deeper difference between these two types of scripts may, however, rest upon the differential magnification of two types of shame, inferiority shame versus immorality shame. The hypochondriacal fear of the ambivalent mother is evoked by having been condemned for doing wrong. The hypochondriacal fear of the older American facing retirement or of the younger American facing the initiation rite of becoming a self-supporting adult involves the fear he may be tested and found wanting, the shame of inferiority and incompetence rather than the shame of the violation of moral norms. Both involve norm violations and shame as a consequence, but the norms violated are moral in one case and achievement and competence norms in the other. Either may be equally shaming, causing the head to be lowered, but for different offenses. As a consequence the evoked fear is also the same "fear" and also different in its "references."

There is, however, yet another difference in these two scripts, namely, the difference between an avoidance script and a negative celebratory script. The person who jogs daily to avoid the fear of immortality and condemnation is, however intermittently, keeping the fear somewhat attenuated or entirely at a distance. The avoidance script serves in varying degrees and for varying periods of time the useful purpose for which it was designed. In the increased hypochondriasis in the late teens and early sixties the script is more properly understood as one of the varieties of negative-affect celebration scripts in which negative affect has been magnified and prompted the response of complaint and distress, of complaint and protest in outrage and in anger, of complaint in helpless terror, or as in this case complaint of terror about the frailties of the body.

Negative celebration is a more reactive response to negative affect than is avoidance, but it need not be regarded as altogether passive, especially when it is used to achieve community of shared suffering, of nurturance from helping others, or, at the least, of pleading with the other not to add to his terror and/or distress or rage or guilt or shame. Negative celebratory scripts may also be invoked not only to protest and to attenuate suffering but also to recast and make the other suffer as the other has made the self suffer. My guilt and my fear are so great I will burden you with guilt for so frightening me, or I will make you afraid of the damage you have done to me by terrorizing me.

With increasing magnification of scene-dependent fear there are increased multiple activators—signs, similarities, and parts of scenes—which evoke multiple saliences of parts of scenes (now the mother, now the bodily hurt, now the guilt, now the fear in ever-increasing varieties of sequences of conscious salience) and which evoke multiple scripted responses to cope with these scenes in the generation of families of scripted response, from celebration to avoidance to counteraction to attempted repair.

The varieties of scene-dependent magnifications of fear are very great, and we sample only a few of them.

The Case of Laura: Scene-Dependent Magnification of Fear via Variation in Scene

Let us briefly reexamine the case of Laura, the young girl studied by Robertson in connection with a study of the effects of hospitalization on young children when they are separated from their parents. Laura was hospitalized for about a week. During this week, away from her parents she was subjected to a variety of medical examinations and procedures and also photographed by a moving picture camera near her crib. She missed her parents; disturbed by the medical procedures, she cried a good deal. We traced the plurideterminate magnification of a fear script through scenes which were magnified not by repetition but by repetition with a difference. Thus, when she first returned home she appeared to be disturbed. But in a few days she was her normal self again. When Robertson unexpectedly invaded her home, she not only became disturbed again, but differently. Before, the main danger had been in the hospital. Now her parents appear to be either unwilling or unable to prevent the dangerous intrusion into what was, till then, safe space. Yet in a few days all is well again. Then she was taken to an art museum and left in a white crib which the museum provided. She did not cry. The deadly parallel to the hospital crib escapes her. A few minutes later, however, a man comes by with a camera and takes a picture of her. And now she does cry. The family of dangerous scenes has now again been critically enlarged. The scene, whether dangerous or not, has been made more dangerous by her own crying. The scenes in the hospital, at home, and at the museum have now become sufficiently similar, as members of a family of dangerous scenes to generate a magnified script which will produce analogs for as yet unexperienced scenes, will become new family members. This is the heart of the process of magnification.

MAGNIFICATION OF FEAR AS INDEPENDENT

In the independent magnification of fear, fear is both the origin and target of the script. Whatever else may be going on in the scene other than fear is of no concern for the responses scripted in independent magnification. Any scene in which fear occurs is likely to be dealt with by a variety of scripts, some of them dealing only with fear as scene-dependent, some of them with fear as scene-interdependent. None of these types of scripts are necessarily mutually exclusive. It is rather that anything which provokes fear often recruits a variety of script resources to deal with the multiple features of scenes which frighten.

Fear-independent scripts address fear as something to be reduced, to be controlled, to be judged and evaluated, to be sought or avoided or escaped as such, independent of what else may be occurring in the scenes which frighten.

In our discussion of the socialization of fear we saw the varieties of types of affect control exerted in any program of affect socialization, with respect to consciousness, display, vocalization, communication and verbalization, and action and consequences of fear-driven action.

We discussed also the ideological scripts which evaluate each of the specific affects and their relative worth compared with each other for example, that men should not be afraid but that women may or should be afraid. Although it is hoped that affect-control scripts will be consistent with ideological scripts, it is also generally understood that there may be failures in affect control but that the evaluation of such failures is governed by separate ideological scripts. In the extreme case ideology may call for suicide for violations of honor, as in exhibiting fear in warfare.

In sedative affect-management scripts the aim is to reduce negative affects by some response. Thus, a fear sedative script might attempt fear reduction by cigarettes, alcohol, drugs, eating, sex, travel, driving, walking, running, TV, conversation, nature, reading, introversion, music, sports, or a favored place or person. The frequency of sedative acts depends on the frequency and intensity and duration of fear and on the relative effectiveness of the sedative act. If it is effective, the act is terminated and its general frequency reduced. If it is relatively ineffective, it will be repeated and the general frequency of sedative responses will increase.

Some fear sedative scripts require the presence of the mother as the sedative response whenever the child feels afraid. Such a child may be able to play endlessly alone or with peers so long as all goes well. As soon as he becomes afraid, however, he runs to or requires that his mother come to him to sedate his fear.

There is another type of negative-affect management script, which I have labeled the preaddictive script. In this case sedation has been magnified by a substantial increment of urgency and required as a necessary condition to remain in a scene or to act in it. The preaddictive fear script is one in which a child will now require the mother's presence before he can start to play, anticipating fear unless the mother's presence is guaranteed in advance. A preaddictive smoker is one who cannot answer the phone until he gets a cigarette. The negative affect has moved forward and is anticipated to need sedation in advance.

Therefore, if the sedative act is to go to a favored place when frightened, the preaddictive script will dictate going to the place whenever fear is anticipated from any source, for example, before having to meet someone feared. If the sedative act is to withdraw into introversion, the preaddictive script will dictate psychological withdrawal in the face of an anticipated frightening scene such as a medical examination for a suspected illness. Another requires a cigarette, a drink, or something to eat, or to masturbate or have sexual intercourse. None of these are intended to cope with the frightening scene but rather to cope with the fear, in the hope that then it may be possible to cope with the scene.

MAGNIFICATION OF FEAR AS INTERDEPENDENT

Although fear may be magnified as independent, as both the source and target of script responses, and may be magnified as dependent, in that both source and target shift away from fear to what is perceived to be the cause of the fear, most scripts in which fear is embedded and magnified are those in which fear is variously scripted as one element among many interdependent elements which must be scripted. In these scripts fear is both of sources of fear and of fear itself as well as one among many affects and many sources and responses which must be integrated and continually transformed in the light of continuing variations in perceived sources and consequences of responses to fear and to other affects.

RECIPROCAL RECRUITMENT AS INTERDEPENDENT MAGNIFICATION OF FEAR

Fear may be magnified by any set of scripts which links fear to any other affect in reciprocal, mutual magnification. Such a case is the fear of shame and the shame of fear.

Warrior cultures bind fear and shame together so that fear as such evokes shame because cowardice in battle violates pride. This bind is further magnified by its inverse: the ever-present possibility of defeat in any contest, with its necessary consequence of shame, makes the warrior ever alert and fearful of any scene which might evoke shame. He becomes just as afraid of shame as he is ashamed of fear. Any honor or pride magnification, whether it involves warfare or not, is vulnerable to the mutual magnification of shame and fear. Paradoxically, under such mutual magnification the enemy within becomes as dangerous and terrifying as the enemy without. This is further heightened by the splitting of the self into a passive, victimized helpless self, an evaluating, disgusted dissmelling, angry, contemptuous self who cannot tolerate that inferior self when the evaluating self acts as an internalized representative of the adversarial culture's values. An adversarial culture or subculture is not less punitive in this regard than a purely warrior culture. Polemic within a profession or within a business or within a sport can be as severe in shame and in fear as in any war or honor culture.

SELF-DISGUST, DISSMELL, AND ANGER AT FEAR VERSUS FEAR OF SELF-DISGUST, DISSMELL, AND ANGER IN RECIPROCAL MAGNIFICATION

To the extent to which the individual holds himself responsible for excessively high standards in work, in interpersonal relations, or in civic duties, or in all these domains, but also fails to commit himself wholeheartedly because of a variety of fears, his own timidity makes him vulnerable to self-disgust, dissmell, and anger. To the extent to which there are secondary defenses against such criticism of oneself by another self, the individual is vulnerable to episodic, intrusive, explosive self-disgust, dissmell, and rage at the offending overly timid self. Thus, an otherwise caring son may, on the occasion of putting an aged, ailing parent into a nursing home, crucify himself for his timidity in not caring for his parent in his own home, invidiously comparing his limited commitment with the unlimited commitment of that same parent to him, as infant and child.

Again, a father who is fearful about his job stability or his professional status may sacrifice his wife and children to what he thinks is demanded by his own and their future. He may indeed guarantee that future even as he loses the enjoyment of the formative years of his children's development and the deepening of his marital and familial relationships out of a haunting fear of disgusting poverty and failure. When finally he arrives at just that degree of success and affluence for which he struggled, the alienation and distance he feels coming from his family may prompt the submerged, punitive, evaluating self to take its revenge on the proud but timid self and turn his success into the deepest failure. His fear of self-disgust about poverty and failure is now transformed into self-disgust at his fear-driven compulsive achievement and its price.

Again, the pure but timid self may sacrifice adventure and risk taking in love, in sexuality, in work, in travel. After an entire lifetime led in timid, chaste, modest, and restricted exploration, that suppressed, underdeveloped, bold, lustful, vivacious, excitement-seeking self may explode in disgust at the overly timid self. This is the occasion for the phenomenon of what has been mislabeled a second childhood. This is more properly understood as a long-delayed childhood and adolescence in protest not at parents or at society but against what one has been all one's life, the divided self in which the underself becomes a militant revolutionary self. Often such a one seeks out the very young as co-conspirators in adventure, travel, work, sex, and friendship and love. Not infrequently, this is occasioned by rapid social change in which the young reject just those values which have been purchased at what is now experienced as too great a price. In the 1960s the derogation by the young of achievement and of war in favor of fun and love eroded the commitments of those of their elders who suspected they had paid an excessive price for their gratifications, suppressed and delayed out of timidity.

Thus, possible self-disgust magnifies fear, which in turn evokes self-disgust and so reciprocally magnifies both.

GREED AND TERROR AS RECIPROCAL INTERDEPENDENT MAGNIFICATION

We have noted earlier that excessive greed is a prime condition for the evocation of rage because the greedy one's demands for more and more can produce sufficient overstimulation from a variety of sources to keep such a one perpetually unsatisfied and overstimulated. But rage is not the only outcome of greed. When greed adds speed to quantity as a demand, then the failure of either the self, the other, or the world is not simply one of insufficiency but rather one of too slow a rate of satisfaction. Such excessive slowness prompts compensatory speedup in demand and performance. Any perceived barrier to such an increase in speed can increase attempted speed and so evoke fear. Just as a claustrophobic can frighten himself by requiring that he escape very quickly and more quickly than is possible from space which is experienced as too constraining, so does a greedy driver who is blocked by a traffic jam from driving as fast as he would like experience fear that he will be unable to accelerate and that he will be late, by virtue of abortive rapid movements to escape his engulfment. It is not unlike the classic terror of the bachelor about to surrender his freedom of movement on the eve preceding his marriage, who is also blocked in simulated rapid, abortive movements to escape engulfment.

The same dynamic occurs in more complex abstract greed. The overachiever whose upward mobility is experienced as painfully slow by virtue of constraints imposed by those higher in the hierarchy can be frightened by his own impatience in accelerating his demands much beyond his capacity to act out their achievement. Perhaps the most universal type of such greed is in the confrontation with mortality. When the aged confront the diminishing amount of time left for them to complete their lives, with its correlated acceleration of passing time, then, paradoxically, there can be terror from the attempt to speed up the tasting of life to the full. Two maxima are conjoined in such a desperate strategy—the greatest quantity of rewarding experience in the smallest possible time. Abortive acceleration of greedy speed may evoke fear by the use of the limbs, by very rapid constructions of possible outcomes, by very rapid retrievals of past scenes, and by very rapid planning, decisions, and impulsive attempts at problem solution.

OBJECTLESS FEAR OF FEAR INTENSIFIES AND MAGNIFIES FEAR AS INDEPENDENT

Any affect may be experienced without a perceived object. One may be angry or sad or happy but at no one in particular. Such freefloating affect may seek an object or not. If I wake feeling very happy, I may accept that state without further incident. There need be no further recruitment of past scenes, plans for the future, or scrutiny of the present for identification of the source of joy. In the case of fear, however, there is always a possibility of the further intensification and duration of fear just because its source has not been identified. In part this will vary as a function of personality. If the demand for mastery and self-control are central, then the experience of objectless fear may add shame, disgust, or anger to the fear. For all individuals, however, objectless fear is a prime source of more fear of fear because the lack of an identifiable frightening object characteristically prompts an accelerated quest for the unknown source. The longer that source cannot be identified, the greater the probability that fear will be repeated and so provide a trigger which is no more likely to be identified than was the original source. In this case one becomes more afraid just because there is now fear of fear and because one doesn't know what one has feared, has tried too hard and too fast to discover the unknown source. Such speeded attempts become additional sources of freefloating fears.

One paradoxical consequence of the magnified need to know what one fears is that a plausible but incorrect interpretation (e.g., in psychotherapy) may temporarily reduce such secondary fear and provide relief simply because one now believes one "understands" why one is afraid. However, if such interpretation is in fact incorrect or incomplete, such relief will be temporary because the original unconscious sources of the fear may continue to operate. A correct interpretation, however, may indeed increase the fear rather than decrease it if the individual is not ready for radical insight and struggles to quickly escape from the consequences and implications of a danger-increasing interpretation. It is only when an interpretation exposes an unconscious source which is immediately intuited to now be entirely nonthreatening that correct interpretation of an unconscious fear is likely to produce both insight and the reduction of the fear rather than its intensification. Thus, an individual who suffered a lifelong inhibition of deep breathing, as a result of painful whooping cough in early childhood, was cured of this inhibition, in a moment, by a correct interpretation. The analyst intuited an unconscious, fear-driven inhibition of deep breathing after the analysand recalled a very vivid and intense joy in witnessing a scene involving deep breathing. The scene was in the moving picture of Remarque's *All Quiet on the Western Front.* The young hero emerges from a visit to his wounded comrade in a military hospital. The hero, obviously anxious at his confrontation with the possible death of his comrade and also relieved that he himself is very much alive, takes a very deep breath, indicating he is both very anxious and very joyful that he is alive. The analysand stressed that it was the extraordinary depth of the inhalation of air by the hero which particularly moved him and that he had never forgotten that scene in the past twenty years. When an interpretation of a breathing inhibition was offered, the analysand immediately had an image of himself as a child in a dark room with a yellow gaslight when he was experiencing great difficulty in breathing because of whooping cough. Immediately thereafter he became conscious that his breathing had for many years been shallow and restricted in inspiration. Thereupon he voluntarily took a very deep breath and experienced intense excitement and then joy in his new-found ability. The power of the fear-driven inhibition of deep breathing had been entirely dissipated.

In objectless fear, the characteristic script of rapid searches for sources of fear as attempted avoidance or escape or attenuation strategies ordinarily further magnify such fear in a circular fashion, in which fear is feared more than any known or knowable object of fear. Such fear may also be scripted for minimal display (by an affect-control script) and for sedation (by an affect-management script).

The magnification of the fear of fear does not, however, depend entirely on its objectlessness. It is as frightening to be frightened as it is to be threatened. Anyone who has had repeated experience of terror, with or without known sources of terror, may become quite as afraid of reexperiencing terror per se as of reexperiencing whatever it is which frightens him. This is in part how it can happen that the belated realization of the harmlessness of a scene may fail to reduce the terror originally evoked by the scene. Such an individual may complain that even though the irrationality of his fear has been exposed, either by psychotherapeutic interpretation or by demonstrated harmlessness of the dreaded scene, he nonetheless continues to fear what he now believes to be a groundless fear. The salience of fear of fear is now more magnified than the fear of any particular object.

There is a position intermediate between objectless fear and specific fears which may also magnify fear. Diven, in an experiment at the Harvard Psychological Clinic many years ago, demonstrated that the intensity and duration of fear depended critically on just how clearly the source of fear was perceived. Subjects who had been given an electric shock to the specific word "barn," in a controlled experiment of association to several words, responded with fear (as indicated by an elevated psychogalvanic skin response) whenever that word was repeated if they had become correctly aware that they had been shocked before on that word. In marked contrast, subjects who were unclear about what word had preceded that electric shock generalized the fear response to all other words which were in any way "rural" in meaning. There appeared to have been a relatively unconscious generalization based on similarity of meaning when subjects were unable to verbalize the specific source of the electric shock. They responded as if they might be shocked on any rural word when they did not know well enough to verbalize it, that it had been one specific rural word on which they had been shocked. Their knowing was real but diffuse, unclear, and uncertain.

THE CONJUNCTION OF HUMILIATION AND DEMANDED SPEED OF PERFORMANCE AS RECIPROCAL MAGNIFIER OF TERROR

Here we consider scenes in which the individual is bombarded with requests and demands for rapid responses at the same time he is threatened with humiliation. Such threats increase the perceived difficulty of the demanded performances sufficiently to slow them down in fact while simultaneously increasing the demand for more competence and more speed. "Hurry up, stupid" is the prototypic message I have found in such cases of recurrent fear. Characteristically, these verbal pressures are "heard" more and more often even in the absence of actual pressure. Such phrases become internal persecutors which panic the individual by urging him to speed up just as his competence is being slowed. He has been taught to demand from himself a rate of response sufficiently rapid to guarantee both the innate activation of fear and dedifferentiation of skill because of the fear of shame and humiliation. One of the classic comic representations of such a scene was Charles Chaplin as a harassed, speeded-up worker on the assembly line in the film *Modern Times*. Such magnification may be produced by either childhood or adult socialization. It does not matter whether it is an overly coercive parent who pushes a child beyond his rate limits or a social or economic system which insists on up-or-out in rate and quantity of productivity, threatening humiliation and loss of status or economic support for failure to "keep up." Publish or perish in academic life is not very different than the bottom-line earnings statement in the quarterly report for the executive, or than the failure of the piece worker to meet the demands of the sweatshop operator. For the child, for the academic, for the executive, or for the lumpen proletariat, terror is critically tied to demanded excessive rate of performance. Under such conditions all become phobic to the "rat race" and therefore dream of and seek the peace of relaxation and the slowdown of the pace of living either in slower space or time, or in drugs, or in quiescence.

RECIPROCAL MAGNIFICATION OF FEAR BY EXCESSIVE AFFECT-CONTROL SCRIPTS AND INCREASED SOURCES OF FEAR

Customary affect-control scripts require the individual to minimize the feeling of fear, its display, its vocalization, and its communication, and to act as if unafraid while he is required to muffle fear and to back it up. The individual may be capable of exerting such control under normal conditions, though at the price of increasing the magnification of backed-up fear. However, when the quantity, intensity, and frequency of fear are increased by emergency conditions, the demand for such control may magnify terror to such an extent that affect control is jeopardized, and in turn increases the fear of loss of control in circular reciprocal magnification. One of the stereotyped symbols of engulfment by psychotic affect is the sudden uncontrolled cry of terror in a public place. Even films produced by psychiatrists have used the uncontrolled cry of terror as a symbol of the sudden onset of psychosis. I have myself witnessed a dozen psychoanalysts suddenly coming out of their offices in a psychiatric hospital, in frightened response to an adolescent's cry when he was receiving outpatient therapy, followed by an enforced hospitalization, as though the failure to control the vocalization of affect made hospitalization mandatory.

INTERDEPENDENT MAGNIFICATION IN PSYCHOTIC FLOODING OF TERROR OVER DISTRESS

As the ratio of the density of negative to positive affect increases, consciousness is more and more flooded, not only with negative affect in general but with terror over distress in particular, because of the perceived helplessness and inability to control the unwanted invasions of negative affect. As this ratio of negative to positive affect becomes less toxic, the ratio of terror over distress diminishes, and distress over terror increases. It is quite possible to tolerate a large density of distress without being overwhelmed because of much less toxicity of distress than of terror. It was my belief that the advantageous ratio of positive over negative affect was a consequence not only of the predominance of rewarding over punishing scenes but also of the magnification of scripts which, in turn, enabled such a ratio to become a stable equilibrium whenever that ratio became extreme in either direction. Such scripts were based on a variety of balancing and compensating rules for the maintenance of such achieved equilibria.

One subset of such rules concerns the remoteness and distance the individual puts between himself and his negative scenes, and the distance he is able to maintain. The more positive affect, the more that quantum is preserved by either delaying confrontation with insoluble negative scenes (e.g., the prospect of one's own death) or by suppressing the consciousness of it, which has the consequence of then invading the dream life. In contrast, as the ratio of the density of negative over positive affect increases, rules for increasing distance and remoteness are either not generated, or if they are attempted, are swamped and fail in their governance. We should therefore expect psychotics to experience not only more negative than positive affect but to experience negative affect equally in both waking and dream life. In contrast we should expect normals not only to experience more positive than negative affect but to relegate more of their negative affect to their dreams. Further, such negative affect as they did experience should favor distress in their waking life and terror in their dreams. In contrast we should expect more terror in the waking life of psychotics because of the inability to segregate and suppress negative affect in general, including both terror and distress.

This possibility was first suggested to me by my analysis of the following case of an individual who had for many years entertained a very vivid and detailed fantasy of becoming a horse trainer. Scarcely a day passed without some part of it being spent in a daydream about horses. Then his father, to whom he was strongly attached and of whom he was also somewhat afraid, forbade him to have anything more to do with horses, in fact or in fantasy. Thereupon, the daydreaming of horses was terminated but as abruptly began to appear in and dominate his dreams. This continued for several years until the death of his father. Thereupon he began once again to daydream about horses and at the same time he ceased to night-dream about horses. This suggested that hot affect and cognition might be handled during the waking state as thought or reverie but that when affect and cognition become too hot to handle and cannot be expressed in overt action, they are banished to the night dream. Inasmuch as terror is much more toxic than distress, there was a presumption that the shifting back and forth between waking fantasies and dreams by an otherwise normal and well-integrated individual represented the suppression of thoughts when his father demanded it and their reappearance when his father's death made them again more exciting, less disobedient, and less frightening. Yet this same individual had carried throughout his life a moderately heavy burden of distress, though predominantly positive in affect.

Our hypothesis then may be stated: The waking life of normal human beings will be characterized, first, by a preponderance of positive affect and, second, by an equal or lesser degree of negative affect, of a relatively nontoxic quality, most typically distress. The dream life of normal human beings will be characterized, first, by a preponderance of negative affect, primarily of a toxic quality, most typically terror, and, second by a lesser degree of nontoxic negative affect, most typically distress. Psychological levels of functioning which are intermediate in remoteness such as in the early memory will be characterized by a more equal representation of positive affect and negative affect and by toxic and nontoxic negative affect. Second, in the severe psychopathology of psychosis there should be no restriction of negative affect to the dream life but rather a flooding of negative affect, with terror in waking life as well as distress and both in the dream life.

All hypotheses were confirmed. The first hypothesis was tested on a group of 135 high school juniors and seniors. The second hypothesis was tested on a group of 60 psychotic depressives and a matched group of 115 older controls. In the recent past, 73 percent of normals said they had experienced enjoyment, and this was the most frequent affect for the group as a whole. The most common negative affect experienced was distress (53 percent of the group). Fear was the least frequent affect experienced (12.1 percent of the group). In marked contrast, in vivid dreams, fear was the affect most frequently experienced by the group—69 percent (compared with 12 percent in recent experience)—and enjoyment was experienced by 20 percent (compared with 73 percent in recent experience). Distress was also greatly reduced—22 percent (compared with 53 percent in recent experience)—but nonetheless the second most frequent affect experienced in dreams after fear.

In the earliest memory enjoyment remains the dominant affect experienced by 36 percent of the group. It is, however, much less frequent than it is in recent experience (73 percent) but more frequent than in dreams (20 percent). The declining frequency—73 percent, 36 percent, 20 percent—indicates that although it is still the most frequent single affect, it is about half as frequent as in recent experience and about twice as frequent as in dreams. The frequency of fear was also midway between most recent experience and dreams. It is the most frequent single negative affect, with a frequency of 26 percent—compared with 12 percent in recent experience and 69 percent in dreams. Fear is almost three times as frequent in dreams as in early memories and over twice as frequent in early memories as in recent experience. Distress is the second most frequent negative affect in dreams, with a frequency of 20 percent—compared with 53 percent in recent experience and 22 percent in dreams. The variation in frequency of distress is a less steep gradient than that of enjoyment. It should be noted that the relative dominance of fear and distress is similar to that in dreams and dissimilar to that in recent experience; that is, in early memories the group as a whole experiences greatly attenuated enjoyment with an increase in fear and a decrease in distress.

To test the hypothesis about the difference between affect in normals and psychotics, we first compared the frequency with which fear and distress appeared in dreams alone compared with their frequency in recent experience alone. For depressives, fear is found in recent experience exclusively 22.9 percent, compared with 2.7 percent among normal controls; whereas in dreams depressives have fear exclusively—6.5 percent, compared with 31 percent among normals. Depressives tend to experience much more fear consciously than in their dreams than do normals, whereas normals restrict their fear to the dream level. In the case of distress the depressives experience this exclusively, just as they do fear, much more in recent experience alone than in dreams alone—31 percent and 1.7 percent, respectively. For normal controls this ratio is more balanced, with only a slightly higher percentage of distress in recent experience than in dreams—12.2 percent and 10.2 percent, respectively. Another test of this hypothesis involved a comparison between the sum of the frequency of affect experienced in early memory alone, in dreams alone, and/or in memory and dreams together. This sum was compared with the sum of the affect experienced in recent experience alone, in recent experience, *and* in early memory, in recent experience *and* in dreams, and finally in recent experience, in dreams, and in early memories. This latter sum is a measure of the *spread* of the affect to all levels of recent experience, early memories, and dreams. The former sum is a measure of the *restriction* of the affect to the more remote levels of dream and memory. For depressives the spread frequency for fear is 72 percent; the restricted frequency is 13 percent. For normals these frequencies are 19 percent and 54 percent, respectively. In other words normals restrict their fear to dreams and early memories—54 percent, compared to 13 percent in depressives—and spread their fear to all levels—19 percent compared to 72 percent in depressives. In the case of distress, however, both normals and depressives spread their distress, although depressives do so by almost a 2 to 1 ratio. Normals spread distress with a frequency of 46 percent, compared to 88 percent in depressives. Normals restrict their distress with a frequency of 25 percent, compared to 5 percent in depressives. The depressive spreads both his fear and his distresses so that he is more consciously aware of both affects, and they also invade his dreams and early memories.

In summary, normals primarily restrict fear to dreams and, to a lesser extent, to early memories. Their waking experience is dominated by enjoyment on the one hand and distress on the other. Psychotics experience a greater spread of negative affect. Their dreams, early memories, and waking experience are all invaded by fear as well as distress.

THE RECIPROCAL MAGNIFICATION OF THE SCHIZOPHRENIC TERROR OF ENGULFMENT AND ABANDONMENT

My analyses of the TATs of schizophrenics have revealed a magnified terror of two mutually dangerous flights, one toward intimacy, one away from intimacy. The terror of being abandoned and alone prompts a precipitate flight toward a rescuing mother. But at the approaching prospect of such salvation he becomes terrified at engulfment by that overcontrolling mother, which prompts a running away from her. Each flight is toward relief from the other flight. As soon as he has temporarily eased his terror of abandonment and isolation by seeking intimacy, he is confronted by the opposite terror of too much of a good thing, from which he must escape to the now preferable scene of being alone. The prospect of salvation seduces at a distance. But the closer he approaches that salvation, the more his savior prompts the panic which cries out for the opposite salvation, producing endless oscillation and terror.

I found a less severe variant of such terror in the neurotic schizoid script in an individual I have referred to as "telegrapher." I was asked for a diagnosis of a candidate who was in training for service in the armed forces during World War II. He had distinguished himself in a prelimary test of his aptitude for training in telegraphy. To the surprise and disappointment of himself and his superior officer he experienced disabling terror as he confronted the requirement of listening to and transmitting ever-faster coded messages. His explanation was that he experienced the speeded-up messages as getting so far ahead of his ability to keep up with them that he felt they wrapped themselves around him, suffocating him so that he had to run out of the room to escape being engulfed.

An analysis of dreams revealed a preponderance of Rankian-type birth imagery, of going down long, dark passageways into the light and then free-falling in space, both of which terrified but in opposite ways. The dark birthlike canal suffocated, but the free fall in the light space terrified by offering no support and had no end but death. In contrast to the psychotic schizophrenic script, however, he had found a haven of security against complete engulfment and complete abandonment. Characteristically, he would oscillate between approaching intimacy and flight away from it. Thus, he had traveled a great deal over the United States. On entering a new town he would be excited by the prospect of possible intimacy with safe strangers; but characteristically, as soon as he found himself on a crowded street, he would feel hemmed in and become claustrophobic and run to the outskirts of the city for fresh air and isolation. But this soon also required salvation, and he would move on to a new town. However, he had also found a danger-free zone, as he described it. This occurred at nightfall blacking out both the crowds and his isolation, revealing a distant but warmly enveloping night sky of beautiful stars under which he could sleep in his equally comforting sleeping blanket. He had found the ideal womb from which he had no need to leave through a suffocating birth canal, nor fall endlessly through space to his death.

THE TERROR OF EMPTINESS OR FULLNESS OR BOTH IN BULIMIA AND ANOREXIA

In contrast to the schizoid oscillation between closeness and distance, the anxious extrovert is more often terrified by oral emptiness or fullness or in the oscillation and mutually magnifying terror of both. Consider first the fear of emptiness, or more precisely the fear of not taking in, of not drinking, not eating, not smoking. In addictive eating there is continuing vigilance against the dread possibility that the mouth is inactive and empty. As soon as this is detected, there are terror-driven efforts to remedy the empty and passive mouth, with accelerating deprivation affect and expected increasing terror until the mouth is once again busy and full. When eating or smoking returns, terror disappears though vigilant monitoring against deprivation continues. Such addiction need not be symbolic of any particular scene other than the addictive scenes themselves. Oral activity has in such a script been transformed from serving the purpose of sedating negative affect to the purpose of guaranteeing against the possible absence of the oral activity itself, as an end in itself which does not satisfy except by its restoration but which has exquisite powers to terrify when it is missing. The oral addict is like the miser who is less interested in money than he is terrified of its absence.

Such addictive eating is likely to be perpetual but nonetheless not excessive in the manner of bulimia. An addictive eater may nibble all day long, as an addictive smoker always has a cigarette in his mouth. But a cigarette addict does not need to smoke two cigarettes at once. When an addictive eater is seized by an invading nuclear script, the symbolic quest for the perfect antianalog swamps the more restricted addictive script and co-opts it for a more desperate aim. The result is an orgy of eating, to the state of bottoming out in vomiting and/or in drinking into unconsciousness. The stakes have been radically magnified for nuclear orality over addictive orality. Symbolic content is now central in the dance between analogs and antianalogs. The good mother may be greedily devoured until she becomes bad and poisonous again.

Such invasion of addictive eating may occur by a massive increase in negative celebratory nuclear scenes by virtue of too many antianalog-analog defeats, which prompt co-opting of oral addictive scenes. Another way is via the acceleration of greedy oral eating after some deprivation, which results in diminishing oral pleasure, which then accelerates eating still more, in quest of a better taste against growing disgust (owing to diminishing hunger). This change from a good taste to a less good taste to a disgusting taste, provoked by trying to accelerate eating and recovering the good taste experienced at the beginning of addictive eating, then recruits the nuclear script, which in turn co-opts addictive eating into nuclear eating for very much more remote magnified scenes so that one eats to complete exhaustion and nausea.

In pure anorexia, terror is restricted to the act of taking in, to becoming full. This may be a consequence of terror at guilt for greedy orality or sexuality, or of pregnancy, or of self- and other disgust at being too fat as well as too full, or of shame at "needing" to take so much from the other, or of inhibited anger at wishing to rob the other, or of defiant anger at not eating what the other gives or insists one eats. In contrast to addictive eating, this is driven by more symbolic purposes than by pure addictive deprivation affect.

In the binge-purge cycles of bulimia-anorexia there is combined both terror and disgust at taking in as well as at having taken in and therefore vomiting forth—what one wanted but also did not want. Such conflict between oral greed and oral disgust may or may not be nuclear. Deep ambivalence or plurivalence generates contamination scripts of many kinds, including nuclear scripts. However, a nuclear script is marked by a sequence of good scenes turning bad. The attempt to recover the good scene in nuclear scripts need not be ambivalent per se. In deep ambivalent conflict or plurivalent turbulence there are desperate efforts to decontaminate good-bad scenes and their conflicted or ambiguous sequences. Such an individual may rarely have experienced pure psychological affluence. Every major positive scene may have had sufficient negative affect from the other and self to make it a mixed blessing at best. "Yes, but" is the primary message. Every carrot reveals a stick: "That's a good job you did, but you might have cleaned up the mess you made." "I am glad you finally did what I asked you to, but why didn't you do it a week ago?" "You have been very helpful, but what have you done lately?" "That's a beautiful gift, but it's too expensive, and besides, I don't really need it." There is no change from a good scene to a bad scene but rather a perpetual variety of good-bad scenes which terrifies by threatening to defeat all attempts at decontaminating the good-evil scene into a pure good scene, or at reducing the turbulence of many plurivalent scenes multiply good-bad-and-indifferent into a more stable, simple, unified good scene. This is a major problem confronting any child whose parent or parents oscillate wildly between indifference, overcontrol, nurturance, and brutality. No scene, whether good, bad, or indifferent, remains long enough to enable the generation of a nuclear script. There is no home or promised land to which to return.

In cyclical bulimia-vomiting-anorexia, there are many different types of reciprocal magnification of fear and nausea and disgust. Very frequent in individuals I have investigated is intense ambivalence and plurivalence toward the mother such that there is a desperate greed for purely good love and food against the deeply disgusting and nauseating bad food which always accompanies or quickly follows good food. It is more a matter of purifying what is contaminated than of integrating competing wishes. Such an individual is not truly conflicted so much as he is disgusted at the contamination of good scenes with parents whose love is always spoiled in some way. Brecht gave expression to this in *The Threepenny Opera* when he has the hero cry out in disgust that his wedding day is turning out to be just as lousy as any other day.

If what seduces you is the promise of good food but you should not have been so greedy, then you will vomit it forth and avoid food until the seduction overwhelms you. Very often both the greed for food and the vomiting are the consequence of heightened sexuality and guilt for having sinned or wished to do so. In this case the contaminated mother has further contaminated sexuality for her daughter. Like the love and the food from her mother, her own sexuality is now also contaminated so that sexual excitement has been made deeply disgusting, and she knows no way of resisting temptation and no way of holding onto her ill-gotten food, and only briefly can she starve herself before she is again seized by irresistible hunger. She has been taught to fear taking in, not taking in, and having taken in, so that she oscillates in terror between lust, sin, and abstinence, as between hunger, nausea, and no appetite, in reciprocal and bonded magnification, since abstinence increases hunger, which increases nausea, which increases abstinence.

INTERDEPENDENT FEAR MAGNIFICATION: THE DANGEROUS STRANGER SCRIPT—FEAR MODULATES ANGER, DISSMELL, AND INTEREST

The stranger, be he a part of the self, an individual, a class, a race, a nation, or a civilization, may be kept at arm's length as bad-smelling. To the extent that the stranger insists on coming closer rather than remaining distant or going away, anger may further be evoked, mixed with dissmell to produce militant contempt against the overly intrusive inferior. Dissmell without anger may be condescending without further militancy and without any deep interest in the stranger so long as he keeps his distance. Bernard Lewis has shown that for over a thousand years, up until the mideighteenth century, Muslims were as ignorant about Europe as they were indifferent and contemptuous of these strange barbarians. Islam was a political religion, embracing the whole of society, providing it with its law and its social order in a single Revelation. It prepared at once to impose itself on the world since all other societies were inferior in every respect to Islam it owed nothing to other societies. By holy war Islam spread its law and doctrine throughout the world and the true believers assumed that their victorious advance had only been interrupted and would one day be completed. After having appropriated Greek philosophy and science by the twelfth century A.D., there was little more that Islam could learn from outsiders other than what might be useful for mundane trade and diplomacy.

But whereas Islam despised Christendom, Christendom feared Islam. Islam did not fear Christian doctrine because it had superseded it, just as it had little fear from Christian arms because (the Crusades excepted) it had successfully defeated Christendom from the seventh to the seventeenth century.

Christendom not only feared the military power of Islam but also feared its religion as either a heresy or schism. It became necessary to study Islam to defeat it. Hence, the Koran was translated in the twelfth century. In contrast there was no Arabic translation of the Bible until the nineteenth century. Only the threat of the increasing military power of Europe brought the beginning of a desire to study a European language to become familiar with European military techniques. Islam learned both fear and thus respect for Europe no earlier than the eighteenth century.

The stranger, then, may be dissmelled and evoke anger so long as he keeps his distance. Whenever he becomes too powerful and intrusive and dangerous as well as strange and bad-smelling, he may then terrorize and next evoke respect and interest in learning the stranger's secrets in order to protect oneself and defeat the other.

A similar dynamic may be seen in the case of Japan, defeated militarily by the United States, identified sufficiently with its feared, dissmelled, angering enemy to respectfully study and improve the methods of its conqueror and then successfully challenge the economic power of its now mutually ambivalent friendly adversary.

Respect, interest, and knowledge may then be magnified as the paradoxical consequence of contempt jeopardized by fear of the stranger and his strange ways. Such interest may or may not itself become sufficiently autonomous to erode the values of the society or the individual. Muhammad had said, "Whoever imitates a people becomes one of them." The contemporary upsurge of Islam fundamentalism may be a forerunner of a future third world backlash against ambivalent "westernization," which seduces by the promise of power and plenty at the price of erosion of long cherished non-Western ideologies.

The seductive strange ideology, evocative of fear, interest, dissmell, and anger, having been swallowed and having in turn swallowed up the ideology which had been threatened, now suddenly proves to be more than a bad smell, a poison, more nauseating than could have been known and therefore must be expelled violently, as occurred in Iran aided by Khomeinei, who rallied Iran against the United States as the Satan who had violated and raped the innocent, too trusting, too curious, faithful members of Islam. Terror, nausea, dissmell, and rage have thereby diminished the seduction of excitement and new knowledge, in a variant of the fall from Eden in which innocence is recovered by blaming it all on Eve and Satan repeating once again purification by projection and the trials of witchcraft and the Inquisition.

At the individual level is a related dynamic exposed by Jung. The successful businessman seduced by the competitive, masculine ethos of capitalism with its amalgam of anger, dissmell, and excitement often suffers a midlife identity crisis in which the stranger is now the softer, more intuitive feminine self within who invades his dreams and frightens him into Jungian therapy. The recovery and integration of this partitioned strange part of himself Jung labeled the quest for individuation—the recovery of the whole by the part. In such a case it is the erosion of excitement *by* success and its diminishing reward, that first distresses and finally frightens, that powers the quest for more knowledge and understanding of parts of the self and of ways of living now strangely seductive as well as frightening.

THE NUCLEAR SCRIPT AS INTERDEPENDENT MAGNIFICATION OF GREED AND COWARDICE

In the nuclear script, terror is magnified by intransigent greed for the recovery of a good scene turned bad, in which terror prevents such recovery and greed prevents giving up the hopeless quest. We will present two examples, first Pascal's terror at the immensity of spacetime and second a review of the case of Sculptor for the magnification of terror as we examined it before for the magnification of anger.

Immensity of Space-Time as Analog of Nuclear Terror

The immensity of space and time, compared with the relative brevity of the lifetime of one small individual, has captured the imagination of all who have observed the beauty of a night sky full of stars, of the boundless deep of a moonlit ocean, of the vast stillness and thrust of a snow-covered mountain peak. But these are scripted and most often nuclear-scripted responses. Such scenes have evoked the entire spectrum of affects depending upon the script. It may excite by an immensity which evokes thoughts of endless rapidly changing potentialities, all of interest. It may evoke deep joy at the relaxation of all other concerns in the face of the eternal immensity. Either excitement or joy or both may be experienced because of the great distance perceived between the small self and the large and enduring other, as between the child and the parent. In radical contrast the same affects of excitement or joy may be experienced because of the reduction of the distance perceived between the small self and the cosmos in a mystical feeling of complete fusion, in the "oceanic" mode. Secondary reactions to either increased or decreased distance may be deep distress and regret at the mundane quality of the everyday world compared either with the distant majesty or the complete immersion in that infinite space and time. Or there may be a secondary or tertiary response of shame at one's own smallness, or self-disgust because the comparison is so invidious, or rage that the self is so small and powerless and above all so mortal.

Less common is terror. The classic statement is Pascal's:

> When I consider the brief span of my life swallowed up in the eternity before and behind it, the small space that I fill, or even see, engulfed in the immensity of spaces which I know not, and which know not me, I am afraid, and wonder to see myself here rather than there; for there is no reason why I should be here rather than there, now rather than then.

We will not examine the particularities of Pascal's nuclear script, here projected into being "swallowed up" and engulfed at the same time that he neither "knows" that other and that other "knows not" him, into the arbitrariness of being "here rather than there." We will stress rather that it is the generation of many, rapid changes in his integrity as an individual (rather than being swallowed up and engulfed), in his accustomed position in space (rather than being arbitrarily placed here and there), in interaction with familiar others (rather than with complete strangers) that generates his fear. More generally, fear in response to the infinite must have been a much more common response in the earliest days of humanity, when control over nature was much more limited. Residues of that terror persist to the present in the response of awe to the infinite. Awe is characteristically excitement with a small admixture of fear at the invidious comparison of the vastness and power of the cosmos compared with humanity.

If it is terror and not excitement or joy that the sight of the infinite evokes, it is the suddenness of realization of rapid unwanted changes in status, in interpersonal relations, in longevity or in power, which are most often implicated.

The Case of Sculptor: Terror of the Return of the Nuclear Scene

When a nuclear scene is deeply contaminated,—for example, by perceived infidelity of the other, as it was for Sculptor—the nuclear script characteristically magnifies the once beloved as more positively ideal than before and more negatively ideal than before. She becomes utterly enchanting and utterly disenchanting. These are reciprocal magnifications, requiring each other, and are constructed illusions. They are illusions in that no human being is in fact as wonderful or as disgusting as the succeeding magnifying responses to betrayal represent them. Such magnification depends critically on the inability either to totally reject or accept the betrayal and the betrayer. The betrayed one is too dependent to reject the other in outrage and too wounded and shamed and outraged to forgive the betrayer, and so is initially suspended in mute backed-up affect and silence. Eventually, however, several nuclear scripts are generated to "solve" the insoluble. These constructed scenes are antianalogs either of the original nuclear scene or of the succeeding bad scenes, which are consequences of ineffective scripts which produce secondary problems.

Thus, as in the case of Sculptor, the betrayed one may attempt a solution by a combined emulation of and hostile surpassing of just that act of betrayal, for example, the creation of an enchanting sibling. A further reparative criterion may be engrafted on the superior product which is to be created, namely, that it endure forever and be appreciated by succeeding generations. Such a criterion is designed to radically improve on the transience of the relationship disrupted by a mother who produced an unwanted child, a child moreover who must be wonderful indeed to have been created by the beloved and to have been preferred to the self. The betrayed one in such a script becomes a better mother, creative of better, more enduring objects of beauty which will never cease to enchant everyone for all time. Such a self is now fortified against the pain of both unrequited love and yearning and unrequited hate. But such a self and such a nuclear script is vulnerable to victimage by the intrusive nuclear scene it is meant to eliminate. Any sign that the self, its products, or its efforts are less than ideal threatens to victimize the creator and reduce him to reexperience the betrayal, not only in its original form but in its magnified sequels.

Because such a self is highly skilled in analog construction, it is also skilled in detecting any remote possibility of the recurrence of the bad scene. It is the suddenness of the signs of possible change and danger which terrifies. This is, above all, the possibility that the nuclear script has been breached by the nuclear scene. If in response to such terror we take evasive action of any kind, that, plus suddenness of the "signs" and the avoidance of a full exploration of and acquaintance with the possible danger can readily produce free-floating terror without an identifiable object, in which one wants to get away from the terror before encountering more fully what it is which terrorizes us. Such terror may, however, be quite unsuccessful in protecting us or in enabling avoidance or escape. The next moment the individual may be swamped by the massive negative affects of the nuclear scene. More often, however, it is the suddenness of the avoidance or escape response itself which continually recycles fear. For example, an individual may recruit a memory of a negative scene which he very quickly stops thinking about. This sudden cognitive response of shutting off further thinking is quite sufficient to innately trigger more fear. If from time to time he encounters other thoughts which promise to return him to the negative scene, he will again try too quickly to think of something else and so recycle the fear endlessly without ever confronting precisely what he fears since now the activator is in fact his own avoidance response. What is most terrifying is what we run away from most quickly. The overly quick avoidance or escape response not only innately activates fear but prevents that full acquaintance with the dangerous scene which is a necessary, but not sufficient condition for its mastery.

Terror That the Nuclear Script Attempt Will Fail, Shame the Self, and Vindicate the Other

Terror is not limited to the possibility of reexperience of the original nuclear scene but arises also from the assumption that others will treat the self as one has treated the victimizer, and the world is partitioned into victims and victimizers. Thus, the heroic vengeful creator will fear that just as he has attempted to steal the fire of the Earth Mother, so will envious others try to steal his creation, to derogate it rather than appreciate it, to try to surpass it, and to make the self envious of the robber. It is a special case of the law of talion—an eye for an eye, a tooth for a tooth. It is a vivid terror because it is based on the keystone of the enduring central intention to redress the wrongs of the nuclear scene.

It is a case of positive and negative idealization followed by heroic vengeful recasting, which then leads to the derivative fear of further recasting by new enemies as analogs of the self, or double recasting.

Mutual terror is inherent in any adversary relationship. One fears the other because one intends to defend oneself against the other if the other objects to the self's offense against the other, and counter-aggresses. This is the dynamic that locks Russia and the United States into mutual escalating deterrence.

Less obviously, it is also the dynamic of the convenant in the Judaic relationship between God and his chosen people, as we have noted before. As in the case of the individual nuclear script of betrayal, there is a continuing reciprocal betrayal and punishment between God and his chosen people, which locks both into recurrent conflict and self-fulfilling prophecies.

Terror That the Nuclear Script Attempt Will Fail, Shame the Self, and Vindicate the Other

There is also the ever-present danger and therefore intermittent terror at the possibility that the heroic, creative, vengeful emulation of the idealized self and other will fail. In this case the individual fears engulfment in humiliation and in self and other diss-mell, disgust, or shame, at the inauthentic exposed fraudulent self. The self is revealed as a fake of the idealized other, an incompetent imitation. This has a further implication of deepening the tragedy of the original nuclear scene in that the blame for the scene would then be shifted from the other to the self. The other's insight, goodness, and beauty is enhanced in invidious contrast to the evil, ugly, and incompetent pretending self. She rejected the self and preferred her own superior created child for good reason. It was not a betrayal. It was the only possible judgment when confronted with her two children, one of whom she had made in her own image, the other an unsuccessful early experiment. Such a judgment might have been entertained from the start in the attempt to understand how such a disaster could have occurred at all, but more often it is a derivative of the later conceived and feared possibility that the attempted recasting will fail.

Freud has invoked a similar explanation of suicide following failure and bankruptcy in business. The bankrupt one is terrified at the exposure of his combined hostility, incompetence, and guilt. He should never have been so greedy, and he was destined to fail, and he deserves to die by his own hand since his internalized super ego no longer can smile upon him.

Terror of Insight Into the Degree of Magnification of Enchantment and Disgust in the Nuclear Script

In contrast to the terror of the reexperience of the nuclear scene is an equal terror at the possibility of insight into the illusory, constructed nature and degree of magnification of both enchantment and disgust in the nuclear script. One must be oriented in the world in which one lives. The nuclear script is not the only source of the maps, programs, and theories which support movement in the life space, but it is nonetheless the major source of orientation about what is sacred and what is profane. It describes where heaven and hell are to be found. As in any strictly religious script, disbelief and possible violation of the sacred through revelation of competing possibilities which expose the illusory nature of our most cherished beliefs is profoundly threatening. If we can be terrified to reexperience a nuclear scene of betrayal, so too can we be terrified to intuit that the betrayer was neither so loving, so wonderful, nor so betraying, so disgusting as we have constructed her in the years of magnification involved in the nuclear script. Such a possibility would suddenly rob a lifetime not only of its orientation but of its meaning and value. It would transform a vengeful heroic victim into a foolish knave who had spent his life tilting at imaginary windmills. It is as though one had savagely hit a man who had bumped into oneself only to discover he was blind. We must keep secret the exaggeration, both positive and negative, of the heroic nature of our lives lest the high tragedy turn to farce. The terror of the exposure of the illusion necessitated by the defense against the terrifying reexperience of the nuclear scene is a deep paradox inherent in nuclear scripts. It arises because we do not wish to suffer again, but neither can we afford the insight that we have devoted much of our lives to exaggerating that suffering and to coping with that exaggeration in such a way that although the total suffering is no longer illusory its source was.

Terror of the Death and Mourning of Illusory Peak Experience and Lesser Progress

There is terror not only at reexperiencing the nuclear scene, at disorientation from insight into its constructed illusory exaggeration, but also at the prospect of the death and mourning of our most cherished peak experiences. These occur when, in the pursuit of script goals, great progress is made, giving visions of entry into the promised land. In the case of the nuclear script of betrayal we have been considering, any evidence that the creator has indeed created an object of everlasting, wondrous beauty, that he has indeed surpassed his enchanting betraying mother, can produce a peak experience of the deepest excitement or enjoyment, or both. Such experiences are episodic, brief, and vulnerable to attenuation and habituation but nonetheless profoundly support the commitment to the nuclear script. Insight into the illusory source of such experience threatens the death of what is most cherished and threatens even more seriously the ultimate attenuation of the intensity of the entire scene. Just as mourning may be delayed and avoided if one cannot renounce the beloved, so too with the most beloved antianalog of the nuclear script. To admit that such engulfing scenes are based on illusion and to thus kill them is also to know that mourning will convert tragic longing to mere affectless remembrance of things past. The intuition of such a possible sequence is as terrifying as the thought that a lump on the skin of the beloved might lead to cancer, death, and worst of all, forgetting.

There is also fear of losing the lesser but more frequent and more enduring sources of excitement and enjoyment in the varieties of nuclear contest and struggle and their evidence of progress or victories over the analogs of the nuclear enemies. The nuclear scene is not only a burden which the individual cannot relinquish, but it is one he does not want to surrender, since the struggle against it is as exciting as are the gains against the enemy, no matter how small. In the case of the nuclear script we are considering, an ideal woman, an antianalog of his unfaithful mother might indeed reward him with one type of peak experience, but she would also rob him of the excitement inherent in wooing a reluctant mother surrogate and rob him also of the excitement of recasting and avenging himself upon her by seducing her and betraying her and rob him of yet another nuclear script, the deep joy of reunion with the mother surrogate who sees the error of her ways and who offers herself completely to her son whom she had not truly appreciated, promising never again to leave him. These are samples of the varieties of nuclear script "work" which defines varieties of different kinds of "progress" great and small, which excite by their promise even when they reward with less than peak experience. En masse, totality of such daily struggles exceeds in affect density the occasional peak experiences in the continuing nuclear script struggle. To lose either would be to impoverish his life.

Terror at Possibility of Forgiveness and Dependency and Reduction of Disgust and Anger in the Nuclear Script

Finally, consider the terror at the radical changes in action, belief, and affect which might be required if there were to be insight into the nuclear scene and the exaggerations inherent in the nuclear script.

In the case we have been considering this would entail a radical reduction in disgust and anger, the necessity of forgiveness and reconciliation, and the reappearance of the long-denied and escaped dependency on the once-beloved mother. This is a much feared endopsychic fifth column within the person which threatens to betray the heroic vengeful creator no less than the mother who originally seemed to betray him. This entails at the very least the terror at the deep shame which such apology and throwing oneself on the mercy of the rejected mother would evoke. There is the projected possibility that she will respond in such a way as to further shame the sinning, now penitent son, that she will seek revenge, just as he did and that she will distance herself from him just as he distanced himself from her. Terror is a response to sudden unknown possibilities and he must be unsure of his welcome after all these years. Resistance to insight is primarily resistance to the changes in behavior, affect, and belief which insight would entail. It is the approximate, sudden intuition of such possibilities which terrify and close off the possibility of self-understanding, whether the teacher be the self or another.

In summary, a nuclear script is a source of multiple terrors, of reexperiencing the original nuclear scene and the succeeding nuclear scenes magnified by the nuclear script; terror at the possibility that others will victimize the self, as the self victimized the original victimizer in a double recasting; terror at the possibility that the desperate attempt to emulate the true hero will fail and expose the self not only to shame but further magnify and justify the original rejection by the other of the self; terror at the possibility of insight into the degree of exaggeration of the original nuclear scene and the illusory nature of the problems constructed by the script; terror of the possibility of the death, mourning, and attenuation of the most cherished peak experiences based on antianalogs; finally, terror at the possibilities of renunciation of anger, disgust, revenge, and autonomy in favor of the long-escaped dependency via forgiveness and seeking of reconciliation. In short, proud, creative, but fearful autonomy is pictured as a failure surrendered for the uncertain tender mercies of the oncetrusted beloved mother, who is now revealed as partly justified in her original rejection of the self.

Epilogue

We have now completed our examination of affect in *Affect, Imagery, Consciousness.* Volume 4 will complete our examination of imagery and consciousness as these are embodied in perception, memory, and action in their interaction as a feedback mechanism. Although Volume 4 is entitled *Cognition: Duplication and Transformation of Information,* I do not regard cognition as a separate mechanism, as I do memory, perception, and the motoric. Rather, I regard it as the system which in interaction orders all the particular subsystems. Cognition, therefore, is to the mind as life is to the body. Life is not the heart, nor the lungs, nor the blood but the organization of these mechanisms. So minding or cognition is the organization of memory, perception, and action as well as of affect. Cognition is the most general ordering principle which governs the human being. The theory of the human being is embodied in these four volumes. My theory of personality will be presented in separate volumes.

Volume IV

COGNITION: DUPLICATION AND TRANSFORMATION OF INFORMATION

Chapter 42
Introduction to the Second Half of Human Being Theory

I have, in Volumes I, II, and III, now completed the examination of the major motivational mechanisms: the homeostatic, the drive, the affect, and nonspecific amplification systems. This constitutes one-half of what I have called human being theory. My excursions into personality theory thus far have been episodic (Volume III, Chapter 26) rather than systematic because I will publish a theory of personality I have called script theory in volumes separate from this prolegomenon to personality theory (Tomkins, 1987). Human being theory is a part of what used to be called general psychology. I have relabeled it because general psychology has been abandoned as a consequence of increasing specialization and because I wish to provide a theory for understanding human beings rather than a more general theory for understanding all animals.

In this second half of human being theory I will examine what I have defined as the cognitive *system*. Before examining the nature of this system, let us briefly review some of the history of cognitive theory.

THE COGNITIVE REVOLUTION

We are in the midst of what has been called the cognitive revolution in psychology. New journals of cognition and cognitive science flourish, and editors and authors alike act as if there were no ambiguity about the nature of this relatively new field. In part this has happened because cognitive theory originated in intellectual combat. When one is certain what one is fighting against, one can afford to believe that one knows precisely what one is fighting for. But like revolutionary movements in general, the defeat of the oppressor characteristically reveals the fragility and ambiguity of the consensus previously cemented by opposition. In the sustained controversy between Hull and Tolman, the issue was joined in the question about the nature of instrumental learning. Did organisms learn because they were driven and reinforced by drive rewards, or did they learn because they thought and generated cognitive maps?

Such a formulation first of all restricted cognition to instrumental learning and disregarded the role of cognition both as an end in itself and in such fusions of cognition and affect as appear in ideology, religion, art, and social life in general. Indeed, it was only as recently as 1979 that Zajonc was prompted to insist that social cognition had characteristics sufficiently different from general cognition to require special theoretical scrutiny. Because the issue was defined as cognitive maps versus drive rewards, one did not need to be too precise about the nature and definition of cognitive maps, apart from operational definition, nor whether this was a necessary and sufficient description of the nature of the cognitive function. The presumed clarity and definability of drives gave a false sense of clarity and definability to its opponent, the cognitive mechanism. In this opposition, cognition is presumed to be *not* like drives. Because Tolman represented himself as a behaviorist, albeit a special kind of behaviorist, the antibehaviorist aspect of cognition was muted in this controversy. Later, however, the cognitive revolution set itself in further opposition to the empty organism behaviorism of Skinner. Cognitive theory then defined itself as centered in the middle of just that black box that Skinner had excluded in favor of the box of his own design, in which rats and pigeons and even infants emitted "behavior." Cognition was thereby further differentiated, not only from drives but from those behaviors that were controlled by Skinnerian schedules of shaping and reinforcement. Thus, cognition became a somewhat autonomous function defined by its difference from being driven from within and from being shaped from without.

This is the most recent instance in a history of favoring man's "reason" as his distinctive glory. Although Genesis equated "knowing" with carnal knowledge, that fateful loss of innocence that exiled him from the Garden of Eden, in both theological and secular thought, reason has been glorified as the divine spark in man.

This perennial idealization of the cognitive function has prejudged its definition. If human beings share sensory and motor equipment as well as drives and passions with other animals, and if reason is represented as both the distinctive and most valued function in man, then the cognitive aspects of the sensory and motor functions are denied by definition. Further, "irrationality" is thereby also denied to be inherently cognitive. "Superstition" and mysticism are prejudged to be different from cognition rather than to be special cases of knowing. In the most extreme derivative of such idealization, even science would fail to meet the criterion of true cognition, inasmuch as today's science can be tomorrow's superstition. In some theologies just this inference was drawn so that only God knew truly and fully.

One might suppose that such idealization of reason no longer plagues psychology. I will attempt to demonstrate, however, that ideology still is and will always be with us, influencing our definitions of basic psychological phenomena. Indeed, the history of American psychology to date can in part be understood in terms of the preferential treatment of particular subsystems and psychological functions, and of the imperfect competition of the conceptual marketplace that overestimates some one function or set of functions to the detriment of others. Drives, affects, memory, perception, cognition, action, consciousness have in varying alliances tended to dominate our theoretical and experimental landscape. If behaviorism and drive theory alike grew out of the characteristic American extraversion, then surely the cognitive movement is an introversive revolt against the major American posture. Indeed, the major theoretical influences here were European, not American. Köhler and Wertheimer introduced rational "insight." Lewin influenced Tolman, and Piaget and Heider further deepened cognitive theory in America. It is not surprising that the older civilization fathered cognitive theory. Introversion has not been the preferred mode of functioning for the descendants of the American activist pioneers even when they have chosen to devote their lives to the study of human beings.

Even within today's cognitive revolution there are deep divisions about the nature of the cognitive function. Consider, for example, the difference between daydreaming, hot cognition, and artificial intelligence. The American pioneer in the experimental study of inner experience, of daydreaming, of imagery and fantasy has been Jerome L. Singer (1955, 1966,1973,1975). His sustained program of research over the past 25 years has illuminated a major mode of experience with which the dominant American culture uneasily coexists. He has continued to remind us that the development of the inner life has been minimized both in American psychology and in American culture generally and that a life lived without fantasy and daydream may be a seriously impoverished life. He has shown that daydreaming is neither trivial nor pathological but an important human ability that requires practice if it is to be developed and that such practice itself requires some degree of privacy.

Yet if all cognitive theorists would resonate to Socrates' dictum that the unexamined life is not worth living, they would part company as soon as "examination" was scrutinized more closely. Are daydreaming and thinking equally "cognitive"?

The introversive conception of thinking as a solitary, inner, autonomous process was, in a fundamental sense, un-American. Such dangerous solipsistic threats were soon to be dealt with in a characteristically American way. The machine and its technology would objectify what might be going on in the black box. "Inner" processes had to be both objectified and operationalized.

Because of the extraverted empirical bias of American psychology, cognitive theory was early on identified with the extraordinary capabilities of the computer. Thinking, as a psychological phenomenon, gained respectability and credibility when it was demonstrated that computers could be programmed to simulate complex thought processes—that they could pay attention to input, consult their past experience, consider alternatives, and make intelligent decisions—in short, that they could mimic the designers who intended they should do so. The theory of automata introduced not only the idea of information processing but also deepened the conception of a feedback mechanism in which a predetermined state is achieved by utilizing information about the difference between the achieved state and the predetermined state to reduce this difference to zero.

Not only did thinking gain respectability from the computer, but so did the conception of "purpose" by exaggerating cerebral purposes. If a chess program could try to win and sometimes succeed in games with a human opponent, it was a small leap to suppose that motivation was really, primarily "cognitive" and that computers could be programmed to simulate their designers. In the "hot" cognition described by Abelson (1963), even distortions of rationalization could be simulated insofar as the underlying affects which power rationalization could be *implicitly* included via their assumed biasing of information processing. Thus, not only was thinking objectified via the computer, but so was purposeful behavior, which appeared to be not only purposeful but surprisingly cognitive. Via computer simulation and artificial intelligence we were promised the best of both worlds. Complex inner processes could be simplified and objectified, at the same time that such objectified cognitive processes could also deal with formidable purposive phenomena. Just as the sea voyage Americanized Freud and Jung, so it did, too, Köhler, Wertheimer, Lewin, Heider, and Piaget.

We have examined a few of the partisans of the cognitive revolution in American psychology. For Tolman, cognitive maps were defined in opposition to drives. The definition of reason by its opposition to drives is a perennial. Its chief liability is its exclusion, by definition, of cognitive processing with vested interests that derive in any way from the drives or from affects. Thus, Marx defined ideology as thought that serves class interests. Such cognition would not be examined with care by any theory that insisted on the autonomy of cognition from drives. Tolman would have insisted that cognitive maps *are* used to find food but that the learning would not be contaminated by hunger; rather that cognition, driven by hunger, might be sharpened by such urgency. Any insistence on the invidious difference between cognition and drives will tend toward an exaggeration of the purity, dignity, and glory of the divine spark in man.

In Singer's (1966) conception of cognition in imagery, daydreaming, and fantasy, the intimate relationships between affect and cognition are central, and he is, in this respect, unique among cognitive theorists. Further, his insistence on the centrality of consciousness is not unique; it *is* unique when the importance of the fusion of affect, consciousness, and cognition is considered. But here too there is selectivity and, in part, definition by exclusion. It is not the enemies within that are excluded by Singer but rather the enemies without. Singer conceives of the stream of consciousness as creative, autonomous, and ever-present. Thus, in one experiment (1966) he found that even in the midst of demanding pressures to meet the task imposed by the experimenter, the subject nonetheless managed to preserve a private retreat within, which freed him from being entirely determined by the demand characteristics of the situation. The importance of the freedom of cognition from external shaping, whether by Skinner or by society, cannot be exaggerated. But this insistence nonetheless would bias our theory of cognition. It is an introversive bias, which is likely to examine external influences on cognition primarily from the point of view of their positive or negative impact on the development of an essentially autonomous and creative cognition. This is to underrate the extent to which cognition is shaped to simulate external and particularly social models, as in language acquisition and in the transmission and preservation of traditions. If society is ever to change, there must be some tension sustained between the society's definition of the situation and the individual's script. If the society is to endure as a coherent entity, its definition of situations must in some measure be constructed as an integral part of the shared scripts of its individuals. Cognition is a major determinant of the scripts that define the world in which we live, and they are amalgams of inner and outer demands and challenges.

As we turn from Singer to artificial intelligence and computer simulation, we have moved a long distance. We are now in the field of cognitive *science* rather than simply cognition. It is precision and objectivity that are now at a premium. What is inside is not good enough. It must be exposed to the daylight of programming and debugging. Consciousness is replaced by statements in computer language. Affect is replaced by its biasing effect on information processing. In artificial intelligence a premium is placed on cleverness. The smarter the chess program is, the better. The only criterion is winning, not playing the game. The situation is much better in computer simulation of problem solving, but the problems are exclusively cerebral. No computer simulation debates whether life is worth living and, if so, how. In Abelson's (1963) computer simulation of rationalization we do have a bridge between Singer and Simon-Newell and artificial intelligence. It is nonetheless a bridge over a deep chasm, as that between artificial intelligence and biological intelligence. Artificial intelligence necessarily relies on a computer that uses few parts and ultra-high-frequency switching processes rather than a biological mechanism that operates at much slower speeds but with greater complexity of parts and circuitry. Computer science has essentially identified cognition with thinking and problem solving, excluding wide ranges of other types of knowing. Some of these excluded types of knowing are essentially aesthetic, in knowing *that* something is so rather than how or why, for example, a face or a place is extraordinarily beautiful. Such knowledge is no less complex than conventional problem solving, but it is generally the consequence of the relatively unconscious coassembly of many past scenes, which converge to endow a momentary scene with the magical power to stop time. Such was the case in the medieval legend of the man who looked up at the sky and beheld God, and when he looked away, it was a few hundred years later. Some thinking is indeed about thinking, but much thinking and knowing has noncognitive referents. Even in the restricted case of thinking that is oriented toward problem solving, there are critical differences between solving mathematical problems and learning how to hit a golf ball effectively. Computer simulation rarely addresses itself to the problem of teaching one's muscles appropriate coordination. These exclusions unduly restrict not only computer simulation but, more important, our conception of what the cognitive system does and can do.

Definition by opposition is hazardous because it limits the multidimensional characteristics of both what is being defined and what is being excluded. Thus, if one were to define joy as the opposite of distress, one would be limited in one's understanding of the role of joy and to the supposition that joy and only joy was the alternative response to distress and only distress; that is, that happy–sad was an adequate delineation of the opposition between positive and negative affects, neglecting the option that, for some, excitement was a viable way of responding positively rather than with joy. Second, it incorrectly describes the range of alternative negative affects that may oppose either excitement or joy. Thus, for one individual joy is experienced as relief from distress, whereas for another, or for the same individual at a different time, the opposition is between joy and anger. Critical differences in personality structure then emerge, depending on the range of positive affects that are put into opposition to a range of negative affects. The individual whose own experience is limited to swings from joy to distress is much less rich than one who alternates in opposition or in relief from either joy or excitement to distress or anger or fear or shame or contempt or disgust. Any theory that employs a restriction of alternatives in its definition of a basic human function, whether it be affect or cognition, unwittingly impoverishes our understanding of such a function.

Role of the Cognitive System in the Human Being: Transformation versus Amplification

We have said that in this second half of human being theory we will be dealing with that set of cognitive subsystems that together constitute the cognitive system. What is the general relation between this *half* and the *motivational half*? It is a set of relations of partial independence, partial dependence, and partial interdependence that vary in their interrelationships, conditional upon the specific state of the whole system at any one moment. Clearly, the system as a whole must satisfy several environmental demands, challenges, and opportunities if the individual, the species, and the genetic pool are to survive and reproduce themselves. Seen in the evolutionary nexus, both the motivational and the cognitive systems must have evolved so that together they guaranteed a viable, integrated human being. It could not have been the case that either "motives" or "cognitions" should have been dominant since both halves of the total system had to be matched, not only to each other but, more important, to the environmental niche of the species. There is a nontrivial sense, then, in which the whole human being could be considered to be "cognitive" (rather than being subdivided into a motivational system and a cognitive system). Because of the high degree of interpenetration and interconnectedness of each part with every other part and with the whole, the distinction we have drawn between the cognitive half and the motivational half must be considered to be a fragile distinction between transformation and amplification as a specialized type of transformation. Cognitions coassembled with affects become hot and urgent. Affects coassembled with cognitions become better informed and smarter. The major distinction between the two halves is that between *amplification* by the motivational system and *transformation* by the cognitive system. But the amplified information of the motivational system can be and must be transformed by the cognitive system, and the transformed information of the cognitive system can be and must be amplified by the motivational system. Amplification without transformation would be blind; transformation without amplification would be weak. The blind mechanisms must be given sight; the weak mechanisms must be given strength. All information is at once biased and informed.

The human being confronts the world as a unitary totality. In vital encounters he is necessarily an acting, thinking, feeling, sensing, remembering person. Consider one of the simplest examples: One begins to cross a street, sees a car coming rapidly; at the same time one becomes frightened at the danger and steps back to the safety of the sidewalk. Cognition here is more than "thinking." It consists in *relating* the car as seen to the danger as felt, to the action of avoiding the danger. It is a momentary environmental, sensory, perceptual, memorial action sequence that is cognitive by virtue of the achieved organized connectedness of these part mechanisms and the *information and urgency* they conjointly generate. If the automobile had traveled much faster, it would *not* have been seen in time to be avoided. The rate at which it traveled produced an abstract fear response, innately, but the interpretation that there was a specific danger unless one took evasive action depends in part on connecting the nature of the danger to appropriate action via retrieval from memory of the relevant pool of information. The innate affect of fear produces only an *abstract urgency*—that something is happening too quickly—by imprinting its own acceleration on both the perceived cause and the necessary responses to that cause, interpretive or motoric, since under fear one thinks fast and acts fast. Such abstractness of the affect amplification is rendered more particular by the combined perceptual, memory, and motor responses. Just as sensory processes achieve enrichment through increased connectedness via memory, so does affect achieve more particularity by being embedded in an ever-widening pool of perceptual and memory-retrieved information.

A very inexperienced child can easily run for a ball in the street despite danger, either due to the distraction of the exciting ball or insufficient knowledge of the possible danger from the car. The motor act is a complex response to a complex set of data provided by interdependent mechanisms, no one of which is more or less specifically "cognitive" than any other one. In such a case, even the affect mechanism provides information—albeit *abstract* information—as well as urgency to both the perceived cause and the appropriate response.

As we have previously shown, even the drive system has some important informational characteristics, telling us when and where both to make consummatory responses and to stop responding. The pain mechanism is equally informative, as place-specific as the drive mechanism but more time-general in that there is not a structural basis for temporal rhythms of activation. Thus, a person may never experience pain or may suffer intractable pain. He enjoys no such freedom of time generality for his primary drives.

The coassembly and fusion of both motivational and cognitive mechanisms is the rule, not the exception. Cognition is sometimes "about" cognition, but this is the special, not the general, case.

Role of Affect and Cognition in the Human Being: A Script Theoretic Formulation

The human being cannot be understood simply as a set of separate motivational and cognitive mechanisms. He is this, but because these are *matched* mechanisms, they necessarily generate with very high probability the emergent phenomena 9 have called scripts. By very high probability I do not mean necessary. Thus, it is very probable that two dice when thrown will unambiguously equal a number between 2 and 12. But this is not necessarily so, inasmuch as one of the dice may land on an edge rather than on one of its flat surfaces. But given the (nonloaded) nature of the dice, the nature of the landing surface, and the nature of the gravitational field, these conjoint conditions make it highly probable (but not certain) that the sum of numbers will be limited in range and unambiguous. It is in this sense that scripts are the very highly probable emergent of the totality of the separate but equal motivational and cognitive mechanisms.

Scripts are not simply actions or thoughts or memories or percepts or feelings or drives but the rules that generate organized scenes made up of these component functions, their processes, and their products. Through his scripts a human being experiences the world in organized scenes, some close to, some remote from, the heart's desire. He does not live to think or to feel but to optimize the world as he experiences it from scene to scene.

Script theory examines the varieties of particular ways of living in the world. Human being theory is concerned with how such phenomena are possible at all.

Script as a Conjunction of Affective Amplification and Cognitive Transformation

If the script is a higher-order organization of affect and cognition, of amplification and transformation, then an ambiguity in the meaning of transformation and cognition is introduced. Such ambiguities in system properties are neither unusual nor peculiar to the human being. I will argue that any organized system is inherently ambiguous at its boundaries, whether these boundaries be at the top or at the bottom, at the part of the system or at the whole of the system, at the most elementary particle or at the outer reaches of space at the time of the big bang. Such ambiguities are in part the consequence of the limitations of our conceptual powers, the "antinomies" of human reason, as Kant called them. Thus, we cannot imagine that space, or time, is either finite or infinite. If it is finite, what is beyond it? If it is infinite, where is its boundary? But the ambiguity of amplification versus transformation is less arcane. Consider an analogue. Language, which has an alphabet as its elements, begins necessarily with ambiguous meaning. An isolated *A* has no meaning, and yet it is an essential element in a language that is to represent meaning. At the top end of the linguistic chain, the outer boundary of language, the zone of pragmatics, there is also ambiguity. As an example, suppose I tell you a lie. There is nothing in linguistic theory that can distinguish such an utterance from a "true" statement. But the ambiguity is deeper than this, because I can tell you a lie with such a statement even if you and I think it is true. Thus, if I say to you, "I think your painting is beautiful" but at the same time lift my upper lip and draw my nose back as from a bad smell, I may be deceiving you and myself by qualifying what I have said by an affective communication in a different "language." So a very precise system of meanings, which we call language, is made up of nonlinguistic elements, letters of an alphabet embedded in a surround that is equally nonlinguistic, producing combinations of language and nonlanguage that are deeply ambiguous—but not necessarily without some extralinguistic meaning. If we define cognition as those mechanisms that have the power to process and transform "information" and oppose this system to the amplifier mechanisms of the reticular formation—drives, pain, and affects that are specialized for amplification of information—then what are we to call the higher-order mechanisms and processes whereby *both* affect and cognition are integrated into scripts?

I propose an ancient term, *mind* in modern dress, the *minding* system. Minding stresses at once both its cognitive process mentality and its caring characteristics. The human being then is a minding system composed of cognitive and affective subsystems. The human being innately "minds" or cares about what he knows.

Scripts are generated by the minding system as rules for that system, including rules for both cognitive and affective ordering as subsets, analogous to the way in which an interpretation of a text presupposes and includes rules of grammar, semantics, pragmatics, and more.

For our purposes in this second half of human being theory we will accept some of the ambiguity of meaning of the cognitive system as a separate system, for analytical purposes, while recognizing that there are higher and more complex ordering principles which integrate *both* the "cognitive" and "motivational" systems. Such ordering principles are the foundations of script theory. They constitute the upper boundary of human being theory, and as such they render human being theory incomplete and ambiguous. It is analogous to the problem of an as yet nonexistent unified theory of alphabet, grammar, semantics, pragmatics, and scripts.

Part I
COGNITION

Chapter 43

Cognition: What Is It and Where Is It?

DEFINITION OF COGNITION AND THE COGNITIVE SYSTEM

I have defined the cognitive system as consisting of the separate specialized mechanisms of the central assembly: perception, the motoric, and memory. These separate mechanisms are cognitive insofar as they all process information in one or another of several different ways: reception, transmission, storage, amplification, translation, coassembly, or transformation of information.

First is the perceptual mechanism, which contains specialized sensory receptors, sensory nerves, and cortical receiving areas. The sensory receptors are also equipped with effector muscles that can move the receptors.

Next is the motor mechanism, which has a cortical sending area, motor nerves, and motor effectors (muscles), as well as sensory receptors embedded in the motor effectors.

The memory mechanism contains short-term reverberating circuits, perhaps intermediate-term reverberating circuits, and receptor areas (such as the hippocampus) for longer-term storage. It also contains afferent and efferent nerves to and from the central assembly and storage receptor areas.

Feedback circuitry is provided all separate systems, as well as the whole system. As examples, the motor mechanisms are supplied with sensory receptors, and sensory receptors are supplied with motor mechanisms (as in the ocular muscles).

The central assembly, the site of consciousness and imagery, is located in a (hypothetical) subcortical center that admits or excludes perceptual and memory messages from all sources on the basis of the relative density of firing of competing messages. Once admitted to this central site, I assume transmitted messages are here further transformed by an as yet unknown process I have called *transmuting*, which changes an unconscious message into a *report*. I define a report as any message in conscious form. Further, I assume that *admitted* messages are in the form of *imagery* and that what is consciously experienced is imagery created by decomposition and synthesis of sensory and stored messages. It is this skill in analysis and synthesis of information that eventually supports the dream and the hallucination.

The glaring omission in this account is language and speech. Theory and research in this area have accelerated at such a rate that it has grown beyond the limits of my expertise. I will, however, refer to it as a metaphor for understanding cognition, as well as for understanding the nervous system and will also examine its role in the theory of imagery and feedback circuitry. It will, however, be an incomplete account of this fundamental subsystem.

I will argue that cognition is as pluralistic as there are ways of "knowing." Consciousness is one way of knowing, but one need not be conscious to know. One inherits, in the gene, much knowledge. In the homeostatic mechanisms there is extraordinary wisdom we also inherit. There are hundreds of feedback loops within the sensory, motor, storage, and amplifier drive mechanisms that know how to maintain equilibria that operate outside of consciousness and permit consciousness to restrict itself to other objects of knowledge. There is knowing in a sensory way that is relatively immediate, which gives a knowing that something is the case. There is, of course, a pluralism of senses, each providing quite different kinds of knowledge. In addition to the familiar differences between tasting, smelling, touching, seeing, and hearing, there are pains of various kinds, drive sensations of various kinds, muscle sensations of various kinds, affect sensations of various kinds, and temperature sensations as well as wakefulness and sleepiness sensations. There are also sensory images that are recognized as imagined rather than sensed. Some of these sensations give us knowledge of what we are doing with our muscles rather than what is out there. Some of these sensations are experienced at a distance, some on the surface of the skin, some on the surface of the tongue, some on the surface of the genitals, some within, some in the viscera.

We also know again by reproductive remembering or by recognizing (as contrasted with knowing possibilities we generate as fantasies), by thoughts, by inner or outer speech to ourselves or to others or from others.

We know with varying degrees of directness and immediacy as contrasted with indirectness and mediation, as in the difference between pain or touch and the awareness of signs and symbols, as in language.

We know with different relationships between thinking and observation, as in the difference between inductive and deductive thought. We know with a great variety of differences in cognitive styles beyond those of induction and deduction. These include breadth versus depth of thought, field dependence versus field independence, introverted versus extroverted, analytic versus synthetic, sharpening versus leveling, to sample some of those types of knowing that have been investigated.

We know differently when we sense *that* something is so—say, that it is raining—compared with knowing *why* or *how* something is so, as in meteorology.

We know differently when we know a particularity or a generality. We may know all there is to know about a particular but little about other members of that class, or all about a class—say, human beings—but little about any particular human being within that class, as one may love humanity but hate human beings, or conversely.

We know differently when we know how and why something is, in general, from when we know how to do something in particular, as in the distinction between basic and applied science.

Within basic knowledge, we know differently when we describe, classify, model, predict, or control, though we may combine any or all of these different ways of knowing.

We know differently depending upon the degree of enrichment of information, by the amount of information brought to bear upon any single bit of information. In the case of perception, this would involve seeing an object from many rather than one or a few perspectives. But enrichment is also a function of comparison with the remembered past as well as an imagined future, immediate and remote, and with possibilities as well as actualities. One's own past life history is continually changing as it is viewed from a constantly changing present. One's appreciation of any person, place, or art or science never ceases to change as information is increasingly enriched through varying coassemblies that compare and contrast and transform perspective. Theoretically, the same life may be experienced in retrospect and in prospect at succeeding moments, in an infinite number of ways. Proust's *Remembrance of Things Past* was but one of many possible perspectives for him. Further, depending on different types of comparisons and integrative transformations, such enrichment of perspectives may yield a cumulative, coherent, unitary perspective; a conflicted, dualistic one; a pluralistic set of perspectives that yield ambiguity or a pluralistic set of perspectives that are orthogonal to each other, experienced as "different."

Differences in knowing may issue from differences in cognitive structures, in the cognitive processes they generate, and in the cognitive products that result, as well as in the varying interrelationships of dependence, independence, and interdependence between cognitive structures, processes, and products. We will examine some of these consequences in greater detail later.

Though each of these mechanisms fulfills distinctive functions, each of which is cognitive, I have nonetheless defined the cognitive system as the totality of these parts and their interrelationships.

I am assuming that structures, processes, and products may each and all be regarded as cognitive and that together they constitute what I am defining as a cognitive system. It is process interrelationships that have been more commonly defined as cognitive rather than either the parts or the totality of parts. Cognition has been more often defined as a process or "operation" than as a mechanism or structure. Thus, some recent theories of memory have been labeled cognitive because they assume that storage is preceded and followed by information transformation processes that are more complex than is assumed in more conventional theories of storage. Again, some perceptual theorists insist that the stimulus has all of the information necessary for valid perception, against those who require that further constructive transformation is needed for stimulus enrichment. The latter is regarded as a more cognitive theory because of the assumption that the perceptual process appears to require more information processing than the sensory apparatus alone can provide. It is somewhat awkward to define the cognitive system as made up of different cognitive subsystems, each with its distinctive cognitive function but nonetheless contributing to a broader cognitive system via the interrelationships between these parts. It is analogous to defining an alphabet as one linguistic structure, syntax as another linguistic structure, semantics as still another, and their combination as constituting language. I will maintain that the eye as a mechanism is as "cognitive" as the messages it receives and processes, and both are as cognitive as the visual memories stored as enduring "products," which may in the future be seen again in the mind's eye.

This definition is unusual in two ways. First is the assumption that the simpler mechanisms and the processes and products they generate are themselves no less cognitive than their more complex interrelationships with the whole system. Second is my assumption that even though the sensory mechanisms are as cognitive as any other mechanism that processes information, yet there is no special cognitive mechanism as such, as one subsystem among many. As Sherrington reminded us in 1906, there is no one "pontifical cell that, on receipt of pertinent data, makes the crucial decision."

Although I am defining the cognitive system as the totality of cognitive parts and their interrelationships, I deny that there is any distinctive cognitive mechanism as such within this system I define as cognitive. One *can* point to relatively separate sensory and motor mechanisms, each with its own distinctive way of processing information. It is my belief, however, that there is no separate mechanism that is distinctively cognitive, in the sense in which the eyes are distinctively sensory mechanisms and the hands and arms are distinctively motor mechanisms. Future neurophysiological investigation may yet disclose such a special mechanism, but as yet there appears no evidence to support the assumption of a cognitive high-command mechanism that knows it all and tells it to all. Rather, it appears to be a more democratic system with no special mechanism completely in charge or, if in charge, able to endure as a stable mechanism.

The distributed "authority" of many cognitive command mechanisms makes cognition as elusive to define as the "power" in a democratic form of government or the "meaning" in a sentence.

The Cognitive System Is Nested in Mind as Language Is Nested in a Representative Government

The relationship between the affect and the cognitive system is the relationship between two parts of a whole, each of which is not only nested in the whole but is mutually interdependent and also partially independent. It may be more readily understood as analogous to the relation between language as a system and representative government as a system. Language is *designed* to be a transparent medium mechanism, to express in an orderly way whatever human beings intend to express. You and I may use such a medium to express quite different meanings. Our shared use of the English language does not require that we express identical meanings to each other, and we could not predict who would say what if we knew only that we shared a common language.

In contrast, a representative government is also governed by rules, but these rules, although designed to order the communication of meanings, including the use of shared language as a major medium, are expressive only as an auxiliary function. The major function is to govern competing, vested interests for the greater good of the whole. Biased action is intended but the representative collective bias rather than any particular bias that is intended to be enacted. The legislature must think and speak, but it must also enact laws that will guarantee satisfaction of the vested interests of the collective. Although one cannot govern without language or thought, one could theoretically have language or thought without government, in the same sense that one could, theoretically, have cognition without affect.

Our analysis of the cognitive system will therefore stress the properties of the nervous system as a language system, as a transparent medium, before examining it as part of a government that represents the more inclusive set of rules that "uses" the cognitive system in the interests of integrating affect and cognition in that larger system we have called mind.

Before proceeding to the detailed analysis of the cognitive system, however, we will attempt to place it within the larger context of matter, life, and mind.

MATTERING, LIVING, AND MINDING

Matter, life, and mind are nouns, suggestive of differences in substances, that we employ because of our incurable visual-mindedness, which favors extended spatial entities that endure in time. Had we no vision but were dependent on hearing, we would conceive the world as a set of audible wave forms endlessly changing in time. I have used process terms—mattering, living, and minding—in order to conceptualize fixed structures as the exceptional special case of rates of change that are relatively slow, rather than essentially static structures that change as a special case.

Further, I use minding rather than knowing to preserve the *function* of knowing as caring, or minding.

Mattering, living, and minding are nested organizations, nested in both space and in time. It has been assumed that life and mind were nested in space but not necessarily in all of time; that is, that the material world antedated the generation of living and of minding organisms and may well postdate them all. It is just this seemingly self-evident assumption that I am calling into question. But just as we do not use the death of any single organism as an argument against the continuity of life and the reproductive ordering principle, so it need not necessarily be the case that the ordering principles of material, living, and minding entities are not contained within the seeds of space-time matter itself.

If matter "obeys" causal ordering principles, then it "had" to legislate itself into becoming in some of itself, alive and self-conscious. The alternative would be to postulate complete discontinuity between causality and life and mind and suppose that the creation of life and mind were "accidental" and somehow miraculously escaped the causal laws that had governed the universe up until the moment of creation of life and of mind. These questions continue at a secular level the great debates in theology about God's relation to the world he created. The classic description of these ambiguities is by Lovejoy (1936) in *The Great Chain of Being*. If God both created the world and its eternal, did he really have any choice, and could he really remain out of time once having created it as a medium for the world he created?

Today the question has been revived in theoretical astrophysics in attempting to estimate how long the universe we know has been in existence. Surprisingly, how "necessary" life and mind are or were makes a difference in how old the universe might be.

Consider how hospitable the earth was for the generation of life and mind. It has abundant water and a restriction of temperature variation, unlike the cold dry environment of Mars or the steaming atmosphere of Venus. The earth's temperature between the freezing point and boiling point of water is just right for life as we know it. Because the circumstances were "right," it "happened." The anthropic principle argues the reverse, that the presence of life explains the conditions.

Clearly, there were an infinite number of possible universes that *would* have made life and mind impossible. Thus, differences in the values of certain physical constants could have produced a universe in which all stars were large, hot, and short-lived, radically reducing the possibility of life and mind. The fact that life and mind do exist places some constraints on the number of ways the universe could have begun and on the physical laws that could have governed its development.

The anthropic principle may be considered to be deductive in reverse. In normal science a theory specifies the initial conditions of a physical system and the laws that govern it and then predicts the subsequent states of the system.

According to Gale (1979),

> The anthropic principle has been invoked in cosmology precisely because the deductive method cannot readily be employed there. The initial conditions are not known, and the physical laws that operated early in its history are also uncertain, the laws may even depend on the initial conditions.

In the extreme form of the anthropic principle, as expounded by Wheeler, the observer is as essential to the creation of the universe as the universe is to the creation of the observer.

The relevance of the anthropic principle for an understanding of mind is that the kind of complex ordering we find in mind and in cognition must be regarded not only as different from the laws that govern nonliving, nonminding matter, but in a deeper sense entirely continuous with the particular kinds of causal ordering found in *this* universe, which might not have occurred in an infinite number of possible other universes. Without *these* causal laws, no life and no mind. The anthropic principle goes further. Without *these* living minds, no universe like *this* one.

We argue, therefore, as did Leibniz that this universe and its laws are a subset of all of the universes that were possible and that the kinds of organizations of life and mind we exemplify are a subset of only that subset. We humans think as we do because the world is as it is and as it was at its beginning. We are not only creatures of causality but of a particularity of causality. Further, if this universe is so particular a universe, we should not be surprised that the ordering principles of life and mind are also quite idiosyncratic as subsets within these causal networks.

What is common to the domains of matter, life, and mind is that all are governed by rules for ordering rates of sameness-change in space-time.

In the ordering of matter, the causal rules have been described by three different general principles: entropy, strong and weak forces, and conservation. Taken together these say that as matter changes it increases in sameness (i.e., decreases in dimensionality), that the rate of change of weak matter is faster than the rate of change of strong matter, and finally, that whatever the rate and direction of change of matter, there is something that is conserved and that does not change.

Victor Weisskopf (1979), in his review of contemporary frontiers in physics, has shown that quantum mechanics has brought about a division of physics into different realms of phenomena. "This is because there exists a threshold of excitation for any dynamical system. The threshold becomes higher as the dimensions of the system decrease." He refers to this as the "quantum ladder." The first rung is the atomic and molecular realm, in which the energy exchanges are so low that the atomic nuclei remain unexcited and therefore all nuclear or subnuclear processes remain dormant. The second rung is the nuclear realm, which becomes active when the energy exchanges between atomic units reach the order of 1 million electron volts (compared with a maximum of a few thousand electron volts for the first rung of the ladder). The third rung is the subnuclear realm, which is activated around energies of 1 billion electron volts. "In general, at a lower rung we can forget about processes at a higher rung . . . thus the quantum ladder divides physics into more or less independent parts, such as atomic physics, nuclear physics, and subnuclear or particle physics."

Thus, strong and weak forces represent radical differences in the rates of change of different forms of matter as a function of the inverse relationship between its dimensionality and its cohesiveness. The simpler the form, the higher the threshold of energy required to change it. The relationships between these forces and all forces has yet to yield to a theoretical unification.

> We still face four different fundamental forces—the strong, electromagnetic, weak, and gravitational interactions. A connection between the second and third kinds has been found. But is there a connection between those two and the others that will lead to a grand unification of all known interactions between particles? (Weisskopf, 1979)

He entertains the possibility. "Will we find an unending series of worlds within worlds when we continue to penetrate deeper into matter to smaller distances and higher energies?"

If the quantum ladder has revealed extraordinary discontinuities within matter itself, which enable a proliferation of different types of organization, we should be less surprised that within such a diversity of types of ordering there should appear under certain conditions those newer types of organization we call life and mind. There is no utterly homogeneous type of "causality" that demands the complete homogenization of elements, as in the classic model of Democritus' atoms. The world appears not to be made up of billiard balls but rather of bursts of waves of energy in time, incessantly expanding and contracting. It is our incorrigible visual-mindedness, which reduces time to space and space to vision, that makes the human being uneasy at the picture of reality emerging from contemporary particle physics and from astrophysics, which seriously entertains the conjunction of explosion and implosion and the razor edge of a universe suspended between endless rapid expansion and contraction, in fragile equilibria that either endlessly expand in time or endlessly alternate in big bangs and collapses. In the ordering of living matter, causal ordering is complicated by rules that produce self-maintaining and self-reproducing entities, which in turn somewhat change the physical environment that supports them.

In the introduction to the first volume of these four, we argued that the most general assumption about the nature of its domain is the most critical single decision of a science, and that the most essential characteristic of a living system is its ability to *duplicate* or repeat itself and its kind in space and time. Duplication is a transformation process in the service of the maintenance and rebuilding of an identity. In order to duplicate a living system, both energy and information transformations are necessary. By means of the genetic process and sexual or asexual reproduction, the species is duplicated over time. The individual duplicates himself in space and time in such a way that the duplicate reproduced is itself capable of reproduction so that, theoretically, an infinite progress becomes possible. In cell division, self-maintenance and species maintenance are both achieved at once.

But such duplication is never perfect, and the introduction of variation together with natural selection enables the continuing stability of reproduction via the better matching to changing environments of what is reproduced. Analogous to the several types of causal ordering, all species stay the same in some ways. All species change in some ways. All species change in different ways at different rates. Thus, cats breed back to a common type, whereas dogs diverge into more and more specialized types.

Mind, and particularly its cognitive system, is ordered not by genes but by a set of *media mechanisms that re-present information* (stable and changing) by ordering in one place and time what happens in another place and time, thus re-presenting reality rather than reproducing the self biologically. It is a more complex type of duplication than selfmaintenance and self-reproduction because it includes *any* aspect of reality—not excluding the infinite re-representation of itself. Mind not only duplicates information but further transforms some of such representation into conscious form. This is critical transformation, not found in all living organisms so far as we know. Thus, plants appear not to be conscious. Life appears to require consciousness to support mobility. The quantity of new information consequent to an organism's moving in space required in the first place a medium mechanism capable of changing its messages in response to environmental change produced by movement, and a heightening and centration of *some* of that information in conscious form to guide mobilized action.

Because matter, life, and mind are governed by causal ordering as well as by reproductive and representational ordering, we will use the concept of *ordering* as the more generic one in our discussion of the cognitive system. We assume that ordering may be simple, as in causal ordering, or may be more complex, as in living or minding ordering. The rules of a game or of a geometry or of a language may be entirely "constructed" but no less strict as ordering principles than causal ordering. In contrast, the laws of causality were constructed a long time ago, not by us but possibly for us, and not so readily changed.

The differential changeability of ordering principles is part of the definition of the varieties of types of ordering. Thus, at the level of matter, strong forces have a much higher threshold for any change than do weak forces, but both types are equally "ordered." At the level of life some types of organisms are more "open," some more "closed."

Ernst Mayer (1974) has distinguished between "closed" behavior programs and "open" ones. He defines a closed program as a genetic program that does not allow appreciable modifications during the process of translation into the phenotype. It is closed because nothing can be inserted in it through experience. A genetic program that allows for additional input during the life-span of its owner is an "open" program. This new information is inserted into the translated program in the nervous system rather than into the genetic program because there is not inheritance of acquired characters. Recent advances in genetic engineering now blur this distinction.

The same type of behavior may be mediated in one species by a closed program, in another species by an open program. Thus, male animals preferentially display to females of their own species, while females normally respond only to the displays of their own males. In most cases only a few key stimuli are crucially involved, the so-called releasers. Most of the mechanisms of animals that guarantee reproductive isolation between related species consist of acts or structures that provide species recognition information.

But in some species—for example, the greylag goose—the freshly hatched chick will follow the first moving object making sounds and adopt it as parent and sometimes even as potential mate. Such imprinting permits enrichment of the innate program with more complex possibilities than would be the case for a closed program.

Under what circumstances is a closed genetic program favored and under what others an open one? Mayer (1974) offers the following generalization: Since much of the behavior directed toward other conspecific individuals consists of formal signals and of appropriate responses to signals, and since there is a high selective premium for these signals to be unmistakable, the essential components of the phenotype of such signals must show low variability and must be controlled genetically. Selection should favor the evolution of a closed program when there is a reliable relationship between a stimulus and only one correct response.

On the other hand, noncommunicative behavior leading to an exploitation of natural resources should be flexible, permitting an opportunistic adjustment to rapid changes in the environment and also permitting an enlargement of the niche as well as a shift into a new niche. Such flexibility would be impossible if such behavior were too rigidly determined genetically.

The longer the life-span of an individual, the greater will be the selective premium on replacing or supplementing closed genetic programs by open ones. A larger nervous system and prolonged parental care favor the development of open programs.

At the level of mind some subsystems of the cognitive system, such as the eye, are more open; some, such as the reflexes, more closed. At the level of amplification some amplifiers, such as the drives and pain, are more closed than others, such as the affects. Causality, we propose, represents a simpler subset of all of the varieties of possible principles of ordering.

OVERVIEW OF MINDING AND KNOWING

Knowing is nested within minding as that is nested in living and mattering. In minding, a society of conversationalists continually enlarges its conversing via multiple interdependent monologues, dialogues, and pluralogues. Conversations include languages as special cases, but a hand that shapes itself around a ball and is itself shaped by that ball is no less a conversational encounter. A scientist who puts an experimental question to nature is awaiting an answer from nature in a conversational encounter in which both talk and listen, though the success of the conversation depends more on the asking of the question than on the initiative of the more taciturn Mother Nature. Although she will give a straight answer to the right question, she will speak somewhat ambiguously to ambiguous questions. Further, her answers may be interpreted so that the conversation enables more and more productive conversation in the future, or they may be so misinterpreted that the questioner is led into a cul de sac, from which he must initiate a radical detour in the conversation if he is to find his way again to more illuminating conversation in theory construction that can be cumulative.

Conversing and conversation's most elementary unit is that type of structure we define as a medium. But a medium must be a member of a society of media to constitute a minding, knowing human being. It takes more than one hand to applaud or to shake hands. In human beings the conversations must be multilingual and also be translatable into one another.

A medium does not represent points in either space or in time but rather represents bursts of information spatially organized in time as well as in space chunks. Chunks of media mechanism information are neither isolated points in space nor fixed in time. They are spacetime wave forms, and as such they are actions rather than snapshots of a momentary pattern on a mirror.

A medium mechanism is itself an assembly capable of receiving and sending assemblies of information. Further, the human being as a whole is an assembly of assemblies of media mechanisms and their messages.

Each medium mechanism is a specialized monad. It is a selfgoverning feedback mechanism, as similar to the whole as a city government is at once a part of, distinct from, and similar to a national government. Anything the whole can do, the part can do and does. At the same time, each medium mechanism is specialized for some activities more than for other activities. Thus, eyes see better than muscles. But each specialized mechanism does embody all other types of specialization with different weights and functions, so the specialized functions are the dominant ones, employing other functions as auxiliaries. Hence, muscles use sensory receptors embedded in muscles for feedback guidance. Eyes use ocular muscles to move the eyes for tracking. The corollary of this is that for every auxiliary function each medium mechanism is capable of representing, there exists another medium mechanism that is better equipped to effect that type of representation of information as a dominant function.

Among the varieties of types of information representation found at every level of the nervous system are receiving, timing, translating, transforming, storing, amplifying, attenuating, partitioning, triangulating, coassembling, disassembling, reassembling, correlating, diverging, converging, compressing, expanding, transmitting, and sending.

Because of the specialization of media mechanisms and their types of representation of information, they have of necessity evolved to be matched to each other. Because each mechanism must be matched to all mechanisms to some degree, they are perfectly matched to no other mechanism. Matching is inherently an imperfect compromise between specialization and integration. We have called this the principle of *play* in design.

The same principles of matching and play hold for the relations between the aggregate of media mechanisms as a whole and the environment. It evolved to be a viable representor of its environment, as well as of its own internal environment. This was achieved by successive re-representation both within and between the internal and external environment by mutiple feedback loops. But feedback circuitry as part of all media mechanisms was not sufficient for evaluating and ordering information. The human being is *not* simply a neutral knower but a biased knower, whose bias has been inherited by a set of variously specialized amplifier mechanisms—such as drives, pain, reticular formation, and, above all, affects—which determine critical abstract increases in loudness or acceleration or deceleration of some information as desirable and some information as undesirable. In the first instance these are governed by changes in the rate of neural firing, either by the level or by the gradient of changes in neural firing. By virtue of the abstractness of these mechanisms, the more particular specifications of their activating and terminating circumstances via cognitive media representations produces affect derivatives that are then further organized as scripts that magnify affect-amplified scenes and govern them by rules of interpretation, evaluation, prediction, and control. Such scripts are at once matched to the world as represented but imperfectly matched because of the multiplicity of mechanisms and messages to be matched and also because of the insistence on being governed by its inherited biassing mechanisms, which press strongly for and against restricted and polarized types of wanted and rejected information.

In contrast to Freud's vision of civilization and its inherently tragic discontents, this is a vision of the equally inherent but less essentially tragic consequences of the differential magnification of a very rich set of potentialities for human civilizations. In such a view there are multiple alternative scripts that are equally rewarding or equally punishing or equally contaminated or both rewarding and punishing but in varying measures. From the standpoint of epistemology, the knowing but biased human being exemplifies a compromise between the principles of correspondence and biased coherence and that of invention, rather than, as in Genesis, between adversaries locked in tragic struggle for dominion and rather than between perfect and imperfect neutral knowers, God and Adam and Eve.

We will argue that the nervous system, at its most elementary level, differs in no essential way from the system as a whole. We will examine the neuron as one such medium mechanism and the eye as another elementary, though more complex, medium mechanism. We will attempt to demonstrate that each monad, while complete and self-governing, is at the same time specialized via the principles of dominant relative to auxiliary functions. We will also argue that there are not only a variety of specialized mechanisms but that within each type of specialization there are also varieties of gradations of such specialization (e.g., nonspecific amplifiers of the whole versus very specific amplifiers). We will examine some of these more complex specialized mechanisms, such as the left-right hemispheric lateralization specialized for partitioning of representation of information; and the varieties of transmission specialists, such as the commissural fibers; the varieties of timing senders, such as the muscle rhythm generators; the varieties of correlating amplifying mechanisms, such as the reticular general alertness amplifier attenuators; and the more specific affect-correlating mechanisms and the still more specific pain and drive-correlating mechanisms.

Then we will explore the varieties of mechanisms for grading the degree of cohesion of information and for grading the degrees of decomposition and recomposition of independently varying components of messages, in some cases of the very same information, held together while another, coordinated mechanism is analyzing and resynthesizing such messages. We will also attempt to show that such specialization of function at the level of mechanism is also found at the level of the enduring informational products achieved by the system as a whole. Thus, we possess both distinctive memories, rich in particularities, as well as the much more independently varying knowledge made possible by language, by maps, by theories, by scripts, culminating in that least redundant species of medium languages, mathematics, which attempts complete combinatorial nonredundancy at a very abstract level. We will show that such differences of graded cohesiveness and independence also exist at the effector level in the rhythmic alternation of the bipedal walker and in the wholistic capacity of both hands to cling at once, to act independently of each other, as in playing the piano, and to act simultaneously in a partitioned manner so that the left hand may hold an object while the right hand manipulates it by independently opposing the thumb and other fingers, in contrast to the left hand, which contracts the fingers as a correlated unit.

We will also propose the hypothesis of variable tuning such that the degree of cohesion or independence may itself be varied, contingent on other information, as we have just noted in the capacity of hands to act either as cohesive coordinated units, as independent units, or as partitioned units.

We will show that the degree of internal cohesiveness of any information is a major mechanism guaranteeing its segregation and relative invulnerability to change, whereas the degree of independent variability of any information guarantees both its ready retrievability and its potentiality for change. Indeed, the coexistence of both types of representation of information is critical for all cumulative learning inasmuch as increments of learning must be preserved in all of their distinctiveness while providing a platform for progressive new learning through decomposition and recomposition of such stabilized chunks of stored information. Further, in cohesiveness of representation such differences promote both variant formation and analogue formation. The variant is an unchanging core with varying attributes, as, for example, a friend with a new suit is not confused with a new friend. The analogue is an invariant set of relations imposed on constantly varying scenes that of necessity requires maximum transformability of each new analogue if it is to be made a special case. Variants organize varying attributes around an invariant core. Analogues organize an invariant relation between varying scenes.

Because each of the several specialized media mechanisms has evolved to be coordinated as a matched mechanism, we have referred to some of these relationships in illustrating the varieties of types of specialization. We next focus more explicitly on how sets of specialized mechanisms function in higher integrations and on how sets of enduring learned products of such integrations are integrated with and control the sets of specialized mechanisms in progressive interdependence, so that a finite set of media mechanisms both produces and is governed by an indefinitely increasing number of messages and products of messages.

The unpacking and explication of these principles will be partitioned between this chapter on the cognitive system as a whole and the succeeding chapters on memory, perception, central assembly, and feedback circuitry.

PRINCIPLE OF THE MEDIUM MECHANISM

We have defined a medium as a mechanism that conjoins and coordinates representation as isomorphic correspondence of source, structure, and product and re-representation as coherence and invention. The simplest medium mechanism is more than a mirror of a source of information. What it faithfully represents it also re-represents, thus generating multiple perspectives of its source and requiring and producing coherence among its several representations and re-representations. It must further transform such re-represented information by operating on it in a variety of ways to create new invented information over and above what it has first received. The actual information represented must in varying degrees be re-represented as a special case of the possible.

In both epistemology and in perceptual theory, correspondence coherence and invention have been polarized as incompatible principles of knowledge. This has been a profitless ideological controversy. Without correspondence there can be no coherence, and without coherence there can be no invention.

It is possible for media mechanisms to produce information that is conjointly and variously correspondent, coherent, and inventive because of the conjunction of three characteristics. Media mechanisms are at once specialized, monadic, and modular. These complementary characteristics we will presently examine in more detail. By specialization some media do some things better than any other media can do. By monadism each medium can do everything that any other medium can do and do anything the whole can do. By modularity each medium can do all things better and more advantageously than any single medium could do without the interactive society of media.

A medium is a mechanism that is capable of representing at one place and time something that exists at another place and time, and then re-representing the representation. It is a mechanism that receives, transforms, and sends patterns of both repeating and changing information. These patterns are assembled as both spatially adjacent and temporally successive and sequential.

A medium is the most elementary component of a cognitive system. It duplicates, not as a living system by self-reproduction, sexual or asexual, but by representation. The eye as one such medium sees something other than itself. This is a many-many relationship in which several features of the world are mapped onto the many receptors of a medium mechanism, for example, as in the visual display on the retina. It represents the epistemological principle of correspondence in its purest form.

Human minding is not immaterial. It is based on the evolution of material structures that are isomorphic with the world and the design of which enables specific functions, which in turn enable specific products that are isomorphic and analogous to each other and to the world in which they are embedded. The simplest case of this type of isomorphism is the cookie mold. Batter stamped by a metal mold enables the production, after baking, of a cookie in the shape of the mold. This is not to say that one would wish to eat the mold. The mold is similar to the product in some but not all ways. Similarly, a medium mechanism such as a neuron, an eye, or a muscle, is a material structure that imposes its own nature and shape on the messages it is designed to receive and send and to do this over and over again with repeated messages. In the case of one critical receptor organ, which we have labeled the central assembly, the shape imposed on messages is an additional one of transmuting into reports, or conscious messages, over and above the customary neural transmission of messages. What the material base of such a transformation might be remains a biophysical problem much more formidable than the decoding of the structure of the helix but nonetheless, we think, fundamentally soluble. It should be remembered that even the understanding of another extraordinary transformation, that of electricity, was long delayed and that the capability of generation of electricity by the dynamo is even more recent. This is not to argue that the entire mind-body problem must be put off into the indefinite future. Most of mind and minding does not require conscious reports but is unconscious. Unconscious mind is the rule, not the exception. Happily, we are unaware of the extraordinary transformations that precede, accompany, and follow that searchlight which illuminates a very small but critical locus of subsets of coassembled messages, which are transmuted into conscious reports. Thus, we rarely become aware of the complex counterpoint between the visual messages from the two eyes or of the complex searches that usually precede the retrieval of specific messages from storage but that sometimes just fail and tell us only that "it is on the tip of my tongue," or sometimes fail us in delivering a phrase or word we quickly correct as not representing what we had "intended" to say. It is not only the biological homeostatic mechanisms that are unconscious. The mind is also largely unconscious. The whole effector system is totally dark, illuminated only by receptor prefeed and feedback information, which informs only how well one has done what one wished to do, not unlike the slip of the tongue. We continue, therefore, always to be at risk in the perfection of retrieval and effector skills because of the unconsciousness of the motor messages themselves.

It should be stressed that a medium mechanism is not restricted to sensory receptors. A hand is an effector medium mechanism for the representation of actions. What such a medium represents is no less ordered information than is externally represented information via sensory media mechanisms.

Media mechanisms are the most elementary "parts" of the cognitive system. It is important to distinguish the most elementary system parts from those parts that are sufficient but not necessary to form the most elementary system parts. As an analogue, consider that the elements of a language are the letters of the alphabet. Any letter itself has parts that are sufficient but not necessary to constitute a letter. It does not matter whether an *A* is large or small, black or colored, saturated or unsaturated, written or spoken or vibrated. Further, whatever the properties of these nonsystem parts, one cannot deduce the essential properties of the subsystem parts from them. The essential properties of the most elementary media mechanisms derive from the relationships between these nonsystem parts. The "A-ness" of an *A* derives from the length and direction of its parts, which together make it a letter of an alphabet. Similarly, any elementary part of a living system need not itself be composed of living parts. When the relationships that exemplify a living system stop, that system dies. So too in the human being as a minding system, one ceases to "have" a mind when the relationships within the most elementary media mechanisms and between the numerous media mechanisms terminate, even though one may remain both a living and a physical system. One of the implications of such an assumption is that neither living nor minding systems are necessarily restricted to the flesh and blood we know. There might be living and minding creatures constituted of very different raw material as long as that material was fashioned into the appropriate relationships of living or minding systems. Conceivably, if we possessed the requisite information, we might invent minding systems that thought just as we do, using quite different raw material, or we might invent minding systems that thought quite differently from ourselves, using either the same or different raw material.

But even the simplest cognitive medium mechanism is more than a mirror of a source of information. What it faithfully represents it also re-represents, thus generating multiple perspectives of its source and requiring and producing coherence among its several representations and re-representations. Thus, Jonides, Irwin, and Yantis (1982) addressed the problem of how visual information from successive fixations of a scene is integrated to form a coherent view of the scene. They demonstrated the existence of a briefly lasting memory in which temporally separate glimpses of a display are stored simultaneously and spatially reconciled with each other. With this memory serving as the basis of perceptual experience, the individual sees a coherent view constructed from the set of glimpses of which it is made.

Further, an elementary medium mechanism not only re-represents multiple, somewhat different copies that must be re-represented in a coherent version of its pluralistic information, but it must further transform that information by operating on it in a variety of ways to create new invented information over and above what it has first received. The actual information represented must also be re-represented as a special case of the possible.

The individual elementary medium mechanism not only gains incremental information about what it is receiving from its source by further transforming that information and sending it back to its origin in the receiver, but it also gains incremental information by amplification, attenuation, and enhancement, by temporary storage in reverberating circuitry, and by transmitting it thus enhanced and sending it thus enhanced not only back to its source but to many adjacent or remote other mechanisms so that it is involved in perpetual dialogue with itself, with its neighbors, and also with its external environment, to which it talks and acts back. Thus, the eye has muscles with several reflexes that move the eyes to track moving objects. This changes the position of the eyes and their relation to the sending world. It is an action on that world by which the individual may increase or decrease the amount and nature of the messages the world sends him, thus changing the nature of the dialogue even if the world is a relatively taciturn conversationalist. The simplest of the medium mechanisms are extra-, intra-, and intercommunication and action networks that reflect all of the subtlety of the total minding human being, who is continually enhancing the information he receives and seeks in an unceasing dialogue.

PRINCIPLE OF CONJOINT MONADISM AND SPECIALIZATION

The most elementary media mechanisms of the cognitive system have all of the essential properties of the whole system and are locally selfgoverning. In this respect they are similar to Leibniz's Monads, for whom what was immediately present in the (conscious and unconscious) awareness was the entire physical universe. We are not making such an assumption between a receptor media mechanism such as the eye and between any single perception and the world but rather between the eye as a mechanism and the whole cognitive system as a mechanism. We propose rather that each subsystem is a self-sufficient organized unit that is capable of processing information in all of the variety of ways that the entire cognitive system can. Each subsystem can receive, translate, transmit, amplify, store, coassemble, send, and transform information as a feedback system. We believe that this is the case not only for such relatively complex structures as the perceptual and motor systems but also for their subsystems (e.g., the neurons). We will examine the extent to which a single neuron is similar to the whole system in which it is such a small part.

Each medium mechanism is a self-governing feedback mechanism as similar to the whole as a city government may be similar to a national government. Anything the whole can do, the part can do, though each is also unique in its jurisdiction.

Despite the fact that a minding human being is an aggregation of media mechanisms, each of which exemplifies all of the properties of the whole, it is also the case that each medium mechanism has evolved to perform unique specialized functions. Thus, receptor mechanisms are specialized to receive specific spectra of energy and information, in contrast to muscle effectors, which are specialized for action. Further, within each type of specialized medium mechanism there are many different unique species of the genus, so we have receptors for vision and audition as well as for taste, smell, touch, temperature, pain, and so on.

But specialization is not achieved by totally specialized mechanisms but by the differential weighting and patterning of the more general elementary media mechanisms into dominant and auxiliary mechanisms.

Thus, the receptor mechanism of the eyes has auxiliary motor effector mechanisms to reflexively move the eyes to track moving objects. In contrast, the muscles, although specialized as effectors, possess receptor mechanisms as specialized auxiliaries to enable the muscles to know where they are and what they are doing; the muscles also possess elongation and tension receptors serving reflexes that govern the muscles on a feedback basis.

The weight of the sensory and motor functions in the eyes is biased toward the sensory and in the muscles toward the motor, even though the eye has auxiliary motor functions and the muscle has auxiliary sensory functions. The motor system, like the sensory system, is also equipped for reception of efferent information, for the transmission of information (over efferent rather than afferent fibers), for transformation of information (of efferent impulses), and for coassembly of information (inasmuch as we are equipped to contract coordinated muscles of fingers, wrist, and arms).

It may be readily granted that the specialization of media mechanisms is a consequence of the differential patterning and weighting of component media mechanisms, in the manner that organic compounds are composed of varieties of chemical elements or that words are compounds of different letters of an alphabet. It may, however, be objected that not all words are composed of the same letters, that *cat* and *dog* have no letters in common even though their letters are drawn from a common alphabet, and that quantum theory has dissipated the once attractive, oversimple picture of an atom as an elementary solar system. To what extent can we document the assumption of monadism, of local self-government in the nervous system in its most elementary components?

This assumption, it should be noted, is not identical with nor, we are arguing, inconsistent with the assumption of emergent specialized media mechanisms, nor with the assumption of further emergent properties of combinations and alliances between specialized media mechanisms, nor with the assumption of radical increases in information gain as a function of the increasingly complex interdependencies of media mechanisms, their messages, and their enduring products. One book is not identical with another book because both utilize the same alphabet and grammar, but neither are two different books entirely independent of either their shared alphabet or their shared grammar. Years ago, German students of philosophy were rumored to have read Hegel in French translation because the greater lucidity of the French language enabled a readier understanding of Hegel's thought than did the compound-ridden structure of the more dense German. We need not be forced to choose between an overly strident reductionism or an imperialistic autonomous centralized authority, between an insistence on complete local self-government or an everexpanding world government. At the biological level we need not be forced to choose between a theory of the helix as our total destiny and a theory of the evolutionary sweep as governing all. Because human beings have an understandable greedy craving for the maximum informational wealth at the lowest possible price, that yearning must not be confused, with the realities of the informational marketplace in which possible profit and risk go hand in hand, inevitably yoked.

Let us examine, then, just how much information has been packed into the most elementary knowers of the nervous system, the neurons.

THE NEURON AS SIMPLE COGNITIVE MECHANISM

The neuron is specialized for the transmission of messages. Inasmuch as the neuron is the most elementary organized unit of the information processing mechanisms, it serves well to illustrate some of the more general features of cognition, as well as the degree to which the simplest parts of a cognitive system share in the characteristics of the more complex cognitive mechanisms, including those of the total cognitive system.

A neuron is an extraordinarily complex structure as it appears under the electron microscope. Its structure contains the cell body, the dendrites, and the axon.

> It has a distinctive cell shape, an outer membrane capable of generating nerve impulses, and a unique structure, the synapse, for transferring information from one neuron to the next. . . . Although synapses are most often made between the axon of one cell and the dendrite of another, there are also synaptic junctions between axon and axon, between dendrite and dendrite and between axon and cell body.
>
> At a synapse the axon usually enlarges to form a terminal button, which is the information-delivering part of the junction. The terminal button contains tiny spherical structures called synaptic vesicles, each of which can hold several thousand molecules of chemical transmitter. (Stevens, 1979)

The cell body contains the nucleus of the neuron and the biochemical machinery for synthesizing enzymes and other molecules essential to the life of the cell. This is another instance of the complex interpenetration of structure and function even at the most elementary level. The neuron, which is specialized for the transmission of information, must nonetheless repair and maintain itself to keep alive. Every organized structure must contain multiple substructures and functions if it is to discharge its primary function. Furthermore, the neuron also requires other structures to keep it alive and functioning. Oxygen and nutrients are supplied by a dense network of blood vessels. There is also connective tissue formed by the glial cells that occupy all of the space in the nervous system not taken up by the neurons themselves. The glial cells provide both structural and metabolic support for the neuronal structures.

So much for the structure of this unit. What process does this structure support? Information is relayed from one neuron to another by means of a transmitter at the dendritic synapse. The firing of a neuron, the generation of nerve impulses, is triggered by the activation of hundreds of synapses with impinging neurons. Some of these synapses are excitatory; others are inhibitory, capable of canceling signals that otherwise would have excited a neuron to fire. Having fired, the axon outer membrane then propagates an electrical impulse to the terminal button adjacent to the dendrite of the next neuron.

What is the product of this process? The product or output is the chemical transmitter. On the arrival of a nerve impulse at the terminal button, some of the vesicles discharge their contents into the narrow cleft that separates the button from the membrane of another cell's dendrite, which is designed to receive the chemical message.

The neuron represents the most elementary unit of a most elementary information-processing mechanism, nervous system transmission, and therefore it is possible to delineate relatively easily and clearly here the fundamental distinctions between cognition as structure, as process, and as product.

In what ways are all of the basic cognitive capabilities of the whole represented at this elementary level? The first, most general cognitive mechanisms represented are reception and translation. The neuron is not only a sensitive receiver of information, but it also has its own code or language by means of which received impulses are systematically transformed and expressed in its own inherited language. We define this as translation since translation both preserves information in one language and expresses it in another language. According to Charles Stevens (1979), the intensity of a stimulus is coded in the frequency of nerve impulses, with all impulses of the same amplitude. Decoding at the synapse is accomplished by two processes: temporal summation and spatial summation. In temporal summation each postsynaptic potential adds to the cumulative total of its predecessors to yield a voltage change whose average amplitude reflects the frequency of incoming nerve impulses. In other words, a neuron that is firing rapidly releases more transmitter molecules at its terminal junctions than a neuron that is firing less rapidly. The more transmitter molecules that are released in a given time, the more channels that are opened in the postsynaptic membrane and therefore the larger the postsynaptic potential is. Spatial summation is an equivalent process except that it reflects the integration of nerve impulses arriving from all of the neurons that may be in synaptic contact with a given neuron.

Such differential coding depends upon a series of steps: transmitter synthesis, storage, release, reaction with receptor, and termination of transmitter actions. These are relatively complex biochemical transformations. According to Iversen and Iversen (1981), the interaction of the transmitter with its receptor alters the three-dimensional shape of the receptor protein, thereby initiating a sequence of events. The interaction may cause a neuron to become excited or inhibited, a muscle cell to contract, or a gland cell to manufacture and secrete a hormone. In each case the receptor translates the message encoded by the molecular structure of the transmitter molecule into a specific physiological response.

A region on the surface of the receptor protein is precisely tailored to match the shape and configuration of the transmitter molecule so that the latter fits into the former with the precision and specificity of a key entering a lock.

Each neuron, then, is both a receiver and a sender of information. It achieves these capabilities by storing, releasing, and transforming information, amplifying some messages and attenuating others. It recognizes and matches messages via lock and key arrangements.

Further, there are feedback processes even at the neuronal level.

According to Stevens (1978), there are reciprocal circuits where one dendrite makes a synaptic contact on a second dendrite, which in turn makes a synaptic contact back on the first dendrite. As Stevens notes, such direct feedback is quite common in the brain. It appears to be a special case of the more general one in which one subsystem influences the way another subsystem transmits information to it. For example, the thalamocortical projections are reciprocated, according to Nauta and Feirtag (1979). The visual cortex projects back to the lateral geniculate body, from which it received its input; the auditory cortex projects back to the medial geniculate body; and the sensory cortex projects back to the ventral nucleus. Nauta and Feirtag suggest that the functional state of the cortex can influence the manner in which the sensory way stations of the thalamus screen the cortically directed flow of information. It is akin to a secretary who is taking dictation asking the dictator to speed up or slow down or speak more loudly or softly.

But the neuron is not quite as isolated a unit as we have thus far represented it.

Even at the neuronal level there is structural, process, and product interrelatedness that is far-reaching in scope. A typical neuron may have anywhere from 1,000 to 10,000 synapses and may receive information from 1,000 or more other neurons. Estimates of the number of neurons in the human brain are on the order of 10^8, a hundred billion. Hubel (1979) has estimated the number of synapses at 10^{14} (100 trillion). It is richly cross-linked, complex, hard-wired circuitry, with elements working at speeds of thousandths of a second. In comparison the computer is much faster (millionths of a second) but with far fewer elements. There are frequent lateral connections and connections in reverse direction, from output to input. According to Schmitt, Dev, and Smith (1976), the older view of one-way information transmission, with the dendrite as a passive receptor surface, has now been transformed via electron microscope evidence to suggest that short-axon or axonless neurons form local circuits transmitting signals through synapses and electrical junctions between their dendrites without spike potentials but via graded electrotonic changes of potential. A crucial feature of such circuits is "their high degree of interaction both through specialized junctional structures and through the extracellular fields generated by local and more distant brain regions." The resulting picture of multiple simultaneous and interactive processes of these systems lends structural support to the known complexity of information processing and its products. The use of graded potentials would provide a discriminatory ability superior to the spike potential all-or-nothing process.

The elementary neuron is also a precise timer of information received, transmitted, and sent. It would not do if the messages were processed at varying speeds of reception, transformation, translation, amplification, reverberation, cross talk, transmission, or sending. All of these processes must be correlated temporally as well as spatially.

But the neuron that correlates messages must also keep different messages distinct from each other. As we will presently see, the neuron is structurally designed to mediate excitatory and inhibitory messages and keep them separate from each other at the same time that many other messages are cumulating excitatory and inhibitory potentials. Thus, the human heart is neuronally modulated by the inhibitory action of cholinergic neurons with their axons in the vagus nerve and the excitatory action of noradrenergic neurons with their axons in the accelerator nerve.

Further, the neuron, like all media mechanisms, is highly redundant in both structure and function. Its components exist by the hundreds and thousands, thus providing large safety factors both structurally and functionally.

Such redundancies not only guarantee a large safety factor but also provide equipotentiality or possible substitutability of one component or process for another under emergency conditions.

Finally, the neuron, like the whole system, exemplifies not only a specialized mechanism but also the principle of partitioning within its own structure and function. The dendrite is a receptor; the axon is a transmitter and sender.

We have argued that the most elementary neurons exhibit all of the essential properties of the whole cognitive system. Does this include specialization? Since there appear to be no fundamental differences in structure, chemistry, or function between the neurons and synapses in human beings and those of a squid, a snail, or a leech, it was for some time assumed that neurons were relatively identical building blocks of all nervous systems.

According to Kandel (1984), this view has now been strongly challenged by studies of invertebrates showing that many neurons can be individually identified and are invariant in every member of the species. This was first proposed in 1912 by Goldschmidt, who showed in his study of the nervous system of a primitive worm, the intestinal parasite *Ascaris,* that the brain of this worm consisted of exactly 162 cells in every animal and that each cell always occupied a characteristic position.

Since then it has been demonstrated that neuronal cells may be excitatory or inhibitory. In invertebrates, Kandel (1984) found that the cell of the neuron mediated different actions through its various connections. The cell excited some follower cells, inhibited others and made a dual connection that was both excitatory and inhibitory to a third kind of cell. Further, it always excited precisely the same cells, always inhibited another specific group of cells, and always made a dual connection with a third group. Its synaptic action depended on acetylcholine, the reaction of which with different types of receptors on the follower cells determined whether the synaptic action would be excitatory or inhibitory.

It would appear then that the nature of the chemical message changes, dependent on the next neuronal "ear" that hears the message. The neuron is therefore not a simple transmitter but has messages that tell different stories depending on the languages of translation of the neurons to which it speaks.

More specifically, the receptors determine the sign of the synaptic action by controlling different ionic channels in the membrane, primarily sodium for excitation and chloride for inhibition. The cells that received the dual connection had two types of receptors for the same transmitter, one receptor that controlled a sodium channel and another that controlled a chloride channel.

In summary, the neuron is at once a specialized cognitive medium mechanism that is also a monadic, self-sufficient, local self-governor, whose specialization is achieved by differentially weighting and patterning the shared properties of all cognitive mechanisms into dominant and auxiliary functions. In common with all media mechanisms, the neuron is structurally and functionally redundant, partitioned, regenerative, and equipotential, capable of receiving information, translating it, transforming it (e.g., via summation and averaging), amplifying it (via temporal and spatial summation), transmitting it, storing and reverberating it, correlating it, keeping it distinct, and timing it, and of sending a product as well as transmitting a message, feeding its messages back to itself, and cross talking with a very large population of neighboring as well as distant neurons.

The neuron proves to be a cognitive system in miniature. If we ask why this should be so, I would suggest it is a consequence of evolution: because we are descended, ultimately, from simpler organisms, and these organisms had to rely on their neurons without the benefit of more highly differentiated subsystems. Therefore, we should expect that at the level of the most elementary animals, their neurons should be capable of supporting learning and remembering without the benefit of information magnification by the complex structure of the human brain.

Such indeed proves to be the case in recent experimentation. Kandel (1984) has demonstrated simple neuronal modifications of some duration that support either sensitization or habituation of simple behavioral responses. Farley and Alkon (1980) have demonstrated, in the *Hermissenda,* behavioral changes dependent on short-term depolarization of the type B cell, which appears to cause associative changes that are retained during the days after training. Simple animals must, of course, base such plasticity as they can achieve upon their relatively simple neuronal equipment. This is not to suggest that more complex nervous systems need to place such a burden upon their simplest components. I cite this evidence rather to attempt an evolutionary answer to the question of why a complex organism should possess such complex, selforganizing, self-sufficient components.

The consequences of such evolutionary pressures have been delineated by Satinoff (1978) in his analysis of the thermoregulatory system. It had been assumed originally that temperature regulation was governed by a central thermostat, which counteracted any deviations from the optimal state via thermosensitive neurons that brought autonomic and behavioral mechanisms into play in a feedback mechanism. This conception proved insufficient to account for the independent variability of behavioral and autonomic responses demonstrated in experiments on behavioral thermoregulation in rats with preoptic lesions. Because thermal stimulation of the preoptic area elicits both autonomic and thermoregulatory responses, it was assumed that lesions of that area, which damage autonomic responses, would also impair behavioral responses. Experiments demonstrated, however, that rats with preoptic lesions used operant responses to turn heat on or off to maintain optimal internal temperature. This indicated that there were sufficient thermosensitive cells and integrative neurons outside the preoptic area to enable rats to regulate their temperature via their behavioral response even though they could not do this via autonomic responses. This indicated that there must be at least two thermostats, neuroanatomically and functionally separate.

Satinoff (1978) has argued further for multiple thermostats to account for more recent experimental evidence. Although there is increasing evidence for multiple parallel systems of thermostats, they are not totally independent of each other. Rather, the activity of lower structures appears to be facilitated and inhibited by those above. However, experiments have also shown that thermostats at the level of the spinal cord can act independently of and even antagonistically to the preoptic area thermostat. Local thermal stimulation can override the normal integration when such stimulation is very intense. Therefore, even the simplest levels of the nervous system can be considered to have set points and to be miniature feedback systems, as we have seen is so even at the neuronal level. Satinoff (1978) attempts to account for this very complex neural architecture on an evolutionary basis similar to the one we have suggested is the general case.

First, he argues that there are many changes needed to evolve from an ecotherm to a well-regulated endotherm—from chemical thermogenesis and shivering, to panting and sweating, to thermal control of peripheral circulation, to the development of fur, feathers, or fat.

Second, evolution takes a great deal of time—millions of years.

Third, all of the changes could not have developed concurrently. No animal has all of them, and some animals have developed one mode of regulation to a much greater degree than other modes (e.g., the arctic fox, an insulation specialist; the shrew, a metabolic specialist; and the elephant, a surface-to-volume specialist).

Fourth, most thermoregulating reflexes evolved out of systems that were originally used for other purposes. Thus, the peripheral vasomotor system, the basic mechanism for changing blood flow at the surface, first served as a supplementary respiratory organ in amphibia. It then became a heat collector and disperser: reptiles regulate the flow of heat from outside the body to inside. Finally, it became an essential temperature regulatory mechanism for endotherms, who regulate heat flow from inside the body to outside. The changes in posture from the sprawling stance of the reptile to the limb-supported posture of the mammal provided the basis for high internal heat production and the need for different kinds of regulation. In changing its posture it coincidentally developed a system for producing heat. Eventually, Satinoff (1978) suggests, the temperature sensors gain control over this new form of heat production and produce another integrating system beyond the simple thermoregulator of the simpler animals. At some point it becomes advantageous to lose some of that heat more quickly. The animal already breathes and for that purpose has a good vasomotor system, so changes in peripheral blood flow and respiratory rate simply need to come under the influence of thermal detectors, thus producing two more integrating systems. The principle is new controls over an already existing mechanism for a *new function.* From an evolutionary point of view, if one function is already perfectly well handled by the midbrain and another by the spinal cord, there would have been no point in transferring all of these separate integrations to the preoptic area of the hypothalamus. But in the event that these functions were not or became not perfectly well handled at lower levels—if, for instance, a narrower set point conferred a selective advantage on the organism that had it—then a higher hierarchically organized set of thermostats would have evolved for the purposes of finer and finer tuning of the thermoneutral zone.

The Gene Is to Life as the Neuron Is to Mind

The discontinuity between matter and life and mind, between simple causality and the more complex ordering principles, appears with the phenomenon of life before its luxuriant takeoff into mind.

Watson and Crick's double helix model, for all of its brilliance, nonetheless obscured both quantum leaps. Crick had radically reaffirmed the billiard ball conception of reality and of life in his "central dogma" for molecular biology that DNA makes RNA and RNA makes protein in a one-way flow of information. But just as quantum physics shattered the oversimplistic conception of matter inherited from Democritus, of a world composed of hard elementary atoms that were mechanically recombined in a giant Tinker Toy universe, so too was the same dogma overturned in molecular biology by the radical work of Barbara McClintock. This revolution required only years rather than centuries.

In the Watson-Crick model all of the complexity of the living organism was accounted for by an inherited program of genes on chromosomes, four bases arranged in groups of three. Evolution was presumed to occur by genetic variation, substituting one nucleic acid base for another, in turn producing a different amino acid in the protein constructed.

This slow, relatively random, and simple process was presumed adequate to account for a sequence of processes of extraordinary complexity. It was a brilliant attempt at simplification and partitioning of variance that "reduced" complexity to simplicity, confirming our deepest yearning that God is an elegant craftsman who used only simple rules and who plays dice only occasionally, if ever, and that the Tower of Babel is at worst a myth to punish excessive hubris. The truth of the matter, as it is told in Genesis, is that God was not satisfied with a simply-run world, so he created a living, minding being in his own image, who had sufficient degrees of freedom to also create novelty. The same divine discontent reappeared in Adam, who insisted on Eve, who in turn insisted on more knowledge. Because God was "creative," he could not help himself. He had to create a world that contained discontented creators.

Life, like mind, once invented, has a life and mind of its own. It is shot through and through with all of the properties of the whole. Living and minding "systems" are composed of similar subsystems, not of parts that are more "elementary." Thus, in the second revolution in molecular biology the gene itself is as "living" as the whole organism of which it is a part. It is *not a* relatively fixed bead on a string but a miniature alive organism, changing itself as well as copying itself and capable of moving to other locations on the string—the so-called jumping genes. Such copies may remain next to their parent or move to other chromosomes. They may regulate other genes, thus controlling the timing of development. Original copies may continue to reproduce the old program conjointly with new copies, which experiment with further possibilities. Some substances, called reverse transcriptase, can read RNA into DNA, inserting new material into genetic programs by running backward along what had been thought to be a one-way street. The emerging picture of the genetic program is that of a fluid, self-regulating feedback system—a conversation, not a monologue. What the gene tells itself it listens to. The product changes subsequent products as well as the producer. The principle of monadic specialized local selfgovernment holds at the genetic level as well as at the neuronal level.

So much for some of the shared characteristics of all media mechanisms found in each specialized, locally self-governing monad. We will now examine some of the varieties of specialization of media mechanisms and some of the varieties of their more complex relationships to each other. We thus pass from the alphabet to the grammar to the semantics of the cognitive system.

Chapter 44

Varieties of Media Mechanisms: A Bottom-Up Perspective

SPECIALIZED SENSORY AND MOTOR MEDIA

According to Hubel and Wiesel (1979), most of the sensory and motor areas contain systematic two-dimensional maps of the world they represent. Destroying a particular small region of cortex could lead to paralysis of one arm; a similar lesion in another small region leads to numbness of one hand or of the upper lip or to blindness in one small part of the visual world; if electrodes are placed on an animal's cortex, touching one limb produces a correspondingly localized series of electric potentials. Clearly, the body was systematically mapped onto the somatic sensory and motor areas, and the visual world was mapped onto the primary visual cortex. This mapping is continuous except for the split of the visual world down the exact middle, with the left half projected to the right cerebral cortex and the right half projected to the left cortex. However, these cortical maps are distorted so that the regions of highest discrimination occupy relatively more cortical area.

In the classic studies of Hubel and Wiesel (1968) it was demonstrated that there are sensory neurons with very specialized functions of specific feature detectors (e.g., to lines and to occular dominance). Since then some cells, and particularly groups of cells, have been discovered that respond to patterns of specific features (e.g., a grate rather than a single line) (De Valois, Albrecht, & Thorell, 1978).

There appears now to be widespread evidence for extreme specificity of structures in the nervous system. Thus, as Dethier (1978) has shown, the specificity of receptors varies widely from species to species and determines the direction in which the individual's window faces the world. Thus, although humans appear to have taste receptors for carbohydrates, acids, salts, and bitter compounds, some animals do not respond to sugars. All animals appear to possess receptors for salts. A caterpillar may have as many as eight primary taste receptors. Specificity of receptors is nonetheless a relative characteristic, according to Dethier, since taste receptors respond to more than one compound (or category of compounds) but better to one than to others. Indeed, differing bandwidths of tuning is the rule in the nervous system. Despite such bandwidths each cell is nonetheless relatively specific compared with other cells with nonoverlapping bandwidths.

Not only are there very specific sensory neurons, but there are also specific motor neurons and specific sensory-motor loops. Thus, Sherrington (1906) introduced the term "proprioception" to describe sensory inputs when the stimuli to the receptors were delivered by the organism itself to provide feedback on the organism's own movements. There are two kinds of proprioceptors. One kind senses elongation, and the other senses tension. The length receptors of muscles send fibers into the spinal cord to form synapses on motor neurons that terminate on the same muscles. Hence, any increased length-receptor activity that results from muscle elongation activates the motor neurons of the elongated muscles. That gives rise to a muscular contraction that opposes the elongation.

The tension receptors sense force rather than elongation. Their activation leads to the inhibition of the associated motor neurons and reduces force in the muscle. Together these two types of receptors maintain a negative feedback control system resisting changes in muscle length and tension.

There appear to be distinct feature analyzers for movement, for upward motion, and for downward motion, so that they balance each other. However, if one looks at a waterfall for a couple of minutes and then turns the eyes to one side, the rocks appear to move upward, presumably because the downward motion detectors have been fatigued. Though the rocks move, they do not move out of sight, presumably because feature detectors other than for movement are still functioning. Hence, upward movement in the absence of sensitivity of the downward movement detectors presents the anomaly of rocks moving upward but continuing to be in view rather than moving out of view.

Specialized Chemical Sender Media Mechanisms

Every neuron "sends" chemical messengers from axon to dendrite as part of the mechanism of neural transmission. However, there are also other specialized sender mechanisms, primarily chemical in nature, that apparently are aimed at specific targets, which they activate, and some that are more global in their effects.

A remarkable feature of the neuropeptides is the global nature of some of their effects. For example, injection of small amounts of angiotensin II into the brain elicits intense and prolonged drinking behavior in animals that were not previously thirsty. Another peptide, luteinizing-hormone releasing hormone, when injected into the brain of a female rat, induces characteristic female sexual behavior. These neuropeptides represent a global means of chemical coding for patterns of brain activity associated with particular functions, such as body-fluid balance, sexual behavior, and pain or pleasure.

Media Specialization for Togetherness and Separateness

The minding mechanisms must be as equally capable of bringing some information together as of keeping some information separate and insulated. This is achieved in a variety of ways.

One way is via open versus closed lines of conduction.

A through line maintains the topography of the sensory periphery from which it comes. A fingertip, for example, can detect two distinct stimuli when it is touched by the points of a pair of drafting dividers no more than 2 or 3 mm apart. This is possible because the conduction paths are independent enough to allow sensory resolution.

Open-line, multimodal conduction paths are open to inputs from other neurons. These are typical of the reticular formation, where relatively few cell groups receive homogeneous inputs.

There are also direct through lines from cortex to spinal cord to motor neurons. The corticospinal tract travels from the cortex to the spinal cord, and 5 percent of these fibers synapse directly on motor neurons thus avoiding the neuronal pools of the local motor apparatus. These animate the musculature of the extremities. This has been called the voluntary or somatic nervous system, as distinguished from the involuntary, or autonomic, nervous system that innervates glands and the smooth musculature of the viscera.

Another way is via the differences in architecture of vertical versus lateral synaptic transmission. The information carried into the cortex by a single fiber can, in principle, make itself felt through the entire thickness in about three or four synapses; whereas the lateral spread, produced by branching trees of axons and dendrites, is limited, to a few millimeters, a small part of the cortex.

Another way in which information is segregated or brought together is by differential magnification and attenuation. Messages that are amplified can, in effect, be at once brought together and separated from messages that either are not amplified, are amplified less, or are attenuated or inhibited.

The receptors generally respond best at the onset or cessation of a stimulus such as pressure on the skin. In the visual system it is contrasts and movements that are important, and much of the circuitry of the early transmission of visual messages is devoted to enhancing the effects of contrast and movement.

Yet another way of connecting or separating information is via timing. Via induction by timing resonance, messages from one system are integrated into the rhythms of a dominant timing sending system. Thus the contagious effect of any marked rhythm in the sound of music to which we resonate by tapping our feet. The rhythmic way in which we alternate our feet in walking is the consequence of specialized central rhythm generators that operate at the level of the spinal cord.

Messages, either sensory or motor, that are too far out of synchrony with dominant timing messages are either excluded or kept separate. Sensory messages result in an evoked potential in the visual cortex only when it is appropriately synchronized with the spontaneous rhythm of the alpha waves, according to Bartley and Bishop (1933).

From the work of Santiago Ramón y Cajal (1928) and Rafael Lorente de Nó (1933) it appears that there is only local analysis possible in some cortical areas. Thus, in the somatic sensory cortex the messages concerning one finger can be combined and compared with an input from a neighboring finger but not with input from the foot or trunk. Similarly, in the visual cortex there can be no correlation of information from left and right parts of the visual field or from above and below the horizon.

Specialized Timing Media Mechanisms

There is now abundant evidence that timed internal clocks control longevity, metabolic rate differences between the sexes, waking and sleeping periodicities, mood swings, jet lag, drive and affect programs, walking rhythms, cortical responsiveness, and sucking rhythms.

Delcomyn (1980), in his review of the neural bases of rhythmic behavior in animals, has argued that the timing of the repetitive movements that constitute any rhythmic behavior is regulated by intrinsic properties of the central nervous system rather than by sensory feedback from moving parts of the body. Such behavior, in which all or part of an animal's body moves in a cyclic, repetitive way, is exemplified in walking, swimming, scratching, and breathing.

The hypothesis of central control was overwhelmed by evidence in the 1930s and 1940s indicating that sensory feedback played an important role. Delcomyn (1980) argues that since then the principle of central pattern generation has been well reestablished by much new work. In a tabular presentation of this evidence, 13 different activities in nearly 50 species of animals are represented.

Such evidence has demonstrated that complete isolation of the nervous system from all possible sources of sensory feedback does not abolish the normal pattern of rhythmic bursts in motoneurons. This evidence derives from isolation, deafferentation, and paralysis experiments. In deafferentation all or some of the sensory nerves that carry information into the nervous system are severed, and the effect on patterned motor output is observed. In the paralysis experiments no muscular contraction can take place, so the lack of movement means that no sensory feedback that is time-locked to the motor activity can be occurring either.

There remains the conflicting evidence that swimming, for example, can proceed in the absence of sensory feedback, and yet phasic sensory input can nevertheless drive that same behavior. Delcomyn (1980) has attempted to resolve this conflicting evidence by suggesting that motor neurons are driven by a network of interneurons capable of generating an alternating or cyclic pattern of output when excited by a continuous input. A network with such a property is referred to as a neural pattern generator, or oscillator, and evidence suggests that each appendage or part of the body with its own cycle of movement is controlled by its own oscillator. If some sensory input is fed back onto components of each oscillator, such feedback could reset the rhythm. A repetitive sensory input provided to one or more oscillators and timed to advance or retard the oscillator's output just a bit could drive oscillators to the frequency of the sensory input. Delcomyn (1980) concludes by urging that systems of oscillators are universal major control systems for general rhythmic behavior.

Sherrington (1906) discovered that within a few months after a dog's spinal cord was severed, a scratch reflex could be elicited by tickling the animal's skin or by pulling its hair. Then Graham Brown showed there are spinal rhythm generators for walking as well as scratching. He severed connections between the brain and spinal cord and showed that rhythmical limb movements similar to those involved in walking were possible in dogs. This led to the contemporary concept of "triggered movement" based on a "central program" involving a spinal rhythm generator.

Wolff (1968) reported that the rhythm of sucking is nearly the same in all normal newborn infants and may be considered a species-specific mechanism for the regulation of motor behavior. Further, he reported that normal newborn infants suck in two distinct rhythms. One is a nonnutritive mode that is characteristically segmented into alternating bursts of sucking and rest periods, that has a basic frequency in the range of two sucks per second, and that can be elicited in all arousal states except sleep and great excitement. There is also a nutritive mode, which usually depends on a flow of milk from the nipple, is organized as a continuous sequence of sucks, and has a basic frequency of about one suck per second.

Peiper (1961) showed that nutritive sucking "drive" swallowing and breathing whenever all three reflexes are simultaneously active in feeding. When nutritive sucking begins, the rate of respiration changes until a 1:1 or a 1:2 ratio is established. The rhythm of sucking can control not only the yoked functions of swallowing and breathing but also can spread to unrelated reflexes that have their own natural rhythm when acting alone but under special motivational conditions are locked in phase with the rhythms of nutritive sucking. Thus, Peiper observed a phase relation between sucking and kneading movements of the front paws in nursing kittens and between sucking and grasping in premature human infants.

The critical role of the circadian body temperature rhythms in the regulation of sleep and wakefulness has been known for some time. It is only recently, however, that the greater dependence of sleep on these rhythms, rather than on the length of prior wakefulness, has been demonstrated by Czeisler, Weitzman, Moore-Ede, Zimmerman, and Knauer (1980).

"Recovery" sleep after 3 to 10 days of total sleep deprivation rarely exceeds 11 to 16 hours, while both longer (15–20 hours) and shorter (6–10 hours) sleep episodes have been observed in subjects not deprived of sleep who lived on a self-scheduled routine. Czeisler et al. (1980) reported that variations in sleep duration depend on when subjects go to sleep, rather than on how long they have been awake beforehand. When bedtimes occurred at the trough of the averaged temperature cycle (that is, near the peak of the averaged sleepiness curve), sleep episodes were short, with wake times occurring on the rising phase of the temperature cycle. When bedtimes occurred at or after the peak of the temperature (and alertness) cycles, the duration of sleep was extended, such that wake times occurred on the next upslope of the temperature curve. Czeisler et al. (1980) report that all human subjects studied to date, living without the knowledge of time in an unscheduled environment for more than 2 months, have progressively developed these same consistent bedrest-activity patterns.

Specialized Translatory Mechanisms

There are a variety of mechanisms specialized for translation. First of all are the specific sensory receptors, each of which has its own code. But each of these codes must eventually be recoded so that messages in these different languages can to some extent be translated into a common language, lest there be a Tower of Babel.

According to Nauta and Feirtag (1979), the thalamus appears to be such a crucial way station, a final checkpoint before messages from all of the sensoria (except olfaction) are allowed entrance to higher stations of the brain. Here the input is transformed, and the code in which the message arrived is fundamentally changed. Translation is needed.

Specialized Variable Tuning Media Mechanisms

Wolff and Simmons (1967) reported that when 4-day-old healthy infants were tickled when sucking on a pacifier in their sleep, they were rendered unresponsive to an external stimulus. A similar but less marked rise in response thresholds was observed when a pacifier was in the baby's mouth but the baby was not sucking. Under these conditions the infant responded to the stimulus of tickling with a new burst of sucking rather than with a burst of diffuse motility as in ordinary sleep.

This would appear to be a special case of variable tuning in which motor action feeds back into the brain and differentially magnifies the focal activity, thus either attenuating or inhibiting competitive activity.

Specialized Convergence-Divergence Media Mechanisms

There are specialized convergence and divergence structures at the sensory, motor, and sensorimotor association levels.

An eye or an ear is designed to receive multiple converging messages from multiple visual or aural senders.

Similarly, at the motor level, motor neurons of the brain and spinal cord receive information from highly convergent channels, from primary sensory neurons, from secondary sensory cell groups in the spinal cord, from the reticular formation of the brain stem, from the red nucleus of the midbrain, and from the motor cortex of the forebrain. The red nucleus and the reticular formation receive inputs from a variety of sources. The entire neocortex, which includes auditory, visual, and somatic sensory and motor fields, as well as other fields, sends projections to the corpus striatum. This cell mass projects its fibers, in turn, to the reticular formation that ultimately acts on motor neurons. What is important at the output end is not the contraction of an individual muscle but the coordinated contraction and relaxation of many muscles. In grasping an object one must flex the fingers by contracting flexor muscles in one's forearm but also contract extensor muscles in the forearm to keep the finger-flexor muscles from flexing the wrist.

Finally, the visual, auditory, and somatic sensory areas represent only a first cortical step in sensory processing. Out from these primary sensory fields come fibers extending to the association areas, which contain the largest fraction of the cortical area. Thus, in these areas there are places where the auditory and visual converge. There are sequences of association area conductions, which terminate in the hippocampus or the amygdala or both.

Specialized Storage Mechanisms

There appear to be a variety of storage mechanisms, varying on both the period of time for which they store—from short-term immediate reverberation to middle-term to longer-term storage—and also in the kinds of information stored. Not all information stored has been learned, nor is all the stored information stored in the brain.

The first step "upward" from the motor neuron is a pool of nearby cells that are usually smaller; together with the motor neurons they form what Nauta and Feirtag (1979) call a "local motor apparatus" that corresponds to the parts of the body: the arms, the legs, the eyes, and so on. Each, it seems, is a kind of file room in which blueprints, each one representing a possible movement of a particular body part, are stored. The brain, with its descending fiber systems, reaches down and selects the appropriate blueprint.

Specialized Amplifying Media Mechanisms

There are several varieties of specialized amplifying media mechanisms. First are varieties of pain receptors, then the varied drive receptors designed to amplify drive appetite, reward, or punishment. Next are the varied specific affect receptors on the face, then the neuropeptides, subserving both drives and moods as with the release of endorphins. More diffuse are the varieties of nonspecific amplifiers, such as the reticular formation. We have previously noted that every medium mechanism, including the neuron, has amplifying capabilities. Thus, all of the senses are equipped for increasing or decreasing the amplification of any messages.

As Kinsbourne (1982) has suggested, the brain "overrepresents" discontinuities in space and time (i.e., boundaries and movements) by lateral inhibition between adjacent neural elements, a "differenceamplifying" servomechanism at the cellular level. He suggests that opponent systems exaggerate contrast.

Wurtz, Goldberg, and Robinson (1980) have described enhanced responses of cells in the posterior parietal cortex as spatially selective, independent of the particular action the monkey takes toward the stimulus. They have demonstrated enhanced brain activity of amplification of information correlated with visual attention.

If the monkey is alert but not attending to anything in particular, the nerve cells respond uniformly. However, as soon as the monkey begins to attend to some object, the nerve cells in the posterior parietal cortex that are related to the object (because it is in their receptive field) begin to discharge more intensely. If the monkey decides to make a saccadic eye movement toward the object to examine it more closely, the cells in the superior colliculus and in the frontal eye field that are related to the object will also discharge intensely. This change happens even if the selected object is no more striking than the rest of the visual field. The only difference is that the monkey has decided to attend to the object.

Specialized Feedback Media Mechanisms

Although each mechanism contains all mechanisms as auxiliary subsets and therefore all contain feedback circuitry, nonetheless some sets of mechanisms are more specialized for feedback control than others are, in that feedback control serves a dominant rather than an auxiliary function. This appears to be the case with the cortex compared with the thalamus. Although the thalamus is specialized for translation of multimodal sensory information before sending such information to the cortex, the latter nonetheless appears to control the conversation.

The thalamocortical projections are reciprocated: The visual cortex projects back to the lateral geniculate body from which it received its input; the auditory cortex projects back to the medial geniculate body, and the somatic sensory cortex projects back to the ventral nucleus. In this way the cortex can influence how the thalamus screens sensory messages going to the cortex.

No line can be drawn between a sensory side and a motor side in the organization of the brain. All neural structures are involved in the programming and guidance of an organism's behavior. Thus, when area 19, a band of neocortex distinct in cell architecture from the neighboring zones and situated not far from the visual cortex, is stimulated electrically, the eyes turn in unison to the contralateral side; that is, the gaze moves to an alignment directed away from the side of the brain receiving the electric current. In this respect it is "motor," but it also reprocesses information that has passed through the visual cortex.

A similar relationship holds for area 22, where electrical stimulation will again cause the eyes to turn to the contralateral side. Yet this area also reprocesses information from the auditory cortex, thus making possible integration of the eyes with sounds.

MODULARITY AND THE CONJOINT PRINCIPLES OF MULTIPLE MATCH AND MISMATCH: PLAY AND SATISFICING

Because each medium mechanism is a monad, sharing all of the essential properties of the whole system and because each mechanism is also modular in design, both internally and in interaction with other media mechanisms, there is widespread matching of all media mechanisms to each other. But because each of the media mechanisms is also specialized by using different elementary functions as dominant and auxiliary, all media mechanisms are to some extent mismatched to each other. As a consequence, matching of media mechanisms is inherently somewhat imperfect. Match is limited by "play"; mismatch is limited by "satisficing."

There are two critical consequences of the evolutionary process for the design of the human being. The first is what I have called play in the design of the system. Each part mechanism must be conjointly adapted to each other part, as well as to the environment and to the demand for reproduction of the gene pool. A necessary consequence of multiple criteria is a very loose fit in the match between one mechanism and every other mechanism, between the system as a whole and its varying environments, and reproductive success. Consider as an example the possible relationships between the affect, perceptual, and motor mechanisms. Let us suppose that the visual system could not resolve information at speeds exceeding 1 mile per hour. Such an animal would suffer a blurred visual field as soon as a predator appeared or as soon as it began to run away from a predator. If the affect mechanism subserving fear were similarly restricted in its range of activation, such a species would not long remain viable, let alone reproducible. So the affect mechanism must be capable of being appropriately activated, by the environment and the visual mechanism, on the one hand, and by changes in perception produced by one's own motor system, on the other. But the affect mechanism must also be adapted differently to predators and to the mother. One must not be excited by the predator and fear one's mother at the outset. One must not be able to move at speeds one cannot "see," nor fail to see and be afraid of threatening others or events. Motoric, perceptual, and affect mechanisms must not only be mutually supportive but multiply supportive. Because each general mechanism must meet many different criteria of the other mechanisms and of varying environmental demands, each mechanism must be mismatched to some mechanisms in varying degrees if it is to be minimally matched to all other mechanisms and to a majority of the changing environmental demands it must meet. "Play" refers to the inevitable looseness of fit in match between mechanisms in the trade-offs between the conjoint criteria of differentiated mechanisms and environmental evolutionary pressures.

If play and looseness of fit between mechanisms and between the system as a whole and its environment is the rule, the second necessary consequence of the evolution of any animal is the inverse of mismatch, the match of each part to the whole and of the whole to its environment. Though the principle of play cautions against the possibility of an ideal fit, the second principle argues for sufficient limitation of mismatch to meet a satisficing criterion, that the system as a whole is good enough to reproduce itself. Though the environment may be grossly tolerant of that "magnificent makeshift" the human being, Mother Nature is not endlessly permissive. The ultimate and ever-present criterion by which both the motivational and the cognitive systems are judged is reproducibility of the species and its gene pool.

There are two competing views on the nature of the evolutionary biology of constraint. In one, the adaptationist program of the "modern synthetic" theory of evolution, constraints are imposed primarily by what "works." Ill-adapted forms simply do not survive. Nature does the best she can. There are thus extreme variations in density of possible biological forms. Many theoretically "possible" types of animals do not exist, while other types swarm with minor variations; hence, over half a million species of beetles.

In the competing view, called "structural integration" by Gould (1989; Gould & Laurantan, 1980) particular solutions are thought to be constrained by the architecture and inherited morphology of ancestors. Thus, while an adaptationist might suppose that land vertebrates had four legs because this was an optimal design for locomotion of a bilaterally symmetrical, elongate body under gravitational conditions, the structural integration view would stress that ancestral fish had four fins, the homologues of our arms and legs, for reasons unrelated to their later invasion of land. Four legs are optimal, but in this view we have them by conservative inheritance, not selected design. In this view minor variations are everywhere, but major reorganizations are rare because of the constraints of inherited structure. It is unlikely that elephants will evolve wings and fly. In this view we are only slightly rebuilt apes. There are thought to be very few distinctively human traits.

In contrast, the adaptationist believes that genetic variation is abundant, small in extent, and available in all directions. Thus, evolution is pictured as a two-stage process of chance (the mutations of random raw material) and necessity (in natural selection among these random changes). Thus, organisms are atomized into parts (characters or traits) that achieve their best configuration for local environments through natural selection. The only divergence from this conception of part-by-part optimization is in a concept of trade-off, in which the demands of an optimized whole may require some concessions among parts. This is similar but not identical to the principle of play I have suggested, since I have argued that it is inherent in the design of any system that every part is constrained by the need to match every other part, as well as to meet the environmental demands on the whole system. The adaptationist views all parts as existing for some function and as best designed to perform it (subject to the above trade-off).

Both views subject the organism to constraints but to different ones. In the adaptationist views, the constraints are primarily environmental. When environments change very rapidly, the much slower evolutionary adaptation exposes human beings to cultural lag, as primitives, for example, in an ultracivilized, internationally interdependent world. In contrast, the structural integration view limits us to being only slightly rebuilt apes, not because the environment has changed faster than evolutionary adaptation but because of the constraints from our genetic ancestors. It is the difference between constraints primarily from the environment and constraints primarily from the past contained in our ancestral genes.

Recent developments in this field appear to favor a resurgence of the structural integration theory against the long-dominant "modern synthetic" adaptationist theory of evolution. These differences were confronted in an international conference held at Chicago, as reported by Lewin (1980).

Both views, however, are consistent with what I have called the principles of play and of satisficing but on different grounds. Both views insist that there are forces toward both conservation and toward change, but they locate these forces in different places and with somewhat different mechanisms.

MODULARITY AND CONJUNCTION OF INFORMATION GAIN: COMBINATION AND RECOMBINATION OF MODULES

The principle of monadism permits all media to do all that the whole society of media can do. The principle of specialization permits each of the media to do something better than all other media. The principle of modularity permits the ensemble of specialized monadic modules to do something together they could not do as individual media mechanisms. Just as media can represent and also re-represent, so too can they combine and recombine and thus achieve information gain for the society of conversationalists. Conversation is enriched communication. Telling and listening is communication. Conversation is interdependent telling, listening, telling and listening, endlessly transforming communication.

By modularity I refer to that property of any system that permits its subsystems degrees of freedom of combination and recombination. The simplest example is a modular language whose elements, plus a grammar plus words, permit the generation of an infinite number of sentences. The modularity of a learned language is possible, I believe, only for human beings who possess a nervous system that is modular in design. Thus, we have receptors, effectors, storage mechanisms, and central assembly mechanisms that enable any information from one receptor—say, vision—to be coassembled with information from other receptors—auditory, smell, or kinesthetic—with information from storage, from affect receptors, and from sensory receptors in hands and limbs, at one moment in time, to guide the entire system in interpretation and in further action. Such combinatorial freedom of coassembly can and does continually recombine succeeding central assemblies so that different mechanisms can be successively brought to bear on the sequences of their recombination. The radical information gain from combining information sources is, of course, at the heart of the potential for cumulative learning. I am here suggesting that such learning depends first of all upon the prior innately endowed modularity and combinatorial flexibility of the entire set of media mechanisms. Modular systems vary in their degree of redundancy, or recombinability. Thus, arithmetic as a formal language is much more recombinable than is the English language. The nervous system is certainly not a maximally recombinable set of modular elements, but it has nonetheless evolved to permit a high degree of recombinability of its mechanisms, as well as of its messages and products.

I distinguish three types of information gain. First is gain by efficiency and simplicity—measured by the decreasing number of messages necessary to describe, explain, predict, or control a domain. Second is gain by power—the increasing number of features described, explained, predicted, or controlled. Third is information advantage—measured by the ratio of power to efficiency. Information advantage increases as the information required to describe or explain is reduced and the information in the domain described or explained increases so that less and less information is required to deal with more and more information effectively.

I propose this as an analogue of mechanical advantage in which the level enables a small force to move a larger force, or as with a valve by which small energy forces are used to control the flow of much larger forces, as in a water distribution system.

There are many types and degrees of informational advantage. The helix possesses very great informational expansion properties of guidance and control. A highly developed scientific theory possesses great informational advantage, being able to account for much with little. The organization of the nervous system, however, exhibits, I believe, the greatest informational advantage in nature as we know it.

Information gain via increased information power alone would not have been an unmixed blessing since it would have overloaded limited channel capacities for handling information. A classic example was described by Angyal (1941)—a woman whose visual imagery was so detailed and vivid she could not readily find her way home for lack of sufficiently reduced and abstract "maps" of her living space. Increased information gain via information power requires increased information gain via efficiency and compression if it is to yield optimal information advantage.

The nervous system possesses many information reducers, compressors, and filters that inhibit and gate some information so that other information may be amplified by contrast. It also possesses integrative mechanisms that take the "best" information from a pool for an accurate and coherent picture, as in the unconscious editing of the information from the two eyes to achieve a unified three-dimensional field. One can experience what an extraordinary amount of work is involved by viewing the alternation as well as fusion that occurs when each eye is presented with excessively conflicting information by means of a stereoscope. We are the beneficiaries of great informational advantage built into our media mechanisms, inherited via evolutionary experimentation. They are structurally embodied theories.

We will now examine some of the varieties of information gain that the modularity of the nervous system permits.

EFFICIENCY AND POWER IN CONJOINT AMORTIZATION AND REDUNDANT PLENITUDE

Any medium mechanism has evolved to generate more substantial information gain than cost. The costliness of such a mechanism is biologically and psychologically justified by amortization. Amortization occurs when the cost that would be excessive for any single information transaction is minimized by being distributed over many instances.

Any duplicating mechanism, such as a mold that creates an isomorphism between itself, its shaping operation, and the final product, need not necessarily exhibit much informational gain. Thus, the casting of the mask of the face of one individual utilizes the isomorphic principle but not the principle of informational gain via amortization because it is used only once.

Amortization occurs either by repeated use of the same medium mechanism to register the same message at two different times or places or by registering different messages but of a set with a limited number of alternatives. Any medium mechanism imposes its own sensitivity spectra on the information it receives or sends, thereby achieving, over and over again, efficiency of representation.

But efficient amortization is also conjoined with power and information gain in representing a plenitude of states of the sending world as these change over space and time. Having an eye does not limit one to seeing the same thing over and over again. The mechanism is invariant Respite variations in the messages it receives.

This plenitude derives from the fact that each component of a medium mechanism is relatively independent of every other component, both spatially and temporally. One rod or cone in the retina is capable of firing relatively independently of an adjacent rod or cone, as well as firing relatively independently of its successive firing in time. This relative independence of receivers within a medium mechanism radically enlarges the possible pool of message sets that may be received and therefore transmitted and sent by a medium mechanism. There is plenitude, not only within each specialized medium mechanism but also between media mechanisms, via the profusion of different varieties of the same general type of medium mechanism. Thus, in the case of sensory mechanisms we are equipped with more than one modality. We hear and smell and touch and taste as well as see. We have a variety of storage mechanisms, from very brief to very long-term reverberators of information. We have a variety of amplifier mechanisms, from those that regulate wakefulness in general, to varied affects, to a variety of more specific pain mechanisms and a variety of drive amplifiers.

Further, as a consequence of the plenitude of supporting media mechanisms there is a parallel but exponential increase in the variety of cognitive messages and products that issue from the combined modular interactions of such a pluralism of similar and different media mechanisms.

PRINCIPLE OF EQUIPOTENTIALITY AND SUBSTITUTABILITY

There are not only redundant parts in the most elementary media mechanisms but also equipotential or substitutable parts. This is not to say that all parts are necessarily substitutable for all parts but rather that some parts are substitutable for some parts. Further, substitutable parts are not necessarily used at all times, any more than reserve power is necessarily employed when customary power is sufficient. As an example, intractable pain is often intractable by virtue of the fact that surgical cutting of the customary transmission nerves fails to offer relief because the pain messages appear to "hunt" and find alternative neural pathways to reach the brain.

This is also the neurological basis for the possibility of retraining individuals who have suffered strokes or other severe neurological insults. The classic experiments of Lashley (1960) demonstrated many years ago some properties of equipotentiality for the brain as a whole. The more recent experiments of Sperry (1982) have demonstrated the equipotentiality and latent function of each half of the cerebral hemispheres.

Until 1960 the bulk of the lesion evidence supported the picture of a leading, more highly evolved intellectual left hemisphere and a relatively retarded right hemisphere that, by contrast, in the typical righthander's brain, was not only mute and agraphic but also dyslexic, word deaf, apronic, and generally deficient in higher mental function. Even a small brain lesion, if critically located in the left, or language, hemisphere, might selectively destroy a person's ability to read while at the same time sparing speech and the ability to converse.

When Sperry (1982) began his experiments on split brain patients who had undergone sectioning of the corpus callosum and the commissural fibers connecting the cerebral hemispheres, he discovered a surprising capacity in the right hemisphere for linguistic competence, both written and spoken. In 6 months after a commissurotomy he found a person would usually go undetected, as a rule, in a conversation or even through an entire routine medical examination. In answer to the question of why the right hemisphere is able to do things after commissurotomy, such as reading, that it fails to do in the presence of focal damage in the left hemisphere, he suggested that left hemisphere lesions in the presence of commissures prevent the expression of latent function, (actually present but suppressed) within the undamaged right hemisphere. This is based on his assumption that, when connected, the two halves work together but with the leading control in one or the other. When this unitary function is impaired by a one-sided lesion, the two hemispheres are both impaired as a result. Only after the intact right hemisphere is released from its integration with the disruptive and suppressive influence of the damaged hemisphere, via the commissurotomy, can its own residual function become effective.

PRINCIPLE OF REGENERATION

Not only do all media mechanisms possess an abundance of redundant parts and equipotential and latent functions, but they also appear capable of regeneration, in varying degrees, after excessive exercise or after insult. Thus, the neuron is not capable of continual transmission without some regeneration. It suffers a "refractory phase," in which it cannot fire until it has recovered its customary competence.

Neurons vary considerably, however, in their capacity for more demanding degeneration following severe insult. Some nerves are capable of regeneration. Others appear not to be so capable.

Conjunction of Segregation and Togetherness of Representation

If all information was permitted to influence all information (as in Gestalt field theory) or kept totally segregated (as, in the telephone switchboard model, which Gestalt field theory regarded as its chief adversary), there would be severe problems of excessive interference in one case and severe problems of isolation and inpoverishment in the other. Clearly, some information has to be capable of enrichment, but so does some information have to be kept free of possible noise. Our nervous system does this by specializing in mechanisms for both segregation and togetherness of representation. Thus, as mentioned earlier, there are both open and closed lines of conduction and transmission.

Connecting and separating information is also controlled by timing-induced resonance, when messages from one system are integrated into the rhythms of a dominant timing sending system. Messages that are too far out of synchrony are usually excluded or kept separate. Thus, sensory messages result in an evoked potential in the visual cortex only when it is appropriately synchronized with the spontaneous rhythm of the alpha waves.

Conjunction of Variable Independence, Dependence, and Interdependent Specialization

In radical contrast to most "machines," in which specialized parts may be variously independent and dependent but not variably independent or dependent, in the human nervous system various kinds of independence, dependence, and interdependence are also capable of variation in their interrelationships. Thus, thermoregulatory mechanisms as well as timing oscillator mechanisms are capable of imposing central control on dependent regulators and also, under special conditions, of being "driven" by these lower control mechanisms. In this way heat regulation and various rhythms are normally preprogrammed but nonetheless capable, under severe environmental stress, of reversing dominance relationships. The relationships between the cortex and subcortical centers appear to be variously independent, dependent, and interdependent. The thalamocortical projections are reciprocated. The visual cortex projects back to the lateral geniculate body form which it received its input. In this way the cortex can influence the way in which the thalamus screens sensory messages going to the cortex. Although the thalamus is specialized for translation of multisensory information before sending such information to the cortex, the latter nonetheless appears usually to control the conversation.

Conjunction of Convergent and Divergent Structures: Gossip Networks

The society of specialized conversationalists is not a simple linear communication system. It is organized like a small-society gossip network in which every member hears all and tells all. This is achieved by the conjunction of convergent and divergent structures in each of the specialized media mechanisms and between them. Thus, each neuron is the target of thousands of connecting synapses converging on it as well as the sender of multiple messages, both to other neurons and backward to its own receptor synapses, thus telling itself what it also tells its many neighbors in dialogue.

Conjunction of Partitioning and Coordination

Inasmuch as each medium mechanism is necessarily specialized, and so partitioned, with respect to other media specialists, there must also be other media specialists whose primary function is coordination. Because of the evolutionary process the specialization of simpler monadic structures is continually being added to, becoming higher and higher structures in order to coordinate what has been partitioned into separate centers for the same function. We have noted this before in the case of thermoregulatory structures. It is also evidenced in the partitioning of the left and right hemispheres with their coordinating structures, the commissural fibres. It is this very feature that prompted Gaylord Simpson's (1949) felicitous characterization of the human being as a "magnificent makeshift."

Conjunction of Reciprocal and Nonreciprocal Cooptive Specialized Media Mechanisms

There is important information gain whenever the same mechanism may coopt another mechanism for its own purposes and at the same time is reciprocally designed to be used by that other mechanism to serve its purposes. However, not all mechanisms permit such two-way reciprocity, in which they may use or be used but not both. Thus, the eyes and the hands are media mechanisms designed for reciprocal cooption. I may use my eyes to guide my hands to bring an object closer so that I can see it better. I use my eyes to locate an object I wish to hold. The eyes make the hand more knowledgeable. The hand makes the eyes better informed. In contrast, the mouth may coopt the eyes to find food for it, but the eyes do not reciprocate and find things to look at by use of the mouth. Infants often use hands and eyes to find objects that can be sensed by mouthing, but they do not use their mouth to see better.

Conjunction of Dominant and Auxiliary Specialization for Representation

We have previously contrasted the principles of monadism and specialization, in that every specialized medium is also capable of all features of the whole and therefore of self-government. We have also contrasted specialization of each medium mechanism as possessing a dominant function aided by auxiliary functions. Here we wish to stress the corrollary of the conjunction of dominant and auxiliary functions in the conjunction of a society of both dominant and auxiliary specializations. In this case we propose that not only are we equipped with different specialized receptors, amplifiers, effectors, and transmitters, but we are also equipped with specialized auxiliary mechanisms whose major function is to serve as aids to all other specialized media mechanisms.

Although any specialized medium mechanism may call on any other specialized medium mechanism for aid (e.g., eye upon the hand or the reverse), each is nonetheless specialized for its own dominant purpose of reception or motor action. In the case of long-term storage, however, we have a medium specialized to be used as a resource for all other mechanisms, as a library or an encyclopedia serves a general reference function. As we have noted before, however, not all stored information is learned information. Thus, there are stored motor blueprints prior to learning, stored in subcortical areas, which may be used as auxiliary information by the cortex.

Conjunction of Inclusion and Exclusion of Assembly, Disassembly, and Reassembly

There are a variety of mechanisms specialized for inclusion and exclusion of information for assembly, disassembly, and reassembly. The most important of these is what I have labeled the central assembly, which accepts information from any sensory receptor, from storage, or from analyzer mechanisms, and transforms it into conscious form. By virtue of rules I will examine later, the most intense messages are favored over less intense messages for inclusion in the momentary central assembly, which is disassembled and continually reassembled from moment to moment, thus guaranteeing alertness and vigilance to the ever-changing internal and external environments.

Unlike the eye, which essentially receives whatever the environment sends, such an assembly receives from many senders and must therefore be more selective in its inclusion by excluding less intense messages. Such exclusion appears to involve various sources (e.g., external sensory versus internal sensory, sensory versus storage, pain versus drive information) and also various options within specific sources. Thus, among pain messages it appears to be only the most intense of a set of pain messages that is included. It is this rule that permits an individual to mask one source of pain by voluntarily inflicting a more intense pain upon himself (e.g., digging his fingernails into his flesh to mask the pain of a toothache or dental drill). The same principle has been used in bombarding the dental patient with intense auditory stimulation to mask the pain of dental procedures. Further, there are rules governing the total amount of density of neural firing that may be permitted inclusion in the central assembly and therefore in consciousness. If these limits are exceeded, the assembly excludes all messages, and the individual faints and becomes unconscious, as happens sometimes under torture.

Coassembly may involve triangulation of information but need not. Indeed, it may provide and pose problems that then require more coassembled information. If I smell something burning and see no flames, these discrepant messages from the visual and olfactory receptors coassembled in the central assembly enrich each other primarily in posing problems rather than in guaranteeing their solution. Incremental interaction is indeed maximized when it enriches information by creating ambiguity in the coassembly. This is not, however, to minimize the significance of immediate information gain as in the triangulation made possible by the coordination of messages from related but disparate sources.

Conjunction of Specialized Fine- and Coarse-Grained Tuning

By variable tuning of specialized media mechanisms, the texture of information received may be systematically varied and combined and recombined for richer representation of the same source.

Thus, the eye may accommodate for either near, fine-grained information or for far, more coarse-grained information and go back and forth between these for a richer knowledge of both detail and the larger frame in which it may be embedded.

Similarly, the hand may close on an object as a whole and also manipulate the same object between its fingers for more fine-grained information or may do both at once by holding the object in one hand and feeling it more finely with the fingers of the other hand.

The same principle may be exercised by selective, successive retrieval of past scenes from memory, examining at one time the details of one scene and then examining the coarser sequential relations between several scenes over extended periods of time, thus uncovering the forest as well as the trees within it.

The same principle may be exercised by alternation between figure and ground in any perceptual field. When these relationships are reversed, both figure and ground may be significantly enriched. This is especially critical when some information has been avoided because of its negative affect potential. Thus, an encounter with someone who is disliked but with whom one must communicate is severely constrained unless and until the groundlike negative information is brought into consciousness as figural. The same applies to the inverse case of the encounter with a hated other, when the ambivalent love for that other is attenuated as ground.

I have experimented with such dynamics utilizing stereoscopic presentation of conflicting information to the left and right eye. If one exposes the same face with a smile to one eye and with a grotesque, menacing expression to the other eye, the smiling face will be seen by all subjects over the grotesque face of the same individual. As this conflict is presented over and over again, however, and the illumination of the smiling face is gradually reduced as the illumination of the grotesque face is increased, there is a reversal of dominance so that the smiling face is now no longer seen, and the grotesque face is seen. In between, however, there are transition perceptions in which the negative face intrudes partially and briefly, contaminating but not displacing the dominant face.

For any given level of the relative ratio of brightness of illumination for the smiling face versus its competitor, I was able to teach the subject not to see the competitor. The hypothesis I tested was that in the competition between disparate sources of information for inclusion in the central assembly, the more intense messages would dominate over the less intense messages. The smiling face dominates all other faces in stereoscopic competition for a variety of reasons I will not examine here. When that same face has a grotesque expression, it loses in competition both at the level of perceptual editing and at the level of the central assembly. However, on repeated presentations the smiling face becomes "older" information and the negative face becomes "newer" relative to the now increasingly familiar face. It has therefore increased its representational power both at the level of perceptual integration and at the level of the central assembly. Eventually, therefore, there is a reversal of dominance relationships, signaled by a transition series in which there is increasing intrusion of the negative face into the smiling face (when illumination is held constant and/or when the ratio of illumination increasingly favors the excluded face). I believed it was possible to interfere with this reversal by decreasing the novelty of the excluded information. This I did by a series of controlled variations in the intensity of illumination on the negative face (while holding the illumination on the smiling face constant). This was accomplished as follows. I instructed the subject to pay special attention to anything that seemed to change in the smiling face, to report whenever this happened, and to describe what it was that seemed to change. Then, unbeknownst to the subject, I gradually increased the illumination on the excluded face until the subject reported any change in the smiling face. Immediately, I would return the illumination to its initial level. I would repeat that same procedure until the subject ceased to report any change in the appearance of the smiling face. I was trying to teach the subject to disregard (unconsciously) what he had seen as some kind of change by making an older story out of it, decreasing its novelty relative to the smiling face. Once accomplished, the illumination on the negative face was then increased again until another change was reported, and then the illumination was returned to the initial level. When this second level of illumination increase was no longer responded to, another series of trials at a higher illumination was carried out. This general procedure could be successively programmed so that extreme illumination on the negative face and very little illumination on the smiling face could be presented and yet preserve the dominance of the smiling face. It was thus possible to teach the nervous system to disregard information that otherwise would have reversed dominance relationships between competing sources of information.

Conjunction of Specialized Mechanisms for Correlation, Cohesiveness, and Independent Variability of Components

In contrast to the conjunction of segregated information and information that is brought together, the contrast of cohesive versus independently variable information is a disjunction within information that is brought together. Is it brought together to be cohesive and to stay together, or is it brought together to be independently varied in perpetual recombination?

The hand is extraordinary in this respect. The hand may close all fingers around an object. The two hands may do the same thing and thus support the whole body swinging on a bar. However, the thumb may be independently innervated. The two hands may be independently innervated, as in playing the piano. Further, the left hand may be used to hold an object by correlated holistic use while the right hand manipulates by opposing the thumb and other fingers independently. The coexistence of both types of representation is critical for all cumulative learning inasmuch as increments of learning must be preserved in all their distinctiveness while providing a platform for new learning through decomposition and recomposition of such stabilized chunks of stored information. A more fragile example is in the reverberation of correlated information via reverberating circuitry as one operates on this to reverse the order, as in a test of reverse memory span. The internal cohesiveness of stored information is a major mechanism guaranteeing its segregation and relative invulnerability to change, whereas the degree of its independent variability guarantees both its readier retrievability and its greater potentiality for transformation. In one form of organization, class membership is minimized. In the other it is maximized. The same distinction underlies the differences between variants and analogues in script formation. In one there is an unchanging core with varying attributes. In the other there is an invariant set of relations imposed on varying scenes.

Conjunction of Specialized Unconscious and Conscious Feedback Mechanisms

We are equipped with several specialized feedback mechanisms that together enable both the unconscious and conscious maintenance of homeostasis: our drives typically conjoin much unconscious feedback circuitry with conscious feedback circuitry. In the case of breathing, the unconscious mode is dominant, and the conscious mode is auxiliary; whereas in most drives it is the conscious mode that is dominant and the unconscious mode that is auxiliary. Thus, vital functions such as those subserving drives contain innate programs that sample the blood stream for varying biochemical balances, which in turn alter taste thresholds and ratios of pain and pleasure dependent on continuing hunger versus eating. As one eats, the pleasure of eating diminishes, as the pain of hunger first diminishes and then the pain of eating increases to the discomfiture of satiety. The drive mechanism itself conjoins correlational programs with feedback circuitry. This can be seen in the contrast between the purely correlational homeostatic control of breathing via sampling by the carotid sinus, which operates outside of consciousness, and the consciously controlled feedback drive mechanisms of suffocation (as in drowning), which enlist violent struggle to get air and breathe.

The contrast between inherited unconscious correlational feedback mechanisms and consciously controlled feedback mechanisms may also be seen in the correlated sequence of the rooting and sucking reflexes in infancy, which early on give way to what I have called autosimulation. In this critical transition the correlated sequence is taken as a model for voluntary feedback controlled simulation. The infant has the requisite conscious feedback circuitry to say to the self, "I'd rather do it myself."

Conjunction of Representation and Biased Amplification of Information

For the human being, increased information gain, whether via power, efficiency, or advantage, is radically enriched by biased amplification as well as by representation per se. The human being is not simply a knower. He is a biased knower whose bias has been inherited by a set of variously specialized amplifier mechanisms, such as drives, pain, reticular formation, and above all, affects that determine critical increases in the intensity and desirability or undesirability of information. We are not governed by an informational democracy in which each bit of information has one free and equal vote. If we wish to be "intellectuals," we must learn to invest affect in representation. This is possible because of the conjoint abstractness and degrees of freedom of the affect mechanisms, but it is necessarily one investment among many. All media mechanisms amplify as well as represent information, since, according to the principle of monadism, each specialized mechanism employs every variety of specialized function but as an auxiliary function. Thus, the neuron amplifies the messages it receives transmits and sends, but its dominant function is transmission rather than amplification. The affect mechanism receives, transmits, and sends information, but its dominant function is amplification. A critical consequence of the conjunction of representation and biased amplification is that informational advantage may vary independently of what I have defined as magnification, the advantaged ordering of biased, amplified information. Of this more later.

Conjunction of Specialized Reception and Production of Information

The individual must not only be able to receive and to send representations, but he must be able to send in a specialized way, to produce effects in his environment via his "effectors." Effectors are not limited, however, to the external environment because in order to receive better, the individual's eyes are also equipped with auxiliary muscle effectors that move them. This is best seen in the hands, which are structurally designed primarily for action and the production of information but are also capable, via their sensory receptors, of being used to sense the texture and shape of objects they explore. The eyes are specialized primarily for the reception of information rather than for production via motor effectors as in the hands.

Conjunction of Spatial and Temporal Media Mechanisms

The "location" of any information is dependent on the conjunction and intersection of at least the coordinates of space and time. An object that is as brief as a momentary flash of lightning or a pistol shot is quite different from an enduring sun and its light or a permanently elevated level of sound. Indeed, inasmuch as we have evolved to live in a changing world, it should not be surprising that the major mechanisms of our living and minding are those that deal with variations in rates of change, in a variety of "spaces"—visual, auditory, smell, pain, drives, proprioceptive, touch.

We have exaggerated the spatiality of mechanisms and their representations because of our disproportionate reliance on the visual sense. It is difficult to exaggerate the widespread consequences of this overemphasis, not the least of which has been the hypostatization of substance and the primary qualities over process and secondary and tertiary qualities. In psychology, the analysis of elaborate time-regulating mechanisms has lagged, despite massive evidence that time and internal clocks control longevity, metabolic rate differences between sexes, waking and sleeping periodicities, mood swings, jet lag, drive and affect programs, walking rhythms, cortical responsiveness, and sucking rhythms. Less obvious is that even such spatial mechanisms as the eye must be temporally coordinated if they are to represent faithfully a source that has sent such simultaneous information. If some of the receptors were to fire with varying random latencies, the possibility of representing simultaneous visual information would be seriously flawed.

Not only are there several "spaces" but there are also several "times." As a consequence, sounds, heats, smells, touches, kinesthesias, pains, hungers, thirsts must be "located" by various mapping and nesting transformations in one overall coordinated space so that we know where a sound might be in visual space, where a smell might be, where a pain or a touch might be, where a hunger or sexual sensation might be, where a phantom limb is located. Because of our utilization of visual space as dominant, translatory codes—some innate, some learned—must be relied on to coordinate these partitioned spaces, to move our fingers in visual space, to turn our face toward sounds, to turn our noses toward burning objects. Were we more smell-dominant we would, like some dogs, take one last smell of our doorway to guarantee a safe return before embarking on a holiday. Two people who smelled the same but looked different would be more similar than two who looked the same but smelled differently. Whenever any ordering principle (for example, of similarity or difference) encounters conflict between spaces of different weight and priority, the secondary space is subordinated to the dominant space, the smaller frame nested and mapped onto the larger frame. Theoretically, translation might be unbiased in either direction, as is the case with a bilingual individual. The radical increase in informational complexity such equal weighting of spaces would produce might, however, seriously overload our channel capacities. Later we will examine the consequences of such reversals of dominance when earlyblinded individuals later become sighted for the first time. Let us suppose we had evolved to be primarily temperature-oriented, so that both the inner and outer world was interpreted in terms of varying gradients and ordering of warm and cold. Then visual space would "look" different to the extent that it looked warmer or colder. Our stomach would move in temperature space as it varied in temperature. The "looming" effect would not be defined by visual looming but by getting suddenly warmer, whether it stayed in the same visual space or got closer or more distant.

This sounds like a much more remote, bizarre possibility than it really is. We have not appreciated the critical importance of temperature in the world we construct, not only because of our excessive visualmindedness but also because of our mapping of time onto space, rather than appreciating their coequal status. Several years ago, Hudson Hoagland (1957), in a brilliant experiment, systematically varied the internal temperature of human subjects. He found that, in accordance with the Arrhenius equation, the rates of all internal processes increased lawfully with increased temperature. The gross consequences of the maintenance or violation of a narrow range of internal temperatures around a mean of 98.6°F have, of course, been known for many centuries. The deterioration of thought and speech in delirium is one obvious case of the intimate interdependence of time, temperature, and knowing, quite apart from visual space. The experience of time itself is radically dependent on the rates of internal processes and the internal temperature. Metabolic rate and temperature are also crucially related, not only to the nature of the world we know but to how long we live in that world. The faster and hotter we live, the shorter time we live. The slower and colder we live, the longer we live. It has been possible to increase the longevity of an animal by slowing down its metabolic rate. Women live longer than men by virtue of a slower metabolic rate. Timing is therefore of the essence, not only of living but of minding. In repayment of our oxygen debt from our higher metabolic rate, we must pay with a cooler, slower 8 hours of sleep for 16 hours of hotter, faster wakeful living.

Coordination of our complex society of living and minding mechanisms is at least as dependent on our various timing media mechanisms as on our visual media mechanisms. A visually blind human being has other senses by which to know the world, but none of these could operate as they do if their several interdependent rates were not coordinated by the conjoint control of temperature and timing clocks.

The consequence of the principle of play is that every other principle of ordering is in some respect less than optimal, whether that be in the matching of parts within the most elementary media mechanisms or between them. Thus, timing and temporal coordination, which is a fundamental ordering principle of the minding mechanism, is less than optimal when messages sent encounter other mechanisms that are slightly out of phase with the sending mechanism.

Visual reaction times vary between 150 and 300 ms. Lansing (1954) examined the relationship between visual reaction times and alpha waves from the occipital and motor areas. He found that the briefest reaction times occurred predominantly when the stimulus message arrived in the cortex at an optimal excitability phase of the occipital alpha wave and that the motor discharge occurred in the motor area in a similar optimal phase of the motor alpha wave. These two phases, however, might be at least 100 ms. apart.

Bartley and Bishop (1933) first demonstrated the significance of timing as a principle of central assembly. They cut the optic nerve of the rabbit and stimulated it electrically. The neural volley resulted in an evoked potential in the visual cortex only when it was appropriately synchronized with the spontaneous rhythm of the alpha waves.

Conjunction of Old and New Information

If the conversation were entirely about the past, or about the present, the possible gain in either informational power or efficiency would be severely constrained. By conjoining present-oriented specialists with past-preserving antiquarians there can be continuing dialogue about shifting relationships in proactive and retroactive transformations. As we have noted, even the neuron conserves and repeats, via reverberating circuitry, what it has just received, transmitted, amplified, and transformed. There also exist redundant structures for longer-term conservation of information that support access and repetition. The eye utilizes not only short-term reverberation circuitry to synthesize the extended present but also has access to past information.

Conjunction of Abstract and Particular Information

To achieve information gain in a changing world that offers possibilities and probabilities in abundance and certainties only occasionally, the human being must conjoin a bandwidth of abstract possibilities and a series of successive approximations of more particular possibilities in a continuing game of Twenty Questions. Every informational encounter has the structure of a program of experimentation in which the world is converted into a laboratory. By the conjunction of the abstract with a converging series of particulars, as more and more probable for identifying the particularity of the more abstract representation, the individual is privileged to enjoy the best of two very different modes of representation.

This is embodied structurally in the specialization of abstract amplifiers conjoined with storage- and receptor-specialized media. The affect mechanism amplifies only the abstraction—in the case of surprise, fear, or excitement—that something is appearing and increasing very fast. Conjoined with the receptors, it may prove to be an automobile, one's own movement, or an increase in heart rate that excites, frightens, or surprises. Should the amplified affective feedback swamp and mask the receptor information, the individual then may experience objectless terror or excitement.

Conjunction of Representation of the Actual and the Possible

In contrast to specialization for the abstract versus the particular, or the past versus the present, is specialization for the representation of the actual versus the possible. The same information that is received in the present from "actual" sources as contemporary representations is conjoined routinely with representations from the past (from long-term storage) and from the immediate past (from short-term storage) as well as from analyzer mechanisms that decompose and recompose the information from both the present and past to enrich these representations with intimations of future possibilities, near and remote.

Thus, one may freeze or jump out of the way of a speeding automobile just because one thinks one "knows" what is about to happen. The possible is, however, in no way restricted to the future. The past is also a candidate for continual reinterpretation as to what it might "mean" and what it portends for the present or future. Was my friend or wife or child tired, indifferent, or angry when acting as he or she did? The generation of the possible need, of course, not be optimal for the system as a whole. Every increase in information gain, whether by efficiency, power, or advantage, is limited by the conjunction of match and mismatch, of play and satisficing. The human being's informational competence is also his vulnerability. In this case he may be overwhelmed by so many possibilities that he suffers cognitive and affective pluralistic turbulence, in confusion, conflict, and indecision.

Conjunction of Isomorphism Between Media Mechanisms, Messages, and Products and an Infinitude of Messages and Products as Operators Upon a Finitude and Limited Number of Media Mechanisms

Every principle that characterizes the basic media mechanisms also characterizes the variety of messages and products using these mechanisms. Thus, the information produced by the minding system is as modular and recombinable as the mechanisms themselves. However, since the messages and products may themselves serve as further input and as operators on the 'system, the ratio of messages and products over mechanisms is an indefinitely increasing number over a fixed number.

The same relationship of finitude of components to infinitude of messages and products holds within some informational products themselves. We have seen this in the principle of amortization, when a ruler may be used to determine the length of any number of objects, a scale to determine the weight of any number of objects, an alphabet to produce any number of sentences, an analytic geometry to solve any number of spatial problems.

The possible information gain in power, efficiency, and advantage, by endlessly recombining not only the ensemble of media mechanisms themselves but also by increasing the variety of messages and products of such recombinations as further operators, enables an increasing information pool without limit.

Consider as one simple example the radical increase in perceptual precision enabled by the combination of the eye, the use of a visual measure of length and a visual measure of weight, and the use of a mathematical formula for the coefficient of correlation. By the use of the eye alone one might guess that taller human beings appear to be heavier, despite the fact that some very short individuals appear to be very heavy and some very tall ones appear to be very light. By independent measurement of the height and weight of each individual and the application of the mathematical operations of the correlation coefficient, one can determine that the degree of correlation is, say, .50, a quantity that cannot be "seen" with the same precision. In such a case four visible quantities have been transformed into one, more precise, visible quantity. The apparent height, the apparent weight, the measured height, and the measured weight (as visible scale readings), together with the mathematical operation, yield the information advantage of a more precise knowledge. In a similar way the "average" height may be attained by adding and dividing the sum of the individual heights. It is very much more difficult to "see" this average or to compare two groups for their average difference by simple visual inspection.

Again, the use of such complex products as microscopes, power tools, and computers may endlessly increase the information advantage of our sensory and motor media mechanisms by amplifying our sensory acuities, our motor strength, and our combinatorial cognitive capacities. Such products of the use of our minding media mechanisms may indeed exceed the information capacities of their creators in several respects. The steam shovel may lift much heavier things than can our arms. The electron microscope can detect much finer visual texture than can our eyes. The computer can execute some recombinations of information much faster than can its inventor. Theoretically, the inventor might one day make himself obsolete, but the distance between himself and his products today is no less than the distance between his most powerful science and the final "truth." That distance is a forever diminishing one, but we have no reason to be confident that it will ever diminish to zero. So long as we do not understand ourselves perfectly, we cannot invent artificial intelligences that enjoy the same informational advantage that we ourselves do. Whether it is theoretically possible for us to invent cognitive systems with greater informational advantage than we possess is a contemporary analogue of Kant's antinomies of human reason, that is, of space or time being either finite or infinite. If we can make ourselves obsolescent, then we are not obsolescent, since we could still endlessly make the superior system itself obsolescent and thus improve ourselves endlessly by our own inventions.

Having completed our examination of some of the varieties of information gain that are consequences of the modular combination and recombination of media mechanisms, we will conclude our examination of the minding and cognitive system by shifting to an analysis of some of the varieties of information gain via transformations of messages and products. As we have argued, these are infinite despite the finitude of the media mechanisms on which they are based. Further, we will include in our analysis such complex cognitive processes as occur in script formation. We are now shifting from a predominantly bottom-up perspective to more of a top-down perspective.

Chapter 45
Varieties of Information Gain and Script Formation: A Top-Down Perspective

INFORMATION ADVANTAGE VERSUS MAGNIFICATION ADVANTAGE

A top-down perspective of the cognitive system shifts the critical questions from the elements and their rules of combination to the question of who governs and by what rules. The elements now become the instruments of higher ordering principles. This is not to say that the more elementary rules are always entirely docile in the face of more comprehensive rules since the system remains essentially conversational in structure. It is, however, to say we are now involved with a more representative than participatory democratic conversation. Some nodes of information now speak more often and with a louder voice, while other speakers now listen more often and speak more softly and in a more acquiescent tone of voice. The principle of reciprocity is now more biased in the direction of cooption. It has to be so for much the same reason that direct, participatory democracy had to give way to representative democracy as the size and complexity of the polity increased.

The top-down view of the minding and cognitive system involves two major governing principles, information advantage and magnification advantage.

In information advantage it is the ratio of efficiency to power that is critical. How much information can be handled with how little information? In magnification advantage the same ratio is involved, but the power of that information is now multiplied and magnified by the density of conscious affect. It is now not simply neutral information but information that matters, that is deeply consequential, in which knowing is transformed into minding and caring. It is no less representational than informational advantage, but it is now more biased representation.

Without the conjoint constraints and sanctions from positive and negative affects, informational advantage would be as directionless as a computer without a program, endless possibilities with minimal actualities. How much the informational efficiency, power, and advantage is to be used and for what depends on what is magnified as seductive and what is magnified as intimidating, on what we cannot have too much of, on what we cannot have too little of. We are not bloodless knowers.

Consider first what I have defined as habitual skill scripts. They have the characteristic of what I have called as-if behavior. City dwellers cross from one side of a street to the other as if they were afraid but with no fear, as if they were curious and interested but with minimal vigilance and monitoring of traffic, quite able to continue an ongoing conversation with one who crosses the street with them because of a minimal claim on consciousness, new learning, and affect in that highly skilled performance. This is even more marked in the part of the skill that governs walking per se. But the automaticity of any such skilled enactment is readily jeopardized by the introduction of consequential novelty. The much overlearned skill of walking loses its automatic features if one is asked to walk a grider of a still incomplete building 25 stories above the street.

In contrast to motor skills, habitual skills that are restricted to the perceptual domain may operate with minimal expansion of compressed retrieved information. Thus, the coins with which I pay a bill are perceived with minimal detail compared with the same act in a foreign land with currency that is relatively unfamiliar. Again, the face of a familiar person is normally seen with retrieval of matching information that is highly compressed, so I am barely aware of that person compared with the high density of monitoring of the face of a person I meet for the first time. Should the face of the familiar person be different from the preprogrammed contingencies anticipated and prepared for meeting, then of course there will be a rapid magnification of monitoring until such a contingency can become incorporated into the network of the habitual skilled perception of that familiar face.

In order to stabilize a habitual skill, every possible contingency that might be encountered must be anticipated, and appropriate, effective strategies for each of such contingencies must be readied and programmed in advance. Only under such conditions will the central assembly not be called on for further affect, further effort, further cognition, and further awareness of such additional information processing.

How can so complex a set of alternative programs operate with minimal dependence on awareness? In general, this necessarily requires great compression of information so that specific expansion of such information is possible where needed but is minimized whenever possible. Thus, in the skilled typewriting from a passage that contains a proofreader's uncorrected error, the individual characteristically corrects the error without knowing that he has done so, in just the same way that the original mistake was not perceived by the proofreader. Here there is quite specific expansion of information that guides the fingers of the typist, expanding the compressions of information perceived from the printed page, which in their compression have incorporated unconsciously corrected information but in which the monitoring of the output is minimally expanded so that the error is again not detected. In skilled performance, monitoring must attain the same high rate of speed as the emission of motor messages. This is usually achieved by monitoring for error only rather than for error and correct responses. In early learning the majority of responses are in error, and one attends both to these errors and to the correct response that matches the intention whenever it occurs. Skill requires a fundamental change, not only in the motor part of the program but in the strategy of monitoring so that awareness can be kept minimal as long as no errors are committed. Since errors are few in comparison with correct responses, as skill increases, monitoring can then afford to be restricted to only those occasions when error has occurred.

Not only is there a simplification of monitoring to error detection, but there is also a transformation of monitoring to parts as family members rather than as independent parts. Thus, if I know a family well, I can recognize any new member of a family by any one of a large number of distinctive features. I recognize one new member by his possession of the chin that is typical of that family and another by the high brow that is distinctive. With respect to any one face I can, in skilled habitual perception, know it is the same familiar face whether I glance at the chin, brow, or haircut, each a member of a distinctive family of features unique to that face.

A habitual skill script involves not only monitoring for error and monitoring for family membership but also a maximizing of the number of repetitions within any class of responses and a minimizing of the number of those classes.

Informational advantage is achieved by the extraction and partitioning of the invariances in otherwise varying information. This enables the more economic description of any series in time as a repeated sequence of something simpler than the totality of the information sets in which the repeated sequences are embedded. Thus, the description of a maze (as a left, left, right, right, left, left set of turns) is much more economical than a series of separate descriptions of each separate turn. It thus enables the motor commands to repeat the same command over and over again while disregarding other information as noise.

A habitual skill script is a minor law of nature in which a small amount of compressed information can be used to be expanded into a larger set of controlled messages, thus producing substantial information advantage. Thus, habitual skill enables simplification via the conjunction of error monitoring alone and alternative family member monitoring and by the fewest number of commands with the greatest number of repetitions of simple responses.

Consider now the differences between such informational advantage and magnification advantage. Learned scripts have been generated to deal with sets of scenes. This entails a difference I have defined as that between amplification and magnification. A single affect is scripted innately to amplify its own activator in a single momentary scene. But when amplified scenes are coassembled, as repeated, the resulting responses to such a set represent magnification or amplification of the already separately amplified scenes. Now it is the set of such coassembled scenes that is then amplified by fresh affect and that I am defining as magnification, in contrast to the simpler script involved in any innate amplification of the single scene. Coassembly of scenes need not be limited either to repeated scenes or to repeated scenes of the same affect, and the affect to coassembled scenes need not be identical with the affect of the coassembled scenes. Further, the coassembled scenes include scenes projected as possibilities in the future, with or without coassembly of past scenes, repeated or sharply contrasted in quality. What is essential for magnification is the ordering of sets of scenes by rules for their interpretation, evaluation, production, prediction, or control so that these scenes and their rules are themselves amplified by affect.

I define magnification as the advantaged ratio of the simplicity of ordering information to the power of ordered information times its affect density:

Magnification Advantage

$$= \frac{\text{Power of Ordered Information} \times \text{Affect Density}}{\text{Simplicity of Ordering Information}}$$

The concept of magnification advantage is the product of information advantage and affect density (Intensity × Duration × Frequency). Information advantage, as I am defining it, is that part of the above formula without the affect. It is fashioned after the concept of mechanical advantage in which the lever enables a small force to move a larger force or as with a valve by which small energy forces are used to control a flow of much larger forces, as in a water distribution system. Informational advantage is an analogue. Any highly developed theory possesses great informational advantage, being able to account for much with little via the ratio of a small number of simple assumptions to a much larger number of phenomena described and explained, which constitutes its power.

But information advantage is not identical with magnification advantage. Contrast the informational advantage of a husband and wife "recognizing" the face of the other with the recognition of the same face in the midst of their initial love affair. When the lover detects the face of the beloved as a figure in a sea of other faces as ground, there is no less informational advantage involved in that recognition of the newly familiar face, but there is a radical magnification of consciousness and affect that, together with all of the significances attributed to the other, make it an unforgettable moment.

In our proposed ratio for script magnification, the denominator represents the compressed (smaller) number of rules for ordering scenes, whereas the numerator represents the expanded (much larger) number of scenes, both from the past and into the indefinite future, that are ordered by the smaller number of compressed rules. In the numerator there are represented both the scenes that gave rise to the necessity for the script as well as all of the scenes that are generated as responses to deal with the initial coassembly of scenes, either to guarantee the continuation of good scenes or their improvement, or the decontamination of bad scenes, or the avoidance of threatening scenes. The compressed smaller number of rules guide responses that, in turn, recruit amplifying affect as well as samples of the family of scenes either sought, interpreted, evaluated, produced, and expanded.

Because there is a mixture of informational advantage and affect-driven amplification, the individual is characteristically much less conscious of the compressed rules than of their expansion scenes, just as one is less aware of one's grammar than of the sentences one utters. Although the compression of rule information in the denominator always involves information reduction and simplification, there may be varying quantities of information in the number of coassembled scenes that give rise to the scripted responses in scenes yet to be played, as well as varying intensities, durations, and frequencies of affect assigned to these scenes and to the scripted response scenes. Thus, a low-degree-of-magnification script may involve a small number of scenes to be responded to by a small number of scripted scenes with moderate, relatively brief affect. In contrast, a high-degree-of-magnification script may involve a large number of scenes to be responded to by a large number of scripted scenes with intense and enduring affect. The magnification advantage ratio of either script might nonetheless be low or high, depending on the ratio of ordering rules to rules ordered.

Any of the values in such equations is susceptible to change. A central, much-magnified script involving someone of vital importance may be first magnified to the utmost via death and mourning and by that very process be ultimately attenuated, producing a series of habitually skilled reminiscences that eventually become segregated and less and less retrieved. Mourning thus retraces in reverse the love affair and is a second edition of it, similar in some ways to the miniversion of such sequences in jealousy, when a long quiescent valley of perceptual skill may be ignited by an unexpected rival.

The most magnified scripts require minimal reminders that the present is vitally connected to much of our past life and to our future and that we must attend with urgency to continually act in such a way that the totality will be as we very much wish it to be and not as we fear it might be. Between such a script and scripts I have labeled "doable" (in which one may pay one's bills as a moratorium in the midst of a task that is critical but, for the time being, "undoable" by any conceivable path) are a large number of scripts of every degree of magnification and type.

Although habitual skill scripts share some overlapping characteristics with magnified scripts, particularly since a magnified script may contain subscripts that are habitual skill scripts, nonetheless there are substantial differences between them.

Magnified scripts, because of their selectivity, incompleteness, and inaccuracy, are continually reordered and changing, at varying rates, depending on their type and the type and magnitude of disconfirmation. The coexistence of different competing scripts requires the formation of interscript scripts.

The incompleteness of scripts necessarily requires auxiliary augmentation. This may be gained via media mechanisms (e.g., vision) that provide relevant contemporary information that cannot be entirely written into any script except in a general way, even the simplest habitual skill scripts (e.g., shaving requires a mirror; driving a car requires constant monitoring no matter how skilled the driver). One cannot begin to use any script without much information that cannot be scripted in advance. Further, one normally requires auxiliary media information, gained by use of the arms and legs, to reach further information as well as to alter perspectives. Again, one requires speech and/or written language as auxiliary sources of information, past as well as present. These are also media mechanisms but culturally inherited media. Next, one requires, as auxiliaries, compressed information in the form of theories, lay and professional, about causal relationships, signs or omens, intentions and consequences. Further, one requires the memorially supported plot, which is a sequentially organized series of scenes of the life one has led and the lives others have led. One also requires maps, which are spatiotemporal schematics that enable the plots to be handled more economically. We possess maps of varying degrees of fineness of texture, normally generated by their usefulness for different scripts. The differences between a duffer and professional tennis player is reflected not only in the differences between their families of tennis scripts but also in the detail of the maps of their opponent's past performances. Finally, one script may use another script as auxiliary. Thus, Calvinism used the entrepreneurial activity of the economic competition script to increase the probability of grace in warding off the hell fires of its vivid version of the life hereafter.

Magnified scripts contain variables as alternatives. Variables are the rules that, as alternatives, depend on auxiliary information to further specify.

A script thus may, for example, differentiate strategy and tactics, conditional upon variable auxiliary information. Thus, Hitler gave orders to his generals to march on the Ruhr but to retreat at any sign of resistance from the French. A child may learn to script a relationship with a parent in which he extorts as much as is possible just within the limits of the patience and power of the indulgent but irascible other. The auxiliary information need not, however, be limited to external information. Thus, an otherwise deeply committed individual may nonetheless exempt himself from his major concern should he become ill or seriously disturbed or depressed. Very few scripts are conceived as completely unconditional, since they are designed to deal with variable selected features of selected scenes. When unanticipated conditions are encountered, the individual has the option of further adding to the script "not when I'm sick" or "no matter what, I must keep at it." Indeed, it is just such encounters and their absorption that are critical in the deepening of a commitment script.

Magnified scripts also have the property of modularity. They are variously combinable, recombinable, and decomposable. The separate scripts may be aggregated and fused, as when a career choice combines scripts that enable an individual to explore nature, to be alone, and to express himself through writing, as in the case of Eugene O'Neill, who chose to live at the ocean's edge in solitude as he wrote his plays. Compare such a set of component subscripts with that of a lumberjack who enjoys nature but in the company of others and also while exercising his large muscles. Contrast both with an archaeologist who is enchanted with the rediscovery of the past, with others, in very special remote nature sites. Not only is each component of a single script endlessly combinable and recombinable, but so are scripts themselves, as when addictive scripts for cigarettes, eating, and drinking are combined in a bottoming-out nuclear script.

Magnified scripts may also be partitioned, as in the classic neurotic split libido and in the characteristically French separation of family and mistress, one cherished for enjoyment and continuity, the other for novelty and excitement.

TRANSFORMATION DYNAMICS OF THE CREATION OF NOVELTY

We have placed an unusually heavy burden on transformation in perception, in memory, in consciousness, and in action governed by the feedback mechanism. Even when the aim is primarily duplicative, as in the perceptual matching of sensory input, we have assumed a central synthesis of imagery. Although we have assumed an innate storage mechanism, we have also postulated the construction of a memory analogue that will make it possible to retrieve past experience. The basic commonality we have assumed in perception, memory, and action is the fabrication and synthesis of components according to some model that is to be duplicated. The general strategy of build and compare, rebuild and compare again, we have maintained, underlies all cognitive functions. In this section our focus will be on transformation dynamics as such, the varieties of changes wrought on messages in the nervous system to enable a human being of demonstrable limitations of channel capacity to better process information. In succeeding chapters we will examine four major types of information transformations: the central matching of sensory input; the monitoring and matching of the Image to feedback information; the matching of past experience by analogues that are retrievable through a series of compression-expansion transformations; and the transformation of transmitted into transmuted, conscious information.

We will now examine language as a model for understanding how a human being processes information in general.

Generation of Novelty through Operations on Simple Elements

We have argued that the nervous system is organized as a language is organized—by incompletely overlapping assemblies that generate endless novelty. Speech and conversation generate and unite diametrically opposed phenomena-exact duplication and real novelty. If I could not respond to your speech in all of its novelty, except with my customary clichés, then conversation would in fact be impossible. Only a predetermined Leibnizian harmony would guarantee that one speaker could respond sensitively to another speaker if each were not capable in response to the other of generating statements he had never made before. On the other hand, conversation would be equally impossible if I refused to use the same alphabet, the same words, the same rules of grammar, ever. Conversation is an extraordinary union of invention and repetition. And so is cognition in general. Let us pursue the commonalities among the structure of language, transformation dynamics, and the nervous system.

The essence of the strategy of creating novelty is transformation rather than duplication. To make something new, something old must be changed in some way. The newer the object invented, the less it will resemble the objects from which it was transformed. Novelty as such may or may not be worth creating, and it need not be either true or useful.

We wish now to examine the human being as a creator of novelty. This should be distinguished at the outset from the domain of problem solving. Many new objects that human beings create produce many more, new problems than they solve. Many new objects are entirely useless, and errors in problem solving are just as new as solutions. Truth may be old and error new. Our interest is in the generation of novelty within which are both intended and unintended consequences, good and bad, true and false. It is because novelty is the domain of the possible that it necessarily entails great risk, the risk of error or of triviality.

The potentialities of any system for the generation of novelty is a function of its complexity. By complexity we mean the number of independently variable states within a system, or what Gibbs called its degree of freedom. We can best understand transformability by examining systems of the highest and lowest complexity. Let us contrast the memory system with what we will call the conceptual system. Both are involved in the transformation of information, but the aim of memory is to duplicate and preserve information, and the aim of the conceptual system is to transform information. Despite the fact that much transformation is involved in learning how to compress and retrieve and how to expand memory analogues, nonetheless the essential aim of these transformations is the preservation of information. At every step of the compression there is an expansion process that is judged successful or not depending on how well it enabled the matching of the retrieved information with the original model.

Ideally, the aim of the memory system is to create a unique object. Ideally, the aim of the conceptual system is to create an infinite set. If one asks another person whether he remembers one's telephone numher, both parties understand that it is critical that the numbers be remembered exactly, that their order be remembered exactly, and that there is only one such combination. If, however, one asks the question of a stranger "Would you try to guess what number I am thinking of?" when one is in fact thinking of one's telephone number, the ultimate aim is to find the same number that might have been retrieved by the memory system, but the strategy of the conceptual system is necessarily radically different than that of the memory system. If the rules of our conceptual game are made particularly severe (e.g., that the player can ask only the one who knows the correct answer whether the number he has guessed is the correct number or not), then the conceptual system of the player must ideally be capable of generating an infinite set of numbers, since under the rules of this game there are no possible strategies that are more economical than any other strategy. It is a needle in a haystack, in which both the needle and the haystack must be generated. In the memory system, transformations are used but only to preserve and duplicaté a model. In the conceptual system, the aim also may be, as in this case, one of matching a model, but the model is not known; and the primary way in which this is achieved in the limiting case is through the generation of an infinite set, one member of which may be a to-be-attained model. The conceptual system is, however, also capable of simply generating new information, with no ulterior model to be matched.

In a low-complexity system uniqueness is the primary characteristic. In terms of class membership there is in the ideal case but one member of a class. In a high-complexity system there is in the ideal case an infinite set, a maximizing of the members of the class. Because there is only one member of the class in a low complexity system, it can be referred to by a unique symbol, what we have defined as its "name." A high-complexity system cannot be referred to by a unique symbol. In the ideal case it would require an infinite number of symbols because it has an infinite number of degrees of freedom, or independently variable states.

In a relatively low-complexity system, such as memory, the chief peril is change. If one of the digits in the telephone number is switched with another digit, this constitutes a memory disturbance. In a highcomplexity system the chief peril is stasis and restriction of variation. Any redundancy or rule that prohibits particular kinds of change is a restriction on the freedom and transformability of a high-complexity system. Thus, in formal systems such as logic or mathematics, where an attempt is made to maximize the degrees of freedom within a system, the discovery that certain combinations might not be permissible creates a state of crisis and finally an enlargement of the freedom of the system.

Imaginary numbers, such as $\sqrt{-1}$, although compounded of three elements, $\sqrt{}$, $-$, and 1, each of which had a specifiable meaning, nonetheless constituted a threat to the generality of mathematics when the permissibility of such a combination was questioned. When such numbers were admitted into good standing, the freedom of the system that could tolerate such novel combinations was enhanced and so, later, were the branches of physics to which these entities were coordinated.

Not only is change a differential threat to low and high-complexity systems and to the memory and conceptual systems, but so also is the existence of similar entities either in the environment or within the system itself. One can undermine memory by flooding the system with members that vary only a little bit from the model. The memory system is most vulnerable to "interference" when exposed to a multiplicity of pseudomodels. In contrast, the more graded the elements of any set that are available for the conceptual system, the more flexibly such a system can operate.

A low-complexity system such as memory is a stable and closed system; that is, it remains constant in a constant environment. In contrast, a high-complexity system such as the conceptual system is both unstable and open; that is, it varies in a variable environment. Conversation is an example of the union of both low and high-complexity characteristics. One may not ever be able to predict what the speech of the other will be, except that it will preserve the constancies of alphabet, words, and grammar. Most subsystems within the human being vary in their degree of complexity or transformability, and none is in fact completely stable or unstable, completely open or closed. Nonetheless, certain systems such as the two we are considering differ radically in their degree of transformability.

Let us consider now what is the nature of the elements and of their relationships to each other in the conceptual system. This is at the heart of the difference between the memory and conceptual systems. First, in an ideal conceptual system any element of a set of elements is itself capable of generating an infinite set of subelements that are equivalent to the element. In a language of communication this is ordinarily not the case. The letters of the alphabet are the elements of the language, but each letter is not itself endlessly divisible into parts of letters though each letter is divisible into component sounds. In arithmetic this condition is met. The number 1 can be subdivided into a set of an infinite number of equivalent fractions (e.g., $2 \times {}^1/_2$, $3 \times {}^1/_3, \ldots, n \times 1/n$. That is, 1 is equivalent to ${}^1/_2 + {}^1/_2$, which is equivalent to ${}^1/_3 + {}^1/_3 + {}^1/_3$ etc. It should be noted that we have used the word *equivalent* rather than *equal*. In arithmetic it is the case that 1 equals ${}^1/_2 + {}^1/_2$, but we have specified only that they need be equivalent, by which we mean equal in some respect but not necessarily in all respects. This means that the subelements may be members of the class of elements without being exactly equal, either to each other or to the element as long as they are equal to the element and to each other in some specifiable respect.

Second, each element of a set is capable of being combined with any other element of the set to form a subset. Thus 1 + 2 may be combined as s subset. In languages of communication, however, not every combination of letters produces a word.

Third, for each subset there are an infinite number of equivalent subsets that can be generated by some operations from the original elements. Thus $1 + 2 = 1.5 + 1.5 = 3 = 0 + 1 + 1 + 1$, etc. In languages of communication any word has a large but not infinite number of equivalents (e.g., species-genus equivalance, singular-plural equivalence, synonym equivalence, and so on).

Fourth, every subset is capable of being combined with every other subset. Thus, if 1 + 2 is a subset and 3 + 4 is a subset, there is a subset 1 + 2 + 3 + 4. In languages of communication words can be combined to generate sentences, sentences to generate paragraphs, and so on.

For each set of subsets there is an infinite number of equivalent sets of subsets. Thus, $1 + 2 + 3 + 4 = 1.5 + 1.5 + 3.5 + 3.5 = 1 + 1 + 1 + 1 + 1 + 1 + 1 + 1 + 1 + 1$. In languages of communication there are an infinite number of sentences that are equivalent, or equal in some respect, to another sentence.

Any system, formal or empirical, that is highly transformable is one in which every part is transformable, independent of the value of every other part of the system. In a formal system the existence of an infinite number of equivalent subsets guarantees both the compressibility of varieties of statements to one statement and the expandability of statements into an infinity of other statements that, among other things, can constitute solutions to problems.

Thus, Descartes in his *Analytic Geometry* remarked:

> But it is not my purpose to write a large book. I am trying rather to include much in a few words, as will perhaps be inferred from what I have done, if it is considered that, while reducing to a single construction all the problems of one class, I have at the same time given a method of transforming them into an infinity of others and thus of solving each in an infinite number of ways.

Not only is problem solving radically enhanced through the infinite transformability of concepts into equivalent concepts, but the very possibility of concept formation rests upon the independent transformability of parts of objects or sets. Only to the extent to which I can order a set of objects to some shared characteristic or set of characteristics can I attain a concept. This characteristic that parts of objects share may itself be identical in all instances, or equivalent—that is, identical in some respects. Thus, the concept of redness is a property that some lollipops and toys may share despite many characteristics in which they differ. But further, it is not necessary that they be equally red for all of them to be red in the sense of equivalence. One may be a yellowish red and the other a more bluish red. It is just as important that a concept be capable of being indifferent to grossly different excluded characteristics as that it be capable of being indifferent to very fine variations of members included within the class. In short, a concept (and the conceptual system) is a mechanism for dealing with classes of objects, not with unique objects. Contrary to the memory mechanism, the aim not the preservation of a unique object with a name but the construction of a class with a "symbol." By a symbol we refer not to a word but to that neurological structure or script that has the capacity to generate or detect similarities in a sea of noise. We use the term in a manner analogous to *name,* by which we meant not a word but a message capable of finding a specific address in the nervous system.

The memory mechanism succeeds to the extent to which an experience in all of its particularity is preserved. The conceptual mechanism succeeds to the extent to which an experience can be ordered to all other experiences, in as many respects as possible.

A picture is worth a thousand words if it is the unique object we wish to preserve, but the same thousand words can be used to describe many thousands of objects.

We are now in a position to examine more closely the relationship between the transformations involved in memory and those involved in conceptual activity. We can best contrast these two types of activity if we examine what on the surface appears to be the same type of transformation, namely, the compression-expansion transformation. It will be remembered that we conceived the learning of retrieval of stored information as dependent on a compression and miniaturization of the to-be-remembered information, which also involved a learned technique of the inverse transformation of expansion so that the individual knew specifically how to recover the original information from the miniaturized analogue plus a transformation. It is not unlike the technique of microfilming information and then recovering the original through the use of a magnifying glass. What has been selected for permanent storage is what is unique in the information. What has been built into techniques of recovery are the nonunique characteristics common to this and other data. In the case of microfilm, it is the absolute size of the print, and in the case of the telephone number we have examined before, it was the speed and volume of the voice in speaking the numbers that was miniaturized. In contrast, when a set of objects is conceptualized, it is just those aspects of the objects that they share in common, in which they are equivalent, that is compressed and miniaturized, and the other relatively unique information about each object is disregarded. One has attained a concept in a series of objects. One has attained a memory to the extent to which one can reproduce or recognize a particular object as distinct from other particular objects. What is unique in the object is preserved in one compression-expansion transformation, whereas what is common in the object relative to other objects is preserved in the other transformation.

We have traced in some detail how the inessential information is compressed out of the memory analogue. What is the nature of the compression in the formation of a concept? It is not simply the learning of a specific word for a particular object that is involved in concept formation. It is rather the production of a neurological structure that we have called a "symbol," which enables the detection of similarity in an indefinite number of new instances or members of a class that may differ radically from previously identified members of the learned class. A concept is, by its nature, not only the consequence of learning but also an instrument of further learning and discovery. It is a means not only of detecting similarities in otherwise disparate entities but also of creating similarities where none may have existed before. A concept, we will argue, is any technique for maximizing the repetitions within a class. With respect to sensory input it refers equally to the techniques for detecting and maximizing what is repeated within the received information as to the techniques for imposing order that may be created entirely by the perceiver. Thus, conceptual responses to sensory input, according to this definition, may vary from responding to only the red objects in the environment to conceptualizing objects as exciting (i.e., objects that are similar according to the affects they evoke). Each concept would maximize the repetitions within the same sensory input but in one case according to a class that is inherent in the received information; in the other, according to one of its repeated consequences.

There are also concepts that govern the motoric system. The fingers of the hand are controlled by sets of messages, some of which are organized as memories are organized (as we have seen in the techniques for the recovery of early handwriting) and some of which are organized by the conceptual system (e.g., in the case of a surgeon performing a new operation). It is our impression that there has been a failure to fully exploit motor performance as a technique of testing the conceptual system. We will presently examine the motoric as a medium of the conceptual system.

Because a concept is a learned technique of maximizing the repetitions within a class, it is, unlike a memory, a continually unfinished business, with the properties of an open rather than a closed system. Whether the next object will be coordinated to one concept or another will depend in part on the competition between concepts and the monopolistic power of one concept over another as well as on the nature of the object. Because of the competition between concepts and between concepts and unique objects, concepts characteristically grow stronger or weaker.

TABLE 45.1 Data on Formation of Concepts in a Two-Concept Mode

Ping	Pong	Votes
Mouse	Elephant	13
Ounce	Pound	13
Inch	Mile	13
Yellow	Black	11
Rubber	Putty	10

Basescu, (1951), comparing high and low-IQ high school students, found that after having attained a concept to a particular criterion, the bright students held the concept successfully on succeeding trials, whereas dull students lost it; that is, they were not capable of recognizing the concept in repetitions of the same material. Every new encounter with the same object has within it the potentiality of destroying the concept that was once achieved in commerce with it.

Because the neurological "symbol" that underlies conceptual activity is a strategy for detecting or generating similarities, it is not only an unfinished business but also unfinishable, inasmuch as new data will necessarily present new challenges for the detection of the concept, and other concepts will also provide competition. A one-track mind or any monopolistic conceptual status is a state of affairs in which particular concepts are regularly attained despite the most unpromising raw material. The one-track mind lives in a world of haystacks wherein it is forever finding a conceptual needle.

If one asks any individual to suspend the competition of concepts in the interests of an arbitrarily chosen concept, one can experimentally simulate conceptual monopolism. Further, we can produce consensus without communication by such a technique.

Gombrich (1960) created a two-word language of "ping" and "pong." He asked 14 subjects to classify a variety of paired words, such as *mouse* and *elephant, ounce* and *pound, mile* and *inch, yellow* and *black, rubber* and *putty.* The results are shown in Table 4.1.

Here we see that subjects not only can be made conceptual monopolists, in which all objects are reduced to two classes, but that in so doing conceptual consensus may be achieved without communication when none of the subjects had ever before attempted to extend the domain of these two concepts. There was apparently sufficient similarity between *ping* and *pong,* on the one hand, and the other words, for the majority of subjects to achieve like-mindedness in this novel extension of the meaning of two words.

We have been able to extend this method to the point of simulating psychotic delusions. If we suppose that a psychotic misinterpretation is the consequence of an underweighting of the common conceptual operations on an object and an overweighting of alternative conceptual operations, then it should be possible to evoke the psychotic interpretation of a picture that unduly threatens the psychotic by asking the normal subject for alternative interpretations in addition to the common one. If we assume that the psychotic individual approaches the task of interpreting reality in much the same way that the normal person does—that is, by weighing the perceptual evidence to find the best conceptual fit—then if the psychotic person encounters a situation that is too terrifying to be confronted, we have two plausible alternatives. Either he flees the scene entirely—perceptually, conceptually, and motorically—or he remains and tries to effect some compromise between the situation, the demands of the investigator, and his own terror. The most common outcome under such circumstances may be understood as a special case of the *Umweg* solution. Confronted with a barrier, he takes a detour, the long way around. Since he is confronted with a picture and since he cannot tolerate seeing it as others see it but wishes, like any subject, to achieve as good an interpretation as he can, he elects the next most reasonable interpretation in the hierarchy of plausible possibilities. In the Picture Arrangement Test there are two types of representations that many paranoid schizophrenics find terrifying. One is to be exposed to and confronted by a group of people. The other is to suffer an injury to the body that produces bleeding. How bizarre and un-understandable are the paranoid's distortions to these situations, shown in Figures 45.1, 45.2, and 45.3?

FIGURE 45.1 Selected plate from the Picture Arrangement Test (Tomkins, Volume II).

FIGURE 45.2 Selected plate from the Picture Arrangement Test (Tomkins, Volume II).

In Figure 45.1 the interpretation may be "a man with a fruit store. He is arranging the apples and oranges." If a normal subject is asked, "What might this be if it were not what it obviously is, a man standing before an audience?" the answer of the paranoid is one of the alternatives given. Again we have consensus without communication if we suspend conceptual competition.

In Figure 45.2 the interpretation may be "a boy playing a violin in the bathtub." Normal subjects have also given this response, and all normal subjects can see it once it has been given to them as a possibility.

In Figure 45.3 the interpretation may be "a man's oil can dripping" or "carving a piece of wood" or "masturbating," all of which have been seen by normal subjects under our particular instructions.

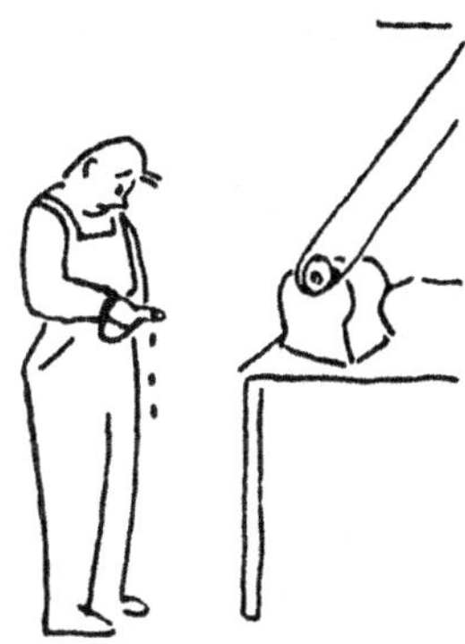

FIGURE 45.3 Selected plate from the Picture Arrangement Test (Tomkins, Volume II).

Ordinarily, there is a brisk competition among concepts. Concepts grow by use, by challenge and by displacing challengers, by the constant reinterpretation of the past to fit the present and the assumed future. We have also noted before that the relative weight of proaction and retroaction vary systematically in youth and senility and that in psychological youth the past is interpreted in terms of the present and the future, in contrast to senility, in which the present and the future are interpreted in terms of past concepts. In youth, retroaction dominates proaction. In senility proaction dominates retroaction. One becomes old psychologically when one suffers "ideosclerosis." In psychological senility each new vintage of information is aged in the same old categories.

The reader is now somewhat puzzled. He may be prepared to agree that concepts are techniques for maximizing the members of a class, that the achievement of such order is hard work, and that it is an unfinishable task, but how does the maximizing of the repetition and equivalence of otherwise disparate information create novelty? Is not the maximizing of the repetitions of instances of a class the exact antithesis of novelty? If I respond to a lollipop and a truck and a red traffic signal in the same way, have I not lost more information than I may have gained? The answer to the latter question may well be affirmative. There can be no guarantee that the quest for novelty will not lose a greater quantity of information than it gains. If I take the carburetors out of two automobiles, I may now have a new class, but I may have lost two members of a larger class. If I took all the *a*'s out of the preceding sentence, I would also have achieved a new class at a somewhat prohibitive cost. The answer to this dilemma is that productive novelty is ordinarily the consequence of combinations of simples, of classes of classes. An industrious monkey working on a typewriter with 26 letters of the English alphabet is capable of producing an occasional masterpiece despite the fact that much of what it writes is rubbish. The human being enjoys certain advantages over the monkey in his production of novelty through the concatenation of simple classes, since he observes the rules of the language, but despite this he also produces much novelty that is trivial.

Any sentence in a language of communication is an instance of the general technique whereby simples can be combined to generate novelty. No matter how familiar I may be with the English language, it remains possible to generate new sentences and new meanings while still employing the same elements, the same words, the same rules of grammer that I have used hundreds of times before. When the same pool of information, received from sensory sources and stored in memory, is continually conceptualized and reconceptualized, it too yields an expanding pool of new information with which to interpret sensory input and with which to guide the motoric system. This novelty, in turn, increases the raw material upon which further transformations can be effected. In general, the greater the number of members of any class and the finer the differences between these members, the more readily can new combinations be constructed. Thus, if one were house building, the number of possible types of houses that could be built, apart from the imagination of the architect, would depend critically on the size and number of the building blocks. The smaller and finer and more numerous these elements were, the greater the number of possible combinations. If the architect had to work only with preasembled rigid wall sections, the number of possible houses that could be built would be radically reduced. Experience begins with primitive huts and only later is decomposed into such components so that it can be rebuilt into a mansion nearer the concept's desire.

The limitation of channel capacity in both perception and action requires constant analysis and resynthesis to enable the human being to enlarge the ability to deal with increasing amounts of information. This process is like a grasping hand that compresses the material it reaches for until it is of such a size that it can be held in the hand while premitting yet another object to be grasped and compressed, and this operation can be repeated cumulatively. This is the same technique humans employ in extending their control over nature through science. Phenomena that appear to be discrete or laws that are about different domains are painfully and slowly reformulated until they become special cases of a more general and simpler theory or law. The general trend of these compressions through analyses and resyntheses is to maximize the number of repetitions in all domains, since once a domain has been conceptualized, the application of these same rules will handle further instances with a reduced claim on the channel capacity. The individual does not constantly increase the complexity of his performance but rather transforms complex information into simpler information, which is to say, he maximizes the number of repetitions within the information he processes.

There is a double maximum implicit in our conception of maximizing of repetitions or duplicates: One is that the components to be duplicated are fewest in number; the other is that the combinations of these duplicates are the largest number. The complexity of any domain cannot be characterized except as we include both the number of different combinations of which the system, whether formal or empirical, is capable of producing and the number of different elements required to produce these different combinations. Thus, a theory may be weak either because it explains little or because it explains much but uses too many different elements to account for what it purports to explain. In elements we include not only the building blocks but the transformations or relational activities required to combine the elements. Two systems might thus have equal power in two different ways: One uses a very small number of building blocks but requires many different kinds of transformations; whereas the other uses a larger number of building blocks but requires a smaller number of kinds of transformations.

Increasing Combinations Through Variants of Components

Let us now examine transformation dynamics and the relative transformability of sets of responses at a more empirical level. We can test the degree of transformability of a set of responses by varying each component of a set and noting the extent to which the variation of each component changes the remainder of the set. The highly transformable set is one in which each component may be varied without changing the residual components of the set. In our examination of the characteristics of handwriting and speaking, we noted that handwriting did not remain invariant under speed transformations but that speaking did, although it did not do so under intensity transformations. As the specificity of a set increases, any change in any component will increasingly disorganize the set. In the limiting case no component of a set can be changed and maintain the identity of the set. In such a case there is no conceptualization of any part of the set, that is, no range of values of, say, the speed components, that can be substituted for the one specific speed with which the entire set of messages subserving the motor performance is tightly linked. In this case it should be noted that we are dealing with the conceptualization of a set of responses to be generated rather than to be detected. In contrast to perceptual conceptualization, in which the same-shape object might be recognized in two instances despite differences in color of two objects of the same shape, in the case of sets of motor responses to be generated, the multiple sets that are to be the same except for the variation in one component must be generated by the individual rather than received from sensory input.

We prefer to exploit motor responses for the study of conceptual activity because the requirement that the individual is responsible for the generation and transformation of information is here undisputed. In the perceptual sphere we think the individual must indeed be equally active to attain both percepts and concepts, but the issue is contaminated by disputes between psychologists about the activity and the passivity of the perceiver. When we ask an individual to write his name and then to alter the speed or the size of the letters, there can be no question that the individual must respond by an act of construction and then of reconstruction. The only disadvantage is that of unfamiliarity, which requires that one must redefine conceptual activity so that concepts are entirely generated rather than simply selected or recognized in presented material. A high degree of conceptualization of handwriting would mean that the individual could write the same at any speed or could write with different pressure and with different sizes and shapes of letters at any speed. If *a* refers to speed, *b* to pressure, *c* to shape, *d* to size, and each of these may vary, let us arbitrarily assume, in 10 equal intervals, then a high degree of conceptualization of such a performance would involve the set of combinations of 10 *a*'s, *b*'s, *c*'s, and *d*'s, a number of combinations of types of handwriting never empirically achieved.

As we have seen before, the ease of producing a set with a somewhat different value of a single component depends on how tightly organized the original set is and how fine the gradations of the component to be altered. If one can write the same at a speed just a little faster than childhood writing, then it may still be possible to write the same with a further slight increase in speed, until finally one has learned to write the same, even, handwriting of one's childhood but at the speed of one's usual adult writing. We also noted that if these steps of increased speed are too great, the total organization will shift to the adult form. Modification of any set of messages that constitutes the guidance of observable responses depends on being able to detach one component from the set and to operate on it to increase the gradations of the isolated variable, by increasing the number of members of that class and by the creation of equal intervals and of small intervals, thus producing a set of scale values of the isolated component, each of which is small enough to be successively combined with the residual members of the set without destroying the original organization.

Interconcept Distance

By interconcept distance we mean the number of transformations on any set that is necessary to modify any set. This distance varies for aach component, for different values of each component, and for different sets of which the component is a subset. Thus, to increase the speed from slow to faster may require fewer transformations than to increase the speed an equal physical interval from the latter to a still faster speed. To increase the pressure of handwriting may not require as many transformations as to increase its speed. Finally, to increase the speed of speech may not require as many transformations as to increase the speed of writing. The interconcept distance is a conjoint function of the correlation between components, the number of gradations of each component that do not change the residual set, and the number of gradations it is necessary to produce so that the residual set will remain invariant under successive transformations.

Increasing Combinations Through the Informational Advantage of Summaries

We have thus far considered conceptual transformations that detect or generate the similarities between components of a number of sets of otherwise disparate characteristics. We will now consider the increased informational advantage of the conceptual transformations which we will call summaries. A summary is the detection or generation of a similarity between a set and an abbreviated or compressed set. Thus, the arithmetic mean is a summary of the central tendency of an array of numbers just as an evaluation, such as "nonsense" or "wonderful" might be a summary of a paper or a speech. A summary need not be a single concept as long as it is more compressed than what is summarized, that is, as long as it enjoys some informational advantage. Thus, a description of an array as having a mean of 25 and a standard deviation of 5 is also a summary describing both the average variability of the numbers and their central tendency. A summary of a paper might be similarly expanded to include some of the general ideas conveyed. A summary, like any concept, loses as well as gains information. In contrast to memory it provides diffusely recoverable rather than specifically recoverable information. If I ask you to guess what numbers I might be thinking of, this is a summary that refers equally well to an infinite set of numbers. If now I characterize these numbers as together equal to 11, there is a reduction in the diffuseness of recoverability of information by this summary. These might be $8+2+1, 11+0, 9+2, 7+2+2$, and so on. If now I say the numbers I am thinking of contain no more than two numbers, then this summary further reduces the diffuseness of recoverable information, since there are fewer possibilities with this summary than with the former. As the diffuseness of members of the summary class increases, there is less and less specific information being given about more and more entities. A combination of summaries, however, provides a powerful remedy for this generality though it falls short of the specificity of a memory. Thus, the combination of mean and sigma give a much more specific, albeit general, summary of the characteristics of an array of numbers.

In contrast to the type of concept we have previously considered (e.g., redness), in which the shape and size of an object might be disregarded and the similarity of the color to that of other objects selected for conceptualization, here it-is rather certain properties of the object as a whole, or of a set of objects as a whole, that are selected for conceptualization, to exclusion of other properties of the object as a whole. In the former case a group of red toys would be conceptualized as red and in the latter case as toys. In the former case other objects that are also red but that are not toys can be instances of the concept, since the concept is indifferent with respect to the nature of the total object.

The informational advantage of summaries is considerable. First, because of channel capacity limitations, information that is much too detailed and complex to be detected or generated can be digested or generated piecemeal if the general outlines can be summarized at the outset. Many forests are lost because of too many trees. Also scientists first detect the meaning of their experimental data when they can convert the hundreds of detailed recorded observations into some summary measure that enables them to see the general trends within the data. In listening to a long speech it would be difficult, if not impossible, to understand unless there were a concomitant compression of the sentences into summaries. In memory exact duplication is a rare achievement. For the most part, summaries play the role similar to but not identical with exact duplications. Thus, if I read a paper today and summarize it to myself as "wonderful" and two weeks later someone stimulated by my expressed enthusiasm asks for a more detailed description of what I found so commendable, I am likely to be embarrassed by an inability to support my affect with hard news.

In beginning to learn to generate complex motor responses, as, for example, in swimming, there are only two major options: either to conceptualize part of the set and to practice kicking the feet while disregarding the remainder of the demands of the total set or to caricature the whole set in a gross but somewhat coordinated flailing of arms and legs. The part-versus-the-whole method in early learning well illustrates the distinction between concepts as summaries and as component concepts. It should be noted, however, that both produce *caricatures* of the model to be attained. Both grossly reject the total demands of the task in the interest of ultimate mastery.

A Set Can Be Organized Into a Combination of General and Specific Concepts

The second great advantage of summaries is that they permit the organization of a set into a combination of components of varying degrees of generality. This is a second way in which the reliance on brute memory is attenuated. If I can organize a set of rules by which I can recover most of the details of a prior percept or action, then I need not store these messages in all of their detail as memory analogues.

Thus, if I know how to multiply, I need not memorize an entire multiplication table. Much of what one appears to have remembered is in fact a rapid relearning from a small amount of fresh information aided and abetted by a great amount of conceptual skill.

Let us now examine the nature of the conceptual skill whereby combinations of summaries of varying degrees of generality enable the detection and generation of sets of relatively unique information.

If learning proceeds through conceptualization of the separate components or through conceptualization of the whole, starting in either direction, the consequence of such transformations is to proceed from the construction of caricatures to an eventual synthesis through the combination of classes. This final synthesis may never entirely attain the object or set of objects it intends, but what it loses in specificity it gains in generality, particularly in economy of organization. Both perceptual organization and motor ogranization are similar to a sentence in a language of communication. A sentence is ordinarily a combination of words of quite different degrees of generality and specificity, and any sentence might have been generated either from combining relatively specific parts and adding relations or by starting with an equivalent sentence that was more general but included relations and then had specific details added to it.

We are suggesting that summary conceptual transformations in a set are stretched to the limit in accounting for as much of the variance of the set as is possible. What one summary cannot account for, another summary is constructed to describe, and so on until the total set can be detected or generated by as few summaries as possible. This process may begin at the level of the most general class and add specifics or begin with the specifics and add more general classes. The word *add* is somewhat misleading since each summary, whether specific or general, is itself changed by adding either more specific or more general classes.

Let us first consider the perceptual problem from this point of view. Hochberg (1957), summarized the Cornell Symposium on Perception as achieving the following consensus among Gibson, Kohler, Metzger, Johansson, and himself: "that perceptual response to a stimulus will be obtained which requires the least amount of information to specify." This is because where an invariable relationship occurs, it is partialed out as a framework, or neutral point, instead of being repeated in each perceptual response. In Johansson's studies on the perception of motion, one can extract a given component from a complex motion and obtain the predicted remainder. In general, there is a figural hierarchy of perceived motion. First there is a static background; then, in reference to this, there is seen the common motion; and finally, the components of motion relative to the common motion. Johansson states that if we abstract the motion components common to all of the moving points, in his experiments the remaining components become the relative motion of the parts, while the common motion becomes the motion of the whole relative to the stationary background.

We would account for such organization of the perceptual field as a maximizing of the repetitions within each class and a minimizing of the number of classes. The general reason for such organization is the limited channel that enforces economy if information is to be processed at all.

Stress should disorganize the more specific classes before the more general classes and produce caricatures of the more general class. If the organization of information tends toward a maximizing of repetitions within each class and a minimizing of classes, then as we go from the more general summaries to the more specific summaries, vulnerability to stress should increase. But under stress the more general class should also revert to its earlier status and exaggerate these early characteristics. This means essentially an increase in distinctiveness or an increased number of repetitions or both. We have tested this derivative by some experiments we will now briefly describe.

We required subjects to print as quickly as they could a series of the letter *N*, so: NNNN NNNNNN NNNN. If we examine the components of the set of messages that must guide this series of responses, it would be as follows: up down up (down, but off the paper) up down up (down, off the paper) up down up (down, off the paper) up down up. This describes approximately the production of the first four letters. The down stroke that is off the paper would look as follows if the pencil were not lifted from the paper: ΛΛΛ/. Since the downstroke that is drawn in the air is similar to the other downstrokes in some respects but different in others, it is organized as a residual class of greater specificity than the more general class of up down up, which contains two successive alternations (from up to down and down to up). When the *N*'s are drawn 10 times, this class contains 20 alternations as opposed to 10 strokes in the air between the letters.

The complete description of the component directions of even the simpliest motor performance is a formidable problem. Consider that the drawing of each of the straight lines is not necessarily a ballistic response but may have to be repeated as the line gets longer. Consider also that the length of two of the lines that go in the same direction is also equal, thus making a correlated repetition in contrast to the diagonal line, which is longer as well as unrepeated in direction. Consider also that the size of the angle of the two uprights is repeated, and the size of the first angle of the diagonal is not. The temporal rhythm tends also to be repeated more within the letter than between letters, aided by the correlated repetitions of length and direction plus the repeated direction alternation with the pencil continuing on the surface of the paper. In contrast, the space between letters lifts the pencil from this surface, often changes the speed, and changes the length of the line as well as the angle from the top of the letter to the beginning of the next letter. As we shall see later, any change in rhythm is the focal point for intrusion effects, since this is where the instructions to simply repeat must be supplemented by either new or additional instructions. Under stress, therefore, we should expect the more specific class of messages to be more disturbed than the more general class, which has the greater number of repetitions. This disturbance should be reflected in an increase in the number of repetitions of the classes of components that already have the most repetitions relative to the residual, more specific classes of components. Such experimentally produced errors should be reflected in either an increase in the number of repetitions or as increase in the degree of difference between classes, or both. Either of these is a caricature that may have occurred earlier in the learning process before the finer differentiations between classes were achieved or may be a new caricature reflecting new stresses not encountered in the original learning.

In the case of the repeated *N*'s one way of increasing the number of repetitions would be to add a downstroke to either the end or the beginning of the letter. Either addition would increase the repetitions by an up-down-up-down repetition instead of an up-down-up asymmetry. These two possibilities are the principal caricatures produced. The more common one is to introduce the additional downstroke at the beginning of each letter as follows:

Less commonly, the additional stroke is added to the end of the letter as follows:

In this case as soon as the error is detected, it is corrected, and the line is rarely completed. The more common error in contrast is frequently not detected at all. This is possible in part because the additional line may be drawn so close to the beginning stroke that it appears only as a thickening of the line. Further, in this and the succeeding experiments that involve speed stress, there are a handful of subjects who cannot comply with the instructions. They are aware that increased speed increases the possibility of error, and they can tolerate error so little that they are unable or unwilling to increase their speed.

A variant of this experiment was designed to evoke an increase in the difference between classes, as well as an increase in the number of repetitions. This was achieved by increasing the degree of similarity between classes that also had a difference that had to be preserved. Thus, the letter *M* has a more symmetrical structure in that it is a series of up, down, up, down, but in addition there is a difference in length plus a repetition of length as follows:

Up	Down	Up	Down
Long	Short	Short	Long

There is a possibility of increasing the number of repetitions by drawing the letters thus:

which would be

Up	Down	Up	Down
Medium	Medium	Medium	Medium

As a counter to such a loss of information, most subjects exaggerate the difference in length, with a maintenance of the symmetry of direction (i.e., up, down, up, down) plus an increase in the number of alternations (an added short stroke at the end) as follows:

The increase of number of repetitions in the letter that serves as a model has entirely reduced the error of adding the stroke at the beginning of the next letter, which would in fact have destroyed the symmetry of the *M*. The continuation of the short stroke at the end appears to be somewhat different from its analogue in the letter *N*. First, it is shorter in average length and is less often regarded as an error to be corrected. It would appear to be a dropping out of the part of the instruction that moves the hand to the next letter rather than an integral part of either letter.

These two experiments highlight a commonplace in the development of handwriting that ordinarily also increases in speed. Early handwriting of all individuals is not only quite homogeneous within itself, but the handwriting of all young people looks more alike than it will ever again. With the increasing skill and speed, handwriting becomes more individualized and more and more of a caricature so that in some cases the signature of a name is no more than a quick thrust with a few distinctive squiggles. We would suggest that an experimental linguistics and graphology could illuminate the nature of language change and language structure through the study of the effect of speed and other stresses on speech and writing. What takes many years to produce linguistic

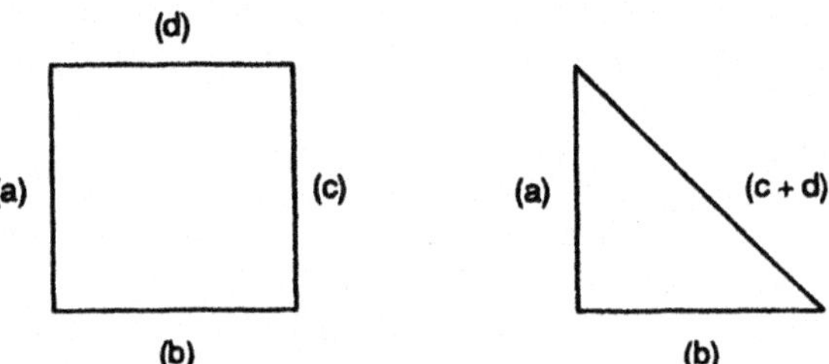

FIGURE 45.4 Error commonly introduced with accelerated drawing of squares.

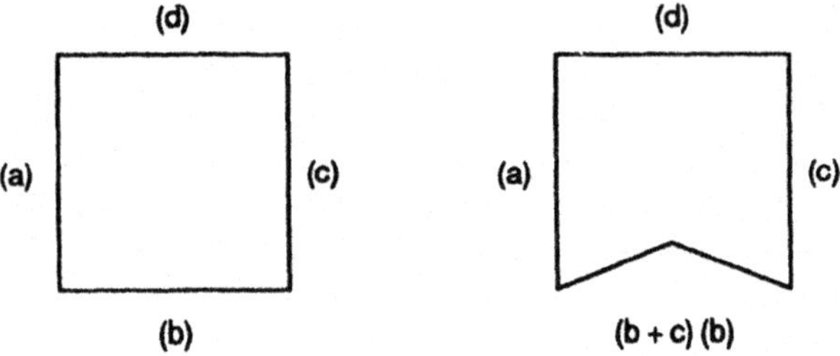

FIGURE 45.5 Another common error in accelerated drawing of squares.

change in actual speech usage should be possible to duplicate under experimental conditions relatively quickly. The utility of such transformations under stress is not simply that it would illuminate the nature of linguistic change, important as this would be, but rather that it would provide a test of the nature of the organization of information within any language and show the continuities between language and other types of information processing.

Just as the structure of matter is most clearly revealed when it is bombarded and stressed, so too would the structure of combinations of classes be revealed when one class must be sacrificed to preserve another or both classes are strengthened not only by an increase in repetitions but by an increased magnificagtion of their salient component characteristics.

The next series of experiments was designed to further illuminate the nature of the loss of information at the critical gaps within any repeated series. Whenever performance is speeded, the central assembly that supports the sequential skill is in danger of losing entirely those classes of instructions that have the weakest organization by virtue of containing the fewest number of repetitions and the smallest number of internal correlations within a class. These are most often the spaces between objects, but not necessarily so if the complexity of the object is increased.

Thus, if the subject is required to speed the drawing of a series of squares, the error most commonly introduced is shown in Figure 45.4. The square becomes a triangle because the messages (c) and (d) are sent simultaneously rather than sequentially and produce a resultant single line instead of two separate lines. Another common error is shown in Figure 45.5.

In this case the same type of resultant of (b) and (c) is begun and then corrected, producing a bowed line. In these cases the instruction is "send (c) and after (c) is finished immediately send (d)." What is lost from the instruction is the delay. Delays are particularly difficult to maintain when the general instruction given by the experimenter is "reduce the time for every operation as much as possible." The operation that is most vulnerable to exaggeration of this directive is the one with fewest repetitions, namely, to wait a given interval since every continuous line has a large number of repetitions with as small a delay as possible. The resultant error in this

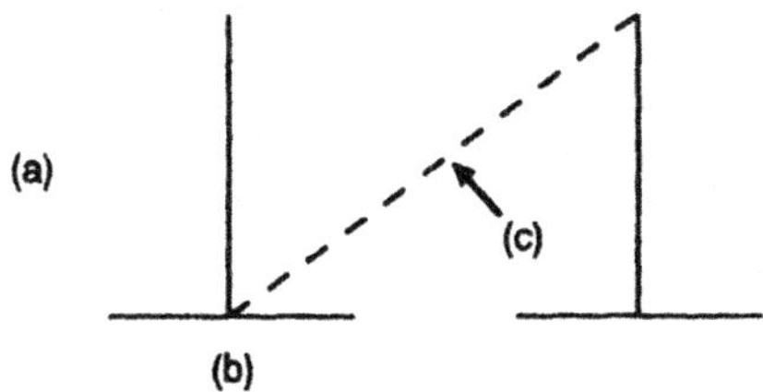

FIGURE 45.6 Illustration of the horizontal and perpendicular lines used in the experiment.

case is to exaggerate time continuity, which thus transforms sequential into simultaneous transmissions.

A variant of this experiment that produces a resultant between the last part of the object and the next movement of the hand through space consists in the repetition of a horizontal and a perpendicular line, in which the vertical line is drawn first (from the top down) and then the horizontal is drawn (from right to left), as shown in Figure 45.6.

The experimentally produced error here is shown in Figure 45.7. The horizontal line creeps upward because it is a resultant of (b) and (c).

Another type of stress that is useful in illuminating the organization of the component classes of a set is to quickly change the organization of the set so that part of the response set is interchanged with part of the stimulus set after these have been forged into a relatively unified new stimulus set. In this way one can experimentally produce the spoonerism. The spoonerism is an extraordinary conservation of order in the midst of chaos. Consider that in the spoonerism a letter has been moved forward to a preceding word and the displaced letter has been moved into the vacated space. John Ross and Harold Schiffman (personal communiction) were able to produce this type of displacement experimentally in what they called the fuddley-duck phenomenon. In this the experimenter instructs the subject to respond to a stimulus (fuddley) with a particular response (duck). After several repetitions so that the response to the stimulus becomes quite automatic, the experimenter alters the stimulus word so that the first letter of the word is now the first letter of the response word. Instead of "fuddley," the experimenter now says "duddley," and the subject almost always responds "fuck." A less dramatic demonstration involves digits. If the experimenter says 86, to which the subject responds 53, and the experimenter then switches to 56, the subject agreeably switches to 83. In most cases these experimentally produced spoonerisms are as unconscious as they are compelling. What is the mechanism whereby a change in the stimulus that is sometimes barely perceived as a change nonetheless produces a rapid substitution of the displaced component to the place in the sequence that was vacated, when these linkages are themselves of recent origin and somewhat weak?

The organization that has been built up in a few repetitions is in the form of an equation specifying that the number of elements are at least four: AB—CD, with each subset possessing at least two components, of which at least the first member of each subset has a specific place in an order. If, when AB is changed to CB, CD is changed to AD, one should first ask why CD is not preserved? The order CB—CD is rejected in favor of CB—AD, we think, because CB—CD is equivalent to C(A)'B—CD, which would mean that one element of the set (A) of four equal elements would have to be sacrificed and another element repeated. This also has the consequence that C's position as the first of one pair would be surrendered in CB—CD since there would be two C's and no A's; whereas in CB—AD, all elements are preserved, and in addition their firstness

FIGURE 45.7 Experimentally produced error based on Figure 4.6.

is preserved. All that is surrendered is the exact first position. What is saved is relative position and number of elements. Given the enforced change in the stimulus, the change in the response would appear to entail change that maximizes the greatest number of possible repetitions of the original stimulus-response set, as a total set. The explanation we have offered here is plausible but not convincing.

We have not pursued this phenomenon much further despite its great interest, except to establish some of the limits of such transformations. The most critical of these appears to be the detachability of the moved component. If a member in the middle of a more complex set is changed, there is no corresponding spoonerism because, we think, it has been insufficiently conceptualized to be very readily transformed further.

Use of Combinations to Find Equivalents That Can Be Operated on to Find Problem Solutions

As in the analysis of memory problems of retrieval, problems can rarely be solved directly through immediate insight. More often they are solved by a series of transformations that are somewhat guided and somewhat blind. Many problems must be solved by a combination of guided randomness. What constitutes guidance is the restrictions imposed on the completely random inspection of all possibilities and all possible transformations on all the possible alternatives. What constitutes the necessary randomness is the generation and inspection of large numbers of sets that are equivalent in some respects to what one needs but are sufficiently different not to be a solution to the problem. These equivalents are generated not because they will necessarily provide the exact solution with one transformation but because they may provide, with a further transformation, still another equivalent, which reduces the transformation distance to the to-be-attained solution so that with a few more transformations "insight" becomes possible. This is yet another example of the utility of the conceptualization of experience, of the increase in transformability of every component and set of components, so that one may build as many bridges as possible between the to-be-attained solution and the present form of knowledge.

In contrast to the utility of increased transformability in the development of motor skills, in which the varieties of combinations themselves constitute part of the skill—as, for example, in the ability to modulate the speed of speech without otherwise changing the organization of sequences of words—in this case the existence of many equivalents is only to serve as scaffolds that enable the individual to more readily move through conceptual space. They are not ends in themselves, nor do they constitute solutions, but they are necessary bridges that enable the construction of solutions.

As in the case of finding words from memory according to a new criterion, such as all five-letter words with the middle letter *u*, it proves useful to be able to examine all words with a *u* somewhere in their middle, as well as all five-letter words whether they have a *u* in them or not, since each of these classes provides words that can easily be transformed into the desired words.

TRANSLATION AS A TRANSFORMATION

We have argued that language is not only a phenomenon that any theory of human cognition must explain but that it also is a valuable paradigm for understanding cognition and the dynamics of the nervous system. Thus far we have examined transformations that produce novelty through increasing combinations of simple components. Now we wish to turn to another type of linguistic transformation, that of mapping the structure of one language upon another. The very possibility of language and indeed all imitation rests upon the fundamental ability of the child to reproduce what he hears. This is a translatory ability whereby the child assembles the appropriate messages that will instruct his tongue to make those motions that will produce the sounds he has just heard and wishes to imitate. Important as the acquisition of language is, we have argued that this

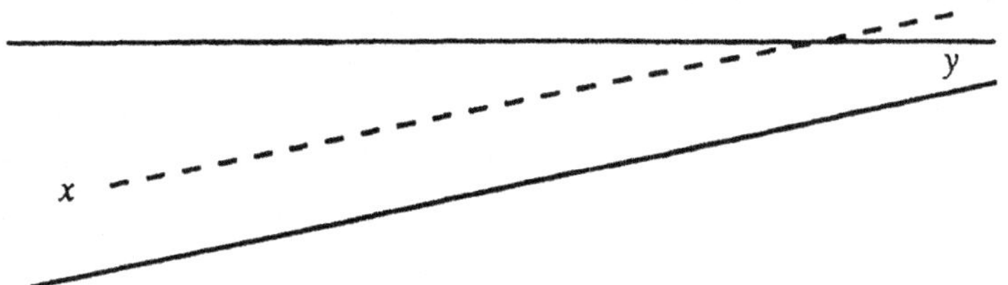

FIGURE 45.8 Representation of altered parallel lines used in the experiment.

ability to translate is fundamental to the control of all motor behavior and that the messages to the motor nerves never become conscious but only the afferent messages are transmuted into conscious form. The translation of the perceptual language into the motor language is an indirect mapping achieved through the correlations between conscious perceptual reports that precede and follow the motor messages. We conceived the efferent system as the space in between a dart thrower and his illuminated target in an otherwise dark room; one can learn to throw a dart to hit an illuminated target in a dark room without ever knowing what the trajectory of the dart might be, as long as one knew how it felt just before the dart was thrown and where the dart landed. The trajectory described by the dart would not and never could become conscious, but the effects of the trajectory could be systematically translated into the preceding conditions in such a fashion that for such a feel or look before throwing one could be reasonably certain that the visual report after the trajectory would be the desired report.

To speak a word, we have argued, one has first to transmit this word to the auditory center and shortly thereafter transmit a translation of this word into the mouth and tongue movements that will produce the sound waves that will then provide the feedback identical to the initial message. This feedback need not be identical as long as it is equivalent. Thus, some individuals transmit visual messages while speaking, rather than auditory messages. We have exposed this chain by interfering with ordinary speech. If one speaks very softly, moving the lips but not allowing the sound to reach an audible level, one will then hear the internal speech that precedes and monitors the feedback. Under these conditions some individuals emit a visual message. The same process can be shown to underlie motor performance, by closing the eyes and drawing a square in the air or writing one's name in the air. One will then see the square or one's name. The visual messages that are translated into motor messages become conscious. That we achieve multiple translations can be easily shown in our capacity to listen and write what we hear, or to read, and write or speak what we read. That these are learned translations is evident from the fact that we may have a speaking knowledge of a language without a reading knowledge or a writing knowledge. The eye, ear, hand, and tongue have learned each other's languages.

We have been able to expose the translation process further by requiring the individual to act without the benefit of correction of his action. Thus, if one asks an individual to draw a straight line through the center of two parallel lines as quickly as he can, this is usually done without gross error. Then if one tilts the bottom line upward so that the space funnels into a smaller opening at the right, as in Figure 45.8, and asks the subject to again quickly draw a line through the middle so that it will pass through the small opening at the right from *x* through *y*, the usual error will be to draw the line through the top line rather than through the opening. We predicted this error on the assumption that the apparent compression of the visual field would be translated into an equivalent motor message.

Triangulation and Translation

Translation ordinarily involves more than the relationship between one sense modality and the motor system. More commonly, there is triangulation in which two or more independent sensory modalities are used to map the motor language. There is some evidence suggesting that visual localization is in part a consequence of a coordination between the language of translation and visual and kinesthetic feedback such that disturbance of the latter impairs the ability to localize visually.

Brain (1958) found a patient with complete inability to localize distant objects in the affected-half fields but who was completely successful with objects within a yard of himself; he had a lesion in the upper part of the parietal lobe. Another patient, who had defects of localization limited to objects within arm's length had a lesion in the posterior part of the temporal lobe. In the first case the lesion would disrupt the neural links between the visual cortex and the leg area of the precentral convolution; the patient had sensory loss of the cortical type in the foot. In the second case the lesion would disrupt the corresponding linkage with the hand area, and the patient's hand was similarly affected.

Brain (1958) suggested that space was built up by exploring space with the limbs. Estimates of the distance and direction of near objects depend to some extent upon the estimation of "grasping distance" and "walking distance."

Visual-motor translation is not identical with motor-visual translation. The researches of Drever and Collins (1928) on pegboard performance of subjects who were early sighted then blind and those early blind and then sighted showed that the former were more proficient in pegboard performance than the latter. Our explanation of these differences would be based on the effect of learned translation from the visual to the motor, from the motor to the visual, and motor relying only on kinesthetic feedback. The sighted subjects' system of translation is primarily from visual to motor. For example, in shaking hands the subject "guides" his hand by visual information until he receives kinesthetic stimulation from the other hand. Therefore, when he has to work with primarily kinesthetic cues, he is at a disadvantage compared with the blind because his differentiation of the purely kinesthetic has not been developed as much as with the early blind. The advantage of late blindness we would explain by the long experience in translating from kinesthetic cues to former visual schemas. Since the latter is a more differentiated sense than the former, the kinesthetic language has been pulled up by visual (imagery) bootstraps and is more differentiated than that of the early blind.

Accent and Translation

There is a special kind of relationship between the perceptual and motor languages, which we have defined as "accent."

We conceive of accent as that state of affairs in which there is a differential rate of change in differentiation of two languages. Thus, many Germans, upon coming to the United States, can "hear" the difference between the German and the American *r* but cannot translate this auditory differentiation into the appropriate message to the tongue. The "sent" American *r* and the German *r* are translated in the same way. The monitoring process (comparison of sent report with obtained report) picks up the error, but it cannot be corrected.

The Ames distorted room also presents a problem in what we have called accent. In the use of a pointer in the Ames room, the visual cues have been changed in such a way that the subject does not perceive the change. He therefore uses the same visual-motor translation, but the feedback doesn't "fit." What actually does not fit is not the visual construction but the visual-motor translations. So there is forced relearning of different transformations on the motor side—the exact opposite of accent in the foreigner's speech, where he "hears" the difference but cannot send the right translations to the motor nerves. In the Ames room he cannot "see" the differences, but he can learn to act differently so that the visual feedback becomes appropriate to his intention.

Induction and Translation

Since translation may itself be conceived as an element in a set, it becomes possible to stress the central assembly by requiring translation of some messages but not translation of other very similar messages.

Many of the pressure symptoms of repression may be understood as special cases of the phenomenon of induction. By induction we mean the tendency of one set of ongoing responses to be transformed by another set of more dominant ongoing responses when both sets have overlapping elements. We have been able to demonstrate this phenomenon experimentally in the following way: A subject is given the task of writing the word *now* over and over again. He is instructed to disregard anything else he sees or hears. While writing *now* over and over again, he is bombarded with a tape-recorded message that repeats the following: "now, now, now is the time for all good men to come to the aid of their party, now, now, now is the time for all good men," etc. This message is repeated over and over again as the subject attempts to continue writing *now.* All subjects report great difficulty in doing this, and a majority show the influence of induction by the introduction of errors, such as *noi* (which is an omission of the *w* and a substitution of the *i* of is) or *nowi.* The error from induction produces corrective attempts, so the overlapping performance is a brief but quite powerful effect. This prediction was derived from our model of motor behavior as dependent on translatory transformations of central eidetically emitted perceptual images. Thus, if a subject is asked to close his eyes and write his name in the air with his finger, a majority of subjects will report visual imagery concurrent with the motor activity. Again, if a subject is asked to move his tongue and lips as though he were speaking "now is the time for all good men to come to the aid of their party" but so softly that it cannot be heard, a majority of subjects report that they hear inner speech. Some, however, "see" what they are pretending to speak. The latter phenomenon illuminates most clearly the fact that there is a translation process between the eidetic image that is "intended" to be achieved and the messages to the tongue or hand that is involved in producing the "intended" act. Therefore, if one involves the subject in emitting the eidetic image "now" and translating it into motor messages to the hand that does the writing, and at the same time involves part of the central mechanism in a perceptual organization that has the word *now* in common with the other process, there will eventually be an induction effect such that the remainder of the perceptual message will be translated into motor messages and produce the characteristic errors we have found, despite the effort of the subject to resist induction effects. The phenomenon of induction is not commonly seen in everyday behavior because the individual ordinarily is capable of maintaining the independent structure of two overlapping responses and ordinarily is not required to execute two such response sets.

We take this to be an experimental paradigm of repression and related intrusion effects, in which one is compelled to act on recurrent thoughts or to say them publicly despite strong counterwishes to resist intrusions. Our subjects in this analogue also report considerable fatigue and distress in their attempts to resist simplification of the field and the translation of ideas into behavior.

This phenomenon may also be considered a special case of the maximizing of repetitions under stress. In this case two different transformations and one similar must be used on two parts of the two message sources, since one "now" must be eidetically emitted and translated and the other eidetically emitted but not translated insofar as the rest of the cliché may not be translated. What makes this particularly difficult is that some of the "now's" of "now is the time" may also be translated if they coincide in time with the beginning of the writing of the word *now* but not if they are a second or two delayed (i.e., if they are heard in the midst of writing *now).* The pressure felt is that of the effect generated by the tendency to simplify the instructions against the instruction to maintain the differentiation.

Translation is thus a special case of the more general relationship of conceptual equivalence. The equivalence in this case is that of two total conceptual structures, such as two languages, rather than between components of sets, as in a concept such as redness, and rather than between subsets of a domain such as the relationship of a summary to what it summarizes.

Part II
MEMORY

Chapter 46
Memory: Defining Characteristics

A human being must learn to answer the basic question: What have I experienced and done before? If he cannot reproduce what he has experienced and produced before, he cannot profit from past experience, and he cannot learn very much of either the outer or the inner world. He will face the world from moment to moment with the same tabula rasa he presented on his first emergence. No cumulative learning is possible without the ability to duplicate the past.

What the individual has duplicated in *consciousness* must be preserved. The environment emits information about both the enduring and the changing aspects of itself from moment to moment. Any organism that is the recipient of such information is threrby more capable of maintaining its life and reproducing itself, but if limited to only this information, it would be an eternally youthful and innocent being. It would look upon the world with continual surprise, and its competence would be sharply constrained by its inherently limited information-processing capacity. By an as yet unknown process, every conscious report is duplicated in some more permanent form. This is the phenomenon of memory. Not all of the information that bombards the senses is, however, permanently recorded. Rather, we think, it is information that, in the competition for consciousness, has succeeded in being transmuted that is more permanently duplicated. An equally critical but different type of duplication is that of information retrieval. Permanently preserved information would be of little utility unless it could be duplicated at some future time, as a report or as a preconscious "guide" to future perception, decision, and action. We have distinguished sharply the storage process, as automatic and unlearned, from the retrieval process, which we think is learned. Both are duplicating processes, but one is governed by a built-in unconscious mechanism, the other by a conscious feedback mechanism.

WHAT MEMORY HAS IN COMMON WITH OTHER MECHANISMS

The memory mechanism cannot be understood entirely in terms of those features that distinguish it from all other information-processing mechanisms. Despite critical distinctive features, it also shares some characteristics with other mechanisms.

Memory, along with every other information-processing mechanism, is a *duplicating* mechanism. The concept of duplication is central not only for biology but also for psychology. This is so because both individual and species duplication is achieved by a set of mechanisms that are themselves essentially duplicative. Thus, the receptors are so constructed that they duplicate certain aspects of the world surrounding the receptors. They may indeed fail to duplicate some aspects of the surround, but if they failed to duplicate *any* aspect of the world, an organism so equipped could not for long duplicate itself in time nor reproduce itself in space. This information is in analogical form, which is duplication that preserves some aspect of the domain in a nonsymbolic, nonconventional manner.

Afferent neural transmission is also duplicative. The sensory nerves stand in the same relationship to the sensory receptors as these do to their surround. Their structure is similar to the receptors, except that they are capable of duplicating what the receptor duplicates, at one point in space, usually deep within the organism, by a chain of duplications or receptions, each of which is spatially contiguous to its neighbor receptor. The dependence of the organism on the integrity of this chain is as great as it is on the integrity of the peripheral sensory receptors. At the terminal of the brain there are multiple receiving stations whose function it is to duplicate those aspects of the world duplicated first at the sensory receptors and then duplicated again all along the sensory nerves.

As we will see later, such duplication is quite different from that in telephonic transmission, since specific feature detectors decompose messages, which are later recomposed at higher centers. Further, these messages are also amplified along the way, just as telephone messages are boosted in gain to preserve the message against noise and attenuation.

Beyond these receiving stations is a central assembly in which there is a type of duplication that is unique in nature. Transmitted messages are here further transformed by an as yet unknown process we call *transmuting*, which changes an unconscious message into a *report.* We define a report as any message in *conscious* form.

Consciousness is a unique type of duplication by which some aspects of the world reveal themselves to another part of the same world. A living system seems to provide the necessary but not sufficient conditions for the phenomenon.

WHAT MEMORY IS NOT

Despite the shared characteristic of duplication with other mechanisms of the cognitive system, memory also possesses some distinctive features. First, it is not *any* duplication of information from one place and time to some other place at some later time. The sensory receptors (e.g., the retina) are duplicators of information that was emitted at some distance at some prior time, and thereby preserve some of the information about an object in another place at a later time. Because of the transience of the information transfer, the sensory receptor is not ordinarily assumed to be a memory mechanism. Neither are afferent nor efferent neural transmissions considered memory mechanisms, despite the fact that they transport information from receptors to cortical areas and from cortical areas to muscles. They, too, are information-moving mechanisms, to sites other than their origin, duplicating information at times later than their beginning. When duplication of information is both *unidirectional* and *brief* there is no memory mechanism.

Second, when information is transported from one site and then transported back again to its origin at some later time, we have an analogue of both storage and retrieval and hence of memory. However, this fails to meet the critical criterion of enduring storage and longdelayed retrieval. When an individual is capable of repeating several numbers after he has heard the last digit, he is said to be exhibiting short-term memory. This is to distinguish it from memory proper, inasmuch as it is presumed to be a transient phenomenon supposedly based upon briefly reverberating circuits that extend the individual's capacity for briefly storing and retrieving information. It is not unidirectional transmission, but it is relatively brief and hence is not memory in the strict sense of the word.

Third, memory is not involved in the storage and retrieval of *misinformation.* There is a presumption that there must be *some fidelity* in the remembered information if there is a memory mechanism. How much fidelity and fidelity *of* what or *to* what is somewhat problematic. But just as we would not speak of a receptor as a receptor if it failed to preserve faithfully *some* order of the information transmitted to it, and would not speak of neural transmission if it did not preserve *some* aspects of the information it transmitted, so a memory mechanism that grossly distorted the information it stored or made available in retrieval would have proved biologically bizarre and useless. An organism equipped to store and retrieve misinformation would be no better off than if it had no memory mechanism, and it might indeed be much worse off. Such a one might think his name was Tom, Dick, or Harry depending on whether it was Monday, Wednesday, or Friday, of this week that he asked himself the question. Next week, however, he might be someone else if he possessed a "memory" in which fidelity was not critical. We will presently examine some of the varieties of fidelity that a memory mechanism must possess.

Suffice it to say that if some fidelity were *not* preserved in storage and in retrieval, such a memory mechanism would not be biologically nor psychologically viable.

Fourth, a memory mechanism is not necessarily involved whenever either experience or behavior is *repeated.* Repetition of experience and/or behavior may be based simply on the reactivation of any of the several innate mechanisms possessed by the individual. A pistol shot at random intervals will elicit essentially the same startle response and the same experience of surprise from the feedback of this response. An infant will cry in much the same way every time he is given an injection, in part because before the age of 6 months he appears *not* to remember and hence not to anticipate the pain to come. In the second half of the first year he will begin to remember and will cry at the *sight* of the physician in the white coat *before* he is injected (Levy, 1960). Indeed, one of the paradoxes of memory is that it is *rarely* revealed by simple repetition. If you laugh just as hard the second time I tell you the same joke, I may well wonder whether you were listening the first time or whether you remembered it if you did listen.

There *are* conditions in which the retrieval of information via the mechanism of memory does result in repetition of either the same experience, the same motor response, or both; but more often than not, the utilization of information from memory storage does not produce repetition, even though the information retrieved may be identical with earlier experience or behavior. This might appear to be inconsistent with the preceding criterion that memory must preserve fidelity of information, inasmuch as a failure to repeat might produce misinformation. Such is not the case, and we will presently examine the matter in more detail.

COGNITION, LEARNING, AND MEMORY

Repetition through activation of innate mechanisms is not the only alternative to repetition through memory retrieval. Consider a man who checks the accuracy of his own addition of a column of numbers that he has just added from the top down. If he now adds the same column from the bottom up and finds that he gets the identical sum in both cases, he has "repeated" substantial elements in both performances. He relies upon the same "remembered" set of rules to do both additions, but they are also in a real sense different component bits of information to which he is applying these rules, and yet he repeats the last, critical response—the sum of the column. There is here *some* reliance on the memory mechanism but not on the same traces, since the cumulative total to which each new member is added is different when one computes from top and bottom. Repetition here and in many other repeated performances may be based in part on memory and in part on cognition, in part on the same traces and in part on different traces. Indeed, most skills require such an organization of rules and traces that there are both explicit alternative instructions prefabricated and stored and alternative past experiences and responses stored and retrievable; so an increasing number of the variations encountered in circumstances in which the skill is exercised have both general strategies and specific tactics as well as concrete instances available for rapid retrieval and application to the shifting demands necessary for skill. Even so simple a skill as driving a nail into wood requires an ever-shifting utilization of different muscle sets to repeat the "same" response when response is defined in terms of the achievement of a class of specific *effects,* rather than specific motor responses.

Memory and learning have shared the same conceptual bed—somewhat uneasily. The memory theorist has stressed the *re*production of behavior. The learning theorist has wavered between a concern for explaining the *recurrence* of behavior and explaining *changes* in behavior. This is proper since learning is necessarily cumulative and involves reproduction of past learning as well as modification that will improve past performance. When learning is errorless, we appear to return to the domain of memory once again, since the repetition of errorless performance seems to require no new learning. So learning is preceded and followed by pure memory. In between there is memory plus modification.

But it is not simply the difference between recurrence and changes in behavior that is critical. Cognition, as we have noted before, aims at understanding the totality of a domain in all of its complex relatedness.

If some phenomenon is left isolated, this constitutes an embarrassment for cognition. But it is just this uniqueness and particularity that memory intends.

In contrast to cognitive transformations whose aim is to maximize the relatedness and similarity of information, memory aims to maximize the distinctiveness of information. Instead of the cognitive maximizing of class membership, memory attempts to minimize class membership, ideally, to one unique member. Shannon's (Shannon & Weaver, 1949) definition of information as the distinctive recognizability of a message from a pool of messages is consistent with the aims of memory. It is, in this case, appropriately quantified as a ratio of the identified message to the number of messages in the pool, from which it is distinctively recognized. As the number of alternatives in the pool increases, the amount of information necessary for the correct identification of any one message increases proportionately. This also implies that recognition (or reproduction) cannot be a stable achievement. Any increase in the pool of possible alternatives decreases the probability of recognition because of the increased amount of information required for correct recognition. Therefore, the greater the number of similar engrams added to the storage pool, the less probable the reliable retrieval of any reproductive specific memory. Similarly, the greater the number of similar exemplars in the perceptual field, the less probable the reliable recognition of any specific object. Thus, a police line-up presents a witness with competing possible criminals to guarantee more veridical recognition by increasing the difficulty of recognition.

We have placed a heavier burden on memory than it ordinarily bears, by virtue of having postulated a central imagery mechanism that is used not only in reconstructing sensory input but also in entering into images and scripts that initiate action and in providing the model for monitoring in the feedback circuit. Further, memory provides not only "interpretation" for the sensory input, it provides prefabricated analogues that, when transmuted, *are* the perceptual experience. If past perceptual reports were not stored, perceptual skill could not increase, since this is achieved through cumulative transformations upon analogues retrieved from memory.

The reasons that prompted us to postulate two independent but close-coupled mechanisms with respect to sensory information are also relevant with respect to stored information. There is, on the one hand, an overabundance of stored information, which would overwhelm consciousness if it were the direct recipient of all such stored past experiences; and at the same time there is insufficient information across time and across separately stored items. Sequential phenomena, trends, and the variety of higher-order organizations of one's past experience that the individual must achieve require a centrally controlled feedback mechanism, which can match the stored information but is not so closely coupled that its matching is limited to the passive reporting of either one isolated memory trace at a time or to the Babel that would occur if all of the stored information were suddenly to become conscious. The inner eye, whether the recipient of information from the outside or the inside, is postulated to be active and to employ feedback circuitry. In the case of both perception and memory, however, there is a more passive nonfeedback registration of information that provides the model for the conscious report. Both the memory traces and the sensory bombardment are primarily duplicating mechanisms, which are primarily nonfeedback in nature. Matching of the past involves retrieval skill, as matching of the present involves perceptual skill. Relating the past to the present is possible because these two skills are based on a shared mechanism that can equally well turn outward to the senses and inward to memory and thought.

The problem of perception is the central duplication of sensory input. The problem of memory is the repetition of this central duplication. In our theory there is no possibility of perception without reliance on a central matching imagery, which must be constructed from analogues that are stored permanently as memory traces. Despite the fact that without memory there can be no perception and without perception there can be no memory, there is nonetheless an important distinction between these two processes. Consider the perception of the number 5923. If we did not have stored in memory each of the digits 5, 9, 2, and 3, the perception of this new combination would not be possible. Perception of novelty always requires some components or aspects of components for which there are exact stored analogues. The novelty consists in some modification of these components, or in some new combination of components or both. If too much novelty is introduced at once, the perceptual achievement is jeopardized. Thus, 5 ɓ ꙅ ɛ is not readily perceived whereas 5 9 2 3 is, though both have unfamiliar changes of position of each digit. Perception is continually novel, but this novelty is achieved only by limited transformation on previously stored memory traces that, when retrieved, enable the central matching of sensory input. In the perception of a series such as 5923 (without the novelty of varied position of each digit) there is also novelty. There usually is not a single memory trace that can be activated to support the perception of such a number. Instead, in such a case, four separate traces are required to construct the central assembly that will match the sensory input. Thus, although memory is required for perception, memory is rarely entirely adequate to meet the perpetually new demands that perception makes upon memory. By meeting these continually changing demands, however, the memory bin is enriched with new traces that are automatically laid down as representatives of succeeding new reports. All of the transformations on past traces by analyzer mechanisms, at the behest of both affects and new sensory challenges, thereby are conserved, and cumulative learning becomes possible.

To understand the mechanisms of memory storage and retrieval we must, then, isolate these from the retrieval and transformation mechanisms that are ordinarily involved in perception.

Chapter 47

The Storage and Retrieval of Imagery: The Nature of These Processes

MEMORY ENGRAMS

There is evidence to strengthen the argument for a theory that the "trace" of past experience produces permanent structural modification at a specific site. First is the evidence against assuming a continuing reverberating circuit as a basis for memory. Gerard (1955) showed some time ago that memory does not depend on the continuing operation of active neuron circuits or assemblies by stopping brain activity with deep cold or by discharging all neurons simultaneously with an electric shock—either of which maneuver should terminate any active patterns of reverberation. Hamsters, so treated after mastering a maze, showed full retention of their learning.

Second, there is abundant evidence from Young's (1955) work on the octopus, as well as from Gerard's (1955) earlier work, that the production of the structural change is not an instantaneous process but takes time. Gerard reported that by altering the interval between each learning experience and electric shock, even though a set of runs and a shock were given every 24 hours, memories required a certain time to become fixed in the nervous system. Thus, when shocks followed trial by an interval of 4 hours or longer, the learning curve was as good as when no shocks were delivered; when the interval between experience and shock was reduced to 1 hour, some defects began to show; at 15 minutes, learning was seriously retarded, and at 5 minutes or less it simply did not occuir.

Gerard (1955) also found that the temperature coefficient of this fixation process is well over 2, perhaps closer to 3, since hamsters kept cool during the interval between experience and electroshock show as great a disruption of learning at an interval of 1 hour as warm ones do at an interval of 15 minutes.

The third source of evidence for a permanent trace is from Penfield's (1937, 1950; Penfield & Boldrey, 1937) explorations. Penfield has shown that during the course of a neurosurgical operation under local anesthesia, electrical stimulation in the temporal lobes has caused the conscious patient to be aware of some previous experience. The experience, though apparently picked out at random, is very detailed. This recollection stops immediately when the stimulation is turned off or the electrode is removed from contact with the cortex. Thus, one patient heard an orchestra playing a tune. When the same spot was restimulated, it always produced the same orchestral experience. The patient believed that a gramophone was being turned on in the operating room on each occasion she was stimulated. Patients characteristically remember when these experiences had occurred in the past.

In contrast are what Penfield (1950) has called interpretive responses, which are evoked from similar stimulation in the same general area. The patient in these cases discovers that, on stimulation, he has changed his interpretation of what he is seeing, hearing, or thinking at the moment. He may say that his present experience seems familiar, as though he had had it before; or, by contrast, things may seem suddenly strange and absurd. These experiences also include affective components. The patient may become afraid, lonely, or aloof. Penfield has suggested that this area in each temporal lobe, to which no special function has been previously assigned by neurologists, be labeled the "interpretive" cortex.

Jackson (1932) had localized the preseizure aura and dreamy state in just this area. Penfield

(1950) describes the case of a girl whose epileptic attacks were always preceded by the same hallucination, in which an experience from early childhood was reenacted. Penfield successfully set off this dream by electrical stimulation in the right temporal lobe while she was under anesthesia. Stimulation at other points on the temporal cortex produced sudden fear without this dream; at still other points the patient saw someone coming toward her; at another point she heard the voices of her mother and brother.

Penfield (1950) claims that in 23 years of such experimental stimulation of the cerebral cortex, which included more than 1,000 craniotomies, organized responses of either the experiential or interpretive kind have been produced only from parts of the temporal cortex.

In contrast, when the neighboring visual sensory area of the cortex is stimulated, patients report seeing stars of light, moving colors, or black outlines, but never organized objects and never as memories experienced before. Stimulation of the auditory sensory cortex may produce ringing, buzzing, blowing, or thumping sounds but no voices that speak or orchestras that play. Stimulation of the motor cortex causes crude movements but no highly organized movement.

On the basis of these observations Penfield (1950) argues that the part of the temporal lobe he has called the interpretive cortex has something to do with a mechanism that can reactivate the vivid record of the past and that can present to consciousness a reflex interpretation of the present. He does not assume that this is necessarily the memory mechanism. He argues that when a man remembers he tends to generalize or else he might be swamped by detail; whereas experimental electrical stimulation produces just such detailed reenactment of a single experience, which normally slips beyond the range of voluntary recall.

Penfield (1950) suggests that the memory record is not laid down in the interpretive cortex but in a part of the brain that is intimately connected with it. He bases this on the following evidence: Removal of large areas of interpretive cortex, on both sides, may result in wild memory defects but does not abolish the capacity to remember recent events. Surgical bilateral interference with the hippocampus, on the other hand, abolishes recent memory but leaves distant memory intact. Penfield cites the earlier work of Bechterew as supporting the hippocampal area as crucial in recording recent experience. Similar memory defects are often reported in patients with hippocampal lesions.

Penfield's (1950) contributions to the theory of memory appear to be of fundamental importance. That the brain has *some* of the properties of a tape recorder seems highly probable from the evidence he amassed over a period of twenty years.

Penfield's (1950) distinction between a mechanism for instant reactivation of the detailed record of the past and a scanning mechanism that compares present experience with the relevant past detailed records is plausible, but it is one with which we do not altogether agree. The interpretive cortex, we would suppose, contains analyzer mechanisms that may operate on any information, whether from memory, sensory sources, or affective feedback. Indeed, Penfield's evidence of the effect of electrical stimulation of this area strongly suggests an equally close linkage with affect arousal as with cognitive transformations, since patients so stimulated report not only a change in interpretation of what they are seeing but also a change in the feeling of familiarity and the activation of fear or distress. Zubin also has presented evidence that one of the major effects of electroconvulsive shock was not so much a memory loss as a change in the feeling of familiarity about experience.

We assume, partly on the basis of such evidence as Gerard (1955), Penfield (1939,1950), Young (1955), and others have reported, that there is a permanent storage of information at specific locations in the temporal and possibly other areas. This structural modification appears to take time to achieve and probably involves transfer of information from short-term storage sites, such as the hippocampus, which in turn involves transfers from even shorter-term memory mechanisms based upon quite transient reverberating circuits. These latter we have to postulate, not only to account for such phenomena as immediate memory span but also to account for the transient holding of sensory and other information that has not yet reached the central assembly and is therefore unconcious. Storage is, we assume, not only relatively permanent, but it is not based on a feedback mechanism. It involves no choice. The individual may not choose what he is to store or not store. He may, however, choose to "memorize" or not to memorize, that is, to learn how to reproduce past experience and to retrieve information that has been permanently stored, without reliance on sensory input. Although there is no choice about whether or not to store, some degree of indirect control of what will be permanently stored is achieved by virtue of the limitation of storage to reports.

Not all of the information with which the individual is perpetually bombarded is permanently stored. It is only the information that, in the competition for the limited channel of consciousness, has succeeded in being transmuted into a report that is automatically sent first to reverberating transient storage, then to longer-term storage, and then to permanent storage. Although the assumed structural stability of the assumed traces has been comforting, the very wide spatial distribution of so many separate records has also been embarrasing for the trace theory. If we assume that the human being contains a small tape recorder in each lobe of the brain, we very quickly are confronted with an embarrassment of riches. It is just as awkward to have too many memories as to have no memory at all. Consider how long it might take to answer the question "What is your name?" On a tape that had run continuously for 50 years, at a conservative estimate of the rate of recordings of, let us assume, 8 a second, there would be 480 a minute, 28,800 an hour, 691,200 a day, 252,288,000 a year, and about 12,614,400,000 separate recordings in 50 years. Access to the part of the tape that contained one's name, if it took 1 second to scan each recording, might take a 50-year-old man 400 years. The problem is analogous to the retrieval of books in a library. There must be some organization of stored information in a card catalog that will permit a librarian to retrieve a particular book more efficiently than scanning sequentially through the whole library every time there is a request for a single book. The problem of accessibility and retrieval of stored information is indeed so troublesome that if we assume a trace theory of memory we must have a supplementary retrieval theory in order to make the traces at all useful. Whether we accept a trace theory or not, the greatest burden will have to be placed not on the passive registration of traces but on the later activity that finds the prior information in the labyrinthine networks of the brain.

A theory of the nature of the retrieval process is a critical requirement for any theory of memory because what is stored may otherwise be entirely wasted. For our model, however, it assumes even greater significance since we argue that no perception, no action, and no monitoring of feedback would be possible without the skilled matching of sensory input by centrally constructed imagery that is in large part permanently stored.

In this chapter we will address three aspects of a theory of memory. First, what information is stored? Second, how is stored information retrieved? Third, how is retrieved information transformed? We will, however, give major attention to the nature of retrieval and, within this topic, to the nature of rote retrieval because we think this is the most severe test of a theory of memory.

WHAT INFORMATION IS STORED?

All of the information in each momentary central assembly is automatically stored, we have said. If this is so, the brain would have to resemble a tape recorder of extraordinary capacity. It implies also that the brain is in some ways capable of dealing with much greater quantities of raw information than we are ever capable of fully utilizing because retrieval is rarely capable of duplicating such an achievement. Rote memorizing, for example, is a very slow and lumbering process. Storage is as profligate, compared with retrieval, as spermatozoa compared with genetic duplication. In the spermatazoa of the male there is a great overabundance of information compared with the information utilized in genetic duplication via the embryo. The relationship between storage and retrieval is collusive in that what is retrieved becomes more and more what is stored, and so becomes more and more what is retrieved, to be then stored again in an ever-expanding family of somewhat similar and somewhat different engrams in storage. In this way the individual becomes slowly both the beneficiary and the victim of the world he has most often experienced and remembered. He is its beneficiary when the stored scenes have been positive-affect scenes. He is its victim when the stored scenes have been negative-affect scenes. He feels "free" when he retrieves (and somewhat transforms) the good scenes. He feels victimized when he retrieves (and somewhat transforms) the bad scenes. Hence, the decisive significance of the ratio of stored positive- and negative-affect scenes for the way in which a life is lived and the way in which the world is experienced. One's freedom is sharply limited by the automatic storage of all of one's experience. This limitation is never nakedly apparent because of the increased degrees of freedom in learning to retrieve from storage and in transforming what has been retrieved. But if the relationship between storage and retrieval is as collusive as we think, then the actual degrees of freedom of the individual is a resultant of the interaction between involuntary storage, voluntary retrieval, and transformation of retrieved information—and therefore a compromise. But it is a compromise that tilts more and more in the direction of the cumulative trends of what has been experienced and then stored and the cumulative ratio of positive- and negative-affect scenes.

What is conscious is stored, and what is conscious is what has survived in the competition for entry into the central assembly. If, then, what survives competition for entry into the central assembly is *retrieved* imagery, we are necessarily involved not only in a collusive relationship between storage and retrieval but also in a bootstrap operation of extraordinary difficulty. Stated most badly, one can "hear" only what one can "speak" to oneself or retrieve from storage for the central assembly as a replica of what has been received via the ear and the auditory nerves.

But the central assembly is the recipient not only of retrieved information but also of that information further transformed in many of the ways possible for the cognitive system. The individual not only can remember, but he can think about and transform both what he remembers and what he perceives and what he does and has done. As he thinks about anything, he may call upon and scan his stored information for retrieval of whatever is relevant for his present purposes. Thus, if another responds "strangely," one may elect to scan storage for any previous signs that might have been underestimated in the past. Since these scenes would not have been experienced as relevant for the other's now strange behavior, retrieval is guided by a search and transform message—that is, look for "something" that *might* match the present scene. Therefore, retrieved information is used as no more than raw data, the significance of which can *only* be determined by complex decomposition and recomposition, by analysis and synthesis. The resultants of successive retrievals, transformed cognitively, are themselves stored and so make cumulative learning possible—including "perceptual" learning as well as motor learning.

Cognitive transformations of retrieved information are responsible for the continually increased ability *both* to accurately match perceptual input and to radically enrich the amount of connected information that can be extracted from perceptual input. In this respect they are similar to the role of theory in science, which enables a small amount of information to become "crucial" in confirming or disconfirming theory. For the individual, his various scripts operate as a set of theories about different kinds of scenes. These various scripts, in some contrast to a highly developed science, may be variously incompatible, orthogonal, or supporting of each other.

What is automatically stored, then, is a constantly changing set of scenes. Since the storage process is automatic, it does not have the burden of making sense of this constantly changing experience. That *is* a problem for the person conscious of these shifting stimulations from without, retrievals from within, and thoughts attempting to relate inner and outer; past, present and future; the particular with the general; and the positive with the negative. Since such complex, shifting experience is only loosely matched with events, and with their sensory and neural representations, the "accuracy" of stored information is limited, though it is capable both of being continually improved and of being continually made worse, in much the same way as a dart thrower may get better or worse in hitting a target. However, there is an additional criterion of "accuracy," which concerns the individual quite as much as accuracy about his environment. That is the continuity and availability of past experience to the individual as he lives his life. Thus, the connected history of his scenes with his mother, father, sibs, lovers, friends, children, and wife as he *experienced them* are most real, and precious or horrible, independent of what they "really" were. One's ability to accurately retrieve a "false" love or hate must be judged by various criteria of "reality" but must not exclude one's life as it was experienced—be that experience illusory, delusory, partially or fully correctly interpreted. The real structure of our experienced scenes is as difficult to discover and describe as the structure of matter. It is least of all a "given."

Our view of automatic storage contrasted with learned retrieval has some implications for present theories of memory that stress the depth of "processing" of information as critical in accounting for the relative memorability of information. We would agree that the retrieval and recruitment of past information, together with its further analysis and synthesis, radically changes what is then *stored* about any scene. We would not agree that this is necessarily critical for retrieval since so much more is continually being stored than can ever be retrieved. No matter what the depth of information processing of some scenes, they may nonetheless be incapable of being retrieved. Thus, how the world looked to us as a 3-year-old, how a lifetime friend's face looked to us the first time we saw him, how a foreign city looked to us on our first visit may later be quite unretrievable except by unusual procedures we will discuss later. Clearly, once we have heard a joke, we cannot retrieve our initial naivete and thus laugh at every repetition. The beginning of the joke has now been hopelessly fused with the end of the joke despite considerable excitement and depth of processing as we first listened to the joke. We now "know" a possible ending quite different from the possibilities we had previously entertained at the beginning of the joke. Knowing *both* the beginning and the end, we cannot readily retrieve the beginning in its detailed pristine innocence. It has fallen into the stream of time. What is now retrievable is *neither* the original innocence nor the fall from innocence which was the essence of the joke, but a much wiser, paler, and more compressed version of both at once. This is a special case of a more general problem of the relationship between storage and retrieval.

How space and time are represented and integrated in consciousness, then in storage, and finally in retrieval are quite separate questions. All significant information in the nervous system is both simultaneous *and* sequential inasmuch as a point at a moment would have insufficient information to be useful for either perception or memory. We will use the distinction at the macro- rather than the microlevel and define simultaneous information as multiple information at a moment (e.g., a musical chord) and sequential information as either singular or multiple simultaneous information over time. Thus, a repeated single note would be sequential information, as would a melody or a series of chords.

Both perception and memory for sequences of events over time clearly require more than the registration of single events in separate engrams at successive moments in time. Even the *perception* of a moving object requires some degree of connectedness of discrete moments as the object changes its position in space. The stored memory of such a connected perception presents a further complication. Are the engrams like a series of billiard balls so that activating one activates the next and so on, thus translating space into time? Or is it, as we think more probable, that sequences are so stored but are *also* compressed and transformed into simultaneous information, as a joke is experienced all at once at the end? The end of the sequence is as devoid of its true meaning without being fused with the beginning as the beginning is misleading without being fused with its unexpected ending. The entire space-time matrix at any *one* moment has all of the ambiguous possibilities of a cosmic joke. We learn only later what really happened before. But *this* knowledge is but *one* moment in time itself, is different from the beginning, and may prove itself to be a misleading beginning of the next succeeding sequence. If, as we think, the entire sequence is stored, it is very rare for it to be so retrieved. More characteristically, what is retrieved is a time-binding integrative summary, which-was achieved only at the end of the sequence. "Trends" of scenes are much more recoverable than the sequences they summarize, but such trends must, in the first instance, have been achieved *within* the experienced sequences. They may later be further transformed, but we think that unless there was a stored summary at the end of the original sequence, such further transformations are less probable. What is stored is the whole sequence of innocence, surprise, and wisdom. What is retrieved is wisdom, which includes transformed versions of innocence and surprise.

Although the relationship between a sequence, storage, and its retrieval is generally one of compression and, to some extent, loss of information, one can nonetheless teach oneself either by rote memorizing or by some transformation of that to recover more specific sequential information. In such a case, prior information may be both simultaneous and retrieved as simultaneous and also may be sequential and retrieved as sequential, as in the exact reproduction of both features by a pianist who has memorized a score. However, prior simultaneous printed visual information may be transformed and translated as a sequential verbal auditory retrieval, either in the original perception or as a transformation upon the retrieved simultaneous visual information. In this case one "speaks" to oneself sequentially what one may have read visually, simultaneously. Further, a sequential display, either heard or spoken, can be compressed so much that it can be retrieved simultaneously and then peeled off and expanded into the original sequential form. We will examine this case in detail later. Complex sequential processes can thus be retrieved by a simultaneous singular compression that can be decomposed via expansion and thus reproduce the original sequential processes. Thus, either simultaneous or sequential prior information (or both) can be retrieved exactly by means of transformations from the simultaneous to the sequential form and then back again, or from the sequential to the simultaneous mode and then back again.

The sequential problem is further complicated by temporal gaps. How are more complex, and especially delayed effects to be remembered? Suppose an individual eats food to which he has a delayed allergic response or a delayed food poisoning. Clearly, he cannot "remember" such a cause-effect relationship without having first perceived or later conceived the critical sequential events. There is evidence suggesting that early human beings were unaware of the relationship between sexual intercourse and pregnancy because of the delayed consequences. Clearly, the integration of information over long time periods requires post facto assemblies and comparisons for analyses and synthesis.

The same problems posed by the complex and varying mixtures of information over time are found not only with respect to the integration of what appears earlier and later in any series but also with respect to the varieties of different kinds of recruitments to different parts of any series with the different transformations they initiate. Thus, there is a waxing and waning of consciousness for different parts of the same field over time. What was figural a moment before can now become ground to some other aspect of the same scene, and the next moment still another aspect becomes figural. If all of these moments are stored sequentially, which one will be most readily retrievable? The favored moment may be the integrated summary *if* such is achieved. If it is not, none of it may be retrievable.

Again any scene may contain varying admixtures of visual, auditory, smell, and temperature information, together with internal speech, and affect and motoric responses, all varying in both figure-ground relationships and their specific content. Both the self and the other constantly change what they say to each other, as well as what they say to themselves. These messages can evoke different affects, which change rapidly in intensity and duration. Such affects are complexly related to their perceived and conceived causes and to possible further responses by the self and others. Generalizations (usually but not necessarily verbal) can coexist with particulars;

for example, "this is a good scene" can coexist in consciousness with all of the vivid details that prompt the verbal generalization. The generalization may vary in level of abstraction so that the good scene then prompts the further affirmation "life is good." At a later point in any continuous series of scenes, the details may drop out entirely to give way to a compression that is part verbal, part affect, part action. "Let me get out of this disgusting scene." This is the analogue of a bad joke plus further response in which the punch line includes summary affect *and* action.

LEARNING TO RETRIEVE INFORMATION

We learn to retrieve from storage different *kinds* of information in a variety of different *ways* for a variety of different *purposes*. What we learn to retrieve reflects the varieties not only of our past experiences but also the varieties of changing *purposes* that prompted the different kinds of searching *quests for* stored information, as well as the different kinds of attempts to intentionally make information *retrievable* in the future, the relatively unconscious *enforced* retrievals of information in recognition, and the constantly *shifting relationships* in competitive strength between inner and outer stimulation and between experience that has been successively magnified and attenuated compared with experience that continues to be magnified.

We may, for example, *intend* to memorize a set of telephone numbers so that we can telephone someone without "looking it up." This requires that the exact digits be remembered in the exact sequence, reproduced at a speed that a telephone operator can understand, with the appropriate decibel level, intonation and so on.

Or we may intend only to "remind" ourselves to do something by tying a string on our finger. But then we must be able to reproduce what the recognition of the string was used to remind us to do. Here we use recognition as an aid to reproduction.

Or we may intend to profit by an experience, teaching ourselves a "lesson"—for example, "Don't ever accept another invitation from the X's, they are crashing bores." Time may soften the impact of the bad scene so that one does repeat the experience and again one reminds oneself—"Never again, don't forget." This second time one may fortify one's resolve by rehearsing particularly punishing aspects of the scene to increase the vividness of the more abstract description of the offenders as "bores." This is motivated not by the wish to remember a boring scene but by the wish not to forget it and not to forget one's decision and one's resolve so that the next time an invitation may be offered one *will* retrieve the details of the scene as well as its more abstract verbal summary and one's previous resolve. In this case *what* we try to learn to retrieve has been changed by the failure of our initial attempt to remember, to be remembered in fact the next time, and our increased resolve to guarantee that we will not forget a third time.

We may bias future retrieval, not by a wish to remember or by an intention to remember, but by magnifying some *part* of a scene by the conjunction of intense affect and cognitive compression, therefore making it more "memorable" for retrieval despite the automatic storage of the *whole* scene. Thus, a scene may be summarized with feeling as an instance of an abstract ideology—"It made me proud of human beings. It showed what human beings can do." It may be cognized as a prototype of affective experience—"It was the most exciting moment of my life." It may be verbalized to the self as proof of a long wished for moment—"I really did it! She really loves me!" Or the same scene might combine all of these interpretations—"I really did it and she really loves me—it was the most exciting moment of my life, and it showed what human beings can do and made me proud of human beings." A parent can make a scene memorable in the same way by responding to the child's behavior with intense affect, ideology, and personal commendation together—"You did it! It's the most exciting thing. I'm proud of you—it shows what human beings *can* do." In such a case the scene and the child's behavior that prompted it is magnified for future retrievability by being embedded in a unique and rich interconnectedness of affect ideology and behavioral specificity.

But much learned retrieval is not intended to be *learned* to be retrievable as such but happens rather through the pressure of perceived information, which requires interpretation and support from memory, as in the recognition of a familiar scene or from searches of memory to solve problems. To become aware that something is being repeated necessarily requires, at the least, supplementary information from storage. Such retrieval is *not* automatic, but requires considerable learning. It is, however, learning that is different in kind from the intended rote memorization of experience.

Recognition Versus Reproduction

The clearest instance of the distribution between intended purposeful learned remembering and unintentionally learned remembering is the difference between recognition and reproduction. Much more of what we do remember is recognized and not reproduced. This difference depends on the origin of the trigger of the prior information and of the trigger of the retrieved information. We can distinguish the origin of the trigger as external or internal. Thus, the distinction between recognition and reproduction is commonly conceived to consist in an external origin for both the prior and retrieved information in recognition and an external origin for prior information, but an internal origin of the trigger for retrieved information in reproduction. Although this is the commonly accepted distinction, we use it for illustrative purposes only; if it were strictly so, there would be no discriminable difference between recognition as conscious familiarity and repetition of experience or response without *awareness* of familiarity or *that* one has *repeated* either an experience or response. In order to recognize someone, one must do more than achieve the identical impression of the face. That alone need involve no memory retrieval at all and no learning. Involved in recognition retrieval is rather the *experienced relationship* that this is the same face one saw before. Although the major origin of the trigger is external in the prior and retrieved recognition experience, yet something internal must have been added from an internal origin (whether in the trace or elsewhere is not certain) to account for the experience of familiarity in repetition, over and above the identity of the early and later experience. Therefore, we can distinguish reproduction from recognition by the exclusively internal origin of its trigger compared with a mixed, but primarily external origin in recognition.

Because we believe that *all* perception depends on internally generated imagery, the distinction between recognition and reproduction is similar to a driver on his own compared with one who is learning to drive side by side with an expert (nature) who, via a dual-control system, provides constant support for what the driver must eventually do entirely on his own, in reproductive memory. In *both* cases he is on his own, but he has more external resources to fall back on in one case than in the other. Therefore, *he* must provide the guidance for memory in reproduction and in recognition, but in the latter case he has a constant external input to support his quest for the *same* memory trace. This is, however, not an all-or-none distinction. Consider the case of a pianist who has memorized a piece versus one who has not. It is true that one can reproduce the same responses without any external support, but the pianist who needs to read the notes to play them combines recognition with reproduction. When he "reads" the notes, he does recognize them for what they are, but he cannot "recognize" what he must do to play these notes. A further set of transformations from the usually recognized to the motoric equivalents must be reproduced *entirely* from within. The distinction between these two pianists is analogous to the distinction between recognition and reproduction. It is easier to reproduce the notes *if* one has the score than if one must *also* be able to reproduce the score and play it. Recognition, therefore, is externally *guided reproduction,* whereas reproduction is externally unguided retrieval. What is critical, in this view, is that *both* are reproductive processes, which vary only in the quantity and location of the trigger or guide—or, as we shall later define it, the "name" of the address in memory.

To return to the question of "intended" versus unintended learning to remember, we propose that unintended learning to remember (i.e., recognition) occurs by the "teacher" instructing the individual to go to the stored information to reproduce the teacher's message or the nearest facsimile thereof. The teacher may be a "score," as in piano playing; a driving instructor, as at a dual control; "nature," as a sensory-neural guide; or a Berlitz language guide in the acquisition of a new language. In the latter case one begins by recognizing and ends by both recognizing and reproducing. There is a continuous set of transition capabilities between these two types of remembering.

Having distinguished between recognition and reproduction as reflecting differences between "intended" purposeful remembering and unintended remembering, we must now soften this contrast. Though one does not consciously "intend" to remember in recognition in the same way as one might intend to rote-memorize a telephone number, yet the unintended *process* of recognition is necessarily embedded in the individual's purposes. The difference here is that his purpose is *perceptual* rather than memorial, so to satisfy his quest for perceptual understanding he is *unconsciously* guided and pushed to the address of the prior experience with the same stimulus and so is enabled to *recognize* it. Retrieval is the relatively unconscious *means* to the end of perception, in recognition, and is learned with minimal *memorial* intention but nonetheless, with perceptual intention.

SEARCHING FOR MEMORY INFORMATION

Different from the "intention" to memorize that enables reproduction, or the usually unconscious instrumental prompting by perception that enables recognition, is the consciously directed *search* for stored material instrumental to problem solution. If someone one knows well acts strangely, one may be prompted to search one's memory for possible data and clues to illuminate that unexpected change in behavior. Such retrieval *may* be a one-time affair and never again be employed either because it solved the problem or proved the problem insoluble. However, unsolved problems may continue to push the individual to seek help from memory. The major problem in such search is that one does not know what to look for. The less one knows how to solve or *pose* a problem, the less such directed searches appear to help. Clearly, given any cognitive problem, there can be no confident matching of stored information and the unsolved problem. The individual simply does not "know" where to look, particularly since the raw data he has in memory are no more than data. What can be analyzed and synthesized *from* such data is necessarily uncertain, so very broad similarities and relevances are generally used in retrieval. One may flounder for a long time "searching" when one doesn't know what one is looking for, especially, if the problem has been poorly posed. Yet such wild searching, if sustained, may finally, amplified by further searching when asleep, reward one with the hoped-for solution.

The situation is somewhat different if the problem is more clearly defined and if the degree of transformation of stored information required is not great.

One can, with appropriate search and transformation procedures, recover stored information one did not know one knew. Suppose an individual wished to instruct himself or wished to comply with the instruction posed to him by someone else: "What are all the five-letter words you know that have the middle letter *u*?" Consider one possible strategy for such search and retrieval:

First, any conjoint set is usually a smaller class than the components of which it is the intersection. There are more traces for five-letter words than for five-letter words with the middle letter *u*. There are also more words with the middle letter *u* than five-letter words with the middle letter *u*.

It is ordinarily easier to find and retrieve larger classes than smaller classes. Thus, it would be easier to retrieve "words I know" than fiveletter words or than words with the middle letter *u*. The first strategy, then, might be to retrieve whatever I was able to retrieve easily enough so that a generous sample might be available for further transformation. In such a strategy, one would have to steer a middle course between wasting time by inspecting any word of no matter what length or composition and wasting time by so strict a criterion that one could not retrieve enough words even to initiate the work of transformation. One such strategy might be to expand the search for five-letter words with middle letter *u* to two instructions that would retrieve somewhat larger classes of words, for example: (1) What are some five-letter words and (2) what are some words with *u* somewhere near the middle with length anywhere between three and seven letters. This might yield for instruction 1: *brick, dick,* and *trick*; and for instruction 2: *but, butter, nut, clumsy.* Having retrieved these words, one would then "operate" on each of them to transform them to successively reduce the distance in order to meet the original instruction. Since the first instruction yielded words that had the right length but not the right middle letter, one possible strategy would be to replace the middle letter with *u* and test whether it is a name for a word you have in storage. By the use of this simple transformation *brick* becomes *bruck*—not a word—but *dick* becomes *cluck*, which is; and *trick* becomes *truck,* which is. At this point the individual has the option of trying to further transform the one failure or to go on with the second list and see what success may be gained with the transformations on this list. The second list contains words with the letter *u* but of varying lengths. The problem therefore is twofold, to increase or decrease the length to five letters and to move the letter *u* to the middle position. The self-instructions therefore might be: "Reduce the longer words and increase the shorter words so that their length is finally five letters in such a way that their middle letter is *u* and test whether this produces any name for a word you have in storage."

By these transformations *but* can be changed to *bute,* which is four letters rather than three, and then this can be changed to *chute*, which is a five-letter word. The next word on the list, *butter*, can be reduced to five letters to give *butte.* The next transformation can move *u* over to the middle but at the cost of increasing length again, to *shutte*, which can then be easily reduced to a five-letter word *shuts.* The next word on the list is *nut.* This can be increased to four letters by adding an *s*—*nuts*, which can be made into a five-letter word by adding two letters as substitutes for the first letter—*sluts.* The next word, *clumsy*, can be reduced to five letters, to *clums*, which can then be transformed to *chums by* changing the letter *l* to *h.* In general, the distance traversed in the second series of words was longer than in the first series.

This example is contrived, but it illustrates the principle that searchplus-transformation procedures can find addresses of information that were originally stored in quite different ways for quite different purposes.

Search of memory may be prompted not only by cognitive problems but also by the experience of objectless affect, when the individual attempts to understand why he is feeling as he is feeling, without apparent cause. He may scan the immediate past for possible clues. Again, as in more purely cognitive quests, he does not know exactly what he is looking for or where it is. Under the circumstances that he feels sad he may search not for causes of his sadness but for happy scenes to comfort himself, and he may thereby unwittingly deepen his depression by the contrast between the retrieved scene and the present. Such searches for the origins of affect or for remedies against affect are different from the relatively unconscious retrivals of relevant scenes prompted by affect, analogous to the general process of recognition. In this case affect is experienced as a probable *part* of a previously experienced scene, which is retrieved in much the same manner as a cliché may be completed upon hearing the first few words of a cliché. This free-floating sadness may contact sad scenes, which can further magnify the original distress. Bower (1981) has recently presented additional evidence for the power of positive affect to retrieve positive scenes and negative affect to retrieve negative scenes.

Search may also be conscious, but minimally so in the execution of any intention to act. Not only is the search minimally conscious, but so is the retrieved program in the case of skilled acts. I walk downstairs intending to do so but barely aware either of the intention, the search, or the retrieved acts. Such skilled searches are possible because they were preceded by learning to achieve skilled performance that involved the *intention* to memorize. Such reduction of consciousness in the search process had to be preceded by the fully conscious intention to practice skilled performance and the retrievals underlying it *until* such minimal drain on consciousness was in fact achieved. Indeed, one cannot *become* skilled unless one can compress the information sufficiently so that the degree of consciousness needed for perceptual, cognitive, and motor integration is minimized. The easiest way to disturb such skill is to slow down that rapid compressed program and flood the central assembly with consciousness. The individual is thereby returned to his earlier lack of skill. He might be forced into stumbling going downstairs if he looks at his feet. In skill, information increases as consciousness decreases.

Much action, therefore, continually requires the skilled retrieval of stored information with minimal conscious representation in contrast to conscious perceptual recognition and in contrast to retrieval in the interest of thought.

Next, there are types of search that are focused but almost entirely unconscious, in which the present is transformed to become an analogue of a stored nuclear scene of a family of such scenes. Differences between the present scene and the nuclear scene are preserved, but similarities are so radically magnified that the individual reacts to the present as if it were more similar to the nuclear scene than it would have been without such analogic transformations upon the stored family of nuclear scenes. An example noted before was the case of the individual who became depressed on a beautiful spring day upon seeing a truck driver intrude upon his communion with Mother Nature. Such search for the meaning of any scene goes well beyond the aim of perceptual recognition, since the difference between the scene as recognized and the scene as analogically interpreted depends upon decomposition and recomposition of one scene to increase its similarity to another scene.

A nuclear scene need not necessarily involve unconscious analogues, nor need it have its origins in early childhood. Any scene that can neither be solved nor renounced will prompt repeated searches for replays closer to the heart's desire, for restitution, for revenge, or for confrontation. These are experienced as "variants," the detection of differences around a stable core.

Thus, I might unexpectedly come upon a scene of betrayal, and elaborate it first by comparing it with my prior innocent reading of the character of the other. Then I may draw multiple conclusions as to the possible reasons for my innocence and the untrustworthiness of the other and generalize about its more general implications for my view of the nature of human beings and of the human condition in general. Then I may consider the possible alternatives for the future of the threatened relationship and the alternative consequences of alternative decisions. I may make a semifirm decision but then question its wisdom, and then fortify this ambivalent decision with vivid present and past scenes to justify my intransigence, as a defense against my known and feared wish to forget and deny the disturbance to the relationship and prior assumptions about the trustworthiness of others in general and of my beloved in particular. What I then must "teach" myself to retrieve in such a case is the final outcome of a set of conflicting purposes that have served to organize what should be remembered, consistent with my last purposes. What I retrieve later will depend on this conclusion and in part on my future purposes and my purposes that change as a consequence of successive retrievals. Thus, if I become lonely, I may instruct myself to search for and retrieve the bittersweet memories of how it was before the betrayal. But having increased my longing by replaying these idyllic memories, I now retrieve the critically wounding scene, further *transformed* by the bitterness that has been accentuated by the contrast with the reward of the remembered good scenes. And so I fall more deeply in hate with that other, supported by my ability to both retrieve and further transform the hated scene with additional fresh, present insights. What one initially chooses to remember one may later choose to forget, to transform so to soften the memory or to harden the memory. The more important the memory, however, and the more nuclear, the more it will continue to support an everincreasing family of remembrances to suit ever-changing purposes. So long, however, as one remains attached to that betraying but still desirable other, there will be unceasing searches for past good and bad scenes in the attempt to solve the insoluble nuclear scenes. The inability either to forgive or forget *may* be entirely contemporary. However, it may *also* be a member of a much longer set of analogue scenes having their origin in early childhood. In such a case the variant scenes are disguised analogues that account in part for the increased difficulty of decisive resolution of the contemporary adult analogue of the childhood nuclear scene.

In radical contrast to increasingly magnified nuclear scenes are the phenomena of romantic love and mourning. In both cases radical magnification characteristically peaks and then becomes attenuated. Consciousness is flooded with both searched-for and unbidden memories as well as anticipations of the future, until the idealization of the beloved (whether in romantic love or in grief) has peaked, characteristically followed by more and more compressed and paler versions of the relationship, ending in what I have called the valley of perceptual skill in marriage, for romantic love, and ending in radically diminished searches or reminders of the lost lover, in grief. Unless a critical scene continues to grow in retrieval, as in the nuclear scene, it will peak and attenuate in its claim upon consciousness.

A type of script intermediate between the nuclear script and the mourning script is the addictive script, in which there is skilled relatively habitual monitoring for possible absence of (say) cigarettes. There is little claim on consciousness *until* a difference is detected, (for example) that one has no cigarettes. Under these limited and specific conditions there is activated a pseudomourning script that mourns the absence of the beloved cigarette but insists upon its resurrection. During that period, memory swamps consciousness as in true mourning as one searches desperately for a cigarette. But this entire process, in contrast to mourning, is short-circuited when the beloved cigarette is once more in one's mouth.

We now wish to address the more general question of how retrieval is possible at all. Consider that some neural message must be capable of finding an address, activating it, and retrieving the activated information for entry into the central assembly *or* being sent directly to a motor nerve. Three distinct processes appear to be involved: discovery, activation, and retrieval. There is at present no compelling theory or evidence for how this is possible. Indeed, many years ago Lashley (1960) concluded that there was no good evidence to believe the engram existed at all at any particular place. It is, of course, entirely possible that memory is *not* recorded as on a tape recorder. It is possible that what is recorded is a synthetic gene—a set of instructions that guide the reconstruction of memory and that no more resemble the "memory" than the helix resembles a person. It is also possible that it is, when activated, a pattern of neural firings that does resemble the original pattern of neural firings in the central assembly and is capable, via some type of resonance, of recreating that original pattern in the central assembly. Again, it is possible that, since the central assembly of the brain is continuously "sending" a carrier wave, the conscious field is a modulation of that carrier wave, first by sensory neural bombardment and later by a stored replica of that pattern as well. Such an arrangement would enable a unitary world to be constructed from the different senses as well as from memory so that touch, kinesthesis, sounds, and smells might, for example, be located in the "same" visual space by permitting comparison of each sense with every other sense by using the *difference* between each memory and sense's firing patterns from the *same* common carrier wave in the central assembly. This would be similar to comparing different world currencies with each other by calculating what each currency is worth in gold. Indeed, there is growing evidence for internal rhythm generators that impose themselves upon many biological subsystems within the body. Some presumptive evidence for such mechanisms at the psychological level is the preemptive nature of rhythms in motor behavior. We cannot readily rub our head and pat our stomach at the same time *unless* we learn to do each one with the same beat. If one rhythm is out of synchrony with the other, there are strong interference and induction effects that argue for a generalized preemptive cortical carrier wave.

This problem must and ultimately will be solved at the neurophysiological level. For the time being, we will examine the phenomenon at the psychological level. At this level we must distinguish the problem of *finding* the address or addresses from the problem of *looking* for the address. Clearly, we may "know" our name if asked (i.e., tell it) but without necessarily trying to find it except *when* asked. Further we may "try" to remember and fail to find an answer to a question we have answered before. So we may look and find, look and not find, find without looking (to our knowledge), and not find unless we do look. The conscious retrieval message appears to be neither a necessary nor sufficient condition for retrieving memory. We have noted before that in skilled action, we retrieve, relatively unconsciously, guidance that silently supports acts that themselves may be monitored with such compressed skill that they reach consciousness only if they fail. Although there are many different kinds of pathways to the address of stored information, we will now address the more general features of the retrieval process.

The Concept of Name

At this point we wish to introduce the concept of a "name." What is a name? It purports to be a relatively unique symbol for something. The emphasis is on difference rather than positive attributes. You and I may both have the same first name, but if we share the same first, middle, and last names, it is an unhappy coincidence. A brand name may refer to as many as a few million automobiles of the same kind, but the intent of the name is not only to identify it as an automobile but to differentiate the automobile made by one manufacturer from that made by his competitor. It is a symbol of limited expansion characteristics, but this is its chief virtue. It is peculiarly appropriate for an organism that wishes to preserve the idiosyncratic reference to an object of its past experience.

We will define a "name" according to this usage but in a somewhat more general way. By a name we will mean a message, conscious or unconscious, that is capable of finding, activating, and retrieving a particular trace at a particular address. We will assume that a "name" itself may or may not have an address and that this address itself may or may not therefore have a "name."

In recognition, as contrasted with reproduction, the sensory input may constitute the only name of the appropriate address insofar as it initiates retrieval processes that activate and retrieve a specific trace at a specific address. In the case of much of our past experience such stimuli are the only names of specific addresses. Unless the individual encounters this stimlus, he may not be able to remember because the name itself has no brain address.

Another case in which the name itself may have no brain address is in sequentially organized memories that depend on external "names." Thus, I may drive home by the same route every day and make all the correct turns by depending on the external cues as they come into view successively. Even when sequentially organized memories depend entirely upon self-reproduced names, these names may nonetheless have no brain address. Thus, when the alphabet is learned by rote, it *may* be learned in such a way that the awareness and *recognition* of the internally reproduced *a* is the *only* name of *b*, and that, when reproduced, is the only name of *c*, and so on. Such a series can, however, be entirely guided by a compressed internal summary that requires no recognition of succeeding letters.

The name may be any *part* of the original message, any *compression* of that message, any *part* of any *compression* of that message, or any *sign, symbol*, or *analogue* of that message.

These do not exhaust the possible types of names. A symbolic name may be no part of or bear no resemblance to the original message if this enables recovery of the original message. The word *Chappaquidick* became a name for the scene involving Ted Kennedy. In classical conditioning, the conditioned stimulus, paired again and again with the unconditioned stimulus as a sign, became a name of the unconditioned response if and when it came to evoke the unconditioned response.

By this definition a natural name may be similar in its evocative power to a symbolic name. Thus, if a particular restaurant is located 1 mile before one crosses a bridge, it may become a sign of the bridge and, by our definition, a name if the person then remembers that the bridge is a mile away when he sees the restaurant.

A name then may be a natural sign, a symbol, an analogue, or something similar to the information stored in the trace, any part of that information or similar to part of that information, any compression of that information or similar to any compression of that information, or similar to part of any compression. As similarity, compression, sign, or symbolic reference become remote, the phenomena become relatively unconscious.

Figure 47.1 shows in a schematic way a number of the major types of names, along with their logical descriptions. We now examine these derivatives and introduce a derivative concept that has properties somewhat different from those of a name. By a "name of a name" we will mean a message, conscious or unconscious, that is capable of activating and retrieving a name. Logically, it has the form $a \supset y \supset x$; *a* activates *y*, and *y* activates the trace.

An example of a name of a name is the typing of a string around the finger to serve as a "reminder" to remember a chore. That it may or may not serve as a name of a name is clear when one forgets what one put the string on the finger to remind one to do. Other examples are sequentially organized skills, in which there is no direct access to any particular part of the set of traces except by retrieval in order, as when one first learns the alphabet. In this case, the message "repeat the alphabet in order" is the name not only of *a* but the name of the name of *b*, since the initial message is the name of the first letter, which is in turn, when retrieved, an instruction or name that locates the second letter. Presumably, this is because we first learned the alphabet as a sequential series, teaching ourselves to use each letter *as* a name for the next letter. In such a series *a* is a name for *b* and only *b*, rather than for the whole alphabet.

Another example of a name of a name, which we will examine in more detail presently, is the instruction to write using very large letters. Because we have never done this before, we do it slowly and thereby activate the traces for early handwriting, which are used together with the operator "write large" to produce new (large) but also old (earlier) handwriting (i.e., as adults we write very large letters in a childishlooking script).

In more complex scene-script relations, if the indifference of a lover is the name of a fight scene, and that is the name of a shame scene, then indifference of the other can become the name of the name of the scene that contains feelings of shame because it is the name of anger, which in turn is the name of shame. Such shame may be evoked at the end of the anger, a move forward to be conjointly experienced with anger, or may even swamp, mask, or attenuate the angry scene.

Next, we define "alternative names" as any set of equivalent names for the same address. Logically, this has the form $(a \vee b) \supset x$; *a* or *b* may activate the trace *x*.

An example is that either John or Mary may be the name of "my child." Either a small triangle or a large triangle may activate the trace "triangle." As learning to retrieve memory information advances, more and more alternative names are learned, so that the same trace is capable of being activated in a variety of ways. Thus, different parts of the same stimulus may be recognized as parts of the same object. In language, the synonym is an example, and so are the varieties of ways the individual may have of expressing the same idea. Different rooms in a house are recognized as rooms in the same particular house. Scenes that begin in different ways may be recognized as ending in the same way. Thus, excitement about the other or sympathy and distress about the other may equally be recognized to end in mutual enjoyment.

We define "alternative names of name" as any set of equivalent names that is capable of activating a name. Logically, it has the form $(a \vee b) \supset y \supset x$. In this case *a* or *b* is the name of a name that can activate a trace at a specific address. An example is that either indifference or criticism by the other may be recognized as evoking anger scenes, which in turn are recognized as evoking shame scenes.

Next, a "distinctive name" is a name that is the only name of a trace and the name of only that trace. The logical form is $a\,x.\ a\,x'.\ a'\,x.\ a\,a'.\ x\,x'$; *a* activates *x*, *a* does not activate any other trace (not *x*), any other name does not activate *x*, *a* does not

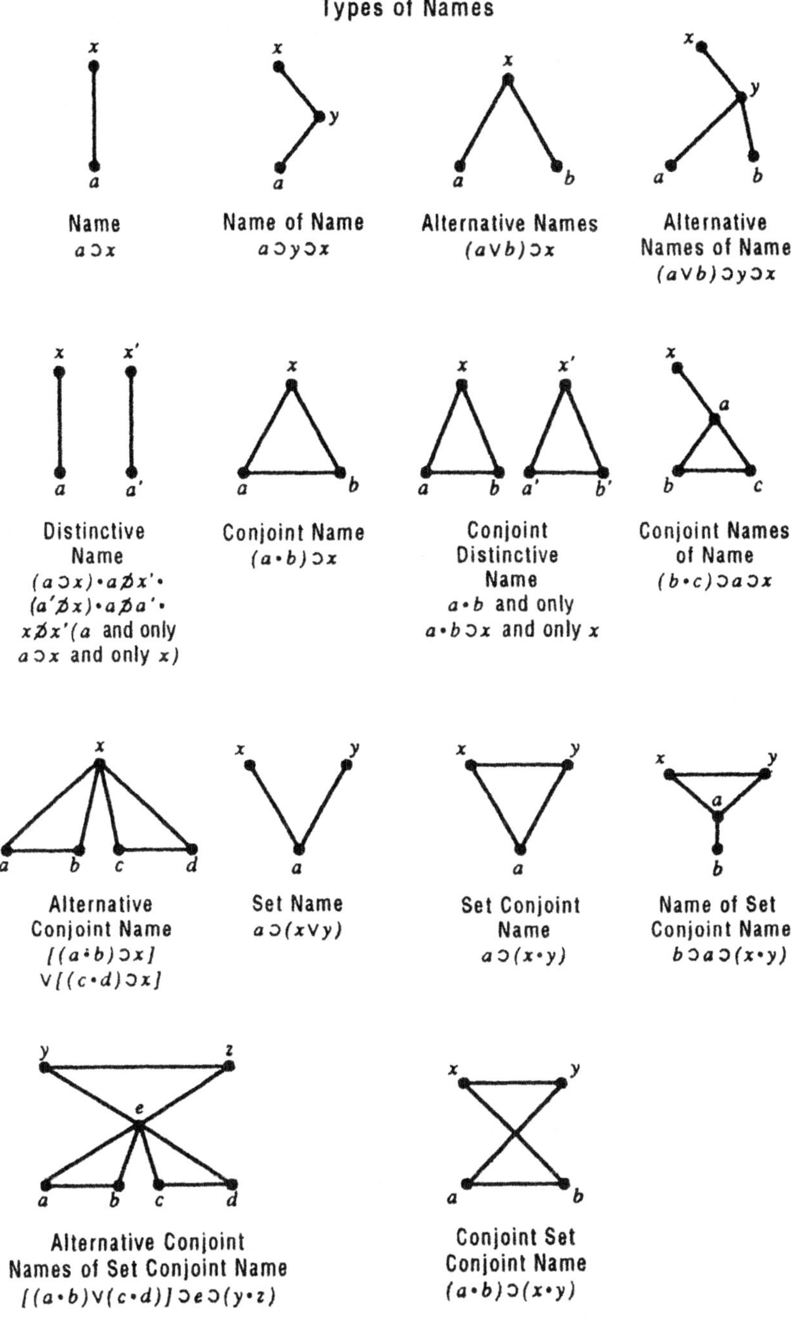

FIGURE 47.1 Types of names.

activate any other time (not *a*), and trace *x* does not activate any other trace (not *x*). An example might be the stimuli a moment ago that assembled the present moment of awareness, which in all probability will never again be retrievable in exactly the same way. These are what we have defined as "transient" scenes.

Next is the "conjoint name," which is defined as any conjoint set of messages, conscious or unconscious, that is capable of activating a particular trace at a particular address. The logical form is (a b) x; both *a* and *b* together activate the trace *x*. Thus, when a child learns that four-footed, furry animals are dogs, he does not necessarily lose this name when he later learns that some four-footed, furry, usually smaller animals are cats. Animals furry and four-footed that are at the same time large is now a conjoint name for dogs, and animals that are furry, four-footed, and small becomes a conjoint name for cats. Sentences in a language also have the structure of a conjoint name, since they are sets of symbols in a particular order that may be uniquely ordered to one trace rather than another.

In scene-script dynamics, either criticism or indifference from the other might evoke a fight scene; but their conjunction, as in a cool and distant criticism, might evoke shame.

Conjoint names may further be distinguished as conjoint distinctive names, conjoint names of name, or alternative conjoint names, as indicated in Figure 47.1.

Next we define the "set name." This is any message, conscious or unconscious, that is capable of activating and retrieving a set of traces at a set of particular addresses. It has the logical form a (x y); a activates traces *x* or y. This activation may be simultaneous or sequential. If it operates in the former fashion, we will refer to it as a "simultaneous set name"; if it operates in the latter fashion, we will refer to it as a "sequential set name." We will use the more general "set name" if we wish to refer to both or either.

An example would be the sight of one's home as a child, which in turn might evoke a memory of the face of one's father or mother or both. In scene-script relations the interest of the other might evoke simultaneous scene possibilities of a casual encounter or a lasting relationship.

Next we define "set conjoint names" as any message that is capable of activating and recruiting a set of traces conjointly (either simultaneously or sequentially). An example is the request by a messenger to acknowledge receipt of a package when he instructs us to "sign here." The movements that constitute the signature may involve several traces that are activated both simultaneously and sequentially.

In scene-script relations a set conjoint name might be indifference from another evoking distress, then both shame and contempt, then mutual reconciliation, which ends the set of scenes. Such a sequence might either be remembered, anticipated, or acted out.

Further complications are, as in Figure 47.1, "name of set conjoint name," "alternative conjoint names of set conjoint names," and "conjoint set, conjoint names."

We define the "conjoint set, conjoint name" as any message set that together activates a set of traces. The logical form is $(a.b)\supset x\ y$; *a* and *b* activate *x* and *y*.

In scene-script relations this would be the case where ambivalence from the other evokes ambivalence from the self.

So much for some of the structural properties of possible name trace relations. Let us return now to the question of the nature of the retrieval process and what makes it possible for there to be messages that have the properties of "names."

Chapter 48

The Possibility and Probability of Retrieving Stored Information

RETRIEVABILITY VERSUS MEMORABILITY

From the question of what makes it *possible* to retrieve stored information we must distinguish sharply the question of what makes it *probable*. This is the distinction we intend by the retrievability of a message versus its memorability. A message may in general be retrievable but nonetheless vary in its probability of retrieval of its memorability, compared with competing *other* stored messages and compared with *itself* from one time to another, or both.

We will first discuss the general possibility of retrievability and then consider the problem of memorability. How could *any* "name," be it sign, symbol, analogue, compression, part, or whole, in the service of conscious cognitive or affective search, perceptual recognition support, rote intention, or skilled act support, *know* where to go and what to do to retrieve the information stored at the correct address?

One way to answer such a question is to examine the phenomenon when it is most self-conscious—when one "intends" to memorize and when this intention succeeds.

Nonredundant Rote Memorization

Let us examine how the human memorizes something so that he may later reproduce it without reliance on the support of external cues.

How *do* human beings go about memorizing? There is no royal common road to the retrieval of information. If memorizing is a technique of learning to remember, we must expect the same variability that is characteristic of any learning sequence, as a function of differences between people and as a function of differences in the nature of what they are trying to memorize. The greatest single source of variability, however, will result from differences in the intention to memorize. It is not ordinarily appreciated how little everyman intends to memorize exactly and how little he does so memorize. Consider the millions of small movements of arms and legs over a lifetime. To duplicate this series or any appreciable segment thereof is well outside the range of possibility. To be able to say what one was doing at this moment a year ago is beyond the memory capacity of most human beings.

We do not intend to and we cannot reproduce exactly very much of our own past behavior, perceptual or motor. Much of our memory skill is recognitive rather than reproductive.

Not only is the intention to achieve reproductive memory relatively rare, but even when it is intended, there are nonetheless many alternative ways of trying to learn how to remember. These alternatives are radically increased with increasing difficulty of the task. We find much less variability in techniques of memorizing a telephone number than of memorizing a lengthy poem. Some of the varieties of techniques of memorizing have been investigated in the classic studies of part-versuswhole methods of learning. For the purpose of illuminating the nature of the memory mechanism, however, it is advisable to study the memorization of simple rather than complex information, since the latter not only increases the variability of technique employed but also involves learning in general as well as that subclass of learning we have called memorizing. This is the difference between learning to remember a telephone number and learning the correct turns in a maze. In the latter case one could not "memorize" the correct turns until one had first learned them. The latter kind of learning involves a detection of the structure of the external world, the former an ability to generate "known" information from reduced information.

A further precaution with respect to redundancy of the task is important. If the material to be memorized is redundant to any marked degree, then what appears to be a pure memory phenomenon may be converted into a learning problem. Thus, a maze of the pattern left, right, left, right, etc., could be remembered by the formula "take the first left turn and then alternate." This formula would indeed have to be remembered perfectly to sustain the ability to reproduce the entire correct performance, but much of what appeared to be rote memory would not be such but rather the consequence of the expansion of such a formula. The human being does in fact constantly maximize his ability to remember by organizing ongoing experience into categories he already knows and thus reduces the amount of new information he must remember. This very important characteristic of the human being nonetheless obscures the essential nature of the rote memory mechanism since it reduces memory to the coordination of new to old information. We need a task recalcitrant to such an efficient technique. The most searching test of any theory of memory retrieval must be based on a task that is at once nonredundant and involves no new learning other than memorizing the information. One ideal task, which meets both criteria, is the memorizing of a number series, such as a telephone number. Each number in such a series is well known—but the relationships are new, although not so demanding as to require extensive new learning nor so structured that they can be reduced to a simpler structure. Thus, 2, 4, 6, 8, 10 would be a poor number series for our purposes because it is easily converted into a simpler series.

We will examine the everyday phenomenon of learning to remember a telephone number. We think this provides a paradigm for pure reproductive memory. It is somewhat surprising that despite thousands of experimental studies of memory we have not taken the trouble to observe the phenomenon as it presents itself to us in our everyday life. Let us scrutinize this sample phenomenon.

First, we find the number in the telephone book. The message is in the first instance a visual one, carried over the retina and optic nerve. The nerve net is the first short-term memory system we employ, since a set of on-off messages is being duplicated as the set is transmitted over the nerve net. Information is being duplicated in successive moments by such a transmission system and may therefore be considered a very limited memory-like system. Since these lines must be kept open for new information, the slightly delayed reproduction by central processes after the input has reached the cortical receptor area 17 now poses a new problem if the person is to be able to repeat the message he has just received. It must be repeated neurologically if the individual is to be able to repeat it just once. It is our assumption that briefly reverberating circuits take up the message conveyed by the optic nerve.

Let us assume that the visual message of the telephone number has been reverberated one cycle, and the person may once again become "aware" of the message just as he was a moment before when it reached the end of the line of sensory transmission. If the sensory line could not repeat the same message but had to be "cleared" for the next message from the retina, the same general problem arises in the case of the reverberating circuits. Although these are operating later than the sensory nerves, yet they must also keep reasonably clear if new sensory information is to be able to be reverberated.

So where can our visual message go to be repeated? One possibility is that the person will continue to "look" at the same number in the telephone book so that both the optic nerve and reverberating circuit will keep repeating the same message. This is not a completely satisfactory solution for a number of reasons. First, the visual system appears to have a built-in mechanism to prevent too much repetition. The eyes are in constant motion, so visual impressions are difficult to repeat exactly. Second, even if the visual input were repeated, the central eidetic process appears as incapable of continuous exact repetition as are the eyes themselves. The span of attention is very limited. It is impossible for the human being to continue for very long to be aware of the same stimulus. He is as incapable of continuously being aware of the same visual message as his eyes are incapable of continually registering the same visual message. These are two built-in sources of instability. Third, the motivational system is coordinated to the sensory input systems in that exact repetition of the same message in awareness reduces the positive affective response of interest or excitement and instigates increasingly intense negative affective responses—boredom, distress, hostility, or fear. This decline in positive affect and rise in negative affect motivates a number of alternatives.

Relief from repetition is sought either in a novel perception or interpretation of the same input, a slight change in the same input (as in moving nearer or farther away from the source of stimulation), in an aggressive attack on the source in order to reduce its impact or change it, in seeking different input, or in going to sleep. In the event of any of these alternatives, it is clear that the motivational system is designed to support only a limited amount of exact repetition and as such is coordinated to the characteristics of the central eidetic mechanism. Depending upon which alternative is elected, repeated stimulation will produce either a set of increasingly novel interpretations of the same input or an abandonment of this input. If the subject elects to reinterpret the input, he has the options of more and more complex organization via conceptual relational activity or of more and more chaotic disorganization of the perceived information in satiation, as he becomes more stimulus-bound.

For all of these reasons our hypothetical subject who wishes to commit the telephone number to memory is beset with barriers to his intended achievement if he were simply to keep looking indefinitely at the number on the page of the telephone book. He cannot even keep looking at it very long, let alone guarantee that he will remember it the next time he needs it.

What does he do? Even if it is only his intention to remember the number long enough to use it once, to give to the operator or to dial it, he keeps repeating it until he has used it. That this is a very precarious achievement, at the outer limits of his capacity, is clear from the great vulnerability of such memory to interference. If someone should speak to him while he is repeating it, he is likely to lose the number and have to look it up again. But how can he repeat it even inexpertly? Have we not just said the system is so unstable that exact duplication is impossible? We have said this is the case of the eidetic response to the repeated sensory message. First, it should be noted that our subject has (usually) translated the visual message, while looking at it, into the spoken word. This he knows how to do if he can read and speak the same language. He did not, however, know his new friend's telephone number before this moment. Here is a case of general knowledge of a language, in two forms, that supports the acquisition of new knowledge by combining old components (i.e., letters and numbers) into new combinations. This is a case of some memory supporting the acquisition of new knowledge. He also brings into this situation the knowledge of how to translate the visual message into the spoken message. These are memories or learned skills with which we shall concern ourselves no longer at this point. Our question is, given these skills how is the new number committed to memory?

The first part of the answer is that the original is used as a model to fabricate an equivalent form, in this case a translation from visual representation of the number to the spoken number. It is not critical to our argument to explain that this translation has been preceded by another equivalent, that is, the motor messages to the tongue, which are in still another language of translation. Nor is it critical that some individuals utilize languages other than the spoken word for the creation of an equivalent form of the original message. Thus, some use a visual image rather than the spoken word to reproduce the number.

What is critical is that the bootstrap memory operation begins with the fabrication of an equivalent form of the information at the same time that the latter is being matched from memory to the information that is retrieved through the sensory nerve transmission, or at latest, when the same message is in consciousness after the completion of a cycle in a reverberating circuit. Contiguity in time is a necessary condition for the first *copy* to be fabricated. This is so because we think there is as yet no retrieval skill to enable recovery of the model from permanent storage. Hence, copies that are to be made must be made while the model is still available. The first copy naturally must stress faithful reproduction, since error introduced at this point is fatal. It is, of course, not always possible to exclude error in this first reproduction. Usually, comparison of the model with the copy will reveal error, but sometimes the error creeps into the awareness of the model itself, as in the proofreader's error. In this, as in all cases, the conscious copy is compared not with the real model but with the conscious model, which was also a "copy" of the sensory input. If there is error in the conscious model, this too will be copied. We have now overcome some of the inherent instability of the system that makes exact repetition difficult. This has been achieved by creating a copy that is an *equivalent*, that is, something that is the same in some respect and different in some respect. What is the same is the numbers, what is different is the language in which the numbers are expressed (i.e., from visual numbers into auditory numbers). So we now have within the human being an equivalent copy of the model that has been constructed. We have a long distance to go before this copy can be of any use to its creator. But a bridge has been built across time, and if he wishes only to use this copy once to make a telephone call, all he needs to do is to make a copy of the copy, and a copy of the copy of the copy, until the operator takes the number from him or he translates the copy into the movements required by the dial telephone.

Let us examine the second step, the fabrication of a copy of the copy. How is it possible for the person to repeat a copy of the copy when we have stressed the difficulty of exactly repeating anything? In the case of copying the model he was creating an equivalent in another language. In using the copy as a model, he is using the same language. How can he do this? He has, after repeating the number once or twice, ceased to look at the number in the telephone book, so the reverberation of the visual model will come to an end; and since the number was spoken concurrently with looking, so will the reverberating feedback from the spoken number. Therefore, when he stops looking at the number he is reduced to one type of reverberating circuit if he continues to repeat the number by speaking. But if there is no more relevant visual information either in the optic nerve or in the reverberating circuits, how can he repeat the spoken number? Remember that he has thus far depended upon the model of the visual number to achieve the translation into the spoken number. When he turns away from this source of stimulation, how is he to reproduce a copy of the spoken number? The number is the same as in the memory span experiment. If the experimenter says 5-8-3, how does the subject repeat this a few moments later? In the case of our subject, he hears himself rather than someone else repeat the number, but the mechanism required is the same. It is an internal feedback mechanism that is required to duplicate one's own speech. After hearing what one has said, one must be able to "send" the appropriate motor message, which will move the tongue so that one will hear the same number again. If instead of actually saying the number over again, he imagines it again by means of auditory or visual imagery, he must also be able to "send" these messages if he is to keep repeating them for himself. We are assuming then that when the auditory copy of the visual model comes off the auditory nerve, it is transmuted into a conscious message and latter transmitted to a reverberating circuit. This reverberated message is also later capable of being transmuted into conscious form and of being reverberated again. We assume that if the reverberated message is not transmuted into conscious form at the end of the cycle, this reverberating circuit is cleared of that message.

The individual then uses the conscious message as a model to "send" a copy of this message, in the case of repeating imagery, or as a model to "send" a translatory message (to the tongue) that will produce an auditory copy of the auditory message.

We have traced the steps from model to copy to copy of the copy. We have thus far an explanation only for immediate, or slightly delayed memory. What are the critical transformations that will produce a memory that will be available at some later time?

Miniaturization

First, the to-be-remembered information must be transformed into a compressed, miniaturized equivalent form. In the case of the telephone number, this means that the informational water and cellulose is squeezed out of the copies. Instead of the exact auditory copy of the visual model, the individual begins to "send" a message that is briefer and more compact. Instead of sending a 5-second, perfectly articulated message—as a telephone operator might say it, "Fyuv–Nyun–Too–Theree," he begins to send something that sounds like "Fivnintoothree," which takes about 1 second to send and receive into consciousness. Then, using this miniaturized copy as a model, he proceeds to send miniatures of the miniatures. The next copy might sound like "Finitothee." As he continues to repeat these numbers in very compressed form, he eventually reaches a form that is completely unrecognizable to anyone but himself—the merest blip, a highly clipped, miniaturized version of the original. If it is very important to our subject that he remember the number, he will continue this miniaturization until the conscious blip is itself miniaturized and finally he knows only that he "knows the number," that is, that he can reproduce it at will from an internal copy that silently supports his recollection. Part of the controversy concerning imageless thought was based on the different degrees of miniaturization and compression utilized in support of thought and memory. This series of compressions is not unlike the complex series of biochemical transformations that make it possible for us to assimilate and store energy from food. But unlike this series it is not as invariant from person to person. There are more degrees of freedom in informational compression. The subject may stop before he has in fact totally assimilated the information, the consequence of which is that he must again refresh his memory by another look at the model. Each individual may miniaturize at a different rate, according to his intelligence and skill, but the general trend of these transformations is essentially the same: to enable the handling of large amounts of information by smaller carriers, which in turn will enable the recovery of the original information.

Before continuing with the next step in this series of transformations, let us examine just how this compression is attained. We have said that the copy of the copy is achieved by sending an internal message, which, when it is received in conscious form, will be a duplicate of the present message, which serves as a model for its successor. We have not looked too closely at the mechanism of such duplication, but we must do that since a more complex demand is now placed on the duplicating mechanism. The message has not simply to be copied in its next transmission but must be altered in such a way that the essentials of the model are preserved while it is miniaturized in its nonessential characteristics. For the visually minded, we can represent this series of transformations in Figure 48.1. To simplify our question, how can numbers that take 2 seconds to say be said first in 1 second, then in $\frac{1}{2}$ second, $\frac{1}{4}$ second, and so on? There are, of course, many parameters of the model other than its speed that must be miniaturized, but the principles involved with the other parameters differ only in complexity.

How is 5923 squeezed from 2 seconds to 1 second? In general, the human being is not born endowed with this type of knowledge. To make a beginning on such transformation he must "intend" to "operate" on what he does know how to do (i.e., repeat the model) by an operator about which he knows something—speed, "to be increased," or "to be doubled." At this point he knows what the operator means in that it is a useful criterion that would enable him to say that this number series has been spoken faster than that number series, but he may not know at all how to produce such a desired change. How does he operate on what he does know by means of an operator whose meaning he also knows? Our answer is that he begins in ignorance and ends in ignorance. He never becomes aware of the vast neurological inner space. We have conceived of this as the space in between a dart thrower and his illuminated target in an otherwise dark room. One can learn to throw a dart to hit an illuminated target in

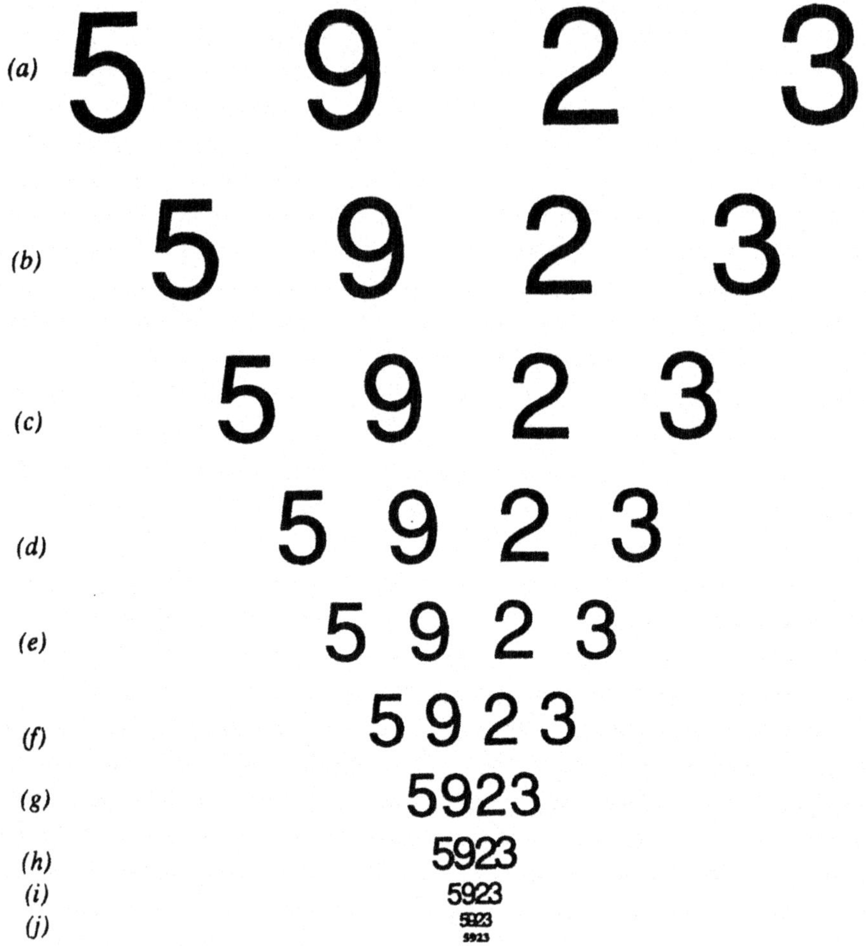

FIGURE 48.1 Representation of the series of transformations.

a dark room without ever knowing what the trajectory of the dart might be, as long as one knew both how it felt just before the dart was thrown and where the dart landed. The trajectory described by the dart would not and never could become conscious, but the visible effects of the trajectory could be systematically translated into the preceding conditions in such a fashion that for such and such a feel or look before throwing one could be reasonably certain that the visual report, after the trajectory, would be the desired report. We have conceived of the efferent messages as the dart trajectory controlled by the afferent reports that precede and follow the efferent messages. We have called this a translation because there are two different languages involved, the motor and the sensory. One must here learn to translate a desired future sensory report into the appropriate motor trajectories. In order, then, to begin learning how to remember we must either know how to use a set of operators on our to-be-compressed model or learn how to do it by neurological experimentation. Thus, our memorizer will try to speed up his duplication of the telephone number. If he does not succeed, he can try again until he does, so long as his failure does produce a recognizable copy of the preceding copy. If it does not, he must refresh his memory from the original model by looking the number up again to produce another useful copy.

But miniaturization involves more than speeded performance. In addition to increased speed, the sounds must be clipped and abbreviated without destroying their essential message. There is a complex relationship between the various parameters of any performance that is to be compressed. In attempting to operate on one it will often happen that other parameters will also be transformed unintentionally. Thus, in speeding up our handwriting we may lose legibility. The original model may be so distorted that only its author can read it at the higher speed. Increased speed may, on the other hand, improve certain performances by so altering the relationships between the parts of the model that it becomes easier to duplicate. This is the case, for example, in learning to ride a bicycle. It takes much more skill to ride a bicycle slowly and expertly, so that one will not fall off, than it does to ride a bicycle at a faster rate. Only vaudeville and circus performers have learned to ride a bicycle very slowly and very skillfully.

So "operating" on any message ensemble can vary from a comparatively simple bit of neurological trial and error to a very complex process in which the original model is transformed in a variety of both intended and unintended ways.

Miniaturization may proceed by the intended transformation of one parameter at a time or by the intended transformation of a set of parameters at once. In the latter case it might be intended to both speed up the numbers and clip them at the same time. In general, the greater the number of conjoint "operations" undertaken at once, the greater the likelihood of unintended consequences that may disorganize the compressed copy so that the whole enterprise has to be started over by looking again at the model.

Expansion

We have concerned ourselves with how we miniaturize the original model. At this point you may ask of what use these miniatures are as their resemblance to the original becomes more and more remote? Each was an "equivalent" to the one just preceding it. But is such a series of increasingly compressed equivalents not like the blurred features of the face of a familiar person as we walk backward farther and farther away from him? Of what utility are they unless they are "recognizable" as compressions of the original model rather than equivalents of the just-preceding miniature? Further, it is not enough that the miniature be "recognized" as a miniature of the original. It must be possible to *reproduce* the original exactly from the miniature. The expansion-compression relationship must be reversible. It would be of no use if our subject were able only to repeat the miniaturized blip to the telephone operator. It would be even less useful as a model for dialing the number since some dialing operations are even slower than the human telephone operator's capacity to receive messages.

How is the reversibility of the miniature achieved? By the inverse of the compression transformation. This recovery of the original by the inverse transformation has been widely used in energy and information transformations in engineering. Thus, it is more efficient to transmit electricity at high voltage and low amperage than at low voltage and high amperage. For this reason electricity is usually transformed from the latter to the former before it is transmitted any great distance. At the receiving station the reverse transformation produces the original form of electrical energy. Another instance is in the recording of music. The low frequencies are reduced in amplitude so that the vibration of the recording stylus will not break down the grooves of the master record. In the amplifying system that reproduces this sound, appropriate compensatory amplification, the inverse of the original attenuation, enables the listener to recover an approximation of the original volume of the low frequencies.

This problem in reproductive skill is similar to an analogue in recognition skill. In the latter case we gradually learn to recognize a familiar person from an increasing variety of perspectives from an increasing number of sequences of parts to the whole. Thus we can recognize a very familiar person from his walk, his talk, his nose, eyes, chin, skin texture, smell, his tempo (whether walking, gesturing, or talking), his clothing, his ideas, or his gestures. Further, smaller and smaller bits of such evidence become sufficient for recognition as less and less information becomes necessary for recognition. Presumably, this is because through increasing contacts in different contexts, different part-aspects of the other are encountered, followed by scanning and recognition of the whole in which these bits are encountered sequentially in different orders. Varieties of part-whole sequences in recognition are achieved over time without planned rehearsal. In achieving rote reproductive memorization, however, the varieties of relationships between miniaturized wholes and expanded wholes must be rehearsed within a much more massed series of trials.

In memorizing we employ inverse transformations by using the operator "decreased speed" on the compressed message set, instead of the "increased speed" operator on the original message set, and by using conjointly the inverse operator "expand" rather than "clip." In this way one can learn to reverse what one has just done. The compression is now the model, and the reverse operation recovers the original expanded model. But if each step (cf. Figure 48.1) from *a* to *b* and from *b* to *c* is a short enough step so that slowing down a little bit and expanding a little bit enables the recovery of *a* from *b*, when *b* is slowed to the original speed, and the recovery of *b* from *c* when *c* is slowed to the speed of *b*, this will not work when speed at (*j*) is slowed to speed at (*a*) because repeating the very miniaturized blip at (*j*) cannot easily be directly expanded to (*a*). To recover the slowed number (a) from (j) a series of bridges must be built from *b* to *a*, then from *c* to *b*; from *c* to *a*; from *d* to *c*, *d* to *b*, *d* to a; from *e* to *d*, *e* to *c*, *e* to *b*, *e* to *a*, and so on so that finally;' can go to *i*, then to *h*, *g*, *f*, *e*, *d*, *c*, *b*, and *a*. This is not a necessary and sufficient series since much depends on the degree of perceived similarity and differences between the series of increasingly miniaturized blips. What is critical is that the recoverability of the original not be jeopardized by too great a difference between the early members of this series and the latter members. One must teach oneself that this gradual set of transitions is more continuous than a comparison between *j* and *a* would suggest.

Let us examine the details of this process more closely. First it should be noted that the compression process is producing a continuing reduction in the density of reports to messages. By continually miniaturizing succeeding copies, the claim on the limited channel of consciousness of the central assembly is continually reduced. The operations of speeding and clipping performed on each copy go on outside consciousness although the "operators" are sent from the central assembly, and the outcome of their transformation of the copy soon reaches the central assembly and is there transmuted into a report. This report, however, by virture of miniaturization, has decreasing conscious detail, although the amount of information it carries may be sufficient to support the performance for which it was constructed. Thus, once we have completely miniaturized a telephone number we can use it to dial the number with so little conscious representation that we may carry on a conversation while translating the miniaturized memory trace into the appropriate hand movements. While we are ordinarily also capable, in this instance, of increasing the density of reports to messages sufficiently to tell someone else, say an operator, the number we are dialing, yet in many types of memorization the original density of reports to messages cannot be easily recovered at will. Thus, if one has learned to touch-typewrite, one may know how to find the letter *q* with one's fingers if one is typing the word *question* and yet not be able to answer the query "Where on the typewriter keyboard is the letter *q?*"

The reduction of the density of reports to messages is critical, not only because of the limited channel of consciousness of the central assembly but because so many skills require such high-speed assembling and sending of motor messages that reliance on detailed, high density of reports to messages is out of the question. The central assembly, with its conscious reports, therefore continually activates operators to transform the information retrieved from storage so that when it enters the next central assembly it will make less of a demand on the limited channel. Consciousness, therefore, increasingly legislates itself out of representation. The process can be verified in any armchair. One had only to repeat a number series to oneself, over and over again, taking care to compress succeeding copies of the original, to discover that soon one knows *that* one knows the number with imageless unconscious thought. Individuals differ, however, in the extent to which they compress their stored information, and some are therefore more aware than others of the information retrieved from their memory traces. Different tasks are also responsible for varying degrees of compression of stored information, as we have seen in the comparison of touch typing and remembering telephone numbers for communication to telephone operators. However, even in the latter instance, prior imagery may not reach conscious form. The individual may become aware of the number for the first time only as he hears himself talk to the operator.

The second feature of this process of reproductive memorizing that should be noted is that the individual is freeing himself from dependence on the external stimulus as a necessary support for his reproductive memory skill and is teaching himself how to retrieve the information from within rather than from the external stimulus. In other words, not only is information being stored in increasingly compressed form at different sites in the brain, but the individual is learning these addresses, where and how to find the stored information and reassemble it. As we have said before, not all information is so retrievable. Much of what we experience is at a brain address unknown to the individual.

The Limitation of Retrieval Ability

The retrieval ability being learned under the conditions of miniaturizing we have described consists, then, not only in the disposition of traces at specific addresses but also in the central assembling of names for each address and the storage of these names at other addresses. This is the basis of the third feature of the process of miniaturization, which should be noted: the sharp limitation of the retrieval ability as thus far achieved. If the telephone number whose memorization we are describing is a new one of an old friend, then there are many older names and names of names that can be recruited to assist in the extension of the fragile new skill in retrieving the number from storage. But let us suppose that the person was looking up the number as a favor to a friend but that the individual himself had never before heard either the telephone number or the name of the person whose number it happened to be. Under these conditions the "name" of the number would itself have no well-established name or "names of names," and these latter would also have to be learned to be retrieved, just as would the telephone number itself. However, how limited retrieval ability may be is still uncertain. It has become clear that previous estimates of memory loss of rote-learned materials must be radically revised. The classical Ebbinghous curve of forgetting is primarily a function of interference from materials learned previously in the laboratory. The similarity of past names and names of names to later names and names of names interferes with the recovery of present names on retest.

Let us return now to our analysis of the memorizing process for further illumination on how the limited retrieval ability that is characteristic of much memory is deepened and consolidated. First, the to-be-remembered information must be transformed into compressed, miniaturized equivalent form. Second, the equivalent compressed form must be capable of being expanded into its original form. Third, the equivalent compressed form must be capable of sequences of further compressions, each of which is capable of being expanded into preceding compressions and into the original form. Fourth, the process must become less and less conscious as compression increases so that *both* the searching process and (in the case of motoric dialing) the retrieved message is relatively unconscious. Thus, names of traces are learned as they are deposited at specific addresses.

In the memorizing of 5923, we have envisioned a series of transformations that successively miniaturize the information and that also successively expand these miniatures by the inverse transformation so that the original model is successively compressed by clipping and accelerating the sending of the copy and recovered through expansion of the clipped information by slowing the sending of the copy to the speed at which the original model was sent.

The ultimate stability of such retrieval skill will depend on several factors: (1) the number of alternative and conjoint names for each member of the set of compressed traces; (2) the number of ways (names) for retrieving each compressed trace from every other more or less compressed member of the set of compressed traces—this enables the individual to retrieve an unrecognizable blip of a trace and use it to support equally rapid and unrecognizable performances (such as in touch typing) or to

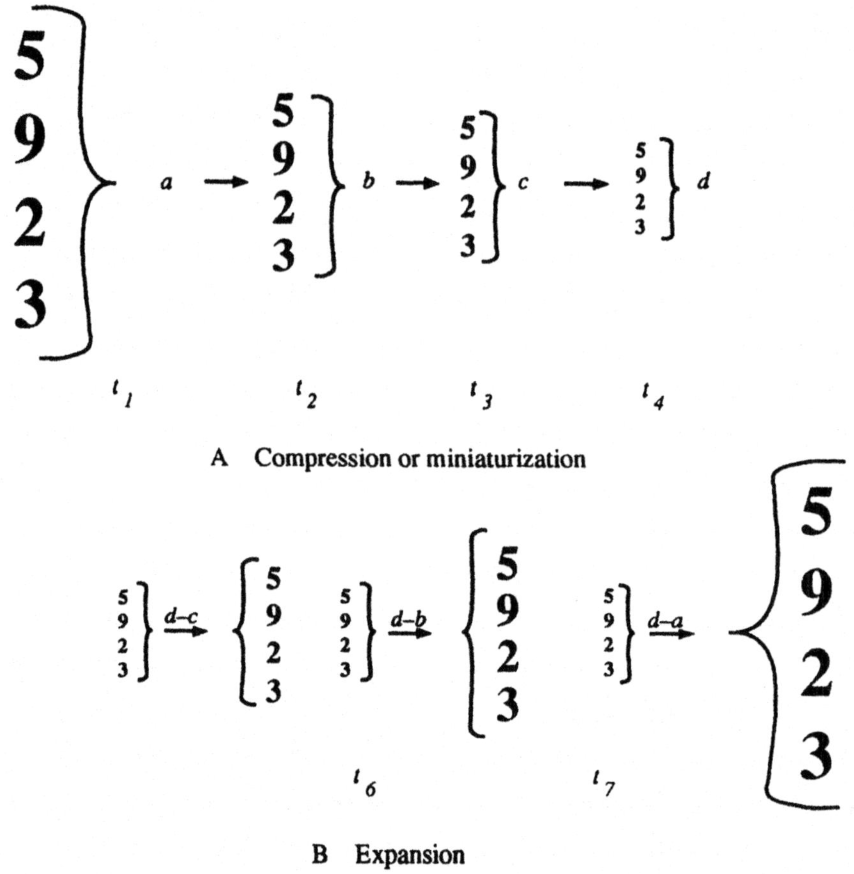

A Compression or miniaturization

B Expansion

FIGURE 48.2 Production of names for (A) compressed and (B) expanded forms of the model.

support slower, more conscious expansions in which the density of reports to messages is as high as in the original reading of the model; and (3) the number of names of names for each compressed trace and for retrieving each compressed trace from every other more or less compressed member of the set of compressed traces. In Figures 48.2, 48.3 and 48.4 we have presented these relationships schematically. Figure 48.2 represents the process we have already described in detail. Figure 48.3 represents the linkage of these names to names of names. The greater the number of already existing linkages of *x*, which number we are learning, the easier to later retrieve the number from internally generated names of names.

In Figure 48.4 we represent one of a variety of possible alternative ways of memorizing the same information. In this case, half of the set is memorized as a whole, the other half is memorized as a whole, and then both halves are combined to form a new name. Theoretically, there is no limit to the number of different ways in which parts may be combined until the whole is assimilated. One consequence of such part models is that such parts, when encountered separately, may become names of wholes, whereas for the whole method this may never occur. If we wished to increase the recognizability of stimuli from varying perspectives or under conditions of partial exposure of the stimulus, this would argue for training methods involving such truncation and variation of the original model.

Even when the names of a trace themselves have no address, as may be the case in recognition when the external stimulus is the only way of

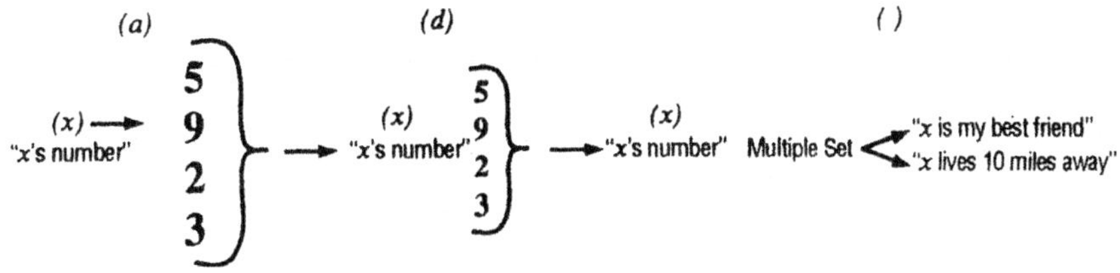

FIGURE 48.3 **Production of names of names.**

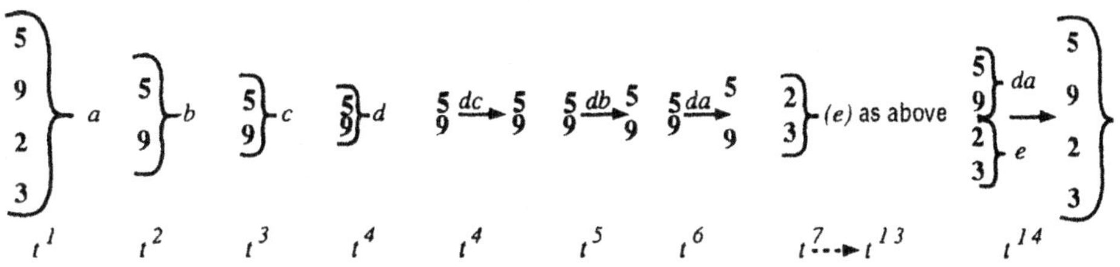

FIGURE 48.4 **Part method of production of names.**

activating memory, there may be varying degrees of skill achieved, depending on the number of alternative names that have been achieved for each part of the stimulus, for changes in its position and distance from the observer, and for changes in the background against which it is viewed.

The great number of alternative names and names of names that are possible in the achievement of recognition or reproduction retrieval skill suggests that we may devise very much more sensitive tests of memory than we now possess, by plotting the proportion of mastered names to the total of possible names or to the total of any specific number greater than that usually achieved with a given frequency of practice.

Although the rote memorization of nonredundant information is a relatively rare phenomenon and does not illuminate the great variety of ways in which retrieval commonly occurs, it does illuminate the extraordinary burden it places upon the retrieval of exact, isolated, and relatively nonredundant information and thereby accentuates the importance of affective amplification and cognitive connectedness in the magnification of information necessary to make it memorable as well as retrievable.

One way, then, of *learning* to retrieve if information is nonredundant is to reduce the amount of information by compression and to *practice*, in a *feedback* manner, how to both *produce* traces and *find* them and *expand* them.

We will next examine a more efficient way of rote memorizing that exploits the redundancy of *already* available names and addresses by depositing new and unique information in already familiar places—places familiar in the external world that have been made familiar in the neurological space of the brain.

Unique Composites, Natural or Constructed, as Another Mode of Providing Memorability

We wish now to examine another kind of memorization, in which redundancy is used heavily in conjunction with its opposite—when the rarity of the information is conjoined with its overlearned typicality. This may happen spontaneously or it may be artificially introduced into attempted memorization.

Frances Yates (1972) in *The Art of Memory* has shown that the Greeks invented an art of memory that was passed on to Rome, whence it descended in the European tradition. This art sought to memorize through a technique of impressing "places" and "images" on memory. In the ages before printing, a trained memory was vitally important. The art belonged to rhetoric as a technique by which the orator could improve his memory, which would enable him to deliver long speeches from memory with unfailing accuracy.

Cicero in his *De oratore* tells how Simonides invented the art of memory. At a banquet given by a nobleman of Thessaly named Scopas, the poet Simonides of Ceos chanted a lyric poem in honor of his host but including a passage in praise of Castor and Pollus. Scopas told the poet he would pay him only half the sum agreed upon and that he must obtain the balance from the twin gods to whom he had devoted half of the poem. A little later Simonides was asked to step outside to see two young men who were waiting to see him. During his absence the roof fell in, crushing to death Scopas and all of the guests beneath the ruins; the corpses were so mangled that the relatives who came to take them away for burial were unable to identify them. But Simonides remembered the places at which they had been sitting at the table and was therefore able to indicate to the relatives which were their dead. And this experience suggested to the poet the principles of the art of memory, of which he is said to have been the inventor. According to Cicero,

> He inferred that persons desiring to train this faculty [of memory] must select places and form mental images of the things they wish to remember and store those images in the places, so that the order of the places will preserve the order of the things, and the images of the things will denote the things themselves, and we shall employ the places and images respectively as a wax writing tablet and the letters written on it.

The first step was to imprint on memory a series of loci, or places. Thus, Quintilian suggests that a building is to be remembered, as spacious and varied as possible. The images by which the speech is to be remembered are then placed in imagination on the places that have been memorized in the building (e.g., an anchor or a weapon in the case of a speech that dealt at one point with naval matters [the anchor] and at another with military operations [the weapon]). This done, as soon as the memory is needed, all of those places are visited in turn as the orator moves in imagination through his memory building while he is making his speech, drawing from the memorized places the images he had placed on them. The method ensures that the points are remembered in the right order, since the order is fixed by the sequence of places in the building. But it is further assumed that we can start from any locus in the series and move either backward or forward from it.

In 86–82 B.C. an unknown teacher of rhetoric in Rome compiled a textbook of rhetoric under the title *Ad Herennium* and (according to Frances Yates) provided the main source for the classical art of memory both in the Greek and in the Latin world.

Let us briefly consider some of the details of his "rules." An unfrequented building is best since crowds of passing people tend to weaken the impressions. There are presumed to be two kinds of images: one for things, the other for words. Memory for words is thought to be much harder than memory for things. What kinds of images should one use?

> Now nature herself teaches us what we should do. When we see in everyday life things that are pretty, ordinary, and banal, we generally fail to remember them, because the mind is not being stirred by anything novel or marvellous. But if we see or hear something exceptionally base, dishonourable, unusual, great, unbelievable, or ridiculous, that we are likely to remember for a long time. Accordingly, things immediate to our eye or ear we commonly forget; incidents of our childhood we often remember best. Nor could this be so for any other reason than that ordinary things easily slip from the memory while the striking and the novel stay longer in the mind. A sunrise, the sun's course, a sunset are marvellous to no one because they occur daily. But solar eclipses are a source of wonder because they occur seldom, and indeed are more marvellous than lunar eclipses, because these are more frequent. . . . We ought, then, to set up images of a kind that can adhere longest in memory. And we shall do so if we establish similitudes as striking

> as possible; if we set up images that are not many or vague but active; if we assign to them exceptional beauty or singular ugliness; if we ornament some of them, as with crowns or purple cloaks, so that the similitude may be more distinct to us; or if we somehow disfigure them, as by introducing one stained with blood or soiled with mud or smeared with red paint, so that its form is more striking, or by assigning certain comic effects to our images, for that, too, will ensure our remembering them more readily."

Rarity *and* affect are here being stressed, 1,900 years ago. Galton rediscovered this in 1880. In his free-association experiment on himself he found that associations that recurred several times over a 4-month period could be traced largely to his boyhood and youth, and associations that occurred only once stemmed from more recent experience. The diagnostic power of this method did not escape Galton. "It would be very instinctive to print the actual records at length, made by many experimenters. . . . but it would be too absurd to print one's own singly. They lay bare the foundations of a man's thoughts with more vividness and truth than he would probably care to publish to the world."

John Ross (Ross & Lawrence, 1968) has tested the effectiveness of the Greek and Roman methods. He instructed his subject to select and commit to memory 52 loci in sequence along a walk through the grounds of the University of Western Australia. Subsequently, he read lists of words with instructions to construct images connecting the words with the loci. Each list was presented only once. After two walks the subject could repeat the loci fluently in forward or backward order. The subject recalled lists of 20 items or more with no errors or very few errors, and pairs of items with similar efficiency even after intervening tasks and no further presentations. Interference effects were virtually eliminated. The single list of 50 concrete nouns in the first session was recalled in its original order with only two errors after a second presentation in a different order. Repeated use of the same set of loci for new stimulus material did not produce detectable proactive inhibition effects or retroactive inhibition effects. Backward association was strong. The subject reported that *any* member of a triple (locus, list word A, or list B word) readily evoked the complete image, which included the locus.

Ross compares his results with reported cases of exceptional recall (e.g., Luria's [1960] series of observations with Shereskewskii). There were several features in common. He too used places on a walk and also forged as striking an image as can be invented, which connects the items to be remembered with the locus. There is little or no attempt at rehearsal. It is common to use symbols or substitutes for words, particularly if they are abstract (e.g., "celery" for "salary"), remembering when the time came to make the appropriate back substitution. Ross offers his experiment and related phenomena as a contribution to understanding the high capacity of memory to supply information promptly and accurately and help to explain why memory is comparatively so poor under normal laboratory conditions.

Although the conjunction of rarity and affect contribute to the increased memorability of Simonides' method, intense affect is not used in Ross's technique, and yet it is as effective. Conceivably, Ross's method, though equally effective for immediate recall, might not be as memorable as a method also employing intense affect in long-delayed recall or in competition with more memorable scenes in the immediate future. However, our concern now is with retrievability rather than memorability.

In contrast to the compression-expansion of nonredundant information, what is here involved is the construction of an *addition* to what one already knows by *transforming* a visual image into a *unique composite*, which is a *variant* of the familiar. The retrievability of *any* information is similar in essence to this case. It is the *conjunction* of the opposite features of *uniqueness* and *commonality* that enable any name to first bracket the general areas where the address is located and then zero in on the unique address where the composite information is located. Every species is *both* a species and a genus, and just as the species is different from its genus to some degree, so is the genus different from other genera.

This is a reformulation of Shannon's (Shannon & Weaver, 1949) original definition of information as proportional to the number of alternative messages in the pool of possible messages from which the identified message has been distinguished. The same message thereby increases or decreases in the information it carries as the pool of messages decreases or increases. It is critical to understand that this definition defines the relevant pool of alternatives as "messages," not as the total population of all possible alternative entities. Because he was in the field of telephonic communication, he was necessarily interested in the measurement of variation in the amount of information achieved in the identification of one message over another message. *All* members of such a pool *shared* common features of being messages, but they were also different messages, as species differ from genus.

Any name therefore must conjoin at least two different kinds of information—the more general, more common reference (which nonetheless distinguishes the message from other general possibilities) and the more specific, less common reference. This conjunction of general and specific, more common and more unique, is a description of *both* the pathway to the address and the message stored at the address. The route is isomorphic with the destination in respect to the conjunction of the general and the specific.

The same dynamic holds for search instructions that are not rote in nature. Thus, to remember the face of a specific person, I must include in the instructions to my memory that I am looking for a living, not an inorganic entity; an animal, not a plant; a human animal, not an invertebrate animal; a male, not a female; a young, not an older man; a member of my family, not all of the young men I know; one of my children, not my wife; the oldest of my sons, not the rest of my sons. Clearly, these conjoint features can be radically compressed in summaries for greater efficiency. No matter how compressed, however, they must describe what constitutes a description of the specific features of the wanted memory together with some features it shows in common with similar entities, plus features that distinguish this immediate class from more general classes. Thus, if I instructed myself to visualize my oldest son, I would not need to add the more general instructions family member, human being, animal, animate entity, since "son" is a summary that implicitly describes these more general characteristics and distinguishes them from all of the varieties of inanimate entities.

To retrieve any symbolic verbal message, then, one must be able to distinguish its class from other classes and to locate the more specific member of the wanted class. In the case of nonsymbolic concrete images we deal not with classes but with individual entities and their "variants"—my wife wearing a red dress or a blue dress, a scene with my wife and son in it or a scene with just my son in it, a scene in which I am happy with my son or a scene in which we are unhappy. In the case of variants the analogue of the genus is the stable core upon which differences are impressed and detected. It is the variable part of the scene that is the analogue of the species in symbolic verbal memory. The power of Simonides' method was to imprint a rare, unique object on the stable core of the building when that building required little new learning to move about it in one's imagination as remembered. It is critical that one place only *one* object in each space for most effective exploitation of this method, since one must conjoin the common and the unique to retrieve information.

One can also generalize such a formulation to deal with sequential action sets. In this case the name of a set must represent a *distinctive discontinuity*, that is, describe conjointly all of the features of a performance that distinguish it from other performances and add a distinctive feature that distinguishes it from all performances of which it is a special case. We will examine this in greater detail in the next chapter, where we will show that the instruction "write slowly" will recover early handwriting, whereas the instruction "write" will recover later handwriting; because slow speed is a distinctive feature of the earlier performance and faster speed is distinctive of later performances. This property of distinctive features accounts in part for the segregation of memory sets. It is governed by a higher degree of intercorrelation within segregated sets than between such sets. The intername distance between sets is defined by the number of transformations necessary to produce a series of transition sets between the segregated sets. In the case of handwriting this would mean learning to write slowly in the adult script and rapidly in the child script through a set of learned intermediate speeds for both scripts.

Whether we are trying to retrieve verbal symbols, images, or actions, the same conjunction of the common and unique is necessary to find the address of the information to be retrieved.

MEMORABILITY

Any stored memory may be retrievable or not, depending on the presence and location of its name. But if it is retrievable, it may nonetheless languish and rarely *be* retrieved. It is the probability and frequency of actual retrieval to which we refer by the concept of memorability.

Memorability is not a fixed characteristic of any stored information. What was once very memorable may cease to be so, for some time and once again become memorable. Or a scene may continually grow in memorability or continually decrease in memorability. Such variability is in part a function of how memorable competing memories are or may become. It is in larger part a function of the waxing and waning of purposes that prompt fewer or more searches for particular memories, the variation in perceptual stimulations that prompt memory support for recognition, variations in scenes that create ambiguities that in turn prompt searches in memory for clues to the interpretation of such scenes. Further, such variability arises from skills that constantly require retrieval of the same memories in support of varied skills. This is particularly critical in speech, which, despite continual novelty, also calls upon invariances in grammar, in style, clichés, words, rate and length of utterances. Analogous invariances occur in gesture, gait, and action, all calling upon specific memory support. Memorability is not unlike the volatile exchange of a complex stock market in which stored memories are constantly being bid for at varying prices and with varying insistences from the central assembly, which needs very different memories for different periods of time with varying urgencies.

Because memorability ranges from the transient to the enduring, from the mildly insistent to the urgency of mania, desperation, or panic, and because duration and intensity of the remembered vary independently, we must again distinguish *amplification* from *magnification.*

Consider the relationships between the immediately amplified scene and its succeeding magnification. Nothing is more immediately "memorable" than a large deviation from a very large class of typical cases. A person who came into a lecture hall full of hundreds of other persons, all of whom had the typical number of heads for a human being, would immediately command the attention of the entire auditorium if he possessed two or more heads on his shoulders. No matter how commonplace an individual he was otherwise—in height, weight, skin color, clothing, and general demeanor—he would constitute for everyone a sight that was memorable, something one *could* neither disregard nor forget. This sight would no doubt be radically amplified by numerous and intense affects. He might startle, excite, frighten, disgust, distress, anger, or make one laugh. Yet although such affective amplification is part of the explanation of the compelling nature of both the perception and the memory, it is not the whole of the matter. It is, in this case, the other way around. The affect is evoked and sustained *because* of the quantity of information to be perceived and conceived. The information in the two-headed person is proportional to the frequency of one-headed human beings, either present or previously encountered and known *and* projected into the foreseeable and indefinite future. It is not simply, either, because of the *difference* between two heads and one head. That difference is in one sense not a large difference. The information concerns both the number of times one has encountered one-headed humans and the theory (both scientific and lay) generated about the genetic mechanism and the general lawfulness of the biological domain, which is being suddenly violated by this one atypical case.

The crucial experiment in professional science is not critically different in its dynamics from this case of the violation of everyman's general theory of how things are. The information in this one case is a function of the quantity of assumed regularity that has been critically put into question. This two-headed visitor from another planet of two-headed persons would find most memorable the very large number of single-headed humans in the lecture hall. But if the conjunction of a human body and an inhuman number of heads startles so by virtue of the quantity of information perceived and conceived, why does this also make it so memorable? Nothing is more commonplace than startling or exciting experiences that eventually habituate, become commonplace, and are forgotten. Yet *some* startling experiences *cannot* be forgotten even when one wishes one could and tries to forget. Differential memorability of some atypical experiences over others has critical sociocultural and political consequences. To the extent to which the previously "unthinkable" (e.g., unusual violence, unusual and offensive sexual behavior, unusual and offensive political totalitarianism, unusual and offensive aesthetic creations) can be rationalized as consistent with an expanded and revised theory of human nature or human society, such previously rare violations of conceptions of reality and value become much less memorable as special events and thus can fade into the ground of all experience. When they occur again, they can be recognized but with much less detail and much less intense affect, until eventually they become totally ground to new experience.

To the extent to which the unthinkable is repeated with diminishing shock and outrage, aided and abetted in a circular incremental attenuation of cognition, affect, and memory, both the individual and his society are changed by imperceptible degrees. To the extent to which the unthinkable can*not* be accepted, there will be magnification rather than attenuation of the nonincreasingly memorable unacceptable scene. Under such conditions a whole society can generate an endlessly magnified nuclear scene, continually punished by an unacceptable violation of its norms, which it cannot accept, cannot avoid, cannot escape, cannot reduce, and cannot forget. Under such conditions an entire society can become obsessed and haunted by variants and increasingly remote analogues of the entire family of scenes, in perpetual outrage and disgust at the invasion of foreign values and in perpetual mourning for a lost golden age, which cannot be worked through as it is in the case of what is believed to be irreversible change or death. Such a society can keep the faith indefinitely, hoping for a return to the promised land, as did the lost tribes of Israel.

Clearly, such intransigence and endurance is most probable the more homogeneous the society and the more discrepant the intrusive foreign scenes. To the extent to which there is strong consensus in any society it will be capable of resisting cultural intrusions that are experienced as unthinkable violations of shared cultural norms.

The same vicissitudes of unwanted "memorable" experiences are found in the life of every individual. The individual who is all of a piece, *monistic* in personality structure, is more vulnerable to the experience of foreign intrusions that create unresolvable and increasingly memorable nuclear scenes.

In contrast, personalities that are already riven by deep *dualistic* conflicts are less vulnerable to the further magnification of alien intrusions in their life space. Similarly, deeply conflicted societies will be less vulnerable to *shared* rejection of foreign intrusions that arise from invasion from without or from internal changes. Each sector of society may experience the invasion as intrusive but in different ways and to different degrees.

Personalities that are more *pluralistic* in their basic scripts are least vulnerable to such bifurcations, being already of a deeply and multiply divided mind. Ambiguity and confusion are compounded if the invasion is experienced in a pluralistic personality characterized by predominantly negative affect. Increased richness of experience is experienced in a pluralistic personality characterized by predominantly positive affect.

Similarly, pluralistic societies are less vulnerable to the intrusion of foreign invasion, since the differences are essentially attenuated by the already highly differentiated and somewhat unshared norms. To the extent that a pluralistic society functions well, the intrusion can enrich the collective. To the extent that the society already suffers from its excessive fractionation, it is further impaired. The most determined resistance to the unwanted, unthinkable scene can be eroded and assimilated and thereby made less and less memorable.

Several years ago, when Liddell (1943) first began to attempt to induce an experimental neurosis in a pig, he encountered failure after failure because the pig was outraged at the assault on its freedom by the experimenter. Rather than attenuation of the memorable unthinkable scene, there was magnification, with the animal becoming more and more resistant and destructive. Eventually, however, Lidell was successful in changing the pig into a submissive compliant animal and then in producing an experimental neurosis in that animal. This was achieved by partitioning the intrusions on the animal's freedom into such finely graded steps that each single procedure did not seem different enough from everyday procedures to arouse resistance. By gradually cumulating these procedures the animal was finally induced to wear the harness and accept all of the restrictions on his freedom that earlier had been entirely unacceptable. Thereafter he became vulnerable to the induction of an experimental neurosis through the introduction of demands for increasingly difficult discriminations, which were conjointly vital and impossible to meet or to reject.

The memorability of any event depends not only on its distinctiveness but upon its magnification, which in turn depends on the ideoaffective connectedness of the event. There is an apparent paradox and inconsistency in this. If the critical feature of memories is their distinctiveness, their *difference* from other events in memory, then how can such distinctiveness be enhanced by increasing the relatedness and connectedness of the event to all other events? The answer to this paradox is that the memorability of any *particular* scene has, in fact, a very limited life span. We *cannot* keep remembering any scene in exactly the same way our entire lives. Characteristically, any particular memory would be less and less retrieved in the daily traffic of trips to and from memory addresses. It is only when some memory becomes a necessary *part* of many different wholes, as in our daily use of language or in our daily use of our arms and legs, that some memories endure almost intact. What appears to be repetition of the same stable core in magnified variants or the same nuclear scene in magnified analogues is not simple repetition but repetition with a *difference.* Magnification of memorability of any scene is based upon the creation of an ever-increasing *family* of somewhat similar and somewhat different scenes.

Where there is real enduring repetition, as in addiction, there is attenuation rather than magnification. A cigarette addict is unaware that he is smoking for most of the time until he stops smoking. He has developed a habitual skill in which smoking is as embedded and unconscious a part of his daily life as is his characteristic rate of speaking, or walking. Addiction is a habitual skill interrupted by occasional memorable intrusions, which, paradoxically, can be controlled and reduced to zero by hoarding cigarettes to guarantee that he will never again experience what was previously memorable in an intolerable way.

Memorability grows through magnification. Magnification requires the development not only of an ever-increasing family of variants and analogues but also an increasing skill in *using* these to detect differences and similarities in ongoing experience. Every time an individual scans a scene for its *possible* similarity or difference to any particular scene, *that* scene has been made more memorable no matter what the outcome of the comparison. This is not to say that this is usually a conscious memory that is retrieved. What *is* conscious is the present scene *transformed* as guided by the variant or analogue. In this respect it is not unlike any perceptual recognition that also may involve some transformation of the stored image in its matching to the perceptual information. The major difference is in the quantity of transformation necessary to perceive a scene and what is necessary to both perceive *and* to interpret it. Interpretation results in re-seeing it from varying perspectives as it continues to be unconsciously compared with retrieved stored variants or analogues, with the resultant magnification of both differences and similarities.

The varieties of internal supports for magnified and especially nuclear scripts are too great to be treated here, but some of these can be indicated briefly. Some individuals learn largely unconscious habitual skills of contracting their muscles to produce either sustained elevations of neural firing that innately trigger distress or anger or with sufficient suddenness to innately trigger interest or fear. Once having triggered any of these affects, these may serve as names or names of names for retrieval of magnified scenes. The same dynamic may also operate through speech volume or rate or cognitive rate or amount, whether by the self or by the other. These are all *contentless* triggers. They may be further magnified by the flooding of consciousness with vivid, detailed replays of prototypic scenes, which in turn retrieve other members of the same family. Again, by continually testing others the individual may, as an *agent provocateur*, produce the magnified scenes he must continually confront.

The dynamics of increased memorability through magnification are complex and will be treated at length in another work on script theory.

Chapter 49

Implications for Human Development: Continuity and Discontinuity

What are some of the consequences of such a theory of memory for human development? The requirement of name formation and reversible compression-expansion transformations must take much time, and this will have two somewhat antithetical consequences: (1) Any human being who is deprived of the opportunity to do this work will be relatively incompetent and will, when first offered the opportunity, require a long period of experience before elementary perceptual and motor skills will be achieved; (2) by virtue of the necessarily long period of incompetence enforced by the slowness of learning how to remember, the impact of experience in early infancy on later life will be limited. Much of early experience will not be remembered and will *not* influence later personality development except under two conditions. Insofar as the infant is kept under *continuous restricted* stimulation, whether positive or negative in kind, so that it results in a condition equivalent to (1) above, that is, sensory deprivation and the associated failure to develop recognition and motor skills for the stimuli the infant did not experience. We are here arguing that an infant who was restricted exclusively to stimuli that produced continuous crying would develop no recognition or skills in dealing with a wide variety of neutral or positively toned stimuli and, conversely, that an infant restricted exclusively to stimuli that produced positive affect would develop no recognition or skill in dealing with a wide variety of negative stimuli. The second condition is that the infantile experience is *continuous* with that of childhood and adolescence. The longer the conditions of infantile experience are continued into later life, the more massive the effect of the earliest experience.

Let us consider each of these hypotheses in turn. There is now abundant evidence that the deprivation of early sensory experience seriously impairs recognition and the development of elementary competence. But if deprivation of experience produces later retardation, there is also evidence that infantile experience per se has limited consequences for later development. Consider first an experiment by Campbell and Campbell (1962), who have reported that in a conditioned fear experiment with rats, retention of fear over four retention intervals, 0, 7, 21, and 42 days, varied directly as a function of the age of the rat at the time of conditioning. Rats conditioned at 18 days of age showed no retention of the fear stimulus 21 days after conditioning, while rats conditioned at 100 days of age showed nearly perfect retention after a 42-day interval. This finding was confirmed by a second experiment using a conditioned suppression technique.

On the other hand, in a third experiment it was found that the rate of extinction of fear, in contrast to retention of fear, did not vary as a function of the age of the rat. These latter results we would account for on an interference basis between the same stimulus as the name of the address of shock fear and as the name of fear, no shock. Since neither the old nor the young rat is capable of developing an experimental neurosis on the basis of a self-reproduced fear but is afraid primarily only on a recognition basis, it is relatively easy to extinguish its fear to the same stimulus. In higher forms, the animal is more capable of generating the name of the fear response from within, on a reproduction rather than recognition basis. In man we should expect that extinction of fear would also be more difficult in adulthood than in infancy.

Let us turn now to evidence from a study on human infants. In a study by David Levy (1960), the infant's memory of inoculation by needle was investigated by means of the infant's cry. It was assumed that the infant who remembered a previous inoculation would cry in anticipation of this painful event when brought back to the place where it occurred and submitted to the same doctor, in the same white coat, repeating the same procedure. The total series of records included about 2,000 infants. Of these, 800 infants completed six of the total series of seven inoculations. Subjected to the most rigorous screening criteria, these 800 records were further reduced to about 52 records. Slightly less rigorous criteria yielded another group of 94 cases, and by eliminating another criterion a third group of 69 cases was obtained. Each group was studied separately and compared with the others.

With the exception (at 6 months), memory cries of inoculation were not found in the first 6 months. There was a rising frequency with age, starting at 1 percent at 6 months of age and rising to 20 percent at 12 months. This frequency also depended on the interval of time elapsing between inoculations; the smaller the interval, the more frequent the crying. Up to 8 months, no memory cry occurred after any interval longer than 1 month; up to 12 months, no memory cry occurred after any interval longer than 2 months.

Here we see further evidence for the failure of early experience, in this case of a painful inoculation, to be remembered but a few months afterward. Before 6 months there is virtually no effect of prior experience. We also see evidence, however, for the second hypothesis above—the continuity and repetition of experience is the critical factor in its later effect, since the shorter the time interval between inoculations, the greater the probability of recognition of the needle or the doctor who administered it before. Even as late as 1 year, however, if the interval between inoculations exceeded 2 months, there was no memory cry.

Rovee-Collier, Sullivan Enright, Lucas, and Fagen (1980) have presented evidence consistent with our position. In their experiment, 3-month-old infants learned to activate a crib mobile by means of operant footkicks. Although forgetting is typically complete after an 8-day retention interval, infants who were given a brief exposure to the reinforcer 24 hours after retention testing showed no forgetting after retention intervals of either 2 or 4 weeks. Their findings supported a conclusion "that procedures that improve accessibility to important retrieval cues will radically alter current views of infant memory" and that failures to observe retention in infants should be discussed in terms of retrieval failures rather than memory deficits. The reader may be alarmed at the slender evidence offered for the second hypothesis, which seems to fly in the face of much contemporary doctrine. It has been possible to verify the basic postulate of the continuity of early and late experience again and again in the consulting room and in scores of studies based on the psychoanalytic hypothesis. We do not reject this evidence but we believe it to be accounted for by the second hypothesis: that whenever the parent-child relationship has been consistent over many years and has played a dominant role in the life of the individual, both when he was very young *and* as he continued to develop, then early personality will be similar to later personality.

The controls necessary to test the psychoanalytic hypothesis have rarely been exercised. The similarity of adult personality to infantile personality needs to be examined as a function of the continuity of the parent-child relationship. Variations in such a control series would consist in using parents who changed their attitudes radically at some point, the introduction of new parents through divorce, or foster parents. Further variations might consist of children who developed strong peer relationships compared with those who did not and for whom the weight of parental influence would therefore be less attenuated by other models. Not the least of the problems in the investigation of the hypothesis are the methodological ones. It is very costly to test any developmental hypothesis when one uses human beings as subjects. Ultimately, this is the kind of evidence we must have in order to answer the fundamental questions about human development. There are, however, some alternatives to costly longitudinal studies. We now present two types of investigation that we think will illuminate this question.

THE USE OF PROJECTIVE TESTS IN THE STUDY OF THE DEVELOPMENTAL SEQUENCE

Adler (1912) was the first to argue that one's earliest memory revealed the style of life. If the earliest memory is, as we think, a symbol, a posticipation of what later became magnified as the most typical and important preoccupations of the adult personality, then there should be a significant relationship between one's present personality and one's earliest memories.

McCarter, Tomkins, and Schiffman (1961) tested this hypothesis by a prediction that the salient characteristics of earliest memories would also appear with unusual strength in the adult personality as measured by a projective test, the Tomkins-Horn Picture Arrangement Test. More specifically, it was predicted that if the subject reported an early memory in which he was not alone, his PAT scales of Sociophilia would be elevated. This was confirmed. There was a correlation of .47, significant at the .005 level (with an *n* of 75 Princeton undergraduates).

If the earliest memory represented the subject persevering in some activity despite environmental opposition, he was also elevated on those keys in the PAT that measure high activity, with a correlation of .44, significant at the .01 level. Other predictions were made and tested, but my own predictions were limited to these two.

That there is some relationship between the present personality and the earliest memory is clear. It is not altogether certain, however, from this investigation what that relationship is. We can clarify these relationships somewhat more by the use of the Thematic Apperception Test (TAT).

If we present a slide of the first card of the TAT to a large group of subjects, these subjects characteristically interpret this card in the light of their idiosyncratic past experience. The scene is a young boy looking at a violin. Although the subjects are not instructed to write a story about their own childhood, there is evidence from Markmann (1943) that this is in fact what they do. They have been instructed to write a story about the boy looking at the violin, not about themselves. Indeed, the power of the projective techniques rests in part on this indirection. Instructions to the same subjects to write about this situation as though they were personally involved produces resistance rather than revelation.

How does it happen that the instruction in fact stimulates memory, which is thereby modified in producing a story? And how does it happen that the same scene is adequate to activate memories that are quite different from subject to subject? Is it the case that the stimulus is identical or that some part of the stimulus is identical with each person's past history? This is extremely unlikely. Yet there must be some essential similarity to each person's overt behavioral past history since if we expose a scene that is less commonplace and more bizarre, the correlation with past overt behavior drops sharply and the variability of themes increases. Such pictures are used in the second half of the test to reveal the innermost recesses of the personality—thoughts and wishes that persons may never express in behavior in their lifetimes. Each type of stimulus activates memory but different kinds of memory, depending on the similarity of the scene to what actually happened in a person's past history or on the similarity of the scene to what he or she wished or feared would happen.

Our theory applied to this problem would suggest that the total scene, or some part of it, must function as an analogue of a specific past situation. There can be a good deal of ambiguity in the picture with respect to the specific past history of each subject as long as the subject will try to interpret it. For one subject, the details of the picture happen to fit exactly—he did in fact practice a violin in his own past. For another, who played the piano, the violin plus the youthfulness of the boy is a sufficient name of a name to activate some of the details of how his parents felt about his practicing the piano and how he in turn accepted or rebelled against their wishes and their authority. In this case the picture is not a name but a name of a name; that is, practicing the violin as a youngster cannot bring back a memory of the subject's own practicing the violin, but it can be transformed into a name. In such a case the story is about a boy who plays a violin (in deference to the tester's request that he tell a story about such a scene), but most of the significant details are slightly modified from his own past experience with the piano rather than the violin.

But suppose our subject did not play a violin or a piano or any musical instrument—how can his story refer to his own past history? If his parents were unusually strict with him, the young boy looking at a violin could be a name of his own parents, transformed into the analogue "parents who insist that he play the violin." Once having recovered insistent parents, further recruitment is now possible, and this interpretation can act as a name for idiosyncratic "insistences" in his own past history, which are then transformed into further analogues to meet the present demands, which is to tell a story about a young boy and a violin.

In all of this the stimulus must be both multivalued and specific enough to instigate different memories from each subject. It is as though we said, "Now is the time for all good men . . ." and this were organized into a different cliché for each subject, or could be transformed into different clichés by different subjects. Memories may be tapped directly by names or indirectly in new ways by learning a new name for an old name, which then transforms the memory into an analog. Our interest, however, should not be restricted to what is overtly observable behavior. The question of the impact of early experience requires, above all, an answer to the question of its impact on the individual's feelings and thoughts as well as his overt behavior. Indeed, the value of the classic situation depicted in the first card of the TAT is that the overt behavior of both parent and child is described along with the feelings and thoughts of both, whether overtly expressed or not.

The unexploited potential of this technique for exploring the developmental sequence relatively painlessly lies in the fact that the storyteller not only identifies with the "hero" but identifies differentially as a function of the apparent age of the hero.

Any changes in the influence of the family during the life of the individual may be directly mentioned within a single story. This is common in the stories of those whose relationship with the family has been marked by dramatic changes, which have not escaped the attention of the individual. He is aware of the changes, and this awareness is reflected in his stories.

Frequently, however, these changes are so gradual and each one so slight that the total change is unnoticed. Wherever these changes have been of such a nature as to escape the awareness of the person, they are rarely reflected in any single story. We can discover whether or not such changes are present in the stories only by a comparison of all of the stories told in which a parent and child are the principal characters. In this comparison two important questions should be kept in mind. The first is the question "Is there a difference in the parent-child relationship when the hero is of different ages?" The second is of equal importance: "Can we be certain that the difference we find is a function of the age of the hero in the stories?"

Is the difference in the age of the hero the only factor to which the change in the parent-child relationship may be traced, or is there some other factor, perhaps unrecognized, to which this change may be attributed? If, for example, we were to find in a protocol one story in which a young child is submissive to parental dominance and another story in which a young adult rebels against parental dominance, we might assume that as the child grew older he became more rebellious. If, however, we were to find a third story in which a "young child" is rebellious to parental dominance, we would question whether our assumption that this rebellion was a function of the age of the hero was true. We would then have to reexamine the stories for some factor other than the age of the hero to account for this difference in the hero's reaction.

I employed this type of analysis only after several years of what I must now regard as serious misinterpretation of TAT material. When confronted, in the past, with a protocol in which the hero expressed intense love for his mother in one story and equally intense hatred for her in another, or rebelled against parental dominance in one story and was submissive in another, I assumed this to be evidence of an ambivalent attitude toward the parent or toward parental dominance. Or, to take another example, if the boy (in picture I) regarded the violin as the instrument through which he would achieve fame and worked hard toward this end, whereas the hero of another story was lazy, preferring the life of a hobo to any kind of work, this was regarded as evidence of ambivalence toward "work" in general. This may be the case, but such fine gradations of delineation of the parent-child relationship were found in so many protocols that I grew suspicious and reanalyzed a long series of protocols previously interpreted in this way. It then appeared that the majority of differences in the parent-child relationship found within each protocol could be better explained as an outgrowth of the individual's development. If the age of the hero in each story was considered, there was to be found in the microcosm of fantasy the impress of the individual's actual developmental sequence. If this proves to be the case, the TAT offers us, in a 2-hour period, the possibility of tracing patterns of growth that would otherwise require years of laborious observation and study. This type of exploration might be more easily accomplished if a special series of pictures were employed depicting the parent and child together in a temporal series, graded from infancy to maturity.

Determination of the generality of this type of projection presents an empirical problem of no small dimension, but we believe that further inquiry along these lines will be rewarding.

MODIFICATIONS

In my experience it is certain that such projection into the past is not in every case a "true" reflection of the sequence of development. There are at least two modifications of this mechanism limiting the inferences that may be made from this type of analysis.

First, there are instances in which important factors shaping the development of the adolescent may be projected back into childhood as though these same factors had been in operation earlier than their actual appearance in the individual's development. This is similar to the relationship we assumed between earliest memories and present personality. This type of modification will be discussed in detail in the case of Helmler.

Second, the individual's projection into the past may be a function of his present condition. This is a special case of a general phenomenon; it is well known that the picture of both the past and the future is to some extent a function of the individual's present condition. Thus, frequently when a person is depressed, he finds it impossible to believe that he ever was happy or that he ever will be happy again. We shall see in the case of Eggman how the present may color the past in the TAT. And when an individual's immediate problems seem insoluble or threaten to overwhelm him, he may see all characters, whatever their age, struggling with the same problems.

This second type of modification places even more serious limitation on the inferences that may be made about the developmental sequence, but this is somewhat counterbalanced by the fact that it is easier to detect if we are familiar with the individual's present state, whereas only through a knowledge of the past history of the individual can we be certain whether or not the TAT faithfully mirrors the sequence of development or whether the image is blurred by the modification first mentioned.

THE CASE OF HELMLER

Past History

In a study by White, Alper, and Tomkins (1945) of the personality of an individual whom we called Helmler, there is an example of telescoping in TAT stories. Helmler was frankly unimpressed with his father but very devoted to his mother until the age of 6. By the age of 6 this cathexis had been tempered by the presence of his brother, $5\frac{1}{2}$ years older, who was "a long way off—a man" and who commanded the respect of both parents. Helmler was "irritated" because his older brother's judgement was listened to, and mine was not." He was always the "baby" and dominated and teased by his older brother. Helmler chose him as his earliest masculine model: "When I was quite young I followed closely in my brother's footsteps." In adolescence, however, he was somewhat disillusioned—his brother turned out to be a "grind." His relationship with his mother was further complicated by the problem of the control of bodily impulses. A slip (enuretic) at the age of 3 or 4 in an automobile was the occasion of humiliation sufficient to create a dread of automobiles, overcome only at the age of 18, when he first learned to drive. It also created a strong sympathy for "dogs not yet housebroken." Continence, he reports, was a matter of pride, but there were several slips (enuretic) at 8 years, which occasioned ridicule from his brother. He also reports being "fortunately scared out of" thumb-sucking at 4 or 5. Fingernail biting continued until he was 11; his mother would slap his hands for this. Control of bodily impulses was not easy, and its significance was somewhat emphasized by the presence of the older brother who was so superior to the "baby" in this as well as other accomplishments. At this time, too, a rich fantasy life appears, charged with anxiety. He had fantasies of being observed by God and great fear of punishment when he did anything wrong. His mother, moreover, was beginning to substitute dominance and more difficult expectations in the place of unquestioned admiration. The baby role, while denuded of its rewards, was nonetheless ascribed to him by mother, father, and brother. Helmler was more than willing to drop the role, but his mother was not so willing to relax her nurturant maternal dominance, and so Helmler seems to have experienced, at the age of 6, a striving for independence more typically adolescent. He sought the solution to this problem in the cultivation of his age equals and began to stay away from home. "I played mostly with people at school, not around home. That's my mother's chief complaint, that I was never at home. If we weren't playing, we were involved in something down at school. I never hang around home. I never could understand being homesick. I was always glad to get out in the country in summer."

Although he acknowledges his mother's influence—"copied her likes and dislikes—tastes, almost unconsciously—clothes, as petty as that—music, movies, small things like that I've noticed . . . never stopped to figure out larger things, probably more influenced than I know"—his struggle for individuality emerges in the following statement in his autobiography: "But by and large, I just grew without anything that seemed to me to be the conscious influences on the part of my parents."

Separation from the family was for some time a successful resolution of his problem. He was an active member of the neighborhood gang and at school "managed to keep honor grades throughout and stood close to the top. They elected me class president a few times and I liked to act in the little skits and plays which we presented." But though he sought out his age equals, this relationship could easily be spoiled if it derived in any way from his parents. "The only thing I can remember is resenting friends when my parents tried to make them for me: here's a nice little boy—why don't you play with him?—I didn't like that."

On entering high school, "I began to take an interest in school affairs. In school politics I attained some success, became president of the assembly, of the honor society, of various social science clubs, editor of the year book, and generally active in student affairs." The high point of this period of his life came with a scholarship to a summer camp dedicated to the development of democratic leadership. "The boys ran the camp as far as they could, with expert advice from a fine staff. There was equipment for the development of all sorts of talent, and encouragement to all. Three summers at this camp had a tremendous effect on my personality. I made about fifteen close friends whom I still call close friends. *And in an environment that lacked the watchfulness of home I began to know what it felt like to shift for oneself.* We were all given responsibility and in my last years I was given a good deal of authority as one of the camp leaders." Helmler's vision of the future, as described in his autobiography, further underlines the importance of this experience in shaping his life. "I visualize a world of a few large complementary powers who will be responsible to some competent world organization. I want the United States to play the chief role in this world, and therefore I want the United States to be ruled by competent men. I hope for a world governed by the modern version of the philospher-king—the well educated statesman-politician who is ultimately responsible to the people. I look for a socialist state where wealth is equalized, opportunities spread, and yet where man is not reduced to the average. The 'wise and the just' must be given enough power to rule effectively but not despotically. I like to picture myself in some position of importance in government, such as justice in a high court. I would like to have some power in enforcing and interpreting this complicated social system which would be necessary."

Helmler's adjustment during these years sprang from native intellectual and social ability, but his striving was greatly reinforced by both familial and endopsychic rejection of the "baby role," made especially intolerable by sibling rivalry. Equally important, however, were the substantial rewards for his independent strivings outside the family.

TAT Stories and Interpretation

In the light of this past history, let us examine a few of his TAT stories:

> This picture would mean, ah, brings up the idea of some sort of a story for children perhaps on the tale of a little boy who had some sort of musical talent which he, he showed at an awfully early age, child prodigy perhaps, in, in the violin, and ah a through some change I will have to work that out—some awfully, ah fortunate happening, for instance accidentally, accidental fiddling with a great violin ah, brought him to the attention of some first-rate musician, took an interest in him and, ah here we have him gazing at this violin, dreaming of how happy he would be if he could have the advantages of good training and possess this violin, and this violin becomes the, the, oh, supreme good thing that ever happened to him and, ah we might have the rest of the story built around a struggle for some sort of recognition against, with a conflict of a family perhaps and, ah lack of money and, ah, the fact that he is such an awfully young fellow and nobody will pay any attention to him and that, at the end perhaps we could have him being awarded as the result of some recital a first-rate violin and ah, perhaps opening up a path toward development of his talent but not, nothing very complete or conclusive in the line of success. I don't mean that the end should have him a great violinist acclaimed by thousands or anything like that.
>
> I walked into this apparent hole in the ground and looking with a good deal of wonder when a man walked up to me and said, "Take this and any time you need any help why merely ask it and take your tool and use it whenever danger approaches." I just walked along this . . . well, it was some sort of a shiny metal instrument and moon-shaped with various embossings on it almost like a shield, a small one. And I walked along through, through what seemed to be the path of life passing these various dangers and for each one assuming different exteriors according to my need and protection, sometimes shell of an armadillo, at other times the spines of a porcupine and the scales of a fish and all sorts of horrible obstacles, sometimes webbed feet sometimes to cross water, other times feet equipped for climbing over huge stones. Finally the path went around and led to a, came to a fork in the road. One side seemed to point outward toward the earth and continuation of life and the other one toward more wandering and more knowledge, more experience in the mysteries that I had been through. I don't know which one I took, though. Do I have to decide that? [laughs] . . . Well, I took the one out to the earth and thought perhaps I could make use of some of the allegory and knowledge that I had picked up in my trip.
>
> Oh Mr. Browdin was a share-cropper down in Alabama and he found that his situation was growing rapidly worse and worse and worse as years went on, and he found, somehow he never seemed to be able to make any sort of a profit, any sort of a subsistence level existence out of his land. His land was always bad and somehow or other there was always something coming up, drought or, or sickness or some special need each year or some new tax always took away any extra money that he might have. Finally there is, finally there is quite a bit of excitement around their village when a radical labor agitator comes in and tries to organize the tenant farmers into some sort of union. There is a lawsuit and the planter tries to compel this, this union to go under and the union behind this ah, find Mr. Browdin is one of the best speaking witnesses of their group so they borrow a, borrow a clean collar and clean shirt and clean suit for him and bring him into court and we find him getting instructions from the union lawyer as to how he should act on the witness stand. He gets on the stand and pleads

> eloquently, ah, for some sort of rehabilitation for his group. As the result of a successful trial, ah the, ah, tenant farmers do form a, a substantial organization, which gets them some improvements and a few guarantees for the next year, and in the last scene we have Mr. Browdin and his wife in the men's store buying their own suit and shirt.

Common to each of these stories is Helmler's concern with the achievement of success. In the first story it is "a struggle for some sort of recognition against, with a conflict of a—family perhaps." In the second story, "thought perhaps I could make use of some of the allegory and knowledge that I had picked up in my trip," and in the final story it is through the hero's efforts that there is a "successful trial" and the "tenant farmers do form a substantial organization which gets them some improvements and a few guarantees for the next year." Common also to these stories are the conditions favorable to this achievement. In the first story it is through the fortunate intervention of a benevolent and gifted outsider ("brought him to the attention of some first-rate musician, took an interest in him") and he is later "awarded as the result of some recital a first-rate violin, and ah, perhaps opening up a path toward development of his talent." In the second story an unknown man "walked up to me and said 'take this and any time you need any help why merely ask it and take your tool and use it whenever danger approaches.'" And in the third story, "a radical labor agitator comes in and tries to organize the tenant farmers into some sort of union . . . and we find him getting instructions from the union lawyer as to how he should act on the witness stand."

Success is achieved through competence, but competence requires the instruction and help of one who is already competent. Further, the instructor is an outsider, certainly someone outside the family. We can understand this in light of Helmler's past history. Most of his successes have been achieved outside the family and with the help of others. His success among his age equals, his experience in the summer camp, and his scholarship to Harvard were achieved "in a struggle for some sort of recognition against, with a conflict of a family, perhaps." But the crucial discrepancy in this projection backward into the story of the boy and the violin is that he *did not* receive this external help in his struggle against the family at the time when he was first breaking away from the family, at the age of 6. As we have seen, it was only when he reached summer camp as an adolescent that "in an environment that lacked the watchfulness of home I began to know what it felt like to shift for oneself," But this gratuitous assistance from the wealthy benefactor who supported the camp is projected into his earlier struggles for recognition against his family.

In Helmler's imagination this difference is of small import. He is telling us in effect, in all of these stories, that through the help of the competent outsider he has been enabled to maintain his individuality against the family. It is, however, important for the theory of interpretation to differentiate between fantasy and the actual course of events if we are to use the TAT as an instrument for diagnosis of the developmental sequence.

In addition to the telescoping of adolescent experience seen in the case of Helmler, this particular theme may represent a wish-fulfillment fantasy. The theme of the fairy godmother, universal in folklore, appears to represent the fulfillment of a need common to all children. Markmann (1943), in her study of the relationship between TAT stories and the past history of the storyteller, found that stories told to Picture 1 most frequently reflected the individual's actual past history. However, the benefactor theme—in which the child, through the help of a benefactor, was enabled to succeed—showed the lowest correlation with the actual past history. This was found in one out of every three stories to have no basis in the past history of the individual who told such a story, whereas other themes told to the same picture faithfully represented the childhood of the storyteller.

THE CASE OF EGGMAN

In the following case of a man of 50 whose problems were very acute and seemingly insoluble, we find attribution of his symptoms to the boy in Picture 3.

> A tired child is sleeping on the floor in a sitting position with one hand and his head resting on a bench. The child has evidently fallen asleep while playing on the floor. The child will awaken sooner or later and resume his playing.

Inability to keep awake was not typical of this individual as a child but is his *present* symptom.

Analysis of the temporal dimension must, then, proceed with caution, since there may be a telescoping of the temporal series in backward projections, juxtaposing elements from later life with those of early childhood; or there may be a complete restructuring of the past in terms of an immediate situation whose pressure is so massive that even the distant past is reinterpreted in terms of it. But despite these limitations we have found much evidence to support the hypothesis that stories told to different pictures frequently do, in fact, represent a reliable picture of the individual's developmental sequence.

THE CASE OF MARNA

Let us now turn to cases where external evidence supports evidence based on the TAT stories. Consider the following sequence:

> The small boy hates to play his violin, and his mother has made him practice because she hopes that someday he'll be a great musician. He gets so angry that he breaks the violin and then is sorry because he knows he'll get whipped—and sure enough he does 'cause it was a genuine Stradivarius.
>
> The boy has come home to tell his mother about his marriage—he was out on a drunken spree and married the town's bad girl. She is heartbroken and refuses to allow him to bring home the girl. He has always been dominated by his mother and is very unhappy at her anger and commits suicide. The mother realizing her failing brings home the wife and makes a lady out of her.
>
> The girl has been so watched by her parents that she feels herself going crazy. She has to tell them to the minute where she goes and what she does. Then her mind collapses, and she spends years in an institution before she becomes normal again.
>
> A man is a great artist and is suddenly hit by a mad hysteria to kill—he shows this in his picture that he paints showing one old man lunging at another—then his desire leaves him and he knows that anything bad he feels can just be brought out in his paintings and he'll never do real wrong.

In the first of these stories the hero is a "small boy"; in the second, a "boy"; in the third, a "girl"; and in the final story, a "man." The differences corresponding to these differences in the age of the hero are representative of similar changes in the personality of the young woman who told these stories.

They represent, roughly, childhood and early and late adolescence. The fourth story has been included, although there is no reference to the child-parent relationship, for the light it throws on the later sequelae of this relationship.

Changes in Parental Dominance

The first three stories show a parent–child relationship based on dominance. But there are changes in time. In the first story the child suffers a dominance somewhat limited in scope and intensity. The mother "has made him practice" and later whips him. In the second story "he has always been dominated by his mother," and the mother "refuses to allow him to bring home the girl"; but in the third story, dominance has increased even more, in both scope and intensity: "The girl has been so watched by her parents that she feels herself going crazy—she has to tell them to the minute where she goes and what she does." Not only does the dominance increase in scope and intensity in time, but there are changes in the reason for dominance. In the first story, the mother is dominant because of the hope she cherished for her son. She makes him practice "because she hopes that someday he'll be a great musician," although she whips him because the violin was a "genuine Stradivarius." There is no dominance for the sake of dominance here. In the second story "she is heartbroken and refuses to allow him to bring home the girl" again because she was the "town's bad girl," presumably frustrating her aspirations for her son. Although in part responsible for her son's suicide, she is able to realize her failing and "brings home the wife and makes a lady out of her." In this story the mother, again, is not pictured as someone who is domineering for the sake of domineering. In the third story, however, the parents—and this time it is not the mother but both parents—are presented as unreasonably domineering and with no other motive clear.

Changes in the Child's Reaction to Dominance

The *child's reaction* to this dominance exhibits more striking changes in time. The most striking change appears between childhood and adolescence. In the first story the child is openly aggressive and "breaks the violin." He also does something of which the mother disapproves in the second story; he marries the town's bad girl. But in the third story there is no evidence of rebellion. Moreover, defiance of the mother's wishes in the second story lacks the spontaneity of expression seen in the first. There is no mention of anger in the second story or even of hating the mother's dominance, and, second, the hero is portrayed on a drunken spree, which seems to be a condition of his defiance. It is explicitly contrasted with his normal state, in which "he has always been dominated by his mother." We see here the beginning of inhibition of selfassertion and aggression that is completed in the third story.

Changes in the Hero's Reaction to His Own Defiance

The *hero's reaction to his own defiance* has also changed. In the first story the hero is not at all worried about the mother's feelings; his only concern is the whipping he may get—"then he is sorry because he knows he'll get whipped." In the second story, however, concomitant with the reduction in spontaneity and freedom of expression of his defiance, his whole concern is with his mother's reaction—"He has always been dominated by his mother and is very unhappy at her anger." It is a concern with the mother's state, rather than the consequences of the state, as it was in the first story. Had the logic of the first story remained unchanged, the *consequences* of her anger, forbidding him to bring the girl home, rather than his unhappiness at her anger as such, would have caused him to commit suicide. Further reactions in this chain show similar changes. In the first story he is punished, and that is all. In the second story he invokes the mother's anger, which is a variety of punishment that makes him unhappy, but the reaction to this is self-destruction. In the third story, extreme parental dominance brings about mental collapse, which is not a striving but the end result of complete submission to extreme dominance.

These changes, then, are from overt aggression against limited dominance and punishment that is tolerated to inhibited aggression against greater dominance and maternal anger that cannot be tolerated, leading to self-destruction; and finally the most extreme dominance and complete inhibition of aggression, complete submission and mental collapse.

The Fourth Story

The end of the third story leads naturally to the fourth. In a mental institution away from the parents, the girl becomes normal again. In the fourth story, with no parent figures present and the hero now a "man," he learns that "anything bad he feels can just be brought out in his paintings and he'll never do real wrong." We are told, then, that in later life aggression that could not be expressed toward the parents without fear of ultimate self-destruction or insanity may be sublimated in painting. The changes delineated in these stories are a faithful picture of this young woman's actual development.

THE CASE OF KAROL

Let us consider the next three stories told by another young woman Karol, in which the hero is a child and then a young adult.

For a long time the little boy has been wishing he could have a violin. His parents have at last bought him one, and he takes great pleasure in just sitting and admiring it. He dreams of the day when he will be older and capable of making beautiful music with it after he has practiced for a long while. The violin will give him pleasure and relaxation when he is older and has mastered it.

Sally has always been a dreamer. When she was small, it didn't matter so much, but now that she is 12 her mother is getting worried about her dreams of greatness and of doing wonderful things. Sally talks about extraordinary things she plans to do someday, and won't keep her mind on the things at hand, such as school. Her mother tries to divert her attention by reading to her and buying her dolls to play with, but though she is polite enough to listen and cooperate with her mother, she finds no joy in ordinary childish pleasures. Sally's father realizes that her dreams may be turned into something practical, so he encourages her to become a nurse, which Sally realizes is a truly great profession. She is willing to study when she grows older with such an aim in view.

Since Peg was a little girl she had been babied by her mother so that when she grew up to be 21 she was dependent on her mother for advice on everything. Peg's father had little to say in the matter, for like most fathers, he was "too busy." After finishing her education, Peg decided she would just stay home and look after her mother. Here is where the father came in. One evening the family was seated in the living room, and the subject of Peg's future came up. The mother said she wanted her daughter to stay home and be domestic. The father walked over to the couch where mother and daughter were sitting, and said to Peg, "What you need is a good spanking to make you wake up to all the opportunities open to girls these days." This speech shocked her mother, but it set Peg to thinking. The more she thought about it, the more she wanted to get out and see what she could do. In spite of her mother she did manage to get out of her over-solicitous control, and she got a job in which she did very well.

Changes in the Characterizations of the Parents

First story. Let us first consider the changes in the characterization of the parents as the individual grows from childhood to maturity. When the hero is a little boy, in the first story, the parents are not differentiated into mother and father. They are "his parents." Their impact on the child's life is a limited one. They neither instigate his wishes nor attempt to control them in any way. Ministering to the wishes of the child is their sole function. This, however, is not done immediately. The child has wished for the violin a long time, and it is not until this wish has endured a "long time" that the parents "at last" bought him one. But having given the child what he wanted, they play no further role in his life.

Second story. In adolescence, as portrayed in the second story, the role of the parents has changed considerably. Not only have they been differentiated into mother and father, but each parent exerts a very different influence on the adolescent's life. Parental impact on the adolescent is much greater than it was in childhood. The continuation into adolescence of childish characteristics is the explanation for this—characteristics that "didn't matter so much" when she was small and that, as we have also seen in the first story, were unnoticed by the parents at that time. But these now mobilize anxiety on the part of the mother and force her to play a more active role toward her daughter. The mother tries to divert her attention but is unsuccessful because she doesn't really understand her daughter. This lack of understanding was not explicit in childhood but might have been inferred from the role attributed to the parents in the first story. But the father has come, in adolescence, to play a new role. This may be explained in part by the influence of puberty, since at that time this young woman saw her father, for the first time, to be a "man," as she expressed it in her autobiography. The father is seen as less anxious and more intelligent in his insight; he encourages her to turn her energies into those channels that will provide the conditions necessary for her further development.

Third story. In the third story, the contemporary picture of the role of the mother and father is presented. This portrayal presents a difficult problem in interpretation. The mother is said to have "babied" her daughter since she was a little girl. Actually, this is not the case. The historical sequence presented by the first two stories represents the actual course of events. Why then, in this story dealing with the contemporary situation, has this sequence, mirrored faithfully to this point, suffered such restructuring? Our hypothesis is that this represents a consequence of her present wish for independence, in the manner in which someone who has just fought with a friend may convince himself that the person now detested was never a true friend, that he never really liked him. We have seen before that this process of reconstruction of the past in terms of the present situation may reach back and distort characteristics of the past as they appear in TAT stories. The process in her case has not spread to those stories in which the picture presents a child, but it has influenced those stories in which the figures in the picture represent a contemporary situation. This, in short, is her present view of her past history. Craving independence, she feels her relationship with her mother is too dependent, that her mother stifles her and, further, that this has always been so. The role of the father has also changed somewhat. He is still the more intelligent of the parents, but now the opposition between the parents has become clearer and more profound. The father not only understands his daughter better, but he appears to have a less selfish attitude toward her future. The mother "wanter her daughter to stay home and be domestic" and to continue her complete dependence. But in adolescence the mother was "worried" about the child and, though not understanding, tried to remedy the arrested development of her childish adolescent daughter. Today, however, the mother is seen to be not only responsible for this arrested development but insistent that her daughter continue in this state of dependence. The father's intervention in adolescence was more successful than the mother's attempts but not in contradiction with the mother's ultimate purpose. Both parents were equally worried about her childlike characteristics. But in the contemporary situation the father's intervention "shocked her mother." These differences in part reflect actual growing opposition between the parents, but they are also derived in part from the fact that she now faces the prospect of cutting the umbilical cord and leaving home and feels her father to be more interested than her mother in her ultimate well-being.

Changes in the Personality of the Hero

First story. Let us consider the changes in the personality of these heroes. The child is full of longing, directed not toward the parents but toward the violin. He is dependent on the parents only insofar as they are instrumental in securing for him what he lacks. But in this respect he is the passive personality who waits for the action of others to satisfy his needs. When granted the object of his wishes, his reaction is on the perceptual level—"sitting and admiring it"—an aesthetic appreciation rather than an active manipulation. His activity is limited in effectiveness by his years. Turning to the level of irreality and daydream, he projects into the future because of his lack of competence as a child. Achievement is thought to be the exclusive possession of the adult or at least the older person. But as a child he possessed the realistic awareness that means-end activity was a necessary prelude to competence and enjoyment of his potentialities "after he has practiced for a long while." Thus, "he dreams of the day when he will be both older and capable of making beautiful music with it." But he recognizes that age and capability are not sufficient conditions of mastery, for these are qualified by "after he has practiced a long while." Thus, although the hero as a child is passive, requiring the activity of the parent on his behalf, and although there is an aesthetic response rather than active manipulation and a turning to the level of daydreaming rather than behavior, he yet envisions a change in his future potentialities and competence. He will work hard when he gets older, and by virtue of both his age and his industry he will be "capable of making beautiful music." But the evaluation of this future achievement contains no social referent; neither the parent nor humanity in general inspires this future effort, nor do they profit from it. It remains a solipsistic venture yielding the future adult "pleasure and relaxation." The achievement of "making beautiful music" is valued for no more than might be achieved through masturbation. It is, in fact, not uncommon for the playing of the violin to symbolize sexual experience. We lack sufficient evidence to know whether it is true in this case.

Second story. In adolescence the hero is still a dreamer and "has always been a dreamer," but this is now symptomatic of arrested development. Puberty did, in fact, intensify her cathexis for the level of irreality. This is, of course, not uncommon in adolescence, but since this adolescent characteristic was superimposed on a long-established habit of daydreaming, the resultant was a withdrawal more marked than is customary at this time. The content of the daydream has become more extravagant and less realistic. It is now "extraordinary things" that she "plans to do someday." Missing is the expectation of hard work and the knowledge of the means-end relationship. Achievement is still put off into the future, but there is a change in her communicativeness; she now "talks" about it to others. But the most important change is in the fact that the daydreaming now has socially conspicuous consequences—"she won't keep her mind on the things at hand, such as school." There is more overt interaction with her mother—"she is polite enough to listen and cooperate with her mother"—but this is a very superficial interaction, for "she finds no joy in ordinary childish pleasures." The wish to enjoy adult pleasures that we saw in her childhood has continued into adolescence, but the path toward the fulfillment of this wish is less certain and less realistic. It is only through her father's intervention that she is restored to the former confidence in her own future and to her previous understanding that means-end activity is necessary for achievement. Finally, she regains her willingness to work "when she grows older."

We see that even as an adolescent she considers herself incapable of beginning the work she feels is necessary to achieve her goal. Since the goal is an adult one and not a "childish pleasure," she cannot begin to strive till she is an adult. The intervention of the father has, however, effected an important difference in this goal. As a child, goal achievement was measured in terms of personal "pleasure and relaxation." This aspiration has been socialized by the father, and she now realizes that nursing "is a truly great profession." If a sexual symbolism is involved, one might suppose that the solitary pleasure of masturbation has been transformed into a sexual aim with a human object, through the agency of puberty and new interest between father and daughter. But whether or not this is the case, the father has been instrumental in turning the adolescent dream toward social reality.

Third story. The daughter as a young adult of 21 is a somewhat different person. We have previously discussed the reasons for this. In part it is the consequence of the hypertrophied level of irreality and daydream. The daydream that inspired her childhood was somewhat responsible for the arrest of development at adolescence, but continuing into adulthood, it has produced a 21-year-old "baby," "dependent on her mother for advice on everything." The heroine attributes this to the fact that "since Peg was a little girl she had been babied by her mother." It is not attributed, as it should be and as it was before, to her own daydreaming but to her mother—the same mother who became worried about her daughter for the first time in adolescence and who, though incompetent, meant to help her daughter escape from infantilism. Although this is her present picture of how her mother has always behaved, we have seen that this restructuring is something the individual does not altogether believe is true—otherwise the actual historical sequence could not have been projected so faithfully in her first two stories. In those cases in which the past is completely restructured, there is no evidence in the backward projections of the actual historical development of the child-parent relationship. Evidence from other sources indicates that in all probability she pictures her mother as responsible for her infantilism because it is now completely unacceptable to her, having reached the age of adulthood, when, according to her childhood dream, she should have been "making beautiful music" and when, according to her adolescent dream, she should have been "willing to study" with "an aim in view." The mother has in effect become a scapegoat, to relieve the daughter of the unacceptable consequences resulting from an excessive immersion in fantasy. But in addition to this, she has been drawing closer and closer to her father, and in her mind this involves rejection of the mother on the part of both father and daughter. The father's suggestions "shocked the mother," but in adolescence the same suggestion had no such effect, since the mother shared the father's interest in helping the daughter establish realistic social contact with her environment. There has been throughout the three stories an identification with the father, which is implicit in the first story, is openly avowed in adolescence, and culminates in opposition between father, daughter, and mother in adulthood. Evidence suggestive of the family romance was also found in the other stories and autobiography. The third story tells us in effect that only as a young adult did she face this conflict openly. As a child there was the dream of playing an adult role. As an adolescent the father sustained the dream, and today her father will help her achieve the dream against the opposition of her mother. Though it shocked the mother and "in spite of her mother," she did manage to get out of her oversolicitous control. With her father's help and openly breaking with her mother, the adult heroine, just come of age, "got a job in which she did very well." This is the first reference to actual achievement. It is no longer placed in the future. This story represents a very recent change in her orientation. She does in fact plan in the very near future to follow the example of her heroine. It is noteworthy that the heroine is 21 years old, whereas Karol is not quite 21.

THE CASE OF LANS

The following three stories show the developmental sequence of an individual's increasing hostility toward his parents.

> Little Johnny looked forward to a pleasant day outside playing baseball with his pals. Before he got halfway to the front door, Mother grabbed him and led him by the arm into the music room, and sat him down in front of a violin. "Practice your lesson for an hour or you can't go out to play today." Johnny sat and looked tearfully at the violin. What will the outcome be? Very simple—he will practice for an hour on the violin.
>
> They were seated around the dinner table. Father and son were violently arguing. Father was very angry. Junior's grades were not what they should be. Father sent Junior from the table when Junior remarked on father's grades during the days of his youth. Junior retired to his room angrily and finally was practically dissolved into tears when he thought of the injustice of it all. He was hungry too. After a while, Father knocked on the door and came in. He put his arm around the boy, and Junior leaned on his shoulder feeling exceedingly sorry for himself. Father did not scold. He talked in a quiet voice and told the boy to please try to work harder in school. Junior relented and promised. He actually believed that he would. And at first he did, but gradually lapsed back into laziness again.
>
> Joel came in the door. He was mad. His father could see that very plainly. The usual chip was on his shoulder. He must have a talk with Joel. He must learn to be more even-tempered and not fly off at any small thing. The father said, "Joel, come here, son, I want to talk to you." Joel said, "I know what you're going to say, Father, but I can't do anything. Please Father, it's no use. Some other time," and left the room.

Changes in the Expression of Aggression

We have seen before that anger, freely expressed in childhood, may later suffer severe inhibition. In these stories the opposite developmental sequence is illustrated. In the first story the hero's reaction to parental dominance is one of tearful compliance. In the second story paternal dominance evokes anger, but the hero retires to his room at his father's insistence. There is again a regression to the original response. He "finally practically dissolved into tears when he thought of the injustice of it all." The father then comes in and puts his arm around the boy, and as a result the boy determines to work harder in school, although he "gradually lapsed back into laziness again." That this individual should be divided within himself between anger and tears is probably a result of his father's oscillation between stern dominance and sympathetic nurturance. In the third story, however, the hero has come to terms with his conflict. He is now capable of expressing more unambivalent anger: "He was mad. His father could see that very plainly. The usual chip was on his shoulder. He must have a talk with Joel. He must learn to be more even-tempered and not fly off at any small thing." In response to his father's dominance he "left the room" but not to dissolve in tears. The hero has accepted his own personality with all of its limitations and will not allow himself to be swayed by his father. "I know what you're going to say, Father, but I can't do anything. Please, Father, it's no use. Some other time," and he left the room.

THE CASE OF BRINT

In the following two stories there is a delineation of the development of an ego ideal.

> Joe has been given one of his greatest wishes. A violin. He had, during his short life, dreamt of becoming a great violinist. Strange, he never knew why, but he did. But now that he had received this precious gift, he realized his future task would not be as easy as his dream. It meant work, hard work, long hours of toil and probably agony for everyone else, but he was still very young, and his mind was set, and his heart and mind were as determined as his face. And he'll reach his goal; I feel sure of that!
>
> It's only natural for a son to want to follow in his father's footsteps—or is it? Well, in the case of young Dick it was so. His father was a surgeon, and Dick had watched many operations. His mother didn't approve of that, but she did wish her son to follow his father. Dick didn't care about being famous; he just wanted to help people, and the sooner he could get to it the better. He was still very young, but he could do it, he would do it—and he did!

The hero in both stories is driven by an ideal that determines his life. It is of little moment that one of these wishes is to be a violinist, and one is to be a surgeon. These differences may be attributed to the fact that the first story was told to the picture of the boy and the violin and the second to the awareness of the origin of the ego ideal. In the first story the child does not know: "Strange, he never knew why but he did." But in the second story he is clearly aware of its origin: "It's only natural for a son to want to follow in his father's footsteps—or is it? Well, in the case of young Dick it was so." Although aware of this origin, the remarks of the subject—"or is it?"—suggest some question of the naturalness of this aspiration. A young woman told these stories, and the fact that "his mother didn't approve of that" may indicate anxiety about identification with the father against the mother's wishes and may further explain why the younger boy did not understand the origin of his dream of becoming a great violinist. Whatever the meaning, it is clear that there has been an important change in both awareness of the origin of his dream and in its direction: "he just wanted to help people, and the sooner he could get to it the better." He is no longer interested, as he was in his career as a violinist, in "being famous." The ideal of becoming a great violinist had a less social meaning; there was no mention either of an audience or of giving pleasure through his playing or pleasing his parents.

There is also an increased confidence that the goal may be attained. In the first story success is placed in the future, and the storyteller is "sure" he'll reach his goal: "He'll reach his goal, I feel sure of that!" But in the second story success is actually achieved in the future: "He was still very young, but he could do it, he would do it, and he did!" These differences again reflect the importance of the avowed identification with the father as the hero matures.

THE CASE OF FRANK

The following two stories are representative of a not uncommon sequence concerning the emancipation of the child from parental ego idealism.

> The little boy has just been told that he must practice on his violin and is looking at it with hatred, for he knows there is a baseball game going on outside. After a while he will pick up the violin and practice without any thought of what he is doing but just go through the motions of it without any thought.
>
> The young man's mother had planned on her son becoming a great physician as his father had been. After going through pre-medical school he realizes that he will never make a good surgeon,

> for he cannot bear to see others in pain. He knows that he will be a great baseball player if he wants to devote his energy to it. He tells his mother of his great chance to become a member of a professional team. When he breaks the news to her, her dreams are shattered. But realizing that her son is at an age where he must make his own decisions, she consents. It, of course, hurts the son to grieve his mother, but he must go ahead with the work he loves to become a great hero on the baseball diamond. Later the mother is to find joy in seeing her son being cheered by millions.

The mother is a dominant figure in both stories. In the first story, "The little boy has just been told that he must practice on his violin"; and in the second story, "The young man's mother had planned on her son becoming a great physician as his father had been." As a little boy he pays lip service to the maternal dictate—"go through the motions of it without any thought." He "is looking at it with hatred," however, because there is a baseball game going on outside. In the second story he realizes that the career planned for him by his mother is not for him. There is neither "hatred" nor mechanical compliance. Although it shatters the mother's dreams, he tells her of his plans to become a professional baseball player, which is what his mother would not allow him to do when he was younger. He eventually not only achieves his goal but proves that he was right and his mother wrong in her plans: "Later the mother is to find joy in seeing her son being cheered by millions." His mechanical compliance with maternal dominance in early childhood has been transformed into an assertion of his own individuality and a realization of the potentialities previously so misunderstood by his mother.

In these few samples of temporal sequences we have seen that, quite apart from later changes in personality, which are a resultant of the diminution of interaction with parents, there may be marked changes in attitudes of both child and parent within the family setting as they adjust to each other's increasing age. Stable inflexible parent-child relationships there are, but development is the typical characteristic of the maturing child and may temper the rigidity of the parent's later years.

What light has the TAT thrown on the theory of memory and on our hypothesis that early experience influences later experience only to the extent to which there is continuity in such experience on the part of both the parent and the child?

First, we have seen that developmental sequences, which in retrospect would certainly have seemed to confirm the psychoanalytic assumption of the continuity of early and late experience, and the dependence of the adult personality on early experience may in fact be negative evidence if we start from childhood and move toward adulthood, rather than conversely. Thus, Lans was tearfully angry as a child but more intensely and overtly angry toward his parents as he grew older.

Marna, in contrast, also begins with open defiance and breaks the violin, albeit with later regret. As this young woman develops, the overt expression of her aggression is more and more curbed but expressed indirectly in painting. The actual developmental sequence in these two cases might easily have been switched with no great violation to psychoanalytic expectation. We are arguing not that the early experience had no effect on the developmental sequence but that this effect was indeterminate until later experience strengthened some possibilities and attenuated others, in accordance with our theory of magnification.

This technique, however, has a serious deficiency for a crucial test of the psychoanalytic hypothesis.

We have seen that there is some element of risk in this procedure owing to the retroactive selective effect of recency on the interpretation and memory of the past. The distortion to which this technique is vulnerable favors the psychoanalytic hypothesis. A negative verdict based on such techniques, however, would constitute crucial negative evidence, since continuity of the past with the present is a consequence of the heavier weight of recency over primacy when memory becomes selective.

The second lesson that may be drawn from this evidence is that the individual may "know" more about his own developmental sequence than he can say to himself or others. Individuals vary very much in the extent to which they have summarized for themselves or others their own developmental sequence. It is the exception rather than the rule that even the major trends of all the changes that together constitute development are logged on a continuous memory drum and trendanalyzed. This is why we must rely on indirect techniques. Only occasionally, when the critical choice points have been illuminated by sustained endopsychic scrutiny, can the individual give a coherent account of his life course. When this has happened, we may find it reflected within the outlines of a single fantasy. In such a case the individual has become his own psychologist, and our work has thereby been reduced. This is, however, a very exceptional state of affairs, and therefore we must ordinarily rely on more indirect techniques. The individual, however, knows more about himself than either he or psychologists have realized. There are many names of names that can be tapped to produce unsuspected retrievals. The picture, which the subject has never before seen in his life, is quite capable of acting as a name of a name, something that will recall something, which will recall something he didn't know he knew. Powerful as the projective technique is in activating long quiescent traces, it is not the most effective method. Let us turn now to another method, which we regard as holding the promise of radically increasing retrieval of isolated memory traces.

Chapter 50

Factors Governing the Activation of Early Memories

THE EXPERIMENTAL PRODUCTION OF REGRESSION

We will assume that the relationship between early memories and later memories may be continuous or discontinuous and that new learning therefore may proceed by transformations upon older memories or by the assembling of relatively new components, which result in the deposition of relatively independent traces and names of traces. Further, accessibility of these traces will vary as a consequence of the relative continuity or discontinuity of learning and the stored traces resulting from learning. We will attempt to delineate the specific conditions under which we should be able to retrieve memories of early experience and the conditions under which this may not be possible. In this connection Freud's view was not altogether dissimilar. He likened the past experience of an individual to an old city that had been successively rebuilt over the centuries. He thought, therefore, that the psychological archaeologist should not expect to find the city as it was before these transformations. But at the same time he elsewhere insisted on the possibility of both continuing fixation and historical regression to objects and stages of fixation.

Before examining our theory in more detail we will present an experimental test of the theory in which we were successful in the prediction of retrieval of early memories. In the light of this evidence we will examine the details of the theory, since in this case it is easier to proceed from the concrete to the abstract than conversely.

The experiment is as follows: The subject is required to write his name very slowly, at a rate approximately three seconds per letter. A metronome may be used to pace the writing if the individual finds it difficult to slow down his writing or to estimate the time accurately. Under these conditions there are two notable consequences. First, the handwriting closely resembles that of childhood rather than his present handwriting, if he is now an adult. Long-forgotten ways of forming letters are reproduced. For example, if the letter *r* is now written *r* and it was formerly written, the latter is reproduced. If the letter *E* is now written and it was formerly written *e*, the latter is now reproduced. Matching of such handwriting to earlier samples has confirmed the general impression of our subjects concerning the similarity of the handwriting, under these conditions, to the actual earlier handwriting. This performance is characteristically unconscious in the sense that it is only after the writing is finished that it is recognized as earlier handwriting. Nor is the handwriting the only set of early memories tapped by this method. Some subjects hold the pencil as they did earlier, more tightly and exerting more pressure on the paper. In some cases there is also retrieval of early memories of the first-grade schoolroom and the firstgrade teacher. In one case the subject looked at me very quizzically. Inquiry finally revealed that I had "reminded" him of his early teacher. The second consequence of this method is a decreased variability of handwriting between all subjects. Most of the idiosyncratic characteristics that distinguish one adult's handwriting from that of another are lost.

Let us now consider a second experiment of this general type. In this experiment a subject is asked to perform before a group. He is asked to shout at the top of his voice the phrase "No, I won't!" In contrast to the handwriting experiment not all subjects are able or willing to do this. Some of these later admitted that the idea produced fear or shame. Some said they didn't know why they couldn't. Some said they would not say why they would not do this. Most subjects, however, do comply with the request, after overcoming varying degrees of reluctance. The consequences of this performance are varied. On the faces of most adults, the lower lip is protruded immediately after speaking, giving the appearance of a defiant, pouting child. Spontaneously emitted reports from many subjects indicate a reexperience of childish affect of distress and anger, with recollection of long-forgotten specific incidents in which such affect was evoked. Other subjects whose faces expressed the smile of triumph rather than a pout reported feelings of joy and anger rather than of distress and anger. These latter frequently reported that the experience was therapeutic and liberating and that in the weeks following the experiment they were often reminded of it and enjoyed these recollections deeply.

So much for the successes of this method. There were also about 5 percent of subjects who complied but in whom the method failed to give any evidence of retrieval of early memories. In the case of handwriting, these were subjects who characteristically wrote very slowly and carefully as adults. In the case of shouting, these were subjects who characteristically shouted as adults (e.g., barkers, and housewives who controlled their children in this way).

Let us now examine the theory of memory upon which these experiments were based.

First, we are dealing here with highly organized performances that have at some time in the life of the individual been under his control and that could be repeated at will.

Second, both skills together have been practiced for the lifetime of the individual, which ensures ready access to memories of these types.

Third, the present form of the performance is discriminably different from the earlier performance. Writing one's name meets this criterion, since the shape of the letters is characteristically different for early and late writing. This is less obvious in the case of speech, though more refined analyses would reveal similar differences. It was our impression that the speech regressed to a higher pitch, but we did not use wave analysis.

Fourth, there are at least two aspects of both early and late performance, which co-vary so that early performance is characterized by one value of each parameter and the later performance by a different value of each parameter. In the case of handwriting the early performance is slow, the late performance more rapid. The other co-varying parameter is in fact a *set* of parameters that produces the more regular script, which we will examine later. In the case of speech, the early performance is louder than the late performance. Pitch appears to be one of a set of co-varying other parameters. If the early and late performance varied in one aspect alone, then this might be used to retrieve the early performance, but this would then be the only difference between the two performances. This would mean that early handwriting would resemble late handwriting except for a difference in speed.

Fifth, each of the names of one parameter must be distinctive for early performance and distinctive for late performance. If speed were not different in early and late handwriting, then speed would not be part of a distinctive name but of an alternative set name. In this case the name of some other parameter would have to be found to retrieve early and late handwriting. If early handwriting was slow or fast or either, and late handwriting was slow but differed in shape, then speed would not be an essential part of a distinctive name and would not enable the retrieval of early handwriting. The differential speed instruction is an essential part of the distinctive name that will retrieve the early handwriting, but it is not a sufficient name. A sufficient name in this case is a distinctive conjoint name that includes at least three components (a) write, (b) slowly, and (c) your name. Whereas (b) is the critical part of the distinctive name, (a) and (b) are also necessary components. None of these components is a sufficient name for early handwriting. Thus, the instruction to write, without further specification, might produce doodling. The instruction "write your name" would ordinarily produce the adult signature. The instruction to write slowly might produce slow doodling but in the adult form. The instruction "slowly," or even "do something slowly," would be insufficient to recover early handwriting. These other components then are not names of the traces we wish to activate. Indeed, one subset "write your name" activates just those traces in which we are not interested. An adequate description of the correct type of name we need in this case is a conjoint distinctive name, which is a group of names that together are capable of activating one and only one trace.

The inclusion in a conjoint distinctive name of subsets that are conjoint distinctive names of the later performance is quite advantageous for ease of retrieval of the earlier traces. Because the subset "write your name" is a conjoint distinctive name for the late performance, the subject who might otherwise have had difficulty in initiating appropriate retrieval processes proceeds boldly and with confidence to a task, most of which, as described, is a familiar everyday achievement. The instruction "slowly" he uses as an operator on the distinctive conjoint name for the *late* performance. If the subject is asked to write his name as he did when he first learned to write, he characteristically disclaims knowledge of how to do this. When he begins to write his name slowly, he has no intention whatever of retrieving the traces of the early performance. He is entirely surprised at the outcome of his slow handwriting. What he tries to do is to use the speed component of the conjoint instruction as an operator on a set with which he is quite familiar. This conjoint instruction happens to be a name of a name. He did not, as a child, use this type of instruction at all, since he did not then know how to write fast and certainly did not know how to write his present adult signature. Therefore, a more accurate description of our instruction is that it is a conjoint distinctive name of a name. That this is so can be shown by a slight variation on our instruction, which produces handwriting that in one respect is different from any past performance but in all other respects is identical with early handwriting. Thus, if we instruct the subject to write his name on a blackboard in giant letters 3 feet high, we also recover early handwriting. The reason for this is that the operator "letters 3 feet high" also produces a slowing of the rate of writing and the high density of reports to messages characteristic of most early learning.

We will now consider why this technique works at all and why the same speed technique does not work with speech, whereas a change in intensity is effective.

It is generally the case that early learning involves monitoring with a high density of reports[1] to messages, and later learning involves monitoring with a lower ratio of reports to messages. In early learning the individual is aware of many more messages, one of which is the set that is potentially available to consciousness, than he is in late learning. This is so because he must examine more possibilities than he will eventually use and because once he has selected the appropriate output and feedback messages to monitor, they will be speeded in emission and reduced in the amount of detail necessary to monitor the process.

It should therefore be possible in general to reintegrate earlier learning by increasing the density of reports to messages. This difference in density of reports to messages between early and late learning is usually linked to differences in speed, since the reduction of reports to messages enables any performance to be speeded. The relationship between speed and density of reports is, however, somewhat more complex than this would suggest. While it is true that a radical discontinuity in density of reports enables an equally radical discontinuity in speed between early and late performance, the converse may also be true. Many performances are reduced in their density of reports only *because* they have been speeded. Thus, most of us learn to ride a bicycle skillfully only if we first speed up our performance. Handwriting is an intermediate case. We must learn it first slowly. The speeded type of writing is in effect a different skill, somewhat discontinuous with the slow, early even handwriting. We have noted before that most individuals write much more alike at slow speed than they will later when they write more rapidly. A handful of individuals, usually very thoughtful, cautious, and somewhat overcontrolled, never do relinquish control over the

[1] Reports are neural messages transformed into conscious form.

steady, even handwriting that must be surrendered to achieve the more individualistic speeded type of handwriting. Among our small sample of signatures at the slow rate that do not differ from the adult form is one university president, one mathematician, and one obsessive neurotic. Ordinarily, however, the two performances are discontinuous in several respects. Since this discontinuity is speed-linked, our particular instruction is effective in retrieving the only set of stored traces that has a program for guiding the slow movements of the hand in writing the name.

Why is a similar instruction not effective in retrieving early speech and its associated affect? First of all, speed in speech, whether early or late, unskilled or skilled, is quite variable. In writing, the variance in speed within early and late performance is quite restricted compared with the variance between early and late performance in speech. In short, one has learned to speak both slowly and rapidly as a child and as an adult. In this respect it differs from both bicycle riding and handwriting. There is a small class of individuals who are somewhat like our adult slow writers. Their speech is characteristically measured and unhurried, and for these an instruction to speak rapidly would probably retrieve early speech if it was possible to evoke compliance. They are different from our slow writers, however, in that their speech was probably more variable in speed during their childhood than it has become in adulthood. The probability is high that these individuals learned to restrict their more impulsive rapid bursts of speech sometime during their childhood. For this reason, in contrast to adult slow writers, it might be possible to retrieve this earlier speech. Generally, however, in order to retrieve the earlier speech of most individuals one must discover a more widely distributed discontinuity, which is uniquely linked to the speech of childhood, on the one hand, and to the speech of adulthood on the other. The most critical such discontinuity is the loudness or intensity of speech. While children speak at varying levels of intensity, the variance of intensity is required to be much reduced in adulthood. Children's loud speech is under steady negative pressure from parents and teachers who insist that the child lower his voice. Eventually, this program is successful in producing an adult who rarely shouts.

Because of this discontinuity, the instruction to shout at the top of the voice is effective, whereas an instruction to speak more slowly or more rapidly is not. It is, however, not effective for those who continue to shout as adults. In general, the more the voice was soft-spoken in adulthood, the more this method unlocked a flood of early memories if there was compliance. This raises the critical question of the nature of the "operator." Just as there are individuals who never "progress" to fast handwriting, there are also those who will not or cannot shout. In the case of handwriting the transition from slow to rapid performance ordinarily involved no massive negative affect. Most of us wanted to write more rapidly. However, most of us did not want to lower our voices, and varying sanctions were employed in teaching us this control. For some, undoubtedly, intense fear or shame was activated as a technique of control. This is particularly likely to have been the case if noisy counteraggression was the first response to the demand for modulation of the voice or the demand for silence. If the increase in intensity of shouting was itself countered by more severe sanctions, which eventually produced terror or humiliation in the child, then the stage is set for a reactivation of this affect when, as an adult, he is confronted with an experimenter who requires that he shout something calculated to reactivate aggressive defiance. If the negative affect that was responsible for the discontinuity in modulation is retrieved by the instruction itself, the individual may be unable to comply. We found several such subjects among our normal sample. More commonly, however, there was shyness, which was overcome when other subjects performed and their performance ended in general laughter. This latter might also have acted as a name that retrieved those happier occasions when the parent was amused at childish caprice. Uniformly, the most reluctant subjects experienced the most therapeutic retrieval of early affect. Some subjects spontaneously volunteered, several weeks later, the information that they found both the experience itself, as well as the aftereffects, surprisingly rewarding.

Let us now examine more closely the interactions between early and late learning. One of the outstanding characteristics of these two performances is their almost complete segregation one from the other. There has been for some years a debate concerning the relative importance of primacy and recency in memory, paralleled in personality theory by a debate concerning the importance of early and later experience in personality development. The evidence from the independent coexistence of two memory skills illuminates a somewhat paradoxical status for early and late memories, for the effect of recency versus primary, and for the effect of early experience on later personality. If we accept the evidence at face value, a good case can be made for our hypothesis that it is not early experience per se that is critical for later personality development but rather experience, early or late, that is continuous and cumulative, so organized that every repetition increases the skill with which it is retrieved in a wide variety of conditions. Late writing easily displaces the individuality-less signature to such an extent that most subjects affirm that they do not know how to write in any other way and that they cannot remember their early signatures.

If we accept this evidence, we might argue for recency over primacy as a critical factor in learning and memory, for functional autonomy in personality development. We would argue rather that apparent interference effects *may* be a function of interference, not with all retrieval ability but with *some* retrieval ability. This is analogous to the need for "warmup" in throwing a baseball skillfully after a lay-off. Many of the components of conjoint names may require approximate retrieval before exact retrieval of all components is possible. Once contact is established with some of the components of a name, these function as names of the name and the correct addresses are zeroed in. Many recency, primacy, retroactive effects are probably name of name effects rather than name-name interference effects. If we stress the skill of retrieval under conditions of supplying the correct instruction, the correct conjoint names of a name, then it is clear that the debate about primacy versus recency, early versus late experience, is a mistaken polarity and that the nervous system is quite capable of supporting two independent sets of traces under certain conditions. Thus, given specific conditions under which we learn early and late handwriting, two quite independent organizations may exist side by side with little interaction in either direction. Early memory here does not influence later memory, nor does later memory alter early memory. There is neither proactive nor retroactive interference. Each address has its own name, and each name has its own address, and peaceful coexistence is the rule. The subject continues to be unable to write as he wrote early at a rapid rate, nor does he appear able to write his adult signature slowly.

This is not to say that he could not learn to write in his early hand with speed, nor that he could not learn to write his adult signature more slowly. The problem is not unlike that of learning to ride a bicycle expertly slowly and unexpertly rapidly. Professionals do learn how to achieve just these skills. We have no doubt that the analogous skills could be learned with handwriting. Characteristically they are not learned. Why not? If one practices a subject in writing his adult signature more slowly, he usually begins to speed up without realizing what he is doing. There is always pressure to slide back into the more efficiently organized adult form unless high-density report-to-message attention can be kept focused on the performance. The moment such vigilance fails to be exercised, the backsliding is automatic. The maintenance of high-density monitoring of such attempted change is further complicated by "pressure," which is consciously experienced as such to "progress" forward to the more unconscious, more efficient organization. The difficulty is partly motivational. Not only does the subject have no good motive to learn these skills, but in addition, the constant intrusion of this later skill seduces the subject into relaxing the vigilance necessary to keep the task under the searchlight of high density of reports to messages; and eventually he speeds up his performance without intending to. Although we have said that the problem is a motivational one, yet the major reason for this difficulty in resisting backsliding or forward sliding (and both can create equally unpleasant pressure) is not motivational. The primary cause of the state of segregation of the two sets of traces and the skills they program is the number of transformations that would be necessary to build a set of bridges between one set of traces and the other set of traces.

INTERNAME DISTANCE

We have defined another derivative of the concept of the name, the "intername distance," as the number of transformations upon a name that are necessary to enable the formation of a modified trace with a modified name.

The primary cause of the state of segregation of the two sets of traces and the skills they program is the number of transformations that would be necessary to build a set of bridges between one set of traces and the other set of traces. Consider that each signature is guided by a set of conjoint messages that, at the least, direct the five fingers of one hand how to move from moment to moment to create the unique tracings that constitute two signatures. For the early signature there is an extended set of complex instructions, all of which are to be emitted at a slow speed. For the later signature there is a quite different set of complex instructions, and all of these are to be emitted at a faster speed. If we grossly simplify the problem, we can represent the first set as composed of a series of three subsets of instructions– one of which, q, is a constant slow speed, another, x, is a set of instructions to proceed to a particular set of points with respect to the abscissa, and the third, y, is a set of instructions to proceed to a particular set of points with respect to the ordinate. The second set we may conceive as another program composed of q', which is a faster constant rate, and x' and y', analogous to x and y but systematically different. The subsets of x and y and x' and y' are very numerous, and each individual instruction has one of two speed markers tightly linked to a particular xy or $x'y'$ reading. Indeed, the empirical correlations between the distinctive components of each signature are critical for how many information transformations will be required to learn the new skills $q'xy$ (fast, early) and $q\,x'y'$ (slow, late). If a very small change in speed produces a large and inappropriate change in an x reading or a y reading, or in both, and if a small change in an x reading produces a very large change in a y reading and conversely, then a great deal of work will be required to build a series of bridges between qxy and $q'x'y'$ and $q'xy$ and $q\,x'y'$ (see Figure 50.1). If, on the other hand, one could change q, say, halfway to q' without disturbing the x y part of the program, and change q' halfway to q without disturbing $x'y'$, then in a few more transformations one might have achieved $q'x\,y$ and $q\,x'y^1$; that is, fast early writing and slow late writing.

The number of intermediate transformations that will be necessary to achieve the new programs and their traces will depend on how much distortion in early writing is caused by how much speedup and how long it will take to learn to correct these distortions at each new intermediate speed. As soon as a faithful signature has been achieved at a slightly faster speed, then the next speed transformation could be attempted. Similarly, with slowing down the speed of the adult signature, one would have to introduce just that amount of reduction of speed that produced a minimal disturbance in the adult signature. When this had been corrected so that the adult signature could be written a little more slowly with no error introduced, then one would be ready for the next transformation. The number of intermediate transformations that would be required to finally reach handwriting skill that was free of speed effects would be a function of the strength of the correlation between all components of each set.

This correlation is purely an empirical matter in the sense that two components may be distinctive in their respective sets but vary in their correlation with other components within their set. Thus, the size of handwriting, within certain limits of variation, may have little effect on speed, and conversely.

Speed of speech, in contrast to handwriting, may be a distinctive component for those whose impulsive utterances are controlled through speaking slowly. If one can induce such an individual to violate his self-control and speak more rapidly, the number of intermediate transformations and the amount of work that are then required for him to speak rapidly as an adult is very much less than in the

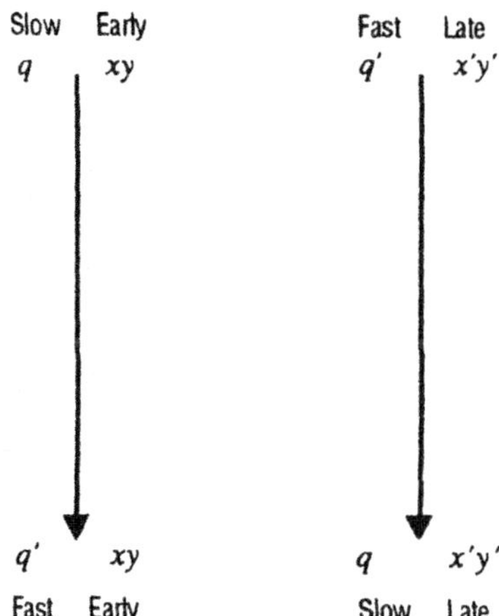

FIGURE 50.1 Transition series needed to free early and late programs from distinctive features.

case of handwriting. Since he once did speak more rapidly in his childhood and since the normal adult normally speaks with a wide spectrum of speeds, either speech skill is usually more highly developed or the tongue is a more differentiated muscle than the fingers, or both.

We have so far accounted for the "backsliding" phenomenon in handwriting, where although there are some motivational pressures, yet the major problem is one of intername distance based on the degree of internal correlation between parameters of the early and late sets of messages involved and the relative ease of transforming each set so that it contains overlapping components of the other set. After these interchangeable components have been used to fabricate alternate sets with varying values of the formerly discontinuous parameters, then the individual is no longer vulnerable to backsliding. In the case of handwriting, it is speed-free because the individual is capable of writing *either* his early or late signature at *any* speed. The instruction to write slowly ceases, therefore, to be part of a distinctive conjoint name. If the correlations between components of the distinctive sets are weak, then relatively simple transformations will bridge the small intername distance, and the intrusion of early memories will be short-lived. If it were, in fact, easy to learn to write early handwriting rapidly and late handwriting slowly, the instruction we used would not provide a stable regressive phenomenon.

Sometimes, for some subjects who shout, "No, I won't!" this proves a similarly unstable phenomenon because it is readily transformed to a variant of adult speech and therefore no longer recovers early memories or affects when shouting.

However, the introduction of negative affect into the distinctive, discontinuous behavior enormously complicates the matter. First of all, the very thought of using a specific parameter that was once relinquished under the threat of negative sanctions is itself sufficient to reactivate the same negative affect. It is not necessaary for our subject, who was frightened or humiliated out of shouting, to shout, to again experience the same fear or shame. This is because he was ordinarily threatened not only when he shouted but also when he did not but only thought of so doing, and because eventually, if he accepted the parental stricture, he experienced negative affect as he entertained the possibility of angrily shouting at his parents. Since speaking softly does not generate negative affect, a critical distinctive component that keeps these two sets discontinuous is the negative affect that was responsible for the initial learning to modulate the voice. Every time the possibility of so behaving is imminent and negative affect is aroused, the discontinuity between the two types of speech is heightened. Under such conditions, the initiation of a set of transformations that would reduce this distinctiveness not only must contend with the potential intername distance that would be there even if there were no anxiety to discourage the work of transformation, but in addition it must be motivated to tolerate the punishing negative affect involved. The individual must want to free himself of his inhibition more than he fears the affect punishment involved if he is even to begin the necessary work. Once having begun he must be prepared to continue to tolerate this negative affect that will be reactivated not only from the past. He must also overcome the secondary pressure of negative affect that we observed resulting from any attempt to modify habits of long-standing and segregated organization, even when the habits themselves are neutral (i.e., do not involve the avoidance of negative affect).

Implications of Psychopathology and Therapy

Behaviors that have been changed to avoid or escape negative sanctions constitute, of course, a large part of the background of psychopathology. Let us now consider the implications of our theory of retrieval for pathology and for therapy.

There are two conditions where negative affect interferes with the ability of the neurotic or psychotic to confront his own past experience. One is when he is on the threshold of confrontation preventing the initiation of behavior that might produce retrieval of earlier experience; in our experiment this appeared in those who were too shy to begin to shout. The other is after it has happened. In our experiment some individuals who experienced momentary awareness of long-forgotten affect were unable to sustain this awareness, changed the subject, and tried to leave the field. This is a commonplace in psychotherapy: Patients not uncommonly work through difficult personal problems and achieve considerable insight that apparently results in great therapeutic gain, only to backslide later to such an extent that one would suppose they had never made any therapeutic gain.

If psychopathology is, above all, as we think it is, a disorder of the affective life, how shall we enable the sick to tolerate their own affects? If our theory of memory is correct, the general outlines of the strategy we must pursue are clear. We must increase the degree of differentiation and the number of graded values of each affect, especially of the negative affects, so that the distinctive discontinuity of each negative affect and the components with which they are linked are successively attenuated. The intername distance between all affects must be sufficiently reduced so that they lose their distinctive features. Just as we can learn to speak at varying speeds, with speed as an independent component of any speech sets, so we must free loudness of voice and intensity of affect to vary independently of whatever assembly it enters.

As an example, suppose an individual is overly shy and overly soft-spoken in the expression of his affect. He would have to be taught to shout in joy as well as in anger and without panic in either event. Insight that he is inhibited in these matters and how he became so will not liberate him unless we begin to push him through a set of procedures calculated to free his affects of their sticky adhesions and their unmodulated and undifferentiated intensity. How can this be done? We must first determine which are the critical affects and the specific forms of their inhibition and lack of modulation. One cannot raise his voice, another cannot glare angrily with his eyes, another cannot clench his fist, another cannot tighten his jaw, another cannot stamp his feet, another cannot use particular words. It is our belief that affect pathology is a set of very specific disabilities and that to liberate these affects and then to enable modulation of varying intensities to be learned and tolerated requires tailormade programs of desensitization not unlike those designed to cope with specific allergies, where the rate of desensitization is critical and where a failure in the diagnosis of the correct rate can produce more pathology and increased sensitization.

As an example of the procedure we are suggesting, consider anger pathology that is expressed through an inhibition of the intensity of speaking. In such a case one could begin with requiring the voice to be used more flexibly in utterly pleasant ways, as in reading the lines of a play. Under such a pretext one could call for a better projection of the voice so that it could be heard in the back of the auditorium. Second, the loud voice can be further differentiated into the competing affect of joy, through the same device of reading prepared scripts, then through exposure to planted subjects who express themselves loudly in delight and who encourage identification by exchanging the telling of jokes in a loud voice and with loud laughter. After such preliminary loosening of the distinctive assembling of the loud voice, a beginning could be made on differentiating its intensity by exposure to arguments between antagonists who expressed intense anger with soft-spoken voices. This could be followed by role playing that imitated one or the other of these models. The therapist might then begin to encourage the indirect expression of moderate anger by taking the lead in expressing his own mild annoyance at something that he knew also annoyed the patient. Such tangential expression of anger could be gradually stepped up in intensity at a rate that was tolerable to the patient. After having reached unaccustomed levels of voice intensity the therapist could experiment with the direct expression of interpersonal discord through the soft-spoken voice to and from the patient and gradually, over time, step up the volume of his own voice as long as it could be countered in kind by the patient. Such a training procedure would require days for some patients, months for others, and years for still others. We doubt whether there can be any substitute for such belated training in the expression and modulation of affect when particular affects have become either so hypertrophied or so underdeveloped that the normal degree of differentiation of the affects is not achieved. When this is so, violent intrusions of ungraded affect and defenses against such intrusions are an inevitable vulnerability. Only the deposition of traces of varying degrees of intensity and duration, particularly of negative affects, can provide the building blocks of sufficient flexibility that they can be assembled into conjoint sets of traces over which the individual can exercise increasing control.

The more continuous the gradations of a distinctive feature within a set, the greater the specificity of name is necessary to retrieve the set and consequently the greater invulnerability to unwanted intrusion.

On the other hand, the increased number of gradations of affect or of any other component increases the ease of retrieval that the individual may self-consciously initiate. To the extent to which there are names of the entire set that can be constructed from alternative components of the set, the entire set becomes increasingly retrievable.

The situation is analogous to the phenomenon of speech that is governed by the intrusion of clichés that the individual cannot control because of their excessive redundancy, compared with the speech of an individual who has at his command subassemblies that are capable of expressing fine shades of difference in the meaning he wishes to convey.

The extraordinary vulnerability of the neurotic to delayed intrusion when the name of the early traces unexpectedly materializes has been described by Bergler (1961) in the case of a patient who developed eye symptoms and depression for the first time in his mid-40s.

At the age of 5 he had a great fear of blindness following an incident in which he had been caught by his mother's sister when peeping into her room and for which he had been severely reprimanded. He did not develop his depression until he found in middle age that glasses were becoming necessary for reading. He interpreted this as the onset of the long-deferred predicted punishment for his voyeurism. Here the normal aging process was sufficient to redintegrate the long-forgotten threat and to confirm it dramatically. It is of interest that at no time prior to this did the man suffer eye symptoms.

Further Extension of the Method

We will now consider how this method we have developed for the retrieval of simple memories may be further exploited for the exploration of the dormant traces of childhood, for both its theoretical and its diagnostic and therapeutic potential.

What are the parameters likely to be unique in childhood? First is relative size. The child is smaller than the adult, and the objects of his environment are functionally much larger to him than they are to the adult. We should therefore fabricate rooms from 2 to

$2\frac{1}{2}$ times normal linear size in all dimensions. Theoretically, no parameters of experience are necessarily continuous or discontinuous. Continuity varies with the culture and with the particulars of the individual's development. Relative size is, however, a discontinuity between infancy and adulthood in the experience of all individuals. The oversize house and rooms should contain furniture, drapery, and accessories to scale.

In addition to living in a space that is relatively larger, there are many types of experience peculiar to infancy and childhood, such as being alone in the dark in a crib; nakedness; being fondled; being tweaked on the face; being wet; being hungry and wet; being sated and cuddled; being in a crib; being looked at intently by adults; smelling urine and feces, talcum powder, mother's body odor; falling while walking; being moved passively; being rocked; being read to sleep at night; being bathed; being undressed; hearing lullabies; being read fairy stories; hearing the variety of talk directed toward infants and children; being tickled and teased; being spanked, being made to stand in a corner as punishment, being made to write 1,000 times "I will not pick my nose," being sent to bed without supper, being subject to castration threats, and so on.

In addition to being the recipient of such distinctive treatments, the infant and child emits a number of types of response peculiar to this period, such as sucking fingers and objects, biting, putting fingers in the mouth, putting objects in the mouth, reaching with both arms and fingers, walking unsteadily, recognizing objects by putting them in the mouth, looking at smiling faces overhead while lying in a crib, slowly dressing, tying shoes, reading slowly, counting slowly, rolling in a crib, gazing intently into the face of a woman for long periods of time, throwing things out of the crib, throwing things down from a high chair, eating in a high chair, walking when one's hand is held by someone else, talking baby talk, crying, screaming, reciting the pledge of allegiance to the flag, singing childhood songs, breaking things, pushing things, tearing things, splashing water in a tub, being dirty, playing with mud pies, rolling in mud, playing with food, pointing, defecating and urinating in the presence of an adult, learning the alphabet, writing on a blackboard by reaching up high, cutting up paper, playing hopscotch and see-saw, rolling a hoop, jumping rope, swinging, climbing poles, bragging, lying, cheating, stealing, fighting, killing animals, engaging in competitive urination, head banging, and so on.

If, then, we place the adult in the milieu of the infant or child, bombard him with the messages peculiar to the milieu, and permit, require, and urge him to emit the behaviors characteristic of infancy and childhood, we should be able to activate traces that have been dormant for most of the individual's lifetime.

For example, in an oversized room, in an oversized crib, we might place the adult clothed only in oversized diapers, surrounded by oversized blocks, looked down upon by a huge face of a giantess mother with a loud and booming high-fidelity voice emitting sweet nothings as she gazes at our subject, pinching, tweaking, poking, and fondling him and from time to time, feeding him milk from a very large bottle. Occasionally, he would hear the taped sounds of the crying of another child or other children from another part of the nursery. Our subject might be deprived of food and left alone in complete darkness, to hear only the crying of a hungry infant, and then be suddenly exposed to the smiling face of the giantess bearing food. After being fed, he might be put into a giant cradle and rocked to sleep to the sound of a gentle lullaby. Or the adult might be held tightly but tenderly in the arms of a heated, foam rubber giantess.

He might be powdered with a large fluffy powder puff all over his body after being washed in a very large tub. After this he might be alternately tickled, chucked under his chin, tweaked on his cheeks, and talked to in baby talk. We might require our subject also to suck a pacifier or his thumb and to put a variety of objects in his mouth. We might encourage him to throw the objects in his crib down to the floor.

Early walking experience could be simulated by requiring the adult to walk on an unstable floor in a dark room that would hurt somewhat when he fell on it. In this environment he might also be given the reassuring hand of a protectress.

Another way in which infantile experience may be more closely approximated would be to increase the weight of the head relative to the rest of the body. The adult in the crib might therefore have a lead-lined helmet strapped onto his head to restrict his ability to sit up and look at the world.

He might also be subjected to the rhythmic sounds of Salk's (1960) simulation of the mother's heartbeat as heard in the womb, as he is swung through space in darkness in a supportive foam rubber cradle that simulates the conditions of the womb for our adult subject.

From the period of childhood we can also prepare appropriate milieus: A peer group made up of planted adults dressed like our subject, as children, in short pants, surrounded by oversize swings and the toys of childhood. We can bombard our child with a variety of the communications peculiar to childhood: full of tenderness or anger, or fear for the safety of the child, or advice and dicta on every aspect of living.

It would not be necessary to be very specific in such "lectures" since each subject would interpret them in ways reminiscent of his own childhood. A sample series would be as follows:

1. Punishment lectures: "I don't want to have to tell you again—or I'm going to give you a good spanking."
2. Cleanliness lectures: "I don't know how a child can manage to get so dirty. Haven't I told you not to get dirty?"
3. Conscience lectures: "Mother doesn't love bad little boys. I am ashamed of you."
4. Achievement lectures: "You must work harder, dear, if you expect to get ahead. Your report card was disgraceful."
5. Respect lectures: "Who is my best boy? Whose boy is the most wonderful boy in the whole world?"
6. Tenderness lectures: "Whom does mother love more than anyone else in the world?"

Sibling rivalry experience might be reactivated through a very large moving picture display of a mother breastfeeding her young infant. Further, we might encourage the subject to make, throw, and play with water and mud pies. We might require him to repeat the pledge of allegiance to the America flag as it was done daily in many schoolrooms.

To reactivate early cognition we might expose our subject to a fulllength taped discussion between two children on their ideas of the nature of the world, of God, of how children are made, of the effects of masturbation, of siblings, of how old old people are. These might constitute names of names for long-forgotten ideas that the adult might retrieve if he could be exposed again to the accent and imagination of childhood as confidences are shared between children.

What may we reasonably expect from the utilization of such methods? We should expect retrievals of varying degrees of fidelity and stability. Retrieval is a function of the uniqueness of certain combinations of messages in the past history of the individual. This uniqueness is, however, a function not only of the particular vicissitudes of an individual's life but also of the general transformability of particular kinds of message sets. If, therefore, messages are too little transformable, there will be insufficient changes from early to late performance to enable retrieval of early performances. Affective responses, for example, have relatively little transformability, compared with motor behavior and cognitive responses. On the other hand, messages may be so easily transformable that the variety of combinations of components produces no distinctive sets that are distinctively discontinuous with respect to time, like the varying combinations of the speed of speech; or if they are distinctively discontinuous, are capable of being easily and rapidly transformed into variants of later performance as soon as they are retrieved. This is true for purely cognitive responses, when compared with motor or affective responses. This is why a patient undergoing insight psychotherapy can readily appreciate and transform his childish ideas, once they are retrieved, but finds it much more difficult to transform the affect they generate. The modification of motor performances, as we have seen, is midway between these two extremes, depending upon the degree of differentiation of the particular muscle system involved and the degree of learned skill attained, as in the difference between writing and speech. We should therefore expect very transient, unstable retrievals of infantile or childhood cognition compared with early motor performance or affect. Early perception should also be relatively unstable in retrieval because of the great transformation skill that is ordinarily developed in this modality.

We may therefore expect retrievals that vary in how stable their components are. Thus, if we speak to an adult as his parent once spoke to him, he may display early affect and some memories from childhood but may easily control his motor behavior and rapidly transform his childish thoughts so that they may drop out immediately upon being retrieved; or they are so altered by adult cognition that their character is radically changed. Again, if an adult is required to do something with his hands with an oversize object, there may be retrieval limited exclusively to the perceptual motor area, with no retrieval of early affect and no retrieval of early cognition. In such a case he might apply adult know-how to the solution of a problem that he would have solved quite differently in childhood.

The second problem that arises in connection with such proposed experimentation is the perennial methodological one—how shall we measure the effects? We are not averse to the utilization of reports from our subjects, but we can also employ more indirect techniques. Thus, we might present objects in the dark for recognition by touch. These objects should be designed to be equally capable of being recognized as familiar objects from childhood or as familiar objects from contemporary experience. Thus, a large glass vase filled with water lifted by the blindfolded adult subject should be recognized as a large flower vase. In the regressed state this same object should be recognized as a drinking glass since the child characteristically must use both hands to lift a drinking glass to his lips.

Similarly, in the regressed state the adult should be able to recognize some objects more readily when they are put into his mouth, in the dark, than when he is in a normal adult environment.

We might also test the relative effectiveness of the early milieu over the normal adult milieu in producing age-linked behaviors under what are otherwise the same experimental conditions. Thus, a child will back into sitting on a chair. Will the instruction to sit down produce differential behavior in accordance with known differences in adult and early modes of motor behavior?

We can test the relative effectiveness of such methods in the evocation of early memories as compared with free association by employing patients who are undergoing protracted psychoanalysis.

We can test the effectiveness of the method in cases of aphasia to see whether retrieval of early experience will also favor the recovery of language traces that do not operate in the normal adult environment. Our basis for supposing that this may be possible is that there are cases where one can communicate with aphasics in the language of their childhood when they learned another language in their adolescence. Also aphasics have been sometimes observed to sing lullabies in the bathtub and to count numbers serially, both of which are suggestive of the retrieval of early achievements.

DISTINCTIVE DISCONTINUITY THEORY OF MEMORY

We will now examine some further implications of the distinctive discontinuity theory of memory.

The Discontinuity of Birth

There is a special distinctive discontinuity that is universal in the experience of all men, the change from the muffled, supportive, claustral environment of the womb to the blooming, buzzing confusion of life in the nursery and thereafter. As we have noted before, Salk (1960) has shown that the simulation of the beating of the heart through a loudspeaker in the nursery is capable of quieting the entire nursery and promoting weight gain in neonates. In our own experience we have noted before that holding a crying infant in one's arms while one is seated does not stop crying, whereas the closer approximation to the womb when one stands up and/or walks with the infant does. To what extent similar retrieval is involved in the widespread delight in underwater skin diving and in sunbathing we cannot be sure, but it would appear that the oceanic bliss, or at least its affective neutrality retrieved by womblike stimulation, is sometimes sufficient to calm the troubled neonate and perhaps his elders.

The Discontinuity of Childhood and Parenthood

A universal discontinuity that is reactivated for every adult is the reliving of infancy and childhood in the role of parent. This is the reason for the sudden massive intrusion of attitudes and affects long forgotten that so often surprise both the parents themselves and their friends. Many a parent is hurled back into his past and held as in a vise. If this was a discontinuous period of positive affect, adults may find themselves reliving a golden age. If it was a discontinuous period of *sturm und drang,* they may have to suffer through it again. If it was a golden age with a sudden decline at the birth of a sibling, this too may be relived. The parents may relive not only the role of themselves as children but also the roles of their own parents. Thus, we find the submissive adult suddenly as domineering a parent as was her parent, the carefree adult suddenly as nurturant and anxious a parent as was her parent, the timid adult suddenly as aggressive a parent as was her parent, the humiliated adult suddenly as contemptuous a parent as was her parent. Some parents' behavior may be understood as a further strategy against these sudden intrusions of unwanted personalities, but others appear to be caught in their social inheritance. The phenomena we are here describing do not apply to the parent-child relationship in general but rather to those adults for whom either their own early personality or that of their parents constitutes a distinctive discontinuity with their adult personalities and life plans.

This can happen whenever there was a sharp polarization between the child and parent in which each played complementary roles or whenever there was a sharp break with the childhood role in the developmental sequence.

The individual is much less vulnerable to such intrusion under other conditions: first, if he had an adequate identification model that resulted in a steady, rewarding progress toward a personality that approximated the personality of the model; and second, if his role as a child, while representing a polarized role (e.g., a submissive personality in response to a domineering parent) has made him too anxious to reverse these roles. In contrast there are parents otherwise submissive who suddenly belatedly find an identification with their own parents because their anxiety at the child's spontaneity is more threatening than the anxiety they may experience in assuming the role of the dominant parent. This is particularly likely to be the case if their own parents buttressed dominance with moralistic postures that were incorporated by the child as justifying submissiveness. An analogue from our experiments with defiant speech may be seen in those subjects who are anxious about shouting but who comply because they are also ashamed to be visible as different from other subjects.

Continuity Distinctively Preserved

There are a variety of experiences and milieus that activate the traces of early experience, not because they are necessarily discontinuous with that experience but because the relationship between the adult and his environment remains essentially unchanged. Thus, although the house he lives in as an adult had become relatively small as he grew larger, the ocean, the mountains, and the starry firmament remain capable of stirring his early wonder—in part because this relationship to nature has not changed, whereas so much of the rest of his experience *has* changed radically.

Further, some manmade edifices, notably the Gothic cathedrals, were designed to preserve the continuity of the smallness of the child in relation to God, the father.

Discontinuity in the Behavior of Others

Much of our posture as adults is achieved and maintained by radical discontinuities in the behavior of others toward us and by the discontinuities of the behavior expected from us as we play the adult role. As long as the adult is treated by other adults as though he were an adult, he is reinforced in the image of himself as an adult. But some of this later adjustment is analogous to our skill in riding a bicycle in that there may be many intermediate steps in the learning process that were simply bypassed rather than mastered. Very few of us have the skill to ride the bicycle slowly, and many of us suddenly feel like children before an overly authoritarian police officer who speaks to us as we might have been spoken to by our parents when we violated their norms. It is, however, always possible to activate earlier feelings and performances by acting toward the adult as though one were his parent and he was the child. This is the source of the power of those who exercise authority—benign or malignant—whether it be as an industrial executive, a police officer, a judge, a teacher, a religious leader, a doctor, a political leader, or a military leader. The exercise of authority can always evoke regressive shame or fear, with submission or defiance, or regressive worship of the good parent, to the extent to which there are radical discontinuities in the behaviors of children and adults and to the extent to which some adults play the role of the powerful parent, good or bad, to other adults, who are thereby pressed into assuming the role of the good or bad child. Only a thoroughgoing democratization of roles, either for the child-parent relationship or for all relationships between adults, or both, would reduce such vulnerability.

The use of giant statues and posters of political leaders also depends for its effectiveness on its potential for evoking the attitudes of the child for his parents. Similarly, any spatial arrangement at political rallies or in lecture halls where the speaker is placed above his audience so that they must look up to him is potentially instrumental in evoking childhood attitudes. This is particularly true when other aspects of the situation reinforce this similarity, as in the elevation of the bar of justice in the judge's bench.

Being Helpless, Loved, and Cared For

There are many types of common adult situations that activate early memories by virtue of their distinctive discontinuity. Thus, all of the situations in which adults are rendered relatively helpless and incompetent are candidates for activating regressive phenomena in those who are characteristically active. Failure, illness, hospitalization, surgery, the prospect of death, rejection, the loss of a love object, defeat by a competitor, and loss of status or money are some of the occasions when the active, ordinarily competent adult may suddenly find himself confronted with early memories and affects he has forgotten for years.

Other types of situations that may have distinctive discontinuity for the adult are those in which he is the recipient of unaccustomed gratuities, such as sudden windfalls of esteem, love or money, or sudden experience of novelty and excitement for those whose adult life has been marked by shame, distress, or boredom. For these the sudden experience of love or money or respect or novelty can produce a massive remembrance of things past. That is why tears come equally to the eyes of adults suddenly struck down into incompetence and helplessness or suddenly lifted up into love, excitement, respect, or affluence.

Linkage of Negative to Positive Affects

There are special conditions under which the evocation of long-dormant positive affects is also capable of paradoxically retrieving negative affects. Thus, many individuals who receive sudden, unexpected praise lower their heads and eyes in shyness and shame. We do not believe that this is simply modesty. When a complex of events that characteristically includes both positive and negative affects is subjected to massive segregation, the retrieval of any part of such a complex may be a name of the total complex. When an individual therefore turns away from the hazards of evoking either praise or blame from others and adopts the posture of becoming his own parent and his own audience, he is vulnerable to the retrieval of blame and shame when he is unexpectedly praised. He is equally vulnerable to the retrieval of longing for approval when criticism and blame penetrate his psychic epidermis. This raises the question of how distinctive is distinctive. It is not the case that all distinctive names are necessarily equally distinctive. A green-haired, 20-foot-tall man with three eyes and two heads would be more distinctive than a three-headed man, distinctive as the latter might be. This is because the former man has a greater number of characteristics any one of which would provide a name for the retrieval of the set of traces. Part of the increased skill in retrieval of traces consists in increasing the number of alternative names of the same trace by increasing the distinctiveness of different aspects of the same information.

Discontinuity as a Basis for Projection

This theory of memory also provides a basis for the understanding of the mechanism of projection. If a particular attitude of a significant other person in one's past history has been the unique activator of a particular response, then the later activation of this response in some other way can be expected to uniquely activate the expected "cause." Thus, if a child has had its anger uniquely aroused by a parent who comes to arouse only anger, then ultimately the activation of anger from any source (e.g., from excessive fatigue or from failure) can activate the commonly expected cause, the hostility of the other.

Discontinuity and Taboos

There are numerous childhood impulses and activities that are ordinarily continuous with adulthood activities, in which their early significance is masked in the manner that late handwriting masks early handwriting. If, however, a serious inhibition was created, sufficient to prevent the continuous development of the wish into adulthood, then the adult who is suddenly confronted with such a wish or activity is vulnerable to the retrieval of the early dread that was responsible for its initial inhibition.

In the past history of most adults is a very archaic set of taboos, utterly inappropriate for any adult by most cultural norms and ordinarily outgrown in normal development. These are not to be confused with the furniture of Freud's superego nor their somber derivatives in Melanie Klein. These are in addition to anything that has been described by these authors. They concern neither sex nor aggressicnor eating, nor being clean. We refer to taboos frequently appropriate to preserve the life of the very young or the comfort of his parents. First is curiosity. The very young child sometimes must be restrained in his philosophic excursions into the nature of things lest he destroy himself and the objects of his curiosity. Second is the fact of self-injury. Whenever a child has, in fact, injured himself, many parents add punishment to this already disturbing fact by their concern and further punishment lest the child not appreciate how he might avoid what he has done to himself. Third is the impulse to cooperate and "help" his parents. A mother who is cleaning the house may be so slowed down by her cooperative child that she punishes the child for his misguided help. Fourth is the identification impulse. There is no other single wish possessed by the normal child that is stronger than the wish to be like the beloved parent. Such a wish, however, produces a great variety of behaviors that may jeopardize the child's life or discomfort his parents. Not all of such behavior is so motivated. The child's curiosity, which may produce the same consequences, is not necessarily motivated by identification. In any event, punishment for identification behavior is often punishment for something other than the impulse itself in the eyes of the parent. To the child, however, it may produce a taboo on his deepest wish.

Fifth is the impulse to cry. To hear an infant or child cry is a discomforting experience for the adult for many reasons. Many children are punished for this display of their own discomfort with sufficient severity to taboo the future expression of the cry and its adult derivative.

Sixth is the smile and laughter of joy. Because the child's delight is noisy and boisterous, it may be punished sufficiently to produce an overly serious child.

Seventh is the generation of noise in general. Apart from explosive laughter there are numerous occasions when the child's spontaneous high decibel level discomfits his parents, who may respond with punishment of varying severity.

Finally, there is the taboo on the most intense form of curiosity, staring into the eyes of the stranger. Although the child is initially shy in the presence of the stranger, once he has overcome this barrier he is consumed with the wish to explore the face of the new person. Since this is a source of discomfort both to the parents and to their guests, this is often forbidden at some point in the development sequence.

In the extreme case the outcome of the imposition of this set of taboos may be catastrophic—an individual unable to explore, to tolerate his own sickness, to express tenderness by helping another, to identify with those closest to him, to express his dissatisfaction, to express his delights, to raise his voice at any time, or to achieve intimacy by looking into the eyes of another person. This set of taboos is ordinarily masked by later learning designed to circumvent the watchful eyes of the parents. The compact of the young had, among its chief aims, the satisfaction of many of these human impulses that parents have appropriately thwarted at certain ages. These parents, however, may never have repealed or sufficiently attenuated these prohibitions or appreciated their collective weight.

To the extent to which they have not been circumvented and outgrown, they are found among our subjects who will not shout at the top of their voice, who are vulnerable to the most massive intrusion effects if and when they are suddenly confronted with these residues of the past. I have known at least three cases in which it appeared that at the age of 60 there was a return to childhood, or rather to a childhood that was never experienced, full of noisy fun, helpfulness, tenderness, and a quest for the intimacy of the interocular experience. It was equally clear that these were responses to the imminence of death and therefore had a desperate undertone. In attenuated form, however, such intrusion may be expected to appear in the senility of any human being who has suffered an unwanted discontinuity in the expression of his positive affects and who therefore has residual affect hunger.

Discontinuity in Adult Experience: Suppression in Grief or Shame

It should be noted that our theory of retrievable memory as distinctive discontinuity is in no sense limited to the discontinuities between childhood and adult experience. There are equally distinctive discontinuities, which when kept segregated from the mainstream of adult experience are capable of being retrieved through confrontation with a name or, more typically, by the name of a name, which intrude in so violent a manner as to overwhelm the individual who belatedly incorporates his own experience.

Thus, the individual who suffers the death of a loved one without grief is thereafter vulnerable to sudden intrusions of painful longing when confronted by fragments of reminders that are so inconspicuous that they do not arouse defensive strategies until it is too late. He is continually subject to the delayed sustained grief reaction that has only been postponed.

Nor is bereavement the only or most conspicuous occasion of violent intrusion of the delayed incorporation of experience. Any behavior that produced regret of any kind, which later was choked off before it could be acknowledged and then progressively attenuated, is a candidate for sudden retrieval that overwhelms. In recent years there has been no more dramatic instance than the spectacular success of *The Diary of Anne Frank* in Germany. This play was a dramatization of a Dutch Jewish girl's tragic chronicle of her family's long hideout from Nazi pursuers. Despite the suffered persecution, this young girl builds a bridge between herself and her German audience in the lines "In spite of everything, I still believe that people are really good at heart." At the end of the play she is dead, but her father reinforces the intrusion from the past in the last line of the play, when, in recalling her courage he says, "She puts me to shame."

The German audience that saw this play had for 10 years resisted the efforts of the occupation forces and of German politicians urging them to admit their responsibility for the persecution and extermination of several million Jews. Another anti-Nazi play, Remarque's *Last Days of Berlin* was a failure the same season that Anne Frank was shown. *The Diary of Anne Frank* did not arouse their defenses, and it did enable them to retrieve the experience they dimly knew they had forced on German Jews and at the same time to expiate their shame.

On the opening night of this play in West Berlin, in 1956, 10 years after the end of the Nazi regime, the curtain went down and stayed down. A. J. Olsen (1958) quotes an eyewitness account as follows:

> For a full two minutes there was no sound in the theatre. Then a spatter of hand-clapping began. It was hissed down immediately. Then seven hundred sophisticated Berliners rose slowly and walked out of the theatre. I saw tear stains on powdered cheeks and men walking as if they were very tired. The people got their coats and went home, still silent. It was like leaving a funeral.

The play opened in six other German cities on the same night. The play everywhere profoundly moved German audiences. Most managements later inserted notes in the programs requesting no applause at the end. It soon established itself as the outstanding dramatic hit of postwar Germany.

The superintendent of schools in Duesseldorf directed his principles to organize attendance by whole classes, writing, "For our children to know 'how it was' and to form the resolution that such never again be permitted to happen is so important that we consider it absolutely necessary that they experience this drama."

Germans ordinarily averse to writing fan letters wrote fan letters by the hundreds, according to Olsen's (1958) account. "I was a good Nazi," one wrote. "I never knew what it meant until the other night." It also produced a resurgence of interest in Jews and Jewish culture. The second stage hit of the same season was a revival of Lessing's drama of Jewish life *Nathan the Wise*. Jewish intellectuals were suddenly much sought as cocktail guests by West Berlin hostesses.

This profound intrusion represents, of course, more than the retrieval of suppressed experience. It represents in addition the consequences of such suppression, the full expansion of self-analysis and self-accusation, which the facts of past acquiescence and past suppression of awareness entailed. What this play did in addition to reminding the Germans of their past was to enable them to confront the consequences of their acquiescence for their victims and the consequences of their acquiescence for their image of themselves as human beings. Finally, it permitted them to recover their images of themselves as good human beings, who had erred, and thereby to forgive themselves.

Discontinuity in Addiction

Another derivative of our theory of memory concerns the dynamics of addiction, and the breaking of addictions. Consider the excessive smoking of cigarettes that cannot be renounced despite an intense wish to do so or that can be renounced only at the cost of suffering intense negative affect. If, given such an addiction, the individual succeeds in breaking it, there arises the practical problem of how long this resolve will be effective and the theoretical question of the conditions under which the older traces may or may not be retrievable.

This problem is essentially a variant of the "backsliding" problem we considered in connection with handwriting and shouting, of the problem of the return of earlier experience in general, and of the grief reaction, in particular, since the breaking of an addiction is equivalent in many ways to loss through death of a love object. The vulnerability to intrusion of the past addiction to smoking or to any past addiction will depend heavily, therefore, on the intername distance and the number of graded intermediate components that can be flexibly combined equally well with the addictive and the nonaddictive set. This latter will in turn depend on the extensiveness or brevity of the addiction-breaking work.

Let us consider first an example of a kind of renunciation that would leave the former smoker quite vulnerable to the reactivation of the earlier traces. Suppose that his method of breaking his addiction had consisted in renting a hotel room in a strange city, locking himself in his room, and easing the transition by looking at television continuously for a week, punctuated by meals and snacks delivered whenever he felt the urge to smoke or when his interest in television flagged. One week later, let us assume our former addict returns home. He now has to fortify himself against his former addiction, despite one week's experience without smoking. Let us contrast him with his friend, an equally heavy smoker, who has spent this week somewhat differently. He has changed none of his habits of daily living. He has in fact continued to buy cigarettes as he has done for years, and has begun the week by "lighting up" whenever he felt like it; but then, instead of smoking, he has confronted the deprivation experience of looking at the lit cigarette with painful longing, of putting it into his mouth and struggling with the impulse to draw on it, of taking it out of his mouth and tolerating the temptation and the anxiety that his unfulfilled longing can only become worse with time. He feels alternately terrified and like crying in distress at this prospect. He wishes to pound his fist and hit and scream in anger at the person nearest him, who playfully lights up and blows smoke under his nose to tease him. The intensity of his affect and his inability to control his thoughts and feelings produce feelings of intense humiliation. He may think that others are aware of his misery and are laughing at him because they are confident that he will never be able to tolerate the deprivation experience and freely predict that eventually he must be defeated in abject surrender. Above all, he can think of nothing but how good a cigarette would taste and how terrible it is not to be able to satisfy this desire. He wonders what good all of this suffering is if he must eventually have a cigarette or be unable to carry on his daily affairs. It seems impossible that he should ever be satisfied without cigarettes when all around him are satisfied smokers. And even if his longing were to abate, how does one become "unaware" of an impulse that is now experienced with increasing frequency as the period of deprivation grows longer? If it is painful now, what will it be a week from now, a month from now, a year from now? Is this not more than the spirit can bear?

About the third day his anguish, his shame, his fear, his longing and his imagination reach a state of crisis. It is truly intolerable, and it is now rapidly getting worse. He clutches at the cigarettes in his pocket, lights up, inhales deeply, is momentarily relieved and then is overwhelmed with shame at his weakness in being unable to withstand his craving. As though to underline his defeat he rapidly smokes one cigarette after another until they become increasingly distasteful and he ends in utter frustration relieved only by long suppressed tears of anguish. And yet from the depths of his misery he resolves he will defeat the enemy within; he will take up the struggle once again. With heavy heart he begins the long vigil again, a little less certain than he was a few days ago but better forewarned of the trials to come. This time he will force the issue. He will seek out the chain smokers and thereby titillate his own longing. To intensify and deepen his anguish he will more frequently light up a cigarette and keep it in his lips for longer and longer periods of time, smelling the aroma of the oh so delicious cigarette. He will not baby himself any longer with respect to other sources of negative affect. He will address himself to all of the problems in his work he has put off because he did not wish to increase the difficulty of breaking the smoking addiction. He will, in short, look for trouble.

His forced posture now brings on the same crisis more rapidly the next day, and again he hovers on the razor edge of tortured decision. But this time he has, fresh in memory, the sweet-bitterness of the consequences of irresolution and frailty in surrendering to his somewhat alien but urgent cravings. This is the moment of truth for him. If he can tolerate himself at such a moment, he can govern himself, grow stronger, and win the reward of the smile of joy that the rapid reduction of negative affect evokes as an incremental bonus. From this point on it will become easier rather than harder as the positive affect evoked by mastery combines with and attenuates each succeeding paler version of negative affect.

At the end of the first week this man's battle is almost won; his vulnerability to backsliding is constantly being reduced by the large number of graded combinations of positive and negative affects that will eventually make it possible for him to retrieve the presmoking traces of looking at a cigarette and being unaware that it is a cigarette, as well as being unaware of the satisfactions of past smoking and the dissatisfactions that such remembered rewards generate during periods of experienced deprivation.

Not so with our first hypothetical addict. Conserved in his memory and readily accessible are all of the traces whose reactivation generated increasing negative affect for our second addict. What he has learned is only that so long as one is distracted by watching television and eating in an unfamiliar environment, one can block access to the numerous other addresses of past desire and satisfaction. But this cannot be his way of life, and as soon as he resumes this, the numerous alternative names of the traces of smoking, which are relatively intact, will reactivate these and generate secondary withdrawal reactions. He still has most of his addiction transformations to achieve before his vulnerability to backsliding is at all attenuated.

Midway between these two extremes are the rank and file of addicts who are vulnerable under some conditions, but not others. Many former smokers, for example, continue to be vulnerable in ways they do not understand because they are shielded from specific kinds of temptations to which they were not desensitized during the period of withdrawal. Thus, most individuals do not subject themselves to the experience of lighting up and holding cigarettes in their hands, or putting them in their mouths during the withdrawal period. I have known smokers who had given up smoking as many as 5 years earlier who have become readdicted under circumstances that confronted the individual with names that had never been transformed. For example, in one case, a wife needing to use her two hands to button her overcoat asks her husband, a former smoker, to hold her cigarette for her a moment. Since the breaking of the addiction did not include withstanding the temptation of smoking with a lit cigarette in the hand, such an individual may suddenly find himself aware of an intense wish to follow through with the rest of the sequence, whose names are still quite retrievable and that activates intense belated affect.

The breaking of addictions involves dynamics similar to what Freud called the work of mourning, by which the individual is enabled to achieve new love objects by freeing himself from his love for former love objects when these must be relinquished following their death. It is similar also, as Janis (1958) has suggested, to the host of anticipatory transformations that enable us to absorb the shock of anticipated negative affect in smaller doses, spread them over time until the dreaded event (as in Janis's study of the effect of an anticipated operation) loses its power to overwhelm the individual.

Nonaffective Perceptual Discontinuity

Not all of the interference between late and earlier experience is based primarily upon affective sources. The examples of the delayed grief reactions and the delayed shame reactions are analogous to our experiments with shouting. There are also analogues with the nonaffective interference, as we saw it between late and early handwriting, that obtain between experiences, all of which may occur in adulthood.

Thus, the city I saw for the first time two weeks ago changes its phenomenological appearance so rapidly that I can remember my first impression of it only with increasing difficulty as I become more familiar with it. The same is true of my recent acquaintances and with my wife, old friends, and parents. It becomes increasingly difficult to recover my earliest awareness as the objects of awareness become more and more familiar.

There is a critical experiment on the kinetic depth effect by Wallach, O'Connell, and Neisser (1953) that we believe, is based upon the masking of earlier names by later names, which would lend itself to a further test of our theory of the conditions under which older experience can be retrieved.

In the experiment by Wallach, O'Connell, and Neisser (1953), the shadows of three different three-dimensional wire figures were shown on a translucent screen. These figures were so chosen that their shadows appeared two-dimensional to the majority of subjects. Turning the wire figures back and forth made the shadows appear three-dimensional, the so-called kinetic depth effect. After intervals that ranged from minutes to a week, the stationary shadows were presented again in the same fashion in which they had been exposed originally and were then reported to appear three-dimensional by a large number of subjects. That these were truly perceptual experiences and not inferences was shown by giving a number of subjects prolonged test exposures, and nearly all of them spontaneously reported reversals of the kind usually seen with a Necker cube. Thus, Wallach, O'Connell, and Neisser conclude that a previous perceptual experience can cause later form perception to be three-dimensional. They believe that in this experiment, as in daily perception, memory effects are responsible for the perception of solid form and the spatial arrangements of the objects in the visual field.

If we assume that the three-dimensionality that is now seen in the same stimulus is due to its now being a name for the activation of the later set of traces, but that the earlier name is as retrievable as the earlier handwriting is, what is the distinctive feature that will permit such a retrieval? We may borrow a suggestion from the technique of the name of the name we used with handwriting, when we required the subject to write letters 3 feet high. Although he had never before written such a signature, it nonetheless retrieved the earlier handwriting because it slowed the writing and increased the density of reports to messages that is characteristic of all early learning. The same technique applied here suggests that any radical increment of novelty to this stimulus should also increase the density of reports to messages sufficiently to activate the earlier traces laid down when one first saw the stimulus. A critical experiment, therefore, would consist in presenting the same stimulus but with some noncritical changes, such as color changes and size radically enlarged. This set of changes should produce a stimulus "new" enough to interfere with the activation of the later traces and reproduce the earlier two-dimensionality.

Everyday instances of the same perceptual phenomenon, while not common, do occur. For example, while I was shopping in a department store with my wife one day, we separated to shop in different sections. A few minutes later I saw, coming down the aisle, a woman of uncommon beauty, so I thought. A moment later I recognized my wife. I had briefly reexperienced the first moment I had seen her.

Theoretically, then, we are suggesting that early perceptual experiences should be no more recalcitrant to retrieval than early motor performances.

Indeed, the same general procedure we suggested in connection with the kinetic depth effect could be applied to interpersonal perception. It should be possible to retrieve the earliest perceptions of familiar persons by one of three techniques: first, by blowing up the size of projected moving pictures of husbands, wives, parents, and old friends and, second, by requiring that a husband and wife, for example, stare at each other for several minutes. Since familiarity produces increasing skill in retrieval of compressed analogues, earlier, less compressed traces may be reactivated by a procedure that increases the density of reports to messages by increasing the detail of the stimulus through enforced looking.

We have also used this technique to reactivate earlier experiences of interpersonal intimacy through requiring two strangers to stare continuously into each other's eyes. Although it is very difficult to exact compliance with this instruction, when it happens, the individuals characteristically report an unexpectedly intense feeling of interpersonal intimacy. The romantic ideology that lovers recognize each other when their eyes first meet is, we think, based upon the distinctive discontinuity created between early and adult experience through the taboo on staring. Adults characteristically learn to look at each other tangentially, at the space between the eyes of the other, above or below the eye, or at the eye of the other when that is not focused on one's own eyes. The early experience with the mother is readily activated by staring at each other, since it was the mother and child who uniquely gazed lovingly at each other in time past. The child may have continued for some years to stare at strangers and others, but it is unlikely it was returned because of the general adult taboo on shared interocular interaction.

There is still a third possible technique of reactivating early perceptual traces based on increasing the density of reports to messages, and this is to reduce anticipatory cues. Much perceptual experience is, of course, organized in time. When the time allowed to anticipate what will be the sequence of stimuli that will follow in succession, is decreased early perceptual experience can be readily retrieved. I first became aware of this when surf bathing in the ocean at night. The reduced illumination produced an extraordinary suddenness and apparent increase in size of the waves, which could be perceived only as they were about to break upon oneself. Experimental reduction and interruption of stimuli in sequences that are ordinarily organized in time should produce a similar type of retrieval of early traces that preceded the development of perceptual skill. A variant of such a technique would be to present a stimulus such as a familiar whole face, which is ordinarily seen as a continuing set, as a sequence of subsets: first a nose, then a chin, then eyes each punctuating a general darkness. This too should impair perceptual retrieval sufficiently to produce the retrieval of earlier traces.

Part III
PERCEPTION

Chapter 51

Perception: Defining Characteristics—Central Matching of Imagery

If the eye is a camera, it is at the very least a moving picture camera. And if it is a moving picture camera, it is in the hands of a very active cameraman, who is assisted by an equally active editing crew that quickly drops out some shots, exaggerates some features, attenuates others, and generally edits sequences so that they become more coherent for constantly shifting purposes.

The researches of Gibson (1959, 1979), Hubel and Wiesel (1962), Johansson, Von Hofsten, and Jansson (1980), and others have disclosed analytical perceptual processes of extraordinary subtlety and complexity.

Several years ago, the physiologist H. J. Henderson raised the fundamental question: what had the physical world to provide in order to make life on earth possible? More recently, Gibson (1979) asked a similar question with respect to information rather than energy: what kind of information had the world to provide for the human being to know the visual world? He has provided an account of this information that is available to humans as they *move* in space. Visual organization emerges as those invariants of light that do not change as we move through space. It is the patterns of light reflected from the ground and from objects at different distances that are invariant, not static momentary pictures on the retina.

Although Gibson (1979) supposes, incorrectly, that the availability of invariant information is a sufficient theory of perception, there can be no doubt that stable invariances are a *necessary* precondition for perception. The analogue with Henderson's question concerning energy is quite close. We could not support life unless the world provided us with the necessary food and energy, but this is nonetheless not a theory of the chemical assimilation and utilization of food. That visual information is decomposed and recomposed before it can be used, emerges from the work of many investigators, beginning with the classical work of Hubel and Wiesel (1968). They showed that brain cells are organized for detection of lines, colors, and other features of the visual world and that successively higher levels of processing occur as the signals reach higher into the brain. Thus, the relatively simple cells that are tuned for responding to distinctive features such as lines and edges pool their output into cells that are specialized for visual shapes and distance. Thus, Hubel and Wiesel established that there are classes of directionally specific neurons. Neurons that fire at a high frequency when a stimulus moves across the visual field in one direction fire at a much reduced rate when the stimulus moves in the opposite direction.

Johansson, Von Hofsten, and Jansson (1980) have further illuminated the decomposition and recomposition of visual information in his studies. Johansson believes that a direct vector analysis is performed on the visual field so that in configurations of moving elements that share common motion components, one common vector becomes the frame of reference for residual component motions.

Perception involves not only the decomposition and recomposition of sensory messages but in addition, centrifugal selection at a distance. From the brain, messages are issued that in effect "decide" between incoming messages—which are to be amplified and which attenuated. It appears that favored entry and exclusion do not wait until all messages are at the gate of the central assembly. Some of this selectivity is achieved at a distance from the brain, as in the work of Pribram (1960).

ROLE OF CONTEXT IN PERCEPTION

Gibson (1979), in his "ecological" theory, revolutionized the theory of visual perception by broadening the pool of information that the perceiver is presumed to sample. He pulled the perceiver and the theorist away from the obsession with the momentary two-dimensional slice of information on the retina. He showed that this obsession had created pseudoproblems (e.g., of object constancy, of how two dimensions can represent three dimensions). But he failed to generalize his great insight to include the more extended past and future as part of the context in which visual messages are necessarily embedded if they are to orient the human being in his personal and sociocultural matrix. To "know" the visual world is an endless open-ended enterprise that can change radically as the "same" input is repeated but coordinated to radically different scenes from the past and the anticipated future. These scenes are no less "real" than the momentary scene. The changing perspectives from within concerning a constant present is no different from the changing perspectives of a piece of sculpture as one walks around it, seeing it now from the "front," then from one side or the other and from the rear. No object can ever be finally achieved perceptually so long as perception can be embedded in the changing perspectives of changing purposes. Although Gibson insisted that the human observer must move through space to extract the invariances embedded in the world which changes *because* he moves, he would not generalize this principle to include the records of the many past movements of exploration.

Just how complex such construction of the visual world is and how long it takes emerges from a critical study by Engel and Douglas (1980). They studied the ability to take viewpoint into account in organizing perception in children of 2½ to 5 years of age. They found, first, a stage in which the child is not yet aware that seeing depends upon the eyes and their access to objects. Second was a stage in which the child is aware of the connection between the eyes and objects but regards seeing as involving mutual facing. Third was the stage in which the child becomes aware of the observer-observed relationship. They conclude "that it is only after the child is four or five that the independence of objects is grasped and that a foundation for perspective-taking exists since it is only then that the system of perceptual relations connecting self, objects and others is at all understood."

THE COORDINATE ROLE OF CORRESPONDENCE AND COHERENCE IN PERCEPTION

The classical debate in epistemology between knowing via correspondence with reality and knowing via coherence within knowledge still continues in contemporary perceptual theory, especially in Gibson's (1979) ecological position that all perceptual information can be found in the invariant features of sequential visual experience. My position is to regard both processes as coordinated, depending upon the degree of success of the matching process. Characteristically, perceiving begins by magnification of the scanning of sensory input for all possible information, stressing correspondence as the chief criterion governing the perceptual feedback process. As perceptual skill in matching is achieved through the deposition of analogues in long-term memory, the skilled monitoring of the sensory input enables the radical reduction of reports to messages. Consciousness and the central assembly now turns to more problematic inputs and converts a correspondence search into a relatively silent coherence scanning. This is accomplished by conjointly compressing the sampling process to a series of homogeneous repetitions, which produces a conscious "difference" signal only when the coherence of homogeneous duplication is violated. At this point the individual switches over to the more fine-grained conscious scanning of the input to determine the precise nature of the suddenly experienced lack of correspondence. When this perturbation has been integrated and assimilated to a larger family of "understood" analogues, the process switches back to the less conscious, more economical coherence mode.

More generally, however, *both* coherence and correspondence are critical because correspondence should not be equated entirely with correspondence to the external world at a moment in time. First, it is a series of moments in time, which must be integrated even when one is perceiving "external" information. But more critically, that series must be integrated with past series stored in memory. Whether one calls that process correspondence of present outer information with past inner information, or one calls that match a coherence match seems to become a matter of the definition of meaning of the two terms. The reality of the present information is not necessarily diminished when it is faithfully retrieved later, to be compared with another present input.

PERCEPTUAL PROCESSES

In 19th-century perceptual theory, a distinction was drawn between sensation and perception, in which the former referred to the brute facts as these were received at the sensory receptors and transmitted to the projection areas and in which the latter referred to this sensory core plus some interpretive activity on the part of the subject. Gradually, it became clear that the concept of sensation, though it referred to real, conceptually separable processes, did not refer to anything a human being could ever experience. In recent years, therefore, we have spoken rather of sensory processes than of sensation. However, we still speak of perception. But no one is more likely to experience a "percept" than a "sensation." This is not to say that there are no conceptually distinguishable perceptual processes. Perceptual processes are quite as distinct as their parents, the sensory processes.

The sensory nerves stand in the same relationship to the sensory receptors as these do to their surround. Their structure is similar to the receptors, except that they are capable of duplicating what the receptor duplicates at one point in space at another point in space, usually deep within the organism, by a chain of duplications or receptions, each of which is spatially contiguous to its neighbor receptor. The dependence of the organism on the integrity of this chain is as great as it is on the integrity of the peripheral sensory receptors. At the terminal of the brain there are receiving stations whose function it is to duplicate those aspects of the world duplicated first at the sensory receptors and then duplicated again all along the sensory nerves.

We have thus far assumed that what is transmuted into a report is the information that has been transmitted step by step from the sensory receptors. What, indeed, would be the point of this laborious reception and transmission of information if it were not to be made available to consciousness? Is there any reason to suppose it is not, or should not be, made directly available to consciousness? It is our belief that the afferent sensory information is not directly transformed into a conscious report. What is consciously perceived is *imagery*. The world we perceive is a dream we learn to have from a script we have not written. It is neither our capricious construction nor a gift we inherit without work. Before any sensory message becomes conscious, it must be *matched by a centrally innervated feedback mechanism*. This is a central efferent process that attempts to duplicate the set of afferent messages at the central receiving station. The individual must learn this skill of matching the constantly changing input as one learns any skill. It is this skill that eventually supports the dream and the hallucination in which central sending produces the conscious image in the absence of afferent support.

Why postulate what appears to be a redundant mechanism? Why not assume that what has been carefully transmitted to the central receiving station is directly transformed into conscious form? Instead of putting the mirror to nature we are suggesting a Kantian strategy, putting the mirror to the mirror. Is this not to compound error? Certainly, the postulation of a feedback mechanism, which will have to learn to mimic what in a sense the eye does naturally, would at first blush appear perverse. But the possibility of error is the inherent price of any mechanism capable of learning. If we are to be able to learn perceptually, we will have to invoke a mechanism capable of learning errors as well as correcting its errors. But, it will be objected, we do not need to learn perceptually. Why may we not use our perceptual system as a mirror put to nature, by means of which we learn what else we need to know to achieve our purposes? Should learning not be restricted to the nonperceptual functions?

There are many reasons why the human being requires a feedback mechanism under central control. First, as a receiver of information, he is at the intersect of an *overabundance* of sensory bombardment. There is an embarrassment of riches, which paradoxically renders him vulnerable to confusion and information impoverishment. The individual must somehow select information to emphasize one sensory channel over another and focus on limited aspects of the incoming information within that channel. There is a large safety factor built into the sensory system, but it represents safety only if it can be optimally used. Brunswick (1947) and Miller (1956), among others, have sensitized us to the limitations of the human being in using all of his received information.

The simplest case of overabundance is the binocular information received from the two eyes. We see one world, though we receive two worlds. By means of a stereoscope we can see these two worlds at the same time or alternating in rivalry from moment to moment. This is the clearest instance of the perceptual feedback system in operation since it is the attained clarity of the perceptual report that appears to govern the organization of the perceptual information. Thus, if the disparity of the two images is increased beyond a critical point, there is commonly a suppression of the information from one eye.

Second, there is *not enough* information in the overabundant sensory bombardment. The world changes over time and so, therefore, does the information it transmits. At any one moment in time the same transmitted information is a subset of a pool of messages that has, in fact, varied from one receiver to another. Perceptual skill is based on such a mechanism, which can select from the flow of sensory messages those redundancies that have occurred before, as well as higher-order trends across time that in a real sense cannot be represented at any one moment of sensory transmission. The study of this mechanism should be restricted neither to the perception of sensory information nor to the most highly developed senses. The nature of the central integrating mechanism should be studied in the more primitive as well as the more complex senses and in the centrally mediated “percepts” as well as in the perception through the senses.

Chapter 52
The Lower Senses

PAIN

Let us first consider some of the "lower" senses for illumination on the nature on the central matching mechanism.

Hardy, Wolff, and Goodell (1952) report, first of all, that the amount of seriousness of tissue damage does not determine the intensity of pain, and therefore the latter may be a poor indicator of the gravity of the subject's plight. This is because, with exposure to noxious forces, the rate of tissue damage rather than the amount or seriousness of such damage determines the intensity of pain. When the injury is slow or not progressive, even though extensive and ominous, little or no pain may be experienced. Further, there is no spatial summation as regards the intensity of pain sensation. Were this not so, intense pain, they suggest, would be omnipresent. Here, then, is a constant bombardment of sensory information of which the central matching mechanism mercifully spares us summation, in marked contrast to visual information. The total intensity of several areas of different intensities of pain is not equal to their sum but to the intensity of their severest pain. Here is a channel limitation based upon an intensity-masking relationship between central matching mechanism and sensory input that would be quite dysfunctional for the visual field (although the latter has similar masking phenomena of a much less marked degree). One of the consequences of this relationship is that, if the pain is of an intensity that cannot be abolished by a specific drug, then no amount of this substance will stop the pain. For example, the intense pain associated with coronary occlusion, though it emanates from a very limited area, is not eliminated by aspirin. The relatively low-grade pain of rheumatic fever, although very widespread in origin, is dramatically abolished.

Next, in contrast with other senses, there appears to be no cortical representation of pain. This may account for two of the most critical characteristics of pain—its insistent claim on attention and its resistance to habituation. If, as we have noted before, the cortex not only receives amplification from the reticular formation but also dampens that amplification, then a bypassing of the cortex might account for its favored entry into consciousness over competing sensory information.

Finally, in contrast to vision, the damaging of tissue may set in motion hyperexcitatory states that require very little additional peripheral stimulation for their maintenance. They may become self-perpetuating. However, once these reverberating circuits are interrupted, they may not be reinitiated. This provides the rationale for the dramatic permanent relief from pain from such injuries as newly sprained ankles by immediate novocain block. Following such transitory interruption of these self-perpetuating hyperexcitatory pain states, the pain characteristically does not return. This phenomenon is primarily a matter of the patterning of stimuli rather than of the central matching mechanism. We have mentioned it for its significance in connection with other lower senses that we will presently consider. It is sufficient at this point to note that the relationship between the external receptors and the central matching mechanism is not always that of the straight-line, relatively isolated, transmission network we find in vision and hearing but rather one of booster networks only loosely associated with external stimuli.

SMELL

If perceptual imagery is centrally innervated and only partially guided by sensory information, then any gross reduction of transmission of such input, or attenuation of it, should, under some conditions, produce a failure of discrimination between imagery and "reality."

One of the conditions under which we should expect difficulty in discriminating imagery from exteroceptive stimulation is with the contact senses, which do not always provide rich, concomitantly changing patterns of stimulation as a function of movement by the subject or object. In contrast to the visual sense, the olfactory sense provides relatively diffuse cues as to its spatial localization. A gas, for example, that was evenly distributed in a room, would offer a subject moving through it no information that would enable him to localize it or to identify it as different from a hallucinated smell.

McKellar (1957) has referred to a colleague who has no visual imagery but who does possess vivid olfactory imagery. He quotes him as follows:

> I seem to have a fairly acute sense of smell but I have learned not to rely on the information it gives me, because I have so often been misled by mistaking imagery for percepts. This olfactory imagery is rather a nuisance, as I now distrust my olfactory experiences unless other people experience them at the same time.

He has confusions over the smell of perfume: "If I am speaking to a man, I know it is an image, but if it is a woman I cannot tell whether she is wearing it or whether I am experiencing an image."

THE BODY IMAGE AND PHANTOM LIMBS

If the exteroceptive olfactory sense can create such problems, we should not be too surprised that confusion can be compounded when the interoceptors and proprioceptors are involved.

Head (1920) first introduced the concept of the body schema to account for the fact that one can become aware of the position of any part of the body at a given moment, even if postural recognition is not constantly in the focus of consciousness. He believed that every change in the position of the body was related to and registered on this plastic schema by the cortex. He did not think of the schema, however, as a conscious image but as a standard against which all postural changes are measured. That there is a conscious body schema, only partly the consequence of afferent stimulation, is most dramatically seen in the phenomenon of phantoms that characteristically occurs with a variety of sudden anatomical or physiological interruptions of the sensory supply of the affected part of the body. There are phantom noses, eyes, nipples, penises, and breasts; however, the best-known phantoms are of those following amputation of limbs. Those who have lost an arm or leg through amputation continue to experience the presence of the limb, though they know it is no longer there. Denervation of a limb will also produce a phantom limb, as will cerebral or thalamic lesions. Partial sensory loss does not produce a phantom limb. Riese and Bruck (1950) examined 24 children with amputations and found no phantoms below the age of 6. Simmel (1956) reanalyzed the data from the 122 amputees of Cronholm (1951) and found no phantoms in his four patients whose amputations had been performed before the age of 5. Two patients with amputations of the right thigh at age 5 still had phantoms 19 and 34 years later.

Simmel herself examined 18 patients with leprosy. Most of these had had *both* surgical amputations of limbs and absorption of digits in other extremities. She found that phantoms appeared following surgical amputation but were absent following loss due to absorption. In this group there was a total of 20 amputations of leg or foot, and in each instance the patient had a vivid phantom of the part removed that, in most cases, had persisted over many years. By contrast, there were 15 instances of absorption of digits without surgical intervention, and none of these had given rise to a phantom at any time. In addition, there were eight instances of surgical amputation of digits—and in one case the nose—after a good deal of absorption had taken place, and in every instance phantoms were present. By contrast, 5 patients who had recent and relatively minor surgery of absorption stumps or had had muscle transplants in a hand in which the fingers were largely absorbed experienced no phantoms in connection with these. These results—that is, phantoms with amputation and absence of phantoms with absorption—are all the more striking as they come from the same patients who experienced phantoms in one case and not in the other.

Phantoms usually appear as soon as the patient becomes conscious after the amputation. The patient, on awakening from the anesthesia, may not be aware that the part has been removed. The foot of the amputated leg may tingle and itch, and, as the patient reaches down to scratch it, he reaches for an empty space. He may not believe his leg has been removed until the covers are removed and he sees for himself. The patient, despite his knowledge of the amputation, may forget and try to get out of bed or out of his chair, step on the foot that has been removed, and fall. The patient experiences reflex movements in the missing arm or leg as he adjusts his position in bed or in the chair, and he feels he can wiggle his fingers or toes and flex or extend the wrist or ankle and that he can perform these movements more or less at will. It is relatively atypical for there to be a delay of a few days, or a few weeks, before a phantom is reported, but such delay does occur.

The duration of amputation phantoms varies from a few months to 30 years or so after surgery. They may disappear and recur many years later due to further surgery on the stump, the wearing of a prosthesis, and sudden emergencies. Thus, if a patient trips over an obstacle, he may reach out for a support with his phantom hand. The ringing of a telephone may waken a patient who jumps out of bed to answer it and falls down because he forgets the missing leg.

There is one respect in which the phantom has characteristics quite different from a real limb. This is the capacity to penetrate solid objects without any sensation of touching them. Simmel reports that a patient with a midthigh amputation lying in bed may feel his phantom leg flexed at the knee, with the lower part hanging down through the mattress yet without experiencing any contact with the mattress. Or, with the patient sitting in a chair, an object may be gradually approximated to the stump until it touches the latter, without either changing the phantom's alignment with the stump or producing a phantom touch sensation. The phantom seems to go blithely through the object, and the experience seems so natural to the patient that it is rarely commented upon spontaneously.

There is also one other respect in which phantom limbs have been reported to differ from real limbs. In patients with high cervical transverse lesions, with lesions in the thalamus and in the cerebral hemispheres, reduplication has been reported. The phenomenon consists of phantoms coinciding with the paralyzed limbs plus extra phantoms of the same limbs. Thus, according to Simmel (1956), one patient with a high cervical transection reported sensations in her stretched-out paralyzed arms and legs and, in addition, a second set of arms and legs, smaller than the first and neatly folded over her chest and abdomen. The existence of stable duplicate phantoms in the case of cerebral lesions suggests that the centrally emitted imagery may, as Gray Walter (1954), has suggested, be duplicated more than once, but ordinarily it will be suppressed before it is transmitted into conscious reports.

Ordinarily phantoms do not disappear suddenly except under unusual conditions such as happened in Henry Head's (1920) classic case. His patient had a phantom limb following amputation of his leg, which disappeared suddenly when the patient suffered a stroke. The ordinary cause of disappearance of the phantom has been best described by Simmel (1956), upon whose vivid and precise observations our report is based.

Fading of Phantom Limb Parts

Although following the amputation, the phantom feels much like the limb before amputation, soon afterward the patient may feel some parts less vividly, whereas other parts continue as vividly as ever. In time these fainter parts tend to fade away altogether, while other parts grow fainter and still others continue to be vividly felt. The parts fade in the following order: first, the upper arm and the thigh while the lower arm, calf, joints, hands, feet, and digits remain; next the lower arm and the calf, followed by the joints, and eventually parts of the hands and feet, leaving perhaps only toes, instep, heel, and the lateral margin of the sole of the foot or the fingers, the palm, and the ulnar part of the hand. Still later, only phantom toes and fingers may be felt, and the great toe and thumb, index finger, and little finger survive longest. According to Simmel (1956), these changes take varying periods of time and, for some patients, never run their full course. This sequence, Simmel notes, follows the Penfield–Boldrey (1937) homunculus, with the possible exceptions of the joints. Parts that have large areas of representation on the homunculus, are richly endowed with sensory fibers, and have high innervation ratios on the motor side, have the longest phantom life. It is noteworthy that it is the parts of the limb that are most skilled rather than most powerful that have the longest life.

Telescoping

The other change is telescoping. When parts of the phantom first begin to fade, the position of the remaining parts is unchanged. Indeed, the patients can report the locus of parts of the phantom with precision and without hesitation. Thus, although he may no longer have a phantom thigh, the rest of the phantom is still in its usual and proper place—there are no holes or empty space between the stump and the remaining phantom limb. Some patients then begin to experience this emptiness of space, with the rest of the phantom limb as floating down there in its normal position. This is a transient stage, not found in all patients. It is followed by the separate parts moving together and approaching the stump. In the absence of a phantom calf, and with both phantom foot and knee present, the foot gradually rises, being felt after a while at a place halfway toward the knee, then just below the knee, then projecting from the knee. As the phantom knee disappears, the phantom foot may be localized where the knee would be, above the place where the knee would be, and eventually at the stump. Once the phantom foot has reached the stump, it begins to fade, leaving the toes. Eventually, these disappear too, at first for brief periods and then for progressively longer periods. In some patients—and Simmel (1956) suggests perhaps in all if they were more carefully examined—the phantom foot may remain intact and gradually slip into the stump, with the toes sticking out longer than the heel. Gradually, the stump comes to enclose the whole foot, which may be felt within the stump for a long time before it disappears.

Simmel cites an experiment she was able to perform with a patient with a high thigh amputation and a phantom foot just outside the stump. She took the hospital chart with the metal backing and moved it toward the stump. The phantom foot seemed to penetrate it just as would be true of the full-length phantom. But at the moment when the metal touched the stump, the phantom slipped inside the stump; but it came out again as soon as the stimulus was removed. Simmel was able to repeat this many times without extinction. This appears to work only with phantoms that have undergone a great deal of telescoping, probably, as Simmel suggests, because the stump cannot accommodate phantoms longer than itself.

Diminution in Size

There is still another transformation of the phantom—the diminution in size of the remaining phantom parts.

All of these changes may be prevented, slowed down, halted or reversed; or after the phantom has disappeared, they can be made to reappear. Pain, peripheral stimulation, the use of a prosthesis, and central stimulation may make it reappear.

Painful phantoms apparently may remain unaltered for a long time. Although 98 percent of all amputees experience phantoms, only 1 percent or 2 percent have painful phantoms. Although the painful phantom may have parts missing, telescoping or change in size does not ordinarily occur. However, in patients with localized pain in the stump and normal painless phantom, the normal phantom undergoes the usual changes except it seems reluctant to disappear into the painful stump. Simmel also cites an interesting case of a patient with a high-thigh painful stump and a normal, nonpainful, and much telescoped phantom when she was relatively free of pain. When she had pain in the stump, however, she was not aware of this phantom at all but experienced a phantom extension of the thigh beyond the stump, apparently as a function of radiating pain, which was provided in this way with a field for the pain to radiate into.

Even in nonpainful phantoms, irritation of the stump by a fall or after reoperation can reverse the telescoping and reconstitute the phantom to its full size and detail even after the phantom had previously totally disappeared. Indeed, occasionally such stimulation may provoke a phantom when there had been none before.

Reappearance of Phantom

When the patient begins to use the artificial limb, the phantom reverts to its full size, even though it may have telescoped or disappeared before this. Phantoms of the lower extremities often coincide with the prosthesis so that it is experienced as a living limb on which he is walking. Thus, one patient on getting home in the evening takes off both her shoes. Other patients have a phantom in parallel with the prosthesis, which moves with it but is clearly distinguished from it. In other patients the phantom leg does not participate in walking at all, and still other patients have no phantom when walking with the prosthesis. The phantom arm and prosthesis, however, rarely coincide, each retaining its autonomy, with the prosthesis being experienced as a tool attached to the stump. Cronholm (1951) has accounted for this difference on the grounds that the leg prosthesis is used for walking much as the leg is used, while the hook is used for manipulations that differ from that of the normal hand, and the dress hand cannot be used at all.

Not only peripheral stimulation provokes the reappearance of the phantom. It may reappear if the patient is forcefully reminded of the original accident or some circumstance in connection with the amputation, seeing another amputee or as a result of dreams. In some cases voluntary concentration may bring it back.

Simmel's Theory

Simmel concludes her extended observations with a theoretical discussion of three basic questions: Why do phantoms occur at all, why do parts drop out selectively, and why is there telescoping?

She accepts Head's (1920) concept of the body schema with its primary emphasis on postural, kinesthetic, and tactile learning. These she regards as of more importance than either visual or emotional factors. She regards the body schema as acquired over a period of time as a function of much peripheral stimulation, which reaches stability at the same age as other complex perceptual activities, at about 6 years. At this age most children are capable of the visual-spatial organization necessary for learning to read and write, and it is also the age at which amputation phantoms first appear. She accounts for the lack of phantoms in patients with leprosy, who have gradual absorption of digits, on a learning basis. Here the body schema, she suggests, can keep up with the changes in body shape through a series of minor changes, and hence no phantom results. Under conditions of amputation the relearning takes time, and the phantom is the result.

She accounts for the differential rate of dropout of parts of the phantom on the basis of the Penfield–Boldrey (1937) homunculus. Large homunculus areas represent highly differentiated sensitivity and movements to which we ordinarily give most attention, while small homunculus representation means low absolute and differential sensitivity and relatively automatic movements. There is a correlative degree of awareness, so those parts of which we were relatively unaware to start with will soon disappear below the threshold of awareness, while those which are very prominent in our experience would offer greater resistance to being abolished.

Simmel's (1954) answer to the problem of telescoping is that because the phantom has lost some parts, it has become disconnected from the rest of the body and can be reconnected in one of two ways. Either the remaining parts could stretch to contact the stump, or they could move toward the stump. She thinks stretching does not occur because it would involve change of shape and thus loss of object identity as well as increasing the size of the phantom parts. Change of position does not abolish object identity, nor prevent reduction in size—which later she seems to regard as one aim of these transformations. As regards the primary origin of the phantom, she sides neither with the earlier writers who favored explanations in terms of the periphery, nor with the later investigators who stressed the importance of the brain; she believes that each is a necessary but not sufficient condition for phenomenal experience.

Further, she argues that the brain-experience relationship necessarily involves a time delay during which learning takes place and that the phantom is a direct outcome of this delay.

Reconsiderations of Simmers Theory

Simmel's (1956) work should now be pursued with attempts to bring the phenomenon under experimental control. Just as the inverted lenses of Stratton (1897) and Kohler (1955) have illuminated visual perceptual theory, we would urge analogous radical experimentation with the body image. After we have considered the theory of the phenomenon in more detail, we will return to possible lines of experimental attack on the problem.

First and foremost it should be noted that the most vivid, precise "perception" is capable of being sustained by peripheral stimulation from a stump that surely lacks the detailed and changing sensory input that would normally be mediated by receptors in the amputated limb. This is not to say that the stump is without sensitivity. Indeed, there is evidence from Haber (1955) that stump sensitivity exceeded that of homologous parts of the sound limb on all three measures he used—light touch, two-point discrimination, and point localization, with the latter giving the largest differences. He believed that central factors were implicated by the finding of better stump sensitivity in amputees who reported telescoped phantoms as compared with those whose phantoms had properties of a normal limb. Since in normal limbs tactile sensitivity is high in distal parts and low in proximal parts, it would appear that when telescoping does not occur, the stump continues to have the lower "normal" insensitivity but becomes more sensitive as the awareness of the phantom begins to overlap with the stump. Here is apparently a reliable change in sensitivity based on a change in imagery rather than a change in peripheral stimulation. We may be overstating the case, however, since it is likely that there are motor innervations to the stump that are different when the phantom telescopes into it than when the phantom is as extended as the normal limb would be.

There is abundant evidence that purely centrally innervated imagery ordinarily also innervates the imagined body area. Jacobsen has shown that imagining any muscle movement evokes recordable muscle potentials in that muscle. Dement and Kleitman (1957) have found eye movements correlated with the visual imagery of dreams. Shagass (1972) has reported that patients whose problems center on sexual conflict have elevated muscle potentials in the thighs, whereas those struggling with the control of aggression have elevated muscle potentials in the arms. It is not unlikely, therefore, that there is increased feedback from the stump created by the increased motor innervations when the phantom limb begins to telescope into the stump.

The Role of Central Factors

The reality of this perception, as we have noted, is such that that the individual has to discover the missing limb not by feel but by looking at it. It is not only very real to the individual, but it is also enduring—in some cases up to 30 years. Dependent as it appears to be on some continuing peripheral stimulation, we would, nonetheless, place more emphasis upon central factors than Simmel (1956) does. Consider first the patient Head (1920) reported, in whom a cerebral stroke suddenly and completely removed a phantom limb that had followed an amputation. The peripheral stimulation presumably remained constant, but the phantom suddenly and atypically disappeared. Second, as Simmel has reported, the sight of another amputee, a reminder of the original accident, or even a dream is capable of restoring the phantom.

It is true that Simmel reports that peripheral stimulation will also make the phantom reappear, but we believe that the latter will not be effective unless it is first transmuted into report. Such a crucial experiment, in which the patient is peripherally stimulated anew while being otherwise distracted, has not, to my knowledge, yet been reported. There is, however, a voluminous clinical literature with which I am not completely familiar.

The Role of Central Imagery

The reality and stability of the phantom limb we regard as evidence that what is normally perceived is a centrally innervated image, guided by sensory input but also by memory, which operates on an internal feedback principle of matching *both* sensory and relevant memory information to produce a report that is in varying degrees similar to and different from the sensory patterns and memory patterns by which it is guided. How else are we to account for a phantom that is neither always the foot it once was nor altogether different, that can play peek-a-boo in and out of the stump? The reality of "imagery" has been known since Galton (1880). Head (1920) and Bartlett both extended our knowledge of imagery and stressed its significance for mental functioning. Bartlett, indeed, urged that what appears to be perceiving is largely the remembering of images. But although such empirical evidence continues to accumulate, psychologists have hesitated to take the final leap into the dark and cold, apparently solipsistic waters.

Only McKay (1956), in a well-disregarded paper in *Studies in Automata,* has taken the logical next step that we are also urging—that perceiving is not partly some mediate process but entirely so and that it uses the feedback-matching principle. Let us be clear on what this does *not* mean. There are many mediate processes in addition to the perceptual process that "guide" and provide a "target" for the final conscious report. If one is trying only to remember someone's face or the appearance of a chess board in blind-fold chess, one is ordinarily aware that one is imagining or remembering and not perceiving.

There are conditions, however, as we have just noted in olfaction, where the individual may be uncertain whether he is imagining or perceiving. Our argument is that in neither case is he simply "perceiving" and that in both cases he is using the same central mediating mechanism. In the case of smell without the stimulus, though we call it hallucinatory, there is a stimulus that the matching mechanism uses as a guide and a target, the patterned impulses from storage. In this case the final report "perceives" the impulses that originate from another internal source rather than from an external source; and when this information compares favorably in detail with the latter and there is no competition from external sources, it then becomes difficult to distinguish a report in which impulses from memory constitute the entire source and target rather than part of the target along with information from external sources.

This view of perception is to be distinguished sharply from the classical view, which has been essentially unchanged since Wundt (1890), that perception is a compound of a sensory core plus an apperceptive mass. Our argument is that this apperceptive mass is a sensory form similar to information received from the sensory receptors and that the final report is to some extent a composite not unlike the composite from the two eyes, (fused into a single image) different, however, in that the composite is constructed by a mechanism other than either of its component mechanisms. Shades of the Wundtian doctrine still are found in all of those theories that emphasize the schematic and categorical nature of perception. We too believe that general schemas, categories—indeed the whole army of cognition—are brought to bear on the mechanism that constructs the perceived object, but we must, nonetheless, eschew the percept as a collection of universals.

Although perception in the absence of universals would be a slow, lumbering, stimulus-bound affair, the perceptual payoff is, nonetheless, neither a word nor a collection of words, nor an assumption, nor a combination of specific values of a set of categories. This, despite the fact that once a word has been invoked in the ordering of the sensory data from a stimulus, that stimulus may bear a closer resemblance to what that word suggests than the stimulus itself would have suggested. There are, in short, many mediational cognitive processes—Wundt's apperceptive mass will still do—that play a central, though usually silent, role in the construction of the perceived object but do not constitute the hard analogical core of the perceptual report. We perceive pictures, smells, and sounds, not categories. The reader will now suppose I have been indulging in the classic avocation of the psychological theorist—cruelty to straw monsters—and in a sense he is right. Who would deny that we seem to sit on chairs rather than a Platonic idea of a chair? Yet I cannot escape the impression that the contemporary winds of perceptual doctrine blow and buffet the percept between the harsh solidity of the physical object and the diaphanous contours of the Kantian categories of the mind.

One final specification of what we do not mean. We do not mean that the total ongoing conscious field is a perceptual field necessarily perceived as an external object. One can and does distinguish the perceived face from the wish to kiss that face, the judgment "what an interesting face," the memory that "it is similar to the face of X whom I have not seen in many years." Although these concurrent responses may have influenced the perceived face more than we know, that face is, nonetheless, phenomenologically somewhat distinct from other reports that are related to it, just as the separate sensory channels are characteristically somewhat distinct from each other.

Varieties of Imagery

We consider that all of these internally mediated processes are transformed into conscious form through the same mechanism that is involved in external perception and that in this important sense *all* conscious experience is some type of imagery but not necessarily the *same* type of imagery. Just as the auditory sense differs in the imagery by which it is reported, so thought, memory, and decisions characteristically differ in quality, detail, intensity, and patterning of the imagery in which they are represented. These are what permit the distinctions to be made between one sense and another and between inner and outer sources. When, however, these characteristics are not sufficiently different, the individual can mistake the primarily inner-guided imagery for the outer-guided imagery.

Penfield (1950), in his studies of electrical stimulation of the brains of human patients undergoing brain surgery, has reported two rather distinct consequences of such stimulation that illustrate well the distinctions we are here attempting. As discussed above, certain spots always yielded a detailed report of something that had been experienced before at a specific time and place. Thus, one patient heard an orchestra playing a melody. When the same spot was restimulated, it always produced the same orchestral experience. This experience was so detailed and vivid that the patient believed that a phonograph was being turned on in the operating room every time she was stimulated at this spot on her brain. This type of experience, though it is confused with reality, is, nonetheless, remembered to have occurred also in the past.

In contrast are what Penfield (1950) has called interpretive responses, which are evoked from similar stimulation in the same general area. In these cases the patient discovers that, on stimulation, he has changed his interpretation of what he is seeing, hearing, or thinking at the moment. He may say that his present experience seems familiar, as though he had had it before; or things may, by contrast, seem suddenly strange and absurd. We see again the possible vividness and detail of memory stimulated by imagery and its consequent confusion with outer stimulated imagery. We see also, however, that memory stimulation can affect the conscious report from outer or inner sources without obtruding itself in the form of detailed imagery but rather as an accompanying awareness that relates the present "percept" to something else that is no more specific than that it is similar to or different from something experienced before. The latter awareness we would characterize as diffuse, schematic imagery that on occasion can lead to the retrieval and consequent construction of a more detailed conscious report.

Phantom as Imagery

Let us return now to the discussion of the phantom limb. This limb, we are supposing, is neither the patterned stimuli from the stump nor the patterned stimuli from memory, except for that relatively brief period immediately following amputation when, despite the change in sensory stimulation, the imagery is primarily patterned on what is available from memory, since the stump offers a too reduced complexity of stimuli to reproduce the same pattern as before. Just as soon as parts begin to drop out of the phantom and telescoping begins, more complex transformations are required to doctor the remaining images into a coherent report that will preserve the unity and identity of the body. Such transformations were produced experimentally by Ponzo (1913). In one of Ponzo's experiments, the subject standing with eyes closed holds a receptacle in his hand with the arms stretched directly up. The receptacle is filled with water. The bottom of the receptacle is connected with a tube through which the water can be drained noiselessly by opening a stopcock. The subject ordinarily does not notice the gradual loss of weight. The first thing he notices is that the receptacle seems to have suddenly lost its complete weight and might fly out of his hand. If attention is directed to the arm rather than the receptacle, marked deformations are experienced. The arm feels elongated, and even the whole body feels as if it were becoming taller.

If the receptacle is placed on the eyeball, as the weight diminishes, the eye is felt to protrude several inches out of the face. Some subjects describe a light substance as apparently emanating from the ocular cavity.

On the basis of these and similar findings, Angyal (1941) believed that some of the somatic delusions in schizophrenia could be understood as a consequence of their impaired body-world differentiation. Fischer and Cleveland (1957) have since then demonstrated that individuals vary in the firmness of the felt boundaries of their body images. Angyal suggested that since schizophrenics characteristically suffered from an impairment of clarity in their body image they were as a consequence more vulnerable to somatic delusions, just as the normal individual could be made to experience similar body deformations if one experimentally restricted his information concerning the conditions of stimulation.

Thus, one of Angyal's patients often complained, as though he were losing something of his body, "They yank out the stuff of my bottom." Angyal had at first supposed this was a classic anal hallucination but then discovered that the "stuff" irradiated from the whole gluteal surface and that the phenomenon always appeared just when the patient arose from the chair or a few seconds later. The patient described his experience as "If I set awhile on the bench and then I stand up, a stuff goes out of my bottom which is ten times lighter than air." Angyal suggests, persuasively, that this is probably based on the same kind of kinesthetic aftersensations as followed the change in weight on the eyeballs and arms.

A similar phenomenon arises with this patient in walking when, in lifting his feet from the ground, he relieves the pressure on the plantar surface. He often complains that he loses his "footprints," that he is leaving something behind himself by walking. He often returns to look on the floor for the "stuff" he lost.

Thus we see that deformations of the body image are relatively easily produced experimentally in the normal individual through alteration of the messages from the periphery at the same time that one somewhat restricts full information concerning these changes. These deformations also include, for some subjects, additional phantoms. What is of interest is that here too is a transformation, which represents faithfully neither the body image as it has been experienced and stored in memory nor the present pattern of unfamiliar afterstimulation. On the basis of these disparate sources there is constructed a new body, taller, with longer arms or much-bulging eyes. The unity of the body is preserved at the cost of familiarity, as it is in the phantom limb. In Simmel's (1956) discussion of telescoping she noted the theoretical possibility of "stretching" to close the gap between the stump and the remaining phantom but supposed it did not happen, in part because this would make the remainder of the phantom larger, and she thought one of the aims of the transformation, in addition to preserving the unity and identity of the limb, was to get rid of and therefore to reduce the size of the phantom. Because denial of impaired parts of the body is usually on an all-or-none basis, we doubt whether size reduction is a critical criterion in this transformation. Since Ponzo's technique has produced just the stretching and elongation that does not happen after amputation, it lends itself well to experimental study of the conditions under which particular deformations of the body image will occur.

What Constitutes Body Image?

Let us turn now to a more general question concerning this plastic body image. What is the stuff of which it is made?

The body image appears to be primarily constituted of a set of kinesthetic and vestibular messages. Within this matrix the information from the skin senses, such as touch, pain, temperature, is fitted, just as the kinesthetic body image itself appears to be contained within the larger visual frame. Orientation may be expected to be based on those sources of information that are most voluminous in quantity and most continuous in time. We should expect sources that are less voluminous, and particularly more intermittent, to be coordinated to the more continuous and voluminous matrix.

There is evidence, according to Ruch (1951), of an important structural differentiation between proprioceptive and skin sensory representation within the brain. He suggests first that sensory and motor areas in the brain are not distinct but constitute a paracentral sensorimotor area. Application of strychnine to the precentral gyrus of the monkey, containing the cortical motor areas, produces signs of sensory activity similar to those following application of strychnine to the postcentral gyrus. Stimulation on conscious human subjects at the time of surgical operation yields sensory responses from the precentral and postcentral gyrus alike, although the responses from the postcentral gyrus are more numerous. Stimulation of posterior spinal roots causes electrical activity in the precentral cortex. Since evoked potentials in the precentral sector are not observed from stimulation of the skin, this may indicate, according to Ruch, that only proprioceptive impulses reach the precentral sector.

As a consequence of the primacy of the vestibular kinesthetic image over touch, pain, temperature, and other intermittent sources of body awareness, we can understand the somewhat shadowy nature of the phantom limb, such as its capacity to penetrate and be penetrated by solid objects without any awareness of touching them. We interpret this to mean that (normally) touch stimulation, when it occurs, is fitted into the kinesthetic image and that when such stimulation is lost through amputation there does not exist a stable touch body image that supplies from within the missing information from without, as happens in the case of the image of stimulation from internal receptors. Although the body moves, phenomenologically, through visual spaces, if the kinesthetic-vestibular stimulation is put into conflict with the visual stimulation by independently varying the angle of the body and the angle of the visual surround, as Witkin (1949) has done, individuals differ radically on the relative weight they attribute to the visual field or to the body image based on kinesthetic and vestibular stimulation. This choice, Witkin has shown in a sustained program of pioneering research, depends on the salience and importance of very general attitudes toward the self and the world.

The contribution of visual factors to the body image proper seems no more important, however, than touch. Both are, in a sense, equally intermittent, psychologically, and hence defer to the more continuous bombardment of internal body stimulation. Vision, we think, is an intermittent source of stimulation for the maintenance of the body image because what is figural in vision is rarely one's own body. One looks out of the body but rarely at it. This is why the visual discovery that the limb is missing has so little immediate effect on the phantom limb and why the "sight" of the phantom limb hanging continuous down through the mattress is only amusing.

The Role of Continuous Inner Stimulation

This, then, is our version of why there are phantom limbs at all. It is not simply because there has been a great deal of past experience with the limb, although it has in fact been touched, seen, and given pain too on numerous occasions, but rather because there has been voluminous, continuous stimulation from the inner receptors both preceding and following purposive action with the limbs. This interplay between stimulation before and after motor innervations, we think, is critical in the formation of those memory images which later support the phantom limb.

We have deferred the discussion of the role of the feedback system until this point. We will now consider the second question Simmel (1956) raised—why there is the selective dropout of parts in the sequence she observed. Her answer is certainly reasonable and persuasive—that it is a function of the homunculus with its varying density of representation of sensory and motor fibers. There is, however, a subtle difficulty with this explanation. Let us suppose that the normal limb had transmitted 5 billion sets of pulses from the periphery prior to amputation and received 2 billion motor impulses during the same period of time. In one sense it would be true that each area of the limb would both send and receive impulses with this combined frequency times the number of individual sensory and motor fibers specific to each area of the limb. Thus, there would, in fact, have been many more innervations to and from some areas than others. Nonetheless, if one describes stimulation frequency in terms of discrete moments in time rather than by the product of moments times number of separate fibers, then every area has been stimulated from the brain and transmits stimulation back to the brain an equal number of times. Simmel's argument, therefore, ultimately depends not on frequency per se but on density or frequency times the number of fibers. Now, it is clear that the difference in density, though large, nonetheless is *relatively* small in comparison with the frequency of firing because of the very large number of times each fiber has been stimulated. The number of sensory and motor nerves, in short, is a much smaller quantity than the number of times they have been fired over a period of 25 years or so. If this argument is sound, we should expect that the original phantom is a good duplicate of the normal limb. This appears to be so and cannot be accounted for by arguing that some areas have greater cortical representation than others. If such an argument is to be used to account for the selective dropout of some areas of the phantom limb, it cannot also be used to account for the initial preservation of normal detail in the phantom.

The second part of Simmel's theory of the selective dropout of parts is not on the basis of frequency of cortical representation but rather on its experiential correlate—the greater awareness of our fingers than of our upper arm, of our toes than of our calf. The less aware to begin with, she argues, the sooner they may be expected to disappear below the threshold of awareness. We would agree that there is a differential degree of awareness to begin with, one that is mediated in part by the structure of the cortical homunculus. It seems reasonable that the less well-defined parts of which we are less aware should be the first to drop out of awareness. But, although reasonable, as all explanations of learning and memory based on frequency have always seemed, why should it happen so? What is necessary here is a theory of memory.

At this point we will argue briefly, on the basis of the theory already presented, that the critical factors in the availability of the memory image are learned skills. These are the skills that so organize sensory input and memory traces that smaller and smaller bits of sensory input are capable of guiding retrieval of memory images. Second, the learning involved in memory so organizes sensory information that there are many alternative, reduced aspects of the stimulus that are capable of steering retrieval strategies to reconstruct the memory image. Third is an organization of memory traces into miniaturized form, so that the individual may be "aware" of the abbreviated information with minimal awareness. Finally, there is an organization of memory traces that is capable of expanding the compressed, miniaturized trace into a more detailed, denser pattern of impulses, which, when transmuted, give a conscious report that is a reasonable facsimile of the original.

These transformations are more likely to be pushed to their most efficient upper limits the more important it becomes to the individual to increase his skill in memory organization and retrieval, or the more he is pushed into the acquisition of such skill by external demands and circumstances. There is ordinarily, but not necessarily, a correlation between such skill and the frequency with which the individual is stimulated to exercise these skills. However, past frequency is an insufficient basis for the prediction of loss of this skill under radical changes of sensory support for the exercise of memory.

Some of the sensory information from the stump is still sufficiently similar to the preamputation sensory information to produce retrieval of the intact memory data. Both of these together, present sensory and past memory, produce the imagery of the phantom limb sufficiently similar to the normal limb that the individual has to learn about the amputation primarily through vision. This is a process not radically different from the proofreader's error, in which some of the sensory information is also missing. Why, then, does the phantom not continue?

It is the production and increasing retrieval skill of *new* phantoms, which are constructed on the basis of the new feedback as this increasingly fails to confirm the old phantom, that gradually destroys reliance on the older memory images. This happens gradually in the case of leprosy patients, whose digits are absorbed, so that, like the clock that is watched, one knows that the hand is moving but not when. That frequency of representation per se is of little account is shown by the continuing vulnerability of the amputee to sudden return of the phantom if circumstances are such that his new retrieval skills are inadequate to block access to the older traces (e.g., the sight of another amputee or a reminder of his accident). Nothing has happened to the memory that supports the phantom except a new set of memories, which gradually change and increasingly block access to the older memory image.

The Phantom Is Never Destroyed

On this view the phantom is never destroyed. Its retrieval is made less frequent because newer and newer versions of the phantom come to be laid down in storage and newer and newer retrieval skills are learned to recover these phantoms rather than the original phantom. These new memories are based on whatever changes are introduced at any time into the awareness of the phantom. Since we believe that all information that reaches conscious form is stored, any difference between the experience of the phantom and the past experience of the normal limb can be the beginning of the destruction of the original memory image. One such difference is the lack of contact sense information. The phantom is never touched, or warm or cold. Such a difference can be the beginning of the systematic changes in the phantom. It should be remembered that a small percentage of phantoms is very painful, so it is not true that all contact sensory information is necessarily absent. This painful stimulation in all probability comes from the stump rather than the memory image, but it is characteristically referred to the phantom. It is of interest that these painful phantoms are frequently the most resistant to extinction. It may be that the continuing pain stimulation from the stump interferes with the disappearance of the phantom because it is responsible for the deposition of new memory images of singular vividness and intensity.

But, in general, it is the lack of some of the accustomed feedback following the attempt to use the phantom that we would hold responsible for the changes in the memory images, which gradually compete more and more with the older set of memories. Why do some parts drop out sooner than others? We would argue that this is a function of the ratio of detail in the phantom to detail in the new feedback. Since the new feedback is almost zero (there is still some feedback from the stump), those parts that were most detailed are less likely to produce changes in the new awareness than those parts that were least detailed. Consider the proofreader's error once again. An error in a longer word is less likely to be seen than the same error in a word half the size, since on a percentage basis there is a smaller error if one letter is wrong in a 10-letter word than if the same letter is wrong in a 5-letter word. On an analogous basis, the difference in actual new feedback from the stump will constitute a bigger difference to those parts of the phantom that are least densely represented. If, however, we could radically exaggerate the difference in feedback, then we might accelerate the formation of new phantoms sufficiently so that even densely represented parts would drop out much more quickly. Such a theory lends itself to experimental test by having a subject wear artificial extensions to fingers or toes or arms or legs, varying the amount and kinds of tasks while wearing false limbs, and then removing these after varying periods of time and practice. In this way one could create new phantoms and study the course of their disappearance as a function of experimentally controlled experience.

The telescoping of parts, we have already noted, represents neither the old phantom nor the new but a transformation of both that appears to have as its aim the preservation of the identity and unity of the body by a compromise that retains the continuity of the old phantom with the remaining parts of the newer phantom. It should also be noted that telescoping itself must play a crucial role in accelerating the disappearance of the phantom limb since the strategy that prompts this transformation is responsible for greater changes in memory images than are produced either by lack of touch or dropout of usually-dimly conscious parts, since, in a sense, both of these have, from time to time, been experienced before with the normal limb. It has happened before that one's limbs were not touched or that one was unaware of some upper part of the limb, but never before has one experienced a shrunken limb. Because of its novelty and relatively infrequent deposition among memory traces, it should offer relatively little resistance to the formation of still more truncated phantoms. In other words, the less similar each new memory trace to the set of past traces that first produces the phantom, the easier it becomes to learn not to retrieve this trace but to retrieve the newest modification and so increasingly rapidly to lose the phantom.

Changes in the phantom could be studied experimentally by varying the degree of difference of size and shape of artificial fingers from the fingers of the subject and studying the speed of loss of this phantom as a function of this difference. Our hypothesis is that the speed of loss of such a phantom would vary with the degree of difference from the normal finger. All new feedback, when transmuted, generates new experience and therefore new memories, which are either identical with past experience and expectation or different from it. For it to be identical with past experience and present expectation is a relatively rare phenomenon. It is more characteristic for new feedback to follow a course of either adaptation or sensitization. In comparison with the memory image, the present experience tends to become more vivid, producing sensitization, or less vivid, producing adaptation. This is due either to contrast or assimilation between the memory image and the new sensory information. Just as a gray object becomes lighter on a black background than on a darker gray background, or becomes darker on a white background, so we postulate similar internal contrast and assimilation phenomena operating between memory information and incoming sensory information.

Since the conscious report is the best possible match the central mechanism is capable of producing, it is possible for conscious reports to become either adapted or sensitized, depending on the relative contrast or assimilation between each new input and the relevant memory image that is retrieved to match it. If the report accentuates the characteristic of the sensory input over the characteristic of the memory image, then the next report may begin adaptation if the repetition of the same sensory input produces a weaker report by contrast to the immediately preceding report if that has become the memory image standard of comparison. This waxing and waning of the vividness of sequential input as it is compared with changing memory images accounts for that difference between the standard and the comparison stimulus that has been called the time error, which may be positive or negative depending on the relative intensity of the decaying immediate memory and the time and intensity of the next input. The second stimulus, though equal in physical characteristics, is judged more or less intense, or heavy, depending on the modality judged. This process could be further pursued by adding extensions to the fingers that left an open space between the fingertip and the tip of the extension of the finger by mounting the latter on a very thin connecting rod mounted on the end of a thimble. Under these conditions the space inbetween should eventually become filled and continuous but should "shrink" more rapidly upon removal than an artificial finger that was solid and continuous, after it was removed.

There is, finally, yet another criterion that governs the telescoping transformations in addition to the preservation of the unity and identity of the body. It is the criterion of maximizing of duplicates, or so organizing the central assembly that repetitions are maximized. This ordinarily governs instrumental sequences rather than the image itself, although the perceptual matching mechanism is governed by this in its goal of matching sensory and memory data with the greatest economy and simplicity. This criterion would produce successive phantoms, much like the yearly model changes of American automobile manufacturers. As much as possible of last year's shell and dies would be used, consistent with fabricating a somewhat new model.

Limbs on and off are not the only way in which we may profitably experiment with the body image. We may also study the separability of the kinesthetic-vestibular body image as a whole from both the visual and tactile body image. This could be done by suspending the subject so that he swings through the air with the greatest of ease in a visual field that is initially unilluminated. By coordinating stereophonic sound over a bank of loudspeakers, one set of which extended indefinitely before and behind him on one side and the other set made to extend similarly on the other side, sound could be started softly at some distance on both sides to increase in volume and speed as it approached the space through which the subject was swinging. This stereophonic moving sound could be coordinated with a parallel bank of lights that moved at the same speed as the sound. If the body image is in fact independent of the touch, visual, and auditory fields, then it should be possible to create a visual-auditory "phi" that would travel through as well as around the body, or a body "phi" in which the visual-auditory field is bisected by the swinging body, depending on the relative dominance of the body percept and the visual-auditory field.

The relative density and contours of the body percept could be mapped by plotting the variations in speed of perceived tactile phi when the body was touched at a constant rate over different surfaces. We would expect in general that phi would move more slowly over sparsely represented skin than over densely populated areas, but we would also expect second-order variations in speed as a function of the more idiosyncratic proprioceptive body image that interacts with the tactile body image.

I have for some years used a simpler technique of evoking the body image. The subject is required to close his eyes and draw a picture of himself, with a pencil. Normal subjects characteristically are somewhat distressed at the outcome since, as they in part correctly insist, the introduced distortions are a consequence of not being able to visually monitor what they are doing. The outcome of this visually unmonitored performance is extraordinarily illuminating. What is produced is a caricature of a caricature. The effect of the closing of the eyes is to exaggerate the salient features of the body image, but since the body image is, to begin with, usually an exaggeration of characteristics about which the individual is hyperaware with pride or shame or fear, the consequence is a caricature of a caricature. It is this exaggeration of the body image that either very much amuses or distresses the subject.

Thus, a woman with a very prominent head drew Figure 52.1A with her eyes closed and Figure 52.1B with her eyes open. In each the head size is much exaggerated. She was, in fact, a very talkative, self-assertive individual. We may note the exaggeration of the size of the mouth in the eyes-closed drawing, which is somewhat reduced when the eyes are open. She was also a rather buxom, bosomy woman. Note the exaggeration of the bust in the eyes-closed drawing, which is somewhat reduced in the eyes-open drawing. Note also the prominence in both drawings of hair on the head. This too represented

FIGURE 52.1A Eyes closed.

FIGURE 52.1B Eyes open.

FIGURE 52.2A Eyes closed.

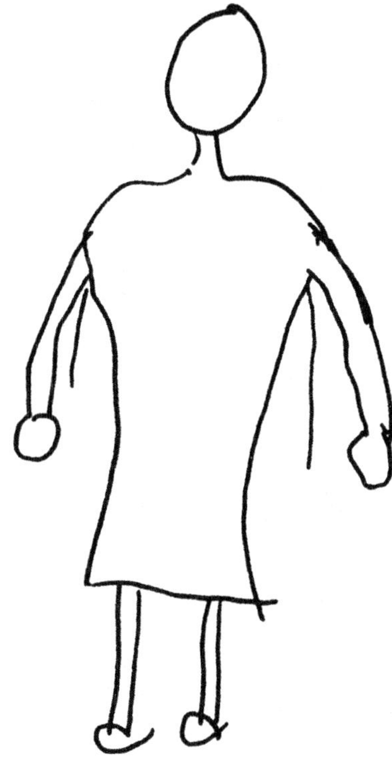

FIGURE 52.2B Eyes open.

rather faithfully a rather unusual growth. It appears to be given somewhat more prominence in the eyes-open drawing. Note also the exaggeration of the fingers in the first drawing and their reduction in the second. She, in fact, used her hands and fingers to gesticulate very actively as an accompaniment to her speech.

The fit here between the actual body and the body image under both conditions was unusually good, and this woman appeared to be a well-integrated personality.

By way of contrast, the young woman who drew Figures 52.2A and 52.2B was 22 years old, equally buxom and bosomy, and was experiencing a severe conflict over her virginity. She wished, and she did not wish, sexual experience. While the head is large, area-wise, in comparison with the body, in the first drawing the body itself is all but denied. There are no fingers, no toes, and no facial detail. The consequence of this conflict was to impoverish all of the organs of communication, mobility, and manipulation as well as to rob the body of its flesh.

With the eyes open there is a determined attempt to remedy these defects. Nonetheless, the face has no eyes, mouth, nose, ears, or hair. The hands have no fingers. The feet have no toes, and the body, despite its massiveness, is wooden, with no suggestion of femininity or the prominent bosom she possessed.

The drawings in Figures 52.3A and 52.3B were those of a normal young woman who was, however, troubled from time to time with a classical syndrome, the twin fears of falling and the claustral one of being shut up in a small space. This type of imagery appears to be a derivative of a birth fantasy in which leaving the womb involves both asphyxiation and falling.

She herself pointed out the lack of legs and feet and commented on her occasional fears of insupport and falling. She also interpreted the outstretched arms as a reaction against unwelcome restraint and said that she had a recurrent dream of being confined in a small space. It is noteworthy that the figure drawn with the eyes open somewhat attentuates the intense quality of the arms but that they are, nonetheless, outstretched in what seems to represent for her a permanent posture of defense against

FIGURE 52.3B Eyes open.

restraint. The feet are now put on the legs, but they have an almost schematic quality.

Figures 52.4A and 52.4B were drawn by a normal young man in his early 20s. Ordinarily, if an individual exaggerates an organ or limb with eyes closed, he will attempt to compensate and correct this exaggeration with the eyes open. Indeed, there are sometimes such gross overcorrections that it appears as protesting too much. In this case I interpreted the drawing to the subject. I suggested that perhaps he felt his arms were too long and too prominent. This evoked an embarrassed acknowledgment that such had been the case for some years. The impact of this public admission of hyperawareness of a specific part of the body, however, was to reverse the usual trend. With eyes open, he exaggerated the length of his arms, although he did correct the elongation and disconnectedness of the neck. The possible phallic significance of the arms is suggested by the unusual introduction of body hair and genitals in this drawing along with the very long arms.

FIGURE 52.4A Eyes closed.

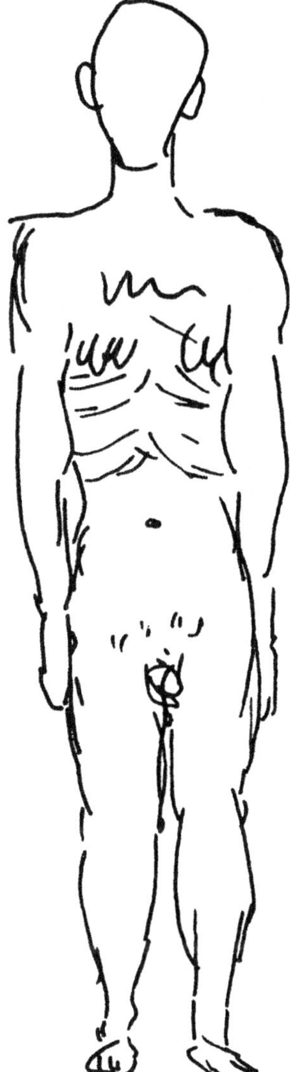

FIGURE 52.4B Eyes open.

Under these conditions each body image is as unique as the fingerprints. It would appear that the phantom body-as-a-whole would have numerous characteristics over and above what the homunculus in the brain would suggest. What impact these idiosyncratic images might have on any radical alteration of sensory input by surgery or by the experimental wearing to artificial limbs, in the manner we have suggested, must await future empirical investigation. In recent years Fischer (Fischer & Cleveland, 1957) has illuminated the significance of the varying degrees of permeability of the body image. The investigation of the body image is of interest, as he has shown, not only for what it tells us of how the individual regards his body. It is also an indirect indication of how he regards himself in the interpersonal domain.

Chapter 53
The Higher Senses

So much for the lower senses. Is there such a difference between such senses as smell, proprioception of the body, and the higher senses such as vision and audition? We think not. We have begun our argument for the central matching mechanism with the lower senses because these senses, by virtue of the relative simplicity, continuity, and homogeneity of information they transmit, provide especially clear evidence of the small differences there may be between imagery from central sources and perception of sensory information. They also provide more evidence of the relative independence of such centrally mediated perception from sensory information than is possible when the latter is radically changed.

These phenomena are less clear in vision and hearing, not because they do not operate but because these senses characteristically handle such an extraordinary traffic of hard news, of continually changing descriptions of the changing surround, that the central matching mechanism is not ordinarily permitted either to confuse internal with external reality for long or to foist stale memory images on an external world that continually challenges this mechanism to keep up with it. There are, nonetheless, visual phenomena that expose a central matching mechanism operating somewhat as it does in smell and body perception.

CONDITIONS UNDER WHICH ILLUSORY VISUAL IMAGES CAN BE PRODUCED

Reed (1963) reported

> . . . a characteristic type of imagery appears to be generated by the visual task of detecting the position of a single line in a uniformly illuminated blank field. Images of the line appear at a number of positions. They exhibit similar features for all observers, and seem to be a function of learning to search the visual field for a particular target. . . . The phenomena reported here . . . are noteworthy for a concrete vividness which competes with the sensory data, for their reliable similarity in all observers tested, and for certain autonomous characteristics. . . . He is not able to turn off or suppress the imagery for the sake of obtaining only "hard news" from the stimulus field.

Reed concludes, in support of my assumption, "We seem to have observed an instance in which a centrally produced template intrudes into the visual experience of the observer."

INVERSION OF VISUAL INFORMATION

Another way of exposing the visual phantoms is to radically and systematically change the visual information and to switch the individual back and forth between these different visual worlds. Under these conditions there are massive aftereffects similar to the phantom limbs, showing that the memory images are playing a dominant role in the conscious report.

The contribution of visual memory to a radical alteration in sensory input by the wearing of lenses that distort either the whole field or half fields is to some extent different from the phantom limb phenomenon. Consider the consequences of inversion of the whole visual field. At first, faces look unfamiliar, the walking of human beings seems mechanical, brightness contrasts are exaggerated, colors more saturated, and as the eyes and head move, the world moves. A good deal of the visual world is quite different from normal. This is in marked contrast to the normal phantom limb. We would attribute the difference to the impoverishment of sensory information in the case of amputation. An analogue for the inverted lenses in the field of body perception would be to radically alter the geography of the terrain that had to be negotiated by the limbs, for example, to walk in a medium of varying texture and position. Something similar, but less radical, occurs on ocean voyages. By the time a new set of memory images has been learned to produce relatively stable locomotion, the voyage is over, and the traveler is plagued with "sea legs," which now incapacitate him for terrestrial exploration. While sea legs are a precise analogue for the adaptation and aftereffects of wearing distorted lenses, neither is a sufficiently simple enough and radical enough alteration in sensory input to expose the complete phantom in all of its detail and purity. As long as sensory input is sufficiently detailed to offer a target to the central matching mechanism, the final report will represent a compromise between the full phantom and present sensory input.

Despite the failure of Ivo Kohler's (1964) experiments in wearing distorted lenses to expose the complete nature of the visual memory image, these experiments are quite impressive. In the case of inverted lenses, the initial gross unfamiliarity of an inverted world eventually gives way to improved motor and locomotor adaptation to what is seen. The subject can walk through town, but despite much improved motor performance his visual world remains inverted.

Next, about a month later the perceived world is much more congruent with geography and head movements. This represents enough deposition of new memories so that when the spectacles are removed, the world appears inverted with normal stimulation. These new retrieval skills sufficiently block the retrieval skills of a lifetime of prior experience, so the old familiar world has to compete with the memory images of the last few months' creation. Ultimately, retrieval of these older traces is achieved. It would be of interest, however, to test the analogy with the phantom limb. Is there a latent vulnerability to seeing the world upside down even after recovery of the familiar world? This could be tested by suddenly and unexpectedly inverting the visual field some months later by rotating either the subject strapped into a chair or rotating the room, as Witkin (1949) had done.

Kohler (1964) had subjects wear distorted prisms for varying periods of time up to 124 days. He was particularly concerned with the question of whether perceptual adaptation can occur in a differentiated manner. By appropriate lenses he therefore divided the visual field into two areas, one distorted, the other normal. Thus, in one experiment, the subject, by looking upward, looked through a distorting prism and by looking downward looked through an undeformed visual field. Differential adaptation occurred over time with increasing compensation for the upward distortion. At the beginning, the normal half of the field appeared distorted in a direction opposite to the distortions induced by the upper half prisms, but these decreased over time. Upon removal of the prisms, there was a difference between the two visual half-worlds. The upper half was more distorted than the lower half, in reverse direction to the distortion that had been induced by the prism.

Kohler (1964) also demonstrated the same bifurcation of the effects of differential visual stimulation with respect to color vision. Subjects wore glasses in which the left half was blue and the right half yellow. Thus, the subject saw everything in blue when looking to the left and yellow when looking to the right. At the beginning there were transitory afterimages in which the blues got bluer at the left after the subject had looked through the yellow glass at the right, and conversely. However, as time went on, the colors became paler and paler. After protracted adaptation there is an eventual disappearance of all color despite eye movements which make light at the fovea blue at one time and yellow at the next—color is seen in neither case. Later, with the spectacles removed, the world looks yellow when the subject looks left, and blue when he looks right. Clearly, there have been systematic alterations in the stimulus, report, and memory relationships, in which, if yellow or blue stimulates the retina when the gaze is to the right or left, the memory image eventually becomes colorless through a series of compromise images that continually halve the difference between the conflicting sensory colors and conflicting supporting memory images. This process is quite similar to the telescoping phantom limb, which is also a continual compromise between the past phantom and succeeding reductions in size that make it smaller and smaller to ultimate disappearance. But these colorless memory images have not been learned to be retrieved for the interpretation of the normal achromatic stimuli of the familiar world. When the spectacles are removed, the same transformation that pulled each color toward neutrality is capable of pulling neutral stimulation toward the opposite color, in what Gibson (1959) many years ago described as adaptation with negative aftereffect.

Visual Perception of the Face

There is another way in which we can expose the central matching mechanism in vision—by examining the perception of that object that is most overlearned: the human face. If we are to examine perceptual skill, then we must pay special attention to those perceptual objects in which all human beings have deep interest and much experience. There exists no other single object about which human beings have had more engaging, diversified, and yet similar perceptual experience. We would offer the rough estimate that each human being has looked with some excitement upon at least 25 new human faces a day as he walks, rides, drives, or flies to and from work each day-. Even farmers and villagers who live in relative isolation from city life now enjoy the facial diversity afforded by television. If these faces were totally different from one another, they would not constitute material for the formation of a stable phantom face. Since, however, they share the same number of ears, eyes, noses, and mouths and approximately the same size and shape, as well as placement on the face, we should expect the formation of a Platonic idea of a face, a generalized phantom based on the general organizational strategy of maximizing of duplicates in received and stored information. This phantom differs from the phantom limb in representing the perception of others rather than self and in regression to a mean that is the common denominator of faces that vary more widely than the proprioceptive feedback from one's own limbs. Despite some variation, however, there is, in fact, sufficient repetition of facial characteristics across faces to afford the ready fabrication of a composite.

One of the most frequently repeated characteristics of the human face is its upright position, and this aspect of the memory image tends therefore to dominate the final conscious report of any perceived face, whether the stimulus is right-side-up or not.

Ivo Kohler (1964) reported that if a subject is wearing lenses that invert the retinal images and is then shown two faces, one upside down alongside an upright face with a smoking cigarette between the lips, both appear upright—but in different ways and in opposite directions. That the facial phantom is much more resistant to deformation appears in the same set of experiments in the finding that we have noted before, that at this stage despite effective motor performance, while wearing inverted lenses, most of the world remains phenomenally inverted. This inversion first disappears for objects connected with the subject's body system—an object grasped, a plumb line, or a face. These are the kinds of objects first seen upright for short periods of time.

The face matrix of Wheatstone (1838) is another instance of the stability of the phantom face. The inside of a mask from a few feet away, viewed binocularly, looks like the outside of a mask. The face continues to look normal under this complete reversal of the binocular cues. Ittelson and Slack (1958) report that this "inside-out" illusion is so striking and gives an impression so strong that it is almost impossible under any circumstances for all parts to appear as one would predict from a knowledge of the stimulus.

I have presented the following line drawings (in Figure 53.1) of the human face to over 100 subjects. Only 10 percent of these failed to identify them as three faces right side up, despite the fact that one is upside down and none contains all of the relevant features. When presented tachistoscopically, each

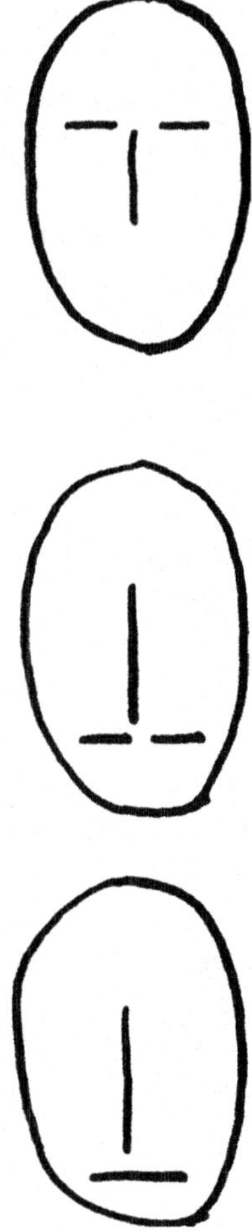

FIGURE 53.1 Line drawings of the human face.

face seems to "borrow" from neighboring faces the missing features that are needed to complete the face.

Engel (1956) has also demonstrated the impressive stability of the human face when, in a stereoscope, one eye is presented with a face right side up and the other eye is presented with a face upside down. Of 48 responses given by the group of subjects, the upright face dominated in 41 and the inverted in 3, and there was no clear dominance in the remaining 4. Each of the subjects reported more upright than inverted pictures. The dominance of the upright figure is shown in two different ways. First, the upright face emerges as an organized figure whose appearance is marred somewhat by isolated and partial details and contours of the inverted face. These details are preceived as conflicting with and extraneous to the dominant impression. Second, there is a tendency for the upright figure to predominate where the two figures are perceived alternately in the field. As Engel (1956) has noted, this experiment differs from previous rivalry experiments in that dominance here is attributable to the residual effects of previous stimulation rather than to differences in physical stimulus attributes. Hastorf and Myro (1959) replicated these findings using briefer exposures of $\frac{1}{10}$ and $\frac{2}{10}$ of a second. This excluded the possibility of comparing alternate appearances of the two faces.

Engel (1956) also demonstrated that if two different but structurally similar human faces are presented in the stereoscope, a fusion occurs, which is a "new" face. Rarely is there any intimation that dissimilar figures are being viewed in combination. When one face is darkened and the subject is asked to describe the other alone, and then this one is darkened and the subject is asked to describe the former and then asked to compare the "monocular" and "binocular" faces, the usual reaction of the subject is that the binocular face is a composite of specific features borrowed from each monocular face. Rather than a combination, however, it is in large part a blending, in which very often the binocular face is reported as more attractive than either of the monocular faces. Further, Engel (1950) noted that when a familiar face was put into one eye and an unfamiliar face into the other, the binocular face was reported as possessing features that were mainly or wholly those of the familiar component.

Still another instance of the stability of the perceived face, despite radical change in the physical stimulus, is reported in another experiment by Engel (1956). A pair of photos of two different faces served as the two monocular targets in a stereoscope. The faces are similar in size and position of facial parts and, by means of a previous adjustment of the apparatus, stimulate corresponding places in the two eyes of the observer. At the outset only one of the monocular targets is illuminated. The observer, viewing binocularly, is asked to describe what he sees. The illumination is then extinguished and a second presentation given, but this time the second monocular target is also illuminated but to a very slight degree. The observer is then asked to state whether any change has taken place in what he sees. Following this report, the illumination is again extinguished and the procedure repeated, but again a slight increment of illumination is added to the second target while the first is kept at the same level. The entire procedure is repeated until the second target reaches the illumination level of the first. Despite these changes, at each step the observer reports that he sees the same face as before! This continues even after the second target reaches the same degree of illumination as the first. Then the reverse procedure is begun. The second target is kept at the same level of illumination while the illumination of the first is brought down in small decrements of each trial. On the last trial only the second target is illuminated. The observer continues to report seeing the same face throughout this series to the end. This occurs despite the fact that on the last trial a clearly different face is shown than on the first.

Ittelson (1973) replicated and extended these findings. With 36 subjects making 108 responses to three pairs of "fusion" faces, in 97 instances the same face was still being reported at the point of equal intensity, that is, when both faces were exposed at the same level of illumination; and in 67 cases the same face was still being reported on the final exposure when the second face alone was being exposed.

Auditory Hallucinations of the Human Voice

In conjunction with the face is a set of auditory stimulations that are equally significant and even more overlearned by all human beings. These are the millions of words emitted and received daily by all nondeaf-mute human beings. Although there are significant differences between individuals in the quantity of words handled and in their skill in the reception and transmission of words, these differences are trivial in comparison with the high order of skill achieved in this domain by even the dullest human being. One of the reasons this skill attains such a notable level is that the same central images used in receiving words are also used in sending them. The message sent to the tongue are translations from a set of images, usually auditory, sometimes visual, sometimes kinesthetic. These can easily be evoked and made conscious by asking the individual to pretend to speak so softly that it cannot be heard. Under these conditions the guiding, predominantly auditory, imagery will be "heard" within. It is this same imagery that is ordinarily reproduced when monitoring the feedback that is created by the individual speaking.

Most of use have not achieved the same skill in retrieving detailed visual imagery as in retrieving auditory imagery except in the case of language. In learning to write we achieve a similar precise detailed visual kinesthetic skill. Writing means we can centrally emit the visual or kinesthetic shapes of letters and the motor translations from these images. We can expose this process in the same manner as with the imaginal guidance in speech by asking the individual to write with his hands but with his eyes closed. The majority of subjects "see" what they are writing under these conditions.

Despite this visual language skill it is nonetheless true that most of us do not learn to reproduce from within the complexities of our visual world. Although it is quite possible for most of us to learn to play blindfold chess and to "see" the chessboard in our mind's eye, relatively few of us learn such skill in the retrieval of visual imagery. Much of our visual skill depends heavily on sensory information.

In the case of words that are heard, the case is radically different. Our skill in fabricating this imagery quite exactly is such that confusion between auditory imagery from within and words received from without is possible if three conditions are met. First, attention must be turned inward, with either a reduction of sensory information at the receptors or by selective inattention or centrifugal attenuation. Second, the voice must be the voice of another person, since one is accustomed to hearing oneself speak all the time in inner speech, muffled outer

FIGURE 53.2 Text used in the perception experiment.

speech, and outspoken words. I know of no data on this point, but I would expect that whether one is talking to oneself or to another is not a distinction that is sharply drawn if one does much of either. But the inner production of the voice of another person is also a commonplace to some extent. Therefore the third condition that must be postulated for the production of an auditory hallucination either in normals or psychotics is the unexpectedness of the particular inner voice that is "heard" and that therefore produces visual and auditory tracking to "confirm" the hallucination. Unexpectedness can be produced by the period of time since one last spoke with the individual, or by circumstance (i.e., since I am alone, what is he doing here, since it is unlikely that he should be here in fact or that I should indulge in an imaginary conversation with him).

Extreme positive or negative affect that accompanies a heard voice is another way in which the voice's vividness and unexpectedness may be increased and the hallucinatory quality produced. We do not believe that *either* normals or psychotics necessarily are hallucinating when they are totally absorbed in the vividness of their internal imagery. The lover who thinks constantly of his beloved may know only too well the difference between real and imaginary conversations. However, for the most part, absorption in vivid imagery can be very similar to absorption in reality, and this means frequently that the distinction between the self and the other is not salient. If one looks at the faces of the audience watching an absorbing play, it is clear that at that moment there is a loss of self-consciousness in their identification with the characters of the play despite the preservation of some aesthetic distance. This absorption is not hallucinatory because this is a "real" perceptual process. What if the individual, upon going to bed, in the darkness of his bedroom sees again and hears again this same play? This need be no more or less hallucinatory than the original deeply absorbing experience.

Holt and Goldberg have also shown that subjects long exposed to sensory deprivation characteristically regard their hallucinations as unreal. Our point is that imagery, to be hallucinatory, must not only be vivid and projected but must be mistakenly regarded as having been stimulated by the presence of an object that is then sought in outer space.

How much of even psychotic preoccupation with self-produced imagery is hallucinatory in this sense we do not know. That the spoken word is capable of producing hallucinations is a consequence of the great skill in emitting such imagery.

It has been possible to produce other auditory illusions experimentally by tying the activation of the memory image of a sound to a memory image of a visual stimulus and then presenting the visual stimulus without the auditory stimulus.

Ellson (1941) presented his subjects with both a light and a buzzer, for many trials. When the light was presented alone, the subjects heard the buzzer too. We would class this as an illusion rather than a hallucination, despite the absence of the stimulus. This is, in principle, no different from the proofreader's error. By embedding the absence of a stimulus in a context in which it usually occurs, the memory image "closes" the gap. One of the most vivid instances of such an illusion is in Figure 53.2 which sometimes resists discovery for several minutes and is usually seen as Figure 53.3.

FIGURE 53.3 Illusion commonly elicited by Figure 53.2.

The Visual Agnosias

Another set of phenomena in which the centrally emitted imagery becomes critical for the perceptual processes is the agnosias, in which familiar visual objects are "seen" but not recognized.

Head and Holmes (1920) described the characteristic changes in tactile perception from cortical lesions as including abnormal persistence of sensations and hallucinations of touch, as well as rapid local fatigue and inconstancy of threshold. This lability of threshold may be a function of persistent afterimages. There is evidence from Cohen (1953), who reported that patients who showed defects of recognition with little or no sensory impairment had both marked lability of thresholds and persistent aftersensations. Such interference between persisting inner imagery and the normal sequence of changing imagery to sequences of sensory input could impair recognition without impairing "perception." This latter has been suggested by Semmes (1953) as a theory of agnosia. We would agree with it in large part but also disagree with respect to the following conclusions she draws. She suggests that in contrast to the traditional view that impulses from the primary sensory areas are organized and patterned in the associative cortex, it may be that impulses from the associative cortex play back on the primary sensory areas, thereby modulating and stabilizing the sensory process.

As we have noted before, the cortex not only receives sensory impulses, amplified by the reticular and other subcortical centers, it also dampens this amplification process. One of the consequences of any interference with this could be an increased inertia of the effect of sensory stimulation on the perceptual process. Although there is increasing evidence that there are important organizational activities that go from the highest central centers down and outward to the periphery in general, yet some degree of independence of sensory transmission from higher centers must be preserved if the partnership is to be profitable. Our view is that the integration that results in the perceptual report occurs *neither* in the sensory projection areas nor in the association areas but in a third site, as yet undetermined, in which information is transformed into reports. We would therefore agree with Semmes (1953) that the lesions are probably responsible for visual agnosia by virtue of the loss of impulses that modulate sensory information but disagree on where this modulation occurs. In our view, it is the final common site to which both association areas and sensory areas converge that is most disturbed in the final integration of information from within and from the sensory receptors.

Visual Anomalies and Synesthesia from LSD

Investigators using LSD have noted similar increases in inertia in the sensory system that have been reported with the agnosias. Bercel, Travis, and Leonart (1958) reported that a marked increase in the average alpha preservation time was observed in almost every instance. This means that, in response to a visual stimulus, the alpha blocking persisted for an inordinately long time. This finding has to be combined with another observation, namely, the markedly long persistence of the afterimage, either positive or negative. Since here the occipital alpha rhythm is involved, there is reason to believe that the disturbance affects those cells responsible for occipital electrogenesis and that some synaptic embarrassment is responsible for the prolonged alpha preservation time and for the long persistence of the afterimage. To what extent LSD operates through the same mechanisms as are involved in lesions that produce visual agnosias is not known, but the similarities in disturbance are suggestive that such might be the case. There is with LSD, however, more extreme synesthesia and interaction between the sense modalities. Thus, the same investigators also report that it was quite striking how often one form of stimulus influenced the perception of another form, suggesting some "cross-talk" mechanism between the individual sensory pathways. Sometimes the synesthesiae were quite primitive and quite simple, for example, the disappearance of the illusion of angular designs and their instant metamorphosis to curved ones upon simply clapping the hands.

A far more complicated synesthesia, however, is the one in which the subject reports that his voice or his perceptual anomaly is influenced by the examiner's voice. We interpret such cross-talk between sensory channels as evidence for the hypothesis that in both the agnosias and LSD disturbance the central matching mechanism is the primary site of disturbance. It would be here that a clap of the hands that has reached the auditory projection area and the sight of a design that has registered in quite a separate projection area could be brought into such intimate interaction. Intersensory influence is not limited to states of druginduced disturbance. Wapner and Werner (1957) have demonstrated in numerous investigations the deformations of the visual field that can be produced by a variety of auditory, vestibular, and kinesthetic stimulations. These phenomena argue strongly that much of the apparent insulation of one sensory channel from another is tenuous in the central assembly and, like other constancies of awareness despite neural variability, is learned and learned only within certain limits. Just as the visual world is reasonably stable despite our moving our head around in space, so it is also stable despite changing vestibular stimulation as we move about in space. Different animals would appear to be endowed innately with varying degrees of constancy of one modality from variation in another modality—witness at one extreme the eagle, who undoubtedly gets less dizzy and less blurred vision as he swoops down at high speed, and at the other extreme the cat, who is easily disturbed by motion in an automobile. This difference would in part depend on how sensitive one modality is, compared with another, as well as how intimately related neurologically. Despite these innate differences, learning also can and does modify these interdependencies, so one does not get dizziness nor blurred vision despite speed of movement for which evolution did not prepare us.

This means that the central matching mechanism must find a fit, not only between one sensory channel and memory data for that channel, but also fits between channels at both the sensory and memory levels. Such matching, for the most part, involves learning to disregard variations in one modality with respect to variations in another modality. This is apparently learned within broad limits of variation of all sensory channels. Nonetheless, it is always possible to exceed these limits, and then intersensory influences are exposed and awareness is disturbed sufficiently so that individuals can become nauseated and quite anxious at the instability of the perceptual, field. One way of exposing the learned component in such intersensory constancy would be to experimentally reverse the visual feedback from head movements. Ordinarily, when one moves one's head and eyes, one is bombarded with a series of visual and vestibular stimulations that vary as the head moves. If we assume that we have learned to interpret the vestibular component and much of the visual changes from memory images that cushion these changes, so that the visual world stands still as our head moves, then, if we were to so arrange viewing that when the eyes and head moved, the visual stimuli did *not,* there would be no memory images for this contingency, and we should produce paradoxical dizziness and visual motion from such movement of the head without correlated movement of the visual field.

Of the nature of imagery and its significance for the life of the individual we know more today than we did when Galton (1880) first published his findings. It is only when the pervasive role of imagery is appreciated, not only in the interpretation of sensory information in the construction of the perceptual world but also in the control of the feedback mechanism via the image, that the problem of imagery assumes a central significance for psychological theory. It is through private images that the individual builds the public world that enables both social consensus and competence in dealing with the physical world.

Part IV

OTHER CENTRALLY CONTROLLED DUPLICATING MECHANISMS

Chapter 54

The Central Assembly: The Limited Channel of Consciousness

In this chapter I propose a hypothetical inner "eye," the central assembly, which receives messages from all sources, both external and internal, and at the same time transforms them into conscious reports. It is assumed that this is a limited channel and therefore necessitates the conjoint admission of some and the exclusion of other neural messages as they compete for entry into this central assembly. I propose that the selection principle is the simple one of the relative density of neural firing of the competing messages. Any mechanism that increases the density of neural firing of one message over another increases the probability of attention and consciousness. Affect is one major amplifier; cross-sensory summation, memory recruitment, especially via scene magnification, are the ways in which competing information achieves favored entry into consciousness and the central assembly.

Finally, I will examine the general role of consciousness, urging that behaviorism and psychoanalysis seriously underestimated the significance of consciousness and its role in a feedback system. I will propose further that consciousness, wakefulness, amplification, and affect are maintained by independent mechanisms. Consciousness is not wakefulness, and wakefulness is not consciousness. Nor is wakefulness a level of amplification nor a level of affective arousal. The empirical correlations between the states subserved by these mechanisms are a consequence of the frequency with which these partially independent mechanisms do in fact enter into combined assemblies.

CONSCIOUSNESS AND THE LIFE PROCESS

If consciousness is distinct from wakefulness and is found even in sleep, it would appear to play a very general role in the life process.

Is life necessary for consciousness? Is consciousness necessary for life? The first question seems to have been answered by the death of every conscious organism. How necessary consciousness is for life is a more difficult question. First, we must ask what kind of consciousness for what kind of life for what kind of organism? If an organism is conscious when it is asleep, the answer must necessarily depend on the specificity and complexity of consciousness we are willing to call "conscious." It is clear that the burden placed upon consciousness is directly proportional to the complexity of the organism. There is increasing encephalization with increasing complexity. Further, the kind of "life" we are prepared to call living will be important in our assessment of the role of consciousness. Complex sensorimotor learning requires more alertness than turning over in bed while asleep. At one extreme, if we are dealing with human animals, the most encephalized of the animals, and speaking of the most alert type of awareness and the most complex type of living, then consciousness would appear to be a necessary condition of life. A man could not drive a car, for example, while asleep, although he appears to be able to walk in his sleep. At the other end, a decerebrate rat might remain alive for some time. The deeply unconscious organism, however, will certainly live on longer than the unattended neonate if for no other reason than that it would starve to death. There is evidence that the decerebrate rat is more viable than the decerebrate dog. With increasing encephalization however the organism is more and more vulnerable to cerebral insult.

Increasing complexity of behavior in general did not necessarily require consciousness. Did nature need a mechanism like consciousness to guarantee the viability of living organisms? Certainly not for all living organisms. The plant lives but appears unconscious. We find consciousness in animals who move about in space but not in organisms rooted in the earth. Mobility is the key. Consider how much information would have been required to be built into an organism that is never twice in exactly the same place in exactly the same world, when that world contains within it complex organisms whose behavior would have had to be predicted and handled. For several million humans to drive an automobile on a Sunday afternoon and return home viable would have required information in advance of an order of magnitude approximating omniscience. Nature did not know enough to build this kind of know-how into living organisms.

There were, of course, many problems that had to be solved before living creatures could be put on their own in space. Not the least of these was the problem of temperature. If an animal were to move around in a world whose temperature changed, it had to be endowed with a mechanism that preserved a relatively optimal and constant internal temperature despite variation in the external temperature as it moved about in space.

But the most complex problem was the magnitude of new information necessary from moment to moment as the world changed, as the organism moved. The solution to this problem consisted in receptors that were capable of registering the constantly changing state of the environment, transmission lines that carried this information to a central site for analysis, and above all, a transformation of these messages into conscious form so that the animal "knew" what was going on and could govern his behavior by this information. There is consequently a correlation between degree and frequency of conscious representation and the structure's pertinence to mobility. There is minor representation of the relatively fixed structures within the body as well as of the fixed external surfaces of the body. Thus, the hands and feet are better represented than the back. There is further a rough match between the type, amount, and rate of information that is received and the type, amount, and rate of information that can be acted on.

The general answer to the question—how necessary is consciousness for life?—is that consciousness becomes more important as the criterion of being alive becomes more complex and as the organism becomes more complex. The general experimental technique that will answer the question more specifically is to remove from the animal those structures essential to consciousness and then attempt to maintain the animal in its normal living state. What the experimenter must do for the animal is what we may presume consciousness did before. We cannot, however, answer the question of the role of consciousness until we can block the specific structures that mediate consciousness. When we can excise these structures and no others, then we can say what is the function of conscious information for the maintenance of life. The answer to this general question must therefore await the outcome of experiments that will establish the site of consciousness.

THE NATURE OF THE TRANSMUTING PROCESS

At the as yet indeterminate site of the transmuting process is a type of duplication that is unique in nature. Transmitted messages are here further transformed by an as yet unknown process we call *transmuting*, which changes an unconscious message into a *report*. We define a report as any message in conscious form.

Consciousness is a unique type of duplication by which some aspects of the world reveal themselves to another part of the same world. A living system seems to provide the necessary but not sufficient conditions for the phenomenon.

It is clear that there are many processes within the organism that are neither conscious nor communicative in nature. There are many processes in the liver, the kidney, and other organs that never become conscious nor play any significant role in the communication network. There are communication processes, afferent, and efferent nerve transmissions that, though they are integral parts of the communication network, nonetheless are not and never become conscious processes. By nonconscious communication processes we refer primarily to the duplication process of "transmission," by which a pattern of events at one place in time is duplicated at another place at another time.

What distinguishes "conscious" duplication from nonconscious duplication? We assume that the process is biophysical or biochemical in nature and that it will eventually be possible to synthesize this process. It must be remembered that this would not be the first time that physical processes yielded to scientific inquiry after centuries of ignorance. The basic nature of electricity for a long time seemed as elusive as consciousness. The dynamo is a relatively late achievement. The dynamo does not exist in nature apart from dynamo manufacturers. We are suggesting that consciousness as a phenomenon might be fabricated by man in a manner similar to but not identical with its present form, just as "organic" substances can be synthesized. Fabricating consciousness is, of course, a very different matter from contructing "thinking" machines. These, we assume, are intelligent but nonconscious. To equate consciousness with discrimination per se is to stand in the way of possible solution of the problem by denying that the problem exists.

The uniqueness of this transformation has been a source of discomfiture for psychologists.

They have sought refuge in words that suggest complexity of transformation, such as organization and integration at the neurological level, and discrimination at the behavioral level. But complexity as such is not peculiar to consciousness. The mechanical chess player is intelligent and discriminating but it is not conscious. It is indeed a great puzzle to guess what is gained by transforming the complex input of transmitted messages into conscious form. If all of the information that is needed by the person is received from the external world and transmitted over afferent fibers, then its further organization and transformation might be sufficient to produce intelligent and discriminating behavior without the benefit of consciousness. Although consciousness represents an increase in complexity, it is clearly not the only way in which nature can increase its complexity.

Yet Descartes' localization of the soul seems less nonsensical today than it did a short while ago. Such studies as the localization of wakefulness centers in subcortical areas and the tracing of the path of the epileptic storm from the cortex to the subcortical areas and back again have focused attention on the subcortical area as a possible site of that transformation we have called transmuting. Further, that series of messages which is most insistent in its claim for attention—pain—is said to have no cortical representation. While it is more than likely that consciousness, like life itself, is an emergent of a complex organization of many parts, it is nonetheless important that we assess the relative contribution to the process of different parts. It is clear that an organism can continue to live despite amputation of limbs and almost complete excision of some of its organs, but certain organs (such as the heart) are truly vital in that they occupy a central position for the support of life. It seems not unlikely that the subcortical centers might play a similar role in the support of consciousness.

To enhance the visibility of the site of transmuting one should reduce sensory input to a minimum and increase the identifiability of the conscious message to a maximum. One way of doing this would be to instruct a subject in a dark, soundproof room to imagine an electric light being turned on and off at a specified rate and to record the change in EEG from different parts of the cortex as the subject turns visual imagery on and off. Because these messages must originate from a central source and be directed toward the transmuting site, this should produce an identifiable pattern and pathway. The limitation of such a method is the difficulty of securing subcortical potentials from human subjects. There has, however, been accumulated over the past decades such a mass of experimental evidence that the site of the transmuting mechanism may be identified in the not too distant future. The information probably exists in the present mass of accumulated records, but it may be masked by the noise of varying amplification, varying wakefulness, and varying affect that accompanies the tranformation of transmitted messages into the transmuted conscious messages we have called reports.

CONSCIOUSNESS AND THE LIMITED CHANNEL

Consciousness is a biologically costly process, requiring as it does in the adult 1 hour of sleep for every 2 hours of wakefulness. If this sleep is itself too conscious and too affect-laden, even more sleep is required to pay the accumulated debt. This energic limitation on the spending of resources in consciousness is one restriction on consciousness. There is yet another restriction on consciousness—whether perceiving, remembering, thinking, feeling, or acting, or all of these at once—the limited channel. By this we mean that the individual is not free to become aware, at any one time, of all he might wish to. He cannot perceive an endless number of objects or equally well with all his senses at once. He cannot remember all he might wish to at any one moment. He cannot become aware of an endless number of thoughts at a moment in time. He cannot always become conscious of all of the feelings emitted momentarily by his face and autonomic system. He cannot easily even rub his stomach and pat his head at the same time. Finally, he could never do all of these at once. The ability to transmute is in this sense like a hand of limited size. If it is to grasp more, it must relinquish its grip on what it presently holds in proportion to the quantity of its new reach. In terms of our language analogy this means that the number of words or letters in the central assembly that can be transmuted into conscious form is a limited finite number. When there is noise, the words and sentences must be shorter, since noise takes up some of the channel capacity. The phenomenon is a commonplace, known for centuries. Nonetheless, its attempted quantification is relatively recent. Not until it was possible to conceptualize "information" and then to quantify it was it feasible to ask what the channel capacity of the human might be.

Equally new is the neurophysiological attack on this problem. The long-disregarded problem of "attention" has become the focus of intensive investigation and has necessitated a radical change in our general conception of the functioning of the nervous system.

Let us begin our discussion of the limited channel with an examination of some of the major findings at the neurophysiological level.

The discovery of the amplifying role of the reticular formation and its importance for consciousness marked the beginning of the rediscovery of the difference between the reception of information that was attended to and information that was not.

In addition to differential amplification by the reticular system as an instrument of differential attention and awareness, centrifugal amplification and attenuation provide a preliminary screening of sensory information at a distance.

There appears to be centrifugal regulation of efferent bombardment by a variety of amplifying and attenuating mechanisms from both the cortical and reticular level. Thus, Eldred, Granet, and Horton (1953) showed that control of the muscle spindle proprioceptor and its sensory discharges takes place at the receptor level through the gamma-efferent system and may be triggered at the reticular level. Similar mechanisms have been demonstrated for the vestibular system, the retina, and the olfactory system. Hernandez-Peon, Scherrer, and Jouvet (1956) showed that a cat sitting quietly and relaxed with electrodes chronically implanted in the cochlear nucleus gives a large response to an auditory click, but when the cat's attention is diverted by putting two mice in a glass jar in front of him, the cochlear nucleus response to the same click is depressed almost to the point of abolition. When the mice are removed, the cochlear response to the auditory click returns to its original level.

The same reduction in amplification and increase in attenuation is reported by Hernandez-Peon and Scherrer (1955) in an experiment in which the repetition of a tone gradually produced a reduction in the cochlear nucleus response. This habituation was quite specific to that tone, and a new tone immediately restored the response. They also demonstrated that direct electrical stimulation of the reticular formation also depresses the cochlear nucleus response.

In both cases when a stimulus loses interest, withdrawal of amplification or direct centrifugal attenuation excludes the component from the central assembly. Either the entire channel may be excluded, if attention turns to another channel (e.g., the cat looking at the mice rather than listening to the auditory clicks), or a specific part of a channel may be excluded as it becomes overly familiar.

Although we have seen that specific channels may be excluded from the central assembly when competing channels are favored and when there is adaptation to the same message being repeated, yet this inhibitory process is itself inhibited if the specific message has been linked to negatively motivating assemblies. Thus, Galambos, Scheaty, and Vernier (1956) showed that if clicks previously used as conditioned stimuli signaling shock were repeated, there was no reduction of the evoked potential in the cochlear nucleus. We are not at this point concerned with the nature of the avoidance mechanism but rather to show that the same stimulus that would normally be excluded from the central assembly because of disinterest and competing interests secures amplification and inclusion in the central assembly by having achieved membership in another component—a set of negative affective responses that provides amplification of both the affect and the stimulus in such a way that habituation does not occur. With respect to the affective response, Bonnvallet, Dell, and Hiebell (1954) have demonstrated that visceral and nociceptive stimuli activate the cortex and through the delayed effect of adrenalin cause a persistence of such activation via the reticular system acting on the cortex. Such an action provides a more sustained arousal than any particular neural message might.

Although there has been increasing evidence for the existence of both sensory and motor control from the center out to the periphery, the work of Hernandez-Peon has not been unchallenged, even by those who agree that there are central mechanisms capable of regulating the flow of sensory information at some distance from the brain.

Horn (1960) postulated a central mechanism capable of regulating the threshold of sense receptors whereby sensory signals into the central nervous system may be augmented by descending facilitation or attentuated by descending inhibition. His criticism of Hernandez-Peon, Scherrer, and Jouvet is as follows:

Hernandez-Peon, Scherrer, and Jouvet (1956) reported that clickevoked responses in the cochlear nucleus of the unanesthetized cat were decreased in amplitude during attention to a nonauditory stimulus—a mouse. They supposed that this provided evidence for an inhibitory mechanism that favored the attended object by the selective exclusion of competing signals. These experiments were then extended to the visual system, and similar results were reported. When an animal's attention was attracted by nonvisual stimuli, photically-evoked responses recorded in the visual cortex, lateral geniculate body and optic trace were reduced in amplitude.

Horn (1960) has criticized these interpretations on the possibility that depression of an evoked response occurs in the modality actually being used for examining the sensory field, that is, that attention to a nonvisual source may have resulted in the cat's searching the visual sensory field for the source of the stimulus. Hernandez-Peon et al. (1956), when using a flash of light, attracted the cat's attention by a call or by sardine odor blown into the cage. Horn suggests that when a cat is called, it usually attends by *looking* toward the source of the voice, and when fish odor is blown into the cage, it attends by sniffing and looking toward the source of the odor. Similarly, with the studies of the auditory system, Horn suggests that when a cat looks at a mouse it may also listen.

By means of implanted electrodes, he investigated these possibilities, among others, in a study of the electrical activity of the visual cortex of six unanesthetized, freely moving cats. The evoked response to a flash of light was recorded when the animal was resting and when it was watching a mouse. He found that the evoked response in the resting animal consists of a primary wave and a secondary wave, followed by a series of oscillations (tertiary waves) lasting at least 500 milliseconds after the completion of the secondary wave. When the cat watches the mouse, the amplitude of all components of the evoked response and the amplitude of the waves of the background electrocortigram are significantly reduced. The cat was then conditioned to receive a shock after a series of tones. It was found that the evoked response to flash was reduced when a series of tones was delivered only if there was some visual searching component in the cat's response to the acoustic stimuli. If there was no visual searching in the behavioral response to the tone, the evoked response to flash was not attenuated.

In one animal an electrode was placed on the auditory cortex, and the response to click was recorded in the relaxed, resting animal and compared with the response when the animal was watching a mouse. On the first few occasions that the mouse was presented, the amplitude of the click-evoked response was reduced. At a later stage, though the cat sat intently watching the mouse, the amplitude of the click-evoked response was increased.

Horn (1960) suggests that at the beginning, the cat was listening as well as watching, that is, searching for auditory cues related to the mouse, even though it sat intently watching the mouse. Horn interprets these results to support his hypothesis that when a cat is called or receives some other nonvisual stimulus, evoked visual responses are attenuated as a correlate of the search for visual information, not because the visual information is irrelevant.

Since the mouse used by Horn was white, the feline retinal receptors that signal information about it would be the same as those that signal information about the flash. The duration of the response in the optic nerve to a flash of 1 millisecond duration is of the order of 25 milliseconds. Insofar as reduction of an evoked response is an index of a net change of sensitivity, the hypothesis that the cat blocks signals concerning the flash but not those concerning the mouse would require that for 25 milliseconds during the time the flash-evoked signals are being conducted, the sensitivity in the visual pathway is reduced, to be increased when the mouse, but not the flash, is present. In one cat, flashes were delivered at half-second intervals, so that fulfillment of this hypothesis would require that for about $\frac{1}{20}$ of the total time the mouse was present, information about the mouse would have to be rejected because information about the flash was being rejected.

What the precise mechanism of attenuation of the evoked potential is, Horn is not certain. He thinks its function is to improve contrast between stimulus and background activity, which would lead to loss of sensitivity in the system but to an increase in specificity. Absence of such an input-attentuating activity in a sensory channel would give a greater absolute sensitivity in that pathway. This would account for this finding that after the cat had watched the mouse for some time, the amplitude of the click-evoked response was increased; that is, when attention to a given modality ceases, evoked responses in that modality are enhanced rather than depressed, as Hernandez-Peon suggests.

Horn (1960) although he rejects the "blocking" hypothesis of Hernandez-Peon, agrees that there is no question but that by some neural process irrelevant information is filtered out during attention to other relevant stimuli. He is inclined to accept Broadbent's (1958) theory of a short-term storage system for signals arriving from one of the channels. Horn is disinclined to believe that such a storage system is situated at the sense organ.

The importance of cooperating senses (e.g., looking at a sound source rather than simply listening to it) has received further attention by Hubel, Henson, Rupert, and Galambos (1959), though they do not relate their findings to those of Horn.

Hubel, Henson, Rupert, and Galambos (1959) have shown that the neural processes responsible for attention play an important role in determining whether or not a given acoustic stimulus proves adequate. They have confirmed and extended the findings of Erulkar, Rose, and Davies (1956) that 34 percent of the units isolated in the auditory cortex cannot be driven by sounds and that only about 14 percent are reliably and securely activated by acoustic stimuli. In the course of examining single-unit responses from the cortex of unrestrained and unanesthetized cats, they found a population of cells that appears to be sensitive to auditory stimuli only if the cat pays attention to the sound source. A typical record is described as follows: The auditory cortex is spontaneously active but can not be driven by clicks, tones, or noise from the loudspeaker. Keys jingled by the experimenters outside the room in which the cat was isolated evoked responses when the animal looked toward the door but not otherwise. The experimenter then entered the room, picked up a small piece of paper between each thumb and forefinger, and held his hands to the right and left of the cat about 12 inches away from its ears. When the paper was rustled in the right hand, no response occurred until the cat looked toward it, whereupon a large burst of firing occurred as long as the sound was produced. If the paper in the left hand was rubbed, nothing happened until the cat turned its head in that direction, whereupon again the unit responded to the sound. Holding the hands out of sight did not change the result: as long as the cat looked in the proper direction the responses occurred.

They have found evidence for some units that do respond reliably for long periods to stimuli presented by means of the loudspeakers, whether the animal is awake or asleep. They have also found pure attention units as described above and attention units that are interspersed among conventional responders. Most puzzling to them, however, was their finding that it proved impossible to discover the stimuli adequate for driving many of our cortical units. "It is not easy to understand why the auditory cortex, in the anesthetized or intact cat, should be populated with so many cells that fail to respond to auditory stimuli." We would suggest the possibility that these areas may be under the control of the memory area and might be activated only from "within." Such a relationship is found, according to Ruch (1951), in the association areas in the frontal lobes, which, he argues, cannot simply elaborate information reaching the primary sensory areas and translate that information into action via the motor areas because they have their own way in and their own way out.

We would suggest the hypothesis that central inhibition of some sensory information in a particular channel is most likely to occur when competing sensory information from the same channel joins another sensory channel to provide attention to this object through converging multiple sensory modalities. This is a special case of magnification by triangulation.

Thus far we have discussed the attenuation of sensory information more than its amplification. Combinations of independent amplifying and attenuating mechanisms provide more subtle regulation than either type of mechanism could in isolation. The existence of independent suppressor and facilitating areas in distinct regions of the reticular formation has been demonstrated. Independent, antagonistic mechanisms are very widely distributed in the nervous system. Let us examine the amplification of component channels.

Under anesthesia the activating reticular action is reduced or abolished. But evoked potentials can be picked up from the primary sensory areas of the cortex. Therefore, anesthesia and the elimination of the reticular amplification do not prevent the normal transmission of sensory messages over the classical afferent pathways to the thalamus and cortex. Since the human being does not appear to respond to sensory stimulation under deep anesthesia, it appears that reticular amplification is at least a necessary condition for the central assembly to transmute sensory information.

So much for the sensory channels. What about amplification and attenuation of other components of the central assembly, of the afferent side, of the effect of memory and cognition? French, Hernandez-Peon, and Livingston (1955) have shown that stimulation of various cortical areas in the monkey gives rise to potentials recorded from the reticular formation. Here is a possible set of mechanisms, facilitating and inhibiting, whereby an activated memory or any other component of the central assembly can amplify or attenuate itself by stimulating the suppressor or facilitating mechanism in the reticular formation, which, in turn, would activate or depress either the whole cortex or amplify or attenuate the special component or process that initiated the circular corticosubcortical amplification/attenuation chain. With respect to the efferent side, Magoun

(1944) and others have demonstrated the existence of independent suppressor and facilitating areas in distinct regions of the reticular formation for inhibition and facilitation of spinal motor neurons and muscles. Elimination of the facilitatory mechanisms produces suppression of the spinal reflexes and cortically induced movements.

In addition to the discovery of the role of the reticular formation and centrifugal regulation of the periphery, a third finding relevant to the limited channel capacity is the importance of timing as a principle of the grammar of the nervous system. In some central assemblies there are wide tolerances for the time of availability of components. The individual may try again and again to retrieve a memory or to practice a motor skill, but just as obviously skill ordinarily involves skill in timing the readying of components for assembly. Let us examine a few of the known facts about the significance of timing for central organization.

Visual reaction times vary between 150 and 300 milliseconds. Lansing (1954) examined the relationship between visual reaction times and alpha waves from the occipital and motor areas. He found that the briefest reaction times occurred predominantly when the stimulus message arrived in the cortex at an optimal excitability phase of the occipital alpha wave and that the motor discharge occurred in the motor area in a similar optimal phase of the motor alpha wave. These two phases, however, might be at least 100 milliseconds apart.

Lansing, Schwartz, and Lindsley (1956) compared visual reaction times and alpha waves under nonalerted and alerted conditions. In the nonalerted condition, there were reactions that occurred with good alpha waves and also when there were no alpha waves. In the alerted condition an auditory warning signal was used to alert the subject to activate the EEG. The mean reaction time in the nonalert condition was 280 milliseconds, 225 for the alerted state. Examination of the reaction times in relation to alpha blocking showed that if alpha blocking is complete, reaction time was at a minimum and that this occurred if the warning signal were 300 to 400 milliseconds before the stimulus proper.

Bartley and Bishop (1933) first demonstrated the significance of timing as a principle of central assembly. They cut the optic nerve of the rabbit and stimulated it electrically. The neural volley resulted in an evoked potential in the visual cortex only when it was appropriately synchronized with the spontaneous rhythm of the alpha waves.

Timing as a principle of inclusion is not entirely as simple as it has thus far been presented. It is quite possible for a component to be displaced by a competing component or competing message within the same channel that comes later to the central assembly site. Thus, Wapner and Werner (1957) showed that the second figure of two, exposed successively to the same retinal area, could displace in consciousness the figure that preceded it. They used a black square and then a white square of the same size, surrounded by a black frame. If the black square was followed after a vacant gray interval of 150 milliseconds by the framed white square, the black square was not seen. When the sequence was reversed, however, both squares were seen. It appeared that either the unseen stimulus never was transmuted into a report or that it was reported but was masked by the report that followed. If a stimulus is weak in some sense, it can be displaced in the assembly either by initial exclusion or rapid reassembly.

A similar phenomenon has been reported by Bull and Girodo-Frank (1950) in the field of affect. In their studies of hypnotically induced affective states, they reported that if an affective facial response is observed to be followed very rapidly by another affective facial response, the individual characteristically is unaware of the first response. It would appear to have been displaced before it could be reported. Thus, a hypnotized subject when instructed to feel disgust was aware of wanting to beat up the person who disgusted him. The observers saw him turn his head away very quickly as if to escape the object of disgust and then respond with anger. The subject, however, was aware only of the anger and not of the wish to escape. The feedback of this reaction was apparently masked by the feedback of the immediately succeeding response of anger.

The fourth finding relevant to channel capacity concerns the optimal level of arousal of the brain. There appears to exist a range of optimal levels of arousal of the brain as well as a range of nonoptimal levels of arousal, mediated by the reticular formation and the limbic system, as well as by the intensity of sensory proprioceptive and autonomic bombardment. The channel capacity of the central assembly would appear to be dependent on an optimal range of arousal values, which lies between an epileptic storm on the one hand and deepest state of coma on the other. Lindsley (1951) and others have shown that behavioral efficiency is at a maximum in states of alert attentiveness, which are in general accompanied by partially synchronized, mainly fast, low-amplitude brain waves. Poorer behavioral efficiency is found as the state of activation goes in the direction of a maximum, with desynchronized, low- to moderate-amplitude and fast mixed-frequency brain waves. Poorer behavioral efficiency is also found as the state of cortical activation goes to a minimum from relaxed wakefulness, with its synchronized alpha rhythm; to drowsiness with reduced alpha and occasional low-amplitude slow waves; to light sleep with spindle bursts and larger slow waves and loss of alphas; to deep sleep, with large and very slow waves; to coma, with irregular large slow waves; to death, with gradual and permanent disappearance of all electrical activity. This is equivalent to varying amounts of noise generated as the central assembly works in varying electrical fields. It is not the case, we think, that there is no central assembly in states of extreme excitement or in states of coma. It is, rather, that the channel capacity declines in a curvilinear fashion as a function of the degree of activation of the nervous system.

We agree, in general, with Hebb's (1949) and Lindsley's (1951) hypotheses concerning the curvilinearity of behavioral efficiency with respect to activation level, but we regard this as a derivative of the changing channel capacity of the central assembly. We do not believe there is a point-for-point correlation between channel capacity and behavioral efficiency. Thus, a grief-stricken individual may be operating at a high point with respect to channel capacity, but since the central assembly is occupied primarily with the feedback of massive affect and a flood of memories, the individual would show low behavioral efficiency with respect to other channels. It has happened that some grief-stricken individuals have been killed by walking into the path of a passing automobile by virtue of indifference to their surround. Under optimal activation levels, then, the central assembly may operate at full channel capacity. At less than optimal activation levels, the channel capacity is reduced, and therefore a smaller number of components may enter into such assemblies. In terms of a language analogy, when there is more noise, sentences must be shorter.

So much for some of the recent neurophysiology that has made attention and channel capacity once again a viable concept. Let us turn now to the problem of measurement of the channel capacity of the human being.

Miller (1956), in his classic paper, "The Magical Number Seven, Plus or Minus Two: Some Limits on Our Capacity for Processing Information," attempted a precise answer to this question. He considers first the information in absolute judgment. If we assume that the human being is a communication channel, then we may measure the amount of transmitted information as a function of the amount of input information. If the observer's absolute judgments are accurate, then most of the input information may be assumed to have been transmitted. Errors represent a loss of transmitted information relative to input information. As the amount of transmitted information approaches an asymptote, despite increases in input information, we have a measure of channel capacity—the maximum amount of information the observer can report about a stimulus on the basis of an absolute judgment.

Miller, in his review of published and some unpublished reports of absolute judgment for a variety of sensory modalities, found a mean value of 2.6 bits, with a standard deviation of 0.6 bit. In noninformation language this means that on the average 6.5 alternative categories can be reliably distinguished, with a standard deviation from 4 to 10 alternative categories. The total range of categories across a wide spectrum of senses, from smell to vision, is from 3 to 15 categories.

We appear to have, as Miller concludes, a finite and small capacity for making unidimensional judgments, which he calls the span of absolute judgment. Adding independently variable attributes to the stimulus increases the channel capacity but at a decreasing rate. By adding more dimensions and requiring crude yes-no judgments on each attribute, he suggests we can extend the span of absolute judgment from 7 to at least 150. On the basis of everyday experience he thinks that the limit is somewhere in the thousands but that we cannot increase dimensions beyond about 10.

In addition to increasing the number of dimensions along which the stimuli can differ, there are two other ways, Miller believes, in which the bottleneck of a limited channel capacity is transcended. One is to make relative rather than absolute judgments, and the other is to arrange the task in such a way that we make a sequence of absolute judgments in a row.

This latter involves memory, immediate and delayed. Miller points out the suggestive similarity between the span of absolute judgment, which is about 7, and the finite immediate memory span, which is also about 7 items in length.

He regards this similarity as spurious, since in memory span the amount of information transmitted is not a constant but increases almost linearly as the amount of information per item in the input is increased. Therefore, Miller concludes, absolute judgment is limited by the amount of information, whereas immediate memory is limited by the number of items. Distinguishing bits from chunks of information, the number of bits is constant for absolute judgment and the number of chunks is constant for immediate memory, which seems to be almost independent of the number of bits per chunk.

Generalizing, Miller suggests that by recoding we can continually increase the amount of information into larger and larger chunks. Thus, one can group the input events, apply a new name to the group, and then remember the new name, rather than the original input events. The most obvious instance is in the learning of telegraphic code, in which at first each *dit* and *dah* is a separate chunk. Soon these are organized into letters as chunks and then the letters are organized into words as chunks and so on. In Miller's opinion, the most customary kind of recoding is to translate into a verbal code—to rephrase "in our own words."

We are indebted to Miller for what is undoubtedly our best estimate of the innate channel capacity of the human being. There are, however, certain residual problems with his estimate, or indeed with any estimate. First, the responses by which the channel is measured themselves constitute part of the channel, first as motor responses that must be assembled and emitted and second as feedback from these responses once emitted. How to measure the varying load of this inherent aspect of measurement is a difficult problem in itself. Second, there is a variable load of information from proprioception and inner and outer stimulation that is incidental to the tasks constituting the measure of channel capacity. This load varies with the energy level, diurnal rhythms, affect, and general body tonus, and most important, with the amount of the channel allocated to such awareness. Its estimation at any moment constitutes a measurement problem of great difficulty. Third, the response by which the channel capacity is estimated is a measure of channel achievement rather than the inherent capacity of the assembly that generates it. This is why, despite a restricted range of estimates of the channel capacity, about 4 distinct concentrations of taste can be reliably distinguished in contrast to up to 15 distinct visual positions, according to the data presented by Miller. It is also why Miller sidesteps the problem (which he mentions) of individuals who can identify accurately any one of 50 or 60 different pitches.

The problem is not unlike that encountered in measuring intelligence. Achievement tests are indeed constructed on principles different from intelligence tests. Nonetheless, any intelligence test is necessarily somewhat contaminated, in unknown amounts, with biases due to the particularities of achievement components. Whether an achievement-free estimate of channel capacity is theoretically possible is not altogther clear. Miller has recognized the problem in connection with sequential performances such as in immediate memory span and in recoding in delayed memory. It is our feeling that the same problem plagues the measurement of channel capacity in unidimensional absolute judgment.

In addition to these problems that beset any empirical estimate, there appears to be a restriction in Miller's estimate to perceptual judgments and to memory. There is a channel capacity problem not only in perceptual judgments and in memory but also in cognition in general, in feeling, in decision, and in action. There are also channel capacity limits on any combination of these functions. An individual who has to both look and act in a coordinate manner faces a rapidly developing channel limit as the complexity of both the perceptual and motor tasks increases.

Someone learning to drive an automobile senses he is close to the boundary of his channel capacity when he complains there are too many things he has to look at, think about, and do with his hands and feet all at the same time.

Limited channel capacity may operate to exclude any component or set of components from the central assembly. Thus, in extreme grief, the central assembly may consist exclusively of memory and affect. Lost in recollection of things past, the aggrieved may hear and see little. In extreme panic, on the other hand, there may be a flooding of awareness, with affect and perceptual information and the feedback of impulsive action. Animals and men who panic in fires have gone to their death because of the unavailability of customary cognitive resources, due not to a limited channel as such but rather to the complete absorption of the channel by affect and action. In the Coconut Grove fire many perished because, in panic, they piled on top of each other in a desperate but self-defeating effort to escape the burning room.

Both motor and cognitive components may be excluded by channel limitations if the central assembly is captured either by overly massive exteroceptive sensory bombardment, or by interoceptive sensory feedback from intense, affective responses. Thus, in acute fear, the individual may be frozen to the spot, unable to think or move. The same immobilization may be the consequence of an overly intense sensory bombardment. A deer may be immobilized by shining a very bright light directly into its eyes. Indeed, its helplessness in the face of such stimulation has prompted the outlawing of "jacklighting" as a technique for hunting this animal. Verheijen (1958) has labeled this the "trapping effect." It is responsible for the death of many insects and birds who become fixated on bright lights in the dark of night.

The seizure of the central assembly by the affective and perceptual mechanisms, as in stage fright, can so block access to the storage mechanism that an inexperienced actor may, for example, forget his overlearned lines on the opening night of a play.

The limited channel principle also appears to be operating in the changing density of reports to messages within any one sensory channel. Thus, when an individual pays closer attention to something within the visual field (e.g., goes from looking casually at a person to examining the face in great detail), this change from a wide angle to a microscopic lens usually sacrifices breadth for density of information. A similar channel limitation appears to be involved in switching from one set to another (e.g., in perceiving the same stimuli in terms of color or form or number, according to prior instruction from the experimenter). Again, when attention shifts from one sensory channel to another (e.g., when one looks at something with intense concentration), there may be a loss of awareness of information received over the auditory channel if the visual channel load is at the boundary of the channel capacity of the central assembly.

Even that part of the central assembly responsible for transmuting the information from other components into reports may be excluded from the central assembly due to overstressing the channel capacity. Thus, if pain stimulation or terror or both exceed a critical maximum, the transmuting apparatus is blocked in transforming messages into reports, and the individual faints into a state of "unconsciousness" or the reduced consciousness of the comatose state. This appears to be a different way of disengaging the transmuting mechanism than in going to sleep, though both eventually result in a much reduced level of activation, which, in turn, reduces the channel capacity of the central assembly.

Consciousness may be reduced in many ways and for many reasons. One way in which consciousness is turned down, in fainting, would appear to be a consequence of a channel limit on the intensity of awareness tolerable for the individual.

Fear is a primary cause of loss of consciousness. Contagious fainting upon witnessing others faint, or suffer, is well known. Physicians who were inoculating soldiers en masse during World War II have reported a group of 15 inductees fainting simultaneously upon seeing the first inductee injected in the arm with a needle. Engel (1950) notes that vasodepressor syncope is a reaction that may occur during the experiencing of fear when action is inhibited or impossible. He cites the case of one subject who fainted when subjected to the rectal insertion of a balloon, but who did not faint when he was able to express his anger at this procedure.

The customary posture of an organism is also of importance in the maintenance of consciousness. In his studies of fainting, Engel (1950) found that if subjects are supported passively on a tilting table in such a way that all weight bearing on the lower extremities is eliminated, many will faint. This was found to be true even among athletes in prime condition. He also cites evidence that many quadrupeds that are not adapted to the upright posture may be killed simply by suspending them in the vertical position. We have already seen some evidence for this plus the arousal of fear operating in Richter's (1949) study of sudden death in wild rats. To what extent changes in customary posture also produce panic and thus also add to the stress on the channel capacity Engel (1950) does not say.

One of the known mechanisms by which consciousness is turned down is the carotid sinus reflex. Lennox, Gibbs, and Gibbs (1935) suggest that an essentially neural mechanism exists in certain persons with hyperactive sinus reflexes to bring about unconsciousness, resembling in this respect cataplexy and reflex epilepsy, without the intervention of a general cerebral anoxia. This reflex operates if the 0_2 tension of the blood flowing to the head falls below 24 percent; a level much above that which interferes with muscular metabolism. This reflex, it is suggested, is adaptive in that by prostrating the body it enlarges the circulation to the brain before the level of blood flow in the circumstances of reduced oxygen tension reaches a level so low as to cause damage to the brain.

Channel acquisition certainly appears to be diminished in the status of coma. Whether channel capacity is similarly reduced is less clear. This lack of clarity is a derivative of the great flexibility of functioning of the central assembly. Consider the hand analogy of the channel capacity. If one tries to pick up more apples than the hand can hold, one runs the risk of dropping all of the apples. Does the central assembly operate under the same gambler's choice? In immediate memory span the individual at times may appear to drop all of the information he has attempted to grasp if he has overreached himself. Yet more sensitive tests would probably reveal some saving. Characteristically, in a test of memory span, the numbers may be remembered but in the wrong position, or they may be recognized if not reproduced. Further, how can we be sure that the drain on the channel in emitting negative affective responses to the failure, and the further drain from the awareness of distress or shame or fear, may not exactly displace informationally the numbers that have been dropped by an ambitious attempt at exceeding the channel capacity?

WHY A CENTRAL ASSEMBLY?

An alternative hypothesis to a central assembly might be that of a transmitting mechanism that operated on the several perceptual areas and several association and memory areas like a scanning searchlight, momentarily "illuminating" messages so that they become conscious simultaneously and sequentially as a conjoint function of the movement of the scanner and the variation in neural inputs. In such a model the scanner would have to have a principle built into it that would accept some and exclude other messages as it swept across all message sites.

We favor the hypothesis of a central assembly for several reasons: first, because we do not think that there is ever consciousness of simple sensory messages. Clearly, we receive visual information from our two eyes yet are aware of one visual world. Somewhere a final resultant of that dual information is consciously represented. In a similar fashion we think there is continual competition between the two visual sets of neural messages and the information stored in memory.

What is finally admitted to the central assembly is neither pure sensory nor pure memory messages. Rather, we think, the centrally produced image that is experienced as a conscious report represents a *compromise* between centrally retrieved information and sensory input. In such a compromise the relative contribution of sensory and central information is presumed to vary. Characteristically, new information is more heavily weighted with sensory input; old, habitually skilled information is more heavily weighted with central information.

What the individual is aware of is neither the sensory input nor what is stored in memory but the centrally emitted imagery that ordinarily attempts to match both sources. For this reason the distinctions between absolute judgment, immediate memory, and delayed memory do not refer to the perceptual process itself but to the relative weight attached by the central mechanism to the different sources of information that it is attempting to match.

As this assembly is disassembled and reassembled from competing sources, then conscious reports continually change from moment to moment.

The independent variability of the components of each and every central assembly constantly changes every semistable psychological structure by providing for storage, ever new perspectives for each separate source brought together a new in every changing central assembly.

The role of the central assembly and of the consciousness of the transmuted information in it is crucial in the prefeed and feedback of information. Only by such a mechanism can the individual know *what* he knows. It is like a psychological test tube in which he learns what happens when he mixes new combinations of information. Like a centrifuge it separates out some components but thereby aggregates others. By putting together both similar and disparate information from several competing channels the individual is enabled to become aware of the consequences of a variety of complex information transformations.

It must be a *central* unitary assembly because of the pluralism of the sources of information which must be capable of being received together at one time. It is *not* necessary that these different sources be integrated there, but it is necessary that all of the information needed *for* integration be assembled together and continue to be so assembled over time. Reassembly presupposes assembly.

PRINCIPLES OF SELECTION AND AVOIDANCE, INCLUSION AND EXCLUSION OF INFORMATION FROM CONSCIOUSNESS

Although channel limitations place severe restrictions on the quantity of information that may be transmuted and stored, it does not constitute a general selective principle. It is rather a restricting condition, which accounts for the quantity of information being processed or excluded at any one time. Additional principles must be invoked to account for why one sees something at a particular moment when the ears have been stimulated at exactly the same moment. First of all, it should be remembered that the human being is not necessarily limited to selecting information from competing simultaneous channels. He has the option of tracking information in the environment so that he will be stimulated with the information he needs, rather than waiting for it to happen and then selecting the most favorable among the given alternatives. Much of the theory of attention and vigilance reflects the peculiar conditions of the psychological experiment—in which it is the experimenter who takes the initiative in putting the question to nature in an optimal form. We should therefore expand the question to the form: what are the principles by which a person seeks or avoids information or selects or excludes it?

When one broadens the question in this way, it is evident that the theory of selective attention and vigilance is a rather special case of motivated behavior in general. Yet, because it is a special case, there may be some special principles involved that are less involved in the broader phenomenon. Broadbent's (1957) suggestions here were fourfold—novelty, biololgical importance, intensity, and innate biases.

Certainly one could not dispute the relevance of such factors in the selection of one or another message to be transmuted into a report. There is a question, however, whether there may not be some redundancy in these principles. We believe there is and that it is possible to account for differential selection of information on a unitary principle—that of the *maximal density of stimulation*. In any competition between message sources, that message or set of messages will be favored for transmuting into a report that has the highest density of stimulation. By density we mean the product of the intensity of firing times the number of firings per unit time. This number may be of a single fiber or a whole set of fibers. The limits of what constitutes a unitary class of firings depend in part on innate structural features of the nervous system and in part on what constitutes a class according to strategies directed from memory, since part of the firing that enters into this density formula is central firing from memory.

Let us first examine some of the structural features that determine relative density of firing. Broadbent (1957) has shown that high pitches are favored over low pitches in humans. This is consistent with a density of stimulation interpretation, since the former fire more frequently than the latter. The perception of pain is another example of innate structural features determining the relative density of stimulation. If an individual's pain receptors are stimulated in several distinct areas, these characteristically do not summate. Only the most dense stimulation becomes conscious, and it masks the other sources of pain. If now pain should increase in density at another site, consciousness shifts to this source. This mechanism makes it possible to mask pain inflicted by dental or surgical procedures by producing greater pain by digging one's nails into one's own flesh. It is clear that there is a structural basis that prevents summation of pain from widely distributed parts of the body—or else, as Hardy, Wolff, and Goodell (1952) have argued, we would be in constant pain most of the time.

There is more involved here than first meets the eye. Let us contrast this structural arrangement with another innate one that is also widely distributed over the body but that does summate. This is the innate startle response. It seems designed to flood consciousness with very dense, widely distributed stimulation that will interrupt almost any ongoing awareness. It achieves this by triggering coordinated massive responses, for a moment, the feedback of which has a high claim on consciousness no matter what the competition. If one were aware of only the most dense of these sets of firings, as is the case with pain messages, the startle response would lose its effectiveness. It is because the density of firing that is transmuted is the totality of this mass of widely distributed messages that it constitutes such an effective competitor. What determines the "unit" whose relative density will determine success or failure in competiton for consciousness is then in some measure itself structurally determined. As what constitutes the unit of firing fibers increases in number, whether on an innate or learned basis, the relative intensity of firing may decline and density remain constant.

Let us examine more generally how this principle might account for selective awareness. The superiority of the more intense over the less intense message would be a special case if the number of fibers involved in each unit were identical or their difference less than a critical amount. The insistence of drives in their claims for conscious attention could be accounted for on a density principle if one includes supportive affect as part of the unit of stimulation. The hierarchy of drives could also be accounted for on such a basis, since the most insistent drive, anoxia, usually has a very steep gradient of activation. When this drive emits signals more slowly and less densely, the drive loses its claim on consciousness. Such a principle would also account for the interference that is possible between dense affective feedback and competing drives, such as the distress or fear that masks the appetite of the hungry one or, in the other direction, as when extreme thirst interferes with reading something in which one is interested.

It would account for the claim on consciousness of the novel, if the latter releases interest or excitement, and would account for the shifting of attention away from the same stimulus as it both lost its affective support and was transformed by analyzers into a form in which the density of reports to messages was reduced. This latter point may seem to be begging the question. It appears as though we are saying that one of the reasons *stimulation* from a particular source becomes less dense is because of a reduced density of reports to messages, when it is the very density of reports that we are trying to explain by a principle of density of stimulation of neural firing. We argue in this way because we assume that one of the ways in which an individual learns to handle increasing amounts of information is by so organizing it that the same goals can be achieved by simpler means. This is analogous to a science that accounts for more and more phenomena with fewer and fewer assumptions, by maximizing duplicates or repetitive operations. The memory traces that are successively laid down as the analyzer mechanism simplifies and miniaturizes the information in the sensory channels are, we assume, less detailed and less dense, compared with the density of the original sensory messages. When these less dense traces are successively used as a guide for central matching, our awareness of the original sensory information also assumes a reduced density of reports to messages if we compare what is in awareness either with what we were aware of a few moments ago when we first perceived the stimulus or if we compare the detail of these reports with the detail of the present sensory messages. Even though the stimulus continues to emit the same stimulation to the receptors and thence to the projection areas, the central matching mechanism is more and more guided by the increasingly simplified and miniaturized traces than by the sensory input so that the density of reports to messages also decreases if by messages we refer to the sum of those from the sensory channels and from the memory traces. This latter is the most exact sense in which our argument holds. On the other hand, the principle of maximal density of firing will also account for the increased awareness of any stimulus that is produced by a growing density of firing from internal sources through increased affect or increased detail and density of analysis, or both. Ordinarily, indeed, the course of a new perception is first an increase in density of firing and awareness, followed by a decrease in both. Should the new percept lead to unresolved or otherwise enduring affect, however, this density of firing and its correlated awareness may constitute a magnified obsession.

By a principle of relative density of neural firing we could also account for such periodic intrusions into awareness as the Zeigarnik effect or any other type of unfinished business that would be transmuted into conscious form the moment more dense competition was reduced by adaptation or any deceleration in the rate of change of information in the environment. The classic instance, of course, is the dream in which visual sensory stimulation is reduced to a minimum so that the relative density of visual traces has no competition from this source and there is a reduced competition from other sensory channels. The combination of little external density of firing (because of reduced reticular amplification), and the relatively dense firing of unfinished business (either from the preceding day or from the cumulative past, or both), could account for the predominantly ruminating and problem-confronting characteristics of dreams and for the rarity of strictly wishfulfilling dreams. We do not mean that wishes may not be gratified in dreams. We do mean that the primary characteristic of the dream is a *continuation* of residual unsolved problems. Sometimes confrontation of problems in the dream produces solutions, and then the dream appears wish-fulfilling; but it need not be wish-fulfilling, as Freud knew but labored to rationalize away. What he regarded as the exceptions to the theory of wish fulfillment we regard as the core of the dream. What he regarded as the core we regard as the exception, or at least as the relatively infrequent outcome of dreams. This is because that which has the highest density of neural firing is most likely to be whatever in the past history of the individual produced the most intense *and* enduring affect. Positive enjoyments ordinarily grow progressively weaker until they reach a stage of adaptation or satiation. Negative affects or incompleted positive transactions are, however, capable of more easily creating enduring, intense inner states whenever the individual finds he cannot either successfully reduce or avoid their negative affect or satisfy the frustrated positive need.

There is one major exception to what we have been saying concerning the predominantly negative qualities of dreams and the reason for their higher density of firing. If an individual goes to sleep while either wrestling with a problem that is exciting to deal with or is on the threshold—the next day or in the near future—of a rewarding experience, or so believes, then the dream would in all probability be positive and wish-fulfilling in nature. Indeed, all who go to sleep in the midst of attempting to solve a soluble problem have reported that frequently they reach a solution, either in the middle of the night, which wakes them from sleep, or, more characteristically, it appears in the morning just after arising. Problem solution under these conditions is not an easy wish fulfillment but is probably the consequence of dream thinking. The closest approximation to pure wish fulfillment is occasioned when sleep is in fact an interruption of an expected positive gratification. We would expect that prisoners, on the night before their expected release from prison, should dream of the morrow.

It will not have escaped the attention of the reader that in every instance of an example of the explanatory power of the concept of density of neural firing we have said that such a concept "could" explain the phenomenon in question. We do not know whether or not it also "would," but the derivations seem to us sufficiently plausible to be considered. There is, however, a serious ambiguity in this criterion as stated, which we illustrated in the difference between the summation of the startle feedback and the independence of the equally widely distributed pain stimulation. This example, however presents no insoluble problem since innate structural features appear to account for the difference, although exactly how this is achieved we do not as yet know. In the case of learned messages, especially those from memory in conjunction with those from the sensory channels, the problem of defining in a general way what constitutes a "unit" of density of neural firing is a difficult one. Despite this, the theory lends itself to ready experimental test since it is comparatively simple to put two message sources from two sensory channels into competition with each other and to vary the relative densities of firing of each channel.

This principle also would permit us to derive consequences, for differential awareness, of any competing sources of sensory information equally matched in density at the outset, which received differential amplification or attenuation either at the periphery or at the reticular level, or if they emerged from central sources and were to receive differential amplification or attenuation. Any increase or decrease in affect, amplification, or cognitive elaboration that accompanied any other message set could be formulated on a neural firing density principle and be used to predict probabilities of attaining awareness or of being excluded from awareness. Its main recommendation is its facile translatability to and from domains that differ widely in nature and content.

So much for the central assembly. Let us next turn to the role of consciousness in general.

CONSCIOUSNESS, BEHAVIORISM, AND PSYCHOANALYSIS

The empirical analysis of consciousness was delayed by two historical developments: behaviorism and psychoanalysis. Behaviorism identified consciousness with the sterile Titchenerian concept and with verbal report. The emphasis on "behavior" submerged the distinctiveness of consciousness as a type of response. Freud also belittled the significance of consciousness. For him it was the epiphenomenal servant of the unconscious. For several decades "behavior" and unconscious hydraulic-like forces dominated the study of the human being. The emergence of ego psychology, the theory of cognition, and significant advances in neurophysiology blunted the excesses of psychoanalytic theory and behaviorism alike.

Man's sovereignty has been challenged and reduced again and again, first by Copernicus, then by Darwin, and most of all by Freud. The paradox of maximal control over nature and minimal control over human nature is in part a derivative of the neglect of the role of consciousness as a control mechanism. The failure of this mechanism in pathological conditions has strengthened the notion of consciousness as an epiphenomenon and of man as the intersect of "forces" essentially beyond his control.

We must study the *transmuting* response as psychologists have studied other responses. We must determine, empirically, the conditions under which messages become conscious and the role of consciousness in the feedback mechanism. This is a critical problem for any theory of the human being. If information is available from an external or internal source but cannot become conscious, it might just as well never have been available. Freud rested his basic theory upon the unavailability of reports—the tactics for avoiding consciousness and the consequences of preventing consciousness. Later, in his theory of trauma, (*Beyond the Pleasure Principle* 1971 [1920]) he concerned himself with the inability of the individual to turn consciousness off.

We are in agreement with Freud that much of psychopathology appears to be concerned with transmuting disabilities—the inability to become *aware* of intolerable content and the inability to become *unaware* of intolerable content. Freud revolutionized the theory of awareness by explaining the process as a derivative motivation. He argued that we become conscious of what we want to know and generally remain unaware of what we do not want to know. The illumination into the remote recesses of the mind this insight provided was revolutionary. The exploration of the strategies dictated by the wish for awareness on the one hand and the wish for unawareness on the other monopolized the energies of a host of theorists and clinicians for over half a century.

At the same time, Freud was haunted all of his life with the discomfiting sense that there existed numerous instances of forced awareness, such as in the traumatic war neuroses where the individual again and again seemed compelled to reexperience the dreaded traumatic incident that had originally overwhelmed him. On the face of it this did not appear to be a wish fulfillment. We do not wish to examine his solution in detail but to note the embarrassment created for a dynamic, motivational theory of awareness by the disregard of the nonmotivated aspects of memory and attention. A general theory must bring back to the problem of consciousness the nonmotivational factors that the revolution minimized but without surrendering the gains won by Freud. The interplay between consciousness and unconsciousness, between motivational and nonmotivational subsystems, must be brought into sharper focus.

The paradox of this second half of the 20th century is that the return to the classical problems of attention and consciousness was not a return by psychologists who had a change of heart. Rather, it was a derivative of the initiative of the neurophysiologists and the automata designers. The neurophysiologists boldly entered the site of consciousness with electrodes and amplifiers. They found that the stream of consciousness from the past could be turned on and off by appropriate stimulation. They found that there were amplifier structures that could be turned up and down, by drugs and by electrical stimulation, and that consciousness varied as a function of such manipulation. They found that seizures and their loss of consciousness were a consequence of excessive stimulation of cortical and subcortical circuitry. They found that there were filter networks that appeared to prevent consciousness by attenuation of sensory input at a distance. In this respect Freud was prophetic, since he conceived of repression as a general process and likened it to the active selective inattention of everyday life.

The renewed interest in the problem of awareness and attention was a consequence also of the extraordinary achievements of automata creators. It appears that the regaining of consciousness is less awkward for behaviorists if it can first be demonstrated with steel and tape that automata can think, can program, can pay attention to input, can consult their memory bins in intelligent sequences—in short, that they mimic the designers, who intended they should do so.

CONSCIOUSNESS AND WAKEFULNESS

Just what consciousness is surely is a grievous question, but one can nonetheless be clear about several things that consciousness is not. It is, first of all, not simply the state of wakefulness. Nor is it the state of "arousal" or "activation."

Just as we have urged that affect be distinguished from amplification, we also urge that consciousness and wakefulness be distinguished from each other and from affect and amplification. There is an increasing confusion created by the indiscriminate lumping together as synonyms the terms *arousal, alerting*, and *activating* with consciousness and wakefulness. We have already examined the distinction between affect and amplification (arousal, alerting, activating). Let us now examine the relationships between these two and consciousness and wakefulness.

The living organism, we think, is never totally unconscious. There is no reason to believe that the mechanisms responsible for transmuting messages are ever completely turned off. When consciousness is at its lowest ebb, the cortex appears to emit no more than a "carrier" wave—like a broadcasting station without a specific message. We do not believe that this carrier wave represents "unconsciousness" but rather a state of reduced specificity of awareness, just as the broadcasting station is not really silent when broadcasting its carrier wave. Sleep, we believe, is the state wherein there is maximal difference between input messages and the central transformation of these messages. The person responds as if all messages said the same thing or that there were very slight differences between messages. It is clear from the phenomenon of dreams, however, that this general diffuseness of reporting can be concurrent with very specific transmuting and elaboration of a subset of centrally emitted messages. Considering the vividness and detail of the dream and the widespread autonomic responses initiated by the dream, as well as the motor responses of the body as a whole (e.g., witness dogs making abortive running movements while asleep), the puzzle is why there are not more sleepwalkers. The difference may be a trival one. It may be that the sleepwalker has learned to get out of bed, whereas most of us do our walking in bed.

The apparent variations in consciousness are only imperfectly related to variations in wakefulness. When the brain goes into a deep state of sleep, the messages of which the individual is conscious are characteristically diffuse and poorly organized. If these messages are sufficiently intense or significant, however, the individual becomes aware enough to either think about them as he sleeps, which we call the dream, or to wake up. If one can dream and be asleep, then awareness and wakefulness are not identical states. One can be asleep and conscious and remember on awakening what one was conscious about. Nor are wakefulness and activation or arousal identical. Amplification is only one of the set of mechanisms that keep the individual in a state of wakefulness. But any massive affective response, such as fear, hostility, distress, shyness, or joy, can serve equally well. One can certainly be kept awake all night by fear or distress as well as by nonaffective amplification. However, it is not only the affective response that can keep one awake. Even a sleepy individual on the point of falling asleep can be kept awake by almost any intense sensory stimulation—loud noise, flashing lights, or self-administered pain (e.g., from biting the lips). It is true that these frequently also activate auxiliary affective responses such as startle or distress, but these are usually secondary responses to the increased stimulation that has broken through the developing state of somnolence. Such intense stimulation requires less amplification from the reticular and other booster mechanisms to maintain the state of wakefulness.

Morris, Williams, and Lubin (1960) report that the sleep-deprived subject showed increasingly frequent shifts of activity to maintain wakefulness, since prolonged attention to any task threatened to put him to sleep. Typically, he would get into a card game, get tired of it, get up and walk about aimlessly, sit a few minutes, join another game or conversation and so on.

Characteristic of the entire group were brief lapses or pauses in ongoing behavior, which increased in frequency, duration, and depth as sleep loss increased. They were interpreted as brief periods of extreme drowsiness or sleep. Between lapses the subject is able to think and act under challenge almost as well as in the control period. Lapses occurred most frequently between midnight and dawn, when body temperature is lowest. They could be *prevented by alerting the subject with intense or rapidly changing stimuli.* During such a lapse in listening to a conversation a subject may be dimly aware that people are talking but not of what they are saying. Intrusive thoughts or dreams may combine with external stimuli to produce distorted perception. The deepest lapses end in sleep. The lapses may last several seconds but are usually self-limiting. It is clear also that affective responses, while they usually keep the individual in a state of wakefulness, can be emitted by a sleeping person and produce a dream or nightmare. The sleeping person, therefore, can be conscious and also experience intense affect, and also have a high amplification (or arousal or activation level) while still asleep. The individual who wakes from a nightmare does so because awareness, affect, and amplification have together passed a critical point with respect to sleep versus wakefulness.

Not only can the sleeping person be aware, affectively excited and amplified, but in insomnia he may be "sleepy," with low amplification, but kept awake by affect. Despite general damping of the cortical and reticular system in "sleepiness," due to the innate wakefulness-sleep cycle and to the increasing depletion of endocrine and other reserves, the cortex and reticular system both act as attenuators rather than amplifiers; but the activation of the sympathetic system in anxious rumination can prevent sleep, even though general neural amplification may be minimal. This is because the affect system is capable of bombarding cortex and reticular system alike with sufficiently intense and numerous messages to keep these systems awake despite generally low amplification of sensory impulses. This is probably mediated by adrenalin, which is known to exert lasting priming influences on the reticular and other systems over and above neural influences.

Kleitman (1963) has also argued that consciousness and wakefulness are not synonymous. In delirium, fugues, or psychomotor epilepsy, a person may be judged to be behaviorally awake, but his level of consciousness is very low and he may have complete amnesia for these events. By contrast, he argues, an individual asleep but dreaming may reach a higher level of consciousness and be able to recall it upon awakening.

He further cites evidence that sleep and wakefulness occur in decorticated dogs, cats, monkeys, anencephalic babies, and normal human neonates. Therefore, sleep and wakefulness cannot be entirely judged by the desynchronization of cortical brain waves—if there is no cortex but there is an innate sleep-wakefulness cycle. Further, in decorticate animals or the anencephalic child the level of consciousness, according to Kleitman (1957), is very low, if not zero, but they nonetheless show the innate sleep-wakefulness rhythms. Hence, he argues that consciousness and wakefulness cannot be identical.

Kleitman (1957) suggests that a "sleep" EEG is without diagnostic significance in the presence of behavioral wakefulness, and a "wakefulness" EEG is not significant when obtained during behavioral sleep. Kleitman reports that such wakefulness EEGs were regularly observed during dreaming, when the subjects were unquestionably asleep.

The criteria he uses to judge the passage from innate wakefulness to innate sleep are, first, a decrease in activity of the skeletal musculature and the assumption of a characteristic posture and, second, a raised threshold of reflex excitability.

The innate sleep-wakefulness cycle in the human lasts from 2 to 4 hours; in the newborn infant there is a 2:1 ratio in favor of sleep, with still shorter sleep-wakefulness cycles with a periodicity of 50 to 60 minutes. On a self-demand feeding schedule the interfeeding periods are usually an integer of these short cycles. If the infant is not waked in the shallow phase of one cycle, it is not likely to awaken until this shallow phase recurs. The mechanism of this cycle is not known, but Kleitman (1957) reports that it lengthens with age. However, the adult sleep-wakefulness cycle, Kleitman suggests, is learned and grafted onto the innate cycles. The acquired once-in-24-hours night sleep differs from the innate cycle in the occurrence of dreaming but resembles innate sleep in the persistence of the primitive rest-activity cycles, which in the adult are of 80 to 90 minutes duration and manifest themselves in oscillations in the depth of sleep. Kleitman did not determine whether the primitive innate cycles also are expressed in fluctuations of alertness during the hours of acquired wakefulness but suggests that the postprandial nap and the 15-minute cat naps in the late afternoon or early evening may be derivatives of the innate cycles.

A number of investigators have found that varying depths of sleep, as measured by the length or intensity of tones required to awaken the subject, are related to increases in amplitude and decreases in frequencies of delta-type EEG patterns. When subjects are awake, subjects characteristically, though not invariably, show alpha rhythms.

Simon and Emmons (1956) have addressed themselves to the relationships between EEG, consciousness, and sleep along the continuum between waking and deep sleep. They pretested 21 normal subjects to see whether they knew the answers to 96 factual questions on history, sports, science, and so on. The subjects then slept in a soundproof air-conditioned room for a normal 8 hours' sleep. The same questions along with the correct answers were played one at a time at 5-minute intervals during the night. Subjects were asked to call out their names immediately if they heard the answer to any question. After the 8-hour training period, all subjects were awakened and given the questions again and were tested to determine which of the answers not known previously could now be recalled.

They found that as the quality and quantity of alpha waves increases, so does the probability that a stimulus will be reported heard when it occurs and recalled correctly later. They point out the obvious exceptions—that lack of alpha does not guarantee lack of consciousness since it disappears during concentration and since many normal individuals show little or no alpha waves. Alpha, they admit, is therefore not a totally reliable index of consciousness. Delta waves are a good index of unconsciousness, however, because when these predominated, subjects neither responded to nor recalled material presented to them, and they appeared deeply asleep. When alpha and delta frequencies are mixed, the probability of recall is related to whichever of these components predominates.

In the light drowsy state the alpha waves are blocked at the onset of stimulation and return when stimulation stops. In the next stage, which Simon and Emmons (1956) call the deep drowsy state, stimulation is followed by the subject's rapid awakening. With presence of the waking alpha rhythm immediately after stimulation, recall still occurs about 50 percent of the time.

Although they found that subjects were roused sequentially through transition phases from sleep to wakefulness following stimulation, there were also instances of skipping phases depending on the speed at which awakening occurred. Despite this lability of wave shift, they also found evidence of an "inertia effect," which they defined as follows: during the presence of any EEG pattern, subjects who have recently been asleep tend to show a lower probability of responding or recalling than do those who have been awake previously. Both responding and recalling were hindered when the preceding period showed no alpha frequencies and were favored when alpha frequencies were present.

They also investigated the concomitants of body movement while asleep. They found that it is possible to have body movement without alpha. In such cases subjects heard and recalled practically nothing. When the subject moved and there was alpha activity, hearing and recalling tended to be high. They conclude that it is therefore the presence of alpha, not movement, that is the critical criterion for conscious responses.

Although Simon and Emmons (1956) have given us valuable information on the relationship between sleep and consciousness and memory, theirs nonetheless is not a definitive study despite their conclusion that their evidence rules out the possibility of learning while asleep.

First, it is limited to information received by the exteroceptors. Much of the mental activity of the night is centrally generated. People do have nightmares that are real enough to waken them. Difficult problems have been solved either in the middle of the night or upon awakening if one has gone to sleep with an unsolved problem. Whether problems are solved or not, sleep can be fitful if one continues to wrestle with problems through the night.

Second, there is abundant evidence that one does not sleep with a complete turning down of the receptor inputs. The cry of a newborn child can easily waken an uneasy mother. Personally relevant information was not used in their experiment. Third, they did not use very intense stimulation. There is little question that as the intensity of stimulation increases, so will responsiveness to it, whether awake or asleep. Finally, they did not compare the effect on the individual of information received while asleep to the effect on that individual while asleep at another time. The difference between the state of wakefulness and the state of sleep is sufficient to create massive interference effects so that, for example, we do not remember all of our dreams upon awakening. Nonetheless, there are dreams that are repeated over a lifetime with little modification, showing at least some effects of past experience in dreaming upon dreaming at a later date. For example, if one were to teach a sleeping person that a tone meant there would soon be a shock, it is entirely possible that such learning might be restricted to the sleep state in the future.

Also there is evidence of habituation to tones of specific frequencies while the experimental animal is asleep. Sherpless and Jasper (1956), using needle electrodes in the brainstem of cats, stimulated them with loud sounds of 3-second duration at intervals every few minutes while the cats were asleep. At first each stimulus evoked a burst of irregular high-frequency waves lasting up to 3 minutes. These waves resembled high-arousal EEG patterns. With succeeding stimulations the arousal reactions became shorter and shorter. By the 30th trial they failed to appear. On the following day the arousal reaction reappeared but habituation was more rapid. A few days rest, however, abolished evidence of habituation. Habituation was highly stimulus-specific. When the reaction to a tone of one pitch was habituated, other pitches would still provoke arousal.

It would thus appear that sleep does not destroy the ability of the brain to respond to, to discriminate, or to habituate to stimulation. One consequence of these findings is that the classical psychophysiological functions would appear to be unduly restricted in range. There should now be an extension of the range of stimuli and an extension of the range of wakefulness to answer the general question of the relationship between the characteristics of the physical stimulus and the response to it. If we should ask the question of the nature of the relationship between the stimulus and awareness when the latter approaches varying degrees of somnolence, we should also extend the range of psychophysical investigation when wakefulness has been increased through the acceleration of metabolism by increasing the internal body temperature. We are indebted to Hudson Hoagland (1957) for the beginning of an answer to the question of the alterations in awareness that are produced by elevated temperature and metabolic rates.

This incessant activity of the brain in sleep is not unlike that of the other vital organ, the heart, which may be slowed but not stopped if life is to be preserved.

Dement and Kleitman (1957) have reported that all of their subjects dream every night for longer periods than we formerly supposed. They found that dreaming occurs in association with periods of rapid, binocularly synchronous eye movements. These eye movements appear to be related to the content of dreams in patterning of direction and amount. They and the associated dreams occur in the lightest phases of cyclic variations in the depth of sleep, as indicated by the EEG records. The length of individual cycles averaged about 90 minutes, and the mean duration of single periods of eye movement was about 20 minutes. Thus, a typical night's sleep, according to their estimate, includes four or five periods of dreaming, totaling about 20 percent of sleep time. It appears also that we not only dream for longer periods of time than we formerly supposed, but that everyone dreams every night, although the dreams are not usually recalled.

For Dement, this raised the question to what extent is it possible for human beings to continue functioning normally if their dream life were completely or partially suppressed? He investigated this question by awakening sleeping subjects immediately after the onset of dreaming and continued this procedure throughout the night. A control group of subjects was awakened an equal number of nights, an equal number of times each night, except that these awakenings were produced during nondream periods.

The subjects in both groups were tested always on consecutive nights so that dream deprivation and being waked (or just awakening for the control group) should be cumulative in its effect. They were asked not to sleep at any other time. After this series all subjects were allowed several "recovery nights" of undisturbed sleep. After a number of nights off these subjects were asked to return and act as their own controls, being awakened during nondream periods. Altogether, from 20 to 30 all-night recordings were made for each subject. The average total sleep time was 6 hours, 50 minutes; total average dream time, 80 minutes; total average percentage of dream time, 19.5.

On the first nights of dream deprivation the return to sleep generally initiated a new sleep cycle, and the next dream period was postponed for the expected amount of time. However, on subsequent nights there was a progressive increase in the number of attempts to dream, and so the number of forced awakenings required to suppress dreaming steadily mounted. All of the subjects showed this progressive increase, although they varied in the starting number and the amount of increase. Actually, this was not a consequence of absolute dream deprivation but of dream *interruption,* or about 65 percent to 75 percent dream deprivation. This was because it took a minute or two of dreaming for the experimenter to make the decision and awaken the subject.

If these were compensatory attempts to dream, then one would expect that the amount of dreaming would increase during the recovery nights, when sleep was undisturbed. Such was the case. The mean total dream time on the first recovery night was 26.6 percent of the total mean sleep time. There was one exception to this rule, and surprisingly this subject showed the largest buildup in number of awakenings required to suppress dreamings. Dement (1960) found that the duration of compensatory dreaming lasted as long as five nights for four or five nights of dream deprivation. These data are meager because he did not expect such enduring consequences, so not all subjects were tested this long during the recovery period.

The effects seem not to be due to awakening as such, since the control group showed no significant increases. Their mean dream time was 20.1 percent. Subsequent recovery nights did not show the marked rise found in the experimental group. The moderate rise found on 4 of 24 recovery nights was interpreted as a response to the slight reduction in dream time on control-awakening nights.

Concomitant with this series of dream deprivation experiences were such general disturbances as increased anxiety, irritability, and difficulty in concentration. One subject quit the experiment in an apparent panic, and two subjects quit on the night before the final night. Five subjects developed a marked increase in appetite, and three of these showed a 3- to 5-pound gain in weight during this period. These changes disappeared as soon as the subjects were permitted to dream. None of the changes occurred in the control group, so these changes cannot be attributed to waking per se.

Dement (1960) has tentatively interpreted these findings as indicating that a certain amount of dreaming each night is a necessity, evident in the increasing frequency of attempts to dream and then in actual dreaming during the recovery period. While sleep is a period of relative muscular rest and inactivity, the body nonetheless continues to change position quite frequently during sleep. The more or less pure carrier wave of consciousness alone is usually emitted during a period of relative rest and mental activity. Nonetheless, it is punctuated by phases of lighter sleep and more active awareness.

Subsequent investigations by others have demonstrated that dreaming is not limited to REM sleep nor is there always dreaming during REM sleep. Further, Dement (1965) himself reported: "The kind of changes that were seen in the early deprivation experiments were not in evidence in the more recent studies." He suggested that inasmuch as these studies showed no serious disturbances in REM-deprived subjects, "it seems likely that the psychological changes observed in earlier studies were an artifact of the experimental procedures and the expectations of the experimenters."

It is now clear that REM deprivation is not necessarily dream deprivation since dreaming also occurs in non-REM periods. Dement (1969) has concluded that the REM phenomenon has a vital role to play even though we do not yet know precisely what that role is, since

> "... the REM phenomenon is so ubiquitous, so complex, and so well represented in terms of brain areas allocated to its structures and mechanisms that it is not likely to have evolved solely as a caprice of nature. We must therefore assume that it does have a vital role to play—a role which we will eventually be able to describe with precision and profit."

The variation in the interdependence of wakefulness, consciousness, amplificaition, and affect has also appeared in cross-species studies of hibernation. Kayser (1961) recorded spontaneous cortical activity in the hibernating and artificially cooled ground squirrel at deep body temperatures of 5°–6°C. Lyman and Chatfield (1953), on the other hand, found that spontaneous cortical electrical activity could not be recorded in the golden hamster arousing from hibernation until the cortical temperature had reached 19°–21°C.

Lyman and Chatfield (1953) then extended their studies to the woodchuck and found large differences between this hibernator and the hamster in regard to the electrocorticogram and in the behavior of the animal during hibernation. Like the ground squirrel, the woodchuck shows spontaneous cortical electrical activity at body temperatures at which the hamster shows none. Also, the woodchuck demonstrates an evoked auditory cortical potential at a cortical temperature as low as 7°C, at which the auditory nerve of the hamster does not conduct. The general pattern of hibernation in the woodchuck also differs from that of the hamster since the woodchuck is capable of responding to auditory and mechanical stimulation by moving about at body temperatures at which the hamster is completely immobile.

Inasmuch as hibernation may be defined as a protracted state of sleep, it *is* clear that there may also be important species differences in the relationships between wakefulness, consciousness, amplification, and affect. We have already examined the evidence for interspecies differences between amplification and affect in the work of Crile (1915) and Richter (1959). A similar exploration of the relationships between the degree of activity of the brain, general wakefulness, and level of amplification has yet to receive attention from comparative psychology.

In summary, consciousness is not wakefulness, and wakefulness is not consciousness. Nor is wakefulness a level of amplification, nor a level of affective arousal. Consciousness, wakefulness, amplification, and affect are maintained by independent mechanisms that are interdependent to the extent to which they constitute an overlapping central assembly. The empirical correlations between the states subserved by these mechanisms are a consequence of the frequency with which these partially independent mechanisms do in fact enter into the combined assemblies.

Chapter 55

The Feedback Mechanism: Consciousness, the Image, and the Motoric

Our final argument for the postulation of a centrally controlled reporting mechanism rests upon the fact that the human being achieves his purposes through a feedback mechanism. His purpose, we think, is primarily a conscious purpose—a centrally emitted blueprint which we shall call the *Image*. Although sensory data becomes conscious as imagery, and memory data must be translated into imagery, and both of these kinds of imagery are the consequence of mechanisms that also employ the feedback principle, there is, nonetheless, a sharp distinction we wish to draw between the operation of imagery in sensory and memory matching and the Image as the blueprint for the primary feedback mechanism. In sensory and memory matching, the model is given by the world as it exists now in the form of sensory information and as it existed once before in the form of memory information. In the case of the Image, the individual is projecting a *possibility* that he hopes to realize or duplicate and that must precede and govern his behavior if he is to achieve it. This image of an end state to be achieved may be compounded of memory or perceptual images or any combination or transformation of these. It may be a state that is vague or clear, abstract or concrete, transitory or enduring, requiring conjoint attainments or permitting alternatives.

Let us examine the feedback system as a duplicating system and the sense in which what is duplicated is a centrally generated Image.

By a feedback system we mean one in which a predetermined state is achieved by utilizing information about the difference between the achieved state and the predetermined state to reduce this difference to zero. The thermostat is a familiar example. As the reading of the thermometer goes above a chosen setting, the fuel supply to the furnace is reduced. As its reading falls below that setting, the fuel flow is started again. A predetermined temperature is maintained by using the amount and direction of departure from the desired condition as a signal to activate the control mechanism in a compensatory manner.

A feedback system commonly employs communication subsystems, whereas a communication system does not necessarily utilize a feedback mechanism. The relationship between the predetermined state and the produced state is duplicative. What is to be produced is a duplicate—in another space at another time of the predetermined aim of the feedback system. A feedback system may or may not employ consciousness.

Let us for the moment simplify the problem of the nature of the Image and its relation to the feedback mechanism and assume that the wish is no more than to repeat something that has just been done successfully. We have assumed that the afferent and efferent channels are relatively fixed circuits whose main function is to duplicate, via transmission, messages from outside in and from inside out and that the individual can never become aware of these messages. Before a transmitted message can become conscious we have assumed that a transformation process was necessary. We have labeled this process transmuting, and called the conscious message a report.

Messages are continually transmitted to muscles and glands, but it is only the afferent messages from these areas that are transmuted into reports. If consciousness is limited to afferent reports, how, then, does the peripheral efferent system come under control? We propose that this is achieved by a *translation* process. We conceive of the efferent and autonomic system as the space in between a dart thrower and his illuminated target in an otherwise dark room. One can learn to throw a dart to hit a target in a dark room without ever knowing what the trajectory of the dart might be, as long as one knew how it felt just before the dart was thrown and where the dart landed. The trajectory described by the dart would and could never become conscious, but the effects of the trajectory could be systematically translated into the preceding conditions in such a fashion that for such and such a feel before throwing one could be reasonably certain that the visual report, after the trajectory, would be the desired report. We conceive of the efferent messages as the dart trajectory, controlled by the afferent reports that precede and follow the efferent messages. We have called this a translation because there are two different languages involved, the motor and the sensory. One must here learn to translate a desired future sensory report into the appropriate motor trajectories.

In addition to a process of translation, a further step is, however, necessary. In the beginning of dart-throwing the translation is after the fact (i.e., such and such a feel led to such a distance off the target). Eventually, the desired report must come before the translation and guide the process or else one would not be able to repeat any performance, good or bad. Therefore, we conceive of the total afferent-efferent chain as follows: the desired future report, the Image, must be transmitted to an afferent terminal and at the same time be translated into a peripheral efferent message. The message that initiated the translation is the same message that must come back if the whole process is to be monitored. The monitoring process is, however, not a comparison between the first message and the feedback but between the first report and the feedback after it has been transmuted into a report. In other words, the individual can be aware only of his own reports, whether they are constructions from memory or his constructions guided by an external source. Let us now examine this mechanism in some detail.

In the conscious feedback mechanism the reports that precede and follow any innervation are the means by which that innervation is brought under control. The report that follows the innervation (when that report is desired and the person wishes to repeat the experience or continue it) must be brought forward in the control series, must be translated into a message that will innervate the nerves that will reproduce the desired report. The report that ordinarily precedes any innervation serves as a "guide" to the site of innervation of the critical message. Clearly, the nearer in space and time the preceding reports are to the site of the critical message, the finer the control possible. Just as with the dart thrower, if he were limited to the "feel" of his body up to 10 seconds before he threw and to the feel only of the muscles in his chest, the achievement of control over the trajectory would be very much more gross than is the case with the human being who has continuous information from receptors all about the sites of the motor nerves plus information from visual distance receptors. Since behavior usually involves sets of muscles and nerves, the achievement of control depends in large part upon an optimal density of receptors to motor nerves. A very large number of independently innervated muscles would be wasted on an organism that had only a small number of receptor cells to guide these motor nerves and muscles. Conversely, we find a reduction in density of receptor cells in those parts of the person that are least mobile, such as the back.

We have said that in any controlled repetition of a response it is the report that is duplicated in the loop; duplicated by a repetition of the same motor message that produced the report in the first place, via a receptor cell at the terminal of the motor nerve. But how can a report about a state of affairs at t^2 produced by an event at t^1 produce an event at t^3 that will duplicate the report of t^2 at t^4? How can an effect reproduce its own cause? Let us first consider the kind of situation in which this will not happen. Suppose we place a subject in a dark room and, taking his hand in our own, we put a pencil in his hand and, guiding his hand, we draw on a piece of paper a Rembrandt etching. Then we ask the subject to repeat this performance on his own. Why is he unable to reproduce what he has just done with our assistance? One of the reasons is that he does not "know" what he has done. The information was registered by the appropriate receptor cells, but the transmuting of this information was limited to relatively gross information such as that the hand was continually moving up, down, and sideways, fairly rapidly, and that it was "guided" movement. So much of his performance he *cannot* reproduce.

The first condition of reproduction then is that the feedback from the receptor cells be sufficiently detailed to support reproduction. What does this mean? Essentially, it means that the complexity of reproduction is limited first of all by the complexity of feedback information. If, for example, the receptors gave the same information if the muscle were moved quickly or slowly, then differences in speed of movement could not be reproduced. In a rationally designed system we should expect to find a matching of receptor information to the information that can be emitted to and transmitted over motor nerves. We should also expect this match to have more "play" in it as the nervous system of the animal became more complex, since with the increased use of symbols, gradients of information from receptors will become useful even if there is not a one-to-one correspondence between sensory and motor systems. Thus, the differentiation of color in the visual system need not have a close match to characteristics of motor messages. The same is true of the differentiated qualities of the auditory system. Indeed, the development of an independent exteroceptive sensory system is critical for any organism that is to utilize information other than it creates by its own movements. Our argument is more pertinent to the proprioceptors and interoceptors than to the relatively external sensory systems, even though to be useful the information from independent sensory systems must be matched to the characteristics of the motor system. Thus, an organism whose threshold for perception of movement was above that of its own speed of movement could not be very competent and would soon perish. It is, however, the existence of such independent sensory systems that reduces the need for a close match between muscle receptors and motor nerves. We argued before that if the receptors gave the same information if the muscle were moved quickly or slowly, then differences in speed of movement could not be reproduced. This is not true when there are other receptor systems (e.g., the visual, which register some of the visual consequences of differences in speed of muscle movement). It is, however, essential that some receptor system convey the information if it is to be brought under loop control.

What we have said thus far is not pertinent to the example of the subject who is unable to reproduce the Rembrandt etching. His receptors did provide the requisite information, yet he was unable to utilize it. There are at least two independent bases for this failure, apart from failure of the receptor cells to provide the necessary information. First there is an incapacity to transmute the receptor information with sufficient detail to support reproduction. The person is faced with too much novel information to be able to keep up with it. He is like a Morse code operator who has not yet learned to receive at fast enough a rate for his "senders." Second, he may be able to "receive" quite complex information at sufficiently rapid rates, but he is incapable, nonetheless, of producing the appropriate motor messages that would allow him to send a duplicate of what he has received. Although we believe it is impossible to send unless one can receive, it is possible to receive but be unable to send.

Our subject who cannot reproduce the Rembrandt etching may be suffering either receiving or sending deficiencies, or both. Let us return to the main thread of our argument: how is the "report" to be duplicated? We see now that before the report can be duplicated at least three conditions must be met. The receptor cells must provide the appropriate information. The transmuting must be sufficiently efficient to keep up with this information. The motor message that originally produced this report must be reproduced. This latter process we have called *translation*. We have defined translation as a duplication of a message in one language by a message in another language. "Dog" is the English translation of "chien." When one listens to a lecture and

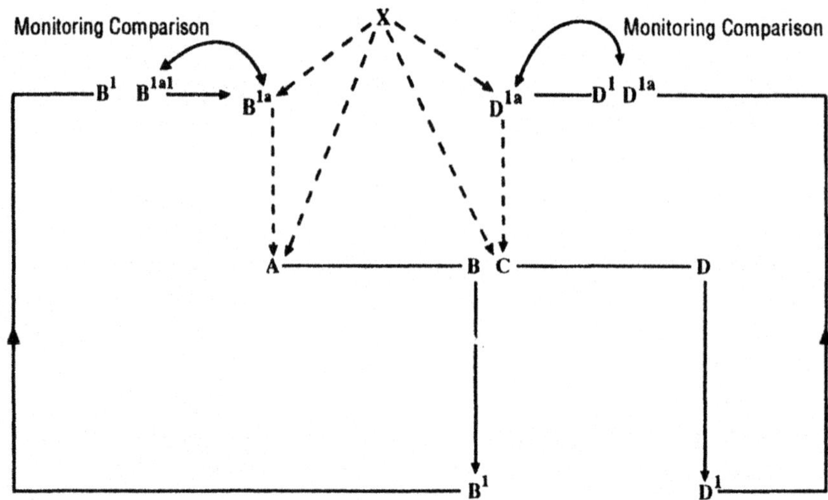

FIGURE 55.1 Diagram of a hypothetical case.

writes down verbatim what one hears, one is not only translating from the aural language into the written language but also translating from the "intended" visual words into a set of motor messages to the hands that will produce the intended visual feedback. That this is a translatory process—from one language to another—is particularly evident when the report is, as in this case, visual in nature and the message that reproduces this is a motor message. It is, however, we are arguing, no less translatory when an intended kinesthetic report is the basis for the motor message. If we assume that Condition 1 is given by genetic endowment, that Condition 2 has been learned, how is Condition 3 learned? Figure 55.1 is a diagram of a hypothetical case.

Let *AB* and CD stand for two motor nerve transmissions.

Let B^1 stand for a receptor cell in the vicinity of B, which is stimulated whenever there is an impulse AB.

Let D^1 stand for a receptor cell in the vicinity of D, which is stimulated whenever there is an impulse CD.

Let $D^1 D^1 a^1$ stand for the transmuted report of the message from D^1.

Let $B^1 B^1 a^1$ stand for the transmuted report of the message from B^1.

Let XD^{1a} stand for the centrally emitted transmission, which at D^{1a} becomes conscious.

Let XB^{1a} stand for the centrally emitted transmission, which at B^{1a} becomes conscious.

Let XC and *XA* be centrally emitted transmissions, which stimulate motor nerves AB at A and CD at C.

Let $D^{1a}C$ and $B^{1a}A$ be centrally controlled transmissions, which stimulate motor nerves AB at A and CD at C.

In terms of this diagram, the question is: how does it happen that CD comes under central control, and thus produces the desired D^{1a}, the "report" of D^1? We have assumed that initially CD can be stimulated by some other motor or association fiber, for example, AB. To answer that CD comes under central control via AB is simply to push the question back, since how AB comes under central control is exactly the same kind of question we have raised in connection with CD.

Our answer is that the "target" (D^{1a}) must be capable not only of being transmuted when D^1 is stimulated by CD but also must be capable of being transmuted for a brief period of time after D^1 has ceased to be stimulated by CD. This is achieved, we think, by recirculating temporary storage circuits. This is the transitory, immediate memory of the kind we see in "memory span" performance. It is a transitory phenomenon that the individual may or may not exploit. If he does not exploit it, however, this report may never again be available. Without memory, both immediate and delayed, loop control cannot be achieved. To return to our diagram, D^{1a} must be capable first of some reverberation if control is even to be attempted. If one does not know what one did, one cannot begin to repeat it; and if what one did cannot be continued in time, first immediately following its occurrence and then at some later time, it cannot serve as a "target" for reproduction. If the control mechanism works as we think it does, it requires some degree of control of the "model" it is trying to reconstruct. This means that one must be capable of centrally emitting and transmuting the "desired" report at such times when CD is *not* stimulating D^1 to produce the report D^{1a}. Further, in the beginning, D^{1a} must continue to be transmuted in order to compare it with the reports that the trial-and-error attempts at reproduction via motor nerve transmission produce by way of receptor cell stimulation. If this were not done, then the second reproduction would be as "accidental" as the first. It would be like a tennis player who accidentally served an "ace" and who, 10 minutes later, achieved the same accidental result.

There is a prior emission and monitoring not only of D^1 via monitoring and comparison of $D^1D^1a^1$ with D^{1a} but also of B^1 (via monitoring and comparison of B^{1a} with $B^1B^1B^1a^1$). What he did before he achieved D^{1a} is the critical information in reproductive learning. This is usually, and particularly so in the beginning, more than one thing. It is a series of responses, some of which are necessary, some of which are not. If one achieves the desired D^{1a} very inefficiently (neurologically speaking), the probability is high that it may never be corrected—like poor "form" in athletics. Now a complication arises in the loop. He may have been successful in closing the loop a second time and yet be unable to do it a third time. This is because the loop within the loop must come under conscious control. This circuitry is not wired in. It must be learned. Now the process of using immediate and delayed memory as a "model" to be reproduced must be repeated with the events that precede D^{1a}. The "end" having been reproduced a second time, the means to this process must now come under more certain control. A bridge must be built backward between D^{1a} as a model and B^{1a} that will activate AB, BB^1, B^1B^{1a}, BC, CD, DD^1, D^1D^{1a1}.

The second reproduction is usually only slightly less "accidental" than the first. It is distinguished from the first production by having been preceded by a report of an "intended" end result. Usually, the series of motor innervations necessary to produce the report D^{1a} is longer than we have included in the diagram. AB is usually preceded by other motor nerve innervations. These innervations inbetween the centrally emitted transmuted report and the peripherally stimulated feedback constitute the "translation" of the report. If this series of intervening events is not too complex and extended in time, the reverberation of the series of reports (D^{1a}, B^{la}) provides a base for conversion of this series into a more enduring memory so that the model is now more detailed, starting with XD^{1a} as the "desired" report, followed now by report $B^1B^1a^1$ and then by report $D^1D^1a^1$ from D. A series of reports in advance now enables firmer control over the final process, since deviations from these reports that are earlier in the series enable correction before the entire process has gotten too far out of hand.

There is, in our explanation, a "gap" that may disturb the reader. How does the individual proceed from the centrally emitted report to transmit a motor nerve impulse? We do not altogether know, nor does the individual. He can know only from later reports *that* he has done so, more or less successfully. We have said only that he will have to "try" to reproduce the report just as a dart thrower tries to achieve the correct trajectory. If he tries and his attempt is poor, he will soon know this from the lack of fit between his model and the feedback, and then he can try again. We assume that by virtue of spatial contiguity some nerve linkages are more probable than others; and that if he tries reproducing D^{1a} via too "remote" innervations, he will fail too often to repeat these efforts indefinitely. The attempts which will succeed most often will be those "nearest" the nerve CD. Since he will ordinarily continue his trial-and-error neurological trajectories until he achieves the ability to repeat D^{1a} perfectly, these trajectories will tend to assume the most efficient topographical pathways.

Although an implicit feedback principle has been employed in learning theory for many years in the concept of trial-and-error learning, the concept of neurological trial and error has not. We regard the learning of the neurological topography under the skin as critical as the acquisition of outer space maps. Paradoxically, it is only by "outer" exploration that the inner space is ultimately mapped. The individual who learns how to achieve outer targets is also learning how to use his neurological networks. To the extent to which his outer aims are attained, his unconscious experimentation with inner networks is also validated. This is one of the critical differences between our present automata and the human being. The automata are instructed to experiment with outer space but not with their own inner space. They are told in advance where their memory data is stored, where their motor printout is, and so on. This is appropriate for purposes of the immediate efficiency of these machines, but it also places a low ceiling on their learning potential. In effect they have been designed to use space (in more built-in wiring), whereas the human has been designed to utilize time to achieve similar ends.

Let us return to our information flow diagram. Eventually, XD^{1a} and XB^{1a} cease to be transmuted, though we believe they never cease to be transmitted centrally. At the same time that XD^{1a} and XB^{1a} are transmitted, the translatory motor impulse is also sent: first AB, followed by CD. In the final stage of learning, XB^{1a} and AB may drop out altogether. XD^{1a} is transmitted but not transmuted, and at the same time an impulse is sent to C from D^{1a} that stimulates D and then D^1. D^1 may then be transmuted in very reduced form. Is there any evidence for the hypothesis that D^{1a} is always transmitted at the same time that C is stimulated? We are usually unaware of such transmission. We can expose this process by interfering with competing feedback (e.g., by asking the person to write his name in the air with his eyes closed). By blocking off the transmuting of incoming visual impulses we expose the centrally transmitted visual "desired" D^{1a}, which is sent at the same time that the motor messages are sent to the fingers. Most individuals characteristically "see" the name they are writing. On the auditory side, we can expose the centrally transmitted words by asking the subject to repeat a sentence without uttering the words aloud (that is, to speak softly). Under these conditions most individuals will "hear" what they are saying. The flexibility of this central process is illustrated by the fact that some subjects use a "translation" even for the central process. These subjects may "see" what they are saying or "feel" what they are writing.

It should be noted that in our diagram there is one dotted line, XC, and another, $D^{1a}C$. We are not certain whether it is one or the other or both of these transmissions that is the correct assumption. It is possible that in the final organization two messages are sent *simultaneously,* one from X to D^{1a} and the other from X to C. It is also possible that the lines of transmission are rather from X to D^{1a} and from D^{1a} to C. Suggestive evidence against the latter alternative is the fact that we may employ auditory imagery without (apparently) moving our tongue and that we may employ visual imagery without (apparently) moving our hands and feet. This independence may, however, be more apparent than real. Lashley (1960) reported many years ago that tongue movements accompanied "thinking" only when the person became emotionally excited. More sensitive recording devices should enable us to answer this question with more certainty today. The question is not whether thinking is subvocal speech, but whether it is possible to emit specific imagery *without* emitting an accompanying translating motor message of some kind. We have presented evidence that leads us to believe that it is not possible to transmit motor messages without supporting imagery, though that imagery may be ordinarily masked by other input.

So much for how, in general, an Image comes to control and monitor the feedback mechanism. This is the third and most critical reason for postulating a central sending imagery mechanism that is capable of translation into motor messages and of matching the feedback messages when they are received from the sensory receptors.

FEEDBACK CONTROL OF INVOLUNTARY PROCESSES

Not all of the reports of which an individual becomes aware are duplicable by the individual. We refer here to the distinction between "voluntary" and "involuntary" behavior. It is possible that the distinction is not a basic one, that what is involuntary is only what has not yet come under conscious control.

The case for the distinction between voluntary and involuntary action has been based on reflexes and the host of bodily processes that are governed without awareness. There can be no question that much of what goes on in the body is "wired in" or at least independent of control by conscious feedback mechanisms. Many of the homeostatic phenomena employ the feedback principle but not awareness of feedback. There is a question whether a process governed by preformed mechanisms independent of conscious control can be brought under conscious control. Clearly, there are processes that are usually nonconsciously controlled that are easily brought under conscious control. Breathing is such a one. One can consciously slow down or accelerate the rate of breathing. One can consciously control the amplitude of breathing. One can, in fact, produce fainting by consciously controlled hyperventilation. In a sense, then, one can "consciously" produce loss of consciousness via this indirect route. If one can tolerate the unpleasant feedback from this conscious intervention, in a process usually governed unconsciously, one can then radically interfere with nonconscious control mechanisms. But one must be prepared to give over most of the channel capacity to this attempt. The moment consciousness goes to another process, the nonconscious mechanisms take over. Biofeedback procedures attempt to substitute a more habitual, efficient type of control for this hyperalert type of control. In the beginning of any learning process consciousness is characterized by high density of reports to messages and gradually is transformed into a more efficient type of conscious control but with a lower density of reports to messages. Can such learning be achieved with involuntary processes, which, unlike breathing, are ordinarily unconscious and generally resist conscious intervention—such as the pupillary reflex, temperature, and so on? First, what is it in the design of the organism that makes these mechanisms relatively inaccessible to conscious control? Second, can they be brought under conscious control by any means?

Why are they relatively inaccessible as compared with a semivoluntary process like breathing? There are at least two possibilities. One, there are no receptors to provide feedback information to consciousness, and, two, there are no motor nerves to the areas that are accessible to innervation from the transmuting center. It is highly probable that where one of these conditions obtains, so will the other. Motor innervation that was guided by conscious processes would be pointless and misguided unless appropriate receptor information were available to monitor the conscious innervations to the motor system. What is the difference between "conscious innervation to the motor system" and feedback information? Basically, there is none. The chief difference we refer to is the site of the receptors. In what we have called feedback information we refer to receptor cells at the terminal of the motor nerves. By conscious innervation to the motor system we refer to receptors prior to the terminal of the motor nerves. It is this prior information that enables a more precise innervation to the terminal site of the motor innervation. This information may come from a receptor either in the vicinity of the pathway of the motor nerve or at the terminal of another motor nerve, which has to be innervated before the next motor nerve can be innervated. In general, the higher the density of receptor cells to motor nerves, the more precise control of the latter should be possible.

Let us consider a relatively inaccessible reflex, such as the pupillary reflex, compared with a more accessible one, the patellar tendon reflex. The latter can be inhibited or augmented by consciously mediated flexing of adjacent muscles. This is possible because there is a high density of receptor cells to motor nerves in this area. In the case of the pupillary reflex, however, there is no direct feedback information about the contraction and expansion of the iris. Previous attempts to condition this reflex were based essentially on Pavlovian theory. This is why we think the efforts to bring this reflex under control at first met with indifferent success. What was necessary was to provide the missing receptor feedback. The question then is, are there sufficient other receptors in the neighborhood of the motor nerves to bring about successful conscious control of those cortical motor processes that in turn might control the sympathetic and parasympathetic dilator and constrictor fibers?

Russian investigators early engrafted the cybernetic model upon the Pavlovian one with little cognitive dissonance and with much profit. Because they added feedback to the "conditioning," they immediately succeeded far more effectively than the American neo-Pavlovian experimenters in bringing normally involuntary processes under conscious control.

What is the limit of such intervention? Should one expect to be able to bring such phenomena as the permeability of cell membranes under conscious control? We do not today know where the limits of such control end. There are very few organs that are unaffected by rage, fear, or love, and these latter may be controlled by "imagining" situations that have made one angry, afraid, or enchanted. Heart rate, blood pressure, blood sugar—the counterpoint of the autonomic symphony is under indirect, conscious control. Psychosomatic disease is essentially a disease of consciousness, the consequence of interpretation of the world in such a way that affective responses are perpetually instigated to the disadvantage of the individual.

It is our belief that the conscious control loop, while it does not ordinarily govern the majority of bodily processes, is nonetheless capable, under appropriate training procedures, of intervening and controlling the most remote bodily processes.

THE FEEDBACK MECHANISM AND INSTRUMENTAL LEARNING

As the number of steps between the desired report and its duplication increases, and as these steps involve changes in the medium outside the skin of the organism, control is less precise, more variable, and more *instrumental.*

Control rests, of course, not only on the mastery of internal neurological circuitry but on the coordination of this knowledge with an equally efficient knowledge of the nature of the external environment. We have stressed the internal circuitry since it is the relatively constant means to the mastery of the great variety of other domains that are variable. It is the language of achievement. If one does not master this language, one masters nothing else. It is paradoxical that it is the external world that is the teacher of the language of the internal world. Again, the external world must be reproduced within this circuitry if it is to be assimilable and useful to the individual so that ultimately the dichotomy between the inner and outer domain becomes a dichotomy within the inner world. We do not embrace solipsism in this any more than does the biochemist who studies the transformations that are necessary before foodstuffs can be used by the body. Because of the great variety of domains that can be learned, the characterization of these domains presents an endless task for analysis, whereas the principal varieties of internal transformation are more limited.

Our hypothetical dart thrower must learn his own neurological pathways from the feedback from the external world and coordinate this derived knowledge of his own body with the information from outside his body. The learning of control is extended and deepened in a variety of ways.

First, even though the neurological pathways are usually constant, except in the case of disease or injury, the environment is not. Our hypothetical dart player is learning in a wind tunnel, with varying velocities of wind turned on and off—at first he knows not when. He has to learn that the neurological skill which hit the bull's-eye once, twice, or any number of times may nonetheless produce error under certain conditions which he does not yet understand. If this happens, trial and error must be undertaken again. He must try to hit the target again. A critical question at this time is the validity of diagnosis of the locus responsible for the loss of control. If it is environmental change that is responsible for his error, and he attributes the error to his own variability (i.e., assumes that he did not exactly repeat what he did when he did it correctly), it would be possible for the individual never to master the problem since he would never attempt to learn what changes in the environment frustrated his control. It has been known since Thorndike that practice without knowledge of results yields no learning.

The question we are raising concerns the locus of this ignorance and its contribution to the learning process. It is one thing to know that knowledge of results is being withheld by the experimenter, or by circumstances, but quite another to assume that there is knowledge when in fact there is not. The former can be corrected; the latter may never be remedied. We could demonstrate this by an experiment in which the subject is encouraged to believe that the source of his failure is his own variability rather than the variability of the environment. Under these conditions we should expect a spotty kind of control that always lagged behind changes in the environment. When a change, unbeknown to the subject, is introduced into the environment, the consequences of which, for performance, are attributed to himself rather than to the variability of environment, then anticipatory control could never be achieved. He is destined to make errors with each shift in the environment, no matter how much practice and skill he achieves, if he incorrectly attributes error to himself. He could develop no higher-order "formula" for coping with either customary or new changes because such a higher-order abstraction would necessarily have to be based on the relationship between changes in the environment that precede his own behavior and changes in the environment following his behavior. In other words, the formula, if put into words, would be of the general form, "when the wind in the tunnel changes in velocity, the force with which the dart is thrown must be increased if the velocity is increased, decreased if the velocity is decreased. If the direction of the velocity shifts, compensatory shift in the direction of the trajectory must be instituted, and so on." It is clear that if the critical changes in the environment were not transmuted, only lower-order formulas of the following type could be achieved: "what I seem to repeat is not actual repetition: therefore, when I fail, I must try again—something slightly different if the error was small, something grossly different if the error was large."

Further, the ability to cope quickly with new changes will be radically impaired since a "formula" that would successfully predict concomitant values of shifts in response for shifts in wind velocity and direction, as the typical formula above would do, cannot be developed with the critical environmental information missing from transmuted reports. It would be possible to further primitivize the second type of formula above, which attempted to abstract correlations between the magnitude of error and magnitude of change in motor message. This could be done as follows: every time an error of large magnitude occurred, it would be followed by a change in environment of such a sort that a compensatory large shift in trajectory would produce an equally large error as the preceding error. Every time an error of small magnitude occurred, it would be followed by a change in environment of such a sort that a small compensatory shift in trajectory would be followed by a large error. Further, these relationships could themselves be made sufficiently variable so that no negative correlation could be abstracted. Under these conditions the final formula would be of the type "when there is error, try again and hope you do it correctly."

The second consequence of such reduced information is that he must await the results of his action anew each time before he can shift his responses, since he does not know enough about the environmental changes ever to be able to learn to "see them coming" or to correctly anticipate them by trend analysis. Even a person who did appreciate the contribution of environmental changes to his own error could be reduced to this status by an environment that had no repetitions of any kind in it. The contingency we have been discussing—ignorance of the locus of error—is rarely as complete as the case we have made. Ordinarily, the individual sooner or later correctly diagnoses the source of error and how much is attributable to himself and how much to the variability of the environment, at least in dealing with the impersonal environment. The major problem every individual confronts in the consolidation of feedback control is the variability of his own response and variability of the environment. This variability can reduce the clarity of the Image so that the individual becomes less clear about what he wants to do, and can reduce the clarity of the feedback so that the answers to his questions become more equivocal and therefore his knowledge connecting means with ends necessarily becomes still more murky. There are, however, numerous sources of half-truth in such diagnosis, and we will examine some of these contingencies, discussing the characteristics of both Images and feedback from attempts to attain the Image, which expedite or hinder the integration of motives and the feedback mechanism in the achievement of one's purposes.

CHARACTERISTICS OF IMAGES AND FEEDBACK THAT EXPEDITE OR HINDER CONTROL

In achieving the correlations between one's own actions and events in the environment there are a number of characteristics of goals and feedback from attempted attainment that can expedite or hinder control. The primary factors are the following: clarity, generality, number of alternatives, number of conjoint characteristics, defining power, credibility, consistency, magnification, the number of duplicates of feedback, and sequential feedback.

Clarity of Feedback and Image

By clarity of feedback we mean the degree of definiteness of either the Image, instrumental knowledge, or feedback with respect to the implicit question in the Image behind the emitted behavior. Thus, if an individual were trying to learn to throw a dart and the lights went out each time he threw, the clarity of the feedback with respect to his goals would be minimal since every attempt would result in the same uninformative feedback. Lack of clarity of feedback more characteristically is a consequence of variability of success, which the individual does not know how to interpret. If the change in results can equally well be a consequence of a change in the environment or a change in his own response, there is reduced clarity of feedback. Or, as in the typical aperiodic reinforcement paradigm, the individual may be unclear as to whether there has in fact been any change. Lack of clarity in the Image would be a dart thrower who was unsure what his target really was (i.e., whether to attempt to hit the bull's-eye or somewhere near it or just throw for the fun of throwing. Lack of clarity of instrumental knowledge is usually a derivative of low clarity of feedback or low clarity of Image, or both. As the individual becomes more unclear about what he wants to do and as the answers to his questions become more equivocal, his knowledge connecting means with ends necessarily becomes still more murky.

Similarly, in social learning, if the child is trying to evoke a specific response from the parent but the parent is busy on the telephone or otherwise preoccupied, the clarity of feedback may be low. The child does not know whether the parent is simply preoccupied or whether this represents a real indifference to his needs. This is one type of lack of clarity of feedback, equivalent in part to the lights going out as he throws the dart. Another type of lack of clarity of feedback is variable answers to the same questions. If the parent is delighted to play blocks with the child on Tuesday, has other things to do on Wednesday, plays on Thursday, and is busy on Friday, the child is not certain what question is being answered in what way. Is it that the parent is atypically busy or characteristically busy one day and idle the next, or grumpy today, or has rejected the child, just doesn't like blocks very much, or what?

Variability and uncertainty also appear in the Image. The child who is overly tired and fretful may not be sure what it is he really wants to do. He may ask his parent to play with him, and no sooner has this request been met than the child's interest is uncertain because he partly wants to play but partly wants to sleep and partly wants to have a tantrum because his fatigue produces mounting distress, which, unrelieved, produces anger. If, now, the parent responds with hostility to the child's uncertainty and hostility, the child's instrumental knowledge becomes more unclear. What did he do that made the parent cooperative a moment ago and hostile now, when in part he still wants to play, and as far as he is concerned is still the same playful, fretful, sleepy child? This is essentially the problem that the scientist faces when he asks a question of nature. The answer is rarely crystal clear unless the question has been asked with unusual clarity. Minimal clarity in the child-parent relationship can produce continual "testing" behavior to determine the exact nature of the relationship or induce the child to renounce searching questions in his interpersonal relationships and ask trivial questions to which he *can* evoke clear answers.

Generality of Feedback

By *generality* of feedback we mean the equipotentiality of feedback with respect to a wide variety of questions asked. The feedback is in no sense unclear with respect to a particular question, but it gives a different answer to different questions.

Consider the person who smiles or laughs pleasantly at another person. The latter may reasonably interpret this as appreciation, that he is an interesting fellow, or that at least he is not a bore, or that he is not alone if he has been feeling lonely, or that he is sexually attractive if his intentions are so oriented, or that he is not inferior if he has been feeling inadequate. Similarly, a frown elicited from another is equally good evidence, depending upon the question asked, for the belief that one is not loved, is not respected, is a bore, is guilty, is dirty, is inferior, is alone, is ugly, will be hurt, and so on.

So-called traumatic experience is sometimes a consequence of feedback of high generality when the question is asked with dread by an individual who has been the recipient of many clear, well-defined, specific answers to the same question. The occasion for suicide is frequently an extraordinarily innocuous response from another, which seems entirely disproportionate to the affect and response it produces. Such general responses have been the basis of the success of the pictorial projective techniques since the respondent "interprets" the very general attitudes portrayed in terms of questions he characteristically puts to others. We are here referring not to representations that are unclear. These also have diagnostic usefulness. We refer rather to representations that show one person smiling at another, or frowning, or showing some clear but general response to the other.

This is, in general, a mechanism of self-confirmation if in addition one is selective in sensitivity and memory. Let us suppose that an individual is either deeply in love or in hate with himself. If there are (as is usually the case) a sufficient number of smiles and frowns from those in his environment, and he minimizes or forgets one or the other, he is relatively easily supported and confirmed in his beliefs by any appropriate feedback of sufficient generality.

Number of Alternatives in Image, Context, and Feedback

By *number of alternatives* in feedback we refer to the phenomenon whereby the *same* question can be answered equally well by a number of alternatives, since the Image permits some freedom of alternative satisfiers and also includes contextual alternatives. In contrast with generality of feedback (the *same feedback* answered a variety of different questions) this introduces a large safety factor in any control loop. These alternatives may be equally characteristic of the goal or the means to the goal or the context of the goal. In the case of number of goal alternatives, the goal may be reached by alternative feedbacks to the extent (in dart throwing) to which there is a broad bandwidth of "hits," any one of which is equally good. Let us assume the target is to hit the center. This may be defined in such a way that an electron microscope would be necessary to determine it or anywhere within a circle of ¼-inch radius, etc. The goal, however, may include more alternatives (e.g., a hit within the center two rings), being equally good answers to the question he puts to nature. Clearly, a skill is easier to develop or a goal easier to achieve when the safety factor is greater, and there is a greater number of possible outcomes that do in fact meet the desired result or the criteria of the Image. One of the important sources of pathology is the reduction of the safety factor in goal setting. The goal may be so specific, either by virtue of addiction or a too demanding level of aspiration, that the individual's probability of success is very slight. This is a particular source of pathology in a competitive society in which there is a limited supply of top targets that can be reached by all who make the attempt. Mental health would, however, be in equal jeopardy if there were so many alternatives that defined goal satisfaction that no effort whatever was necessary other than the transmuting of sensory input. Such extreme degrees of freedom of alternatives would result in failure to develop any response skills. This would be the best of all possible worlds as it presented itself to the individual over his sensory channels.

As Helson has shown, magnification can produce *new* dissatisfaction with a skill that, until a new scale was introduced, was entirely satisfactory to the individual. The converse is also possible and might be used as an adjunct to therapy—coarsening the scale used by the individual to judge his own skill. In the case of children this usually means changing the standards set by parents. Children who are disturbed by too high standards set by parents may be helped by submitting them to supervised achievement-oriented play therapy in which the therapist attempts to "implant" lower standards. In general, this can be achieved by the expression of genuine satisfaction and enthusiasm for whatever the child *does* achieve and a dramatic turning away from continued striving *after* such a display, with the implication that there is nothing more to strive for. Difficult striving will here be followed by satisfaction and enthusiasm and then by "easy" play that has minimal achievement aspects.

In the case of contextual alternatives, the dart thrower would find that a variety of features of the environment might be changed and yet give the right answers to enable the skill to be exercised. Thus, the color of the light in the room or large differences in brightness of illumination might yet permit the same degree of control. It is, indeed, by such changes in the context that the skill eventually achieves its peak development. It is when an individual can control a process despite considerable variation in the context of feedback that we properly speak of a skill.

Those aspects of feedback that the individual has to learn to control so that they make no difference, enrich and deepen the skill. The attitudes of others toward the skill one is trying to achieve are of particular significance for the individual's development. Some measure of autonomy must *be* learned if the individual is to master skills of which particular individuals or society at a particular moment in history disapproves. These are problems of "noise" in the acquisition of information.

The number of alternatives from the feedback of the means to the goal refers to two classes of feedback. One is the number of possible paths to any goal. Thus, independent of whether the goal is defined as hitting the target within a ⅛-, ¼-, or ½-inch circle, there may be a great variety of ways of holding the dart or throwing the dart (high trajectory with little energy, straight trajectory with more, etc.), each of which will hit the target equally well. The same variety of alternatives is found on the neurological level. There are usually many sets of alternative neurological pathways and innervations that will produce the same pathway or trajectory in the environment.

Further, there are integrated alternative pathways in which, if part of either a neurological or space-time pathway is altered, there is a compensatory alternative, either in the neurological network or in spacetime, that will still produce the same final control. These alternatives, judged by the achievement of the final goal, may be equally effective. To the extent to which this is inherently the case or learned there is a safety factor in the control process. The impressive equipotentiality of the cortex guarantees this safety factor at the neurological level. The infinite number of pathways between any two points in space guarantees it in the world. It is only when other criteria are brought to bear (energy, time, safety) that some of these alternatives are ruled out as undesirable.

Learning ordinarily consists in creating a large number of possible alternatives in feedback at every stage of the control loop so that control can become more and more habitual and mechanized. Thus, to pick up an object would require considerable attention if the object had to be right side up and so many inches from the fingers. It is because great variations all along the way provide feedback, which is equally satisfactory to achieve the goal of picking up the object, that it can be done with so little attention. This is the difference between finding the house of someone for the first time in an otherwise familiar town and finding it a second time. The second time very much less attention is necessary and a number of alternative routes *is* equally possible. The same familiarity with the internal networks, we think, is responsible for the very rapid transformation (neurologically speaking) that is possible after a single trial with an act that is unfamiliar when it is executed by an organism that is quite familiar with its own internal network. The so-called reduction of cues is, we believe, somewhat misleading. It is true that the monitoring of the control loop proceeds from detailed monitoring with hyperalertness to very great reduction in detail with a habitual, more peripheral awareness; but the total number of possible alternative cues upon which the highly skilled actor may rely *increases*. In other words, if in one performance the actor uses the cues a_1, c_2, e_1, and d_3 and in the next performance uses a_2, e_2 and f_1 and next uses a_1, g_2, h_3, and so on, he is increasing the total number of cues while reducing the number he uses for any one performance, which may originally have utilized b_1, b_1, c_1, d_1, e_1, f_1, g_1, h_1. The total in the former performance is a_1, a_2, a_3, b_1 b_2, $b_3 \ldots h_1$, h_2, h_3.

The same increase in number of alternatives and decrease in sets used at any one time is also going on neurologically, which is one reason for the extraordinary resistance of the cortex to interference. Basically, it is no different from the detours that a driver in his hometown makes when a particular street is crowded or torn up. We know from the retraining of patients with cortical lesions that alternative pathways can almost always be found.

In social learning the number of alternative skills the individual possesses in interacting with other individuals is in part a function of the number of different kinds of people he has had to deal with. There is a tendency for this skill to be somewhat underdeveloped in all individuals since it is easy to dislike those with whom we don't know how to interact. Shyness is a premature acceptance of limitation in such competence.

Number of Conjoint Characteristics of Image and Feedback

By the *number of conjoint characteristics* of feedback we refer to the phenomenon whereby the same feedback contains the answers to more than one question at once, all meant for the same individual. In generality of feedback, in contrast, we referred to that characteristic of feedback that answers different questions put by different people, or the same person at different times, in a different fashion.

A question may be put in such a way that a single answer gives very little or very much information. Thus, in the game of Twenty Questions, the questions at the beginning ordinarily evoke more information than the questions at the end, even though it is the latter answers that finally solve the problem. It is the answer to the beginning questions—such as "Is it living?"—which with a single answer establishes that it is in one large domain, to be sure, but it is not in an equally large other domain.

The more information in the question, the more information in the answer, or put differently, the same feedback may say more depending on what the individual has asked. The more compressed the question, the more the answer can support expansion.

The number of conjoint characteristics in the feedback is again inherent and/or learned. It may be there and communicated with little work necessary by the questioner, or it may require years of study in order to be found.

Learning consists, among other things, in so organizing experience that the questions that are always being asked extract the greatest yield of conjoint characteristics in the answers they receive from the domain of interest. Thus, in psychoanalysis a mountain can be, and frequently is, made of a molehill. The molehill may or may not be a "sign" of a mountain, but it becomes so only after mountainous labor by the questioner. The same is true of any crucial experiment. The experiment itself is the clipping of the coupon of an investment made by the clipper's ancestors in a company that is still a going concern.

The "reduction" of cues that is so necessary to expert control depends in part on the achievement of an organization such that the information necessary for control is coaxed *conjointly* out of fewer and fewer separate questions. Monitoring, for example, can only be reduced with safety (say, in driving an automobile) when the briefest occasional hyperalert monitoring can inform the individual of whether everything is as it should be. At the beginning of driving not only is much attention necessary for the execution of the necessary responses, but the monitoring process tends to ask one question at a time—am I shifting correctly, is the wheel straight, is the gas being fed correctly, and so on. At the end all of this, information can be gotten from occasional questions asked with a moderate degree of alertness. Further, it is so organized that even with minimal alertness the driver knows *when* to *become* more alert. There are also questions and answers that indicate that more searching questions had better be asked and quickly.

Goals may also be organized so that they have conjoint characteristics, that one achieves not *x* or *y* or *z* but *x* and y and z. It is entirely possible in this way to overload the human being. There are pathologies that result from exposure to and seduction by too many ideals, each one of which might have provided a way of life capable of integration and control.

Pathology apart, the conjoint characteristics of goals are, of course, among the most distinctive characteristics of the human being. He is capable of striving for, and somewhat attaining, many goals in one. He demands, or should demand, that his primary work be interesting, socially useful, socially respected, remunerative, secure, and so on. He may demand that his wife and friends have a number of conjoint characteristics. With respect to his total life, he may demand that he achieve a number of goals conjointly and that he himself be a complex person, playing a variety of roles at once.

In the achievement of simpler control, we find the same necessity for conjoint characteristics. In picking up a moving object the goal is to be at the right place at the right time. The means to achieve a goal that has conjoint characteristics must also have conjoint characteristics that are integrated. In picking up the moving object, feedback from the hand and from the object must give both space and time information at once. This necessity for conjoint response based on feedback that has conjoint characteristics makes early learning seem to the beginner to necessitate keeping so many things in mind. The change from early to late learning is achieved by increasing the number of answers per question asked and asking the question and receiving the answers in as compressed a form as possible.

Defining Power of Feedback

By the *defining power* of feedback, we refer to the converse of generality. Instead of the feedback answering many different questions in many different ways, the feedback doesn't answer questions at all. It rather informs the individual of what he has just done, from the point of view of another person or from some point of view other than he has been acting on. In our dart model, nature cooperated with the dart thrower in yielding consistent signs that indicated when he was and when he was not doing the right thing. In this sense, nature was answering questions put by the dart thrower. Let us suppose, however, that every time he threw the dart, the target moved toward him and said, "Just what do you think you're doing to my face—stop it!" Such a feedback would have great defining power. The individual who heard it would not know whether he was making progress or not in his attempt at control, but he would have defined for him by another what he was doing from the point of view of that other. He may now try to control this other, attack him, or avoid him, but he cannot simply continue his prior behavior without reference to the goals of the other.

This is a prime method for producing the "other-directed" individual. In the extreme case, the individual has no self-initiated goals.

As soon as language skill is developed, the scope of social definition of acts is unlimited. A single act by a child may encounter an extraordinary diversity of interpretation, which then constitutes a "target" that did not exist before this interpretation. Consider the following examples of behavioral interpretation commonly found in the socialization process:

1. Personality evaluations:
   "That's a good boy"—"That's a bad boy" (i.e., the act is one that would come only from a specific kind of person)
2. Act evaluation:
   "That's a good way of doing it."
3. Affecteffects—with personality evaluation:
   "I love you—you are such a good boy."
4. Affecteffects—with act evaluation:
   "I love you for doing such a nice thing."
5. Consequence evaluations—self-referent:
   "Don't do that—do you want to lose your eye?"
6. Consequence evaluations—other referent:
   (a) affect induced; (b) action consequences
   "Don't do that—you make Momma unhappy."
   "Don't do that—I'll beat you."

In short, language enables the socializer to connect the behavior of the child with anything he or the culture thinks it is or should be connected with. This kind of connection is much more efficient and subtle than could possibly be achieved without language. Such interpretation is limited only by the imagination. Characteristic differences in the locus of evaluation will tend to produce concern about different loci.

Children whose parents evaluated their "personality" will become more concerned with what kind of a personality they have. Children evaluated for their acts will be concerned not with their egos but with their acts. Children evaluated by the consequences of their acts will be even less interested in their immediate personality. Children evaluated primarily on an affect basis will be concerned with the affect of other individuals—to evoke it and to experience it themselves.

There is yet another way in which feedback has defining power. Consider our dart thrower again, and let us suppose that after hours of attempting to hit the bull's-eye he achieves only repeated failure. The repeated fact of failure and the probably negative affective responses to his repeated failures also have defining power—the power of delineating attempted control as nothing more than misery and failure and hard work. If this is what practice at control really is, then the individual will in all probability renounce his goal. The process is not basically different from an external definition of his behavior since the consequences are external to his attempt at control. Any feedback that is capable of radically modifying the goal striving that produced the feedback has *defining power.* It should be noted that unexpected positive consequences of goal seeking have the same defining power. Reward over and above what was attempted can intensify the original goal.

Credibility of Feedback

By *credibility* of the feedback we mean its trustworthiness. In nonsocial learning, one learns quickly that although one may be ignorant of all of the critical factors in a domain, nature is taking no sides—she does not willfully deceive, nor is she interested in the effect of her communications. In social learning, human beings learn that they may expect deception as well as practice it, and that they may expect communication for the sake of some purpose other than communication per se. Another person may wish to impress, to threaten, to please, to be kind, to be cruel—in short, his communications are purposeful.

Understanding, prediction, and control of social communications therefore necessitates interpretation of the motives and intentions of the communicator.

Credibility is a derivative of a theory about a person and his intentions toward oneself. If this theory can be strengthened *or* weakened by events that fly in the face of the theory, credibility may be expected to change.

Consistency of Feedback

By *consistency of feedback* we refer to the extent to which the same question appears to evoke the same answer every time it is asked. We have already discussed this at some length in connection with the dart model. What of its application to social learning? Here, consistency is a much more scarce commodity.

To the extent to which a child wishes to please his parents, or to the extent to which his parents suggest that this is an appropriate goal for little human beings, the child may vary his behavior to evoke smiles, approval, and love from the parents. If this should work for the most part, then when it does not work—for example, mother has had a hard day at home and/or father has suffered in the office, and the little boy suddenly finds that his old behavior evokes not love but hostility—then he has several options of interpretation: (1) he has somehow failed to duplicate what always works, so he will try again; or (2) his parents have changed, so he must learn new techniques of winning their approval; or (3) there is no difference in what he is trying to do, but there is a difference within himself (his internal environment has changed rather than his external environment) since he has failed in some way to repeat what he has always been able to repeat before.

The more consistent the parents have been in the past, the more the first option will be elected, since (2) and (3) have not occurred before, and they are radical discriminations unlikely to be made at first in any event and are frightening in their implications when the possibility does occur. Therefore, like the dart thrower who doesn't realize that the wind may suddenly have become variable in the tunnel, he simply repeats his performance in the hope that he will do it right this time. The paradox of the situation is that the longer the history of consistency in this parent-child interaction, the less likely the child is to perceive the change in the parent. If the next day the parents are their old selves again, the child will be confirmed in the hypothesis that the source of variability was internal. As long, then, as there is a preponderance of successful evocations of attitudes from parents, the failures will be interpreted as internal "noise" failures. This, we think, is why success in interpersonal relationships can produce beliefs extremely resistant to modification by the behavior of the other. This is also why a long history of success in problem-solving followed by occasional failure leads to simple repetition of the same general efforts, since the belief that the self has radically changed or that the world has radically changed is unlikely to be entertained.

What will happen in the above situations if the parents continue to be hostile and failure continues to follow previously successful effort? Eventually, the simple assumption of identical repetition will yield to the interpretation that new trial-and-error learning needs to be instituted. The child will try new tricks to win the parents' approval, just as the dart thrower, after apparently repeating the former successful throws, will begin to try different trajectories. If these continue to fail, the child is faced with the hypothesis that he has changed radically himself, or his parents have, or both he and his parents have changed. In the case of problem solving after repeated failure, following many success experiences, the same essential options are faced: either I have changed radically or the world has changed or both have happened. The most common instance of this phenomenon in the history of those other than only children, or last children, is the birth of a sibling.

Magnification of Feedback

By *magnification* of feedback we refer to an increase in detail or relative density of reports to messages. Early learning is usually characterized by high-density monitoring, which is unnecessary in late learning. Any interference with late learning usually prompts the individual to return to magnification of feedback. Thus, if one is walking down a dark corridor at a rate customary for walking generally, and one walks into an object, one will slow down so that there will be a magnification of feedback that will permit awareness of the next object before the damage is done. This will increase the density of reports to messages.

It is our impression that this principle, which the individual ordinarily uses in early learning, has not been sufficiently appreciated and exploited in the

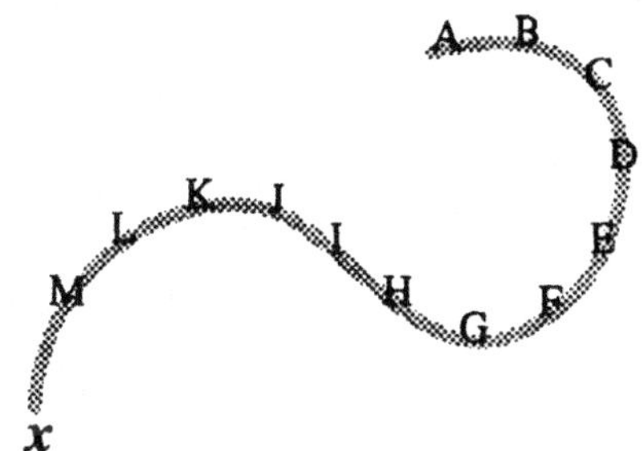

FIGURE 55.2 Illustration of the path.

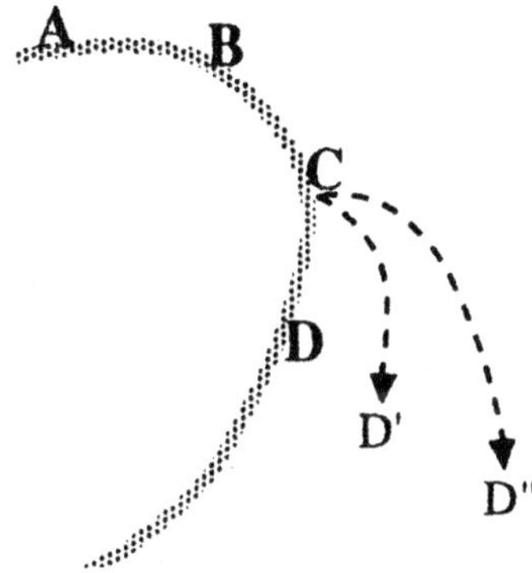

FIGURE 55.3 Illustration of the path with error magnification.

educational process generally and in the teaching of skills specifically.

It would be profitable to experiment with magnification techniques for purposes of general education, acquisition of skills, and psychotherapy.

To illustrate what we mean, let us suppose we wish to teach a person how to move his hand and arm through space in a particular path (to hit a tennis ball, say) and let us suppose the path is as shown in Figure 55.2. Let us suppose that we record his movement so that the actual path of his arm as he moves it through the air is made visible to him on a screen. This is a minor order of magnification, since the visual field has more detail than the kinesthetic feedback. Now suppose that at the moment he deviates from the path we wish him to learn, we greatly magnify, on the same screen, the extent of his error in the following way. Suppose that his movement was perfect till he reached C. At that point the visual representation, as shown in Figure 55.3, would dramatically go off into space in the *direction* of his error but with a magnified *distance* and *velocity,* C to D′. In other words, we want him to learn CD. He actually does CD′, a slight deviation of curvature over a part of the path. We magnify the error just after it is made at C by flashing a path CD′ which is *not* his actual path but an exaggeration of precisely where he made what kind of error, forgetting for the time being the other errors he made and the return to the correct path at D.

An alternative technique would be a device that holds his hand and arm and at the point of error magnifies the consequences by pulling his arm rapidly through space in the same way as the visual display would. By such a technique we would make errors highly "visible" and their exact nature more easily reported than by reproducing what he actually did. The extent of magnification should be suited to the optimal rate at which the human being can utilize such information at different stages of the learning process. We are convinced that part of the difficulty of early learning and its inefficiency comes from insufficient magnification of feedback. Every *step* of the learning process must be blown up before it can be reduced.

The same general technique can be used as an aid to psychotherapy. Group therapy, indeed, seems to us to be just such a "magnifier"—via the overly intense reactions of other disturbed individuals to the smallest details of the behavior of members of the group. Such magnification, however, is contraindicated for those who are already oversensitized to the effect of their behavior on others. Overly exquisite self-consciousness is one of the group therapy-created pathologies in certain individuals, but the use of magnification by the disturbed reactions of disturbed members of a group therapy is, we think, useful in quickening self-consciousness and the breakdown of defenses in those who are particularly unaware of their personalities and their effect on other individuals.

It should be noted that this has been a technique employed in socialization, somewhat unwittingly and unself-consciously. Thus, the belaboring of a child with the possible consequences of a trivial act is an instance of magnification; for example, "Do you realize what might have happened if that ball had broken that window and there was someone standing under the window?" Children socialized under the technique of magnification are often similar in personality to those who have been overanalyzed.

Number of Duplicates in Feedback

By *number of duplicates* of feedback we refer to the number of characteristics in the feedback that are the same, both at a moment in time and in a series. The greater the number of duplicates, the more "visible" new classes of information can become. By means of maximizing of duplicates, further transformations of feedback become possible. Characteristics that were not transmuted because of channel limitation can now be responded to and transformed into further sets of duplicates, and the same process begun again.

As in all of the other characteristics of feedback, there are *inherent* and *learned* differences in the number of duplicates in any feedback. If there is an inherent homogeneity of the field, compared with another field, that field is more quickly and easily transmuted. Specific perceptual fields (e.g., visual) are inherently more homogeneous than fields that include *all* input channels, although cross-modality similarities do exist.

Clearly, the transformability of a field is a function of the number of duplicates that are inherent or can be imposed according to some system of classification. Learning consists in maximizing the number of duplicates so that the formulas or theories that are distilled from experience enable more and more experience to be understood, predicted, and controlled as variations in an equation.

The complexity of control of input and output possible for the human being is essentially governed by the same capacity for maximizing of duplicates as we find in science. This is because of a limitation of channel capacity. Man must make a virtue of necessity. He is pushed toward increasing simplification of information. Any discovery of novelty therefore requires a continuing reduction of novelty to new redundancies. The power of new information is proportional to the quantity of older homogenized information it violates and interrupts. Thus can a feedback mechanism overcome its channel limitations at the same time it erodes the power of its perfected images.

In summary, the human feedback mechanism requires a centrally constructed Image that guides a translatory process, which returns a report for monitoring that informs whether the individual has in fact achieved his purpose. The simplest kind of feedback circuitry is that implicated in the ability to repeat any motor act. This requires the individual to master the internal neurological networks in his body. Paradoxically, such mastery can be achieved only indirectly by mastering external space in simple motor skills.

When such mastery of the internal networks has been achieved, the individual is faced with the more variable space of his environment, both physical and social. Since variability and sameness can never be diagnosed with complete assurance or correctness, the individual is forever vulnerable to assuming change in one locus, when in fact it has occurred in another locus, and to assuming stability when in fact there has been change.

The simplicity of the feedback mechanism is vulnerable to endless complication in the social world because the clarity of both feedback and Image may be jeopardized by variable answers to the same questions. It may be complicated by the generality of the feedback by giving a different answer to different questions. It may be complicated by the number of alternatives in Image, context, or feedback, thus introducing expansion or contraction of safety factors in achieving purposes. It can be complicated by the number of conjoint characteristics of Image and feedback so that the same feedback is forced to answer an increasing number of questions at once. It may be complicated by the defining power of feedback that does not answer questions but imposes an unasked question and answer. It is complicated by the credibility of feedback that arises from the competing and independent purposes of others who may and can mislead and deceive. It is complicated by the consistency of feedback arising from changes in the purposes and feelings of others, which cannot always be predicted, understood, or accepted. It is complicated by the magnification of feedback that may either exaggerate or minimize the significance of the feedback. Finally, it is complicated by the compression and homogeneity of the feedback, which is a necessary condition both for skill and for the detection and generation of novelty—and for the creative expansion of the many purposes of the human being.

Epilogue: Rate Change and Dimensionality as Fundamental Axiom

Affect, imagery, and consciousness have all been grounded in our model in rates of change as fundamental and mutually interdependent.

Consciousness appears in animals who move about in space but not in organisms rooted in the earth. Mobility is the key, requiring ever changing information for an organism which is never twice in exactly the same world when the world contains within it complex organisms whose behavior would have had to be predicted and handled.

Consciousness is a report about affect-driven imagery. Since affect in our view amplifies varying rates of change (its innate activities), the images within the control assembly represent only such information as is urgent that reports significant, vital, new changing information.

We had also said that the most essential characteristic of a living system is its ability to *duplicate* or repeat itself in space and time. We had urged that the concept of duplication was central not only for biology but also for psychology, because individual and species duplication is achieved by a set of mechanisms which are themselves essentially duplicative.

Between the one extreme of duplication, which consists largely in the transportation of energy and material from outside to inside the organism, and the other extreme, which consists of the reception and transmission of linguistic symbols, there are many duplicative phenomena which vary in their relative composition of energy and information. However, all duplicative processes whether biological or psychological deal necessarily with rates of change of either energy or information. Affect amplification is a special case of making some rates of change urgently rewarding or punishing as privileged, vital information which provides a set of blue prints for conscious, imagined ways of orienting and behaving in a world whose constant change varies only in its rate. Stability is that very rare special case of a rate of change which is extremely slow compared with the totality of the environment.

If rate of change is the fundamental axiom of our model of affect, imagery, and consciousness, then we must also specify what the fundamental ordering principle of rate change is. That has proven to be surprisingly simple, elegant, and powerful—the dimensionality of the domain.

As Victor Weisskopf (1979) has shown in his review of quantum mechanics, "There exists a threshold of excitation for any dynamical system. The threshold becomes higher as the dimensions of the system decrease." This he refers to as the "quantum ladder."

Thus strong and weak forces represent radical differences in the rates of change of different forms of matter as a function of the inverse relationship between its dimensionality and cohesiveness. The simpler the form, the higher the threshold of energy required to change it.

What is common to the domains of matter, life, and mind is that all are governed by rules for ordinary rates of sameness–change in space-time.

The subnuclear particles which proved to be such "strong" cohesive forces, obeying non-Newtonian "laws," were as different as the Newtonian "weak" forces in their increased rate of change of weak matter proportional to their increased dimensionality.

Stated positively, for any dynamic system, the rate of change is a function of the dimensionality of its components. The "more" going on, the "faster"

(**Publisher's Note**–The following epilogue by Silvan Tomkins was left unfinished at the time of his death. Even though he left behind notes as to how he intended to complete it, we are publishing only the portion which he actually did complete.)

the rate of change. I encountered this formulation a decade ago and it provided a fundamental axiom for the integration of my model into the nature of the cosmos as it has yet been revealed.

If matter itself has exhibited such discontinuities while at the same time revealing the ordering principle of dimensionality as its root, we should not be surprised that life and mind exhibiting increasing dimensionality should also exhibit increased rates of change, and that affect, imagery, and consciousness have evolved to cope with just such increasing dimensionalities is revealed also in perception, memory, and feedback circuitry. The "more" that had to be dealt with was the radical increase in information produced by the movement of animals through space, thus requiring consciousness of changing information, central imagery to change with the constantly changing information, integrating past, present, and possibly future change, and above all an innate affect mechanism which amplified particular rates of change as rewarding and punishing and therefore vital biases towards and away from such sources. . . .

References—Volumes III and IV

Abelson, R. (1963). Computer simulation of "hot cognitions." In S. S. Tomkins & S. Messick (Eds.), *Computer simulation of personality.* New York: Wiley.

Abelson, R. (1975). Concepts for representing mundane reality in plans. In D. G. Bobrow & A. Collins (Eds.), *Representation and understanding.* New York: Academic Press.

Abraham, K. (1952). *Selected papers.* London, Hogarth.

Adler, A. (1912). *The Neurotic Constitution.* Trans. B. Gluck & J. E. Lind. New York: Moffit, Yard, 1917.

Alexander, F., & Portis, S. (1944). A psychosomatic study of hypoglycaemic fatigue. *Psychosomatic Medicine, 6,* 195–205.

Allport, G. W. (1924–1925). Eidetic imagery. *British Journal of Psychology, 15,* 99–120.

Ambrose, J. (1960). *The smiling and related responses in early human infancy: An experimental and theoretical study of their course and significance.* Unpublished doctoral dissertation, University of London.

Angyal, A. (1935). The perceptual bases of somatic delusions in a case of schizophrenia. *Archives of Neurology and Psychiatry, 34,* 270–279.

Angyal, A. (1936). The experience of the body-self with schizophrenia. *Archives of Neurology and Psychiatry, 35,* 1029–1053.

Angyal, A. (1941). *Foundations for a science of personality.* Cambridge: Harvard University Press

Aristotle. *Rhetoric,* by W. Rhys Roberts.

Asch, S. E. (1956). Studies of independence and conformity: 1. minority of one against a unanimous majority. *Psychological Monographs, 70*(9), 1–70.

Atwood, G. E., & Tomkins, S. S. (1976). On the subjectivity of personality theory. *Journal of the History of the Behavioral Sciences, 12,* 166–177.

Averill, J. (1980). The emotions. In E. Stuab (Ed.), *Personality: Basic aspects and current research.* Englewood Cliffs, NJ: Prentice-Hall.

Bartley, S. H., & Bishop, G. H. (1933). The cortical response to stimulation of the optic nerve in the rabbit. *American Journal of Physiology, 103,* 159–172.

Bartley, W. W. (1985). *Wittgenstein.* LaSalle, IL: Open Court.

Basescu, S. (1951). *Concept formation in high and low I.Q. subjects.* Unpublished doctoral dissertation, Princeton University.

Beach, F. A. (1948). *Hormones and behavior.* New York: Hoeber.

Bercel, N. A., Travis, L. E., Olinger, L. B., Dreikurs, E. (1958). Model psychoses induced by LSD-25 in normals. In C. F. Reed, I. E. Alexander, & S. S. Tomkins, *Psychopathology: A source book.* Cambridge, MA: Harvard University Press, pp. 605–639.

Bergler, E. (1961). *Curable and incurable neurotics.* New York: Liveright.

Bower, G. A. (1981). Mood and memory. *American Psychologist, 36*(2), 129–148.

Bowlby, J. S. (1973). *Attachment and loss: Vol. 2. Separation, anxiety and anger.* New York: Basic Books.

Brain, R. (1958). The psychological bases of consciousness. *Brain, 81,* 426–455.

Broadbent, D. E. (1953). Classical conditioning and human watch keeping, *Psychological Review, 60,* 331–339.

Broadbent, D. E. (1957). A mechanical model for human attention and immediate memory. *Psychological Review, 64*(3), 205–215.

Broadbent, D. E. (1958). *Perception and communication.* New York: Pergamon Press.

Bruner, J. (1968). *Process of cognitive growth: Infancy.* Worcester, MA: Clark University Press.

Brunswick, E. (1947). *Systematic and representative design of psychological experiments.* Berkeley, CA: University of California Press.

Bulgakov, V. (1971). *The last year of Leo Tolstoy.* New York: Dial.

Bull, N., & Girodo-Frank, L. (1950). Emotions induced and studied in hypnotic subjects. Part 2. The findings. *Journal of Nervous and Mental Disease.*

Campbell, B. A., & Campbell, E. H. (1962). Retention and extinction of learned fear in infant and adult rats. *Journal of Comparative and Physiological Psychology, 55*(I), 1–8.

Carlson, R. (1981). Studies in script theory: 1. Adult analogs of a childhood nuclear scene. *Journal of Personality and Social Psychology, 40,* 501–510.

Christian, R. F. (Ed.). (1978). *Tolstoy's letters: Vol. 1. 1828–1879;* Vol. 2. 1880–1910. New York: Scribner.

Coale, A. J., Fallers, L. A., Levy, M. J., Schneider, D. M., & Tomkins, S. S. (1965). *Aspects of the analysis of family structure.* Princeton, NJ: Princeton University Press.

Cohen, G. (1926). Stereognostische Störung. Deutsche Zeitschnift für Nervenbeilk, *93,* 228–244.

Cohen, R. (1953). Role of "body image concept" in pattern of ipsilateral clinical extinction. (1953). *Archives of Neurology and Psychiatry, 70,* 503–510.

Crile, G. (1915). *The origin and nature of the emotions.* Philadelphia: W.B. Saunders.

Crile, G. (1916). *Man—an adaptive mechanism.* New York: Macmillan.

Crile, G. (1941). *Intelligence, power and personality.* New York: McGraw-Hill.

Czeisler, C. A., Weitzman, E. D., Moore-Ede, M. C, Zimmerman, J. C., Knauer, R. C. (1980). Human sleep: Its duration and organization depend on its circadian phase. *Science, 210*(12), 1264–1267.

Darwin, C. (1965). *The expression of emotions in man and animals,* Chicago: University of Chicago Press. (Original work published 1872).

Delcomyn, F. (1980). Neural bases of rhythmic behavior in animals. *Science,* 210(31), 492–498.

Dement, W., & Kleitman, N. (1957). The relation of eye movements during sleep to dream activity: An objective method for the study of dreaming. *Journal of Experimental Psychology, 53,* 339–346.

Dement, W. C. (1965). Dreams and dreaming. *International Journal of Neurology, 5,* 168–186.

Dement, W. C. (1969). The biological role of REM sleep (circa 1968). In A. Kales (Ed.): *Sleep: Physiology and pathology.* Philadelphia: Lippincott.

Dethier, V. G. (1978). Other tastes, other worlds. *Science, 201,* 224–228.

De Valois, R. L., Albrecht, D. G., & Thorell. (1978). Spatial tuning of LGN and cortical cells in monkey visual systems, In H. Spekreijsel (Ed.), *Spatial contrast.* Amsterdam: Royal Netherlands Academy of Sciences.

Dollard, J., & Miller, N. E. (1950). *Personality and psychotherapy.* New York: McGraw-Hill.

Drever, J., & Collins, M. (1928). *Performance tests of intelligence: A series of nonlinguistic tests for deaf and normal children.* Edinburgh: Oliver & Boyd.

Eden, M., & Morris, H. (1959). The characterization of cursive writing. *Quarterly Progress Report of the Research Laboratory of Electronics,* 152–155.

Ekman, P. (1972). Universal and cultural differences in facial expression of emotion. In J. R. Cole (Ed.), *Nebraska Symposium on Motivation* (Vol. 19). Lincoln: University of Nebraska, 1972.

Ekman, P., & Friesen, W. V. (1978). *Facial action coding system.* Palo Alto, CA: Consulting Psychologists Press.

Ekman, P., Friesen, W. V., & Tomkins, S. S. (1971). Facial affect scoring technique: A first validity study. *Semiotica, 1,* 37–53.

Ekman, P., Sorenson, E. R., & Friesen, W. V. (1969). Pancultural elements in facial displays of emotions. *Science, 164*(3875), 86–88.

Eldred, E., Granit, K., & Horton, P. A. (1953). Observations on "intact" de-afferented and de-efferented muscle spindles. *Acta Physiologica Scandinavica, 29,* 83–85.

Eliade, M. (1978). *A history of religious ideas: Vol. 1. From the Stone Age to the Eleusian mysteries.* Chicago: University of Chicago Press.

Elias, N., & Dunning, E. (1986). *Just for excitement.* Basil Oxford: Blackwell.

Elliott, R. (1964). Physiological activity and performance: A comparison of kindergarten children with young adults. *Psychological Monographs, 78* (10, Whole No. 587).

Ellson, D. G. (1941). Hallucinations produced by sensory conditioning. *Journal of Experimental Psychology, 28,* 1–20.

Eisner, R., Franklin, D. L., Von Citters, R. L., & Kennedy, D. W. (1966). Cardio-vascular defense against asphyxia. *Science, 153,* 941–949.

Emde, R. N., Gaensbauer, I. J., & Harmon, R. J. (1976). Emotional expression in infancy: A biobehavioral study. *Psychological Issues* (Vol. 10). New York: International Universities Press.

Engel, E. (1956). The role of content in binocula resolution. *American Journal of Psychology, 691,* 87–91

Engel, E., & Douglas, E. C. (1980). *Visual viewpoint development.* Washington, DC: Southeastern Psychological Association Meetings.

Engel, G. L. (1950). *Fainting: Physiological and psychological considerations.* Springfield, IL: C. C. Thomas.

English, O. S. (1949). Observation of trends in manic-depressive psychosis. *Psychiatry, 12,* 125–134.

Erulkar, S. D., Rose, J. E. & Davies, P. W. (1956). *Bull. Johns Hopkins Hospital, 99,* 55.

Evarts, E. V. (1979, September) Brain mechanisms of movement. *Scientific American,* 164–178.

Farley, J., & Alkon, D. L. (1980). Neural organization predicts stimulus specificity for a retained associative behavioral change. *Science, 210*(4476), 1373–1375.

Fisher, S., & Cleveland, S. E. (1957). An approach to physiological reactivity in terms of a body image schema. *Psychological Review, 64,* 26–37.

Foulds, G. A. (1949). Variations in the intellectual activities of adults. *American Journal of Psychology, 62,* 238–247.

Frankenhaeuser, M. (1979). Psychoendocrine approaches to the study of emotion. *Nebraska Symposium on Motivation* (Vol. 26). Lincoln: University of Nebraska Press.

French, T. M., Alexander, F., et al. (1941). Psychogenic factors in bronchial asthma. *Psychosomatic Medicine.* Monograph No. 2.

Freud, S. (1971). *Beyond the pleasure principle.* Standard Edition, 18. Original work published 1920.

Freud, S. (1933). *New introductory lectures on psychoanalysis.* New York: Norton.

Fried, E. (1976). *The impact of nonverbal communication of facial affect on children's learning.* Unpublished doctoral dissertation, Rutgers University, 1976.

Friedman, J., & Schiffman, H. (1962). Early recollections of schizophrenic and depressed patients. *Journal of Individual Psychology, 18,* 57–61.

Fries, M. E. (1944). Psychosomatic relationships between mother and infant. *Psychosomatic Medicine, 6,* 159–162.

Gale, G. (1979, September). The anthropic principle. *Scientific American,* 154–171.

Gallup, G., & Hill, E. (1959). *The secrets of long life.* New York: Bernard Geis Associates.

Galton, F. (1880). *Brain, 2,* 149–162.

Gerard, R. B. (1955). Biological roots of psychiatry. *Science, 122,* 225–230.

Geschwind, N. (1974). *Selected papers on language and the brain.* Boston: D. Reidel Publishing Co.

Gibson, J. J. (1959). Perception as a function of stimulation. In S. Koch (Ed.), *Psychology: A study of a science* (Vol. 1, pp. 456–501). New York: McGraw-Hill.

Gibson, J. J. (1979). *The ecological approach to visual perception.* Boston: Houghton Mifflin.

Gombrich, E. H. J. (1960). *Art and illusion.* New York: Patheon Press.

Gould, S. J. (1989). *Wonderful life: The Burgess Shade and the nature of history.* New York: Norton.

Gould, S. J., & Lawantan, R. C. (1980). The spandrels of San Marco and the Panglossian paradigm: A critique of the Adaptationist Programme. *Proceedings of the Royal Society,* London.

Haber, W. B. (1955). Effects of loss of limb on sensory functions. *Journal of Psychology, 40,* 115–123.

Hardy, J. D., Woff, H. G., & Goodell, H. (1952). *Pain sensation and reactions.* Baltimore: Williams & Wilkins.

Harlow, H. F. (1963). The formation of learning sets. *Psychological Review, 56,* 51–65.

Hastorf, A., & Myro, G. (1959). The effect of meaning on binocular rivalry. *American Journal of Psychology, 72*(3), 393–400.

Head, H. (1920). *Studies in neurology.* London: Oxford University Press.

Head, H., & Holmes, G. (1920). Sensory disturbances from cerebral lesions. In *Studies in neurology* (Vol. 2). London: Frowde & Hodder & Stoughton.

Hebb, D. (1949). *Organization of behavior.* New York: John Wiley & Sons.

Hernandez-Péon, R., & Scherrer, H. (1955). "Habituation" to acoustic stimuli in cochlear nucleus. *Federation Proceedings, 14,* 71.

Hertz, R. (1973). The pre-eminence of the right hand: a study in religious polarity. In R. Needham (Ed.), *Right and left.* Chicago: University of Chicago Press.

Hoagland, H. (1957). *Hormones, brain function, and behavior: Proceedings of a Conference on Neuroendocrinology, held at Arden House, Harriman, NY, 1956.* New York: Academic Press.

Hochberg, J. R. (1957). Effects of the Gestalt revolution; The Cornell Symposium on Perception. *Psychological Review, 64,* 73–84.

Horn, D., & Waingrow, S. (1966). *Behavior and attitudes questionnaire.* Bethesda, MD: National Clearinghouse for Smoking and Health.

Horn, G. (1960). Electrical activity of the cerebral cortex of the anaesthetized cat during attentive behavior. *Brain, 83,* 57–76.

Hubel, D. H., Henson, C. O., Rupert, A. A., & Galambos, R. (1959). "Attention" units in the auditory cortex. *Science, 129,* 1279–1280.

Hubel, D. H., & Wiesel, T. N. (1968). Receptive fields and functional architecture of monkey striate cortex. *Journal of Physiology, 195,* 215–243.

Hubel, D. H., & Wiesel, T. N. (1977). Ferrier Lecture: Functional architecture of Macaque monkey visual cortex. *Proceedings of the Royal Society of London, 198,* Series B, 1–59.

Hubel, D. H., & Wiesel, T. N. (1979). Brain mechanisms of vision. *Scientific American, 214*(3), 150–162.

Huber, E. (1930). Evolution of facial musculature and cutaneous field of trigeminus. *Quarterly Review of Biology, 5,* 133–188. 389–437.

Huber, E. (1931). *Evolution of facial musculature and facial expression.* Baltimore: Johns Hopkins University Press.

Ikard, F., & Tomkins, S. (1973). The experience of affect as a determinant of smoking behavior: A series of validity studies. *Journal of Abnormal Psychology, 81,* 172–181.

Ittelson, W. H., & Slack, C. W. (1958). The perception of persons as visual objects. In R. Tagiuri & L. Petrullo (Eds.), *Person perception and later personal behavior.*

Iverson, L. L., & Iverson, S. D., & Snyder, S. H. (1975–1978). *Handbook of psychopharmacology.* New York: Plenum Press.

Iverson, S. D., & Iverson, L. L. (1981). *Behavioral pharmacology.* Second Edition. Oxford: Oxford University Press.

Izard, C. E. (1968). The emotions and emotion constructs in personality and culture research. In R. G. Cattell (Ed.), *Handbook of modern personality theory.* Chicago: Aldine.

Izard, C. E. (1971). *The face of emotion.* New York: Appleton-Century-Crofts.

Izard, C. E. (1977). *Human emotions.* New York: Plenum Press.

Izard, C. E. (1981). Differential emotions theory and the facial feedback hypothesis of emotion activation: Comments on Tourangeau & Ellsworth's "The role of facial responses in the experience of emotion." *Journal of Personality and Social Psychology, 40,* 350–354.

Izard, C. E., & Tomkins, S. S. (1966). Affect and behavior: Anxiety as a negative affect. In C. D. Spielberger (Ed.), *Anxiety and behavior.* New York: Academic Press.

Jackson, J. H. (1932). *Selected writings of].H. Jackson.* Edited by James Taylor. London: Hodder & Stoughton.

Jackson, M., & Sechrest, L. (1962). Early recollections in four neurotic diagnostic categories. *Journal of Individual Psychology, 18,* 52–56.

Jackson, R. L. (1958). *Dostoevsky's underground man in Russian literature.* The Hague, Netherlands: Mouton & Co.

Janis, I. L. (1958). *Psychological stress.* New York: Wiley.

Johansson, G., von Hofsten, C. & Jansson, G. (1980). Event perception. *Annual Review of Psychology, 31,* 27–63.

Jonides, J., Irwin, D. E., & Yantis, S. (1982). Integrating visual information from successive fixation. *Science, 215*(8), 192–194.

Kandell, E. R. (1984). Steps toward a molecular grammar for learning: Explorations into the nature of memory. In K. J. Isselbacher (Ed.), *Science and Society.* New York: John Wiley & Sons.

Kant, I. (1929). *Critique ofpure reason.* London: Macmillan.

Karon, B. P. (1958). *The Negro personality.* New York: Springer Publishing Co.

Karon, B. P. (1964). Suicidal tendency as the wish to hurt someone else, and resulting treatment technique. *Journal of Individual Psychology, 20,* 206–212.

Kayser, C. (1961). *The physiology of natural hybernation.* Oxford, New York: Pergamon Press.

Kinsbourne, M. (1982). Hemispheric specialization and the growth of human understanding. *American Psychologist, 37*(4), 411–420.

Kleitman, N. (1963). *Sleep and wakefulness.* Chicago: University of Chicago Press.

Kohler, I. (1955). Experiments with prolonged optical distortion. *Ada Psychologica, 11,* 176–178.

Kohler, I. (1964). *The formation and transformation of the perceptual world.* New York: International University Press.

Landis, C, & Hunt, W. A. (1939). *Tire startle pattern.* New York: Farrar, Straus & Giroux.

Lansing, R. W. (1954). *The relationship of rhythms to visual reaction time.* Unpublished doctoral dissertation, UCLA.

Lansing, R. W., Schwartz, E., & Lindsley, S. B. (1956). Reaction time and EEC activation. *American Psychologist, 11,* 433.

Lapidus, L. B., & Schmolling, P. (1975). Anxiety arousal and schizophrenia: A theoretical integration. *Psychological Bulletin, 82,* 689–710.

Lashley, K. S. (1960). The problem of serial order in behavior. In F. A. Beach and others (Eds.), *The neuropsychology of Lashley* (pp. 506–528). New York: McGraw-Hill.

Lebow, N. (1980). *Causes of war.* Baltimore: Johns Hopkins Press.

Levin, H., & Baldwin, A. C. (1959). Pride and shame in children. In M. Jones (Ed.), *Nebraska symposium on motivation* (pp. 138–173). Lincoln: University of Nebraska Press.

Levy, D. M. (1960). The infant's earliest memory of innoculation: A contribution to public health procedures. *Journal of General Psychology, 96,* 3–46.

Lewin, R. (1980, November). Evolutionary theory under fire. *Science, 210,* 883–887.

Lewis, B. (1982). *The Muslim discovery of Europe.* New York: Norton.

Lewis, M., & Brooks, J. (1978). On the ontogenesis of emotions and emotional-cognition relationships in infancy. In M. Lewis & L. Rosenblum (Eds.), *The development of affect.* New York: Plenum Press.

Lidell, H. S. (1943). The alteration of instinctual processes through the influence of conditioned reflexes. In S. S. Tomkins (Ed.) *Contemporary psychopathology: A source book.* (pp. 445–553). Cambridge, MA: Harvard University Press.

Lindsley, D. B. (1951). In S. S. Stevens (Ed.), *Handbook of experimental psychology.* New York: Wiley.

Lomax, A. (1968). *Folk song style and culture.* Washington, DC: American Association for the Advancement of Science.

Lorente de N6, R. (1933). Studies on the structure of the cerebral cortex. *J. of Psychiat.* U. Neurol., Bd. xiv, p. 381.

Lorenz, K. Z. (1950). The comparative method in studying innate behavior patterns. *Symposia of the Society for Experimental Biology, 12,* 221–268.

Lorenz, K. Z. (1965). Preface. In C. Darwin (Ed.), *The expression of the emotions in man and animals.* Chicago: University of Chicago Press.

Lovejoy, A. O. (1936). *The great chain of being.* Cambridgc: Harvard University Press. [Reprinted 1960 New York: Harper & Row].

Luria, A. R. (1960). Verbal regulation of behavior. In *Third Macy Conference: The central nervous system and behavior.* Bethesda, MD: National Institutes of Health.

Lyman, C. R., & Chatfield, P. O. (1953). Hibernation and cortical electrical activity in the woodchuck. *Science, 117,* 533–534.

Lynn, K. S. (1987). *Hemingway: The life and the work.* New York: Simon & Schuster.

Magarshack, O. (1952). *Chekhov the dramatist.* New York: Auvergne.

Magoun, H. W. (1944). Bulbar inhibition and facilitation of motor activity. *Science, 100,* 549–550.

Malmo, R. B. (1959). Activation: A neurophysiological dimension. *Psychological Review, 66,* 367–386.

Markmann, R. (1943). *Predictions of manifest personality trends by a thematic analysis of three pictures of the Thematic Apperception Test.* Unpublished doctoral dissertation, Radcliffe College.

Maslach, C. (1978). The emotional consequences of arousal without reason. In C. E. Izard (Ed.), *Emotion and psychopathology.* New York: Plenum Press.

Mayer, E. (1974). Behavior programs and evolutionary strategies. *American Scientist, 62,* 650–659.

McCarter, R., Tomkins, S. S., & Schiffman, H. (1961). Early recollections as predictors of Tomkins-Horn Picture Arrangement Test performance. *Journal of Individual Psychology, 17,* 177–180.

McKay, D. M. (1956). The epistemological problem for automata. In C. E. Shannon & J. McCarthy (Eds.), *Automata studies. Annals of Mathematical Studies,* Study 34. Princeton, NJ: Princeton University Press.

McKellar, P. (1957). *Imagination and thinking.* New York: Basic Books.

Meltzoff, A. N., & Moore, M. K. (1977). Imitation of facial and manual gestures by human neonates. *Science, 198,* 75–78.

Miller, G. A. (1956). The magical number seven, plus or minus two: Some limits on our capacity for processing information. *Psychological Review, 63,* 81–97.

Miller, P. (1961). *The New England mind: The seventeenth century.* Boston: Beacon Press.

Moruzzi, G., & Magoun, H. W. (1949). Brain stem reticular formation and activation of the EEC. *Electroencephalography and Clinical Neurophysiology, 1,* 455–473.

Mosher, D. L., & Tomkins, S. S. (1988). Scripting the macho man: Hypermasculine socialization and enculturation. *Journal of Sex Research, 25*(1), 60–84.

Mowrer, O. H. (1950). *Learning theory and personality dynamics.* New York: Ronald Press.

Nauta, W. J. (1958). Hippocampal projections and related neural pathways to the mid-brain in the cat. *Brain, 81,* 319–340.

Nauta, W. J. & Feirtag, M. (1979). The organization of the brain. *Scientific American, 241*(3), 88–111.

Needham, J. (1954). *Science and civilisation in China: Vol. 1. Introductory orientations.* Cambridge: Cambridge University Press.

Needham, R. (1973). Right and left in Nyono Symbolic Classification. In R. Needham (Ed.), *Right and left* (pp. 299–341). Chicago: University of Chicago Press. 1973.

Nesbitt, M. (1959). *Friendship, love and values: A project on "Mathematical techniques in psychology."* ONR Technical Report. Princeton, NJ: Educational Testing Service.

Nussbaum, M. C. (1986). *The fragility of goodness: Luck and ethics in Greek tragedy and philosophy.* Cambridge: Cambridge University Press.

Oken, D. (1960). An experimental study of suppressed anger and blood pressure. *Archives of General Psychology, 2,* 441–456.

Olds, J., & Milner, P. (1954). Positive reinforcement produced by electrical stimulation of septal area and other regions of rat brain. *Journal of Comparative and Physiological Psychology, 47,* 419–427.

Olsen, A. J. (1958, February 17). Anne Frank speaks to the Germans. *New York Times.*

O'Neill, E. (1956). *Long day's journey into night.* New Haven, CT: Yale University Press.

Pascal, B. (1946). *Pensées.* New York: Peter Pauper Press.

Peiper, A. (1961). *Cerebral function in infancy and childhood.* New York: Consultants' Bureau.

Penfield, W. (1937). *The cerebral cortex and consciousness.* Harvey Lectures, Jenis, xxxii, 35–69.

Penfield, W. (1950). Observation on the Anatomy of Memory, *Fol. Psychiat. Neurolog. Neurochimergies Neerl. 53,* 349–351.

Penfield, W., & Boldrey, E. (1937). Somatic and Motor Representation in the Cerebral Cortex of Man as studied by electrical stimulation. *Brain, 60,* 389–443.

Ponzo, M., & August, A. (1933). Zur Systematik der Gewichtsempfindungen. *Archiv fuer die Gesamati Psychologic, 88,* 630.

Pratt, C. C. (1956). The stability of aesthetic judgments. *Journal of Aesthetics and Art Criticism, 15,* 1–11.

Pribram, K. H. (1960). Theory in physiological psychology. In *Annual Review of Psychology* (pp. 1–33). Palo Alto, CA: Annual Reviews.

Ramon y Casal, S. (1928). *Degeneration and Regeneration of Nerve Tissue.* Oxford: Oxford University Press.

Redl, F. (1951). The concept of ego disturbances and ego support. *American Journal of Orthopsychiatry, 21,* 273–284.

Reed, C. F. (1963). Illusory images consequent to search in a visual task. *Confin. Psychiat. 6,* 67–70.

Remarque, E. M. (1929). *All quiet on the western front.* Boston: Little, Brown, & Co.

Richter, C. P. (1949). Domestication of the Norway rat and its implication for the problems of stress. *Proceedings of the Association for Nervous and Mental Disease, 29,* 19–47.

Richter, C. P. (1959). Rats, man and the welfare state. *American Psychologist, 14,* 18–28.

Riese, W., & Bruck, G. (1950). Les membres fantomes chez l'enfant. *Revue Neurologique, 83,* 221–222.

Robertson, J. (nd). *Case history of a child undergoing short separation from mother in a hospital.* Unpublished report, Tavistock Institute, London.

Ross, J., & Lawrence, K. A. (1968). Some observations on memory and artifice. *Psychonomic Science, 13,* 107–108.

Rovee-Collier, C. K., Sullivan, M. W., Enright, M., Lucas, D., & Fagen, J. W. (1980). Reactivation of infant memory. *Science, 208*(6), 1159–1161.

Ruch, T. C. (1951). Sensory mechanism(s). In S. S. Stevens (Ed.), *Handbook of experimental psychology.* New York: Wiley.

Rustow, A. (1980). *Freedom and domination.* Princeton, NJ: Princeton University Press.

Salk, L. (1960). The effects of normal heartbeat on the behavior of the newborn infant: Implications for mental health. *World Mental Health, 12,* 168–175.

Sanday, P. R. (1981). *Female power and male dominance.* Cambridge: Cambridge University Press.

Satinoff, E. (1978). Neural organization and evolution of thermal regulations in mammals. *Science, 201,* 16–22.

Schacter, S., & Singer, J. E. (1962). Cognitive, social, and physiological determinants of emotional state. *Psychological Review, 69,* 379–399.

Schank, R., & Abelson, R. (1977). *Scripts, plans, goals and understanding.* Hillsdale, NJ: Lawrence Erlbaum Associates.

Schiff, W., Caviness, J. A., & Gibson, J. S. (1962). Resistant fear responses in Rhesus monkeys to the optical stimulus of "looming." *Science, 136,* 982–983.

Schmitt, R. O., Dev, P., & Smith, B. H. (1976). Electronic processing of information by brain cells. *Science, 193*(4248), 114–120.

Semmes, J., (1953). Agnosia in animal and man. *Psychology Review, 60,* 140–147.

Seneca. (1969). *Letter from a stoic.* Baltimore: Penguin.

Shagass, C. (1972). *Evoked brain potential in psychiatry.* New York: Plenum.

Shannon, C. E., & Weaver, W. (1949). *The mathematical theory of communication.* Urbana: University of Illinois Press.

Sherpless, S., & Jasper, H. (1956). Habituation of the arousal reaction. *Brain, 79,* 655–680.

Sherrington, C. S. (1906). *The integrative action of the nervous system.* New Haven, CT: Yale University Press.

Simmel, M. C. (1956). Phantoms in patients with leprosy and in elderly digital amputees. *American Journal of Psychology, 69,* 529–545.

Simon, C. W., & Emmons, W. (1956). EEG, consciousness and sleep. *Science, 124,* 1066–1069.

Simpson, G. G. (1949). *The meaning of evolution: A study of the history of life and of its significance for man.* New Haven, CT: Yale University Press.

Singer, J. L. (1955). Delayed gratification and ego development: Implications for clinical and experimental research. *Journal of Consulting Psychology, 19,* 259–266.

Singer, J. L. (1966). *Daydreaming: An introduction to the experimental study of inner experience.* New York: Random House.

Singer, J. L. (1973). *The child's world of make-believe: Experimental studies of imaginative play.* New York: Academic Press.

Singer, J. L. (1974). *Imagery and daydream methods in psychotherapy and behavior modification.* New York: Academic Press.

Singer, J. L. (1975). Navigating the stream of consciousness: Research in daydreaming and related inner experience. *American Psychologist, 30,* 727–738.

Smelser, N. J., & Halpern, S. (1978). The historical triangulation of family, economy, and education. In J. Demos & S. S. Boocock (Eds.), *Turning points.* Chicago: University of Chicago Press.

Solomon, R. L., Kamin, L. J., Wynne, L. C. (1953). Traumatic avoidance learning: The outcomes of several extinction procedures with dogs. *Journal of Abnormal and Social Psychology, 48,* 291–302.

Sperry, R. (1982). Some effects of disconnecting the cerebral hemispheres. *Science, 217,* 1223–1226.

Spielberger, C. D. (Ed.), (1966). *Anxiety and behavior.* New York: Academic Press.

Sprague, J. M., Chambers, W. W., & Stellar, E. (1961). Attentive, affective, and adaptive behavior in the cat. *Science, 33,* 165–173.

Stevens, C. F. (1978). Interactions between intrinsic membrane protein and electric field: An approach to studying nerve excitability. *Biophysical Journal, 22*(2), 295–306.

Stevens, C. F. (1988). The neuron. In: R. R. Llinás (Ed.), *The biology of the brain: From neurons to networks* (pp. 1–19). New York: W.H. Freeman.

Stratton, G. M. (1897). Vision without inversion of the retinal image. *Psychological Review, 4,* 341–360.

Tacitus. (1907). Germania. In *Works of Tacitus,* The Oxford translation/revised. (Vol. 14, p. 305). London: G. Bell. Vol. I & II.

Tolstoy, I. (1972). *Reminiscences of Tolstoy, by his son.* New York: Cowles.

Tolstoy, L. (1959). *Anna Karenina.* New York: Harper.

Tolstoy, L. (1960). *The death of Ivan Ilych.* New York: New American Library.

Tolstoy, T. (1977). *Tolstoy remembered.* London: Michael Joseph.

Tomkins, S. S. (1946). *The Thematic Apperception Test.* With the collaboration of E. J. Tomkins, BA. New York: Grune and Stratton.

Tomkins, S. S. (1956). La conscience et l'inconscient représentés dans une modéle de l'etre humain. In J. Lacan (Ed.), *La psychoanalyse* (Vol. 1). Paris: Presses Universitaires de France.

Tomkins, S. S. (1962). *Affect, imagery, consciousness* (Vol. 1). New York: Springer Publishing Co.

Tomkins, S. S. (1963a). *Affect, imagery, consciousness* (Vol. 2). New York: Springer Publishing Co.

Tomkins, S. S. (1963b). The right and the left: A basic dimension of ideology and personality. In R. W. White (Ed.), *The study of lives.* New York: Atherton.

Tomkins, S. S. (1965). Affect and the psychology of knowledge. In S. S. Tomkins & C. E. Izard (Eds.), *Affect, cognition, and personality.* New York: Springer Publishing Co.

Tomkins, S. S. (1971). A theory of memory. In J. Antrobus (Ed.), *Cognition and affect.* Boston: Little, Brown.

Tomkins, S. S. (1975). The phantasy behind the face. *Journal of Personality Assessment, 39,* 550–562.

Tomkins, S. S. (1979). Script theory: Differential magnification of affects. In H. E. Howe, Jr., & R. A. Dienstbier (Eds.), *Nebraska Symposium on Motivation* (Vol. 26). Lincoln: University of Nebraska Press.

Tomkins, S. S. (1981a). The quest for primary motives: Biography and autobiography of an idea. *Journal of Personality and Social Psychology, 41*(2), 306–329.

Tomkins, S. S. (1981b). The rise, fall and resurrection of the study of personality. *Journal of Mind and Behavior, 2*(4), 443–452.

Tomkins, S. S. (1982). Affect theory. In P. Ekman, W. V. Freesen, & P. Ellsworth (Eds.), *Emotion in the human face* (2nd ed.). Cambridge: Cambridge University Press.

Tomkins, S. S. (1987). Script theory. In J. Aronoff, A. I. Rubin, & R. A. Zucker (Eds.), *The emergence of personality* (pp. 147–216). New York: Springer Publishing Co.

Tomkins, S. S., & Izard, C. E. (1965). *Affect, cognition, and personality.* New York: Springer Publishing Co.

Tomkins, S. S., & McCarter, R. (1964). What and where are the primary affects? Some evidence for a theory. *Perceptual and Motor Skills, 18*(1), 119–158.

Tomkins, S. S., & Messick, S. (Eds.). (1963). *The computer simulation of personality.* New York: Wiley.

Tomkins, S. S., Miner, J. B. (1956). *The Tomkins-Horn Picture Arrangement Test.* New York: Springer Publishing Co.

Tomkins, S. S., & Miner, J. B. (1959). *PAT interpretation.* New York: Springer Publishing Co.

Tourangeau, R., & Ellsworth, P. C. (1979). The role of facial response in the experience of emotion. *Journal of Personality and Social Psychology, 37,* 1519–1531.

Twain, M. (1882). *The prince and the pauper.* New York: Harper & Brothers.

Underwood, B. J. (1957). Interference and forgetting. *Psychological Review, 64,* 49–60.

Valentine, C. W. (1956). *The normal child.* London: Penguin Books.

Vasquez, J. (1975). *The face and ideology.* Unpublished doctoral dissertation, Rutgers University.

Wallach, H., O'Connell, D. N., & Neisser, U. (1953). The memory effect of visual perception of three-dimensional form. *Journal of Experimental Psychology, 45,* 360–368.

Walter, G. (1954). The electrical activity of the brain. *Scientific American, 190,* 54–63.

Wapner, S., & Krus, D. (1959). Behavioral effects of lysergic acid diethylamide. *Archives of General Psychiatry, 1,* 417–419.

Wapner, S., & Werner, H. (1957). *Perceptual development: An investigation within the framework of sensory-tonic field theory.* Worcester, MA: Clark University Press.

Wapner, S., Werner, H., & Krus, D. M. (1957). The effect of success and failure on space localization. *Journal of Personality, 25,* 752–756.

Wasiolek, E. (1978). *Tolstoy's major fiction.* Chicago: University of Chicago Press.

Weisskopf, V. F. (1979). Contemporary frontiers in physics. *Science, 203,* 240–244.

Wheatstone, C. (1838). On some remarkable, and hitherto unobserved phenomena of binocular vision. Part I. *Philosophical Transactions, 128,* 371–394.

Wheatstone, C. (1852). On some remarkable, and hitherto unobserved phenomena of binocular vision. Part II. *Philos. Mag. Series, 4*(3), 504–523.

White, R. W., Alper, T. G., & Tomkins, S. S. (1945). The realistic synthesis: A personality study. *Journal of Abnormal and Social Psychology, 40,* 228–248.

Witkin, H. A. (1949). Perception of body position and of the position of the visual field. *Psychological Monographs* No. 302, *63*(7), 1–46.

Wolff, P. H. (1968). The serial organization of sucking in the young infant. *Pediatrics, 42*(6), 943–956.

Wolff, P. H., & Simmons, M. A. (1967). Nonnutritive sucking and response thresholds in young infants. *Child Development, 38*(3), 631–638.

Wurtz, R. H., Goldberg, M. E., & Robinson, D. L. (1980). Behavioral modulation of visual responses in monkeys. *Prog. Psychobiol. Physiol. Psychol., 9,* 42–83.

Wurtz, R. H., Goldberg, M. E., & Robinson, D. L. (1981). Behavioral modulation of visual responses in the monkey: Stimulus selection for attention and movement. *Progress in Psychology and Physiological Psychology,* 46(4), 755–772.

Wundt, W. (1890). *Compendium of psychology.* Translation of 3rd edition. Torino: Clausen.

Yates, F. A. (1972). *The art of memory.* Chicago: University of Chicago Press.

Zajonc, R. B. (1980). Feeling and thinking: Preferences need no inferences. *American Psychologist, 35,* 151–175.

Author Index

Subject Index

CPSIA information can be obtained
at www.ICGtesting.com
Printed in the USA
BVOW10*0337170816
459234BV00002B/2/P